JUDGES
Canada
J	Justice
JA	Justice of Appeal
JJ	Justices
CJ	Chief Justice

United Kingdom
LJ	Lord Justice
MR	Master of the Rolls

CASELAW REPORTERS
Canada
AR	Alberta Reports
BCDLA	British Columbia Decisions, Labour Arbitration
BCLR	British Columbia Law Reports
BLR	Business Law Reports
CBR	Canadian Bankruptcy Reports
CCC	Canadian Criminal Cases
CCEL	Canadian Cases on Employment Law
CCLT	Canadian Cases on the Law of Torts
CELR	Canadian Environmental Law Reports
CPR	Canadian Patent Reporter
CTC	Canada Tax Cases
DLR	Dominion Law Reports
DTC	Dominion Tax Cases
Ex CR	Canada Law Reports: Exchequer Court of Canada
FC	Federal Court Reports
FTR	Federal Trial Reports
LAC	Labour Arbitration Cases
NBR	New Brunswick Reports
Nfld & PEIR	Newfoundland and Prince Edward Island Reports
NSR	Nova Scotia Reports
OLR	Ontario Law Reports
OLRB Rep	Ontario Labour Relations Board Reports
OR	Ontario Reports
OTC	Ontario Trial Cases
OWN	Ontario Weekly Notes
PPSAC	Personal Property Security Act Cases
Sask R	Saskatchewan Reports
SCR	Supreme Court Reports
WWR	Western Weekly Reports

United Kingdom
AC	Appeal Cases
All ER	All England Reports
App Cas	Appeal Cases
Ch D	Chancery Division
ER	English Reports
HL Cas	House of Lords Cases
KB	King's Bench
LR	
Lloyds Rep	
QB	
WLR	Weekly Law Reports

United States
F	Federal Reporter
F Supp	Federal Supplement
NE	Northeastern Reporter
NY	New York Reports
P	Pacific Reporter
So	Southern Reporter
WL	Westlaw

Quicklaw Databases
BCJ	British Columbia Judgments
OJ	Ontario Judgments
YJ	Yukon Judgments

Australia and New Zealand
CLR	Commonwealth Law Reports
SR (NSW)	State Reports (New South Wales)
Qd R	Queensland Reports

STATUTES
Canada
RRO	Revised Regulations of Ontario
RSC	Revised Statutes of Canada
RSA	Revised Statutes of Alberta
RSBC	Revised Statutes of British Columbia
RSM	Revised Statutes of Manitoba
RSN	Revised Statutes of Newfoundland
RSNB	Revised Statutes of New Brunswick
RSNWT	Revised Statutes Northwest Territories
RSNS	Revised Statutes of Nova Scotia
RSO	Revised Statutes of Ontario
RSPEI	Revised Statutes of Prince Edward Island
RSQ	Revised Statutes of Quebec
RSS	Revised Statutes of Saskatchewan
RSY	Revised Statutes of Yukon
SOR	Statutory Orders and Regulations

United Kingdom
Vict	Victoria
Cha	Charles

United States
USC	United States Code

PERIODICALS
Berkeley Tech LJ	Berkeley Technology Law Journal
Can Bar Rev	Canadian Bar Review
Cornell LQ	Cornell Law Quarterly
Osgoode Hall LJ	Osgoode Hall Law Journal

MANAGING THE LAW
THE LEGAL ASPECTS OF DOING BUSINESS

FOURTH EDITION

MITCHELL MCINNES
FACULTY OF LAW, UNIVERSITY OF ALBERTA

IAN R. KERR
FACULTY OF LAW, UNIVERSITY OF OTTAWA

J. ANTHONY VANDUZER
FACULTY OF LAW, UNIVERSITY OF OTTAWA

PEARSON

Toronto

Vice-President, Editorial Director: Gary Bennett
Editor-in-Chief: Nicole Lukach
Acquisitions Editor: Megan Farrell
Marketing Manager: Claire Varley
Developmental Editor: Karen Townsend
Project Manager: Marissa Lok
Production Editor: Sheena Uprety and Rajni Pisharody, Cenveo Publisher Services
Copy Editor: Deborah Cooper-Bullock
Proofreader: Barbara Kamienski
Compositor: Cenveo Publisher Services
Photo and Permissions Researcher: Tara Smith
Art Director: Julia Hall
Cover and Interior Designer: Miguel Acevedo
Cover Image: Halfdark/Getty Images

Credits and acknowledgments of material borrowed from other sources and reproduced, with permission, in this textbook appear on the appropriate page within the text and on page xxxiv.

If you purchased this book outside the United States or Canada, you should be aware that it has been imported without the approval of the publisher or author.

10 9 8 7 6 5 4 3 CKV

Library and Archives Canada Cataloguing in Publication

McInnes, Mitchell
      Managing the law : the legal aspects of doing
business / Mitchell McInnes, Ian R. Kerr, J. Anthony
VanDuzer. —4th ed.

Includes bibliographical references and index.
ISBN 978-0-13-216442-9

      1. Commercial law—Canada—Textbooks. I. Kerr, Ian
R. (Ian Randall), 1965- II. VanDuzer, J. Anthony (John
Anthony), 1958- III. Title.

KE919.M38 2013   346.7107   C2012-904558-6
KF889.M38 2013

ISBN 978-0-13-216442-9

Brief Contents

Contents

About the Authors

Mitchell McInnes, PhD (Cambridge), LLM (Cambridge), LLB (Alberta),
BA (Alberta), of the Alberta Bar, Professor

Professor McInnes joined the Faculty of Law at the University of Alberta in 2005. He previously taught at the University of Western Ontario, the University of Melbourne, and Deakin University. He has clerked at the Supreme Court of Canada and served as a Legal Research Officer with the Alberta Court of Appeal.

Professor McInnes' research focuses on Unjust Enrichment, Restitution, Remedies, Trusts, Contract, and Tort. He has published more than one hundred papers in leading journals, including the *Canadian Bar Review*, the *University of Toronto Law Journal*, the *Cambridge Law Journal*, and the *Law Quarterly Review*. He is a co-author of three casebooks: *Cases and Materials on the Law of Torts* (Carswell), *Oosterhoff on Trusts: Text, Commentary and Cases on Trusts* (Carswell), and *Cases and Materials on the Law of Restitution* (Emond Montgomery). He has also published two collections of essays on the law of unjust enrichment: *Restitution: Developments in Unjust Enrichment* (Law Book Company) and *Understanding Unjust Enrichment* (Hart). His work has been relied upon by a number of courts, including the Supreme Court of Canada and the High Court of Australia.

Professor McInnes has received a number of teaching awards and he has been recognized by *Maclean's* magazine as one of Canada's leading university teachers.

Ian R. Kerr, PhD (Western), MA (Western), LLB (Western), BA Hons (Alberta),
BSc (Alberta), of the Bar of Ontario, Full Professor

As Canada Research Chair in Ethics, Law, and Technology, Ian Kerr is Canada's leading authority on how legal and ethical issues intersect with electronic commerce. Ian plays a significant role in the development of national and international laws in e-commerce, privacy policy, and digital copyright reform. He has advised various Canadian agencies on legal policy for online activities, and has served as a Canadian delegate to the United Nations' Special Working Group on e-Commerce, a project of the United Nations Commission on International Trade Law. Ian teaches at the Faculty of Law, University of Ottawa, where he co-designed a new graduate program in law and technology. He holds cross-appointments to the Faculty of Medicine, the Department of Philosophy, and the School of Information Studies, and has won numerous awards for teaching excellence.

Ian's previous research projects include *On the Identity Trail*, a multi-disciplinary project supported by one of the largest-ever grants from the Social Sciences and Humanities Research Council, which studied the impact of information and authentication technologies on identity and anonymity. He also co-lead *An Examination of Digital Copyright*, a large private sector grant from Bell Canada and the Ontario Research Network in Electronic Commerce examining the implications of copyright reform on Canadian values including privacy and freedom of expression. With his background in philosophy, technology, and private law, Ian has published numerous articles and papers and has edited and contributed to several books and journals on the legal implications of doing business online, including the *Canadian Business Law Journal* and the *Electronic Commerce Research Journal*. He has also contributed scholarly articles and chapters in several books on a range of other subjects, including cyberspace law, nanotechnology, bioethics, robo-ethics, contract law, information ethics, and the philosophy of law, and has lectured world-wide on these topics. His most recent book, *Lessons From The Identity Trail*, is published by Oxford University Press and available for free download through a creative commons licence at idtrail.org.

J. Anthony VanDuzer, LLM (Columbia), LLB (Ottawa), BA (Queen's), of the Bar of Ontario, Professor

Tony VanDuzer has taught and practised extensively in the area of corporate and commercial law for more than 25 years. Following five years in private practice, he joined the Faculty of Law at the University of Ottawa. He teaches a variety of advanced business law subjects, for which he has received several teaching awards. He has taught in the University of Ottawa's Executive MBA program as well as at universities in the UK, Germany and New Zealand. Since 2003, he has been an Adjunct Research Professor at the Norman Paterson School of International Affairs at Carleton University.

Tony has published over 60 articles and papers on subjects ranging from pharmaceutical patents and health care to corporate law. He has also written several significant books on business law, including *The Law of Partnerships and Corporations*, 3d ed. (Concord: Irwin, 2009); and *Merger Notification in Canada* (with Albert Gourley, Toronto: CCH Canadian, 1994). His work has been cited by the Supreme Court of Canada as well as provincial superior courts and courts of appeal.

Over the past decade, he has often been called on to advise Canadian government agencies and organizations on business and trade law issues. He completed a study for the Canadian Competition Bureau in 1999 on anti-competitive pricing practices. Many of his recommendations for reform of the *Competition Act* were included in amendments to the *Act* in 2009. His study for the Department of Foreign Affairs and International Trade of the impact of the WTO General Agreement on Trade in Services on the delivery of health, education, and social services in Canada was presented to the Standing Committee on Foreign Affairs and International Trade in 2005.

Tony has worked with international development agencies around the world, such as the Canadian International Development Agency and the World Bank, delivering workshops, drafting new laws, and providing other forms of technical assistance to foreign governments on issues related to business and trade. He played a key role in the drafting of Russia's foreign trade law and business registration law.

Tony is also the Chair of the Centre for Trade Policy and Law, an institute jointly established by the Faculty of Law and the Norman Paterson School of International Affairs and engaged in trade policy research and international technical assistance.

Preface

Managing the Law: The Legal Aspects of Doing Business aims to equip students with the conceptual tools and intellectual skills needed to identify, assess, and manage the legal risks that arise in the course of doing business. Students who study this text will achieve the following:

- A basic understanding of the function of law.
- A basic understanding of the structure of the Canadian legal system.
- A basic understanding of legal sources, concepts, and principles.
- A sound understanding of the specific areas of the law that are especially important to business.
- The ability to identify legal problems that arise in business contexts.
- The ability to formulate opinions on important socio-legal issues that affect business.
- The ability to apply basic legal principles to problems that arise in business contexts.
- The ability to critically evaluate legal arguments put forth by others.
- The ability to devise arguments and present them persuasively.

Training students "to think like lawyers" (to use a favourite phrase of law professors) has long been the main purpose of law courses, even those designed for business students. But although this book provides valuable insight into legal thought processes, we have written this text to address a different primary goal. With *Managing the Law*, we aim to help students learn how "to think like successful business people." The key concept here is **risk management**. Business people should know enough about the law to identify legal issues and arrange their affairs so as to avoid difficulties. Moreover, they should know enough about the law to recognize when it is appropriate to obtain expert advice from a legal professional. Success in the business world often depends on thoughtful delegation.

This book was written with these considerations firmly in mind. As a result, *Managing the Law* differs from other books on the market in two important ways. First, it is a book for business students, not law students. *Managing the Law* provides a thorough and current picture of the legal rules that are relevant in the business world. It does not sacrifice important information for the sake of simplicity. At the same time, however, it does not overwhelm the business student with unnecessary detail or impenetrable jargon. The tone is intelligent and student-friendly. The text is accessible and comprehensible, regardless of the reader's background.

Second, the text's recurring theme is *risk management*. That focus is reflected in both the choice and the presentation of material. Legal topics are chosen for their relevance to the commercial context. Furthermore, they are presented in a manner that fosters the development of effective risk-management skills. Through the extensive use of discussion boxes, review exercises, cases and problems, and the like, the text draws students into the business law world and requires them to actively resolve practical problems. Sometimes, of course, the proper resolution of a problem involves recognition of the need for a lawyer's assistance.

Canadian business students, like Canadians in general, are an increasingly diverse group. They come from a variety of backgrounds in terms of personal characteristics, past qualifications, and professional aspirations. Some are new Canadians; others have long-established roots. Some are embarking on post-secondary education for the first time; others are engaged in advanced degrees. Some have little experience in the business world; others are retraining after successful careers. Some are seeking a generalized education; others are more focused on a particular career. This book is appropriate for them all.

Law texts are invariably dense and uninviting, not only in substance and language but also in appearance. By extension, business law texts often suffer the same flaw. In contrast, *Managing the Law* has been specifically designed with the full breadth of its target audience in mind. It is visually engaging. Its use of colour, boxes, icons, figures, and layout draws readers in and provides them with room to breathe intellectually.

Managing the Law has also been designed for use in any course that deals with legal issues in a "business context" (using that phrase broadly). Consequently, without limiting its scope, it is appropriate for students who are studying the legal aspects of any of the following areas:

- Accounting
- Business administration
- Commerce
- Finance
- Management
- Marketing
- Office administration

Organization

This text is divided into nine parts.

- **Part 1 (Introduction to Law)** consists of two chapters. The first chapter, dealing with risk management and sources of law, opens with an explanation of why business people should study law explaining the core concept of risk management. The chapter then sketches the essential features of the Canadian legal system, including:
  - The nature of law
  - Branches of law
  - Sources of law

  The second chapter, dealing with litigation and alternative dispute resolution, explains various mechanisms for the resolution of legal disputes:
  - The litigation process
  - The court system
  - Alternative dispute resolution
- **Part 2 (Torts)** is divided into four chapters. The focus throughout is on risk management in the business context. Here we introduce such key concepts as vicarious liability and liability insurance. And we examine business torts such as nuisance and defamation. The final chapter, which deals with the tort of negligence, places special emphasis on professional negligence as it arises in commercial matters.
- **Part 3 (Contracts)** consists of eight chapters dealing at length with the central concept of contracts. Because of the significance of enforceable

agreements in the commercial context, separate chapters are devoted to each of the following:

- Formation of contracts
- Consideration and privity
- Terms and representations
- Contractual defects
- Discharge and breach
- Remedies

The final chapters focus on two particularly important types of contracts:

- Sales of goods
- Negotiable instruments

- **Part 4 (Property)** consists of three chapters on the law of property. The discussion, as always, places the reader at the heart of practical business-law problems. The examination of personal property, for instance, centres on the institution of bailment and the means by which various forms of insurance can be used to manage legal risks

- **Part 5 (Business Law in the Digital Age),** consisting of two chapters, provides an unprecedented introduction to business law in the digital age. It deals with:
  - Intellectual property rights
  - Electronic commerce

- **Part 6 (Business Organizations)** deals with various types of business organizations. Its three chapters examine sole proprietorships, partnerships, corporations, agency relationships, joint ventures, and franchises. The principles of risk management are highlighted throughout.

- **Part 7 (Practical Business Decisions)** addresses specific decisions that affect business. Its two chapters focus on issues arising from:
  - Secured transactions
  - Bankruptcy and insolvency

- **Part 8 (Sources and Forms of Public Law Regulation)** moves the discussion out of the purely private realm and into the world of public regulation and international relations. Its one chapter examines the various means by which Canadian governments regulate commercial conduct. It considers, for example, competition law, consumer protections laws, and environmental protection laws.

- **Part 9 (Employment and Labour Law)** is divided into two chapters. The first focuses on individual employment. Risk management issues are highlighted at all stages of the employee/employer relationship, ranging from pre-employment matters (such as advertising and hiring) to post-employment matters (such as dismissal and severance packages). The second chapter focuses on organized labour. It includes a discussion of collective agreements, grievances, and industrial conflicts.

Taken together, those nine parts provide a thorough examination of the legal issues that generally affect Canadian businesses. At the same time, we have organized the material to offer instructors the utmost flexibility in matching the book to their course designs. We recognize that time is usually tight in business law courses. Therefore, we have adopted a modular approach in organizing the chapters and units. After covering the introductory Chapters 1 and 2 and the core material on contracts in Chapters 7–12, instructors can feel free to cover the remaining chapters in the order that best suits their needs.

Features

Students learn effectively when they are interested, enthusiastic, and engaged. As a result, we have designed this text to encourage students to participate actively, rather than merely read passively. A large number of features ensure that the materials are both accessible and stimulating.

Objectives. Each chapter opens with a list of 10 objectives that stress key issues and highlight risk-management skills that students should aim to develop. By providing a roadmap at the beginning of each chapter, the objectives help students to read and understand the material more efficiently and more effectively.

Key Terms. Key terms are boldfaced where they are defined in the body of the text. They are also restated with their definitions in the margins.

Discussion Boxes. Each chapter contains at least one instance of each of five distinct types of discussion boxes. These boxes provide instructors with additional opportunities to stimulate critical thinking and engage students in classroom debate. With the exception of the Case Briefs, each discussion box ends with Questions for Discussion. (Model answers appear in the *Instructor's Resource Manual*.) Each type of box fulfils a particular pedagogical goal.

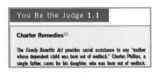

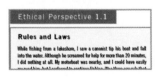

- **Case Briefs** illustrate how the courts have formulated and applied legal rules in specific business contexts. They also introduce students to many of the leading cases in the common law system.
- **Business Decision** boxes ask students to respond as business people to common legal problems. They are designed to foster the development of sound commercial judgment. Accordingly, they focus less on purely legal concepts and more on practical matters that influence decisions in the commercial world.
- **You Be the Judge** boxes ask students to respond as judges to legal problems that commonly arise in the business world. They are designed to give students insight into legal thought processes.
- **Ethical Perspective** boxes ask students to assess morally contentious business-law scenarios. They compel students to place both business considerations and legal concerns into a larger social context, and to develop an appreciation of the fact that alternative solutions often pull in different directions. These boxes are particularly effective in generating classroom discussions.

Concept Summaries. Every chapter contains at least one Concept Summary; most chapters contain many more. Presented in tabular form, the Concept Summaries provide succinct and easily understood reviews of difficult concepts and rules. They are often used to compare and contrast related areas of law.

Figures. Every chapter contains at least one figure. Various diagrams and drawings are used to illustrate and clarify important concepts. Aside from their inherent pedagogic value, they contribute to the visual appeal of the book and therefore draw students into the material.

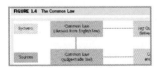

Chapter Summaries. Each chapter ends with a chapter summary that briefly reviews the important concepts of the chapter. These summaries help prepare students for the end-of-chapter exercises.

Review Questions. Twenty review questions appear at the end of each chapter. In some instances, students are required to define and explain key concepts and terms. In others, they are asked to respond to short problems. The review questions can be discussed in class or assigned to students for independent study. (Model answers are provided in the *Instructor's Resource Manual*.)

Cases and Problems. Each chapter concludes with 12 Cases and Problems (with the exception of the first and second chapters, which each contain six), at least two of which are new to this edition. These exercises vary in both length and difficulty. They are ideally suited to classroom discussion, but they too can be assigned to students for independent study. (Model answers are provided in the *Instructor's Resource Manual*.)

Canadian Case Studies. A special Canadian Case Study is provided at the end of each of Parts 2, 5, 8, and 9. Each of these cases provides an in-depth opportunity to apply the lessons learned from the text. Students are able to identify issues within practical business contexts and then propose possible solutions. The Canadian Case Studies readily lend themselves to both classroom discussion and independent study. (Model answers are provided in the *Instructor's Resource Manual*.)

MyBusLawLab

The moment you know

Educators know it. Students know it. It's that inspired moment when something that was difficult to understand suddenly makes perfect sense. Our MyLab products have been designed and refined with a single purpose in mind—to help educators create that moment of understanding with their students.

MyBusLawLab delivers **proven results** in helping individual students succeed. It provides **engaging experiences** that personalize, stimulate, and measure learning for each student. And, it comes from a **trusted partner** with educational expertise and an eye on the future.

MyBusLawLab can be used by itself or linked to any learning management system. To learn more about how MyBusLawLab combines proven learning applications with powerful assessment, visit MyBusLawLab **www.pearsoned.ca/mybuslawlab**.

MyBusLawLab —the moment you know
MyBusLawLab is our online component for the 4th edition of *Managing the Law: The Legal Aspects of Doing Business*. This valuable tool provides **students** and **instructors** with personalized Study Plans and the opportunity for unlimited practice. MyBusLawLab also includes Pearson eText, a robust eBook version of the textbook that enables both students and instructors to highlight specific sections, add notes, share notes, and magnify any of the images or pages without distortion. MyBusLawLab also makes additional materials available to students. These materials include: topics of interest as they relate to business law practices in British Columbia, Alberta, Saskatchewan, Manitoba, the Atlantic Provinces, and Ontario; the *Charter of Rights and Freedoms*; and sample mortgage documents.

- MyBusLawLab features:
    - **Self-study questions** for extra practice and review (the questions do not duplicate any of those in the *Test Item File*).
    - **Provincially specific material,** aimed at British Columbia, Alberta, Saskatchewan, Manitoba, the Atlantic Provinces, and Ontario.
    - **Additional materials** that could not be incorporated into the book, such as the text of the *Charter of Rights and Freedoms*, and sample mortgage documents.

New to This Edition

While retaining the strengths of the previous editions of *Managing the Law*, this fourth edition introduces several important changes.

- **Risk Management.** The focus on the management of legal risks is strengthened throughout the book.
- **Paralegals.** The coverage of paralegals in Chapter 2 is expanded and includes discussion of paralegals outside Ontario.
- **Judicial Review.** Chapter 2's discussion of Adminsitrative Law is updated and now includes a discussion of judical review.
- **Invasion of Privacy.** The emerging tort of invasion of privacy is now discussed in greater detail, including a look at *Jones v Tige*.
- **Land Owners' Rights.** Chapter 4 features a new discussion of the extent of land owners' rights, and an expanded discussion of right of defence of property.
- **Defamation.** Chapter 5 features a new Case Brief discussing online defamation.
- **Negligence.** Chapter 6 features a new discussion of the application of negligence in the workplace.
- **Contract Law.** Chapter 9 now features a new section dealing with boilerplate clauses, and includes an example of a boilerplate contract.
- **Electronic Payments.** Chapter 11 includes a new discussion of electronic payment systems, including PayPal.
- **Damages.** Chapter 12 contains a new section on calculation of expectation damages.
- **Intellectual Property.** Chapter 18 is expanded to include a discussion of new forms of expression (literary, artistic, and dramatic works).
- **Copyright Infringement. Chapter 18** includes a discussion of the new *Copyright Modernization Act*. Figure 18.4 lists all the major new provisions in The *Copyright Modernization Act* and explains the effect of such changes. One of the significant changes in the Act deals with new "technological protection measures" or "digital locks". This change is explained in order to have students consider whether the new law will help maintain copyright's balance or whether it will impair citizens' ability to access information
- **Electronic Commerce.** The discussion of jurisdiction in electronic tort cases is updated to include new Supreme Court rulings in Chapter 19. "You be the Judge 19.2" features the Heartleand Payment processing case—a case many consider to be the largest security breach in history.
- **Identity Theft.** The discussion in Chapter 19 of identity theft is extended with a discussion of new legislation that focuses on the preparatory stages of identity theft.
- **Internet Spam.** Chapter 19 now includes a discussion of Bill C-28, *Fighting Internet and Wireless Spam Act* (FISA). The text provides an explanation of the Act and the penalties that it imposes on violators.
- **Corporate Social Responsibilty.** Chapter 22 is heavily revised to include an expanded discussion of corporate social responsibility, featuring real-world examples of companies that have failed or excelled.
- **Securities Law.** The discussion of securities law in Chapter 22 is expanded with a longer introduction and new material concerning environmental disclosure rules.

- **Taxation.** The taxation coverage in Chapter 25 is revised to include a new section on the taxation of corporations and shareholders, to discuss taxation of small businesses, and to provide a discussion of the legal basis for federal and provincial taxation
- **Contractors.** The section on contractors in Chapter 26 is expanded to include information on a new category of worker, the dependent contractor.
- **Discrimination.** The coverage of human rights and discrimination, in Chapter 26, is changes to include updates to the Human Rights Code of several provinces.
- **Boilerplate Contractual Clauses** is a new appendix that contains a variety of examples of clauses that are discussed in Chapter 9.

Supplements

All the supplements that instructors need to teach and test their students are available on both our MyBusLawLab, and on our easy-to-access Instructor's Resource Centre, available at **http://catalogue.pearsoned.ca/**.

We have carefully prepared the following resources to aid instructors in presenting lectures, fostering class discussion, and administering examinations:

- **Instructor's Resource Manual.** The *Instructor's Resource Manual* is designed to enhance the organization and presentation of course materials. It includes **model answers** for all of the questions that appear in the discussion boxes, Review Questions, and Cases and Problems. Where appropriate, the answers explain the pedagogic purpose of their associated questions. The Manual also provides **case briefs** for every judicial decision that is mentioned in the text or its footnotes. In addition, the Manual includes **teaching tips and suggestions** that instructors might find useful in tailoring the materials in the textbook for their students.
- **PowerPoint® Presentation Slides.** The PowerPoint slides for each chapter can be used in electronic form to present materials in class or in printed form to guide the preparation of new lecture notes.
- **Image Library.** An electronic version of all the figures, tables, and concept summaries from the textbook.
- **MyBusLawLab.** Pearson Canada's online resource, MyBusLawLab, offers instructors and students all of their resources in one place. With MyBusLawLab, you will be able to enliven your lectures with a variety of material. Your students will be able to prepare and perform better on assignments and exams with customized study plans. MyBusLawLab is available to instructors by going to **www.pearsoned.ca/mybuslawlab** and by following the instructions on the opening screen. Students receive access to MyBusLawLab when they purchase their new text.
- **Pearson eText.** Pearson eText gives students access to the text whenever and wherever they have access to the Internet. eText pages look exactly like the printed text, offering powerful new functionality for students and instructors. Users can create notes, highlight text in different colours, create bookmarks, zoom, click hyperlinked words and phrases to view definitions, and view in single-page or two-page view. Pearson eText allows for quick navigation to key parts of the eText using a table of contents and provides full-text search. The eText may also offer links to associated media files, enabling users to access videos, animations, or other activities as they read the text.

MyBusLawLab

- **MyTest.** MyTest from Pearson Canada is a powerful assessment generation program that helps instructors easily create quizzes, tests, exams, and homework or practice handouts. Instructors can author questions and tests online, which allows ultimate flexibility and efficiency in managing their marking and assessments.

Technology Specialists. Pearson's Technology Specialists work with faculty and campus course designers to ensure that Pearson technology products, assessment tools, and online course materials are tailored to meet your specific needs. This highly qualified team is dedicated to helping schools take full advantage of a wide range of educational resources, by assisting in the integration of a variety of instructional materials and media formats. Your local Pearson Education sales representative can provide you with more details on this service program.

CourseSmart for Instructors

CourseSmart goes beyond traditional expectations–providing instant, online access to the textbooks and course materials you need at a lower cost for students. And even as students save money, you can save time and hassle with a digital eTextbook that allows you to search for the most relevant content at the very moment you need it. Whether it's evaluating textbooks or creating lecture notes to help students with difficult concepts, CourseSmart can make life a little easier. See how when you visit **www.coursesmart.com/instructors**.

CourseSmart for Students

CourseSmart goes beyond traditional expectations–providing instant, online access to the textbooks and course materials you need at an average savings of 60%. With instant access from any computer and the ability to search your text, you'll find the content you need quickly, no matter where you are. And with online tools like highlighting and note-taking, you can save time and study efficiently. See all the benefits at **www.coursesmart.com/students**.

Acknowledgments

We wish to thank a number of people who were instrumental in the production of this book.

Several members of Pearson Education's team made vital contributions. Megan Farrell brought tremendous enthusiasm in her role as acquisitions editor; Karen Townsend guided the work carefully through its various stages of development; Sheena Uprety efficiently guided the book through production. We also thank Deborah Cooper-Bullock for her expert review of the manuscript.

The Faculties of Law at the University of Ottawa and the University of Alberta provided stimulating and supportive work environments. A number of students at these institutions served as research assistants: Adam Barker, Beatrice Bozinovski, Goldie Bassie, Katie Black, Marcus Bornfruend, Eliot Che, Mysty Clapton, Charlotte Freeman-Shaw, Robert Gazdag, Heather Gray, Vanessa Gruben, Greg Hagen, Brett Harrison, John Hoben, Nikiforos Iatrou, Carole Johnson, Alesia Kachur, Cherolyn Knapp, Kathryn Kirkpatrick, Corey Levin, Todd Mandel, Trevor McGowan, Michelle McLean, Meghan Murtha, Bernard Sandler, Linda Smits, Byron Thom, Kristen Thomasen, Peter Waldkirch, Katie Warfield, James Wishart, and Hilary Young.

The focus, content, and style of this book reflect the comments—often challenging and always insightful—that we received from external reviewers.

We are grateful to each of the following for providing formal reviews of parts of the manuscript:

George Allen (Red River College)
Pnina Alon-Shenker (Ryerson University)
Bruce Anderson (Saint Mary's University)
Jeff Bone (University of Alberta)
Peter Bowal (University of Calgary)
Barbara Cox (University of British Columbia)
Barbara H. Eccles (Lakehead University)
Weldon Green (NBCC)
Bill Farr (Red Deer College)
Murray Horowitz (Humber College/University of Guelph-Humber)
Murray Kernaghan (Assiniboine College)
Lori Larsen (Red Deer College)
Douglas H. Peterson (University of Alberta)
Mark Schwartz (York University)
Brian Sugg (Douglas College)
Don Valeri (Douglas College)

Mitchell McInnes
Ian Kerr
Tony VanDuzer

Dedication

For Alison: *durate et vosmet rebus servate secundis.*

M.M.

To my sweet little Ruby Tuesday, who turned two in June—*yum, yum bubba yum, bubba yubba bubba gum"*

I.R.K.

Jodie—for her continuing indulgence and support; Taylor and Eli—for their patience with their too often absent father; and Shirley—for being my biggest fan.

J.A.V.

Table of Statutes

Table of Cases

Credits

Text

Chapter 18; 443 Source: Industry Canada A Guide to Copyrights (2010) at 4.; **444** Source: Industry Canada A Guide to Copyrights (2000) at 3–4.; **446** Source: Industry Canada A Guide to Copyrights (2000) at 3–4.; **452** Tom's House of Pizza; 457 Source: Industry Canada A Guide to Patents (2010) at 4; **458** Reproduced by permission of Ardashus A. Aykanian.

Photos

Chapter 1; 1 © Zack Frank/Shutterstock; **Chapter 2; 28** © aiok/Shutterstock; **Chapter 3; 62** © Evgeny Murtola/ Shutterstock; **Chapter 4; 82** © Brandon Bourdages/Shutterstock; **Chapter 5; 105** © Martin Haas/Shutterstock; **Chapter 6; 134** © Woman/Alamy; **Chapter 7; 161** © Lordprice Collection/Alamy; **Chapter 8; 183** © Viktor Gladkov/ Shutterstock; **Chapter 9; 207** © StockLite/Shuttertock; **Chapter 10; 236** © lichtmeister/ Fotolia; **Chapter 11; 262** © hin255/Shutterstock; **Chapter 12; 288** © Jeff Greenberg/Alamy; **Chapter 13; 312** © Yuri Arcurs/Shutterstock; **Chapter 14; 324** © alexskopje/Shutterstock; **Chapter 15; 364** © Elena Elisseeva/Shutterstock; **Chapter 16; 389** © Mark Sykes/Alamy; **Chapter 17; 415** © Gunnar Pippel/Shutterstock; **Chapter 18; 438** © vector_master/Fotolia; **Chapter 19; 470** © Digital Genetics/Shutterstock; **Chapter 20; 514** © Andrey Yurlov/ Shutterstock; **Chapter 21; 534** © Hannamariah/ Shutterstock; **Chapter 22; 556** © Morgan Lane Photography/Shutterstock; **Chapter 23; 584** © Brinkstock/Shutterstock; **Chapter 24; 608** © Rob Byron/Shutterstock; **Chapter 25; 631** © James A. Kost/Shutterstock; **Chapter 26; 658** © Bateman Photo/Shutterstock; **Chapter 27; 687** © Igor Vidyashev/ Shutterstock

Risk Management and Sources of Law

1

LEARNING OBJECTIVES

After completing this chapter, you should be able to:

❶ Explain why it is important for business people to study law.

❷ List four basic strategies for managing risks.

❸ List three strategies for risk management that businesses often use in different situations.

❹ Provide a general definition of the word "law."

❺ List four areas of public law and three areas of private law. Provide examples that demonstrate how each one of those areas is relevant to business people.

❻ Outline one way in which tort and contract law are similar and two ways in which they are different.

❼ Explain how federalism is related to the division of powers.

❽ Describe the *Canadian Charter of Rights and Freedoms* and provide several examples of how it can help or hurt a business.

❾ Explain two meanings of the term "civil law" and three meanings of the term "common law."

❿ Explain the historical development of equity. Briefly explain the relationship between law and equity today.

Law is essential to any society. It both shapes and reflects how people interact. As we will see in this textbook, it can affect a person even before birth (can you sue someone for injuries that you suffered as a fetus?) and even after death (what happens to your property after you are gone?). It also governs the most important issues that arise in between: the freedom to choose a lifestyle, the right to marry, the ability to create and raise children, the obligation to pay taxes, and so on.

Not surprisingly, the law is an enormous subject. As a whole, it cannot be studied in a single course. Indeed, as a whole, it cannot be mastered in an entire lifetime. Therefore, we have to make choices. We must examine some topics and leave others to the side. To a large extent, those choices depend upon our reason for studying law in the first place.

L.O. ❶ ❷ ❸

Why Study Law?

We therefore begin with the obvious question: Why study law? The answer depends upon who you are. As consumers, we all need to be aware of the rules that govern commercial transactions. In terms of employment, you may intend to work in the public sector. If so, you need to understand not only the nature of government organizations, but also the different types of laws that may affect you. Chances are, however, that you are a business student. And as you know, businesses exist primarily to make money. The goal is to maximize gains and minimize losses. Of course, there are many factors in that equation: hard work, natural talent, good luck, and so on. But for the most part, success and failure are the results of choices. A business must choose, for example, a product, a price, a location, and a marketing strategy. And every one of those *business* choices has *legal* consequences. Some consequences are profitable; others are financially disastrous. The difference between winning and losing in the business world often depends upon the ability to make good choices from a legal perspective. That fact suggests, in general terms, both *why* you should study law and *which* parts of the law you should study.

It is important to realize that the law can both hurt *and* help. Many people think of laws only in terms of prohibitions and punishments. For example, if you break the rule against murder, you may be sent to jail. But the law can also allow you to do things that you could not otherwise do. Generally speaking, for instance, I am entitled to ignore my promises. I can stay home and read even if I agreed to meet you at the movies. Beyond the fear of making you angry, there is nothing that compels me to keep my word. In the business world, however, that sort of behaviour simply cannot be tolerated. If I promise to provide materials to your factory, you may act on the assumption that I will deliver. For instance, you may hire extra staff or promise to re-sell the materials to someone else. You therefore need some way of holding me to my word. Your best bet is to persuade me to enter into a *contract*. As we will see in a later chapter, a contract is a legal concept that allows people to create *enforceable* promises. In that situation, you would not have to worry (as much) that I might ignore my promise.

RISK MANAGEMENT

risk management is the process of identifying, evaluating, and responding to the possibility of harmful events

Throughout this book, we will see a number of other ways in which businesses can positively benefit from the law. Much more often, however, we will be concerned about avoiding losses. The main theme of our discussion is that legal education plays a critical role in *risk management*. **Risk management** is the process of identifying, evaluating, and responding to the possibility of harmful events. Business Decision 1.1 provides a simple example.

Business Decision 1.1

Risk Management

One of your ex-employees is hoping to join another company. She has asked you to write a reference letter on her behalf. She obviously does not know that you have a very low opinion of her, largely because you believe that she stole money from your business. Furthermore, since the company that she wants to join is one of your best customers, you are tempted to write a candid letter.

Questions for Discussion

1. Will you write a reference for your ex-employee? If so, what will it say?

Unless you know something about the law of torts, you are not in a position to answer those questions properly. You need to identify, evaluate, and respond to the legal risks involved.

- **Identification:** If you accuse your ex-employee of theft, she may sue you for defamation because your statement would cause a reasonable person to think less of her.[1] More surprisingly, if you unreasonably refuse to write a letter, or if you write an unreasonably brief letter, you may be held liable for reducing the ex-employee's job prospects. In any event, you need to be concerned about *liability*, about actually being held legally responsible. But you also need to be concerned about the possibility of being sued. As we will see in the next chapter, litigation is time-consuming and expensive, even when you win.

- **Evaluation:** Having identified the risk of being sued for defamation, you may decide that a candid letter would nevertheless be legally acceptable. Your allegations may be true. Even if they are not, you may be justified in sharing your suspicions with the other company. Furthermore, you may believe that the arguments in your favour are strong enough to discourage your former employee from suing you.

- **Response:** Finally, having identified and evaluated the risks, you need to formulate a response. You have several options. You can refuse to write a letter. You can write a letter that does not mention your suspicions. Or you can write a letter that accuses your former employee of theft. The choice is still yours. Significantly, however, you are now in a position to make an informed decision. A basic understanding of the law makes you a better business person.

Business Decision 1.1 demonstrates risks that are largely legal and private in nature. While court cases are public events, very few cases ever go before a judge. Most are settled by the parties themselves. As a result, you were mainly concerned about being held liable to your ex-employee. Quite often, however, extra-legal concerns may prove even more important. In addition to potentially leading to liability, an accident may generate bad publicity and damage consumer confidence. Canadians have seen many examples in recent years. In 2008, for example, contamination at a Maple Leaf meat packing plant in Ontario resulted in at least six deaths and dozens of injuries from listeriosis.

---

[1] The tort of defamation is discussed in Chapter 5. As we will see, a reference letter is protected by the defence of qualified privilege, meaning that an inaccurate and harmful statement will not trigger liability if the writer acted in good faith.

Although the company's response to the tragedy was considered by many to have been a textbook example of corporate responsibility, millions of dollars were lost to suspended operations, recalled products, and loss of consumer confidence. Those risks also need to be managed.

Notice that we have been talking about risk *management*. There are potential costs associated with nearly every form of behaviour, and that includes doing nothing at all. A business probably cannot exist, and certainly cannot profit, unless it is willing to take some chances. The goal therefore is not necessarily to eliminate risks; it is to *manage* them. The appropriate strategy depends upon the circumstances.

- **Risk avoidance:** Some risks are so serious that they should be avoided altogether. An automobile that regularly explodes upon impact should be removed from the market. Aside from issues of morality, the financial costs of being held liable will probably outweigh any sales profits.[2]

- **Risk reduction:** Some risks can be reduced to an acceptable level through precautions. For example, a bank that lends $500 000 to a manufacturer realizes that the loan may not be repaid if the economy goes into recession. The bank can, however, protect itself by requiring the business to grant a *mortgage* over its factory. In that case, if the bank does not get its money, it may at least get the property.

- **Risk shifting:** Even if a risk cannot be avoided or reduced, it may be shifted onto another party. We will very shortly introduce two exceptionally important strategies for shifting risks: *insurance* and *exclusion clauses*. There are others. Suppose, for example, that a construction company requires the temporary use of a crane. It has two options. First, it may rent a crane and have it operated by one of its own employees. Second, it may rent a crane and hire an *independent contractor* to operate it.[3] An independent contractor is a person who performs services on behalf of a company, but who is not a regular employee of that company. Although it is often difficult to distinguish between an employee and an independent contractor, there is a crucial difference in terms of risk management. Suppose the worker operates the crane carelessly and injures a bystander. The bystander will certainly be able to sue the person who was actually in control of the equipment. Furthermore, if that person was an employee, then the bystander will also be entitled to sue the company. Even if it did not do anything wrong, a company is *vicariously liable* for the actions of its employees. (We will examine the doctrine of vicarious liability in Chapter 3.) A company is not, however, vicariously liable for an independent contractor. In some situations, it is therefore prudent to have work done by an independent contractor, rather than an employee.

- **Risk acceptance:** It is sometimes appropriate to simply accept a risk. Imagine a golf course that operates behind a factory. It is possible that a wild shot might hit a factory window, and that the golf course might be held responsible for the resulting damage. Nevertheless, if the likelihood of such an accident is small, the club might decide to do nothing at all. It certainly would not close the course to avoid the risk altogether. It might also find that the costs of reducing the risk by erecting a large safety net,

---

[2.] *Grimshaw v Ford Motor Co* (1981) 119 Cal App (3d) 757.

[3.] We will examine the difference between employees and independent contractors in Chapters 3 and 26.

or shifting the risk by buying an insurance policy, are too high. The most sensible approach might be to hope for the best and pay for any windows that are broken.

As we have seen, it sometimes is possible to deal with individual problems as they arise. Many of the most effective forms of risk management, however, apply more broadly. Some are fairly obvious. Businesses should, of course, ensure that employees are carefully selected and properly trained. Other strategies are more legal in nature. We will discuss those strategies in greater detail in later chapters. At this point, it is enough simply to introduce three important concepts.

- **Insurance:** Insurance is a contract in which one party agrees, in exchange for a price, to pay a certain amount of money if another party suffers a loss. There are many types of insurance. For now, we will mention two. Liability insurance provides a benefit if the purchaser is held liable for doing something wrong.[4] Property insurance provides a benefit if the purchaser's property is damaged, lost, or destroyed. (We will examine property insurance in Chapter 17.) In either situation, insurance shifts the risk. For instance, while millions of Canadians buy liability insurance every year, only a fraction of those people are actually sued. Insurance works by spreading the cost of that liability over the entire group.

- **Exclusion and limitation clauses:** Many businesses make money by selling goods or services. Those sales are created by contracts. And those contracts very often contain exclusion or limitation clauses. (We will examine exclusion and limitation clauses in Chapters 9 and 12.) Such a clause is a contractual term that changes the usual rules of liability. The clause may attempt to exclude all risk of liability, or it may exclude liability for certain types of acts or certain types of losses, or it may limit the amount of compensation that is available. For instance, a courier company's contract may say that it cannot be held liable at all, or for more than $100, if it loses, damages, or destroys a package. In another example, if parties conducting business do not create a written contract, a company may attempt to exclude or limit liability by posting a notice somewhere on its premises. The entrance to a car park, for instance, may contain a large sign telling customers that they park at their own risk. While exclusion and limitation clauses are subject to certain rules and restrictions, the law generally allows people to sign away their right to sue.

- **Incorporation:** There are many ways to conduct business. An individual who chooses to act in a personal capacity may be held personally liable for any debts or liabilities incurred by the business. To avoid some of those risks, many businesses are set up as corporations or companies. (We will examine corporations, and others ways of carrying on business, in Chapter 21.) The most significant benefit of incorporation is limited liability. That means that it is usually only the company itself, and not the directors or shareholders, that may be held liable for debts. The company may be lost, but the people behind it will be safe. It is important to realize, however, that the concept of limited liability does not protect individuals from *all* risks. For example, employees, directors, and officers may be held personally liable for the torts that they commit.

[4.] Liability insurance also creates a *duty to defend*. That means that the insurance company is responsible for the litigation, including the costs of hiring lawyers, if its customer is sued by a third party. We will examine liability insurance in Chapter 3.

Risk management does not require you to become a lawyer. It may, however, require you to hire a lawyer. As a business person, you need to know enough about the law to recognize potential problems. In some situations, you will be able to resolve those problems yourself, preferably by taking steps to avoid them in the first place. But in other situations, it makes sense to call in an expert. Although lawyers' fees can be quite high, you may end up paying much more in the long run if you do not seek professional advice at the outset. Compared with the cost of losing a lawsuit or watching a deal collapse, a lawyer's bill is often a bargain. In fact, many businesses have *in-house counsel*. Instead of hiring lawyers from time to time as the need arises, a company may create its own permanent legal department. While that option creates an additional expense, it also provides more efficient risk protection. Lawyers will be on hand not only to resolve legal problems, but also to help identify and prevent them.

L.O. ❹ ❺ ❻ ❼ ❽ ❾ ❿

An Introduction to the Legal System

In the chapters that follow, we will examine various areas of law, including tort, contract, and property. But first, we must discuss the Canadian legal system as a whole. We can do so quite quickly. While it is important for business people to understand the basic structure of the courts, for instance, most of the details can be left to the lawyers.

THE NATURE OF LAW

What are laws? Most people would say that they are rules. That may be true, but it is also clear that not every rule is a law. Sometimes that point is obvious. For example, there is a rule against moving a bishop horizontally across a chessboard, but there certainly is not any law to that effect. Sometimes, however, it is much more difficult to determine whether a rule is also a law. Consider Ethical Perspective 1.1.

Ethical Perspective **1.1**

Rules and Laws

While fishing from a lakeshore, I saw a canoeist tip his boat and fall into the water. Although he screamed for help for more than 20 minutes, I did nothing at all. My motorboat was nearby, and I could have easily rescued him, but I preferred to continue fishing. Was there any rule that required me to get involved? Assuming that the canoeist drowned, can I be held legally responsible?

Most people would agree that I had an obligation to rescue the canoeist, especially since I could have done so safely and easily. However, that rule may exist only in *morality*, and not in *law*. According to an old American case, I could not be held legally responsible even if I had rented the boat to the deceased when I knew that he was drunk.[5] In the same situation today, a Canadian court would undoubtedly impose liability.[6] But if I did not have a business relationship with the canoeist,

the answer would be less clear. The courts traditionally drew a distinction between moral obligations and legal obligations, and generally said that there was no duty to rescue in law. Recently, however, Canadian judges have begun to adopt a different attitude. Consequently, while we now know that there is sometimes both a moral duty *and* a legal duty to rescue, we do not know exactly when that is true.

Questions for Discussion

1. How would you, as a business person, decide when to follow a moral rule, even if you were not obligated to do so by a legal rule?

2. Does your answer depend entirely upon morality? Are there also important business consequences to acting morally or immorally?

[5.] *Crocker v Sundance Northwest Resorts Ltd* (1988) 51 DLR (4th) 321 (SCC). This case is discussed in Chapter 6 (Case Brief 6.5 on page 155).

[6.] *Osterlind v Hill* (1928) 160 NE 301 (Mass).

Ethical Perspective 1.1 demonstrates that it is occasionally difficult to distinguish between moral obligations and legal obligations. However, it also helps us define the word "law." Although philosophers have debated the issue for thousands of years, it is enough for us to say that a **law** is a rule that can be enforced by the courts. If I had merely broken a moral obligation by refusing to rescue the canoeist, then I might be punished, but only through public opinion. Colleagues might stop talking to me, and newspapers might print unflattering articles. However, if I had also broken a legal obligation, then I would have more serious things to worry about. Depending on the precise nature of the legal obligation, a court might put me in jail or require me to compensate the victim's family for his death.

> a **law** is a rule that can be enforced by the courts

Of course, moral issues may arise even if a rule is identified as a law. For instance, as a clothing manufacturer, you may be legally entitled to reduce production costs by using child labour in developing nations. If so, you may be faced with a difficult choice between your heart and your wallet. The Ethical Perspective boxes throughout this book provide many more examples.

A MAP OF THE LAW

Even after it has been distinguished from other types of rules, the law remains an enormous topic. To make sense of it all, we need to organize it into different parts. There are many ways of doing so. In Canada, for example, it is necessary to distinguish between *civil law* and *common law*.[7] **Civil law** systems trace their history to ancient Rome. Since the Roman Empire covered most of Europe, most countries on that continent are still *civilian*. The only civil law *jurisdiction* in Canada, however, is Quebec, which initially borrowed its law from France. (Although it has many different meanings, **jurisdiction** in this situation refers to a geographical area that uses the same set of laws.) **Common law** systems trace their history to England.[8] Consequently, most jurisdictions that were settled by English colonists continue to use the common law. That is true of the rest of Canada, as well as jurisdictions such as Australia, New Zealand, and most of the United States.[9] Since there are significant differences between civil law systems and common law systems, there are also significant differences between the laws that apply in Quebec and the laws that apply in the rest of this country.[10] It is for that reason that we will focus on Canadian laws that apply outside of Quebec. At the same time, however, it is important to recognize that some types of laws are the same across the entire country. That is true, for example, of criminal laws and constitutional laws. We will therefore occasionally consider cases from Quebec.

> **civil law** systems trace their history to ancient Rome

> a **jurisdiction** is a geographical area that uses the same set of laws

> **common law** systems trace their history to England

[7.] There are other systems of law as well, such as Aboriginal law and Islamic law.

[8.] The phrase "common law" refers to the fact that the rules in question were used throughout ancient England, in contrast to the various systems of localized rules that had developed over time.

[9.] The exception in the United States is Louisiana. Like Quebec, it was settled by France and therefore uses a civil law system.

[10.] "Civil law" is a confusing phrase. While it often refers to a legal system that can be traced to ancient Rome, later in this chapter we will encounter another definition of that phrase. Within a common law system, "civil law" may refer to private law rather than public law. For example, when Canadian lawyers talk about "civil litigation," they are usually referring to cases involving contracts or torts. "Common law" is also a confusing phrase. While it often refers to a legal system that can be traced to England, later in this chapter we will see that it may also refer to rules that are made by judges, rather than by legislators. And within the context of rules made by judges, "common law" may refer to those made by judges who sat in the courts of law, as opposed to the courts of equity. (The concepts of "law" and "equity" are explained at the end of this chapter.)

FIGURE 1.1   A Map of the Law

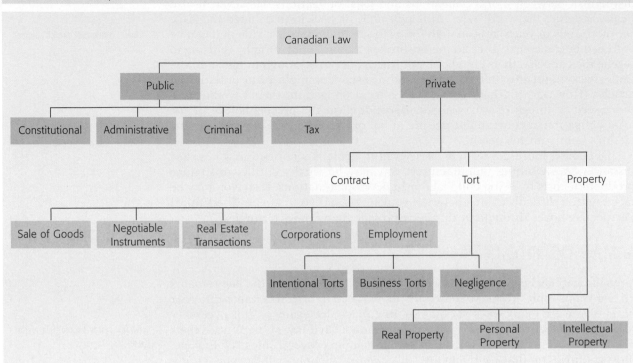

Within Canada's common law system, we can further organize legal rules on the basis of the topics they address. Although it does not cover every possibility, Figure 1.1 represents some of the most important areas that we will discuss in this book.

Public Law

Figure 1.1 shows that the major division is between *public law* and *private law*. **Public law** is concerned with governments and the ways in which they deal with their citizens. It includes

- constitutional law
- administrative law
- criminal law
- tax law

Constitutional law provides the basic rules of our political and legal systems. It determines who is entitled to create and enforce laws, and it establishes the fundamental rights and freedoms that Canadians enjoy. We will discuss the Constitution in more detail in a later part of this chapter.

In the past 50 years, Canadians have grown to expect more and more from their elected officials. To manage the workload, governments regularly *delegate* or *assign* responsibility to a variety of agencies, boards, commissions, and tribunals. **Administrative law** is concerned with the creation and operation of those bodies. It has a profound impact on business. For instance, a human rights tribunal may decide that a corporation discriminated against women by paying them less than it paid men for work of similar value. If so, the company

public law is concerned with governments and the ways in which they deal with their citizens

constitutional law provides the basic rules of our political and legal systems

administrative law is concerned with the creation and operation of administrative agencies, boards, commissions, and tribunals

FIGURE 1.2 Administrative Bodies Affecting Business

Federal	
Canadian Radio-television and Telecommunications Commission	regulates broadcasting and telecommunications systems
National Energy Board	regulates pipelines, energy development, and trade in the energy industry
Canadian International Trade Tribunal	investigates possible violations of international trade regulations
Competition Tribunal	resolves disputes under the *Competition Act* (discussed in Chapter 25)
Provincial or Territorial	
Workers' Compensation Board	promotes workplace safety and rehabilitates and compensates injured workers
Labour Relations Board	assists in the resolution of labour disputes
Environmental Appeal Board	assists in the resolution of environmental disputes
Professional Society (*eg* Law Society of Alberta)	regulates and licenses the practice of a particular profession (*eg* law)
Municipal	
Zoning and Planning Board	regulates the use of land
Building and Inspections Department	regulates and licenses building projects
Licence Division	regulates and licenses business operations

may be ordered to pay millions of dollars in compensation.[11] Even if a particular business never becomes involved in that sort of landmark case, it probably has to deal, in the normal course of operations, with a number of administrative bodies. There are literally hundreds. Figure 1.2 lists a sampling of federal, provincial (or territorial), and municipal bodies that regularly affect business.[12]

Criminal law deals with offences against the state. In other words, it is concerned with people who break rules that are designed to protect society as a whole. For instance, if you punch me, you have committed a *tort* because (as discussed below) you have done something wrong to me personally. However, you have also committed a *crime* because you have done something wrong to the entire community. Even if I am not particularly upset about being hit, society may want to discourage and punish your behaviour. Consequently, the police and the prosecutor may bring you to court even if I would prefer to drop the matter. Although we tend to think of criminals as violent individuals, it is important to know that crime can happen in the business world as well.

criminal law deals with offences against the state

- *White-collar crimes*, as the name suggests, are committed by people in suits. A manager who steals money from the petty-cash drawer is a white-collar criminal.
- A crime can even be committed by a company itself. A *corporate crime* occurs, for instance, when a used-car dealership adopts a policy of rolling

---

[11.] *Bell Canada v Canadian Telephone Employees Association* (2001) 199 DLR (4th) 664 (FC CA).

[12.] This list is not exhaustive. Some bodies serve more than one function. Note that, below the federal level, the name of a particular body may vary from place to place.

back the odometers on its vehicles. That company is guilty of fraud.[13] Case Brief 1.1 discusses another exceptionally important example.

Case Brief 1.1

R v Transpavé Inc 2008 QCCQ 1598 (Ct of Que)

Traditionally, a company could be convicted of a crime only if the criminal acts were performed by the company's "directing mind." In 2004, Parliament amended the *Criminal Code* in an effort to improve workplace safety. Under section 217.1, a company can now be convicted on the basis of acts performed by a long list of individuals, including directors, officers, managers, partners, employees, and agents. The new law states

> Every one who undertakes, or has the authority, to direct how another person does work or performs a task is under a legal duty to take reasonable steps to prevent

bodily that person, or any other person, arising from that work or task.

Although that amendment did not save Steve L'Écuyer's life, it did allow his employer to be punished. Transpavé Inc manufactures concrete products. Steve was killed after being crushed beneath a pallet loader. The evidence indicated that he had not been properly trained and that a safety device on the machine, a motion detector, had been turned off. The court imposed a fine of $110 000. The amount would have been much higher if the company had not spent more than $750 000, after the accident, to upgrade worker safety.

---

tax law is concerned with the rules that are used to collect money for public spending

The various branches of government, such as Parliament, administrative bodies, and courts, require a great deal of money to operate. **Tax law** is concerned with the rules that are used to collect money for public spending. This is an area of great interest to the business community.

Private Law

private law is concerned with the rules that apply in private matters

Although we will occasionally discuss public law, our focus is on *private law*. **Private law** is concerned with the rules that apply in private matters. Both parties in a private dispute are usually private *persons*, either individuals or organizations such as corporations. For instance, your theatre company might sue me if I failed to perform a play as promised. However, private law can also apply to the government. First, it is possible for a private person to sue a public body.[14] Suppose the municipal government carelessly forgot to inspect the foundations of your house while it was being built. If your basement later develops cracks, you could sue the construction company for providing shoddy work, but you could also sue the City for its failure to enforce its own building regulations.[15] The government is also subject to private law rules when it enters into private transactions, such as when a government contractually agrees to purchase paper from a store.

Private law is usually divided into three main parts:

- the law of torts
- the law of contracts
- the law of property

---

13. *R v Waterloo Mercury Sales Ltd* (1974) 49 DLR (3d) 131 (Alta Dist Ct). Corporate crime is discussed in Chapter 22.

14. And vice versa. If you accidentally burned down City Hall, the municipal government could sue you.

15. *Neilson v City of Kamloops* (1984) 10 DLR (4th) 641 (SCC).

We have defined a crime as a public wrong, an offence against society as a whole. A **tort**, in contrast, is a private wrong, an offence against a particular person. The law of torts covers a great deal of territory. For the purposes of discussion, we will split the category into three: (i) *intentional torts*, such as assault and false imprisonment, (ii) *business torts*, such as deceit and conspiracy, and (iii) *negligence*, which covers most situations in which one person carelessly hurts another.

a tort is a private wrong

The **law of contracts** is concerned with the creation and enforcement of agreements. For business people, this is a tremendously important area of law. Business is based on transactions, and the law of contracts governs virtually every one of them. For instance, even if we limit ourselves to the headings in Figure 1.1, we can see that contracts are involved in (i) *the sale of goods*, such as cows and computers, (ii) the use of *negotiable instruments*, such as cheques, (iii) *real estate transactions*, such as the purchase of land, (iv) the operation of *corporations*, and (v) the *employment* relationship that exists between a business and its workers. We will see many more examples throughout this book.

the law of contracts is concerned with the creation and enforcement of agreements

We will have much more to say about torts and contracts in later chapters. Given the tremendous importance of those two subjects, however, you may want to turn to page 64 now for a comparison between those two areas of law.

As the name suggests, the **law of property** is concerned with the acquisition, use, and disposition of property. The discussion is once again divided into three main parts: (i) *real property*, which involves land and things that are attached to land, (ii) *personal property*, which involves things that can be moved from one place to another, and (iii) *intellectual property*, which involves things that consist of original ideas, such as patents and copyrights. All three forms of property are important in business. Every company owns personal property; most have interests in real property; and a growing number rely heavily on intellectual property. There are also several areas of law that deal with all forms of property. For instance, (i) the law of *succession* deals with the distribution of a person's property after death, and (ii) the law of *trusts* deals with a situation in which one person holds property on behalf of another.

the law of property is concerned with the acquisition, use, and disposition of property

Overlap

Before leaving this section, we must stress that different areas of law can overlap. There are at least two possibilities.

- First, a single event can trigger more than one set of rules. We have already mentioned one example. If you punch me, you may commit both a crime and a tort. Other illustrations are more common in the business world. For instance, if you hire lawyers who provide poor work and bad advice, you may have the option of suing them for both the tort of negligence (because they carelessly caused you to suffer a loss) and breach of contract (because they did not act as promised).[16]

- Second, some situations involve various types of laws. For example, an employment relationship is based on a contract between the employer and the employee. Nevertheless, the parties should also have some knowledge of administrative law (in case a company discriminates against ethnic minorities), criminal law (in case a boss sexually harasses an employee), and tort law (in case one worker injures another).

[16.] *Central Trust Co v Rafuse* (1986) 31 DLR (4th) 481 (SCC).

SOURCES OF LAW

In the last section, we organized laws according to topics. In this section, we organize them according to sources. Broadly speaking, there are three sources:

- the Constitution
- legislation
- the courts

As we will see, not all laws are created equal. Some are more important than others.

The Constitution

the **Constitution** is the document that creates the basic rules for Canadian society, including its political and legal systems

The most important source of law is the **Constitution**. This document creates the basic rules for Canadian society, including its political and legal systems.[17] The fact that it provides the foundation for everything else has two significant consequences.

First, every other law in the country must be compatible with it. Section 52 of the Constitution states, "The Constitution of Canada is the supreme law of Canada, and any law that is inconsistent with the provisions of the Constitution is, to the extent of the inconsistency, of no force or effect."

Second, the Constitution is very difficult to change. It is one thing to tinker with, say, the rules that govern the enforcement of contracts. It is a far more serious matter to alter the fundamental rules of Canadian society. Most laws can be changed by a legislature or a court. The Constitution is different; as a general rule, it can be changed only through a special *amending formula*. This requires the consent of Parliament plus the legislatures of at least two-thirds of the provinces, where those consenting provinces represent at least 50 percent of the country's population. Not surprisingly, Constitutional amendments are rare.

Canada is a **federal** country because it has two levels of government

DIVISION OF POWERS   Many parts of the Constitution are important to business people. We will look at two. The first concerns the *division of powers*.[18] To understand that concept, it is necessary to appreciate that Canada is a **federal** country because it has two levels of government.[19]

- **Federal:** The Parliament of Canada, which is located in Ottawa, governs the country as a whole. It is composed of two parts. The House of Commons consists of members of Parliament (MPs), who are elected from every province and territory. The Senate consists of senators, who are appointed to their jobs. Since Canada began life as a British colony and is still part of the British Commonwealth, the Queen of England remains our head of state.[20] In reality, however, the country is run by the political party that has the most MPs. The leader of that party is the prime minister.

- **Provincial and territorial:** In addition to electing MPs to represent them nationally in Ottawa, Canadians also elect politicians to represent

---

[17] *Constitution Act 1982*, being schedule B to the *Canada Act 1982* (UK), 1982, c 11. Although our current Constitution came into force in 1982, it is virtually identical to the *British North America Act*, which contained Canada's first Constitution in 1867: see Constitution Act 1867, 1867 (UK), 30 & 31 Victoria, c 3. The most notable feature of the new Constitution is that it includes the *Canadian Charter of Rights and Freedoms*.

[18] Chapter 25 examines the division of powers as it affects business regulation in Canada.

[19] There is, in fact, a third level of government. Section 92 of the Constitution allows provinces and territories to create municipalities.

[20] The Queen is represented by the governor general.

them within their own provinces and territories.[21] The elected body, or *legislature*, is usually called the Legislative Assembly.[22] And for the most part, each of the 13 legislatures is similar to Parliament. Once again, even though the official head of state is the Queen, power really is held by the party with the most elected members, whose leader is the premier.[23]

Wherever you live in Canada, you are subject to two sets of laws: federal and provincial (or territorial). With respect to any particular issue, however, there is generally only one law. Our system would not work very well, for instance, if Parliament required you to drive on the right side of the road at the same time that your provincial or territorial legislature required you to drive on the left. Sections 91 and 92 of the Constitution therefore establish a **division of powers** by identifying the areas in which each level of government can act. Concept Summary 1.1 lists some areas that are particularly important to business people. Note the last item on the left side of the chart. The federal government has the **residual power**, the power over everything that is not otherwise mentioned. Consequently, Parliament now has authority over a number of topics that did not exist when our original Constitution was written in 1867, such as telecommunications and air travel.

the **division of powers** states the areas in which each level of government can act

residual power gives the federal government authority over everything that is not specifically mentioned

Concept Summary 1.1

Division of Powers

Federal	Provincial or Territorial
criminal law	property and civil rights (*eg* contracts, torts)
taxation	direct taxation to raise money for provincial purposes
employment insurance	the creation of municipalities
banks	matters of a local or private nature within a province
bankruptcy and insolvency	
money	
negotiable instruments (*eg* cheques)	
international and interprovincial trade and commerce	
navigation and shipping	
copyright	
any matter that is not exclusively given to the provinces	

A government sometimes tries to create a law outside of its own area. When it does so, it acts *ultra vires*, which literally means "beyond the power." As a result of section 52 of the Constitution (which we quoted earlier), such laws have "no force or effect." In other words, they are not really laws at all. In one famous case, the federal government tried to create a law that prohibited people from importing or manufacturing margarine. It did so to protect the dairy industry from competition. The Supreme Court of Canada found that that law

---

[21.] Provinces and territories do not have senators.

[22.] There is some variation. Newfoundland and Labrador, for instance, has a House of Assembly, while Quebec has a National Assembly.

[23.] The Queen is represented by a lieutenant governor in each province and by a commissioner in each territory.

was partially invalid.[24] The federal government was entitled to ban the *importation* of margarine because it had authority over international and interprovincial trade. It could not, however, ban the *manufacture* of margarine. Because a province has authority over "property and civil rights," it has the authority to regulate the production or sale of margarine within its own borders.

A different type of problem arises if both levels of government create legislation that conflicts. Consider the example of workplace health and safety aboard a cargo ship. The federal government may create legislation on the basis of its authority over navigation and shipping. A province may create legislation on the basis of its authority over working conditions and labour relations. If a court finds that the issue in a particular case really has more to do with an area of provincial power, then the provincial legislation will be effective.[25] But if the court finds that the two statutes truly are in conflict, then the dispute will be decided by the *doctrine of federal paramountcy*. The **doctrine of federal paramountcy** determines which law is pre-eminent based on the Constitution's division of powers. The federal law wins.

the **doctrine of federal paramountcy** determines which law is pre-eminent based on the Constitution's division of powers

CHARTER OF RIGHTS AND FREEDOMS Traditionally, as long as a government acted within the scope of its power (or *intra vires*), its laws were generally valid. The situation changed dramatically in 1982, when the *Canadian Charter of Rights and Freedoms* was written into the Constitution.[26] As its name indicates, the *Charter* was introduced to protect basic rights and freedoms. As Case Brief 1.2 demonstrates, a law may now be attacked in different ways.

Case Brief 1.2

Irwin Toy Ltd v Quebec (Attorney General) (1989) 58 DLR (4th) 577 (SCC)

Quebec created a law that generally prohibited advertisements aimed at pre-teens. Irwin Toys wanted to advertise its products on television. It argued that the law was unconstitutional because (i) it dealt with television, which is a federal matter, rather than a provincial matter, and (ii) it violated the *Charter* right to freedom of expression.

Division of powers: The Supreme Court of Canada agreed that the federal Parliament has authority over telecommunications as part of its residual power. However, the court also said that the disputed law affected television only in an indirect or incidental way. The province's goal was not to regulate broadcasters; it was to regulate advertisers.

And since the regulation of advertisers is a provincial matter, the law was acceptable under the division of powers.

Charter of Rights and Freedoms: The Supreme Court of Canada agreed that the disputed law violated the right to freedom of expression under section 2(b) of the *Charter*. After all, it prevented the toy company from using television to tell children about its products. However, the court also held that under section 1, the province was justified in placing restrictions on the ability to advertise. Society has an interest in protecting young children from commercial exploitation. Furthermore, the ban was reasonable. For instance, it applied only to toys aimed at children under 13 years of age.

The *Charter* has had a profound impact on virtually every aspect of life in this country. It has, for example, led to the recognition of same-sex marriages,[27] and it may dramatically affect the availability of health care by allowing people to receive treatment outside of the public system.[28] Indeed, it is difficult to understand Canadian law, Canadian politics, or Canadian society without some appreciation of the *Charter*. We will therefore consider it in some detail.

[24.] *Reference Re Validity of s 5(a) of the Dairy Industry Act (Canada)* [1949] 1 DLR 433 (SCC).

[25.] *R v Mersey Seafoods Ltd* (2008) 295 DLR (4th) 244 (NS CA).

[26.] Part I of the *Constitution Act, 1982*, being Schedule B to the *Canada Act, 1982* (UK), 1982, c 11.

[27.] *Reference Re Same-Sex Marriage* (2004) 246 DLR (4th) 193 (SCC).

[28.] *Chaoulli v Quebec (Attorney General)* (2005) 254 DLR (4th) 577 (SCC).

FIGURE 1.3 *Canadian Charter of Rights and Freedoms*

Topic	Section(s)	Illustration or Example
Guarantee	1	"guarantees the rights and freedoms . . . subject only to such reasonable limits prescribed by law as can be demonstrably justified in a free and democratic society"
Fundamental freedoms	2	freedom of religion, expression, peaceful assembly, and association
Democratic rights	3–5	right to vote in House of Commons and Legislative Assembly elections
Mobility rights	6	right to leave and enter Canada; right to live and work in any province
Legal rights	7–14	"right to life, liberty and security of the person"; "right to be secure against unreasonable search or seizure"
Equality rights	15	right to be free from discrimination
Official languages	16–22	"English and French are the official languages of Canada"
Minority language education	23	limited right to have children educated in either official language
Enforcement	24	a court may respond to a *Charter* violation with any "remedy [it] considers appropriate and just in the circumstances"
General	25–31	the *Charter* shall be interpreted for the "preservation and enhancement of the multicultural heritage of Canadians"
Application	32–33	the *Charter* applies to federal and provincial governments

The *Charter* covers a great deal of territory. Figure 1.3 identifies and illustrates all of the rights and freedoms. (A complete copy of the *Charter* is available through MyBusLawLab.)

For present purposes, we will focus on three sections of the *Charter* which, in addition to affecting Canadians generally, sometimes have an impact on businesses.

Fundamental Freedoms

2 Everyone has the following fundamental freedoms:
  (a) freedom of conscience and religion;
  (b) freedom of thought, belief, opinion and expression, including freedom of the press and other media of communication;
  (c) freedom of peaceful assembly; and
  (d) freedom of association.

Mobility Rights

6 (1) Every citizen of Canada has the right to enter, remain in and leave Canada.
  (2) Every citizen of Canada and every person who has the status of a permanent resident of Canada has the right
    (a) to move to and take up residence in any province; and
    (b) to pursue the gaining of a livelihood in any province. . . .

Equality Rights

15 (1) Every individual is equal before and under the law and has the right to the equal protection and equal benefit of the law without discrimination and, in particular, without discrimination based on race, national or ethnic origin, colour, religion, sex, age or mental or physical disability.

(2) Subsection (1) does not preclude any law, program or activity that has as its object the amelioration of conditions of disadvantaged individuals or groups including those that are disadvantaged because of race, national or ethnic origin, colour, religion, sex, age or mental or physical disability.

A court may be able to choose from amongst several remedies if the *Charter* has been violated. We will consider some of those remedies in greater detail below. For now, it is enough to know that since the *Charter* is part of the Constitution, any law that is inconsistent with it has "no force or effect." From a business perspective, the results can be quite dramatic. A few examples, based on the rights that have been quoted, demonstrate that point.

- To protect Christian beliefs, Parliament created a law that required most stores to close on Sundays. That law was declared invalid because it discriminated against non-Christians.[29] It violated their freedom of religion under section 2(a).

- Alberta created a law that prohibited law firms in that province from creating partnerships with law firms in other provinces. That law was declared invalid because it prevented lawyers from working in different parts of the country.[30] It violated their mobility rights under section 6(2).

- British Columbia passed a law that prevented people who were not Canadian citizens from practising law in that province. That law was declared invalid because it discriminated against people on the basis of their national origin.[31] It violated their right to equality under section 15(1).

property rights are rights to own and enjoy assets

economic rights are rights to carry on business activities

Although the *Charter* may affect business people, it is important to realize that it does not contain **property rights** (to own and enjoy assets) or **economic rights** (to carry on business activities). On the contrary, the people who drafted the *Charter* expressly rejected a right to "the enjoyment of property." They worried that such a right would, for instance, hamper the government's ability to protect the environment, regulate the use of property, control resource-based industries, or restrict foreign ownership of Canadian land. They also worried that economic rights would allow wealthy individuals to frustrate government policies aimed at helping the less fortunate. As a result, the Supreme Court of Canada has said that there is no *Charter* right to "unconstrained freedom" in economic activities, nor is there an "unconstrained right to transact business whenever one wishes."[32] Against that backdrop, it is ironic that the general denial of economic rights has actually made it *more* difficult for disadvantaged Canadians to force governments to provide social assistance.[33] The courts, for instance, have refused to interpret the *Charter* in a way that ensures that every person enjoys accommodation or a certain standard of living. They also have held that poverty does not sit alongside ideas such as race, sex, or religion, as a prohibited ground of discrimination under section 15 of the *Charter*.[34]

Leaving aside the general exclusion of property rights and economic rights, the *Charter* is also subject to a number of other important restrictions. Those restrictions reveal a great deal about the *Charter*'s role in Canadian society.

---

[29] *R v Big M Drug Mart Ltd* (1985) 18 DLR (4th) 321 (SCC).

[30] *Black v Law Society of Alberta* (1989) 58 DLR (4th) 317 (SCC).

[31] *Andrews v Law Society (British Columbia)* (1989) 56 DLR (4th) 1 (SCC).

[32] It had been argued that economic and property rights were protected by section 7 of the *Charter*, which states that everyone "has the right to life, liberty and security of the person." The court denied that "liberty" generally includes economic liberty.

[33] *Gosselin v Quebec (Attorney General)* (2002) 221 DLR (4th) 257 (SCC).

[34] *Boulter v Nova Scotia Power Inc* (2009) 307 DLR (4th) 293 (NS CA).

- **Government action:** The *Charter* was introduced to govern the relationship between the individual and the state. Section 32(1) states that the document applies to "Parliament" and "the legislature . . . of each province." Consequently, the *Charter*'s rights and freedoms have full effect only if a person is complaining about the government's behaviour.[35] The *Charter* does not directly apply to disputes involving private parties. For instance, the right to freedom of expression that is found in section 2(b) does not entitle a union to picket a private corporation.[36] Interestingly, however, the Supreme Court of Canada has said that private law should be developed in a way that is consistent with *Charter* values.[37] It is not yet clear exactly what that means.

- **Corporations:** The *Charter* generally does not apply *against* private corporations. It may not apply in *favour* of them either. It depends on the circumstances. It has been decided, for example, that a corporation enjoys freedom of expression under section 2(b), but not equality rights under section 15. Section 2(b) extends to "everyone," whereas section 15 applies only to "every individual." A corporation is a type of person, but it is not an "individual."[38] Furthermore, while a corporation has a need to express itself, it does not possess the sort of dignity and sense of self-worth that lies at the heart of equality.[39]

- **Reasonable limits:** Section 1 of the *Charter* states that its rights and freedoms are subject to "such reasonable limits prescribed by law as can be demonstrably justified in a free and democratic society." The Constitution therefore recognizes that it is occasionally acceptable to violate a person's rights. In one famous case, the Supreme Court of Canada held that a shop owner's freedom of expression was infringed by a law that prevented him from selling violent pornography.[40] However, the judges also held that society was justified in banning that sort of material because it is degrading, dehumanizing, and harmful to women. The law was therefore enforceable, and the shop owner was prohibited from selling the offending material.

- **Notwithstanding clause:** Section 33 may allow Parliament or a legislature to create and enforce a law "notwithstanding" the fact that it violates the *Charter*.[41] That is, of course, a serious matter. It requires the government to expressly declare that it is overriding fundamental rights and freedoms. Canadians generally oppose such a move. As a result, section 33 has been used only once in the common law of provinces

---

[35] In this context, "government" refers to Parliament, the legislatures, and other organizations that are closely controlled by the government, including the police and community colleges, but not universities and hospitals. *Pridgen v University of Calgary* (2010) 325 DLR (4th) 441 (Alta QB).

[36] *RWDSU Local 580 v Dolphin Delivery Ltd* (1986) 33 DLR (4th) 174 (SCC).

[37] *Dobson v Dobson* (1999) 174 DLR (4th) 1 (SCC).

[38] Although "everyone" includes both people and corporations, not all of the freedoms listed in section 2 are available to companies. For instance, while a corporation will benefit from freedom of expression, it cannot have religious beliefs that deserve protection. The employees of a corporation, however, may hold religious beliefs, which is why Sunday closing laws can be declared invalid (as discussed above).

[39] *R v Rockwood* (2007) 287 DLR (4th) 471 (Nfld CA).

[40] *R v Butler* (1992) 89 DLR (4th) 449 (SCC). As we saw in Case Brief 1.2, the court also relied on section 1 in finding that a law restricting advertising to pre-teens was justified as a limitation on the right to freedom of expression.

[41] The notwithstanding clause is not available for all of the rights and freedoms listed in the *Charter*. Parliament or a legislature can override section 2 (fundamental freedoms) or section 15 (equality rights), for instance, but not section 6 (mobility rights). Furthermore, the notwithstanding clause can be used for only five years at a time. At the end of that period, the clause must be re-applied. This rule ensures that significant constitutional rules are re-examined on a regular basis.

and territories.[42] The situation has been different in Quebec, perhaps because of the feeling that the *Charter* was introduced without sufficient regard to that province's special status. An interesting example arose in connection with Bill 101, which prohibited the use of languages other than French on outdoor signs. Although that law violated the *Charter's* right to freedom of expression, Quebec's government used section 33 so that its law applied notwithstanding the *Charter*.[43]

CHARTER REMEDIES   What happens if the *Charter* has been violated? We have already seen that any law that is inconsistent with the *Charter* is "of no force or effect." Section 24 of the *Charter* further states that a court may award "such remedy as [it] considers appropriate and just in the circumstances." The precise nature of the court's response therefore depends upon the situation.

We can list a few of the more important possibilities. Notice that some remedies are more active than others. Judges try to strike a balance between respecting the legislature and respecting the *Charter*. They are, nevertheless, sometimes criticized for going too far—for *making* laws rather than *applying* them. (See You Be the Judge 1.1 on the following page.)

- **Declaration:** A court may simply *declare* that the *Charter* has been violated. The legislature must then find some solution to the problem.[44]

- **Injunction:** A court may take a more active role. It may impose an *injunction* that requires the government to address the problem in a certain way. (We will examine injunctions in more detail in Chapters 3 and 12.) The choice therefore lies with the judge, rather than the legislature.[45]

- **Striking down:** Going even further, a court may *strike down* or eliminate a statute that violates the *Charter*. That decision may take effect immediately or it may be *temporarily suspended*.[46] A temporary suspension is appropriate where the immediate elimination of a statute would create substantial problems.[47]

- **Severance, reading down, and reading in:** Sometimes, a court may save a statute by re-writing part of it. If only one part of a statute is offensive, it may be *severed* or cut out.[48] If a statute is written too broadly, it may be *read down* so that it applies only where it can be justified.[49] In contrast, if a statute is written too narrowly, the court may *read in* a broader interpretation, so that certain people are not excluded from its benefits.[50]

- **Damages:** A plaintiff who wins a private lawsuit usually receives damages for the injuries or losses that have been suffered. (We will examine damages in more detail in Chapters 3 and 12.) The same remedy may

---

[42.] The province of Saskatchewan applied section 33 to protect back-to-work legislation from potential *Charter* attack. Interestingly, however, the notwithstanding clause was not actually necessary, since the Supreme Court of Canada later held that the legislation was valid in any event: *RWDSU v Saskatchewan* (1987) 38 DLR (4th) 277 (SCC).

[43.] *Ford v Quebec (Attorney General)* (1988) 54 DLR (4th) 577 (SCC). A Parti Québécois government had previously applied the notwithstanding clause to all of Quebec's legislation: *Alliance des professeurs de Montréal v Quebec (Attorney General)* (1985) 21 DLR (4th) 354 (Que CA).

[44.] *Eldridge v British Columbia (Attorney General)* (1997) 151 DLR (4th) 577 at 631–632 (SCC) ("there are myriad options available to the government that may rectify the unconstitutionality of the current system" and it was "not this Court's role to dictate how this is to be accomplished").

[45.] *Marchand v Simcoe County Board of Education* (1986) 29 DLR (4th) 596 (Ont HCJ).

[46.] *R v Big M Drug Mart Ltd* (1985) 18 DLR (4th) 321 (SCC).

[47.] *Reference Re Manitoba Language Rights* (1985) 19 DLR (4th) 1 (SCC).

[48.] *Canada (Employment and Immigration Commission) v Tétreault-Gadoury* (1991) 81 DLR (4th) 358 (SCC).

[49.] *R v Sharpe* (2001) 194 DLR (4th) 1 (SCC).

[50.] *Miron v Trudel* (1995) 124 DLR (4th) 693 (SCC).

be awarded to a person who has suffered a *Charter* violation.[51] *Charter* damages are intended to compensate the plaintiff's loss, vindicate the plaintiff's rights, and deter or discourage future wrongdoing.[52]

You Be the Judge 1.1

Charter Remedies[53]

The *Family Benefits Act* provides social assistance to any "mother whose dependent child was born out of wedlock." Charles Phillips, a single father, cares for his daughter, who was born out of wedlock. Phillips applied for benefits under the statute but was denied assistance because he is a father, rather than a mother. He has shown that the Act violates his right to equality under section 15(1) of the *Charter*. You are now required to decide the appropriate remedy.

Questions for Discussion

1. The province argues that it should have the right to determine which citizens receive social assistance, and that the only appropriate remedy is to strike down the entire statute. Do you agree? If so, what will happen to single mothers who care for children born out of wedlock?

2. Phillips argues that he should be entitled to receive benefits under the Act. Do you agree? If so, which remedy will you use? Is it possible to achieve the desired result through severance, reading down, reading in, or damages?

As we have seen, judges have a great deal of power under the *Charter*. It is important to appreciate, however, that the *Charter* was not intended to destroy the doctrine of *parliamentary supremacy*. **Parliamentary supremacy** means that while judges are required to interpret constitutional and statutory documents, they must also obey them. For that reason, Canadian judges present their decisions as part of an ongoing *dialogue*. Even when they strike down a law, they are merely indicating that the legislature failed to follow the rules. The government is often able to respond by creating a new law that properly respects the *Charter*. Case Brief 1.3 illustrates the idea of a dialogue.

parliamentary supremacy means that while judges are required to interpret constitutional and statutory documents, they must also obey them

Case Brief 1.3

RJR MacDonald v Canada (Attorney General) (1995) 127 DLR (4th) 1 (SCC)

Canada v JTI—Macdonald Corp (2007) 281 DLR (4th) 598 (SCC)

The federal government introduced legislation that imposed a *complete* ban on virtually all tobacco advertisements. One of the major tobacco companies complained that the statute violated its right to freedom of expression under section 2(b) of the *Charter*. The Supreme Court of Canada agreed and struck down the legislation. However, the court also indicated that a *partial* ban on advertising would be acceptable. In effect, it invited Parliament to try again.

The government accepted that invitation and enacted new legislation. The tobacco company once again made a constitutional challenge, but this time, the Supreme Court held that while certain legislative provisions violated the *Charter*'s guarantee of free speech, the whole statute could be justified under section 1. Parliament therefore is entitled to ban advertising that is false or misleading, that is aimed at children, or that suggests a connection to attractive lifestyles. The government is also entitled to require that at least half of every cigarette package be given over to health warnings.

[51.] *Jane Doe v Metropolitan Toronto (Municipality) Commissioners of Police* (1998) 160 DLR (4th) 697 (Ont Gen Div).

[52.] *Ward v Vancouver* (2010) 321 DLR (4th) 1 (SCC).

[53.] *Phillips v Nova Scotia (Social Assistance Appeal Board)*(1986) 27 DLR (4th) 156 (NS SC TD), aff'd (1986) 34 DLR (4th) 633 (CA).

Legislation

legislation is law that is created by Parliament or a legislature

The Constitution, including the *Charter*, is the first source of law. *Legislation* is the second. **Legislation** is law that is created by Parliament or a legislature. The most important kinds of legislation are *statutes*, or *acts*. For example, every jurisdiction in Canada has an act that allows companies to be created.[54] And the *Criminal Code*, which is a federal statute that applies across the country, determines when a crime has been committed.[55]

THE LEGISLATIVE PROCESS The legislative process provides an important opportunity for risk management. That may seem surprising. After all, when we talk about risk management, we are usually worried about laws that already exist. Sometimes, however, the best strategy is either to prevent the creation of a law or to make sure that it is written in a way that causes as little trouble as possible.

We will focus on the legislative process at the federal level.[56] As we saw earlier, Parliament consists of the House of Commons and the Senate. In most cases, a *bill* is introduced into the House of Commons by an MP.[57] If the majority of MPs support it, it passes the *first reading*, usually without much discussion. Some time later, the bill re-appears for *second reading*, when it is the subject of debate amongst the MPs. If it once again enjoys majority support, it is sent to a legislative committee for detailed study. After that, the bill re-appears for a *third reading*, when the MPs take a final vote. If the bill passes that stage, it is sent to the Senate, where the three-stage process is repeated. If all goes well, and the bill is passed by Parliament, it simply requires one last formality. Since the head of state in Canada technically is the Queen, the bill must receive *royal assent*, which is Her Majesty's approval. That approval is given on her behalf by the governor general.[58]

Members of Canadian society may influence the legislative process during at least three stages. First, although you cannot introduce a bill into Parliament, you may *lobby*, or encourage, an MP to do so. Because of the influence that some lobbyists have, their activities are controlled by legislation. Those rules are, however, difficult to enforce. Politicians often meet with business people, and it is difficult to know when a conversation crosses the line between casual chat and improper lobbying. Second, before a bill appears for second reading, you may contact an MP and express any concerns that you may have. The MP may then raise those concerns during debate. And finally, legislative committees often receive advice and assistance from people outside Parliament. If you are concerned about any particular aspect of a bill, you may have a chance to be heard in committee.

SUBORDINATE LEGISLATION AND MUNICIPALITIES It is impossible for Parliament and the legislatures to constantly monitor all of their legislation to make sure that it is effective and up to date. Therefore, statutes often set

---

[54] The usual name is the *Business Corporations Act*, the *Corporations Act*, or the *Companies Act*. Those statutes are examined in Chapter 21.

[55] *Criminal Code*, RSC 1985, c C-46.

[56] The process is much the same at the provincial and the territorial level. The main difference is that the provinces and territories do not have senates.

[57] A bill sometimes is introduced in the Senate, where it must pass before being sent to the House of Commons.

[58] In a province or territory, the Queen's royal assent is given by her lieutenant governor or commissioner.

up a basic structure but allow someone else (such as a government minister, a commission, or a tribunal) to create specific rules without the need to go through the entire legislative process. Those regulations are known as **subordinate legislation**.[59] For example, Parliament created the Canadian Radio-television and Telecommunications Commission (CRTC) and gave it the power to regulate broadcasting in Canada. It is the CRTC, rather than Parliament, that decides which channels appear on your television.

One of the most important types of subordinate legislation involves *municipalities*. The Constitution is concerned with only two levels of government: federal and provincial (or territorial). However, a third level is needed. For instance, neither Parliament nor the legislature will decide whether cats can roam free in a particular town. That decision must be made locally. The Constitution gives the provinces the power to create **municipalities**, which are towns or cities. And when a province creates a municipality, it gives that new body the authority to pass **by-laws**, which are a type of subordinate legislation. Although municipalities are the lowest level of government, their impact on business can be significant.[60] Amongst other things, by-laws are used to license businesses, impose some sorts of taxes, plan commercial developments, and regulate parking. City Hall is a powerful place.[61]

> **subordinate legislation** is the term given to regulations that are created with the authority of Parliament or the legislature

> a **municipality** is a town or city

> a **by-law** is a type of subordinate legislation that is created by a municipality

The Courts

The *courts* are the third source of law. Judges certainly play a crucial role in connection with the other two sources of law. They must *interpret* and apply the words that appear in the Constitution and in legislation. At this point, however, we are concerned with rules that courts actually *create*.

The process that courts use to create laws is too large to fully consider in this section. We will therefore return to that topic in the next chapter. For present purposes, it will be enough to introduce two important concepts: *common law* and *equity*.

COMMON LAW Although lawyers often refer to judge-made rules as "the common law," that phrase has at least three different meanings, depending upon whether it refers to a *system of law*, a *source of law*, or a *type of court*.

- **Systems:** We previously used the term "common law" to refer to legal systems that can be traced to England, and compared the common law system that operates throughout most of Canada to the civil law system that Quebec borrowed from France.

- **Sources:** Within a common law system, the term "common law" can also be used in a more specific way to refer to rules that are created by judges rather than by legislators or the drafters of the Constitution. Most of the rules in contract law, for instance, are common law rules because they were developed by the courts. Statutes apply only to certain small areas of contract. The law of taxation, in contrast, is almost completely based on statutes. For the most part, judges simply interpret and apply the legislation.

[59.] There are various types of subordinate legislation, including regulations, by-laws, statutory instruments, ordinances, and Orders-in-Council. The appropriate one depends on the circumstances.

[60.] *Adult Entertainment Association of Canada v Ottawa* (2007) 283 DLR (4th) 704 (Ont CA).

[61.] *1254582 Alberta Ltd v Edmonton (City)* (2009) 306 DLR (4th) 310 (Alta CA).

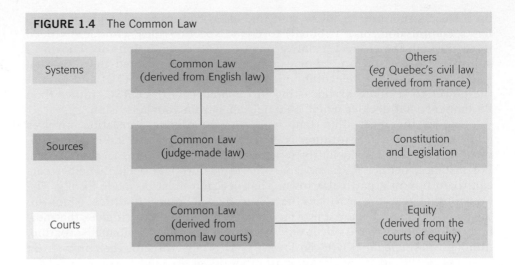

FIGURE 1.4 The Common Law

- **Courts:** Finally, if we limit our discussion to judge-made rules, we can use the phrase "common law" in an even more specific way. England traditionally had two sets of courts: the *courts of law* and the *courts of equity*.[62] Lawyers sometimes still talk about the "common law" when referring to rules developed in the first type of court, and about "equity" when referring to rules developed in the second type of court. We will examine that difference in greater detail in the next section.

Figure 1.4 uses a diagram to explain the various meanings of the term "common law."

LAW AND EQUITY The legal system that developed in England originally had only one type of court: *courts of law*. And because those courts usually insisted on applying the strict letter of the law, they were often rigid and harsh. At the same time, however, the king (or queen) was seen as the ultimate source of law.

Consequently, people who were unhappy with decisions they received in the courts could ask the king for relief. Not surprisingly, the king was too busy to deal with all of those *petitions* personally. He therefore asked the *chancellor*, who was his legal and religious adviser, to act on his behalf. As the number of petitions continued to increase, the chancellor asked other people to act on his behalf. The chancellor and the people under him eventually became recognized as a separate court that was known as the *court of equity* (or the *court of chancery*).

That name reflects the way in which the new court originally decided cases. The king, the chancellor, and the chancellor's men simply did what they believed was right. Unlike the courts of law, they were much less concerned with rigid rules and much more concerned with justice. In other words, their decisions were based on **equity**, which, in a general sense, means fairness.

equity is, in a general sense, fairness

[62.] The ancient courts of law in England consisted of the Court of Common Pleas (which largely dealt with civil disputes between commoners), the Court of Exchequer (which largely dealt with cases involving questions of revenue and the king's property), and the Court of King's Bench (which dealt with criminal cases, cases involving the king, and appeals from the other courts).

Equity continues to play an important role in our legal system. However, it is much different from when it was first created. Two changes are especially significant.

- **The nature of equity:** The concept of equity no longer allows judges to decide cases simply on the basis of fairness. Like the courts of law, the courts of equity eventually developed and applied a consistent set of rules. Equity may still be slightly more flexible than law. But for the most part, those two systems are different only because they occasionally apply different rules. For instance, if I break a contract by refusing to transfer a house to you, the law says that you are entitled only to the *monetary value* of that house, not to the property itself. Equity, however, may be willing to grant *specific performance* and force me to actually transfer the house to you.

- **One set of courts:** Initially, the courts of law and the courts of equity were completely separate. They occupied different buildings; they used different judges; they heard from different lawyers. At the end of the nineteenth century, however, the two court systems were joined into one. Consequently, nearly every Canadian court is now a court of law *and* a court of equity. The same judges apply both sets of rules.[63]

Given that there has been a "fusion" of the courts of law and equity, it may seem strange that we continue to draw a distinction between them. And, in fact, in some circumstances, Canadian courts have begun to ignore the historical differences. A good example occurs in connection with the protection of secrets. If you stole secret information that I had regarding the location of a gold mine, I traditionally would go to a court of equity and sue you for breach of confidence. Recently, however, the Supreme Court of Canada has said that breach of confidence is neither equitable nor legal, but rather a unique combination of the two.[64] Nevertheless, the distinction between law and equity remains critically important for some purposes.

The division between law and equity is especially important with respect to a *trust*. A **trust** exists anytime that one person owns property for the benefit of another. A trust may arise in a variety of ways. The most common type is an express trust, which is created when one person, called the *settlor*, transfers property to another person, called the *trustee*, to hold on behalf of the *beneficiary*. The trustee legally owns the property, but more importantly, the beneficiary is the equitable owner. Assume, for example, that a set of grandparents wants to give $500 000 to a grandchild, but are worried that the grandchild, still young and occasionally foolish, may waste the money. They therefore transfer the money to a trustee to hold on behalf of the grandchild. The grandparents may tell the trustee to use the fund to pay for the grandchild's education and to hand over any money that remains when the grandchild reaches the age of 30. An express trust also may be used for business purposes, as explained in Business Decision 1.2.

a **trust** exists anytime that one person owns property for the benefit of another

---

[63] If there is any inconsistency, the equitable rules apply.

[64] *LAC Minerals Ltd v International Corona Resources* (1989) 61 DLR (4th) 14 at 74 (SCC). We will consider breach of confidence again in Chapters 4 and 18.

Law, Equity, and the Trust

You own a small airline. Like other airlines, your airline does most of its business through travel agents. Those agents attract passengers, issue tickets, and receive payment on your behalf. Unfortunately, a travel agent may become bankrupt. And if that happens, you may not receive all of the money that customers have paid to the agent for seats on your planes. Even if you can show that the money from the customers is still sitting in the agent's bank account, there will be many other people, just like you, who are demanding payment. The amount of money that you receive will depend upon whether your relationship with the agent exists in law or in equity.

Law: If your relationship with the agent exists only in law, you will receive little, if any, money. Although the agent sold tickets on your behalf, they received payment from the customers for *themself*. The money belonged entirely to the agent as soon as it was received. The agent merely promised that they would pay the appropriate amount to you when asked to do so. Of course, the agent also promised to pay a

number of other people as well. And unfortunately, there is not enough money to go around. Each of you might receive a few cents on each dollar.

Equity: The result will be much different if you entered into an equitable relationship with the agent. If so, then when the agent sold tickets on your behalf, they received payment from the customers on *trust* for you. Although the common law will say that the agent owns the money, equity will say that you are the real, or *beneficial*, owner. It will also say that the agent cannot pay their debts with your money. You therefore are entitled to take everything in the bank account—perhaps leaving nothing behind for anyone else.

Questions for Discussion

1. We will consider trusts again in Chapter 8. As you can already see, however, they can be very useful. Is there any reason why you would not always insist upon receiving payment by way of a trust?

Chapter Summary

The study of law is important to business because of the need for risk management. Risk management is the process of identifying, evaluating, and responding to the possibility of harmful events. Depending on the circumstances, a business can pursue various strategies for risk management, including risk avoidance, risk reduction, risk shifting, and risk acceptance.

A law is a rule that can be enforced by the courts. It is important to distinguish laws from other types of rules, including rules of morality. With the exception of Quebec, Canada is a common law country because its legal system was adopted from England. Canadian law can be divided into public law and private law. Public law is concerned with governments and the ways in which they deal with people. Examples of public law include constitutional law, administrative law, criminal law, and tax law. Constitutional law provides the basic rules of our legal system. Administrative law is concerned with the creation and operation of administrative bodies. Criminal law deals with offences against the state. And tax law is concerned with the rules that are used to collect money for public spending. Private law is concerned with the rules that apply in private matters. Examples include tort law, contract law, and property law. The law of torts is concerned with private wrongs; the law of contracts is concerned with the creation and enforcement of agreements; the law of property governs the acquisition, use, and disposition of property.

The three sources of law are the Constitution, Parliament and the legislatures, and the courts. The most important is the Constitution, which is the document that creates the basic rules for Canadian society. Section 52 of that document says that any law that is inconsistent with the Constitution is "of no force or effect." Canada is a federal country because it has two levels of government: federal and provincial or territorial. Sections 91 and 92 of the Constitution create a division of powers by stating the areas in which each level of government can create laws. A government that tries to create a law outside of its own area acts *ultra vires*. The *Canadian Charter of Rights and Freedoms* is a part of the Constitution that protects basic rights and freedoms. Although many of its provisions are quite broad, the *Charter* is also subject to several restrictions. It applies only against government behaviour; it may not apply in favour of corporations; it is subject to reasonable limits; and some of its sections can be overridden by the notwithstanding clause. If a *Charter* right or freedom has not been respected, a court may award a number of remedies, including a declaration, an injunction, striking down, severance, reading down, reading in, and damages.

Legislation is law that is created through the authority of Parliament or a legislature. As a matter of risk management, it is sometimes possible for business people to affect the creation of a law during the legislative process. Subordinate legislation, which is law that is created by someone on behalf of Parliament or the legislature, is important to municipalities.

Parliamentary supremacy requires that the courts obey the Constitution and elected officials. Nevertheless, in some areas, the courts do have the authority to create laws. Historically, there were two court systems: courts of law and courts of equity. Equity was developed in response to the harsh nature of law. Today, there is only one court system. Every Canadian judge applies both legal rules and equitable rules. The concept of equity no longer allows judges to decide cases simply on the basis of fairness. In some situations, however, equity is different from law. Equity recognizes a trust, which exists when a settlor transfers property to a trustee to hold on behalf of a beneficiary.

MyBusLawLab   ADDITIONAL RESOURCES FOR CHAPTER 1

MyBusLawLab provides students with an assortment of tools to help enrich the learning experience, including a Study Plan with Pre- and Post-tests, mini-cases with assessments, and provincial content material, which provides links to relevant cases, legislation, and additional resources.

MyBusLawLab provides the following resources for Chapter 1:

- *Constitution Act 1867*, sections 91 and 92
- *Canadian Charter of Rights and Freedoms*

Provincial Material

- **British Columbia:** British Columbia's Legislative Process, Statutory Interpretation, Municipal By-laws, British Columbia's Electoral System, Government Lobbyists
- **Alberta:** *Adult Interdependent Relationships Act*, *Alberta Human Rights Code,* Civil Enforcement, *Civil Enforcement Amendment Act (2009)*, *Human Rights, Citizenship and Multiculturalism Amendment Act,* Jurisdiction, *Notice to the Attorney General Act (2011)*
- **Manitoba and Saskatchewan:** Charter Cases, Ethics and the Law, Government Made Law—Statutes, Human Rights, Lawyers and Ethics
- **Ontario:** Agreements to Share Power, Business Ethics, *Charter of Rights and Freedoms,* Corporate Codes of Ethics, Human Rights Legislation, Jurisdiction, Legislation, Same-Sex Marriage, Public Liability Insurance
- **Atlantic Provinces:** Human Rights, Law Societies

Review Questions

1. Briefly define the term "risk management." Why is risk management important in the business world and how is it related to the study of law?

2. What are the three steps that are involved in risk management? Illustrate your answer with an example.

3. Briefly explain how incorporation may be used for the purposes of risk management.

4. What is "in-house counsel"? Identify an advantage and a disadvantage of in-house counsel.

5. "'White-collar crime' and 'corporate crime' are two phrases that mean exactly the same thing." Is that statement true? Explain your answer.

6. What is the difference between public law and private law? Can the government ever be involved in a private law case?

7. What is administrative law? Explain how it is relevant to business.

8. Briefly explain the nature and significance of section 217.1 of the *Criminal Code*.

9. Briefly outline three areas of private law. Provide an example of each that is important to business.

10. What is the significance of section 52 of the Constitution? How is that section related to the concept of *ultra vires* legislation?

11. "The Constitution provides the basic rules for Canadian society. And because it needs to continually reflect the nature of that society, the Constitution is easy to amend or change." Explain whether or not that statement is accurate.

12. "People usually have a closer connection to their provincial government than to their federal government. As a result, although the doctrine of paramountcy favours the federal government, the residual power gives the provinces authority over topics that are not

expressly granted to the federal government." Is that statement true? Explain your answer.

13. Briefly explain how the introduction of the *Canadian Charter of Rights and Freedoms* changed Canadian constitutional law. Did it increase or decrease the grounds upon which laws can be declared invalid?

14. Does the *Charter* contain general property or economic rights? Explain why the drafters of the *Charter* did or did not include such rights.

15. Describe four restrictions to the application of the *Charter*.

16. "Damages require one person to pay money as compensation for another person's loss. Damages are therefore a private matter. Since the *Charter* is part of public law, damages cannot be awarded in response to a *Charter* violation." Is that statement true? Explain your answer.

17. "Subordinate legislation is a type of law that only a municipality can create." Is that statement true? Briefly explain the nature of subordinate legislation.

18. What is a "by-law"? Which level of government creates by-laws?

19. Does a trust arise under the "common law" or under "equity"? Explain your answer.

20. Explain the historical difference between law and equity. Are law and equity still separate systems of law?

Cases and Problems

1. The Nagatomi Corporation is Canada's largest manufacturer of farm machinery. It specializes in custom-designing equipment to meet its customers' individual needs. Inga Raimani operates a farm in the foothills of Alberta. Because the terrain in the area is quite uneven in places, she cannot use a standard harvesting machine. Unfortunately, the custom-built harvester that she has used for the past 23 years was destroyed in a fire last winter. Immediately after the accident, she contacted Nagatomi and ordered a replacement. She stressed to the sales representative that she absolutely needed the machine by the first day of September. The parties drafted a contract, which contained the following provisions:

   (5) The Nagatomi Corp shall deliver the unit by the last day of August of the current year.

   (6) Inga Raimani shall pay the full price of $150 000 before delivery.

   (9) In the event that payment is not received by the last day of August of the current year, Inga Raimani shall lose the right to demand possession of the machine and the Nagatomi Corp shall have the right to sell the machine to another customer. If the machine is re-sold to another customer, Inga Raimani shall compensate the Nagatomi Corp for any expenses or losses that it incurs as a result.

   In the middle of August, Nagatomi contacted Inga and informed her that the machine was ready for delivery. At that point, however, Inga informed the company that she did not have $150 000 and that she was unable to obtain a bank loan. She explained that her financial situation had been badly damaged by a number of health problems and by a sharp increase in the cost of farm supplies. But she also further explained that her crop was particularly good and that she would easily be able to pay the full price, with interest, *after* the harvest. She therefore pleaded with the company to deliver the machine first and to accept payment later.

   Nagatomi realizes that Inga cannot harvest her crop without the machine. It also realizes, in light of her recent problems, that Inga would probably be forced into bankruptcy if she could not bring in the harvest. At the same time, however, it knows that it is not under any legal obligation to deliver the machine before payment. Furthermore, it has received an order from a farmer in Colorado for a custom-built harvester with exactly the same specifications as Inga's. That harvester does not need to be delivered until the end of next summer.

   Is Nagatomi under any obligation to deliver the machine to Inga? Does it have a legal obligation? A moral obligation? Even if it does not have any obligation, should it agree to Inga's proposal? What factors influence your answer?

2. Rabby Industries Ltd manufactures computer software. Late last year, it launched Budget Smart, a program that allows users to manage their finances from their home computers. It shipped 1 000 000 units to stores around Canada. As a result of an extensive advertising campaign and favourable reviews in the media, sales have been very good. About 600 000 units have already been sold, and the rest are moving quickly from store shelves. Recently, however, Rabby's engineers discovered a problem. After 18 months in use, the program causes damage to some types of home computers. At this point, the full extent of the problem remains unknown. For instance, it is not clear which types of systems will be affected. It is clear, however, that in at least some situations, the defect will irreversibly erase the entire hard drive, and all of the computer's information will be lost.

   Rabby has not yet received any customer complaints. The company knows, however, that the situation will soon change. It is therefore concerned about a number of things. It is distressed by the thought of damaging customers' computers. It is worried that it might be forced into bankruptcy if it is held liable in a large number of cases. And it is worried that it might even be financially ruined by a small number of claims. Since it is still a relatively new company in a highly competitive field, it could be wiped out by bad publicity.

Discuss Rabby's situation from a risk management perspective. Explain the process of risk management and identify several responses that the company might consider.

3. Lafarge Canada Inc developed plans to build a new set of docks in Vancouver's harbour. The land was owned by a federal body named the Vancouver Port Authority (VPA). The VPA was created under a federal statute called the *Canada Marine Act*. The VPA's purpose was to ensure that various aspects of the shipping industry worked effectively in Vancouver's harbour. The VPA gave its approval to Lafarge. The project was opposed, however, by a citizens' group, which argued that the project could not proceed because it had not received city planning approval. Such approval normally is required under municipal law. Is the citizens' group right? Must Lafarge comply with municipal law? Explain your answer.

4. Prime Minister Chrétien visited Vancouver in August 2002 to commemorate the opening of a new gate to the city's Chinatown. City police received a tip that an unidentified man intended to throw a pie at the prime minister. The plaintiff, a lawyer in his mid-40s, attended the event, acted in a suspicious manner, and loosely fit a broad description given to the police. The police, mistakenly believing that the plaintiff was the would-be assailant, handcuffed him and took him to a police station. He was subjected to a strip search and held in a police cell for approximately four and a half hours. When the error eventually was discovered, the plaintiff was released. The plaintiff then sued the government on the basis of the police actions. Although he has not proven that the police committed any torts, he has convinced the court that the police violated his rights under section 8 of the *Charter*, which says that "Everyone has the right to be secure against unreasonable search or seizure." What remedy would be best in this case? Explain your answer.

5. You live in the City of Peterborough. City Council recently created By-law 2720, which states

1. No bill, poster, sign or other advertisement of any nature whatsoever shall be attached to any public property, including any pole, post, or other object which is used for the purpose of carrying the transmission lines of any telephone, telegraph, or electric power company within the limits of the City of Peterborough.

2. Every person who contravenes this by-law is guilty of an offence and liable to a penalty not to exceed two thousand dollars ($2,000.00) exclusive of costs for each and every such offence.

You operate a nightclub that regularly features live musical performances. You advertise those performances by posting signs on telephone poles. You have been charged under By-law 2720. You are worried about the possibility of paying a fine, but you are more worried about the general effect that the by-law will have on your business. You simply cannot afford to buy advertising space in newspapers or on television. If you cannot attach your advertisements to City-owned poles, you will not be able to effectively advertise at all.

Is it possible for you to successfully challenge By-law 2720 under the *Charter of Rights and Freedoms*? Explain the arguments that you would make to a court. Explain how the City would likely respond if the court agreed that the by-law violated your *Charter* rights.

6. Macca Enterprises Ltd sells various types of insurance. To streamline its operations, it hopes to eliminate its "collections department," which contains a large number of employees who have the task of collecting money from customers who buy insurance. Macca would much prefer to hire another company, Ramon Inc, to perform that service on its behalf. Ramon is willing to act as Macca's collection agent and the parties have worked out most of the terms of their proposed agreement. Macca, however, still has one big concern. "What happens," asks Macca's general manager, "if Ramon collects a lot of money on our behalf, but then goes bankrupt before paying that money over to us?" As the general manager knows from painful past experience, it is impossible to get full payment—if anything—from someone who is bankrupt. Suggest a way in which Macca can retain Ramon's services without exposing itself to risk if Ramon goes bankrupt. Explain the role played by each party under that arrangement.

2 Litigation and Alternative Dispute Resolution

LEARNING OBJECTIVES

After completing this chapter, you should be able to:

❶ Describe class actions and explain when they can be used.

❷ List the advantages and disadvantages of hiring lawyers and paralegals.

❸ Define "pleadings" and list five types of pleadings.

❹ Explain the difference between winning a lawsuit and enforcing a judgment.

❺ Define "costs," and identify two situations in which a court may award costs that are higher than usual.

❻ Describe contingency fee agreements.

❼ Identify different types of trial courts and appeal courts.

❽ Explain the advantages and disadvantages of small claims courts.

❾ Describe the court hierarchy and explain how it is related to the doctrine of precedent and the rule of law.

❿ Identify forms of alternative dispute resolution and explain how they compare to litigation.

When people think about the law, they usually think about courts—about lawyers standing up and making arguments, and about judges sitting back and making decisions. One side wins and the other side loses. And indeed, that is an important part of Canadian law. In this chapter, we will examine the *litigation* process in more detail. **Litigation** is the system of resolving disputes in court. As always, our discussion will focus on issues of risk management. We will see how a business person can reduce the risks that are associated with litigation. We will, however, also look outside of the litigation system. Many types of issues and disputes are taken not to courts, but rather to administrative tribunals. We will briefly discuss how tribunals are different from courts. Furthermore, as successful business people realize, litigation is often a poor way to settle disputes. Amongst other things, it is usually expensive, often unpredictable, and frequently fatal to business relationships. We will therefore examine several types of *alternative dispute resolution* (ADR) that allow people to settle their disputes without going to court.

> **litigation** is the system of resolving disputes in court

We need to stress one point at the outset: Very few cases actually go to trial. It is easy to overlook that fact. We seldom hear about disputes that are settled out of court.[1] Our focus instead is on those relatively rare cases that are decided by judges. Because a judgment is a public document, it may be reproduced in a case reporter and perhaps even mentioned in a newspaper.[2] Those cases are, however, the exception. By some estimates, fewer than 1 percent of private disputes are decided by judges.

The Litigation Process

L.O. ❶ ❷ ❸ ❹ ❺ ❻

This section provides an introduction to litigation.[3] We will look at some of the people who are involved in that system, the steps that have to be taken in order to win a case, and the different types of courts that may be involved. As we will see, it is sometimes possible for business people to deal with lawsuits by themselves. As a general rule, however, it is a good idea to hire an expert to help out with more serious matters. For that reason, we will focus on the big picture, rather than the details.

WHO CAN SUE AND BE SUED?

In discussing who can sue and be sued, it is helpful to draw a distinction between people and organizations. As a general rule, all adults are free to use the Canadian courts, whether or not they are Canadian citizens. It is, for example, possible for an American consumer to sue a Canadian company for delivering shoddy merchandise. An adult who is suffering from a mental incapacity, however, must use a court-appointed representative. Children similarly must be represented by a parent or *litigation guardian*.

[1.] In fact, settlement agreements are often made confidential, so that neither party can reveal the details. Confidentiality allows the injured party to receive compensation without generating adverse publicity for the guilty party.

[2.] Case reporters are books containing court judgments. A list of the most important case reporters can be found on the inside cover of this text.

[3.] We will focus on civil litigation. The procedures that are used for criminal cases are somewhat different.

The situation is somewhat more complicated with organizations. As a matter of law, a corporation is a type of person. A company may therefore sue or be sued.[4] In contrast, unincorporated organizations, such as clubs and church groups, are not classified as legal persons. As a result, they normally cannot sue or be sued. Instead, it is necessary to sue the individual members of those organizations. In some provinces, however, there is an important exception to that rule. Although trade unions are unincorporated organizations, they can sue and be sued directly.

Special rules may also apply when the government is sued. Because of the traditional rule that said that "the King can do no wrong," the Crown could not be sued without its consent. The traditional rule has now been changed by legislation.[5] The statutes are, however, complicated and they often introduce unusual restrictions. They need to be read very carefully.

Class Actions

Sometimes it makes little sense for people to individually sue, even if they have clearly suffered some sort of legal wrong. If so, there is a danger that wrongdoers may profit from their own misconduct. Consider the case against the Consumers' Gas Company.[6] It sold natural gas in Ontario. As part of its pricing scheme, it imposed a penalty of 5 percent on bills that were paid late. That late payment penalty violated the *Criminal Code*. For most people, however, it was not worth a fight—it was easier to pay the small penalty (say, $25) than to start a lawsuit. But because there were as many as 500 000 of those people, Consumers' Gas was able to illegally collect as much as $150 million. The law fortunately has a way to deal with that sort of problem. A **class action** allows a single person, or a small group of people, to sue on behalf of a larger group of claimants. In the case of Consumers' Gas, that individual was Gordon Garland. Although he had paid only about $75 in late payment penalties, he was able to hold the corporation accountable through a class action.

Class actions are becoming increasingly common in Canada. Concept Summary 2.1 lists some of the situations in which they are frequently seen. The primary attraction is obvious: They allow small individuals to take on large organizations. While it is difficult to find a lawyer to fight a large corporation for $75, it is much easier to find a law firm willing to take on a case that may be worth $150 million. The threat of a class action may also prevent a wrong from occurring in the first place. A company may not worry about thousands of claims worth a few dollars each, but it will worry about a single claim worth $150 million. Finally, class actions may also save society money. If there are thousands of claims, and each one is almost identical, it is cheaper to deal with them all at once. Court time is very expensive.

a **class action** allows a single person, or a small group of people, to sue on behalf of a larger group of claimants

---

4. There are, however, restrictions on foreign corporations, which may need to be provincially licensed before they can use Canadian courts.

5. See *Canada Crown Liability and Proceedings Act*, RSC 1985, c C-50 (Can); *Proceedings Against the Crown Act*, RSA 2000, c P-25 (Alta); *Crown Proceeding Act*, RSBC 1996, c 89 (BC); *Proceedings Against the Crown Act*, CCSM, c P140 (Man); *Proceedings Against the Crown Act*, RSNB 1973, c P-18 (NB); *Proceedings Against the Crown Act*, RSNL 1990, c P-26 (Nfld); *Proceedings Against the Crown Act*, RSNS 1989, c 360 (NS); *Crown Proceedings Act*, RSPEI 1988, c C-32 (PEI); *Proceedings Against the Crown Act*, RSO 1990, c P.27 (Ont); and *Proceedings Against the Crown Act*, RSS 1978, c P-27 (Sask).

6. *Garland v Consumers' Gas Co* (2004) 237 DLR (4th) 385 (SCC).

Concept Summary 2.1

Class Action Claims

- product liability (eg prescription drugs that have disastrous side effects)
- mass torts (eg contaminated water that affects an entire town)
- workplace discrimination (eg a corporation pays female employees less than male employees)
- clubs and churches (eg sexual abuse of children by clergy)
- banking law (eg improper service charges)
- business law (eg price fixing amongst companies that sell similar products)
- company law (eg misleading information that attracts investors)
- securities law (eg insider trading that hurts shareholders)

Seven provinces have legislation dealing with class actions.[7] Although the details vary from place to place, the basic ideas are the same.

- **Common issues:** There must be common issues amongst the various members of the class. For instance, they may all be women who received defective breast implants from the same manufacturer, or they may all be medical patients who received tainted blood from the same source. It is not necessary, however, for every claim to be identical. Even if the court allows a class action to occur, it may set up a process to deal with the special circumstances that affect some claimants.

- **Representative plaintiff:** The plaintiff must qualify as a *representative plaintiff*. They must demonstrate a workable plan for fairly representing the interests of the class members. That will not be true, for instance, if the plaintiff wants the court to rely on a rule that will help some claimants, while hurting others.

- **Notification:** A representative plaintiff must also have a workable plan for *notifying* potential class members. It is not unusual, for instance, to see class action notices in newspapers or magazines. Those notices are very important. In most situations, a class action automatically includes every claimant who has not expressly *opted out* within a certain length of time.[8] And every member of that class will be bound by the decision that the court gives at the end of the trial. People who have not opted out cannot bring separate actions on their own.

[7.] *Class Proceedings Act*, SA 2003, c C-16.5 (Alta); *Class Proceedings Act*, RSBC 1996, c 50 (BC); *Class Proceedings Act*, CCSM, c C130 (Man); *Class Actions Act*, SNL 2001, c C-18.1 (Nfld); *Class Proceedings Act*, 1992, SO 1992, c 6 (Ont); *Class Actions Act*, SS 2001, c C-12.01 (Sask); Code of Civil Procedure, RSQ, c C-25, ss 999–1051 (Que). Class actions are also possible in the Federal Court: *Federal Court Rules*, 1998, SOR/98-106, ss 299.1–299.42, as amended by Rules Amending the *Federal Court Rules*, 1998, SOR/2002-417, s 17.

[8.] In most provinces, *residents* of the province in which a class action is brought are automatically included in the class. Out-of-province claimants, however, must expressly *opt in* within the relevant time period. Otherwise, they are excluded. In Ontario and Quebec, however, there is no residency requirement. Both in-province and out-of-province claimants are automatically included in the class.

- **Preferable procedure:** The court must be convinced that a class action is the *preferable procedure* for dealing with the claims. It will, for instance, consider whether a class action will become too complicated, and whether there are enough similarities between the class members.

- **Certification:** Assuming that the previous requirements are met, the action will be *certified*. **Certification** represents the court's decision to allow the various claims to be joined together and to proceed as a class action. It is usually the most important step in the entire process. It demonstrates that the court believes that there is a serious and genuine claim to be considered. As a result, certification of a class action is often enough to persuade the defendants in a class action lawsuit to settle.

certification represents the court's decision to allow the various claims to be joined together and to proceed as a class action

As we have seen, most provinces now have class action legislation. Those statutes have done a great deal to clarify the applicable rules. It is important to appreciate, however, that class actions are also possible in jurisdictions that have not yet enacted legislation. Case Brief 2.1 discusses the Supreme Court of Canada's position on the issue.

Case Brief 2.1

Western Canadian Shopping Centres v Dutton (2000) 201 DLR (4th) 385 (SCC)

Muh-Min Lin and Hoi-Wah Wu, along with 229 other individuals, invested in a company that was controlled by Joseph Dutton. Some time later, Lin and Wu became convinced that their investments were being mismanaged and that Dutton was acting improperly. They attempted to bring a class action in Alberta on behalf of themselves and the other investors.

Although Alberta now has class action legislation, the statute was not in force at the relevant time. The Supreme Court of Canada nevertheless held that the judge was entitled to allow a class action to occur under the *Rules of Court*. Chief Justice McLachlin established certain requirements:

- The class must be clearly defined.
- There must be issues of fact or law that are common to every class member.
- Success for one class member must mean success for all.
- The representative plaintiff must represent the interests of the entire class.
- The advantages to a class action must outweigh the disadvantages.

LEGAL REPRESENTATION

Assuming that you want to sue, or that you have been sued, you need to make a decision regarding *legal representation*. Who will argue for your side? That question raises an important risk management issue.

Self-Representation

You have the right to represent yourself. You can go into court and argue your case before a judge, even if you are not a lawyer. And in some situations, it makes sense to do so. As we will see later in this chapter, for example, small claims courts have been set up to encourage people to deal with some sorts of disputes by themselves. There is, however, a great deal of truth in the old saying: If you represent yourself, you have "a fool for a lawyer and a fool for a client." Litigation is often very complicated. While it is expensive to hire a lawyer, it may be far more expensive in the long run to lose a lawsuit because of your own lack of experience.

Lawyers

If you do not want to represent yourself in court, you may hire someone to act on your behalf. The obvious choice is a lawyer.[9] There are advantages to doing so. Hiring a lawyer obviously does not guarantee success, but it does provide you with competent help and it may increase your likelihood of success.

Each province and territory has legislation to deal with the legal profession. That legislation restricts the practice of law to people who have met certain requirements. People cannot act as lawyers until they have graduated from law school, completed an apprentice period known as a *period of articles*, and *passed* the bar by successfully writing a number of examinations. The legislation also establishes a body, usually called the Law Society, to regulate the profession.[10] The Law Society imposes codes of conduct and punishes members who act improperly. For instance, a lawyer who misleads a client may be fined, suspended, or disbarred.

Law societies also require every lawyer to hold *professional liability insurance*. If your lawyer acts carelessly, and you suffer a loss as a result, you may sue for professional negligence. (We will consider the tort of professional negligence in Chapter 6.)

The lawyer, however, may not have enough money to pay for that loss. **Professional liability insurance** allows you to receive compensation from the lawyer's insurance company. Law societies also create **assurance funds**, which provide compensation to people who have been hurt by dishonest lawyers.

There are a number of other advantages to hiring a lawyer. For instance, conversations with your lawyer are generally *confidential* and *privileged*. That means that your lawyer cannot share your information with anyone without your consent and that your discussions cannot be used against you in court.

> **professional liability insurance** allows a client to receive compensation from a lawyer's insurance company if the lawyer has acted carelessly

> an **assurance fund** provides compensation to people who have been hurt by dishonest lawyers

Paralegals

Depending upon your particular circumstances, you may hire a *paralegal* instead of a lawyer. A **paralegal** is not a lawyer but provides legal advice and services. Paralegals are an important part of the Canadian legal system. It is occasionally difficult to find a lawyer to work in a certain area or at an affordable price. Consequently, paralegals are particularly common in small claims courts and landlord and tenant tribunals.

In the past, some people—including some judges—were concerned that paralegals were not subject to the same types of rules and regulations that govern lawyers.[11] For instance, paralegals were not regulated by a governing body, they were not subject to a code of conduct, and they were not required to carry liability insurance. As a result of those concerns, the provinces and territories have increasingly created legislation for paralegals.

The situation in Ontario provides a good example. Because of the large number of paralegals operating in that province, the Law Society of Upper Canada introduced a licensing scheme in 2007.[12] As a result of that reform, lawyers and paralegals in Ontario now have much more in common. Just as a lawyer must

> a **paralegal** is not a lawyer but provides legal advice and services

---

[9.] As we saw in Chapter 1, many large businesses have *in-house* counsel. Instead of hiring a lawyer every time that a problem occurs, a company may create a permanent legal department within its organization. While that approach may be more expensive, it also increases the chances that potential problems will be identified before they become major difficulties.

[10.] There are exceptions. In Nova Scotia, the body is called the Barristers' Society.

[11.] *R v Romanowicz* (1999) 178 DLR (4th) 466 at 495 (Ont CA).

[12.] *Law Society Act*, RSO 1990, c L.8, s 25.1 (Ont).

hold a law degree, a new paralegal must have trained at an approved institution. Specialized programs are offered at several colleges within the province. The new rules also require paralegals to pass rigorous examinations, just as lawyers must write bar exams. Furthermore, members of both professions must abide by a *Code of Conduct*, which allows the Law Society to punish wrongdoers. A formal process has been established to receive complaints from the public, and anyone who suffers a loss as a result of dishonesty by a lawyer or a paralegal may be entitled to compensation. And, finally, just like lawyers, paralegals must now carry liability insurance.

Some differences, however, do remain between lawyers and paralegals. Perhaps most significantly, paralegals are confined to certain types of work. In Ontario, for example, licensed paralegals may appear in administrative tribunals, the Small Claims Court, the Ontario Court of Justice under the *Provincial Offences Act*, and some criminal cases in which the maximum penalty is less than six months in jail. They may also provide advice and draft documents in connection with those cases. They cannot, however, appear in other types of cases, nor can they perform services, such as drafting wills or handling real estate transactions or estates, that are restricted to lawyers only. Paralegals who act outside the permitted areas of practice may be prosecuted for practising law without a licence.[13] Other distinctions also remain. For instance, in contrast to lawyers, paralegals cannot work on a contingency fee basis.[14]

PLEADINGS

Whether you act for yourself or hire someone to represent you, a great deal must be done before your case can appear in court. In this section, we will look at *pleadings*. **Pleadings** are the documents used to identify the issues and clarify the nature of a dispute. Some are prepared by the *plaintiff*, while others come from the *defendant*.[15] The **plaintiff** is the person who is making the complaint. The **defendant** is the person about whom the complaint is being made.

It is important to start the pleadings process promptly. Most types of claim are subject to *limitation periods*. A **limitation period** is a period of time within which an action must be started. The details vary depending upon the nature of the claim and the place in which it is started. We will discuss limitation periods at several places in this book. For now, we can offer a few general observations.

■ Canadian limitation statutes traditionally drew a distinction between claims in contract (which had to be commenced within six years) and claims in tort (which had to be commenced within two years). That remains true in some jurisdictions.[16] More recently, however, there has been a move toward a simplified system in which most claims must be started within two years from the day on which the plaintiff discovered, or should have discovered, the cause of action.[17]

pleadings are the documents used to identify the issues and clarify the nature of a dispute

the **plaintiff** is the person who is making the complaint

the **defendant** is the person about whom the complaint is being made

a **limitation period** is a period of time within which an action must be started

---

[13] *Law Society of Upper Canada v Boldt* 2007 ONCA 115 (Ont CA).

[14] *Koliniotis v Tri Level Claims Consultants Ltd* (2005) 257 DLR (4th) 297 (Ont CA).

[15] In a criminal case, the *Crown* (or government) makes the complaint against the *accused*.

[16] *Limitation of Actions Act*, CCSM, c L150 (Man); *Limitation of Actions Act*, RSNWT 1988, c L-8 (NWT); *Statute of Limitations*, RSPEI 1988, c S-7 (PEI); *Limitation of Actions Act*, RSY 2002, c 139 (Yuk).

[17] *Limitations Act*, RSA 2000, c L-12 (Alta); *Limitations Act*, RSBC 1996, c 266 (BC); *Limitation of Actions Act*, CCSM, c L150 (Man); *Limitation of Actions Act*, SNB 2010, c L-8.5 (NB); *Limitations Act*, SNL 1995, c L-16.1 (Nfld); *Limitations Act*, 2002, SO 2002, c 24, Sched B (Ont); *Limitations Act*, SS 2004, c. L-16.1 (Sask).

- Outside of the general limitation provisions, periods vary considerably. Depending upon the circumstances, the relevant period may vary from days to decades.[18] For instance, it is usually necessary to act *very* quickly if you intend to sue a municipality or the Crown.[19] But you may have 20 years to sue someone who has been improperly occupying your land.[20]

- The consequences of missing a limitation period deadline may also vary. The general rule in contract is that while the debt still exists, it is *unenforceable*. The money should still be paid, but the courts will not compel the debtor to do so. In other circumstances, however, the plaintiff's rights may die along with the limitation period. That may be true, for instance, if you let me occupy your property for 30 years. At the end of that time, I may become the owner of that land.

- It may seem harsh that the mere passage of time can prevent the enforcement of an otherwise valid claim.[21] Limitation periods are necessary, however, for at least two reasons. First, after a time, memories fade and evidence is lost. The courts do not want to resolve disputes on the basis of unreliable information. Second, it would be unfair to allow the plaintiff to hold the threat of litigation over the defendant forever. At some point, it should be possible for the defendant to get on with life.

In most jurisdictions, a lawsuit starts with a *statement of claim*.[22] A **statement of claim** is a document in which the plaintiff outlines the nature of the complaint. It states the facts that the plaintiff intends to rely upon and the remedy that it wants to receive. Like all pleadings, it must be issued by a court and served on the other party.[23]

Once a party is served with a statement of claim, they must react quickly. If the defendant does nothing within the relevant period (usually less than one month), the plaintiff may go to court alone and receive a *default judgment*. If so, the defendant will lose by default, without having said a word.[24] Assuming that the defendant intends to deny liability, they should therefore prepare a **statement of defence**, which is a document in which the defendant sets out their version of the facts and indicates how they intend to deny the claim. Depending upon the circumstances, the defendant may also include a *counterclaim* along with the statement of defence. A **counterclaim** is a claim that the defendant makes against the plaintiff. For instance, if the plaintiff sues for the price of goods that they delivered to the defendant, the defendant may counterclaim if they believe that those goods are defective.

> a **statement of claim** is a document in which the plaintiff outlines the nature of the complaint

> a **statement of defence** is a document in which the defendant sets out its version of the facts and indicates how it intends to deny the claim

> a **counterclaim** is a claim that the defendant makes against the plaintiff

---

[18.] Limitation periods are contained in a number of statutes. Claims that are not caught by statutory limitation periods may be caught by the equitable *doctrine of laches*. A court may refuse to award a remedy if you waited for an unreasonable length of time and if the other party would be hurt by the delay.

[19.] For instance, if you want to sue a municipality in Ontario for an injury that was caused by a road in poor repair, you may need to give notice within seven days and start your action within three months: *Municipal Act*, 2001, SO 2001, c 25, s 44(10) (Ont).

[20.] See *eg Real Property Limitations Act*, RSO 1990, c L15 (Ont).

[21.] The rules regarding limitation periods are sometimes softened. For instance, a period may not start until a reasonable person in the plaintiff's circumstances could have discovered a cause of action and taken steps to act on it.

[22.] In some jurisdictions, a writ comes before the statement of the claim. A writ notifies the defendant that the plaintiff intends to sue.

[23.] Although the pleadings are written by the parties, they must be stamped and recorded by a court official before being put to use.

[24.] It may be possible to have a default judgment set aside later, but it is obviously better to do things right in the first place.

a **reply** is a document in which a party responds to a statement of defence

a **demand for particulars** requires the other side to provide additional information

an **examination for discovery** is a process in which the parties ask each other questions to obtain information about their case

a **settlement** occurs when the parties agree to resolve their dispute out of court

a **pre-trial conference** is a meeting that occurs between the parties and a judge

mediation is a process in which a neutral person—called a *mediator*—helps the parties reach an agreement

The plaintiff is entitled to respond to the defendant's pleadings. They may use a **reply** if they want to dispute anything in the statement of defence. And if they received a counterclaim, they may use a *statement of defence to the counterclaim*. After receiving the basic pleadings, the parties may still not be entirely sure what the other side has in mind. They may therefore use a *demand for particulars*. A **demand for particulars** requires the other side to provide additional information.

PRE-TRIAL ACTIVITY

A case does not normally go to court immediately after the pleadings have closed. The parties will first conduct *examinations for discovery*. **Examination for discovery** is a process in which the parties ask each other questions to obtain information about their case. For instance, in a case involving a vehicle that exploded on impact, the victim's lawyer may ask the car manufacturer's chief engineer about the company's product safety studies. Although discoveries occur outside of court, they are conducted under *oath*, and the answers that they generate may be used as evidence during the trial.

While discoveries may be time-consuming, that time is better spent outside of court than in front of a judge. Court time is remarkably expensive and difficult to schedule. Discoveries, in comparison, are cheaper and more flexible. Discoveries may also serve another important function. By revealing the strengths and weaknesses of a claim, they may indicate which side is likely to lose if the case goes to trial. If so, it may be foolish for that party to press on. Further proceedings will simply add to the eventual cost. Discoveries therefore encourage *settlement*. A **settlement** occurs when the parties agree to resolve their dispute out of court. In the earlier example, for instance, the chief engineer might have been forced to reveal that the car company knew about the risk of explosion. If so, the company might agree to pay for the plaintiff's injuries in exchange for her promise to drop her claim.[25]

The vast majority of claims (more than 95 percent) are settled out of court. That is not surprising. The rules are designed to encourage settlements. Every jurisdiction has a system for *pre-trial conferences*. A **pre-trial conference** is a meeting that occurs between the parties and a judge. After the parties outline their positions, the judge may indicate which of them is likely to win if the case goes to trial. If so, the likely loser may be persuaded to settle. Depending upon the jurisdiction, a pre-trial conference may be required, or it may be initiated by either the parties or the judge. Some jurisdictions, including Ontario and Alberta, have gone even further. In an effort to settle disputes outside of court, those provinces have adopted a system of mandatory mediation. **Mediation** is a process in which a neutral person—called a *mediator*—helps the parties reach an agreement.[26] Under a system of mandatory mediation, the parties cannot go to trial until they have gone through mediation, and a party who refuses to co-operate may, for instance, be required to pay costs. Even if that process does not produce a settlement, it often speeds up the litigation process.

THE TRIAL

If a lawsuit does go to trial, it will normally be decided by a judge. While a person who is accused of a crime generally has the option of appearing before

---

[25.] The company will also want the plaintiff to promise that she will keep quiet about the case. Negative publicity is bad for business.

[26.] We will discuss mediation in greater detail at the end of this chapter.

a jury, civil litigation is almost always decided by a judge alone. If there is a jury, the judge is responsible for finding the law, and the jury is responsible for finding the facts and applying the law.

The court will hear first from the plaintiff and then from the defendant. Each side will present arguments and *evidence*. **Evidence** consists of the information that is provided in support of the arguments. To get that evidence in front of the court, each side will call *witnesses*. *Ordinary witnesses* testify about facts that they know first-hand (for instance, a pedestrian may describe a car accident that they saw happen). *Expert witnesses* provide information and opinions based on the evidence (for instance, a physician may suggest how the defendant's ability to drive was affected by the alcohol that they were drinking). The party who calls a particular witness will ask questions and receive answers during a process known as *examination-in-chief*. The other party will then have an opportunity to vigorously *cross-examine* the same witness. Canadian law is based on the belief that an *adversarial system* is the best way to get to the truth. Each side is encouraged to present its own version of events and to attack the other side's story. The truth of the matter usually lies somewhere in between.

> **evidence** consists of the information that is provided in support of an argument

There are strict—and often complicated—rules that determine which types of evidence are *admissible*. For instance, the courts generally insist on hearing only *direct evidence*. They normally will not listen to *hearsay evidence*. **Hearsay evidence** is information that a witness heard from another person, rather than directly from the source. Going back to an example in the previous paragraph, the court is not interested, for instance, in what the pedestrian's father heard about the accident from his daughter. The main problem with hearsay evidence is that it cannot be tested in court. The pedestrian's father does not have direct knowledge of the facts. He cannot explain precisely where the pedestrian was standing, what she saw, what she heard, and so on.

> **hearsay evidence** is information that a witness heard from another person, rather than directly from the source

On the basis of their arguments and evidence, the plaintiff has to prove their claim on a *balance of probabilities*. That means that every important part of their claim must be *probably* true. While it is impossible to accurately measure these things, it may help to think of a set of scales. At the end of the trial, the defendant will be held *liable* only if the scales are tipped in the plaintiff's favour. If the scales are either evenly balanced or tipped in the defendant's favour, then the defendant will be *not liable*. In criminal cases, the standard of proof is much higher. The Crown has to prove the accused's guilt *beyond a reasonable doubt*. If that standard is met, then the accused will be found *guilty*. If not, the verdict will be *not guilty*.

THE REMEDY

Various punishments may be available if a person is convicted of a crime. The court may, for instance, impose a *fine* or a *prison sentence*. Canadian courts also frequently use *conditional sentences*, which allow criminals to serve time in their own houses, rather than in prisons. A different variety of remedies is available if the plaintiff wins a civil lawsuit. We will look at some of those remedies in more detail in later chapters. For now, Concept Summary 2.2 will introduce a few of the more important possibilities.

ENFORCEMENT

There is a difference—sometimes a very disappointing difference—between winning a lawsuit and enforcing a judgment. A defendant who has been found liable and ordered to pay money to the plaintiff is called a **judgment debtor**. Unfortunately, even if the court has said that the plaintiff is entitled

> **a judgment debtor** is a defendant who has been found liable and ordered to pay money to the plaintiff

Concept Summary 2.2

Remedies in Civil Litigation

Name of Remedy	Purpose	Example
Compensatory damages	financially compensate the plaintiff for a loss	provide an injured person with the amount they spent on medical bills
Punitive damages	punish the defendant for acting very badly	punish an insurance company that fabricated an allegation of arson in an attempt to avoid paying a benefit under an insurance policy
Nominal damages	symbolically recognize that the defendant acted wrongfully, even though the plaintiff did not suffer any loss	recognize the right of a store that sued for trespass, even though the unwanted customer did no harm
Specific performance	requires the defendant to fulfill a promise	compel performance by a vendor who contractually agreed to sell a piece of land to a purchaser
Injunction	requires the defendant to act in a particular way	compel a construction company to remove its equipment from a neighbour's property
Rescission	terminates a contract	eliminate a contract that a con artist tricked an elderly couple into signing

to a remedy, the judgment debtor simply may not have any assets available. For instance, it may be a company that is bankrupt. And even if the judgment debtor does have enough money to pay its debt, it may be reluctant to do so. There are, fortunately, several ways to deal with that second sort of problem.[27]

For instance, it may be possible to *garnishee* a judgment debtor's income by forcing their employer to pay money to the plaintiff. Or it may be possible to *seize and sell* some of the judgment debtor's assets, such as computers, vehicles, and land. (There are, however, limits to that type of remedy. The judgment debtor cannot be stripped bare or left without any way to earn an income.) Court officials and other types of public authorities, such as the sheriff, are available to help with those enforcement procedures.

Business Decision 2.1 demonstrates that it is important to know, even before starting a lawsuit, whether the judgment that you hope to receive will be enforceable.

APPEALS

an **appeal court** decides whether a mistake was made in the court below

the **appellant** is the party who attacks the decision of the lower court

the **respondent** is the party who defends the decision of the lower court

A lawsuit does not necessarily end after a trial. The losing party is often entitled to *appeal* to a higher court. An **appeal court** (or appellate court) decides whether a mistake was made in the court below. The party who attacks the decision of the lower court is called the **appellant**, and the party who defends that decision is called the **respondent**. An appeal must be started promptly, normally within 30 days after the trial court gave its decision.

There are a number of significant differences between trials and appeals. First, while there is only one judge at trial, most appeals are heard by three judges

[27.] In some circumstances, at least, there may also be ways of dealing with the problem of the defendant's bankruptcy. As we saw in Business Decision 1.2 (see page 24), it may be possible to use a *trust* to avoid the unfortunate consequences of the defendant's bankruptcy. We will see several other possibilities in Chapter 23 when we look at secured transactions.

Business Decision 2.1

Judgment Debts and the Decision to Sue

Your company sells ebooks over the Internet. The business was recently brought to a standstill for three days as a result of a computer virus that infected your system. The overall cost of that incident, including the loss of sales and the expense involved in repairing your equipment, is about $750 000. After some investigation, you discovered that the virus was sent to you by a hacker in Whitehorse. As is common in this type of situation, that hacker is a high-school student who lives with his parents.

Further investigation and a brief discussion with your lawyer revealed additional information:

- The precedents consistently state that a hacker in this type of situation is legally responsible for the damage that has been caused.

- Experience suggests that this type of litigation tends to be quite expensive because of the technical nature of the evidence. Furthermore, your investigation indicates that while the boy is

remarkably lazy and unlikely to make much of his life, he is also very knowledgeable about computers. He has threatened to "create as much trouble as possible" if he is sued.

- Parents are generally not liable for their children's behaviour. Consequently, although the hacker was living at home when he sent the virus, he is the only person your company can sue. You could not bring an action against the boy's mother or father.

Questions for Discussion

1. Should you sue the boy?

2. From a risk management perspective, what is the major argument against doing so?

(and sometimes more). Second, appellate courts do not listen to witnesses or receive evidence. Instead, they simply hear and read arguments from the parties or their lawyers. Third, appellate courts normally deal with law, but not facts. They correct any mistakes that the trial judge made regarding the law. But they overturn a finding of fact only if the trial judge made a *palpable and overriding error*. A palpable and overriding error is a clear and indisputable error. It is a mistake that is completely unreasonable or entirely unsupported by the evidence. Those rules are sometimes surprising. As long as the trial judge acted reasonably, a simple error of fact cannot be overturned on appeal.

The majority rules in an appellate court. For that reason, appeals are almost always heard by an odd number of judges, in order to avoid tie votes. If the majority believes that the decision in the court below was correct, it *affirms* the lower court's decision. If it believes that the lower court decision was wrong, it may have a number of options, depending upon the circumstances. It may *reverse* the lower court decision (for instance, by saying that the defendant was liable rather than not liable), *vary* some part of it (for instance, by saying that the defendant was liable, but for $15 000 rather than $10 000), or send the case back for a *re-trial* (if it does not have enough information to make the right decision itself). An appellate judge who disagrees with the majority is entitled to write a separate judgment called a *dissent*. A dissent often calls attention to some weakness in the majority's decision. And because the law is continually evolving, today's dissent may become tomorrow's law.

As we will see below, it is sometimes possible to appeal the decision of an appellate court. The most obvious example occurs when a case goes from a trial court, to a Court of Appeal in a particular province or territory, and then to the Supreme Court of Canada.

COSTS

Litigation is expensive and somebody has to pay for it. To a large extent, the government supports the court system (including judges' salaries and the construction of courthouses) through the collection of taxes. Courts also charge fees for filing documents and other services. Most expenses, however, show up on lawyers' bills. Lawyers routinely charge hundreds of dollars per hour for services, plus substantial amounts of money for *disbursements* (such as the cost of mailing letters and hiring expert witnesses). The final bill at the end of a long case can easily run to many thousands of dollars. (If the client believes that the fee is excessive, a court official—called a *taxing officer*—may order the lawyer to reduce the amount.)

Depending upon the outcome of a case, a litigant may get some relief from those expenses. Judges have the discretion to order one party to pay *costs* to the other. **Costs** are the expenses that a party incurred during litigation. As a general rule, they are awarded to whichever side wins the lawsuit. As a result, losing a case usually hurts twice. If the plaintiff loses, then they will be denied the remedy that they wanted *and* will have to pay the defendant's costs. If the defendant loses, then they will have to pay for both the judgment *and* the plaintiff's costs.

It is important to realize, however, that there is a substantial difference between court costs and actual costs. A judge will normally order the losing party to pay costs on a *party-and-party* basis. The amount that the winning party is entitled to receive is determined by regulations. And that amount is almost always less than the winning party must pay their own lawyer. Suppose, for example, that I wrongfully cause you to suffer a loss of $10 000. You win your lawsuit. The court orders me to pay $10 000, plus costs of (say) $2000. Your lawyer, however, actually charges you $4000. While you will be better off than if you had not sued me, you will not be put back into your original position—as if the accident never happened. At the end of the day, your experience with the court system will still cost you $2000.

Depending upon the circumstances, a different rule may apply. A judge may award costs on a *solicitor-and-client* basis. If so, the loser will have to pay for a much greater share of the winner's *actual* costs. Solicitor-and-client costs are, however, awarded only in exceptional circumstances. That might be true if a lawsuit was *frivolous and vexatious* (for example, if the plaintiff knew that it did not have a good claim but sued the defendant anyway as a form of harassment).[28]

Costs may also be affected by an offer to settle. Although the specific rules vary from place to place, they are generally designed to encourage litigants to accept reasonable offers to settle out of court. Suppose, for instance, that you sue me for $20 000. Before the trial actually begins, you offer to settle your claim in exchange for $15 000. I refuse. If you win the case and the court finds that I am liable for *more* than $15 000, I may be ordered to pay solicitor-and-client costs, rather than party-and-party costs.[29] The same rules may also work in the other direction. You sue me for $20 000. I immediately offer to settle the case for $15 000. You refuse. Even if you eventually win the case, you may be

costs are the expenses that a party incurred during litigation

---

[28.] Ontario adopted a different system in 2002. Instead of party-and-party costs and solicitor-and-client costs, it now offers *partial indemnity* and *substantial indemnity*. Partial indemnity usually provides the winning party with about 40 to 50 percent of their actual costs. Substantial indemnity usually covers about 70 to 80 percent. A second change involves the calculation of costs. Ontario has abandoned its old tariff for a new system in which costs are based on the number of years that the lawyer has been in practice, the number of hours they spent on the case, and the type of proceedings that were involved (such as a discovery or a trial).

[29.] The rules that apply in the Federal Court are even harsher. A judge may award *double* party-and-party costs (excluding disbursements) from the time that the offer was made if the defendant is held liable for at least the amount contained in the plaintiff's offer: *Federal Rules of Court*, SOR 98-106, Rule 420(1).

ordered to pay my costs on a party-and-party basis if the court finds that I am liable for *less* than $15 000.[30]

Contingency Fees

The fear of losing a case and paying for one set—and quite possibly *both* sets—of lawyers may discourage a person from suing. That problem may be overcome, however, through the use of a *contingency fee agreement*. A **contingency fee agreement** requires a client to pay their lawyer only if the lawsuit is successful. Contingency fees are allowed across the country.[31] Although such arrangements were banned in Ontario for many years, they are now possible in that province.[32]

Contingency fee agreements undoubtedly serve a useful purpose. Many people cannot otherwise afford to litigate. Consider the situation of a small business that has been wrongfully injured by a much larger corporation. The small business certainly does not have enough money to pay a monthly lawyer's bill as the case (slowly) makes its way through the system. And even if the law firm is prepared to *defer* collection of its bill until after the case is finished, the small business may not be willing to accept the risk of losing the case and eventually being required to pay a massive bill. A contingency fee agreement would help. Assuming that the lawyer is willing to work on such a basis, the small business would be able to sue without the fear of being financially ruined.

Contingency fee agreements, however, are not necessarily as attractive as they may seem. They cut both ways. While the client may not be required to pay anything if the case is lost, it will be required to pay much more than usual if the case is won. Lawyers are, after all, in the business of making money. If they lose money in some cases, they want to make it up in others. As a result, it is not unusual for a contingency fee agreement to allow a lawyer to keep 25 to 40 percent of everything that is won.[33] The precise amount will depend upon the circumstances.[34] A contingency fee agreement may also encourage a lawyer to settle a claim quickly and cheaply. Both of those concerns can be seen in Ethical Perspective 2.1.

a contingency fee agreement requires a client to pay their lawyer only if the lawsuit is successful

---

[30.] The rules in the Federal Court are again even harsher. If the defendant is held liable for less than the amount contained in its offer, then the plaintiff may be entitled to party-and-party costs up until the time of the offer, but the defendant may be entitled to *double* party-and-party costs from the time of the offer. And if the court finds that the defendant is not liable at all, then the plaintiff may be ordered to pay party-and-party costs from the time that the case started, plus *double* party-and-party costs from the time that the offer was made: *Federal Rules of Court*, SOR 98-106, Rule 420(1).

[31.] The governing rules often prohibit contingency fee agreements in certain types of cases, such as criminal prosecutions and family matters. In addition, even when contingency fee agreements are allowed, they are subject to certain requirements. For instance, they usually need to be written, dated, and signed. If a contingency fee agreement is found to be invalid, a court normally orders the client to pay a reasonable fee to the lawyer.

[32.] *Contingency Fee Agreements*, O Reg 195/04, under *Solicitors Act*, RSO 1990, c S.15 (Ont).

[33.] In most jurisdictions, there is no set limit. British Columbia is an exception. In that province, a contingency fee generally cannot exceed 33 percent in a case of personal injury or death arising from a motor vehicle accident, or 40 percent for other causes of personal injury or death: *British Columbia Law Society Rules*, Rule 8-2. There are no limits for other types of claims.

[34.] For instance, contingency fee agreements often apply only to the lawyer's fee, so that the client is required to pay for disbursements (expenses) in any event.

Ethical Perspective 2.1

Contingency Fee Agreement

You have become seriously ill. You believe that the problem was caused by toxic waste that a company illegally dumped into a lake near your home. You require expensive prescription drugs and you will probably never be able to return to a full-time job. The evidence indicates that your damages amount to $1 000 000. Because you have little money, and because toxic waste claims are difficult to prove (especially against wealthy corporations with teams of high-priced lawyers), it is difficult to find someone to take your case. You did, however, recently meet a lawyer who is willing to work for a contingency fee of 40 percent. Unfortunately, he also appears to be down on his luck and a bit desperate.

Questions for Discussion

1. Should you accept the lawyer's offer? Even if you win your case and the judge orders the defendant to pay $1 000 000, you will receive only $600 000 after the lawyer has taken his share. Will you buy only 60 percent of the medication that you require? How will you live?

2. Assume that you signed the contingency fee agreement. Early in the case, the defendant's lawyers offers to pay $200 000 if you will drop the claim and keep quiet (since the company is worried about bad publicity that may encourage other people to sue). You ask your lawyer for his advice. He strongly suggests that you should accept the offer. You are not sure that you can trust him. Is he perhaps subconsciously motivated by a desire to earn an easy $80 000, rather than face the risk of being paid nothing?

L.O. ❼❽❾   The Court System

We have already seen the general structure of the Canadian court system: There are trial courts, appeal courts, and the Supreme Court of Canada. We can now describe some of those courts in more detail.

THE SUPREME COURT OF CANADA

The Supreme Court of Canada is the highest court in the country. It has nine members: the Chief Justice and eight others (called *puisne* judges).[35] They are all appointed by the federal government,[36] and like most Canadian judges, they are entitled to keep those jobs until they turn age 75.[37] In recent years, that appointment process has become increasingly controversial. As we saw in the last chapter, the Supreme Court of Canada's interpretation of the *Charter of Rights and Freedoms* significantly affects Canadian society. At the same time, however, the appointment process remains highly secretive. Although there have been minor reforms, the power to select judges is still effectively held by the prime minister. In contrast to the United States, that process is mostly closed to the public, and the opposition parties in Parliament do not have an opportunity to fully question candidates. Should the public have

---

[35.] Pronounced "puny." The term is derived from a Latin word meaning "later born" or "younger." The Chief Justice is not, however, necessarily the oldest (or largest) person on the court, or the one who has been on the court the longest. The Chief Justice is selected by the federal government (or, more specifically, by the prime minister).

[36.] Some types of American judges are elected. Canadian judges are never elected—they are always appointed by the government.

[37.] Judges "hold office during good behaviour." That means that they may be removed for serious misconduct. The removal process is, however, very cumbersome (it must pass through the House of Commons, the Senate, and the governor general), and it has never been used to remove a member of the Supreme Court of Canada.

more say in selecting the people who may fundamentally change the way that the country operates?

The Supreme Court of Canada is not a trial court. With rare exceptions, it hears only appeals from other appellate courts.[38] Furthermore, it is generally entitled to choose which appeals it will hear.[39] If you want to take your case to the Supreme Court, you must successfully apply for *leave*, or permission, to appeal. That is not easy to do. Most leave applications are *denied*. The Supreme Court of Canada will generally not *grant* leave to appeal simply because the lower courts made a mistake. It normally agrees to hear an appeal only if a case raises an issue of national importance. Appeals are almost always heard by five, seven, or nine *justices* (as the judges are properly called). As previously explained, an odd number is required in case some of the justices *dissent*, or disagree, on the outcome. In that situation, the majority opinion prevails.

COURT OF APPEAL

Every province and territory has a court of appeal. Although each one is concerned with the law in its own jurisdiction, its members are appointed by the federal government, not by the provincial or territorial government. Appeals at this level are usually heard by three justices, but the number is sometimes higher. The name of the court varies among jurisdictions, as Concept Summary 2.3 shows.

Concept Summary 2.3

Court Names

Province or Territory	Superior Court	Appeal Court
Alberta	Queen's Bench	Court of Appeal
British Columbia	Supreme Court	Court of Appeal
Manitoba	Queen's Bench	Court of Appeal
New Brunswick	Queen's Bench	Court of Appeal
Newfoundland and Labrador	Supreme Court, Trial Division	Supreme Court, Court of Appeal
Northwest Territories	Supreme Court	Court of Appeal
Nova Scotia	Supreme Court	Court of Appeal
Nunavut	Court of Justice	Court of Appeal
Ontario[40]	Superior Court	Court of Appeal
Prince Edward Island	Supreme Court, Trial Division	Supreme Court, Appeal Division
Quebec	Superior Court	Court of Appeal
Saskatchewan	Queen's Bench	Court of Appeal
Yukon	Supreme Court	Court of Appeal

[38] It occasionally hears *references*, which occur when the government asks for an opinion as to whether a statute is constitutionally valid.

[39] Some exceptions exist for criminal cases.

[40] In addition to the Superior Court and the Court of Appeal, Ontario has a Divisional Court. It consists of the Chief Justice of the Superior Court and other Superior Court judges. It acts as a court of appeal for provincial courts and administrative tribunals.

SUPERIOR COURT

The federal government also appoints judges to the superior court in each province and territory. The main job of the superior courts is to hear trials. However, they also occasionally hear appeals from lower courts. The names vary across the country, as Concept Summary 2.3 shows.

FEDERAL COURT

Finally, the federal government appoints the members of three specialized courts that deal only with cases that affect the federal government.[2] (The Federal Court's role in the government's regulation of business is discussed in Chapter 25.)

The Tax Court allows a person to dispute the government's demand for the payment of a tax. The Trial Division of the Federal Court hears trials concerning issues that the Constitution assigns to the federal government, such as copyright, bills of exchange, and telecommunications. Concept Summary 1.1 (see page 13), which appeared in the last chapter, listed some of the subjects that are federal matters.) And the Appeal Division of the Federal Court hears appeals from its own Trial Division and from the Tax Court.

PROVINCIAL COURT

The provincial governments appoint the members of the provincial courts. These are trial courts. Although the details vary from place to place, they generally deal with four types of cases: (i) small claims, which are private disputes involving small amounts of money (we will discuss small claims courts in more detail below); (ii) family matters, such as support payments; (iii) youth matters, such as young offenders and neglected children; and (iv) most criminal cases. More serious trials are usually moved up to a superior court. That is true, for instance, of private claims involving large amounts of money and criminal cases involving crimes such as murder. Decisions in the provincial courts can be appealed to the superior court or, in some circumstances, directly to the court of appeal.

Small Claims Courts

a **small claims court** is a type of court that deals with disputes involving limited amounts of money

It will be useful to say something more about small claims courts. A **small claims court** is a type of court that deals with disputes involving limited amounts of money. In most parts of the country, small claims courts are a branch of the provincial courts. Ontario, however, uses a slightly different system.[41] Although the basic ideas are the same everywhere, some of the other details vary from one jurisdiction to the next. You should therefore check the rules before suing. Fortunately, because these courts are designed for easy access, basic information is often readily available on the Internet.[42]

---

41. In Ontario, the small claims courts are a branch of the Superior Court. Small claims disputes, however, are not heard by the Superior Court judges, who are appointed by the federal government. Instead, they are heard by deputy judges, who are lawyers or retired judges who have been appointed under the authority of Ontario's provincial government.

42. There are also several "how-to" manuals that are aimed at non-lawyers. See *eg* M Celap & P Larmondin *Small Claims Court for the Everyday Canadian* (2000).

Small claims courts are very popular with business people because they are faster, simpler, and less expensive than regular courts.[43] Since the rules and procedures are less complicated than usual, many parties act on their own behalf (though they are entitled to use lawyers or paralegals). Although the parties must pay court fees, the amounts are fairly modest.[44] Furthermore, small claims courts are, by their very nature, well-suited to deal with a variety of situations that frequently arise in the business context. Concept Summary 2.4 lists a few examples of claims that are brought to small claims courts.

Concept Summary 2.4

Small Claims Courts—Common Business Disputes

Disputes Dealing with Money Owed	Disputes Dealing with Wrongful Losses
• repayment of loans	• losses arising from a breach of contract
• payment for goods delivered	• losses caused by poor workmanship
• payment for services provided	• delivery of shoddy merchandise
• payment of rent	• damage to goods being moved or stored
• payment of wages	• personal injuries caused by defective products
• charges associated with not sufficient funds (NSF) cheques	• losses occurring under a *Parental Responsibility* Act[45]

There are, however, certain drawbacks to small claims courts.

■ **Geographical limits:** Small claims courts exist in many cities and towns across Canada. As a general rule, the plaintiff must sue either where the relevant event happened (for example, in the town where they slipped on the defendant's icy sidewalk) or where the defendant lives or carries on business. If the claim is started in the wrong location, it may be transferred to another court, which will involve additional expenses.

■ **Types of claims:** Small claims courts can deal with most cases in which the plaintiff is suing for either a limited amount of money or the return of property that they already own. There are, however, several restrictions. The precise rules vary from place to place. In some provinces, for instance, a dispute arising from a defamatory statement or a false imprisonment must be taken to a superior court. Small claims courts are also incapable of dealing with federal statutes, including the *Income Tax Act* and the *Copyright Act*. Nor can they evict tenants or grant divorces.

---

[43] In 2000, approximately 132 000 new civil claims (excluding divorces) were started in Ontario. Over 62 percent of those claims (82 000) appeared in small claims courts. See JF Kenkel & WS Chalmers *Small Claims and Simplified Procedure Litigation* 4th ed (2002) 1.

[44] Although the amounts change from time to time, it is helpful to note, as an example, the fees that are currently charged in the Ontario small claims court. The regular fee for filing a statement of claim is $75, but the amount is increased to $145 for "frequent" claimants (*ie* claimants who had filed more than 10 claims in the preceding 12 months). That category may include home renovators who regularly sue for the value of their work, and lending agencies who regularly sue for repayment of loans. A statement of defence costs $40 to file.

[45] As we will see in Chapter 6, several provinces have enacted statutes that allow a person who has suffered a loss as a result of a child's wrongful behaviour to use a special procedure to sue that child's parents.

- **Types of remedies:** Small claims courts cannot award equitable relief, such as specific performance and injunctions.[46] You therefore must go to a different court if, for instance, you want to force someone to perform a contractual obligation or you want to stop a neighbouring factory from polluting your water. As a general rule, small claims courts are limited to ordering the payment of money. As an exception, however, a judge may order a defendant to hand over property that already belongs to the plaintiff.

- **Monetary limits:** The most significant drawback to suing in a small claims court is that the court can hear only *small claims*. The size of the claim is determined by the amount of money at stake. The limit varies, sometimes quite widely, between jurisdictions. Concept Summary 2.5 states the limit that applied in each province and territory at the time that this chapter was written.[47] While a claim that is worth more than the limit may be brought in a small claims court, the excess amount has to be abandoned. It is not possible to split a single large claim into two smaller ones. For instance, if you live in Ontario and are owed $30 000 on a contract, you cannot sue twice in the small claims court, once for $20 000 and again for $10 000. Nor can you sue for part of the money in a small claims court and the rest in a superior court.

Concept Summary 2.5

Small Claims Courts—Monetary Limits

Province or Territory	Maximum Amount
Alberta	$25 000
British Columbia	$25 000
Manitoba	$10 000
New Brunswick	$6000
Newfoundland and Labrador	$25 000
Northwest Territories	$135 000
Nova Scotia	$25 000
Nunavut	no separate small claims court
Ontario[48]	$25 000
Prince Edward Island	$8000
Saskatchewan	$20 000
Yukon	$25 000

COURT HIERARCHY

courts are arranged in a **hierarchy** according to their importance

As we have already noted, Canadian courts are arranged in a **hierarchy** according to their importance. We need to look at that concept in greater detail. The court hierarchy does not merely determine where a party needs

---

46. The concept of equity was explained at the end of Chapter 1. We introduced the equitable remedies of specific performance and injunctions in Concept Summary 2.2 (see page 38). We will consider these in more detail in Chapter 3 and Chapter 12.

47. The limits change from time to time. Before suing, you should double-check the rules.

48. In Ontario, claims valued between $25 001 and $50 000 are resolved *outside* of the small claims court, but on the basis of a special set of simplified rules. The goal, again, is to make it easier and less expensive to deal with disputes involving limited amounts of money.

FIGURE 2.1 The Court Hierarchy

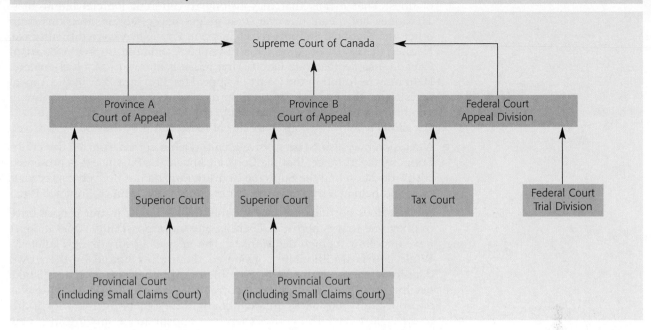

to go for the purposes of a trial or an appeal. It also determines which rules each court must apply.

Figure 2.1 illustrates the concept of a court hierarchy. The first thing to notice is that we should be talking about court *hierarchies*, rather than just a single court *hierarchy*. There is a separate hierarchy for each province and territory, and another for the federal courts. To simplify matters, however, we have limited Figure 2.1 to the systems that exist in two provinces (Province A and Province B) and the Federal Court.[49] The second thing to notice is that even though there are 14 separate court systems in this country, each one ends in the same place: the Supreme Court of Canada.

To fully understand the importance of that scheme, we need to introduce a second concept: the *doctrine of precedent*. The **doctrine of precedent** requires a court to follow any other court that is above it in a hierarchy.[50] We can demonstrate that idea by taking a few examples from Figure 2.1.

the **doctrine of precedent** requires a court to follow any other court that is above it in a hierarchy

- Since it is at the top of the entire court structure, the Supreme Court of Canada is not required to obey any other court.[51] (It is, however, required to obey the Constitution and legislation.)

- The Superior Court of Province A must obey both the Court of Appeal of Province A and the Supreme Court of Canada. Those courts stand above it in the same court hierarchy. They are connected by the same set of lines.

- However, the Superior Court in Province A does not have to obey the Court of Appeal in Province B or the Appeal Division of the Federal Court.

---

[49] Figure 2.1 is simplified in another way as well. It does not list *every* court that may exist. As we previously noted, for example, Ontario has a separate level of court called the Divisional Court. Furthermore, some courts are divided into different divisions. The provincial courts, for example, contain small claims courts, youth courts, and so on.

[50] Lawyers sometimes refer to that doctrine by the Latin *stare decisis*, which means "to stand by decided matters."

[51] Until 1949, it was possible for Canadians to send their appeals to the Judicial Committee of the Privy Council in England, which the Supreme Court of Canada was therefore required to obey.

Figure 2.1 illustrates that these courts are not connected by the same set of lines. That means that they belong to different judicial hierarchies. That does not mean, however, that judges never rely on decisions from other jurisdictions. Suppose a trial judge in Province A has a difficult case. Neither the Court of Appeal for Province A, nor the Supreme Court of Canada, has decided one like it. That judge is allowed to look elsewhere. Help may be found in the Court of Appeal for Province B or in the Appeal Division of the Federal Court. Help also may be found from a court in another country, such as England, the United States, or Australia.[52] Decisions from those courts are not *binding*, but they may be *persuasive*.

■ A decision may also be persuasive even though it comes from a *lower* court. Suppose, for instance, that the Court of Appeal for Province A is presented with a question that the Supreme Court of Canada has not yet answered. It may find help in a trial judgment from either Province A or Province B.

■ A court does not have to obey a court that is below it, but it does have to obey one that is above it. There is one more possibility. Does a court have to follow its *own* decisions?[53] The answer is surprisingly unclear. While courts traditionally considered themselves bound by their own decisions, there is an obvious problem with that rule.[54] If a mistake occurs, there may be no way to correct it. And even if the old rule was appropriate when it was created, changes in society may call for a different rule today. The courts therefore appear to be moving in a new direction. The Supreme Court of Canada will now overrule itself in the right circumstances,[55] and lower courts sometimes do the same.[56]

the **rule of law** states that disputes should be settled on the basis of laws, rather than personal opinions

Having looked at the court hierarchy and the doctrine of precedent, we can now introduce a third concept. The **rule of law** states that disputes should be settled on the basis of laws, rather than personal opinions. The concept of a hierarchy and the doctrine of precedent support the rule of law by requiring judges to follow the courts above them. That system has a number of benefits. One of the most important benefits is consistency. For instance, the Supreme Court of Canada has decided that a mother cannot be sued for carelessly injuring her child before birth.[57] If that issue arises again in British Columbia, Saskatchewan, or the Yukon, it must be resolved in the same way. And that sort of consistency creates another important benefit: respect for the legal system. Even if you disagree with the trial judge's decision in one of those jurisdictions, you can be confident that it was based on law, and not on the judge's personal preference.

As a review of this section, consider how you would answer the questions in You Be the Judge 2.1.

---

52. As we saw in Chapter 1, Canada is a common law country. We inherited our legal system from England. The same is true for many other countries, such as the United States and Australia. As a result, Canadian judges can look abroad, especially to English courts, for help with difficult cases.

53. The question is interesting largely because each court has many judges. Consequently, for example, although two very similar cases may be heard in the Court of Appeal for Province A, they may be heard by entirely different *panels*. In other words, each case may be heard by a different set of judges. Of course, that will certainly be true if the second case is heard years after the first one.

54. In England, the Court of Appeal is still bound by its own decisions. Since 1966, however, the House of Lords (or Supreme Court, as England's highest court is now called) has been entitled to overrule itself: Practice Note (Judicial Precedent) (1966) 1 WLR 1234.

55. *Harrison v Carswell* (1975) 62 DLR (3d) 68 at 71–72 (SCC).

56. There may be less need for a Court of Appeal to correct its own mistakes. The Supreme Court of Canada can do that job for it. Nevertheless, the modern view tends to allow lower courts to correct their own mistakes. That view reflects the fact that the Supreme Court of Canada grants leave to appeal to very few cases.

57. *Dobson v Dobson* (1999) 174 DLR (4th) 1 (SCC).

You Be the Judge 2.1

Court Structure

Oscar Reynes has sued the company that owns the Alberta Fire, a professional soccer team. Because of an administrative error, the team sold 20 000 tickets to a game even though its stadium contains only 10 000 seats. A riot erupted in the stands as fans fought with one another and with the police. Twelve people were killed, and many more were severely injured. Although Oscar did not attend the game and did not personally know anyone who did, he watched the entire spectacle on television. He claims that he has suffered psychological distress as a result of the incident.

As a member of the Court of Queen's Bench in Alberta, you heard Oscar's trial in Edmonton. You are convinced that he has, in fact, suffered emotional harm as a result of watching the riot. You are also convinced that the soccer club acted carelessly by selling too many tickets. However, you are not sure if the defendant is legally responsible for the plaintiff's injury. On the one hand, neither the Supreme Court of Canada nor the Alberta Court of Appeal has discussed that precise issue. On the other hand, several other courts in the country have dealt with very similar cases. Both the Supreme Court of British Columbia and the Saskatchewan Court of Appeal *have* imposed liability. In contrast, both the Superior Court in Quebec and the Ontario Court of Appeal have *refused* to impose liability.

Questions for Discussion

1. Are any of those precedents binding on you? If not, are any of them relevant?

2. Given that consistency is one of the goals of our legal system, what can be done to make the law the same across the country?

Administrative Tribunals

As we saw in Chapter 1, governments now have a much bigger impact on day-to-day life than ever before. To manage that enormous workload, they often delegate decisions and responsibilities to a variety of boards, commissions, agencies, and tribunals. The basic process is fairly simple. Parliament or a provincial legislature will enact a statute that sets out very broad policies for a particular field. The same statute also creates an administrative body and gives it responsibility for actually putting the broad policies into effect. That body may perform a variety of functions. The National Parole Board, for instance, determines whether a prisoner may be released from jail before a full sentence has been served. Within the business world, an egg-marketing board may be given responsibility for formulating rules for the production and sale of eggs, just as an energy board may regulate the price of natural gas. In some situations, a statute may require an administrative body to fulfill a number of roles in a specific field. Ontario's *Securities Act*, for example, created the Ontario Securities Commission (OSC) and gave it responsibility for regulating the industry within the province.[58] It is important that securities are traded in a fair and efficient manner, that investors are protected from shady dealers, and that the public has confidence in the system. Therefore, the OSC establishes rules for the purchase and sale of securities, licenses investment dealers, requires the disclosure of "inside" information, and investigates suspicious transactions.

Another type of administrative body is a *tribunal*. An **administrative tribunal** is a body, somewhere between a government and a court, that resolves issues and disputes that arise in administrative law. There are countless examples. The Canadian Human Rights Tribunal hears allegations of discrimination. The Canadian Artists and Producers Professional Relations Tribunal deals

an **administrative tribunal** is a body, somewhere between a government and a court, that resolves issues and disputes that arise in administrative law

---

58. *Securities Act*, RSO 1990, c S-5 (Ont).

with complaints that arise in that context. Similarly, the Employment Equity Review Tribunal, established under the *Employment Equity Act*, may step in when an employer is accused of paying male employees more than female employees for doing work of similar value.[59] Many tribunals deal with commercial matters. For instance, the Competition Tribunal, which exists under the *Competition Act*, hears complaints of unfair business practices, such as price fixing.[60]

When they make decisions that affect people's rights, administrative tribunals are said to be "*quasi*-judicial." And indeed, some tribunals look and act very much like courts. They hear witnesses, receive evidence, and provide detailed reasons for their decisions. There are, however, important differences. Although a great deal depends upon the circumstances, the rules and procedures that apply in administrative tribunals are generally more flexible and less detailed. Certain types of evidence that can not be heard in court may be permitted in an administrative tribunal. Perhaps most significantly, the people who sit on administrative tribunals are seldom judges. Instead, tribunal members are usually selected, either by the parties or by a statutory process, based on their experience in an area. A tribunal under the *Competition Act*, for instance, includes at least one judge, along with several other individuals chosen by the Minister of Industry on the basis of their expertise in economics, accounting, marketing, and business.

Administrative bodies, like courts, may have a huge impact on a person's life. As a general rule, a person who is unhappy with the decision of a judge may appeal, at least once, to a higher court. The situation within administrative law, however, is different. Legislators often delegate authority to a commission, board, agency, or tribunal because they want specific issues to be resolved quickly and efficiently. Those goals would not be met if every decision could be appealed to a court. Furthermore, administrative bodies usually are staffed by people with specialized knowledge and extensive experience in an area. It therefore makes sense to leave some matters with them.

Because judges recognize that administrators are often experts, courts are generally *deferential* to administrative tribunals. Administrative decisions may be further protected by *privative clauses*. A **privative clause** is a statutory provision that attempts to prevent a court from exercising judicial review over a tribunal decision. A statute may say, for example, that the decision of a tribunal "is final and conclusive and is not open to question or review in a court on any grounds." A person who is dissatisfied with an administrative decision will then be prevented, for the most part, from bringing the matter to court. As always, however, the Constitution is the ultimate authority. Even if a decision is protected by a privative clause, it may be struck down by a court if either the administrative body or the legislature was *ultra vires* ("beyond the authority") by acting outside the scope of authority that it received under the Constitution.

If a court does become involved in an administrative matter, it does not provide an appeal. An appeal usually asks whether the right decision was made. Instead, a court involved in an administrative matter provides *judicial review*. **Judicial review** is a process aimed at determining whether an administrative body's decision is valid. Depending upon the circumstances, judicial review may be available on an issue of *substance* or on an issue of *procedure*.

a **privative clause** is a statutory provision that attempts to prevent a court from exercising judicial review over a tribunal decision

judicial review is a process aimed at determining whether an administrative body's decision is valid

---

[59] *Employment Equity Act*, SC 1995, c 44 (Can).

[60] *Competition Act*, RSC 1985, c C-34 (Can).

JUDICIAL REVIEW OF SUBSTANTIVE DECISIONS

As previously mentioned, courts generally defer to administrative bodies. That statement actually needs to be refined. The *standard* of judicial review that applies in any given case depends upon the circumstances and the nature of the issue.[61] There are two possibilities:

- **Reasonableness:** The *reasonableness standard* requires judicial deference. The court cannot substitute its view for the administrator's view simply because it believes that a question was answered incorrectly. The administrative decision is allowed to stand as long as it was reasonable. Not surprisingly, it is fairly rare for a judge to find that an administrative decision was so wrong as to be unreasonable.

- **Correctness:** The *correctness standard* does *not* require judicial deference. Even if it was reasonable, an administrative decision will be overturned if it is found to be incorrect. The court then acts on its own view of the matter.

The two standards are very different. How, then, do we know which test governs a particular case? Sometimes, that question is answered by precedent. An earlier court may have decided, on similar facts, that a certain kind of issue attracts either the reasonableness standard or the correctness standard. If that precedent is binding, then it must be followed.

If the standard of review cannot be decided by precedent, then a court must consider four questions.[62] (i) Is the administrative decision protected by a *privative clause*, and if so, how strict is that clause? Does it state that the administrative decision is absolutely final and binding, or does it provide protection in only some respects? (ii) How much *expertise* does the administrative body possess in comparison with the court? For instance, while judges seldom come into contact with the highly technical world of securities regulation, they resolve human rights matters every day. (iii) What *purpose* did the legislature intend the administrative body to serve? Does the board, agency, commission, or tribunal actually formulate or develop policy for a particular area, or does it merely apply well-settled rules to specific circumstances? (iv) What is the *nature* of the issue under review? Did the administrative body either exercise a discretion or sift through a mountain of evidence in order to reach a finding of fact? Or does the dispute centre on the administrator's application of a general law?

That four-part test is easily applied if, by a stroke of good fortune, all of the elements point in the same direction. Usually, however, some criteria favour the reasonableness standard while others support the correctness standard. In that situation, it is not enough to simply add up the competing factors and let the majority rule. The court must instead *weigh* and *balance* the individual considerations. Some may be much more significant than others. Not surprisingly, different judges may reach different conclusions in the same case.[63]

---

[61] *Dunsmuir v New Brunswick* (2008) 291 DLR (4th) 577 (SCC).

[62] In the text, each of the four main questions is followed by a pair of subordinate questions. A positive answer to the first of those subordinate questions tends to support the reasonableness standard; a positive answer to the second tends to support the correctness standard.

[63] In *Monsanto Canada Inc v Ontario (Superintendent of Financial Services)*, the lower courts, and even the parties, were agreed that the reasonableness standard applied. The Supreme Court of Canada, in contrast, unanimously preferred the correctness standard: (2004) 242 DLR (4th) 193 (SCC).

JUDICIAL REVIEW OF PROCEDURAL DECISIONS

the **rules of natural justice** require that, in some circumstance, a decision must be the product of a fair process

As an alternative to attacking the substance of a decision made by an administrative body, a person may complain that the *rules of natural justice* were not followed. The **rules of natural justice** require that, in some circumstance, a decision must be the product of a fair process. Some lawyers therefore refer to the idea as the rules of *procedural fairness*. If the process leading up to a decision was unfair, then an aggrieved party may be entitled to a remedy even if the decision itself is otherwise perfectly acceptable.

Not all administrative bodies are bound by the rules of natural justice. To decide whether those rules apply in a particular case, the courts apply a two-part test. (i) The governing legislation may settle the matter. In setting up a tribunal, for instance, a statute may say that the affected parties are entitled to be heard at an oral hearing. That hearing must be conducted fairly. (ii) If the answer is not clear from the legislation, then the court must consider several factors: (a) What is the *nature* of the decision? Did the tribunal formulate a broad policy, or did it resolve a specific dispute? (b) What is the *relationship* between the decision-maker and the affected party? Did the tribunal act with the entire community in mind, or was its decision directed at the affected party personally? (c) How does the decision *affect* the complainant's rights and interests? Is the affected party unhappy for the same reason that many people are unhappy, or did the tribunal's decision eliminate or diminish some right or interest that is special to the affected party?

In each case, the court must weigh all the factors. It nevertheless is possible to offer some general observations. The rules of natural justice probably do not apply if a tribunal exercises a "legislative" function by formulating general policies or rules. That is true, for instance, when a municipal council passes a by-law that prohibits smoking in public parks. In contrast, a tribunal that exercises a "judicial" function likely must respect procedural fairness. That might be true if a human rights tribunal resolved an allegation that an employer discriminated against women by paying male employees a higher salary.

REMEDIES ON JUDICIAL REVIEW

certiorari brings an administrative decision into a court to have it struck down

prohibition orders an administrative body not to proceed with a matter

mandamus directs an administrative body to perform its duties correctly

a **declaration** is issued by a court to provide an enforceable statement of a parties' rights and obligations

Judicial review allows the courts to supervise administrative bodies. The remedies that are available reflect the nature of that exercise. Historically, relief was awarded in the form of *prerogative writs*. Three of those ancient writs are most important: *certiorari*, *prohibition*, and *mandamus*.[64] A writ of **certiorari** ("to prove or to ascertain") is used to bring an administrative decision into a court and to have it *quashed* or struck down. A writ of **prohibition** orders an administrative body not to proceed with a matter. And a writ of **mandamus** ("we command") directs an administrative body to perform its duties correctly. A court can also issue a **declaration** that provides an enforceable statement of the parties' rights and obligations.

Case Brief 2.2 discusses an important case involving administrative law and a business person.

[64.] Some provinces have enacted legislation to simplify the remedies. The basic ideas, however, remain the same.

Case Brief 2.2

Roncarelli v. Duplessis (1959) 16 DLR (2d) 689 (SCC)

Frank Roncarelli owned and operated a very successful, upscale restaurant in Montreal during the 1950s. He was also a firm believer in a form of Christianity known as Jehovah's Witness. At the time, there was great deal of tension within Quebec between Catholics and Jehovah's Witnesses. Members of Roncarelli's church were often arrested for selling a magazine, called *The Watchtower*, even though they were not licensed to do so. Roncarelli used his wealth to bail out nearly 400 Jehovah's Witnesses over a three-year period. Maurice Duplessis, the premier of Quebec, decided to put an end to that practice. The premier talked to the Chairman of the Quebec Liquor Commission, who promptly revoked Roncarelli's licence to sell alcohol in his restaurant. The tactic worked. The restaurant quickly lost business and Roncarelli was forced to sell it within six months. Roncarelli then sued the premier.

The trial judge upheld the claim, but the Quebec Court of Appeal found in favour of the premier. On further appeal, the Supreme Court of Canada reinstated the trial decision. By interfering in the case, the premier acted *ultra vires*. He had no authority or power to direct the Quebec Liquor Commission to revoke Roncarelli's licence. Furthermore, although the Quebec Liquor Commission was entitled to decide who could hold a liquor licence, it had to make that decision honestly and in good faith. In fact, its decision-making process was flawed because it was based on an irrelevant consideration: Roncarelli's support for fellow Jehovah's Witnesses. The Court awarded Roncarelli a total of $33 123: $8123 for business losses and $25 000 for personal losses.

Alternative Dispute Resolution

L.O. ⑩

Courts are essential to a civilized society. Judges provide a way of peacefully resolving disputes when all else fails. As most lawyers will tell you, however, you should go to court only as a last resort. The litigation process has a number of drawbacks. Because it is usually necessary to hire a lawyer to work through the various stages of a lawsuit, litigation is time-consuming and expensive.[65] Because of the number of factors that go into a trial, the result may be difficult to predict.[66] Because the process is adversarial—with both sides attacking each other—it tends to be harmful to ongoing business relationships. And because the courts are open to the public, litigation may generate bad publicity.

There is another reason why it may not be desirable to go to court. In most situations, the only thing that a court can do to help a successful plaintiff is to award damages against the defendant. It's all about the money. The plaintiff may realize, however, that no amount of money will bring a lost loved one back to life. The real goal may be to receive an explanation and an apology. Of course, a court generally cannot compel the defendant to provide such things, and before trial, most defendants are unwilling to do anything that may be seen as an admission of responsibility. Some provinces have taken steps to allow apologies to occur, without any admissions of liability, but the problems largely remain.[67]

For all of those reasons, many Canadians—especially business people—are turning to *alternative dispute resolution (ADR)*. **Alternative dispute resolution (ADR)** is any process that allows the parties to resolve their dispute without going to court. ADR is *required* in some situations. As we already have seen,

alternative dispute resolution (ADR) is any process that allows the parties to resolve their dispute without going to court

---

[65.] It is not at all unusual for a case to wait two years before getting to trial. In 2012, lawyers' fees for a two-day trial were, on average, nearly $25 000 per party. The average cost of an appeal was $21 600: "The Going Rate" *The Canadian Lawyer* (June 2012) 34.

[66.] Litigation has been likened to a lottery: T Ison *The Forensic Lottery* (1968); P Atiyah *The Damages Lottery* (1997).

[67.] *Apology Act*, SBC 2006, c 19 (BC); *The Apology Act*, SM 2007, c 25 (Man); *Apology Act*, SO 2009, c 3 (Ont); *Evidence Act*, SS 2006, c E-11.2, s 23.1 (Sask).

for example, litigants in Ontario and Alberta usually have to pass through the mandatory mediation program before they are allowed to go to court. And as discussed below, it is common for a written contract to include a term that requires disputes to be resolved outside of the courts. For the most part, however, ADR is *voluntary*. The parties choose it because they want to avoid a trial. ADR may be used in almost any type of case. It is very common in family matters (because of the damage that the adversarial process may do to the parties' relationship), and it may even be used in criminal cases (as when criminals of Aboriginal heritage opt for *sentencing circles*). Our focus, of course, is on the use of ADR in business disputes. There are many examples:

- *international sales*—a manufacturer claims that the buyer failed to make suitable shipping arrangements
- *franchises*—local outlets in a chain of fast-food restaurants claim that they are entitled to control their own advertising campaigns
- *employment*—an employee claims discrimination on the grounds of a disability
- *consumer protection*—a group of customers claim that they were hurt by a defective product
- *leases*—a department store claims that it is entitled to renew its lease without an increase in rent
- *professional fees*—a client claims that its lawyer has charged too much for services
- *intellectual property*—a band claims that its songs were sold without permission
- *sports*—an Olympic athlete claims that a test for performance-enhancing drugs was improperly conducted

There are three major types of ADR:

- negotiation
- mediation
- arbitration

We will look at each of those possibilities in more detail. By way of introduction, however, Concept Summary 2.6 suggests how they compare to litigation.

Concept Summary 2.6

Alternative Dispute Resolution—A Comparison

	Quick and Inexpensive	Parties Select Decision-Maker	Parties Control Outcome	Likely to Maintain Ongoing Relationship	Confidential	Conclusive
Litigation	✗	✗	✗	✗	✗	✓
Negotiation	✓	✓	✓	✓	✓	✗
Mediation	✓	✓	✓	✓	✓	✗
Arbitration	✓	✓	✗	✓	✓	✓

NEGOTIATION

A **negotiation** is a discussion aimed at settling a dispute. It is the most common form of ADR. Business people routinely settle their differences by doing what they do best—they make deals. It happens all the time, usually without much fuss. For instance, if a purchaser is unhappy with the quality of the merchandise, the vendor may simply agree to reduce the price. If the situation is more complicated, the parties may negotiate through their lawyers or representatives.[68]

Like the other forms of ADR, negotiation often has several advantages over litigation.

- It tends to be quicker, less complicated, and less expensive.
- It allows the parties to control the process and decide the outcome themselves.
- It often helps the parties to remain on good terms with each other.
- Since it is a private procedure, it can be used to avoid bad publicity.

It is important to realize, however, that negotiation may also have disadvantages.

- Since negotiation requires co-operation, it may not be possible if a dispute has already turned ugly.
- One party may take the opportunity to simply drag the matter out—possibly in the hope that the other side will eventually lose interest or run out of resources.
- If the parties do not have equal bargaining power—perhaps because one side is represented by a team of lawyers, while the other side is small and inexperienced—then negotiations may not result in a fair settlement.
- Confidentiality may be undesirable—a consumer who has been hurt by a defective product may want to go to trial in order to publicize the manufacturer's poor safety standards.
- There is no guarantee of success—negotiations may collapse after years of effort, and the parties may have to go to court after all.
- If a dispute is covered by an insurance policy, the insured party may lose the benefit of the policy unless it immediately hands the matter over to the insurance company.

MEDIATION

Mediation is a process in which a neutral party—called a *mediator*—helps the parties reach an agreement. Mediation is different from negotiation because it involves an outsider. In other respects, however, the two processes are quite similar. The parties still control the process because they select the mediator. And they still control the outcome because mediation is *non-binding*. The

a negotiation is a discussion aimed at settling a dispute

mediation is a process in which a neutral party—called a *mediator*—helps the parties reach an agreement

---

[68.] Earlier in this chapter, we saw that costs may be awarded against a party who rejected a *formal* offer to settle that was filed with the court. That rule does not apply, however, to an *informal* offer made during negotiations.

mediator brings the parties together, listens to their arguments, outlines the issues, comments on each side's strengths and weaknesses, and suggests possible solutions. Often, the end result is an outcome that benefits both parties. But the mediator does *not* give a decision, and the parties are *not* required to obey any orders.

ARBITRATION

arbitration is a process in which a neutral third person, called an arbitrator, imposes a decision on the parties

Arbitration is a process in which a neutral third person—called an *arbitrator*—imposes a decision on the parties.[69] As Concept Summary 2.6 suggests, it sits somewhere between mediation and litigation. It is faster and cheaper than going to trial. It allows the parties to control the process by selecting their own arbitrator. It helps them to maintain an ongoing relationship. And it is confidential. At the same time, however, it shares two important features with court proceedings. The parties do *not* control the outcome, and they *are* (usually) required to obey someone else's decision.

The parties may decide to go to arbitration after a dispute has already erupted. It is, however, very common for business people to agree to arbitration in advance. A fruit producer in Honolulu promises to deliver pineapples to a beverage manufacturer in Vancouver. A Russian hockey star signs a long-term deal to play with a Canadian team. A construction company agrees to erect an office tower for a building mogul. The parties hope that things will go smoothly, but they are sophisticated enough to realize that problems may occur. If so, the parties want to have easy access to definite results. They therefore insert an *arbitration clause* into their contract. In a typical case, that clause will require the parties to *submit to binding arbitration* (perhaps after an attempt at mediation). It will also set out as much information as possible regarding the actual arbitration process. It may, for instance, create a process for selecting the arbitrators and it may state that the arbitrator's decision is final. If necessary, it is usually possible to take an arbitrator's decision to court and enforce it in much the same way as a judgment.

The actual arbitration process will vary with the circumstances. It may occur anywhere in the world that is convenient for the parties. It may be fairly informal or it may closely resemble court proceedings. The arbitrator may, for instance, hear arguments from lawyers and receive evidence from witnesses who are under oath. But even when an arbitration looks a great deal like a trial, there will often be one important difference. An arbitrator will usually have greater expertise than a judge. The government selects people to become judges for a variety of reasons. And once those people are *on thebench*, they generally hear every type of case. Sometimes they have considerable experience in an area; sometimes they have none at all. After working as a criminal defence lawyer for many years, a person may become a judge and be assigned to a case involving a complicated international sales contract. In contrast, the parties will select an arbitrator on the basis of experience and expertise. Arbitrators are often lawyers or professors who have spent decades dealing exclusively in specific areas of law. They earn their reputations by consistently delivering decisions that are fair and well-informed.

Business Decision 2.2 examines the operation of an arbitration clause.

[69.] It is not unusual for the parties to select more than one arbitrator. For instance, arbitrators often sit in panels of three.

Arbitration Clause

Frozen Pond Inc, a Canadian company, operates a wide range of manufacturing businesses around the world. One of those businesses is a car manufacturing plant in South Korea. Frozen Pond recently entered into a contract with Deutsch GmbH, a German company that produces steel. The contract will run for a period of 10 years and it may, depending upon the circumstances, involve over $50 000 000.

The parties have agreed to use arbitration for any disputes that may arise. They have included the following clause in their contract: "All disputes arising out of, or in connection with, this contract shall be settled by arbitration."

Question for Discussion

1. The primary purpose of an arbitration clause is to set up a procedure that will allow disputes to be resolved quickly and easily. Have the parties selected an appropriate clause? What additional information should the clause include? What questions might arise if the parties eventually go to arbitration?

Chapter Summary

Legal disputes may be resolved either through litigation or through alternative dispute resolution. Litigation is the system of resolving disputes in court. As a general rule, any adult can sue or be sued. Certain restrictions do apply, however, to children and people with intellectual disabilities. Corporations are treated like human beings, but other types of organizations are not. Special rules may apply when the government is sued. A class action may allow a single person, or a small group of people, to sue on behalf of a larger group of claimants. Parties to a legal dispute may represent themselves, or they may hire lawyers or paralegals.

Pleadings are the documents that are used in a lawsuit. They identify the issues and clarify the nature of the dispute. There are various types of pleadings, including statements of claim, statements of defence, counterclaims, replies, and demands for particulars. Pleadings must be filed within certain time periods. The plaintiff's rights may be lost or unenforceable if the claim is not made within the limitation period. The plaintiff may receive a default judgment if the defendant does not react quickly to a statement of claim. The plaintiff is the person who makes the complaint. The defendant is the person about whom the complaint is made.

Before the parties go to trial, they usually conduct examinations for discovery. They may also go through a pretrial conference or a mandatory mediation program. Most lawsuits are heard by a judge alone, but some are heard by a judge and a jury. Each side will present evidence. There may be ordinary witnesses or expert witnesses, who go through examinations-in-chief and cross-examinations. The court normally will not allow hearsay evidence. The litigation process is adversarial. In a civil trial, the plaintiff must prove the claim on a balance of probabilities. (In a criminal trial, the Crown must prove the accused's guilt beyond a reasonable doubt.) In a civil trial, the judge will find that the defendant is either liable or not liable. (In a criminal trial, the court will normally find that the defendant is either guilty or not guilty.) If the plaintiff wins a lawsuit, the court may award a number of remedies, including compensatory

damages, punitive damages, nominal damages, specific performance, injunctions, or rescission. A defendant who has been found liable and ordered to pay money to the plaintiff is called a judgment debtor. It is sometimes more difficult to enforce a judgment than to win a case.

A party who is unhappy with a trial judgment may appeal. Appellate courts usually have at least three judges. The party who attacks the decision of the lower court is called the appellant and the party who defends that decision is called the respondent. An appellate court will correct any mistakes of law, but they will correct mistakes of fact only if the trial judge made a palpable and overriding error. The appellate court may affirm, vary, or reverse a trial judgment, or it may send the case back for a re-trial. An appellate judge who disagrees with the majority's decision may dissent.

Costs are the expenses that a party incurs during litigation. As a general rule, costs are awarded to whichever side wins the lawsuit. Costs may be awarded on a party-and-party basis or a solicitor-and-client basis. A judge may award costs either to punish a party for acting improperly or for rejecting a settlement offer. A party who is concerned about the costs of litigation may find a lawyer to work on a contingency fee basis. A contingency fee agreement requires a client to pay its lawyer's fees only if the lawsuit is successful.

There are several types of courts in Canada, including the Supreme Court of Canada, courts of appeal, superior courts, federal courts, and provincial courts. A small claims court is a type of provincial court that uses simplified procedures for claims involving limited amounts of money. Canadian courts are arranged in a hierarchy according to their importance. The doctrine of precedent requires a court to follow any other court that is above it in the same hierarchy. The concept of a court hierarchy and the doctrine of precedent support the rule of law.

To help manage its enormous workload, Parliament and the provincial governments often delegate authority to formulate or apply policies and rules to various boards, commissions, agencies, and tribunals. A decision made by an administrative body is ultra vires and void if that body or the legislature that created it acted beyond the scope of its constitutional authority. An **administrative tribunal** is a body, somewhere between a government and a court, that resolves issues and disputes that arise in administrative law. Tribunals that affect people's rights are quasi-judicial. However, although they may receive evidence, hear from witnesses, and deliver reasons for their decisions, administrative tribunals generally operate in a more flexible and informal manner, as compared to courts. Courts generally defer to administrators' expertise. A privative clause is a statutory provision that attempts to prevent a court from exercising judicial review over a tribunal decision. If a court does become involved in an administrative matter, it provides judicial review by determining whether an administrative body's decision is valid. Judicial review may be applied to substantive decisions. If so, the court will apply either the reasonableness standard or the correctness standard. In deciding which standard applies, a court will look for a binding precedent. If it finds none, it will consider a privative clause, the extent of the administrators' expertise, the purpose of the administrative body, and the nature of the disputed issue. Judicial review may also apply to procedural decisions. Rules of natural justice require that, in some circumstances, a decision must be the product of a fair process. In deciding whether those rules apply, a court will look for a binding precedent. If it finds none, it will consider the nature of the decision, the relationship between the decision-maker and the affected party, and the manner in which the decision impacted upon the affected party. After judicial review, a court may award a variety of remedies, including certiorari, prohibition, mandamus, or a declaratory judgment.

Alternative dispute resolution (ADR) is any process that allows the parties to resolve their dispute without going to court. Although ADR often has significant advantages over litigation, it may be inappropriate or undesirable in some circumstances. The parties usually *choose* to use ADR, but they are sometimes *required* to use it. There are three major types of ADR: negotiation, mediation, and arbitration. Negotiation is a discussion that leads to the settlement of a dispute. Mediation is a process in which a neutral party, called a mediator, helps the parties reach an agreement. Arbitration is a process in which a neutral third person, called an arbitrator, imposes a decision on the parties. Business contracts often contain arbitration clauses that set out the procedure that will be used to resolve any disputes that arise. Arbitration is generally binding on the parties and the arbitrator's decision often cannot be appealed.

MyBusLawLab   ADDITIONAL RESOURCES FOR CHAPTER 2

MyBusLawLab provides students with an assortment of tools to help enrich the learning experience, including a Study Plan with Pre- and Post-tests, mini-cases with assessments, and provincial content material, which provides links to relevant cases, legislation, and additional resources.

MyBusLawLab provides the following resources for Chapter 2:

- Sample Contingency Fee Agreement
- Sample Arbitration Clause

Provincial Material

- **British Columbia:** Court Structure in British Columbia, Small Claims Court, Federal Court, Lawyers Fees, Law Society of British Columbia, Notaries, Paralegals, Sheriffs and Bailiffs, Class Action Lawsuits, Limitation Periods, Litigation Guardian, Mediation and Arbitration, International Arbitration, Juries for Civil Actions, Practice of Law, Proceedings Against the Crown, Administrative Tribunals, Judicial Review, Comity in the Enforcement of Foreign Judgments, Commercial Arbitration and Mediation Centre for the Americas, International Investment, Reciprocal Enforcement, Rules of Court—Revised, Supreme Court of BC Self Help Centre (SHC)

- **Alberta:** *Class Proceedings Amendment Act (2010),* Class Actions, Contingency Fees, Costs, International Arbitration, Small Claims Court, *Provincial Offences Procedure Amendment Act,* Reciprocal Enforcement, *Rules of Court Statutes Amendment Act (2011)*

- **Manitoba and Saskatchewan:** Alternative Dispute Resolution, Court Rules, Small Claims, Trial Courts of the Provinces, Costs, Courts in the Province, Pre-Trial Process Differences

- **Ontario:** Alternative Dispute Resolution, Administrative Law, Arbitration, Case Management, Class Actions, Commercial Arbitration, Consumer Arbitration, Consumer Class Actions, Contingency Fees, Costs, Court System, Enforcement of Foreign Judgments, Inter-provincial Enforcement, Jurisdiction, Legal Aid, Legal Profession, Paralegals, Mandatory Mediation, Security for Costs, Simplified Procedure, Small Claims Court, Solicitor–Client Privilege, Trial Process

- **Atlantic Provinces:** Arbitration Clauses, Class Action Certification, Contingency Fees, *International Commercial Arbitration Act,* Reciprocal Enforcement of Judgments

Review Questions

1. "An organization can always be sued in the same way as a person." Is that statement true? Explain your answer.

2. What is a "class action"? Describe a situation in which a class action may be desirable.

3. "'Certification' refers to a process or decision that always brings a lawsuit to an end." Is that statement true? Explain your answer.

4. "A paralegal is someone who works outside the legal system. While paralegals may be able to provide practical help to their clients, they cannot perform any of the services or functions that a lawyer provides." Is that statement true? Explain your answer.

5. "A provincial Law Society is entitled to set standards and suggest how lawyers ought to act. A Law Society, however, does not have any actual control over lawyers and it cannot offer any form of help for people who are hurt when lawyers act badly." Is that statement true? Explain your answer.

6. "All lawsuits are governed by the same limitation period. Once the defendant receives a statement of claim, they must respond in 14 days or less. If they fail to do so, a court may award default judgment." Is that statement true? Explain your answer.

7. Explain the concept of *laches*.

8. What is the difference between a statement of claim and a counterclaim?

9. What is an "examination for discovery"? What purposes do examinations for discovery serve?

10. Explain the purpose of a pre-trial conference.

11. Explain the meaning of these two phrases: "the balance of probabilities" and "beyond a reasonable doubt." In what type of case will each phrase be used?

12. What is "hearsay evidence"?

13. Describe four different results that an appellate court may reach.

14. "Winning in court is often the easy part—enforcing the judgment may be much more difficult." Discuss that statement.

15. Explain how the courts use the concept of costs to encourage the parties to behave appropriately.

16. "A contingency fee is a special type of penalty that a court may award against a defendant. The 'contingency' part of the phrase refers to the fact that the penalty is used only if the defendant acted very badly. The 'fee' part of the phrase refers to the fact that the penalty requires the defendant to pay the fee that the plaintiff's lawyer charged the plaintiff." Is that statement true? Explain your answer.

17. Explain the advantages and disadvantages of suing in a small claims court.

18. Describe the "doctrine of precedent." Explain how it is related to the court hierarchy and to the rule of law.

19. What is "judicial review"? Briefly explain the manner in which a court will approach the decision of an administrative tribunal during judicial review.

20. Define the term "alternative dispute resolution." Name three forms of ADR and identify some of the advantages and disadvantages of each.

Cases and Problems

1. Salazar Construction Inc (SCI) is a badly run company. As a result of a poor business model, insufficient resources, inadequate training, and insensitive managers, it has generated a remarkable level of ill will amongst its workers. Antonio Salazar founded the company 30 years ago, but he long ago sold his interest in the business and he consequently no longer plays any role within the corporation. It nevertheless bothers him to see the workers at SCI suffer and he recently decided that "enough is enough—someone's got to do something." He wants to bring a class action claim against SCI on behalf of its current and former employees. He believes that there are at least three sets of claims. First, although they do not realize it, one group of workers has been systematically underpaid for the past decade. Second, many former employees were forced into early retirement as a result of injuries that they suffered because SCI forced them to work in dangerous conditions. And third, Antonio Salazar knows that a small number of female employees—three or four secretaries—have dealt with various forms of sexual harassment over the years. Is Antonio Salazar entitled to bring a class action claim against SCI on those bases? What benefits do class action proceedings generally create?

2. Nine years ago, Papandreou Financial Services Inc entered into a long-term contract with Merkel Gratuities Ltd. Until recently, both parties performed faithfully, and both were very happy with their arrangements. Last week, however, Merkel alleged that Papandreou had committed various forms of misconduct within the past year. Papandreou has angrily denied all of those allegations, and it insists, on the contrary, that Merkel owes it a great deal of money. Merkel would like to sue Papandreou, but it is worried about several things. First, it is concerned that since the contract is quite old, any legal action would be barred by the passage of time. Second, Merkel is worried that the law may not be on its side. The most important allegation against Papandreou raises a difficult question of law. Different Canadian

courts have given different answers to that question. Merkel and Papandreou created and performed their contract in a single province. The courts of that province have not yet addressed the issue. Trial judges in some other provinces have held in favour of parties in Merkel's position. Appellate judges in a third set of provinces have held in favour of parties in Papandreou's position. Third, Merkel is concerned that it does not have all the information that it would need to prove its case, and Papandreou has said that it would never provide that information. Fourth, Merkel knows that lawsuits are expensive. It is worried that if it sues Papandreou, then Papandreou will turn around and sue it. Merkel therefore is concerned that it may have to pay for two completely separate sets of lawyers, two completely separate sets of documents, and so on. Should Merkel really be worried about any of these four issues? Explain your answer.

3. Malcolm Poole is unhappy. He recently won his claim against a corporation for breach of contract, and the court awarded him damages of nearly $400 000. The company paid the damages almost immediately. Today, however, his lawyer, Ellie Little, presented Malcolm with her final bill. Two years ago, when he hired her, Malcolm explained that since he was broke, he would not be able to pay Ellie very much money if his claim failed. After a long discussion, the parties came to a verbal agreement. Although Ellie would not charge anything if the case was lost, she would be entitled to 75 percent of any money that she won on Malcolm's behalf. Ellie therefore insists that Malcolm must pay $300 000 for her services. He agrees that she did a good job, but he believes that she is demanding far too much money. Is Ellie entitled to $300 000? If not, is she entitled to anything? Explain your answer.

4. After being subjected to various complaints by customers and competitors, Acme Inc was called before an administrative tribunal. Following a surprisingly informal procedure, in which the tribunal received hearsay evidence and refused to apply the rules of evidence that normally apply in court, Acme was ordered to pay a large fine. The tribunal reached that conclusion largely by applying its experience and expertise to the facts.

After reviewing the case and doing more research into the substantive issues, Acme's lawyer has formed the opinion that while the tribunal's decision is not far-fetched or unsupported by the facts, it probably was not the best decision that could have been reached. The lawyer has also observed that while the complaints made against Acme were all closely tied to an issue of international trade, the tribunal purported to act under the authority of a provincial statute.

Finally, in trying to determine whether the tribunal's decision might be overturned in court, Acme's lawyer discovered that the provincial statute in question provides a provision that states, "All tribunal decisions are final and shall not be subject to judicial review on any ground whatsoever." Is there much chance that Acme will be able to persuade a judge to overturn the tribunal's decision? Explain your answer. (To fully answer that question, you may find it helpful to review some parts of Chapter 1.)

5. Glenn Brendel is a classical musician. Although he is now internationally famous for his work with symphony orchestras, he began his career by recording piano pieces by Bach and Beethoven. Those recordings sat unnoticed for many years in the basement of the Vancouver studio where they were made. Recently, however, Trilby Svengali, the owner of that studio, rediscovered the recordings and realized that they had economic value. She quickly released them on a series of CDs, which have since topped the charts.

While he is delighted with the public's reaction to his early work, Glenn Brendel is quite upset that the recordings were released without his knowledge, and he is very upset that he has not been paid for them. Svengali has responded by pointing to a contract that Brendel signed in 1971. Svengali believes that that contract gave her ownership of the recordings.

Brendel sued Svengali in the Federal Court for breach of copyright. While each party was confident that they would win, neither was anxious to go to court. Consequently, at the beginning of the dispute, Brendel formally offered to settle his claim for $400 000. Svengali immediately responded by formally offering to settle the claim for $200 000. Unfortunately, the parties were unable to reach an agreement and the case has now gone to trial. Both sides have run up very large lawyers' bills.

Consider the issue of costs. What will the result likely be if the judge finds that (i) Svengali is liable for $500 000, (ii) Svengali is liable for $100 000, or (iii) Svengali is not liable at all?

6. Carpathian Blood Services Inc (CBSI) entered into a contract two years ago with Vlad Tepes. The relationship was unhappy from the outset and CBSI has decided that it would like to bring matters to an end. It believes that it may do so on a number of grounds. First, it appears that Tepes may have duped the company into creating the agreement in the first place. Second, it is quite likely that Tepes breached several terms of the contract. Tepes insists that even if he is in breach (which he denies), CBSI has not suffered any loss. That may be true—a court would have to decide the issue. CBSI, however, feels that it has lost money as a result of Tepes's breach of contract. Furthermore, it believes that Tepes not only breached the contract, but also acted so badly that he ought to be punished somehow. (The president of CBSI has gone so far as to call Tepes the "Dark Prince"!) And third, CBSI says that even if Tepes is not in breach as alleged, he clearly has not fulfilled his promise to transfer a piece of land to the company. In any event, CBSI is worried that it would have a difficult time collecting on a judgment, even if a court did find in its favour. Tepes has warned the company that it "can't get blood out of a stone" and he has vowed that he would never voluntarily pay a cent. The case obviously is still at an early stage. Nevertheless CBSI would like to know what sort of remedies it might receive if it defeated Tepes in court. It also would like to know whether there are any means of forcing a defendant to pay money as ordered by a court. Please advise the company.

Power to the People

Nova Scotia Power Inc (NSPI) holds a virtual monopoly on the sale of electricity in Nova Scotia. To ensure that NSPI does not abuse its position by inflating prices or by unfairly discriminating between different groups of consumers, the province has enacted several statutes to regulate the sale of electricity. The aim is to limit NSPI to the revenue stream that it would enjoy if it sold electricity in a competitive market. In effect, the amount that NSPI receives from its various categories of customers cannot exceed a combination of (i) the cost of supplying the electricity, and (ii) a "reasonable rate of return" or profit margin.

The regulatory regime requires NSPI to have its rate (or pricing) schemes approved by the Nova Scotia Utility and Review Board (the Board). In deciding whether or not it will grant such approval, the Board must apply the rules created by the *Public Utilities Act*, RSNS 1989, c 380. Section 67(1) of that Act states that "all tolls, rates and charges shall always, under substantially similar circumstances and conditions in respect of service of the same description, be charged equally to all persons and at the same rate." In accordance with section 67(1), the Board recently approved a price scheme proposed by NSPI, under which all residential consumers will be charged the same rate for the electricity that they consume.

Although it may seem fair for every residential consumer to pay the same rate, a number of individuals, calling themselves the Affordable Price Coalition, see things differently. The members of the Coalition come from a variety of backgrounds, but they all share one important characteristic: they all earn less than ~$20 000 annually. As a result, they all find it very difficult to find enough money to buy electricity from NSPI. And that, they say, simply is not fair. While they do not expect to receive electricity for free, they argue that they have the right to purchase the necessities of life at prices that they can afford.

The Coalition members offer a simple comparison to make their point. Assume that NSPI charges residential customers 10¢ per kilowatt hour. Customer A, a wealthy lawyer with a large house, spends $1500 a year on electricity. Customer B, a low-income single mother who lives in a small apartment, spends $750 per year on electricity. Although he uses more electricity, Customer A can easily afford to pay the bill he receives from NSPI because he earns $150 000 per year. In contrast, even though she uses less electricity, Customer B struggles to pay her bill because her annual income is only $15 000.

The Coalition members realize that even though their bills come from NSPI, the real problem lies with section 67(1) of the *Public Utilities Act*, which requires the Board to ensure that all customers pay the same rate. That provision, the Coalition members say, discriminates against them on the basis of their economic status. As the example has shown, a single-rate pricing scheme creates hardship for poor people, but not for others. The Coalition members consequently intend to argue that section 67(1) violates their rights under the *Charter of Rights and Freedoms*.

Questions to Consider

1. As a general matter, does the *Charter* apply in this situation? If so, precisely which feature of the case attracts the *Charter*?

2. Assuming that the *Charter* does generally apply in this situation, what section of the *Charter* will the Coalition members most likely rely upon in complaining about discrimination? Is that argument likely to succeed? Does the *Charter* provide protection against discrimination on the basis of economic status?

3. As a matter of policy, *should* the members of the Coalition be protected in this sort of situation? Suggest some arguments for and against a right to be free from discrimination on the basis of economic status.

4. Assume that the members of the Coalition have suffered unfair discrimination and that, by way of remedy, they are individually entitled to be re-paid to the extent that they were overcharged. Also assume that while the Coalition includes between 250 and 300 people, the amount of re-payment varies from one person to the next. What sort of lawsuit would be most appropriate in the circumstances?

ADDITIONAL RESOURCES

Nova Scotia Court of Appeal—*Boulter v Nova Scotia Power Inc*
www.canlii.org/en/ns/nsca/doc/2009/2009nsca17/2009nsca17.html

This website contains the Nova Scotia Court of Appeal's decision in the case upon which this case study is based.

Nova Scotia Power Inc **www.nspower.ca/en/home/default.aspx**

This website is home to the company involved in this case. It provides information about the company and its pricing schemes.

The Court—(Mis)Construing *Kapp* to Preclude the Impoverished **www.thecourt.ca/2009/05/08/misconstruing-kapp-to-preclude-the-impoverished/**

This website contains a case comment on the Nova Scotia Court of Appeal's decision in *Boulter v Nova Scotia Power Inc*. The author suggests that the court applied the wrong test in deciding that section 15(1) of the *Charter* does not prohibit discrimination on the ground of economic status.

Social Rights Advocacy Centre **www.socialrights.ca**

This website belongs to the Social Rights Advocacy Centre. The Centre is a not-for-profit, non-governmental organization aimed at providing relief from poverty. It provided expert evidence in the early stages of *Boulter v Nova Scotia Power Inc*. Such organizations attempt to level the playing field when disadvantaged individuals seek legal remedies.

3 Introduction to Torts

LEARNING OBJECTIVES

After completing this chapter, you should be able to:

❶ Define the word "tort."

❷ Explain the similarities and differences between torts and crimes.

❸ Explain the similarities and differences between torts and contracts.

❹ Distinguish between intentional torts, negligence torts, and strict liability torts.

❺ Explain the circumstances in which tort law will adopt a rule of strict liability.

❻ Describe the nature of liability insurance and explain why it is important to business people.

❼ Describe the concept of vicarious liability and explain how it affects business people.

❽ Use the concept of risk management to explain how the difference between employees and independent contractors is important to the doctrine of vicarious liability.

❾ Outline the types of remedies that are generally available in tort law.

❿ Describe two important types of alternative compensation schemes and explain why they have been created.

There are two main sources of obligations in private law: contract and tort. Part 3 of this book is devoted to contract. We begin in this part, however, with tort. Our discussion is split into four sections. The current chapter provides a general introduction to tort law. Chapter 4 considers intentional torts; Chapter 5 considers a variety of torts that affect business people; and Chapter 6 considers the most important tort of all—negligence.

Introduction to Tort Law

L.O. ❶ ❷ ❸ ❹ ❺

"Tort" is not a word that people often use outside of the law. It is derived from the French word *"tort"* (meaning "wrong"), which came from the Latin word *"tortus"* (meaning "twisted or crooked"). While it is difficult to precisely define the term, we can say that a **tort** generally consists of a failure to fulfill a private obligation that was imposed by law.

a **tort** generally consists of a failure to fulfill a private obligation that was imposed by law

TORTS AND CRIMES

That definition of "tort" contains a number of important ideas. Notice, for instance, that it refers to the breach of a *private* obligation.[1] An obligation in tort law is owed to a person.[2] For instance, I owe an obligation to you personally to not make defamatory statements about your past.[3] That obligation will be broken if I falsely tell your employer that you were once convicted of murder. I will be a **tortfeasor**—a person who has committed a tort. You will then be entitled to sue me.[4] If you win that lawsuit, the court will hold me liable and it will probably order me to pay damages to you.

a **tortfeasor** is a person who has committed a tort

    A tort can be compared with a crime. Whereas a tort occurs when a person breaks a *private* obligation, a crime occurs if a person breaks a *public* obligation. A public obligation is owed to society as a whole, rather than to any particular person. Consequently, if something goes wrong, the government will prosecute the accused on behalf of the whole community. That is true even if the crime was one (such as theft) that affected a specific person. Finally, if the court agrees with the government, then the accused will be found guilty and may be subject to some form of punishment (such as a fine or imprisonment).[5]

    Concept Summary 3.1 (see below) summarizes the differences between torts and crimes.

    Although it is important to distinguish between torts and crimes, it is also important to appreciate that the two concepts often arise from the same facts. If I hit you, I will commit the tort of battery and the crime of assault; if I take your car without permission, I will commit the tort of conversion and the crime of theft; if I sneak into your house, I commit the tort of trespass to land and the crime of break and enter; and so on.

---

[1] The definition also refers to a private obligation that was "imposed by law." As discussed below, a contract also contains private obligations. Contractual obligations are different from tort obligations, however, because they are created by the parties, rather than imposed by law.

[2] As we will see in Chapter 21, the legal definition of a "person" generally includes a corporation.

[3] The tort of defamation is discussed in Chapter 5.

[4] As we saw in the last chapter, you have to prove your tort claim on a *balance of probabilities*—the judge has to be satisfied that your version of events is *probably* true.

[5] As we saw in the last chapter, the government in a criminal prosecution has to prove its case *beyond a reasonable doubt*—the judge has to be satisfied that the accused almost certainly committed the crime.

Concept Summary 3.1

Tort Law and Criminal Law

	Private law or public law?	Which parties are involved in the obligation?	Who are the parties to the action if that obligation is broken?	What is the usual remedy?
Tort Law	private law	the defendant owes an obligation to the plaintiff	the plaintiff sues the defendant	compensatory damages
Criminal Law	public law	the accused owes an obligation to society	the government prosecutes the accused	punishment (such as a fine or imprisonment)

That overlap between tort and crime is not surprising. Those two areas of law share a common history. Every society has to respond to misconduct. Those responses tend to become more sophisticated over time. For instance, the common law long ago abolished the rule of *blood feud*, which allowed the family of a murder victim to take revenge by killing the murderer or someone in the murderer's family. In place of that rule, local communities began the practice of requiring a murderer to pay money to the victim's family. The same process also applied to other types of wrongs (such as breaking a person's arm or killing a person's horse). Over time, those basic ideas branched off in two directions. The idea of allowing a victim to demand compensation from a wrongdoer developed into the system of private tort law. The idea of allowing the community to punish a wrongdoer developed into the public system of criminal law.[6]

TORTS AND CONTRACTS

Just as torts may be confused with crimes, they may also be confused with contracts. We will look at contracts in much more detail in Part 3. For now, it will be enough to outline one similarity and four differences between torts and contracts.

- **Structure:** Both tort and contract involve *primary* and *secondary* obligations. Primary obligations tell people how they ought to act. For instance, the tort of battery says, "Do not touch another person in an offensive way." (Battery is discussed in more detail later in the next chapter.)The law of contract says, "Keep your promises." Secondary obligations are remedial. They tell people how they must act *after* primary obligations have been broken. In most cases, the defendant is told, "Pay money to the plaintiff as compensation for the losses that you caused." That is true whether the case involves a tort or a contract.

- **Source of Primary Obligations:** There are, however, some fundamental differences between tort and contract. The first is concerned with the source of primary obligations. Obligations in tort are simply imposed by law.[7] Even though you never promised to behave yourself, even though we are complete strangers, and even if (remarkably) you never heard of

---

[6.] For an excellent summary of tort law's historical connection to criminal law, see M Kerr, J Kurtz & L Olivo *Canadian Tort Law in a Nutshell* (1997) at 1–11.

[7.] The same is true of public obligations in criminal law.

such a law, you must not commit a battery against me. Obligations in contract, on the other hand, are created by the parties. If you have an obligation to deliver a car to me, it is only because you voluntarily agreed to do so.

- **Privity:** When two people enter into a contract, they create a special relationship for themselves. Consequently, as we will see in Chapter 8, the doctrine of *privity* states that the only people who can sue, or be sued, on a contract are the parties themselves. In contrast, because obligations in tort are simply imposed by law, there is no need for the parties to create a special relationship for themselves. I can sue you for battery, for instance, even if you never promised to not hit me.

- **Compensation:** Compensation is available in both tort and contract. As a general rule, however, it is calculated differently in each. The purpose of imposing obligations in tort law is to prevent harm. The tort of battery prohibits you from hurting me with punches and kicks. Consequently, if you have breached your primary obligation, then you will have a secondary obligation to put me back into the position that I enjoyed at the outset. If I had to spend $5000 on medical treatment, I am entitled to recover that amount from you. In contrast, the purpose of creating obligations in contract is usually to provide benefits. I paid $10 000 to you because I wanted your car. If you breach your primary obligation, then you will once again be required to compensate me. This time, however, the goal is to put me into the position that I expected to enjoy once you fulfilled your promise. Consequently, if the car was really worth $13 000, then you will have to pay that amount to me. We therefore can say that while tort looks *backward*, contract looks *forward*.

- **Risk Management:** The fact that primary obligations in tort and contract arise for different reasons also has a significant impact on the issue of risk management. Because tort obligations are imposed by law, they are more likely to take a person by surprise, and they may require more than a person is actually capable of providing.[8] In contrast, because obligations in contract are created voluntarily, they should never take the parties by surprise, and they should never require more than the parties believe they can actually provide.

Concept Summary 3.2 (see page 66) summarizes our discussion of tort and contract.

TYPES OF TORTS

So far, we have distinguished between tort law and other types of law. It also is important to distinguish between different types of torts. As we will discover in the next three chapters, tort law covers a great deal of territory. It includes almost every sort of private law wrong outside of breach of contract.[9]

[8.] For instance, as we will see in Chapter 6, the tort of negligence requires people to act with "reasonable care." That is true even if a particular person suffers from a mental incapacity and therefore cannot possibly meet the legal expectation.

[9.] As we saw in Chapter 1, our legal system was divided into courts of law and courts of equity until the end of the nineteenth century. Torts were developed in the courts of law. Courts of equity also developed a small number of private law wrongs, including breach of confidence and breach of fiduciary duty. Although those equitable wrongs look a great deal like common law wrongs, they are usually excluded from the category of "tort" on entirely historical grounds.

Concept Summary 3.2

Comparing Tort and Contract

	Source of Obligation	Privity	Compensatory Damages	Risk Management
Tort	imposed by law	enforceable regardless of any agreement between the parties	place the plaintiff as if the tort had not occurred	• may take a person by surprise • may require more than a person is able to give
Contract	voluntarily created by the parties	enforceable only by or against a party to the contract	place the plaintiff as if the contract had been performed	• always possible to know the obligations in advance • always possible to limit the obligations to promises that can be fulfilled

Not surprisingly, different situations call for different rules. Tort law has to strike a balance between competing interests. While it wants to respect freedom of choice, it also wants to discourage dangerous behaviour. While it wants to allow businesses to be innovative and efficient, it also wants to compensate consumers who are hurt by manufactured goods. While it wants to tightly control activities that threaten physical safety, it also wants to adopt a more lenient approach where the only risk is to financial well-being. And so on.

Tort law responds to those challenges in a variety of ways. One of its most important strategies focuses on *mental culpability*. Because tort law needs to strike a different balance in different circumstances, some torts require proof that the defendant acted with a *guilty mind*, while others do not. There are three possibilities.

- *Intentional torts* occur when a person intentionally acts in certain ways. As we will see in the next two chapters, however, the law often uses a rather odd definition of "intention." Some torts require proof that the defendant intended to hurt the plaintiff. Others are satisfied by proof that the defendant merely intended to act in a certain way, even if they did not realize that the plaintiff would be hurt.

- *Negligence torts* occur when a person acts carelessly.

- *Strict liability torts* occur when a person does something wrong without intending to do so and without acting carelessly. It is enough that the defendant was responsible for the situation that resulted in the plaintiff's injury.

Concept Summary 3.3 (see p. 67) classifies the intentional torts, negligence torts, and strict liability torts that we will examine in this book.

Strict Liability

We will discuss intentional torts and negligence torts in considerable detail over the next three chapters. At this point, however, it is important to say something about strict liability torts, which are unusual and often misunderstood.

Strict liability torts create special problems for risk management. They do not require proof of any sort of intentional or careless wrongdoing. Liability is imposed simply because the defendant was responsible for the situation that

Concept Summary 3.3

Forms of Tortious Wrongdoing

Intentional torts	• assault
	• battery
	• false imprisonment
	• trespass to land
	• interference with chattels
	• conspiracy
	• intimidation
	• interference with contractual relations
	• unlawful interference with economic relations
	• deceit
Negligence torts	• occupiers' liability
	• nuisance[10]
	• negligence
	• professional negligence
	• product liability
Strict liability torts	• animals
	• *Rylands v Fletcher*[11]

injured the plaintiff. As a result, while special precautions may reduce the danger of liability, effective risk management may require the defendant to simply avoid the relevant activity altogether.

Strict liability torts consequently may substantially affect behaviour. It would be wrong, however, to overestimate that possibility. As indicated in Concept Summary 3.3, tort law is dominated by intentional torts and negligence torts. Strict liability is rare.[12] The reason is clear. In most situations, it would be unfair to impose liability on a person who did not intentionally or carelessly cause the plaintiff's injury. Strict liability is therefore limited to situations in which the defendant is involved in some extraordinarily dangerous activity. Tort law strikes a balance. It allows the defendant to engage in that activity, but it also requires the defendant to pay for any damage that occurs. That is the idea behind the rule that holds the owner of livestock strictly liable for any damage that the animals cause by trespassing on someone else's

---

[10.] As we will see in Chapter 5, nuisance and occupiers' liability are not always classified as negligence torts.

[11.] Some people also consider *vicarious liability* to be a form of strict liability. As we will see later in this chapter, however, an employer who is held vicariously liable has not really committed a tort. Instead, the employer is held liable for a tort that their employee committed. In contrast, as we will see in Chapter 5, the rule in *Rylands v Fletcher* (1868) LR 3 HL 330 is true strict liability. The defendant is held liable for doing something wrong even though they did not act intentionally or carelessly.

[12.] The only one that we will discuss in detail is the rule in *Rylands v Fletcher*, which appears in Chapter 5.

property.[13] As Case Brief 3.1 illustrates, a similar rule applies to the owner of a wild creature.[14]

Cowles v Balac (2005) 29 CCLT (3d) 284 (Ont SCJ)

David Balac and Jennifer Cowles began dating in 1996. He worked as an accordion player and studied at Sheridan College; she worked as an "exotic dancer." On a warm spring day, they visited African Lion Safari (ALS). ALS offers a unique wildlife experience. In a typical zoo, the animals are enclosed and the customers roam freely from one exhibit to the next. But at ALS, the roles are reversed. The animals roam freely within their reserves and it is the customers who are enclosed (in their own vehicles) as they drive through the park. Not surprisingly, ALS has become very popular with people who want a close encounter with wildlife. Where else can a family sit in safety while their van is swarmed by monkeys!

Jennifer and David's wildlife encounter was, tragically, *too* close. Shortly after they had entered the tiger reserve, their car was attacked by the big cats. Although the facts were rather sketchy, the judge found that the initial attack startled David, who accidentally hit a button that rolled down Jennifer's window. A Siberian tiger named Paca then lunged through the window and mauled the pair. The injuries were severe. Because of permanent scarring to her scalp and hip, Jennifer was unable to work as a "featured dancer." David fared even worse. In addition to physical injuries that prevented him from playing the accordion, he suffered psychological injuries that further limited his employment prospects.

The Court awarded $1 701 032 to David and $813 169 to Jennifer. It offered two explanations for holding ALS liable.

- **Negligence:** The trial judge held that an ALS employee had carelessly created the accident by driving through the area with a young tiger cub in the cab of her truck. The employee should have realized that by doing so, she would cause Paca to become excited and aggressive.

- **Strict Liability:** The trial also held that ALS would have been responsible for the accident even if its employee had taken every conceivable precaution. A special rule applies to certain types of extraordinary risks. As Justice MacFarland explained, a business that displays "dangerous, unpredictable, wild predators... in out of control settings. . . should be strictly liable for any damage" that occurs. Consequently, a person who is hurt by a wild animal is not required to prove that the animal's owner intentionally or carelessly did something wrong. It is enough for victims to show that their injuries were caused by the danger in question.

The threat of strict liability obviously creates a tremendous problem for zoos and wildlife parks. That is not to say, however, that they will be held liable to *every* customer who is injured by one of their animals. They may have a defence. Most importantly from a business perspective, the trial judge suggested that Jennifer and David would have lost their case if they had been sufficiently warned about the risk of attack and if they had consented to that danger. It was not enough, however, for ALS to simply post warning signs. It should have taken steps to ensure that Jennifer and David were fully aware of those warnings. (The defence of voluntary assumption of risk is discussed in Chapter 6.)

L.O. ❻❼❽❾❿

General Principles of Tort Law

Having identified different types of torts, we can now begin to look at several general principles that apply throughout tort law. In this section, we will concentrate on three concepts:

- liability insurance
- vicarious liability
- remedies

[13.] The same explanation applies to the rule in *Rylands v Fletcher*, which we will examine in Chapter 5.

[14.] Tort law draws a distinction between wild animals (such as tigers) and tame animals (such as dogs). As a general rule, the owner of a wild animal is liable for any damage that it causes. In contrast, the owner of a tame animal is usually liable only if the animal was known to be unusually dangerous. In other words, tame animals are entitled to "one free bite." Recently, however, some governments have enacted legislation that allows the victim of a dog bite to recover damages without proving that the owner knew that the animal was especially dangerous: see *eg Stray Animals Act*, RSNS 1989, c 448, s 12 (NS); *Dog Owner's Liability Act*, RSO 1990, c D.16, s 2 (Ont).

LIABILITY INSURANCE

Because torts can occur unexpectedly, risk management is especially important. Business people should know enough about tort law to predict potential problems and develop strategies for avoiding liability. They should also protect themselves with *liability insurance*.(Other types of insurance are considered in Chapter 17.) **Liability insurance** is a contract in which an insurance company agrees, in exchange for a price, to pay damages on behalf of a person who incurs liability.[15] Figure 3.1 provides an illustration. Liability insurance also includes a *duty to defend*. A **duty to defend** requires the insurance company to pay the expenses that are associated with lawsuits brought against the insured party.[16] That is significant. As we saw in the last chapter, litigation costs can be very high, even if you win your case.

Liability insurance creates an interesting tension between two of tort law's most important functions.

- On the one hand, liability insurance contributes to the *compensatory function* of torts. The **compensatory function** aims to fully compensate people who are wrongfully injured. If a tortfeasor cannot personally afford to pay damages, the plaintiff will not receive full compensation unless the defendant is insured.

- On the other hand, liability insurance undermines tort law's *deterrence function*. The **deterrence function** discourages people from committing torts by threatening to hold them liable for the losses that they cause. People have little reason to be afraid, however, if they know that their insurance companies will pay if something goes wrong. That is one reason why tort law has surprisingly little deterrent effect.[17]

liability insurance is a contract in which an insurance company agrees, in exchange for a price, to pay damages on behalf of a person who incurs liability

a **duty to defend** requires the insurance company to pay the expenses that are associated with lawsuits brought against the insured party

the **compensatory function** aims to fully compensate people who are wrongfully injured

the **deterrence function** discourages people from committing torts by threatening to hold them liable for the losses they cause

FIGURE 3.1   Liability Insurance

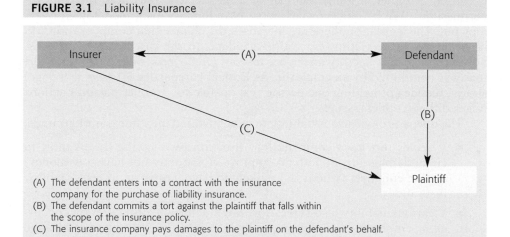

(A) The defendant enters into a contract with the insurance company for the purchase of liability insurance.
(B) The defendant commits a tort against the plaintiff that falls within the scope of the insurance policy.
(C) The insurance company pays damages to the plaintiff on the defendant's behalf.

[15.] Strictly speaking, liability insurance is not a general principle of tort law. It is a form of risk management. The topic nevertheless is addressed here because it is critically important and because it involves a number of other ideas that are undoubtedly general principles of tort law, such as the *compensatory function* and the *deterrence function* (as discussed below).

[16.] *Scott v Wawanesa Mutual Insurance Co* (1989) 59 DLR (4th) 660 (SCC).

[17.] M Trebilcock & D Dewees "The Efficacy of the Tort System and Its Alternatives: A Review of Empirical Evidence" (1992) 30 *Osgoode Hall LJ* 57.

Liability insurance plays an important role in tort law.[18] It is important to understand, however, that liability insurance policies do not usually cover *all* torts. Case Brief 3.2 provides an illustration.

Case Brief 3.2

Non-Marine Underwriters, Lloyd's of London v Scalera (2000) 185 DLR (4th) 1 (SCC)

The plaintiff, a young teenager, worked in a corner store that was located at the end of a city bus line. The defendant, a bus driver, sexually abused her on a number of occasions. She later sued him for battery. He claimed coverage under his liability insurance policy. His insurance company rejected his claim, however, by pointing to a clause in that contract that excluded coverage for injuries inflicted through "intentional or criminal acts."

The Supreme Court of Canada held that the defendant was not protected by his insurance policy because he had committed the tort of battery with the intention of injuring the plaintiff. As a result, the plaintiff's chances of recovering full damages were reduced. While the insurance company was wealthy, the defendant was not.

VICARIOUS LIABILITY

vicarious liability occurs when one person is held liable for a tort that was committed by another person

Liability insurance is always a good idea, especially for businesses that have employees. That additional need for insurance arises from the doctrine of vicarious liability. Vicarious liability occurs when one person is held liable for a tort that was committed by another person. Vicarious liability may arise in a variety of ways. For public policy reasons, a statute may hold one person responsible for another's torts in particular circumstances. For example, there is legislation that generally holds the owner of a vehicle liable if an accident is caused by either a family member or a person who borrowed the car with permission.[19] While vehicle owners must have liability insurance, some drivers may not. The legislation therefore increases the chance that compensation will be available to the victim of a traffic accident. In the vast majority of cases, however, vicarious liability arises because an employer is held liable for a tort that was committed by an employee. As Ethical Perspective 3.1 (see next page) shows, the idea of holding one person responsible for another person's actions raises difficult ethical issues.

The doctrine of vicarious liability may be justified on a number of grounds.

- It serves tort law's compensatory function by allowing the plaintiff to claim damages from both an employee (who may not have any money) and an employer (who is more likely to have money or, at least, liability insurance).

- Vicarious liability also serves tort law's deterrence function by encouraging employers to avoid unusually hazardous activities and to hire the best people available.

[18.] It is also possible to purchase insurance for liabilities arising outside of tort. For example, a company may obtain coverage for liabilities arising through breach of contract.

[19.] See, for example, *Motor Vehicle Act*, RSBC 1996, c 318, s 86 (BC); *Highway Traffic Act*, RSA 2000, c H-8, s 181 (Alta); *Highway Traffic Act*, CCSM c H60, s 153 (Man); *Highway Traffic Act*, RSO 1990, s H.8, s 192 (Ont); *Motor Vehicle Act*, RSNB 1973, c M-17, s 267 (NB); *Highway Traffic Act*, RSNL 1990, c H-3, s 200 (NL); *Motor Vehicle Act*, RSNS 1989, c 293, s 248 (NS); *Highway Traffic Act*, RSPEI 1988, c H-5, s 287 (PEI).

■ As a matter of fairness, it may be appropriate to require a business to bear responsibility for the losses that its activities create, even if those losses are caused by misbehaving employees.

Ethical Perspective 3.1

Bazley v Curry (1999) 174 DLR (4th) 45 (SCC)

The defendant was a charitable organization that operated a residential care facility for emotionally troubled children. It employed a number of people, including a man named Curry, to act as substitute parents (for example, by bathing children and putting them to bed at night). Although the defendant conducted a reasonably thorough investigation before hiring Curry, it failed to discover that he was a pedophile. Sadly, Curry sexually assaulted a number of children, including the plaintiff, within the defendant's facilities. The plaintiff sued the defendant organization on the basis that it was vicariously liable for Curry's actions.

The Supreme Court of Canada held that an employer is vicariously liable for both (i) acts that it authorized an employee to do, and (ii) other closely connected acts.

On the facts of the case, the court found that Curry's actions fell within the second category.[20] While recognizing that the employer certainly did not want its employees to sexually abuse the children, the court held that the nature of the employer's operation significantly increased the risk of wrongdoing.

Questions for Discussion

1. Is it fair to impose liability on an employer that acted reasonably?

2. Why should an innocent person be responsible for someone else's wrongs?

You should note several other points about vicarious liability. First, an employer is not liable *every time* an employee does something wrong. As the Supreme Court of Canada stressed in *Bazley v Curry*, an employer is not vicariously liable if an employee's tort occurred completely outside of the employment relationship.

Second, an employer may be held vicariously liable for employees, but not for *independent contractors*. An **independent contractor** is a worker who is not as closely connected to the employer's business as is an employee. Consequently, as a matter of risk management, it is sometimes preferable for a business to have work performed by an independent contractor rather than by an employee. (There may be other benefits, as well. For instance, a business may be required to contribute to a workers' compensation scheme if it employs an employee, but not if it retains an independent contractor.) (We introduced the distinction between employees and independent contractors in Chapter 1. The issue is considered in more detail in Chapter 26.)While it is often difficult to distinguish between those two types of workers, the courts are more inclined to find that a person is an employee if (i) the employer generally controls what is done, how it is done, when it is done, and where it is done, (ii) the worker uses the employer's equipment and premises, (iii) the worker is paid a regular wage or salary rather than a lump sum at the end of each project, and (iv) the worker is integrated into the employer's business and does not own their own business. Significantly, however, there is no magic in words. A worker will not be classified as an independent contractor, rather than an employee, merely because an employer uses that language.

an **independent contractor** is a worker who is not as closely connected to the employer's business as is an employee

---

20. It is often difficult to determine whether an employee's tort falls within the second branch of the test. On the same day that it held the employer responsible in *Bazley v Curry*, the Supreme Court of Canada refused to impose vicarious liability in a similar case: *Jacobi v Griffiths* (1999) 174 DLR (4th) 71 (SCC).

Third, vicarious liability does not relieve the employee of responsibility. Rather, it allows the plaintiff to sue both the employer *and* the employee, and to recover all or some of its damages from either defendant. Furthermore, if the employer actually pays damages to the plaintiff, they are usually entitled to claim that amount from the employee. In practice, however, employers seldom do so. Aside from the fact that an employee is unlikely to have much money, employers usually realize that morale would drop if employees were worried about being held liable.

Fourth, an employer may be both *vicariously liable* and *personally liable* in the *same situation*. Vicarious liability occurs if the employer is responsible for an *employee's tort*. Personal liability occurs if the employer is responsible for their *own tort*. Business Decision 3.1 provides an illustration.

Business Decision 3.1

Vicarious Liability and Personal Liability

You suffer a serious injury after falling out of a chairlift at a ski resort. The evidence indicates that the accident was caused by the fact that the lift was operated carelessly by Alberto, an employee of the resort. The evidence also indicates that the resort failed to properly train Alberto.

Liability could arise in three ways. First, Alberto might be *personally* liable, under the tort of negligence, because he operated the chairlift carelessly. Second, the resort might be *vicariously* liable because it was Alberto's employer. Third, the resort might also be *personally* liable, under the tort of negligence, because, carelessly, it failed to train its employee.

Questions for Discussion

1. Why should you sue both Alberto and the resort?

2. Who would pay for your injuries if (i) Alberto alone was liable, (ii) both Alberto and the resort were liable, and (iii) the resort alone was liable?

Figure 3.2 summarizes our discussion of vicarious liability. It assumes that the only tort was committed by the employee.

REMEDIES

A variety of remedies are available in tort, depending upon the circumstances. We will see several examples in the next three chapters. This section simply provides an introduction to the most important possibilities:

FIGURE 3.2   Vicarious Liability

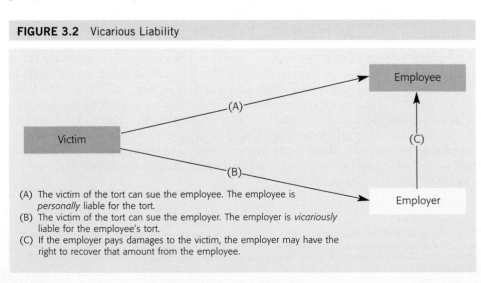

(A) The victim of the tort can sue the employee. The employee is *personally* liable for the tort.
(B) The victim of the tort can sue the employer. The employer is *vicariously* liable for the employee's tort.
(C) If the employer pays damages to the victim, the employer may have the right to recover that amount from the employee.

- compensatory damages
- punitive damages
- nominal damages
- injunctions

Compensatory Damages

As previously mentioned, most private law obligations arise in either tort or contract. Compensatory damages are the standard remedy in both. In either situation, the defendant is required to pay for the losses that they caused the plaintiff to suffer. As we also saw, however, there is a significant difference between contract and tort. While compensation in tort is designed to put the plaintiff back into the position that that party enjoyed before the tort occurred, compensation in contract is usually designed to put the plaintiff forward into the position that that party expected to enjoy after the contract was performed.

The distinction that exists between compensation in contract and tort is important because it is sometimes possible for the plaintiff to sue in both tort *and* contract. The plaintiff can recover damages for only one of those actions, even if both are successful. They will, of course, choose whichever option provides the most money.[21] To better understand these issues, consider You Be the Judge 3.1.

You Be the Judge 3.1

Compensation in Tort and Contract[22]

Pippa is in the business of buying and re-selling cultural artifacts. During the negotiations that led up to a contract, David made a number of comments and promises regarding a particular item. On the basis of those negotiations, Pippa paid a purchase price of $5000 and took possession of the item. When she attempted to re-sell the piece, however, she discovered that David's pre-contractual statements were untrue and inaccurate. The actual market value of the item, both at the time of sale and now, has been appraised at $2000. Pippa's disappointment, however, runs deeper than that. As she had explained to David at the outset, an art collector had offered her $7000 for the type of item that David had described during negotiations. Given the circumstances, of course, that re-sale has fallen through and Pippa is stuck with the item.

David now admits that he is guilty of both (i) a breach of contract, because his promises were untrue, and (ii) the tort of deceit, because he lied to Pippa. The parties also agree that, for a variety of reasons, it would be impossible to *rescind* the contract by simply giving back the land and the purchase price. (The remedy of rescission is discussed in Chapter 9.) They therefore want you, as the judge, to determine how much money Pippa is entitled to receive as damages.

Questions for Discussion

1. How much money would be required to place Pippa in the position that she would have enjoyed if the contract had turned out as expected?

2. How much money would be required to place Pippa in the position that she would have enjoyed if she had not entered into the contract?

3. Given that the plaintiff ultimately can recover compensation for either breach of contract or tort, but not both, how much will Pippa receive?

REMOTENESS Compensation is not available for *every* loss that the plaintiff suffered. First, the defendant is responsible only for losses that they in fact *caused*. Second, even if the defendant's tort caused the plaintiff to suffer a loss, the court will not award damages if the connection between the tort and the

---

[21.] *Central Trust Co v Rafuse* (1986) 31 DLR (4th) 481 (SCC).

[22.] *Goldstar Management Ltd v Varvis* (1995) 175 AR 321 (Alta QB).

a loss is **remote** if it would be unfair to hold the defendant responsible for it

loss is too *remote*.[23] A loss is **remote** if it would be unfair to hold the defendant responsible for it. The judge will ask whether a reasonable person in the defendant's position would have realized that a particular activity might cause the sort of harm that the plaintiff suffered.[24] Suppose one of your employees develops a rare disease after coming into contact with rat urine. You might not be liable even if you carelessly allowed rats to run loose in your warehouse. A judge once held that a reasonable person would recognize the danger of *rat bites*, but not *rat urine*.[25]

There is an important limitation on the remoteness principle. The concept of remoteness applies to most types of torts, but not to intentional torts. (We will examine intentional torts in the next chapter.) People who intentionally do wrong do not deserve any leniency in tort law.[26]

mitigation occurs when the plaintiff takes steps to minimize the losses that result from the defendant's tort

MITIGATION Compensatory damages are also limited by the principle of *mitigation*.[27] Compensation is not available for a loss that the plaintiff unreasonably failed to mitigate. **Mitigation** occurs when the plaintiff takes steps to minimize the losses that result from the defendant's tort. Suppose a customer was bitten by a rat that you negligently allowed to run around your warehouse. You advised the customer to get a tetanus shot, but they refused. As a result, the customer developed lockjaw and was unable to work for eight months. If the person had received a tetanus shot, they would have missed only three days of work. We can use that example to illustrate four aspects of mitigation.

- First, the plaintiff is responsible only for taking *reasonable* steps to mitigate a loss. A court therefore would not expect the customer to receive a tetanus shot if they would be at risk of developing serious side effects.

- Second, although lawyers sometimes refer to a "duty to mitigate," there is not really a *duty*. The plaintiff is not *required* to mitigate. The plaintiff will, however, be denied compensation for losses that they could have reasonably avoided. Mitigation therefore is a question of risk management.

- Third, damages are denied *only to the extent* that the plaintiff unreasonably failed to mitigate. Even if the plaintiff had received a tetanus shot, they still would have missed work for three days. The plaintiff consequently is entitled to compensation for that loss.[28]

- Finally, the plaintiff can recover the costs associated with mitigation. If the plaintiff had received a tetanus shot, and if they had been billed $100 for it, they would be entitled to compensation for that amount.

Punitive Damages

punitive damages are intended to punish the defendant

Damages are usually intended to compensate the plaintiff for a loss. *Punitive damages* serve a different purpose. **Punitive damages** are intended to punish the defendant. If the defendant has done something particularly outrageous or

---

[23.] Compensatory damages in contract are also limited by a principle of remoteness. We will look at the special rules that apply in contract in Chapter 12.

[24.] *Overseas Tankship (UK) Ltd Morts Dock and Engineering Co Ltd, The Wagon Mound (No 1)* [1961] AC 388 (PC).

[25.] *Tremain v Pike* [1969] 3 All ER 1303.

[26.] *Bettel v Yim* (1978) 88 DLR (3d) 543 (Ont Co Ct).

[27.] As we will see in Chapter 12, the principle of mitigation also applies in contract.

[28.] *McAuley v London Transport Executive* [1957] 2 Lloyds Rep 500 (CA).

reprehensible, the court may impose both compensatory damages *and* punitive damages.

Punitive damages are important, but they also are unusual. There is a popular perception, based on American movies and news programs, that they are awarded very often and in very large amounts. In fact, Canadian courts take a much narrower view of the matter. In this country, punitive damages are available only in exceptional circumstances. The Supreme Court of Canada has said that, in addition to committing a tort, the defendant must have acted in a "harsh, vindictive, reprehensible and malicious" manner. For example, punitive damages have been awarded against an elderly doctor who committed the tort of battery by demanding that a young woman provide him with sex in exchange for drugs, against a reform school that committed the tort of negligence by failing to fire a predatory employee who sexually abused a young inmate, and against a land developer who committed the tort of trespass to land by cutting down trees on a neighbouring lot in order to enhance the view from their own property.[29] In the leading case of *Whiten v Pilot Insurance Co*, the Supreme Court of Canada confirmed a jury's decision to award $1 000 000 in punitive damages against an insurance company that deliberately concocted a false allegation of arson after a family home burned down.[30]

Nominal Damages

Nominal damages can be awarded for *some* torts. **Nominal damages** symbolically recognize that the defendant committed a tort even though the plaintiff did not suffer any loss. Since nominal damages are merely symbolic, they are awarded in very small sums, say $10.[31] Furthermore, because they are usually awarded only if the plaintiff did not suffer any loss, they are generally restricted to torts that are actionable *per se*. Most torts (such as negligence) occur only if the defendant inflicted a loss upon the plaintiff. However, some torts (such as the intentional torts) occur as long as the defendant acted wrongfully. They are therefore actionable *per se*, that is, in themselves, rather than being actionable upon proof of a loss.

nominal damages symbolically recognize that the defendant committed a tort even though the plaintiff did not suffer any loss

Injunctions

Compensatory damages provide a substitute for the thing that the plaintiff has lost. For instance, they may allow the plaintiff to replace a car that has been destroyed, or they may provide the equivalent of an income that has been lost. Sometimes, however, damages are inadequate because they cannot truly replace what the plaintiff has lost. If so, the court may award an *injunction*. An **injunction** is a court order that requires the defendant to do something or refrain from doing something. For instance, the defendant may be told to close a foul-smelling pig farm that is operating in a residential area, or it may be told to tear down a billboard that it wrongfully erected on the plaintiff's property. Of course, it is often too late to impose an injunction. If the defendant carelessly kills the plaintiff's horse, the court cannot bring the animal back to life.

Concept Summary 3.4 briefly explains the tort law remedies.

an **injunction** is a court order that requires the defendant to do something or refrain from doing something

[29] *Norberg v Wynrib* (1992) 92 DLR (4th) 449 (SCC) ($10 000 in punitive damages); *Roose v Hollett* (1996) 139 DLR (4th) 260 (NS CA) ($35 000 in punitive damages); *Horseshoe Bay Retirement Society v SIF Development Corp* (1990) 66 DLR (4th) 42 (BC SC) ($100 000 in punitive damages).

[30] *Whiten v Pilot Insurance Co* (2002) 209 DLR (4th) 257 (SCC). The case was actually concerned with a claim for breach of contract. The court nevertheless discussed punitive damages in tort as well.

[31] *Bowen Contracting Ltd v BC Log Spill Recovery Co-operative Assn* (2009) 99 BCLR (4th) 59 (BC CA).

Concept Summary 3.4

Tort Law Remedies

Remedy	Purpose
Compensatory damages	monetarily repair plaintiff's loss
	• not required if loss is too remote
	• not required if plaintiff failed to mitigate loss
Punitive damages	punish defendant's outrageous and reprehensible conduct
Nominal damages	symbolically recognize that defendant committed tort even though plaintiff did not suffer any loss
Injunction	prevent commission or continuation of a tort

ALTERNATIVE COMPENSATION SCHEMES

Tort law is not the only source of compensation. In fact, in recent years, the number of *alternative compensation schemes* has increased considerably. An **alternative compensation scheme** is a system that allows a person who has suffered an injury to receive compensation without bringing an action in tort. Two such systems are especially important:

an **alternative compensation scheme** is a system that allows a person who has suffered an injury to receive compensation without bringing an action in tort

- workers' compensation
- no-fault insurance

Because job-related injuries are so common, workers' compensation schemes exist across the country. While the details vary between jurisdictions, the basic ideas are always the same. The schemes involve a series of trade-offs. Workers generally lose the right to sue in tort for workplace injuries, but in exchange, they gain the right to claim compensation from a fund without having to prove that anyone was at fault for their injuries. The loss of tort law is the price that workers pay to enjoy access to a far simpler and much quicker system of compensation.[32] Likewise, while employers are required to contribute to the compensation fund, they escape the risk of being held liable in tort for workplace injuries. Furthermore, while the employers' compulsory contributions undoubtedly are substantial, they generally can be passed onto consumers in the form of higher prices.

The second major type of alternative compensation scheme applies to injuries that are caused by automobile accidents. Several provinces have adopted some form of no-fault system.[33] In Manitoba and Quebec, for example, victims of traffic accidents cannot sue in tort, but they are entitled to receive compensation from the scheme without having to prove that another driver was at fault. Other provinces have enacted less extensive schemes. In British Columbia, the right to no-fault benefits exists alongside the right to sue in tort. In Saskatchewan, people can choose between tort and no-fault insurance coverage. And in Ontario,

---

[32.] *Béliveau St Jacques v Fédération des Employées et Employés de Services Publics Inc* (1996) 136 DLR (4th) 129 (SCC).

[33.] For a useful summary of automobile accident compensation schemes, see AM Linden & LN Klar *Canadian Tort Law* 11th ed (1999) at 754–757.

the no-fault system prevents an action in tort unless the victim's losses are especially serious.

There are two main reasons for the rise of alternative compensation schemes.

- First, tort law provides compensation only if a person is injured as a result of a *wrongful* act. From the victim's perspective, however, the physical and financial consequences of being injured are the same, even if an injury occurs *innocently*. Consequently, it is sometimes desirable to allow that person to collect compensation regardless of fault.

- Second, tort law is inefficient. Since it is based on an adversarial system in which lawyers compete on behalf of clients, it requires a great deal of time and expense. Studies suggest that less than one-third of all the money involved in the tort system is actually used for compensating injuries.[34] Because alternative compensation schemes operate on a no-fault basis, there is far less need for costly investigations and lengthy disputes.

While alternative compensation schemes have many advantages, they also have a major disadvantage. They provide compensation more often, but they also provide less of it. In tort law, the plaintiff is usually entitled to recover the full value of a loss. In alternative compensation schemes, however, the level of compensation is almost always capped. Because such schemes include many more claimants, the schemes would quickly go broke if they provided full compensation for every loss.

[34.] *Ontario Ministry of Financial Institutions Ontario Task Force on Insurance, Final Report* (1986) at 66. Part of the remaining money is paid to lawyers; part is paid to simply operate the system.

Chapter Summary

A tort generally consists of a failure to fulfill a private obligation that was imposed by law. It is important to distinguish between torts and crimes. Torts involve private obligations; crimes involve public obligations. It also is important to distinguish between torts and contracts. Torts generally involve obligations imposed by law; contracts generally involve obligations that the parties voluntarily create for themselves.

Tort law needs to strike a balance between competing interests in a variety of situations. It therefore includes three types of torts: intentional torts, negligence torts, and strict liability torts. Strict liability torts are unusual. The defendant may be held liable even though they did not act intentionally or carelessly. Strict liability torts are limited to situations in which the defendant was involved in an extraordinarily dangerous activity.

Liability insurance is a contract in which an insurance company agrees, in exchange for a price, to pay damages on behalf of a person who incurs liability. It is

critically important in tort law, especially in the business context. Liability insurance furthers tort law's compensatory function, but undermines its deterrence function.

Even if an employer did nothing wrong, they may be held vicariously liable for a tort committed by their employee.

The victim of a tort usually receives compensatory damages. Compensation in tort looks backward. It is intended to place the plaintiff in the position that that party enjoyed before the tort occurred. It is not available for losses that are remote, or for losses that the plaintiff failed to mitigate. In unusual situations, a court may award punitive damages or nominal damages, or impose an injunction.

The tort system does not provide compensation to people whose injuries are innocently caused. It is also expensive and inefficient. Therefore, alternative compensation schemes have been introduced in some jurisdictions for some purposes.

MyBusLawLab   ADDITIONAL RESOURCES FOR CHAPTER 3

MyBusLawLab provides students with an assortment of tools to help enrich the learning experience, including a Study Plan with Pre- and Post-tests, mini-cases with assessments, and provincial content material, which provides links to relevant cases, legislation, and additional resources.

MyBusLawLab provides the following resources for Chapter 3:

Provincial Material

- **British Columbia:** Insurance Corporation of British Columbia (ICBC), Motor Vehicle Insurance, Parental Liability, Workers' Compensation, WorkSafeBC
- **Alberta:** Automobile Insurance, *Maternal Tort Liability Act, Auto Insurance Act*
- **Manitoba and Saskatchewan:** No-fault Insurance, Vicarious Liability
- **Ontario:** No-Fault Liability Insurance, Parental Liability, Strict Liability, Vicarious Liability, Workers' Compensation
- **Atlantic Provinces:** Workers' Compensation

Review Questions

1. What is a "tort"?

2. To whom is the obligation owed in tort law and in criminal law? Identify the person or party entitled to complain in court about a tort or a crime.

3. Is it ever possible for the same set of events to be both a tort and a crime? Explain your answer.

4. Is it ever possible for the same set of events to be both a tort and a breach of contract? If so, why would it ever be desirable to sue for both?

5. "Tort law does not punish acts alone. A court will never impose liability if the defendant did not act with a guilty mind." Is that statement true? Explain your answer.

6. Explain the "one free bite" rule.

7. How is liability insurance related to the concept of risk management?

8. When does a "duty to defend" arise? Why is it important?

9. "Liability insurance creates an interesting tension between two of tort law's most important functions." Explain the meaning of that statement.

10. Is it possible to purchase liability insurance as protection against liability for *every* type of tort? Explain your answer.

11. What is the difference between vicarious liability and personal liability?

12. On what grounds can vicarious liability be justified?

13. When will an employer be held vicariously liable for torts committed by their employees? When will an employer be held vicariously liable for torts committed by their independent contractors?

14. How does the vicarious liability of an employer affect the personal liability of an employee?

15. Are compensatory damages calculated in the same way in both tort and contract? Explain your answer.

16. Explain the relationship between compensatory damages and the concept of remoteness.

17. "Courts often refuse to award punitive damages. In most cases, they refuse to do so because the defendant failed to fulfill the duty to mitigate." Is that statement true? Explain your answer.

18. Identify and explain three types of damages that are available in tort.

19. What is the difference between damages and an injunction?

20. Explain how workers' compensation schemes create both advantages and disadvantages for workers and for employers.

Cases and Problems

1. Francesca owns and operates a small stereo store. That store was robbed last night after Francesca had locked up and gone home. The thief broke a window, entered the premises, and stole a dozen portable disc players. Francesca fortunately had installed a security camera several weeks ago. After discovering the theft in the morning, she reviewed the tape and recognized that the thief was her neighbour Ned. Francesca now has several concerns. She believes that Ned should be responsible to her

personally, but she also believes that he owes a debt to society. Briefly describe two types of proceedings that may be brought against Ned.

2. Kwik Office Supplies hired Jackson to act as its manager. The employment contract spelled out, in substantial detail, the various rights and obligations that the parties assumed under the agreement. Two years later, Jackson was fired after the company received an angry letter from a dissatisfied company that had been defrauded by Jackson. To protect its reputation, and in recognition of the validity of the allegation, Kwik Office Supply is prepared to settle the customer's tort claim. As part of that same process, however, it believes that once it has compensated the customer, it is entitled to receive reimbursement from Jackson. Jackson rejects that claim. He insists that his only relationship with the company is contractual and he correctly notes that the employment contract did not deal with the situation that has actually occurred. Will Jackson be required to reimburse the company for the money that it pays to the customer? How can he be held liable for an obligation that he never accepted as part of his contract?

3. Rochard owns and operates a drug store. Because business is often slow during the day, and because he worries about robberies, Rochard regularly brings his dog, Sid, to work with him. Sid has been a bit of a mixed blessing over the years. He has provided good companionship and his aggressive nature has discouraged teenagers from hanging around the store. At the same time, Sid has occasionally frightened customers and on a couple of occasions he has tried to bite small children. Rochard's luck recently ran out when Sid did, in fact, attack and severely injure Sarah, a young girl who was visiting the store with her father. Although Rochard feels very sorry for Sarah, he denies that he is responsible for her medical bills. As he correctly points out, he did not intentionally cause Sid to attack Sarah. On the contrary, he took every reasonable precaution to prevent the incident from occurring. Rochard therefore insists that he cannot be held liable in tort. Is he correct? Explain your answer.

4. Toronto's SkyDome was owned and operated by Sportsco. The Toronto Blue Jays rented the building for their home games. One of those games, against the Kansas City Royals, was cancelled after portions of SkyDome's retractable roof broke off and fell to the ground. The Blue Jays sued Sportsco in tort for its loss of profits. Sportsco was worried that the lawsuit might become very expensive, not only because of the need to hire lawyers, but also because of the need to hire expert witnesses to explain why the roof fell apart. Sportsco did, however, have an insurance policy that it had purchased from ING Insurance Company of Canada. Explain the significance of that policy.

5. Amrhein Developments Inc (ADI) is a large real estate developer with a reputation for bullying and boorish behaviour. That reputation was earned during its construction of the Buffalo Park Project, a large residential complex that it built on a waterfront site. The owners of two neighbouring properties, Paul Law and Judith Skool, opposed the project and refused to sell their land to ADI. The evidence shows that ADI's subsequent actions were motivated, in part, by a desire to take revenge against Law and Skool. First, despite knowing where the boundaries fell, ADI deliberately constructed a large fence 10 metres inside of Law's land. Second, despite knowing that Skool had not consented, ADI cleared away a number of trees that were located on her land. The trees were mature and the evidence indicates that even minimal success at reforestation would require decades. Briefly explain the remedies that may be available to each of the claimants.

6. Dave Woodstock was hired to clean and deliver vehicles for EconoCar, a car rental agency. Although Dave drives very safely in his own vehicle, he tends to be rather careless when he is behind the wheel of one of his employer's vehicles. Not surprisingly, then, he was recently involved in an accident while driving a truck owned by EconoCar. Although that truck did not suffer any serious damage, the car that Dave crashed into requires $10 000 in repairs. Dave has admitted that he was at fault, but as he explained to his girlfriend, he was not worried. "What's the worst that could happen? I've already quit my job and found a new one. And obviously, EconoCar is on the hook for repairing the other guy's vehicle. I'm totally out of the picture." Is Dave correct? Explain your answer.

7. Paul owns Walrus Music Inc. He is also a car enthusiast, and since business has been quite good, he has purchased several vehicles for both business use and personal use. Unfortunately, Paul has been indirectly involved in a number of car accidents recently. First, while transporting company goods in the company van, an employee named Harrison mistakenly ran through a red light and crashed into another car. The driver of the other vehicle is seeking damages for the injuries that she suffered, but Harrison honestly says that he cannot possibly afford to pay in full. The second case involves Mimi, an independent contractor who occasionally does work for Walrus Music. After completing a particular project for the company, she asked Paul if she could use his car to run a few errands that she needed to complete in a hurry. He agreed but was very upset when he learned that Mimi had crashed into a neighbouring fence while using his vehicle. The owner of the fence wants to hold both Mimi and Paul responsible for the damage. Finally, while Paul slept in late one Sunday morning, his daughter, Stella, grabbed the keys to one of his cars and sneaked out of the house. As she raced from the house, she crashed into a stop sign. The city is now suing for the cost of replacing the sign, but Stella has no job and no money. Is Paul or Walrus Music responsible for paying damages for any of the accidents? Explain your answer.

8. For 14 years, Leon Brick was employed as a commissioned sales agent for La-Z-Boy Canada Ltd, a furniture manufacturer. In an effort to avoid contributing to the Employer Health Tax and Workplace Safety and Insurance Board schemes, however, the company informed Brick that, if he wished to continue working for La-Z-Boy, he would be required to sign a document in which he expressly declared that he was an independent contractor and not an employee. That document further stated that La-Z-Boy was entitled to terminate Brick's services, at any time and for any reason, as long as it provided two months' notice. The new arrangement also brought a few other changes. The company encouraged Brick to create a corporation and to provide his services through that corporation. It also required him to register for the goods and services tax (GST), and it encouraged him to share office space with other individuals in the same position. In most respects, however, the parties' relationship was unchanged. Brick's responsibilities and compensation remained the same as in the past. The company continued to provide training and promotional materials, it continued to control the products being sold, and it continued to restrict Brick's sales efforts to a certain territory. Nine years after that new arrangement had been created, the parties' relationship suddenly came to an end. The precise reasons are unclear. Brick suspects that the company decided to sever ties after it learned that a prospective customer had filed a statement of claim alleging that Brick had committed a harmful tort. If successful, that tort claim will trigger damages in excess of $500 000. A second source of tension involves the circumstances surrounding Brick's termination. La-Z-Boy insists that, under the terms of the signed contract, Brick was entitled to only two months' notice. In contrast, Brick believes that, after 23 years with the company, he deserves a much more generous severance package. And, in fact, the evidence indicates that an employee in Brick's position normally would be entitled to a severance payment equal to 18 months' income. Discuss the legal issues raised in this case.

9. Syd recently was injured while attending a concert. During the performance, the band's guitarist, Arnold Layne, unexpectedly leaped from the stage while carrying his instrument. Syd, who was sitting in the second row, suffered a serious head injury when the guitar struck him. The concert was immediately stopped and paramedics took Syd to the nearest hospital. The wound was treated, but a week later, Syd began experiencing blinding headaches that prevented him from working. After further investigation, a team of specialists agreed that Syd required surgery. The operation was simple enough and it carried a 95 percent chance of a complete cure. Like all operations, it also carried a slight risk of additional injury. Although his family and friends unanimously urged him to undergo surgery, Syd refused. He insists that since the original accident was not his fault, he should not be required to expose himself to danger in order to find a cure. Discuss the rights and obligations of Arnold Layne and Syd. (You should not discuss liability of any other parties.)

10. Dominion Tankship owned a large tanker ship called *The Erie Mistake* that it operated on the Great Lakes. The ship arrived at the Port of Toronto carrying a cargo of Flamonol, a synthetic lubricant used by manufacturers. As a result of the captain's carelessness, *The Erie Mistake* rammed into a dock that Mortimer Docking owned. In addition to causing some structural damage to the dock, the accident punctured a hole in the side of the ship, which caused several thousand litres of Flamonol to leak into the water. The manager for Mortimer Docking asked if there was any danger that the Flamonol might catch fire. The captain of *The Erie Mistake* gave his assurance that Flamonol was entirely non-flammable. Mortimer Docking therefore began repair work on its dock. During the course of those repairs, sparks from a welding gun fell onto the Flamonol, which was still floating on top of the water. The Flamonol almost immediately burst into flames and the ensuing fire completely destroyed the dock. Mortimer Docking has sued Dominion Tankship. The company admits that the captain of *The Erie Mistake* committed a tort when he rammed into the dock, and it is willing to pay for that original damage. However, Dominion Tankship has also established that, at the time of the accident, there was no scientific evidence that Flamonol could be set on fire. It therefore refuses to pay for the additional damage that the fire caused. Is Dominion Tankship liable for destruction of the dock or merely for the damage caused by the original ramming accident? Explain your answer.

11. Jessica worked as a courier for Pony Express Deliveries. Although Pony Express had no way of knowing it when they hired her, Jessica has a pathological hatred for Simone. The source of that hatred is not clear, but it seems to stem from a dispute between the two women dating back to high school. Three months ago, Pony Express asked Jessica to deliver a package to an office in the Dominion Tower. After making that delivery, Jessica went to the cafeteria in the basement of the building, where she knew Simone worked as the manager of a fast-food restaurant. Jessica jumped Simone from behind and administered a severe beating. The unprovoked attack has left Simone in constant pain and unable to work. Simone therefore intends to sue in tort. She wants compensation for her losses, but she also wants to see Jessica punished for her actions. Although she realizes that Jessica has very little money, Simone believes that she should be entitled to payment from Pony Express or from Western Insurance (which sold a general liability insurance policy to Jessica). Explain the remedies that Simone may be entitled to receive, and identify the party or parties who are most likely to pay for those remedies.

12. Bickle's Cab Company owns and operates a fleet of taxis. Last autumn, one of its cars was involved in an unfortunate incident. The driver almost ran into Jody DeNiro, a bike courier, as she emerged from an alleyway. Although DeNiro was entirely at fault for that near-accident, she was the one who became furious. She kicked the taxi's door repeatedly before being restrained by a passerby. The damage to the car consisted of a large dent and scraped paint. Bickle's Cab Co then parked the damaged vehicle in an outdoor lot for the winter. When it re-examined the car in the spring, it found extensive rust damage. That damage would not have occurred if the car had been promptly repaired. It is clear that DeNiro intentionally interfered with the car. There is, however, a disagreement regarding the amount of compensation that she will have to pay. The evidence indicates a number of things. Immediately before the accident, the car was worth $7000. Immediately after the accident, the car was worth $5000. The cost of repairs at that time would have been $3000. Because of the rust damage, the car is now worth $2000. It would now cost $6000 to fully repair it. A new car of the same model can be purchased for $15 000. How much is Bickle's Cab Co entitled to receive?

4 Intentional Torts

LEARNING OBJECTIVES

After completing this chapter, you should be able to:

❶ Explain the general nature of intentional torts and define "intention" as it applies to those torts.

❷ Describe and distinguish the torts of assault and battery.

❸ Identify a situation in which battery presents a particular danger for business people who occasionally attract undesirable customers.

❹ Explain why the concept of reasonable force is important to the tort of battery.

❺ List four reasons why tort law does not yet contain a separate tort of invasion of privacy.

❻ List five ways in which tort law may indirectly protect privacy interests.

❼ Explain the tort of false imprisonment and describe how a business can protect itself against liability.

❽ Describe the tort of malicious prosecution.

❾ Describe the tort of trespass to land and explain when a business is entitled to prohibit people from coming onto its premises.

❿ Identify and explain four complete defences and two partial defences.

A number of torts require proof of the defendant's intention. We will see several examples in the next chapter. In this chapter, however, we will focus on the torts that traditionally have been labelled the "intentional torts":

- assault
- battery
- invasion of privacy
- false imprisonment
- trespass to land
- interference with chattels

Intentional torts involve intentional, rather than merely careless, conduct.[1] For instance, the defendant may be held liable for battery if they deliberately punched the plaintiff. Somewhat surprisingly, however, tort law's definition of "intention" goes even further. It is enough if the defendant knew that a particular act would have particular consequences. The plaintiff does *not* have to prove that the defendant intended to either cause harm or commit a tort. For example, if you build a fence on my property, you commit the intentional tort of trespass to land, even if you think that the land belongs to you. It is enough that you know that your actions will result in a fence being constructed on *that* piece of ground. The courts have adopted that broad definition of "intention" because they want to strongly protect the interests that I have in myself and in my property. From a risk management perspective, the lesson is clear. Before acting in a particular way, you should know as much as possible about the consequences of doing so.

intentional torts involve intentional, rather than merely careless, conduct

Assault and Battery

L.O. ❶ ❷ ❸

It is easy to confuse the ideas of assault and battery. People often use those terms interchangeably. And even lawyers use the word "assault" to describe the crime that occurs when one person physically attacks another. In tort, however, "assault" and "battery" have very different meanings. An **assault** occurs when the defendant intentionally causes the plaintiff to reasonably believe that offensive bodily contact is imminent. There are several important points in that definition.

the tort of **assault** occurs when the defendant intentionally causes the plaintiff to reasonably believe that offensive bodily contact is imminent

- First, the tort is *not* based on physical contact. It is based on a reasonable belief that such contact will occur. The tort is designed to keep the peace by discouraging people from alarming others. As a result, you may commit an assault by swinging your fist at me, even if you do not actually make contact. But if you punch me from behind, you do not commit the tort of assault if I did not know that the blow was coming (although you do commit the tort of battery).

- Second, it is enough if the plaintiff *reasonably believed* that bodily contact would occur. As a result, you may commit an assault by pointing a gun in my direction, even if the gun is not really loaded. It is enough that a reasonable person would have thought that a gunshot was possible.

---

[1] Confusingly, Canadian courts occasionally say that an intentional tort can consist of either intentional *or* careless conduct: *Cook v Lewis* [1952] 1 DLR 1 (SCC). Our discussion, however, can be limited to intentional acts. The intentional torts are also characterized by a requirement of *directness*—the plaintiff's injury must flow naturally from the defendant's conduct and must not depend upon the intervention of some outside factor. That requirement is complicated, but it seldom creates problems in practice. There is no need to explore it in this book.

- Third, the plaintiff must have believed that bodily contact was *imminent*. Although that requirement is rather vague, you probably would not commit an assault if you threatened to kick me two weeks from today. The threat must be more immediate.

- Fourth, an assault can occur even if the plaintiff was not frightened. It is enough that the defendant threatened some form of *offensive contact*. You therefore may commit an assault by swinging your fist at me, even if I know that you are far too small to do any harm.

People seldom sue for assault alone. It normally is not worth the trouble and expense of litigation. A claim for assault is usually joined with a claim for *battery*. A **battery** consists of offensive bodily contact.[2] There are several points to note about this definition.

the tort of **battery** consists of offensive bodily contact

- First, the requirement of "bodily contact" is not strictly applied. It is enough if the defendant causes something, such as a knife or a bullet, to touch the plaintiff. It also is enough if the defendant makes contact with the plaintiff's clothing or with something that the plaintiff is holding.

- Second, not every form of contact is offensive. Normal social interaction is allowed. Consequently, you do not commit a battery if you gently brush past me in a crowded elevator or if you tap my shoulder to get my attention. At the same time, however, contact may be offensive even if it is not harmful. Consequently, you will commit a battery if you kiss me despite my objections. You may even commit a tort if your actions are highly beneficial (as when a physician performs a life-saving blood transfusion against a patient's wishes).[3]

Understanding the tort of battery is especially important for businesses that control crowds or remove rowdy customers. Bouncers and security personnel often injure patrons whom they eject from taverns, concerts, and sporting events. Given the doctrine of vicarious liability and the need for risk management, such employees should be carefully trained. Case Brief 4.1 serves as a warning.

Case Brief **4.1**

Vasey v Wosk's Ltd [1988] BCJ No 2089 (BC SC)

The plaintiff was escorted out of a bar after becoming drunk and belligerent. Once outside, he struck one of the bouncers from behind. In retaliation, that bouncer knocked him to the ground with a kick to the head. Another bouncer then climbed on top of the plaintiff and punched him in the face for about five minutes. The plaintiff suffered a number of injuries and consequently sued the company that owned the bar.

The court held that the bar's employees were entitled to use reasonable force to remove the obnoxious customer from the prem-

ises. It further held that the plaintiff was partially to blame for the disturbance because he had struck one of the bouncers from behind. However, the court also found that the employees used excessive force. It therefore allowed the plaintiff to recover compensation for the losses that he suffered, minus a reduction of 30 percent to reflect the fact that he had provoked the attack. The bouncers were held personally liable and the company that owned the bar was held vicariously liable.

[2.] A person who commits the tort of battery often commits a crime at the same time.

[3.] *Malette v Shulman* (1990) 67 DLR (4th) 321 (Ont CA). But see *Hobbs v Robertson* (2004) 243 DLR (4th) 700 (BC SC).

As we shall see, the concept of reasonable force is important in other situations as well. While you may be entitled to make a citizen's arrest, or remove a trespasser from your property, or recover your goods from a thief, you can never use anything more than reasonable force. You cannot, for instance, set a deadly trap to catch a burglar or viciously beat a bike thief. If you go overboard, you may be sued in tort or prosecuted for a crime.

Invasion of Privacy

L.O. ❹ ❺ ❻

The traditional torts of assault and battery focused on the risk of physical injury. As new technologies continue to emerge, however, people are becoming more concerned with their privacy interests. A telephoto lens can capture a photograph from far away; a camera-equipped cellphone can secretly record images from inside a public restroom. Tort law has not yet caught up with those technological advances. There is no general tort of *invasion of privacy*. Consequently, a business that owns land next to a racetrack is entitled to erect a high platform, watch the races, and broadcast the events over the radio.[4] As the court explained in that case, people are not required to look away or to keep quiet about what they see.

There are several reasons why the courts traditionally have been reluctant to recognize a tort of invasion of privacy. They want to support freedom of expression and freedom of information. They are concerned about defining the concept of privacy in a way that strikes a fair balance between the parties.[5] They are reluctant to award damages in favour of celebrities who seek out publicity but then complain when they are shown in a bad light. And they find it difficult to calculate compensatory damages for the kinds of harm, such as embarrassment, that an invasion of privacy usually causes.

That is not to say that tort law does not provide any protection at all. Privacy is *indirectly* protected by several torts.

- A photographer who sneaks onto someone's property to obtain candid pictures commits the tort of *trespass to land*.[6]

- Employees who publish embarrassing details about their employer's private life may be liable for *breach of confidence*.[7] That action also allowed an English court to award damages against a magazine that published unauthorized photographs taken by a guest at a private wedding between two Hollywood heavyweights, Michael Douglas and Catherine Zeta-Jones.[8]

- Despite rejecting a tort of invasion of privacy, English courts have recognized a tort of abuse of *private information*. Consequently, supermodel Naomi Campbell was able to sue a newspaper that published a photograph of her coming out of a Narcotics Anonymous meeting.[9]

---

[4] *Victoria Park Racing and Recreation Grounds Co Ltd v Taylor* (1937) 58 CLR 459 (HCA).

[5] *Wainwright Home Office* [2004] 2 AC 406 (HL).

[6] The tort of trespass to land is considered later in this chapter.

[7] *Stephens v Avery* [1988] Ch 449 (Ch). The action for breach of confidence is examined in Chapter 18.

[8] *Douglas v Hello! Ltd* [2001] QB 969 (CA).

[9] *Campbell v Mirror News Group* [2004] 2 AC 457 (HL). Interestingly, the court relied upon the action for breach of confidence even though the photograph was taken while the plaintiff was emerging from a public building. The element of secrecy was provided by the fact that the newspaper added a caption explaining that Ms Campbell was leaving a substance abuse meeting.

- A company that makes unauthorized use of a celebrity's image to sell its own products may commit the tort of *misappropriation of personality*.[10]

- A newspaper that ignores a judge's instructions and publishes the name of a police officer who had been sexually assaulted during an undercover investigation may commit the tort of negligence.[11]

While those torts provide some protection, many people believe that there is room for a separate tort of invasion of privacy. New Zealand's highest court recently accepted that argument, and Australia's highest court seems inclined to follow suit.[12,13] Canadian courts may not be far behind. A cause of action has been recognized in certain situations. A judge imposed liability upon a couple who, as part of a petty feud, installed a surveillance camera that continuously monitored their neighbours' backyard. While recognizing that the law generally does not prohibit one person from watching another, the judge held that an intentional invasion of privacy will not be permitted.[14] Another judge was prepared to impose liability after a woman violated her nephew's reasonable expectation of privacy by telling his family that he was HIV positive.[15] The Supreme Court of Canada pointed in the same direction in *Aubry v Éditions Vice-Versa Inc.*[16] A photographer took a picture of a young woman sitting on the steps of a building in Montreal. When the photograph was published in an arts magazine, the young woman was teased by her school friends. The court awarded her $2000 in damages for invasion of privacy. It explained that a

Case Brief 4.2

Jones v Tsige (2011) 333 DLR (4th) 566 (Ont SCJ), varied (2012) 108 OR (3d) 231 (Ont CA)

The plaintiff and the defendant worked at separate branches of the Bank of Montreal (BMO). The plaintiff had a personal bank account at the same branch where the defendant worked. Although the parties did not know each other, the defendant was romantically involved with the plaintiff's ex-husband.

Over a four-year period, the defendant abused her position with BMO to view the details of the plaintiff's bank account 174 times. When the bank confronted the defendant about the issue, she admitted that she had no legitimate reason for looking at the plaintiff's information. Her only explanation was that she wanted to see if her boyfriend—the plaintiff's ex-husband—was paying child support to the plaintiff. She then apologized and promised not to misbehave again. The plaintiff, however, believed that she was entitled to more. She sued the defendant for invasion of privacy and demanded compensatory and punitive damages.

Although the trial judge rejected that claim, the Ontario Court of Appeal recognized a limited version of a tort of invasion of privacy. Sharpe JA listed four possible types of privacy torts: (i) intrusion into the plaintiff's seclusion or private affairs, (ii) public disclosure of embarrassing information, (iii) publicity that places the plaintiff in a bad light, and (iv) unauthorized use of the plaintiff's likeness or image. The facts of *Jones v Tsige* fell into the first category.

The new tort of *intrusion upon seclusion* requires the plaintiff to prove that the defendant (i) *intentionally* (ii) *invaded the plaintiff's private affairs* without legal justification (iii) in a way that a *reasonable person* would consider *highly offensive*. As long as those three elements are satisfied, it does not matter that the plaintiff did not suffer any economic harm. The tort is aimed at preventing distress, humiliation, or anguish. For that reason, damages will usually not be very large. In *Jones v Tsige*, the Court of Appeal awarded $10 000.

[10.] *Athans v Canadian Adventure Camps Ltd* (1977) 80 DLR (3d) 583 (Ont HCJ).

[11.] In *LR v Nyp* (1995) 25 CCLT (2d) 309 (Ont Gen Div), the court was anxious to protect sexual assault victims from embarrassment by preserving their privacy. The tort of negligence is considered in Chapter 6.

[12.] *Hosking v Runting* [2005] 1 NZLR 1 (CA).

[13.] *ABC v Lenah Game Meats* (2001) 208 CLR 199 (HCA).

[14.] *Lipiec v Borsa* (1996) 31 CCLT (2d) 294 (Ont Gen Div).

[15.] *Caltagirone v Scozzari-Cloutier* (Unreported, 21 Sept 2007, Ont SCJ).

[16.] (1998) 157 DLR (4th) 577 (SCC).

balance must be struck in each case between the right to privacy and freedom of expression. It then imposed liability because the plaintiff was not merely part of a larger scene—she was the focus of the picture. *Aubry*, however, was decided under Quebec's civil law and therefore is not precedent in the rest of Canada. Case Brief 4.2 looks at another important development.

Because the courts are moving slowly in this area, legislators are becoming more involved. In 2005, Parliament enacted section 162 of the *Criminal Code*. The crime of "voyeurism" is committed by secretly observing or recording a person "in circumstances that give rise to a reasonable expectation of privacy," if that person is engaged in sexual activity or is partially or fully nude.[17] A crime also is committed by anyone who "prints, copies, publishes, distributes, circulates, sells, advertises or makes available" a prohibited recording.[18] That law could, for instance, catch the sort of unscrupulous paparazzi who earned millions of dollars by secretly photographing supermodel Claudia Schiffer as she sunbathed topless in her parents' garden in Majorca, and the Duchess of York Sarah Ferguson as she lounged topless beside a private pool in St Tropez.

In addition, several provinces have created statutory causes of action to protect privacy interests.[19] While those statutes vary from jurisdiction to jurisdiction, they generally impose liability if a person "wilfully" violates another's privacy by doing something that they know to be wrong.[20] The definition of "privacy" has been left open so that the courts can flexibly respond to different types of situations. Case Brief 4.3 illustrates the statutory action.

Case Brief **4.3**

Hollinsworth v BCTV [1999] 6 WWR 54 (BC CA)

The plaintiff entered into a contract with the defendant, Look International Enterprises (LIS), to have a hairpiece surgically attached to his scalp. Under the terms of that contract, LIS was allowed to videotape the procedure for instructional purposes only. Seven years later, without the plaintiff's knowledge, LIS allowed a television station to use the videotape during a news feature on hair grafts. When the station's reporter asked if the patient had consented to such use, LIS wrongly said, "Yes." The plaintiff suffered great embarrassment as a result of the broadcast. He sued both LIS and the television station under British Columbia's *Privacy Act*.

The court awarded damages of $15 000 against LIS for its "wilful" invasion of privacy. The plaintiff's claim against the television station failed, however, because the station had not acted "wilfully." Given the information that its reporter had received from LIS, the station believed that the plaintiff had consented to the use of the videotape.

False Imprisonment

L.O. ❼ ❽

False imprisonment occurs when a person is confined within a fixed area without justification. That would clearly be true if the plaintiff was physically dragged to a prison and thrown into a locked cell. The scope of the tort is, however, considerably wider than that.

the tort of **false imprisonment** occurs when a person is confined within a fixed area without justification

---

[17.] RSC, c C-46, s 162 (Can).

[18.] A defence exists if the accused's actions "serve the public good and do not extend beyond what serves the public good."

[19.] *Privacy Act*, RSBC 1996, c 373 (BC); *Privacy Act*, CCSM, c P125 (Man); *Privacy Act*, RSNL 1990, c P-22 (Nfld); *Privacy Act*, RSS 1978, c P-24 (Sask).

[20.] *Heckert v 5470 Investments Ltd* (2008) 299 DLR (4th) 689 (BC SC); *Wasserman v Hall* (2009) 87 RPR (4th) 184 (BC SC).

- An actual prison is not necessary. The tort can be committed if a person is trapped in a car, locked in a room, or set adrift in a boat. But in any event, the confinement must be practically complete. The defendant does not commit a false imprisonment by obstructing one path while leaving another reasonable path open. Nor is the tort committed if the plaintiff can easily escape.

- Perhaps surprisingly, physical force is *not* necessary. The detention may be *psychological*. A tort may be committed, for example, if a shopper accompanies a security guard to a backroom in order to avoid public embarrassment.[21] Confronted by a person in uniform who is making a serious demand, many people feel that they have no choice but to do as they are told. That perception may be reinforced if, for example, a theft detection device triggers an alarm when a customer leaves a store.[22] In that type of case, the judge has to decide whether the plaintiff voluntarily chose to go to the backroom (no liability) or whether the plaintiff believed that there really was no other option (liability).

- Because a police officer has a wider power of arrest than a private citizen, a business person may *reduce* the risk of liability by calling a police officer, instead of directly arresting a suspect. That tactic will not, however, *eliminate* the risk. The business may still be held liable if it *directed* the officer to make the arrest, rather than merely stated the facts and allowed the officer to draw a conclusion.[23]

- Even if the business did not direct a police officer to make an arrest (and therefore cannot be held liable for false imprisonment), it may be liable for the tort of *malicious prosecution*.[24] **Malicious prosecution** occurs when the defendant improperly causes the plaintiff to be prosecuted. The focus is not on detention or imprisonment, but rather on being subject to criminal proceedings.[25] That might be true, for instance, if a business concocted a story about shoplifting and persuaded the government to lay charges against the plaintiff. Malicious prosecution is difficult to prove, however. The court has to be satisfied that (i) the defendant started the proceedings (ii) out of malice, or for some improper purpose, and (iii) without honestly believing on reasonable grounds that a crime had been committed, and that (iv) the plaintiff was eventually acquitted of the alleged crime.[26]

the tort of **malicious prosecution** occurs when the defendant improperly causes the plaintiff to be prosecuted

Although the tort of false imprisonment is quite wide, the defendant will not be held liable if the plaintiff agreed to be confined. *Consent* is a complete defence to all intentional torts. Consequently, bus passengers cannot complain

---

[21.] *Chaytor v London, New York & Paris Assoc of Fashion Ltd* (1961) 30 DLR (2d) 527 (Nfld SC TD).

[22.] *Naujokaitis v Dylex Ltd* (Unreported, 17 March 1982, Ont Co Ct).

[23.] *Valderhaug v Libin* (1954) 13 WWR 383 (Alta CA); *Lebrun v High-Low Foods Ltd* (1968) 69 DLR (2d) 433 (BC SC).

[24.] *Roberts v Buster's Auto Towing Service Ltd* (1976) 70 DLR (3d) 716 (BC SC). The same tort may be used by an aggrieved employee: *McNeil v Brewers Retail Inc* (2008) 66 CCEL (3d) 238 (Ont CA).

[25.] Aside from the tort of malicious prosecution, liability may arise under the tort of *negligent investigation*. Although that tort was first applied to police officers, it now extends to private investigation firms that are hired by businesses who suspect employee misconduct. Significantly, however, the tort does not apply to employers themselves: *Correia v Canac Kitchens* (2008) 294 DLR (4th) 525 (Ont CA). The tort of negligence is discussed in Chapter 6.

[26.] *Nelles v Ontario* (1989) 60 DLR (4th) 609 (SCC); *Kvello Estate v Miazga* (2009) 313 DLR (4th) 330 (SCC).

if the driver refuses to make an unscheduled stop.[27] A company that operates a mine is generally entitled to leave a worker underground until the end of a shift.[28] And a traveller at an airport may be detained for the purpose of a search. The same rule may apply to a customer in a store, at least if the store gave advance warning. Likewise, although a false imprisonment can be committed by wrongfully detaining someone's valuable property, the tort does not arise if the plaintiff agreed to that arrangement. Consequently, a person cannot remove a vehicle from a car park without paying the appropriate fee.

An imprisonment is false only if it is done *without authority*. That statement raises an important question for business people. When is there authority to make an arrest? Unfortunately, the law is complicated. The basic rules are found in the *Criminal Code*.

- A *police officer* may arrest anyone who is reasonably suspected of (i) being in the act of committing a crime, or (ii) having committed a *serious* crime in the past.[29] If that test is satisfied, the police officer cannot be held liable, even if the person who was arrested was actually innocent.

- The rules[30] are much narrower for *private citizens*—including *security guards*.[31] A private citizen is entitled to make an arrest only if a crime is *actually being committed* by the suspect.[32] If, in fact, no crime was being committed, the arrest is unjustified. And whoever made the arrest may be held liable in tort, even if they acted honestly and reasonably. The law generally favours a customer's freedom of movement over a store's desire to protect its property. The law's restrictive attitude toward security guards, bouncers, doormen, and crowd control personnel is further reflected in a growing trend toward statutory regulation. Ontario's *Private Investigators and Security Guards Act*, for instance, requires such individuals to complete mandatory training and to be certified on an annual basis.[33] A person convicted of any one of eighty-four crimes is ineligible for certification. And any establishment that employs uncertified personnel may be shut down for up to a year.

[27.] *Martin v Berends* [1989] OJ No 2644 (Ont Prov Ct).

[28.] *Herd v Weardale Steel, Coal & Coke Co Ltd* [1915] AC 67 (HL).

[29.] *Criminal Code*, RSC 1985, c C-46, s 495 (Can).

[30.] The rules in this section are found in the *Criminal Code*. As discussed below, some provinces have additional legislation that allows occupiers, and their security personnel, to arrest trespassers.

[31.] Not only do security guards lack the authority given to police officers, they may be held to a higher standard than regular citizens. An Ontario Provincial Court judge once explained that since "security guards should be expected, by the nature of their work, to be more aware of the limitations on their powers than ordinary citizens," an especially strong punishment is required, when they exceed their authority, "as a strong reminder... that their powers are circumscribed by the law." *R v JC* [1995] OJ No 1637 at 23 (Ont PC).

[32.] *Criminal Code*, RSC 1985, c C-46, s 494 (Can); *Hayward v FW Woolworth Co Ltd* (1979) 98 DLR (3d) 345 (Nfld SC TD). A private citizen may also arrest a person who is reasonably believed to have committed a crime *and* who is being chased by a police officer. If that test is satisfied, the citizen will not be liable in tort, even if no crime was actually committed.

Section 494(2) of the *Criminal Code* recently was expanded slightly. The statute previously said that a property owner could arrest a person caught "committing a criminal offence on or in relation to... property" (such as stealing goods), but the arrest had to happen at the same time as the offence. Today, however, an arrest can be made "within a reasonable time after the offence is committed," as long as the property owner reasonably believes that it is not "feasible" or practical for a peace officer to make the arrest.

[33.] RSO 1990, c P-25 (Ont). Legislation of the same name, and with much the same effect, exists in several other provinces: RSA 2000, c P-23 (Alta); SS 1997, c P–2601 (Sask); CCSM 132 (Man); RSPEI 1988, c Q–1 (PEI); RSY 2002, c175 (Yuk). See also *Security Service Act*, SBC 2007, c 30.

Business Decision 4.1

The Lucky Moose Case: *R v Chen* 2010 ONCJ 641 (Ont CJ)

David Chen immigrated to Canada and established the Lucky Moose grocery store in Toronto's Chinatown and Kensington area. Like many shopkeepers, he grew frustrated not only by shoplifters, but also by his belief that the legal system does not take that type of crime seriously. In an effort to protect himself, he installed video surveillance cameras in his store. On 23 May 2009, his cameras captured images of Anthony Bennett taking several plants from the Lucky Moose, loading them onto the handlebars of his bike, and riding away. That was business as usual for Mr Bennett, a lifelong criminal with 43 convictions for theft.

About an hour later, Mr Bennett returned to the Lucky Moose with the intention of shoplifting more goods. Before he could do so, however, Mr Chen calmly confronted him. When Mr Bennett dropped his bike and attempted to escape, Mr Chen and two colleagues called 911 and went after Mr Bennett. After catching up to him, they tied his feet and hands, placed him in the back of a van, and headed back to the Lucky Moose. The police then arrived, but to Mr Chen's surprise, he and his friends were arrested, strip-searched, held overnight in jail, and eventually charged with criminal assault and false imprisonment.

In separate proceedings, Mr Bennett was convicted of theft as a result of his actions at the Lucky Moose. The case against Mr Chen, however, is far more interesting. He relied upon section 494(1) of the *Criminal Code* for his defence against the criminal charges.

494. (1) Any one may arrest without warrant

(a) a person whom he finds committing an indictable offence, or

(b) a person who, on reasonable grounds, he believes

  (i) has committed a criminal offence, and

  (ii) is escaping from and freshly pursued by persons who have lawful authority to arrest that person.

Questions for Discussion

1. Based on the law, do you believe that the *Criminal Code* allowed Mr Chen to arrest Mr Bennett? At the time of the arrest, did

Mr Chen "find [Mr Bennett] committing an indictable offence" of theft? Did the shopkeeper "on reasonable grounds . . . believe" that Mr Bennett "had committed a criminal offence" and was "escaping from and freshly pursued by persons who have lawful authority to arrest" Mr Bennett? And even if Mr Chen was entitled to make an arrest under section 494(1), did he and his colleagues use unreasonable force?

2. How would you have reacted in Mr Chen's position? What if Mr Bennett returned to your store a week after you had seen him shoplifting? If you simply called the police, how quickly do you think they would respond? Do you think that if you asked him nicely, Mr Bennett would wait with you until the police arrived?

3. How would you react if people in your store were acting suspiciously and heading for the exit? Would you be entitled to arrest them as long as you honestly believed that they had stolen goods stuffed into their jackets? Would it be safer to have your security guards arrest the people?

4. As a result of the Lucky Moose case, Parliament changed the law to give property owners a greater power of arrest. Section 494(2) of the *Criminal Code* now says:

The owner or a person in lawful possession of property, or a person authorized by the owner or by a person in lawful possession of property, may arrest a person without a warrant if they find them committing a criminal offence on or in relation to that property and

  (a) they make the arrest at that time; or
  (b) they make the arrest within a reasonable time after the offence is committed and they believe on reasonable grounds that it is not feasible in the circumstances for a peace officer to make the arrest.

Would that section have helped Mr Chen? Was it "feasible" for Mr Chen to have the police arrest Mr Bennett?

The rules that apply to private citizens often create difficulties for business people. For instance, a person who objects to the price of a meal and tries to leave the restaurant without fully paying the bill usually commits a breach of contract, but not a crime.[34] In that situation, the law is faced with a difficult choice. [35] It could allow the business to detain the customer (or the customer's property) until it receives payment. That approach, however, would violate the

---

[34.] A crime of fraud or false pretences will be committed only if, for instance, the customer intended to refuse payment from the outset, tried to sneak out of the restaurant, gave a false name, or provided a worthless cheque: *Criminal Code*, RSC 1985, c C-46, ss 362, 364, 380 (Can). A crime is also committed if, for instance, a shopper switches price tags, or puts a more expensive item into the carton of a less expensive item, in order to obtain a "discount."

[35.] One solution is for the business to require payment *before* providing service. Aside from gas stations, however, most businesses find that approach to be inconvenient and off-putting to the customer.

customer's freedom of movement. Alternatively, the law could merely allow the business to sue the customer for breach of contract. Quite often, however, the amount in question would be too small to justify the expense of a lawsuit. Although neither solution is perfect, the law prefers the latter. Consequently, while the restaurant is entitled to take down the patron's name and sue for breach of contract, it may be liable for false imprisonment if it tries to detain the customer.[36]

As we previously suggested, even if a business is authorized to make an arrest, it should not use more force than is necessary. In most situations, the customer should be given an opportunity to surrender peacefully. And in any event, the arrested person should be turned over to the police as soon as possible. Business Decision 4.1, which is based on a case that received a great deal of publicity, illustrates the difficult decisions that business people sometimes have to make.

Trespass to Land

L.O. ❾

A **trespass to land** occurs when the defendant improperly interferes with the plaintiff's land. Interference can take several forms. A trespass is obviously committed if a vandal sneaks onto someone's property. However, the tort can also arise quite innocently. That is true, for instance, if I kick a ball into your yard (even if I do not walk onto your property to retrieve the ball), or if a lawn care company mistakenly cuts your grass instead of your neighbour's. If that seems surprising, remember our earlier discussion of "intention." It is enough if I intended to do the act, even if I did not intend to do wrong or cause damage. The law wants to protect property interests. As the old saying goes, "A man's home is his castle."

The person who has the right to a particular piece of property also has rights to the air above it and the ground beneath it. Those rights are sometimes discussed in terms of the "giant carrot" theory of ownership.[37] That theory suggests that the landholder's rights extend from the centre of the Earth and up through the skies. Modern courts, in contrast, generally say that the rights are available to a reasonable extent. A property owner, for example, normally cannot successfully sue simply because a jet flies overhead. Damages may be available, however, if a construction company allows its building crane to swing over the plaintiff's land, or if metal rods are inserted beneath the plaintiff's land in order to support a building on a neighbouring plot.[38]

The tort of trespass is not committed, however, by a person who has legal authority to be on a property. Police officers are entitled to enter premises under a search warrant. Likewise, a number of other public officials, such as building inspectors and meter readers, may do whatever is reasonably necessary to carry out their duties.

More significantly for our purposes, a trespass does not occur merely because a customer walks into a place of business during regular hours. Under normal circumstances, it is assumed that the business *consented* to the intrusion; indeed, it implicitly *invited* the customer onto the property. However, a business can usually revoke its consent, as long as it does not violate human

the tort of **trespass to land** occurs when the defendant improperly interferes with the plaintiff's land

---

[36.] *Bahner v Marwest Hotel Ltd* (1969) 6 DLR (3d) 322 (BC SC); *Perry v Fried* (1972) 32 DLR (3d) 589 (NS SC TD).

[37.] The Latin phrase is "*cuius est solum, eius est usque ad coelum et ad inferos*," which means "whoever owns [the] soil, [it] is theirs all the way [up] to Heaven and [down] to Hell."

[38.] *Atlantic Aviation Ltd v NS Light & Power Co* (1965) 55 DLR (2d) 554 (NS SC); *Austin v Rescon Construction (1984) Ltd*(1989) 57 DLR (4th) 591(BC CA); *Bocardo SA v Star Energy UK Onshore Ltd* [2011] AC 380 (UK SC).

rights legislation (for example, by excluding a person on racial grounds).[39] Consequently, the owner of a shopping mall is not required to allow mall employees to set up a picket line on its premises as part of a labour dispute.[40] Similarly, the owner of a racetrack may exclude a highly successful gambler.[41] And once a business has revoked its consent, a customer who remains on its property becomes a trespasser. If the customer still refuses to leave, the business may use reasonable force to eject them. However, as we discussed under the tort of battery, it should be very careful when doing so.[42]

Quite often, a business will deal with an unwelcome visitor by simply removing the trespasser. In some situations, however, the business may want to do more—it may want to arrest the trespasser. There is legislation in most jurisdictions that allows an occupier to arrest a trespasser who refuses a request to leave the premises.[43] And indeed, Intelligarde, one of Ontario's largest security guard companies, has made more than 30 000 arrests during the past 20 years. Nevertheless, it only recently became clear that an occupier is entitled to use *reasonable force* in making such an arrest. In *R v Asante-Mensah*, Binnie J explained that since the legislature granted the special power of arrest, it must have intended to protect people who exercise that power in a reasonable way. However, he also stressed the need for private citizens to use caution.

> Many trespasses are of trivial importance... They are best handled by means short of arrest.... An arrest is a grave imposition on another person's liberty and should only be attempted if other options prove ineffective. Further, an arrest may lead to a confrontation that is more serious than the initial offence of trespass.... Excessive force, or improper use of the arrest power, may leave the occupier... open to both criminal charges and civil liability.[44]

The usual remedy for a trespass to land is compensation for the harm that it caused. However, a court may also award nominal damages if there was no loss, or punitive damages if the defendant's conduct was shockingly bad. Furthermore, if the defendant's wrong is ongoing, the plaintiff may be entitled to an injunction to stop the trespass. For example, if a company constructs a billboard on a person's land without permission, the judge will likely demand that it be torn down. In some circumstances, however, the courts are faced with

---

[39]. The business will not always be able to revoke its consent. For example, a customer who had paid to attend a baseball game and had not broken any of the conditions attached to their ticket could not be ejected merely because they refused to show their ticket to an attendant during the game: *Davidson v Toronto Blue Jays Baseball Ltd* (1999) 170 DLR (4th) 559 (Ont Gen Div).

[40]. *Harrison v Carswell* (1975) 62 DLR (3d) 68 (SCC). In some provinces, legislation now allows picketing in such circumstances: for example,see *Petty Trespasses Act*, CCSM, c P150 (Man).

[41]. *Russo v Ontario Jockey Club* (1987) 46 DLR (4th) 359 (Ont HCJ).

[42]. *Aspden v Niagara (Regional Municipality) Police Services Board* [2005] OTC 187 (Ont SCJ).

[43]. *Trespass to Premises Act*, RSA 2000, c T-7, s 5 (Alta); *Trespass Act*, RSBC 1996, c 462, s 10 (BC); *Petty Trespasses Act*, CCSM, c P50, s 2 [rep and am 1992, c 21, s 3] (Man); *Trespass Act*, SNB 1983, c T-11.2, s 7 [am 1985, c 70, s 5; 1989, c 42, s 5; 1990; c 22, s 51] (NB); *Petty Trespass Act*, RSNL 1990, c P-11, s 4 (Nfld); *Protection of Property Act*, RSNS 1989, c 363, s 6 (NS); *Trespass to Property Act*, RSO 1990, c T.21, s 9 (Ont); *Trespass to Property Act*, RSPEI 1988, T-6, s 5 (PEI). The wording of those statutes sometimes varies. In British Columbia, Nova Scotia, and Prince Edward Island, for instance, the legislation gives a power of arrest to police officers but not to occupiers. In Ontario and New Brunswick, an occupier (or an occupier's security personnel) is entitled to arrest anyone believed "on reasonable and probable grounds" to be a trespasser. In Alberta and Manitoba, in contrast, an occupier's power of arrest exists only if the detained person actually is a trespasser.

[44]. *R v Asante-Mensah* (2003) 227 DLR (4th) 75 (SCC). Although the Supreme Court of Canada's decision technically applies only to the Ontario statute, the court's reasoning will apply in some other jurisdictions as well.

a difficult choice between protecting the plaintiff's property interests and avoiding economic waste. In deciding whether to grant an injunction, a judge will consider a number of factors, including the defendant's motivation for committing the wrong, the extent to which monetary damages would adequately protect the plaintiff, and the costs associated with removing the trespass. How would you decide the case in You Be the Judge 4.1?

You Be the Judge 4.1

Trespass to Land and Injunctions

Vista Inc, a real estate developer, built a 20-storey apartment complex. Unfortunately, as a result of an innocent error, a corner of the building extends two metres onto the neighbouring lot, which is owned by Paolo. Vista admits that it committed the tort of trespass and it is willing to either pay compensatory damages or buy the affected land from Paolo. Paolo, however, insists that he should be able to exercise complete control over his property. He therefore wants an injunction to prevent Vista's ongoing trespass. If successful, Paolo will be able to force Vista to tear down a substantial part of its building.

Questions for Discussion

1. Would you grant the injunction?

2. Would your answer be different if the cost of removing the trespassing portion of the apartment complex were $50 000? What if it were $5 000 000?

3. Would your answer be different if Paolo suffered no financial loss as a result of the trespass? What if, for some reason, he suffered a substantial loss of $50 000 or $5 000 000? What if he was simply very upset that his rights had been infringed?

4. Would your answer be different if Vista had committed the trespass on purpose? What if Vista knew at the outset that it was committing a tort but was confident that, even if Paolo noticed the trespass, a court would award only nominal damages for the minor infringement?

5. If a court awards an injunction, the power of enforcement lies with the plaintiff. In this case, the court's order would *allow* Paolo to compel Vista to remove the offending building, but it would not *require* him to do so. How would an injunction change the parties' bargaining positions? How might Paolo act if he were granted an injunction?

Concept Summary 4.1

Communication Rules

Tort	Protected Interest	Elements of Proof
Assault	freedom from fear of offensive bodily contact	• intentional act • causing a reasonable belief that offensive bodily contact is imminent
Battery	freedom from offensive bodily contact	• intentional act • causing offensive bodily contact
False imprisonment	freedom of movement	• intentional act • involving physical or psychological forces • causing person to be confined within fixed area without justification
Malicious prosecution	freedom from improper prosecution	• criminal proceedings commenced for malicious or improper purpose, without honest belief on reasonable grounds that crime was committed • resulting in acquittal of accused
Trespass to land	right to exclude trespassers from land	• intentional act • causing person or object to interfere with land

Before moving on to the final sections of this chapter, dealing with interference with chattels and defences to intentional torts, it will be useful to review the torts that we have discussed. Concept Summary 4.1 identifies the essential elements of each of those torts.

Interference with Chattels

chattels are moveable forms of property

Tort law protects not only land, but also *chattels*. **Chattels** are moveable forms of property, such as horses, books, and cars. The rules are quite complicated, largely because the courts have developed a number of torts to protect chattels. We will outline the most important of those torts:

- trespass to chattels
- conversion
- detinue

Concept Summary 4.2 lists the essential features of those torts.

Concept Summary 4.2

Intentional Interference with Chattels

Tort	Basis of the Tort	General Remedy
Trespass to chattels	defendant's interference with chattels in plaintiff's possession	compensation for loss
Conversion	defendant's interference with chattels in plaintiff's possession—serious enough to justify forced sale	forced sale of chattel from plaintiff to defendant
Detinue	defendant's failure to return chattels that plaintiff has right to possess	compensation for loss or return of chattels

the tort of **trespass to chattels** occurs when the defendant interferes with chattels in the plaintiff's possession

Trespass to chattels occurs when the defendant interferes with chattels in the plaintiff's possession. The element of interference is satisfied if the defendant damages, destroys, takes, or uses the plaintiff's goods. There may even be a trespass if the defendant merely touches the plaintiff's property, at least if that property is, for example, a priceless painting that requires protection.[45] As a general rule, the remedy for trespass to chattels is compensatory damages.[46] If you completely destroyed my car, you would be required to pay the vehicle's market value. In contrast, if you merely damaged my car, you would be required to pay either for the value that it lost or for its repairs, whichever is less.

the tort of **conversion** occurs when the defendant interferes with the plaintiff's chattels in a way that is serious enough to justify a forced sale

The tort of **conversion** occurs when the defendant interferes with the plaintiff's chattels in a way that is serious enough to justify a forced sale. That may be true if the defendant takes, detains, uses, buys, sells, damages, or destroys

---

[45]. JG Fleming *The Law of Torts* 9th ed (1998) at 59.

[46]. In exceptional cases, the plaintiff may receive nominal damages or punitive damages.

the plaintiff's property. If so, the defendant will be required to buy the item by paying the market value that the chattel had at the time of the tort. In exchange for that payment, the defendant acquires the property.

The main difficulty with the tort of conversion is that it is often hard to know whether the defendant's actions are serious enough to justify a forced sale. The courts consider all of the facts, including:

- the extent to which the defendant exercised ownership or control over the chattel
- the extent to which the defendant intended to assert a right that was inconsistent with the plaintiff's right to the property
- the duration of the defendant's interference
- the expense and inconvenience caused to the plaintiff[47]

Conversion is clearly committed if a thief steals my property or if a vandal destroys it. The tort may also occur if you habitually use my umbrella without my permission, but not if you use it only once because you were caught in a downpour.[48] Notice, however, that even though you do not commit a conversion if you borrow my umbrella for a short time, you do commit the tort of trespass to goods. Although trespass can be used for very serious matters, it is usually used for less serious ones. Conversion, in contrast, can be used only for serious matters.[49]

Once again, the tort may be committed even if the defendant did not intend to do anything wrong. It is enough, for instance, that you intended to exercise control over a particular piece of property, even if you thought that you were entitled to do so. That rule presents a particular danger for business people. As a matter of risk management, it means that you should use every reasonable effort to ensure that you buy goods from people who are actually entitled to sell them. And even that may not be enough to protect you from liability. Ethical Perspective 4.1 illustrates the rules.

The tort of conversion can be unusually harsh. In the business world, however, it is subject to one very important exception. While an innocent purchaser of goods (such as cattle, cars, or jewellery) may be held liable, an innocent purchaser of money has nothing to fear. For example, if a thief steals my watch and sells it to you for $100, you have committed a tort against me. But if a thief steals my $100 bill, and sells it to you in exchange for your own watch, you are not liable for conversion. The law treats money differently than other assets.[50] It does so to ensure that money flows freely through our economy. The business world quickly would grind to a halt if every shopkeeper felt compelled to ensure that every customer actually owns the money being offered as payment.

The tort of **detinue** occurs when the defendant fails to return a chattel that the plaintiff is entitled to possess. The word "detinue" is derived from the old French word "*detenue*," which means "detention." Because the tort is based on a wrongful detention, the plaintiff is normally required to demand possession of the property before bringing an action. That requirement is

the tort of **detinue** occurs when the defendant fails to return a chattel that the plaintiff is entitled to possess

---

[47] W Prosser "The Nature of Conversion" (1957) 42 *Cornell LQ* 168 at 174.

[48] *Canadian Orchestraphone Ltd v British Canadian Trust Co* [1932] 2 WWR 618 (Alta CA).

[49] Although trespass and conversion can also overlap with detinue, that tort is somewhat different. As explained below, it is not so much concerned with the *interference* with property rights. It deals instead with the wrongful *detention*, or failure to return, a chattel.

[50] The rule generally is limited to cash money—notes and coins. Similar rules also apply to negotiable instruments, as explained in Chapter 14.

PART 2

Ethical Perspective 4.1

Conversion and Innocent Purchasers[51]

John stole a herd of cattle from Katherine and sold the animals to you for $50 000. Before you paid, you checked the cattle and noticed that they were not branded. You asked John about the herd and were convinced that he owned the animals. Unfortunately, he has disappeared, and Katherine has sued you for conversion. You protest that you had acted honestly.

While an unsuspecting buyer or seller of goods is sometimes protected by a special defence, a court would probably hold you liable for conversion. In buying the cattle and treating them as your own, you seriously interfered with Katherine's rights. Consequently, you would have to pay her $50 000, which was the market value of the animals. Notice that while you will be entitled to keep the herd, you have now paid $100 000 for it. You could try to recover $50 000 from John, but he has disappeared, as rogues often do.

Questions for Discussion

1. Are the rules for conversion fair?

2. Why do you think that the law of conversion is so strict?

removed, however, if the demand would obviously be refused. The fact that detinue consists of a wrongful detention also affects the remedies that may be available to a plaintiff.

■ First, the tort comes to an end as soon as the defendant returns the property to the plaintiff. At that point, the plaintiff is normally limited to compensation for losses that they suffered during the detention, as well as for any harm done to the item.

■ Second, if the property has not been returned by the time of trial, the plaintiff can ask the court to compel the defendant to do so.[52] The court usually gives the defendant the option of either giving the property back or paying damages. However, the judge may require the property to be returned if it is special or if damages would not satisfy the plaintiff.

Detinue is the only tort that generally allows a court to order the defendant to return a chattel to the plaintiff. In some situations, however, the plaintiff may not need the court's help. The right of **recaption** allows a person to take their own property back. For instance, a shopkeeper may be entitled to grab a stolen watch away from a shoplifter who is trying to leave the store. That right should, however, be exercised very carefully. The owner is entitled to use only reasonable force while recovering the property. Anything more will expose the owner to the risk of liability for battery.

the right of **recaption** allows a person to take their own property back

L.O. ❿

Defences to Intentional Torts

At several points in this chapter, we have referred to certain defences in connection with certain torts. We have seen, for instance, that damages for battery may be reduced if the victim *provoked* the attack, that a false imprisonment does not occur if the plaintiff *consented* to being confined, and that a public authority does not commit a trespass by entering onto a property with *legal authority*. Before leaving this topic, it will be useful to draw those strands

---

[51.] *Nilsson Bros Inc v McNamara Estate* [1992] 3 WWR 761 (Alta CA).

[52.] That option does not exist under trespass to chattels or conversion. Those torts generally support only monetary damages.

together with a brief overview of the defences to intentional torts.[53] Although special rules apply under some torts, most of the defences apply across the board. You should notice, however, that it is never a defence to plead *mistake*. A trespass to land occurs even if the defendants thought that they owned the property, conversion is committed even if the defendants honestly thought that they were buying goods from the true owners, and so on. The lesson is clear. As a matter of risk management, the intentional torts require you to be not only careful, but also correct.

COMPLETE DEFENCES

Most defences to intentional torts are classified as *complete defences*.

A **complete defence** protects the tortfeasor from all liability. Even though the plaintiff has demonstrated the existence of a tort, the defendant will not be held responsible. We will focus on four defences:

- consent
- legal authority
- self-defence
- necessity

> a **complete defence** protects the tortfeasor from all liability

Consent

Consent is by far the most important defence. **Consent** exists if a person voluntarily agrees to experience an interference with their body, land, or goods. That defence applies in a wide range of circumstances. For instance, it allows a person to borrow a friend's car without committing the tort of conversion; it ensures that a company's clients do not commit a trespass to land when they visit the company's premises; and it explains why a bus company is not liable for false imprisonment when it refuses to let a passenger out between scheduled stops.[54] Perhaps more surprisingly, since every sexual act involves interference with another's body, it is only the defence of consent that protects lovers from being held liable in battery![55]

Consent may be *express* or *implied*. At one extreme, a surgeon will insist upon a detailed, signed consent form before operating. Far more often, however, consent is implied by the circumstances. By participating in a hockey game, for instance, a person agrees to being hit in the normal course of the play (but not to a vicious attack that goes beyond the sort of behaviour that referees normally penalize).[56] Whether consent is express or implied, however, it is effective only if it is *free and informed*. The defence consequently will not apply if the apparent consent was given because the plaintiff was threatened or tricked. Nor can consent be given by a person who lacks legal capacity because they are too young or because they suffer from a mental illness. Likewise, a medical consent form is effective only if the physician properly informed the

> **consent** exists if a person voluntarily agrees to experience an interference with their body, land, or goods

---

[53.] Our discussion is limited to the most important defences. There are several others that seldom apply in business situations. That is true, for instance, of the defence of *discipline* that allows parents and possibly teachers to punish children without fear of committing the tort of battery: *Criminal Code*, RSC 1985, c C-46, s 43 (Can). For very different reasons, which are discussed in Chapter 6, the defence of *illegality* is seldom seen in Canadian courts.

[54.] Consent to enter onto land is often called a *licence*.

[55.] *Non-Marine Underwriters, Lloyd's of London v Scalera* (2000) 185 DLR (4th) 1 (SCC), discussed in Case Brief 3.2 (see page 70).

[56.] *R v McSorley* [2000] BCPC 116 (BC SC); *R v Bertuzzi* (2004) 26 CR (6th) 71 (BC Prov Ct).

patient of the risks and benefits involved in a certain procedure. And finally, consent is *revocable* in most circumstances. For instance, even if you allowed a person onto your property, you may withdraw your consent, so that they will become a trespasser if they refuse to leave.[57]

Legal Authority

legal authority provides a person with a lawful right to act in a certain way

After consent, the most common defence to an intentional tort is *legal authority*. **Legal authority** provides a person with a lawful right to act in a certain way. Acts that are legally authorized cannot lead to liability in tort. We already have seen several examples. In the context of false imprisonment, legal authority allows police officers, and sometimes other individuals, to exercise a power of arrest. Similarly, in the context of trespass to land, public officials, such as meter readers and by-law enforcement officers, are entitled to enter onto land to perform their jobs. Although many of those situations traditionally involved common law rules, legal authority today is more often provided by statute.

Self-Defence

self-defence consists of the right to protect oneself from violence and the threat of violence

Some defences are closely connected with only a few of the intentional torts. Most importantly, *self-defence* naturally is tied to battery and assault. **Self-defence** consists of the right to protect oneself from violence and the threat of violence. As might be expected, the courts strike a balance between respecting the natural reaction to fight back and the danger of giving people an excuse to cause harm. The defence therefore is entirely defensive. It is available only if a person was at immediate risk. Furthermore, the acts of self-defence must be reasonable, having regard to the nature of the threat, the presence of weapons, the possibility of a non-violent resolution, and so on. At the same time, however, a person under attack "is not required to 'measure with complete nicety' the force necessary to repel the attack."[58] The defence therefore may apply even if, in the heat of the moment, the defendant reasonably used more force than was strictly necessary. Although there are very few cases on this point, the same rules generally apply if the defendant, having been sued for battery or assault, pleads *defence of a third party*. The precise scope of that defence is unsettled, but it is clear, for instance, that a parent may use reasonable force to protect a child. In the remarkable case of *Gambriell v Caparelli*, a mother, honestly believing that her son was being choked, was not liable for hitting the attacker on the head with a garden rake.[59]

Some interests are more important than others. Self-defence and defence of a third party are broadly defined because they are aimed at protecting human life and well-being. Because property interests are considered less important, the rules regarding the *defence of property* are less generous. As previously explained, non-threatening trespassers normally must be given an opportunity to leave peacefully before any force is used. Likewise, fences, barbed wire, and guard dogs may be used to keep intruders out, but a landowner will likely be held liable for injuries that trespassers suffer as a result of loaded traps or attack dogs. If the only threat is to land or chattels, it may never be reasonable to deliberately cause death or serious injury. The Supreme Court of Canada

---

[57.] If the person paid for the right to be on your land, however, you may be in breach of contract if you attempt to revoke your consent.

[58.] *Wackett v Calder* (1965) 51 DLR (2d) 598 (BC CA).

[59.] (1974) 54 DLR (3d) 661 (Ont Co Ct).

applied those rules in *R v Szczerbaniwicz*.[60] During a heated argument, a woman grabbed her husband's diploma and smashed it to the ground. The man became enraged and in an effort to protect his property, he pushed his wife hard against a staircase. He was convicted of criminal assault. The court held that while he was entitled to defend his diploma, he used excessive force in doing so.

Necessity

Necessity is a rare, but important, defence. The defence of **necessity** applies if the defendant's actions were justified by an emergency. The concept consequently is restricted to situations in which immediate action is required in order to avoid some calamity. The court must consider all the circumstances and decide whether the benefits flowing from the defendant's conduct outweigh the harm that was caused.[61] The defence may protect, for example, a physician who provides urgent medical care to an unconscious patient, or a person who tore down a neighbour's house in order to prevent the disastrous spread of a fire.

the defence of **necessity** applies if the defendant's actions were justified by an emergency

Because the defence of necessity, by definition, seldom applies, there are very few cases. As a result, some of the rules remain unclear. Most significantly, although we generally classify necessity as a complete defence, the defendant may not entirely escape responsibility in every instance. In one famous case, a terrible storm blew in while the defendant's boat was moored at the plaintiff's dock.[62] Since the defendant did not dare sail away from shore, he tightly fastened his ship to the dock. By doing so, he saved his vessel, but damaged the plaintiff's property. The American court attempted to balance the parties' interests. It first held that even though the he normally had no right to trespass on the plaintiff's property, the emergency created by the storm entitled the defendant to tie his boat to the dock. However, the court then held that even though the defendant's actions were justified, he was liable for the plaintiff's loss. In effect, the defendant was allowed to trespass, but he had to pay for any damage that he caused. Normally, of course, the defendant is either justified *or* liable, but not both.

PARTIAL DEFENCES

A **partial defence** allows a court to reduce damages on the basis of the plaintiff's own responsibility for a loss or an injury. Even though the defendant committed a tort, the plaintiff is partly to blame. We will look at two such defences:

a **partial defence** allows a court to reduce damages on the basis of the plaintiff's own responsibility for a loss or an injury

- provocation
- contributory negligence

Provocation

The concept of *provocation* is closely tied to the torts of assault and battery. **Provocation** consists of words or actions that would cause a reasonable person to lose self-control. In a typical case, the defendant "snaps" after being taunted

provocation consists of words or actions that would cause a reasonable person to lose self-control

---

[60.] (2010) 317 DLR (4th) 586 (SCC).

[61.] Those benefits may apply to the defendant, the plaintiff, a third party, or the general public.

[62.] *Vincent v Lake Erie Transport Co* (1910) 124 NW 221 (Minn SC).

and insulted by the plaintiff. The defendant is held liable for the physical attack, but the plaintiff is not entitled to full compensation.[63] The defence therefore strikes a balance. Because the legal system cannot condone violent behaviour, it imposes liability. Nevertheless, because the legal system recognizes that the plaintiff's boorish behaviour caused the attack and that even a reasonable person can be pushed only so far, it reduces damages.

Contributory Negligence

contributory negligence occurs when the plaintiff is partially responsible for the injury that the defendant tortiously caused

Provocation is often seen as a narrower version of the general defence of *contributory negligence*. As will be explained in more detail in Chapter 6, **contributory negligence** occurs when the plaintiff is partially responsible for the injury that the defendant tortiously caused. Because responsibility is shared between the parties, the defendant is held liable, but damages are reduced to reflect the plaintiff's contribution to the injury. That defence, however, is not equally available across the country. Different legislation exists in each province and territory. Some statutes *apportion*, or divide, responsibility on the basis of the parties' "fault." That term is broad enough to cover every type of tort. Other statutes refer instead to the parties' "negligence." And since that term does not naturally fit the intentional torts, some courts have found it difficult to apply the defence of contributory negligence to cases of battery, trespass, and so on.

Concept Summary 4.3 reviews the essential elements of the defences to intentional torts.

Concept Summary 4.3

Defences in Intentional Torts

Complete Defences	
Consent	voluntary choice to allow acts that otherwise would be tortious
Legal authority	statutory or common law right to perform acts that otherwise would be tortious
Self-defence	right to protect oneself, or a third party, or perhaps property, from an attack by a person
Necessity	right to protect oneself, or a third party, or perhaps property, from a natural disaster or general threat
Partial Defences	
Provocation	words or actions that cause a reasonable person to lose self-control
Contributory negligence	plaintiff is partially responsible for the injury that the defendant tortiously caused

---

[63.] The precise rules are inconsistent across the country. The Courts of Appeal for Ontario and Manitoba have held that provocation leads to a reduction in only *aggravated* and *punitive* damages. In contrast, appellate courts in British Columbia, Alberta, Nova Scotia, and Newfoundland and Labrador have relied upon the defence in reducing *compensatory* damages. See P Osborne *The Law of Torts* 2d ed (2003) at 261–262.

Chapter Summary

Intentional torts involve intentional conduct. It is enough if the defendant knew that particular conduct would have particular consequences. The plaintiff does not have to prove that the defendant intended to either cause harm or commit a tort.

Several types of intentional torts may be committed against a person. An assault occurs when the defendant intentionally causes the plaintiff to reasonably believe that offensive bodily contact is imminent. A battery consists of offensive bodily contact. False imprisonment occurs when a person is confined within a fixed area without justification. Malicious prosecution occurs when the defendant improperly causes the plaintiff to be prosecuted.

Although there traditionally has not been a separate tort of invasion of privacy, Canadian courts may be in the process of developing one. In the meantime, certain aspects of privacy are protected by other torts, including breach of confidence, abuse of private information, trespass to land, misappropriation of personality, and negligence. Some provinces have introduced statutory actions for invasion of privacy.

Several types of intentional torts may be committed against a person's property. Trespass to land occurs when the defendant improperly interferes with land that the plaintiff possesses. An occupier may use reasonable force when removing or arresting a trespasser. Trespass to chattels occurs when the defendant interferes with chattels that the plaintiff possesses. Conversion occurs when the defendant interferes with the plaintiff's chattels in a way that is serious enough to justify a forced sale. Detinue occurs when the defendant fails to return goods that the plaintiff has the right to possess. In some circumstances, a person may be entitled to recover property by recaption.

Special defences for intentional torts may be either complete or partial. A complete defence entirely protects the defendant from liability. That may be true if the plaintiff consented to the defendant's actions, if the defendant acted with legal authority, if the defendant acted in self-defence or defence of a third party or defence of property, or if the defendant acted in response to a necessity. A partial defence merely reduces the damages that the plaintiff is entitled to receive from the defendant. That may be true if the plaintiff provoked the defendant, or if the plaintiff was guilty of contributory negligence that combined with the defendant's tort to cause a loss or injury.

MyBusLawLab   ADDITIONAL RESOURCES FOR CHAPTER 4

MyBusLawLab provides students with an assortment of tools to help enrich the learning experience, including a Study Plan with Pre- and Post-tests, mini-cases with assessments, and provincial content material, which provides links to relevant cases, legislation, and additional resources.

MyBusLawLab provides the following resources for Chapter 4:

Provincial Material

- **British Columbia:** Trespass to Land
- **Alberta:** Trespass to Land
- **Manitoba and Saskatchewan:** Trespass to Land
- **Ontario:** Trespass

Review Questions

1. In what sense do the intentional torts require intentional conduct? Is tort law's definition of "intention" fair? Explain your answer.

2. Explain the difference between assault and battery. Describe a situation in which there is assault but not battery. Describe a situation in which there is battery but not assault.

3. Identify and explain a situation in which the concept of reasonable force is important to the removal of a person who is trespassing on business property.

4. "The tort of battery exists to protect people from injury. If the defendant's actions did not actually cause any physical harm, the plaintiff's claim must fail." Is that statement correct? Explain your answer.

5. "The tort of false imprisonment does not require proof that the defendant actually locked the plaintiff into a prison, but it does require proof that the defendant physically prevented the plaintiff from leaving an enclosed area." Is that statement true? Explain your answer.

6. Describe how privacy statutes generally operate.

7. List four ways in which tort law indirectly protects privacy.

8. "A business person is at liberty to use any amount of force to remove or arrest an undesirable customer." Is that statement true? As a business person, what factors would you consider before making an arrest or removing a customer from your place of business?

9. "Police work for the public good. As a result, they cannot be held liable if, as a result of carelessly collected evidence, they mistakenly cause the plaintiff to be prosecuted for a crime. Similarly, because criminal charges are brought against a person by a Crown prosecutor, a private citizen cannot be held liable in tort for wrongly causing criminal charges to be brought against the plaintiff." Are those statements true? Explain your answer.

10. Describe the tort of malicious prosecution and explain how it is related to the tort of false imprisonment.

11. Do police officers, security guards, and private citizens have the same rights when it comes to arresting criminals and suspected criminals? Explain the special dangers that arise when a business person arrests a suspected shoplifter.

12. Is it generally possible for a restaurant owner to arrest a person who refuses to pay the full amount of a bill? Explain your answer.

13. Identify and explain two types of statutes that may allow a private citizen to arrest a person.

14. "Trespass to land is an all-or-nothing idea. Assume that the defendant was not a trespasser when she walked onto the plaintiff's property. Although the plaintiff may ask the defendant to leave, the defendant cannot be considered a trespasser simply by remaining on the property." Is that statement true? Explain your answer.

15. Does a person commit a trespass to land by walking into a store if the owner of the store actually did not want any visitors? Explain your answer.

16. "The tort of trespass to land is based on the 'giant carrot' theory." Is that statement true? Explain your answer.

17. When will a court impose an injunction to stop a continuing trespass to land?

18. Explain the special dangers that the tort of conversion presents when a business person buys chattels.

19. "The tort of conversion operates differently depending upon whether the plaintiff's property consists of money or other types of goods." Is that statement true? Explain your answer.

20. What is the difference between a *complete defence* and a *partial defence*? Provide examples of each.

Cases and Problems

1. Marjorie, a middle-aged entrepreneur, was involved in a terrible, single-car accident. When she was taken to a nearby hospital, the attending nurse discovered that Majorie's purse carried a card that contained the following statement: "NOTICE: I am a Jehovah's Witness. Because of my religious beliefs, I do *not* consent, under any circumstances, to any emergency medical procedures that involve blood transfusions." The nurse brought the card to the attention of the emergency room physician, Dr Curtis. He immediately appreciated the dilemma. If he failed to perform a blood transfusion, Marjorie certainly would die within an hour. But if he proceeded with the transfusion, he would be overriding her religious beliefs. How should Dr Curtis proceed? Aside from moral considerations, what should he be told regarding the law? Can he be held liable, under an intentional tort, for performing an operation that will save Marjorie's life?

2. Debra Fairweather, a fashionabl e college student, went shopping for bargains on Boxing Day with her mother. As Debra walked through the front doors of Stylz Ladies Boutique, an alarm was set off. Deb turned around to find two older women, whom she assumed were security guards, looking at her suspiciously. Deb continued shopping with her mother, but neither found anything to buy. As they were leaving the store, the alarm again sounded as Deb went through the front doors. After she and her mother reached the sidewalk, the two older ladies—who were indeed acting as security guards for the store—approached Deb. One of the ladies touched Deb lightly on the shoulder and the other asked Deb to return to the store. Deb believed that she had no choice. As she walked back into Stylz, the alarm once again went off. One of the ladies then instructed Deb to pass through the security door without her jacket. The alarm did not sound. On inspection, one of the security guards located a Stylz security tag, which triggers the door alarm, inside one the jacket's sleeves. The store manager then confiscated the tag, wrote down Deb's name and address, and told Deb that she could take her jacket and leave. The entire episode was witnessed by at least two dozen people, who were also shopping in Stylz. Deb was terribly embarrassed at the time, but she is now angry. After she returned home,

she remembered that she had purchased the jacket, a month earlier, at another branch of Stylz. That explains the presence of the security tag. Deb wants to sue. Which tort should she use? Whom should she sue? What are her chances of success? If she wins her case, what remedies might the court award?

3. Although Jasmine Bhasin usually rode the bus to work, a one-day transit strike required her to drive instead. Not surprisingly, she was unable to find a parking space when she arrived at her office tower. She therefore simply parked in front of a fire hydrant and hoped for the best. At the end of the day, she was disappointed, but not particularly surprised, to find that her car had been towed away. After a few phone calls, she determined that her vehicle was being held in a compound that belonged to Buster's Towing Service. She went to the compound, paid the towing charge, and collected her car. As she approached the exit gate, she rolled down her window and expressed her displeasure to the attendant—in rather colourful and abusive language. The attendant tried to close the gate to prevent Jasmine from leaving, but he was too late. Jasmine slipped past him without difficulty. She thought nothing more of the incident until the police appeared at her office the next day and charged her with a crime. In the criminal case that followed, the attendant accused Jasmine of trying to run him over after collecting her car from Buster's compound. The judge rejected that evidence, however, and found that the attendant had concocted the whole story out of anger. Jasmine was therefore acquitted on all charges. She now believes that she should be entitled to sue the attendant in tort. Is she correct? Explain your answer.

4. Reverend Baldasaro, a gentleman in his late 50s, is a member of both the Church of the Universe and the Marijuana Party of Canada. He regards cannabis as part of the holy sacrament. He also hopes to be elected to Parliament during the current federal election. Two weeks ago, he visited Eastgate Square Shopping Mall in Hamilton with a view to attracting voters. A security guard employed by the mall told the Reverend that his activities were prohibited and asked him to leave. Reverend Baldasaro left without incident. Yesterday, however, he returned with a collection of pamphlets and buttons, and a colleague, Reverend Tucker (aged 72). The candidate and his friend were then approached by two security guards, who told them that they were trespassing and that they would be arrested if they did not leave immediately. The guards claim that Reverend Baldasaro replied, "Go ahead and arrest us because we're not leaving." The Reverend denies that statement, and claims instead that he indicated that he would leave after Reverend Tucker had purchased a book from a nearby store. In either event, the security guards forcibly arrested both gentlemen and detained them in a mall office. A police officer, who could have been called at the outset, was already present in the office. He then assumed control of the situation and later escorted the two Reverends out of the mall. Reverend Baldasaro was not hurt during the incident, but the security guards' actions caused Reverend Tucker injury and considerable pain. Discuss the legal issues that are raised by the facts.

5. As part of a promotional campaign, the Blacksox Baseball Club ran an advertisement in a local newspaper that featured a picture of about three dozen fans who were cheering wildly at a recent home game. In one corner of the picture, a man and a woman were hugging and kissing, apparently delighted with their team's success. The man's wife, however, knew better. When she saw the photo, she realized that her husband had resumed an affair with a woman he had promised to never see again. Angry that the Blacksox had exposed his infidelity, the man wants to sue the organization for invasion of privacy. Assuming that no relevant conditions were attached to the ticket that the man had purchased, and assuming that the relevant events occurred in Alberta, can the man successfully bring an action against the team on the basis of an intentional tort? Explain your answer.

6. Indira, an employee of Speedit Delivery Service, left a package at the front door of 57 Rollingwood Drive. In fact, she was supposed to leave it at the front door of 75 Rollingwood Drive. Late that night, when Anton arrived home at 57 Rollingwood Drive, he tripped over the box and suffered serious injuries. Is he entitled to sue for an intentional tort? If so, whom should he sue? Explain your answer.

7. Elaine and Latka each operate a stall in a market. During a particularly busy day, Elaine noticed that she had nearly run out of coins. She normally walked to a nearby bank to obtain change. However, since business was so brisk, she did not want to leave her stall unattended for long. She went to Latka's stand to ask if she could borrow his vehicle. He was out for lunch, but she noticed that he had left his car keys under his counter. While she did not really know Latka very well, Elaine assumed that he would not mind if she borrowed his car for a few minutes. When she returned, however, Latka was furious to learn that she had taken his car without permission. Has Elaine committed an intentional tort? If so, which one? Explain the remedy that Latka may receive.

8. Peter and Elizabeth are neighbours in a rural area. They are also brother and sister. Peter was unhappy with the small size of a pond on his property. He wanted to enlarge it for the purposes of swimming, fishing, boating, and skating. The only possibility for expansion, however, required the use of part of his sister's land. Elizabeth refused to give her consent to that plan. Peter then offered to buy the relevant portion of his sister's property, but she rejected that offer as well. Peter then remembered a piece of advice he once received from his father: "It's easier to get forgiveness than permission." While Elizabeth was away on vacation, Peter simply went ahead with the expansion. When she returned from her holiday, Elizabeth was furious to discover that her property now contained half of a very large pond. Peter hoped

that she would calm down after a few days, but she instead sued him in tort. What cause of action would Elizabeth use against Peter? What remedies might she receive from a court?

9. Strand Rentals Inc is in the business of renting electrical equipment for use in the entertainment industry. Some time ago, it rented an electronic switchboard to Brisford Entertainments Ltd. The rental period covered two weeks, at a price of $5000 per week. Brisford required that equipment for the purpose of staging a concert. Under the terms of the parties' rental agreement, Brisford was required to return the switchboard to Strand immediately after the concert. Nevertheless, because the initial concert turned out to be a great success, Brisford decided to hold a second show three weeks later. It therefore failed to return the switchboard as expected. Strand called repeatedly to demand the return of its property, but Brisford ignored those calls. It was only after the second concert, which earned Brisford a net profit of $50 000, that Brisford returned the switchboard to Strand. In all, Brisford had held the property for five weeks—two under contract and three after the lease had expired. Strand insists that it should be paid for that extra period. Brisford, however, has established that, during the period in question, Strand had far more switchboards than customers. Even if Brisford had performed as promised, the switchboard in question would have sat idle for the next three weeks. As a result, Brisford insists that Strand did not really lose anything as a result of the episode and therefore should not be entitled to any relief. Is that correct? Has Brisford committed any tort? How much, if anything, is Strand entitled to receive from Brisford as damages? How would you classify those damages? In the alternative, assume that Brisford is correct in saying that Strand suffered no compensable loss. Is there any other way in which a court might calculate relief? Does it matter that Brisford earned a huge profit as a result of its actions?

10. Madeleine sees Hugh stealing her car. Because she does not know who he is or where he lives, she realizes that she would have little chance of successfully suing him in tort. She also realizes that if she does not act immediately, she may lose her car permanently. What can Madeleine do?

11. Mary operates a convenience store. Much to her dismay, it has become a hangout for teenagers. She hired Frank to act as a security guard between the hours of 3:00 pm and 5:00 pm, when the store is at its busiest. Mary noticed that a young woman named Shelley, whom she had previously suspected of shoplifting, was acting suspiciously. She notified Frank, who approached Shelley and said in a loud voice and an accusing tone, "Come here. I've got a few questions to ask you." Shelley realized that Frank was acting on instructions from his employer and shouted over his shoulder at Mary, "If you've got a problem, come over here and speak to me yourself! I'll smack you silly!" At that point, Frank lunged at Shelley in an attempt to determine whether she was concealing stolen goods in her jacket. He grabbed her arm, but she managed to wrestle free and run out of the store. A number of Shelley's classmates saw the fracas and later teased her about it. Angry that Frank and Mary had humiliated her, Shelley returned to the street outside the store later that night and threw a garbage can through the shop window. Discuss the intentional torts that the parties may have committed.

12. Hannah's Holiday Foods Inc (HHF) operated a slaughterhouse where it killed, butchered, and packaged "exotic" animals, including rabbits and possums. HHF's business was fully licensed and entirely legal. An unknown animal rights group nevertheless believed that the public would be horrified to learn about the conditions under which the animals were killed. It therefore sneaked onto the premises one night and installed video surveillance cameras. The end product was a film showing rabbits in great distress before being slaughtered. That film was then delivered to a national television station, which announced its intention to broadcast the footage during its nightly news program. HHF has now gone to court and asked a judge to grant an injunction prohibiting the broadcast. While admitting that the television station acquired the film innocently, HHF insists that the film violates its right to privacy and almost certainly will hurt its business. Assuming that an injunction will be available if HHF can persuade the judge that there is, or should be, a right to privacy in private law, explain how you expect the case will be decided.

Miscellaneous Torts Affecting Business

5

LEARNING OBJECTIVES

After completing this chapter, you should be able to:

❶ Describe the tort of conspiracy and explain the risks that arise when two or more companies plot together against another business.

❷ Explain the two ways in which a business can commit the tort of intimidation.

❸ Distinguish between direct inducement to breach of contract and indirect inducement to breach of contract.

❹ Describe the tort of unlawful interference with economic relations.

❺ Outline the elements of the tort of deceit.

❻ Explain the rules that apply to occupiers' liability in your province or territory.

❼ Outline the range of situations in which the courts may impose liability on a business for committing the tort of nuisance.

❽ Describe the elements of the rule in *Rylands v Fletcher* and explain how that tort involves strict liability.

❾ Explain why businesses are frequently in danger of committing the tort of defamation.

❿ Describe the tort of injurious falsehood.

In Chapter 4, we began our consideration of specific torts by examining several intentional torts that commonly affect business people. In this chapter, we continue our discussion by looking at a number of other torts that are important in the business context:

- conspiracy
- intimidation
- interference with contractual relations
- unlawful interference with economic relations
- deceit
- occupiers' liability
- nuisance
- the rule in *Rylands v Fletcher*
- defamation
- injurious falsehood

As you will have gathered by now, tort law is something of a grab bag. With a few exceptions, it covers every type of private wrongdoing (as opposed to criminal wrongdoing) that is not a breach of contract.[1] Consequently, while some of the torts that are included in this chapter overlap with one another, many of them have very little in common.

You should also notice that many of the torts discussed in this chapter require proof of the defendant's *intention*. That requirement may be confusing. In the last chapter, we saw that when courts deal with intentional torts, they adopt a very broad definition of "intention." It is enough that the defendant intended to act in a certain way. The plaintiff does not have to prove that the defendant intended to either commit a tort or cause harm. Consequently, for example, you will commit the tort of trespass by walking on my lawn as long as you intend to walk on *that* piece of ground—even if you mistakenly believe that you own it. In the topics discussed in this chapter, in contrast, the courts often use a much different concept of intention. Although the precise requirements vary from one tort to the next, the court normally must be satisfied that the defendant either intended to hurt the plaintiff or at least knew that such an injury was reasonably foreseeable. You should ask yourself why the meaning of "intention" changes between Chapter 4 and Chapter 5. Why are some torts easier to prove than others? What sorts of interests (such as physical well-being, protection of property, and protection of business assets) do the various torts protect?

L.O. ❶   Conspiracy

As a general rule, there is no tort if *one person* deliberately inflicts an economic injury on another.[2] Somewhat surprisingly, however, the same act may trigger liability if it is performed by *several people* working together. That is true even though the act in question is otherwise perfectly lawful. The tort of **conspiracy** usually occurs when two or more defendants agree to act together with the primary purpose of causing the plaintiff to suffer a financial loss. The lesson is clear.

the tort of **conspiracy** usually occurs when two or more defendants agree to act together with the primary purpose of causing the plaintiff to suffer a financial loss

---

[1.] Those exceptions include the equitable wrongs of breach of confidence and breach of fiduciary duty, which we examine in other chapters.

[2.] *Allen v Flood* [1898] AC 1 (HL). In Chapter 25, we will look at statutes that control unfair business practices that improperly affect competition.

While the law generally condones aggressive competition between individuals, its sense of fair play may be offended if several people conspire against another.

The tort of conspiracy is hard to prove.[3] The courts are reluctant to find that the defendants co-operated for the *primary purpose* of hurting the plaintiff. In one recent case, a number of people organized a consumer boycott of a paper company's products to draw attention to Aboriginal land claims.[4] Although the company lost a lot of money when many of its customers were persuaded to buy elsewhere, the boycott organizers were not liable. The court held that the protestors' main purpose was not to hurt the company, but rather to raise public awareness of a political issue.

The tort of conspiracy raises difficult issues, both legally and ethically. Consider Ethical Perspective 5.1.

Ethical Perspective 5.1

Conspiracy to Injure a Plaintiff by Lawful Means

Do the rules governing the tort of conspiracy make sense from an ethical or a legal point of view?

Questions for Discussion

1. Should a single person, acting alone, be entitled to intentionally hurt another person's business interests, as long as lawful means are used? What arguments can be made for and against the current law?

2. If it is ethically permissible for one person, acting alone, to intentionally harm another person's economic interests, why should the situation be any different merely because several people act together to achieve the same result? Is the plaintiff more vulnerable if they are targeted by two small local businesses, rather than a single, but enormous, multinational corporation?

If the defendants' actions were otherwise *lawful*, then conspiracy is difficult to establish because the court will require proof that the defendants' *primary purpose* was to hurt the plaintiff. The situation is different, however, if the defendants conspired to perform an otherwise *unlawful* act. They might agree to commit a tort, or to violate the *Criminal Code*, labour relations legislation, or licensing regulations.[5] If so, then the court will merely require proof that the defendants *should have known* that their actions might hurt the plaintiff.[6]

Intimidation

L.O. ❷

The tort of *intimidation* is concerned with unethical business practices. **Intimidation** occurs when the plaintiff suffers a loss as a result of the defendant's threat to commit an unlawful act against either the plaintiff or a third

the tort of **intimidation** occurs when the plaintiff suffers a loss as a result of the defendant's threat to commit an unlawful act against either the plaintiff or a third party

---

[3.] In some jurisdictions, the tort of conspiracy has been statutorily restricted or abolished with respect to actions performed by members of trade unions during trade disputes: see *eg Labour Relations Code*, RSBC 1996, c 244, s 69 (BC); *Rights of Labour Act*, RSO 1990, c R 33, s 3(1) (Ont); *Trade Union Act*, RSS 1978, c T-17, s 28 (Sask); but see *Labour Relations Act*, RSNL 1990, c L-1, s 103 (Nfld).

[4.] *Daishowa Inc v Friends of the Lubicon* (1998) 158 DLR (4th) 699 (Ont Gen Div).

[5.] If the unlawful act also constitutes a separate tort, such as deceit, the plaintiff can bring an action in that tort, without relying on the tort of conspiracy.

[6.] *Canada Cement LaFarge Ltd v BC Lightweight Aggregate Ltd* (1983) 145 DLR (3d) 385 (SCC).

FIGURE 5.1 Intimidation

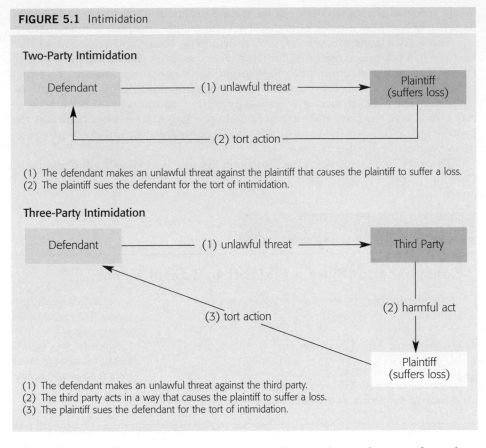

Two-Party Intimidation

Defendant ——————— (1) unlawful threat ——————→ Plaintiff (suffers loss)

(2) tort action

(1) The defendant makes an unlawful threat against the plaintiff that causes the plaintiff to suffer a loss.
(2) The plaintiff sues the defendant for the tort of intimidation.

Three-Party Intimidation

Defendant ——————— (1) unlawful threat ——————→ Third Party

(3) tort action

(2) harmful act

Plaintiff (suffers loss)

(1) The defendant makes an unlawful threat against the third party.
(2) The third party acts in a way that causes the plaintiff to suffer a loss.
(3) The plaintiff sues the defendant for the tort of intimidation.

party. As that definition suggests, the tort of intimidation has two branches, which are represented in Figure 5.1.

> **two-party intimidation** occurs when defendant directly coerces the plaintiff into suffering a loss

- **Two-party intimidation** occurs when the defendant directly coerces the plaintiff into suffering a loss. For example, the manager of a supermarket might use threats of physical violence to frighten the owner of a small convenience store into closing down.

> **three-party intimidation** occurs when the defendant coerces a third party into acting in a way that hurts the plaintiff

- **Three-party intimidation** occurs when the defendant coerces a third party into acting in a way that hurts the plaintiff. In the leading case of *Rookes v Barnard*, the plaintiff was an employee of an airline.[7] The defendant, a trade union, was angry with him as a result of a labour dispute. The union threatened the airline with an illegal strike unless it fired the plaintiff. The plaintiff successfully sued the defendant after the airline gave in to that pressure and fired him.

Whether intimidation involves two or three parties, the basic rules remain the same.

- First, the plaintiff must prove that the defendant threatened to commit an unlawful act, such as a crime, a tort, or even a breach of contract.[8]

[7.] *Rookes v Barnard* [1964] AC 1129 (HL).

[8.] It is not clear whether two-party intimidation can ever be based on the defendant's threat to break a contract with the plaintiff. The courts have sometimes said that the plaintiff should resist that sort of pressure by simply suing for breach of contract. That tactic is not possible in a three-party situation, however, because the plaintiff cannot sue on a contract that exists between the defendant and the third party. Furthermore, the Supreme Court of Canada has indicated that a threat to break a contract is not intimidation in either a two-party or a three-party situation if the defendant reasonably believed that such a threat was lawful: *Central Canada Potash Co v Saskatchewan* (1978) 88 DLR (3d) 609 (SCC).

- Second, the tort does not occur unless the threatened party gave in to the intimidation. For example, the plaintiff would not have won in *Rookes v Barnard* if the airline had ignored the union's threat.

- Third, as long as the other elements of the tort are established, there is no need to prove that the defendant intended to hurt the plaintiff. For instance, intimidation may occur even if the tortfeasor was motivated by a desire to benefit themself, rather than injure the plaintiff.

Interference with Contractual Relations

One of the most effective ways of gaining an advantage over a competitor in the business world is to hire away its best workers or otherwise prevent those people from performing their jobs. That is especially true in professions and industries that employ highly skilled personnel. However, that tactic can trigger the tort of *interference with contractual relations*. As its name suggests, **interference with contractual relations** occurs when the defendant disrupts a contract that exists between the plaintiff and a third party. Figure 5.2 illustrates the basic process that underlies both forms of the tort:

the tort of **interference with contractual relations** occurs when the defendant disrupts a contract that exists between the plaintiff and a third party

- direct inducement to breach of contract
- indirect inducement to breach of contract

A **direct inducement to breach of contract** occurs when the defendant directly persuades a third party to break its contract with the plaintiff. Liability requires four factors:

a **direct inducement to breach of contract** occurs when the defendant directly persuades a third party to break its contract with the plaintiff

- First, the defendant must *know about the contract* that exists between the third party and the plaintiff. The defendant does not, however, have to know all the details of that contract.

- Second, the defendant must *intend to cause* the third party to breach that contract. However, the defendant does not have to intend to hurt the plaintiff. The tort may be committed even if the defendant is motivated by a desire to benefit itself.

- Third, the defendant must *actually cause* the third party to break its contract with the plaintiff. For instance, the defendant might hire the third

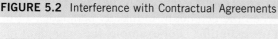

FIGURE 5.2 Interference with Contractual Agreements

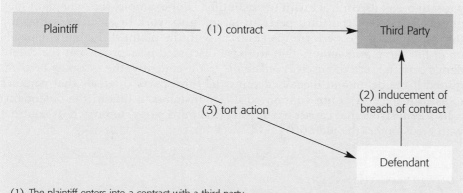

(1) The plaintiff enters into a contract with a third party.
(2) The defendant causes the third party to break its contract with the plaintiff.
(3) The plaintiff sues the defendant for interference with contractual relations.

party for a job that makes it impossible for that person to work for the plaintiff. The issue is much more difficult, however, if the defendant simply *informs* the third party about the advantages and disadvantages of working for the plaintiff. In that situation, the judge will ask whether the defendant actually *encouraged* the third party to commit a breach of contract.

■ Fourth, the plaintiff must suffer a *loss* as a result of the defendant's conduct. In most cases, that requirement is satisfied by the fact that the third party does not perform its contract with the plaintiff.

Note that in addition to suing the defendant in *tort* for inducing breach of contract, the plaintiff can also sue the third party in *contract* for the actual breach. However, the plaintiff cannot recover full damages under both actions. (We will discuss the possibility of concurrent actions in tort and contract in Chapter 6.) Finally, if the defendant's conduct is particularly outrageous, the plaintiff may be entitled to recover punitive damages, as well as compensatory damages, under the tort.

Case Brief 5.1 illustrates the rules for inducing breach of contract.

Case Brief 5.1

Lumley v Gye (1853) 118 ER 749 (QB)

An opera singer named Johanna Wagner agreed to sing for one season with the plaintiff's company, Her Majesty's Theatre. Ms Wagner broke that promise after being offered a higher fee to sing with the defendant's company, the Royal Italian Opera. The plaintiff suffered a financial loss as a result of losing Ms Wagner's services. He sued the defendant for inducing breach of contract.

The plaintiff was able to satisfy most of the requirements of that tort: (i) the defendant knew of Ms Wagner's contract with the plaintiff, (ii) the defendant persuaded Ms Wagner to break her contract with

the plaintiff, and (iii) the plaintiff suffered a loss as a result of the defendant's intervention. The court nevertheless rejected the claim on the ground that the defendant had acted in *good faith*. He honestly believed that Ms Wagner had not been paid by the plaintiff and that she therefore was entitled to terminate her contract to sing at Her Majesty's Theatre.

In another case arising from the same facts, however, the court awarded an injunction to prevent Ms Wagner from singing for the defendant's company.[9]

---

an indirect inducement to breach of contract occurs when the defendant indirectly persuades a third party to break its contract with the plaintiff

As we have seen, a tort may be committed if the defendant *directly* interferes with a contract that exists between the plaintiff and a third party. A tort can also be committed through *indirect* interference. An **indirect inducement to breach of contract** occurs when the defendant indirectly persuades a third party to break its contract with the plaintiff.[10] For example, the defendant may physically prevent the third party from going to work or steal tools that the third party needs to perform the contract with the plaintiff. Liability depends upon the same four factors that we have discussed *plus* proof that the defendant's actions were themselves *unlawful*.[11] Consequently, the tort may be committed if the defendant illegally detains the third party or steals that person's tools. But the tort is not committed if, for instance, a union (the defendant) calls a *legal* strike that causes a company (the third party) to breach its contract with a customer (the plaintiff).

[9.] *Lumley v Wagner* (1852) 42 ER 687 (Ch D).

[10.] *DC Thompson & Co Ltd v Deakin* [1952] Ch 646 (CA).

[11.] Note that the defendant must have intended to induce a breach of contract, even if they did not intend to hurt the plaintiff.

Unlawful Interference with Economic Relations

L.O. ❹

We have already seen several torts that may occur if the defendant performs an *unlawful* act and causes the plaintiff to suffer a loss: intimidation, interference with contractual relations, and conspiracy.[12] The existence of those torts leads to a larger question. Even if it is impossible to satisfy the requirements for those torts, can the defendant still be held liable for committing an unlawful act that hurts the plaintiff? Although that possibility was traditionally overlooked, Canadian courts have begun to recognize a general tort of *unlawful interference with economic relations*. The tort of **unlawful interference with economic relations** may occur if the defendant commits an unlawful act for the purpose of causing the plaintiff to suffer an economic loss. The leading case is discussed in Case Brief 5.2. Notice that the Ontario Court of Appeal adopted a very broad approach to two of the tort's three elements.

the tort of **unlawful interference with economic relations** may occur if the defendant commits an unlawful act for the purpose of causing the plaintiff to suffer an economic loss

Case Brief 5.2

Reach MD Inc v Pharmaceutical Manufacturers Association of Canada (2003)
227 DLR (4th) 458 (Ont CA)

The plaintiff sold calendars to health care professionals. The calendar in question was called "Herman MD" because it featured the cartoon character named "Herman" in various medical settings. The venture was remarkably successful, largely because the calendars also contained advertisements that had been purchased by drug companies.

The plaintiff's business suffered a devastating blow, however, when its calendars caught the defendant's attention. The defendant is an organization of companies that are involved in the drug industry. It told its members that the advertisements contravened its Code of Conduct. In fact, that was not true. While the defendant could have prohibited its members from purchasing advertising space in the plaintiff's calendars, its Code of Conduct did not actually do so.

The Ontario Court of Appeal held that the defendant was liable for the tort of unlawfully interfering with the plaintiff's economic relations. The court set three requirements.

■ First, there must be *intent to injure*. The defendant argued that liability should depend upon proof that its primary purpose was to hurt the plaintiff. Significantly, however, the court said that it was enough that the defendant's unlawful act was in some way directed against the plaintiff.

■ Second, there must be an *unlawful or illegal act*. The defendant argued for a narrow reading of this requirement. It suggested that it should be held liable only if it committed a crime, broke a contract, or violated some other tort. The court disagreed. It was enough that the defendant had done something that it was not entitled to do. Since the Code of Conduct did not actually prohibit the purchase of advertising space on the calendars, the defendant did not have the authority to tell its members to stop advertising. (More recently, however, the Ontario Court of Appeal sometimes has taken a narrower view, by requiring proof that the defendant committed an "actionable wrong."[13])

■ Third, the plaintiff must suffer an *economic loss*. That requirement was met because the plaintiff lost the revenue that it otherwise would have earned from advertisements on "Herman MD."

The court awarded damages equal to the value of the lost revenue. However, it limited liability to a one-year period to reflect the fact that the defendant was entitled to change its Code of Conduct to prohibit the advertisements.

[12.] Liability may also be imposed, in limited circumstances, if the defendant hurts the plaintiff by doing something that is otherwise *lawful*. That is true if the defendant *directly* induces a breach of contract or if the defendant is part of a conspiracy that has the *primary purpose* of hurting the plaintiff.

[13.] *Barber v Vrozos* (2010) 322 DLR (4th) 577 (Ont CA); *Alleslev-Krofchak v Valcom Ltd* (2010) 322 DLR (4th) 193 (Ont CA).

Before going on to the next section, it will be useful to briefly summarize the torts that we have already considered. Conspiracy, intimidation, interference with contractual relations, and interference with economic relations are commonly referred to as "the business torts." They all deal with situations in which one business may try to gain an advantage over another. Because they overlap, however, they are easily confused. Therefore, Concept Summary 5.1 compares how those torts deal with two important questions:

- Must the tort involve behaviour that is otherwise unlawful?
- Must the defendant intend to harm the plaintiff?

Concept Summary 5.1

Business Torts—A Summary

Name of Tort	Unlawfulness	Intent to Harm
Conspiracy	defendant's act may be lawful or unlawful	*lawful act*—hurting plaintiff must be defendant's primary purpose *unlawful act*—hurting plaintiff must be foreseeable
Intimidation	defendant must threaten unlawful act	defendant's act must be directed at plaintiff—but hurting plaintiff need not be defendant's primary purpose
Interference with contractual relations	*indirect* inducement to breach of contract—defendant's act must be unlawful *direct* inducement to breach of contract—defendant's act may be lawful or unlawful	defendant's act must be directed at plaintiff—but hurting plaintiff need not be defendant's primary purpose
Interference with economic relations	defendant's act must be unlawful or unauthorized	defendant's act must be directed at plaintiff—but hurting plaintiff need not be defendant's primary purpose

L.O. ❺ Deceit

The tort of *deceit* encourages ethical behaviour in the business world.[14] **Deceit** occurs if the defendant makes a false statement, which they know to be untrue, with which they intend to mislead the plaintiff, and which causes the plaintiff to suffer a loss.[15] There are four parts to that definition.

First, the defendant must make a *false statement*. That requirement is easily met if the defendant says or writes something that is positively untrue. It may be satisfied in other ways as well.

- The defendant may be held liable for a *half-truth*. For example, if I am selling my business to you, I may provide figures representing gross profits as if they reflect net profits.
- The defendant may be held liable for *failing to update information*. For example, if I am selling my business to you, I may provide information that is accurate when I give it, but that later becomes inaccurate because

the tort of **deceit** occurs if the defendant makes a false statement, which they know to be untrue, with which they intend to mislead the plaintiff, and which causes the plaintiff to suffer a loss

---

[14.] As we will see in Chapter 9, the concept of fraud or deceit is also important in the law of contract. For example, it may allow one party to rescind an agreement.

[15.] *Derry v Peek* (1889) 14 App Cas 337 (HL).

of a dramatic change in the market. If that change happens before our deal closes, I may have to tell you about it. If I do not, my silence may amount to a representation that the circumstances have stayed the same.

■ The general rule in the commercial world is *caveat emptor*: "let the buyer beware." Consequently, the seller is usually not obligated to volunteer information. The buyer is responsible for asking questions and making investigations. There are, however, exceptions to that rule. For instance, if I am selling a house to you, I am required to warn you about hidden defects that make the building dangerous or unfit for habitation. If I fail to do so, I may be held liable for silently deceiving you. Similarly, if I am buying an insurance policy from you, I have a duty to disclose important information. If I fail to do so, I may be unable to claim a benefit under the policy.

The lesson is clear. As a matter of risk management, business people must not only avoid lying; they must also avoid creating the wrong perception.

Second, the defendant must *know*, at the time of making a statement, that it is false. It is enough if the defendant acted recklessly, without regard to the truth. But it is not enough if the defendant was merely careless.[16]

Third, the defendant must make the statement with the *intention of misleading* the plaintiff. The statement does not have to be made directly to the plaintiff. However, the court must be satisfied that the defendant intended to deceive the plaintiff, or at least was substantially certain that the plaintiff would be misled. Suppose you and I are involved in complex commercial negotiations. I may be liable for deceit if I make a false statement to your banker with the intention of tricking you into signing a contract.

Fourth, the plaintiff must suffer a *loss* as a result of *reasonably relying* upon the defendant's statement. The plaintiff's reliance is "reasonable" if a reasonable person might have reacted to the defendant's statement in the same way. That rule has several consequences:

■ The defendant's statement normally has to refer to a *past or present fact*. Liability is usually not possible if the defendant offered an opinion, predicted the future, or made the sort of boastful claim (called a "puff") that salespeople often make. Reasonable people do not rely on those kinds of statements.

■ Occasionally, however, a statement of fact may be *implied* by an opinion, a prediction, or a puff. Suppose I persuade you to buy my car by lying: "This little miser will go 300 kilometres between fill-ups." A court might find that my prediction includes a statement of existing fact regarding the vehicle's current rate of gas consumption.

In terms of remedies, it is important to remember that we are dealing with a tort, rather than a contract. As we saw in Chapter 3 (see page 73), that means that compensatory damages look backward, rather than forward. The plaintiff is entitled to be put into the position that they would have enjoyed if the defendant had not lied—not into the position that they would have enjoyed if the defendant's statement had been true. Suppose I tricked you into buying an apartment complex from me for $600 000. The building is actually worth $500 000. But if my deceitful statement had been true, it would have been worth $750 000. In tort, you are entitled to $100 000—not $250 000. (We will look at the calculation of compensatory damages for breach of contract in Chapter 12.)

[16.] The next chapter discusses how the plaintiff may be held liable under the tort of negligence as a result of carelessly making a false statement.

L.O. ❻

Occupiers' Liability

The tort of **occupiers' liability** requires an occupier of premises to protect visitors from harm.

- An **occupier** is any person who has substantial control over premises. Note that the critical element is *control*, not *ownership*. A tenant, for instance, can control an apartment without owning it.

- A **visitor** is any person who enters onto premises. We will discuss different types of visitors later.

- **Premises** include more than land. Apartments and offices certainly count, but occasionally, so do elevators, vehicles, ships, trains, and airplanes. The scope of occupiers' liability is therefore quite wide and potentially very dangerous for business people.[17] Although there has been a sharp rise in electronic commerce, most businesses still occupy premises that are visited by customers, suppliers, sales representatives, cleaners, government officials, trespassers, and so on. If one of those visitors trips over a step, slips on spilled food, falls through a decrepit floorboard, crashes into a plate-glass window, or is beaten by another visitor, the business may be held liable as result of being the occupier.

The law of occupiers' liability is complicated, partly because it differs between jurisdictions. Legislation has been enacted in every jurisdiction *except* Newfoundland and Labrador, Saskatchewan, and the three territories. We will therefore separately consider:

- the common law rules (which were made by judges)
- the statutory rules (which were made by legislators)

Even if you live in a jurisdiction that now has a statute, it is useful to understand the traditional common law rules in order to appreciate why legislation has been introduced.

COMMON LAW RULES

The traditional common law rules recognized four categories of visitors: *trespassers*, *licensees*, *invitees*, and *contractual entrants*. Each type of visitor was owed a different type of obligation. Concept Summary 5.2 (on page 115) summarizes the traditional approach. As we will see, however, that approach is now being changed.

There are a number of problems with the traditional system of occupiers' liability.

- First, it can lump together different types of people. For example, a person who breaks into an office is a trespasser, but so is a child who curiously wanders onto a construction site. It seems unfair that the occupier should not have to do more for the child than for the criminal.

- Second, it is often difficult to distinguish between the different categories. That is especially true for licensees and invitees. For example, does a visitor to a municipal library or a provincial park provide an economic benefit to the occupier?[18] Should the visitor's ability to recover compensation for a loss depend upon the answer to that narrow question?

[17.] The law of occupiers' liability is not restricted to the business world. Any person who controls premises (including residential premises) falls within the tort.

[18.] *Nickell v City of Windsor* (1926) 59 OLR 618 (CA); *Coffyne v Silver Lake Regional Park Authority* (1977) 75 DLR (3d) 300 (Sask QB).

- Third, a visitor's status may change from one moment to the next. For example, a customer who refuses a request to leave a store is transformed from an invitee into a trespasser.
- Fourth, it often is difficult to decide whether a danger is *hidden* or *unusual*. Does an icy parking lot during a Canadian winter satisfy either requirement?[19]

Concept Summary 5.2

Traditional Rules for Occupiers' Liability

Type of Visitor	Description of Visitor	Occupier's Obligation
trespasser	a person who does not have permission to enter the premises (*eg* a burglar)	not to *intentionally or recklessly injure* a trespasser (*eg* by setting a trap for a burglar)
licensee	a person who has permission to enter the premises but who does not further the occupier's economic interest (*eg* a social guest)	to protect a licensee from *hidden dangers* that were *actually known* to the occupier
invitee	a person who has permission to enter the premises and who furthers the occupier's economic interests (*eg* a business customer)	to take reasonable care to protect an invitee from *unusual dangers* that the occupier *knew or should have known* about
contractual entrant	a person who enters into a contract to use the premises, rather than to receive services that are offered on the premises (*eg* a hotel guest, but not a restaurant diner)	a contractual obligation to make sure that the premises were as safe as *reasonably possible*

Business Decision 5.1 illustrates some of the difficulties associated with the traditional rules.

Business Decision 5.1

Common Law Categories of Occupiers' Liability[20]

In the course of describing the law of occupiers' liability, a judge once posed this question:

A canvasser who comes onto your premises without your consent is a trespasser. Once he has your consent, he is a licensee. Not until you do business with him is he an invitee. Even when you have done business with him, it seems rather strange that your duty toward him should be different when he comes to your front door than when he goes away. Does he change his colour in the middle of the conversation?

Questions for Discussion

1. Does the judge believe that it is possible to determine the precise moment when a person changes from a trespasser into a licensee and then into an invitee?

2. If your answer to the last question was "no," then how do courts actually decide cases? Might they intuitively decide an appropriate result and then characterize the plaintiff in a way that achieves that result?

---

[19] *cf Francis v IPCF Properties Inc* (1993) 136 NBR (2d) 215 (QB) and *Waldick v Malcolm* (1991) 83 DLR (4th) 114 (SCC).

[20] *Dunster v Abbott* [1953] 2 All ER 1572 at 1574 (CA) *per* Lord Denning.

Because of those difficulties, the jurisdictions that still use the common law rules have modified them.[21] They have generally moved away from categorizing visitors and toward increasing the occupier's obligations.

- First, an occupier must do more than simply refrain from intentionally or recklessly hurting a trespasser. The law now uses a duty of common humanity that strikes a balance between the parties.[22] The occupier's obligations are determined by a number of factors, including:
  - the age of the trespasser
  - the reason for the trespass
  - the nature of the danger that caused the injury
  - the occupier's knowledge of that danger
  - the occupier's cost of removing that danger
- Second, licensees and invitees are now generally treated the same. An occupier must protect them both from *unusual* dangers. Previously, a licensee was protected from only *hidden* dangers.[23]
- Third, the courts in Newfoundland and Labrador have gone even further. An occupier in that province is required to use *reasonable care* toward all *lawful* visitors.[24]

STATUTORY RULES

Because of the problems associated with the common law rules, six provinces have enacted legislation to govern occupiers' liability.[25] Although the statutes vary somewhat between jurisdictions, the basic principles are the same. We can note the most important differences between the common law and the legislation.

- First, the common law generally applies only to dangers that are created by the *condition* of the premises. The legislation also applies to *activities* that occur on the premises. For example, under a statute, the occupier of a campsite can be held liable not only for failing to remove a rotten tree that collapsed on a visitor, but also for failing to prevent one drunken guest from attacking another.[26]
- Second, as a general rule, the standard of care no longer depends upon a visitor's classification. Nor are special distinctions drawn between, say,

---

[21.] Newfoundland and Labrador, the Northwest Territories, Nunavut, Saskatchewan, and the Yukon.

[22.] *Veinot v Kerr-Addison Mines Ltd* (1974) 51 DLR (3d) 533 (SCC).

[23.] There may still be a slight difference. It may be that a licensee can sue only for a danger that the occupier *knew* about, while an invitee can also sue for a danger that the occupier *should have known* about: *Yelic v Gimli* (Town) (1986) 33 DLR (4th) 248 (Man CA).

[24.] *Stacey v Anglican Church of Canada (Diocesan Synod of Eastern Newfoundland and Labrador)* (1999) 182 Nfld & PEIR 1 (Nfld CA).

[25.] *Occupiers' Liability Act*, RSA 2000, c O-4 (Alta); *Occupiers' Liability Act*, RSBC 1996, c 337 (BC); *Occupiers' Liability Act*, CCSM, c O8 (Man); *Occupiers' Liability Act*, SNS 1996, c 27 (NS); *Occupiers' Liability Act*, RSO 1990, c O.2 (Ont); *Occupiers' Liability Act*, RSPEI 1988, c O-2 (PEI). New Brunswick has gone even further by doing away with a separate tort of occupiers' liability altogether: *Law Reform Act*, SNB 1993, c L-1.2, s 2. In that province, the courts simply use the general tort of negligence, which is discussed in Chapter 6.

[26.] *McGinty v Cook* (1991) 79 DLR (4th) 95 (Ont CA); *cf Coleiro v Premier Fitness Clubs (Erin Mills) Inc* 2010 ONSC 4350(Ont SCJ).

hidden or unusual dangers. An occupier must use *reasonable care*, which depends upon a number of factors, including:

- the potential danger to the visitor
- the occupier's cost of removing the danger
- the purpose of the visit
- the nature of the premises

There are special exceptions to that general rule in some provinces.

- In Alberta, occupiers are not required to protect adult trespassers from danger. They are merely prohibited from wilfully or recklessly hurting them. In contrast, reasonable care must be taken to protect child trespassers who the occupier knows, or ought to know, are on the property.

- Likewise, an occupier in Ontario or Prince Edward Island does not have to use reasonable care to protect some types of trespassers. It is enough to simply refrain from intentionally hurting them. A similar rule applies in Manitoba, but only to trespassing snowmobilers.

- Third, the statutes generally allow an occupier to avoid liability by issuing a warning. For example, the occupier of a ski resort might conspicuously post signs that state:

As a condition of using these facilities, you assume all risk of personal injury, death, or property loss resulting from any cause whatsoever. (Exclusion clauses will be discussed in Chapter 9.)

An occupier's liability may also be affected by other statutes.[27]

- Fourth, under the common law, a landlord generally cannot be held liable for injuries that a person suffers while visiting a tenant. The primary reason is that a landlord has ownership but not control over the premises and therefore is not an occupier. A different rule applies under the legislation. A landlord may be liable to a visitor if they fail to make repairs under their lease with the tenant. For example, a landlord may be held responsible if a tenant's guest falls in a stairwell because of the absence of a handrail.[28]

Nuisance

L.O. ❼

The tort of *nuisance*, like the tort of occupiers' liability, involves land. Generally, a **nuisance** occurs when the defendant unreasonably interferes with the plaintiff's use and enjoyment of their own land.[29] There is a tension between the way in which the defendant wants to use *their* property and the way in which the

the tort of **nuisance** occurs when the defendant unreasonably interferes with the plaintiff's use and enjoyment of their own land

---

[27.] For example, innkeepers in Ontario need to take less care than usual: *Innkeepers Act*, RSO 1990, c I.7.

[28.] *Zavaglia v MAQ Holdings Ltd* (1986) 6 BCLR (2d) 286 (CA); *Taylor v Allard* (2010) 325 DLR (4th) 761 (Ont CA); cf *Blount v H Corp Coiffures Ltd* (Unreported, 17 September 2008, Ont SCJ).

[29.] Our discussion is limited to the tort of *private nuisance*. There is also a less important tort of *public nuisance*. A public nuisance occurs when the defendant commits the crime of common nuisance against the public, but creates a special loss for the plaintiff: *Criminal Code*, RSC 1985, c C-46, s 180(2) (Can). That tort can arise, for instance, if the defendant creates a hazard on a street that not only interferes with the general public's right to use that roadway, but also causes the plaintiff to be injured in a traffic accident: *Ryan v Victoria (City)* (1999) 168 DLR (4th) 513 (SCC).

plaintiff wants to use *their* property. The courts have a great deal of flexibility in resolving a dispute between neighbours.[30]

A nuisance occurs if the defendant *interferes* with the plaintiff's use of their land. Interference can happen in a variety of ways. Simple cases involve *physical damage* to the plaintiff or their property. For instance:

- the defendant's factory may emit chemical particles that drift with the wind and destroy the paint on the plaintiff's building, or
- the defendant's construction project may create a heavy vibration that cracks the foundations of the plaintiff's store.

A nuisance can also occur if the defendant creates a smell or a sound that *impairs the enjoyment* of the plaintiff's property. For instance:

- the defendant may operate a pig farm that causes a stench to waft over the plaintiff's outdoor café, or
- the blaring music from the defendant's nightclub may keep nearby residents awake at night.

It may even be possible to commit a *non-intrusive* nuisance, without causing anything to travel onto the plaintiff's property. For instance:

- the defendant may install a sewer system on their own property that drains water *from* the plaintiff's land in a way that damages the foundations of the plaintiff's building, or
- the defendant may operate a brothel that brings traffic and criminals close to the plaintiff's home.

Note, however, that certain types of activities generally will *not* support a claim in nuisance. For instance, it is unlikely that a tort is committed if:

- the defendant builds something on their own property that ruins the plaintiff's view of a lake or reduces the amount of sunshine that enters the plaintiff's house, or
- the defendant paints their building a colour that reduces the market value of the plaintiff's house.[31]

A nuisance occurs only if the defendant's interference is *unreasonable*. In deciding that issue, the courts look at a number of factors. The most important is the nature of the interference. The defendant's conduct is almost always considered unreasonable if it causes substantial *physical damage*. In contrast, the courts are less likely to hold the defendant liable if the interference merely *impairs the enjoyment* of the plaintiff's property, especially if the defendant's interference is *non-intrusive*. Beyond that, the courts also consider:

- the *nature of the neighbourhood* (for example, the smell of livestock may be reasonable in the country but not in the city)
- the *time and day* of the interference (for example, construction sounds that are reasonable at noon on a weekday may be unreasonable late at night or on the weekend)

---

[30] Strictly speaking, it is not necessary for *both* parties to have an interest in land. While the plaintiff can sue only if their land is affected, the defendant does not have to commit the nuisance from their own property. In practice, however, most nuisance cases arise between neighbours.

[31] It may be different if the defendant *intentionally* annoys or hurts the plaintiff.

- the *intensity and duration* of the interference (for example, a barking dog or a foul odour may have to be tolerated if it occurs occasionally, but not if it is nearly constant)

- the *social utility* of the defendant's conduct (for example, the late-night sound of screeching tires may be reasonable if it is caused by an ambulance, but not if it is caused by drag racing)

- the defendant's *motivation* (for example, the sound of a gun may be reasonable if it occurs in the course of normal activities, but not if it is made to terrify the plaintiff's foxes and ruin his breeding business)[32]

DEFENCES TO NUISANCE

There are several defences to the tort of nuisance, but they are generally interpreted very narrowly.[33] The courts are reluctant to allow the defendant to escape liability despite unreasonably interfering with the plaintiff's property.

The defence of *statutory authority* provides a good example. **Statutory authority** means that the defendant caused a nuisance while acting under legislation. Significantly, that defence applies only if the defendant's nuisance was an *inevitable result* of the statutorily authorized activity. Business Decision 5.2 illustrates that rule.

statutory authority means that the defendant caused a nuisance while acting under legislation

Business Decision **5.2**

Nuisance and the Defence of Statutory Authority[34]

Legislation allowed the Town of Sepsis to build a sewage system that conformed to industry standards. Such systems usually use pipes that are between 1 metre and 1.5 metres in diameter. In the course of construction, the mayor of Sepsis decided, for financial reasons, to use 1-metre pipes. Several months after the project was completed, the town received a lot of rain. While the system generally performed quite well, it backed up in one neighbourhood and pumped raw sewage into your restaurant. As a result, you were required to replace all of your kitchen equipment, which had been ruined by the mess. The evidence indicates that the problem was caused by the fact that the pipes were too narrow to accommodate the rainfall. It also indicates that the problem would not have occurred if 1.5-metre pipes had been used.

Since litigation is expensive, you do not want to sue the Town of Sepsis unless there is a good chance that you will win your case. How would you make that decision?

Questions for Discussion

1. Did Sepsis commit the tort of nuisance?

2. If Sepsis did commit the tort, could it nevertheless avoid liability by pleading the defence of statutory authority? Given the legislation and the evidence, was a nuisance inevitable?

Before leaving the issue of defences, it is important to note that the defendant is not relieved of liability merely because the nuisance already existed when the plaintiff arrived in the neighbourhood. For instance, a physician can complain that the noise from a factory disrupts his practice, even though the person who previously occupied his building was not affected by that sound.[35]

[32.] *Hollywood Silver Fox Farm v Emmett* [1936] 2 KB 468 (QB).

[33.] For example, the plaintiff cannot complain if they *consented* to the defendant's activity. However, consent usually requires proof that the plaintiff encouraged the defendant's activity, not that they merely failed to complain.

[34.] *Tock v St John's (City) Metropolitan Area Board* (1989) 64 DLR (4th) 620 (SCC); *Ryan v Victoria (City)* (1999) 168 DLR (4th) 513 (SCC).

[35.] *Sturges v Bridgman* (1879) 11 Ch D 852.

REMEDIES FOR NUISANCE

The most common remedies for nuisance are compensatory damages and injunctions. The usual rules regarding compensation apply and do not have to be repeated here. Injunctions are more complicated. A judge will usually grant one to stop a nuisance. For example, the defendant may be required to close a chemical plant that is emitting noxious fumes, or they may be ordered to refrain from dumping toxic material into a river. Occasionally, however, the court may exercise its discretion to refuse an injunction. That is clearly true if the nuisance causes relatively little damage to the plaintiff and if damages can provide an adequate remedy. It may also be true if an injunction would create an intolerable hardship for the defendant or, more importantly, for the community as a whole. Consequently, if a town's entire economy revolves around a single factory, a judge would be reluctant to grant an injunction that would have the effect of closing that factory. Finally, the courts sometimes award both compensatory damages and an injunction. The damages take care of past losses, and the injunction prevents harm in the future.

The Rule in *Rylands v Fletcher*

L.O. ❽

the **rule in** *Rylands v Fletcher* states that the defendant can be held strictly liable for their non-natural use of land if something escapes from their property and injures the plaintiff

The rule in *Rylands v Fletcher* is a third tort that deals with land.[36] The **rule in *Rylands v Fletcher*** states that the defendant can be held strictly liable for their non-natural use of land if something escapes from their property and injures the plaintiff. (We discussed the idea of *strict liability* in Chapter 3.) We need to examine three aspects of that rule.

First, the defendant must have made a *non-natural use* of their land. Courts have interpreted this in two ways. Some courts say that it refers to any use of land that creates a *special* danger; others say that the defendant must create a *special and unusual* danger. Judges have recently preferred the second interpretation.[37] As a result, the defendant cannot be held liable simply because they install a gas appliance in their building, or deliberately start a fire to burn away scrub grass in the normal course of their farming operations. While those activities are non-natural, they are not unusual. It is therefore irrelevant that they endangered the plaintiff. However, the tort may be committed if the defendant collects an unusual amount of water in a reservoir, or stacks fireworks in a store display. Those activities are not only especially dangerous; they are also unusual.

Second, something associated with a non-natural use must *escape* from the defendant's land and cause the plaintiff to suffer a loss. For instance, water may break through a reservoir and flood a neighbour's house, or explosives in a warehouse may ignite, shoot onto the sidewalk, and injure a pedestrian. The need for an escape may create problems if the plaintiff suffers an injury *on the defendant's property*. A spectator who is hit by flying debris at a racetrack may not be able to use *Rylands v Fletcher* since nothing *left* the defendant's premises. It would not be surprising, however, if a judge ignored the requirement of an escape in order to avoid an unfair result.

Third, most torts are based on some form of *fault*. The defendant is usually liable only if they intentionally, or at least carelessly, caused the plaintiff's injury. The rule in *Rylands v Fletcher*, in contrast, is *strict*. The defendant may be held

36. *Rylands v Fletcher* (1868) LR 3 HL 330.
37. *Tock v St John's (City) Metropolitan Area Board* (1989) 64 DLR (4th) 620 (SCC).

liable even though they acted as carefully as possible. Strict liability does not, however, mean that liability is imposed *every time* there is a non-natural use, an escape, and an injury. A defence may be available in exceptional circumstances. For example:

- the plaintiff may have *consented* to the defendant's non-natural use of their land
- the escape may have been caused by a *third party* or a *natural force* (such as a tornado or an earthquake) that the defendant could not have guarded against
- the plaintiff's injury may have been the *inevitable result* of an activity that the defendant was *statutorily authorized* to do

Those defences, however, are difficult to prove. Consequently, business people should learn an important lesson from the rule in *Rylands v Fletcher*: They should take special precautions whenever they use land in a non-natural way.[38]

We have seen four torts that involve the use of land. We discussed trespass to land in Chapter 4 and occupiers' liability, nuisance, and the rule in *Rylands v Fletcher* in this chapter. Concept Summary 5.3 shows the most important features of those torts.

Concept Summary 5.3

Torts Involving the Use of Land

Tort	Basis of Liability
Occupiers' liability	the defendant, who is the occupier of the premises, fails to take adequate precautions to protect the plaintiff, who is visiting those premises
Nuisance	the defendant unreasonably interferes with the plaintiff's use and enjoyment of their own land
Rule in *Rylands v Fletcher*	the defendant uses their land in a non-natural way with the result that something escapes and injures the plaintiff
Trespass to land	the defendant intentionally interferes with the plaintiff's land

Defamation

L.O. ❾

Communication is essential to the success of any business. However, it also creates the risk of *defamation*. **Defamation** occurs when the defendant makes a false statement that could lead a reasonable person to have a lower opinion of the plaintiff.[39] As Case Brief 5.3 illustrates, a business faces a special risk when it tries to enhance its own reputation by disparaging its competitors' abilities.

the tort of **defamation** occurs when the defendant makes a false statement that could lead a reasonable person to have a lower opinion of the plaintiff

---

[38.] The potential danger that the tort creates for businesses is illustrated by a class action used by the members of a community that were affected when an unusual substance (nickel dust) escaped from the defendant's refinery. Although liability was denied on the facts, the claim was valid in principle: *Smith v Inco Inc* 2010 ONSC 3790 (Ont SCJ), rev'd 2011 ONCA 628 (Ont CA).

[39.] Some parts of defamation have been modified by legislation. Nevertheless, the most important issues are governed by the common law rules that are discussed below.

Case Brief 5.3

WeGo Kayaking Ltd v Sewid 2007 BCSC 49

The Broughton Archipelago, located off the coast of Vancouver Island, is amongst the most beautiful locations on Earth. In addition to having an abundance of wildlife, it also is relatively protected from ocean waves. Not surprisingly, two types of businesses have become established in the area. First, Thomas Sewid, a member of the Kwakwaka'wakw First Nation and the Mamalaleqala Band, conducts cultural tours of the archipelago. Second, a large number of companies cater to the tremendous demand for kayaking tours. Northern Lights Expeditions (NLE) is one of those companies.

Mr Sewid operated a popular website that provided information and access to prospective tourists. The website contained a page that purported to list "Good Kayak Companies" and "Bad Kayak Companies." NLE's name was included on the latter list. Mr Sewid's official explanation was that the company treated "First Nations [as] token Indians who are needed only as items of attraction or convenience." He also claimed to have "environmental concerns with their operating practices." As a result of that adverse publicity, NLE suffered a substantial loss in business.

The trial judge found that Mr Sewid's comments were not only untrue and defamatory, but also maliciously motivated. The real reason for NLE's inclusion on the "Bad Kayak Companies" list was revealed in a series of emails that Mr Sewid sent to the company. He explained that he intended to use the website to coerce kayaking companies, such as NLE, to include him in their operations. Unless they directed their customers to his cultural tours, they would be "taken down." "The bottom line," he threatened, was to "stay away from my people's traditional territories or find a way to work with me."

Macaulay J found in favour of NLE and WeGo Kayaking, another company that Mr Sewid had defamed. Because the claimants were corporations, rather than human beings, damages were not available for personal distress. Substantial relief was available, however, for the loss of business reputation and the associated loss of profits. The judge also awarded punitive damages to punish and deter the defendant's reprehensible behaviour. In total, Mr Sewid's misguided strategy cost him $257 500, plus costs. (Costs were explained in Chapter 2.)

A statement is defamatory only if a reasonable person would have thought that it referred to the plaintiff. That requirement is quite broad.

- First, it can be satisfied even if the defendant did not *intend* to refer to the plaintiff. The purpose of the tort is to protect reputations. It is therefore enough if a reasonable person would have *thought* that the defendant was referring to the plaintiff. Reputations are often hurt by mistake.

- Second, a claim for defamation can be made by any sort of *living person*. As we will see in Chapter 21, the term "person" refers not only to human beings, but also to things such as corporations.

- Third, defamation may be difficult to prove if the defendant made a statement about a *group of individuals*. Each person must prove that the statement can be reasonably interpreted as referring to them *personally*. That is unlikely if the group is large and if the statement is a generalization. Consequently, I probably could not sue you for saying "All lawyers are liars!"[40]

slander is a defamatory statement that is spoken

libel is a defamatory statement that is written

Lawyers sometimes draw a distinction between *slander* and *libel*. **Slander** is a defamatory statement that is spoken; **libel** is a defamatory statement that is written.[41] While that distinction is important for technical reasons in some parts of Canada, the general rule is that defamation can occur through any

---

40. *Bou Malhab v Diffusion Métromédia CMR inc* (2011) 328 DLR (4th) 385 (SCC).

41. The distinction between libel and slander has been abolished in several provinces, including Alberta, Manitoba, New Brunswick, Nova Scotia, and Prince Edward Island. Where it has not been abolished, the difference is important mainly because the plaintiff in a slander action (though not in a libel action) is usually required to prove *special damages*. That distinction is based on the belief that libel is usually more serious than slander. Written words normally last longer and reach more people. Special damages for the purpose of a slander action may include a financial loss, but not mere embarrassment. However, even in a slander action, there is no need to prove special damages if the defendant made a false statement that (i) the plaintiff had committed a crime serious enough to result in imprisonment, (ii) the plaintiff was an "unchaste" woman, (iii) the plaintiff suffers from a contagious disease that people would want to avoid, or (iv) the plaintiff is unfit to carry on their profession or business.

sort of communication, including spoken words, written documents, gestures, photographs, and puppet shows.

Almost any uncomplimentary statement can be defamatory, as long as it could hurt a person's reputation. You will defame me if you suggest, for example, that I am incompetent, racist, lazy, dishonest, infected with a communicable disease, or involved in criminal activity. Furthermore, even a seemingly harmless statement may be defamatory once it is considered in context. For example, although I would not normally be defamed if you said that I sold pork chops, it might be different if I owned a kosher deli.

There cannot be defamation without *publication*. **Publication** occurs when a statement is communicated to a third party. Remember that the tort is concerned with the protection of reputations. If I say something uncomplimentary to you in private, I may hurt your feelings or upset you, but I cannot damage your reputation, which is based on what *other people* think of you. The rule about publication can, however, work in your favour. A new tort may occur every time that a statement is *repeated*. Consequently, if I write a defamatory book about you, I commit a tort when I deliver the manuscript to my publisher. But my publisher may also commit a tort against you when it sells the book to the public.

publication occurs when a statement is communicated to a third party

The combination of defamation liability and social media is especially troubling for employers. For whatever reason, communication on the Internet tends to be very informal. People often say things in emails or blogs, or on *Twitter* or *Facebook*, that they would never write in a traditional letter or report. Employers are at risk not only because of the rules of vicarious liability (which we examined in Chapter 3), but also because anyone who "publishes" a defamatory statement may be held liable. Although the courts have not yet given a clear answer, it is quite possible an employer will be considered a "publisher" if an employee uses a company device (such as a computer or BlackBerry) to make a defamatory statement. In order to manage that risk, an employer should educate employees about defamation laws and encourage them to think before they write.[42]

DEFENCES TO DEFAMATION

The tort of defamation is broadly interpreted. In some situations, however, the defendant will not be held liable even though they published a statement that hurt the plaintiff's reputation. We will briefly look at several important defences to the tort of defamation:

- justification
- privilege
- fair comment

Justification occurs if the defendant's statement is true. Note that the statement must *actually* be true. The defendant will not avoid liability simply because they *honestly believed* that the statement was true. Note also that the defendant has the burden of proof. Once the plaintiff satisfies the requirements that we discussed, a judge will assume that the defendant's uncomplimentary statement was false. The defendant must prove otherwise.

justification occurs if the defendant's statement is true

The courts want people to speak freely on important issues. Consequently, they sometimes grant a *privilege*. A **privilege** is an immunity from liability. It takes two forms. First, an *absolute privilege* provides a complete immunity. It applies even if the defendant knowingly made a false statement for a malicious purpose. That defence is available only when the law needs to encourage people

privilege is an immunity from liability

---

[42] The Supreme Court of Canada has held that the requirement for publication is not met simply because the defendant's Internet page contains a hyperlink to another page that contains a defamatory statement about the plaintiff: *Crookes v Newton* 2011 SCC 47 (SCC).

to communicate without *any* fear of being sued. It is therefore usually limited to statements made:

- during parliamentary proceedings
- among high government officials who are dealing with government business
- by a judge, lawyer, litigant, or witness in the context of legal proceedings
- between spouses

The second form of the defence is a *qualified* privilege. Rather than being limited to specific situations, it may apply whenever (i) the defendant has a legal, moral, or social obligation to make a statement, and (ii) the statement is made to someone who had a similar duty or interest in receiving it. Both of those elements must be satisfied. Consequently, a qualified privilege may be recognized if:

- a manager makes an unfair statement about a former employee to the personnel director of a company that is considering hiring that individual—but not if the manager makes the same statement to a friend during idle gossip, or
- a department store discreetly posts a notice instructing its employees not to accept cheques from a customer who is wrongly suspected of fraud—but not if the notice is large enough to be noticed by other customers, who have no interest in the matter.[43]

The defence of qualified privilege is also limited to statements that the defendant made in good faith. It is not available if the defendant knew that its statement was untrue or if the defendant was motivated by some malicious purpose.

An important application of the qualified privilege defence arises under the label of *public interest responsible journalism*. **Public interest responsible journalism** occurs when a journalist, despite getting some facts wrong, acted in accordance with the standards of responsible journalism in publishing a story that the public was entitled to hear. As Sharpe JA said in the case that first adopted the new defence, "the focus of defamation law shifts away from the truth and towards the conduct of the defendant."[44] Protection of the plaintiff's reputation is restricted in order to encourage journalists to speak out on important issues. In deciding whether the defence ought to apply in a particular case, the courts are guided by 10 factors: (i) the *seriousness* of the allegation made against the plaintiff, (ii) the *importance* of the subject matter for public debate, (iii) the *reliability* of the defendant's information, (iv) the *steps taken to verify* the defendant's information, (v) whether the subject matter has already been *investigated and reported*, (vi) the *urgency* of the matter, (vii) whether the publication offered the *plaintiff any input*, (viii) whether the publication presented the *plaintiff's side of the story*, (ix) the *general tone* of the publication, and (x) the *timing* and *overall circumstances* of the publication.

The defence of *fair comment* is intended to encourage useful debate on significant social issues.[45] A **fair comment** is an expression of an opinion

public interest responsible journalism occurs when a journalist, despite getting some facts wrong, acted in accordance with the standards of responsible journalism in publishing a story that the public was entitled to hear

a fair comment is an expression of an opinion regarding a matter of public importance

---

[43.] *Pleau v Simpson-Sears Ltd* (1977) 75 DLR (3d) 747 (Ont CA).

[44.] *Cusson v Quan* (2007) 286 DLR (4th) 196 (Ont CA), rev'd (2009) 314 DLR (4th) 55 (SCC). See also *Grant v Torstar Corp* (2009) 314 DLR (4th) 1 (SCC).

[45.] Although they may seem very similar, the defences of privilege and fair comment are different. A privilege protects statements of fact, but fair comment protects opinions based on facts. For instance, a privilege may protect you if you say, "Mr Jones is a thief," whereas fair comment may provide a defence if you say, "Mr Jones was once convicted of theft and therefore he is not fit to serve as our mayor." Furthermore, the privilege defence is limited to certain situations that have been recognized by a statute or a judge. Fair comment, in contrast, can apply anytime that the defence can prove the elements of the defence.

regarding a matter of public importance. As long as the defendant did not act *maliciously*, the defence may apply if the court is satisfied on three elements.

- First, the defence is intended to protect *informed opinions*. The defendant has to prove that a reasonable person would have interpreted the statement as an opinion based on fact, rather than as a fact. Consequently, the defence may apply if a newspaper columnist accurately describes a politician's behaviour and suggests that "the leadership of this country is morally corrupt"—but not if that statement is made without the support of any background information.[46]

- Second, the defendant's opinion must concern an issue of *public interest*, such as a cultural, religious, or political matter. Consequently, while it is possible to criticize the public activities of poets, priests, and politicians, the defence does not allow personal attacks on their private lives.

- The Supreme Court of Canada recently changed the third element of the defence. [47] A comment traditionally was not considered "fair" unless it was *honestly held* by the defendant.[48] That requirement created considerable difficulty, especially when newspapers printed letters to the editor. The rule consequently has been revised. The defence now applies as long as the opinion in question *could honestly be held*. The focus falls not on the defendant's actual beliefs, but rather on the beliefs that could honestly be held by *some* person—even if that person is prejudiced or opinionated. The new rule accordingly is a victory for freedom of speech.

It is not yet clear how defamation laws will adjust to new forms of electronic media. Political blogs, for instance, routinely involve statements that might be considered tortious if made in other contexts. Do the usual laws apply or is it appropriate for a judge to consider such statements from the perspective of someone who regularly reads or participates in blogs? That question was raised in Case Brief 5.4.

Concept Summary 5.4 identifies the most important elements of the defamation defences.

REMEDIES FOR DEFAMATION

The usual remedy for defamation is compensation. Actual financial losses are always recoverable. Furthermore, if the plaintiff is a human being, rather than a corporation, compensation also is available for personal distress. Punitive damages may also be awarded if the defendant's conduct was particularly

---

[46.] The background information may be expressed or implied.

[47.] *WIC Radio Ltd v Simpson* (2008) 293 DLR (4th) 513 (SCC).

[48.] The Supreme Court of Canada previously held that a newspaper was entitled to use the defence of fair comment only if the publisher honestly shares the opinion that is contained in such a letter: *Cherneskey v Armadale Publishers Ltd* (1978) 90 DLR (3d) 321 (SCC). That was a very narrow rule. As a result, several provinces enacted legislation that allows a newspaper to use the defence as long as an honest person could have held the opinion in question, even if the publisher did not: *Defamation Act*, RSA 2000, c D-7, s 9 (Alta); *Defamation Act*, CCSM, c D20, s 9 (Man); *Defamation Act*, RSNB 1973, c 58, s 8.1(1), as amended by *An Act to Amend the Defamation Act*, SNB 1980, c 16, s 1 (NB); *Libel and Slander Act*, RSO 1990, c L.12, s 24 (Ont).

Case Brief 5.4

Baglow v Smith 2011 ONSC 5131 (Ont SCJ), rev'd 2012 ONCA 407 (Ont CA)

The parties were involved in a debate on a political blog. The debate focused on the treatment of Omar Khadr, a Canadian citizen who, as a 15 year old, allegedly killed an American soldier in Afghanistan. The plaintiff argued that Khadr's trial for murder was contrary to international law. The defendant responded by saying that the plaintiff was "one of the Taliban's more vocal supporters." The Taliban is a fundamentalist Muslim organization that has been linked to terrorist activities. The plaintiff sued the defendant for defamation.

The claim was rejected on summary judgment.[49] Annis J doubted that the defendant's statement would lead any reasonable person to have a lower opinion of the plaintiff. Furthermore, the court held that even if the statement was defamatory, it was protected by the defence of fair comment. The judge explained that many of the niceties of polite discussion are abandoned for the purposes of political blogging. The plaintiff himself had referred to his debating opponents as "yokels with pitchforks." As a result, within the context of the parties' debate, a reasonable person would interpret the defendant's insult not as a statement of fact, but as an opinion based on fact. In effect, the defendant was saying that he forcefully disagreed with the plaintiff's political analysis of Mr Khadr's situation.

The Ontario Court of Appeal, however, allowed the appeal. It held that the case was too important to be decided by summary judgment. Since the idea of defamation by blog is new, a full trial was necessary. The Court of Appeal also said that in deciding whether a blog comment is defamatory, the trial judge should consider the full context, including the dialogue between the parties, the position each took during the debate, and way in which a reasonable person might view the debate.

Concept Summary 5.4

Defamation Defences

Defence	Elements
Justification	• statement must be *true*

Absolute privilege	• any statement made in circumstances where people must speak *without fear of liability*:
	   • parliamentary proceedings
	   • high government officials discussing government business
	   • judges, lawyers, parties, and witnesses during court proceedings
	   • spouses

Qualified privilege	• statement made *without malice* • by a person with a legal, moral, or social *duty to speak out* • to a person with a *duty to receive*
Public interest responsible journalism	• statement *by a journalist* • meets *standards of responsible journalism* • story that *public was entitled to hear*
Fair comment	• statement made *without malice* • regarding issue of *public interest* • statement of *opinion* rather than fact • opinion *could be honestly held* by someone

---

[49.] In order to save time, the defendant may apply for summary judgment by arguing that the plaintiff cannot possibly win. The court then assumes that all of the plaintiff's allegations are true and asks if there is any chance of liability. If not, then the defendant wins summary judgment and the case comes to an end.

outrageous.[50] And in truly exceptional circumstances, a court may impose an injunction to prevent a person from even making a statement—but only if it is clear that the statement would be defamatory. In most situations, judges are reluctant to restrict freedom of speech in that way.

Injurious Falsehood

L.O. ❿

Our legal system protects personal reputations through the tort of defamation.[51] The tort of **injurious falsehood** occurs when the defendant makes a false statement about the plaintiff's business that causes the plaintiff to suffer a loss.[52] That tort may take a variety of forms.

the tort of **injurious falsehood** occurs when the defendant makes a false statement about the plaintiff's business that causes the plaintiff to suffer a loss

- **Slander of Title:** The defendant may falsely say that the plaintiff does not own a particular piece of land, therefore making it difficult for the plaintiff to sell that property for its full value.

- **Slander of Quality:** The defendant may falsely disparage the plaintiff's products in a way that causes potential customers to take their business elsewhere. The tort is not committed, however, if the defendant merely suggests that its products are better than the plaintiff's; nor if the defendant's statement about the plaintiff's business is true; nor if the defendant tries to gain an advantage by making a false statement about the high quality of its *own* products.[53]

- **Other Situations:** Even if there is no slander of title or slander of quality, the defendant may be held liable for making some *other* type of false statement about the plaintiff's business. For example, in the bizarre case of *Manitoba Free Press v Nagy*, the defendant newspaper said that the plaintiff's house was haunted, and therefore made it difficult for the plaintiff to sell that property.[54]

Regardless of the precise form of the injurious falsehood, the plaintiff must prove three elements.

- **False Statement:** The defendant must make a *false* statement about the plaintiff's business or property. Because the tort is concerned with reputations, that statement must be made to a third party.

- **Malice:** The defendant must have acted out of *malice*. Although the word generally means "spite" or "ill will," its precise legal effect is somewhat unclear. The defendant certainly may be held liable if they made the false statement for the purpose of hurting the plaintiff. However, it also appears to be enough if the defendant either knew that the statement was false or was reckless as to the truth of the assertion, and if the defendant either intended to hurt the plaintiff or knew that the plaintiff was likely to be injured.

---

[50] *Hill v Church of Scientology of Toronto* (1995) 126 DLR (4th) 129 (SCC).

[51] The tort of injurious falsehood is easily confused with the tort of defamation. It may also be confused with the tort of deceit, which we considered earlier in this chapter. There is, however, a critical difference between those two torts. Injurious falsehood occurs when the defendant makes a false statement that misleads the plaintiff's *customers*; deceit occurs when the defendant makes a false statement that misleads the *plaintiff*.

[52] Another related tort is *passing off*. As we will see in Chapter 18, that tort occurs when the defendant makes it seem as if its own goods were manufactured by the plaintiff.

[53] In that situation, however, the defendant may be held liable for misleading advertising.

[54] *Manitoba Free Press v Nagy* (1907) 39 DLR 340 (SCC).

Concept Summary 5.5

Elements of Business Torts

Tort	Elements of Proof

Conspiracy	• *two or more* people *act together* to cause *economic injury* to plaintiff
	• if otherwise *lawful* acts . . .
	   • defendants' *primary purpose* is to hurt plaintiff
	• if otherwise *unlawful* acts . . .
	   • defendants *should know* that acts might hurt plaintiff

Intimidation	• defendant *threatens* to commit an *unlawful act* • threat *directed* against *plaintiff or third party* • threatened party *gives in* to the threat • plaintiff *suffers* a loss

Interference with contractual relations	• defendant *induces* a *third party* to *break contract* with plaintiff
	• if defendant *directly* induces third party . . .
	   • defendant *knows* of contract
	   • defendant *intends* for third party to *breach* contract
	   • defendant *actually causes* third party to breach contract
	   • plaintiff *suffers* loss
	• if defendant *indirectly* induces third party . . .
	   • same four elements *plus*
	   • defendant's actions are otherwise *unlawful*

Unlawful interference with economic relations	• defendant performs *illegal, unlawful, prohibited,* or *unauthorized* act • defendant *intends* to hurt plaintiff • plaintiff *suffers* economic loss
Deceit	• defendant makes *false statement* • defendant *knows* that statement is false • defendant *intends to mislead* plaintiff • plaintiff *suffers a loss* as a result of *reasonable reliance* on the statement
Nuisance	• defendant *unreasonably interferes* with plaintiff's use of land
The rule in *Rylands v Fletcher*	• *strict liability* • defendant makes *non-natural use* of their land • something associated with that use *escapes* from defendant's land • plaintiff *suffers* harm
Defamation	• defendant makes *false statement* • *publication* to a third party • plaintiff's *reputation lowered* in eyes of *reasonable person*
Injurious falsehood	• defendant makes *false statement* about plaintiff's *business* or *property* • *publication* to a third party • defendant acted with *malicious intent* • plaintiff *suffers* economic loss

- **Loss:** The defendant's false statement must have caused the plaintiff to suffer a loss. The plaintiff may prove, for example, that a customer broke a contract to purchase the plaintiff's goods, or that a customer took their business elsewhere, or that a customer was willing to pay only a reduced price. It is not enough, however, for the plaintiff to merely show that their profits began to decline *after* the defendant uttered the false statement. A business may fall on hard times for a variety of reasons. A court will therefore insist upon persuasive evidence that the defendant's injurious falsehood actually *caused* the plaintiff's loss.

The 10 torts discussed above cover a great deal of territory. By way of review, Concept Summary 5.5 identifies the elements of those torts (with the exception of occupiers' liability, which differs between provinces).

Having reviewed the business torts, consider how you would decide the case that appears in You Be the Judge 5.1.

You Be the Judge **5.1**

Secondary Picketing[55]

The employees of Pepsi-Cola were legally on strike. In an attempt to put pressure on their employer, they set up secondary pickets. As well as picketing their employer's premises, the employees also picketed (i) stores that sold Pepsi-Cola, in an effort to disrupt the delivery of the employer's products and to discourage people from buying those products, (ii) a hotel where replacement workers were staying, and (iii) houses belonging to the employer's managers, where they chanted slogans, screamed insults, and threatened bodily harm.

Questions for Discussion

1. Have the employees committed any of the torts that we examined in this chapter (or in the last chapter)?

2. Should the courts allow secondary picketing? By setting up a picket in front of a store, for instance, the employees may have discouraged customers from going into that store. Why should the store have to suffer simply because the employees have a dispute with their employer?

[55.] *Pepsi-Cola Canada Beverages (West) Ltd v RWDSU, Local 558* (2002) 208 DLR (4th) 385 (SCC).

Chapter Summary

In this chapter, we examined 10 torts that are particularly important for business people.

Conspiracy usually occurs when two or more defendants agree to act together with the primary purpose of causing a financial loss to the plaintiff. The conspiring parties can be held liable even if their actions are otherwise lawful. However, the courts are more willing to impose liability if the defendants acted in an otherwise unlawful way.

Intimidation occurs when the plaintiff suffers a loss as a result of the defendant's threat to commit an unlawful act against either the plaintiff or a third party. Two-party intimidation occurs when the defendant directly coerces the plaintiff into suffering a loss. Three-party intimidation occurs when the defendant coerces a third party into acting in a way that hurts the plaintiff.

Interference with contractual relations occurs when the defendant disrupts a contract that exists between the plaintiff and a third party. A direct inducement to breach of contract occurs when the defendant directly persuades a third party to break its contract with the plaintiff. An indirect inducement to breach of contract occurs when the defendant indirectly persuades a third party to break its contract with the plaintiff.

Unlawful interference with economic relations occurs when one person intentionally does an unlawful (or unauthorized) act that causes the plaintiff to suffer a loss.

Deceit occurs if the defendant makes a false statement, which it knows to be untrue, with which it intends to mislead the plaintiff, and which causes the plaintiff to suffer a loss.

The law of occupiers' liability requires an occupier of premises to protect visitors from harm. Some provinces and territories rely on the traditional common law rules. Others rely upon occupiers' liability statutes.

Nuisance occurs when the defendant unreasonably interferes with the plaintiff's ability to use and enjoy its own land. The defence of statutory authority may protect a defendant from liability, but it has been narrowly interpreted by the courts. The courts often award injunctions to stop or prevent nuisances.

The rule in *Rylands v Fletcher* states that the defendant may be held strictly liable for its non-natural use of land if something escapes from its property and injures the plaintiff.

Defamation occurs when the defendant makes a false statement that could lead a reasonable person to have a lower opinion of the plaintiff. Liability may be avoided through the defences of justification, privilege, and fair comment.

Injurious falsehood occurs when the defendant makes a false statement to a third party about the plaintiff's business in a way that causes the plaintiff to suffer a loss.

MyBusLawLab   ADDITIONAL RESOURCES FOR CHAPTER 5

MyBusLawLab provides students with an assortment of tools to help enrich the learning experience, including a Study Plan with Pre- and Post-tests, mini-cases with assessments, and provincial content material, which provides links to relevant cases, legislation, and additional resources.

MyBusLawLab provides the following resources for Chapter 5:

Provincial Material

- **British Columbia:** Occupiers' Liability, Defamation
- **Alberta:** Defamation, Occupiers' Liability, Social Hosts
- **Manitoba and Saskatchewan:** Occupiers' Liability—Trespass to Land, Farming and Nuisance, Defamation
- **Ontario:** Defamation, Occupiers' Liability

Review Questions

1. Many of the torts examined in Chapter 5 require proof of the defendant's "intention." Is "intention" defined the same way for all torts? If not, suggest a reason why different torts use different meanings of the word "intention."

2. "The tort of conspiracy always requires proof that the plaintiff and the defendant agreed to commit a crime together." Is that statement accurate? Explain your answer.

3. The courts sometimes say that the tort of intimidation cannot be based on a threat to commit a breach of contract. Why does that apparent rule apply to two-party intimidation but not to three-party intimidation?

4. The defendant has threatened to breach an existing contract. When, if ever, can that threat provide the basis for a successful claim under the tort of intimidation?

5. "A company is in danger of committing a tort every time it hires a person away from a rival company." Explain the extent to which that statement is true.

6. "There is really no difference between interference with contractual relations and unlawful interference

with economic relations." Explain the extent to which that statement is true.

7. It is sometimes said that the tort of deceit requires a statement of fact. How is a statement of fact different from an opinion, a prediction, or a puff? Why is a statement of fact necessary?

8. "The courts do not like liars. Consequently, damages are available in tort law for every loss that the plaintiff suffered as a result of relying on something that a liar said." Is that statement true? Explain your answer.

9. Describe the main problems created by the common law's traditional approach to occupiers' liability. How have Canadian courts improved that tort?

10. Explain the general approach of occupiers' liability legislation. In what ways are the statutory rules significantly different from the common law rules?

11. Can a landlord ever be held liable under the tort of occupiers' liability if a claimant is injured while visiting a property that is being rented by a tenant? Explain your answer.

12. What factors do the courts consider in deciding whether the defendant has committed the tort of nuisance? What is the most important factor?

13. What remedies are available for the tort of nuisance? How does a judge decide which remedy to award in any particular case?

14. What do the courts mean when they say that a person can be held liable under the rule in *Rylands v Fletcher* only if there has been a "non-natural use" of land? Why is the meaning of that term important?

15. Why is the rule in *Rylands v Fletcher* considered a strict liability tort?

16. Explain three defences that may be available against the rule in *Rylands v Fletcher*.

17. Why is publication critically important to the tort of defamation? Why do I not commit the tort of defamation if, in the course of a private conversation, I wrongly accuse you of some horrible crime?

18. Explain the defences of absolute privilege and qualified privilege. Outline the situations in which those defences will apply.

19. Describe the defence of fair comment. Why is that defence especially important to businesses such as newspapers, magazines, and television broadcasters?

20. The tort of defamation protects reputations. Does it protect the reputation of a person's property or business as well? If so, explain how it does so. If not, does any other tort do so? Explain your answer.

Cases and Problems

1. The federal government operated a program under which it leased land to Aboriginal Canadians. It entered into one such lease with David Cardinal, a member of the River Valley Band. Shortly afterwards, however, several other members of that band began to harass Cardinal by using their trucks to block access to that property, allowing their cattle to stray onto the land, and, despite his repeated objections, hunting on his land. Cardinal believes that they did so to frighten him into terminating his lease with the government. If that happened, the other members of the band would be able to lease the land themselves. When he confronted them with that allegation, one of their group replied, "We haven't done anything wrong. But if you can't stand the heat, maybe you should just get out of the kitchen!" Does Cardinal have a cause of action in intimidation? Do you have enough information to answer that question?

2. DeJohnette Developments was in the process of building a recording studio. It agreed to purchase about $5 000 000 worth of sound equipment from Peacock Electronics Inc. Jarrett Koln, who custom builds sound equipment, heard that DeJohnette was planning a new recording studio. Koln did not know that DeJohnette had already entered into a contract with Peacock. He sent a letter to DeJohnette that said:

> You should not, under any circumstances, buy equipment from Peacock. Although that company has been around for years, the quality of its merchandise is vastly inferior compared to mine.

DeJohnette knew that Koln was correct. Recent studies had shown that Peacock's equipment was second-rate. DeJohnette nevertheless honoured its contract with Peacock and refused to buy from Koln. Peacock, however, is upset that Koln jeopardized its agreement with DeJohnette. Can Peacock successfully sue Koln for inducing breach of contract? Provide several reasons for your answer.

3. The cement-manufacturing business is a cutthroat industry. For many years, a small number of large companies, including Ash Inc and Izzy Supplies Ltd, have enjoyed a virtual monopoly. They have strongly resisted the emergence of new competitors. Two years ago, Roxel Corp attempted to break into the business. Because of certain technological advances that it had developed, Roxel was able to produce a much better product than was currently available in the market. Although Roxel's product was initially available only in the Atlantic provinces, Ash and Izzy were worried that their profits might drop sharply if Roxel became successful and expanded across the country. They therefore agreed to sell their own cement in the Maritimes at a drastically reduced price. That agreement had two effects: (i) It allowed Ash and Izzy to maintain their traditional share of the market across the country, and (ii) it incidentally drove Roxel out of the cement business. The agreement between Ash and Izzy was unlawful under the *Competition Act* because it involved regional price discrimination. Can Roxel successfully sue Ash and Izzy for the tort of conspiracy? Explain your answer.

4. By early July, Arvid had become quite nervous about his ability to afford the upcoming school year. Fees, tuition, and books were estimated to cost $10 000. Leaving aside money needed for rent and living expenses, his budget contained only $5000. His problem seemed to be solved, however, when an acquaintance, Miriam, offered Arvid a "remarkable, short-term investment opportunity," as she put it. She explained that while she had developed a "fail-safe" business plan for selling T-shirts to tourists over the summer, she was short of funds. She further said that she could guarantee that Arvid would "at least double his money" if he invested between

$3000 and $6000 in the scheme. Although Arvid was skeptical at first, he eventually was persuaded after Miriam provided him with an impressive document, containing charts showing profits from past ventures and projected revenues from the current project. He therefore invested his $5000 with Miriam. Sad to say, the business failed miserably and, instead of doubling his money, Arvid lost his entire investment. It is now early September and he has no money for school. A friend has suggested that Arvid should sue Miriam for the tort of deceit. Is Arvid likely to win such an action? If so, how much would he likely receive from Miriam?

5. The Alkabe Corporation owned a large piece of land on which it planned to develop a shopping mall. When the starting date of that project was delayed, the company erected a one-metre-high fence around the site and posted a notice: "absolutely no trespassing." The site nevertheless became a very popular play area for local children. A number of young teens created a large ramp that they used for jumping their bikes. Alkabe learned of that fact, but it took no steps to stop the children from playing on the site. Some time later, Jyoti, a 13 year old, was seriously injured when she flipped her bike while racing over the ramp. Would Alkabe be held liable for the tort of occupiers' liability under the traditional common law rules? Assuming that the accident occurred in the jurisdiction in which you live, will Alkabe be held liable for the tort of occupiers' liability? Explain your answer.

6. Hamilton House is a charming country home, situated on a small piece of land, several kilometres from a nearby city. It was built about a century ago. Until quite recently, it sat next to empty crop land. Ten years ago, however, Carlos Aguiar and his family moved onto that neighbouring property. A short time after doing so, he made a number of substantial changes to his land: (i) he elevated an area, on which he constructed his own house, by just over one metre, (ii) he built a large pond a short distance from Hamilton House, and (iii) he channelled a stream, which had run across the entire area for centuries, into narrow PVC piping, with the result that the stream no longer ran through its natural course. Five years ago, Barb Howlett bought Hamilton House. She soon regretted the purchase. Although Hamilton House had traditionally had few flooding problems, the changes that Aguiar introduced had created enormous difficulties. In short, by altering the natural topography of his own property, Aguiar caused water to flood from his land to Hamilton House during times of heavy rain. One particular serious incident not only damaged the house itself, but also contaminated Hamilton House's water supply for one year. To make matters worse, although he could have prevented much of the damage by activating a flood pump that he had installed on his own property, Aguiar refused to help in any way. Which tort or torts, considered in this chapter, might allow Barb Howlett to recover damages from Carlos Aguiar? Explain your answer.

7. The Putrescible Food Company operates a plant that processes and packages a wide variety of foods, including meats and vegetables. In the course of doing so, it generates a large amount of waste product. It has long been in the habit of burying that waste in a ravine that is located just inside the boundary of its property. (A residential district is situated on the other side of the ravine.) The company knew that the buried waste might generate methane gas, but did nothing to prevent that from happening. Consequently, an invisible cloud of that gas recently drifted out of the ravine, across the company's property, and into the nearby residential district. Alonzo suffered terrible injuries after striking a match to light a cigar. The flame from the match ignited the cloud of gas and caused a fireball that engulfed him. At the time of the accident, Alonzo was standing on a public street in front of his house. Which of the torts, if any, discussed in this chapter provides him with the best possibility of successfully suing the Putrescible Food Company? Explain your answer.

8. A new runway was added to the Vancouver International Airport. As usually occurs with large infrastructure projects, the development was governed by statutes and regulations. That legislation determined, amongst other things, the location and direction of the new runway. The final result has been a mixed blessing. The new runway has created hundreds of jobs and further added to the city's reputation as a desirable holiday destination. Unfortunately, it has also "ruined" several neighbourhoods. Until recently, for example, Bridgeport was a peaceful community in which residents spent a great deal of time enjoying the outdoors. As a result of the air traffic associated with the new runway, however, life has become unpleasant, if not intolerable. It is impossible to conduct a conversation outdoors if a jet is passing overhead, and in some situations, it is even difficult to hear a television or radio while indoors. The noise regularly keeps some residents awake at night. Those problems have caused property values to plummet. It is very difficult to find a buyer for a home in Bridgeport. Has a tort been committed? If so, what remedy will the residents of Bridgeport likely receive?

9. Dina Papadopoulos is a journalism student at Metro University. Since her goal is to become an investigative reporter, she joined her university's newspaper—the *Metro Squawker*—as a writer. Jiang Lee, another student at the university, occupies the position of Treasurer on the Student Union. The Union received several anonymous allegations that Jiang was spending the Student Union's money for his own benefit. Carl Polano, an art history major and the President of the Union, carried out an informal investigation of Jiang. Although Carl has no experience in financial matters and although he did not have access to all of the relevant documents, he became convinced that Jiang was indeed stealing money from the Union. Carl then called Dina, as well as three members of the Student Union, to his dorm room to talk about

the matter. Carl presented his evidence and accused Jiang of financial misconduct. The other members of the Union insisted that the issues would have to be raised during the next Student Union meeting. Dina, who has some experience with financial fraud, came to her own conclusion that Jiang was almost certainly guilty. The next issue of the *Metro Squawker* contained her report in which she called upon Jiang Lee "to resign from the Student Union and refund the money that he has stolen." Jiang has sued for defamation. Discuss the case.

10. Tony Twist was a professional hockey player with the Quebec Nordiques and the St Louis Blues. During his career, he was known as an enforcer—while playing in the NHL for a decade, he amassed only 10 goals, but over 1100 minutes in penalties. Todd McFarlane is the publisher of a number of comic books. One of those publications, *Spawn*, features a vicious gangster named Antonio Twistelli, who also goes by the nickname of "Tony Twist." The real Tony Twist's mother became very upset when she discovered that such a character shared her son's name. She was worried that *Spawn* would lead people to think badly of her boy. McFarlane insists that he did not base his comic book villain on any real person and argues that if he wanted to borrow a hockey player's name, he would have called the gangster Wayneatelli Gretzkytello. Can the real-life Tony Twist successfully sue McFarlane for defamation? What test would a court apply in these circumstances?

11. Malcolm Maxwell is the host of a popular radio program. The program's popularity is largely based on Maxwell's reputation for making outrageous statements. Maxwell was in rare form during a recent broadcast. He was discussing what he believed to be the very poor quality of taxi service in his city. He focused on the fact that many taxi drivers are immigrants who came to Canada from the small, impoverished country of Ruritania. Most people in Ruritania speak the Esperantuc language. Maxwell said:

> Why is it that there are so many incompetent people and that the language of work is Esperantuc in a country that's French and English? I'm not very good at speaking "donkey." Taxis have really become the Third World of public

transportation around here. My suspicion is that the driving exams, well, they can be bought. You can't have such incompetent people driving taxis, people who know so little about the city, and think that they took actual exams. Our taxi drivers are really arrogant, especially the Ruritanians. They're often rude, you can't be sure at all that they're competent and their cars don't look well maintained. Most of them stink.

The plaintiff is a taxi driver in the same city. He hails from Ruritania and his first language is Esperantuc. He has started a class action, on behalf of himself and approximately 1500 other city taxi drivers from Ruritania, that claims that they have been defamed by Maxwell. Identify and explain the strongest defence that Maxwell can use against the claim.

12. Canaural Inc was a small Canadian company that manufactured audio components. Until recently, the brains behind the operation were two key employees: Jurgen Ballack and Karl Heinz. DeutscheSonic GmbH is a large German company that trades around the world. Its success is due in part to its tactic of ruthlessly "squeezing out" its competitors. A year ago, it set its sights on Canaural. DeutscheSonic realized that Ballack and Heinz were the key players in Canaural. It therefore secretly approached them with lucrative job offers. Ballack and Heinz initially resisted. They explained that their contracts required them to give six months' notice to quit, and that Canaural was a small operation that was unlikely ever to challenge DeutscheSonic. DeutscheSonic, however, was not to be denied. Its president explained the situation to Ballack and Heinz: "Wake up boys! Canaural is going to die. You can either be my assassins, or you can be buried along with the rest of your little company. Get rich or get dead!" It turned out to be an easy choice. Ballack and Heinz quickly experienced a change of heart, abruptly quit their jobs with Canaural, and joined DeutscheSonic. Without Ballack and Heinz, Canaural soon crumbled beneath DeutscheSonic. The Canadian company has, in effect, been wiped out. Explain the causes of action and the remedies that are available to Canaural.

6 Negligence

LEARNING OBJECTIVES

After completing this chapter, you should be able to:

❶ Describe the nature and function of the concept of a duty of care.

❷ Explain the term "reasonable foreseeability" and explain the ways in which that concept is relevant to the tort of negligence.

❸ Explain why the concept of proximity is important to the duty of care, especially in the context of claims for negligent statements.

❹ Explain the role of policy under the duty of care concept, especially as it applies to the regulation of professions.

❺ Describe the reasonable person and explain how that person is relevant to the standard of care.

❻ Outline the special considerations that arise when a court decides whether a professional has acted carelessly.

❼ Outline the nature and function of the but-for test.

❽ Briefly describe the defence of contributory negligence.

❾ Explain why and how the courts have limited the defence of voluntary assumption of risk.

❿ Outline the scope of the defence of illegality.

In this chapter, we finish our discussion of torts by examining the most important tort of all: negligence. In non-legal terms, that word usually means "carelessness." Its legal meaning is much the same. The tort of **negligence** determines whether the defendant can be held liable for carelessly causing the plaintiff to suffer a loss or injury. That issue can arise in numerous ways: a manufacturer may produce a beverage that makes a consumer sick; an investment counsellor's bad advice may lead a client to purchase worthless stocks; a golfer may hit an errant shot that cracks a spectator's skull; a builder may construct a defective bridge that collapses onto a motorist's vehicle; an employer may write an inaccurate report that prevents an employee from receiving a promotion; and so on.

the tort of **negligence** determines whether the defendant can be held liable for carelessly causing injury to the plaintiff

The tort of negligence requires the plaintiff to prove that the defendant:

- owed a *duty of care*, in that they were required to act carefully toward the plaintiff
- *breached the standard of care* by acting carelessly
- *caused harm* to the plaintiff

Even if the plaintiff proves those three elements, the defendant may be able to avoid liability by proving a defence. Three possibilities are especially important. The defendant may show that the plaintiff:

- was guilty of *contributory negligence* that caused or contributed to the injury
- *voluntarily assumed the risk* of being injured by the defendant
- was injured while engaged in some form of *illegal* behaviour

Those elements are represented in Figure 6.1.

Before examining those elements, we must discuss two preliminary matters. First, people sometimes talk about *professional negligence*. That phrase is misleading because it suggests that there is a separate tort by that name. In fact, the term "professional negligence" simply refers to negligence that is committed by a professional person, such as a banker, a lawyer, or an accountant.[1] However, it *is* true that the cause of action in negligence is flexible enough to reflect different types of situations. For example, the standard

---

FIGURE 6.1   The Cause of Action in Negligence

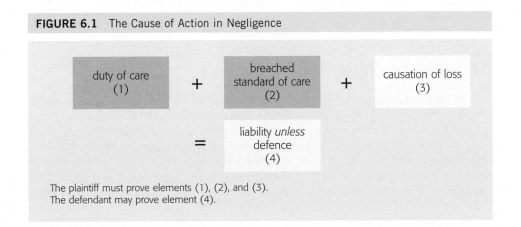

The plaintiff must prove elements (1), (2), and (3).
The defendant may prove element (4).

---

[1] Chapter 22 explains how a professional may also be held liable on other grounds, such as breach of contract and breach of fiduciary duty.

of care always requires the defendant to act as a reasonable person would act *in similar circumstances*. The precise meaning of that requirement therefore depends upon the circumstances. An architect who is drafting plans for an office tower must act much more carefully than a gas station attendant who is washing a car. And in that way, the idea of "professional negligence" makes sense. It refers to the special considerations that shape the general cause of action in negligence when it is applied to professional people. The topic of professional negligence is discussed later in this chapter.

Second, the law of negligence contains a tension between two important values. On the one hand, the courts want a wide scope of liability in order to compensate people who suffer injuries. On the other hand, the courts recognize that liability sometimes hurts society. If a business had to fully compensate every person whom it injured, it might be forced out of business. Admittedly, in some situations, that would be a good thing. An especially hazardous industry that produces few social benefits perhaps should be shut down. In other situations, however, it may be in society's best interests to protect certain types of activities from liability. For example, it is quite difficult to successfully sue a physician, partially because judges do not want to discourage doctors from practising in risky areas, such as obstetrics.[2] The tension between the desire to provide compensation and the desire to encourage socially useful activities appears in all areas of tort law. It is particularly noticeable in negligence, however, because that cause of action is so flexible. It is not much of an exaggeration to say that a judge, with a bit of ingenuity, can often reasonably find for either the plaintiff or the defendant. The actual decision frequently depends on which interests the judge finds more compelling. As we discuss the action in negligence, notice how the courts view the societal role of different types of business activities.

Duty of Care

L.O. ❶❷❸❹

a **duty of care** exists if the defendant is required to use reasonable care to avoid injuring the plaintiff

The courts use the concept of *duty of care* to control the scope of liability under the cause of action in negligence. A **duty of care** exists if the defendant is required to use reasonable care to avoid injuring the plaintiff. Without a duty of care, there cannot be liability, even if the defendant carelessly injured the plaintiff. Ethical Perspective 6.1 (on the next page) provides an interesting illustration.

TEST FOR DETERMINING THE EXISTENCE OF DUTY OF CARE

A duty of care is required for an action in negligence. But how does a judge decide when to impose such a duty? Traditionally, there was no general answer—a duty of care was restricted to certain types of relationships, such as innkeeper and traveller, lawyer and client, railway company and passenger, and surgeon and patient. A plaintiff could win only if they fell within one of those relationships. Eventually, however, the courts replaced those individual categories with a single test. A duty of care can now be recognized any time that certain conditions are met. Case Brief 6.1 discusses one of the most famous cases in our legal system.

---

2. *Reibl v Hughes* (1980) 114 DLR (3d) 1 (SCC); *ter Neuzen v Korn* (1995) 127 DLR (4th) 577 (SCC).

Ethical Perspective 6.1

Duty of Care[3]

The Supreme Court of Canada has held that a pregnant woman does not owe a duty of care to her unborn child. Consequently, if a pregnant woman carelessly causes a traffic accident that results in damage to her unborn child, that child cannot sue in negligence despite being born later with a disability.

Interestingly, the same rule does *not* apply between an unborn child and other people. Anyone, except a mother, can owe a duty of care. For example, if a father carelessly causes a child to suffer an injury before birth, he can be held liable if that child is later born with a disability. Furthermore, everyone, including a mother, can be held liable for carelessly causing an injury to a child *after* birth.

The rule that denies the existence of a duty of care between a pregnant woman and her unborn child reflects the court's attempt to strike a balance between the desirability of providing compensation for the injured child and the desirability of protecting the woman's freedom of action. Because nearly everything that a woman does can affect her unborn child, it has been argued that a duty of care would unfairly require her to be on guard for nine months.

Questions for Discussion

1. Has the Supreme Court of Canada struck a fair balance?

2. From a legal and moral perspective, should a pregnant woman be entitled to carelessly injure her unborn child?

When answering those questions, consider that the mother would usually want to be held liable to her injured child. More precisely, she would want her child to be able to recover compensatory damages from her insurance company.

Case Brief 6.1

Donoghue v Stevenson [1932] AC 562 (HL)

The plaintiff, Mrs Donoghue, visited a café with a friend. Her friend bought her a bottle of ginger beer that the defendant had manufactured. After drinking some of the beverage, the plaintiff poured the remainder into her glass. She then noticed that the bottle contained, along with ginger beer, a decomposed snail. The event made her sick, and she sued the defendant for carelessly allowing a snail to get into the drink.

The issue before the court was whether a manufacturer owes a duty of care to a person who consumes, but did not personally buy, a particular product. Lord Atkin said "yes."

You must take reasonable care to avoid acts or omissions which you can reasonably foresee would be likely to injure your neighbour. Who, then, in law, is my neighbour? The answer seems to be—persons who are so closely and directly affected by my act that I ought reasonably to have them in contemplation as being so affected when I am directing my mind to the acts or omissions which are called in question.

That decision is important to business people for two reasons.

- First, it created a general test for determining the existence of a duty of care. It is no longer necessary to bring a case within one of the traditional categories.

- Second, it established that a manufacturer can be held liable to any consumer. Manufacturers therefore have to worry not only about the people who buy their products, but also about the people who use their products. We will discuss the second point later.

Based on *Donoghue v Stevenson,* the Canadian courts have developed a unique test for the creation of a duty of care.[4]

- The judge will first ask whether or not the duty of care question has already been answered for the particular type of case that is being litigated. We already know, for instance, that the bottler of a beverage owes

---

[3.] *Dobson v Dobson* (1999) 174 DLR (4th) 1 (SCC).

[4.] *Nielsen v Kamloops (City)* (1984) 10 DLR (4th) 641 (SCC); *Cooper v Hobart* (2001) 206 DLR (4th) 193 (SCC).

a duty of care to a consumer, and that a mother does not owe a duty of care to an unborn child.

- If the duty of care question has not already been answered for the particular type of case, then it will be necessary to ask three questions in order to determine whether or not a duty of care *should* exist.

  - Was it *reasonably foreseeable* that the plaintiff could be injured by the defendant's carelessness?

  - Did the parties share a relationship of sufficient *proximity*?

  - If an injury was reasonably foreseeable, and if the parties shared a relationship of sufficient proximity, then a duty of care presumably will exist. The judge might still deny a duty of care, however, on the basis of *policy* reasons.

We will look at the concepts of *reasonable foreseeability*, *proximity*, and *policy* in more detail.

Reasonable Foreseeability

The reasonable foreseeability test is *objective*. The issue is not whether the defendant *personally knew* that its activities might injure the plaintiff. It is whether a *reasonable person* in the defendant's position would have recognized that possibility. That test is intended to strike a balance between the parties. It would be unfair to deny compensation simply because the defendant was unaware of a danger. The plaintiff should not have to suffer simply because the defendant was not paying attention. But at the same time, it would be unfair to hold the defendant liable for *every* injury that it creates, even those that were unforeseeable. A person cannot take precautions against a hidden danger. Similarly, it is difficult to arrange liability insurance for an unpredictable event. To better understand the reasonable foreseeability test, consider Business Decision 6.1.

Business Decision **6.1**

Reasonable Foreseeability and Risk Management[5]

Hermes Holdings Ltd sold a piece of land to Mercury Developments Inc for $500 000. Mercury intended to build a shopping mall on that property. To do so, however, it needed certain documents to be delivered to a government office by December 31. If it failed to do so, it would not be able to proceed with its project and it would suffer a loss of $1 000 000. Hermes still had possession of those documents. Mercury therefore told Hermes to send them to the government office by courier.

Hermes contacted your courier company. You agreed to deliver an envelope to the government office by December 31 in exchange for $10. Hermes did not, however, tell you what the envelope contained, nor that Mercury would suffer an enormous loss if delivery was late. Unfortunately, because you were very busy, you did not actually deliver the envelope until January 3.

Hermes is not particularly concerned about the late delivery. Mercury, however, is very upset. Your carelessness cost it $1 000 000. Nevertheless, you probably would not be held liable. A reasonable person in your position might not have appreciated the consequences of late delivery.

Questions for Discussion

1. Why would it be unfair to hold you liable if Mercury's loss was not reasonably foreseeable?

2. If the situation had been fully explained to you at the outset, would you still have charged only $10? Would it make good business sense to expose yourself to a risk worth $1 000 000 in damages in exchange for such a small price?

[5.] *BDC Ltd v Hofstrand Farms Ltd* (1986) 26 DLR (4th) 1 (SCC).

Proximity

Reasonable foreseeability is only a start. A duty of care will not be recognized unless there was also a relationship of *proximity*. The concept of proximity is hard to define. The basic idea is that there must somehow be a close and direct connection between the parties. In simple situations, the court will focus on *physical* proximity (as when the defendant carelessly swings a baseball bat while standing next to the plaintiff). In more complicated situations, however, the court will look at the issue of proximity from a variety of perspectives. Depending upon the circumstances, it may ask:

- whether the parties shared a *social relationship* (for example, a parent is required to look after a child, but a stranger is not)

- whether the parties shared a *commercial relationship* (for example, a tavern may be responsible if a drunken customer later causes a traffic accident, but the host of a house party may not be responsible if a drunken guest injures a pedestrian on the way home)[6]

- whether there was a *direct causal connection* between the defendant's carelessness and the plaintiff's injury (for example, a motorist who rams into a bridge will be liable for the damage to the bridge, but probably not for the profits that were lost when customers could not reach a store that was located on the other side of the bridge)[7]

- whether the plaintiff *relied* on the fact that the defendant *represented* that they would act in a certain way (for example, a railway company may have a duty to continue operating a safety gate that it voluntarily installed and that pedestrians have come to rely upon)[8]

As you can see, the concept of proximity is very broad and very open-ended. It allows the court to look at all of the circumstances before deciding whether or not it would be appropriate to recognize a new duty of care.

DUTY OF CARE FOR PROFESSIONAL STATEMENTS Although it is difficult to define, the concept of proximity often plays a crucial role in determining whether or not a duty of care exists. In the business context, the best example concerns *negligent statements*.[9] The Canadian economy is increasingly based on the supply of information and advice, rather than on the production of physical goods. Inevitably, some of the statements that are made by professionals (such as financial advisers, business consultants, lawyers, stockbrokers, and bankers) will be inaccurate. And inevitably, consumers and clients will suffer as a result. The law of negligence must strike a balance between the need to compensate people who are hurt by negligent statements and the need to protect businesses from the potentially disastrous consequences of being held liable.

Special rules are needed because *careless statements* are different from *careless actions* in at least three ways.

[6.] *Jordan House Ltd v Menow & Honsberger* (1973) 38 DLR (3d) 105 (SCC); *Childs v Desormeaux* (2006) 266 DLR (4th) 257 (SCC).

[7.] *Star Village Tavern v Nield* (1976) 71 DLR (3d) 439 (Man QB).

[8.] *Soulsby v Toronto* (1907) 15 OLR 13 (Ont HCJ).

[9.] Courts also are reluctant to recognize a duty of care to avoid acts that cause *psychological*, rather than *physical*, injury. Broken bones can be proven by X-rays, but it is far more difficult to be sure that a person has suffered a broken mind. Furthermore, while a single careless act may physically hurt one or two people, it may cause many more to suffer "nervous shock" if, for instance, the incident is broadcast on television. See *Mustapha v Culligan Canada Ltd* (2008) 293 DLR (4th) 29 (SCC).

- Since the dangers associated with physical conduct are usually obvious, the need for precaution is normally clear as well. You know that if you swing a baseball bat in a crowded room, you may hurt someone. In contrast, because the risks associated with statements are often hidden, the need for care is usually less apparent. Consequently, people tend to speak loosely, especially in social settings.

- "Words are more volatile than deeds."[10] In most situations, the risk created by a careless action is limited in time and space. Drunk drivers pose a real threat, but generally only for the motorists and pedestrians in their path. Furthermore, they will likely be stopped once the first accident occurs. In contrast, if a duty of care exists for a careless statement, there is a possibility of "liability in an indeterminate amount for an indeterminate time to an indeterminate class."[11] Suppose a financial report that was created for personal purposes is mistakenly distributed to the public. If it contains inaccurate information, many people may later rely upon it and suffer financial loses when they make bad investments.

- Careless actions usually result in property damage or personal injuries. A negligent driver may crash through your fence or run you down. Careless statements, however, usually result in *pure economic losses*, financial losses that are not tied to any property damage or personal injuries. For example, if you follow your stockbroker's negligent advice and make a poor investment, you will simply lose money. And significantly, the law is more reluctant to provide compensation for pure economic losses than for property damage or personal injuries.[12] Some things in life are more important than others.

For those reasons, Canadian courts apply special rules when deciding whether to recognize a duty of care if the defendant's *careless statement* caused the plaintiff to suffer a *pure economic loss*.[13] Case Brief 6.2 discusses a simplified version of a leading case.

Case Brief 6.2

Hercules Managements Ltd v Ernst & Young (1997) 146 DLR (4th) 577 (SCC)

The defendant was an accounting firm that prepared audited financial statements for a company. Those statements were required by statute and were intended to allow shareholders to supervise the management of the company. The plaintiff, who was one of the shareholders in the company, claimed that the defendant's carelessness caused those statements to contain inaccurate information. He further claimed those statements caused him to continue his investment in the company, and therefore caused him to suffer a loss when the company later collapsed.

The Supreme Court of Canada first asked whether it was *reasonably foreseeable* that the plaintiff would suffer a loss by relying upon the

(Continued)

[10.] *Hedley Byrne & Co v Heller & Partners Ltd* [1963] 2 All ER 575 at 602 (HL).

[11.] *Ultramares Corp v Touche* 255 NY 170 (CA 1931).

[12.] This is true whether a pure economic loss is caused by careless words or by careless conduct. In contrast, the courts generally do not feel the need to apply special rules if the defendant's careless statement causes the plaintiff to suffer property damage or physical injury. In one case, a model suffered physical injuries as a result of falling off a stage while following a director's instructions: *Robson v Chrysler Corp (Canada)* (1962) 32 DLR (2d) 49 (Alta CA). The director clearly owed a duty of care.

[13.] The courts are more willing to impose liability if the defendant's inaccurate statement was intentional rather than merely careless. In this section, we are discussing the law of *negligent statements*. However, as Chapter 5 explained, liability can also be imposed under the tort of *deceit* if the defendant intentionally misled the plaintiff.

(continued)

defendant's statement. A duty of care is more likely to be imposed with respect to a statement if:

- the statement was communicated on a *serious occasion*—it is often reasonable to rely upon information that is provided during a business meeting, but not during an informal party
- the defendant's statement was made in response to *an inquiry*—a person who is specifically asked for information should realize that the answer may be relied upon
- the defendant received a *financial benefit* in exchange for the statement—reasonable people do not usually pay for information unless they intend to rely upon it
- the defendant communicated a *statement of fact*, or an *opinion or prediction based on fact*, rather than a purely personal opinion—it is often reasonable to rely upon a professional evaluation of certain stocks, but not upon a prediction as to the outcome of a horse race

However, a duty of care is less likely to be imposed if:

- the defendant issued a *disclaimer* along with its statement—a reasonable person does not generally rely upon a statement if the speaker was unwilling to assume responsibility for it

Given the facts of the case, including the lack of a disclaimer, the court held that it was reasonably foreseeable that the plaintiff would reasonably rely upon the defendant's statement.

At the second stage of the duty of care analysis, however, the court was worried about "indeterminate liability." The defendant prepared the statements for a specific purpose—to allow shareholders to monitor the management of the company. It did not intend for those statements to be used as investment advice by people like the plaintiff.[14] The Court was also worried that the fear of widespread liability would cause businesses in the defendant's position to substantially increase their prices to offset the risk of being held responsible. The Court therefore held that a duty of care will be recognized only if:

- the defendant knew that the plaintiff, either individually or as a member of a defined group, might rely upon the statement, and
- the plaintiff relied upon that statement for its intended purpose

Because he was a shareholder, the plaintiff was a member of an identifiable class. He did not, however, use the statement for its intended purpose. He used it as investment advice, rather than for management of the company.

The defendant therefore did not owe a duty of care to the plaintiff.

As a business person, you should be very careful about providing information and advice. Second, if you do not wish to be held liable for your statements, you should clearly disclaim responsibility. Third, you should be careful about relying on statements made by others. While you may be entitled to compensation, your claim may also be rejected for lack of proximity.

Policy

A duty of care will not necessarily exist even if there was reasonable foreseeability and proximity. The court will also ask whether liability should be denied on *policy* grounds. It is often difficult to distinguish the issues of proximity and policy.[15] Broadly speaking, however, proximity deals with the relationship that exists between the parties, whereas policy is concerned with the effect that a duty of care would have on the legal system and on society generally. For example, depending upon the circumstances, a court may ask whether the recognition of a duty of care would:

- "open the floodgates" by encouraging a very large number of people to swamp the courts with lawsuits (that is one reason why the courts are reluctant to recognize a duty of care for negligent statements)[16]

[14.] Financial statements may be relied upon for many reasons by many types of people, including creditors, customers, competitors, and employees.

[15.] Canadian courts previously used a *two-part* test to determine the existence of a duty of care. If they were satisfied that harm was reasonably foreseeable, they asked whether any policy factors prevented a duty of care from arising. Those policy factors included the idea of proximity. As previously explained, the new *three-part* test deals separately with proximity and policy (as well as reasonable foreseeability). It is, however, often difficult to draw that distinction in practice. In Case Brief 6.2 (see page 140), was a duty of care rejected in *Hercules Managements Ltd v Ernst & Young* because the connection between the parties was not close and direct enough (proximity) or because the court was worried about indeterminate liability (policy)? Does it really matter?

[16.] We saw this in Case Brief 6.2 (on page 140).

- interfere with political decisions (that is why a government may be able to escape responsibility for deciding that it could not afford to frequently check a stretch of road for fallen trees)[17]
- hurt a valuable type of relationship (that is one reason why a mother does not owe a duty of care to her unborn child)[18]

Policy considerations may affect the application of the negligence action in a business context. Of course, the basic rules of negligence usually apply regardless of the precise situation. If the defendant becomes drunk and seriously injures the plaintiff while carelessly attempting to dance with them, damages almost certainly will be awarded. It does not matter that the parties are co-workers and that the injury occurs during an event held by their employer.[19] In more unusual circumstances, however, policy may prevent the recognition of a duty of care in a business context.[20] It has been held, for example, that an employee cannot sue an employer in tort for carelessly causing mental distress on the job. The recognition of a duty of care would be "a considerable intrusion . . . into the workplace," it would limit a business's ability to increase efficient production, and it would create a great deal of uncertainty.[21]

DUTY OF CARE AND POLICY: REGULATION OF PROFESSIONS Another excellent example of the importance of policy appears in cases dealing with the *regulation of professions*. Many professions are governed by regulatory bodies. As we saw in Chapter 2, for instance, every jurisdiction in Canada has a Law Society that sets standards, imposes a code of conduct, and punishes members who misbehave. The same is true for accountants, mortgage brokers, stockbrokers, physicians, psychiatrists, dentists, architects, and so on. A difficult question may arise, however, if a person is hurt by a professional's incompetence or dishonesty. It is usually obvious that the professional will be held personally liable. But what if the regulatory body is sued as well? The plaintiff may argue that if that body had done its job properly (for example, by rigorously enforcing its code of conduct and imposing a suspension), the professional would not have been in a position to commit the tort. Case Brief 6.3 illustrates how the courts decide whether or not the regulatory body owes a duty of care.

Case Brief 6.3

Cooper v Hobart (2001) 206 DLR (4th) 193 (SCC)[22]

Like thousands of other people, Mary Cooper invested money in Eron Mortgage Corporation. And like the rest of them, she lost her money as a result of crimes committed by Eron's managers. Cooper sued the Registrar of Mortgages, who was responsible for investigating complaints, freezing funds, and suspending delinquent brokers. She claims that the Registrar negligently allowed Eron to carry on business, even after he knew that Eron was in serious violation of the *Mortgage Brokers Act*. The question for the courts was whether the Registrar owed a duty of care to Mary Cooper.

The Supreme Court of Canada said "no." It was willing to accept that the plaintiff's loss was reasonably foreseeable. However, it denied that there was proximity between the parties. The Registrar's job was to serve

(Continued)

[17.] *Swinamer v Nova Scotia (Attorney General)* (1994) 112 DLR (4th) 18 (SCC).

[18.] We saw this in Ethical Perspective 6.1 (on page 137).

[19.] *Danicek v Alexander Holburn Beaudin & Lang* (2010) 8 BCLR (5th) 316 (BC SC).

[20.] *Design Services Ltd v Canada* (2008) 293 DLR (4th) 437 (SCC).

[21.] *Piresferreira v Ayotte* (2010) 319 DLR (4th) 665 at 683 (Ont CA).

[22.] See also *Edwards v Law Society of Upper Canada* (2001) 206 DLR (4th) 211 (SCC).

(continued)

the general public—not individual investors. His function was to promote integrity and efficiency within the profession—not to protect Mary Cooper's money.

The Court further held that even if there had been a close and direct connection between the parties, policy considerations would have prevented a duty of care from arising. It mentioned several concerns:

- The Registrar fills a largely political and judicial role by creating policies and deciding when to suspend brokers—and the

courts are generally reluctant to interfere with political or judicial decisions.

- Recognition of a duty of care could open the floodgates—aside from Mary Cooper, thousands of other people who lost money on Eron would also sue the Registrar.

- The Registrar is a public official, and if he was held liable, the judgment would actually have to be paid with tax dollars—in effect, taxpayers would have to insure Mary Cooper's investment.

Breach of the Standard of Care

L.O. ❷ ❺ ❻

The first element of the cause of action in negligence requires the plaintiff to prove that the defendant owed a duty of care. The second element requires the plaintiff to prove that the defendant breached the *standard of care*. The **standard of care** tells the defendant how they should act. It is **breached** when the defendant acts less carefully.

The standard of care is based on the **reasonable person test**—the defendant must act in the same way that a reasonable person would act in similar circumstances. The reasonable person is a *fictional character*. One judge provided this description.

> I shall not attempt to formulate a comprehensive definition of "a reasonable man.". . . I simply say that he is a mythical creature of the law whose conduct is the standard by which the Courts measure the conduct of all other persons. . . . He is not an extraordinary or unusual creature; he is not superhuman; he is not required to display the highest skill of which anyone is capable; he is not a genius who can perform uncommon feats, nor is he possessed of unusual powers of foresight. He is a person of normal intelligence who makes prudence a guide to his conduct. He does nothing that a prudent man would not do and he does not omit to do anything that a prudent man would do. He acts in accord with general and approved practice. His conduct is guided by considerations which ordinarily regulate the conduct of human affairs.[23]

The reasonable person test gives the courts a great deal of flexibility in deciding whether the defendant acted carelessly. Although it is impossible to list all of the relevant factors, we can identify some important ones.

- The reasonable person test is said to be *objective*.[24] It does not make allowances for the defendant's *subjective*, or personal, characteristics.

the **standard of care** tells the defendant how they should act

the standard of care is **breached** when the defendant acts less carefully

the **reasonable person test** requires the defendant to act in the same way that a reasonable person would act in similar circumstances

---

[23.] *Arland v Taylor* [1955] 3 DLR 358 (Ont CA) *per* Laidlaw JA.

[24.] By applying an "objective" test, the courts create the appearance of approaching tort law without making value judgments. A judge who is criticized in a particular case might respond by insisting that the decision simply reflected the views of the "reasonable person," rather than a personal political perspective. Feminist scholars, in contrast, have long argued that the "reasonable person" usually bears a striking resemblance to the judges themselves, most of whom continue to be white males from wealthy backgrounds. They further argue that tort law consequently tends to unfairly favour white, affluent males: L Bender "A Lawyer's Primer on Feminist Theory and Tort" (1988) 38 *J of Legal Education* 3. On a deeper level, however, it might be asked whether it is really possible to create an objective reasonable person, or whether judges will always decide disputes according to their own views of right and wrong, reasonable and unreasonable.

For example, I cannot avoid liability by simply proving that I did my best. I may be held liable even though my carelessness was caused by the fact that I suffer from a mental disability.[25] The courts are more concerned with providing compensation to my victims than with showing sympathy for my shortcomings. Nevertheless, judges do lower the standard of care somewhat for children. A child is generally not required to act like a reasonable adult.[26] It is enough to act like a reasonable child of similar age, intelligence, and experience.[27]

- The reasonable person takes precautions against *reasonably foreseeable risks*. Notice that the test does not refer to "probable" or "likely" risks. As long as it is not fanciful, something may be reasonably foreseeable even if it is unlikely to occur. A 1-in-100 or 1-in-1000 chance may be sufficient. At the same time, however, there is no need to take precautions against unforeseeable risks. The reasonable person does not guard against every conceivable danger.

- The reasonable person is influenced by both the *likelihood of harm* and the *potential severity of harm*. Greater care is required if the chance of injury is 90 percent rather than 10 percent. Likewise, greater care is required if the relevant injury is death rather than a light bruise.

- The reasonable person is more likely to adopt *affordable precautions*. For example, a taxi company that regularly carries children should certainly pay $50 for tamper-proof door locks. But it does not have to spend an enormous sum by purchasing the safest vehicles on the market.

- The reasonable person may act in a way that has great *social utility*, even though it creates a risk. For instance, it is sometimes appropriate for an ambulance driver to speed through a red light to save a dying patient.

- The standard of care requires the defendant to act as the reasonable person would act "in similar circumstances." Consequently, less care is required during emergencies. The *sudden peril doctrine* states that even a reasonable person may make a mistake under difficult circumstances.

THE STANDARD OF CARE FOR PROFESSIONALS: PROFESSIONAL NEGLIGENCE

We previously discussed the rules that determine when a *duty of care* will be imposed on a professional. We stressed two particularly important factors: first, the existence of a close *relationship* between the parties, and second, the extent to which the client *relied* upon the professional. We now need to consider the *standard of care* that professionals are expected to meet. The basic rule is the

---

[25.] I might be able to avoid liability, however, if my mental disability was so severe that I effectively had no control over my actions: *Buckley v Smith Transport Ltd* [1946] 4 DLR 721 (Ont CA) (the defendant caused a traffic accident because he believed that his vehicle was being operated by remote control). Likewise, I might be able to avoid liability if I suffer from a severe physical disability. The law does not expect me to see if I am blind. It does, however, require me to recognize my limitations and to avoid dangerous activities, such as driving.

[26.] The rule is different if a child participates in an adult activity, such as driving a boat.

[27.] *McEllistrum v Etches* (1956) 6 DLR (2d) 1 (SCC). There are relatively few cases in this area, largely because there is seldom anything to be gained from suing a child. Furthermore, parents are not *vicariously liable* for their children's torts. That is true even under "parental responsibility" legislation: *Parental Responsibility Act*, CCSM, c P-8 (Man); *Parental Responsibility Act 2000*, SO 2000, c 4 (Ont); *Parental Responsibility Act*, SBC 2001, c 45 (BC). Parents may, however, be held personally liable for failing to properly supervise their children.

same as always: A professional must act as a reasonable person would act in similar circumstances. The courts do, however, pay special attention to five factors when they are dealing with professionals.

First, it is not enough for a professional person, while engaged in a professional activity, to meet the standard that would be applied if a layperson performed the same task. A professional must act as the *reasonable professional* would act in similar circumstances.

- Professional people must live up to the training that they received or claim to have received. The last part of that sentence is important: If people claim to have special expertise, they cannot avoid liability by later confessing that they lied about their qualifications.

- Even within the same profession, more may be expected of a specialist than of a generalist. For example, an accountant who specializes in a particular type of transaction must perform to a higher level when acting within that area than an accountant who does not claim to have the same expertise.

- Special allowances are *not* made for beginners. Even an inexperienced professional must conform to the standard of a reasonably competent and experienced professional.

Those rules are based on the reasonable expectations that people have about professionals.

Second, by the time a case gets to trial, it is often easy to say what the defendant could have done to avoid injuring the plaintiff. It would be unfair, however, to judge the defendant's actions in *hindsight*. That is especially significant in scientific or technical fields, where knowledge often develops very quickly. The standard of care is therefore based on information that was reasonably available to the defendant at the time of the accident.[28]

Third, carelessness is different from mere *errors of judgment*. The former can result in liability; the latter cannot. A professional does not have to be perfect. As long as the defendant's mistake is one that a reasonable professional might make, the standard of care is not breached. For example, a surgeon will not be held liable for incorrectly choosing one procedure over another if a reasonable physician might have done the same.

Fourth, a professional who follows an *approved practice* generally cannot be held liable. Consequently, the standard of care is usually met if the defendant either complies with requirements established by a professional organization or follows the same procedures that are used by other members of the profession. But sometimes, an approved practice is itself careless. A court will reach that conclusion, however, only if the relevant activity can be judged by common sense and does not involve technical or complex matters. As the Supreme Court of Canada explained:

> [C]ourts do not ordinarily have the expertise to tell professionals that they are not behaving appropriately in their field. . . . As a general rule, where a procedure involves difficult or uncertain questions of medical treatment or complex, scientific or highly technical matters that are beyond the ordinary experience and understanding of a judge or jury, it will not be open to find a standard medical practice negligent. On the other hand, as an exception to the general rule, if a standard practice fails to adopt obvious and reasonable precautions which are readily apparent to the

---

[28.] *Walker Estate v York Finch General Hospital* (2001) 198 DLR (4th) 193 (SCC).

ordinary finder of fact, then it is no excuse for a practitioner to claim that he or she was merely conforming to such a negligent common practice.[29]

Fifth, just as compliance with a professional standard usually protects a professional from liability, so too compliance with a *statutory standard* may protect a defendant. The issue of *breach of a statutory duty* actually extends beyond the context of professional negligence. In fact, the leading case arose after the Saskatchewan Wheat Pool violated the *Canada Grain Act* by delivering beetle-infested wheat to the Canadian Wheat Board.[30] When the Wheat Board sued to recover the cost of fumigating the grain, the Supreme Court of Canada held that breach of a statutory duty *may*—not *must*—provide evidence that the standard of care in negligence was not met.[31] And on the facts, the court decided that, even though the statute had been broken, the defendant had acted with reasonable care in delivering the grain and therefore was not liable. The same analysis often applies in connection with professionals.[32] Breach of a statutory duty is merely one factor that a judge will consider in deciding whether a professional acted with reasonable care.

THE STANDARD OF CARE FOR MANUFACTURED PRODUCTS: PRODUCT LIABILITY

product liability can occur when a person is injured by a product

Like professional negligence, the topic of *product liability* falls within the general action in negligence. However, it also requires special attention. **Product liability** can occur when a person is injured by a product. As we will see in Chapter 11, it may be possible to sue for breach of contract if the victim was the person who actually bought the item. (And, as we will see in Chapter 13, that action for breach of contract may be made even easier by the *Sale of Goods Act*.) Liability for breach of contract is *strict*. The plaintiff does not have to prove that the defendant *carelessly* provided a defective product. It is enough that the contract was defective in a way that caused harm.

Sometimes, however, the parties are not linked together by a contract. In *Donoghue v Stevenson* (Case Brief 6.1 on page 137), for example, the defective bottle of ginger beer was purchased for the plaintiff by her friend. Mrs Donoghue therefore had to sue for the tort of negligence. And, as always, that tort required Mrs Donoghue to prove that her injury was caused by the manufacturer's *carelessness*. That rule continues to apply in Canada: Tortious liability for defective products is *not* strict.[33] The situation is different in the United States. The American law of product liability *is* strict. The plaintiff does not have to prove that the defendant was careless. It is enough to show that a defective product caused an injury. Some people believe that Canadian law should similarly adopt strict liability. Such a rule would (i) better ensure that

---

[29.] *ter Neuzen v Korn* (1995) 127 DLR (4th) 577 (SCC).

[30.] *R v Saskatchewan Wheat Pool* (1983) 143 DLR (3d) 9 (SCC). See also *Galaske v O'Donnell* (1994) 112 DLR (4th) 109 (SCC).

[31.] In contrast, most American courts say that a statutory duty creates the standard of care for the purposes of negligence, so that a breach of the statute provides proof of the defendant's carelessness.

[32.] *Varcoe v Sterling* (1992) 7 OR (3d) 204 (Gen Div), aff'd (1992) 10 OR (3d) 574 (CA).

[33.] SM Waddams *Product Liability* (2001) c 11. Several Canadian statutes introduce elements of strict liability, but do not create a general rule that allows a person who is injured by a defective product to claim damages without proving negligence: *Consumer Protection Act*, SS 1996, c C-30.1, s 64 (Sask); *Consumer Product Warranty and Liability Act*, SNB 1978, c C-18.1, s 27 (NB). As we will see in Chapter 13, consumers are also protected by the *Sale of Goods Act*.

consumers are compensated for injuries that are caused by defective products, (ii) encourage manufacturers to develop safer products, and (iii) require manufacturers to pay for the losses that they cause as a result of selling their products and earning their profits. On the other hand, there are concerns that a rule of strict liability would (i) unfairly require a manufacturer to pay for an injury even though it had used reasonable care, (ii) increase the number of lawsuits against manufacturers, (iii) increase the cost of liability insurance for manufacturers, and (iv) eventually increase the cost of products. Which approach do you prefer?

Under current Canadian law, a person who wants to sue in tort for product liability must use the action in negligence. The courts almost always find that a duty of care was owed to a person who was injured by a defective product, whether that person was the purchaser, a consumer, or simply a bystander. It is reasonably foreseeable that a defective product may hurt someone; there is sufficiently close proximity between the manufacturer and the victim; and there are no policy reasons for generally denying relief. Liability therefore usually turns on the standard of care. We divide that discussion into three parts:

- manufacture
- design
- failure to warn

Manufacture

The courts usually impose liability if the defendant carelessly *manufactured* a product that injured the plaintiff. *Donoghue v Stevenson*, which we discussed in Case Brief 6.1, is the classic case. Mr Stevenson was required to compensate Mrs Donoghue because he negligently allowed a snail to crawl into a bottle of ginger beer that he manufactured.

Design

The courts are more cautious if the plaintiff's injury was caused by the *design*, rather than the *manufacture*, of a product. A manufacturing defect usually affects only a few items. Not every bottle of Mr Stevenson's ginger beer contained a decomposed snail. A design defect, in contrast, usually affects every item that is produced. For instance, if a system of headlights is poorly designed, *every* vehicle that uses that system will create a danger. The courts are therefore more concerned about imposing a tremendous burden on the defendant. In the headlights case, the judge demanded proof that the product's disadvantages outweighed its advantages.[34] He carefully balanced the probability and severity of harm against the difficulty and expense of using an alternative design.

Failure to Warn

Even if a product is carefully designed and manufactured, liability may arise if consumers are not reasonably *warned* about its dangers. For instance, ladders should carry stickers that caution people against using them on slippery surfaces, just as some electrical appliances should alert people to the risk of electrocution in water. Several more points should be noted.

[34.] *Rentway Canada Ltd v Laidlaw Transport Ltd* (1989) 49 CCLT 150 (Ont HCJ).

- The nature and extent of the warning depends upon the circumstances. Greater care is required if the danger is severe or if the consumers are unsophisticated. Less care is required if the risk is marginal or if the product is invariably sold to professionals who are specially trained to use it. And no warning at all is required if a danger is obvious. People are assumed to know that knives cut and matches burn.

- A warning is usually needed only for a product's intended use. Sometimes, however, a warning may be required for a use that is unintended, but foreseeable. Glue is not meant to be sniffed, but manufacturers realize that their product is often abused.

- A warning may be required even though the manufacturer discovers the danger *after* the product has been sold. In that situation, it should take reasonable steps to contact consumers and, if necessary, recall the dangerous items.

- A warning may be required not only by a manufacturer, but also by someone who sells, distributes, or installs a product. The key question is whether the particular person knew, or should have known, of the danger.

- In some situations, the defendant can avoid liability if they provided a warning to a *learned intermediary*. The law in this area is complicated. For our purposes, it is enough to know that the rule may apply if a product is always sold to a professional rather than directly to the intended consumer. Breast implants, for instance, are not bought off store shelves. They are supplied to physicians, who then insert them into patients. If a manufacturer does not warn a doctor, it may be held liable if the implants later rupture inside a woman.[35]

Claims for product liability often raise difficult issues of personal responsibility. A consumer may use a product that is obviously dangerous, but then expect the manufacturer to provide compensation when something goes wrong. Ethical Perspective 6.2 raises some tough questions about tobacco litigation.

Ethical Perspective **6.2**

Tobacco Litigation

Tobacco is big business in Canada. The three major tobacco companies annually earn profits of approximately $4 billion. Few products, however, are more controversial. Although there is some disagreement on the statistics, one commonly cited figure states that tobacco products kill 45 000 Canadians every year.

Not surprisingly, the tobacco industry has increasingly become the subject of litigation. And perhaps predictably, Americans have led the way. In 1998, the major tobacco companies entered into a settlement with 46 states. In addition to accepting new advertising restrictions, the tobacco industry agreed to pay $25 billion over the course of a quarter century. That money will be used to reimburse the state governments for the financial burden that tobacco products place upon the health care system. Tobacco companies have also been sued in tort law by private individuals. In one case, non-smoking flight attendants received $300 million after contracting diseases caused by inhaling second-hand smoke during flights. And in a third line of cases, liability has stretched beyond the cigarette companies. An asthmatic corrections officer won $300 000 after his employer failed to provide a smoke-free work environment; a court declared that it was "cruel and unusual punishment" to expose a prisoner to a smoke-filled jail; and a tenant was entitled to withhold rent as long as his landlord allowed smoke to seep into his apartment from a downstairs nightclub.

That trend has begun to move north into this country. British Columbia has enacted legislation that allows the province to sue

(Continued)

---
35. *Hollis v Dow Corning Corp* (1995) 129 DLR (4th) 609 (SCC).

(continued)

tobacco companies for the expenses that they generate for the health care system.[36] Within the context of private litigation, a court in that same province recently certified a class action against cigarette companies.[37] That class action claims that the companies fraudulently misled consumers by suggesting that "light" cigarettes were somehow less harmful than regular cigarettes. The plaintiffs are not asking to be compensated for their own losses. Instead, as in the American case that won $25 billion, the Canadian claimants are demanding that the tobacco companies disgorge (give up) the profits that they earned by deceiving the public.[38]

Canadian courts will eventually be required to decide whether or not tobacco companies should be held liable in tort law for manufacturing products that cause disease and death. Consider a typical case. Carey, a 45-year-old Canadian, is dying of lung cancer. The medical evidence strongly suggests that his condition was caused by smoking. He began smoking when he was 15, as a result of peer pressure and the attractive images (such as the Marlboro Man) that tobacco companies used to promote their products. Carey had heard the health warnings but did not pay any attention to them at first. By the time he reached his early 20s, and fully appreciated the potential effects of smoking, he had become addicted and was unable to kick his habit. He now insists that the company that manufactured his brand of cigarettes should be held liable for his illness and impending death. The defendant responds with two arguments. First, they deny that there is any connection between cigarettes and poor health. And second, they say that since Carey knew about the risks allegedly associated with cigarettes when he began smoking, he must accept responsibility for his own behaviour.

Questions for Discussion

1. How should tort law strike a balance between Carey's claim that he has been injured by the company's products and the company's claim that Carey should have to live with the consequences of his own lifestyle?

2. We will consider the defences of contributory negligence and voluntary assumption of risk at the end of this chapter. Would either of those defences apply in this case? Have the Canadian courts formulated those defences too narrowly?

3. Assuming that Carey sues in the tort of negligence, how should he phrase his specific allegation? What exactly did the cigarette company do wrong? Were the cigarettes carelessly manufactured or carelessly designed? If so, is there something that the cigarette company could have done to produce a safe product? Or did the company fail to issue an adequate warning? If so, is there any reason to believe that a more explicit warning would have prevented Carey from smoking? (Indeed, given the fact that people continue to smoke despite the gruesome appearance of cigarette packages today, is it reasonable to believe that warnings are really effective?)

4. Carey has a health condition that requires treatment. Who should pay for that treatment? Should you and I, as taxpayers, be required to provide care to people who are hurt by the tobacco companies' dangerous products? Or should the legal system find a way of imposing those costs on the tobacco industry? In that respect, are cigarettes significantly different from other unhealthy products? What about alcohol, fast foods, and chocolate? What about other products that obviously create health risks, such as motorcycles and skateboards?

Causation of Harm

L.O. ❷ ❼

The third element of the claim in negligence is *causation of harm*. Even if they owed a duty of care and breached the standard of care, the defendant will not be held liable unless their carelessness caused the plaintiff to suffer a loss.[39] Although causation can be a difficult issue, we will highlight only the basic principles. The reason is simple. From a risk-management perspective, much can be done to avoid liability under the first two stages of the negligence action. But once a business has come under a duty of care and has acted carelessly,

---

[36] *Tobacco Damages and Health Care Costs Recovery Act*, SBC 2000, c 30 (BC); *Tobacco Damages and Health Care Costs Recovery Act*, SO 2009, c 13 (Ont); *Tobacco Damages and Health Care Costs Recovery Act*, SNB 2006, c T-75 (NB) . The validity of that legislation was upheld by the British Columbia Court of Appeal: *British Columbia v Imperial Tobacco Canada Ltd* (2004) 239 DLR (4th) 412 (BC CA), and the Supreme Court of Canada (2005) 257 DLR (4th) 193 (SCC). See also *Ontario v Rothmans Inc* 2011 ONSC 5356 (Ont SCJ); *New Brunswick v Rothmans Inc* (2010) 373 NBR (2d) 157 (NB QB).

[37] *Knight v Imperial Tobacco Canada Ltd* (2005) 250 DLR (4th) 357 (BC SC). The action is based on the *Trade Practice Act*, RSBC 1996, c 457, rather than the tort of negligence.

[38] Disgorgement is the opposite of compensation. Compensation is measured by the plaintiff's wrongful loss. Disgorgement is measured by the defendant's wrongful gain.

[39] As we have already seen, that loss may take many forms. The plaintiff may suffer a physical injury, property damage, or a pure economic loss.

the **but-for test** requires the plaintiff to prove that they would not have suffered a loss but for the defendant's carelessness

there is relatively little that it can do to avoid causing harm. As a matter of luck, its carelessness either will or will not hurt somebody.

The issue of causation is usually decided by the *but-for test*. The **but-for test** requires the plaintiff to prove that they would not have suffered a loss but for the defendant's carelessness. It is based on a simple question: "If the defendant had not acted carelessly, would the plaintiff have still suffered the same loss?" If the answer is "yes," the defendant cannot be held liable. If the answer is "no," the defendant may be held liable. To better understand that test, consider Concept Summary 6.1 and answer the questions in You Be the Judge 6.1.

Concept Summary 6.1

The But-For Test

Question	Answer	Result in Fact	Result in Law
But for the defendant's carelessness, would the plaintiff have suffered the same loss?	Yes—the plaintiff would have suffered the same loss even if the defendant had not acted carelessly.	The defendant did *not* cause the plaintiff's loss.	The defendant *cannot* be held liable.
	No—the plaintiff would not have suffered the same loss if the defendant had not acted carelessly.	The defendant *did* cause the plaintiff's loss.	The defendant *may* be held liable.

You Be the Judge 6.1

The But-For Test[40]

A man went to a hospital complaining of stomach pain. The doctor on duty believed that there was nothing seriously wrong with the patient and simply told him to go home and sleep. The man later died of arsenic poisoning. His widow has shown that the doctor (i) owed a duty of care to her husband, and (ii) carelessly failed to realize that her husband's stomach pains were due to arsenic poisoning.

Questions for Discussion

1. Will the doctor be held liable if the evidence indicates that the man would have lived but for the doctor's carelessness?

2. Will the doctor be held liable if the evidence indicates that the man's arsenic poisoning was so serious that he could not have been saved even if he had been properly diagnosed?

There are several other things to note about causation of harm. First, as we saw in Chapter 2, the plaintiff generally has to prove all of the elements of the tort of negligence, including causation, on a *balance of probabilities*.

Second, the law generally adopts an *all-or-nothing* approach. If there is at least a 51 percent chance that the defendant's carelessness caused the plaintiff's loss, then the court will award damages for *all* of that loss. In contrast, if there is less than a 51 percent chance that the defendant's carelessness caused the plaintiff's injury, then the court will not award damages for *any* of that loss.

---

40. *Barnett v Chelsea & Kensington Hospital Mgmt Committee* [1969] 1 QB 428.

Third, the plaintiff has to prove only that the defendant's carelessness was *a cause*—not necessarily *the only cause*—of a loss. Suppose my back pain was caused mostly by poor posture but partly by the fact that you pushed me off my bike. I may be entitled to receive 100 percent of my damages from you.[41]

Fourth, if *different defendant*s cause the plaintiff to suffer *different injuries*, then each one is responsible accordingly. For example, if you break my arm and Mary breaks my leg, you can be held liable only for my arm and she can be held liable only for my leg.

Fifth, the situation is more complicated if *different defendants* create a *single injury*. Suppose you slip on my neighbour's sidewalk after leaving my party. You lost your balance and fell only because (i) I secretly drugged your drinks, *and* (ii) my neighbour, Shannon, failed to shovel her sidewalk. Shannon and I will be held *jointly and severally liable*.[42] That means that you can recover all of your damages from her, *or* all of your damages from me, *or* some of your damages from each of us. The choice is yours, because Shannon and I are responsible in proportion to our share of the blame. Suppose the court said that Shannon was 30 percent to blame and that I was 70 percent to blame. If you recovered all of your damages from Shannon, she could demand 70 percent of that money from me.

Sixth, a court may reject the but-for test if it would lead to an unfair result. Suppose you and I went hunting with Akbar. When you made a rustling sound in a bush, he and I both turned and shot because we carelessly mistook you for a deer. You were hit by a single bullet, but you have no way of knowing whose. The but-for test seems to suggest that neither Akbar nor I will be held liable. You cannot prove on a balance of probabilities (that is, at least 51 percent) that he fired the relevant shot. Nor can you prove on a balance of probabilities (that is, at least 51 percent) that I fired the relevant shot. For each of us, there is only a 50 percent chance. A court, however, would probably hold both of us liable and allow you to recover all of your damages from either one or both.[43]

REMOTENESS

Even if the defendant caused the plaintiff to suffer a loss, liability will not be imposed if that loss was too *remote* from the careless conduct. A loss is **remote** if it would be unfair to hold the defendant responsible for it. We already examined that concept in connection with intentional torts in Chapter 4. We can now add a few more points.

a loss is **remote** if it would be unfair to hold the defendant responsible for it

In negligence, the basic issue is whether the *type of harm* that the plaintiff suffered was a *reasonably foreseeable* result of the defendant's carelessness. As always, the phrase "reasonably foreseeable" does not mean "probable" or "likely." It simply refers to a possibility that is not far-fetched. Furthermore, if the *type of harm* that the plaintiff suffered was reasonably foreseeable, it is irrelevant that the *manner in which it occurred* was not. To understand that distinction, consider Case Brief 6.4.

[41.] *Athey v Leonati* (1996) 140 DLR (4th) 235 (SCC).

[42.] "Joint" liability means that all of the defendants are liable for the same tort. "Several" liability means each defendant is individually liable to the plaintiff for the entire amount. "Joint and several" liability therefore means that while all of the defendants are liable for the tort, the plaintiff is entitled to decide which of the defendants they will collect from.

[43.] *Cook v Lewis* [1952] 1 DLR 1 (SCC); *Clements v Clements* 2012 SCC 32.

Case Brief 6.4

Hughes v Lord Advocate [1963] AC 837 (HL)

The defendant's employees had been working in a manhole. They left the cover off the manhole when they went for lunch. They also left a paraffin lamp nearby. A young boy crawled down the manhole with the lamp. He was badly burned when the lamp fell and exploded.

The explosion occurred because vapours escaped from the lamp and were ignited by the flame. The court held that the series of events was entirely unforeseeable. It nevertheless imposed liability because the *type* of injury that the plaintiff suffered, a burn, was reasonably foreseeable. It did not matter that the source of that burn was a bizarre accident rather than direct contact with the lamp's flame, as might have been expected.

---

a **thin skull** case occurs if the plaintiff was unusually vulnerable to injury

The remoteness principle is used to resolve *thin skull* cases. A **thin skull** case occurs if the plaintiff was unusually vulnerable to injury. In a literal example, suppose I am injury-prone because my skull is very thin. If you carelessly hit me on the head with a stick, are you responsible for all of my losses? What if a normal person would not have suffered any injury? What if a normal person would have suffered a minor injury, but not one as serious as mine? The law tries to strike a balance between its desire to compensate me and its desire to treat you fairly. You are *not* responsible at all if a normal person would not have suffered *any* harm. But you are fully responsible for *all* of my losses if it was *reasonably foreseeable* that a normal person would have suffered *some* damage.[44] For instance, if your carelessness would have bruised a normal person, I can fully recover for the fact that I also suffered brain damage.[45]

Significantly for business people, the courts traditionally refused to apply a *thin wallet* principle. The defendant was not responsible for the fact that the plaintiff suffered to an unusual extent because the victim was poor. More recently, however, the courts have begun to suggest that the defendant may be fully liable if it was reasonably foreseeable that the plaintiff's poverty would cause them to suffer more than usual.[46] Business Decision 6.2 explores those issues (see p. 153).

an **intervening act** is an event that occurs *after* the defendant's carelessness and that causes the plaintiff to suffer an additional injury

The remoteness principle is also used to deal with *intervening acts*. An **intervening act** is an event that occurs *after* the defendant's carelessness and that causes the plaintiff to suffer an additional injury. Suppose you carelessly broke my leg. A week later, I suffered another injury, either because I fell while walking down stairs on crutches or because I was hit by lightning in my physician's parking lot. In either event, you are *factually responsible* for my second injury. But for your initial negligence, I would not have been using crutches, nor would I have been visiting my physician. The crucial question, however, is whether you are *legally responsible*. In light of the intervening act, is my second injury too *remote* from your carelessness? A judge would ask if it was reasonably

---

[44.] The same principles could apply, for example, if I drive a type of vehicle that is unusually vulnerable to damage in an accident: *Oke v Weide Transport Ltd* (1963) 41 DLR (2d) 53 (Man CA).

[45.] While the thin skull doctrine may hold the defendant fully liable for the plaintiff's injury, damages are reduced if the plaintiff's skull was not only thin but also *crumbling*. In other words, the plaintiff is denied compensation to the extent that his condition was so fragile that he eventually would have suffered the same injury, even without the defendant's carelessness. In that situation, the defendant merely caused the plaintiff's injury to happen sooner than expected. Damages are therefore available only for the period leading up to the time when the plaintiff would have suffered the loss in any event.

[46.] *Alcoa Minerals of Jamaica v Broderick* [2000] 3 WLR 23 (PC); *Lagden v O'Connor* [2004] 1 AC 1067 (HL). A leading Canadian textbook ignores those cases and still supports the traditional rule on the basis that "a thin pocketbook is less worthy of protection than a thin skull": A Linden & B Feldthusen *Canadian Tort Law* 8th ed (2006) 385.

Business Decision 6.2

Remoteness and Thin Wallets[47]

You had a contract with Acme Goods Ltd to carry several loads of timber between Vancouver and Halifax. Unfortunately, Darva carelessly caused an accident that destroyed your truck. You therefore needed to use another vehicle to fulfill your agreement with Acme. The purchase price for a replacement was $100 000, but you were unable to buy one because you did not have immediate access to that much money and because your credit rating is very poor. Consequently, you were forced to lease a truck. You were able to afford that option because you could periodically meet the rental charge after being paid for each delivery of timber. That option, however, eventually cost you $150 000, which is $50 000 more than the purchase price of a truck.

Assuming that Darva is liable in negligence, you are entitled to compensation for your loss. However, you might recover only $100 000, rather than $150 000. Even though the loss of your truck was reasonably foreseeable, a court might say that Darva is not responsible for the fact that you suffered to an unusual extent because of your own financial problems.

Questions for Discussion

1. Would it be fair if the court rejected the thin wallet principle in your case? Explain your answer.

2. The courts have historically accepted the thin skull principle but rejected the thin wallet principle. What does that contrast say about the law's attitude toward personal injuries on the one hand and economic losses on the other? Which sort of harm is considered more important?

foreseeable that your initial carelessness would cause my later injury. As usual, that test may be flexible enough to allow a judge to decide my case on policy grounds. As a general rule, however, liability will be imposed if your original negligence *increased the risk* of my subsequent injury. By causing me to use crutches, you made it more likely that I would fall, but you did not increase my chance of being struck by lightning.

Defences

L.O. ❽ ❾ ❿

The plaintiff is usually entitled to compensatory damages once the court is satisfied that there was (i) a duty of care, (ii) a breach of the standard of care, and (iii) a causation of harm. Occasionally, however, the defendant can avoid liability, at least in part, by proving a defence. We will briefly consider the three most important defences:

- contributory negligence
- voluntary assumption of risk
- illegality

Concept Summary 6.2 introduces the essential elements of each defence.

Concept Summary 6.2

Defences to Negligence

Defence	Basis	Effect
Contributory negligence	loss is caused partly by the defendant's carelessness and partly by the plaintiff's carelessness	apportionment—damages reduced to extent of contributory negligence
Voluntary assumption of risk	plaintiff freely agreed to accept the factual and legal risk of injury	complete—defendant not liable
Illegality	plaintiff suffered a loss while participating in an illegal act	complete—defendant not liable

---

[47.] *The Dredger Liesbosch v SS Edison* [1933] AC 449 (HL).

CONTRIBUTORY NEGLIGENCE

the defence of **contributory negligence** occurs when a loss is caused partly by the defendant's carelessness and partly by the plaintiff's own carelessness

The most important defence is *contributory negligence*. **Contributory negligence** occurs when a loss is caused partly by the defendant's carelessness and partly by the plaintiff's own carelessness. In deciding whether the plaintiff is guilty of contributory negligence, the courts generally consider the same factors that they use when deciding whether the defendant breached the standard of care: foreseeability of harm, likelihood of injury, severity of harm, and so on. The cases tend to fall into three groups. Contributory negligence may arise if the plaintiff:

- unreasonably steps into a dangerous situation (as when a sober person accepts a ride from a drunk driver, who then drives into a wall)
- unreasonably contributes to the creation of an accident (as when a passenger in the back of an open bed truck is thrown to the ground after carelessly standing while the driver turned a corner too quickly)
- unreasonably contributes not to the creation of an accident, but to the damage that it causes (as when a passenger in a carelessly driven car suffers unusually severe head injuries after refusing to wear a seatbelt)

Contributory negligence was traditionally a complete defence. If it applied, the plaintiff could not recover *any* damages. That rule was often unfair. The plaintiff could be denied compensation even though the defendant was mostly responsible for causing the injury. Consequently, modern legislation allows for *apportionment*.[48] A court can assign responsibility for the plaintiff's loss between the parties and award damages appropriately. Suppose you broke your wrist and suffered $10 000 in damages after falling over a package that I carelessly dropped onto the sidewalk. The evidence indicates that you were 25 percent responsible because you did not watch where you were going. A judge could reduce your damages by 25 percent and require me to pay only $7500.

Although judges can apportion the blame between the parties in whatever way is appropriate, they usually place contributory negligence at less than 30 percent. A court is normally reluctant to further reduce the amount of compensation that is available to the plaintiff, especially since the defendant often has liability insurance.

VOLUNTARY ASSUMPTION OF RISK

the defence of **voluntary assumption of risk** applies if the plaintiff freely agreed to accept a risk of injury

The defence of **voluntary assumption of risk** applies if the plaintiff freely agreed to accept a risk of injury. Unlike contributory negligence, *volenti*, as it is sometimes called, remains a complete defence. If it applies, the plaintiff cannot recover *any* damages. The courts therefore interpret it very narrowly. The defendant has to prove that the plaintiff expressly or implicitly agreed to accept both the physical *and* the legal risk of injury. The last part of that test is not satisfied unless the plaintiff agreed to give up the right to sue the defendant for negligence. Consequently, that defence rarely succeeds.[49]

---

[48] *Contributory Negligence Act*, RSA 2000, c C-27 (Alta); *Negligence Act*, RSBC 1996, c 333 (BC); *Tortfeasors and Contributory Negligence Act*, CCSM, c T90 (Man); *Contributory Negligence Act*, RSNL 1990, c C-33 (Nfld); *Contributory Negligence Act*, RSNB 1973, c C-19 (NB); *Contributory Negligence Act*, RSNS 1989, c 95 (NS); *Contributory Negligence Act*, RSNWT 1988, c C-18 (NWT and Nun); *Negligence Act*, RSO 1990, c N.1 (Ont); *Contributory Negligence Act*, RSPEI 1988, c C-21 (PEI); *Contributory Negligence Act*, RSS 1978, c C-31 (Sask); *Contributory Negligence Act*, RSY 2002, c 42 (Yuk).

[49] *Dubé v Labor* (1986) 27 DLR (4th) 653 (SCC).

Although it is quite narrow, the defence is an important tool for risk management. The best way of proving the voluntary assumption of risk is to show that the plaintiff signed an *exclusion clause*. We will examine exclusion clauses in more detail in Chapter 9. The most important point for now is that they must be drawn to a customer's attention. Case Brief 6.5 demonstrates that fact.

Case Brief 6.5

Crocker v Sundance Northwest Resorts Ltd (1988) 51 DLR (4th) 321 (SCC)

The defendant organized an event in which contestants raced down a snow-covered mountain on inner tubes. Before being allowed to compete, the plaintiff was presented with a form that released the defendant from liability for negligence. Although the plaintiff signed that document, he had not read it, nor had it been explained to him. He was later injured after being thrown from his tube during the race. He sued the defendant on the basis that it carelessly allowed him to compete even though he was obviously very drunk. The defendant responded by pleading the *volenti* defence.

The Supreme Court of Canada held that the plaintiff had not voluntarily assumed the risk of injury.

[T]he waiver provision in the entry form was not drawn to the plaintiff's attention... he had not read it, and, indeed, did not know of its existence. He thought he was simply signing an entry form. In these circumstances [the defendant] cannot rely upon the waiver clause in the entry form.

The Court did, however, reduce the plaintiff's damages by 25 percent to reflect his own contributory negligence.

ILLEGALITY

The defence of **illegality** may apply if the plaintiff suffered a loss while participating in an illegal act. Like voluntary assumption of risk, however, illegality is unpopular with the courts because it is a complete defence. It does not allow for the apportionment of liability. The courts have therefore interpreted it very narrowly. Case Brief 6.6 considers the leading case on the defence of illegality. Notice, however, that the facts raised the issues of contributory negligence and voluntary assumption of risk as well. That often is true.[50]

the defence of **illegality** may apply if the plaintiff suffered a loss while participating in an illegal act

Case Brief 6.6

Hall v Hebert (1993) 101 DLR (4th) 129 (SCC)[51]

The plaintiff and the defendant went out for a night of drinking and driving. The defendant stalled his car and allowed the plaintiff to try to start it. The plaintiff lost control of the vehicle, drove it off a steep embankment, and suffered serious injuries. He claimed that the defendant was negligent in allowing him to drive while drunk. In response, the defendant pointed to the fact that the plaintiff was injured while he was drunk driving, and argued the defences of contributory negligence, voluntary assumption of risk, and illegality.

Only the first defence was successful. The Supreme Court of Canada reduced the plaintiff's damages by 50 percent to reflect his own contributory negligence. With respect to the *volenti* defence, the court

once again said that the plaintiff "must not only consent to accept the risk of harm but also must bargain away his or her right to sue for injuries that may result from the dangerous activity." On the facts, however, there was no evidence of any such agreement between the parties.

The Court also rejected the illegality defence on the facts. It held that that defence applies only when the plaintiff attempts to use the tort system in a way that would undermine the integrity of the law. And that occurs only if the plaintiff tries to either profit from their illegal act or avoid a criminal penalty. The defence does not apply if, as in *Hall v Hebert*, the plaintiff merely seeks compensation for the injuries that were caused by the defendant's negligence.

---

50. See also *British Columbia v Zastowny* (2008) 290 DLR (4th) 219 (SCC).
51. See also *British Columbia v Zastowny* (2008) 290 DLR (4th) 219 (SCC).

Chapter Summary

Negligence is the most important tort. It requires proof of three elements: (i) a duty of care, (ii) a breach of the standard of care, and (iii) the causation of harm.

A duty of care requires the defendant to use reasonable care to avoid injuring the plaintiff. A duty will be imposed if (i) it was reasonably foreseeable that the defendant's carelessness might hurt the plaintiff, (ii) there was proximity between the parties, and (iii) there are no compelling policy reasons for refusing to impose a duty.

The defendant cannot be held liable unless they breached the standard of care, which is based on the reasonable person test. A court must ask whether the defendant acted as a reasonable person would have acted in similar circumstances. That test is flexible and allows the courts to consider all of the circumstances of a case. Judges use special considerations in applying the standard of care in a case of professional negligence or product liability.

The defendant cannot be held liable unless their carelessness caused the plaintiff to suffer a loss. Causation is usually decided by the but-for test. Causation normally has to be established on a balance of probabilities, but once it is, the courts generally adopt an all-or-nothing approach to the issue of liability. The plaintiff merely has to prove that the defendant's carelessness was a cause of a loss. If two or more defendants combine to inflict a single injury on the plaintiff, they may be held jointly and severally liable. Even if the defendant caused the plaintiff to suffer a loss, liability will not be imposed if that loss was too remote from the breach of the standard of care. The remoteness principle is used to resolve cases involving thin skulls and intervening acts.

Even if the plaintiff proves duty, breach, and causation, the court may limit or deny liability if the defendant establishes a defence. Damages may be reduced if the plaintiff was guilty of contributory negligence. Damages may be denied entirely if the plaintiff either voluntarily assumed the risk of injury or was engaged in an illegal activity at the time of the accident. The last two defences, however, are interpreted very narrowly by the courts.

MyBusLawLab   ADDITIONAL RESOURCES FOR CHAPTER 6

MyBusLawLab provides students with an assortment of tools to help enrich the learning experience, including a Study Plan with Pre- and Post-tests, mini-cases with assessments, and provincial content material, which provides links to relevant cases, legislation, and additional resources.

MyBusLawLab provides the following resources for Chapter 6:

Provincial Material

- **British Columbia:** Good Samaritans, Contributory Negligence, Parental Liability, *Apology Act,* The Law Society of British Columbia, Self-Regulating Professional Bodies
- **Alberta:** *Charitable Donation of Food Act,* Contributory Negligence, *Emergency Medical Aid Act, Fatal Accidents Amendment Act (2010), Maternal Tort Liability Act,* Professional Liability, Professional Liability Insurance, *Podiatrists Act*
- **Manitoba and Saskatchewan:** Contributory Negligence, Codes of Professional Conduct, Negligent Misrepresentation
- **Ontario:** Causation, Codes of Conduct, Conflict of Interest, Contributory Negligence, Disclaimers, Duty of Care, Fiduciary Duty, Lawyers, Multi-disciplinary Partnerships, Parental Liability, Private Investigators and Security Guards, Professional Discipline, Professional Organizations, Reverse Onus
- **Atlantic Provinces:** Contributory Negligence

Review Questions

1. Although tort law is generally concerned with striking a balance between the desire to provide compensation and the desire to protect socially useful activities from liability, that issue is particularly important in the context of the tort of negligence. Why?

2. How will a court decide whether or not a duty of care will exist in a particular case?

3. Does the duty of care analysis differ if the plaintiff complains about psychiatric injuries rather than physical injuries? Explain your answer.

4. "The tort of negligence normally is not available if an employee wants to complain that they suffered mental distress as a result of an employer's carelessness." Is that statement true? Explain your answer. At which stage of the negligence analysis would a court resolve that issue?

5. Explain the concept of reasonable foreseeability. How is that concept related to the issue of risk management? At which stage(s) of the negligence analysis does the concept arise?

6. "The standard of care requires everyone to act like a reasonable adult would act. That rule may seem harsh when it is applied to a child. The rule is acceptable, however, because it allows the victim of a child's tort to recover damages from the child's parents. Once a child is held liable, the child's parents can be held vicariously liable." Are those statements true? Explain your answer.

7. Summarize the factors that a judge considers in deciding whether the defendant breached the standard of care.

8. Will a court find that professionals breached the standard of care if they complied with an approved practice? Explain your answer.

9. "Causation is determined on a balance of probabilities in an all-or-nothing manner." What does that statement mean?

10. In the context of product liability, identify three ways in which the defendant's carelessness may create an intolerable risk of injury for consumers. Are the courts equally willing to impose liability on all three grounds? Explain your answer.

11. Is the but-for test always applied to resolve the issue of causation? Illustrate your answer with an example.

12. Explain the meaning of the phrase "joint and several liability." Provide an example in which that concept would apply.

13. What is the basic test for resolving the issue of remoteness? Must the plaintiff prove that a reasonable person would have foreseen both the type of harm that occurred *and* the manner in which it occurred?

14. What is the difference between a "thin skull" and a "crumbling skull"? When does each of those concepts apply? Explain your answer.

15. When will an intervening act cause a court to find that the plaintiff's loss is too remote?

16. What is the main reason why Canadian courts prefer the defence of contributory negligence to the defences of voluntary assumption of risk and illegality?

17. Outline three situations in which the defence of contributory negligence can arise.

18. What is "apportionment"? Why was that principle introduced into Canadian tort law? Was it introduced by judges or by legislators?

19. Outline the steps a business should take to ensure that it will be protected by the defence of voluntary assumption of risk.

20. What is a "learned intermediary"? Explain the significance of that concept in the context of the tort of negligence.

Cases and Problems

1. Dean Zastowny began taking drugs when he was in Grade 9, and he was addicted to crack cocaine by the time he was 18. After committing a string of crimes to support his habit, he was convicted and sent to prison. While in prison, he was sexually assaulted by a prison officer. The evidence indicates that those assaults caused Zastowny to develop low self-esteem, anti-social behaviour, and sexual anxiety. Those conditions remained even after he was released from prison. Zastowny found comfort in heroin and, in order to afford his drugs, he once again led a life of crime. He consequently spent 12 of the next 15 years in jail. Zastowny has now sued the prison guard and the province (as the guard's employer). The defendants have admitted liability and the only issue concerns the remedy. The trial judge has found that but for the sexual assaults, Zastowny would not have become addicted to heroin, and he consequently would not have committed the crimes that led to his return to prison. The judge also has found that but for the sexual assaults, Zastowny would not have developed the personality disorders that prevented him from finding work during the brief periods that he was not in jail. Zastowny therefore argues that he is entitled to be compensated for all of the income that he has lost during the past 15 years. He also argues that, since his personality problems continue to exist, he is entitled to be compensated for the fact that he probably will have difficulty holding a job in the future. Should the judge award damages for all of those losses? Explain your answer.

2. John Brokaw was interested in purchasing an apartment building. He was, however, very concerned about the price. Since he did not trust the revenue figures that the vendor had provided, he hired Lonnie Hauser, a property value appraiser. Brokaw explained in great detail that he needed to know, as precisely as possible, how much the apartments would generate in rent. Hauser's final report indicated that the building was worth $1 400 000. Brokaw accepted that information and purchased the property at that price. He soon discovered, however, that the building was actually worth considerably less. The tenants were all on social assistance. The basic rent that the government was willing to pay was set at $325 per month, and each apartment contained two tenants. Hauser therefore had simply assumed that each apartment would produce $650 per month. In fact, however, whenever the two tenants were related, then the government set the rent at $520 per month. A number of apartments were occupied by married couples. As a result, the actual value of the property was $1 000 000. Hauser

nevertheless says that he should not be held responsible because he had reasonably assumed that the same rent would apply to every apartment. Will Brokaw be successful if he sues Hauser in negligence? Explain your answer.

3. Frank Carra drives a truck for Weide Transport Ltd (WTL). During an otherwise routine journey, a deer jumped onto the highway and caused Carra to swerve out of his lane and onto a strip of gravel that divided northbound and southbound traffic. Carra's truck collided with a signpost, which was left bent over and protruding about 50 centimetres from the ground. Carra could not remove the post and while he thought about notifying the police, he failed to do so. About a day later, Samuel Oke was travelling in the opposite direction on the same highway. Although the solid yellow lines on the road prohibited such a manoeuvre, Oke attempted to pass a slow-moving vehicle by driving on the gravel divider. As he did so, the bent post rammed through his car's floorboards and impaled his chest. Oke died instantly. His widow has now sued Carra and WTL. In defence, they rely on three arguments. First, they say that Oke's death was the result of a "freak accident." Second, they say that Oke was carelessly responsible for his own death. And third, they argue that since Carra was not legally responsible for colliding with the post (which is true), they did not do anything wrong. Discuss those arguments and explain the likelihood that a court would impose liability.

4. Renata owns an importing business. She sought legal advice regarding the possibility of obtaining government approval to enter into a particular contract to purchase widgets from a company in Peru. Because her regular lawyer, a specialist in trade law, was away on vacation, she brought her file to Franz, whom she found in the telephone book. Although Renata did not know it, Franz was not really a lawyer. While he had attended two years of law school, he never graduated and never passed the bar exam. Furthermore, although he is a distinguished-looking 50-year-old, he only recently began to hold himself out as a lawyer. Franz prepared the necessary documents but, because he failed to read the governing statute carefully, he did not instruct Renata to place her corporate seal on them. Renata's application was consequently rejected by the government, and she lost the $75 000 profit that she expected to earn under her contract with the Peruvian company. She has sued Franz, claiming that her loss was caused by his professional negligence. He has responded by arguing that since he was not really a lawyer, he was not really a professional and therefore could not be held to a professional standard of care. He also has argued that even if he can be treated as a professional, he never claimed to have special expertise in the area of trade law and therefore should not be expected to fulfill the standard that would be applied to Renata's regular lawyer. Will either of those arguments succeed?

5. In February 1983, Pia entered the hospital for a simple operation. During that procedure, she received a blood transfusion. Although the operation was entirely successful, Pia was diagnosed with HIV several years later. The blood she had received had come from Everett, a carrier of HIV. He had donated that blood to the Canadian Red Cross Society (CRCS) at a blood donor clinic in January 1982. When it became well known that HIV could be transmitted through blood, the CRCS started using a detailed questionnaire to prevent people in high-risk groups from making donations. Because of his lifestyle, Everett would have fallen into one of those groups. At the time of donation in January 1982, however, there was very little medical information available about HIV, and there was no reasonable basis for believing that it could be spread through blood transfusions. The CRCS therefore did not take any steps to screen out potentially harmful donors. Pia sued Everett and the CRCS in negligence shortly after learning that she was infected. Sadly, both Pia and Everett have since died of AIDS. Pia's widower has nevertheless continued the lawsuit against the CRCS. He claimed that the CRCS was careless in allowing a person of Everett's lifestyle to donate blood. Would that claim succeed? Explain your answer.

6. Arthur Fairchild contracted mesothelioma, an incurable and fatal disease, as a result of inhaling an asbestos fibre. He had been repeatedly exposed to asbestos fibres while working for five different employers over a period of 30 years. Each employer had breached the standard of care by failing to prevent the inhalation of asbestos fibres. Significantly, however, the medical evidence indicates that the disease was caused by the inhalation of a *single* fibre. Fairchild was not at all hurt by the countless *other* fibres that he inhaled. The evidence also indicates that it is impossible to determine precisely *which* fibre caused the disease or *when* it was inhaled. Mesothelioma may lie dormant for many decades after a harmful fibre has taken effect. Fairchild therefore cannot prove on a balance of probabilities that his condition was caused by the carelessness of one of the five employers. Does that mean that Fairchild will not be entitled to any compensation under the tort of negligence?

7. For many years, the Funch Gum Company sold a product that it called "aspargum," a low-calorie gum made from asparagus and other ingredients. Although aspargum never enjoyed great success in the market, it did prove very popular with a small number of people. Clint was one such person. He chewed aspargum almost daily for nearly two decades. Several years ago, however, aspargum was taken off the market when it was discovered to cause several forms of cancer, including mouth cancer. Clint was recently diagnosed with mouth cancer and has sued Funch. Funch admits that it owed a duty of care to Clint, and that it had carelessly sold a product that it should have known was

carcinogenic. It insists, however, that Clint's cancer was not caused by the aspargum but by the cigarettes that he smoked over the same period. In fact, the evidence indicates that there is a 60 percent chance that the cancer was caused by the aspargum and a 40 percent chance that it was caused by smoking. Assuming that Clint's damages are valued at $1 000 000, how much should he actually receive? Should Funch's liability be reduced to $600 000 to reflect the possibility that the cancer was caused by cigarettes? Explain your answer.

8. The plaintiff was a fastidiously clean man with a fastidiously clean house. For health reasons, his family consumed only purified, bottled water, which he purchased from the defendant company. While replacing an empty bottle, the plaintiff discovered that the new bottle contained the remains of a fly. Although the contaminated water was not consumed and did not cause anyone to suffer any physical injury, the plaintiff became obsessed with the event and its "revolting implications" for the health of his family. He constantly thought of flies crawling across garbage or animal feces and then swimming in his supposedly pure water. His personality changed dramatically. His hairstyling business lost clients because he was depressed and no longer had a sense of humour. He was unable to have sex with his wife. He could not properly shower because he could not bear the thought of water on his face. He was so sickened by the thought of contaminated water that he could no longer drink tea or coffee. He often felt like he was going to vomit. The defendant, however, proved that the plaintiff's reaction to the tainted water was unusual and extreme. A normal person, in the same circumstances, might have been angered or mildly disgusted by the sight of the fly, but those feelings would have passed within a few hours and there would be no real lasting harm. Discuss the various elements of the plaintiff's claim in negligence against the defendant. Is a court likely to impose liability? Explain your answer.

9. Claire brought her truck to Darius's garage for repairs. In the course of the job, Darius carelessly punctured the gas tank. Fuel leaked onto the floor of his garage and was ignited when he carelessly threw a cigarette butt away. When he noticed the small blaze, he was in the process of carrying a heavy piece of equipment over to the truck. He instructed Claire, who was waiting for her vehicle, to use a nearby fire extinguisher. Unfortunately, she panicked. Instead of grabbing the fire extinguisher, she tried to douse the small, but rapidly growing, flame by throwing snow on it. Her effort was unsuccessful and within a short time, her entire truck was destroyed. Darius has admitted liability, but he insists that Claire was contributorily negligent and should shoulder part of the blame for the damage. Is he correct? Explain your answer.

10. Mr Aldous Lagden owns a 10-year-old Honda Civic. The vehicle was badly damaged in a collision with a car owned by Ms Georgia O'Connor. Lagden took his car to an auto body shop for repairs, which charged $5000 to restore the Honda to its prior condition. O'Connor admits that the accident was entirely her fault and there is no doubt that she is liable in negligence for at least the cost of repair ($5000). A difficult issue arises, however, because Lagden required a vehicle while his Honda was in the repair shop. Unfortunately, because he is unemployed, in bad health, and a poor credit risk, he was unable to pay for a temporary replacement vehicle by paying with existing funds, borrowing money, or obtaining credit. He felt compelled instead to use the services of Diamond Rentals Inc (DRI). Unlike other car rental agencies, DRI operates a special service under which it provides replacement vehicles, to people like Lagden, without immediate charge. It instead receives payment only after its customer (in this case Lagden) has successfully sued the person responsible for the accident (in this case O'Connor). Not surprisingly, although it postpones payment, DRI charges an additional fee for that valuable service. Is O'Connor liable for that fee, in addition to the usual cost of a car rental? What is her best argument against liability? Will that argument be successful?

11. Casey has a well-earned reputation for being immature and irresponsible. She works in a warehouse that is owned by Finnegan Inc. Two weeks ago, she spent much of a workday goofing off and hiding in the restroom. Near the end of her shift, she sneaked into a restroom stall and smoked a marijuana cigarette. When the time bell rang, she punched the clock, left the warehouse, jumped into her car, and opened a bottle of vodka. Halfway home, she finished the bottle as she waited at a red light. The combined effect of the marijuana and the vodka dulled Casey's senses. When her light turned green, she shifted her vehicle into gear and slowly began to drive through the intersection. While she was doing so, however, she was blindsided by a car driven by Rusty. Until that moment, Rusty had a perfectly clean driving record. Despite having a licence for more than three decades, he had not received a single ticket and had never been involved in an accident. He always drove carefully, cautiously, and within the law. On this occasion, however, his attention was distracted by a rabbit. As he watched the animal hopping through a nearby field, he failed to notice that his light was red. When the police arrived on the scene, they observed three facts about Casey: (i) she had suffered a broken leg during the accident, (ii) she was impaired by drugs and alcohol, and (iii) she had an unregistered pistol hidden under her front seat. Casey will be facing criminal prosecution. For the purposes of this question, however, you should focus entirely on the negligence action between Casey and Rusty. Who is likely to win that lawsuit? Will the defendant be able to avoid liability, in whole or in part, on the basis of some defence? Explain your answer.

12. Jake was stopped in his car at a red light. A pair of teenagers unexpectedly ran up to the vehicle and smashed the windshield with a baseball bat. Jake put his car into park and leaped out to chase the teenagers. Unfortunately, he did not catch them. Worse yet, upon returning to the traffic light, he found that his car had been stolen. A few minutes later, several blocks away, the thief rammed Jake's vehicle into Mysty's truck. The teenagers and the thief have never been identified. Mysty has therefore sued Jake. She claims that if Jake had not left his keys in the ignition while he chased the vandals, the thief would not have been in a position to steal his car and crash into her truck. Jake admits that he should have taken the keys with him but denies that he committed the tort of negligence. Who is right? Explain your answer.

The Nature and Creation of Contracts

7

After completing this chapter, you should be able to:

❶ Identify three essential elements of most contracts.

❷ Outline the situations in which people generally do or do not have an intention to create legal relations.

❸ Distinguish between an offer and an invitation to treat.

❹ Explain five ways by which an offer may cease to exist.

❺ Explain the effect of a firm offer.

❻ Outline the role of offer and acceptance in the tendering process.

❼ Explain how the courts resolve a battle of the forms.

❽ Distinguish between bilateral contracts and unilateral contracts, and explain the difference between acceptance by promise and acceptance by performance.

❾ Explain whether an offer can ever be accepted by conduct or by silence.

❿ Describe the postal rule and explain when it will apply.

Most people are unaware of the vast number of contracts they create every day. Consider your acquisition of this textbook. You may have found it, borrowed it, or received it as a gift; but most likely you bought it. Try to recall that transaction. At that time, did you know that you were creating a contract? Did you realize that your conduct generated a number of legal rights and obligations?

You may have had a choice in how you purchased this book. You probably bought it from your university or college bookstore, but you also may have bought it directly from the publisher via telephone, fax, or the Internet. Or you may have acquired a used copy from a former student. In any event, you probably paid with cash, a credit card, or a debit card. Those, however, were not the only possibilities. For example, if you bought this book from a former student, you may have acquired it in exchange for a set of computer discs. Or if you were industrious, you may have convinced the owner of a bookstore to give you a copy in exchange for your promise to work a weekend at the store.

Whichever option you used, you presumably became party to a **contract.**[1] You and the other person entered into an agreement that contained legally enforceable rights and obligations. You were able to enter into that agreement because you both experienced a **meeting of the minds**, a shared decision to enter into a legal transaction on a particular basis.[2] And the most obvious feature of that contract is that it involved a mutual **exchange of value**. You both gave up something as part of the deal.[3] You probably paid cash in return for the book, while the other person provided the book text in return for cash.

It is important to realize that a contractual relationship can continue even after there has been an exchange of value. Indeed, one reason for entering into a contract may be to reserve some rights and obligations for the future. The choices that you made yesterday may affect you even today. For example, if you paid with a promise to work in the bookstore, you limited your options for the future. You will have to spend your weekend stocking shelves. Or consider what would happen if your book becomes unglued during the semester and pages fall out. If you bought this book "as is" from a used bookseller, you might not have any remedy. The situation would be different, however, if you purchased it from a bookseller who offered a "satisfaction or money back" guarantee. You would enjoy the right to a refund.[4] Having already given the guarantee, the bookseller no longer has a choice about returning your purchase price. The law of contract would require them to do so. As an aside, consider why some booksellers are willing to give such guarantees. While they presumably value freedom of choice as much as you do, they also know that guarantees generate goodwill and increase the price that customers are willing to pay. By limiting their choices in the future, booksellers hope to attract more business.

Fortunately, textbooks seldom come unglued. Because the book that you bought almost certainly is of satisfactory quality, the seller's guarantee will probably never be enforced. The same is true for most contractual terms. Right and obligations usually lie quietly beneath the surface while the future unfolds as the parties expected. In that sense, contract law represents the pathology of commerce. Legal issues usually arise only if a commercial relationship becomes unhealthy.

a **contract** is an agreement that contains legally enforceable rights and obligations

a **meeting of the minds** is a shared decision to enter into a legal transaction on a particular basis

an **exchange of value** occurs when the parties each give up something

---

[1] Not every acquisition involves a contract. There would be no contract in this case if you received the book as a gift or if you found it as abandoned property.

[2] Lawyers sometimes refer to this as *consensus ad idem*, or "agreement on that previously mentioned."

[3] Lawyers sometimes refer to this as *quid pro quo*, or "something for something."

[4] As we will see in Chapter 13, the law imposes a number of obligations on a person who sells goods (such as books) even if the parties' contract does not expressly do so.

It would be dangerous, however, to assume that business people do not really need to know about the law. It is true that most contracts are performed without problems. But it is also true that most of the problems that do arise are avoidable. They occur because the parties failed to think carefully about the legal implications of their actions. Bear this in mind as you read the chapters on contract. Most of the cases that you will encounter are unusual precisely because they went to court. People need the help of a judge only when something has gone terribly wrong. By knowing your rights and obligations, you can almost always avoid that situation.

Of course, when something does go wrong, it may be preferable from a business perspective to avoid the court system. We discussed that proposition in Chapter 2. While a clear understanding of your legal rights and obligations allows you to litigate more effectively, it may be better to resolve a dispute informally. Legal proceedings tend to signal the end of a relationship. The long-term benefits of retaining a healthy commercial relationship are often more important than winning a particular dispute.

So far, we have been discussing the creation of contracts in very general terms. As we will see, however, every contract actually requires a number of distinct steps or elements. Three are especially important:

1. The parties must have an *intention to create legal relations*.
2. They must reach a mutual agreement through the process of *offer* and *acceptance*.
3. They must enter into a bargain by each giving *consideration*.

We will discuss the first two elements in this chapter and the third in Chapter 8. As you may have noticed, our list does *not* include the *writing* of a contract. In fact, most contracts do not have to be written in order to be enforceable. In Chapter 10, we will discuss some exceptions to that rule. At the same time, we will also consider other factors that may render a contract ineffective, such as *illegality* and *incapacity to contract*.

Comparing Torts and Contracts

L.O. ❶

Before turning to a detailed examination of the creation of contracts, it is important to consider one more introductory issue: the difference between torts and contracts. We previously addressed that issue in Chapter 1 and again in Chapter 3. You should take a moment to review that material, especially Concept Summary 3.2 (see page 66).

Intention to Create Legal Relations

L.O. ❷

A contract will not arise without an **intention to create legal relations**. The parties must have intended to create a legally enforceable agreement. To decide that issue, a court asks whether a "reasonable person" would have believed that the parties intended to enter into a contract. (The concept of a reasonable person is discussed in detail in Chapter 6). Notice that the test is objective rather than subjective. The judge is concerned with what a reasonable person would have thought, not necessarily with what the parties themselves actually thought. There are two reasons for that rule. First, a test of subjective intentions would be difficult to apply because a person could easily lie at trial. Second,

an **intention to create legal relations** arises if a reasonable person would believe that the parties intended to create a legally enforceable agreement the law of contracts aims to protect reasonable expectations. If you and I enter into an apparent contract for the sale of certain components, I will reasonably expect to receive those components even if, during the sale negotiations, you secretly planned to keep them for yourself. Furthermore, on the basis of my reasonable expectation, I may have arranged to resell the components to someone else, who may have arranged to sell them to yet another person, and so on. The business world could not function smoothly unless people were entitled to rely on outward appearances.

The presence or absence of an intention to create legal relations is usually obvious. A reasonable person simply ignores unrealistic and exaggerated proposals. For instance, a lecturer's sarcastic promise to pay $5000 for a correct response in class cannot be taken at face value. To further simplify matters, the courts usually presume that an intention to create legal relations exists in a commercial context, but not between friends or family members.[5] However, those presumptions can be *rebutted*, or disproved. For example, a business person may be able to convince a judge that while a commercial agreement was contained in a formal document, it *was not* really intended to be legally binding.[6] Likewise, a son may be able to persuade a judge that while his mother's promise to pay his tuition at business school was given within a family setting, it really *was* intended to create contractual obligations.[7]

In the business world, the issue of intention to create legal relations can arise in a variety of ways. For example, the parties may create a document that looks very much like an enforceable agreement, except for the fact that it contains a clause that says that their apparent agreement is "subject to formal contract" or "subject to further negotiation." A court will likely find that although the parties *could* have created a contract, they did not yet do so. Neither party can be forced to perform the deal. However, if the parties then go ahead and actually perform, a court may decide that a contract *has* come into existence—on the basis of their actions, rather than their document. The issue of intention to create legal relations may also be important in a case that involves a *comfort letter*.[8] Suppose, for example, that a small company borrows money from a bank. If the bank is afraid that the company may not be able to repay the loan, it may ask the company's director for a personal *guarantee*. That guarantee is a separate contract that would allow the bank to collect from the director if the company did not repay the loan. If the director is not willing to be held responsible for the company's debt, they may persuade the bank to accept a comfort letter that contains an informal promise to help out if necessary. A comfort letter creates a *moral* obligation, but not a *legal* one. It is valuable, in a practical sense, because many business people fulfill their promises—even if they are not *legally* liable—in order to protect their reputations.

The issue of intention to create legal relations is most difficult when the circumstances involve a combination of both social relations and business transactions. How would you decide the case in You Be the Judge 7.1?

[5] *Balfour v Balfour* [1919] 2 KB 571 (CA).

[6] *Rose & Frank Co v JR Crompton & Rose Ltd* [1923] 2 KB 261 (CA).

[7] *Jones v Padavatton* [1969] 2 All ER 616 (CA).

[8] *Toronto-Dominion Bank v Leigh Instruments Ltd (Trustee of)* (1999) 178 DLR (4th) 634 (Ont CA).

You Be the Judge 7.1

Fobasco Ltd v Cogan (1990) 72 OR (2d) 254 (HCJ)

When major league baseball came to Toronto in 1976, Eddie Cogan bought eight season's tickets in a prime location—field level, behind first base. At that time, he agreed to sell four of his tickets to Fobasco Ltd, a company owned by his friend and business associate, David Fingold. David, in turn, gave the tickets away to Fobasco's prospective customers, in an effort to drum up business. Although that arrangement lasted for many years, Eddie decided in 1986, around the same time that the Blue Jays became contenders and shortly before they moved into SkyDome, that he would prefer to sit next to his own sons rather than Fobasco's clients. He told his old friend that their arrangement was at an end. David was upset because he could not otherwise get good seats for the games. He therefore sued for breach of contract, claiming that Eddie had contractually agreed to sell tickets to Fobasco on an annual basis.

Questions for Discussion

1. Would a reasonable person believe that the parties had entered into contractual relations? Or did they merely have a social arrangement?

2. While contracts generally do not need to be written to be effective, do you believe that the lack of writing in this case is significant? What if the parties, as business people, normally put all of their contracts into writing?

3. If you believe that a contract should be recognized, should Eddie be required to make tickets available to Fobasco Ltd forever?

Offer

L.O. ❸ ❹ ❺ ❻ ❼

THE NATURE OF AN OFFER

A contract requires more than an intention to create legal relations. The parties must also enter into a mutual agreement through the process of offer and acceptance. An **offer** is an indication of a willingness to enter into a contract on certain terms. A person who offers to enter into a contract is called the **offeror**. A person who receives an offer is called an **offeree**.

An offer creates a risk because a contract comes into existence as soon as an offer is accepted. At that point, both parties become obligated to fulfill the promises contained in the agreement. And once a contract comes into existence, neither party, acting alone, can alter its contents or bring it to an end.

Consider the dangers that can arise from making an offer. Suppose you sent a message to your class website offering to sell your cars. If 10 people simultaneously show up at your door wanting to buy a vehicle, are you contractually obliged to honour 10 contracts even though you have only two cars to sell? The courts recognize that it would be impractical if every proposal could be classified as an offer that can be transformed into a contract through acceptance. Therefore, judges have developed guidelines for deciding which types of statements qualify as offers. They have also placed limits on how long offers will last.

an **offer** is an indication of a willingness to enter into a contract on certain terms

an **offeror** is a party who offers to enter into a contract

an **offeree** is a party who receives an offer to enter into a contract

INVITATION TO TREAT

The courts classify some statements not as offers, but rather as *invitations to treat*. An **invitation to treat** is not an offer but an indication of a willingness to receive an offer. In other words, it is an invitation for *others* to make offers. In such circumstances, a person who responds to the invitation is an offeror, and the person who initially presented the invitation is the offeree.

The distinction between an offer and an invitation to treat depends on an objective test. A court will look at all of the circumstances and ask how a reasonable person would interpret a particular statement. Would a reasonable person believe that the person making the statement was prepared to enter into

an **invitation to treat** is an indication of a willingness to receive an offer

a contract as soon as an acceptance was received? Or would it be more reasonable to believe that the person making the statement was simply prepared to receive and consider offers?

Those questions are often difficult to answer, but the courts are guided by certain presumptions. Most significantly, they usually say that the display of an item on a store shelf, even if it carries a price tag, is an invitation to treat.[9] Similarly, a statement placed in a newspaper advertisement or a catalogue is usually not an offer. There is a very good reason for those presumptions. Recall our example in which 10 people see your advertisement and they each want to buy a car. If your ad is classified as an offer, you might be held liable to fulfill 10 contracts, even though you have only two cars to sell. However, if your ad is classified as an invitation to treat, each response is an offer, which you are free to accept or reject. The presumptions regarding advertisements and displays generally protect business people from overexposing themselves. There are, however, exceptions to those presumptions. An advertisement may be considered an offer if a reasonable person would read it that way. That may be true, for example, if it expressly indicates that a limited number of items are available while supplies last. Your ad therefore might be an offer if it said, "Cars for sale. $10 000 each. First come, first served." In that situation, you would not be in danger of being bound to an unmanageable number of contracts.[10]

COMMUNICATION OF AN OFFER

A statement is not an offer unless it is communicated and received *as* an offer. The issue is not as simple as it might appear. Suppose the directors of a company decide during a meeting to offer a $10 000 bonus to a long-serving secretary in exchange for her early retirement. The directors ask the secretary to type the handwritten notes of their meeting. In doing so, she learns of the proposed bonus, completes the task at hand, and promptly tenders her resignation. She is probably not entitled to the bonus payment. The minutes of the meeting were communicated to her, not as a contractual offer, but rather as a typing assignment. In those circumstances, the reasonable person would not believe that the directors intended to be bound by their communication.[11]

However, as long as a proposition is communicated and received as an offer, it usually does not have to take any particular form.[12] It may be contained in a written document. For example, if you buy a television from a department store on credit, you will probably be asked to complete a lengthy application that contains countless terms and conditions. That is your offer to the store. Alternatively, an offer may be made verbally. For example, if you go to a restaurant and say, "A cheeseburger and a milkshake, please," you are offering to enter into a contract for the purchase of a meal. An offer may even be inferred from conduct alone.

---

9. *Pharmaceutical Society of Great Britain v Boots Cash Chemists (Southern) Ltd* [1953] 1 QB 401 (CA).

10. Business people occasionally try to take advantage of that rule by advertising items they do not have to sell in the hopes of attracting customers who can be persuaded once they are in the store to buy other items. In most jurisdictions, such practices, known as "bait and switch," are prohibited by statute: *Competition Act*, RSC 1985, c C-34, s 52 (Can); *Fair Trading Act*, RSA 2000, c F-2, s 9 (Alta); *Trade Practice Act*, RSBC 1996, c 457, s 2 (BC); *Trade Practices Inquiry Act*, CCSM, c T110, s 2 (Man); *Trade Practices Act*, RSN 1990, c T-7, s 5 (Nfld); *Consumer Services Act*, RSNS 1989, c 94, s 6(1)(c) (NS); *Business Practices Act*, RSO 1990, c B.18, s 2 (Ont); *Business Practices Act*, RSPEI 1988, c B-7, s 2 (PEI); *Competition Protection Act*, RSQ, c P-40.1, ss 224–225 (Que); *Consumer and Commercial Affairs Act*, RSS 1988, c C-29.2, s 8 (Sask).

11. *Blair v Western Mutual Benefit Association* [1972] 4 WWR 284 (BC CA).

12. In Chapter 10, we will discuss situations in which a contract must be written to be enforceable.

For example, if you enter a barbershop, sit silently in the chair, and get a trim, you have offered, and the barber has accepted, a contract to cut your hair.[13]

THE LIFE OF AN OFFER

An offer does not last forever. If it is accepted, it gives way to a contract. And if it is not accepted, it may cease to exist in a variety of ways:

- revocation
- lapse of time
- death or insanity
- rejection
- counter-offer

Revocation

Revocation occurs if the party who made an offer withdraws it. The offeror is the master of the offer and is generally entitled to revoke it at any time.[14] As a matter of risk management, however, there is some need for caution. Revocation is not effective unless it is reasonably communicated to the offeree. Until that occurs, the offer remains open, and the offeree can create a contract through acceptance.

> **revocation** occurs if the offeror withdraws an offer

FIRM OFFERS Although the basic rules regarding revocation are quite simple, two types of situations call for special attention. The first involves a **firm offer**, which occurs when the offeror promises to hold an offer open for acceptance for a certain period. Do not be misled by the terminology. A firm offer is not very firm at all. As a general rule, the offeror can revoke it at any time. The reason, as Ethical Perspective 7.1 shows, turns on the fact that a firm offer is not contained in a

> a **firm offer** occurs when the offeror promises to hold an offer open for acceptance for a certain period

---

Ethical Perspective **7.1**

Dickinson v Dodds (1876) 2 Ch D 463 (CA)

George Dickinson was one of several people interested in buying a piece of land from John Dodds. On Wednesday, John wrote to George, offering to sell the property and promising to hold that offer open until Friday morning. While George was considering his options on Thursday, he learned that John was negotiating with another potential buyer. George immediately tried to find John to accept the offer. Although George failed to locate John that night, he did manage to leave a letter of acceptance with John's mother-in-law. Moreover, he caught up with John the next morning and expressed his desire to buy the property. By that time, however, George had learned from a third party that the land had already been sold to someone else. George sued John for failing to fulfill his promise to keep the offer open.

The lawsuit failed. The court held that John's promise was unenforceable because it was entirely *gratuitous*.[15] He had not received anything of value in exchange for his promise to hold his offer open until Friday.

Questions for Discussion

1. Do you approve of John's behaviour? What do you think of the fact that the law allowed him to break his promise? Is the legal rule pertaining to firm offers morally acceptable?

2. Although firm offers are revocable, most successful business people honour such promises. What reasons might motivate them to do so?

[13.] If the parties to a contract do not stipulate a price, the courts may require the purchaser to pay a reasonable price. Lawyers sometimes refer to this as *quantum meruit*, or "as much as it is worth."

[14.] Generally, an offeror can communicate revocation in the same way that they communicated the offer. For instance, if the offer appeared in a newspaper advertisement, the revocation can appear there as well.

[15.] Lawyers use the word "gratuitous" to describe an act that was not required by law—in effect, a gift. Of course, no one is required to give a gift, just as no one is obligated to hold open an offer unless one has been paid to do so.

contract and therefore is not enforceable in law. Nevertheless, as you read that case, consider how you, as a business person, would act in such circumstances.

Despite the general rule, a firm offer *cannot* be revoked if the offeror's promise was placed under *seal* or if the offeree paid for the right to accept within a certain period. (We discuss seals in Chapter 8.) For example, if you think that you might want to buy a particular piece of land in the future, but are not prepared to commit yourself to that transaction just yet, you might try to purchase an *option* from the owner. An **option** is a contract in which the offeror is paid in exchange for a binding promise to hold an offer open for acceptance for a specific period. That option would accomplish two things. First, it would allow you and the offeror, at some point in the future, to create a contract for the sale of land. Second, it would immediately create an entirely separate contract requiring the offeror to wait while you decided whether to buy the land. As you might expect, one must take special care in granting options. Consider the situation in Business Decision 7.1.

an **option** is a contract in which the offeror is paid in exchange for a binding promise to hold an offer open for acceptance for a specific period

Business Decision 7.1

The Granting of Options

ABC Corporation is investigating the possibility of developing a shopping mall in a certain neighbourhood. To do so, it will need to buy your land. It also will need to obtain zoning approval for its proposal. Although you have offered to sell your property for $100 000, ABC Corporation does not want to be locked into a contract unless its zoning application is allowed. However, it also knows that other companies may offer to buy your land to develop their own projects. It therefore wants to buy an option that will require you to hold your offer open for 90 days.

Questions for Discussion

1. Will you grant the option? If so, on what terms and at what price?

2. How does the existence of other potential buyers affect your decision?

3. How will your expectations about the future market value of your land affect your decision?

TENDERS The second special situation involving the revocation of offers is more complicated. It is also very important in the business world. Suppose a city wants a new library built. It will probably call for *tenders*. A **tender** is an offer to undertake a project on particular terms. In calling for tenders, the city issues an invitation to treat and promises to award the project to the company that submits the best offer. If the general rule applied, each bidder would be entitled to withdraw its offer any time before acceptance. The city, however, needs some assurance that that will not happen. It needs to know that the offers will remain open while it considers them. Otherwise, the process would not work—at least not very well.

a **tender** is an offer to undertake a project on particular terms

To avoid that problem, a court will probably find that the bidding process immediately creates a special contract between the city and each company that submits an offer.[16] Thus, the city's call for tenders serves two purposes:

1. It constitutes an offer to enter into a special contract, called "Contract A," to hold a fair tendering process in exchange for the submission of an irrevocable bid.

2. It also constitutes an invitation to treat to receive offers to enter into a contract, called "Contract B," for the construction of the library.

A company's tender also serves two purposes:

1. It constitutes acceptance of the city's offer to enter into a fair and irrevocable tendering process under Contract A.

[16.] *R v Ron Engineering & Construction (Eastern) Ltd* (1981) 119 DLR (3d) 267 (SCC); *MJB Enterprises v Defence Construction* (1999) 170 DLR (4th) 577 (SCC).

2. It also constitutes an offer to enter into a contract for the construction of the library under Contract B.

There will be many Contract As (one for each company that submits a tender to the city) but only one Contract B (between the city and the company that submits the winning tender). Concept Summary 7.1 illustrates this view of the tendering process.

Concept Summary 7.1

The Tendering Process

Stages	Contract A (Contract to Enter Process)	Contract B (Contract to Build Library)
Call for Tender by City to Company	offer by city to hold a fair tendering process	invitation to treat issued by city
Submission of Tender by Company to City	acceptance by company of offer	offer by company to build library
Award of Project by City to Company		acceptance by city of offer

Lapse of Time

An offeror is entitled to limit the lifespan of an offer, possibly by stating that acceptance must occur by a specific date. That is almost always true with an option. But even if no time period is stated, an offer is open only for a "reasonable period." In deciding what constitutes a reasonable period, a court will look at many factors, including the subject matter of the proposed contract, the nature of the agreement, the volatility of the market, and the usual practice in the industry. An offer to sell farmland in a financially depressed region may be open for many weeks; an offer to sell shares in a wildly fluctuating market may be open for mere hours or minutes.

Death or Insanity

It is often said that an offer is automatically revoked if either the offeror or the offeree dies. A dead person does not have the capacity to enter into a contract, and there cannot be a meeting of the minds if only one person is alive. An exception may apply, however, if the proposed contract does not call upon the affected party to perform personally. For example, that may be true if the offer pertains to the sale of land rather than the performance of a concert. In that situation, the offeree may communicate acceptance to the deceased offeror's estate, or the deceased offeree's estate may communicate acceptance to the offeror.[17] The same analysis generally holds true for insanity.

Rejection

Rejection occurs when the offeree refuses an offer. An offer is terminated once it is rejected. Suppose Bruno offers to sell his business to Helga for $100 000. If

rejection occurs when the offeree refuses an offer

---

17. In this context, "estate" refers to the person representing the interests of the deceased.

she says, "No, thank you, I'm not interested," the offer is dead. And because it is dead, Helga cannot later accept it if she changes her mind and decides that she really would like to buy the business after all. Unless Bruno repeats his initial offer, Helga must make an offer to him and hope that he accepts it.

Counter-Offer

a **counter-offer** occurs when an offeree responds to an offer by indicating a willingness to enter into a contract but on different terms

A similar rule applies to *counter-offers*. A **counter-offer** occurs when an offeree responds to an offer by indicating a willingness to enter into a contract but on different terms. A counter-offer has the effect of rejecting an existing offer and creating a new one. Consequently, as Concept Summary 7.2 shows, a counter-offer causes the parties to switch roles.

Concept Summary 7.2

Offer and Counter-Offer

Event	Party A	Party B
Offer	Offeror ⟶	Offeree
Counter-offer	Offeree ⟵	Offeror

To create a contract, an offer must be *entirely* accepted. Any attempt to accept on modified terms constitutes a counter-offer. Returning to our previous example, suppose Helga responded to Bruno's offer by saying, "You've got yourself a deal, but I can pay only $50 000." Her statement is a counter-offer. It kills Bruno's offer to sell for $100 000 and replaces it with her own offer to buy at $50 000. If Bruno rejects Helga's offer, she cannot revive his initial offer by saying, "Okay, I'll pay the full $100 000." If she wants the business, she must hope that Bruno repeats his original offer. He may do so expressly or implicitly by responding to her counter-offer by saying something like, "No, I won't take less than $100 000."

Because the general rule regarding counter-offers can be harsh, the courts sometimes characterize an offeree's statement as a harmless inquiry rather than a counter-offer. Therefore, if Helga had said, "I'd love to buy your business, but I'm just wondering if you'd take $50 000 for it," she might be able to persuade a judge that even if Bruno had said, "No," his original offer would still be open for acceptance.

a **battle of the forms** occurs when each party claims to have entered into a contract on the basis of its own standard form document

A judge will also try to avoid the general rule regarding counter-offers in a case involving a *battle of the forms*. A **battle of the forms** occurs when each party claims to have entered into a contract on the basis of its own standard form document. It is common for a business to create a complicated contractual form, containing many terms, which it will insist upon using for every transaction. This only makes sense, as it would be too difficult and expensive to constantly negotiate new contracts. Problems arise, however, if both parties insist upon using their *own* forms and if those forms contain *different* terms.[18]

---

18. Problems can also arise if only one party uses a standard form contract. Corporations often try to use such documents to force complicated and harsh terms on their customers. That problem is addressed in Chapter 9.

To decide which contractual form, if either, applies, a judge will consider several factors, including the usual practice in the industry, past dealings between the parties, the precise sequence of events, and the forms, if any, that the parties actually signed. Consider the example in Business Decision 7.2.

Business Decision 7.2

Battle of the Forms

For years, Vendor Inc has been selling computer chips to you without any problems. During that time, it developed a standard form document, which it uses to offer its goods for sale. That document contains a clause that allows unsatisfactory goods to be returned for a refund within seven days. You also developed a standard form document, which you use for accepting offers of sale. That document, however, contains a clause that allows unsatisfactory goods to be returned for a refund within 21 days. In fact, most businesses that buy and sell computer chips use a 21-day return period. You and Vendor purport to create a contract for the sale of 5000 computer chips. As always, you each use your own form and, as always, neither of you realizes that those forms have different terms. If, after 10 days, the chips are found to be defective and you want your money back, are you entitled to a refund?

Strictly speaking, because it did not exactly match the terms of Vendor's offer, your document seems to be a counter-offer rather than an acceptance. And if there has been no offer and acceptance, there cannot be a contract.

Nevertheless, since the agreement is executed (already performed) rather than executory (not yet performed), and since you both reasonably believed that a contract existed, a judge might be persuaded to find that a contract was created. For example, if Vendor signed and returned a copy of your document before shipping the computer chips, the judge might hold that Vendor agreed to the terms contained in your counter-offer, especially since those terms reflect industry practice.[19] In some situations, however, it will simply not be possible to save the transaction, and you will be without a contractual remedy for the defective goods.[20]

Questions for Discussion

1. What does this example demonstrate about the need to carefully read every document that affects your business?

2. How can you avoid the sort of difficulties that arise in this case?

Acceptance

L.O. ❽ ❾ ❿

In discussing acceptance, it is important to distinguish two situations:

- acceptance by promise
- acceptance by performance

ACCEPTANCE BY PROMISE

Many contracts are *bilateral*. A **bilateral contract** occurs when a promise is exchanged for a promise. The offer consists of the offeror's promise to do something; the acceptance consists of the offeree's promise to do something. Therefore, when the contract comes into existence, both parties have promises to fulfill. Suppose, for example, that you offer to sell your car for $7500. To accept your promise to transfer ownership of the vehicle, I promise to pay the price. As Figure 7.1 (on the next page) illustrates, we have a bilateral contract. That would be true whether we expected to complete the exchange immediately or next week.

a **bilateral contract** occurs when a promise is exchanged for a promise

We can define the element of acceptance even more precisely. **Acceptance** occurs when an offeree agrees to enter into the contract proposed by the offeror. Acceptance generally has to be communicated to the offeror. It must

acceptance occurs when an offeree agrees to enter into the contract proposed by the offeror

---

[19.] *Butler Machine Tool Co v Ex-cell-O Corp* [1979] 1 All ER 695 (CA); *Tekdata Interconnection Ltd v Amphenol Ltd* [2010] 1 Lloyd's Rep 357 (CA).

[20.] In some situations, however, the court may rely on the cause of action in unjust enrichment if one party has conferred a benefit on the other party. That possibility is discussed in Chapter 12.

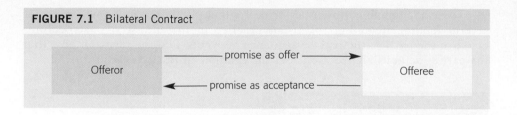

FIGURE 7.1   Bilateral Contract

be unequivocal and it must correspond precisely with the terms of the offer. If the offeree changes the terms, it does not create an acceptance but rather a counter-offer, as we saw in the last section. An acceptance must also be a *response* to an offer. For that reason, no contract is formed if I send you a letter that says, "I will sell you my car for $5000," at the same time that you send me a letter that says, "I will buy your car for $5000." This situation is sometimes described as a "cross-offer"—each letter contains an offer and neither contains an acceptance. Therefore, there is no meeting of the minds.

Words

Acceptance usually occurs through written or spoken words. The offeror, as master of the offer, can dictate how those words must be communicated. It is possible to insist that acceptance be communicated to a particular location or provided in a particular form. For example, if an offeror states that "acceptance *must* be sent in writing to my office," a contract is not formed if acceptance is communicated orally or if it is sent to the offeror's home. Often, however, the offeror does not impose any restrictions, and the offeree can accept by any reasonable means. If so, it is usually best to avoid complications by responding in kind, for example, by providing written acceptance to a written offer. It may be possible, however, to use any equally effective method, for example, by responding to a faxed offer with a telephoned acceptance.

Conduct

In some circumstances, an offer may be accepted by conduct. Suppose I offer $5000 in exchange for your promise to develop a software program for me. If you accept, you will probably say, "Yes," either orally or in writing. However, you might also nod agreeably and silently shake my hand. A reasonable person would likely interpret your conduct as acceptance.

Silence

While acceptance may occur without words if the offeree acts in a certain way, silence alone cannot be acceptance. That rule can be very important. An unscrupulous company may send goods to you along with a note that says, "You will be charged for these items unless you tell us that you do not wish to purchase them." Generally speaking, you will not be required to pay, even if you completely ignore the offer.[21]

The courts developed that basic rule. Some jurisdictions also have statutes that discourage businesses from foisting goods on unsuspecting consumers. In Ontario, for example, the *Consumer Protection Act* allows recipients of unsolicited goods to use them without fear of being charged.[22] However, those rules

---

[21.] *Felthouse v Bindley* (1862) 142 ER 1037 (Ex Ch).

[22.] *Consumer Protection Act*, RSO 1990, c C.31, s 36.

apply only to *unsolicited* goods. The situation may be different if you did something in the past that allows a company to treat your silence as acceptance. For example, by joining a book club, you may enter into a contract that requires you to pay for a monthly selection unless you return it within a specified time. In such circumstances, your acceptance of the book will consist of your silence *plus* your earlier promise to abide by your agreement with the company. The result may be the same if you regularly accept goods from a company and pay for them.

Acceptance at a Distance

Special problems can occur when people do not deal face to face. Practically speaking, contracts cannot always be created in person. Business people often deal with each other across vast distances. And even when they are neighbours, they may not have the time or desire to arrange a meeting. Furthermore, individual consumers are increasingly entering into transactions and paying bills not only through the mail, but also over the telephone or by various electronic means, such as ATMs and the Internet.

Two issues arise when parties deal with each other at a distance. First, if the lines of communication break down, it is necessary to decide whether a contract was formed. Suppose an insurance company, in exchange for a certain payment, offers to protect your business against the risk of property damage. As required by the offer, you mail your letter of acceptance and a cheque to the insurer. The letter is lost in the postal system and never arrives. If your property is later damaged by a flood, do you have insurance coverage? Is the insurer liable even though it never received your letter?

Second, even if the lines of communication work properly, it may be necessary to determine where and when a contract was formed. Returning to the previous example, suppose your business is located in Alberta, but the insurance company is located in Manitoba. Assume that the insurance company is required to pay a fee to the Government of Manitoba if a contract is formed there, but not if it is formed in Alberta. Where was your contract formed? Is the insurer liable for the fee?

THE GENERAL RULE The law in this area is complicated, partly because the courts have not yet decided how to deal with many of the newer forms of technology, such as smartphones and the Internet. The courts have, however, used a pair of basic rules for many years. First, the **general rule** states that acceptance by *instantaneous communication* is effective when and where it is received by the offeror. That rule was initially formulated at a time when people typically conducted business face to face. There was **instantaneous communication** because the parties' interactions involved little or no delay. Courts today hold that many modern forms of communication, including the telephone and the fax machine,[23] are also instantaneous. (The rule that applies to email is discussed in Chapter 19.)

The general rule governing instantaneous communications can be illustrated with our previous example. Suppose that while you are in Alberta, you telephone your insurer, which is located in Manitoba, and accept its offer of coverage. Your acceptance takes effect when and where it is received. Your contract is therefore formed in Manitoba when your insurer hears you say, "I accept." However, if your statement was inaudible because you happened to be driving through a tunnel while talking on your cellphone, a contract would not be formed. Acceptance is effective only when and where the offeror *actually* receives it.

the **general rule** states that acceptance by instantaneous communication is effective when and where it is received by the offeror

an **instantaneous communication** is any form of communication in which there is little or no delay in the interaction between the parties

---

[23.] *Rolling v Willann Investments Ltd* (1989) 63 DLR (4th) 760 (Ont CA).

PART 3

a **non-instantaneous communication** is any form of communication that involves a substantial delay between the time that it leaves one person and reaches another

THE POSTAL RULE The general rule works well for instantaneous communications. It can cause problems, however, for *non-instantaneous communications*. A **non-instantaneous communication** is one that involves a substantial delay between the time that it leaves one person and reaches another, such as when a letter is mailed or a package is sent by courier.[24]

The courts refuse to rigidly classify communications as instantaneous or non-instantaneous. Even if a form of communication *appears* to be instantaneous, it may be considered non-instantaneous if, in the circumstances, it involves a substantial delay between transmission and receipt. For example, although a fax is usually received without delay, not every faxed communication is classified as instantaneous. A judge would consider the parties' objective intentions, usual business practices, and the fairness of placing the risk on one person rather than the other. Therefore, if an offer states that "acceptance must be conveyed by means of instantaneous communication no later than Friday," you should not fax an acceptance letter at 11:59 pm on that day. If you know that the offeror's office always closes for the weekend at 5:00 pm and that no one will be there to receive a late-night fax, your communication is not really instantaneous. It will not be effectively received until Monday morning. Given the circumstances, the acceptance would be late, and a contract would not be formed.

Consider why the courts draw a distinction between instantaneous and non-instantaneous communications. If a non-instantaneous acceptance were effective only when and where it was actually received, the offeree would be required to frequently check with the offeror in order to know whether a contract was formed. And until the receipt of the acceptance was confirmed, the offeree would be reluctant to perform the contract. Suppose I mail a letter from Saskatoon accepting your offer to pay me $5000 to deliver a series of lectures in Charlottetown. Unless I can be sure that we have a contract as soon as I put my letter in the mailbox, I will hesitate to book a flight, even if airfare will be much more expensive if I delay. I would be afraid that if I bought a ticket today, you might revoke your offer tomorrow before receiving my acceptance. If so, I would have a ticket to Charlottetown and no real reason to go there.

the **postal rule** states that an acceptance that is communicated in a non-instantaneous way is effective where and when the offeree sends it

For those reasons, the general rule does not apply to non-instantaneous forms of communication. Instead, according to the **postal rule**, an acceptance that is communicated in a non-instantaneous way is effective where and when the offeree sends it.[25] Continuing with our example, a contract is formed in Saskatoon as soon as I drop my acceptance letter into the mailbox, even though you will not receive that letter in Charlottetown for several days. Figure 7.2 illustrates the general rule and the postal rule.

By holding that my acceptance takes effect as soon as I send it, rather than when you receive it, the postal rule prevents you from revoking your offer while my letter is in the postal system. After all, you cannot revoke an offer that I have already accepted. In fact, the postal rule may work against you in an even stranger way. As long as the judge believes that I actually sent the letter, a contract can be formed between us even if my letter is lost in the mail and never reaches you.

Notice that the postal rule imposes certain risks upon you as the offeror. Until you actually receive a clear acceptance or rejection from me, you cannot be sure whether a contract has been created. There are, however, ways around

---

[24.] *Nova Scotia v Weymouth Sea Products Ltd* (1983) 149 DLR (3d) 637, aff'd 4 DLR (4th) 314 (NS CA).

[25.] Of course, the postal rule will not apply if the offeree's letter was not capable of being delivered. That will be true, for instance, if the offeree used the wrong address or failed to place sufficient postage on the envelope.

FIGURE 7.2 General Rule and Postal Rule

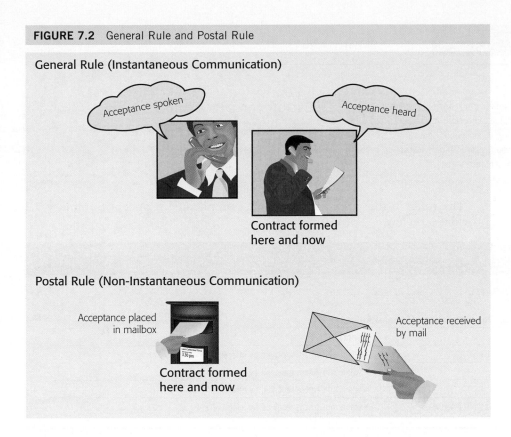

the postal rule. First, you could carefully draft your business proposals to ensure that they are invitations to treat rather than offers. If so, any replies that you receive will be offers seeking your acceptance rather than acceptances of your offer. You remain in control of the process. Second, the postal rule applies only if it is consistent with the parties' objective intentions. Even if you make an offer and are willing to receive acceptance by mail, you are entitled, as master of the offer, to eliminate the postal rule. You could, for example, say that a letter of acceptance is effective only when and where you actually receive it. You would therefore not be bound by an acceptance letter that was lost in the mail.[26] Third, even if you have not used your authority as master of the offer to limit the offeree's ability to accept an offer by mailing an acceptance, the postal rule will not apply where it would be unreasonable. For instance, a court might decide that in the particular circumstances of a case, no reasonable person would be willing, as an offeror, to be bound by a contract simply because the offeree dropped an acceptance letter into a mailbox.

We emphasize one more point about the postal rule: It applies only to acceptances. It does not apply to an offer, a revocation, a rejection, or a counter-offer. An offer or a revocation is effective only when and where it is received by the offeree. And a rejection or counter-offer is effective only when and where it is received by the offeror. Consider the situation in Business Decision 7.3.

[26.] *Saskatchewan River Bungalows Ltd v Maritime Life Assurance Co* (1994) 115 DLR (4th) 478 (SCC).

PART 3

Business Decision 7.3

The Postal Rule

On June 1, Maria sent you a letter offering to sell you her watch for $50. On June 3, she sent another letter that supposedly revoked her offer. On June 5, you received Maria's offer and immediately put an acceptance letter into a mailbox. On June 7, you received Maria's revocation letter. And on June 9, she received your acceptance letter.

Question for Discussion

1. Assuming that the usual rules apply, do you and Maria have a contract?

The rules in this area are somewhat complicated. Concept Summary 7.3 provides a review.

Concept Summary 7.3

Communication Rules

Rules Governing Instantaneous Communications (General Rule)	
Type of Communication	**Effective**
• offer by offeror	• when and where received by offeree
• revocation by offeror	• when and where received by offeree
• rejection by offeree	• when and where received by offeror
• counter-offer by offeree (who becomes the offeror)	• when and where received by initial offeror (who becomes the offeree)
• acceptance by offeree	• when and where received by offeror
Rules Governing Non-Instantaneous Communications (Postal Rule)	
Type of Communication	**Effective**
• offer by offeror	• when and where received by offeree
• revocation by offeror	• when and where received by offeree
• rejection by offeree	• when and where received by offeror
• counter-offer by offeree (who becomes the offeror)	• when and where received by initial offeror (who becomes the offeree)
• acceptance by offeree	• when and where sent by offeree

ACCEPTANCE BY PERFORMANCE

a **unilateral contract** occurs when an act is exchanged for a promise

We have discussed bilateral contracts in which a promise is exchanged for a promise. One party offers to do something in the future, and the other party accepts by similarly promising to do something in the future. The rules are different for *unilateral contracts*. A **unilateral contract** occurs when an act is exchanged for a promise. In that situation, the offeror promises to pay a reward to anyone who performs a particular act. As Figure 7.3 illustrates, the offeree accepts by actually performing its part of the agreement. You should notice

FIGURE 7.3 Unilateral Contract

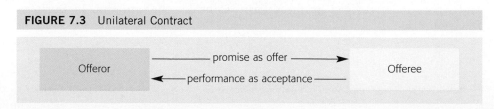

two things about unilateral contracts. First, no contract exists unless and until the offeree *fully* performs. Second, if the offeree performs and the contract is created, the offeror is the only one with an outstanding obligation to perform.

For example, suppose I offer to pay $100 to anyone who finds and returns my lost cat. At that point, we do not have a contract, and you are not required to look for her. However, a contract may be created if and when you bring her home to me. If so, you will not be obligated to do anything more, but I will be expected to pay the reward. Notice that we said that a unilateral contract *may* be created if you return my cat to me. That will be true only if you acted with the *intention of accepting* my offer. If you did not, then we did not have a meeting of the minds, and there is no contract. Perhaps you had not seen my offer but returned my cat out of the goodness of your heart. Although your actions took the proper form for acceptance, they were not performed in *response* to my offer.[27] Therefore, you are not entitled to the reward.

Case Brief 7.1 provides a famous illustration of a unilateral contract.

Case Brief 7.1

Carlill v Carbolic Smoke Ball Co [1893] 1 QB 256 (CA)

In the 1890s, England was plagued by two related phenomena: an influenza epidemic and quack medicine. The Carbolic Smoke Ball Co was one of many companies that tried to capitalize on the country's ill health. It produced a hand-held gadget that, when squeezed, emitted a small cloud of carbolic acid dust. The company claimed that if one inhaled the dust regularly, it would prevent a long list of ailments ranging from diphtheria and bronchitis to snoring and sore eyes. As part of its marketing ploy, it published an advertisement that offered to pay £100 to any person who contracted influenza while using the Carbolic Smoke Ball. Mrs Carlill saw the ad, bought the product, and used it as directed. When she later came down with the flu, she claimed to be entitled to £100. The company refused to pay. It said that there was no contract because she had not told them that she had accepted their offer and was using their product.

The court, undoubtedly put off by the company's unsavoury practices, rejected that argument. It held that the contract was unilateral and that the company, as offeror, had implicitly dispensed with the usual need for the communication of acceptance. Consequently, Mrs Carlill, as offeree, effectively accepted the offer by using the product as directed. As a result, she was entitled to collect £100.

The courts generally prefer bilateral contracts over unilateral contracts.[28] Bilateral contracts provide more protection. Neither party has to worry about wasting time and expense. The offeree knows that if it performs, it will be entitled to the offeror's performance, and *vice versa*. In contrast, a unilateral contract might operate unfairly. Consider a twist on the facts of *Carbolic Smoke Ball*. The company said that it would pay £100 to anyone who caught the flu despite using the device three times a day for two weeks. What if Mrs Carlill had gone to the trouble and expense of buying and using the ball three times a day for 13 days, but just as she was about to complete the treatment, a company representative knocked on her door and said, "Sorry, the deal's off"? Acceptance of a unilateral offer is not effective until the stipulated act is completed, and, as we saw earlier, an offeror is generally free to revoke an offer any time before acceptance. Consequently, it might appear that Mrs Carlill could not collect the reward even if she became sick after continuing to use the smoke ball.

A court would struggle to avoid that result. It would want to give Mrs Carlill an opportunity to inhale the dust for one more day and claim the money if she became sick. Its approach to the problem might be quite complex. For example, a judge might hold that the company's notice actually contained offers for *two*

---

27. *R v Clarke* (1927) 40 CLR 227 (HCA).

28. *Dawson v Helicopter Exploration Co* [1955] 5 DLR 404 (SCC).

unilateral contracts. The main contract would involve the company's promise to pay £100 to anyone who became sick despite using the smoke ball. The other contract would involve the company's promise to not revoke its offer once a customer began using the device.[29] Alternatively, the judge might simply say, as a matter of fairness, that the company was not entitled to revoke its offer while Mrs Carlill was in the process of accepting.[30]

[29.]*Errington v Errington* [1952] 1 KB 290 (CA).

[30.]*Ayerswood Development Corp v Hydro One Networks Inc* (2004) 39 CLR (3d) 288 (Ont SCJ).

Chapter Summary

A contract is an agreement that creates rights and obligations that can be enforced in law. The formation of a contract usually requires three things: an intention to create legal relations, a meeting of the minds, and an exchange of value. The first two requirements were discussed in this chapter; the third is considered in the next chapter.

The courts presume an intention to create legal relations in commercial contexts but not in family or social settings. However, these presumptions can be rebutted.

A meeting of the minds occurs through the process of offer and acceptance. Not every statement regarding a proposed transaction is an offer. The courts will not recognize a contract if a reasonable person would have interpreted the parties' communications as involving mere inquiries or invitations to treat.

Contractual offers must be communicated and received as offers. An offer may be made orally, in writing, or through conduct. The life of an offer is usually limited. To create a contract, acceptance must occur before the offer is terminated. An offer can be brought to an end through revocation, lapse of time, death or insanity, rejection, or counter-offer. A counter-offer creates a new offer in which the person who originally was the offeree becomes the offeror. The process of offer and acceptance requires special attention in the case of an option, a tender, or a battle of the forms.

A bilateral contract occurs when a promise is exchanged for a promise. Acceptance arises when an offeree agrees to enter into the contract proposed by the offeror. Acceptance usually occurs through words, but it may also occur through conduct. Mere silence generally cannot be acceptance, but silence may be sufficient if it is coupled with other factors. In any event, acceptance must be unequivocal and correspond precisely with the terms of the offer. Generally, it must be communicated to the offeror. With instantaneous forms of communication, acceptance is effective and a contract is formed when and where the communication is received by the offeror. The same is not true for non-instantaneous forms of communication, where acceptance occurs when and where it is sent, whether it is received or not. The general rule and the postal rule can be altered or eliminated by the offeror. The offeror, as master of the offer, can set special rules for acceptance.

A unilateral contract occurs when performance is exchanged for a promise. The offeree accepts by performing its part of the agreement. No contract exists unless and until the offeree performs. And if the offeree performs and the contract is created, the offeror is the only one who has an outstanding obligation. The courts generally prefer bilateral contracts over unilateral contracts.

MyBusLawLab   ADDITIONAL RESOURCES FOR CHAPTER 7

MyBusLawLab provides students with an assortment of tools to help enrich the learning experience, including a Study Plan with Pre- and Post-tests, mini-cases with assessments, and provincial content material, which provides links to relevant cases, legislation, and additional resources.

MyBusLawLab provides the following resources for Chapter 7:

Provincial Material

- **British Columbia:** Government Procurement and Tenders, Cooling-Off Period, Electronic Transactions
- **Alberta:** *Consumer Protection Acts,* Cooling-Off Period, Electronic Contracts, Form of Contract
- **Manitoba and Saskatchewan:** *Internet Consumer Contracts and the Consumer Protection Act*, Negative Marketing
- **Ontario:** Acceptance, Consumer Agreements, Cooling-Off Periods, *Consumer Protection Act 2002*, Exemption Clauses, Electronic Contracts, Standard Form Contracts, Terms Requiring Notice
- **Atlantic Provinces:** Internet Sales Contracts, Public Tenders

Review Questions

1. What is meant by the term "meeting of the minds"? How is it significant to the formation of contracts?

2. What is a "comfort letter"? What rights and obligations do the parties have under a comfort letter?

3. What risks are associated with offers? Describe two techniques by which the courts reduce those risks.

4. Provide a translation of the phrase *quantum meruit*. Briefly explain the significance of the phrase in connection with the law of contracts.

5. Why do the courts generally rely upon an objective test rather than a subjective test when deciding contractual issues?

6. What is an "option"? When and why is an option important?

7. Distinguish between an offer and an invitation to treat. Give an example of each. How does the distinction help to promote commercial activity?

8. Briefly discuss the commercial and ethical implications of revoking a firm offer.

9. What is a "cross-offer"? Can two cross-offers create a contract? Explain your answer.

10. Describe how the tendering process works. Explain the two types of contracts that are involved.

11. Identify and briefly explain the various ways in which an offer may come to an end.

12. "As long as it is communicated to the offeror, acceptance is always effective, even if it is communicated in a different manner than the original offer." Is that statement true? Explain your answer.

13. What is the effect of rejecting an offer? Why do you think the rule is set up this way? If you change your mind after rejecting an offer, what can you do to revive the transaction?

14. What is a "counter-offer"? What effect does a counter-offer have on an offer?

15. Describe the problems that arise from a "battle of the forms."

16. What is the difference between a bilateral contract and a unilateral contract? How is each type of contract accepted?

17. Can an offer ever be accepted through the offeree's silence? Why or why not?

18. What is the difference between instantaneous and non-instantaneous forms of communication? How is that difference relevant to the formation of contracts?

19. "An offeror who is willing to receive an acceptance by mail always runs the risk of being bound by a contract without knowing it." Is that statement true? Explain your answer.

20. "An offer of a *unilateral* contract is *always* accepted through the performance of some act. An offer of a *bilateral* contract is *never* accepted through the performance of some act." Are those statements true? Explain your answer.

Cases and Problems

1. Ziggy Sounds Ltd is a music production company. It frequently needs to update its equipment as technology develops and styles change. For many years, it has contracted with David Jones Inc (DJI) to create and supply all of its computerized components. A new contract was created each time that Ziggy required something new from DJI, but those contracts always were based on DJI's standard form contract (a pre-prepared document that sets out the parties' rights and obligations) and they always included precisely the same promises regarding the quality of the goods. DJI, however, recently came under new ownership and the owners are very cautious people. They generally want to carry on business as usual, but they are not yet sure that they are willing to provide the same promises regarding the quality of their company's goods. Ziggy recently sent a purchase order to DJI. DJI responded by sending back its usual standard form contract, containing all of the usual promises, but with one new phrase added: "This agreement is subject to formal contract." Although DJI's new owners intended to redraft its standard form contract, its workers immediately went ahead by creating the requested component and sending it to Ziggy. Ziggy paid, but within a few days, it discovered that the component was defective. When Ziggy indicated that it intended to sue for breach of contract, DJI's owners said that there was no contract. Are they right? Did the parties create a contract? Is Ziggy entitled to sue for breach of contract? Explain your answer.

2. Danuta Swinton was unhappy with a very large maple tree in her front yard. She therefore contacted West End Tree Service (WETS) to discuss the problem. At the end of their discussion, WETS's manager wrote up a document, entitled "Tree Removal," that provided an estimated price of $1950. That price was broken down into three elements: $950 to cut down the tree, $800 to remove the logs and debris, and $200 for a city permit. The work could not be done without the permit. During the same meeting, Danuta signed an application for

a tree removal permit. Acting on Danuta's behalf, WETS sent the application to the city along with a cheque for $200. Two weeks later, after the city had issued the permit, WETS went to Danuta's house during the middle of the day, cut down the tree, and hauled it away. When she returned home from work that evening, however, Danuta paid $200 for the permit, but refused to pay anything more. She has persuaded the court that she never actually asked WETS to do anything more than obtain the permit, and that she never thought that they had a contract to actually perform the work. In contrast, WETS has explained that it would never simply obtain a permit on behalf of a customer. Unless it gets paid to actually remove a tree, the job is not worth the hassle. All of WETS's competitors have the same policy. Does Danuta have to pay for WETS's services in removing the tree? Did the parties have a contract?

3. The City of Darlington, which wants to build a new recreational centre, places an advertisement in a local newspaper requesting that contractors submit tenders. The newspaper advertisement states that tenders must be received by 4:00 pm on June 15 and that tenders are irrevocable after they have been received by the city. Ronaldo is amongst the contractors who submit tenders. At 4:15 on June 15, however, he realizes that he had miscalculated the expenses that would be involved in the project and that his bid consequently is grossly understated. He telephones the city and asks it to remove his tender from consideration. Even though the city has yet to select the winning tender, it rejects Ronaldo's request and informs him that it will select his bid if that bid offers to build the recreation centre for the lowest price. Explain whether Ronaldo will be able to revoke his bid.

4. Parktown Realty Inc developed an upscale condominium complex. On October 1, Miranda Wine signed an offer to purchase one of the units. Part of that document said, "This offer is irrevocable by the Purchaser until one minute before midnight on the fifteenth day after its date, after which time if not accepted, this offer shall be null and void." As both parties were aware, the real estate market was highly volatile at the time that Miranda signed her offer to purchase. In the preceding months, prices had gone up and down, quite unpredictably. On October 10, Parktown signed that document with the intention of accepting Miranda's offer. Because of an oversight, however, the company did not mail the signed document back to Miranda until October 14. Miranda eventually received the letter on October 20. By that time, the real estate market had collapsed and she was no longer interested in buying a condominium unit at the original price. She therefore insists that her offer lapsed before it had been turned into a contract by Parktown's acceptance. Is she correct?

5. Birinder was considering the purchase of a laptop computer, but he was not yet sure exactly what he needed. He visited Singh's Computer Shop and explained his situation to the saleswoman. She said that she would try to find something appropriate. The next day, she sent a laptop to Birinder's home, along with a note that said, "Take a look at this one. If it suits your needs, you can buy it. If not, just let us know and we'll come around to collect it. We have to insist, however, that you not use it until you've decided to purchase." After examining the unit, Birinder was impressed, but he decided that he would try to find the same model at a different shop for a lower price. He therefore telephoned Singh's and left a message on the answering machine: "Many thanks for the suggestion. I have, however, decided that I don't want the laptop that you sent over. You can come by to retrieve it." Immediately after hanging up, however, Birinder realized that he would need a computer to write a major assignment for his business law course. He therefore used the laptop that he had received from Singh's. Once that was done, he packed up the computer and returned it to the computer shop. The saleswoman seemed surprised to see him. "Didn't you get my message?" Birinder asked. "No," she said, "our answering machine broke. Why, don't you want the unit?" Birinder then explained the whole story, including his use of the computer. "Well, then," said the saleswoman, "it's too late. You've already bought yourself that computer." Is she right? Do the parties have a contract?

6. Ahmad owned Regent Arms, an apartment block in downtown Vancouver, which he wished to sell. He knew that Felicity, a real estate developer, was interested in such properties. Therefore, on Thursday, he faxed this offer to her: "I will sell Regent Arms to you for $5 000 000. If you wish to accept this offer, please do so as soon as possible. I promise that I will not make a similar offer to anyone else while you are considering this proposal." Felicity was very interested in the offer but received it just as she was about to leave for a meeting in Medicine Hat. When she returned on the following Monday, she immediately faxed a letter purporting to accept Ahmad's offer. He replied that since he had not heard from her earlier, he had sold Regent Arms to another party on Saturday. Felicity now claims that because Ahmad had done nothing to communicate the revocation of his offer, his offer was still open for acceptance when she sent her fax to him. Is she correct? Has the offer lapsed or been revoked? Explain the arguments that Ahmad and Felicity might make if their dispute goes to court.

7. Mack Darin owns and operates a store in a rough downtown neighbourhood. Last week, he received a shipment of switchblade knives. He placed one of the knives in his store window, alongside a small notice board that said, "Switchblade Knives—$25 each." That display soon caught the attention of Constable Boot, a member of the local police department. Darin was arrested and charged with a crime under section 7 of the *Prohibited Weapons Act*, which says that it is illegal to "manufacture, sell, rent, or offer for sale or rent. . . any knife. . . which has a blade

that opens automatically by hand pressure applied to a button, spring, or other device in or attached to the handle of the knife." There is no doubt that the switchblade that appeared in Darin's store window falls within that description. Is it therefore safe to assume that Mack Darin has committed a crime? Explain your answer.

8. On October 15, Olaf mails a letter in Winnipeg offering to sell widgets to Simone. The next day, before Simone receives Olaf's offer, he sends another letter from Winnipeg revoking his offer. Simone receives Olaf's offer letter in Kelowna on October 21 and immediately sends a letter of acceptance. The next day, she receives Olaf's revocation letter in Kelowna. Applying the rules summarized in Concept Summary 7.3, on page 176, determine if, when, and where the parties formed a contract.

9. Ten years ago, Edgar's daughter, Tina, married Hussein. Because the young couple could not afford to buy a house by themselves, Edgar placed a down payment of $90 000 on a home and told his daughter and son-in-law that they could live in the house and that if they paid monthly mortgage instalments of $1000 until the mortgage was satisfied, he would transfer the clear title into their name. Unfortunately, Tina and her parents recently had a falling out. Although Tina and Hussein have regularly paid the monthly mortgage instalments and wish to continue doing so until the mortgage is paid off (which they predict will occur in about seven years), Edgar has purportedly revoked his offer and stated that he intends to pay the remaining mortgage instalments and permanently live in the house himself. Did the parties act with an intention to create legal relations? Was the contract proposed by Edgar's initial offer a bilateral contract or a unilateral contract? Have Tina and Hussein fully accepted Edgar's offer? If not, can Edgar revoke his offer? If it was a unilateral contract, were Tina and Hussein obligated to pay the full mortgage once they began to make instalment payments?

10. Five years ago, Arvid and Dora were involved in an amorous relationship while they studied business together at college. Since that time, they have gone their separate ways and have moved to different cities, but they are still intimate on those rare occasions when their paths cross. Unfortunately, while Arvid's business has flourished, Dora's has foundered and she has fallen on hard times. Last month, Arvid wrote to Dora to offer her a job with his company. The relevant portion of his letter stated, "Given all that we have been through together and given the generous salary that I am offering, I just know that you'll accept. I'm considering the deal done and I'll begin setting up an office for you tomorrow." Arvid's letter did not mention that his offer was also motivated partly by a secret desire to rekindle their old romance into a permanent and stable relationship. When Dora received the letter, she decided to definitely take the job and began making arrangements to join Arvid's company. She did not, however, inform her old friend of that decision. She wanted to surprise him by simply appearing at his door the next week. However, three days later, her own company received an unexpected financial grant from the federal government. At that point, she reconsidered her earlier decision to work for Arvid and telephoned him to say that she would not be joining him after all. Because he had already spent a considerable amount of money preparing for Dora's arrival and because he was upset that she spurned his offer, Arvid reacted angrily. He insisted that a contract had been created and that she was his employee. Is he correct? Did Arvid act with an intention to create legal relations? Does it necessarily matter that both Arvid and Dora firmly believed that they had formed an enforceable agreement? Has there been valid acceptance?

11. Ekaterina owned a farm in a remote region of Saskatchewan, which she had been trying to sell for several years. In late November, Rasheed faxed her an offer to purchase the property for $50 000 and asked that she quickly reply by fax or telegram. Two weeks later, Ekaterina responded with a letter that stated that, by coincidence, another person had recently expressed interest in the farm and that, in the circumstances, she would not sell for less than $60 000. Her message stated that if that price was satisfactory, the deal "could be completed immediately," and suggested January 1 as a closing date. Ekaterina's letter also asked Rasheed to reply by telephone or email to avoid delay. A week later, Ekaterina's letter was delivered to Rasheed's house. As he was abroad on business, his wife, Naima, opened it in his absence. Without Rasheed's authorization, Naima immediately sent a telegram to Ekaterina, stating that Rasheed would return in 10 days and asking that the offer be held open until that time. The telegram also indicated that Rasheed had earlier expressed interest in the property and stated that if he purchased the farm, he would not require the land until March, as it would not be possible to commence farming operations until the spring. Ekaterina did not reply to that telegram. Ten days later, Rasheed returned from abroad and promptly emailed Ekaterina to accept her offer to sell the farm for $60 000. She replied that she had sold the property to a third party the previous day and that her offer consequently was no longer open. Rasheed believes that since his acceptance was communicated before he was informed of the sale to the third party, a contract was formed between himself and Ekaterina. Is he correct? Was Ekaterina's offer still open when Rasheed purported to accept it? What factors would a judge consider in deciding that issue?

12. Connie and Michael Fikowski owned Saskatchewan River Bungalows Ltd (SRB). That company purchased an insurance policy on Michael's life and named Connie as the beneficiary. The policy was purchased from Maritime Life Assurance Co (MLA). The policy was renewable each year according to the terms of the insurance contract. The relevant terms stated:

The obligations contained in this contract are conditional upon payment of the premiums as they become due.

Each premium is payable on or before July 26 at the head office of the Company in Halifax, Nova Scotia.

If any premium remains unpaid at the end of the grace period, this policy automatically lapses (terminates because of non-payment of premiums).

Near the end of the first year of coverage, in late June, SRB mailed a cheque and a renewal request to MLA's head office in Halifax. In the normal course of events, that letter would have reached Halifax within five business days. In fact, for reasons unknown, the letter has never been received by the insurance company. The Fikowskis did not realize that their letter had gone missing until nearly a year later. At that point, they presented a new cheque to the insurance company and requested reinstatement of their policy. By that time, however, Michael had been diagnosed with cancer, so the insurance company refused to accept the payment. Michael recently died and the insurance company denies any liability. Connie Fikowski, in contrast, insists that she is entitled to a benefit under the policy. Discuss the parties' dispute.

Consideration and Privity

8

LEARNING OBJECTIVES

After completing this chapter, you should be able to:

❶ Explain the nature of consideration and the role it plays in the formation of contracts.

❷ Describe past consideration and explain why it cannot support a contract.

❸ Distinguish between (i) pre-existing public duties, (ii) pre-existing contractual obligations owed to a third party, and (iii) pre-existing contractual obligations owed to the same party.

❹ Describe the nature and effect of a seal.

❺ Define promissory estoppel and identify its four requirements.

❻ Describe the concept of privity of contract and explain its relationship to the concept of consideration.

❼ Distinguish between equitable assignments and statutory assignments and explain how assignments provide an exception to the privity of contract rule.

❽ Explain how a trust can be used to create an apparent exception to the privity of contract rule.

❾ Identify two types of statutes that provide exceptions to the privity of contract rule.

❿ Explain when and why employees will be entitled to enforce exclusion clauses that are contained in contracts to which they are strangers.

In Chapter 7, we looked at some of the ingredients required to form a contract: intention to create legal relations, offer, and acceptance. In this chapter, we examine another: *consideration*. As we will see, "consideration" refers to the thing that each party provides under a contract. This is critical—unless consideration exists on both sides of a bargain, the courts will usually not enforce the parties' agreement.

We will also examine the concept of *privity of contract*. Consideration, offer and acceptance, and intention to create contractual relations are required to create a contract. "Privity of contract" identifies the parties to a contract. It determines who can sue or be sued.

L.O. ❶❷❸❹❺

Consideration

The main goal of contract law is to enforce bargains. And as business people know, a bargain involves more than an offer and an acceptance. It also involves a *mutual exchange of value*. Without that sort of exchange, a contract usually cannot exist. Suppose I offer to give you a computer and you simply agree to receive it. I have made a **gratuitous promise**—I did not receive anything of legal value in exchange for it. I have promised to give you something, but you have not promised to do anything in return. Consequently, while you will be entitled to keep the computer if I actually give it to you, you cannot force me to hand it over to you. Because we did not have a bargain, we did not have a contract. And because we did not have a contract, I am entitled to change my mind.[1]

The creation of a contract therefore generally depends on an exchange of value. *Consideration* must be provided by both parties. While that term is notoriously difficult to define, we can generally say that **consideration** exists when a party either gives (or promises to give) a benefit to someone else *or* suffers (or promises to suffer) a detriment to themself.[2] Consideration must move *from* each side of a contract but not necessarily *to* the other side. For example, you and I will have a contract if I promise to give $5000 to your brother, and you promise to give a car to my sister. In that situation, it is enough that we have both promised to provide a benefit to *someone*; we did not have to promise to provide benefits to each other.[3]

Because the idea of consideration is so broad, it seldom causes problems. Difficulties do, however, occasionally arise. It is therefore important to examine the concept in some detail.

SUFFICIENT AND ADEQUATE CONSIDERATION

A contract must be supported by *sufficient consideration*. That requirement is, however, easily met. **Sufficient consideration** may be almost anything of value. It is, for instance, sufficient if a person promises to give up smoking, drinking, or swearing.[4] There are nevertheless exceptions. "Love and affection"

---

a **gratuitous promise** is a promise for which nothing of legal value is given in exchange

consideration exists when a party either gives (or promises to give) a benefit to someone else *or* suffers (or promises to suffer) a detriment to themself

sufficient consideration may be almost anything of value

[1.] An interesting application of that rule may occur if you promise to give money to a charity. Unless the charitable organization promised to do something in exchange for your promise, you are entitled to change your mind: *Dalhousie College v Boutilier Estate* [1934] 3 DLR 593 (SCC).

[2.] *Currie v Misa* (1875) LR 10 Ex 153 (HL).

[3.] As we will see, however, even though the contract is made for their benefit, your brother and my sister lack "privity of contract" and therefore may find it impossible to enforce our agreement.

[4.] *Hamer v Sidway* 27 NE 256 (1891 NY CA).

is not enough to support an enforceable agreement. Consequently, if an elderly gentleman promises to pay $10 000 to his wayward niece in exchange for her promise to "always be kind and caring," the parties will not have a contract. The reason for this rather surprising attitude is not entirely clear. It probably arises from the fact that during the nineteenth century, when many of the rules in law of contract were created, judges generally wanted to avoid becoming involved in intimate matters.[5]

Although consideration must be sufficient, it does not have to be *adequate*. **Adequate consideration** has essentially the same value as the consideration for which it is exchanged. For example, if I promise to give you a computer worth $5000, and you promise to give up smoking, drinking, and swearing for a year, it would seem that I have made a very bad bargain. In economic terms, I will be giving up far more than you will be providing in return. Nevertheless, we probably have a contract, and it is unlikely that a judge will save me from my own foolishness. Because the law presumes that people are able to look after their own interests, it generally allows them to decide what price they will demand under a contract.[6] Lawyers sometimes refer to that set of rules as the *peppercorn theory*. In the traditional example, two people create an agreement by exchanging a peppercorn for a horse. The peppercorn has *some* value (and therefore is *sufficient* consideration), but it certainly is not worth as much as a horse (and therefore is not *adequate* consideration). The contract nevertheless is enforceable.

adequate consideration has essentially the same value as the consideration for which it is exchanged

Forbearance to Sue

For business people, the difference between sufficient consideration and adequate consideration is particularly important in the context of *forbearance to sue*. **Forbearance to sue** is a promise not to pursue a lawsuit. Because lawsuits are expensive and unpredictable, very few are actually decided by judges, as we saw in Chapter 2. In the vast majority of cases, the parties settle their dispute out of court. They often enter into a contract for that purpose. The plaintiff promises not to bring the matter into court and the defendant agrees to pay less money than they allegedly owed. If the plaintiff's action would have won in court, there obviously is consideration on both sides of the contract. The plaintiff surrendered the right to claim full damages, and the defendant paid money.[7] But what if it is later discovered that the plaintiff would have lost the case if it had gone to trial? In that situation, it might appear that the plaintiff did not give consideration. After all, they merely agreed not to pursue a lawsuit that they would have lost. Nevertheless, a judge would likely hold the parties to their agreement. As you read You Be the Judge 8.1, consider the possible reasons for enforcing such contracts. Also consider the importance of receiving advice from a lawyer before agreeing to forbear on a possible action.

forbearance to sue is a promise to not pursue a lawsuit

[5] Furthermore, as Chapter 7 explained, the courts generally assume that there is no intention to create legal relations between family members and close friends.

[6] However, as Chapter 10 will explain, when one party exercises an unfair advantage over the other, the courts may become concerned about the inadequacy of consideration. For example, if a con artist tricks a senior citizen into trading her home for his essentially worthless share certificates, a judge may strike down the parties' agreement because it is "unconscionable" or grossly unfair. (The concept of unconscionability is examined in Chapter 10.)

[7] The term "damages" refers to the money that the court may order the defendant to pay to the plaintiff. Chapter 12 discusses the damages thatmay be awarded for a breach of contract.

PART 3

You Be the Judge 8.1

Forbearance to Sue[8]

Igor works as a stockbroker for a company. Following procedures that he remembered reading in the company's official policy, he purchased $100 000 worth of shares on instructions from a client. Unfortunately, despite Igor's repeated demands, the client refused to pay for those shares. Worse yet, during that time, the value of the shares dropped by 60 percent. Eventually, the company took control of the account, sold the shares for $40 000, and threatened to sue Igor for $60 000. In the company's view, the whole fiasco was his fault. Igor vigorously denied liability, but he was worried that a lawsuit would damage his professional reputation. He was also unable to find the policy document that he had relied on. Consequently, he agreed to pay $50 000 in exchange for the company's promise to drop the matter. Two weeks later, however, before actually making the payment, Igor located the lost document. It proved that he could not be held liable in the circumstances.

Questions for Discussion

1. Can the company force Igor to pay the $50 000? Did he incur a contractual obligation to do so? Did the company provide consideration in exchange for his promise?

2. Even if the company did not actually have a valid claim against Igor, is it true to say that it gave nothing of value when it agreed to drop its lawsuit against him?

3. As a matter of policy, why are the courts eager to find the existence of a contract, even if the underlying claim is invalid? If they refused to do so, would it ever make sense for a party to forbear? Consider the general consequences that would follow from such an approach.

In some situations, the courts will not enforce forbearance agreements, especially if the party that threatened to sue did not honestly believe that they had a valid claim in the first place. Case Brief 8.1 provides an interesting illustration.[9]

Case Brief 8.1

DCB v Zellers Inc (1996) 138 DLR (4th) 309 (Man QB)

A teenager was caught allegedly stealing a number of items from a Zellers store. The store sent a letter to the boy's mother, threatening to exercise its "legal right to claim Civil Restitution" from her unless she paid $225. She promptly paid that amount, but later realized that while the store was entitled to sue her son, it did not actually have any right to sue her. (As we discussed in Chapter 6, parents are not vicariously liable for their children. In other words, parents cannot be sued simply because their child broke the law.) The woman therefore insisted that she was entitled to repayment of the $225. The store eventually agreed that it did not, in fact, have a right to sue the teenager's parent. It nevertheless argued that it was entitled to

the money because it had honestly thought otherwise when it received the payment.

The store would have been entitled to keep the money if it had truly believed that it was entitled to sue the boy's parent. In that situation, the parties would have had a binding contract. In exchange for the mother's payment of $225, the store would have given its forbearance to sue. The court held, however, that the lawyer who wrote the initial letter on behalf of the store could not have "seriously thought that this claim could succeed." Consequently, since the store had not given consideration, there was no contract. And since there was no contract, the woman was entitled to recover her money.

PAST CONSIDERATION

mutuality of consideration requires that each party provide consideration *in return* for the other party's consideration

Because the law views a contract as a bargain, consideration must be provided by both sides. There must also be **mutuality of consideration**. Each party must provide consideration *in return* for the other party's consideration.

---

8. See also *Moss v Chin* (1994) 120 DLR (4th) 406 (BC SC).

9. The facts are based on *Stott v Merit Investments Inc* (1988) 48 DLR (4th) 288 (Ont CA).

The requirement of mutuality is important to the idea of *past consideration*. **Past consideration** consists of something that a party did *prior to the contemplation of a contract*. In that situation, there is no mutuality. Past consideration is not given *in exchange for* the other party's consideration. And for that reason, past consideration is not really consideration at all. It therefore cannot support a contract.

Sometimes it is difficult to determine whether something is past consideration. Consider two situations. In the first, you arrive home to find that a landscaping company has worked on your lawn. Although you had not asked the company to do so, you are delighted with the result. You therefore promise to pay $250. You are not legally obligated to keep that promise. There is no contract. One reason is that the company provided its services *before* you promised to pay the money. The company did not work *in exchange for* your promise.[10]

Now suppose you see the landscapers working on your neighbour's lawn and ask them to work on your lawn as well. The company's manager agrees to do so, but neither of you says anything about the price. After the company finishes the job, you promise to pay $250. It might appear, once again, that there is no contract. After all, your promise to pay came *after* the company provided its services. Those services therefore might seem like past consideration. A court, however, would view the matter differently. A reasonable person would have interpreted your initial request to include a promise to pay the company for its services. A judge would therefore require you to pay a "reasonable price."[11] A judge would also find that your *subsequent* promise to pay $250 merely provided evidence of a reasonable price. (If you had not subsequently promised to pay $250, the judge would determine the value of the company's services after considering all of the circumstances.) In other words, although the terms of the contract were not entirely settled at the outset, there was a sufficient meeting of the minds. And on that view, the company's actions were good consideration, rather than past consideration. They were provided *in return* for your implicit promise that you would pay.[12] They were part of a bargaining process.

The rule on past consideration may produce results that do not easily fit with basic notions of fairness and morality. Consider the situation in Ethical Perspective 8.1.

past consideration consists of something that a party did prior to the contemplation of a contract

PART 3

Ethical Perspective **8.1**

Past Consideration[13]

While strolling on a beach, you discover Heena unconscious and face down in the water. You pull her ashore, administer first aid, and bring her back to life. Shaken, but grateful, she promises to pay you $500 every year for the remainder of your life. However, when you attempt to collect the first payment, she states that she has changed her mind and refuses to pay anything.

Questions for Discussion

1. Does Heena have a moral obligation to pay any money to you? Does she have a legal obligation to do so?

2. Leaving aside the rule governing past consideration, do you believe that Heena should be required to pay anything to you?

[10.] *Eastwood v Kenyon* (1840) 113 ER 482 (CA). As we saw in Chapter 7, a court could also refuse to recognize a contract on the basis that there was no offer and acceptance. There was, rather, simply a promise to pay for work that had already been done.

[11.] Lawyers sometimes refer to the reasonable price for services as *quantum meruit,* or "as much as it is worth."

[12.] *Lampleigh v Braithwait* (1615) 80 ER 255 (KB).

[13.] The facts are based on *Webb v McGowin* 168 So 2d 196 (Ala CA 1935).

PRE-EXISTING OBLIGATION

Because past consideration is no consideration at all, an act that was *actually performed* before a contract was proposed cannot provide consideration for that agreement. But can a contract be supported by a *promise* to fulfill a **pre-existing obligation**, that is, an obligation that existed, but was not actually performed, before the contract was contemplated?

We must distinguish three types of pre-existing obligations:

- a pre-existing public duty
- a pre-existing contractual obligation owed to a third party
- a pre-existing contractual obligation owed to the same party

a **pre-existing obligation** is an obligation that existed, but was not actually performed, before the contract was contemplated

Pre-Existing Public Duty

A person who owes a *pre-existing public duty* cannot rely upon that obligation as consideration for a new contract. For example, firefighters and police officers who are called to your office during an emergency cannot sell their services to you under a contract. One reason for this is that when they became public servants, they already promised to help people like you in times of need. Therefore, they do not have anything more that they can offer as part of a new agreement. An even stronger reason, which is not tied to the idea of past consideration, is that it would be against *public policy* to allow public servants to take advantage of your misfortune by charging for their services. It would also be undesirable if public servants were tempted to pass by poor citizens and enter into lucrative contracts with wealthy citizens.

However, by becoming a public servant, a person does not promise to protect citizens around the clock. For example, after police officers finish their shifts, they can generally do as they please. They are certainly not required to guard your house during their "off" hours, even if you are worried that thieves might be lurking in the area. If you want that type of protection, you have to pay for it.

Pre-Existing Contractual Obligation Owed to a Third Party

We have seen that a promise to perform a pre-existing *public duty* is not good consideration for a new contract. In contrast, a promise to perform a pre-existing obligation that previously arose under a *contract with a third party* can be good consideration for a new contract. That rule is often important in business, as Case Brief 8.2 shows.

In one sense, there is an advantage to using the same consideration for two different contracts. Despite promising to do only one thing, you may be able to extract valuable promises from two different parties. However, there is also a danger in that sort of arrangement. Suppose a classical quartet agrees with a promoter to perform a concert in exchange for $15 000. The quartet subsequently persuades a music publisher, under a separate contract, to pay $20 000 for the right to record the concert. If all goes well, the quartet will receive $15 000 from the promoter *and* $20 000 from the publisher, even though it essentially did only one thing. However, if the quartet refuses to perform, it will be held liable to both the promoter *and* the publisher, even though it essentially failed to do only one thing.

Case Brief 8.2

Pao On v Lau Yiu Long [1980] AC 614 (PC)

The plaintiff bought 4 200 000 shares from a company called Fu Chip. Under the terms of that agreement, the plaintiff promised Fu Chip that it would not resell more than 60 percent of those shares within one year. Resale of a larger number of the shares would hurt Fu Chip's financial situation. The plaintiff later realized, however, that it might suffer a financial loss itself if, for some reason, the value of the shares dropped. It would be required to retain the shares while their value declined. The plaintiff therefore approached the defendants, who were the majority shareholders in Fu Chip, and persuaded them to enter into a separate, *indemnification* contract.[14] Under that agreement, the plaintiff promised to honour its earlier sale contract with Fu Chip, and the defendants promised to compensate the plaintiff for any loss that it suffered as a result.

The plaintiff therefore used the same consideration twice. It separately promised both the defendants and Fu Chip (which, as a stranger to the indemnification contract, was classified as a *third party* to that agreement) that it would not resell 60 percent of the shares within one year.

As feared, the value of the shares dropped, and the plaintiff claimed indemnification under its contract with the defendants. The defendants argued that the plaintiff had merely promised to fulfill the first (sale) contract and had not provided good consideration for the second (indemnification) contract. The court, however, held that the plaintiff's promise to perform the contractual obligation that it already owed to Fu Chip (the third party) was good consideration for its later contract with the defendants.

Pre-Existing Contractual Obligation Owed to the Same Party

We have seen that a promise to perform a pre-existing obligation that previously arose under a contract with a *third party* can be good consideration for a new contract. But what if the pre-existing obligation arose under an earlier contract with the *same party* that is on the other side of the new contract? Perhaps surprisingly, a different rule applies in that situation. The courts usually hold that the *same* person cannot be required to pay twice for the same benefit. If a promise is merely repeated, it does not provide anything new. Furthermore, the courts want to prevent a person from threatening to breach one contract in order to get the other party to enter into a second contract at a higher price. The leading case is discussed in Case Brief 8.3.

Case Brief 8.3

Gilbert Steel Ltd v University Construction Ltd (1976) 67 DLR (3d) 606 (Ont CA)

The plaintiff contractually agreed to sell several shipments of steel to the defendant at a set price. After that agreement was partially fulfilled, the plaintiff's own supplier raised its prices. The defendant then promised to pay the plaintiff a higher price for the remaining shipments of steel. The plaintiff delivered the rest of the steel, but the defendant refused to honour their promise to pay the extra amount. The defendant argued that

the plaintiff had already promised to deliver the steel under the initial contract and therefore did not provide anything in exchange for the later promise of the higher price.

The court agreed. It held that the defendant was not required to pay the extra price because they had not received anything new in exchange for its promise to do so.

The court's analysis may seem appropriate in *Gilbert Steel*, but it does not sit so well in other situations. Parties sometimes fail to appreciate the effort and expense that will be involved in the performance of their contract. If so, they

---

14. Indemnification occurs when a party receives compensation for a loss that it suffered.

may genuinely agree that the terms of their original contract should be revised to ensure that the deal benefits both of them, especially if they want to develop and maintain goodwill. Successful business people often recognize that a small sacrifice in the short term can lead to larger benefits in the long term. For those reasons, many scholars argue that a party's promise to revise the terms of a contract should sometimes be enforceable if the revision accurately reflects an unexpected change in circumstances. That argument was accepted in England and may eventually be adopted in Canada as well.[15]

In the meantime, there are other ways in which Canadian business people can avoid the rule in *Gilbert Steel*. First, they can use the process of *novation* to discharge their initial contract and enter into a new agreement that includes a higher price.[16] Second, they can agree that something new is to be done in exchange for the extra price. For example, in *Gilbert Steel*, the plaintiff could have promised to deliver either somewhat more steel or the same amount of steel somewhat earlier. Third, as we will discuss in the next section, the defendant's promise in *Gilbert Steel* would have been binding, despite the lack of any new consideration from the plaintiff, if it had been made under *seal*. And finally, as previously suggested, business people can simply ignore the rule in *Gilbert Steel*. They may be unaware of it. And even if they are aware of it, they may realize that financial success in the long run sometimes requires short-term flexibility.

Concept Summary 8.1 lists the general rules regarding pre-existing obligations and consideration.

Concept Summary 8.1

Pre-Existing Obligations and Consideration

Situation	Can a Pre-Existing Obligation Generally Provide Consideration for a New Contract?
Pre-existing public duty	No
Pre-existing contractual obligation owed to a third party	Yes
Pre-existing contractual obligation owed to the same party	No

PROMISE TO FORGIVE AN EXISTING DEBT Before leaving this topic, it is important to discuss one more set of cases. The question in *Gilbert Steel* was whether a pre-existing obligation can be used to support the enforcement of a new promise between the same parties. Similar issues arise when a creditor promises to forgive a debt in exchange for something less than full payment.

Suppose you lend me $100 000, which I promise to repay in cash on June 1. (To keep things simple, assume that the loan is interest free.) When the repayment date arrives, however, I honestly explain that I do not have that much money. You recognize the reality of the situation and promise to discharge my entire debt in exchange for $70 000. I pay that amount, but after receiving the money, you insist that I still owe $30 000. Are you entitled to do so?

Your promise to accept the lesser amount is, as usual, enforceable only if it was supported by fresh consideration. I therefore have to prove that I provided

---

15. *Williams v Roffey Bros & Nicholls (Contractors) Ltd* [1990] 1 All ER 512 (CA); *cf Greater Fredericton Airport v Nav Canada* (2008) 290 DLR (4th) 405 (NBCA).

16. *DeLuxe French Fries Ltd v McCardle* (1976) 10 Nfld & PEIR 414 (PEI CA). The concept of novation is discussed in Chapter 11.

something *new*. I will argue that even though I had previously *promised* to pay $100 000 under our original agreement, my *actual* payment of $70 000 provided you with a new benefit. If you had not accepted that amount, you would have been put to the trouble and expense of suing me. Furthermore, if my financial situation continued to deteriorate, I might have declared bankruptcy. And if that happened, you would have been required to share my assets with my other creditors and you therefore might have received far less than $70 000. (Bankruptcy is discussed in Chapter 24.) As a practical matter, then, it would appear that I did provide fresh consideration. As a matter of law, however, my argument will fail. A court will say that my payment of $70 000 was merely part performance of my earlier promise, and that I did not provide any fresh consideration for your promise. You are therefore entitled to demand the remaining $30 000.[17]

That analysis is often criticized as being unfair and unrealistic. Not surprisingly, the courts have developed several exceptions. First, a promise to accept a smaller sum is enforceable if it is placed under *seal*. Second, a promise to accept less money is enforceable if the debtor gives something new in exchange for it. Returning to our earlier example, I might have promised to give you $70 000 *plus* a vehicle that I own. Or I might have promised to pay $70 000 on May 31 instead of $100 000 on June 1. If you agreed to that arrangement, you effectively would have purchased one day for $30 000. Perhaps most surprisingly, your promise might even be enforceable if I promised to pay $70 000 by *cheque* instead of $100 000 in *cash*.[18]

In addition to those judicially created exceptions, an important statutory exception exists in many parts of Canada. Several jurisdictions have legislation that allows a debt to be extinguished upon payment of lesser amount.[19] Section 16 of the *Mercantile Law Amendment Act* of Ontario is typical:[20]

> Part performance of an obligation either before or after breach thereof when expressly accepted by the creditor or rendered in pursuance of an agreement for that purpose, though without any new consideration, shall be held to extinguish the obligation.

While that provision is important, it is also subject to certain restrictions. First, it requires *part performance*—part of the debt must have been paid. Therefore, it would apply if you *actually received* $70 000 from me. In contrast, if you merely received my *promise* to pay that amount, you could change your mind and insist upon full payment any time before I handed over the $70 000. Second, a court will not allow the statute to be used in an unconscionable manner. (The concept of unconscionability is examined in Chapter 10.) Suppose, for instance, that I had enough money to pay my full debt of $100 000. However, I also knew that you were desperate for cash and that if you did not receive at least $70 000 soon, you would be ruined. I tried to exploit the circumstances by telling you that I would either pay $70 000 or nothing at all. Even if you accepted payment of the lesser amount, you can still sue for the remainder of the original debt.[21]

[17.] *Foakes v Beer* (1884) 9 App Cas 605 (HL).

[18.] *Foot v Rawlings* (1963) 37 DLR (2d) 695 (SCC). But see *D & C Builders v Rees* [1965] 3 All ER 837 (CA).

[19.] *Judicature Act*, RSA 2000, c J-2, s 13(1) (Alta); *Law and Equity Act*, RSBC 1996, c 253, s 43 (BC); *Mercantile Law Amendment Act*, CCSM, c M120, s 6 (Man); *Judicature Act*, RSNWT 1988, c J-1, s 40 (NWT); *Judicature Act*, SNWT 1998, c 34, s 37 (Nun); *Queen's Bench Act*, 1998, SS 1998, c Q-1.01, s 64 (Sask); *Judicature Act*, RSY 2002, c 128, s 25 (Yuk).

[20.] *Mercantile Law Amendment Act*, RSO 1990, c M.10 (Ont).

[21.] *Graham v Voth Bros Construction* (1974) Ltd [1982] 6 WWR 365 (BC Co Ct).

PART 3

PROMISES ENFORCEABLE WITHOUT CONSIDERATION

Generally speaking, a promise is enforceable only if it is contained in a contract that is supported by consideration. That rule is subject to two major exceptions:

- seals
- promissory estoppel

Seals

a **seal** is a mark that is put on a written contract to indicate a party's intention to be bound by the terms of that document, even though the other party may not have given consideration

A **seal** is a mark that is put on a written contract to indicate a party's intention to be bound by the terms of that document, even though the other party may not have given consideration. The essential purpose of a seal is to draw the parties' attention to the importance of the occasion and to ensure that they appreciate the seriousness of making an enforceable promise outside the usual bargaining process. Before you affix your seal to a document, you should therefore think carefully about the fact that you may be agreeing to do something for nothing. One of the most common uses of the seal occurs in connection with guarantees. A bank may be willing to lend money to me, but only if you *guarantee* my loan by promising to repay the bank if I fail to do so. The loan agreement is between me and the bank, and you take no benefit. The bank therefore will likely require you to put your promise under seal. The guarantee will then be enforceable even if you received no consideration.

The process of placing a seal on a document is subject to a loose rule and a strict rule. On the one hand, the seal need not take any particular form. Historically, a seal was applied by pressing an insignia (usually of a family crest or a coat of arms) into a drop of hot wax on a document. The usual practice today is to affix a red adhesive wafer to a document. However, it is also acceptable to simply write the word "seal" on the paper. On the other hand, the courts insist that the seal must be applied at the time that a party signs the document. It is not sufficient, for example, to use a form that already has the word "seal" written on it or to add the word "seal" after the fact.[22]

Promissory Estoppel

estoppel is a rule that precludes a person from disputing or retracting a statement that they made earlier

To explain the concept of *promissory estoppel*, we need to first define the term "estoppel."[23] **Estoppel** is a rule that precludes a person from disputing or retracting a statement that they made earlier. In a variety of situations, a court may hold that a person is "estopped" from unfairly denying the truth of a prior statement if the person to whom the statement was made relied on it. For example, suppose you trick me into building a house on your property by saying that the land is mine. When I complete the project, the law will not allow you to unfairly assert your ownership of the property. You will be estopped from denying the truth of your earlier statement that I owned the land. I therefore may be entitled to keep the property along with the house.[24]

promissory estoppel is a doctrine that prevents a party from retracting a promise that the other party has relied upon

Traditionally, the concept of estoppel applied only to statements regarding *past* or *present* facts.[25] More recently, however, it has been applied to statements regarding *promises* and *future* facts as well. **Promissory estoppel** is a

---

22. *Royal Bank of Canada v Kiska* (1967) 63 DLR (2d) 582 (SCC).

23. The term is derived from the Latin word meaning "to stop" or "to prevent."

24. *Willmott v Barber* (1880) 15 Ch D 96.

25. *Jorden v Money* (1854) 5 HL Cas 185 (HL).

doctrine that prevents a party from retracting a promise that another party has relied upon. That doctrine therefore creates an important exception to the general rule that enforces only promises that were acquired in exchange for consideration. Case Brief 8.4 discusses the decision that established the modern principle of promissory estoppel.

Case Brief 8.4

Central London Property Ltd v High Trees House Ltd [1947] KB 130 (KB)

The defendant leased an apartment block in London, England, from the plaintiff. The lease began in 1937 and was to run for 99 years, at a yearly charge of £2500. The defendant intended to rent out the individual apartments to other tenants. However, it became apparent after World War II began that the defendant could not rent out enough apartments to cover their obligations under the main lease. The plaintiff was sympathetic and therefore promised that they would reduce the rent to £1250 per year. That was a gratuitous promise because the defendant did not give any consideration in exchange for it. The parties proceeded on that basis for several years. By 1945, however,

the war had ended, and the building was fully occupied. The plaintiff then brought an action to determine (i) whether they could charge the original rent of £2500 in future years, and (ii) whether they could recover as back rent the amount that they had allowed the defendant to not pay during the war.

The court held that while original rent could be reinstated in *future years*, the plaintiff was estopped from retracting their promise that they would charge only half rent during the war. In other words, for the *past years*, the plaintiff's promise was enforceable even though it was not supported by consideration.

As Case Brief 8.4 shows, the doctrine of promissory estoppel will apply only if four requirements are met.

1. The *representor* (the party making the promise) must clearly indicate that they will not enforce their legal rights against the *representee* (the party receiving the promise). Therefore, promissory estoppel will not apply if, for example, one party is simply slow in collecting money that they are owed. Accepting late payment is not the same thing as clearly saying that future payments need not be made on time or that they need not be made at all.[26]

2. The representee must *rely* upon the statement in a way that would make it unfair for the representor to retract their promise. For example, the representee might have rearranged their business plans because of the promise. However, if the promise was not relied upon in any way, then it is not enforceable.

3. The representee must not be guilty of *inequitable behaviour*. This means that the doctrine of promissory estoppel does not apply, for example, if the representee unfairly pressured the representor into making the statement.[27]

4. The representor's statement must be made in the context of an *existing legal relationship*. Although American courts use the similar doctrine of "injurious reliance" to *create* rights, Canadian courts usually hold that promissory estoppel can be used only to *vary* existing rights. (As lawyers in this country sometimes say, promissory estoppel can be used as a shield, but not as a sword.) Consequently, unless a legal relationship already exists between the parties, our courts will not enforce a gratuitous promise even if the representee has relied upon it.[28]

---

[26] *John Burrows Ltd v Subsurface Surveys Ltd* (1968) 68 DLR (2d) 354 (SCC).

[27] *D & C Builders Ltd v Rees* [1965] 3 All ER 837 (CA).

[28] *Maracle v Travelers Indemnity Co of Canada* (1991) 80 DLR (4th) 652 (SCC); *cf Re Tudale Exploration Ltd v Bruce* (1978) 20 OR (2d) 593 (HCJ).

If these four requirements are met, the representor cannot assert their original rights with respect to the *past*. However, that party may be allowed to enforce their original rights in the future if they give reasonable notice of their intention to do so. As we saw, this occurred in *High Trees*. That possibility does not exist, however, if it would result in an unfair hardship for the representee.

Before moving on to the next section, take a minute to study Concept Summary 8.2, which lists the various grounds upon which a person may be held to a promise to forgive an existing debt.

Concept Summary 8.2

Enforcing a Promise to Forgive a Debt

Fresh Consideration

- a promise to give something new
- a promise to pay a lesser sum early
- a promise to pay the same sum by cheque instead of cash

Legislation (some jurisdictions only)

- actual acceptance of a lesser sum with intention to discharge whole debt

Seal

- symbolic indication of intention to create gratuitous obligation

Promissory Estoppel

- a representation that rights will not be enforced
- reasonable reliance upon the representation
- absence of inequitable behaviour by the representee
- variation of existing relationship—not creation of new rights

---

L.O. ⑥⑦⑧⑨⑩

Privity of Contract

Consideration is necessary for the *creation* of a contract. The concept of *privity of contract* is different. It identifies the people who can be involved in the *enforcement* of a contract. Nevertheless, we address it in this chapter because it is closely tied to the idea of consideration.

It is often important to determine who can sue or be sued on a contract. In a simple two-party situation, each party enjoys the right to enforce the agreement against the other. Suppose, for example, you agree to sell your car to me for $5000. You can sue me if I fail to pay the money, and I can sue you if you fail to transfer the car.

> a **stranger** is someone who did not participate in the creation of the contract

Complications can arise, however, if the facts involve a *stranger*. A **stranger** is someone who did not participate in the creation of the contract. Suppose you agreed to transfer your car to me if I paid $5000 to your sister. If I get the vehicle but refuse to pay the price, the real complaint lies with your sister. She is the one who suffers from my broken promise. Can she compel me to fulfill the contract that I made with you?

A court would probably answer "no." A contract is used to distribute benefits and burdens *amongst the parties*. The last part of that sentence is important. You and I cannot impose an obligation on someone who is not part of our agreement. Likewise, someone who is not part of our agreement generally cannot take advantage of it. Those rules are reflected in *privity of contract*.

Privity of contract refers to the relationship that exists between the individuals who create a contract. Only those people *are parties* to the agreement, and in most situations, only parties can sue or be sued on the contract.[29]

Although the two concepts are technically distinct, privity of contract is often expressed in terms of the consideration doctrine. That approach emphasizes the bargaining aspect of contracts and says that, generally speaking, only a person who has provided something of value can sue or be sued on the contract. Returning to our illustration, we can see why your sister cannot compel me to fulfill my promise. Although she expected to take the benefit of that promise, she did not bargain for it. She gave nothing in return for my agreement to pay $5000. If you are surprised by that result, consider what might happen if *you* tried to enforce my promise against me. You provided consideration when you promised to transfer the car to me. You therefore have the right to sue me *in theory*. But *in practice*, I might be able to persuade a court that I do not have to pay the money to you either.[30] After all, I was supposed to pay $5000 to your sister rather than to you. Why should you now be able to demand payment from me?

As our discussion suggests, the privity of contract rule sometimes seems unfair. As a result, a number of common law jurisdictions around the world, including one in Canada, have abolished that doctrine.[31] In those places, a stranger who was intended to enjoy the benefit of a promise can generally enforce it. In other jurisdictions, the privity doctrine sometimes can be avoided on the basis of much narrower exceptions (or apparent exceptions). We will examine several:

- assignment
- trusts
- statute
- employment
- Himalaya Clause[32]

As we do so, notice the business contexts in which these issues arise, as well as the ways in which business people can prevent problems from arising in the first place.

ASSIGNMENT

A business person who wants to allow a stranger to enforce a contract will usually use an *assignment*. **Assignment** is a process in which a contractual party transfers their rights to a third party. The contractual party who assigns their rights is called the **assignor**; the stranger to whom the contractual rights are assigned is called the **assignee**; and the original contracting party against whom the assigned rights can be enforced is called the **debtor**. In effect, as Figure 8.1 (on the next page) illustrates, the assignee steps into the assignor's shoes to enforce the promise against the debtor.

Assignment often provides the best way to avoid the harsh consequences of the privity doctrine. The process is, however, quite complex. This section merely provides a basic overview of the rules. A business person who is faced with a complicated assignment issue should consult a lawyer.

[29.] *Dunlop Pneumatic Tyre Co Ltd v Selfridge & Co Ltd* [1915] AC 847 at 853 (HL).

[30.] *Woodar Investment Development Ltd v Wimpey Construction UK Ltd* [1980] 1 WLR 277 (HL).

[31.] *Contracts (Rights of Third Parties) Act 1999*, c 31 (UK); *Law Reform Act*, SNB 1993, c L-1.2, s 4 (NB).

[32.] Several other exceptions to the privity doctrine are examined in other chapters: promises that run with the land (Chapter 15), negotiable instruments (Chapter 14), and agency (Chapter 20).

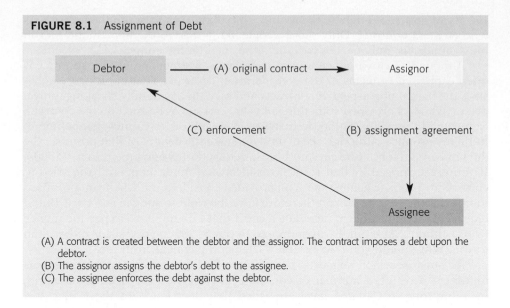

FIGURE 8.1 Assignment of Debt

(A) A contract is created between the debtor and the assignor. The contract imposes a debt upon the debtor.
(B) The assignor assigns the debtor's debt to the assignee.
(C) The assignee enforces the debt against the debtor.

Equitable Assignments

We start with the fact that the assignment can occur either as an *equitable assignment* or a *statutory assignment*. An **equitable assignment** is an assignment that was traditionally enforced by the courts of equity, which we discussed in Chapter 1. It is usually possible to make an equitable assignment of a contractual right, although there are some exceptions. First, the parties to a contract can agree that their rights are non-assignable. Furthermore, the courts sometimes refuse to allow an assignment on policy grounds. For example, contracts for matrimonial support cannot be assigned.

In some respects, the process involved in an equitable assignment is very simple. No particular documents are required, and the assignment can even be completed orally. As a matter of risk management, however, it is best to avoid complications and disputes by using written documents whenever possible.

A valid assignment does not depend on the debtor's consent. Nevertheless, if you are an assignee, there are several reasons why you should provide *notice* of the assignment to the debtor as soon as possible. A debtor has to pay a debt only once. Consequently, if they pay the assignor before receiving notice from you, you cannot demand a second payment for yourself. (You can, however, sue the assignor.) A similar danger occurs if the assignor improperly assigns the same debt to you and then to another person. If that person is unaware of your assignment, they are entitled to payment if they provide the debtor with notice before you do. And again, since the debtor has to pay only once, you could not demand a second payment for yourself. (You could, however, sue the assignor.)

TAKING AN ASSIGNMENT SUBJECT TO THE EQUITIES There is another reason why you should give notice as soon as possible. An assignment is **subject to the equities**, which means that the debtor can generally use the same defences and counterclaims against the assignee that they could have used against the assignor. That is a fair rule. The debtor should not be in a worse position simply because the original creditor has assigned the debt to the assignee. The rule is also fair to the assignee. If the debtor is able to avoid paying the full amount of

---

an **equitable assignment** is an assignment that was traditionally enforced by the courts of equity

subject to the equities means that the debtor can generally use the same defences and counterclaims against the assignee that they could have used against the assignor

the original debt, the assignee will probably have the right to sue the assignor for breach of contract. After all, the assignee received less than they expected to receive under the assignment.

It is, however, important to draw a distinction between (i) defences and counterclaims that arose out of the *same contract* that is the subject of assignment, and (ii) defences and counterclaims that arose out of *other transactions* between the debtor and the assignor. The debtor can *always* rely on the first category of defences and counterclaims against the assignee. But the debtor can rely on the second category of defences and counterclaims only if their transaction with the assignor occurred *before* they received notice from the assignee. These rules are rather complex. The examples in Business Decisions 8.1 and 8.2 help to illustrate them (see below).

Business Decision 8.1

Equities Arising from the Assigned Contract

In January, Stetson Construction agreed to build a cottage in May in exchange for Ahmad's promise that he would pay $60 000 in August. Since Stetson needed money up front to buy supplies, it assigned its rights to you in March for $55 000. You immediately notified Ahmad of the assignment.

After you gave notice, Stetson broke its contract with Ahmad by using inadequate materials in the construction of the cottage. As a result, Ahmad was required to spend $40 000 to hire another contractor to repair the problem. It is now September.

Question for Discussion

1. If you bring an action against Ahmad under the equitable assignment, how much will you probably be able to collect?

Although equitable assignments of contractual rights are quite flexible, they can also create problems for the assignee. Most significantly, if they want to sue the debtor, the assignee may have to include the assignor as a party to that action.[33] That may be difficult to do, however, if the assignor is no longer available. For example, the assignor may have been a company that ceased to exist after it made the assignment.

Business Decision 8.2

Equities Arising from Other Transactions

Citron Used Cars sold a vehicle to White Stationery Inc for $7000. When White failed to pay the purchase price, Citron assigned its contractual right to recover that money to you. White later delivered $5000 worth of paper products to Citron under a separate contract. Citron has not yet paid that price.

Questions for Discussion

1. How much would you be entitled to collect from White if you gave notice *before* Citron became indebted to White for the receipt of the paper products?

2. How much would you be able to collect from White if you gave notice after Citron became indebted to White for the receipt of the paper products?

[33.] The assignor is included in the action as a co-plaintiff if they are willing to co-operate with the assignee, or as a co-defendant if they are not.

Statutory Assignments

a **statutory assignment** is an assignment that conforms to the requirements of a statute

Because of the problems associated with equitable assignments, legislation has been introduced across Canada that creates an alternative form of assignment.[34] A **statutory assignment** is an assignment that conforms to the requirements of a statute.

While they generally follow the same principles as equitable assignments, statutory assignments are subject to three special requirements:

1. While an equitable assignment may be oral, a statutory assignment must be *written*.

2. While notice to the debtor is merely advisable under an equitable assignment, *written notice* is required for a valid statutory assignment.

3. Unlike an equitable assignment, a statutory assignment must be *absolute* at the time that it is created. An assignment is not absolute if it is *conditional*, for example, because it depends on some uncertain event in the future. That situation would arise if the assignor continues to deliver goods to the debtor on credit and therefore alters the amount of the debt. Nor is an assignment absolute if it is *incomplete*, for example, because it covers only part of a debt. That situation would arise if the assignor assigned $3000 of a $5000 debt to the assignee.

A statutory assignment is simply an alternative to an equitable assignment. Consequently, even if the requirements of the statute are not met, an assignment can still be effective in the equitable sense. In fact, equitable assignments are sometimes preferred for that very reason. For example, the assignor may intend to have ongoing transactions with the debtor, with the result that the amount of debt will vary from time to time. If so, an assignment of the right to receive payment from the debtor would be conditional. The assignment would therefore have to be equitable, rather than statutory.

Assignments by Operation of Law

Equitable and statutory assignments arise from the assignor's intention. Other types of assignment, however, occur by operation of law. The best examples involve bankruptcy and death. When a contractual party becomes bankrupt, all of its rights and liabilities are placed under the administration of a *trustee in bankruptcy*. (The process of bankruptcy is discussed in detail in Chapter 24.) When a person dies, all of their contractual rights and liabilities are placed under the administration of a *personal representative*. In either event, the assignee has the responsibility of collecting and paying the person's debts. For reasons that are explained in the next section, however, the assignee is not required to satisfy obligations of a *personal* nature that were owed by the bankrupt or the deceased.

Vicarious Performance

So far we have discussed the assignment of contractual *rights*. We have not considered the assignment of contractual *obligations*. In fact, contractual obligations cannot be assigned. The general rule is that a party must personally

---

[34.] *Judicature Act*, RSA 2000, c J-2, s 20(1) (Alta); *Law and Equity Act*, RSBC 1996, c 253, s 36 (BC); *Law of Property Act*, CCSM, c L90, s 31 (Man); *Conveyancing and Law of Property Act*, RSO 1990, c C.34, s 53(1) (Ont); *Judicature Act*, RSNB 1973, c J-2, s 31 (NB); *Judicature Act*, RSNL 1990, c J-4, s 103 (Nfld); *Judicature Act*, RSNS 1989, c 240, s 43(5) (NS); *Choses in Action Act*, RSS 1978, c 11, s 2 (Sask). The legislation in Manitoba and Saskatchewan is slightly broader in scope; the discussion in the text focuses on the position in the other common law jurisdictions.

perform. That is clearly true if the party's personal skills are essential to the fulfillment of the contract. For example, if a Broadway producer hires a famous actress to star in a production, she is not entitled to send her understudy to play the role. The contract is intended to secure *her* services.

In many situations, however, *vicarious performance* is allowed. **Vicarious performance** occurs when a contractual party arranges to have a stranger perform their obligations. That is possible if the contractual party's personal skills are not essential to performance. For instance, if you enter into a contract with a house builder, you cannot reasonably expect that individual to *personally* undertake the work alone. It is clear that the contractor will use employees or subcontractors. However, vicarious performance is not a form of assignment. The obligation to build the house remains on the builder. Consequently, if the house is defective because the employees or subcontractors were careless, you will still sue the builder.[35]

> **vicarious performance** occurs when a contractual party arranges to have a stranger perform their obligations

TRUSTS

An apparent exception to the privity doctrine involves the equitable concept of the *trust*. We discussed trusts in Chapter 1. As we saw, a **trust** occurs when one person holds property on behalf of another. The person who holds the property is the **trustee**, and the person for whom the property is held is the **beneficiary**. For example, suppose an elderly couple want to provide for their grandchildren's education but are afraid that the money may be wasted. They may give the money to a trustee, who will sensibly spend it on the grandchildren's behalf. The trustee may, for example, pay for the grandchildren's tuition or accommodation while they are at school.

> a **trust** occurs when one person holds property on behalf of another
>
> the **trustee** is the person who holds the property on behalf of the other
>
> the **beneficiary** is the person on whose behalf the property is held

A trust can be used to avoid the consequences of the privity doctrine. Suppose you and I enter into a contract. I promise to pay $10 000 to you and you promise to transfer a car to my sister. Without more, my sister is merely a third party beneficiary and therefore cannot sue if you refuse to honour your promise. To eliminate that problem, I may receive your promise *on trust for* my sister. As we will see in Chapter 17, a contractual promise is a type of property.[36] Although it cannot be held or seen, the courts treat it as something that exists and that can be transferred from one person to another. Under a trust, I will have legal ownership of your promise, but my sister will have *equitable* or *beneficial* ownership of the promise. Consequently, if you refuse to transfer the car to her, she is entitled to sue you even though she did not participate in the creation of the contract. Figure 8.2 illustrates that situation.

The trust was once quite commonly used to avoid the privity doctrine. Judges were quite willing to assume, on the basis of thin evidence, that if the parties to a contract wanted a third party to take a benefit, they also wanted the third party to equitably own the relevant promise. In *Vandepitte v Preferred Accident Insurance Co*, however, the Privy Council severely restricted that use of the trust when it declared that the courts should insist upon very clear proof that a trust was actually intended.[37] And since it is rather odd for parties to think in terms of trusts and equitable ownership, trusts are seldom used today as a way around the rules of privity. Case Brief 8.5 (on page 200) provides a relatively rare exception.

---

[35] The builder, in turn, may have a contractual action against the workers. Moreover, as we saw in Chapter 3, you may have actions in tort against both the builder and the workers.

[36] That type of property is called a "chose in action," which means "a thing in action." Unlike a *chose in possession*, such as a computer or a car, that can be enjoyed through physical possession, a *chose in action* can be enjoyed only by taking legal action on it—by suing, if necessary.

[37] [1933] AC 70 (PC).

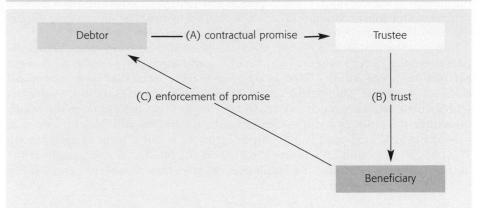

FIGURE 8.2   Privity of Contracts and Trusts

(A) A contract is created between the debtor and the trustee. The debtor gives its promise under that contract.
(B) When that contract is created, the trustee acquires the debtor's promise on behalf of the beneficiary.
(C) The beneficiary enforces the promise against the debtor.

Case Brief 8.5

Burton v FX Music Ltd [1999] All ER (D) 621 (Ch)

Gina G, an Australian singer, hit the top of the charts with a song called "Ooh Aah Just a Little Bit." The song was written by a man named Taube and was produced by a company called FX Music. It was only FX, however, that signed a contract with Warner Music to have the song pressed onto discs and distributed. The contract that was created between FX and Warner said that Taube was to receive certain royalties. At the same time that the contract was created, FX also directed Warner, by way of a separate letter, to (i) pay Taube's royalties directly to Taube, and (ii) suspend payment to Taube if a dispute arose regarding his precise share of the royalties.

Some time later, the parties fell into dispute and it became necessary to determine the nature of Taube's interest (if any) under the contract. At first glance, he appeared to be a simple third party beneficiary, who consequently was unable to sue on the contract in order to demand payment of his royalties.

The court, however, held that Taube actually enjoyed equitable ownership of the relevant promise. FX did not merely receive Warner Music's promise to pay Taube. Instead, FX received Warner Music's promise *on trust for* Taube. Ownership of that promise was split—FX received legal ownership and Taube received equitable ownership.

The trust existed because the court, after considering all the circumstances, believed that FX and Warner Music *intended* to create such an arrangement. The contractual parties did not simply want Taube to take a benefit. They instead wanted him to *own* the right to take a benefit. That is why FX required Warner Music to make payment directly to Taube. That is also why Warner Music was to withhold payments to Taube if a dispute arose. It would be wrong, for example, for Warner Music to pay the relevant amount to FX and for FX to then pay it over to Taube. Since Taube was the equitable owner, he should receive the royalties directly.

STATUTE

A person who wants the benefit of a trust must show that the contractual parties truly did intend to enter into such an arrangement. Canadian law, however, has increasingly recognized that the privity doctrine often creates injustice. The Supreme Court of Canada has therefore questioned the attitude of the Privy Council in *Vandepitte v Preferred Accident Insurance Co.*[38] For the same reason, the legislatures have created a number of true exceptions that allow strangers to enforce promises. The clearest illustrations arise in the context of insurance contracts. Suppose, for example, that a father

---

[38.] *Fraser River Pile & Dredge Ltd. v Can-Dive Services Ltd* (1999) 176 DLR (4th) 257 (SCC).

buys automobile accident insurance for the purpose of protecting himself and his daughter. Because the daughter is a third party beneficiary to the contract, and therefore does not have a right to enforce the insurance policy under the common law, legislation now allows her to do so.[39] Similar provisions have been introduced for life insurance.[40] The primary purpose of a life insurance policy is to benefit someone who is not a party to that contract, usually a grieving family member. It would be grossly unfair if an insurance company could invoke the privity doctrine and refuse to make payment to that person after an insured party died.

EMPLOYMENT

The same reasoning has led the courts to create exceptions to the privity doctrine in other situations. Judges, however, proceed more cautiously than legislators, and the judicial exceptions are much narrower in scope. The clearest example arises in the employment context. When a company agrees to do work for a customer, it is usually obvious that the actual task will be performed by the company's employees. Furthermore, the contract that is created between the customer and the company may include an exclusion clause that expressly says that the customer cannot sue either the company *or* its employees if something goes wrong. (Exclusion clauses are discussed in Chapters 9 and 12.) However, if the employees do perform carelessly, the customer may sue them in tort and argue that they cannot rely upon the contractual exclusion clause. After all, they were not parties to that contract. As explained in Case Brief 8.6, however, the Supreme Court of Canada has held that employees may be entitled to rely upon an exclusion clause that was created for their benefit, even though they lack privity of contract.[41]

HIMALAYA CLAUSE

The decision in *London Drugs* was driven largely by the court's desire to reach a fair and commercially realistic result. In the circumstances, it was fair to the employees, and not unfair to the plaintiff, to extend the exemption clause beyond the immediate parties to the contract. Essentially the same ideas led to the creation of the *Himalaya clause*. A **Himalaya clause** is a special term of contract that protects a third party beneficiary from liability. The somewhat strange name comes from the case in which the rule was first formulated.[42] Although that decision was delivered by an English court, the Supreme Court of Canada has adopted the analysis.[43]

a **Himalaya clause** is a special term of contract that protects a third party beneficiary from liability

---

[39.] *Insurance Act*, RSA 2000, c I-3, s 616 (Alta); *Insurance Act*, RSBC 1996, c 226, s 159 (BC); *Insurance Act*, CCSM, c I40, s 258 (Man); *Insurance Act*, RSNB 1973, c I-12, s 250 (NB); *Automobile Insurance Act*, RSNL 1990, c A-22, s 26 (Nfld); *Insurance Act*, RSNWT 1988, c I-4, s 28 (NWT); *Insurance Act*, RSNS 1989, c 231, s 133 (NS); *Insurance Act*, RSNWT 1988, c I-4, s 151 (Nun); *Insurance Act*, RSO 1990, c I.8, s 258 (Ont); *Insurance Act*, RSPEI 1988, c I-4, s 240 (PEI); *Saskatchewan Insurance Act*, RSS 1978, c S-26, s 210 (Sask); *Insurance Act*, RSY 2002, c 119, s 157 (Yuk).

[40.] *Insurance Act*, RSA 2000, c I-3, s 583 (Alta); *Insurance Act*, RSBC 1996, c 226, s 53 (BC); *Insurance Act*, CCSM, c I40, s 172 (Man); *Insurance Act*, RSNB 1973, c I-2, s 156 (NB); *Life Insurance Act*, RSNL 1990, c L-14, s 26 (Nfld); *Insurance Act*, RSNWT 1988, c I-4, s 93 (NWT and Nun); *Insurance Act*, RSNS 1989, c 231, s 197 (NS); *Insurance Act*, RSO 1990, c I.8, s 195 (Ont); *Insurance Act*, RSPEI 1988, c I-4, s 143 (PEI); *Saskatchewan Insurance Act*, RSS 1978, c S-26, s 157 (Sask); *Insurance Act*, RSY 2002, c 119, s 100 (Yuk).

[41.] See also *Fraser River Pile & Dredge Ltd v Can-Dive Services* Ltd (1999) 176 DLR (4th) 257 (SCC).

[42.] *Adler v Dickson (The Himalaya)* [1955] 1 QB 158 (CA).

[43.] *ITO—International Terminal Operators Ltd v Miida Electronics Inc* (1986) 28 DLR (4th) 641 (SCC).

PART 3

Case Brief 8.6

London Drugs Ltd v Kuehne & Nagel International Ltd (1992) 97 DLR (4th) 261 (SCC)

The plaintiff delivered an expensive piece of machinery, called a "transformer," to the defendant for storage. The storage contract contained a clause that limited the defendant's liability to $40. The plaintiff rejected the defendant's offer to raise that limit in exchange for an additional price.

The defendant's employee damaged the plaintiff's transformer while moving it for storage purposes. The plaintiff sued the employee personally for $34 000. The employee argued that he was covered by the limitation clause contained in the storage contract. In response, the plaintiff argued that the employee was not a party to that contract and therefore could not rely upon it for protection.

The Supreme Court of Canada found in favour of the employee by creating an exception to the privity rule. That new rule states that an employee is covered by a limitation clause contained in an employer's contract with a third party if:

■ the employee was expressly or implicitly contained within the clause, and
■ the employee performs the work that was required by the contract.

The court based that rule on commercial reality. On the facts of the case, the plaintiff knew that their equipment would be handled not by the defendant (which was, after all, a corporation), but rather by the defendant's employees. The court also explained that the purpose of a limitation clause is to allocate the risk of damage to one of the parties, and to alert that party to the need for insurance. Consequently, the plaintiff should have either accepted the defendant's offer to raise the amount in the limitation clause or purchased protection from an insurance company.

The Himalaya clause arose in the context of maritime shipping. A special set of international rules, known as the *Hague Rules*, strictly limit liability (to $500 per package) for any losses that a carrier may cause to a property owner.[44] Although that may seem unfair, limiting liability makes a great deal of sense in the business world. Accidents are bound to happen. The real question deals with insurance: Which party is in a better position to obtain insurance?[45] The law could impose full liability and encourage the carrier to purchase liability insurance. Or the law could limit the carrier's liability and encourage the property owner to purchase property insurance. In practice, the second option is preferable. Unlike the carrier, who knows nothing about the goods, the property owner has all the information required to purchase insurance. That solution also has the benefit of preventing the costs of shipping contracts from escalating as liability insurance prices increase.

The benefit of that scheme would be lost, however, if a property owner was unable to effectively sue the carrier, but could successfully sue the various people—such as stevedores—who actually handle the goods.[46] Carriers therefore began to insert a special term or clause into the contract of carriage. That term contained two important features. First, it extended the limitation on liability not only to the carrier, but also to stevedores (and others who handle goods). Second, it said that the carrier acted not only for itself, but also as an agent, for the purpose of connecting the property owner to the stevedores. (Agency is discussed in Chapter 20.) Courts soon accepted that a separate contract—limiting liability—arose between the property owner and the stevedore once the stevedore began the task of handling the goods.[47] A Himalaya clause therefore is not really an exception to the privity rule. Instead, it involves a process that leads to a new contract being created for the benefit of the stevedores.

[44.] Like many countries, Canada now uses a newer set of rules known as the *Hague-Visby Rules*. However, some countries, including the United States, continue to use the old *Hague Rules*.

[45.] Insurance is discussed in Chapter 17. Property (or first party) insurance compensates a policyholder whose goods have been damaged, lost, or destroyed. Liability (or third party) insurance essentially pays damages on behalf of a policyholder who is held liable for another's loss.

[46.] A stevedore is a person who loads and unloads goods from a ship.

[47.] *New Zealand Shipping Co v AM Satterthwaite & Co (The Eurymedon)* [1975] AC 154 (PC NZ).

Chapter Summary

Consideration is an essential element in the formation of most contracts. Because the law of contract is based on the concept of a bargain, gratuitous promises are generally not enforced. There must be an exchange of consideration between the parties. The bargain between the parties need not be a good one; as long as there is an exchange of value, a contract will be created. Consideration must be sufficient but it need not be adequate. An important application of the rules governing the sufficiency and adequacy of consideration arises in the context of forbearance to sue.

Past consideration is no consideration at all because it fails to satisfy the requirement of mutuality. Good consideration can be based on a pre-existing contractual obligation owed to a third party. However, good consideration cannot be based on a pre-existing public duty and usually cannot be based on a pre-existing contractual obligation owed to the same party.

As a general rule, a creditor's promise to accept less than full payment from a debtor is not binding. That rule is, however, subject to several exceptions.

A promise may be enforceable even if it is not supported by consideration if it was placed under seal or if it falls under the doctrine of promissory estoppel. In Canada, the doctrine of promissory estoppel is used to vary existing contractual rights but not to create new ones.

The doctrine of privity of contract is closely associated with the doctrine of consideration. A person who has not provided consideration and who is not a party to a contract generally cannot sue or be sued on the contract.

Privity of contract is subject to several exceptions and apparent exceptions. A stranger to a contract can enforce a contractual promise that has been assigned to it. An assignment of a contractual right may be either equitable or statutory and may arise either from the assignor's intention or by operation of law. A beneficiary can enforce a contractual promise acquired on their behalf by a trustee. In a number of situations, statutes allow strangers to enforce contractual rights created for their benefit. Likewise, the courts have recently allowed employees to take advantage of exclusion clauses that are contained in contracts for which they have not provided consideration and with respect to which they lack privity. A Himalaya clause is a special term of contract that protects a third party beneficiary from liability.

MyBusLawLab   ADDITIONAL RESOURCES FOR CHAPTER 8

MyBusLawLab provides students with an assortment of tools to help enrich the learning experience, including a Study Plan with Pre- and Post-tests, mini-cases with assessments, and provincial content material, which provides links to relevant cases, legislation, and additional resources.

MyBusLawLab provides the following resources for Chapter 8:

Provincial Material

- **British Columbia:** Statutory Assignment
- **Alberta:** Seals, Partial Payment of Debt, Trusts, Statutory Assignments, *Wills and Succession Amendment Act (2011)*
- **Manitoba and Saskatchewan:** Statutory Override of the Rule in *Foakes v. Beer*
- **Ontario:** Assignment of Rents, Equitable Estoppel, Partial Payment of Debt, Seals, Death Without a Will, Executors, Statutory Assignments, Trusts, Consumer Credit
- **Atlantic Provinces:** Probate Legislation, *Public Trustee Act*

Review Questions

1. What is a "gratuitous promise"? Is a gratuitous promise ever enforceable in the law of contract? Explain your answer.

2. Is it possible for a person to enter into an enforceable contract without receiving any benefit from the agreement?

3. Explain the difference between "sufficient consideration" and "adequate consideration." Will either type of consideration support the creation of a valid contract? Explain your answer.

4. What is a "forbearance agreement"? Why do the courts generally uphold such agreements? Are such agreements supported by consideration?

5. What is the "requirement of mutuality"? How is it related to the bargain theory of contract?

6. What is "past consideration"? In light of the bargaining process that underlies a contract, explain why judges hold that past consideration is no consideration at all.

7. "There is a difference between past consideration on the one hand and a promise that indicates the reasonable price for work that was previously performed under a contract on the other hand." Explain the meaning of that statement. Provide an example to illustrate your answer.

8. Explain why a pre-existing public duty cannot be good consideration under a new contract. Does your explanation rely entirely on the doctrine of consideration, or does it also include other factors?

9. "Good consideration usually cannot be based on a pre-existing contractual obligation owed to the same party." Describe three ways by which business people can avoid that rule. What commercial reasons might motivate them to do so?

10. Explain the relationship between the doctrine of consideration and the concept of *quantum meruit*.

11. List and briefly describe the non-statutory exceptions to the general rule that payment of a lesser sum does not discharge a debt of a larger amount.

12. In your province or territory, does legislation ever allow you to discharge a debt by paying your creditor a lesser amount than you actually owe them?

13. "A seal is a type of consideration." Is that statement true? Explain your answer.

14. Describe the doctrine of promissory estoppel. What does it mean to say that promissory estoppel can be used to vary, but not create, contractual rights? Give examples to illustrate your answer.

15. Explain the relationship between the requirement of consideration and the privity of contract doctrine.

16. Explain why it would be undesirable if contractual parties were free to assign contractual obligations, even though contractual rights generally can be assigned. Illustrate your answer with examples. Discuss the extent to which the doctrine of vicarious performance provides an exception to the general rule precluding assignment of contractual obligations.

17. Provide an example of a statute that allows a contract to be enforced by or against a person who would not normally be classified as a "party" to a contract. Explain how that statutory provision operates.

18. What is a "Himalaya Clause"? What effect does such a clause have on privity of contract?

19. Explain the concept of taking an assignment subject to the equities.

20. Why do you think judges allow employees to take advantage of exclusion clauses to which they are strangers? Give at least two reasons for your answer.

Cases and Problems

1. Douglas Dixie and Millie Grace, both aged 43, have known each other since high school. Their adult lives, however, followed very different paths. After earning a college business degree, Douglas established a pet supply company. The company now operates several dozen stores across Canada and earns large profits. Douglas has amassed a fortune. Millie, in contrast, never earned a higher degree and has bounced from one low-paying job to another. The pair recently became reacquainted during their high school class's 25-year reunion. Millie described her sad situation to Douglas and, after learning that he was worth millions, asked if he would give her enough money to open a small bakery, which she had always dreamed of owning and operating. Douglas explained that he had no interest in that sort of business and said that he was not in the habit of simply giving money away. Millie nevertheless kept asking and, before the evening was done, Douglas promised that he would give her $100 000 within a month. The next day, Douglas received a document from Millie. The document contained Millie's seal and it said, "I, Millie Grace, hereby acknowledge that I will receive $100 000 from Douglas Dixie within one month." It is now

two months later. Douglas refuses to pay any money to Millie, but she insists that he is legally obligated to do so. She is especially eager to receive the money because, in reliance upon Douglas's promise, she has already entered into a contract with another company to buy bakery supplies and equipment. Is there any basis upon which Millie can force Douglas to fulfill his promise? Explain your answer.

2. The Goldberg Conservatory, a music school, ran a notice in several newspapers to announce that it had decided to have a new organ built and installed on its premises. The notice also asked for donations to help fund the project. John Sebastien, a local businessman and patron of the arts, responded to the notice by immediately promising the Conservatory that it would donate $100 000. He explained that a cheque would be sent within a month, after he had made suitable arrangements with his accountant. Before he was able to send a cheque, however, Sebastien's finances suffered a severe setback as a result of several failed business ventures. He therefore informed the Conservatory that, with regret, he would not be able to make a donation after all. The Conservatory insists that he no longer has a choice in the matter. While admitting that it had planned to acquire the organ in any event, it says that it would be unfair if it were to be deprived of the money that Sebastien had promised. It also says that Sebastien is legally obligated to fulfill his promise. Is Sebastien's promise enforceable?

3. Hardy Construction Ltd contractually agreed to build an office complex for Schtick Corp. Under the terms of that contract, Hardy Construction would incur a financial penalty if it failed to complete the project on schedule. Hardy Construction hired Laurel Electric Co as a subcontractor to install wiring in the building. The terms of that subcontract required payment of $50 000 on completion. Laurel Electric began work immediately but later discovered that it had honestly underestimated the cost of performance. Accordingly, it approached Hardy Construction and stated that unless it was promised an additional $20 000, it simply would not be able to complete the job. Hardy Construction realized (i) that it could not possibly find a replacement for Laurel Electric on such short notice, and (ii) that any delay in completion of the project would trigger the penalty provision contained in its contract with Schtick Corp. Hardy Construction consequently agreed to Laurel Electric's request. Nevertheless, although Laurel Electric subsequently completed its performance on schedule, Hardy Construction refuses to pay more than $50 000. Does it have a right to do so in law? Regardless of its legal position, why might Hardy Construction consider honouring its promise to pay an extra $20 000? Explain whether you believe that the law should more closely reflect business practice.

4. After being charged with a serious crime, Anthony Lampleigh wrote to Tammy Braithwait, a lawyer, asking for assistance. After setting out the facts of the case and the precise nature of the allegations against him, Lampleigh asked in his letter to Braithwait, "Will you please help me avoid prosecution on these charges?" Braithwait wrote back in very simple terms, stating merely that she would "do everything possible to achieve the desired result." Braithwait then used considerable ingenuity, and expended considerable time and expense, in persuading the government to drop the charges against Lampleigh. When Braithwait conveyed that news, Lampleigh gratefully said, "Thank you so much. For your efforts, I will prepare a cheque for $25 000 and have it delivered to your office tomorrow." In fact, Lampleigh never sent any cheque to Braithwait. After the initial joy and relief wore off, Lampleigh felt far less thankful and he now refuses to pay anything at all. Braithwait insists that she is entitled to a contractual payment of $25 000, but Lampleigh argues that his promise of that amount was given in exchange for past *consideration* and therefore is not enforceable. How would a court resolve the parties' dispute?

5. Mr Chin ran down Mrs Moss at a pedestrian crosswalk. Because she suffered severe brain damage, her interests were represented by the Public Trustee. The Public Trustee sued Mr Chin in the tort of negligence and claimed, amongst other things, compensatory damages for the cost of Mrs Moss's future medical expenses. Over time, as negotiations between the parties progressed, Mrs Moss's physical condition deteriorated, and she eventually died. The Public Trustee, however, chose not to reveal that fact to Mr Chin. Based on his belief that Mrs Moss would require ongoing medical treatment, Mr Chin eventually settled the case out of court for more than $300 000. He has now discovered the truth. He therefore demands payment. The Public Trustee, on the other hand, points to the settlement contract that it had persuaded Mr Chin to sign. It insists that the money was given in exchange for good consideration. Which party is correct?

6. The Blacksox Baseball Club and Roark Designs Corp conducted extensive negotiations concerning the development of a new ball park. During those negotiations, the owner of the Blacksox said to the owner of Roark, "Look, we both know that this stadium will eventually be built. The lawyers will have to work out the details, and of course nothing will be official until we sign a formal contract. But as far as I'm concerned, we might as well get started. I can promise you right now that if you draft the plans, we'll pay you $100 000 for your efforts." Roark spent a considerable amount of time and money preparing a blueprint for a new stadium. Unfortunately, the entire proposal collapsed when, through no fault of either the Blacksox or Roark, the local government denied zoning approval for the project. Roark nevertheless insists that the Blacksox abide by the promise made by their president. Will the doctrine of promissory estoppel assist Roark in that regard?

7. Christine Robinson owed a debt of $25 000 to Black Crow Music Inc (BCMI). Because she genuinely could not pay the full amount, Christine asked the company whether it would be willing to accept $15 000 in complete discharge of the obligation. The company initially took pity on Christine after she demonstrated her seriousness by placing her request in a document under seal. It therefore agreed to her proposal, on the condition that she pay $15 000 within one week. Three days later, however, BCMI had a change of heart and told Christine that it expected to receive the full sum of $25 000. Three days after that, Christine presented $15 000 to BCMI. The company took the cash, but only after repeating its intention to collect on the entire debt. Christine, however, believes that she is debt-free and that BCMI no longer has any claim to the outstanding $10 000. Which party is correct? Explain your answer.

8. Everlast Tire Co, which manufactures automobile tires, sold a shipment of tires to Automotive Wholesaler Inc. Under the terms of that contract, Automotive Wholesaler was allowed to resell the tires below the price suggested by Everlast if (i) the sub-buyer was a business in the car industry, and (ii) the sub-buyer promised not to resell below the price suggested by Everlast. Automotive Wholesaler then sold the tires to AJ's Used Cars Ltd. Under the terms

of that contract, AJ's, which was engaged in the car industry as a used car dealer, promised Automotive Wholesaler that it would not resell the tires below the price suggested by Everlast. AJ's also promised Automotive Wholesaler that if it broke that promise, it would pay $100 to Everlast for each tire that was sold below the manufacturer's suggested price. In fact, AJ's did sell 10 tires to individual customers at prices that were well below the price suggested by Everlast. Everlast now argues that it is entitled to recover $1000 from AJ's. Is that true? If not, does the result seem fair? And if not, what are the simplest means by which Everlast could have arranged the resale of its tires so that it would be able to enforce the promise that AJ's made to Automotive Wholesaler?

9. Ann agreed to provide a car to Bruno in exchange for his promise to pay $8000 to her sister, Claire. Ann actually delivered the vehicle as promised, but Bruno refuses to pay any money to Claire. Is Claire entitled to compel Bruno to honour his undertaking? If not, does Ann have the right to recover the $8000 from Bruno? Is there anything that Ann can now do that would allow Claire to enforce Bruno's promise?

10. Fraser River Inc owned a boat called *The Squamish*. Fraser River did not actually use the boat. Instead, it chartered (rented) the boat to other people. Until recently, it had chartered *The Squamish* to Can-Dive Corp. The boat unfortunately was badly damaged as a result of Can-Dive's negligence. In normal circumstances, Fraser River would have sued Can-Dive in either tort or contract for compensation. In fact, Fraser River did not need to do so. It had purchased an insurance policy from London Insurance Inc. That policy required the insurance company to pay for the repairs. As we will see in Chapter 17, an insurance company that provides compensation to a policyholder is normally "subrogated" to the rights of that policyholder. In the present situation, that would mean that London Insurance could "step into the shoes" of Fraser River and sue Can-Dive for the damage that Can-Dive created. Can-Dive, however, points to a provision that was contained in the insurance contract that Fraser River bought from London Insurance. That provision states, "It is agreed that the insurer waives any right of subrogation against any charterer." Can-Dive therefore argues that it cannot be sued by London Insurance. Is that correct?

11. During the summer months, Ontario Cruises Inc (OCI) operates pleasure cruises around Lake Ontario, one of the Great Lakes. The purchase of a ticket, for $50, entitles a customer to enjoy an informative and enjoyable cruise that lasts for about three hours. At the time of purchasing a ticket, a customer must sign a "Waiver of Liability." The relevant part of that document states, "The passenger accepts all physical and legal risks of loss or injury. Neither Ontario Cruises Inc nor its employees shall be responsible or liable for any loss or injury suffered by any passenger that is caused by the negligence of Ontario Cruises Inc or its employees." Ms Rose Adler purchased a ticket, read the "Waiver of Liability," and signed the document. The cruise was to be conducted aboard *The Spirit of Ontario*, which is one of OCI's ships. The boat sat alongside a pier that was owned and operated by the provincial government. Wallis Boatswain, a college student, was working during the summer for the province. It was his job to make sure that individuals—like Rose Adler—safely got on and off boats that were next to the pier. Unfortunately, when Rose was about to board *The Spirit of Ontario*, Wallis's attention was focused entirely on an attractive young woman who was walking by. As a result of his carelessness, Rose stumbled, hit her head, and fell into the water. She suffered serious injuries. Rose has now sued OCI and Wallis Boatswain. If the company did anything wrong, it is protected by the "Waiver of Liability." Wallis argues that he is protected by the same document. Is that correct? Explain your answer.

12. The province intended to have a highway built in an otherwise undeveloped area. Its first step was to hire ND Lea & Associates, a firm of architects, to draft a basic plan for the project. The province then incorporated those plans into the tender documents that it used when it called for bids on the construction project. The tender documents also contained an exemption clause that stated, "The Province shall not be subject to any liability for any damage which the Contractor may sustain by reason of any delay or delays, from whatever cause, arising in the progress of the work." The province received a number of tenders and eventually hired Edgeworth Construction Ltd (ECL) to build the highway. ECL very soon realized that the plans provided by the province (and created by the architects) were inaccurate and ineffective. It ultimately suffered a loss of $2 000 000 on the project as a result. ECL believes that it should not have to bear that loss, but it also knows that the province is protected by the exemption clause. ECL therefore has sued the architectural firm under the tort of negligence. The architects admit that they acted carelessly and that their carelessness caused ECL's loss. ND Lea & Associates insist, however, that it is entitled to be protected by the exemption clause by virtue of the *London Drugs* case. Will that argument succeed in court? Explain your answer.

Representations and Terms

LEARNING OBJECTIVES

After completing this chapter, you should be able to:

❶ Identify pre-contractual and contractual statements.

❷ Distinguish misrepresentations from other false statements made during contractual negotiations.

❸ Identify the various circumstances when silence, half-truths, or actively concealed facts might amount to misrepresentation.

❹ Explain the differences between innocent, fraudulent, and negligent misrepresentation.

❺ Describe the legal effects of innocent, fraudulent, and negligent misrepresentation.

❻ Outline the rules associated with proving the existence of express terms.

❼ Summarize and apply the various judicial approaches to interpreting express terms.

❽ Discuss when, how, and why a court might imply a term into a contract.

❾ Outline the advantages and disadvantages of standard form agreements and describe why a business should use plain language in contracts.

❿ Identify various boilerplate terms and appreciate their significance in a contract.

We have considered how a contract is formed. Now we will examine the legal effect of statements made or adopted by parties in connection with their contracts. First, we will investigate statements made by the parties during the negotiation of a contract. Second, we will consider what happens when those statements are false. Third, we will consider how terms can be incorporated into a contract. Fourth, we will consider standard form agreements in consumer transactions, including reasons to use plain language in contracts.

L.O. ❶   Pre-Contractual and Contractual Statements

Because the communication of an offer and its acceptance can be accomplished in a number of ways, it is sometimes difficult to identify which of the parties' statements are part of the negotiations and which are part of the actual contract. We therefore need to distinguish between *contractual terms* and *pre-contractual representations*.

Not every statement communicated during the negotiation process is a *contractual term*. A statement becomes a **contractual term** only if it is included in the agreement as a legally enforceable obligation. A contractual term is, by its very nature, a *promissory statement*. The person who makes it voluntarily agrees to do something in the future.

In contrast, a **pre-contractual representation** is a statement one party makes by words or conduct with the intention of inducing another party to enter into a contract. By definition, it does not impose a contractual obligation. Although a pre-contractual representation may induce the creation of a contract, it does not form part of that contract. Figure 9.1 illustrates some of the differences between contractual terms and pre-contractual representations.

> a **contractual term** is a provision in an agreement that creates a legally enforceable obligation

> a **pre-contractual representation** is a statement one party makes by words or conduct with the intention of inducing another party to enter into a contract

FIGURE 9.1 Pre-Contractual Statements: Terms and Representations

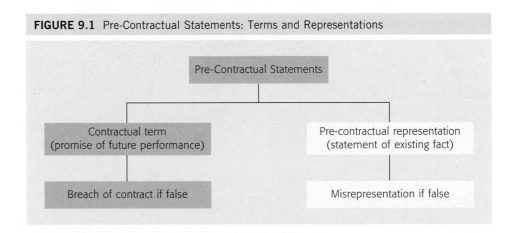

L.O. ❷❸❹❺   Misrepresentation

The distinction between contractual terms and pre-contractual representations is especially important if a statement is false. If a non-contractual statement is false, we say that one of the parties has made a *misrepresentation*. When a contractual statement is not fulfilled, we say that one of the parties is in *breach of contract*. That distinction is important because misrepresentation and breach of contract have different legal effects. Pre-contractual representations may result in a form of legal liability, such as actionable misrepresentation, but not in an action for breach of contract. In this section, we will focus on misrepresentation. (We consider the remedies for breach of contract in Chapter 12.)

THE NATURE OF MISREPRESENTATION

A **misrepresentation** is a false statement of an *existing* fact that causes a recipient to enter into a contract. Whether it is a statement about the past or the present, its main feature is that it is false when it is made. In contrast, a contractual term is not meant to describe an existing state of facts, but rather it provides a promise of *future* performance. Given its promissory nature, a contractual term cannot be false when it is given. Nor can a breach of contract occur as soon as such a promise is made. A breach occurs only when one of the parties fails to perform precisely as promised.

a **misrepresentation** *is a false statement of an* existing *fact that causes a recipient to enter into a contract*

Misstatement of Fact

Not every misstatement during pre-contractual negotiations is a misrepresentation. A misrepresentation occurs only if the speaker claimed to state a *fact*. The difficulty with that requirement is that people often make *non-factual* statements during negotiations. For example, they sometimes state their own *opinions*. An **opinion** is the statement of a belief or judgment. For example, a person offers an opinion when they estimate the potential future revenue of an income-earning property. Opinions can range from carefree speculations to deliberate assessments based on a substantial body of evidence.

an **opinion** *is the statement of a belief or judgment*

A personal opinion is not usually a misrepresentation, even if it is false. There are, however, situations in which it is risky to offer an opinion. If you state an opinion in a way that leads me to think that it *must* be true, a court may find that your statement includes not only an opinion, but also an implied statement of fact that can be treated as a misrepresentation. That is true especially if you offer an opinion within your area of expertise. It is also risky to offer an opinion if you have no reason to believe that it is actually true. Suppose you are trying to persuade me to buy a particular vehicle from your used car lot. When I explain that I know nothing about gas consumption but am very concerned about fuel costs, you say, "I think that you'll find this model to be very thrifty, indeed." In fact, you know that the car in question is a notorious gas guzzler. Because the fuel consumption of the car is within your area of expertise, a court may decide that it was reasonable for me to rely on your statement as an implied statement of fact, and not merely as a personal opinion.

During pre-contractual negotiations, a person may describe how they (or someone else) will act in the future. A statement of **future conduct** is not a statement of fact. Rather, it is a statement about a person's future intentions. Such statements are not usually treated as misrepresentations. However, a statement of future conduct *is* a misrepresentation if it is made fraudulently or if the future conduct is described in terms of a present intention. For instance, to persuade me to buy your farm, you might say, "I certainly do not intend to sell the neighbouring land to Herb's Sewage Treatment Facility." That statement contains an indication of your *present* state of mind, meaning that it will be characterized as an implied statement of present fact. If it is false, it may be classified as a fraudulent misrepresentation.

a statement of **future conduct** *is not a statement of fact; it is a statement about a person's future intentions*

People sometimes discuss the law during pre-contractual negotiations.[1] A misrepresentation does not arise merely because you inaccurately describe a

---

[1] *cf Rule v Pals* [1928] 2 WWR 123 (Sask CA) and *Graham v Legault* [1951] 3 DLR 423 (BC SC).

particular *law itself*. We all are presumed to know the law. However, the court may find a misrepresentation if you inaccurately describe the *consequences of a law*, because those consequences are treated as a matter of fact rather than law. Suppose you are trying to persuade me to buy your land. It is not a misrepresentation if you incorrectly tell me that zoning laws do not apply to the property. That is a matter of law. However, it may be a misrepresentation if you inaccurately tell me that zoning approval has been granted and that I therefore would be able to develop the land. That is a matter of fact.[2]

Concept Summary 9.1 shows that expressions of opinion, descriptions of future conduct, and statements of law—even when they are inaccurate and induce the creation of contracts—are not normally treated as misrepresentations. To prove misrepresentation in those circumstances, a party must prove that the speaker implicitly claimed to state some fact. It is often difficult to tell when a factual statement has been made. Consider the case in Business Decision 9.1.

Concept Summary 9.1

Types of Pre-Contractual Statements Inducing Contracts

Non-Factual Statements (not actionable as misrepresentation)	Factual Statements (actionable as misrepresentation)
Opinion based on speculation	Expert opinion
Description of another's future intent	Description of one's present intent
Statement of law	Statement of legal consequences

Business Decision 9.1

Statement of Fact or Opinion?[3]

Mrs and Mr Perry decided to construct a building, which they could rent out to stores as part of a shopping complex. In order to make a proper return on their investment, they determined that their development had to be constructed for less than $120 000. The Perrys met with an architect who "guesstimated" that he could design a plan that could be constructed for $120 000 or less. The Perrys agreed to have the architect draw up the design plans for a fee of $5000. When the Perrys later brought the architect's plans to a contractor, they were told that construction of that building would in fact far exceed their spending limit. The Perrys now refuse to pay the architect the agreed fee for his plans on the basis of what they claim to be a pre-contractual misrepresentation about the cost to implement his construction plans.

Questions for Discussion

1. Should the architect's "guesstimate" be characterized as a statement of fact or opinion? Explain your answer.

2. Does the fact that the architect is an expert make any difference to your answer?

3. Would your answer change if you knew that the Perrys regularly commissioned buildings like this one?

---

[2] *Hopkins v Butts* (1967) 65 DLR (2d) 711 (BC SC).

[3] These facts are based on *Salo v Komadowski and Komco Ltd* [1981] MJ No 294, 8 Man R (2d) 134, 7 ACWS (2d) 513.

Silence as Misrepresentation

As a general rule, parties are not required to disclose material facts during pre-contractual negotiations, no matter how unethical non-disclosure may be. Suppose a company director is negotiating to buy shares from a shareholder. The director does not have to reveal that he knows certain information that will cause the value of the shares to increase within a few months.[4] There are, however, at least six occasions when the failure to speak will amount to misrepresentation:

- when silence would distort a previous assertion
- when a statement is a half-truth
- when the contract requires a duty of utmost good faith
- when a special relationship exists between the parties
- when a statutory provision requires disclosure
- when facts are actively concealed

WHEN SILENCE WOULD DISTORT A PREVIOUS ASSERTION As Ethical Perspective 9.1 illustrates, a party's silence sometimes has the effect of falsifying a previous statement or a presumed set of circumstances. When a change in circumstances affects the accuracy of an earlier representation, the party that made that statement has a duty to disclose the change to the other party. Failure to do so amounts to a misrepresentation.

WHEN A STATEMENT IS A HALF-TRUTH A misrepresentation may also occur if a party tells half the truth and remains silent on the other half. Despite the right to remain silent, a party cannot give a *partial* account if the unspoken words would substantially alter the meaning of the actual statement, even if the actual words are literally true. Suppose you take your cotton shirts to the dry cleaner. You are asked to sign a claim ticket, which, the cleaner tells you, "excludes liability for damage caused to silk and crushed velvet during the dry cleaning process." That is true. But the ticket *also* excludes liability for any other damage to any kind of fabric. The half-truth is a misrepresentation.[5]

WHEN THE CONTRACT REQUIRES A DUTY OF UTMOST GOOD FAITH By their very nature, some contracts require a party to make full disclosure of the material facts. These are known as *contracts of utmost good faith*. The requirement of utmost good faith arises when one party is in a unique position to know the material facts. The best example involves insurance contracts. In order to assess the risk that a particular type of loss might occur, and to determine how much to charge for coverage, an insurance company needs to know as much as possible about the situation. Of course, the only person who has that information is the customer. The law therefore imposes an obligation of utmost good faith that requires the customer to disclose all of the relevant facts. A breach of that obligation is usually treated as a misrepresentation that allows the insurance company to avoid the contract.

WHEN A SPECIAL RELATIONSHIP EXISTS BETWEEN THE PARTIES When the relationship between two parties is one of trust, or when one of the parties has some other form of special influence over the other, a duty of disclosure may arise.

4. *Prudential Insurance Co Ltd v Newman Industries Ltd* [1981] Ch 257.

5. *Curtis v Chemical Cleaning and Dyeing Co Ltd* [1951] 1 KB 805.

PART 3

Ethical Perspective 9.1

Misrepresentation and Silence[6]

Johnny Grievor has always wanted to be a firefighter but he is functionally blind in his left eye. Knowing that the City of Ottawa would not hire him if it knew about his visual impairment, Grievor applied to be a firefighter but did not mention his disability. He also remained silent about the fact that he had arranged for a friend to take the required medical examination. On the basis of his resumé and the results of his friend's medical examination, the city offered Grievor a position.

One day, while responding to a fire alarm, the fire truck that Grievor was driving collided with a van, killing two people. A short time later, the fire chief received an anonymous tip that Grievor was blind in his left eye. As a result, the city persuaded Grievor to resign and then had charges pressed against him under the *Criminal Code*. Although he had resigned from the fire department, Grievor relied on a clause in his old employment contract that required the city to pay for "any and all damages or claims for damages or injuries or accidents done or caused by [him] during the performance of [his] duties." He therefore argued that, since the accident had occurred while he was working, the city was required to pay any legal fees that arose during the criminal proceedings. The city responded by arguing that Grievor had misrepresented the facts regarding his eyesight and that it consequently did not incur liability under the agreement.

The court held that the failure to disclose his visual impairment amounted to a misrepresentation that *would have* justified Grievor's dismissal. But the court also said that since the city accepted Grievor's resignation, rather than terminate his contract, it was obliged to pay his legal fees.

Questions for Discussion

1. Do you agree that Grievor had a duty to disclose his disability? Would these facts have given rise to misrepresentation if Grievor had not used a friend to pass his medical examination? Explain your answer.

2. Do you agree that the city should be required to pay Grievor's legal fees? What if circumstances were different and money was owing to the families of the car crash victims? Should the city be required to pay the families if Grievor cannot? Explain your answer.[7]

Suppose your accountant is selling her cottage. If she sells it to a stranger, she is not obliged to disclose information about its structural defects if the purchaser does not ask the relevant questions. But she cannot remain silent if she is selling it to you. Because you would otherwise trust her on the basis of your special relationship, she has to fully disclose all material facts, whether or not you asked questions about the building's structure.

WHEN A STATUTORY PROVISION REQUIRES DISCLOSURE Some statutes require the disclosure of material facts in a contractual setting.

- Insurance legislation in many provinces contains statutory conditions that are deemed to be part of every insurance contract and must be printed on every policy. Many provinces have statutes that automatically insert certain conditions into every insurance contract. One of those conditions requires the disclosure of relevant information by those seeking insurance. If a customer does not satisfy that obligation, the contract may be unenforceable.[8]

- Some financial officers have a duty to disclose material facts. For instance, an officer or director has to speak up if they (or someone close to them) have an interest in a contract with their own company. If they fail to do so, the company may be entitled to set aside the contract.[9] The

---

[6.] *Ottawa (City) v Ottawa Professional Fire Fighters* (1985) 52 OR (2d) 129 (Div Ct).

[7.] You may want to review the discussion of vicarious liability that we presented in Chapter 3.

[8.] *Eg Insurance Act*, RSBC 1996, c 226, s 89 (BC); *Insurance Act*, RSO 1990, c I.8, s 148 (Ont).

[9.] *Securities Act*, RSO 1990, c S.5, s 75 (Ont); *Securities Act*, RSA 1981 c S-6.1, s 119 (Alta); *Securities Act*, RSBC 1996, c 418, s 85 (BC); *Securities Act*, CCSM, c S50, ss 50, 72 (Man).

same holds true for some Crown corporations.[10] A similar disclosure requirement arises in securities law.[11]

- Many provinces have legislation regulating the formation of domestic contracts. If a party failed to disclose significant assets or significant liabilities that existed when the domestic contract was made, the court can set aside the agreement or a provision in it.[12]

WHEN FACTS ARE ACTIVELY CONCEALED If a party to a contract actively conceals the truth it may be treated as a misrepresentation. For example, if a building vendor takes steps to hide evidence of structural damage to the building, a court will consider the act of concealment as a form of misrepresentation and the sale may be rescinded on that basis.[13]

Inducement

For a statement to be actionable as a misrepresentation, the deceived party must prove that the false statement induced the contract. In other words, the statement must have misled its recipient into creating the contract. The statement does not have to be the *only* inducing factor. A party can claim relief for misrepresentation even if other factors were also influential. However, a statement will not be actionable if it did not affect the recipient's decision, even if the other party made the representation with an intention to deceive. Nor will a statement be actionable if the recipient conducted an independent inquiry into the matter. In that situation, the contract is induced by the results of the party's own investigation, rather than the other party's representation.

What happens if the recipient of a false representation has an opportunity to test its accuracy but fails to do so? Should that failure to investigate preclude a claim of misrepresentation? Consider the situation in You Be the Judge 9.1.

THE LEGAL CONSEQUENCES OF MISREPRESENTATION

There are two possible consequences of an actionable misrepresentation. The deceived party may receive:

- the remedy of rescission
- the right to damages

Rescission is the only *contractual* consequence of misrepresentation.

Rescission

Rescission is the cancellation of a contract with the aim of restoring the parties, to the greatest extent possible, to their pre-contractual state. It can be done by the parties or, if necessary, through the courts. However, it is often difficult to know in advance whether a court will grant rescission because it

rescission is the cancellation of a contract, by the parties or the court, with the aim of restoring the parties, to the greatest extent possible, to their pre-contractual state

---

[10.] *Eg Bank Act*, SC 1991, c 46, s 206 (Can); *Credit Unions and Caisses Populaires Act*, 1994, SO 1994, c 11, s 148 (Ont); *Credit Union Act*, 1985, SS 1985, c C-45.1, s 74 (Sask).

[11.] *Financial Administration Act*, RSC 1985, c F-11, s 118 (Can).

[12.] *Eg Family Law Act*, RSO 1990, c F.3, s 56 (Ont); *Family Law Act*, SNWT 1997, c 18, s 8(4) (NWT).

[13.] *Gronau v Schlamp Investments Ltd* (1974) 52 DLR (3d) 631 (Man QB).

You Be the Judge 9.1

Motkoski Holdings Ltd v Yellowhead (County) 2010 ABCA 72, [2010] A.J. No. 243

A group of business partners decided to look for land on which to build a motel and gas station. They identified a promising parcel of land in Yellowhead County. Both the county and the business partners were aware that a landfill had once existed in the area where this parcel of land was located. Prior to selling the land, the county commissioned a report confirming that the land had been previously used as a landfill. Nevertheless, the report concluded that the sale could go ahead with the land to be sold "as is." The county put the land on the market and the business partners purchased it. The partners never made any inquiries as to the state of the land and did not see the report prior to purchasing the land. In fact, it was only after the sale was complete that they learned from the provincial environment ministry that the land was not suitable for development. The business partners sued the county for fraudulent misrepresentation for its

failure to show them the report. The county claimed *caveat emptor* ("buyer beware"), stating that there was no misrepresentation as the land was sold "as is."

Questions for Discussion

1. If you were the judge, how would you decide the outcome of this case?

2. From a business perspective, do you think that the developers, as experienced buyers of land, ought to have been responsible for making better inquiries as to the state of the land that they wished to purchase?

3. Was the county's failure to bring the report to the attention of the developers a form of "silence" amounting to a misrepresentation?

---

restitution involves a giving back and taking back on both sides

is a *discretionary remedy*, one that is not available *as of right*. The remedy is awarded on the basis of the court's judgment about what is best according to the rules of reason and justice.[14]

The remedy of rescission is often accompanied by an order for *restitution*. **Restitution** involves a giving back and taking back on both sides. (We will discuss restitution in more detail in Chapter 12 under the heading of "Unjust Enrichment.") Suppose you manufacture snowboards and need to order a steady supply of waterproof paints. A supplier represents that it has waterproof paints to sell but insists that you agree to purchase four shipments over the next two years to take advantage of a special rate. You agree to those conditions, requisition a cheque, and send it to the supplier. When the first shipment arrives, you discover that the paint is not waterproof and is therefore useless to you. You ask for your money back, but the supplier refuses. Assuming that the shipments of paint are worth thousands of dollars, it might be wise to seek an order of rescission from the courts rather than simply disregard the contract. Merely setting aside the contract will not be sufficient. You paid thousands of dollars that you will want back. Likewise, the supplier delivered a truckload of paint that it will want back. Restitution is therefore the appropriate remedy. The court will try to restore the pre-contractual situation by allowing you to recover the money at the same time that it allows the supplier to recover the paint.

affirmation occurs when the misled party declares an intention to carry out the contract or otherwise acts as though it were bound by it

The victim of a misrepresentation may be barred from rescission in certain circumstances. First, if the misled party *affirmed* the contract, then rescission is not available. **Affirmation** occurs when the misled party declares an intention to carry out the contract or otherwise acts as though it were bound by it. A person who has been misled is said to "affirm" the contract only if the person discovered the misrepresentation prior to the declaration or act of affirmation. To continue the earlier example, suppose you discover that the first shipment of

---

[14.] *Wrights Canadian Ropes Ltd v Minister of National Revenue* [1946] 2 DLR 225 (SCC).

paint is not waterproof but do nothing about it. Six months pass, and the next shipment arrives. You then complain that neither shipment contained waterproof paint. The six-month *lapse of time* suggests you affirmed the contract.[15]

Second, rescission may be barred if restitution is impossible. If the parties cannot be substantially returned to their pre-contractual positions, a court is reluctant to grant rescission. The more that has been done under the contract, the less likely a court is to grant rescission. To further continue our example, if you used a substantial portion of the paint supply before discovering that it was not, in fact, waterproof, restitution is not possible in a strict sense. Since you cannot give the paint back, rescission may not be available.

Third, rescission may be unavailable if it would affect a third party. In this case, it is the rights of a third party that make restitution impossible. Suppose you buy a strip mall on the basis of certain representations about its earning potential. You lease portions of the mall to tenants but are unable to earn enough to pay down your mortgages on the building, let alone make anywhere near the profits you were promised. If you seek an order for rescission against the vendor of the mall, you would probably fail. The tenants have acquired a right to occupy the premises. Those third-party rights therefore preclude the court from forcing the vendor to give back your purchase price in exchange for an empty shopping mall.

Damages

A court may respond to a misrepresentation by awarding *damages* against the party that made the statement. In this situation, **damages** are intended to provide monetary compensation for the losses that a person suffered as a result of relying upon a misrepresentation. It is important to understand the precise reason for those damages. As we will see in Chapter 12, damages may be awarded for a breach of contract. Nevertheless, if damages are awarded for a misrepresentation, the plaintiff's claim arises not in contract, but rather in tort. (That is true even though the plaintiff is complaining that the misrepresentation induced the creation of a contract.) As Part 2 of this book explained, tort law is based on the principle that "a person who by his or her fault causes damage to another may be held responsible."[16] There are many types of tort. The one that is relevant for present purposes depends upon the nature of the misrepresentation.

> **damages** are intended to provide monetary compensation for the losses that a person suffered as a result of relying upon a misrepresentation

TYPES OF MISREPRESENTATION

The law distinguishes between three types of misrepresentation: innocent, negligent, and fraudulent. The rules are somewhat different for each.

Innocent Misrepresentation

An **innocent misrepresentation** is a statement a person makes carefully and without knowledge of the fact that it is false. If the speaker is innocent of any fraudulent or negligent conduct, the general rule is that the deceived party is not entitled to recover damages. The only legal remedy available for innocent misrepresentation is rescission, and rescission is available only when there is a substantial difference between what the deceived party had bargained for and what was, in fact, obtained.

> an **innocent misrepresentation** is a statement a person makes carefully and without knowledge of the fact that it is false

---

[15.] *Leaf v International Galleries* [1950] 2 KB 86 (CA).

[16.] *Canadian National Railway v Norsk Pacific Steamship* (1992) 91 DLR (4th) 289 (SCC).

Negligent Misrepresentation

a negligent misrepresentation is a false, inducing statement made in an unreasonable or careless manner

Even a person who acts honestly may *carelessly or unreasonably* make a statement that is inaccurate and that induces the creation of a contract. The party making the statement does not need to know that it is false in order to be liable. Such statements are known as **negligent misrepresentations**. Until recently, the law did not distinguish between innocent misrepresentations and negligent misrepresentations. In either event, the only possible remedy was rescission. However, the courts have now recognized that a negligent misrepresentation may also amount to a tort that supports an award of damages. (Chapter 6 covers the tort of negligent misrepresentation.)

Fraudulent Misrepresentation

a fraudulent misrepresentation occurs when a person makes a statement they know is false *or* that they have no reason to believe is true *or* that they recklessly make without regard to the truth

A **fraudulent misrepresentation** occurs when a person makes a statement that they know is false *or* that they have no reason to believe is true *or* that they recklessly make without regard to the truth.[17] Liability will arise under the tort of deceit. (The tort of deceit was discussed in Chapter 5.) Fraud is, of course, a very serious matter, especially in the business world. A person who is held liable for fraud will find it difficult to attract investors, partners, or customers. For that reason, the courts require an allegation of fraud to be supported by very clear evidence.[18] At the same time, however, if fraud is proven, then the courts are particularly eager to award damages.[19]

Concept Summary 9.2 summarizes the types of misrepresentation and their legal effects.

Concept Summary 9.2

Types of Misrepresentation and Their Legal Effect

	Elements of Proof	Available Remedies
Innocent misrepresentation	• false statement of fact or misleading silence • inducing contract	• rescission of contract
Negligent misrepresentation	• false statement • made in an unreasonable or careless manner • inducing a contract • causing a loss that is not always sufficiently remedied by rescission	• rescission of contract • damages in tort
Fraudulent misrepresentation	• false statement or misleading silence • made without honest belief in its truth • made with intent to induce contract • inducing contract • causing a loss not always sufficiently remedied by rescission	• rescission of contract • damages in tort

---

[17.] *Derry v Peek* (1889) 14 App Cas 337 (HL).

[18.] In order to discourage improper allegations of fraud, the courts often award costs against people who fail to prove such claims. The concept of costs was discussed in Chapter 2.

[19.] A court may award not only compensatory damages, but also punitive damages. The concept of punitive damages was discussed in Chapter 3.

Contractual Terms

L.O. ❻ ❼ ❽ ❾

Having considered pre-contractual statements, we can now turn to statements that actually become part of a contract. Unlike representations and misrepresentations, contractual terms arise from statements that impose obligations under the contract. The intention of the parties is key to understanding the difference between representations and terms. If a statement is intended by both parties to form a part of the contract, then it is a term of the agreement. If it is made by one party to induce the other to enter into an agreement, and the party understands it that way, then it is a representation or a misrepresentation.[20] We will consider two types of contractual terms: terms expressed by the parties and those that are implied by a court or a statute.

EXPRESS TERMS

An **express term** is a statement made by one of the parties that a reasonable person would believe was intended to create an enforceable obligation.

an **express term** is a statement made by one of the parties that a reasonable person would believe was intended to create an enforceable obligation

Proof of Express Terms

When the contract is formed on the basis of an oral agreement, it is first necessary to determine what words were actually spoken. That is primarily a question of evidence. Written contracts produce different difficulties. For example, what if the formation of a contract involves the exchange of several conflicting documents? (In Chapter 7, we discussed the possibility of the "battle of the forms.") Perhaps even more difficult is the situation that arises when a combination of written and spoken words are used during the formation of a contract. We consider each of these situations.

It is often difficult to prove the terms of a contract that was created orally. When an agreement is unwritten and unwitnessed, a court is required to determine whose version of events is more believable. Still, as long as there is no formal writing requirement and all of the other conditions of contract formation have been met, oral agreements are binding. As a matter of risk management, however, it is usually a good idea for a business person to "get it in writing." Aside from issues of proof, the writing process encourages the parties to contemplate the terms more carefully.

If an agreement is written, oral evidence generally cannot be used to add to, subtract from, qualify, or vary the terms of the document.[21] That is known as the *parol evidence rule*. **Parol evidence**, in this context, refers to evidence that is not contained within the written contract. Knowledge of that rule is an important element of risk management. Business people often sign a written agreement on the assurance that some of its terms will not be enforced, or on the assurance that certain items discussed during negotiations are part of the deal even though they are not mentioned in the written document. One should be extremely suspicious of such oral assurances. The parol evidence rule generally means that such oral assurances are unenforceable.

parol evidence is evidence that is not contained within the written contract

There are several exceptions to the parol evidence rule. Parol evidence is admissible:

- to rectify or fix a *mistake* in a contractual document
- to prove that a contract was *never really formed* or is somehow *defective*

[20.] GHL Fridman *The Law of Contract in Canada* 5th ed (2006) at 439.

[21.] *Goss v Lord Nugent* (1833) 110 ER 713 at 715.

- to *resolve ambiguities* in the document
- to demonstrate that a document does not contain the parties' *complete agreement*

There is one other way around the parol evidence rule. A statement may be characterized as a *collateral contract* that independently exists alongside the main contract. A **collateral contract** is a separate agreement one party makes in exchange for the other party's entry into the main contract. Suppose you want to buy oil of a certain quality. The seller's standard written contract contains a clause indicating that it *does not* warrant the quality of its oil.[22] You therefore offer to enter into a contract for the purchase of oil under the seller's standard form contract, but only if the seller enters into a collateral contract that *does* warrant the quality of the oil. You have avoided the parol evidence rule. The seller's promise regarding the quality of the oil is inadmissible under the main contract but it is enforceable as a separate agreement.

Concept Summary 9.3 summarizes the exceptions to the parol evidence rule.

> a **collateral contract** is a separate agreement one party makes in exchange for the other party's entry into the main contract

Concept Summary 9.3

Exceptions to the Parol Evidence Rule

- Parol evidence is admissible to rectify a mistaken contractual document.
- Parol evidence is admissible to prove that a contract was never formed or is defective.
- Parol evidence is admissible to resolve contractual ambiguities.
- Parol evidence is admissible to demonstrate an incomplete agreement.
- The parol evidence rule is not applicable to a collateral contract.

Interpretation of Express Terms

Even if the parties agree on particular terms and write them into a document, they may disagree on the interpretation of those words. Consider Business Decision 9.2.

A great deal of contractual litigation turns on differences in interpretation. In resolving such disputes, the courts ask how a reasonable business person in the parties' positions would have interpreted the relevant clause. Nevertheless, the issue can still be difficult.

The business school in Business Decision 9.2 would likely take a **literal approach** to the words and stress their *ordinary meaning*. They would argue that the contract plainly stated that "the university reserves the right to change fees without notice."

The students would interpret the contract somewhat differently. They would take a *contextual approach*. The **contextual approach** goes beyond the four corners of the document by looking at the parties' presumed intentions and their circumstances. The students would argue that the intent of the clause was to contemplate an "adjustment"—that is, a slight alteration, not a 400 percent increase. They would further argue that if the university had intended to

> the **literal approach** assigns words their *ordinary meaning*

> the **contextual approach** goes beyond the four corners of the document by looking at the parties' presumed intentions and their circumstances

---

[22] *LG Thorne & Co Pty Ltd v Thomas Borthwick & Sons (A'asia) Ltd* (1956) 56 SR (NSW) 81 at 94.

Business Decision **9.2**

Contractual Interpretation[23]

On the heels of a six-year tuition freeze put in place by the previous provincial government, the Dean of Vancouver Business School was relieved to see a change in provincial power. For quite some time the business school had been planning to raise its tuition gradually over several years in order to meet its basic costs. Precluded by the freeze from doing so, the school now found itself in the awkward position of having to quadruple the price of admission for its 15-month MBA program to $28 000 in order to recover costs incurred during the freeze. Even worse, because the newly formed government had not yet lifted the tuition freeze, offer letters sent to students who had been accepted into the program were legally precluded from implementing the new fee structure. Consequently, the offer letters included the following term:

> Tuition Fees: $7000* for the 15-month program (payable in four instalments of $1750).

> * Student activity fees are also assessed. Fees for the year are subject to adjustment and the university reserves the right to change fees without notice. Please see attached information sheet and fees section of the university calendar.

A number of applicants received and accepted the offer of admission between November and February. In March, as expected, the provincial government officially lifted the tuition freeze and the business school swiftly approved an increase in tuition, raising the price from $7000 to $28 000. Shocked to later learn about the spike in tuition, a number of applicants claimed that they had accepted admission offers at the old tuition rate. The school replied that the contract students accepted clearly and expressly permitted changes that would allow for the new fee structure. Both parties agreed that the contract contained the fee adjustment clause. They disagreed, however, on its proper interpretation.

Questions for Discussion

1. .Do you think the fee adjustment clause is ambiguous?

2. Who should win this case and why?

3. How might Vancouver Business School have minimized its risk of litigation when sending the offer letters, assuming that it knew there would likely be a significant tuition hike?

charge nearly $30 000 per year, it would not have stipulated a meagre $7000 amount. The students receiving offers had no way of knowing that the faculty was always planning a significant increase and the contract would not have been understood by a reasonable person to give that much leeway on the stipulated amount, which, from a student perspective, is clearly an important term in the contract.

Which of these two interpretations is more plausible? If you are inclined to side with the students, you should also consider the golden rule of interpretation. According to the **golden rule**, words will be given their plain, ordinary meaning unless to do so would result in absurdity. If we were to adopt a strict, literal reading of the sentence—"Fees for the year are subject to adjustment and the university reserves the right to change fees without notice"—it would not be absurd to imagine a significant fee hike, especially in light of the economic circumstances plaguing the business school as a consequence of the six-year tuition freeze.

the **golden rule** says that words will be given their plain, ordinary meaning unless to do so would result in absurdity

At the same time, another rule of interpretation may operate in favour of the students: the *contra proferentem* rule. The ***contra proferentem* rule** ensures that the meaning least favourable to the author will prevail. That rule is justified by the fact that the author, in this case the university, is in the best position to create a clear and unambiguous term.

the *contra proferentem* rule ensures that the meaning least favourable to the author will prevail

IMPLIED TERMS

Even if the parties carefully write out their agreement, that document may not contain all the relevant terms. A contract may contain both express terms and *implied terms*. An **implied term** arises by operation of law, either through the common law or under a statute.

an **implied term** arises by operation of law, either through the common law or under a statute

---

[23.] *MacDonald v University of British Columbia* (2005) 47 BCLR (4th) 325 (BCCA).

Terms Implied by a Court

Unlike representations and express terms, implied terms do not arise from the parties themselves. They are inserted into a contract by the law. And since people are generally entitled to create their own agreements, a court will normally not imply a term unless that term is necessary to implement the parties' presumed intentions. In other words, courts will not interfere with people's bargains unless there is a gap or omission in the agreement that can be fixed only by way of an implied term. An implied term is "necessary" in this context if (i) it is an obvious consequence of the parties' agreement, or (ii) it is required for the purpose of business efficacy.

Those two criteria often overlap. Suppose you are in the business of leasing equipment. A customer returns some leased equipment to you on time but in damaged condition. What if your contract did not expressly say anything about the condition of the equipment? That sort of term was presumably intended by both parties. After all, the whole point of a rental agreement is that the thing must be returned at the end of the lease. Consequently, a court will imply a term that requires the equipment to come back in the same condition in which it went out, subject to reasonable wear and tear.[24]

Courts will not imply a term simply because it is reasonable or would improve the contract. On the contrary, a term generally will be implied only if it is reasonable, necessary, capable of exact formulation, and clearly justified with regard to the parties' intentions when they contracted. Of those considerations, the last one is the most important.[25] A contract may also contain an implied term that reflects a standard practice that has evolved within a particular field, as long as that term would not be inconsistent with the parties' express intentions. Return to our example in which you created a lease with a company that regularly rents equipment. Even though your contract is silent on the point, it may contain a term that people in your trade habitually include in their agreements.[26]

The courts sometimes imply a term on the basis of a contract's legal characteristics. Certain kinds of agreements, by their very nature, involve certain obligations, even if the parties did not intend them. The Supreme Court of Canada, for example, has held that an employment contract contains a term that requires the employer to provide reasonable notice before dismissing the employee, even if a contract is silent on the issue or even if the agreement expressly says that the employee can be dismissed without notice.[27]

Terms Implied by Statute

Terms are often implied by statute. In Chapter 13, we will see several examples that arise under the *Sale of Goods Act*. Likewise, consumer protection laws in Manitoba, the Northwest Territories, and the Yukon imply a term that the goods being sold are new and unused, unless otherwise described.[28] Whenever a statute implies a term into a contract, the term is incorporated automatically

---

[24.] *Con-force Prods Ltd v Luscar Ltd* (1982) 27 Sask R 299 (QB).

[25.] *Canadian Helicopters Ltd v Interpac Forest Products Ltd* [2001] BCCA 39.

[26.] *British Crane Hire Corp Ltd v Ipswich Plant Hire Ltd* [1975] QB 303.

[27.] *Machtinger v HOJ Industries* (1992) 91 DLR (4th) 491 (SCC). Employment contracts are discussed in Chapter 26.

[28.] *The Consumer Protection Act*, CCSM c C200, s 58(1)(d) (Man); *Consumer Protection Act*, RSNWT 1988, c C-17 s 70(1)(d) (NWT); *Consumer Protection Act*, RSY 2002, c 40, s 58(1)(d) (Yuk).

without judicial intervention. If a dispute comes before the courts, the term is treated as if the parties expressly created it. In some cases, however, a statutory term will not apply if the parties have expressly excluded it. In these instances, the statutory term is merely a default rule. From a risk management perspective, it is important for parties negotiating contracts to determine whether there are relevant statutory terms and whether they are mandatory or merely default terms.

STANDARD FORM AGREEMENTS

The terms of many business transactions are dictated by *standard form agreements*. **Standard form agreements** are mass-produced documents usually drafted by a party who is in an economic position to offer certain terms on a "take-it-or-leave-it" basis. Standard form agreements are most often used for transactions that occur over and over again. A bank, for instance, does not want to negotiate a completely new contract every time it lends money to a customer. As a matter of risk management, it is better to avoid the risk of trouble by using a model that has been refined and tested over the years. Furthermore, it would be time-consuming and expensive to allow each customer to negotiate new terms. Those additional costs would, of course, translate into higher interest rates. The same general principles apply to any business that enters into similar agreements on a repetitive basis.

> **standard form agreements** are mass-produced documents usually drafted by a party who is in an economic position to offer certain terms on a "take-it-or-leave-it" basis

There is, however, a downside to standard form agreements. Such contracts are often so long and complex that few customers actually read and understand them. Furthermore, because they tend to be offered on a take-it-or-leave-it basis, customers have no realistic opportunity to bargain for better terms. In a sense, the customer is at the mercy of the other party. In such cases, the nature of the standard form agreement is different from a contract negotiated by parties with equal bargaining powers in that it may lack the usual *consensus ad idem* (the meeting of the minds). If customers refuse to accept the standard terms, they cannot purchase the goods or services in question.

One type of term that customers are often required to accept in standard form agreements is an **exclusion clause**—or *limitation clause* or *waiver*—which is a contractual term that seeks to protect one party from various sorts of legal liability. For example, an outdoors adventure company might try to use an exclusion clause to preclude the risk of being sued by customers who are injured during their expeditions. Such a term is perfectly legitimate if the following three things can be demonstrated:

> an **exclusion clause** is a contractual term that seeks to protect one party from various sorts of legal liability

- First, the term must have been drafted in clear, *unambiguous language*. If an exclusion clause is ambiguous, it will be interpreted as strictly and as literally as possible, and it will be given the meaning that is least favourable to its author.

- Second, the party against whom the exclusion clause is meant to operate must be given *reasonable notice* of the term and its effect.

- Third, it must be shown that the party against whom the exclusion clause is meant to operate *agreed* that the exclusion clause is part of the contract. A signature is usually the best evidence of that agreement.

An exclusion clause will not be invalidated merely because one party was in a stronger bargaining position than the other. A judge will, however, consider such an imbalance when deciding whether the weaker party truly did agree to the clause.

Ticket Contracts

Standard form agreements sometimes take the form of a ticket or a receipt. As a business person, you might try to incorporate certain terms, including exclusion clauses, into your contract by having them printed on the back of a ticket you issue to your customers. Whether those clauses are valid depends on how they are presented. As with exclusion clauses, the general rule is that the terms must be brought to the customer's notice either before or when the contract is made. As usual, the question is not whether the customer actually read those terms, but whether they were given *reasonable notice*. If the reasonable person would not have known about the printing on the back of the ticket, then the customer probably will not be bound by those terms. On the other hand, if the customer knew that the back of the ticket contained terms, those terms will be incorporated into the contract even if the customer chose not to read them. Business Decision 9.3 illustrates some of the issues associated with ticket contracts that contain limitation of liability clauses.

Business Decision **9.3**

Ticket Contracts[29]

Mr Malayko decided to spend the day skiing at Snowy Valley Ski Hills. In order to access the ski lifts, he purchased a lift ticket that he affixed to the outside of his coat. Before he could enjoy his day on the slopes, though, Malayko was injured by a ski lift. While standing in position waiting for the next lift, he was struck on the knee from behind by a handle which, instead of hanging straight down from the lift was improperly protruding in a horizontal position. He suffered a serious ligament tear and brought an action against Snowy Valley alleging that it was negligent in its maintenance, operation, and supervision of the lift.

On the front of Malayko's lift pass is printed:

PLEASE READ THE EXCLUSION OF LIABILITY AND ASSUMPTION OF RISK NOTICE ON THE BACK.

On the back of the ticket is printed:

NOTICE TO ALL USERS OF THESE FACILITIES: EXCLUSION OF LIABILITY—ASSUMPTION OF RISK. THESE CONDITIONS WILL AFFECT YOUR LEGAL RIGHTS—PLEASE READ CAREFULLY!

As a condition of the use of the ski area facilities, the Ticket Holder assumes all risk of personal injury from any cause whatsoever including but not limited to the risks, dangers and hazards of skiing; the use of ski lifts; and negligence. The Ticket

Holder agrees that the ski area operator shall not be liable for any such personal injury, death or property loss and releases the ski area operator and waives all claims with respect thereto.

Snowy Valley had also posted brightly coloured signs containing these terms in the lift ticket purchase area and in various other locations throughout the ski area. In addition, an Alpine Responsibility Code was also posted throughout the area, including the ticket purchase area. One of its provisions said, "You must have sufficient dexterity, ability, and knowledge to safely load, ride, and unload lifts."

Malayko claims that this limitation of liability clause does not form part of his contract with Snowy Valley because he had no knowledge of it.

Questions for Discussion

1. Do you think Snowy Valley took reasonable steps to bring the limitation of liability to Malayko's attention? What more could Snowy Valley have done?

2. How does the fact that Malayko's injury was caused by a mechanical fault in the ski lift rather than the "use of the ski lift" (which is the language used in the limitation of liability clause) affect the scope of the limitation? If you ran Snowy Valley, what would you change about the clause, if anything?

Signed Forms

As a general rule, people who sign standard form agreements are bound by all of the terms expressed in them, even if they have not actually read or understood those terms. There is a rationale for this rule. By signing a document, a customer indicates a willingness to be bound by its terms, and the other party receives some assurance that the agreement is enforceable.

---

29. These facts are based on *Pelechytik v. Snow Valley Ski Club* 2005 ABQB 532, [2005] AJ No 875, 53 Alta LR (4th) 117.

Many standard form agreements are, however, extremely long and complicated. A judge therefore may apply an exception to the general rule if the customer is required to quickly sign the document without enjoying a reasonable opportunity to study its terms. In such circumstances, there is an onus on the party relying on the document to prove that the customer was given reasonable notice of its relevant terms. That exception prevents a more powerful party from burying onerous or unusual terms in the small print of a difficult document. Case Brief 9.1 provides an illustration.

Case Brief **9.1**

Tilden Rent-a-Car Co v Clendenning (1978) 83 DLR (3d) 400 (Ont CA)

While filling out a car rental application at the Vancouver airport, Mr Clendenning was asked by the rental agent at Tilden Rent-a-Car whether he wanted to purchase collision insurance for an additional, modest fee. After agreeing to pay extra, Clendenning was handed a complicated rental contract. Being in a hurry, he signed the document without reading it. The rental agent neither asked him to read the contract nor mentioned that it included an unusual term that excluded insurance coverage if the driver had consumed *any* amount of alcohol.

During the rental period, Clendenning got into an accident and damaged the vehicle. He admitted to drinking a small quantity of alcohol that day, but it was unclear exactly how much he had consumed. Not having read the agreement, Clendenning was unaware of the term that excluded coverage if *any* alcohol was consumed. That

term did not appear on the face of the contract; it was found on the back in small print. Clendenning claimed he was led to believe that the insurance provided complete coverage. Tilden, on the other hand, argued that Clendenning's signature was sufficient to bind him to the terms of the contract. Tilden also claimed that Clendenning's previous dealings with Tilden provided him with ample opportunity to read the terms of the contract despite the fact that he signed it that day in a hurry.

The Court of Appeal held that Clendenning's signature did *not* represent a true acceptance of the terms in the contract. Because the relevant term was onerous and unusual, Tilden was required to provide Clendenning with reasonable notice of it as well as a reasonable opportunity to understand and appreciate what he was signing.

The clause that was contained in the standard form contract that Mr Clendenning signed is an example of a *boilerplate clause*. A **boilerplate clause** is a standard provision that can be reused in various contractual settings in a virtually unchanged form.[30] As we have seen, businesses often use boilerplate clauses to quickly and efficiently allocate contractual risks, manage exposure to liability, and highlight the need to purchase insurance (amongst other things). The final section of this chapter contains a survey of some of the more significant types of boilerplate clauses.

a **boilerplate clause** is a standard provision that can be reused in various contractual settings in a virtually unchanged form

Concept Summary 9.4 lists how businesses can manage the risk associated with standard form contracts.

Concept Summary 9.4

Managing Risk in Association with Standard Form Contracts

- Use standard form contracts that have been tested and have a proven record of use, over a period of years if possible.
- Use clear, unambiguous language for onerous terms and consider using plain language throughout the contract.
- Give reasonable notice of onerous and unusual terms, and instruct staff to draw customers' attention to such terms.
- Require customers to clearly indicate their agreement to be bound by onerous or unusual terms, perhaps by requiring their initials in a box next to the term itself.

[30.] The source of the phrase is not entirely clear. It may refer to sheets of metal that were used by newspapers in the first half of the twentieth century. Those sheets were very strong and very durable.

USING PLAIN LANGUAGE IN CONTRACTS

There is an old joke that asks, "What do you get when you cross *The Godfather* with a lawyer?" Answer: "An offer you can't understand." Contracts and other legal documents are sometimes difficult to decipher. More often than not, this is the result of unnecessary *legalese*. **Legalese** is a slang expression designating the formal and technical language of traditional legal documents. The early history of English law provides a stark example of the importance of using understandable language in legal matters. Following the Norman Conquest of England in 1066, all legal proceedings and documents were required to be in Latin or French, even though most of the law's subjects spoke only English. It took nearly 500 years to correct this, when the Archbishop of Canterbury publically complained, "I have heard suitors murmur at the bar because their attorneys pleaded their cause in the French tongue which they understood not."[31] Using another language in those times was strategic though unjust; it intentionally limited court access to a select group of people. The same holds true today. The often archaic and circular language used by many companies in their legal documentation is just as unintelligible and inaccessible to the general public—even to those who are perfectly fluent in English. The Archbishop's complaint was perhaps the earliest "plain language" movement in law, a movement that culminated during the Commonwealth, when the king was executed and a law passed requiring all legal documents to be written in English.

> **legalese** is a slang expression designating the formal and technical language of traditional legal documents

Although its history is interesting, the modern notion of the plain language movement has its roots in the contemporary business setting. In 1973, First National City Bank (now Citibank) became alarmed at the rate at which it was forced to sue its own customers to enforce debts. A committee within the bank determined that part of the problem was its own standard form "promissory note"—a legal document that was confusing even to the bank's own lawyers. After revising the document, including a name change to "customer loan note," the bank found that the increased comprehensibility of its terms and conditions led to a reduction in lawsuits and an increase in market share. As this example illustrates, by using plain language, businesses can increase the likelihood that the documents they use will be understood by everyone, including people who do not have legal training. Many public and private sector entities are now moving in this direction. For example, the official *Communications Policy of the Government of Canada* requires the use of plain language in all government communications, both internally within government and externally by the public.[32] Likewise, the Canadian Bankers Association aims to ensure that mortgage documents are written in understandable plain language.[33] Some laws even make it mandatory to use plain language in certain circumstances.[34]

The use of plain language in contracts is clearly a consumer protection issue, as discussed in Chapter 19. However, businesses can also benefit from the use of plain language in contracts and other documents, as it can lead to a reduced need for employee training (regarding the meaning of different business documents), improved communication with customers, and reduced time

---

[31.] PM Tiersma *Legal Language* (1999) at 35.

[32.] *Communications Policy of the Government of Canada* (1 August 2006; updated 1 April 2012), www.tbs-sct.gc.ca/pol/doc-eng.aspx?id=12316&section=text.

[33.] Canadian Bankers Association, *Plain Language Mortgage Documents—CBA Commitment* (7 March 2000).

[34.] See, *eg*, the *Bank Act*, 1991, c 46, s 459.1(4.1): "A bank shall disclose the prohibition on coercive tied selling set out in subsection (1) in a statement in plain language that is clear and concise, displayed and available to customers and the public at all of its branches . . ."

spent answering customer questions that arise from confusion about documents. These effects can lead to tremendous cost savings, improved customer relations, and the reduction of unnecessary disputes.[35]

With the above in mind, it is important for those in business to work with lawyers to minimize legalese and ensure plain, comprehensible language in their business documents. The basic approach is the same as other forms of business writing: You should *write for your audience*. The main goal is to ensure that legal documents are understood by all of those who are affected by them, including business personnel who use the documents and the customers with whom they interact. Steps can be taken to increase the comprehensibility of legal documents. Archaic terms, such as "herein" or "aforesaid," can be avoided completely. Sentences and paragraphs should be short. The passive voice should be avoided. In terms of style, pomposity is a poor substitute for formality and only obscures meaning. Structurally, legal documents should begin with the most important terms of the contract at the beginning, so that readers immediately understand their primary rights and obligations. Although entrepreneurs and risk managers will not usually draft these documents themselves, it is important to have a clear sense of the difference between traditional legalese and the modern plain language approach. Figure 9.2 offers some illustrations.

FIGURE 9.2 Shedding the Weight of Legalese

Before (Traditional Legalese)	After (Plain Language)
Title to property in the goods shall remain vested in the Company (notwithstanding the delivery of the same to the Customer) until the price of the Goods comprised in the contract and all other money due from the Customer to the Company on any other account has been paid in full.	We shall retain ownership of the goods until you have finished paying for them.[36]
The said Lessee covenants, promises, and agrees that it will not carry on or suffer to be carried on any business in the herein demised premises under a name or a style other than the name of the said Lessee as designated herein, nor call or suffer the herein demised premises or any business carried on therein to be called by any name other than such name, without the written consent of the Lessor first had and obtained.	You must not carry on business or let business be carried on in the leased premises by any name other than your own (as described in this lease), without first getting our written consent.[37]
In the event of failure of Purchaser to pay any instalment when due, whether such failure be voluntary or involuntary, the only right of Seller arising thereunder shall be that of termination of this Agreement and retention of all sums previously paid as liquidated damages and not as a penalty, because Seller has taken the property off the real estate market, incurred expenses in selling the property to Purchaser, turned away other prospective purchasers and incurred or will be incurring development and other expenses in connection with the property. Upon such termination, any and all rights Purchaser may have in the property shall immediately terminate and Seller may return the property to its inventory and resell it free and clear of any claims, liens, encumbrances, or defects arising out of this Agreement or Purchaser's rights in the property.	If you miss even a single payment, we can cancel this contract and keep all the money you've paid us. You'll lose all your rights.[38]

[35] CM Stephens *Plain Language Legal Writing* (2008).

[36] *Unfair terms in consumer contracts*, Plain English Campaign, www.plainenglish.co.uk/legal/unfair_terms.html.

[37] RC Dick *Legal Drafting in Plain Language* 3d ed (1995) p. 184.

[38] R Flesch *How to Write Plain English: A Book for Lawyers and Consumers* (1979) at 120.

L.O. ⑩   Boilerplate Clauses

Standard form agreements often include a number of *boilerplate clauses*. As described above, a boilerplate clause is a standard provision that can be reused in various contractual settings in a virtually unchanged form. Boilerplate clauses often help to provide a framework for commercial agreements. Without them, many of the parties' substantive rights that are contained in an agreement would have little meaning. Lawyers have come to rely on boilerplate clauses to satisfy clients who require contracts to be drafted in a hurry at as little expense as possible. Because boilerplates play such an important role in many business transactions, we will briefly consider some of the more common types of boilerplate clauses:

- exclusion clauses
- *force majeure* clauses
- confidentiality clauses
- arbitration clauses
- jurisdiction clauses
- entire agreement clauses

Exclusion Clauses

Many standard form agreements contain exclusion clauses, terms that are designed to protect one party from various sorts of legal liability. (See the example of an exclusion clause on the following page.) As already discussed in this chapter, exclusion clauses can be perfectly legitimate as long as they meet certain requirements.

A difficult question arises if the party trying to rely on an exclusion clause acts in a way that deprives the other party of substantially the whole benefit of a contract. Suppose you own a factory and enter into a contract with a security company to patrol your building on a regular basis. The security company's standard form contract excludes liability against "burglary, theft, fire or any other cause." Although these are the very things that you are seeking to avoid in your decision to hire security, you figure that the low monthly fee makes the risk of agreeing to exclude liability seem reasonable. While making the required rounds one day, a security guard decides to light a small fire, which eventually burns out of control and destroys your entire factory. Should the security company be able to take advantage of the exclusion clause, even though it failed to perform the fundamental term of the contract—to secure, rather than to destroy, your factory? To allow the security company to rely on the clause seems unjust, since it was the security company's misperformance of the contract that ultimately deprived you of its entire benefit.

The Supreme Court of Canada has held that an exclusion clause should generally be enforced according to its true meaning, even if the party relying on the exclusion clause has failed to live up to its end of the bargain and thereby deprived the other party of substantially the whole benefit to be obtained under the contract. However, it also held that an exclusion clause will not be enforced if it is "unconscionable" or if it would be "unfair or unreasonable" to enforce the exclusion clause.[39]

[39.] *Hunter Engineering Co v Syncrude Canada Ltd* (1989) 57 DLR (4th) 421 (SCC).

EXCLUSION CLAUSE

The Great Canadian Adventure Company

The Great Canadian Adventure Company:

I, _____, hereby acknowledge and agree that in my participation in adventure activities by The Great Canadian Adventure Company:

1. I will not hold The Great Canadian Adventure Company, its officers, directors or employees responsible for any injury, death, accident, illness, delay, personal loss, personal property damage or other loss sustained by me and hereby release The Great Canadian Adventure Company, its officers, directors and employees due to any cause whatsoever, including, without limitation, negligence on the part of The Great Canadian Adventure Company or its employees. I further agree to indemnify The Great Canadian Adventure Company and its employees for any and all legal fees (on a solicitor and his own client basis) or costs that may be incurred in defending any lawsuit or claim I may bring against them.

2. AND I DO HEREBY ACKNOWLEDGE AND AGREE THAT:

   (a) I will participate in adventure activities entirely at my own risk. Participation in any outdoor activity and travel in natural, outdoor environments involves inherent risks, dangers and hazards. These risks may include, but are not limited to: natural disasters, forces of nature, weather conditions, rugged or steep terrain, avalanches, rock fall, slippery footing, water, isolation from medical facilities, difficult evacuation, equipment failure, mechanical breakdown, human error and accidents. These and other risks may cause serious injury, illness, death, personal property damage or personal losses.

   (b) this Waiver of All Claims, Release from Liability and Assumption of Risk is binding on myself, my heirs, my executors, administrators, personal representatives and assigns.

   (c) the term "adventure activities" as used in the Waiver of All Claims, Release from Liability and Assumption of Risk includes, without limiting, the generality of that term, training sessions, programmes and events that are in any way authorized, sanctioned, organized or operated by The Great Canadian Adventure Company.

   (d) I understand that by signing this release I may be forever prevented from suing or otherwise claiming against The Great Canadian Adventure Company, its officers, directors or employees for certain loss or damages, whether for property loss or personal injury, that I may sustain while participating in adventure activities.

   (e) I understand that the included itinerary is a general guideline of what can be expected on my adventure trip, but is NOT a contract. Factors such as weather conditions, mechanical breakdown, flight cancellations, medical emergencies, political unrest, natural disasters or other uncontrollable circumstances can alter my trip.

   (f) I will not hold The Great Canadian Adventure Company responsible for extra costs incurred by me, which include, but are not limited to: extra meals, personal costs or rebooking of commercial transportation in the event of unforeseen or uncontrollable circumstances.

I confirm that I have carefully read this agreement and understand its terms as acknowledged by my signature below.

Dated at _____ on _____, 20___.

Participant's Name: _____   Participant's Signature: _____

Witness's Name: _____   Witness's Signature: _____

* Minors under 18 years of age must have a parent or legal guardian witness the form. Note: All participants in your party are required to read and sign a waiver before a booking/reservation can be confirmed. All waiver forms must be witnessed and dated. Any participants under 18 years of age must also have their parent or legal guardian sign the waiver.

Force Majeure Clauses

a **force majeure** clause aims to protect the parties when part of the contract cannot be performed because of some event that is outside of their control

Another way for the parties to limit their potential liability is through the use of a *force majeure* clause. *Force majeure* literally means a superior or irresistible force, such as a flood, stormy weather, or war. A **force majeure** clause aims to protect the parties when part of the contract cannot be performed because of some event that is outside of their control and could not have been prevented by their exercise of due care. Sound risk-management principles dictate the use of such clauses. Unlike exclusion clauses, which ought to be drafted as narrowly as possible, an effective *force majeure* clause will be drafted as broadly as possible to include as many unpredictable events as are imaginable. The following is an example of a *force majeure* clause:

FORCE MAJEURE CLAUSE

O'Brien's Encyclopedia of Forms:[40] Where the Seller is unable to make delivery of any portion of the Items covered by this contract due to a labour dispute, accident, fire, war, government regulation or any cause whatsoever beyond the control of the Seller, the Seller shall not be liable for such liability to make delivery if, within a reasonable time, it notifies the Buyer by prepaid post of the cause of such inability and that the contract for the undelivered portion of the Items is cancelled or that it will make delivery of such Items at a future date to be named in the notice of. The Buyer may, within _____ days after the date of mailing of such notice, notify the Seller by prepaid post that it will accept the delivery of the Items pursuant to the terms of the Seller's notice or cancel the undelivered portion of the contract. But upon the Buyer's failure to so notify the Seller, the undelivered portion shall be cancelled.

Confidentiality Clauses

a **confidentiality clause** prevents disclosure of certain information about the agreement to third parties

In many business transactions, one or both parties want to prevent the disclosure of certain information to third parties. Business people generally do not want competitors or other customers to learn about such things as payment schedules, business operations, or trade secrets. When confidential treatment is warranted, the parties might choose to include a **confidentiality clause**. Unlike the *force majeure* clause, an effective confidentiality provision should be drafted narrowly to apply to only specific, limited information. A good confidentiality clause requires that materials be expressly designated as confidential by the party seeking confidential treatment and that the other party to the agreement have a sufficient time to register objections. It provides that information is presumed not to be confidential and that the burden lies with the party seeking confidential treatment to justify such treatment. The following is an example of a confidentiality clause:

CONFIDENTIALITY CLAUSE

Liblicense, Yale University Library
It is understood and agreed by the parties that specific reports and other disclosures required by this agreement, and any changes that may be effected thereto,

---

[40.] *O'Brien's Encyclopedia of Forms: Commercial and General*, 11th ed looseleaf vol 4 (1998) 39.21–39.22.

are considered by both parties to be sensitive. Such information will not be disclosed by either party to third persons except as may be required by law.

Arbitration Clauses

Parties often recognize that future disputes about the terms of an agreement could result in costly litigation. To avoid having to litigate such disputes, they sometimes insert an arbitration clause into a contract. (Arbitration was discussed in Chapter 2.) An **arbitration clause** outlines who should act to resolve the dispute and what method of arbitration should be used. Business people should consider these features of arbitration clauses:

1. Like exclusion clauses, a well-drafted arbitration clause is drafted in a clear, straightforward manner. By keeping the clause simple, one reduces the risk of hindering the arbitration process.
2. An effective arbitration clause stipulates how the expenses incurred in the course of arbitration are to be divided.
3. The clause determines, in advance, the number, qualifications, and role of the arbitrators.
4. An effective clause settles the procedural aspects of the arbitration, including the order in which the parties will present their cases and the amount of time allowed for each presentation.
5. A well-constructed clause ensures that any information discussed at the arbitration will be kept confidential.
6. The clause contemplates whether the parties will require written reasons in support of the decision and whether there are avenues of appeal available to the parties.

Most of these details may not be specifically enumerated in the arbitration clause itself. They are often prescribed by reference to a document external to the contract, such as a set of rules or guidelines published by some arbitration institute. The following is an example of an arbitration clause:

ARBITRATION CLAUSE
BC International Commercial Arbitration Centre
All disputes arising out of or in connection with this contract, or in respect of any legal relationship associated therewith or derived therefrom, shall be referred to and finally solved by arbitration under the rules of the British Columbia International Commercial Arbitration Centre. The appointing authority shall be the British Columbia International Commercial Arbitration Centre. The case shall be administered by the British Columbia International Commercial Arbitration Centre in accordance with its "Procedures for Cases under BCICAC Rules." The place of the arbitration shall be Vancouver, British Columbia, Canada.

Jurisdiction Clauses

Parties that are not interested in arbitration as an alternative method of dispute resolution might still decide that it is worthwhile to contemplate where the court battle will take place, should there be one. A **jurisdiction clause** predetermines the locale of the court and whose law will apply in the event of a legal dispute between the parties. Such a clause is especially useful for situations where the parties are not governed by the same jurisdiction. As will be discussed in Chapter 19, jurisdiction issues are particularly important for the e-commerce aspects of a business, and there a number of steps a business should take to manage risk in this area. If a business has a centralized structure, based in a single jurisdiction, it is usually wise to insert a jurisdiction clause.

an **arbitration clause** outlines who should act to resolve a dispute and what method of arbitration should be used

a **jurisdiction clause** predetermines the locale of the court and whose law will apply in the event of a legal dispute between the parties

PART 3

Such a clause will help to ensure that those involved in the litigation process, whether as lawyers or witnesses, are not required to travel to other jurisdictions to sue or be sued. The following is an example of a jurisdiction clause:

JURISDICTION CLAUSE
Typical Website
This user agreement is governed by the laws of the Province of Ontario, Canada. You hereby consent to the exclusive jurisdiction and venue of courts in Middlesex County, Ontario, Canada, in all disputes arising out of or relating to the use of this website. Use of this website is unauthorized in any jurisdiction that does not give effect to all provisions of these terms and conditions, including, without limitation, this paragraph.

Entire Agreement Clauses

When parties to a contract negotiate both orally and in writing, it is sometimes difficult to know which communications are to be incorporated as terms of the contract. One way to avoid uncertainty is to use an *entire agreement clause*. An **entire agreement clause** is a provision stating that the entire agreement between the parties is contained within the four corners of the contract. Such a clause ensures that none of the exceptions to the parol evidence will operate to defeat the written document. The principles of risk management therefore require business people to determine whether the standard forms they are signing contain an entire agreement clause. If so, they must ensure that every single aspect of the agreement is captured in the written document. The following is an example of an entire agreement clause:

an **entire agreement** clause is a provision stating that the entire agreement between the parties is contained within the four corners of the contract

ENTIRE AGREEMENT CLAUSE
O'Brien's Encyclopedia of Forms[41]
This Agreement constitutes the entire agreement between the Lessor and Lessee and the Lessee acknowledges that there are no promises, inducements, representations, collateral warranties, warranties, conditions, options or terms, oral or written, express or implied or otherwise made by or on behalf of the Lessor or operating in favour of the Lessee with respect to any aspect of the Equipment including, without limitation, its condition, design, capabilities, operation, use, suitability, fitness, durability, quality, merchantability or history (new, used, reconditioned) or with respect to the appropriate treatment of this Agreement or payments to be made pursuant thereto for the Lessee's accounting or tax purposes, other than as may be expressly stated in this Agreement.

[41.] *O'Brien's Encyclopedia of Forms: Commercial and General,* 11th ed looseleaf vol 4 (1998) 39.21–39.22.

Chapter Summary

Not every statement made during pre-contractual negotiations becomes a contractual term. Pre-contractual representations are assertions of fact made with the intention of inducing another party to enter into a contract that do not form part of the contract. Contractual terms, on the other hand, are provisions in an agreement that create legally enforceable obligations. If necessary, a court will determine whether a statement is a representation or a term, based on how a reasonable person would have understood the statement and the parties' intentions.

A misrepresentation is a false pre-contractual statement that induces the recipient of the statement into a contract. Inaccurate expressions of opinion, descriptions of future conduct, and statements of law are normally not treated as misrepresentations. To prove misrepresentation in those circumstances, a party must prove that the speaker implicitly claimed to state some fact. Silence, half-truths, and acts that conceal the truth can amount to misrepresentation in certain circumstances.

For a false statement to be actionable misrepresentation, the deceived party must be able to prove that it induced the contract. The two possible consequences of an actionable misrepresentation are (i) the remedy of rescission, and (ii) the right to damages. The remedy of rescission usually coincides with restitution, requiring a giving back and taking on both sides. Its aim is to return the parties to their pre-contractual state. Rescission may be barred if (i) the misled party ultimately affirms the contract, (ii) restitution is not possible, or (iii) a third party's rights are affected. Damages are an award of money meant to compensate the loss suffered by the misled party because of the misrepresentation.

An innocent misrepresentation involves a statement made carefully and without knowledge that it is false. A negligent misrepresentation is a false statement made in an unreasonable or careless manner. A fraudulent misrepresentation is made without any belief in its truth or with reckless indifference. All three types of misrepresentation can give rise to rescission. Only fraudulent and negligent misrepresentation can give rise to tort damages.

An express term, whether oral or written, is a statement intended to create a legally enforceable obligation. When an agreement has been reduced to writing, the parol evidence rule states that oral evidence is inadmissible to vary or qualify the written contract unless it meets certain requirements. Parol evidence can also be used to demonstrate the existence of a collateral contract.

Courts use several approaches to resolve business disputes over the interpretation of contractual terms. The literal approach assigns words their ordinary meaning. The contextual approach takes into account the parties' intentions, as well as the surrounding circumstances.

The golden rule suggests that words be given their plain meaning unless doing so would result in absurdity. Courts imply a term only if it is necessary to implement the parties' presumed intentions. Some statutes imply certain terms into particular types of contract.

Standard form agreements are mass-produced documents drafted by the party who is in an economic position to offer those terms on a take-it-or-leave-it basis. A person who signs a standard form agreement is generally bound by its terms, whether or not they ever read or understood those terms. Courts require that the existence of onerous or unusual terms in a standard form agreement be brought to the attention of the other party. Businesses should use plain language in their contracts with consumers. Plain language helps ensure that consumers understand contracts and can result in cost savings and improved customer relations for businesses.

Standard form agreements often include a number of boilerplate terms, which can be reused in various contractual settings. Exclusion clauses seek to protect one party from various sorts of legal liability. To be effective, they must be drafted in unambiguous language; the party against whom the exclusion clause is meant to operate must be given reasonable notice; and both parties must agree that the clause is part of the contract. *Force majeure* clauses aim to protect the parties from events beyond their control. Confidentiality clauses prevent disclosure of certain information to third parties. Arbitration clauses outline who should resolve a dispute and what method of arbitration should be used. Jurisdiction clauses predetermine the locale of the court and whose laws will be applied in the event of a legal dispute between the parties. Entire agreement clauses state that the entire agreement between the parties is contained within the contract, preventing the assertion of oral terms.

MyBusLawLab ADDITIONAL RESOURCES FOR CHAPTER 9

MyBusLawLab provides students with an assortment of tools to help enrich the learning experience, including a Study Plan with Pre- and Post-tests, mini-cases with assessments, and provincial content material, which provides links to relevant cases, legislation, and additional resources.

MyBusLawLab provides the following resources for Chapter 9:

- Boilerplate Clauses

Provincial Material

- **British Columbia:** Terms Implied by Statute
- **Alberta:** Implied Terms, Legislative Interpretation
- **Manitoba and Saskatchewan:** Negligent Misrepresentation
- **Ontario:** Credibility, Misrepresentation
- **Atlantic Provinces:** *Interpretation Act*

Review Questions

1. Distinguish between a pre-contractual representation and a contractual term, giving examples of each. Why is that distinction important?

2. Define "misrepresentation" in your own words. Can a statement be a misrepresentation if neither party is aware that the statement is false? What must one be able to demonstrate to prove misrepresentation?

3. What is the difference between an opinion and a statement of fact?

4. Under what circumstances might a true statement be treated by the courts as a misrepresentation?

5. Provide suggestions of steps a person should take to avoid affirming a contract if misled during pre-contractual negotiations.

6. When would you seek an order for restitution? What does restitution give you?

7. What is meant by the term "rescission"?

8. List three circumstances that may preclude the victim of a misrepresentation from seeking restitution. Why is restitution unavailable in these circumstances?

9. What is an "express term"? Why is it sometimes difficult to determine the meaning of an express term?

10. Why is it important for business people to know and understand the parol evidence rule?

11. Given the parol evidence rule, what is the most reliable method by which two parties can change the terms of a standard form contract?

12. When is a contractual term ambiguous? Describe how courts resolve disputes over ambiguous terms.

13. When might you prefer that the court take a literal rather than contextual approach to contractual interpretation? When might you prefer a contextual approach?

14. State and explain the "golden rule" of interpretation.

15. State and explain the "*contra proferentem* rule."

16. What is the business reality that leads the court (or legislation) to recognize implied terms in a contract?

17. When will a court find that a contract contains an implied term? When will a court be reluctant to do so?

18. If a business wants to limit its liability using a standard form contract, what steps should it take?

19. What measures can a company take to ensure that the terms on a ticket form part of its contract with customers?

20. Describe a boilerplate clause. When might a business want to use a boilerplate clause and when is it inappropriate to do so?

Cases and Problems

1. Seymour is a supplier of custodial cleaning products. While negotiating a contract to sell a crate of floor wax, Seymour makes the statements below. Categorize each statement as (i) a pre-contractual representation, (ii) a mere opinion, (iii) a contractual term, or (iv) a collateral contract. Give reasons for your answers and describe the legal effect of each statement.

   a. "This floor wax is the best made anywhere in the world."

   b. "I personally truly believe this floor wax is the best made anywhere in the world."

   c. "Studies have shown that this floor wax is the best made anywhere in the world."

   d. "If, after trying this floor wax, you don't agree that it is unquestionably the best made anywhere in the world, I'll come and polish your floors myself for a month."

   e. "If, after trying this floor wax, you don't agree that it is unquestionably the best made anywhere in the world, I'll eat my hat."

2. Shawna and Sheila live in a small northern community where the roads are not always plowed in the winter. After getting stuck in the snow one too many times, they decided their best option for a reliable vehicle was a used 4 × 4 truck. Within a few minutes of stepping onto the lot of Farmer Jane's Cars Ltd, Shawna and Sheila spotted a truck they liked and Shawna asked the sales manager, Baltar, for some more information. While Baltar was telling Shawna about the truck's features, Sheila noticed that a decal was missing from the back of the truck. When asked about the missing decal, Baltar told her, "When we received the truck at the dealership, there were a few scratches and other marks that we touched up and painted, but that's about it." Baltar also told Shawna and Sheila that the truck had new wheels and tires. Shawna and Sheila talked about the truck for a few hours that evening and decided to buy it. The next day they finalized the paperwork and drove the truck home.

   A few months later, Sheila lost control of the truck on a snowy road and crashed into a ditch. She was fine, but the truck required repairs costing a total of $5000. When the local mechanic, Tanya, had the truck on a hoist, she noticed some damage to the body that she thought was from a previous accident. Tanya told Sheila about the older damage. Sheila phoned the provincial insurance company and had a representative look into the claims history of the truck. The insurance company representative told her that the record showed the truck had been reported stolen a few years ago and had sustained $1900 worth of damage at that time. It turns out that these damages were repaired by the mechanics at Farmer Jane's.

Shawna and Sheila are upset that they were not told about the full repair history of the truck and want their money back. Will the couple be successful in proving that Baltar's statement about the scratches on the truck amounted to a misrepresentation that induced them to enter into the purchase contract? If so, are they entitled to rescission?

3. Maria and Joe are married and co-own a construction supply business. They are also employees of the construction business and participate in the employee group insurance plan. A salesperson for Peace of Mind Insurance approached the company management and convinced them to change their insurance coverage to his company. As part of the new insurance plan, the employees could apply for long-term disability coverage. Maria did so. In order to qualify for coverage, Maria had to meet with a medically trained representative of Peace of Mind Insurance to review her medical history. During that interview, she mentioned several visits to doctors over the past several years but didn't get into the details. Based on the interview with the Peace of Mind representative and on the financial statement forms she filled out, Maria was insured for $4000 per month in case she should become disabled.

Several years later, Maria found herself unable to work because of vertigo and back problems. She applied to receive her long-term disability benefits but, after investigating her case, Peace of Mind Insurance denied her claim, stating that it was previously unaware of these facts:

■ Maria had talked to five different medical doctors in the four years before she signed up with Peace of Mind Insurance. The reason for each visit was either that she was concerned about frequently being dizzy or had back pain that was interfering with her daily life.

■ Maria's financial statements showed that she had not made $100 000 in annual taxable income as she had claimed. Instead, her annual income as an employee of the family business never exceeded $45 000.

■ Maria had not disclosed that she had disability coverage from a different insurance company at the time she signed up for Peace of Mind Insurance.

Will Peace of Mind Insurance be able to avoid its long-term disability contract with Maria? Should the original insurance contract stand even if no payment is to be made on this particular claim?

4. QwikSlim published advertisements at various dates in newspapers. The statements published in the newspapers are reproduced below:

LOSE: UNWANTED FAT IN ONLY 90 MINUTES. No costly pills. No tiring exercises. No strict diet. Our method has proven itself in the art of making you beautiful. Lose Unwanted Fat. All you have to do is sit back and relax while QwikSlim does the work for you. You get sensational results in 90 minutes. RESULTS GUARANTEED.

Several individuals saw this advertisement and purchased QwikSlim. However, they never saw any results and decided to sue QwikSlim for misrepresentation. They claim that the advertisement amounts to statement of fact. QwikSlim says it only intended the advertisement to reflect an opinion.

Is this a statement of fact or opinion? If it is an opinion, could the unhappy customers still sue QwikSlim? Explain. Redraft this advertisement in a way that better manages the risk associated with a product that might not work for all customers.

5. Mike decided to put his farm up for sale in January. After seeing the listing, Shirley, an experienced farmer, came to look at the property. During the tour of the farm, Shirley told Mike that her main concern was about sources of water. Mike told her that there was no shortage of water on the property. He said that he already had one well that produced a steady flow of water and more could easily be dug. Shirley bought the property and took possession in April. One of the first things she noticed was that the well was producing only a trickle of water. Thinking that it must be blocked, she cleaned it out, but it still produced a minimal amount of water. As the water flow was insufficient to water her crops, she proceeded to dig two more wells in likely places on the property. Again, neither produced more than a trickle of water. Shirley made arrangements to purchase water from a neighbouring farm and continued farming throughout the summer and fall. Over the winter, as she was planning her crops for spring, Shirley found herself more and more frustrated by the water situation. She decided that she would speak to a lawyer about it.

Assuming that Shirley can prove that she was induced to buy the property by Mike's misrepresentation as to the amount of water available, what remedy do you think a court should grant? If Shirley gave up on farming and, instead, paved over half of the property (to create a revenue-generating parking lot for a nearby park-and-ride transit system), will it change the remedy that might be available to her?

6. Mac's Machines Ltd, an importer of high-tech German industrial equipment, had an ongoing shipping arrangement with Take Care Tankers Inc. According to Clause 4 of Take Care Tankers' standard form agreement:

Subject to express instructions in writing given by the customer, Take Care Tankers reserves to itself complete freedom in respect of means, routes, and procedures to be followed in the handling and transportation of the goods.

Although the parties had done business before on several occasions, a representative from Mac's telephoned Take Care Tankers to request that a particular shipment of machines be stored below deck. Although the machines were usually transported in waterproof plastic containers that were amenable to deck transportation, the shipment in question was packaged in wooden crates and was therefore susceptible to rust if left on deck. The shipping manager at Take Care Tankers assured the Mac's representative over the phone that the special arrangement would be no problem. Despite that promise, the shipment was inadvertently stored on deck. During the voyage, the crate fell overboard, and the machines were lost at sea. On the basis of the telephone call, Mac's claims that Take Care Tankers was not merely negligent but also in breach of contract. Relying on Clause 4 of its standard form agreement, Take Care Tankers claims that the oral assurances made over the telephone were not part of the contract. Leaving aside the issue of negligence, apply your understanding of the parol evidence rule to determine how a court would resolve the contract issue in this case.

7. Sperry Rand makes farm machinery. To promote its products, Sperry published a sales brochure that includes the following representations:

> You'll fine-chop forage to one centimetre season after season! You'll harvest over 45 tonnes per hour with ease. Under test conditions, the big New Holland harvesters have harvested well over 60 tonnes per hour. And Micro-Shear cutting action gives you a choice of crop fineness—from one to six centimetres.

Induced by the brochure, John decided to buy one of Sperry's machines from a third-party dealer. As a result of the failure of the machine to live up to its description in the brochure, John lost his entire season's crop. Aiming to recover damages for breach of contract, John attempted to sue the dealership. Unfortunately the dealership had gone bankrupt. John decided that he would try to sue Sperry Rand. Assume that his contract with the dealership excluded any possible tort liability against Sperry Rand. Does John have a contractual remedy against Sperry? Is the parol evidence rule relevant to your determination?

8. Mr Anwar, a taxi driver, signed an agreement with Tip Top Cabs that provided him with the use of a van-taxi licence in exchange for a monthly licence fee. He also paid a "dispatch system fee" for the use of Tip Top's dispatch services. Under the agreement, the monthly dispatch system fee was set at $1175. Other operators, who drove regular taxis, paid the same dispatch fee.

A short while later, Tip Top advised only its van operators that their dispatch fees would be increased by $500 per month. Anwar objected to the increase as being contrary to his understanding of the meaning of "dispatch system fee" in the agreement. Anwar argued that a fee that applied only to van-cabs did not fit within the term "dispatch fee." All cabs access the dispatch service and therefore the fee should be the same for all cab drivers. Tip Top claims that this is not the case, and that the term allows for different fees for different types of cabs as deemed appropriate by Tip Top.

Do you think the phrase "dispatch system fee" is ambiguous? From a business perspective, how might Tip Top have altered the wording in its contract to minimize the risk of litigation, assuming it knew it might one day wish to increase its fees?

9. Clinton was 14 years old when his mother entered into a written agreement with the town library on his behalf. According to the agreement, Clinton would obtain full borrowing privileges and his mother would become "responsible for any fines, loss, or damage occasioned by the use of the library card." Shortly after Clinton lost his library card, a stranger used it to borrow more than 30 items. Those items were never returned. The library issued a bill to Clinton's mother for $1570, the replacement value of those items. Do you think Clinton's mother should have to pay? How might the library have better managed its affairs?

10. The Upper Crust Academy, an exclusive boarding school, has inserted the following clause into its standard form agreement:

> The parents of _____ hereby authorize the Principal to ensure that said child shall receive a proper social and academic education in accordance with the highest standards of personal conduct and that said child will be kept free from danger while in the custody of Upper Crust Academy.

Like everyone else whose child attended the academy, Manjunath's parents signed the agreement. One evening, Manjunath was returned to the academy by the local police after he was found stealing pylons off the street. In addition to the mischief he caused in the streets, Manjunath was in breach of the curfew rule at the academy. After unsuccessfully attempting to contact Manjunath's parents by phone, the principal decided to sentence Manjunath to 20 hours of peeling potatoes in the academy kitchen to dissuade him from repeating such inappropriate behaviour. When his parents found out that the potato peeling had caused Manjunath to develop unsightly calluses on his hands, they quickly removed their darling son from the academy. The principal of the academy responded by issuing a bill for the remainder of the year's tuition plus an additional fee for boarding. The academy claims that the disciplinary action taken by the principal was within its contractual rights. Manjunath's parents disagree. Given that the agreement makes no specific mention of discipline, how could the principal persuade a court to side with the academy? Explain your reasoning.

11. Lila and Binyamin decided that they would like to spend the first few years of their retirement sailing around the world. Because they would be spending so much time on the boat, they decided they should order a new model from the manufacturer so that they could have the exact options and features they wanted. After doing a lot of research and talking to several dealers, they finally picked their dream boat and sat down with a salesperson, Ned, at Sam's Yachts to sign the purchase contract.

   The purchase contract was on a single sheet of paper. Its front side included a description of the boat, the $170 000 purchase price and agreed method of payment, and a space for the parties to sign. Directly above the space for signatures was clearly printed, "It is agreed and declared that the terms and conditions set forth on reverse hereof are part of this contract and are binding upon the parties hereto." On the back were terms and conditions.

   Lila reviewed the front side of the contract and then flipped the page over to read the terms and conditions. "Oh, don't worry about those," Ned told her. "That's just the manufacturer's warranty that we pass on to you." Lila hesitated, at which point Binyamin told her that if it was just the manufacturer's warranty, then there was no point in the two of them wasting their time reading the fine print. Ned handed a pen across the desk and both Lila and Binyamin signed the purchase contract.

   In fact, the terms and conditions on the back contained the following clause (clause 9):

   > Manufacturer reserves the right to change the price to Dealer of new Equipment and Dealer reserves the right to change the total sale price of Equipment Purchased and so **TOTAL BALANCE DUE** to Purchaser.

   Several months later the boat was finally ready and Lila and Binyamin went to pick it up. They were completely shocked when Ned handed them a final invoice for $198 200. The manufacturer's costs had gone up and, based on clause 9 in the terms and conditions, Sam's Yachts expected Lila and Binyamin to pay the additional $28 200. Anxious to finally get the boat in the water, the couple paid the full price under protest and then went home and phoned their lawyer to see if they could get the $28 200 refunded to them.

If Lila and Binyamin sue Sam's Yachts for the return of the additional fee, will they be successful? What arguments should they make to convince the court that they should not have had to pay the money?

12. You work at a company called CuddleTech (CT). CT operates a website where users can play 3-D interactive video games online. When users create an account for the CT website, they are required to agree to a standard form contract. You have been assigned the task of reviewing and rewriting this contract. Under the contract, users are required to disclose any physical disabilities or medical conditions that might cause them to react negatively in CT's online 3-D game environment. CT is concerned that users with certain medical conditions may be prone to negative reactions in the 3-D game environment. This obligation to disclose any disabilities applies continuously so long as users continue to use their accounts to play games at the CT website. You have been asked to ensure that CT's standard form contract contains a term that gives CT the right to immediately terminate the account of any user who does not comply with this disclosure obligation. You have been presented with the following two options for this clause. Which option would you recommend CT use in its contracts and why?

   Option 1:

   If at any time the user intentionally or unintentionally, or fraudulently, or negligently, or otherwise fails in any direct or indirect manner to comply with their obligation to disclose any and all physical disabilities that might in any direct or indirect way cause them to react negatively in CT's 3-D gaming environment, then CT shall have the right and be entitled to declare that this contract is null, void, and unenforceable immediately or at any time, at its sole discretion.

   Option 2:

   CT is concerned about your health. Throughout the duration of your account with CT, you must disclose to CT any physical disability or medical condition that might cause you to react negatively in CT's 3-D game environment. If at any time you do not disclose such a condition or disability to CT, CT may immediately terminate your account.

10 Contractual Defects

CHAPTER OVERVIEW

Incapacity to Contract
Personal Incapacity
Business Corporations
Associations
Indian Bands and Aboriginal
  Persons
Public Authorities

Absence of Writing
Statute of Frauds
Consumer Protection and Writing
  Requirements

Mistake
General Principles
Mistakes Preventing the Creation
  of Contracts
Mistakes Rendering Impossible
  the Purpose of the Contract
The Doctrine of Frustration
Documents Mistakenly Signed

Unfairness during Bargaining
Duress
Undue Influence
Unconscionable Transactions

Illegality
Agreements Prohibited by Statute
Common Law Illegality
The Doctrine of Public Policy

LEARNING OBJECTIVES

After completing this chapter, you should be able to:

❶ Identify six types of parties that lack capacity or have limited capacity to contract.

❷ Distinguish between voidable and enforceable contracts with a minor.

❸ Explain what it means for a corporation to act beyond its capacity.

❹ Outline the types of contracts that must be evidenced in writing, state the basic writing requirements that must be proved, and summarize the legal effect of non-compliance.

❺ Explain how writing requirements protect consumers.

❻ Determine when a contract is or is not frustrated.

❼ Define duress of goods and economic duress.

❽ Distinguish between undue influence and unconscionable transactions, and identify when a presumption is created in each case.

❾ Summarize the traditional factors that courts take into account in determining whether an agreement is illegal.

❿ Discuss the doctrine of public policy and its effect.

Contractual defects are particularly significant because they often provide one of the parties with a defence when the other party commences a lawsuit. In this chapter, we survey five different contractual defects and their legal consequences: incapacity to contract, absence of writing, mistake, unfairness during bargaining, and illegality.

Incapacity to Contract

A person cannot enter into a contract unless they have the legal power to give consent. For example, although 10 year olds may be able to read, understand, and sign a contractual document, they may not be legally bound by it. The same is true for adults who, for some reason, lack the ability to consent. To protect specific groups of people, the law has drawn a distinction between those who have the *capacity* to contract and those who do not. **Capacity** is the legal power to give consent. Sometimes the question of capacity depends on a person's ability to understand the nature and consequences of their acts. At other times it does not.

capacity is the legal power to give consent

We will consider seven groups of persons who may have no capacity or only limited capacity to create a contract:

- minors
- mentally incapacitated persons
- intoxicated persons
- corporations
- associations
- Indian bands and Aboriginal persons
- public authorities

PERSONAL INCAPACITY

Minors

The law distinguishes between *minors* and those who have reached *the age of majority*. The **age of majority** is the age at which a person is held fully accountable in law. Those who have not reached the age of majority are **minors**. The law simply says that everyone under the age of majority lacks capacity. In some jurisdictions, including Alberta, Saskatchewan, Manitoba, and Ontario, the age of majority is 18 years.[1] In other provinces, including the Yukon, Nunavut, Newfoundland and Labrador, New Brunswick, and British Columbia, it is 19 years.[2] Though perhaps overprotective in some instances, the law's approach shields minors from exploitation and the consequences of their own inexperience. It is therefore important for businesses that transact with minors to understand how the law operates.

the **age of majority** is the age at which a person is held fully accountable in law

minors are people who have not reached the age of majority

Some contracts are voidable at the minor's option. A contract is **voidable** if a minor is entitled to avoid the legal obligations that the contract would have

a contract is **voidable** if a minor is entitled to avoid the legal obligations that the contract would have otherwise created

---

[1] *Age of Majority Act*, RSA 2000, c A-6, s 1 (Alta); *Age of Majority Act*, RSS 1978, c A-6, s 2(1) (Sask); *Age of Majority Act*, CCSM c A7, s 1 (Man); *Age of Majority and Accountability Act*, RSO 1990, c A.7, s 1 (Ont).

[2] *Age of Majority Act*, RSY 2002, c 2, s 1(1); (Yuk) *Age of Majority Act*, RSNWT 1988, c A-2, s 2 (Nun); *Age of Majority Act*, RSNB 1973, c A-4, s 1 (NB); *Age of Majority Act*, RSBC 1996, c 7, s 1 (BC).

otherwise created. Note an important legal subtlety here. *Some* contracts with minors are voidable; not *every* contract with a minor is *void* at the outset. If a contract is voidable, minors may elect to avoid contractual liability. If so, they are relieved of all future liabilities under the contract. However, minors may also choose to carry out the contract, making the obligations binding.

A minor who wants to avoid contractual liability should do so as soon as possible. Suppose a 15-year-old boy rents stereo equipment for a year. If he elects to avoid the contract after two months, he cannot be sued for the other ten. He can, however, be sued for the rent that accumulated before he avoided the agreement. Furthermore, if there is a substantial delay, a court may say that the boy *affirmed* the contract and therefore lost the right to avoid it. Finally, once a person reaches the age of majority, they must decide, within a reasonable time, whether they want to avoid a contract that they created as a minor.

The ability to avoid certain contracts does not mean that a minor can take the benefit of a contract and then cancel it with impunity. Minors who elect to avoid contracts must give back any benefits that they received under them.

These rules regarding contracts with minors have been modified by statute in some cases. In British Columbia, for example, the *Infants Act* states that a contract with a minor is unenforceable unless certain prescribed circumstances are met.[3] A contract with a minor can be enforced only if it is either affirmed or has not been repudiated within a year of the minor attaining the age of majority. There are some contracts that minors cannot avoid—contracts for necessary goods and services such as food, clothing, education, medical treatment, and legal advice, which are to their benefit.[4] Minors cannot avoid contracts of employment that are to their benefit. Case Brief 10.1 demonstrates one important implication of the *Infants Act* that companies need to be aware of.

Mental Incapacity

Regardless of age, a person may also lack capacity because of a deficient intellect. We need to distinguish two situations. First, if a court has declared a person to be lacking in mental capacity, their contracts are *void* and cannot be enforced at all. Second, even if there is no court declaration, a person may still be considered mentally incompetent if they lack the mental capacity to contract at the time the contract is formed. If so, their contracts are *voidable*, just as in the case of a minor. They can avoid the agreement within a reasonable time of becoming competent. There is, however, an important difference between mental incapacity and minority. A minor's contract is voidable even if the other party was unaware of the age issue. In contrast, so long as it is fair to do so, the contract of a person with a mental incapacity is voidable only if the other party should have recognized the problem.

It is sometimes difficult to tell whether a person is legally incapacitated. Courts often rely on the testimony of a family doctor for this purpose, though

---

[3.] *Infants Act*, RSBC 1996, c 223 (BC).

[4.] This rule aims at ensuring that people are willing to sell such goods and services to minors. Goods that are considered "necessaries" are usually enumerated by statute. See *Sale of Goods Act*, RSPEI 1988, c S-1, s 4 (PEI); *Sale of Goods Act*, CCSM, c S10, s 4 (Man).

Case Brief 10.1

Wong v Lok's Martial Arts Centre Inc. 2009 BCSC 1385, [2010] 2 WWR 729

At age 12, Victor Wong commenced martial arts training at Lok's Martial Arts Centre Inc in British Columbia. In order to register Victor in classes, Victor's mother had to sign a membership contract. The contract included a provision that waived Victor's right to sue should he be injured. Shortly afterwards, Victor was injured during his training. He asked the court to find that his mother's signature on the membership contract did not bind him to the provisions in the contract and that he could still sue the defendant for his injuries.

The court determined that in British Columbia the *Infants Act* establishes the sole means of creating contractual obligations that bind minors. According to section 40(1.1) of the *Act*, parents can contract away a minor's rights only with the consent of the Public Trustee or the court. Therefore, the court concluded that the Act does not permit Victor's mother to bind him to an agreement that waives his legal rights. Victor was allowed to sue Lok's Martial Arts Centre for his injuries.

they may equally draw an inference themselves where evidence is scanty or competing.[5] A person may obviously lack capacity because of extreme age or because of some kind of impairment in mental function. Often, however, it requires a careful examination of the circumstances, which may be further complicated by the fact that an incapacitated adult may later regain capacity. As a matter of risk management, employees should be trained to identify potential problems.

Intoxication

The rules for drunkenness are similar to those for mental incapacity. An otherwise capable person may enter into a contract while intoxicated. That agreement is voidable if two conditions are met. First, the person must have been so drunk that they could not know or appreciate what they were doing. Second, the other contractual party must have been alerted to that fact. Often, the courts are as much concerned with the possibility of fraud or unfairness as they are with the issue of incapacity. To set aside a contract, the intoxicated party must make a prompt election to avoid it once sober. A failure to do so will be taken as affirmation of the agreement. Case Brief 10.2 illustrates one court decision regarding the effect of intoxication on the ability to contract.

BUSINESS CORPORATIONS

Corporations are treated as legal persons. (Corporations and other types of business organizations are considered in detail in Chapters 21 and 22.) The law distinguishes between *chartered corporations* and *statutory corporations*. In the context of contractual capacity, **chartered corporations** are treated the same as individuals who have reached the age of majority. If a chartered corporation enters into contracts in breach of its charter, its charter may be forfeited, but the contracts made in breach of the corporate charter will still be binding. **Statutory corporations**, on the other hand, have more limited contractual capacity. Because they are statutory creations, their capacity to contract is

chartered corporations are treated the same as individuals who have reached the age of majority

statutory corporations have limited contractual capacity

[5.] *Hart v Cooper* (1995) 2 ETR (2d) 168 (BC SC).

Case Brief 10.2

Bawlf Grain Co. v Ross [1917] SCJ No 22, 37 DLR 620

Ross had been drinking heavily for hours and entered an agreement to sell wheat to the plaintiff while he was intoxicated. The plaintiff was well aware of Ross's intoxication when the contract was formed. Once sober, Ross realized that he was therefore entitled to terminate his obligations under the contract. However, Ross also knew that the price of wheat fluctuates on an almost daily basis. So, he decided to wait and see whether the market price of wheat would increase, in which case he would avoid the contract and sell the wheat at a better price, or whether the price would decrease, in which case he would keep the contract with the plaintiff. When the price of wheat increased shortly thereafter, Ross decided to avoid the contract with the plaintiffs. The plaintiffs brought Ross to court to enforce their contract.

The court recognized that intoxication could give rise to a contractual defect. However, it held that the intoxicated party must exercise their right to repudiate the contract within a reasonable time. In this case, Ross waited over a month to see what would happen to the price of wheat. In light of the regular fluctuation in the price of wheat, the court found that a reasonable time for repudiation would be within a few days of Ross becoming sober, not weeks. Ross's delay in repudiating the contract was tantamount to an express ratification of the contract. He was therefore bound to deliver the wheat to the plaintiffs at the agreed upon price, despite his having been intoxicated during the formation of the contract.

limited by the powers given to them through legislation. If a statutory corporation attempts to contract in a manner that exceeds its statutory powers, it acts *ultra vires*, literally "beyond the authority." When a corporation acts *ultra vires*, it lacks the capacity to contract. Those agreements are consequently unenforceable. Generally, the question is whether the purported transaction is in line with the legal objects and purposes of the corporation. To understand the importance of this, read Business Decision 10.1.

Business Decision **10.1**

Drafting Articles of Incorporation

Reva is named a director of a statutory corporation. While drafting the constitutional documents of the corporation, she and the other directors enter into a discussion about how best to characterize its objects. According to its current business plan, the corporation will focus exclusively on the business of constructing the exterior of buildings. For this reason, one of the directors, Ling, recommends the following characterization: "To carry on in the business of pouring concrete foundations and erecting building exteriors." Reva expresses concerns about Ling's characterization and counters with the suggestion of a much broader description: "To carry on in the business of construction."

Questions for Discussion

1. Assume that you are also on the board of directors. In what sense is the capacity issue relevant to your decision about whether to adopt the recommendation made by either Reva or Ling?

2. What are the advantages and disadvantages of Reva's broader statement of the objects of the corporation?

3. Could Reva's and Ling's stated objects be met through an unincorporated association?

ASSOCIATIONS

associations are usually unincorporated business organizations that lack contractual capacity

Capacity issues arise more frequently with another type of business structure—*associations*. **Associations** are usually unincorporated business organizations, including private clubs, charities, and religious societies. Although they share some features with corporations, most associations do not enjoy independent legal existence and are thus incapable of contracting.[6] Therefore, some provinces have legislation that gives contractual capacity to associations involved in such activities as education, religion, and charity. Trade unions may also be given capacity. (Trade unions are examined in Chapter 27.) Those statutes define an association's capacity in much the same way as a statutory corporation's constitution. If an association attempts to contract outside of those limits, it lacks capacity, and its agreement is ineffective.

Because an association generally lacks capacity, one of its members may enter into a contract for its benefit. Significantly, it is that individual member who becomes liable under the agreement. Unlike corporate officers and directors, individuals cannot escape liability by pleading that they were merely contracting on the association's behalf. On the other side of the bargain, if your business intends to contract with someone who claims to act on behalf of an association, you can manage the risk by ensuring that the association has capacity or that the individual personally has the resources to perform the obligations.

INDIAN BANDS AND ABORIGINAL PERSONS

One kind of unincorporated association that *does* have legal capacity is an *Indian band*. According to the *Indian Act*, an **Indian band** is a body of Aboriginal people whose land and money are held by the Crown.[7] Nevertheless, despite the Crown's role, Indian bands have contractual capacity in much the same way as corporations.[8] They can sue or be sued.

an **Indian band** is a body of Aboriginal people whose land and money are held by the Crown

The same is not always true, however, of individual Aboriginal persons who qualify as "Indians" under the Act. There are some restrictions on their capacity to contract, principally in relation to reserve land. For instance, property on a reserve cannot be used as security for a credit transaction, nor can it be transferred to another member of the band without the Crown's consent.[9] Under section 28 of the *Indian Act*, any deed, lease, contract, instrument, document, or agreement purporting to permit a person other than a member of a band to occupy or use a reserve, or to reside or otherwise exercise any rights on a reserve, is void, unless approved by the Crown. Other than these special restrictions in the *Indian Act*, Aboriginal persons generally have capacity and are free to contract just like any other person.

Having canvassed the various forms of incapacity to contract, Concept Summary 10.1 encapsulates several approaches to risk management where issues of capacity arise.

PUBLIC AUTHORITIES

Many contracts are created on a daily basis by public authorities at the federal, provincial, and municipal levels. Generally speaking, a public authority acting on behalf of a governmental body has the capacity to contract, independent of any specific statutory authority to do so.[10] The only limit on a particular official's capacity to contract is the division of powers section of the *Constitution Act 1867*—in order to have capacity, the action must be consistent with that division of powers.

[6.] *Nesbitt v Vander Kooi* (2003) BCSC 194.

[7.] *Indian Act*, RSC 1985, c I-5, s 2 (Can).

[8.] *Wewayakum Indian Band v Canada and Wawayakai Indian Band* (1992) 42 FTR 40 (FC TD).

[9.] *Indian Act*, RSC 1985, c I-5, s 24 (Can).

[10.] PW Hogg *Liability of the Crown* 2d ed (1989) at 161–162.

Concept Summary 10.1

Managing Risk in Association with Incapacity

- Train employees to identify potential capacity problems in the contracts that your business enters into.

- Be aware of the rules governing contracts with minors, particularly if your business is likely to enter into contracts with minors.

- In potential cases of contracts involving minors, mental incapacity, or intoxication, take steps that will help to show that the other party has affirmed the contract. For example, you might attempt to have the other party commence performance of their obligations under the contract or pay them money under the contract. If they begin performance or accept the payment, then these may be taken as signs of affirmation of the contract. These steps should be taken at a time when you know they are no longer a minor, mentally incapacitated, or intoxicated.

- Be aware of whether your company may contract with statutory corporations, associations, Indian bands, individual First Nations people, and public authorities, and act accordingly.

- Where you are not certain about the other party's capacity, you might consider requiring a written representation from the other party in the contract, which states that it has the capacity to enter into and fulfill the contract. If it later turns out that the party did not have capacity, then you may have an action against it in tort for misrepresentation.

L.O. ❹❺ Absence of Writing

For most contracts, there are no formal requirements. However, certain types of contracts must be *evidenced* in writing. That requirement first arose as a result of an old piece of English legislation—the *Statute of Frauds*.[11] More recently, consumer protection legislation has required certain types of contracts to be made in writing. Both are discussed below.

STATUTE OF FRAUDS

The *Statute of Frauds* required some contracts to be evidenced in writing as a way of reducing the risk of perjury, or lying in legal proceedings. The requirement was intended to discourage people from falsely claiming the existence of oral contracts. That rationale is less persuasive today. Electronic and paper documents can now be produced, altered, and reproduced with a few clicks of a mouse. For that reason and others, many jurisdictions have amended their legislation.[12] And some jurisdictions, such as British Columbia and Manitoba, have replaced or repealed the Statute altogether.[13] As electronic commerce continues to expand, the issue may be examined even more broadly.

Despite such law reform, risk management still requires an understanding of the *Statute of Frauds*, even for businesses in British Columbia and Manitoba. After all, a company in Kamloops or Brandon may enter into a contract with a party in another jurisdiction where the Statute is still in force. We will therefore discuss the types of contracts that must be evidenced in writing, the basic writing requirements that must be proved, and the legal effect of non-compliance.

[11.] *Statute of Frauds*, 1677 (29 Cha 2), c 3.

[12.] Law reform has been recommended in other provinces, including Ontario and Newfoundland and Labrador. See Ontario Law Reform Commission, *Report on the Amendment of the Law of Contract* (1987) c 5; M Bridge "The *Statute of Frauds* and the Sale of Land Contracts" (1986) *64 Can Bar Rev* 58.

[13.] For instance, British Columbia replaced the *Statute of Frauds* with the *Law and Equity Act*, RSBC 1996, c 253, s 59. Manitoba repealed the Statute by adopting its *Act to Repeal the Statute of Frauds*, SM 1982-83-84, c 34, CCSM c F158, s. 1.

Types of Contracts That Must Be Evidenced in Writing

Only certain types of contracts fall under the *Statute of Frauds*. In Chapter 13, we will examine the circumstances in which an agreement for the *sale of goods* must be evidenced in writing. For now, we will look at three other types of contracts: guarantees, contracts for the sale of an interest in land, and contracts not to be performed within a year.[14]

GUARANTEES   The Statute applies to *guarantees*. A **guarantee** is a contractual promise by a third party, called a *guarantor*, to satisfy a debtor's obligation if that debtor fails to do so. (Guarantees are examined in Chapter 23.) For example, you may apply for overdraft protection that allows you to withdraw more than your bank account actually contains, which is, in effect, a bank loan. The bank may refuse that arrangement unless you find a third party (such as your parent or your spouse) to guarantee repayment.

The guarantor does *not* promise to pay, no matter what. Rather, the guarantor gives a *conditional* promise. For example, if your mom signs on as a guarantor, she is not agreeing to pay the overdraft in any event. Because her promise is conditional on your inability to pay, she is required to discharge the debt only if you fail to do so.

A guarantee can be distinguished from an *indemnity*. An **indemnity** is an *unconditional promise* to assume another's debt completely. To continue with our example, if your mom promises to indemnify the bank for your overdraft, the bank is entitled to collect payment from her as soon as the overdraft amount becomes due, even if the bank has not bothered to ask you for payment first. An indemnity is therefore not a promise to answer for another's debt. It is a promise to assume another's debt altogether.

In a number of provinces, the *Statute of Frauds* applies to contracts of guarantee but not to contracts of indemnity. Consequently, the bank will not be able to demand payment from the guarantor unless that agreement was evidenced in writing. However, a bank may be able to enforce an indemnity even if the agreement was entirely oral. In British Columbia, the judicial distinction between a guarantee and an indemnity has been rendered inoperative by the *Law and Equity Act*. This legislation requires both forms of promises to be evidenced in writing to be enforceable unless the guarantor or indemnitor has acted in a manner that indicates a guarantee or indemnity.[15]

CONTRACTS FOR THE SALE OF AN INTEREST IN LAND   Contracts for the sale of an interest in land are unenforceable unless they are evidenced in writing. (The sale of interests in land is discussed in Chapter 16.)

Other cases are more clear-cut. For example, a contract to repair a building need not be evidenced in writing, nor must an agreement for room and board. On the other hand, a long-term lease of land clearly must be evidenced in writing.

CONTRACTS NOT TO BE PERFORMED WITHIN A YEAR   Contracts that are not to be performed within a year of their creation are unenforceable unless they

a **guarantee** is a contractual promise by a third party, called a *guarantor*, to satisfy a debtor's obligation if that debtor fails to do so

an **indemnity** is an *unconditional promise* to assume another's debt completely

---

14. Most provincial statutes require writing in other circumstances, including (i) ratifications of contracts made by minors upon reaching age of majority, (ii) promises by executors or administrators to be personally liable for the debts of a testator or intestate, (iii) contracts made upon consideration of marriage, (iv) assignment of express trusts, (v) creation of trusts of land, and (vi) leases or agreements to lease land for a term exceeding three years.

15. *Law and Equity Act*, RSBA 1996, c 253 s 59 (BC).

are evidenced in writing. This extends the writing requirement to all sorts of agreements of indefinite duration regardless of their subject matter. Because the Statute applies so broadly, it can catch parties by surprise. Contrary to their expectations, parties may not have an enforceable agreement. The courts therefore tend to interpret this part of the Statute quite narrowly. For instance, they usually say that a contract is not caught if it could *possibly* be performed within one year. And sometimes they go to great lengths to enforce oral agreements, notwithstanding the existence of the Statute. Consider how you might apply this requirement to the example in You Be the Judge 10.1.

You Be the Judge 10.1

Boutilier v Everett [1979] 40 NSR (2d) 527, 73 APR 527 (NSSC)

Boutilier made an oral agreement to loan several thousand dollars to Everett. The agreement stipulated that Everett could repay the loan through $300-per-month instalments, or whenever he was capable of repaying. Boutilier could also request repayment of part or the entire loan. Within less than one year, relations between Boutilier and Everett broke down. Boutilier bought an action for the outstanding balance. Everett claims that because he could feasibly take more than one year to repay the loan, the *Statute of Frauds* applies to render this oral contract invalid. Everett therefore claims that he does not have to repay the outstanding balance.

Questions for Discussion

1. Do you think the contract entered into by Boutilier and Everett amounts to a contract "not to be performed within a year," such that the *Statute of Frauds* would render it invalid? Why or why not?

2. Should individuals be able to escape their contractual obligations simply on the basis that their contract *could* take longer than one year to perform?

Writing Requirements

If a contract falls within the Statute, the court must decide if the writing requirement was satisfied.

FORM AND CONTENT OF THE NOTE OR MEMORANDUM Either the contract must be in writing or there must be a note or memorandum that provides evidence of it. The document does not have to take any particular form, but has to (i) provide evidence of the essential elements of the contract (such as the parties' names, the subject matter of the agreement, and the price), and (ii) be signed by the party against whom the agreement is being enforced. The courts are often lenient. For instance, they sometimes allow the signature requirement to be satisfied by a name on letterhead or an invoice. Furthermore, they are sometimes satisfied by the combined effect of several documents, even if they do not expressly refer to each other.[16]

Effect of Non-Compliance

The *Statute of Frauds* renders some contracts *unenforceable* unless they are sufficiently evidenced in writing. Such contracts therefore cannot support an action for breach of contract where the defendant pleads the *Statute of Frauds* as a defence. If one party does not perform, the other cannot demand a remedy. This does not mean that their agreement is entirely irrelevant. Their contract is not void; it is merely unenforceable. It can therefore be used to pass property

---

[16.] *Harvie v Gibbons* (1980) 109 DLR (3d) 559 (Alta CA).

and may provide a defence. The difference is somewhat obscure but can be demonstrated through examples. Suppose someone pays you $5000 as a down payment under an oral contract for the sale of land. A down payment acts as part of the purchase price, but it also provides an incentive to perform. If the payor does not go through with the deal, the payee can keep the money. Now suppose the other party refuses to complete the transaction. Although your contract is unenforceable, it still provides a valid explanation as to why you do not have to repay the $5000. To use another example, if a party provides goods under an oral contract and the other party accepts the goods, and the contract is found unenforceable under the *Statute of Frauds*, then the doctrine of *quantum meruit* may require the party who accepted the goods to pay for the benefit it received.

CONSUMER PROTECTION AND WRITING REQUIREMENTS

Some consumer protection laws require certain types of agreements to be made in writing to protect consumers' interests. By requiring agreements to be in writing, and in some cases, that a copy of the agreement be provided to the consumer, these laws can help prevent exploitation of consumers and prevent disputes about the terms of the contract. Reducing disputes about the terms of an agreement is good for consumers, who are often the weaker party to the contract and who do not have the resources to fight disputes, but it is also good for business.

Under Ontario's *Consumer Protection Act 2002*, for example, all personal development services contracts must be made in writing in cases where the consumer's payment in advance is required under the contract.[17] Personal development services contracts are service contracts in the areas of health, fitness, diet, modelling, talent, martial arts, sports, and dance. If such contracts are not made in writing, then the business is not permitted to require or accept payment from the consumer. Ontario's consumer protection law also requires businesses to deliver a written copy of an Internet contract in cases where the consumer is required to pay more than a prescribed amount under the contract in advance.

Concept Summary 10.2 explains ways in which businesses can manage the risk associated with writing requirements.

Concept Summary 10.2

Managing Risk in Association with Writing Requirements

- Ensure that guarantees, contracts for the sale of an interest in land, and contracts not to be performed within a year are always made in writing.
- To meet the writing requirement, you should, as a minimum, (i) provide evidence of the essential elements of the contract (such as the parties' names, the subject matter of the agreement, and the price), and (ii) ensure that the party against whom the agreement is being enforced has signed the written document.
- To avoid the uncertainty and debate that oral agreements can create, all contracts should be written whenever possible.
- Businesses should ensure that they understand the requirements that may exist under provincial consumer protection laws to put certain agreements in writing and to provide consumers with a copy.

---

17. *Consumer Protection Act*, 2002, SO 2002, c 30, Sch A, s 30 (Ont).

L.O. ❻

Mistakes

We have examined incapacity and the absence of writing. A third kind of contractual defect arises from *mistakes*.

GENERAL PRINCIPLES

Contracts are based on agreements. As discussed in Chapter 7, contracts require a meeting of the minds, or *consensus ad idem*, which is a shared mutual agreement to enter into an enforceable transaction on a particular basis. However, anyone involved in business knows that people sometimes are mistaken about their agreements at the time that they are made.

■ Some mistakes occur when an error affects the basic process of contract formation. When that happens, the mistake may negate the existence of an agreement between the parties. And without an agreement, there cannot be a contract.

■ Other mistakes make it impossible for the object of the contract to be achieved. Here, the mistake does not affect the process of contract formation but rather pertains to the very existence of the contract's subject matter. In that case, the contract may be defective.

MISTAKES PREVENTING THE CREATION OF CONTRACTS

Two types of mistakes prevent the creation of a contract: mistaken identity and mistake about subject matter.

Mistaken Identity

Many business relationships are based on trust and reliability. People are more willing to invest in institutions that are known to be reliable. Financial institutions are more willing to lend money or give credit to people who have a history of paying their debts. Therefore, a mistake about corporate or personal identity may become a contractual issue. The situation is even more difficult if a con artist obtains goods under a contract and then resells them to a third party. The person who was duped under the first transaction may try to recover the goods from the third party on the basis of the mistake.

Sometimes that approach succeeds; sometimes it does not. The courts are required to weigh the interests of the seller against those of the innocent purchaser. Mistaken identity will therefore not render a contract defective unless (i) the mistake was known to the other contractual party, and (ii) the mistake was *material*. A **material mistake** is one that matters to the mistaken party in an important way.

It is difficult to always be clear about the difference between mistakes and a lack of *consensus ad item*. The difficulty in this distinction is revealed in Business Decision 10.2.

a **material mistake** is one that matters to the mistaken party in an important way

Mistake about Subject Matter

Some mistakes put the parties at cross-purposes and therefore prevent the formation of a contract. This often occurs when the parties are mutually mistaken about the subject matter of an agreement. Suppose you enter a contract to buy

Business Decision 10.2

Lewis v Averay [1971] EWCA Civ 4, 3 WLR 603

Lewis was hoping to sell his car when a man claiming to be Richard Green approached him with an offer to buy. Green was a famous actor, well known in England at the time. The buyer who approached Lewis, however, was a fraudster simply pretending to be Green. He even showed Lewis a studio pass to convince Lewis that he was indeed the famous actor. Lewis eventually agreed to sell the car to the fraudster. Because he believed the buyer to be a famous actor, Lewis was willing to accept a non-certified cheque as payment for the car. The fraudster took the car and quickly resold it to Averay before disappearing. The cheque bounced when Lewis attempted to deposit it, so Lewis brought an action against Averay claiming that the car still belonged to him because he had not been paid.

The court found that Lewis would not have released the car to the buyer had he not been under the mistaken impression that the buyer was a well-known actor. Therefore, the effect of this mistaken identity was to render the contract voidable, such that Lewis could repudiate the contract with the fraudster and get his car back. However, until Lewis communicated his repudiation, the contract remained valid. The fraudster sold the car to Averay before the contract was repudiated and while he still had a valid contractual right to the vehicle. The court therefore found that Averay was entitled to keep the car as an innocent purchaser under English legislation.

Questions for Discussion

1. Do you think that the decision of the court is fair to Mr Lewis?

2. Setting aside your views about the fairness of the decision to Mr Lewis, if you encountered a similar situation, what measures would you implement to prevent this kind of fraud from occurring?

cotton that will arrive on a ship called the *Peerless*, which you believe will arrive in October. However, neither you nor the seller knows that there is actually more than one ship called *Peerless*. One is set to arrive in October and another in December. The seller, not knowing of the earlier ship, sends the cotton on the later ship. By the time the cotton arrives, you no longer have a use for it and refuse to purchase it. In the circumstances, there was a mutual mistake about a material issue—which *Peerless* the cotton was to be shipped on—which prevented a true agreement or the creation of a contract.[18]

MISTAKES RENDERING IMPOSSIBLE THE PURPOSE OF THE CONTRACT

Even if a mistake does not pertain to the process of contract formation, it may be relevant if it makes the contract impossible to perform. We will consider one possibility and a related scenario: mistake about existence of the subject matter and frustration.

Mistake about Existence of the Subject Matter

The parties' mistake may render the contract impossible to perform. In this situation, both parties make the *same* mistake, one that is usually based on a false assumption. Suppose you agree to lease your beach house to me for the summer. We draft a contract, sign it, and exchange keys for money. The next day, however, we learn that the house was completely destroyed by fire a week ago. Consequently, when we created our contract, we both made the same mistake—we believed that the house existed and that our agreement could be performed. The contract is therefore defective. You have to return

---

[18.] These facts are derived from *Raffles v Wichelhaus* (1864) 159 ER 375.

my money, and I have to return your keys. And neither one of us can sue to enforce the deal.[19]

However, a common mistake about the existence of the subject matter of a contract does not *always* prevent the enforcement of the agreement. A business should therefore protect itself by inserting into the contract a *force majeure*, or "irresistible force," clause, that states which party bears the hardship if the subject matter of the contract is destroyed or if some other unexpected event occurs. The affected party should then arrange insurance against the potential loss.

THE DOCTRINE OF FRUSTRATION

We have considered situations involving a mistake about an existing fact. Sometimes, however, the parties may make an erroneous assumption about the *future*. Even if they are fully informed when they create their contract, subsequent events may make it impossible for them to perform as anticipated. In such a case, we say that the contract is frustrated. Unlike a contractual mistake, where a mistake takes place at or during contract formation, a frustrating event takes place sometime after the contract is already in place.

Going back to our earlier example, I agree to rent your beach house for the summer. We create a contract and exchange keys for money. At that time, the building is in excellent shape and I mistakenly assume it will stay that way. During the spring, however, it is completely destroyed by a fire. I could still occupy the empty lot for the summer, but that is not what we had in mind. The purpose of our agreement has been *frustrated* by an unexpected occurrence. A contract is **frustrated** when some event makes performance impossible or radically undermines its very purpose.

It is important to note that a contract is not frustrated merely because it becomes more expensive or somewhat more difficult to perform. For instance, our agreement would still be effective even if, because of heavy rains, you were required to spend a considerable amount of money cleaning up the beach house to make it fit for habitation during the summer. In some cases, an agreement will still be effective where performance of the contract is still possible, but slightly delayed on account of circumstances beyond the control of both parties. For example, in a contract for a six-day guided wilderness tour, a court has held that no frustration takes place when an airline cancels flights because of terrorist attacks (delaying the arrival of the guest) in circumstances where the guest can arrive two days later and the guide offers to take the guest on the tour two days later than originally planned.[20]

The doctrine of frustration, like the law of mistake, tries to strike a fair balance between the parties. Ultimately, however, it requires a decision about who will bear the risk of a loss. In some situations, the parties themselves supply the answer.

■ The doctrine of frustration applies only if neither party is responsible for the relevant event. If one party is responsible, then that party bears the loss. For instance, I would not be entitled to a refund if I carelessly burned the beach house down during the first night of my stay.

a contract is **frustrated** when some event makes performance impossible or radically undermines its very purpose

---

[19.] Provincial consumer protection legislation often deals with this type of mistake. See, *eg*, *Sale of Goods Act*, RSA 2000, c S-2 (Alta) ("where there is a contract for the sale of specific goods and the goods without the knowledge of the seller have perished at the time that the contract is made, the contract is void").

[20.] *Allen v Taku Safari* [2003] BCJ No 754 (BC SC).

■ Even if neither party is at fault, they may have agreed that one of them would bear the risk of loss. For instance, as a business that is aware of potential risks, you may have inserted a *force majeure* clause into our agreement. If so, I could not demand a refund of the rent even though the house is gone.

If the parties themselves cannot settle the issue in some way, a judge must do so. First, however, we must draw a distinction between provinces that use the common law rules and those that have legislation on point.[21] Common law jurisdictions use an all-or-nothing rule. A purchaser can recover *all* of their contractual payments if they have not received *any* benefit from the seller. However, if the purchaser has received *some* benefit, they cannot recover *any* payments. In neither event can the seller actually demand payment from the purchaser, even if the seller incurred substantial expenses under the agreement.

In other jurisdictions, the effect of the legislation turns upon the existence of a contractual payment or a benefit.

■ If the purchaser paid an advance or a deposit under the contract, the court has discretion to divide that money between the parties as it sees fit. Consequently, if the seller incurred some expense under the contract, they may be entitled to retain an appropriate amount as compensation. In other circumstances, the purchaser may be entitled to a complete refund.

■ If the purchaser received some benefit from the seller, the seller is entitled to either retain money that they have received or make a fresh claim for compensation against the purchaser. That compensation, however, cannot exceed the value of the benefit.

■ If the purchaser neither paid money nor received a benefit under the contract, the entire burden of the frustrating event falls on the seller. In that situation, the seller cannot claim compensation, regardless of how much expense they incurred under the agreement.[22]

DOCUMENTS MISTAKENLY SIGNED

Another type of mistake occurs when a person signs a contractual document in error. As a general rule, that sort of mistake is irrelevant. A person is usually bound by a signature, even if they did not read the document. The other party is normally entitled to assume that a signature represents an acceptance of the agreement. There are, however, exceptions to that rule. As we saw in Chapter 9, unusual or onerous terms are not binding unless they are reasonably drawn to the attention of the person who signed the contract. There is another exception—*non est factum*.

Non est factum, literally "this is not my deed," allows the mistaken party to avoid any obligations under the contract. The plea is available only if there is a *fundamental*, *total*, or *radical* difference between what a person signed and what that person thought they were signing. This is a high threshold and will rarely be met. It may happen if the document was presented as a sale of land, when it was actually a purchase of shares. However, if the issue is merely misrepresentation, then the contract may be only voidable, not void. Similarly, the doctrine

non est factum literally means "this is not my deed"

---

21. Legislation has been enacted in Alberta, British Columbia, Manitoba, Newfoundland and Labrador, New Brunswick, Ontario, and Prince Edward Island.

22. An exception exists in British Columbia, where the seller can claim compensation for half of its expenses.

does not apply if the difference is merely a matter of degree. Consequently, a signatory cannot plead *non est factum* simply because they were mistaken about the quantity of goods that were sold under the contract. Furthermore, the doctrine cannot be used by someone who, through carelessness, failed to take steps to understand the document. This means that the doctrine cannot be used by someone who could read a contract but did not because their glasses were broken at the time. It may also mean that someone who cannot understand a contract in English, but who could have asked a friend to translate, cannot rely on *non est factum*.

Although the plea of *non est factum* will not apply in situations where a mistaken party signs an agreement without carefully reading it, it is important to be aware that courts will invoke the rules of equity to ensure fair outcomes whenever a business knows that its customer is operating under a mistaken impression but tries to "snap up" the deal anyway. Consider this approach to doing business from an ethical perspective. See Ethical Perspective 10.1 for an example.

Ethical Perspective 10.1

Performance Industries Ltd v Sylvan Lake Golf & Tennis Club Ltd [2002] 1 SCR 678

TerranceO'Connor stood firm. He had a signed agreement from Frederick Terrance Bell. Although Bell had in mind a development of a double row of housing totalling 58 homes on about 11 acres, the signed contract specified only 3.6 acres. Bell was shocked to realize this and learned the hard lesson about signing a contract without reading it. The agreement, as Bell had understood it, had been arrived at on the basis of several discussions. After a number of preliminary meetings, O'Connor spent about two-and-a-half hours at Bell's home. The two men met at length in O'Connor's truck a day or two later. Amongst other things, they agreed to a land deal of 110 yards (100 metres) in width east to west and approximately 480 yards (440 metres) in length north to south. They also agreed that O'Connor would have his lawyer reduce the verbal terms to writing. Shortly thereafter, a document was produced. Clause 18 accurately specified the 480-yard length of the proposed development, but instead of sufficient width to permit a double row of houses (approximately 110 yards [100 metres]), clause 18 allowed only enough land for a single row of houses (110 feet [33 metres]). O'Connor knew from Bell's comments during the negotiations that Bell was unwilling to sign an agreement without the option for sufficient land to create the layout development with two rows of housing. According to Bell, anything less would be "a waste." O'Connor therefore knew that when Bell signed the document that he had not detected the substitution of 110 feet for 110 yards.

The Supreme Court of Canada invoked the equitable remedy of rectification to render the written document consistent with what it held to be a definite and ascertainable prior oral agreement. Although the Supreme Court recognized that the remedy of rectification was traditionally available only in situations where both parties were mistaken

and wanted to fix the mistake, the court confirmed that rectification is also available in cases where one party is mistaken so long as (i) the mistaken party can establish that the terms agreed to orally were not accurately reflected in the written document, (ii) the other party knew or ought to have known about the error when the mistaken party signed the written document, and (iii) the other party's attempt to rely on the erroneous written document amounts to "fraud or the equivalent of fraud." In this case the rectification resulted in Bell, the plaintiff, being awarded over $600 000 in damages in compensation for his losses at the hands of O'Connor. As a result of his "misbehaviour" in the conduct of the trial, O'Connor also had to pay Bell's legal costs, which would have been in the hundreds of thousands of dollars.

Questions for Discussion

1. Although courts will now rectify written contracts induced by unilateral mistakes where the other party knew about the mistake but snapped up the deal anyway, the law does not otherwise penalize or punish parties for doing so. Should there be some form of penalty or punishment?

2. What should a business do if it learns that one of its salespersons has tried to snap up a contract where the other party is clearly mistaken about its terms?

3. What should an employee do if they are instructed by a superior to snap up a contract where the other party is clearly mistaken about its terms?

Concept Summary 10.3

Managing Risks Concerning Mistake and Frustration

- Ensure that contracts clearly describe the object, purpose, and conditions of the contract. Providing as much detail as possible reduces the risk of unilateral and mutual mistakes.

- Ensure that all parties carefully read, understand, and indicate that they have both read and understood the terms of the contract prior to agreeing to be bound by its contents.

- Include a *force majeure* clause ("irresistible force") that clearly indicates which party will bear financial responsibility if the subject matter of the contract is destroyed or an unforeseen event transpires.

- If the contract indicates that one party will assume a substantial risk, consider including an additional clause articulating that the party assuming the risk understands the nature and scope of the risk. It is prudent to require that party to sign their initials beside this clause.

- When entering into a contract, ascertain the other party's ability to understand the language in which the contract is written. If the contracting party does not understand the language in which the contract is written, offer them an opportunity to have the contract translated.

Concept Summary 10.3 encapsulates several approaches to risk management in the cases of mistake and frustration.

Unfairness during Bargaining

L.O. ❼ ❽

As we saw in the discussion on incapacity, weaker parties are not always required to complete their agreements. If a disadvantaged party is pressured into an agreement or placed in an unfair position during the bargaining process, the contract may be ineffective. We conclude this chapter with a brief examination of three types of unfair bargaining: duress, undue influence, and unconscionable transactions.

DURESS

Duress of person refers to physical violence or the threat of violence against a person or that person's loved one. If a contract is the product of duress, it is *voidable*. The innocent party may choose not to perform, and to recover any payments they made under the agreement. Similar rules apply to *duress of* goods. **Duress of goods** occurs when one person seizes or threatens to seize another person's goods to force that person to create a contract. The innocent party can avoid the contract if they can show that the pressure was practically irresistible.

Fortunately, the courts seldom hear cases involving duress of person or of goods. Unscrupulous business people do, however, occasionally resort to a more subtle form of pressure—*economic duress*. **Economic duress** arises when a person enters into a contractual arrangement after being threatened with financial harm. For example, a contractual party, claiming that the cost of performance is higher than expected, may indicate that it will not fulfill its obligations unless it receives additional money.

Economic duress is more difficult to determine than duress of person or duress of goods. It is always wrong to put a gun to someone's head; it is not always wrong to exert economic pressure over them. Indeed, that sort of thing regularly happens in the business world. Courts look at several factors before determining that a pressure was an illegitimate threat.

- Economic pressure is more likely to be considered illegitimate if it was made in *bad faith*. It is one thing for a party to honestly say that it cannot

duress of person refers to physical violence or the threat of violence

duress of goods occurs when one person seizes or threatens to seize another person's goods to force that person to create a contract

economic duress arises when a person enters into a contractual arrangement after being threatened with financial harm

perform without more money; it is another to apply pressure on some-one simply because they are vulnerable.

- The victim of the pressure must show that they *could not have reasonably resisted*. Sometimes, it is reasonable to resist by bringing the matter to court; sometimes the situation requires a much quicker response.
- The courts are more sympathetic if the victim started *legal proceedings promptly* after the effects of the pressure passed.
- The courts are more likely to become involved if the victim *protested* when presented with the pressure. However, a failure to protest is not necessarily fatal if that course of conduct was obviously futile in the circumstances.
- A contract is more likely to be considered voidable if the victim *succumbed to the pressure without legal advice*; otherwise, agreement to a contractual proposal tends to look more like a sound business decision.

UNDUE INFLUENCE

Even if the elements of common law duress cannot be established, relief may be available under the equitable principle of *undue influence*. Whereas duress flows from the conditions under which a contract is formed, undue influence focuses on the power relationship between the parties. **Undue influence** is the abuse of a relationship in order to influence someone and induce an agreement. Influence refers to "the ability of one person to dominate the will of another, whether through manipulation, coercion, or outright but subtle abuse of power."[23] Cases involving undue influence are usually one of two types: the parties can be in a *fiduciary relationship* or there may be no special relationship between the parties. Figure 10.1 illustrates the differences.

A **fiduciary relationship** occurs when one person is in a position of domi-nance over the other. That power imbalance usually exists in a relationship that is based on trust or confidence. Fiduciary relationships generate a special kind of duty that requires the more powerful party to subordinate its personal interests in favour of the weaker party. Whenever parties in a fiduciary relation-ship enter into a business transaction, there is good reason to suspect undue influence on the part of the more powerful party. For this reason, the law imposes a *presumption of undue influence* whenever a fiduciary is involved in a transaction.

Not every transaction involving a fiduciary is defective, and the presump-tion of undue influence can be rebutted. If the fiduciary can prove that the transaction was fair, the contract will stand. Often, the best tactic for a fidu-ciary is to ensure that the other party receives independent legal advice before entering into the agreement.

The second type of undue influence scenario arises when there is no special relationship between the parties. In such a case, there will be *no presumption* of undue influence. The party seeking relief from such a contract must prove that

undue influence is the abuse of a relationship in order to influence someone and induce an agreement

a fiduciary relationship is a relation-ship in which one person is in a posi-tion of dominance over the other

---

23. *Geffen v Goodman Estate* [1991] 2 SCR (SCC) at 377 *as per* Wilson J. More recently, in *National Commercial Bank (Jamaica) Ltd v Hew* [2003] UKPC 51 (PC), at para 32, Lord Millet suggested that actual abuse of the relationship is a necessary element of proof: "However great the influence which one person may be able to wield over another, equity does not intervene unless that influ-ence has been abused. Equity does not save people from the consequences of their own folly; it acts to save them from being victimized by other people." While the judicial question of whether to focus on the weaker party's impaired capacity to consent or the act of exploitation by the stronger remains open, the answer may lie in a complex middle ground.

FIGURE 10.1 Undue Influence

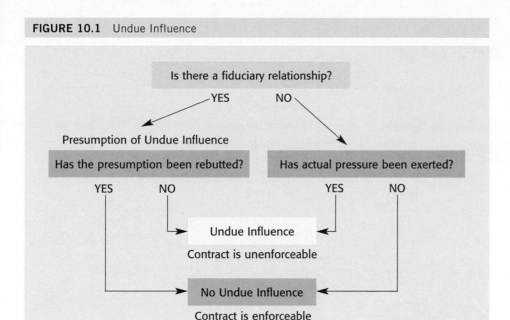

undue pressure was applied. When a business is not in a position of domination, it will be much harder for the other party to have the transaction set aside for undue influence. As a matter of risk management, a business can avoid that possibility by refraining from using bullying tactics and, in appropriate circumstances, by suggesting independent legal advice.

UNCONSCIONABLE TRANSACTIONS

Equity also provides relief from *unconscionable transactions*, which are characterized by their one-sidedness. An **unconscionable transaction** is an agreement that no right-minded person would ever make and no fair-minded person would ever accept. The weaker party must prove (i) that there was an **improvident bargain**, one that was made without proper regard to the future, and (ii) that there was an inequality in the bargaining position of the two parties. (Figure 10.2 distinguishes the differences.) If those elements are satisfied, the court presumes that the transaction was unconscionable. The stronger party must then rebut the presumption of unconscionability. Even if the contract does not provide a benefit for the weaker party, the agreement may stand if the stronger party shows that the bargaining process was fair, right, and reasonable after all.[24] As usual, the risk can be managed, most notably by ensuring that the weaker party receives independent legal advice. Ethical Perspective 10.2 illustrates the problem.

Several provinces have legislation governing unfair transactions. Some is preventive, using such devices as disclosure requirements or "cooling-off" periods to reduce the risk of a stronger party taking advantage of a weaker one.[25]

an **unconscionable transaction** is an agreement that no right-minded person would ever make and no fair-minded person would ever accept

an **improvident bargain** is a bargain made without regard to the future

[24.] *Turner Estate v Bonli Estate* [1989] 5 WWR 730 (Sask QB), aff'd [1990] 5 WWR 685 (Sask CA).

[25.] *Business Practices and Consumer Protection Act*, SBC 2004, c 2, s 212 (a), and BC Reg 274 2004; *Consumer Protection Act*, CCSM c C200, s 62(1) (Man); *Consumer Protection Act*, RSO 1990, c C.31 s 21 (Ont); *Direct Sellers Act*, RSNB 1973, c D-10, s 17 (NB).

FIGURE 10.2   Unconscionability

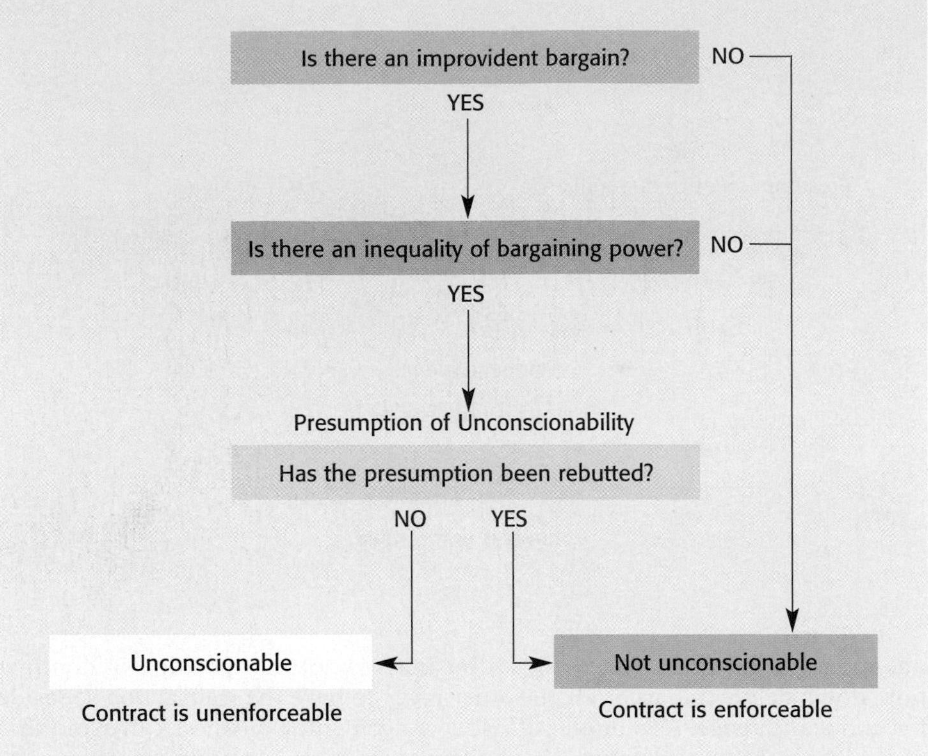

Ethical Perspective **10.2**

Waters v Sun Route Tours Inc [1994] BCJ No 16, 1994 CarswellBC 2428

Mr Waters owned a travel company that his friend Mr Kinney was interested in purchasing. Kinney told Waters that he wanted to incorporate Waters' company into his own company, Sun Route Tours. The two discussed a possible sale. However, at the time of discussions, Waters was suffering from anxiety and insomnia and was taking medication that clouded his judgment.

Prior to closing, Waters met with a lawyer, who communicated to Kinney that Waters was not in a position to make decisions about the sale of his company. Nevertheless Kinney and his lawyer proceeded to meet with Waters and finalize an agreement for the sale of Waters's company. Neither Kinney, nor his lawyer contacted Waters's lawyer prior to the meeting, and they proceeded with the sale in the absence of any legal representation for Waters. In the end, Waters sold all the shares in his business in exchange for $14 600 and discounts on travel through Sun Route Tours. Waters had purchased five-sixths of the shares in his company only a few years earlier for $30 000. Waters had been eager to leave for Australia in hopes of recovering from his distress, and he departed immediately upon completion of the sale.

While in Australia, Waters recovered and ceased taking medication. He returned to Canada and tried to book a discounted vacation through Sun Route Tours when Kinney informed him that he had no right to travel discounts. Waters had never received a copy of the sale agreement from Kinney, so he had no document with which to counter Kinney's claim. Waters promptly brought an action to set aside the sale agreement, stating that he was incapable of consenting to an agreement at the time when the transaction was completed.

Questions for Discussion

1. Did Kinney do anything wrong or was he simply conducting an ordinary business deal? Explain.

2. If you were in Kinney's position, how would you conduct this transaction?

3. If you were the judge in this case, how would you respond to this incident?

Other statutes prohibit the use of particular unfair terms, such as exclusion or forfeiture clauses.[26] Still other statutes give the court a broad discretion to render harsh or unconscionable agreements ineffective, typically in legislation regulating moneylending institutions and insurance companies.[27]

Illegality

A contract may be ineffective because it violates the law. There are several variations on that theme. **Illegal agreements** are expressly or implicitly prohibited by statute and are therefore void. Other agreements, though not strictly prohibited, come into conflict with a common law rule or offend public policy. They too are often unenforceable.

AGREEMENTS PROHIBITED BY STATUTE

Most statutes that prohibit particular types of agreements are *regulatory* in nature. The purpose of a **regulatory statute** is not to punish individuals for wrongdoing, but rather to regulate their conduct through an administrative regime. For example, there are statutes that prohibit the sale of apples that have not been graded in accordance with provincial regulations.[28] Other statutes require licences to be obtained prior to engaging in certain kinds of transactions. Contracts that do not adhere to certain statutory regimes are not automatically set aside. Instead, courts will generally assess their legality by examining the seriousness of the consequences of invalidating the contract, the social utility of those consequences, and a determination of the class of persons for whom the prohibition was enacted.[29] Sometimes a court will invalidate certain aspects of a contract but not others. Typical examples of this occur in the context of business loans that are illegal because their rate of interest contravenes provisions in the *Criminal Code*. Although courts will set aside contracts with criminal interest rates, they will not set aside such contracts in their entirety in cases where doing so would enable the borrower to keep the principal.[30]

COMMON LAW ILLEGALITY

Some agreements are illegal even if they do not contravene a particular statute. The common law is unwilling to recognize agreements that are contrary to public policy. For example, a mobster may hire a thug to kill a politician. If the thug decides instead to take the money and run, the mobster cannot sue for breach of contract. The same is true of any agreement that is aimed at committing a crime or tort.

The common law will not recognize several other types of agreement, including those that damage a country's safety or foreign relations, interfere with the administration of justice, promote corruption, or promote sexual immorality. Each type of agreement is contrary to public policy.

L.O. ❾ ❿

illegal agreements are expressly or implicitly prohibited by statute

the purpose of a **regulatory statute** is not to punish individuals for wrongdoing, but rather to regulate their conduct through an administrative regime

PART 3

---

[26] *Consumer Protection Act*, CCSM, c C200, s 58 (Man); *Consumer Protection Act*, RSO 1990, c C.31, s 34 (Ont); *Sale of Goods Act*, RSBC 1996, c 410, s 20 (BC).

[27] *Money-lenders Act*, RSNS 1989, c 289, s 3 (NS); *Unconscionable Transactions Act*, RSA 2000, c U-2, s 2 (Alta); *Insurance Act*, RSO 1990, c I.8 (Ont); RSPEI 1988, c I-4, s 92 (PEI); RSNWT 1988, c I-4, s 46 (NWT).

[28] *Kingshott v Brunskill* [1953] OWN 133 (CA).

[29] *Royal Bank of Canada v Grobman* [1977] OR (2d) 636 (Ont HCJ); *Eha v Genge* (2007) 239 BCAC 313.

[30] *Eha v Genge* (2007) 239 BCAC 313; *Alexopoulos v Rescinity* (2004) Carswell-Ont 3156.

THE DOCTRINE OF PUBLIC POLICY

It may seem odd that a court can strike down a contract simply because it is contrary to public policy. After all, the law of contract is intended to facilitate stable and predictable business relationships by allowing people to enter freely into whatever bargains they choose. The notion of public policy, however, is notoriously vague. It may allow judges to make or unmake contracts on the basis of their own personal views as to what is best for society. Public policy, according to an old saying, becomes "an unruly horse" if it is let out of the barn.

Covenants in Restraint of Trade

> a **covenant in restraint of trade** is a contractual term that *unreasonably restricts* one party's liberty to carry on a trade, business, or profession in a particular way

An agreement may be ineffective on the grounds of public policy if it contains a *covenant in restraint of trade*. A **covenant in restraint of trade** is a contractual term that *unreasonably restricts* one party's liberty to carry on a trade, business, or profession in a particular way. Such covenants often require a person to (i) trade or *not* trade with someone in particular, or (ii) work for someone in particular or, at least, *not* work for anyone else. In its most unreasonable form, a broadly drafted restraint of trade provision comes close to slavery. In that situation, the covenant will be presumed contrary to public policy unless the party seeking to enforce it can demonstrate that the restriction is reasonable. However, even if an unacceptable provision is struck down, the rest of the contract may remain.

Many restrictive covenants are perfectly reasonable and therefore not contrary to public policy. Suppose you are thinking about buying a convenience store. You may legitimately insert a provision into the contract that prevents the current owner from opening or operating another convenience store within a six-block radius. That provision merely ensures that the current owner does not steal all of your expected customers. It would be different, however, if the contract prohibited the current owner from operating another convenience store *anywhere* in Canada. A convenience store in another neighbourhood, let alone another city, does not create a threat to your business. The contractual term would therefore be an unreasonable restraint of trade, contrary to public policy, and hence ineffective.

Restraint of trade clauses are often found in employment contracts. As a matter of risk management, employers should consider drafting such provisions as narrowly as possible to achieve the desired goals while maximizing the likelihood of enforcement. This issue is discussed in more detail in Chapter 26.

Chapter Summary

A contract may be defective because of (i) incapacity to contract, (ii) absence of writing, (iii) mistake, (iv) unfairness during bargaining, and (v) illegality.

A contract cannot normally be created by a person who lacks the legal power of consent. With the exception of a limited class of contracts concerning employment and the purchase of necessaries, a minor's contracts are voidable. Similarly, an agreement created by a mentally incapacitated adult may be set aside. Intoxicated persons who seek to avoid contractual liability can do so only if they can prove that they were incapable of knowing or appreciating what they were doing, and that the other party was

aware of this incapacity. A statutory corporation, unlike a chartered corporation, has a limited contractual capacity. Although associations are generally incapable of contracting, some provinces have enacted legislation that enables associations involved in specific purposes to enter into contracts. Generally, a public authority acting within its powers has the capacity to contract independent of any specific statutory authority to do so.

The *Statute of Frauds* requires the party seeking to enforce contracts such as guarantees, contracts for the sale of an interest in land, and contracts not to be performed within a year to have evidence in the form of a written and signed memorandum or note. Some consumer protection laws contain similar requirements that certain agreements be made in writing, with a copy provided to consumers.

A mistake can interfere with the parties' attempt to reach an agreement or make it impossible for the object of the contract to be achieved. A mistake of identity or a material mistake about the terms of a contract may preclude its formation if the mistake is known to the other party. A material mistake about the subject matter of a contract may also negate consent. A common mistake about the existence of the subject matter renders it impossible for a contract to be fulfilled and will sometimes operate as a defence. A mistaken assumption that one or both parties make about the future can result in frustrating a contract.

A contract is frustrated when some event occurs that makes further performance of the contract impossible or radically undermines its very purpose.

When a party is pressured into an agreement or placed in an unfair position during the bargaining process, the agreement may be defective. Economic duress arises when a party enters into a contractual arrangement after being threatened with financial harm. Undue influence occurs when pressure is exerted by a stronger party to overpower the will of a weaker party and thereby induce an agreement. The law imposes a rebuttable presumption of undue influence whenever a fiduciary is involved in a transaction. The presumption is usually rebutted if the stronger party shows that the weaker party had the opportunity to seek independent advice. An unconscionable transaction is an agreement that no right-minded person would ever make and no fair-minded person would ever accept. Although it is generally up to the parties to make their own bargains, courts will interfere if a contract was the result of duress, undue influence, or unconscionability.

Illegal agreements are those that are expressly or implicitly prohibited by statute. Illegal agreements, along with other agreements that come into conflict with a common law rule or public policy, are often unenforceable. An example of an agreement that conflicts with public policy is a covenant in restraint of trade, which is enforceable only if it is reasonable.

MyBusLawLab ADDITIONAL RESOURCES FOR CHAPTER 10

MyBusLawLab provides students with an assortment of tools to help enrich the learning experience, including a Study Plan with Pre- and Post-tests, mini-cases with assessments, and provincial content material, which provides links to relevant cases, legislation, and additional resources.

MyBusLawLab provides the following resources for Chapter 10:

Provincial Material

- **British Columbia:** Minors, Mentally Incompetent Persons, Committee, Public Guardian and Trustee, Business Corporations, Societies and Associations, Form of Contract, Power of Attorney, Adult Guardianship, Representation Agreement, Identity Theft, Parental Liability, Wills, Estates and Succession

- **Alberta:** *Consumer Protection Acts* Identity Theft, Guardianship, Legality, Limited Capacity, Minors/Infants, *Statute of Frauds*, Unconscionable Transactions, Undue Influence, Personal Directives, Powers of Attorney

- **Manitoba and Saskatchewan:** Age of Majority, Majority Rules, Necessaries, *Parental Responsibility Act*, Sale of Goods Act Implied Terms, *Statute of Frauds*, Statutory Requirements for Written Contracts, Statutory Right to Cancel Contracts, Unconscionable Transactions

- **Ontario:** Age of Majority, Confidentiality Agreements, Consumer Agreements, *Consumer Protection Act 2002*, Identity Theft, Implied Terms, Independent Legal Advice, Insurance Legislation, Incompetence, Lotteries, Necessaries, Non-Competition Clauses, Powers of Attorney, *Sale of Goods Act*, *Statute of Frauds*, Unconscionable Transactions, Undue Influence, Unfair Business Practices

- **Atlantic Provinces:** Adult Protection Legislation, Age of Majority, Independent Legal Advice, Statute of Frauds

Review Questions

1. What is meant by the term "contractual capacity"?

2. Why does the law treat minors differently than adults?

3. Give examples of contracts that will be enforced even if a person has not attained the age of majority.

4. What is the key difference in how the law treats contracts entered into by a minor as compared to contracts entered into by a person lacking mental capacity?

5. Under what circumstances will a person be liable for a contract that they entered into while intoxicated?

6. Explain how the contractual capacity of a chartered corporation differs from that of a statutory corporation.

7. Why must a business person be particularly careful when contracting with or on behalf of an association?

8. Do Indian bands have the legal capacity to contract? Under what circumstances do Aboriginal persons have the capacity to contract? Explain.

9. What types of contracts must be evidenced in writing?

10. Does the *Statute of Frauds* have effect throughout Canada? Briefly explain the rationale for the writing requirement.

11. If a contract does not comply with the *Statute of Frauds*, making it unenforceable, does it follow that the agreement has no legal effect? Explain your answer.

12. What is the difference between a mistake about the existence of the subject matter of a contract and frustration?

13. How might a case of mistaken identity provide a contractual defence?

14. How can you determine who bears the risk when the subject matter of a contract is frustrated?

15. Explain why the plea of *non est factum* is part of the law of mistake.

16. What makes a contract illegal? Will every illegal contract be set aside in its entirety?

17. Describe the doctrine of public policy. Why might it be a concern for risk management?

18. Outline three bases upon which a court might set aside an unfair contract. Is there a common thread underlying the rationale in each?

19. What are the five factors that courts will assess when determining whether economic pressure exerted during the formation of a contract was illegitimate?

20. When two people enter into a contract for the sale of goods, do they establish a fiduciary relationship? Why or why not?

Cases and Problems

1. Erin had always been independent. Shortly before her seventeenth birthday, she moved out of her parents' house and bought a used car, which she needed for her fledgling chocolate-covered-cranberry enterprise. She agreed to pay $15 000 for the car, $5000 as a down payment and the rest in monthly instalments over one year. She used the car mostly to make deliveries and pick up supplies. After she had driven the car for three months, the bearings burnt out. Since Erin was in a position to hire a delivery person, she decided that she no longer wanted the car. Having studied the basics of contract law in high school, Erin attempted to return the vehicle to the car dealership, claiming that she had elected to avoid the contract. The dealership refused, having received an opinion from its lawyer that a contract for necessaries is enforceable against a minor. Erin replied that the car was not a necessary, and that the contract was therefore not enforceable. Do you think that Erin will be permitted to avoid her contract with the dealership? Give reasons to support your position.

2. Elwood is a pig farmer who is known to enjoy a drink or two. One day in July, after a weekend of particularly heavy drinking, he staggered into the office of Pork Bellies of America and offered to sell all of his piglets. He promised to deliver them in October, as soon as they were fattened up. Hank, Pork Bellies' purchasing agent, saw that Elwood was extremely drunk, but decided to write up the contract anyway since the price was a fair one.

After the deal was signed, Hank and Elwood went to the neighbourhood saloon to play darts and have lunch. The next day, after sobering up, Elwood was reminded about their agreement. In fact, over the course of the next two weeks, Hank and Elwood ran into each other on a number of occasions. Each time, Hank mentioned the deal, and Elwood acknowledged it. In September, the price of pork nearly doubled. Consequently, Elwood sent Pork Bellies of America a registered letter saying that he would not be delivering the pigs. He had decided to sell them to someone else at a higher price. Pork Bellies has sued Elwood. Will the court allow Elwood to avoid contractual liability? Give reasons to support your position.

3. Michael is a young man with a long psychiatric history. One day he decided to apply for a credit card from his local bank. He filled out the forms, submitted them to the bank and soon after received a credit card. Not fully understanding the consequences of using the card for purchases, he quickly racked up thousands of dollars of debt. After numerous missed payments, the bank brought an action in court to sue Michael for the balance owing. Michael's lawyer argued that the contract was voidable because of mental incompetence. He submitted medical evidence to show that Michael was incompetent at the time he entered into the credit card contract. Will the bank be able to sue for the outstanding balance? What additional piece of information would be helpful to make a conclusive determination here?

4. The General Manager of Nunzio's Kosher Pizzeria has hired you to wash dishes in the evening. On your third shift, you are finally introduced to Nunzio. He seems like a nice guy as he welcomes you aboard. You are paid weekly by a cheque drawn from the account of a numbered company called 551999 Alberta Ltd. Nunzio's name is one of the two signatures on the cheques. Things go well for the first two months. Then you are not paid for three weeks in a row. The following week, the pizzeria is shut down. After finding out that the numbered company has gone bankrupt, you see your lawyer about suing Nunzio personally. After reviewing the corporate records, your lawyer tells you that there has been a mistake of identity—your employment contract was with the numbered company, but Nunzio is neither an officer nor a shareholder in that company. What does your lawyer mean by mistaken identity, and how will it apply in your case?

5. Hole-In-One Mini Donuts Co (HIO) was knee-deep in negotiations with Lemon Chicken Enterprises (LCE) for the sale of its deep-fryer machine factory and the adjacent 345 acres of land. HIO presented to LCE an Agreement of Purchase and Sale. While both parties had already agreed to the price of $39 000 000 and many of the other key terms, LCE returned the agreement the next day with a couple of suggested amendments that it felt were essential changes. Before the final version of the agreement was signed, LCE was suddenly told that HIO had sold the factory and adjacent land to a third party. Extremely miffed, the CEO of LCE telephoned the CEO of HIO, wherein the latter admitted that HIO had indeed concluded an agreement but that he had simply changed his mind before the paperwork was done. What HIO's CEO did not know was that LCE recorded the call. LCE has now commenced an action for breach of contract. Assuming that the recorded conversation is admissible as evidence, will LCE succeed in enforcing the agreement? Provide clear and convincing reasons one way or the other.

6. Waggles Farm grows grains and legumes. This past year, it planted a large crop of lentils. Part of Waggles's business plan is to get commitments from purchasers in advance of the harvest by way of contract. To that end, once the entire crop had been planted, Waggles entered into a significant contract with Lentils and Lima Beans Inc (L&L), a Canadian distributor of legumes known for selling exclusively to high-end health food stores. Partway through the season, a period of unusual rain prevented Waggles from spraying down the crop. This was an important part of the lentil growing process and it put the entire crop in jeopardy. Waggles decided not to mention this to any of its customers, hoping that the crop would come through as originally planned. The failure to spray had significant consequences. The lentils, although successfully harvested, were not fit for human consumption and could be used only as cattle feed. When L&L found this out, it tried to renege on the contract. It claimed that Waggles knew very well that L&L was in the business of selling human food, not cattle feed. The terms and conditions of the contract did not contemplate what would happen in the event of a crop failure. Waggles decided to sue for breach of contract, claiming that the contract was for lentils and L&L got their lentils. L&L made a counterclaim, alleging that it was Waggles that was in breach of the contract since it never got what it ordered and now it was stuck without a supply of lentils for the season. Analyze the facts of this case and determine whether there are any contractual defects and, if so, what will be the likely outcome at trial.

7. Several years back, Golden Joe's Geology bought a 1000-acre package of land in the Northwest Territories. When he purchased the property, Joe was sure to purchase the mineral rights as well. For years, Joe spent his summers panning for gold on the property. Recently, quite by accident, Joe discovered that his land is at the heart of a potentially lucrative diamond stash. Joe is overjoyed and has decided to sell his property so that he can retire to a tropical locale. He has agreed to sell the property and mineral rights to Prospectus Prospecting, which will invest the money needed to mine and process the diamonds. The agreement is drawn up and signed by both parties, and everyone is satisfied. However, when the actual land transfer is about to take place, it is discovered that the Crown grant of property to Joe has been substantially revoked. As a result, the land available for sale is in fact reduced by 90 percent. Is Joe still entitled to performance of the contract with Prospectus? Explain why or why not. As a prudent business manager, could Joe have better protected himself against such a possibility? Explain how.

8. Emond is an experienced fisherman. A local restaurant hired Emond to procure 500 kilograms of herring, which it would freeze and serve to customers over the coming months. The restaurant's herring dishes are popular amongst its customers, and it was imperative that Emond return with a good catch so that the restaurant could meet its demand. Emond set out to sea, only to learn that the area where he normally goes for fish contained very few herring. It was a poor fishing year, and other fishers had already taken the bulk of the herring. There were other areas where Emond could fish for herring, but they were much farther away and Emond did not care to venture so far off course just to get fish for the restaurant. Emond returned empty-handed and the restaurant sued for loss of profits. Emond claimed in his defence that the lack of fish meant that the contract was frustrated and therefore Emond was relieved of his obligations. Will Emond succeed in this argument? Why or why not?

9. Bundy had lived and worked on a farm his entire life. For the past 20 years or so, he had rented most of the farmland to his extended family, since he is no longer fit to work the land himself. Eventually, his family sought to buy the farm from him. After

a couple of years of discussing the purchase, Bundy finally agreed to sell the farm to his nephew for $100 000. An Agreement of Purchase and Sale was drawn up and eventually signed by both parties. A few days later, the nephew paid the 10 percent deposit as required by the contract. He wrote a $10 000 cheque for Bundy and personally drove him to the bank so that he could cash it. Bundy did so but, after a couple of days, he told his nephew that he had made a huge mistake, claiming that the price was too low. Consequently, he refused to transfer title. His nephew brought an action for specific performance. One of Bundy's central claims in the lawsuit was that he was taken advantage of because he never actually read the Agreement of Purchase and Sale prior to signing it. Is the fact that the poor old farmer never read the agreement significant? How will a court respond if Bundy pleads *non est factum*?

10. Mind Games Inc hires CompuNerd to overhaul its entire computer network for a flat fee of $350 000. Marinka, Mind Games's general manager, stresses that the computer upgrades must be finished by the end of July so that there is enough time for Mind Games to complete a large consulting project before its fall deadline. Marinka explains to CompuNerd that a failure to meet these deadlines would cause Mind Games severe financial hardship. From the start, the computer overhaul seems jinxed. Because of several delays, the software upgrades are not quite half finished by the beginning of August. Bernie, the nerd in charge of the upgrades, meets with Marinka that afternoon. He claims that the delays were unavoidable and that CompuNerd is incurring unexpected costs. He insists on renegotiating their agreement to include additional payment for "time and materials." He threatens Marinka by saying that, unless she agrees to the new terms, he will reduce his staff by half. Marinka realizes that such a reduction would mean that the computer upgrades would not be completed for two additional months. Finding herself in a serious bind, Marinka reluctantly agrees to alter the terms of the original flat-fee contract to include additional payment for time and materials. But after the job is finished, Mind Games pays only the originally agreed-upon amount. CompuNerd sues to recover the amount owing under the renegotiated terms. Marinka asks you to determine whether Mind Games is obligated to pay the additional amount. How did you arrive at your conclusion?

11. Coby and Maya immigrate to Canada. Unlike her doctor husband, Maya speaks no English and misses her friends and family terribly. She becomes depressed. Her husband, Coby, prescribes an antidepressant in ever-increasing dosages. Eventually, the couple separates. Maya continues to take her medication. They enter into a separation agreement whereby Coby pays Maya support, but the monthly sum barely covers her rent and living expenses. During divorce proceedings, Maya claims that she was forced into the separation agreement by her overbearing husband and that she was heavily sedated at the time. What is the legal basis of her claim? What must her husband prove to ensure that the separation agreement contract is enforceable?

12. In 1995, Oli Bonli was 88 years old. He owned some land that he agreed to lease to Mr Turner for five years with an option to purchase the land when the lease expired. The purchase price for the land at the end of the five-year lease term was set at $100 000, payable over 20 years at $5000 per year. No interest was payable under the agreement. In fact, the value of the land in 1995 was $167 000, much higher than the purchase price. Land prices in the area were skyrocketing at this time and Mr Turner knew it. At that time, Mr Turner was 47 years old and he personally drafted a written contract on the terms agreed to. He had Mr Bonli come to his office to sign the contract at 7:00 am, when no one was likely to be around. Mr Bonli did not obtain independent legal advice before entering into the contract. Despite being a long-time farmer on the same piece of land, Mr Bonli made two errors in the legal description of his land on the contract. At that time, age was catching up to Mr Bonli—he had good days and bad days when he was very confused. Very shortly after signing the contract, Mr Bonli denied that he had sold his land and told someone that he thought he had actually *bought* land from Mr Turner. In 1996, Mr Bonli was taken to a nursing home as he could no longer care for himself properly. By the end of the lease term in 2000, the value of Mr Bonli's land had risen to $418 000. Mr Turner then sought to exercise his option to purchase the land for $100 000 pursuant to the payment terms of the contract. Mr Bonli's estate refused to sell the land to Mr Turner, claiming that the contract was unconscionable. If you were the judge deciding this case, would you find the contract to be unconscionable? Why or why not?

Discharge and Breach

LEARNING OBJECTIVES

After completing this chapter, you should be able to:

❶ Explain the nature and effect of a discharged contract.

❷ Discuss the manner in which a contract may be discharged by performance.

❸ Describe the circumstances in which a contract can be discharged if a party has not performed in a timely manner.

❹ Explain the difference between a condition subsequent, a true condition precedent, and a condition precedent.

❺ Explain the difference between rescission, accord and satisfaction, and release.

❻ Explain the difference between a variation and a novation.

❼ Describe the circumstances under which a contractual right is waived.

❽ Discuss three situations in which a contract may be discharged by operation of law.

❾ Describe the differences between conditions, warranties, and intermediate terms. Explain the situations in which a contract may be discharged for breach.

❿ Describe three different types of breach.

We have considered the formation of contracts, the contents of contracts, and the ways in which contracts may be defective. We will now finish our general discussion of contracts by examining the end of the contractual process. In this chapter, we will examine the ways in which a contract may be brought to an end. In the next, we will examine the remedies that may be available to the innocent party if a contract is wrongfully brought to an end.

A business person is often keenly interested in knowing whether a contract has been brought to an end. Suppose a manufacturer contractually agrees to deliver 500 computers to a business. Do the manufacturer's obligations come to an end after it delivers the five-hundredth item? If the purchaser wants more computers, does the manufacturer have to supply them? What if some of the computers that have been delivered are defective? Is the manufacturer obligated to repair or replace them? To answer those questions, we must examine the discharge of contracts.

> a contract is **discharged** when the parties are relieved of the need to do anything more under the contract

As we saw in Chapters 9 and 10, some contracts come to an end when they are voided or rescinded. Most contracts, however, are brought to an end through discharge. A contract is **discharged** when the parties are relieved of the need to do anything more under the contract. We will look at a number of ways in which a contract can be discharged. (See Figure 11.1 on the next page.) Some involve performance; others reflect the parties' agreements or intentions; still others arise by operation of law; and one particularly important type of discharge occurs when one party fails to perform as expected. Finally, although there are various ways to bring a contract to an end, it is important to appreciate that a contract generally will not cease to exist merely because the parties largely ignore it. A person who believes otherwise may be in for an unpleasant surprise.[1]

L.O. ❶❷❸

Discharge by Performance

> **performance** occurs when the parties fulfill all the obligations contained in the contract

When parties enter into a contract, they generally assume that everything will go well. And, in fact, the most common method of discharge is *performance*. **Performance** occurs when the parties fulfill all the obligations contained in the contract. In some situations, however, it may be difficult to determine whether proper performance has occurred. Occasionally, it may be possible for a party to perform a contractual obligation in more than one way. For example, a contract may require a security company to check a particular property for intruders between two and four times a night. As long as the company performs twice a night, it is not in breach even if the property owner would have preferred the premises to be checked four times a night.[2] Normally, however, a contract calls for performance in one particular way. As a general rule, the parties must perform *exactly* as the contract requires. Any deviation from the terms of the contract, however small, is considered a breach, rather than performance, and will entitle the innocent party to a remedy.

[1.] *Jedfro Investments (USA) Ltd v Jacyk Estate* (2007) 289 DLR (4th) 385 (SCC).

[2.] *Hamilton v Open Window Bakery Ltd* (2004) 235 DLR (4th) 193 (SCC).

FIGURE 11.1 Methods of Discharge

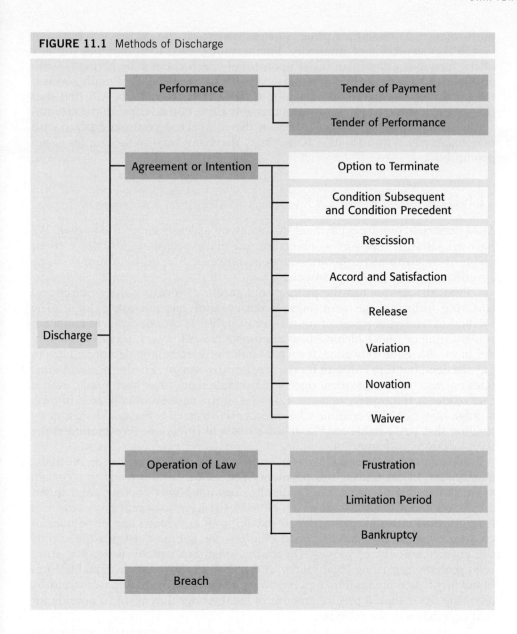

TIME OF PERFORMANCE

Although the parties generally have to perform exactly as the contract says, as a general rule *time is not of the essence*. To say that **time is not of the essence** means that a party is entitled to perform late even if the contract sets a specific date. However, if a party does perform late, it can be held liable for losses that the other party suffers as a result of the delay. Suppose I contractually agree to deliver a vehicle to you by June 1. Although our agreement stipulates that date, I may be allowed to discharge our contract by delivering on June 8. But if I do so, I may be required to compensate you for the fact that you had to rent a car for a week.

In some situations, however, time *is* of the essence. If so, late performance can be refused, and if that happens, the contract will not be discharged by

time is not of the essence means that a party is entitled to perform late even if the contract sets a specific date performance. For example, time is of the essence if the parties agree to that fact, either expressly or impliedly. Furthermore, even if time is not initially of the essence, a party can insist upon timely performance by giving reasonable notice that performance must occur by a specific date. Finally, even if the parties do not agree on a specific time or date, the courts will find that performance must occur within a reasonable time, considering all the circumstances, including the subject matter of the contract. A contract dealing with perishable goods or a volatile market may therefore require the parties to act promptly.

TENDER OF PAYMENT

Most contracts require a payment of money by at least one of the parties. We have all satisfied that sort of obligation on many occasions, usually without giving it much thought. Business people, however, should be aware of some specific rules that govern payments.

First, the debtor has the primary obligation of locating the creditor and *tendering* (offering) payment, even if the creditor has not asked for it. The method of tendering payment must be reasonable. It cannot occur at an inconvenient time or under inconvenient circumstances. However, a reasonable tender has to be made only once. If such a tender is rejected, the debtor still has to pay the debt, but they can wait for the creditor to come by. Furthermore, interest does not accrue on a payment once a reasonable tender has been made, even if that tender is improperly rejected. Likewise, if the case eventually goes to trial, a judge may punish a creditor who improperly rejected a reasonable tender by holding that party liable for the debtor's costs of litigation. (We examined the issue of costs in Chapter 2.)

Second, unless a contract says otherwise, a creditor can insist on receiving *legal tender*. **Legal tender** is a payment of notes (bills) and coins to a certain value.[3] Consequently, a creditor generally does not have to accept payment by way of a cheque or electronic debit. Nor does it have to accept payment from a disgruntled customer who tries to pay with an enormous bag of pennies. A creditor does not even have to make change—the debtor must provide exactly the correct amount of money. Of course, creditors usually waive the strict requirements regarding legal tender and happily receive any acceptable form of payment. As a precaution, however, a business person who intends to pay by anything other than a precise amount of legal tender may want to provide for that possibility in the contract.

Third, despite the usual rule, a debtor does not have to actually tender payment if it would obviously be refused. Consequently, if the creditor indicates beforehand that they intend to reject payment, the debtor does not have to waste time on a useless gesture.

Discharge of a contractual debt by payment of money has both advantages and disadvantages. Money is advantageous because it is absolute. The recipient of money has nothing more to do. Unlike a debit card, a credit card, or a cheque, money is not a means to an end, but rather an end in itself. For much the same reason, however, money carries a significant disadvantage. (The risks associated with money are discussed in more detail at the beginning of Chapter 14.) It is

legal tender is a payment of notes (bills) and coins to a certain value

---

[3.] *Currency Act*, RSC 1985, c C-52, s 8 (Can). In terms of coinage, legal tender consists of up to $40 in two-dollar coins, $25 in one-dollar coins, $10 in quarters, $10 in dimes, $5 in nickels, and 25¢ in pennies.

risky. If money is misplaced or stolen, the owner usually cannot do anything about the loss. Individual coins have no identifying marks. Every note ($5 bills, $10 bills, and so on) does have a unique serial number, but it rarely is known or used.[4] As a result, it is very difficult to locate lost or stolen cash. Furthermore, a person who finds or steals money can easily use it to buy land, goods, or services. And once money passes into the hands of a *bona fide* purchaser for value, it is wiped clean.[5] Even if the original owner miraculously locates the bills or coins, the money cannot be recovered.[6] Because of the risks associated with money, it has become common to discharge a contractual debt by other means. We therefore will briefly look at four common options:

- debit cards
- credit cards
- cheques
- PayPal

Payment by Debit Card

Although they are now very common, debit cards are quite new. The Interac Association, a private corporation that owns and operates the network of automated banking machines (ABMs), was created in 1984, and the Interac system was opened up to general use in 1996. As a result, there are very few cases dealing with the legal aspects of debit cards. For the most part, the basic rules are well settled.

A **debit card** is a plastic card that allows a person to debit, or withdraw, funds from a bank account. The key feature, of course, is that while a debit card can be used at the bank where the account is held, it usually is used at some distant location, such as a store. By swiping the card through a device and typing in a secret personal identification number (PIN), the account holder electronically directs the bank to transfer funds to the merchant. Upon receiving that message, the bank either authorizes or refuses the customer's request, and immediately sends a return message to the merchant. The actual transfer of funds occurs a short time later through the *clearing and settlement system*. At the end of each day, all the information entered into the Interac system is compared and then funds are added or subtracted from each participant's bank account.

Like a payment by cash, a payment by debit card is *final*. Once a bank authorizes or refuses payment, the system no longer plays any role in the transaction that occurs between the merchant and the debit card holder. Any dispute that arises between the other parties (because, for example, the cardholder is unhappy with the goods or services that the merchant provided) must be resolved independently of the debit card system. The cardholder cannot, for instance, *revoke* or cancel the request for payment. In that sense, a debit card is different from a cheque, which the customer can *countermand*, through a "stop payment order," before the merchant "cashes" the cheque.

a **debit card** is a plastic card that allows a person to debit, or withdraw, funds from a bank account

---

[4.] Cash is said to be *fungible*, which means, for example, that one $20 bill is the same as the next. All $20 bills are (virtually) identical and there normally is no advantage or disadvantage to holding one particular $20 bill rather than another.

[5.] A *bona fide* purchaser for value is a person who honestly acquires money in exchange for something else of value.

[6.] The original owner likely has a good action against the person who found or stole the money, but that person usually is impossible to identify.

The most common issue regarding debit cards concerns unauthorized use. Who is responsible if someone other than the cardholder (such as a thief) uses a debit card to obtain cash or buy goods and services? Although the courts are still working out the rules, the answer appears to depend upon the circumstances, including the terms of the contract that was created between the cardholder and the bank. As a general rule, the cardholder is liable if the cardholder is to blame. That is true, for instance, if the cardholder carelessly keeps the card and a record of the PIN number in the same wallet or desk drawer. Cardholders are also responsible if they fail to promptly report the loss or theft of the card to the bank. In contrast, the bank must bear the loss if the cardholder is not to blame for the unauthorized use.[7] That is true, for instance, if the cardholder was forced at knifepoint to give up the card and the PIN number.[8]

Payment by Credit Card

The difference between a debit card and a credit card can be seen by focusing on their names. A debit card works by *debiting*, or withdrawing funds from, the cardholder's bank account. The entire process is completed almost immediately. In contrast, a **credit card** operates by allowing the cardholder to obtain *credit*, or a loan, for the purpose of paying for goods or services. In effect, *credit* is the ability to enjoy value now, with a promise to pay for it later. By providing a credit card to a merchant, the cardholder asks the credit card company, or *card issuer* (often Visa or MasterCard), to arrange credit for a purchase. The merchant usually sends details of the purchase, by electronic means, to the card issuer. The card issuer may accept or reject the customer's request. If the request is accepted, then the credit card company arranges for the merchant to be paid. Later, the card issuer will require the cardholder to repay the credit. In practice, of course, credit card companies seldom demand full repayment immediately. Because they earn money mostly by charging interest on their cardholders' debts, card issuers are happiest when repayment occurs over a very long period.[9]

The use of credit cards involves three relationships, each one governed by contract.[10] It is important to understand how those relationships operate.

- **Card Issuer and Cardholder:** The contract between the cardholder and the card issuer involves a long list of rights and obligations. The essence of that relationship, however, is relatively simple. The card issuer arranges credit by paying for goods or services on the cardholder's behalf.[11] The cardholder, in exchange, promises to repay both the value of each purchase and an agreed-upon rate of interest. The cardholder also promises to pay a minimum amount each month (depending on the size of the total debt), to keep the credit card safe, and to report promptly (usually within 24 hours) the loss or theft of a card.

- **Card Issuer and Merchant:** A customer can pay for a purchase with a credit card only if the merchant has an agreement with the card issuer.

a **credit card** operates by allowing the cardholder to obtain *credit*, or a loan, for the purpose of paying for goods or services

---

[7.] The bank obviously can sue the thief, but most thieves disappear after committing their crimes.

[8.] *MH Ogilvie Bank and Customer Law in Canada* (2007) at 354–355.

[9.] A credit card company may also earn money by charging cardholders annual fees or by requiring merchants to pay a small percentage on each credit card purchase.

[10.] Because of the complexity of the area, as well as the potential for abuse, governments have become involved in credit cards through a web of legislation. Credit card companies are limited, for example, in the rate of interest that they can charge to cardholders.

[11.] The situation is slightly simpler if the card issuer and the merchant are the same party. For example, instead of buying goods at a Zellers store by using a MasterCard, a customer may use a Zellers card.

Most merchants, however, do accept credit cards because of the substantial benefits that they receive. By offering customers another payment option, a merchant increases sales. Even more significantly, in exchange for small fees and a promise to fulfill a number of other obligations, the merchant is relieved of the need to chase after customers for payment of goods and services.[12] Once a transaction has been authorized by the card issuer, that credit card company is obligated to transfer funds to the merchant. If it later becomes clear that the cardholder cannot actually afford the purchase, the loss falls on the card issuer. The merchant is paid in any event.

■ **Cardholder and Merchant:** Aside from providing a means of payment, the relationship between the cardholder and the merchant is not affected by the use of a credit card. Most significantly, once a transaction has been authorized by the card issuer, the cardholder cannot revoke payment if the merchant's goods or services turn out to be defective. The merchant is entitled to retain the funds received from the card issuer and the cardholder remains liable to the card issuer. The cardholder's only option is to sue the merchant on the underlying sales contract.

As with debit cards, one of the most important legal issues for credit cards involves unauthorized use. Some provinces have legislation that generally limits the cardholder's liability to $50.[13] Other provinces, including Ontario (home to more than half of all credit card holders in Canada), rely instead on judge-made rules. The law in that area remains unsettled, but it seems clear that in deciding whether the loss falls upon the cardholder or the card issuer, the courts will look for signs of fault. A cardholder, for example, may be to blame for dealing with a card carelessly or for failing to report a lost or stolen card. Alternatively, the card issuer may be to blame for failing to monitor card use in order to detect a suspicious pattern of use.[14]

Payment by Cheque

Finally, though less popular today than in the past, cheques remain a fairly common source of payment. Because of their importance, cheques (along with other types of negotiable instruments) are discussed in detail in Chapter 14. For now, it is enough to observe that, in contrast to cash or a credit card or a debit card, payment by cheque *conditionally* discharges a contractual debt. Suppose Susan buys goods from a store and pays by cheque. That cheque discharges her debt to the store *unless* something goes wrong. By accepting the cheque, the store agrees to look for payment from Susan's bank. Most likely, the bank will *honour* the cheque, make payment to the store, and then *debit* Susan's chequing account by the same amount. Occasionally, however, a problem may arise and the bank may refuse to honour the cheque. For example, the cheque may be *forged*, Susan may have issued a *stop payment order*, or the bank may realize that Susan's account is *overdrawn* because it does not contain enough credit to cover the cheque. If so, the bank will refuse to pay the store. Susan's original debt will then be revived and the store once again will look to her for payment.

[12.] For instance, the agreement with the card issuer usually requires the merchant to submit documents promptly, provide an invoice to the cardholder, display the credit card company's logo, and so on.

[13.] *Fair Trading Act*, RSA 2000, c F-2, s 89 (Alta); *Consumer Protection Act*, CCSM c C200 (Man).

[14.] Card issuers now often contact cardholders to inquire about sudden or unusual changes in patterns of use.

PART 3

Payment by PayPal

As electronic commerce continues to reshape the way that the world does business, new forms of payment have been developed to allow goods and services to be purchased easily online. (Chapter 19 examines electronic commerce in more detail.) There are many possibilities. One of the most important is PayPal. Although it can be used for many purposes, PayPal is best known from its association with eBay. It is estimated that PayPal has 100 000 000 users worldwide, and that 95 percent of transactions on eBay are completed through PayPal.

PayPal is an example of a third party payment system (3PPS). The company acts as a trusted third party, or "middleman," to facilitate the transfer of funds from the buyer to the seller. The system actually is quite simple. Suppose that you want to buy or sell goods online. You create an account with PayPal by providing the company with your credit card details and information about your bank account. Once your PayPal account is open, you can transfer funds into it from either your credit card or your bank. When PayPal receives your funds, it places them into the company's own (very large) bank account and keeps a record of the amount that is held in your name. You can access your funds by logging onto PayPal's website and typing in your email address and your secret password.

After your account is set up, you can purchase an item you see online through PayPal as long as the seller also has a PayPal account. The transaction can be completed quickly and safely. You simply provide PayPal with the amount of the purchase and the identity of the seller. PayPal then electronically *debits* your account and *credits* the account of the seller.[15] Neither you nor the seller ever has to disclose personal financial details to the other party. And because of its size and reputation, you may be reasonably confident that your funds with PayPal are secure.

TENDER OF PERFORMANCE

Many of the same principles apply when a contract requires the provision of goods or services rather than money. For instance, while the party who owes the obligation is required to properly tender performance, it has to do so only once. Furthermore, that party is discharged of its duty to perform if the other party renders performance impossible. For example, the owner of a piece of land may improperly refuse to allow a building contractor onto the work site. In that situation, the builder, as the innocent party, is entitled to begin a lawsuit immediately to recover *damages*. **Damages**—the amount of money that the court may order the defendant to pay to the plaintiff—are discussed in Chapter 12.

damages are the amount of money that the court may order the defendant to pay to the plaintiff

Substantial Performance

A tender is usually effective only if the goods or services conform precisely to the terms of the contract. Occasionally, however, a party may be discharged from further obligations if it provides *substantial performance*.[16] **Substantial performance** generally satisfies the contract but is defective or incomplete in some minor way.

substantial performance generally satisfies the contract but is defective or incomplete in some minor way

---

[15.] If the price of the purchase exceeds the funds that are contained in your PayPal account, PayPal will charge the additional amount to your credit card.

[16.] *H Dakin & Co Ltd v Lee* [1916] 1 KB 566 (CA).

In deciding whether substantial performance has occurred, a court will consider a number of factors, including the nature of the defect, and the difference between the contract price and the cost of curing the defect. For example, many building contracts state that payment is due only once construction is completed. Nevertheless, if a builder leaves a work site without having installed, say, several doorknobs, they will likely be discharged from their obligations and entitled to payment.

Of course, if a contract is discharged by substantial performance, the innocent party is not required to pay for work that was not done. Continuing on with our example, while the builder might not be required to install the doorknobs, they obviously will not be entitled to be paid for that task. On the contrary, the contract price will be reduced by the amount that the innocent party reasonably paid a third party to install the knobs. That is true even if, for example, the third party reasonably charged $250 for work that the builder could have performed for $100.

A difficult issue may arise if a builder leaves a work site *without* providing at least substantial performance. There are two possibilities. First, the parties may have used a single contract to deal with a series of tasks. In that situation, part of the overall price is earned each time a task is performed. For instance, if the defendant agreed to cut the plaintiff's lawn 10 times in exchange for $100 but performed only twice, a court will likely say that the defendant is entitled to $20.[17]

The second situation is more difficult. Even if their agreement requires a number of tasks to be performed, the parties may create an *entire contract*. An **entire contract** says that *no* part of the price is payable unless *all* of the work is done. The results of that rule are sometimes surprising.[18] Assume, for instance, that a builder agreed to construct a house in exchange for $100 000. After doing half of the job, he ran out of money and stopped work. The landowners then used materials (such as lumber and nails) that the builder had left behind and finished the house themselves. The builder now wants to be paid for both the materials that he left behind and the work that he performed. He will probably be disappointed. According to the traditional rule, the landowners are liable only for those benefits that they *chose* to accept after the builder breached the contract. Since the landowners *chose* to use the discarded materials, they will have to pay for them. But they probably will *not* be liable for the work that the builder performed.[19] The landowners had agreed to pay for a whole house—not half of one. And when the builder abandoned the work site, the landowners were not in a position to accept or reject the work that had been done. As one judge explained, "What is an owner to do? He cannot keep the buildings on his land in an unfinished state forever."[20]

an **entire contract** says that *no* part of the price is payable unless *all* of the work is done

---

[17.] *Kemp v McWilliams* (1978) 87 DLR (3d) 544 (Sask CA). Of course, the innocent party will be entitled to counterclaim for breach of contract. Consequently, if the innocent party had to spend $15 to find another lawn care company to work on the same terms, it will be entitled to damages of $15. By off-setting the price and the damages, the innocent party will therefore pay the difference of $5.

[18.] Not surprisingly, the courts sometimes try to avoid finding that the parties' agreement is an entire contract. They often prefer to find that a party earned part of the overall price each time that part of the contract was performed.

[19.] *Sumpter v Hedges* [1898] 1 QB 673 (CA). The builder's right to payment for the materials did not arise under the contract. Instead, it arose under the cause of action in unjust enrichment, which we will briefly consider in Chapter 12.

[20.] *Sumpter v Hedges* [1898] 1 QB 673 at 676 (CA).

L.O. ❹❺❻❼

Discharge by Agreement

In some situations, one or both parties can discharge a contract even though it was not fully performed. That type of discharge can occur in several ways.

OPTION TO TERMINATE

an **option to terminate** is a contractual provision that allows one or both parties to discharge a contract without the agreement of the other

When creating a contract, the parties can insert an **option to terminate**, which allows one or both of them to discharge the contract without the agreement of the other. That sort of provision is often found in employment contracts. Each party may be permitted to end the relationship on, say, two months' notice.[21] In principle, however, an option to terminate can be inserted into any type of contract.

Options to terminate are frequently subject to restrictions. For example, a party may be entitled to terminate only after giving reasonable notice that it intends to do so. Similarly, the contract may require the party that exercises the option to compensate the other party for the losses that it suffered as a result of the early termination.

CONDITION SUBSEQUENT AND CONDITION PRECEDENT

a **condition subsequent** is a contractual term that states that the agreement will be terminated if a certain event occurs

When creating a contract, the parties can also insert a **condition subsequent**, a contractual term that states that the agreement will be terminated if a certain event occurs. A condition subsequent is different from an option to terminate because it does not have to be exercised by either party to be effective. Under a condition subsequent, a contract may be automatically discharged as soon as the relevant event happens. For example, the contract represented by a ticket to an open-air concert may state that the musicians' obligation to perform is discharged in the event of rain. If so, the contract will probably also entitle the disappointed ticket holder to either a refund or a ticket to another event.

a **true condition precedent** is a contractual term that states that an agreement will come into existence only if and when a certain event occurs

A contract that is subject to a condition subsequent exists until the relevant event occurs. It is also possible, however, to make a contract subject to a true condition precedent. A **true condition precedent** is a contractual term that states that an agreement will come into existence only if and when a certain event occurs.[22] Suppose you and I want to deal in a specific type of weapon, but we are concerned that such a contract may be illegal. We can settle the terms of the agreement but state that our contract will actually be created only if it receives government approval. In that situation, we would not have a contract, and therefore would not break the law, if government approval were refused.

a **condition precedent** is a contractual term that states that while a contract is formed immediately, it does not have to be performed unless and until a certain event occurs

Strictly speaking, a condition subsequent causes an existing contract to come to an end if a certain event occurs, whereas a true condition precedent allows a contract to come into existence only if a certain event occurs. Unfortunately, Canadian courts also use the phrase **condition precedent** to refer to a contractual term that states that while a contract is formed immediately, it does not have to be performed unless and until a certain event occurs. As we will see in Chapter 16, that type of condition precedent is very common in contracts for the sale of land. Consider the example in Business Decision 11.1.

[21.] As discussed in Chapter 26, if an employment contract does not contain such a provision, the courts will allow the contract to be terminated on "reasonable notice."

[22.] *Pym v Campbell* (1856) 119 ER 903 (KB).

Business Decision 11.1

Condition Precedent[23]

Yuri offers to sell his house to you for $250 000. You are eager to accept that offer, but you do not want to completely commit yourself to the purchase until you are sure that you can sell your own cottage for at least $200 000. You and Yuri therefore agree on the terms for the sale of Yuri's house, but state that the performance of that contract is conditional on your ability to find a buyer for your cottage within 30 days.

Although the relevant term of your agreement will be called a "condition precedent," it will not affect the *existence* of the contract between you and Yuri. It will merely *suspend* your obligations to perform. In other words, your contract occurs immediately, but unless and until you are able to find a buyer for your cottage, you do not have to pay $250 000 to Yuri and he does not have to transfer his house to you. Furthermore, if you cannot find a buyer for your cottage within 30 days, your contract with Yuri will be discharged.

Questions for Discussion

1. Why would you want to enter into such an agreement?

2. Why would Yuri agree to such an agreement?

Notice two more things about the type of condition precedent discussed in Business Decision 11.1. First, because a contract exists from the outset, Yuri is not entitled to sell his house to another person during the 30-day period. If he does, he will be in breach of his contract with you. After all, he has only one house to sell and he has already agreed to sell it to you. To avoid that problem, Yuri probably insisted on having another term inserted into your contract. That term will be activated if Yuri receives an offer from another potential purchaser. In that situation, you will have a limited amount of time (say, three days) to either find a buyer for your cottage or somehow come up with the money to buy Yuri's house. If you fail to do so, your contract with Yuri will be discharged and he will be free to sell his house to the other purchaser.

Second, while a condition precedent may suspend the *primary* obligations under an existing contract, one or both parties may have *subsidiary* obligations that they are required to perform right away. For example, while you would not have to pay the purchase price for Yuri's house immediately, you probably would have to make a reasonable effort to satisfy the condition precedent by finding a purchaser for your cottage. If you failed to do so, you could be held liable for the losses that you cause by breaching that subsidiary obligation.[24]

Concept Summary 11.1 shows the differences between conditions subsequent, true conditions precedent, and conditions precedent.

Concept Summary 11.1

Conditions Subsequent, True Conditions Precedent, and Conditions Precedent

Type of Condition	Time of Creation of Contract	Effect of Condition
Condition subsequent	immediate	discharge of existing contract
True condition precedent	if and when condition is satisfied	creation of contract
Condition precedent	immediate	suspension of primary obligations

---

23. *Wiebe v Bobsein* [1986] 1 WWR 270 (BC CA).

24. *Dynamic Transport Ltd v OK Detailing Ltd* (1978) 85 DLR (3d) 19 (SCC).

RESCISSION

Options to terminate, conditions subsequent, and conditions precedent are ways in which the parties can agree, *when initially creating a contract*, that their obligations will be discharged in certain circumstances. The same sort of agreement can also be reached *after* a contract has been created.

First, we must distinguish between *executory contracts* and *executed contracts*. A contract is **executory** if a party has not fully performed its obligations. A contract is **executed** if a party has fully performed its obligations.

If a contract is executory on both sides, it can be discharged through *rescission*. **Rescission** occurs when the parties agree to bring their contract to an end.[25] That agreement may be express or implied. For example, the parties may enter into a new contract that necessarily implies the discharge of an earlier one. Suppose I agree to sell my car to you for $5000. If, before executing that agreement, we enter into another contract that calls upon me to deliver my car and my boat to you in exchange for $7500, the second contract necessarily implies the rescission of the first. After all, we both know that I have only one car to sell.

As Chapter 8 explained, an agreement is usually enforceable only if it is supported by *consideration*. Each party must provide a benefit or suffer a detriment. If an executory contract is rescinded, that requirement is easily satisfied. Each party suffers a detriment by giving up the right to insist upon performance of the original contract.

> a contract is **executory** if a party has not fully performed its obligations
>
> a contract is **executed** if a party has fully performed its obligations
>
> **rescission** occurs when the parties agree to bring their contract to an end

ACCORD AND SATISFACTION

The situation is more difficult if one party has fully performed, or *executed*, the contract. In that case, a mere agreement to discharge a contract may be unenforceable for lack of consideration. The party that has not performed cannot suffer a detriment by giving up the right to insist upon performance. After all, the other party has already performed. Consider the case in You Be the Judge 11.1.

You Be the Judge 11.1

Accord and Satisfaction

Miles and Sudevi entered into a contract. He agreed to repair her roof and she promised to drill a water well on his farm. Miles immediately fulfilled his obligation by repairing Sudevi's roof. Sudevi later discovered, however, that contrary to her initial assumption, Miles's farm is situated on rock rather than sand. She also realized that she did not have the type of equipment required to drill a well through rock. Miles took pity on her and generously agreed to simply discharge their contract.

Questions for Discussion

1. Did Sudevi provide consideration in exchange for Miles's agreement to discharge the contract? Could she provide consideration by releasing Miles from his obligation to repair her roof?

2. Is Miles required to honour his promise to discharge the contract?

[25.] This use of the term "rescission" must be distinguished from the way in which "rescission" was discussed in Chapter 9. The word has a very different meaning depending upon the situation. In this chapter, the word refers to a *bilateral*, or two-party, agreement to discharge a contract. In the context of contracts induced by fraud, misrepresentation, or mistake, the same word refers to a *unilateral*, or one-party, decision by the innocent party to terminate a contract. In the one case, the parties effectively create a new contract to get rid of an old contract. No one has done anything wrong. In the other case, the innocent party decides to escape a contract that the other party wrongfully created. It would be better, of course, if a completely different word were used in one of those situations.

The agreement to discharge the original contract in the last exercise would have been enforceable if there had been *accord and satisfaction*. **Accord and satisfaction** occurs when a party gives up its right to demand contractual performance in return for some new benefit. "Accord" refers to the parties' new agreement; "satisfaction" refers to the new consideration provided by the party that is relieved of the need to perform the original contract. Suppose Miles's second agreement with Sudevi (the accord) required her promise to build a water tank on his property (the satisfaction). If so, he could not require Sudevi to perform the original contract. In effect, by promising to build a water tank, she would have bought the right to not drill the well.

accord and satisfaction occurs when a party gives up its right to demand contractual performance in return for some new benefit

Accord and satisfaction requires fresh consideration. It is, however, sometimes difficult to determine whether or not a party has given anything new. In that regard, we must remember some of the rules that we saw in Chapter 8. It is especially important to appreciate that, as a general rule, a promise to pay a smaller sum cannot discharge an obligation to pay a larger amount. For example, if I am contractually obliged to pay $5000 to you, but do not have that much on hand, I might ask if you would agree to take $4000 in satisfaction of my entire debt. Even if you agree to that proposal, you probably are still entitled to sue for the remaining $1000. There are, however, exceptions to that rule.

RELEASE

The parties can agree to discharge a contract without fresh consideration if they enter into a *release*. A **release** is an agreement under seal to discharge a contract. As we saw in Chapter 8, a seal serves as a substitute for consideration. As a result, an agreement can be enforceable even if it is not supported by an exchange of value.

a **release** is an agreement under seal to discharge a contract

VARIATION

Parties usually use an accord and satisfaction, or a release, when they want to terminate a contractual relationship. In some situations, however, they may want to retain their agreement, but in a modified form. **Variation** involves an agreement to alter the terms of an existing contract.

variation involves an agreement to vary the terms of an existing contract

A variation requires fresh consideration on both sides of the agreement. A party usually provides consideration either by giving up rights that it held under the original terms of the contract, or by accepting new obligations under the modified terms of the contract.

Suppose Stefan and Nicole enter into a contract. He promises to cut her lawn 20 times during the summer, and she agrees to pay a lump sum of $200 at the end of the season. However, spring arrives unusually late, and Nicole's lawn will not require as much attention as expected. The parties might agree to vary their contract by requiring Stefan to perform only 15 times and by requiring Nicole to pay only $150. If so, Stefan provides consideration by giving up the right to $50 and Nicole provides consideration by giving up the right to lawn care on five occasions.

NOVATION

Variation can be used to introduce small changes to an existing contract. However, if the parties want to introduce substantial changes that go to the root of their agreement, they can use *novation*. Broadly speaking, **novation** is a process in which one contract is discharged and replaced with another.

novation is a process in which one contract is discharged and replaced with another

The new contract may differ from the old one because it imposes significantly different obligations on the same parties. Suppose Lucy owns two neighbouring properties, called Blackacre and Whiteacre. She initially agrees to sell Blackacre to Ricardo. If she later discovers that she is unable to perform that contract, she might offer to sell Whiteacre instead. If Ricardo agrees to that proposal, the parties could discharge their original agreement for Blackacre and replace it with a new agreement for Whiteacre.

Usually, however, novation involves a substitution of parties rather than obligations. The Supreme Court of Canada has defined novation as "a *trilateral* agreement by which an existing contract is extinguished and a new contract is brought into being in its place."[26] In that situation, the parties under the new contract essentially adopt the rights and liabilities that existed under the old contract. For instance, in order to purchase a piece of land, you might have borrowed money from a bank and given it a mortgage over your new property. If you later decided to sell the land to me, and if I also required a mortgage in order to afford the property, the bank might agree to a novation. In effect, I would step into your shoes. I would acquire the land, but I would also assume the debt under the mortgage.

There are several things to notice about novations. First, a novation cannot occur unless all of the affected parties consent to the new arrangement. Second, whether new obligations or new parties are introduced, the agreement to discharge the old contract is supported by consideration. The parties to the original contract agree to give up their rights under that agreement. Third, although novation can be achieved either expressly or impliedly, as a matter of risk management, the agreement should always be clearly written.

WAIVER

We have seen a number of situations in which the parties agree to discharge their contractual obligations. In each instance, the agreement is enforceable only if it is supported by consideration or a seal. However, a promise to discharge or suspend a contractual obligation may be enforceable even without consideration or a seal.

waiver occurs when a party abandons a right to insist on contractual performance

Waiver occurs when a party abandons a right to insist on contractual performance.[27] There are several points to notice. First, waiver does *not* require consideration or a seal. It operates as an exception to the general rule that the courts will not enforce gratuitous promises. Second, waiver does not have to take any particular form. It can be either written or oral, and either express or implied. Third, because waiver allows a contractual party to obtain a benefit without providing anything in return, the courts require clear evidence that the other party intended to waive its rights. Fourth, although the cases are somewhat inconsistent, the better view is that waiver is effective only if the party who received the waiver relied upon it. And finally, a party can retract its own waiver if it gives reasonable notice of its intention to do so *and* if retraction is not unfair to the other party. Case Brief 11.1 illustrates these rules.

---

[26] *National Trust Co v Mead* (1990) 71 DLR (4th) 488 at 500 (SCC).

[27] Waiver is similar to the concept of promissory estoppel, which we examined in Chapter 8. Some commentators suggest that the main difference between the two is simply jurisdictional. Waiver was developed by the courts of law, and promissory estoppel was developed by the courts of equity. The distinction between law and equity was discussed in Chapter 1.

Case Brief 11.1

*Maritime Life Assurance Company v Saskatchewan River
Bungalows Ltd* (1994) 115 DLR (4th) 478 (SCC)

Maritime Life Assurance (MLA) sold an insurance policy to Saskatchewan River Bungalows (SRB) on the life of Mr Fikowski. The contract required the premium (that is, the price) to be received at the insurer's head office in Halifax by July 26 of each year. In 1984, SRB sent a cheque for the premium on July 24, but that letter was lost in the mail. At that point, MLA was entitled to terminate the policy for non-payment. Nevertheless, it sent a number of notices that offered to accept late payment. By February 1985, however, it ran out of patience and sent a letter stating that the policy had been cancelled. In April, SRB collected its mail for the first time in many months and finally became aware that MLA had not received the cheque for the premium. It then waited another three months before delivering a replacement cheque. Unfortunately, by that time, Mr Fikowski had

fallen ill and died soon after. SRB then claimed a benefit under the life insurance policy and argued that MLA had waived its right to timely payment because it had not insisted on strict performance under the contract.

The Supreme Court of Canada held that MLA had implicitly waived its right to timely payment when it offered to accept late payment. However, the court also held that MLA was entitled to retract its waiver. Furthermore, because SRB received notice that the policy was cancelled at the same time that it received the insurer's earlier offer to accept late payment (April 1985), it had not relied upon that offer. Consequently, MLA was not required to give reasonable notice of its intention to retract its waiver. The result was that SRB could not collect a benefit under the life insurance policy when Mr Fikowski died.

We have considered a number of ways in which a contract may be discharged before it is complete. Concept Summary 11.2 reviews two essential features of those various possibilities.

Concept Summary 11.2

Discharge by Agreement

	Consideration	Usual Effect on Contract
Option to terminate	part of original contract	contract terminated
Condition subsequent and condition precedent	part of original contract	contract terminated
Rescission	each party gives up rights under contract	contract terminated
Accord and satisfaction	one party gives up old right—other party provides new consideration	contract varied
Release	seal	contract terminated
Variation	each party either gives up old rights or provides new consideration	contract varied
Novation	each party gives up rights under old contract	contract varied or replaced
Waiver	none	contract varied

Discharge by Operation of Law

L.O. ❽

We have examined contracts that are discharged by performance or by agreement of the parties. However, a contract may also be discharged by operation of law. In this section, we will briefly consider three situations in which that frequently happens:

- frustration
- lapse of limitation period
- bankruptcy

FRUSTRATION

As Chapter 10 explained, a contract is *frustrated* when it becomes impossible to perform or when the circumstances change so much that performance would be something much different from what the parties initially expected. One result of frustration is that the parties are, as a matter of law, discharged from performing any remaining obligations.

LAPSE OF LIMITATION PERIOD

statutes of limitation require a party who has suffered a breach of contract to sue within a certain period

The need to perform a contractual obligation can also be displaced by the passage of time. **Statutes of limitation** require a party who has suffered a breach of contract to sue within a certain period (usually either two or six years, depending upon the jurisdiction). (Additional information regarding limitation periods can be found in Chapter 2.) There are two main reasons for that legislation: First, the courts do not want to deal with claims if the evidence is old and unreliable. Second, it is unfair to hold the threat of a lawsuit over a person's head for a very long time.

Technically speaking, a contract is not usually discharged if a person fails to sue within the required time. That person is simply prevented from starting legal proceedings. There are, however, exceptions to that rule. Most significantly, the right to sue may be revived, even after the lapse of the limitation period, if the party that broke the contract acknowledges that it is still liable. It might do so by paying part of its outstanding debt. Consider Ethical Perspective 11.1.

Ethical Perspective **11.1**

Limitation Periods

Twelve years ago, you entered into a contract with Estevan Flooring Inc for the installation of a hardwood dance floor in your tavern. Estevan Flooring completed the work and delivered a bill for $7500. Unfortunately, your tavern had fallen on hard times and you were able to pay only $2500. In the circumstances, the owner of Estevan Flooring saw little point in suing you for the rest of the money. In the past two years, however, your tavern has become very popular and prosperous. Estevan Flooring therefore has asked you for the remaining $5000, plus interest.

It has done so despite being informed by its lawyer that the statutory limitation period has expired.

Questions for Discussion

1. Will you pay the remainder of the bill that you initially received from Estevan Flooring?

2. Is your decision based strictly on legal considerations? Is it influenced by commercial considerations? By moral considerations? To what extent do those different considerations overlap?

BANKRUPTCY

Bankruptcy is discussed at length in Chapter 24. Here, it is enough to note that a bankrupt debtor is discharged from outstanding contractual obligations *if* the bankruptcy was caused by misfortune rather than by misconduct.[28]

[28.] *Bankruptcy and Insolvency Act*, RSC 1985, c B-3, s 175 (Can).

Discharge by Breach of Condition

L.O. **9** **10**

Finally, a contract may be discharged if one of its *terms*, or promises, is broken. As we saw in the discussion on discharge by performance, a contract must be strictly performed. Consequently, a **breach** occurs whenever a party does not perform precisely as promised. However, not every breach will result in the discharge of a contract.

a **breach** occurs whenever a party does not perform precisely as promised

TYPES OF TERMS

According to the traditional approach, the law distinguishes between two types of contractual terms. First, a term is a **condition** if the innocent party would be substantially deprived of the expected benefit of the contract if a breach occurred.[29] For example, if a rental company delivers a minivan, instead of a large moving truck as it promised, the customer receives something much different than expected. Furthermore, given the serious consequences of the company's breach, it would be unfair to require the customer to carry on with the contract by accepting the vehicle and paying for it, even at a reduced price. Since the customer is deprived of the essence of what they expected to receive, they should not be required to uphold their end of the bargain. Consequently, the customer enjoys an option. They can choose to continue on with the contract and merely claim damages for the losses that they suffered because they received a minivan instead of a large moving truck. Or they can choose to discharge the contract and claim damages for the losses that they suffered as a result of the breach. Notice, then, that the breach of a condition does not automatically discharge a contract. Nor can a party generally bring a contract to an end simply by breaching a condition. The right of discharge lies with the innocent party.

a term is a **condition** if the innocent party would be substantially deprived of the expected benefit of the contract if a breach occurred

Second, a term is a **warranty** if the innocent party would *not* be substantially deprived of the expected benefit of the contract if a breach occurred. Suppose a rental company properly delivers a large moving truck but, contrary to its promise, the vehicle has not been fully cleaned. Given the relatively insignificant nature of that breach, it is fair to require the customer to carry on with the contract. They are, after all, still receiving the essence of what they expected to receive. Consequently, a breach of warranty does *not* provide the innocent party with the option of discharging the contract. Although that party can claim damages for any losses that they suffered as a result of the breach (for example, by cleaning the truck before using it), they must continue on with the contract.

a term is a **warranty** if the innocent party would *not* be substantially deprived of the expected benefit of the contract if a breach occurred

While the courts generally continue to follow the traditional approach, they have recently recognized that some contractual terms cannot be treated so simply. Historically, it was thought that every term could be classified, as soon as a contract was formed, as either (i) a condition, which would support the right of discharge if breached, or (ii) a warranty, which would not. That view can lead to unfair or inconvenient results. It is sometimes clear that the breach of a particular term will, or will not, substantially deprive the innocent party of the expected benefit of a contract. But often, a seemingly important term may be breached in a trivial way, or a seemingly unimportant term may be breached in a significant way. For example, the courts have occasionally held that the date of shipment is a condition of a contract, and that if goods are shipped one day earlier or later than agreed, the innocent party is entitled to discharge the contract, even if they did

PART 3

---

29. We must carefully distinguish "condition" as it is used in this context from the same word as it was used in the context of "conditions subsequent" and "conditions precedent."

not suffer a loss as a result of the breach.[30] That result may be difficult to justify, especially if the innocent party discharges the contract only because they wanted a way out of a contract that they realized was unprofitable.

To avoid that sort of situation, the courts now recognize a third type of term that applies when the consequences of a breach are not obvious at the outset. A term is **intermediate** if, depending upon the circumstances, the innocent party may or may not be substantially deprived of the expected benefit of the contract in the event of breach.[31] As you would expect, the innocent party may or may not have the right to discharge the contract if an intermediate term is breached. The existence of that right depends upon whether the breach *in fact* substantially deprived that party of the expected benefit of the agreement. In that sense, intermediate terms are "wait-and-see" terms. Case Brief 11.2 provides an excellent example.

a term is **intermediate** if, depending upon the circumstances, the innocent party may or may not be substantially deprived of the expected benefit of the contract in the event of breach

Case Brief 11.2

Hong Kong Fir Shipping Co v Kawasaki Kisen Kaisha Ltd [1962] 2 QB 26 (CA)

The plaintiff owned a ship that they chartered (rented) to the defendant for 24 months. The defendant wanted the ship so that they could conduct a business of transporting goods for others. A term of the contract required the plaintiff to provide a "seaworthy" vessel. The contract also stated that if the ship was out of service for repairs during the life of the agreement, the defendant would be entitled to extend the duration of the contract by the appropriate length of time. In fact, the ship was out of commission for four months near the beginning of the contract because its engines required extensive repairs. The defendant therefore attempted to discharge the agreement on the basis of the plaintiff's breach of condition. The plaintiff, however, denied that they had breached a condition. Indeed, they claimed that the defendant had breached a condition of the contract when they tried to discharge the agreement.

The English Court of Appeal held for the plaintiff. It said that the seaworthiness term could be breached in a variety of ways, some serious and others trivial. For example, a ship might be unseaworthy either because its hull was irreparably pierced or because its toilets did not work quite right. The disputed term therefore was classified as an intermediate term, which would support a right of discharge only if its breach substantially deprived the defendant of the expected benefit of the agreement. And in the circumstances, the court held that the defendant could still enjoy the essence of the agreement even though the vessel required extensive repairs during the initial part of the contract. Despite the period of repair, the contract still provided the defendant with an opportunity to act as a carrier for 24 months. As a result, the defendant became liable for a breach of contract when they wrongfully claimed to discharge the agreement.

Concept Summary 11.3 shows the basic differences between conditions, warranties, and intermediate terms.

Concept Summary 11.3

Conditions, Warranties, and Intermediate Terms

Type of Term	Effect of Breach on Innocent Party	Rights of Innocent Party
Condition	substantially deprived of benefit of contract	discharge contract and claim damages or continue with contract and claim damages
Warranty	not substantially deprived of benefit of contract	continue with contract and claim damages
Intermediate	depends upon circumstances—may or may not be substantially deprived of benefit of contract	depends upon seriousness of breach—discharge contract and claim damages or continue with contract and claim damages

---

[30] *Bowes v Shand* (1877) 2 App Cas 455 (HL).

[31] Lawyers sometimes use the phrase "innominate term" instead. That type of term is innominate, or unnamed, because it is not named either a "condition" or a "warranty."

It is often difficult to distinguish between conditions, warranties, and intermediate terms. The parties can expressly state that the breach of a certain term will or will not support a right of discharge. A statute may also classify a term as either a condition or a warranty.[32] Usually, however, a judge must decide the issue by examining all of the circumstances. In essence, the court asks whether the parties, as reasonable people, would have intended to allow the innocent party to bring the contract to an end in the particular situation. In doing so, the judge may be influenced by the portion of the total performance that is defective, the likelihood that the breach will be repeated in the future if the contract calls for performance by instalments, and the seriousness of the breach to the innocent party.

As a matter of risk management, notice that uncertainty regarding the classification of terms often creates the sort of dilemma that arose in *Hong Kong Fir Shipping*. You may believe that the other party breached the contract in a way that allows you to discharge the agreement and sue for damages. But if you are wrong about that, *you* may commit a breach that allows the other party to discharge the contract and sue *you* for damages. Consequently, in a doubtful case, you should seek legal advice before attempting to discharge a contract for breach. You should also be aware, however, that even your lawyer may not be able to predict how a judge will interpret the situation. Business Decision 11.2 illustrates that difficulty.

Business Decision 11.2

Discharging for Breach

You wanted to operate a live-bait kiosk during a week-long fishing competition at Lake Katenben. Although you expected to sell some of the worms to recreational anglers, you assumed that most of your sales would be to the competitors. You entered into a contract with LJ, a local farmer, which required him to deliver 10 kilograms of worms to you each morning at 3:00 am for the seven days that the fishing competition was scheduled to run. LJ properly performed on the first day, but he did not deliver the second day's box of worms until 9:30 am. Although you were able to sell a small portion of the second day's shipment to recreational anglers, you sold nothing to the competitive anglers, who had all left the dock before sunrise.

You are in a dilemma. On the one hand, you know that if you miss another day of trade with the competitive anglers, you will probably not earn a profit during the week-long competition. You also know that if you discharge your contract with LJ, you can arrange an alternative supply of worms without difficulty. On the other hand, you are worried that if LJ's single late delivery does not really justify discharge, you will be liable to him in breach of contract.

Questions for Discussion

1. Should you attempt to discharge your contract with LJ?

2. Would it be relevant that LJ's breach was caused by his difficulty in finding 10 kilograms of worms on the second night? What if his breach was caused by the fact that he was involved in an automobile accident at 2:00 am while driving to deliver the load of worms to you?

3. Would it be relevant if the competition lasted one month rather than one week?

TYPES OF BREACH[33]

Whether it applies to a condition, a warranty, or an intermediate term, a breach can occur in one of four ways:

- defective performance
- deviation
- anticipatory breach
- self-induced impossibility

[32.] That is true under the *Sale of Goods Act*, which is discussed in Chapter 13.

[33.] We will consider the issue of "fundamental breach" in the next chapter when we discuss exclusion clauses.

Defective Performance

defective performance occurs when a party fails to properly perform an obligation due under a contract

Most breaches take the form of *defective performance*. **Defective performance** occurs when a party fails to properly perform an obligation due under a contract. That idea is quite broad. It includes a complete lack of performance. For example, a photographer may entirely fail to attend a wedding that he was expected to capture on film. It also includes a relatively trivial departure from the terms of a contract. For example, a wedding photographer may take 475 pictures, rather than the promised minimum of 500. Significantly, a departure from the terms of a contract will create a breach, even if it does not cause the performance to be any less valuable. Consequently, a vendor who agrees to deliver 3000 tins of canned fruit in cartons containing 30 tins each commits a breach of contract by delivering the same number of tins in cartons of 24. The buyer is entitled to reject the delivery.[34] An exception is made only if the defect in performance truly is trivial. *De minimis non curat lex* ("the law does not concern itself with trifles").

Deviation

deviation occurs when a ship, train, or truck departs from the route agreed upon by the parties

A particular type of defective performance takes the form of *deviation*. Although that term sometimes is used to refer to any failure to act precisely in accordance with contractual obligations, it also carries a narrower definition in the context of a contract for the carriage of goods by land or sea. **Deviation** occurs when a ship, train, or truck departs from the route agreed upon by the parties. In one leading case, goods were to be shipped, by sea, from Singapore to New York. The goods instead were taken by sea from Singapore to Seattle, and then by train to New York. The contract was broken.[35]

The effect of deviation can be dramatic. Not only is the carrier in breach of contract, but it may lose the benefit of any contractual limitation or exclusion clause that normally would reduce or eliminate liability. The same may be true if, for instance, a carrier breaks a promise to place goods below deck by storing them instead above deck. A contract may also be breached if goods are not shipped within a stipulated time period or if goods are not shipped by a designated carrier.[36] While that rule may seem harsh, it is justified by the parties' allocation of risks. In contracts of carriage, insurance is all-important. Because the owner of goods may lose insurance coverage if a shipment deviates from its expected course, it is appropriate to shift the risk of loss onto the carrier, who is responsible for the deviation.

Anticipatory Breach

anticipatory breach occurs when a party indicates in advance, by words or conduct, that it does not intend to fulfill an obligation when it falls due under a contract

Defective performance applies to an obligation that is already due. An *anticipatory breach* occurs before an obligation is scheduled to be performed. **Anticipatory breach** occurs when a party indicates in advance, by words or conduct, that it does not intend to fulfill an obligation when it falls due under a contract. Generally, the same rules apply to an anticipatory breach as to other types of breach. For example, depending upon the seriousness of the situation, the breach may or may not entitle the innocent party to discharge the contract. And even if an anticipatory breach is serious enough to support discharge, a contract will not actually be brought to an end unless the innocent party chooses to do so. As an English judge poetically said, "An unaccepted repudiation is like a thing writ in water and of no value to anybody."[37]

---

34. *Re Moore & Co and Landauer & Co* [1921] 2 KB 519 (CA).
35. *Re L Sutro & Co and Heilbut Symons & Co* [1917] 2 KB 348 (CA).
36. *California Prune and Apricot Growers Inc v Baird and Peters* [1926] 1 DLR 314 (SCC).
37. *Howard v Pickford Tool Co* [1951] 1 KB 417 at 421 (CA) *per* Asquith LJ.

The innocent party is entitled to seek relief *immediately* if there is an anticipatory breach. There is no need to wait until the time when the obligation was to be performed. Suppose you enter into a contract to rent a cottage for the summer months. If the landlord contacts you in February and states that the premises will not be available, you do not have to wait until June before suing.

If an anticipatory breach is serious enough to support discharge, the innocent party must make a decision. They may reject the breach, claim damages, and carry on with the contract. Or they may accept the breach, claim damages, and discharge the other party from future performance. In either event, however, the innocent party will be held to the choice that they make. Suppose you agreed to carry my cattle on your truck at the beginning of September. In July, I called to say that the animals would not be ready on time. You rejected my breach and insisted that we perform as planned. We each receive a surprise at the end of August: I am delighted to discover that my cattle are ready after all, but you are saddened to discover that your truck requires repairs and will not be available until October. Now *you* are liable to *me* for breach of contract.

Self-Induced Impossibility

As we saw in Chapter 10, a contract is discharged for frustration if, through no fault of either party, it becomes impossible to perform. However, if the impossibility is caused by one of the parties, then that party will be held liable for breach. Suppose I agree to deliver a specific cord of firewood to you by January 1. If I burn that wood in my own fireplace during December, I have made the contract impossible to perform. Consequently, you will be entitled to discharge our contract and claim damages from me.

THE EFFECT OF DISCHARGE

It is important to understand the consequences of discharge. In Chapters 9 and 10, we examined contracts that were rescinded or voided. In those situations, the contracts are wiped out altogether, as if they had never existed. The effect of discharging a contract for breach is quite different. The parties are merely relieved of the need to perform their primary obligations in the future. For example, once the contract in *Hong Kong Fir Shipping* was discharged, the owner no longer had to provide a seaworthy ship, and the charterer no longer had to pay for the use of the ship. Discharge does not, however, wipe out the contract altogether. The agreement survives for the purposes of contractual liability. Returning to *Hong Kong Fir Shipping*, the owner would have to rely on the contract to sue the charterer for damages. Similarly, if the contract contained an exclusion clause that limited the charterer's liability, that clause would have effect because the contract would still be alive for that purpose. (Exclusion clauses were examined in Chapter 9. We will consider them again in Chapter 12.)

Factors Affecting the Right to Discharge

Even if a contract is breached in a way that would normally support a right of discharge, that right may be lost if, for example, the innocent party chooses to continue on with the agreement. Discharge may also be impossible if the party in breach provided a benefit that the innocent party cannot return. In that situation, the innocent party must perform their own obligations under the contract and be content with a claim for damages. Suppose a lawn care company breaches a contract by spreading an inferior grade of fertilizer on your lawn. Because the fertilizer cannot be returned, you do not have the option of discharging the contract. You can, however, claim damages for the fact that you received an inferior product.

Chapter Summary

A contract may be discharged by performance if both parties completely or substantially fulfill their obligations. Time is usually not of the essence, but it may be in some circumstances. A tender of payment or performance must be reasonable; but, once done, it need not be repeated. Payment and performance do not have to be tendered if a tender would clearly be rejected. In some situations, a contract may be discharged if one party has provided substantial performance.

A contract may be discharged by agreement in a number of ways:

■ A contract may contain an option to terminate that allows one or both parties to bring that contract to an end without the agreement of the other.

■ A contract may be automatically discharged on the basis of a condition subsequent if a specified event occurs. In contrast, a contract that is subject to a condition precedent does not exist unless and until the specified event occurs.

■ An executory contract can be rescinded if both parties agree to do so. Each party provides consideration by releasing the other from the obligation to perform the original contract.

■ A partially executed contract may be discharged by accord and satisfaction. If so, the party that has yet to fully perform must provide new consideration.

■ A contract may be discharged by a release if the parties make an agreement under seal to terminate the contract.

■ The terms of a contract may be subject to variation if each party provides consideration for the alterations.

■ A contract may be discharged and replaced with a new contract under the process of novation. If so, consideration for the new contract consists of the parties' agreement not to enforce the terms of the original contract.

■ Performance of a contractual obligation may be waived by the party that was not required to perform the obligation.

A contract can be discharged by law if it is frustrated or if a contractual party becomes bankrupt. Similarly, although the passage of time does not technically discharge a contract, it may prevent a party from suing for breach of contract.

Breach of contract may involve the breach of a condition, a warranty, or an intermediate term. Classification of a term generally depends on whether a breach substantially deprives the innocent party of the expected benefit of the contract. The innocent party is entitled to discharge a contract only if the breached term is a condition or an intermediate term that has resulted in a substantial deprivation. A term may be breached through (i) defective performance of an obligation that has fallen due, (ii) deviation from the strict terms of the contract, (iii) anticipatory breach of an obligation that has yet to fall due, or (iv) self-induced impossibility.

MyBusLawLab   ADDITIONAL RESOURCES FOR CHAPTER 11

MyBusLawLab provides students with an assortment of tools to help enrich the learning experience, including a Study Plan with Pre- and Post-tests, mini-cases with assessments, and provincial content material, which provides links to relevant cases, legislation, and additional resources.

MyBusLawLab provides the following resources for Chapter 11:

Provincial Material

■ **British Columbia:** Tender of Payment, Tender of Performance, Frustrated Contracts, Limitation Periods, Credit Cards

■ **Alberta:** Credit Cards, Fundamental Breach, Frustration, Limited Periods, Substantial Performance

■ **Manitoba and Saskatchewan:** Conditions and Warranties, *Frustrated Contracts Act*, *Limitations Act*

■ **Ontario:** Effect of Frustration, Exemption Clauses, Fundamental Breach, Limitation Periods, Options to Terminate, Substantial Performance

■ **Atlantic Provinces:** *Frustrated Contracts Act*, Limitations Statutes

Review Questions

1. "Given the need for speed, contractual obligations must be performed on time. It is impossible for an agreement to be discharged by performance if a party either pays late or delivers goods late." Is that statement true? Explain your answer.

2. Briefly explain the effect of discharging a contract.

3. "A contract automatically comes to an end if both parties simply ignore it even though the time to perform has come and gone." Is that statement correct? Explain your answer.

4. Explain how and why the *Currency Act* is important to the issue of tender of payment.

5. "Cash is dangerous for the same reason that it is useful." Think about the concept of tender of payment and provide the best explanation for that statement.

6. Explain how a debit card works.

7. Explain the basic difference between a debit card and a credit card.

8. Explain the operation of a condition precedent and the operation of a condition subsequent.

9. Explain the nature and effect of the concept of an "entire contract."

10. Explain the difference between rescission, accord and satisfaction, and release. Why does the issue of consideration cause problems for accord and satisfaction but not for rescission or release?

11. Describe the process of novation as it applies between two parties and as it applies between three parties.

12. Identify and explain two different meanings of the word "rescission."

13. What test do the courts use to distinguish between conditions, warranties, and intermediate terms?

14. Why does the breach of a condition support the right to discharge?

15. Why does the breach of a warranty not support the right to discharge?

16. When will the breach of an intermediate term support the right to discharge?

17. What is an "anticipatory breach"? How does it differ from a normal breach?

18. Describe the circumstances in which a breach will arise from self-induced impossibility. How do those circumstances differ from circumstances involving frustration?

19. If a contract is discharged for breach of a condition, does that contract completely cease to exist? Explain your answer.

20. Under what circumstances will the right to discharge be lost even if there has been a breach of a condition?

Cases and Problems

1. Closed Door Bakery Inc (CDBI) is a large company that produces and sells a variety of baked goods. Because of its success in Canada, the company wants to sell its goods abroad as well. It therefore hired Jane Burlington to act as its exclusive marketing agent for Japan. The contract was set to run for 36 months. However, there were two ways in which the contract might be brought to an early end: (i) CDBI was entitled to terminate Jane's employment at any time, without notice, if she improperly acted in a way that hurt the company; (ii) After 18 months of performance, CDBI had an unconditional right to terminate Jane's employment for any reason at all, as long as it gave her one month's notice. The contract worked well for 12 months. CDBI then formed two opinions. First, it correctly concluded that Japan was not a good market for its products. It therefore wanted to get rid of Jane as soon as possible. Second, it honestly came to believe that Jane had taken a bribe from another baked goods company and that she was directing Japanese consumers to the competitor's products. Although it insisted that it was entitled to fire her immediately, CDBI told Jane that she had one

month to leave the company. One month later, she did so. Unfortunately, it is now clear that CDBI was terribly mistaken and that Jane had never done anything wrong. Jane consequently claims that CDBI is liable for breach of contract. Is that correct? Explain your answer. If CDBI has breached the contract, it is liable to pay damages for each month that Jane was out of work as a result of the company's breach. Jane claims that she is entitled to damages for 23 months. Is that correct? Explain your answer.

2. Tadpole Inc wanted to sell a warehouse that it owned. It therefore entered into a contract with Bentley Properties Inc, a real estate agent. That contract contained a number of important terms. First, it gave Bentley the exclusive right to list and advertise the warehouse for 90 days. Second, it stated that Bentley would be entitled to receive a sales commission of 10 percent on "any successful sales contract created within the exclusive listing period." Eighty days into the listing period, Bentley showed the property to Janhelene Inc. Janhelene was seriously interested in the warehouse, but since it thought that it could get a better price by dealing directly with the owner, it sent

an offer to Tadpole rather than to Bentley. After further communications, Tadpole and Janhelene signed a document, according to which Janhelene agreed to buy the warehouse "subject to the availability of suitable financing." That document was created on the eighty-eighth day of the listing period. A week later, Janhelene informed Tadpole that it had arranged financing, and the sale was completed two days later. When Bentley eventually discovered the details of the sale, it demanded the payment of a commission from Tadpole. Is Tadpole obligated to pay? What should Bentley have done to better protect itself in its contract with Tadpole?

3. Dennis and Carmen entered into a contract under which he agreed that, in one week's time, he would pay $10 000 in exchange for her motorcycle. Three days later, however, he contacted her and said, "Look, as it turns out, my financial situation isn't as strong as I thought it was. I wonder if you'd be willing to just call off our agreement?" She replied, "Fine. You keep the money and I'll keep the motorcycle." After considering the matter further, however, Carmen called him back and said that she wanted the contract to be performed as initially planned. Dennis refuses to comply. In fact, he insists that the contract no longer exists. Is he correct? If the parties' contract did come to an end, explain the process that was used to achieve that result.

4. Rabby Computer Inc agreed to design a networking system for Pendulum Publishing Ltd. The contract called for Pendulum to pay $50 000 after Rabby completed its performance. However, when Rabby finished designing the system, Pendulum stated that it could not afford to pay that amount of money in cash. Pendulum therefore asked Rabby if it would agree to discharge the contract upon receipt of $35 000. Although Rabby initially agreed to the proposal, it later insisted upon full payment. It did so before it actually received any money from Pendulum. Is Pendulum entitled to have the contract discharged if it pays $35 000? Would your answer be different if Rabby had promised under seal that he would discharge the contract upon receipt of $35 000? Would your answer be different if Rabby had initially agreed to discharge the contract in exchange for $35 000 plus a set of encyclopedias from Pendulum? Explain your answers.

5. The Darjeeling Tea Company hired Hans Rooibos, an artist and carpenter, to produce and deliver 10 tea chests ornately carved from teakwood. The tea chests were intended to decorate the company's various offices around the world. The parties' contract was very detailed in terms of expectations. Amongst the many obligations that Rooibos undertook was a promise to complete the tea chests with varnish finish. The total price was $25 000. Rooibos worked long and hard on the project. As the delivery date drew near, however, he realized that he would not have time to both finish the tea chests for the Darjeeling Tea Company and begin a new contract for another customer. Rooibos therefore delivered the 10 chests to the company without varnish. The company now

points to the contract, insists that Rooibos is in breach, and refuses to pay any part of the price. It does so even though it is using the tea chests, as intended, in its various offices. The chests were put to use after Earl Grey, another craftsperson, was hired to varnish them. Somewhat curiously, given its tight-fisted attitude toward Rooibos, the company paid Grey $2500 for a job that normally would cost only $500. The company has not explained that extravagance. How much money, if any, is Rooibos entitled to receive from the Darjeeling Tea Company?

6. The defendant owns and operates DiNardo's Mansion, a luxurious building that is available for conferences, parties, and whatnot. The plaintiffs, Ellen and Richard, wanted to hold their wedding at the mansion. The defendant's sales manager told the young couple that, by the time of their wedding in November, the facility would have a new, heated glass canopy over an outdoor courtyard, as well as a new two-tier fountain and waterfall that would be ideal for photographs. The couple was impressed with the plans and emphasized the need for outdoor facilities that would be suitable even near the end of autumn. They also indicated that the new improvements to DiNardo's Mansion were very important to them. The parties then agreed on a total price of $14 000 for 280 guests (at a cost of $50 per person). The situation then went downhill. Instead of a glass canopy, the defendant installed a canvas covering over its courtyard. Likewise, the planned waterfall was never built and the fountain was simpler than expected. Worst of all, after the defendant's manager left the organization, the defendant realized that the agreed-upon price was far too low. The defendant contacted the plaintiffs, explained that the price should have been doubled, and insisted that the "contract is impossible to execute." However, after the plaintiffs told the defendant that they were discharging the contract on the basis of his breach, he changed his mind and said that he would honour the agreement. Unwilling to deal with DiNardo's Mansion any longer, the plaintiffs took their wedding elsewhere. Because the alternative venue was arranged at the last minute, it cost $18 000 and it could accommodate only 200 guests. The plaintiffs have sued for breach of contract, but the defendant argues that he is not to blame because he was willing to perform. Are the plaintiffs likely to win their case? Explain your answer.

7. Debbie Krawchuk wanted to buy a horse for her 11-year-old daughter to ride around their ranch. She agreed to purchase an eight-year-old Anglo-Arabian gelding, named Omar, from Eva Ulrychova. The contract was conditional upon Eva's ability to provide a veterinarian's certificate of good health. Eva therefore had the horse checked by Dr Rach, who issued a clean bill of health. Debbie then paid $3000 and took Omar home to her daughter. A short time later, however, she noticed that Omar was cribbing. Cribbing occurs when a horse bites onto a fence rail and breathes deeply. This action gives the animal a sort of high. Depending upon the severity of the condition, a horse may suffer

a number of side effects, including a loss of appetite, weight loss, and colic. When Debbie complained about the situation, Eva provided her with a "cribbing collar," which effectively prevented Omar from continuing his bad habit. Debbie nevertheless wants to return Omar to Eva for a full refund. Eva refuses to comply. She believes that Debbie actually wants to get rid of Omar because he has an occasional tendency to buck. Eva also says, quite correctly, that while cribbing is a condition that affects a horse's health, bucking is not. The fact that Omar bucks therefore cannot possibly constitute a breach of contract. Is Debbie entitled to get her money back? If not, is there any other remedy that she may receive?

8. Bettini entered into a contract with the Vancouver Opera Company under which he agreed to perform for the company twice a month for one year. A term in the contract required Bettini to arrive in Vancouver at least three days before each performance to attend rehearsals. As a seasoned professional, however, he believed that he did not need that much rehearsal and he therefore arrived only one day before his first scheduled performance. The director of the opera company was furious and tried to discharge the agreement on the basis that Bettini had committed a serious breach of the contract. Was the director entitled to do so? Would your answer be the same if Bettini had arrived as scheduled for the first 10 performances, but had arrived only one day before the eleventh? Would your answer be different if Bettini was not a seasoned professional, but rather a novice? Explain your answers.

9. Ivan entered into a contract with Poe Paperback Inc, a small publishing company, to write a mystery novel in exchange for $5000. Under the terms of the contract, Ivan was to deliver a manuscript to Poe within 18 months. However, after three weeks of staring hopelessly at a blank computer screen, Ivan reached the conclusion that he had developed irreparable writer's block and that he would not be able to produce the promised novel. He sent a letter to Poe that said, "I am terribly sorry, but I will have to withdraw from our contract. Since you have not made any payments to me yet, I cannot imagine that you have any objections and I will assume that my proposal is acceptable to you." Ivan received no response from Poe. After another 12 months, however, he suddenly found the inspiration to write a brilliant mystery novel in the space of two weeks. He then entered into negotiations with Christie Mysteries Ltd, a large publishing company, to sell the completed manuscript for $100 000. At that point, Poe contacted Ivan and insisted that the book belonged to it. Ivan, however, insists that he was relieved of his contractual obligations to Poe. Did Ivan breach his contract with Poe? If so, describe the nature of the breach. If there was a breach of contract, is Poe entitled to rely upon it and to seek legal relief from Ivan? Explain.

10. Anita is a gun dealer. Brad informed her that he wished to purchase an Uzi machine gun. She had none in stock but presented Brad with a document that contained the following passage, which both parties read and signed: "Anita agrees to sell one Uzi to Brad in exchange for payment of $5000. This contract is subject to government permission for the sale." As Anita explained to Brad before either party signed, the terms of the document were written to reflect the following provision in the *Prohibited Weapons Act*, RSC 1985, c P-23, s 12. That section states, "Any person who enters into a binding contract for the purchase or sale of a prohibited weapon is liable for an offence regardless of whether or not the sale is ever executed." The next day, Anita consulted the government department that administers the *Prohibited Weapons Act* and was informed that the Uzi is classified as a prohibited weapon under the statute. Briefly explain whether or not Anita and Brad have violated the *Prohibited Weapons Act*.

11. Gerry and Harlan both have lawn-care businesses. For a number of years, they agreed to take care of each other's clients for a two-week period while the other took a family vacation. Seven years ago, while Harlan was away, Gerry fully performed his part of the agreement. That same summer, just as Gerry was about to leave for his vacation, Harlan fell off his riding lawn mower and broke his leg. Harlan was no longer able to perform under their arrangement and, although Gerry was upset to miss his vacation, he agreed to discharge their contract and do his own maintenance. Harlan was uncomfortable about being indebted to Gerry, so he proposed a number of solutions to clear the debt:

1. He offered to have his young son, Jeb, complete the work. Gerry, however, was not confident that the quality of Jeb's work would meet his high standards. Gerry thanked Harlan for his offer, but told him that he would do the work himself.

2. Harlan offered to pay Gerry market value for his earlier work, but Gerry told him not to give it another thought.

3. Harlan also tried to give Gerry three bags of top-of-the-line fertilizer, but it was not the brand Gerry liked to use, so he politely declined the offer.

Harlan decided he had done what he could to fulfill his obligations and gave up trying.

For many years, Gerry and Harlan maintained the same arrangement. This past summer, the day before leaving for his vacation, Gerry told Harlan that he intended to take an extended four-week holiday but expected that Harlan would not charge anything more under their agreement on account of the incident that had happened seven years earlier. Harlan acknowledged his indebtedness to Gerry and agreed to work one extra week, but simply refused to do Gerry's lawn maintenance for the two additional weeks on such short notice. Gerry is furious at Harlan's refusal and insists that he will sue Harlan if Harlan does not perform. Is Harlan legally obligated to perform under the seven-year-old agreement? Would Gerry succeed in court? Give reasons for your answer.

12. Dolores Van de Laer and her husband, Harry, recently had an in-ground pool constructed in their backyard. To protect their seven children, they hired Ruth, a certified lifeguard, to teach the family proper swimming techniques and basic rescue procedures. From the beginning, Ruth had difficulty keeping the older children in line while she assisted the younger ones. She complained to Dolores and Harry, and even though they spoke to the children, the situation did not improve. After a few lessons, Ruth told the Van de Laers that she could not take it anymore and that she had arranged to have her friend Kirk, also a certified lifeguard, replace her as their swimming instructor. Dolores and Harry grudgingly agreed to the new arrangement. They soon discovered that Kirk was great with all of the children and that he was also experienced at pool maintenance. Neither Dolores nor Harry had much luck keeping the pool's pH balanced, so they instructed Kirk to take over that responsibility as well.

Later that summer, Kirk bumped into Ruth at a friend's pool party. When she asked how the job was going, Ruth was surprised to learn that Kirk was disappointed with the pay. Ruth had thought the pay was quite good, but apparently the Van de Laers were paying Kirk $50 less per week than they had promised Ruth. When Kirk learned this, he was outraged that the Van de Laers had taken advantage of him. The next day, before beginning the lesson, Kirk spoke with Dolores and demanded to receive the money she owed him under the original agreement with Ruth. Additionally, he asked for an extra $25 per week as payment for the pool maintenance. Dolores refused to pay Kirk any extra money. She claims that the original agreement with Ruth was discharged by agreement and that a new one with different rights and obligations was created with Kirk. Kirk, however, argues that there was a novation and that he adopted the same rights and obligations that existed under the old contract. Analyze each party's argument. Do you think Kirk is entitled to more money? Explain your answer.

Contractual Remedies

12

LEARNING OBJECTIVES

After completing this chapter, you should be able to:

❶ Define the term "damages" and explain why the courts will generally award only damages for a breach of contract.

❷ Describe expectation damages and explain how they are calculated.

❸ Explain two important limitations on the availability of expectation damages.

❹ Explain the nature of reliance damages and distinguish them from expectation damages.

❺ Explain the concept of account of profits and suggest when that sort of remedy may be available for a breach of contract.

❻ Describe nominal damages and punitive damages and explain how they are calculated.

❼ Distinguish liquidated damages from penalties.

❽ Describe specific performance and injunctions and explain when they are awarded.

❾ Explain how exclusion clauses apply under contracts that are discharged for breach.

❿ Describe the cause of action in unjust enrichment and the remedy of restitution, and explain when those concepts are applicable in a contractual context.

One or more remedies may be available if a contract is breached. As we saw in Chapter 11, the innocent party usually enjoys the option to discharge the agreement if breach substantially eliminates the expected benefit of the contract. Other remedies may also be available, whether or not a contract is discharged. Figure 12.1 outlines the possibilities that we will discuss.

FIGURE 12.1   Remedies for Breach of Contract

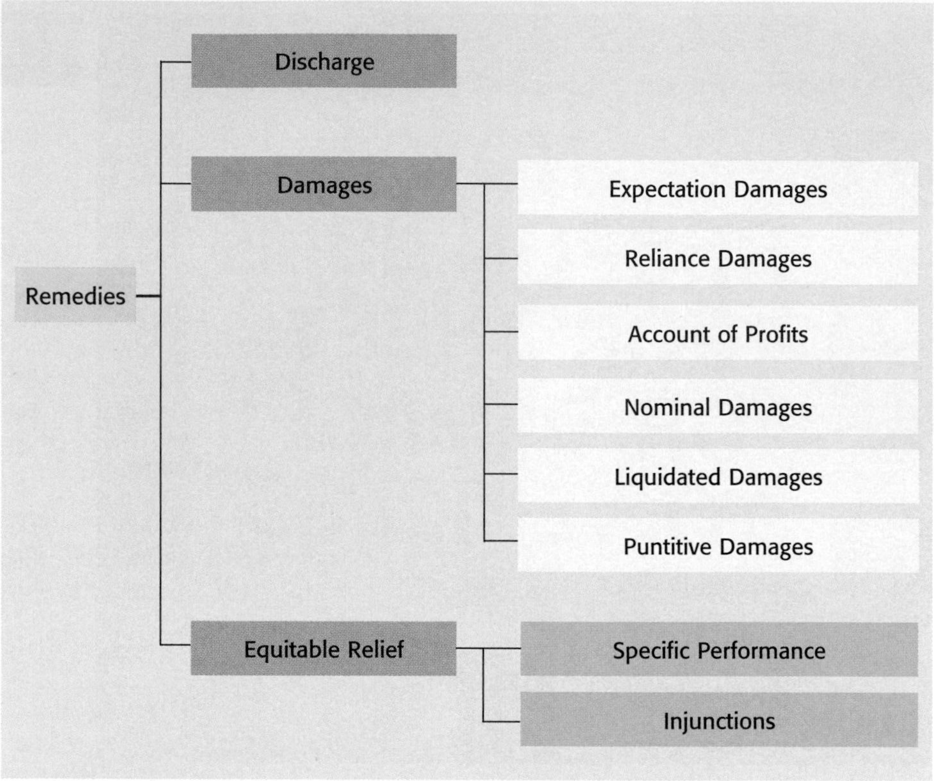

Damages

In the vast majority of cases, the remedy for a breach of contract is *damages*. **Damages** is an award of money that is intended to cure a wrongful event, such as a breach of contract. The nature of that remedy needs to be stressed. Except in rare cases, the plaintiff is *not* entitled to receive the *exact thing* that they expected to get under the agreement. They are entitled to only the *monetary value* of that thing. For example, if I agree to sell my car to you, but later break my promise after you have paid the price, you are probably not entitled to get the car itself. Instead, you are entitled to the monetary value of that car.

There are several reasons for that rule. First, the courts of law historically did not have the authority to compel a defendant to do anything other than pay money.[1] Second, contracts traditionally were seen as commercial arrangements between business people. And even today, money is often the only thing that

L.O. ❶❷❸❹❺❻❼

damages is an award of money that is intended to cure a wrongful event, such as a breach of contract

---

[1] In contrast, the courts of equity did have the authority to compel a defendant to do other things. As we discuss below, courts can still use their equitable powers to award specific performance and injunctions, instead of monetary damages, in some situations. The difference between law and equity was explained in Chapter 1.

matters in the commercial world. Consequently, there is no need to award any other sort of remedy. Third, especially in the business world, it would often be inconvenient to award something other than monetary damages. Returning to our earlier example, suppose I am a used car dealer and that I agreed to sell a specific car to you. What would happen if, as a result of my breach, you could sue me and demand the delivery of that particular vehicle? It could be several years before our dispute was resolved. And in the meantime, I would not be able to deal with the car. I would have to set it aside in case you won the case. An efficient economy, however, requires the free flow of goods.

EXPECTATION DAMAGES

Within the broad category of damages, there are many different *measures of relief*, or ways in which the courts can calculate the amount of money that the plaintiff is entitled to receive from the defendant. The most common measure of relief in contract law is *expectation damages*. **Expectation damages** represent the monetary value of the benefit that the plaintiff expected to receive under the contract.

expectation damages represent the monetary value of the benefit that the plaintiff expected to receive under the contract

That definition contains an important idea. Expectation damages are *forward-looking* because they are intended to place the plaintiff in the position that they expected to be in *after* the contract was properly performed. In contrast, as discussed in Chapter 3, compensatory damages in tort law are *backward-looking* because they are intended to place the plaintiff in the position that they were in *before* the defendant acted wrongfully. Consider the difference:

■ Backward-looking damages are easily justified. They allow the plaintiff to recover the value of something, such as a favourable reputation or a properly functioning machine, that they previously enjoyed but lost as a result of the defendant's wrongful act.

■ Forward-looking damages go further. They allow the plaintiff to recover the value of something that they never previously enjoyed but merely expected to receive under their contract with the defendant. Nevertheless, forward-looking damages can be justified in contract law. The business world operates largely on the basis of credit, which is a promise to do something in the future. Such a promise is valuable only if the person who receives it can be confident that it will be fulfilled. Expectation damages therefore provide an assurance that if a promise is not actually fulfilled, the innocent party will at least be able to recover the monetary value of that promise.

As Figure 12.2 shows, expectation damages are equal to the value of the benefit that the plaintiff expected to receive under the contract *minus* the value of the costs that it expected to incur.

That calculation may seem difficult whenever a sales contract deals with something that may go up or down in value. The parties agree on a price, but they cannot know what the thing will be worth when the time for performance

FIGURE 12.2 Calculation of Expectation Damages

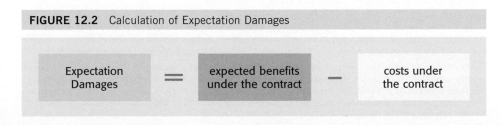

| Expectation Damages | = | expected benefits under the contract | − | costs under the contract |

arrives. The expectation value is calculated at *that* time. The buyer hopes that the thing will go up in value. The seller hopes that it will go down in value. Notice, then, that while each party has *some* expectation when the contract is created, neither knows how that expectation will turn out. In effect, the contract is a gamble. The buyer has agreed to pay the agreed price for something of unknown value; the seller has agreed to trade something of unknown value for the agreed price.

Take a simple example. I agree to pay $75 for a bale of cotton, which you agree to deliver in two months. When the time comes, you fail to deliver. You are liable for breach of contract, but how much are damages? That depends upon the value of the cotton on the agreed day of delivery.

- *Increased Value* If the market price has increased to $100, then you must fulfill my expectation of receiving that amount. If I already paid the price, you owe me $100. If I have not paid the price, you owe me $25. Since the $75 that I intended to spend on the cotton is still in my pocket, my expectation will be fulfilled once you pay me $25. How much would you owe if I had already paid part of the purchase price, say, $50 out of $75?[2]

- *Same Value* If the market value of the cotton is still $75, then neither one of us wins or loses. If I have already paid the price, you simply pay it back. If I have not paid anything, you owe me nothing. The $75 still in my pocket fulfills my expectation value.

- *Decreased Value* If the market value has dropped to $50, then it is clear that I entered into a bad bargain. I agreed to pay $75 for something that turned out to be worth $50. I may be entitled to some reliance damages,[3] but I cannot receive anything as expectation damages. In effect, my expectation is a loss.[4]

The examples in You Be the Judge 12.1 and 12.2 will help you understand how expectation damages are calculated. As you work through them, ask yourself

---

You Be the Judge **12.1**

Calculation of Expectation Damages

José agreed to sell a car to Maria for $5000. Although she made a down payment of $4000, he refused to deliver the vehicle because he discovered that it was really worth $7500. Assuming that José has breached the contract, Maria will be entitled to recover expectation damages of $6500.

Questions for Discussion

1. As a judge, how would you arrive at that conclusion?

2. Does that conclusion seem fair?

[2.] I agreed to pay $75 for cotton that turned out to be worth $100. Since I already paid $50, I still have $25 in my pocket. You therefore have to pay expectation damages of $75: $25 (in my pocket) + $75 (expectation damages) = $100 (my expectation value).

[3.] As explained below, reliance damages are available only *to the extent* that a contract is not unprofitable. Suppose I pre-paid the full price of $75. Since I agreed to pay $75 for cotton that turned out to be worth $50, I am stuck with a loss of $25. Reliance damages therefore are available for only $50: $75 (paid in reliance) – $25 (extent of my bad bargain) = $50 (reliance damages).

[4.] Although you "won" the contract, by persuading me to pay $75 for cotton that turned out to be worth only $50, you also are the party in breach. The court therefore will not enforce the contract for your benefit. As a result, if I have not yet paid the purchase price, I am not entitled to expectation damages, but I also am not required to perform my side of the bargain by actually paying the money to you.

You Be the Judge **12.2**

Calculation of Expectation Damages

José agreed to sell a car to Maria for $5000. Although she made a down payment of $4000, he refused to deliver the vehicle. He did so despite the fact that the car was really worth only $1000. Assuming that José has breached the contract, Maria will not be entitled to recover any expectation damages. (However, she may be entitled to restitution, as explained at the end of this chapter.)

Questions for Discussion

1. As a judge, how would you arrive at that conclusion?

2. Does that conclusion seem fair?

these two questions. How much did the plaintiff *expect* to have at the end of the contract? How much does the plaintiff *actually* have after the defendant's breach? Expectation damages should be equal to the difference between those two numbers.

As we have seen, it is usually fairly easy to calculate expectation damages. In some situations, however, the exercise is much more difficult. We will consider six issues:

- difficulty of calculation
- cost of cure or loss of value
- alternative performance
- intangible losses and emotional distress
- remoteness
- mitigation of damages

Difficulty of Calculation

Expectation damages are usually available even if they are very difficult to calculate. The courts will do the best they can. In one famous case, the defendant breached a contract by depriving the plaintiff of an opportunity to win a beauty contest.[5] While the plaintiff's actual chance of winning the contest was largely guesswork, the court awarded expectation damages based on its best guess as to how she would have fared in the competition. In contrast, if the calculation of the plaintiff's loss is not merely difficult, but entirely speculative, a court will not award damages. A court of law is not a proper place for a stab in the dark.[6]

Cost of Cure or Loss of Value

Sometimes, it is difficult to decide exactly what the plaintiff expected to receive from the defendant. There may be a question as to whether the plaintiff expected to receive a *service* or the *value of the end product* of that service. Consider the illustration in Case Brief 12.1 (on the next page).

That result may seem surprising, especially when you learn that the plaintiff did not actually use the damages that they received from the defendant to level the land.[7] Nevertheless, the court's decision may be justifiable. The defendant's promise to level the land was part of the price that they agreed to pay in exchange

---

[5.] *Chaplin v Hicks* [1911] 2 KB 786 (CA).

[6.] *McRae v Commonwealth Disposals Commissioners* (1951) 84 CLR 377 (HCA).

[7.] A plaintiff is generally entitled to spend their damages as they choose.

Case Brief 12.1

Groves v John Wunder Co (1939) 286 NW 235 (Minn CA)

The plaintiff rented a piece of land to the defendant for $105 000. The defendant was entitled to operate a sand and gravel mine on that property, but they were also required to level the ground at the end of the lease. After removing a great deal of sand and gravel, the defendant left huge craters on the property. They did so for economic reasons. It would have cost $60 000 to level the land. But even if the land had been level, it would have been worth only $12 000.

The plaintiff claimed that expectation damages should be measured by the cost of cure. It argued that they expected to receive a level piece of land at the end of the lease and that they were therefore entitled to receive the amount of money that would be required to put the land into that condition. In response, the defendant claimed that expectation damages should be measured by the *loss of value*. They argued that what the plaintiff really expected to receive under the contract was land worth $12 000.

The court agreed with the plaintiff and awarded $60 000 in expectation damages.

for the right to mine sand and gravel from the property. If the plaintiff had known that the land would be left with huge craters, they probably would have insisted on a different deal. For instance, instead of asking for $105 000 plus level land, they might have asked for $165 000.

The courts often follow the approach taken in *Groves*. They are most likely to do so if the plaintiff has a legitimate interest in having the work done or if the plaintiff has actually already spent money curing the defendant's defective performance.[8] However, judges usually refuse to award damages on a "cost of cure" basis if the difference between the cost of cure and the benefits of that cure is unreasonably large. In an important English case, the defendant breached a contract by building a swimming pool to a depth of 6 feet 6 inches (198 centimetres), rather than 7 feet 6 inches (228 centimetres). The cost of curing that defect was £22 000. The value of the swimming pool, however, was the same in either event. The evidence also indicated that the defendant's breach did not make the pool any more dangerous for diving. The court therefore refused to award expectation damages on a "cost of cure" basis.[9]

Alternative Performance

As a general rule, expectation damages allow the plaintiff to fully recover the anticipated benefits of the contract. A difficulty may arise, however, if the contract allowed the defendant to perform in a variety of ways, some of which involved more or fewer benefits to the plaintiff. Case Brief 12.2 explains how damages will be calculated in such circumstances.

Case Brief 12.2

Hamilton v Open Window Bakery Ltd (2004) 235 DLR (4th) 193 (SCC)

Jane Hamilton was hired by Open Window Bakery (OWB) to act as its marketing and sales agent in Japan. The term of the contract was 36 months. However, the contract allowed OWB to terminate the agreement early in the following two situations: (i) OWB could terminate the contract at any time, without notice, if Hamilton acted in a manner that was "detrimental to the reputation and well-being" of the company; and (ii) OWB

(Continued)

---

8. *Nu-West Homes Ltd v Thunderbird Petroleum Ltd* (1975) 59 DLR (3d) 292 (Alta CA).

9. *Ruxley Electronics & Construction Ltd v Forsyth* [1996] 1 AC 344 (HL). The court did, however, award £2500 for "loss of amenity" or "intangible loss."

(continued)

could terminate the contract, anytime after 18 months, by giving three months' notice. After the contract had been in operation for 16 months, OWB repudiated the agreement by alleging that Hamilton had acted dishonestly. That allegation, in fact, was unfounded—OWB had no grounds for using the first option. When Hamilton sued for breach of contract, it was necessary to determine the correct basis for calculating damages.

The trial judge awarded damages for the full term of the contract, minus a deduction of 25 percent to reflect the possibility that OWB, at some point, might have relied on the second option to end the agreement early. The Supreme Court of Canada disagreed. It held that if a party may perform a contract in several different ways,

damages should be calculated on the basis of the least onerous option. The trial judge incorrectly asked, "What most likely would have occurred if the defendant had not breached the contract?" The proper question instead asks, "What was the minimum acceptable performance?" In addition to reflecting the parties' expectations, that approach is simpler and more predictable.

Applying that test to the facts, the court held that Hamilton had no right to expect that OWB would allow the contract to run for anything more than the minimal period, under the second option, of 18 months plus three months' notice. Damages were calculated accordingly.

Intangible Losses and Emotional Distress

Expectation damages are also difficult to calculate when the plaintiff suffers an intangible loss as a result of the defendant's breach. An **intangible loss** is a loss that does not have any apparent economic value. Examples include the anger, frustration, sadness, or disappointment that may occur when a promise is broken. Those losses are very real, but they do not carry a price in the marketplace.

Historically, the courts generally were not interested in intangible losses. As we discussed earlier, contracts were seen as commercial arrangements between business people who were concerned with finances rather than feelings. Furthermore, the courts traditionally were uncomfortable assigning dollar figures to personal emotions. What is the monetary value of your sense of disappointment if a courier company breaks its promise to deliver a birthday gift to your grandmother on time? How can a court put a price tag on the sadness that a person feels after being fired from a job? For all of those reasons, contractual damages were restricted to *pecuniary* losses (that is, losses that have clear monetary value), such as lost income.

In the last quarter of the twentieth century, however, the courts began to recognize that "peace of mind" is one of the things that a person may expect to receive under a contract. Accordingly, while the cases remained somewhat inconsistent, relief may be available if the defendant performed the contract in a way that disappointed the plaintiff's expectations and caused distress.[10] For example, expectation damages have been awarded for the disappointment caused by a ruined holiday and for the grief that was experienced when a beloved pet dog was suffocated to death during air travel.[11]

The more modern attitude toward intangible losses has now led to a fundamental change. The traditional rule that simply rejected claims for emotional distress no longer applies in Canada. The Supreme Court of Canada has decided instead that intangible losses generally should be treated in the same way as other types of losses. Case Brief 12.3 explains that dramatic shift.

an **intangible loss** is a loss that does not have any apparent economic value

Remoteness

The plaintiff cannot recover expectation damages for *every* loss that they suffer after the defendant's breach. The loss must, as a matter of fact, have been *caused*

[10.] *Honda Canada Inc v Keays* (2008) 294 DLR (4th) 371 (SCC); *Farley v Skinner* [2002] 2 AC 732 (HL); *Turczinski v Dupont Heating & Air Conditioning Ltd* (2004) 246 DLR (4th) 95 (Ont CA).

[11.] *Jarvis v Swan Tours Ltd* [1973] QB 233 (CA); *Newell v Canadian Pacific Airlines Ltd* (1976) 74 DLR (3d) 574 (Ont Co Ct).

PART 3

Case Brief 12.3

Fidler v Sun Life Assurance Co of Canada (2006) 271 DLR (4th) 1 (SCC)[12]

The plaintiff bought a long-term disability insurance policy from the defendant. Several years later, she claimed benefits under the policy after being diagnosed with chronic fatigue syndrome and fibromyalgia. The insurance company denied liability until the very eve of trial, when it accepted that the plaintiff had indeed suffered a loss under the policy. The case consequently proceeded on the issue of damages only. The trial judge awarded $20 000 in "aggravated damages" for the mental distress that the plaintiff suffered as a result of the insurance company's earlier refusal to accept responsibility. That result was affirmed on appeals to the British Columbia Court of Appeal and the Supreme Court of Canada. The Supreme Court of Canada's decision is very important. It held that there was no need for special rules in connection with

intangible injuries. It said mental distress is merely another type of loss and therefore is governed by general principles. "The law's task is . . . to provide the benefits contracted for, whatever their nature, if they were in the reasonable contemplation of the parties. . . . The basic principles of contract damages do not cease to operate merely because what is promised is an intangible, like mental security." That test was satisfied on the facts. The purpose of long-term disability insurance is to provide both monetary benefits and "the prospect of continued financial security." The defendant should have realized, at the outset, that their refusal to honour the policy could cause the plaintiff to suffer not only material need, but also stress and anxiety. They therefore were fully liable.

---

*a loss is **remote** if it would be unfair to hold the defendant legally responsible for it*

by the breach. Furthermore, the loss must not be *remote* from the breach. A loss is **remote** if it would be unfair to hold the defendant legally responsible for it.

A loss is *not* remote if the defendant either *should have known* or *actually did know* that it was the sort of loss that might occur if the contract was breached. That test has two parts:

■ First, liability may be imposed if *a reasonable person would have known* that the plaintiff's loss might result from a breach. That is true even if the plaintiff did not draw the defendant's attention to that possibility.

■ Second, liability may be imposed if the defendant actually knew that the plaintiff's loss might result from the breach. That is true even if a reasonable person would not have normally expected such a loss.

Case Brief 12.4 illustrates the two parts of the remoteness test.

Case Brief 12.4

Victoria Laundry (Windsor) Ltd v Newman Industries Ltd [1949] 2 KB 528 (CA)

The defendant agreed to deliver a boiler to the plaintiff on June 5. When the contract was created, the defendant knew in a general sense that the plaintiff operated a laundry, but they did not know the specific details of the plaintiff's business. The defendant broke the contract by delivering the boiler 20 weeks late. As a result of that breach, the plaintiff suffered two types of losses: First, it lost £16 per week because they were unable to perform ordinary laundry operations, such as cleaning and pressing shirts. Second, it lost £262 per week because they were unable to obtain an enormously profitable and highly unusual dyeing contract from the government.

As a matter of fact, the defendant's breach caused both types of losses. Liability therefore turned on the issue of remoteness.

Even though the plaintiff had not specifically mentioned the possibility of the first type of loss when the contract was created, the defendant was liable for £16 per week in expectation damages. The court held that any reasonable person, even without being told, would have known that that type of loss might occur. In contrast, the court held that the second type of loss was remote. Because the government contract was highly unusual, a reasonable person would not have known about it without being told. And furthermore, the plaintiff had not told the defendant about it. The plaintiff therefore could not recover the additional £262 per week.

---

12. See also *Honda Canada Inc v Keays* (2008) 294 DLR (4th) 577 (SCC). The issue of intangible loss is especially important in the employment context, where unfair dismissal may have devastating effects upon a person's dignity and sense of self-worth. That issue is discussed in Chapter 26.

Remoteness is a principle of fairness. It is applied to the time when the parties created their contract, not to the time when the defendant committed the breach, nor to the time when the judge hears the case. Before entering into a contract, a party should consider all the costs potentially associated with the agreement, including the risk of being held liable as a result of breaking a promise. As that risk increases, the party will ask for a higher price. And at some point, the risk will become too much and the party will refuse to enter into the contract altogether. Of course, the party can be expected to perform that calculation only on the basis of information that they *should know* or that they *do know*. It would be unfair to impose liability for a loss that a party could not have predicted.

Victoria Laundry provides a good example of this. It was fair to impose liability for £16 per week because the defendant must have realized that if they delivered the boiler late, the plaintiff would be unable to conduct their ordinary laundry business. However, the defendant had no way of knowing that the breach might cause the plaintiff to lose the government contract. And if they had known of the possibility of being held liable for £262 per week, they almost certainly would have demanded a higher price from the plaintiff.

As a matter of risk management, the lesson is clear: Before entering into a contract, you should make sure that the other party is aware of any unusual losses that you might suffer as a result of its breach. The other party may demand a higher price or even refuse to enter into the agreement.[13] But if you do not draw attention to the possibility of an unusual loss, you will not be able to recover expectation damages if that loss occurs.

Mitigation of Damages

Even if remoteness is not a problem, the plaintiff cannot recover damages for a loss that it unreasonably failed to *mitigate*.[14] **Mitigation** occurs when the plaintiff takes steps to minimize the losses flowing from the defendant's breach. Consider the example in Business Decision 12.1.

mitigation occurs when the plaintiff takes steps to minimize the losses flowing from the defendant's breach

Business Decision 12.1

Mitigation of Damages

Manfred agreed to deliver a shipment of potato chips to you each week for a year. If he had fulfilled that promise, you would have been able to earn a net profit of $1000 per week by reselling the chips in your convenience store. Unfortunately, Manfred breached the contract at the outset and refused to make any deliveries. Instead of ordering the same number of chips from someone else, you simply complained for the next 52 weeks. At the end of the year, you brought a claim against Manfred for $52 000 in expectation damages.

Questions for Discussion

1. Assuming that your loss is not remote, is Manfred liable for all of your loss?

2. Assuming that you could have arranged an alternative supply of chips within three weeks of the breach, how much will you receive in damages?

Business Decision 12.1 can be used to illustrate four more points about mitigation.

- First, lawyers sometimes say that there is a "duty to mitigate." In fact, there is not really a *duty* in the sense of something that *must* be done.

[13] The other party could also enter into the contract at a lower price but insist on the insertion of an "exclusion clause." Exclusion clauses are discussed later in this chapter.
[14] *Asamera Oil Corp v Sea Oil & General Corp* (1978) 89 DLR (3d) 1 (SCC).

The plaintiff is not required to mitigate. Failing to do so is, however, a poor business decision. As we saw, you are unable to recover damages for losses that you could have mitigated.

- Second, the plaintiff is responsible only for taking *reasonable* steps to mitigate a loss. Expectation damages will not be denied if the only way to mitigate a loss was unreasonably difficult, inconvenient, or risky. That does not mean, however, that mitigation will always be a pleasant experience. In some circumstances, at least, the plaintiff may be expected to mitigate the breach of an old contract by agreeing with the defendant to create a new one.[15]

- Third, damages are denied *only to the extent that* the plaintiff unreasonably failed to mitigate. Although you, the plaintiff, did not take any steps toward mitigation, you are still entitled to $3000 in damages. You would have suffered that loss even if you had acted reasonably.

- Fourth, the plaintiff can recover the costs associated with mitigation. For example, if you had spent $500 arranging the alternative supply of chips within three weeks, you would have been entitled to $3000 in lost profits, plus $500 as the cost of mitigation.

RELIANCE DAMAGES

Expectation damages are the usual remedy for a breach of contract. In some situations, however, other types of damages may be awarded. *Reliance damages* are the most common alternative. **Reliance damages** represent the monetary value of the expenses and opportunities that the plaintiff wasted under a contract.

In one sense, reliance damages are the opposite of expectation damages. If you ask for expectation damages, you are saying, "Give me what I expected to get. Put me in the position that I would have enjoyed if the contract had been properly performed." If you ask for reliance damages, you are saying, "Give me what I lost. Put me in the position that I would have enjoyed if I had not wasted resources under this contract." Expectation damages look *forward* in an attempt to fulfill a contract; reliance damages look *backward* in an attempt to undo the effects of a contract.[16]

The plaintiff is generally entitled to recover either expectation damages or reliance damages, but not both. Expectation damages represent the benefit that the plaintiff expected to receive under the contract; reliance damages represent the cost that they incurred. If the plaintiff wants the benefit, they must be willing to pay the cost. As a result, the plaintiff should sometimes carefully consider which measure of damages is preferable.[17] Business Decision 12.2 provides an illustration.

Reliance damages are subject to an important limitation. They can be awarded only to the *extent* that a contract is *not unprofitable*.[18] That does not mean that reliance damages are entirely unavailable under a bad bargain, but

reliance damages represent the monetary value of the expenses and opportunities that the plaintiff wasted under a contract

---

[15.] *Evans v Teamsters Local Union No 31* (2008) 292 DLR (4th) 557 (SCC).

[16.] In that sense, reliance damages in contract are similar to the damages that are awarded in tort. Tort damages were explained in Chapter 3.

[17.] The plaintiff is entitled to sue for both expectation damages and reliance damages. However, if they successfully prove that the defendant committed a breach of contract, the plaintiff must elect by telling the trial judge which measure of relief they want to receive. Likewise, if the facts support a claim in contract and a claim in tort, the plaintiff is entitled to plead and prove both. They must make an election, however, if they win on both counts.

[18.] *Bowlay Logging Ltd v Domtar Ltd* (1982) 135 DLR (3d) 179 (BC CA).

Business Decision 12.2

Expectation Damages and Reliance Damages

As a music promoter, you hired Ursula to perform a piano concert in exchange for $5000. Based on your experience in the music business, you expected to personally receive a net profit of $7000 from the concert. Ursula received full payment when she signed the contract but told you a week later that she was not willing to perform. You reluctantly cancelled the concert. You are now doubly unhappy. Not only did you pay $5000 for a piano recital that never occurred, you were also deprived of your expected revenue.

Question for Discussion

1. Assuming that Ursula has breached the contract, will you claim expectation damages or reliance damages?

it does mean that the plaintiff cannot use reliance damages to avoid a loss that they would have suffered if the contract had been performed. The rule therefore requires the claimant to bear responsibility for having made a poor deal. While that rule may seem complicated, it can be easily illustrated. Consider Ethical Perspective 12.1.

Ethical Perspective 12.1

Reliance Damages and Bad Bargains[19]

You agreed to pay $14 000 to Anwar in exchange for a shipment of steel. Although you provided $5000 as a down payment, he refused to deliver the goods. You sue for breach of contract. At trial, the evidence indicates that you had entered into a bad bargain. Although you agreed to pay $14 000, the steel was really worth only $11 000. If the contract had been fully performed, you would have suffered a net loss of $3000.

Because you did not expect to earn a profit under the contract, you cannot recover any expectation damages. Furthermore, although you paid $5000 under the contract, you cannot recover reliance damages to the extent that your contract was unprofitable. Since you would have suffered a net loss of $3000 if the contract had been performed, you can recover only $2000 in reliance damages. In effect, you are responsible for the $3000 that you expected to lose as a result of entering into a bad bargain.[20]

Questions for Discussion

1. Does that result seem fair to you?

2. Suggest a reason why the courts have adopted that rule.

ACCOUNT OF PROFITS

The usual remedy for breach of contract is compensation. Damages are measured by the plaintiff's loss. Occasionally, however, the plaintiff may prefer to complain about the defendant's gain. As a result of breaking a promise, the defendant may have received a substantial benefit for themselves. It may seem unfair to allow a party to profit from their own wrongdoing. Nevertheless, the courts have traditionally rejected such claims: "The question is not one of making the defendant disgorge what he has [received] by committing the wrong, but one of compensating the plaintiff."[21] As explained in Case Brief 12.5, however, the British House of Lords created a new rule more recently.

[19.] *Bush v Canfield* 2 Conn 485 (1818).

[20.] We will examine the cause of action in unjust enrichment later in this chapter. When we do so, return to Ethical Perspective 12.1 and calculate the amount of money that you would be entitled to receive as restitution rather than as expectation damages or reliance damages.

[21.] *Tito v Waddell* [1977] Ch 106.

PART 3

Case Brief 12.5

Attorney General v Blake [2001] 1 AC 268 (HL)

George Blake was a double agent during the Cold War. While pretending to be a spy for the British, he actually worked for the Soviets. After his treachery had cost countless lives, he was caught, tried in a British court, and sentenced to 42 years in Wormwood Scrubs Prison in London. Five years later, however, he made a daring escape and fled to Moscow. While still in Russia, he entered into a contract with an English publisher for the release of his memoirs, *No Other Choice*. The publisher agreed to pay him an advance of £150 000. It had already paid £60 000 of that amount when the British government began legal proceedings.

The government sued for breach of contract. When Blake initially joined the British secret service in 1944, he signed an agreement that contained a promise "not to divulge any official information gained by me as a result of my employment." He clearly broke that promise by writing his memoirs. On the question of remedies, however, the government could not prove that it had suffered any loss. It is impossible to put a monetary value on the protection of state secrets. Furthermore, by the time of publication, the Berlin Wall had fallen and the Cold War was over. Consequently, much of the information contained in Blake's book had become public knowledge.

The House of Lords nevertheless held in favour of the government. While recognizing that contractual remedies usually focus on the plaintiff's loss, Lord Nicholls insisted that they may, "in exceptional circumstances," focus on the defendant's gain. Consequently, instead of awarding damages, he applied the equitable remedy of *account of profits* or *disgorgement*.[22] The government was entitled to the profits that George Blake received as a result of breaking his contract.

Attorney General v Blake is a landmark decision. It means that the remedy for breach of contract may focus on either the plaintiff's loss or the defendant's gain.[23] The scope of the decision is, however, unclear. Lord Nicholls said that it was impossible to establish "fixed rules." By way of guidance, he merely suggested that a judge must consider all the circumstances before asking "whether the plaintiff had a legitimate interest in preventing the defendant's profit-making activity and, hence, in depriving him of his profit." More precise rules will have to be "hammered out on the anvil of concrete cases." Consequently, it will be many years before we are able to confidently predict when an account of profits will be given for a breach of contract.

NOMINAL DAMAGES

nominal damages symbolize the fact that the plaintiff suffered a wrong when the defendant broke a promise

If a court finds that a breach of contract did not result in any loss to the plaintiff or any gain to the defendant, it may award *nominal damages*. **Nominal damages** symbolize the fact that the plaintiff suffered a wrong when the defendant broke a promise. Because they are merely symbolic, nominal damages are awarded in very small amounts, such as $10.

It is usually a bad idea to bring an action to recover nominal damages. Judges do not like to waste time on trivial matters. If a court believes that the plaintiff did not have a legitimate reason for suing the defendant, it may require the plaintiff to pay the costs associated with the trial. And as we saw in Chapter 2, the value of those costs will be much greater than the value of the nominal damages that the plaintiff is entitled to receive from the defendant.[24]

---

22. The concept of equity was discussed in Chapter 1. We will look at other equitable remedies later in this chapter.

Although the House of Lords referred to an "account of profits," a variety of labels have been applied to the same remedy. Gain-based relief is sometimes called "disgorgement" or "restitution." That second possibility should, however, be avoided. As we will see at the end of this chapter, "restitution" is the name of the remedy that is triggered by the cause of action in unjust enrichment. It would be confusing to use the same label to describe two different remedies. In this situation, the question is whether the defendant received a benefit from anyone as a result of committing a breach of contract against the plaintiff. Under the action for unjust enrichment, the defendant is liable only for those benefits that he received from the plaintiff.

23. The Supreme Court of Canada has accepted the possibility of gain-based relief: *Bank of America Canada v Mutual Trust Co* (2002) 211 DLR (4th) 385 (SCC).

24. In one famous case, the artist James Whistler sued the art critic John Ruskin for £1000 under the tort of libel (or defamation). In reviewing an exhibit that contained a painting entitled *Nocturne in Black and Gold: The Falling Rocket*, Ruskin accused Whistler of "flinging a pot of paint in the public's face." The jury held Ruskin liable, but awarded Whistler nominal damages of only one farthing (a quarter of a penny). To make matters worse, the court took the unusual step of refusing to award costs in favour of the winning side. The result bankrupted Whistler and forced him to auction off his paintings and his home.

LIQUIDATED DAMAGES

At the time of creating a contract, the parties may want to avoid the risk of becoming involved in a complicated and expensive lawsuit in the future. They may also want to provide each other with an incentive to properly perform. If so, they can include a *liquidated damages* clause in their agreement. **Liquidated damages** represent a genuine attempt to estimate the value of the loss that may occur as a result of a breach. If the contract is in fact broken, the innocent party is entitled to recover the liquidated amount, even if that amount turns out to be more than the loss that they actually suffered. Liquidated damages also work the other way. The innocent party is usually entitled to recover only the liquidated amount, even if they suffered a larger loss as a result of the breach.

Liquidated damages must be distinguished from *penalties*. A **penalty** requires a party to pay an exorbitant amount if they breach the contract. Unlike liquidated damages, a penalty is not a genuine attempt to estimate the loss that may be caused by a broken promise. It is merely an attempt to bully a person into performing. While the courts enforce liquidated damages, they do not enforce penalties. If a contract contains a penalty clause, the court will ignore it and calculate damages in the usual way.

A liquidated damages clause is very often inserted into a consumer contract. If you have a cellphone, you probably will find a liquidated damages clause in your service contract. If so, it will be unenforceable if it actually amounts to a penalty. A California court came to that conclusion.[25] American cellphone contracts routinely required customers to pay $150–$200 as *early termination fees* (ETF) if customers terminated their service agreements ahead of schedule. When Sprint's customers complained, a judge held that the ETF was not a genuine attempt to estimate the company's loss. It was a penalty. Sprint was allowed to receive a reasonable sum, but it had to pay back all the additional money that it had collected over the years.

PUNITIVE DAMAGES

Damages are usually intended to compensate the plaintiff for a loss. *Punitive damages*, however, have a different purpose. **Punitive damages** are intended to punish the defendant and discourage other people from behaving badly. Consequently, if the defendant has done something that the court thinks deserves punishment, the plaintiff may be entitled to recover both compensatory damages (either expectation damages or reliance damages) *and* punitive damages.

Because of the influence of American media, it is important to appreciate that punitive damages are quite different in this country. In comparison to American courts, Canadian courts award punitive damages far less often and in far smaller amounts. That is especially true if the plaintiff is relying upon a breach of contract, rather than a tort. The Supreme Court of Canada has said that two conditions generally must be met in order for it to award punitive damages.[26] First, the defendant must not only commit a breach of contract, but also act in a "harsh, vindictive, reprehensible and malicious" manner. Second, in committing that breach of contract, the defendant must have also committed another independently actionable wrong, such as a tort or another breach of contract. Those requirements can be satisfied only in very unusual circumstances. In one famous

liquidated damages represent a genuine attempt to estimate the value of the loss that may occur as a result of a breach

a **penalty** requires a party to pay an exorbitant amount if they breach the contract

PART 3

punitive damages are intended to punish the defendant and discourage other people from behaving badly

---

[25.] *Cellphone Fee Termination Cases* 193 Cal App 4th 298 (2011 Cal CA, First District).

[26.] *Whitenv Pilot Insurance Co* (2002) 209 DLR (4th) 257 (SCC); *cf Royal Bank of Canada v W Got & Associates Electric Ltd* (1999) 178 DLR (4th) 385 (SCC).

example, a professional hockey team broke its contract with a player by refusing to allow him to visit a physician for treatment of an injury.[27] In that situation, the team (i) breached its contract, (ii) in a morally reprehensible way, and (iii) in a way that also created the tort of negligence. The player was therefore entitled to both compensatory damages and punitive damages.

Concept Summary 12.1 reviews the different remedies that we have discussed.

Concept Summary 12.1

Monetary Relief

Type	Purpose
Expectation damages	place the plaintiff in the position that they would have enjoyed if the contract had been performed
Reliance damages	compensate the plaintiff for the costs that they incurred in reliance upon the contract
Account of profits	strip the defendant of a benefit that they received as a result of breaking a contract
Nominal damages	symbolically demonstrate that the defendant breached their promise to the plaintiff
Liquidated damages	enforce the parties' estimate of the loss that the plaintiff would suffer if the defendant breached the contract
Punitive damages	punish the defendant for breaching the contract in an outrageous way

L.O. ❽

Equitable Relief

As we discussed earlier, a person who suffers a breach of contract usually receives monetary damages. In most situations, that sort of remedy is adequate. Suppose a car dealer breaks a promise by refusing to deliver a particular vehicle to you. If you are limited to monetary damages, you will not receive that specific car. But with the money that you recover from the defendant, you can buy another car that is virtually identical. Furthermore, by limiting you to monetary relief, the law allows the car dealer to carry on with business as usual. He does not have to hold onto the disputed vehicle while your lawsuit slowly works its way through the court system. In some situations, however, money is not enough. The courts of equity have therefore developed other types of remedies. (The courts of equity were explained in Chapter 1.)

SPECIFIC PERFORMANCE

specific performance occurs when the court orders the defendant to fulfill a contractual obligation to do something

The most common type of equitable relief is *specific performance*. **Specific performance** occurs when the court orders the defendant to fulfill a contractual obligation to do something.[28] The plaintiff becomes entitled to *actual* performance, rather than just the monetary value of that performance.

It is sometimes said that specific performance, like other equitable remedies, is *discretionary*. The plaintiff does not have a *right* to receive it simply because the defendant breached the contract. The court has to be convinced that specific performance would be *appropriate* in the circumstances. That discretion is, however, exercised on the basis of settled rules. For example, a judge will not order the defendant to specifically perform a promise unless the

---

[27.] *Robitaille v Vancouver Hockey Club Ltd* (1981) 124 DLR (3d) 228 (BC CA).

[28.] If the defendant refuses to obey the court's order, they can be held in contempt of court. A court will then order the defendant to pay a fine or to be held in prison.

plaintiff came to court with "clean hands." The plaintiff has dirty hands if, for instance, they somehow took advantage of the defendant. Specific performance will also be refused if it would create unfair hardship for the defendant, or if the plaintiff unreasonably delayed before starting the lawsuit.

Specific performance depends on four other factors:

- adequacy of damages
- mutuality
- judicial supervision
- personal services

The first limitation is the most important. Specific performance is awarded only if monetary damages would provide an *inadequate* remedy. In our earlier example, you could not get specific performance against the car dealer, because monetary damages were sufficient for your purposes. You could use those damages to buy a virtually identical vehicle from someone else. The situation would be different, however, if the specific car that the dealer promised to deliver was unique, and if you had a legitimate reason for wanting to receive that car in particular. For instance, you might be entitled to specific performance if your contract with the dealer concerned John Lennon's infamous psychedelic Rolls-Royce. Other types of goods occasionally support a right to specific performance as well. A court may decide that a family heirloom, such as a great-grandmother's wedding ring, cannot be replaced by money.

In contrast to a contract for the sale of goods, a contract for the sale of an interest in land almost always triggers a right to specific performance. Every piece of land is thought to be unique. And if that is true, then monetary damages will not allow the plaintiff to buy an adequate substitute from someone other than the defendant. That traditional approach was, however, recently modified. The Supreme Court of Canada said that, in the modern world, "residential, business and industrial properties are all mass-produced much in the same way as other consumer goods."[29] Consequently, if the plaintiff wants specific performance of a promise to transfer land, they now have to prove that they really do have a substantial interest in receiving that property.

The concept of *mutuality* provides a second important limitation on the availability of specific performance. **Mutuality** means that specific performance can be awarded *to* a party only if it could also be awarded *against* that same party. It would be unfair to award specific performance to one person but only monetary damages to the other. For example, the courts generally will not award specific performance *against* a child. Consequently, they also generally will not award specific performance *to* a child. If a person who enters into a contract with a child cannot be assured of getting anything more than monetary damages, they should not be compelled to give anything more in return.

Third, specific performance generally will not be awarded if it would require ongoing *judicial supervision*. Judges want to resolve disputes once and for all. They do not want the parties repeatedly coming to court. Furthermore, they are not willing to constantly monitor a situation to ensure that the defendant is behaving properly. For those reasons, a court may refuse to order specific performance of a promise to keep a grocery store in operation.[30]

mutuality means that specific performance can be awarded *to* a party only if it could also be awarded *against* that same party

---

29. *Semelhago v Paramadevan* (1996) 136 DLR (4th) 1 (SCC).

30. *Co-operative Insurance v Argyll Stores Ltd* [1998] AC 1 (HL).

Finally, the courts generally will not order specific performance of a promise to perform a *personal service*. For example, an actress will not be compelled to appear in a movie even if she promised to do so. Aside from the fact that specific performance would require ongoing judicial supervision, it would require the actress to work for the movie studio against her will.

The factors that determine the availability of specific performance are reviewed in Concept Summary 12.2.

Concept Summary 12.2

Criteria for Specific Performance

Inadequacy of damages	Specific performance will not be ordered if monetary damages will adequately protect the plaintiff's expectations.
Mutuality	Specific performance will not be ordered in favour of someone unless it could also be ordered against that same person.
Judicial supervision	Specific performance must not require ongoing judicial supervision to ensure compliance.
Personal services	Specific performance must not require the provision of services of a personal nature.

INJUNCTIONS

an **injunction** occurs when the court orders the defendant to *not do something* that is prohibited by the contract

Specific performance compels a person to fulfill a contractual obligation to *do something*. An *injunction* usually operates in the opposite direction. That term is used in a variety of ways. For now, we will say that an **injunction** occurs when the court orders the defendant to *not do something* that is prohibited by the contract. Suppose you enter into an agreement with a manufacturer that allows you to sell its product in only one province. If you try to sell in another province, the manufacturer may obtain an injunction to prevent you from doing so.

The same rules generally govern specific performance and injunctions. For example, neither type of remedy is available if monetary damages are sufficient to protect the plaintiff's interests. There are, however, some differences. The courts are much more willing to award injunctions than specific performance. That rule is based on the courts' desire to restrict freedom of action as little as possible. Specific performance requires a party to *do* something. And while they are doing that thing, they cannot do anything else. In contrast, an injunction usually requires a party to *not do* something. And while they are not doing that thing, they remain free to do anything else.

That difference between the two types of equitable remedies creates an interesting tension in some situations. As we saw, the courts generally refuse to order specific performance of a promise to provide personal services. A court, therefore, will not compel an actress to appear in a movie. Nevertheless, it may impose an injunction to prevent her from breaching a contractual promise to *not* perform for anyone else. Consider the decision in Case Brief 12.6.

Although the court awarded an injunction in *Warner Bros Pictures Inc*, it also stressed that injunctive relief is subject to an important restriction. An injunction will not be granted if it would compel the defendant to choose between working for the plaintiff and not working at all. That rule is seen in Case Brief 12.7.

Case Brief 12.6

Warner Bros Pictures Inc v Nelson [1937] 1 KB 209

Early in her career, Bette Davis signed a contract with Warner Bros movie studio.[31] That agreement contained positive and negative undertakings. Positively, Davis promised to act in the studio's films. Negatively, she promised not to act for anyone else. By 1937, however, she had enjoyed great success in *Of Human Bondage* with Leslie Howard, *The Petrified Forest* with Humphrey Bogart, and *Dangerous*, for which she won an Academy Award. She therefore decided that her contract with Warner Bros did not pay enough for someone of her stature. She wanted to work elsewhere for more money.

Warner Bros did not seek specific performance of Davis's positive promise to perform in its movies. And, indeed, the court said that such an order would not have been granted. The studio did, however, obtain an injunction with respect to the actress's negative promise not to appear in anyone else's movies. The court held that if Davis wanted to appear on film during the life of her contract with Warner Bros, she had to work for that studio. The court also held, however, that she was free to earn a living in other ways if she chose.

Case Brief 12.7

Page One Records Ltd v Britton [1968] 1 WLR 157 (Ch D)

The defendants, four young English musicians who played as The Troggs, had a hit song in 1966 with "Wild Thing." Several years earlier, they had signed a contract with the plaintiff. Under the terms of that agreement, the defendants gave a positive promise to employ the plaintiff as their manager and a negative promise to not employ anyone else in that capacity. Unfortunately, the relationship between the parties deteriorated, and the group decided that it could no longer work with the plaintiff. The plaintiff sought an injunction preventing The Troggs from hiring anyone else to act as their manager.

The court refused to grant an injunction for several reasons. Most significantly, the judge recognized that an injunction would effectively prevent the defendants from earning a living. Bette Davis could have made money by doing things other than acting in film. The Troggs, in contrast, had no skills outside of music. And they could work as musicians only if they had a manager. It therefore would have been unfair to make them choose between unemployment and working with the plaintiff.

Exclusion Clauses

L.O. **❾**

Before completing our discussion of contractual remedies, it is important to stress that the parties are generally entitled to create whatever contract they want. Consequently, they are free to reject or modify the remedies that are usually available for breach of contract. We have already seen that they can agree to *liquidated damages* (but not *penalties*). They can also insert an *exclusion clause* into their contract. An **exclusion clause** excludes or limits liability for breach of contract. The clause may apply to certain types of breach. For example, the parties may agree that liability will arise if a promise is intentionally broken but not if it is carelessly broken. Or the clause may limit the amount of damages that are available. For example, the parties may agree that an action cannot be brought for more than $500. In either event, the exclusion clause will apply even if the parties' contract has been discharged for breach.

an **exclusion clause** excludes or limits liability for breach of contract

Exclusion clauses play an important role in the commercial world. Because they allow a business to limit its liability, they create a crucial form of risk

---

[31.] The style of cause refers to "Nelson" because Bette Davis was married to Harmon Nelson at the time of the case.

management. They also allow for the efficient allocation of risks. If the parties know who will be responsible for a certain type of loss, they also know which of them should arrange insurance.[32] In some situations, however, exclusion clauses may produce unfair results, especially when they are contained in *standard form contracts*. Consequently, as we saw in Chapter 9, they are subject to certain rules and restrictions:

- An exclusion clause is strictly enforced against the party that drafted it. For instance, a sign in a restaurant that excludes liability for "lost and stolen clothes" may not protect the restaurateur if a diner's briefcase is stolen. Similarly, an exclusion clause that limits liability in contract may not be effective against a claim in tort.[33] Exclusion clauses should therefore be written in clear, *unambiguous language*.

- A business that wants to limit its liability must provide *reasonable notice* of its exclusion clause. The effect of that requirement depends upon the circumstances. In some situations, a court may simply assume that the clause in question is so common that the customer must have known about it. Often, however, the business must actually draw the customer's attention to the clause *before* entering into the contract. For instance, a large, easily read sign may need to be posted at the entrance of a parking lot. Or a car rental agent may be required to specifically identify and explain an unusually onerous clause in a rental contract.[34]

- If a business wants to rely upon an exclusion clause, it must prove that the other party *agreed* to it. Although that agreement may take any form, the best evidence is usually a signature.

- Finally, even if all those requirements have been met, an exclusion clause will not apply to a *fundamental breach* if the effect of enforcing the clause would be unfair. Although the law remains somewhat unclear, a **fundamental breach** essentially consists of a breach that goes to the very "core" of the contract. If a breach of that sort were protected by an exclusion clause, then the contract would become radically different from what the parties had initially agreed upon. Assume, for example, that the plaintiff paid to store his car in the defendant's garage. The defendant required the plaintiff to sign a contract that excluded liability "for any loss or damage, however caused, either intentionally or by accident." That clause would not protect the defendant if he deliberately destroyed the plaintiff's vehicle.

a **fundamental breach** consists of a breach that goes to the very "core" of the contract

L.O. ⑩

Unjust Enrichment

If an agreement is broken, the innocent party usually complains about the breach of contract and asks for damages, specific performance, or an injunction. In some situations, however, that party may bring an action in *unjust enrichment* and ask for *restitution*. The rules for unjust enrichment and restitution are quite complex. We will consider them briefly.

---

[32] *Fraser Jewellers (1982) Ltd v Dominion Electric Protection Co* (1997) 148 DLR (4th) 496 (Ont CA).

[33] As we saw in Chapter 3, the same set of facts may support claims in both contract and tort.

[34] *Tilden Rent-a-Car Co v Clendenning* (1978) 83 DLR (3d) 400 (Ont CA).

Unjust enrichment is a cause of action that requires proof of three elements:

- an enrichment to the defendant
- a corresponding deprivation to the plaintiff
- the absence of any juristic reason for the defendant's enrichment[35]

The remedy for unjust enrichment is always *restitution*. **Restitution** requires the defendant to give back the enrichment that they received from the plaintiff. We earlier said that expectation damages allow the plaintiff to demand, "Give me what I expected to get," and that reliance damages allow the plaintiff to demand, "Give me what I lost." Following the same pattern, we can now say that restitution allows the plaintiff to demand, "Give me what you received from me."

We must stress one point about the relationship between the law of contract and the law of unjust enrichment. Unjust enrichment usually can be claimed only if the parties' transaction is *not* governed by an enforceable contract. Unjust enrichment therefore can be used if there *never was* a contract between the parties. For example, if I mistakenly pay $1500 in rent to you, rather than to my landlord, there is no contract between us and I can demand restitution from you. Unjust enrichment can also be used if an apparent contract between the parties is either *void* because its terms are uncertain or *unenforceable* because it is not in writing.[36] Finally, unjust enrichment can be used if a valid contract has been *discharged* on the basis of a breach.

Since the law of unjust enrichment is very complicated, a business person should consult a lawyer whenever a problem arises in that area. As Case Brief 12.8 demonstrates, however, an action for unjust enrichment is sometimes much more effective than an action for breach of contract.

unjust enrichment is a cause of action that requires proof of an enrichment to the defendant, a corresponding deprivation to the plaintiff, and the absence of any juristic reason for the defendant's enrichment

restitution requires the defendant to give back the enrichment that it received from the plaintiff

Case Brief 12.8

Boomer v Muir (1933) 24 P 2d 570 (Cal DC)[37]

The plaintiff agreed to build a dam for the defendant in exchange for a price that they later realized was well below market value. The plaintiff worked on the project and received a number of payments during the first 18 months of the contract. However, as the project neared completion, the defendant refused to honour their obligation to supply materials. The plaintiff therefore discharged the contract on the basis of that breach.

At that point, the plaintiff had an option. They could have claimed expectation damages under the cause of action in breach of contract. However, because they had entered into a bad bargain, that choice was not very appealing. In light of the payments that the defendant had already made, the plaintiff would have received only an additional $20 000.

The plaintiff therefore claimed restitution in unjust enrichment for the value of the construction services that they had rendered:

- the defendant was *enriched* because they had received the value of the plaintiff's services,
- the plaintiff suffered a *corresponding deprivation* because they had supplied the services, and
- since the defendant was unwilling to perform their own obligations under the contract, there was *no juristic reason* why they should be able to retain the value of the plaintiff's services.

Significantly, once the plaintiff established the cause of action in unjust enrichment, they were entitled to restitution of the *actual value* of their services. Because the plaintiff's claim was not breach of contract, their remedy was not limited by the terms of their contract with the defendant. Consequently, after taking into account the payments that the defendant had already made, the court awarded $257 000 to the plaintiff. That was $237 000 more than they expected to receive under the contract.

---

[35] *Pettkus v Becker* (1980) 117 DLR (3d) 257 (SCC); *Garland v Consumers' Gas Co* (2004) 237 DLR (4th) 385 (SCC).

[36] *Clarke v Moir* (1987) 82 NSR (2d) 183 (CA); *Deglman v Guaranty Trust Co of Canada* [1954] 3 DLR 785 (SCC). As we saw in Chapter 10, most contracts do not have to be written.

[37] See also *Lodder v Slowey* [1904] AC 442 (PC), and *Komorowski v Van Weel* (1993) 12 OR (3d) 444 (Gen Div).

Chapter Summary

If a contract is breached, the innocent party may be entitled to a variety of remedies. If the breach is serious, the innocent party may be allowed to discharge the contract. Whether or not a contract is discharged for breach, the innocent party may be entitled to damages.

Expectation damages allow the innocent party to recover the monetary value of the benefit that they expected to receive under the contract. The calculation of expectation damages is complicated if the defendant was entitled to perform in various ways, or if the plaintiff claims the cost of cure or the value of intangible losses. Expectation damages are subject to two important restrictions: remoteness and mitigation. Instead of expectation damages, the innocent party may be entitled to reliance damages, which allow them to recover the monetary value of expenses and opportunities that they wasted in reliance upon the contract. Reliance damages are available only to the extent that the contract was not unprofitable. In exceptional circumstances, a court may impose an account of profits in order to compel the defendant to disgorge a benefit that they acquired in breach of contract. The courts will enforce a contractual term regarding liquidated damages, but they will not enforce a penalty. If the innocent party did not suffer any loss as a result of a breach, the court may award nominal damages. Punitive damages are occasionally awarded to punish the defendant and discourage other people from behaving badly.

Equitable remedies are sometimes available for a breach of contract. Specific performance occurs when the court orders the defendant to fulfill a contractual obligation to do something. An injunction occurs when the court orders the defendant to refrain from doing something that is prohibited by the contract. Specific performance and injunctions are subject to special limitations.

Even if a contract has been discharged for breach, an exclusion clause contained in that contract may continue to limit the defendant's liability.

In some situations, it may be possible to sue for unjust enrichment rather than breach of contract. The cause of action in unjust enrichment requires proof that (i) the defendant received an enrichment, (ii) the plaintiff suffered a corresponding deprivation, and (iii) there was an absence of any juristic reason for the defendant's enrichment. The remedy for unjust enrichment is always restitution.

MyBusLawLab   ADDITIONAL RESOURCES FOR CHAPTER 12

MyBusLawLab provides students with an assortment of tools to help enrich the learning experience, including a Study Plan with Pre- and Post-tests, mini-cases with assessments, and provincial content material, which provides links to relevant cases, legislation, and additional resources.

MyBusLawLab provides the following resources for Chapter 12:

Provincial Material

- **British Columbia:** Enforcement of Judgments, Garnishment, Injunction, Seizure and Sale, Specific Performance, Writ of Execution
- **Alberta:** Exemption Clauses (Breach), Fundamental Breach, Garnishment
- **Manitoba and Saskatchewan:** Collection of Judgments
- **Ontario:** Debt Collection Processes, Equitable Remedies, Executions, Exemption Clauses, Foreign Judgments, Fundamental Breach, Garnishment, Judgment Debtor Examination
- **Atlantic Provinces:** Garnishment, Seizure and Sale

Review Questions

1. Is it ever possible to receive and enforce more than one remedy for the same breach of contract? Explain your answer and provide examples.

2. Identify and briefly explain the types of monetary relief that may be available for a breach of contract. What purpose is served by each type of relief?

3. How are expectation damages calculated?

4. What is the difference between loss of value damages and cost of cure damages? Present arguments for and against cost of cure damages.

5. Briefly explain the Supreme Court of Canada's most recent approach to the issue of compensation for intangible losses.

6. The calculation of damages often requires the court to estimate the value of the plaintiff's loss. When, if ever, will a court refuse to speculate on the appropriate amount?

7. Under what circumstances will damages be considered remote and therefore unavailable?

8. Briefly outline the rules regarding mitigation of loss.

9. Do the rules governing mitigation seem fair to you? Is there any justification for requiring the plaintiff to minimize the losses that are caused by the defendant's breach? Explain your answer.

10. Can a party escape the consequences of a bad bargain by claiming reliance damages rather than expectation damages?

11. What is "disgorgement"? When it is available as a remedy for a breach of contract?

12. What are "nominal damages"? How are they calculated? What purpose do they serve?

13. Does the "duty to mitigate" apply if the plaintiff claims an account of profits? Explain your answer.

14. What are "liquidated damages"? How do they differ from penalties? Are liquidated damages recoverable? Are penalties recoverable?

15. What are "punitive damages"? How are they calculated? Under what circumstances are they available? What purpose do they serve?

16. Explain the main reason why the courts prefer to award monetary damages rather than specific performance.

17. Why are the courts more willing to grant injunctions than specific performance?

18. What is an "exclusion clause"? Identify and briefly explain the rules that govern exclusion clauses.

19. When will the courts allow a party to bring a claim in unjust enrichment?

20. "Once a contract is discharged, the plaintiff has the option of suing for breach of contract or for unjust enrichment. The remedy for unjust enrichment, however, can never be more valuable than the remedy for breach of contract." Is that statement true? Explain your answer.

Cases and Problems

1. Redwood Inc, which owned a parcel of land that contained dense forests, entered into a contract with Bunyon Corp. Bunyon was required to cut and remove the trees from a 40-hectare area. In exchange, Redwood was required to pay $150 000 and provide trucks to Bunyon to transport the cut logs from the work site. After Bunyon had cleared about 20 hectares, Redwood breached a condition of the contract by failing to provide a sufficient number of trucks. Bunyon therefore discharged the contract for breach and claimed damages. At trial, the evidence indicated that Bunyon had entered into a bad bargain. It had cleared about half of the designated area and had received $75 000 in payment from Redwood. In doing so, however, Bunyon had actually incurred $300 000 in expenses. That amount represented the true market value of the services rendered and was not at all attributable to incompetence or mismanagement. If Bunyon claims expectation damages, what amount of money should it receive? If Bunyon claims reliance damages, what amount of money should it receive? Is there any other basis upon which Bunyon could claim relief? If so, what amount of money would it receive?

2. Pacific Guano Ltd wanted to mine phosphate on Ocean Island in the South Pacific. The small population of that island formed the Ocean Island Residents Co (OIRC) and entered into an agreement with Pacific Guano. Under the terms of that contract, Pacific Guano received the right to extract unlimited quantities of phosphate from the island for 20 years in exchange for its promises to pay $20 000 000 and to undertake an extensive reforestation project at the end of the 20-year term. Shortly after signing the contract, the members of the OIRC, which consisted of all the residents of Ocean Island, permanently resettled to another nearby island. Pacific Guano carried out its mining operations and paid $20 000 000. However, at the end of the lease, it refused to replant the property and left the island resembling a lunar landscape. The reforestation project that the contract required would have cost about $3 000 000, but it would have improved the value of the land by only $600 000. Is the OIRC entitled to recover $3 000 000 as cost of cure damages? Leaving aside the legal rules, do you think that the OIRC should be able to recover $3 000 000 as cost of cure damages? If, at the time of forming the contract, the OIRC had known that Pacific Guano would not reforest the land as promised, would the OIRC have entered into the same contract? Explain your answers.

3. Classique Cars Ltd rents out limousines for $200 per day, almost invariably to people arranging wedding parties. It is one of several companies to do so. On one occasion, Classique found that it was overbooked and did not have enough limousines to meet its rental obligations. It therefore called Adam, with whom it had entered into a rental contract a week earlier, and informed him that he would not be provided with a vehicle. Adam responded by informing Classique for the first time that he did not want a limousine for a wedding party. He needed the car to film a scene in a movie that he was directing. Adam also told Classique that if he did not receive a limousine, the filming schedule for his movie would be set back one day at a cost of $50 000. If Adam sues Classique, identify two reasons why he may not be entitled to recover $50 000 in expectation damages.

4. Marta Ferreira is a hard-working and very talented investment adviser. Until recently, she worked for

Globo Finance Inc, one the leading companies in the field. She earned approximately $750 000 a year and she consistently received very positive reviews from her clients. Because she always remained calm and cool even in the most stressful situations, her co-workers gave her the nickname "Ice." The company, unfortunately, was less happy with Marta's performance. After discovering that she had broken a number of rules and policies, it decided to fire her. The terms of her employment contract contained two relevant provisions. The first provision said that the company was entitled to fire Marta, at any time and without notice, if she committed a "serious" breach of her obligations. The second provision said that if Marta was not guilty of a "serious" breach, the company could fire her by providing either three months' notice or "payment in lieu" (that is, payment of three months' salary). The company explained the first option to Marta and then told her to get out and stay out. Marta understandably was upset and angry at the time. Somewhat surprisingly, she continues to be very distressed. Because of her emotions, she has not been able to find a new job. It is now one year later. Marta has sued the company for damages under two headings. First, since the company now admits that Marta's various misdeeds did not include a "serious" breach, she believes that she is entitled to damages for lost income. Second, she claims that she is entitled to damages because of all of the stress and unhappiness that the company has caused her. Explain the damages that Marta is likely to receive from a court.

5. Paolo owns an apartment complex in a poor area of town. The building contains a large number of identical apartments. Because demand is low, there are always several empty apartments. Paolo leased an apartment to Dhalia for one year at a rent of $1000 per month. After two months, however, Dhalia broke the lease, moved out, and refused to pay the remaining rent. The next day, Paolo convinced Xavier to live in the apartment that Dhalia had occupied. In doing so, did Paolo mitigate the loss that resulted from Dhalia's breach? Would your answer be the same if Dhalia had introduced Xavier to Paolo? What if Dhalia had introduced Xavier to Paolo only because she was moving out? In answering those questions, place yourself in Paolo's position and ask whether Xavier's contract really made up for the loss that Dhalia caused when she broke her lease.

6. Cornwall Gravel wanted to submit a tender (offer) for a government contract. It contacted Purolator Courier to arrange delivery of the offer to the government office. Purolator collected the envelope at 6:00 pm on October 1. At that time, Cornwall Gravel told Purolator's employee that the envelope contained a "tender" and stressed that it had to be delivered by 3:00 pm on October 2. It then signed a bill of lading, which was presented by Purolator's employee, and which created a contract between Cornwall and Purolator. That contract contained a paragraph that said, "Purolator's liability for any loss or damage to the package shall be limited to $1.50 per kg based on the weight of the envelope." Because of the employee's carelessness, Cornwall's envelope was not delivered to the government office until 3:17 pm on October 2. As a result, the government refused to consider Cornwall's offer. The evidence indicates that if the envelope had been delivered on time, Cornwall would have received the government contract and would have earned a net profit of $700 000. Cornwall has therefore sued Purolator for breach of contract. In defence, Purolator says that (i) since the package weighed only 1 kilogram, damages must be limited to $1.50, and (ii) even if the exclusion clause does not apply, it should not be held liable for $700 000 because it did not know all the details concerning the contract that Cornwall hoped to receive from the government. What will the court decide?

7. Donald Evans Inc (DEI) supplies materials to the oil industry in Alberta. Although the company deals in several types of equipment, the vast majority of its profits are generated by a device called a heavy oil extraction coupler (or, more simply, a "coupler"). The manufacture of those couplers required the use of widgets purchased from Harjat Machine Corp (HMC). HMC is the only source of such widgets. Two years ago, the parties created a contract that obligated HMC to provide widgets to DEI for 10 years. One year ago, however, HMC breached that contract by refusing to perform the contract unless DEI promised to pay a higher price. As it was entitled to do, DEI immediately discharged the contract for breach of condition. HMC now concedes that it had acted wrongfully and that it is liable to DEI. The more difficult question pertains to the measure of relief. There are three possibilities. (i) Because DEI cannot manufacture its couplers without HMC's widgets, DEI is entitled to the full value of the profits that it will lose for the remainder of the full life of the parties' 10-year contract. (ii) DEI could have rearranged its manufacturing process, within two years, to produce its couplers without widgets from HMC. Damages could be confined to DEI's lost profits during that period. (iii) Within a very short time of its own breach, HMC admitted that it had acted wrongfully. It therefore offered to create a new contract with DEI to supply widgets for either (a) the remainder of the time contemplated by the original contract, or (b) the length of time that DEI would require to develop a manufacturing process that did not involve widgets. Which solution would a court most likely adopt? Explain your answer.

8. CanPro, a Canadian film company, hired Alan Smithee, a relatively unknown actor, to star in a biographical movie about Pierre Trudeau. Although the contract called for payment of only $15 000 in exchange for four months of work, Smithee accepted the role because he believed that the film would be widely publicized in Canada and consequently would give his career an invaluable boost. The evidence supports that belief. In similar circum-

stances, other actors have seen their annual income rise to an average $100 000 in the year following the release of a major motion picture. Given the other factors involved in the movie industry, however, it is almost impossible to predict the longer-term effects of starring in a major motion picture. Unfortunately, Smithee never actually tasted glory. Just days before filming was scheduled to begin, CanPro decided to replace Smithee with another actor. The movie has now been made and Smithee is unhappy. CanPro has not given any reason for its decision to replace him, but it insists that its breach of contract did not really cause him to suffer much of a loss. Although Smithee is trained as an actor, he has spent the last four years working as a waiter for $2000 per month. Out of "generosity," CanPro is willing to pay $2000 to Smithee on the assumption that he stopped working a month before filming was scheduled to begin to rehearse his part. Would a court agree with that conclusion? Explain your answer.

9. In September, Marcy's Department Store placed an order with Fuego Toys Inc for the upcoming holiday season. While it is difficult to predict which toys will be popular with children, both parties expected that the Squiggles line of giggling squirrels would be amongst the market leaders. Marcy's therefore agreed to buy 50 000 Squiggles at $20 each. From that stock, the department store expected to earn a gross profit of $1 000 000 by charging $40 per item. Marcy's was concerned, however, because it knew that Fuego's overseas manufacturing operations were experiencing labour difficulties. Marcy's therefore persuaded Fuego to insert the following clause into the contract.

> Fuego Toys Inc promises to deliver 50 000 Squiggles to Marcy's Department Store by December 15. If Fuego is unable to meet that obligation, it will pay liquidated damages of $40 for each Squiggle that it is unable to deliver on schedule.

As the holiday season drew closer, the Squiggles fad grew much more dramatically than the parties had anticipated. By mid-December, their market value reached $100 per item. Unfortunately, Fuego's overseas labour problems also grew unexpectedly. As a result, it was unable to deliver any Squiggles to Marcy's. Furthermore, it was impossible for Marcy's to obtain an alternative source of Squiggles so close to the holidays. Assuming that Marcy's paid the purchase price at the time of signing the contract, how much can it recover in damages? Explain your answer.

10. Five years ago, Vladimir Ulyanov, a professional hockey player, signed a contract with the Rebels Hockey Club, which contained these terms:

- Vladimir Ulyanov agrees to perform for the Rebels Hockey Club and not to perform for any other hockey club for the duration of this contract.

- This contract shall run for 10 years from the date of signing.

- The Rebels Hockey Club agrees to pay Vladimir Ulyanov a base salary of $6 000 000 per year for the duration of this contract.

Last year, the Rebels hired a new coach, who changed the club's style of play by focusing far more on intimidation and far less on skill. Vladimir, a highly talented, but slightly built, player, wants no part of the new approach and has signed a contract to play with a rival team. The Rebels have brought an action against him for breach of contract. The team argues that monetary damages would not be an adequate remedy because (i) no amount of money would allow them to hire another player of Vladimir's calibre, and (ii) it is impossible to accurately predict the loss of merchandising and ticket revenue that would be caused by Vladimir's defection to a rival team. In response, Vladimir says that his only employment prospects outside of professional hockey lie in the food service industry, and that if he is required to take a job in a restaurant, his annual income would drop from $6 000 000 to $25 000. Will a court order specific performance against Vladimir? Will a court order an injunction against Vladimir? What do you believe would be a fair result in this case?

11. Rodeo & Blue Inc (RBI) has been a remarkable success story over the past four years. Starting from a small basement operation, it has quickly grown to a worldwide leader in the music industry. It is now valued at $500 000 000 and shows little sign of slowing down. Not surprisingly, shares in the company are very much in demand. Aside from their intrinsic value, those shares entitle their shareholders to enormous dividends (profits) on an annual basis. Furthermore, unlike many successful companies, RBI's shares are not available to the general public. The company continues to be private, rather than public, and the list of shareholders is jealously guarded. Four years ago, when the company was still small, it contractually sold an option, for the purchase of 20 000 shares, to Greg Cuddy. The company, however, has refused to honour that agreement. As a result, Cuddy feels doubly aggrieved. He has been denied the shares, and he has been deprived of $2 000 000 that he would have received as dividends if the contract had been performed as promised. Needless to say, he will continue to miss out on dividends as long as he does not hold the shares. At this point, however, it is impossible to determine the eventual value of those losses. Assuming that RBI is liable for breach of contract, what remedies should Cuddy receive?

12. The city has a set of by-laws that control the availability and operation of taxi cabs. To be a taxi driver, a person must hold both (i) a special driver's licence and (ii) a special permit for their vehicle. The driver's licence is relatively easy to acquire. A person must simply pay a fee and pass a series of examinations. The vehicle permit, in contrast, is very difficult to obtain. The by-laws strictly limit the number of permits that exist at any time. The city occasionally

increases that number, but there is always a long waiting list (usually about four years in length) for anyone wishing to purchase a new permit. There is only one other option for a person who hopes to begin operating a taxi. A driver who already owns a permit is entitled to sell it privately. That situation, however, occurs only rarely, and when it does, there is always a huge demand. Rich McTiernan recently decided to retire after driving a taxi for more than 30 years. After considering several offers, he contractually agreed to sell the permit to William Dixon for $50 000. Dixon immediately paid a deposit of $5000 and the parties agreed that the sale would be completed at the end of the year. In early December, however, McTiernan learned that, as a result of a recent turn in the stock market, his pension was worth much less than he had believed. He therefore decided that he would need to continue driving his taxi for five or ten years. He then told Dixon that the sale would have to be called off. Dixon is furious. He insists that McTiernan is required to complete the sale by handing over the vehicle permit in exchange for the agreed price. What result would a court most likely reach? Explain your answer.

Special Contracts: Sale of Goods

13

LEARNING OBJECTIVES

After completing this chapter, you should be able to:

❶ Explain why knowledge of the *Sale of Goods Act* is important for risk management.

❷ Define the term "sale of goods" and explain when it applies.

❸ Outline the rules that determine when property and risk pass under a sale of goods.

❹ Summarize the rules that the Act implies with respect to the seller's title to sell.

❺ Summarize the rules that apply when goods are sold on the basis of a sample.

❻ Explain the extent to which the Act requires goods to match their description. Explain the difference between merchantability and fitness for an intended purpose.

❼ Describe the rules that the Act implies with respect to delivery and payment.

❽ Outline the situations in which an action for the price is available and explain how that sort of action is different from a claim for damages under a breach of contract.

❾ Explain the difference between a lien and a stoppage in transit, and describe the situations in which each can apply.

❿ Explain when the seller can exercise a right of repossession.

We have completed our basic examination of contracts. Before leaving the topic, however, we will look at several types of contracts that are subject to special rules. We will discuss a number of these in other chapters, including leases, mortgages, insurance, agency, electronic commerce, and employment. In this chapter and the next, we will briefly consider two types of special contracts that are especially important in the business context: *sales of goods* and *negotiable instruments*.

The *Sale of Goods Act*

The Canadian economy was traditionally based on the sale of tangible (physical) goods, such as beaver pelts, timber, oil, and grain. The situation has changed. We now depend much more on intangible things, such as information and services. The sale of goods nevertheless remains vitally important. First, as individual consumers, we will always need to buy things such as food and clothing. Second, many businesses in this country continue to deal primarily in goods, buying or selling, for example, bicycles, apples, and cows. Third, even those businesses that do focus on information occasionally find it necessary to participate in the sale of goods. For example, although accountants are paid to provide analysis and advice, they cannot do so without first buying calculators, computers, and pens.

Because sale of goods contracts are so significant, they are governed by a special statute, the *Sale of Goods Act*. Interestingly, that statute was initially introduced as a *codification*. Over several hundred years, judges had developed a large number of rules that applied when goods were sold. They did this to ensure the smooth flow of commerce. Business people do not want to spend time or money in court. They want clear and comprehensive laws that allow them to quickly deal with potential problems and get on with the job of making money. With that same goal in mind, the British Parliament transferred, or *codified*, the judge-made rules into the *Sale of Goods Act* in 1893. Since then, all the common law jurisdictions in Canada have adopted virtually identical legislation.[1]

The history of the Act continues to be significant. Judges never intended to force contractual parties into certain types of agreements. They merely wanted to provide *default rules* that would apply if the parties did not deal with particular issues themselves. The general concept of freedom of contract meant the parties were usually free to make up different rules if they wished. That generally remains true today. While some exceptions do exist, the *Sale of Goods Act* is typically intended to fill in gaps. Goods can be bought and sold quickly because the parties do not have to negotiate and agree on a long list of terms. The Act does much of that work for them. At the same time, however, the Act also gives parties the freedom to create contracts with different terms, which better serve their purposes. All of that remains true even as an increasing amount of business is achieved through the Internet. We will address electronic commerce in

---

[1] *Sale of Goods Act*, RSA 2000, c S-2 (Alta); *Sale of Goods Act*, RSBC 1996, c 410 (BC); *Sale of Goods Act*, CCSM, c S10 (Man); *Sale of Goods Act*, RSNB 1973, c S-1 (NB); *Sale of Goods Act*, RSNL 1990, c S-6 (Nfld); *Sale of Goods Act*, RSNWT 1988, c S-6 (NWT); *Sale of Goods Act*, RSNS 1989, c 408 (NS); *Sale of Goods Act*, RSO 1990, c S.1 (Ont); *Sale of Goods Act*, RSPEI 1988, c S-1 (PEI); *Sale of Goods Act*, RSS 1978, c S-1 (Sask); *Sale of Goods Act*, RSY 2002, c 198 (Yuk). Because the statutes are almost identical, references in this text will be made to the Ontario legislation. A table of concordance, which provides a comparative listing of section numbers for all of the statutes, can be found in GHL Fridman *Sale of Goods in Canada* 4th ed (1997) at 3–5.

detail in Chapter 19. For now, it is enough to know that the same rules generally apply whether a sale of goods is created in person, over the telephone, or via the Internet.

It is important to understand how the *Sale of Goods Act* affects risk management. Because the Act provides default rules, a contract may include terms that the parties did not even discuss. Suppose you sell a conveyor belt to a mining company that is involved in a large and expensive project. If the belt is defective and causes the mining operation to shut down for several weeks, you may be held responsible for an enormous loss. Whether or not you were aware of the fact, your contract with the mining company may have included a condition that the conveyor belt was of *merchantable quality* or *fit for its intended purpose*. And if one of those conditions was breached, you might be liable for, say, $500 000 even though you charged only $500 for the belt. Knowledge of the *Sale of Goods Act* is therefore critically important. You cannot effectively manage a risk unless you are at least aware of it. If you are buying or selling goods, you should know the rights and obligations that the statute implies. And if you are unwilling to accept those rights and obligations, you should either walk away from the deal or persuade the other party to adopt different terms. If you do enter into a contract, you should use your knowledge of the Act to ensure that you are properly covered by insurance.

A Sale of Goods

L.O. ❶ ❷

The *Sale of Goods Act* applies only to a *sale of goods*. It defines a **sale of goods** as "a contract whereby the seller transfers or agrees to transfer the property in goods to the buyer for a money consideration, called the price."[2] We stress four points:

> a **sale of goods** is a contract whereby the seller transfers or agrees to transfer the property in goods to the buyer for a money consideration called the price

- The Act applies only to a *sale*.
- The Act applies only to a sale of *goods*.
- The Act applies only to a sale of goods for *money*.
- The Act is sometimes enforceable only if the contract is *evidenced in writing*.

First, the Act usually applies only to a *sale*.[3] That term covers two situations: *sale* and *agreement to sell*. A **sale** occurs if the buyer obtains ownership of the goods as soon as the contract is created. An **agreement to sell** occurs if the buyer does not obtain ownership of the goods until some time after the contract is created. For example, the buyer may agree to purchase a car that has not yet been manufactured or a bicycle that has not yet been separated out from an inventory of several dozen bikes. However, a sale of goods does *not* occur if the buyer is not intended to eventually obtain ownership. Consequently, the Act does not apply, for instance, if goods are leased (because ownership is not transferred), if they are given as a gift (because there is no contract), or if they are provided as security for a loan (because ownership is not transferred for the purpose of a sale).[4] And, as usual, a court will be guided by the substance,

> a **sale** occurs if the buyer obtains ownership of the goods as soon as the contract is created

> an **agreement to sell** occurs if the buyer does not obtain ownership of the goods until some time after the contract is created

---

[2.] *Sale of Goods Act*, s 2(1) (Ont).

[3.] The situation is different in British Columbia, where the *Sale of Goods Act* has been amended to include contracts in which goods are leased primarily for personal, family, or household purposes.

[4.] The Act is not excluded merely because goods are sold on credit. For instance, when goods are sold under a *conditional sales contract*, the buyer obtains possession immediately, but the seller retains ownership until the full price is paid. The Act nevertheless applies because the ultimate purpose of that transaction is to transfer ownership in exchange for money.

rather than the form, of a transaction. Consequently, the parties cannot turn a lease into a sale simply by calling it "an agreement to sell."[5]

Second, the Act applies only to a sale of *goods*. Goods are tangible (physical) things that can be moved.[6] These include cars, books, pigs, and crops that will be harvested from the land. It does not include land or things that have already been attached to land, such as houses and fences, because those things are not moveable. Nor does the definition of "goods" include things that are not tangible. For that reason, the Act does not apply to the sale of trademarks, shares, debts, or negotiable instruments.[7] And finally, services are not caught by the legislation. A difficult question often arises, however, when goods are sold together with services. In such circumstances, a judge must determine whether the essence of the contract was the performance of a service on the one hand or the transfer of property on the other.[8] Although the courts are not always consistent in their approach, Case Brief 13.1 provides a common illustration.

Case Brief 13.1

Gee v White Spot Ltd (1987) 32 DLR (4th) 238 (BC SC)

Mr Gee developed botulism after eating a meal at the defendant's restaurant. Claiming that the food he had purchased fell within the definition of "goods," he sued for damages under the *Sale of Goods Act*. The restaurant responded by arguing that the contract was really based on services, that is, the preparation of the meal.

The judge stressed that a contract does not have to deal exclusively with goods to fall within the Act. He then found in favour of Mr Gee for two main reasons. First, he held that a customer's primary purpose in ordering a meal in a restaurant usually is not to receive the services of a cook and a waiter, but rather to receive the food itself. Second, the judge was influenced by the fact that consumers like Mr Gee are better protected from defective goods if they are allowed to sue under the *Sale of Goods Act*.

Third, the Act applies only if the buyer provides consideration in the form of money. It does not apply if the parties simply trade goods, say, a car for a boat. However, the buyer does not have to pay entirely with cash. "Money" includes both cash and other forms of payment, such as cheques and credit cards, that allow the seller to receive cash. Furthermore, the Act may apply even if the buyer pays with money and goods. For example, you may purchase a new bicycle by paying $200 and trading in your old bike. That transaction would be considered a sale of goods.

Finally, a sale of goods is sometimes enforceable only if it is *evidenced in writing*. That requirement is limited in several ways. First, it applies only in some jurisdictions and only if the price is over a specific amount.[9] Second, a

---

[5] *Helby v Matthews* [1895] AC 471 (HL).

[6] *Sale of Goods Act*, s 1(1) (Ont).

[7] Those things are intangible even though they can be represented by something tangible, such as a share certificate.

[8] As we will see, one of the Act's most important functions is that it implies a number of terms regarding quality. Even if a contract involves services rather than goods (so that the Act does not apply), the courts may imply similar terms. For example, in *Maple Leaf Construction (1978) Ltd v Maloney* (1987) 34 BLR 93 (Man QB), a contract to build a tennis court was not a sale of goods, but it did contain an implied condition as to quality.

[9] The dollar value varies: $50 (Alberta, Newfoundland and Labrador, Northwest Territories, Nunavut, and Saskatchewan), $40 (Nova Scotia), $30 (Prince Edward Island), and $1000 (Yukon). There is no writing requirement in British Columbia, Manitoba, New Brunswick, or Ontario.

lack of writing does not mean that a contract is invalid, but rather that a court will not enforce it. As long as neither party needs to sue on the agreement, the transaction is perfectly effective. And third, the rule does not apply if the buyer (i) accepts part of the goods, (ii) pays part of the price, or (iii) provides something "in earnest." The first two exceptions are straightforward. The third occurs when the buyer gives something valuable, other than part of the purchase price, to make the agreement binding. That is an ancient idea that is seldom used today.

Passing of Property

If a contract involves a sale of goods, the Act implies a number of terms. A particularly important one is concerned with the *passing of property*. **Property passes** when the ownership or title in goods is transferred from the seller to the buyer. At that point, the property stops belonging to the seller and starts belonging to the buyer. Significantly, however, there is often a difference between *property* and *possession*. The seller may still possess the goods, in the sense of having physical control over them, even though the buyer has become the owner. Likewise, the buyer may obtain possession of the goods even though the seller is still the owner. As we will see, that separation of ownership and possession can cause considerable problems.

> **property passes** when the ownership or title in goods is transferred from the seller to the buyer

The passing of property is important for several reasons. It may affect the remedies that are available if a contract is breached.[10] It may also be important if one party becomes bankrupt. Suppose you pay for goods that the seller promises to deliver in a week. If the seller declares bankruptcy before having a chance to deliver, you will want to prove that you already acquired ownership of the goods. Otherwise, they may form part of the seller's bankrupt estate, and you will have to share them with the other creditors.[11] The passing of property is most important, however, because the Act states that *risk* passes with property unless the parties otherwise agree.[12] **Risk** is any loss or damage that may occur to the goods. Consequently, the party who bears the risk suffers the loss if, for example, goods are destroyed in a fire or stolen by a thief. From a risk management perspective, the lesson is clear: If you are buying valuable goods, you should make sure that you have an insurance policy that protects your investment from the moment that the risk passes to you.

> **risk** is any loss or damage that may occur to the goods

The Act provides rules for determining when property and risk pass under five situations.[13] We will quote each rule and follow it with a brief illustration.

RULE 1 Where there is an unconditional contract for the sale of specific goods in a deliverable state, the property in the goods passes to the buyer when the contract is made and it is immaterial whether the time of payment or the time of delivery or both is postponed.

[10.] In particular, the seller may bring an action for the price if property has passed.

[11.] As we will discuss under the heading of "Repossession," different rules may apply if a buyer becomes bankrupt after receiving title but before paying the price. The seller may be protected from the buyer's bankruptcy.

[12.] *Sale of Goods Act*, s 21 (Ont). Business people often use certain types of contracts that allocate property and risk in different ways. That is true for bills of lading, as well as cost, insurance, and freight (CIF) and freight on board (FOB) contracts.

[13.] *Sale of Goods Act*, s 19 (Ont).

Business Decision 13.1

Passing of Property—Rule 1

After closing a major deal and earning your first $1 000 000 in business, you decide to reward yourself by buying something special. You therefore visit Clouseau's jewellery store, pick out a diamond, and agree to buy it for $50 000. However, because you want to go straight to the gym afterwards, you persuade Clouseau to place the diamond in his safe. You promise that you will pick it up the next morning when you bring in the purchase price. Unfortunately, Clouseau's store is burglarized that night, and the thief makes off with the diamond.

Because there was an unconditional sale of a specific item that was already in a deliverable state, the property and the risk passed to you as soon as the contract was made. It is irrelevant that Clouseau still had possession of the diamond and that you had not yet paid the price. Consequently, the theft is your problem. You are still required to pay $50 000 to Clouseau, even though he no longer has the diamond. To protect yourself, you should have bought an insurance policy from an insurer at the same time that you bought that diamond from the jeweller.

RULE 2 Where there is a contract for the sale of specific goods and the seller is bound to do something to the goods for the purpose of putting them into a deliverable state, the property does not pass until such thing is done and the buyer has notice thereof.

Business Decision 13.2

Passing of Property—Rule 2

Assume the same facts as before, except that you agree to pay $50 000 for a particular diamond on the condition that Clouseau recut it. He agrees, estimates that the job will take between one and two weeks, and says that he will call you when he is finished. Eight days later, Clouseau recuts the diamond, places it in his safe, and leaves a reminder for himself to call you the next day. However, before he can call you, his store is burglarized, and the thief makes off with the diamond.

There was a sale of goods that required Clouseau to do something to put the diamond into a "deliverable state," that is, to put it into a condition that would require you to accept it under the contract. Consequently, property did not pass to you. While Clouseau had recut the diamond, he had not yet notified you. The theft is therefore his problem. You do not have to pay the purchase price and, unless he had insurance, he will suffer the loss.[14]

RULE 3 Where there is a contract for the sale of specific goods in a deliverable state but the seller is bound to weigh, measure, test, or do some other act or thing with reference to the goods for the purpose of ascertaining the price, the property does not pass until such act or thing is done and the buyer has notice thereof.

Business Decision 13.3

Passing of Property—Rule 3

Assume the same basic facts, except that you leave the diamond with Clouseau so that he can weigh it to determine its exact price. After doing so, he calls and tells you that the diamond is ready to be collected. Before you can get to his store, however, it is burglarized, and a thief makes off with the diamond.

There was a sale of goods that required Clouseau to do something to determine the price of the diamond. Consequently, property did not pass to you immediately. It did, however, pass as soon as Clouseau weighed the diamond *and* notified you of that fact. The theft is therefore your problem. Unless you bought insurance for the diamond, you will have to pay $50 000 to Clouseau for nothing.

[14.] If you already paid the purchase price, you would be able to recover it from Clouseau either under the contract or under an action for unjust enrichment, as explained in Chapter 12.

RULE 4 When goods are delivered to the buyer on approval or "on sale or return" or other similar terms, the property therein passes to the buyer,

   (i) when the buyer signifies approval or acceptance to the seller or does any other act adopting the transaction;

  (ii) if the buyer does not signify approval or acceptance to the seller but retains the goods without giving notice of rejection, then if a time has been fixed for the return of the goods, on the expiration of such time, and, if no time has been fixed, on the expiration of a reasonable time; what is a reasonable time is a question of fact.

Business Decision 13.4

Passing of Property—Rule 4

Assume the same basic facts, except that Clouseau allows you to take the diamond away on a trial basis because you are not sure that you really want to buy it. He is hoping that you will be persuaded to finalize the sale once your friends see the item and express their envy. Ten days later, a thief breaks into your house and steals the diamond.

More information is required to determine who will bear the loss of the diamond. Property would have passed if you had told Clouseau that you had chosen to keep the diamond or if you had done something that was inconsistent with his ownership of it (such as having it set into your own ring). Property also would have passed if you had agreed to return the diamond within three days, or if 10 days was more than a reasonable length of time.

RULE 5

   (i) Where there is a contract for the sale of unascertained or future goods by description and goods of that description and in a deliverable state are unconditionally appropriated to the contract, either by the seller with the assent of the buyer, or by the buyer with the assent of the seller, the property in the goods thereupon passes to the buyer, and such assent may be expressed or implied and may be given either before or after the appropriation is made.

  (ii) Where in pursuance of the contract the seller delivers the goods to the buyer or to a carrier or other bailee (whether named by the buyer or not) for the purpose of transmission to the buyer and does not reserve the right of disposal, the seller shall be deemed to have unconditionally appropriated the goods to the contract. (Bailees are discussed in Chapter 17.)

Business Decision 13.5

Passing of Property—Rule 5

Assume the same basic facts, except that Clouseau does not have an appropriate diamond in stock. You therefore pay $50 000, and he agrees to obtain a diamond from his dealer, which he will then deliver to you within a month. A week later, Clouseau receives an appropriate diamond from his supplier. He places it in his safe with the intention of delivering it to your office the next day. Unfortunately, his store is burglarized that night, and the thief makes off with the diamond.

Because there was a sale of unascertained goods, property would pass to you only after Clouseau obtained *and* unconditionally appropriated

a particular diamond to your contract. The courts have interpreted that requirement narrowly. Unconditional appropriation occurs only if the seller has lost the ability to use the goods for any purpose other than fulfilling the buyer's contract. Very often, that happens only when the goods are actually delivered to the buyer. Consequently, although the courts are somewhat inconsistent, the stolen diamond was probably *not* unconditionally appropriated to your contract.[15] After all, Clouseau could have changed his mind overnight and ordered another diamond for you. If so, property did not pass and the theft is his problem, not yours.

---

15. If Clouseau's actions *do* amount to unconditional appropriation, the court would probably find that you had given your "assent" (agreement) beforehand when you asked him to obtain an appropriate diamond.

PART 3

Concept Summary 13.1 reviews the rules regarding the passing of property.

Concept Summary 13.1

Passing of Property—Default Rules

Type of Contract	Property Passes
RULE 1: an unconditional contract for the sale of specific goods that are already in a deliverable state	• at the time of the contract, even if delivery and payment occur later
RULE 2: a contract for specified goods that requires the seller to do something to put the goods into a deliverable state	• when the seller has done that thing *and* the buyer has been notified
RULE 3: a contract for specified goods that requires the seller to do something to the goods (such as weigh, measure, or test them) in order to determine the price	• when the seller has done that thing and the buyer has been notified
RULE 4: a delivery of goods "on sale or return"	• when the buyer has signified approval *or* adopted the transaction *or* retained the goods beyond a reasonable time
RULE 5: a contract for unascertained or future goods by description	• when goods of that description, that are in a deliverable state, are unconditionally appropriated to the contract by one party with the other party's assent

Before leaving the issue of property passing, note two more points.

- First, it bears repeating that the Act merely provides default rules. The parties are generally entitled to override the Act and adopt other rules for the passing of property and risk.[16] Suppose you take possession of a specific diamond after promising to pay $50 000 to Clouseau. According to Rule 1, property has passed to you even though he has not yet received any money. However, if Clouseau is worried about your ability to pay, he might insert a *retention of title* clause into your contract that specifically says that he will continue to own the diamond until you have paid the full price. Otherwise, if you became bankrupt, he might lose the jewel *and* he might not be paid in full.

- Second, even if property has passed to the buyer, the risk is still on the seller if that party creates a loss by improperly delaying delivery.[17] Suppose Clouseau agrees to deliver a specific diamond to you on Monday. He carelessly forgets to do so and the diamond is stolen early Tuesday morning. Although property passed to you under Rule 1 when the contract was made, he bears the risk of the loss. The theft is his problem.

L.O.❹❺❻❼ Terms in Contracts of Sale

The *Sale of Goods Act* implies a number of terms in addition to the rules that determine the passing of property. We will look at three types:

- terms regarding the seller's title to sell
- terms regarding the nature of the goods themselves
- terms regarding delivery and payment

[16.] *Sale of Goods Act*, s 18 (Ont).

[17.] *Sale of Goods Act*, s 21 (Ont). Likewise, a party who possesses goods that are owned by someone else can be held responsible as a "bailee" for wrongfully causing those goods to be damaged or lost. We will examine bailees and bailors in Chapter 17.

Before we do so, it is important to review a distinction that was explained in Chapter 11. A contractual term is either a condition or a warranty. If a condition is breached, the innocent party substantially loses the whole benefit of the agreement, and therefore has the option of discharging the contract. If a warranty is breached, the innocent party does not substantially lose the benefit of the agreement, and therefore must carry on with the contract. In either event, however, the innocent party is entitled to damages. The *Sale of Goods Act* adopts those rules. Some of the implied terms under the Act are classified as conditions, while others are classified as warranties.

TITLE TO SELL

When you are buying goods, you want some assurance that the seller actually has *title to sell*. A person who does not actually own the goods cannot normally transfer ownership to you.[18] You may end up paying for nothing; or worse, you may commit a tort by attempting to buy property that belongs to someone else. (The tort of conversion was examined in Chapter 4.) The Act therefore implies a condition that the seller either has the right to sell the goods or will have the right to do so when the time comes to pass property.[19]

Similarly, you normally want some assurance that the seller is the *only* person who has an interest in the goods. Even if the seller is the owner, you do not want to buy property that is, for instance, the subject of a mortgage in favour of a third party. The Act therefore implies warranties that the buyer will receive clear title.

NATURE OF THE GOODS

The Act implies a number of conditions dealing with the goods themselves:

- Goods sold by description must match that description.
- Goods sold by sample must correspond with the sample.
- Goods must be of merchantable quality.
- Goods must be fit for their intended purpose.

Description

The Act implies a condition that goods sold by description will match that description.[20] Suppose you want to buy a stereo that can hold six CDs. You see such a product advertised on a website and place an order. When the equipment arrives, however, you discover that it can hold only three CDs. The seller has breached a condition, and you are entitled to reject the goods and discharge the contract.

Note that the term "description" refers to the *identity* of goods rather than to their *quality*. Consequently, there would not be a breach of contract (at least not under this heading) if the stereo you received could hold six CDs but

---

[18.] Lawyers often use the Latin phrase *nemo dat quod non habet*, which means "no one can give what they do not have." There are some exceptions to that rule. For example, the *Sale of Goods Act* says that a buyer who possesses goods, but who has not yet obtained ownership from the seller, can sell the property to an innocent person who was unaware of the seller's rights. The same basic rule applies to a seller who has possession of goods but no longer owns them. Those rules are intended to protect innocent people who honestly believe that they are dealing with property owners.

[19.] *Sale of Goods Act*, s 13 (Ont).

[20.] *Sale of Goods Act*, s 14 (Ont).

was not as loud as you had hoped. You still received an item that matched its description: a six-CD stereo.

Note also that goods can be sold by "description" even if a sale occurs in person. Suppose you bought a stereo from a store rather than over the Internet. There were 20 identical boxes on a shelf and you picked one. You could still discharge the contract for breach of a condition if you got home and discovered that the stereo did not really hold six CDs as the box had promised. You relied on the description of the goods even though you also selected one particular box for yourself.

Sample

a **sale by sample** occurs when the parties agree to deal in goods that match a particular specimen

A special set of conditions applies if goods are *sold by sample*. A **sale by sample** occurs when the parties agree to deal in goods that match a particular specimen. Suppose after seeing a circular saw being demonstrated in a hardware store, you read a brochure about that tool and tell the salesperson that you want to buy 10 units for your construction company. Four rules will apply to the sale:[21]

- First, if you bought by description as well as by sample, the store is required to deliver goods that correspond to both the description *and* the sample. Consequently, the saws must be the same kind that was demonstrated *and* they must have the features that were listed in the brochure.

- Second, the store must deliver saws that are of the same *quality* as the sample. Consequently, you would be able to discharge the contract if they did not cut as quickly or as accurately as the saw that was used in the demonstration.

- Third, the store must give you a *reasonable opportunity to compare* the saws to the one that was used during the demonstration.

- Fourth, the saws must be free from any defect that would make them *unmerchantable* and could not have been discovered by a *reasonable examination*. Consequently, you will have a strong incentive to inspect the saws when they are delivered. If they later turn out to be defective, you will not be able to complain if you could have discovered those defects at the outset. However, you are expected to conduct only a *reasonable* inspection. You would not have to take the saws apart or perform complicated tests on them.

Merchantable Quality

caveat emptor means "let the buyer beware"

The general rule in sales is ***caveat emptor:*** "let the buyer beware." Therefore, unless the seller made specific promises, you cannot complain if you are disappointed by the goods that you bought. The law expects you to be responsible for yourself. If you want to be protected from defective goods, you should either inspect them before you enter into a contract or pay the seller to guarantee their quality. At the same time, however, the law recognizes that those options are unrealistic in many circumstances. Suppose you visit a major electronics store to buy a new computer for your office. You will probably not have much opportunity to actually inspect or test a specific unit before taking it away. Furthermore, the store will probably be reluctant to draft a new contract that reflects your particular needs or concerns. It will want to use the standard document that it uses for all of its sales. For those reasons, to protect buyers like you, the *Sale of Goods Act* creates certain exceptions to the general rule of *caveat emptor*.[22]

[21.] *Sale of Goods Act*, ss 14, 16(2) (Ont).

[22.] *Sale of Goods Act*, s 15 (Ont).

First, the Act implies a condition that goods are of a *merchantable quality* if they are purchased by description from someone who normally deals in those sorts of goods. That rule requires four comments.

■ First, goods are **merchantable** if a reasonable person would buy them without a reduction in price despite knowing their imperfections. Goods do not have to be perfect to be merchantable. Returning to our example, a reasonable person might pay the full price for a computer even if a couple of pads on the keyboard are a bit sticky. However, no sensible person would pay full price for a computer with a cracked hard drive. Note that the implied condition can apply to both manufactured goods (such as computers) and natural products (such as milk). It can also apply to both new and used goods, although the expected quality of used goods is usually lower. And finally, the implied condition can apply to both the quality of the goods themselves and to such things as their labelling and packaging.[23] In any event, it is enough for the plaintiff to prove that the goods are not of merchantable quality. There is no need to prove the precise cause of the defect.[24]

> goods are **merchantable** if a reasonable person would buy them without a reduction in price despite knowing their imperfections

■ Second, the implied condition applies only if the *seller normally deals* in those sorts of goods. Consequently, a requirement of merchantability would arise if you bought a computer from an electronics store, but not if you bought it from me. I am not in the business of selling computers.

■ Third, the implied condition of merchantability does not cover *defects that the buyer should have noticed* if they examined the goods. Although the cases are somewhat inconsistent, it appears that the buyer is not actually required to conduct an examination. But if an inspection does occur, the seller is no longer responsible for problems that the buyer should have noticed. The seller does remain liable, however, for defects that could not have been discovered even with a reasonable examination. Consequently, if you spent 40 minutes thoroughly inspecting a computer without noticing any defects, you would still be able to discharge the contract if you later discovered that the machine overheats if it is left running for more than six hours.

■ Fourth, it is unclear whether the implied condition of merchantability (or fitness for purpose) includes a requirement that the goods be durable for a reasonable length of time. The answer is clearly "yes" if the lack of durability is due to some defect that existed, but was hidden, at the time of delivery. But what if the goods were merchantable when they were delivered but soon fell apart? Buyers in that situation seldom win in court. Consequently, some provinces have amended their legislation to include an implied condition of durability. In British Columbia, section 18(c) of the *Sale of Goods Act* says that "there is an implied condition that the goods will be durable for a reasonable period of time having regard to the use to which they would normally be put and to all the surrounding circumstances." Other provinces have adopted similar rules in their consumer protection legislation.[25]

[23.] *Sale of Goods Act*, s 1(1) (Ont).

[24.] *Schreiber Brothers Ltd v Currie Products Ltd* (1980) 108 DLR (3d) 1 (SCC).

[25.] *Eg Consumer Protection Act*, SS 1996, c C-30.1, s 48(g) (Sask). Also, *Sale of Goods Act*, RSBC 1996, c 410, s 18(c) (BC), and *Consumer Protection Act*, RSNS 1989, c 92, s 26(3)(j) (NS).

Fit for Intended Purposes

The requirement of merchantability is concerned with quality: The goods must not be defective. In some situations, the Act also implies a condition that goods must be *fit for their intended purpose*. Although those two requirements often overlap, they are different. Even if goods are not defective, they may not be suitable for the buyer's needs. For example, a computer is not defective simply because it does not have a DVD player. However, it is not fit for your purpose if you require a DVD player for use in your business.

Although the implied condition of fitness is potentially very useful, it applies only in certain circumstances:

- First, the *seller must normally deal* in the sorts of goods that the buyer purchased.

- Second, the *buyer must rely on the seller's skill or judgment* in selecting goods for a particular purpose and the *seller must be aware* of that fact. The buyer does not have to expressly mention a purpose that is obvious. It can be assumed that a personal computer will be used for word processing at least part of the time. However, the buyer does have to stipulate less obvious purposes. For instance, if you are relying on the seller to select a computer that is capable of operating a small Internet business, you must say so. Indeed, as a matter of risk management, you should specify your purpose whenever there is any doubt.

- Third, the implied condition does not apply if the buyer purchases goods on the basis of a *trade name*, rather than relying on the seller's judgment.

    The condition is intended to protect someone who relies on a vendor's skill and experience in selecting appropriate goods. Consequently, if you simply tell a store that you want a specific model of computer, you cannot later complain if that machine does not suit your needs. You made the choice for yourself. However, the implied condition is not barred every time you mention a trade name. The court has to decide whether you were relying on your own judgment or whether you were seeking the store's advice as to the suitability of a particular product.

Exclusion Clauses

The implied conditions and warranties that we have considered impose substantial burdens. For that reason, a person who sells goods will often try to avoid those obligations by writing an *exclusion clause* into the contract. (We examined exclusion clauses in Chapters 9 and 12.) Such clauses may, however, allow the seller to unfairly escape responsibility for shoddy goods. The courts and legislatures have therefore developed several techniques for controlling exclusion clauses. First, judges read exclusion clauses very narrowly. For instance, a clause that excludes "all implied *warranties*" may not affect the Act's implied *conditions*. Second, an exclusion clause will not be enforced if it would be unfair or unconscionable. (See Chapter 10.) Perhaps most significantly, however, the *Sale of Goods Act* may itself forbid an exclusion clause. As a general rule, the Act allows the parties to exclude or vary any of the implied terms.[26] Nevertheless, in some provinces, an agreement to vary or negate a condition or warranty under the *Sale of Goods Act* will be void and of no effect.[27]

[26.] *Sale of Goods Act*, s 53 (Ont).

[27.] See *eg Sale of Goods Act*, RSBC 1996, c 410, s 20 (BC); *Consumer Product Warranty and Liability Act*, RSNB 1973, SNB 1978, c 18.1, ss 24–25 (NB); *Consumer Protection Act*, RSO 1990, c 31, s 34 (Ont); *Consumer Products Warranties Act*, RSS 1978, c C-30, s 7 (Sask).

DELIVERY AND PAYMENT

The Act implies a number of terms dealing with *delivery* and *payment*.

■ First, unless the parties otherwise agree, *delivery and payment should occur concurrently*.[28] The buyer should take possession of the goods at the same time that the seller receives the money. Very often, however, the parties agree that delivery and payment will be separated, such as when the price is paid immediately for furniture that will be delivered several days later.

■ Second, although the Act is rather vague, the courts usually say that the *time of delivery is a condition*, whereas the *time of payment is a warranty*.[29] Consequently, the buyer may be able to discharge the contract if delivery is late, whereas the seller may have to settle for damages if payment does not occur promptly. The parties are entitled to stipulate when payment and delivery must occur. If they fail to do so, the contract must be performed within a "reasonable time." As always, the courts determine "reasonableness" in light of all the circumstances.[30]

■ Third, *delivery normally occurs at the seller's place of business*, unless the parties agree to some other arrangement.

■ Fourth, there is an implied condition that the *seller will deliver goods that conform with the contract*. That requirement is quite broad. For example, you are entitled to reject a shipment of peas if you ordered carrots. Similarly, if you ordered 50 cartons of peas for $500, you do not have to accept more or less. If the seller delivers 48 cartons of peas, you have the option of either rejecting them all *or* paying at the reduced price of $480. And if the seller delivers 52 cartons, you have the option of rejecting them all *or* accepting 50 at the price of $500 *or* accepting them all and paying at the contract rate of $520.

Concept Summary 13.2 reviews the terms that are implied under the Act.

Concept Summary 13.2

Implied Terms—Default Rules

Title to sell	• condition that the seller has title to sell • warranty that the buyer will receive clear title
Nature of the goods	• condition that goods sold by description will match that description • condition that goods sold by sample will match the sample in quality *and* that the buyer will have reasonable opportunity to compare the goods to the sample *and* that the goods are free from unmerchantable defects • condition that goods are of a merchantable quality if they are purchased by description from someone who normally deals in such goods • condition that goods will be fit for their intended purpose if the buyer relies on the skill or judgment of a seller who normally deals in such goods *and* if the seller knows of that reliance
Delivery and payment	• delivery and payment shall be concurrent • condition that delivery will occur on time and warranty that payment will occur on time • delivery will occur at the seller's place of business • condition that seller will deliver goods that conform with the contract

---

[28] *Sale of Goods Act*, s 27 (Ont).

[29] *Sale of Goods Act*, s 54 (Ont).

[30] *Sale of Goods Act*, s 11 (Ont).

L.O. ⑧ ⑨ ⑩   Remedies

If there is a breach of a contract for the sale of goods, several remedies may be available. The *Sale of Goods Act* provides a number of special remedies for an unpaid seller.[31] However, it also allows the parties to use the general remedies that we saw in the last two chapters. We will consider four special remedy possibilities.

GENERAL REMEDIES

First, the innocent party generally has the right to discharge a contract if there has been a breach of a *condition*. Suppose you agree to pay $50 000 to Nordic Furniture for the delivery of five oak desks to your office on June 1. You will be able to discharge the contract if, for instance, Nordic delivers desks on June 10 (late delivery), or if it delivers the wrong number of desks (wrong quantity) or pine desks (failure to correspond to description) or desks that topple over (unmerchantable and unfit for intended purpose). If you do discharge the contract, you will not have to pay the price, and if you have already paid the price, you will be able to recover it. In other circumstances, the seller would have the right to discharge the agreement. For instance, Nordic would be able to bring the contract to an end if, contrary to the usual rule, the time of payment were a condition, which you breached by failing to provide $50 000 on June 1 (late payment).

Second, the innocent party always has the right to claim compensatory damages. That is normally the only remedy that is available if there is a breach of a *warranty*. However, if there is a breach of a *condition*, the innocent party usually has the ability to discharge the contract in addition to claiming damages. In other words, that party can treat the term as either a condition (discharge plus damages) or a warranty (damages alone). Sometimes, however, that option is lost.[32] The Act states that a condition *must* be treated as a warranty if:

- the contract is not severable (in other words, if delivery is not made in instalments) and if the buyer has accepted at least some of the goods, or
- property in specific goods has already passed to the buyer.

In any event, the general purpose of compensatory damages is to put the innocent party in the same financial position that they would have enjoyed if the contract had been properly performed. Consider the case in You Be the Judge 13.1 (on the next page).

Third, as we saw in Chapter 12, the courts will enforce a contractual term for *liquidated damages*.[33] The parties are allowed to agree in advance that a certain amount will be paid if their agreement is breached. In the context of sale of goods, the most important illustration of that rule concerns *deposits*. A **deposit** is a sum of money that the buyer pays when entering into a contract

a **deposit** is a sum of money that the buyer pays when entering into a contract and that the seller is allowed to keep if the contract is not performed

---

[31.] This section discusses remedies that may be available for a breach of contract. Note that a contractual party may occasionally be entitled to rely on a different cause of action. For instance, it may be possible to rescind a contract that was induced by a misrepresentation (Chapter 9), to sue for damages under the torts of deceit (Chapter 5) or negligence (Chapter 6), or to claim restitution for unjust enrichment (Chapter 12).

[32.] *Sale of Goods Act*, s 12 (Ont).

[33.] However, the courts will not enforce a *penalty*, which is an amount of money that is completely out of proportion to the consequences of a breach.

You Be the Judge 13.1

Compensatory Damages and the *Sale of Goods Act*

The Town of Noix holds an annual, one-day nut festival, which attracts a large number of tourists. Helene, who operates a restaurant in Noix, contacted Ranjit, who owns a dry goods supply company, and ordered 50 kilograms of walnuts. As she explained to him, she intended to devote her entire menu during the festival to dishes prepared with walnuts. She paid $2500, and Ranjit promised to deliver the goods on May 30. Ranjit delivered on time, but the nuts were almost all mouldy. As she was entitled to do, Helene rejected them on the ground that they were unfit for their intended purpose. They would have made her customers sick.

Unfortunately, given the circumstances, Helene was unable to arrange an alternative supply of nuts and therefore was forced to remain closed during the festival. She consequently lost $10 000 in net profits from that day.

Question for Discussion

1. How much will Helene receive in damages from Ranjit? Explain how you reached that decision.

and that the seller is allowed to keep if the contract is not performed. Suppose you promise to pay within one week for a television that is worth $1000. The store clerk may demand a deposit of $100. If you return within a week and pay the remaining $900, you will be allowed to take the television home. But if you fail to pay the outstanding balance, the store will be entitled to keep the television *plus* the $100.

Fourth, in exceptional circumstances, a court may award *specific performance* of a contractual promise.[34] However, as we saw in Chapter 12, that remedy is available only if monetary damages would be inadequate. As a result, a buyer will not be entitled to specific performance unless the goods in question are special or unique, such as a family heirloom or a priceless painting.

SPECIAL REMEDIES FOR THE SELLER

An unpaid seller has a number of special remedies under the Act. We will consider four:

- an action for the price
- a lien
- stoppage in transit
- repossession

Action for the Price

The *Sale of Goods Act* states that the seller can sometimes bring an *action for the price*.[35] An **action for the price** occurs when the seller sues the buyer for the price of the goods. To help you understand how that type of action is different from a claim for damages under a breach of contract, consider Ethical Perspective 13.1 (on the next page).

Although the action for the price is an important remedy, it is available in only two situations: (i) if property has already passed to the buyer, or (ii) regardless of whether or not property has passed, if the contract requires payment to be made on a certain day and the buyer fails to pay on that day.

an **action for the price** occurs when the seller sues the buyer for the price of the goods

---

[34] *Sale of Goods Act* s 50 (Ont).

[35] *Sale of Goods Act*, s 47 (Ont).

PART 3

Ethical Perspective 13.1

Action for the Price and Expectation Damages

You own a used car dealership. One afternoon in late September, Conchita came onto your lot. She explained that she had moved to town to study for a business degree and that she needed a small vehicle for shopping. She looked at a number of cars before settling on a particular convertible. Because you were concerned about her financial circumstances, you persuaded her to sign a contract that required her to pay the full price of $8000 on October 1, even though she would not actually take possession of the car until October 4.

On September 29, however, Conchita informed you that she had dropped out of school because she needed to return home to care for a sick relative. She also asked if you would consider letting her out of the contract. You told her that you would think about it overnight. Later that same day, Logan wandered onto the lot and offered to pay $7000 for the same convertible.

You have three main options: First, you could simply release Conchita from the contract. She would not pay anything, and you could sell the car to Logan. Second, you could rely on the Act and bring an action for the price against Conchita. She would have to pay $8000, and you would have to deliver the car to her. Third, you could discharge your contract with Conchita and sue her for damages. Under the normal rules, you would be entitled to recover only $1000 from her. As Chapter 12 explained, if you sue for damages, you are expected to mitigate (or minimize) your loss. You could do so by selling the car to Logan. And in that situation, you would lose only $1000 as a result of Conchita's breach, since you would have sold the car for $7000 instead of $8000.

Questions for Discussion

1. Which of those three options would you choose? Why?

2. Is it fair that you have the ability to force Conchita to pay for a car that she no longer wants? Would your answer be different if you could not find anyone else to buy that particular vehicle?

Lien

a **lien** allows a person to retain possession of something until another person fulfills an obligation

The Act allows the seller to exercise a *lien* in some circumstances.[36] A **lien** allows a person to retain possession of something until another person fulfills an obligation. In the context of sale of goods, the seller may have the right to hold the goods until the buyer pays the price. That right can arise whether or not property has already passed.[37] It can also arise even if the time of payment is a warranty rather than a condition. In that case, while the seller cannot discharge the agreement if they do not receive the price on time, they may be able to hold onto the goods until the money is paid.

The right to exercise a lien is limited in several ways. First, a lien requires possession.[38] Consequently, once the buyer legitimately takes control of the goods, the seller loses the right to apply a lien. Second, the seller normally cannot exercise a lien if the buyer enjoys credit under the contract. Suppose you agree to deliver furniture to Leon on February 14, even though the contract does not require him to pay until October 31. You could not enforce a lien on Valentine's Day. You would have to deliver the goods and then wait until Halloween for the money.[39] The situation would be different, however, if Leon became *insolvent* before February 14. **Insolvency** occurs when a person is unable to meet their debts as they become due. (The issue

insolvency occurs when a person is unable to meet their debts as they become due

---

[36.] *Sale of Goods Act* s 39 (Ont).

[37.] Technically, the seller cannot exercise a lien unless property has passed. A person cannot have a lien over their *own* goods. However, a seller can exercise a similar right to *withhold delivery* if property has not passed and if payment has not been received: *Sale of Goods Act*, s 38(2) (Ont).

[38.] The lien that operates under the *Sale of Goods Act* is *possessory* because it allows the creditor to retain possession of an asset until a debt is paid. Other types of liens are discussed in Chapters 16 and 17.

[39.] A lien can be exercised, however, if the time for credit has *expired*. Consequently, if you agreed to deliver some of the furniture on Valentine's Day and the rest on New Year's Eve, you would not have to make the second delivery if Leon failed to pay the price on Halloween.

of insolvency will be discussed in Chapter 24.) In that case, the Act allows a lien to be exercised, even if goods were sold on credit. However, sometimes it is dangerous for a seller to use a lien in such circumstances, as Business Decision 13.6 shows.

Business Decision 13.6

Seller's Lien and Insolvency

You agree to sell 100 dictionaries to Erykah, who operates a small bookstore. Under the terms of that agreement, you are required to deliver the dictionaries on July 31, and she is required to pay $5000 before October 15. You know that she intends to eventually re-sell the books for $75 each.

On July 29, you hear a rumour that Erykah has experienced severe financial difficulties and has stopped paying her debts. For the next two days, you unsuccessfully try to contact her to determine if that rumour is true.

When July 31 arrives, you find yourself in a dilemma. You do not know whether you should deliver the books as promised.

Questions for Discussion

1. Explain the dilemma. What will happen if you deliver the books and later learn that Erykah is insolvent? What will happen if you refuse to deliver the books and later learn that the rumour was false, and that Erykah was not insolvent?

2. How will you resolve the dilemma? As you continue to read through the rest of this section on remedies, consider your other options.

Stoppage in Transit

The remedy of *stoppage in transit* is similar to a lien, but it is even more remarkable.[40] It can be exercised even if the seller no longer has property *or* possession. **Stoppage in transit** occurs when an unpaid seller instructs a carrier to not deliver goods to a buyer. Suppose you agree to sell a bull to Festus. Under the terms of that contract, you are required to send the animal to him by train, and he is required to pay $7500 when it arrives. During the course of the trip, however, you learn that Festus has become insolvent. In that situation, the Act allows you to contact the train company and prevent it from delivering the bull as initially directed. You can also demand that Festus pay within a reasonable time.[41] If he does so, he will be entitled to the bull. If not, you are free to sell the animal to another buyer and claim damages from Festus for any loss that his breach caused.[42]

stoppage in transit occurs when an unpaid seller instructs a carrier to not deliver goods to a buyer

Like a lien, stoppage in transit cannot be exercised if the buyer has already acquired possession of the goods.[43] Furthermore, it can be exercised only if the buyer has actually become insolvent. Consequently, the dilemma covered in Business Decision 13.6 can again arise.

Repossession

Section 81.1 of the *Bankruptcy and Insolvency Act* provides the most remarkable remedy of all. A seller is sometimes entitled to *repossess* goods from a

---

[40.] *Sale of Goods Act*, ss 42–44 (Ont). Stoppage in transit is no longer used very much. Many people believe that it unfairly favours the seller over the buyer's other creditors. Furthermore, payment today is often made by way of bankers' confirmed credits. Consequently, there is less danger that the seller will be unpaid.

[41.] If the goods are perishable, the seller can re-sell them immediately without first demanding payment from the buyer: *Sale of Goods Act*, s 46(3).

[42.] The same right of re-sale arises in connection with a lien and (presumably) with a repossession.

[43.] The right of stoppage in transit is also lost if a "document of title" (such as a *bill of lading*), is transferred to the buyer, who then uses that document to sell the goods to a third party who is unaware of any stoppage: *Sale of Goods Act*, s 45 (Ont).

buyer. That right may be available even though the buyer has already obtained property *and* possession. The remedy of repossession is, however, limited to very narrow circumstances. It can be used only if

- the goods are purchased for use in the buyer's business (and not for personal use)
- the seller delivers the goods to the buyer without receiving full payment
- the buyer becomes bankrupt or insolvent
- the seller provides written notice to the buyer's trustee in bankruptcy, within 30 days after delivery, that the goods are being repossessed
- the goods remain in the buyer's possession, have not been resold to an innocent third party, and are in the same condition as when they were delivered[44]

The effect of repossession is significant. Rather than being forced to bring an action and stand in line with the buyer's other creditors, the seller is allowed to recover the goods and simply walk away from the purchaser's financial problems.[45]

Concept Summary 13.3 reviews the extraordinary remedies that may be available to an unpaid seller of goods.

Concept Summary 13.3

Special Remedies for Unpaid Sellers

Remedy	Nature
Action for price	The seller is entitled to sue for the price of the goods, even if that price exceeds the damages arising from the buyer's breach
Lien	The seller is entitled to retain possession of the goods until payment is made, even if property has passed to the buyer
Stoppage in transit	The seller is entitled to prevent a carrier from delivering the goods to the buyer, even if property has passed to the buyer
Repossession	The seller is entitled to recover possession of the goods from the buyer, even though property and possession have passed to the buyer

---

[44] The requirement that the goods remain in the same condition as when they were sold may be applied flexibly. The remedy may be available, for instance, if the plaintiff sold grain to the defendant, who then mixed it with other grain of the same kind and quality. The plaintiff may be allowed to take the appropriate amount of grain from the larger mass. See *Port Alice Specialty Cellulose Inc (Trustee of) v ConocoPhillips Co* (2005) 254 DLR (4th) 397 (BC CA).

[45] Special remedies apply in favour of farmers, fishers, and aquaculturists: *Bankruptcy and Insolvency Act*, RSC 1985, c B-3, s 81.2 (Can).

Chapter Summary

Sale of goods contracts are governed by a special statute called the *Sale of Goods Act*. That Act supplies default rules that apply unless the parties have agreed otherwise. Knowledge of the Act is therefore necessary for the purposes of risk management.

The Act applies only to a sale of goods. There must be a sale that transfers property from the seller to the buyer. The contract must substantially deal with goods rather than services. The buyer must provide money as consideration. In some jurisdictions, some sale of goods contracts must be evidenced in writing.

The Act provides a number of default rules regarding the passing of property. The passing of property is important for several reasons. First, it may affect the remedies that are available to the parties. Second, it may allow one party to avoid financial complications if the other party becomes insolvent. And third, the party who has the property usually also bears the risk.

The Act implies several default terms. Some terms are conditions, and others are warranties. There is an implied condition that the seller has title to sell and an implied warranty that the buyer will receive clear title. There is an implied condition that goods sold by description must match their description. A number of conditions may apply if goods are sold by sample: (i) the goods must correspond to the sample, (ii) the buyer must be given a reasonable opportunity to inspect the bulk and compare it to the sample, and (iii) the goods must be merchantable. If goods are sold by description, there may be an implied condition that the goods are merchantable or fit for their intended purpose. Implied conditions or warranties can sometimes be avoided through exclusion clauses.

The Act implies a number of terms regarding delivery and payment. As a general rule, delivery and payment should occur at the same time. Time of delivery is normally a condition, but time of payment is normally a warranty. Delivery should usually occur at the seller's place of business. The seller must deliver goods that conform with the contract.

In addition to allowing general contractual remedies, the Act provides a number of special remedies for unpaid sellers. If property has passed, or if the buyer has not paid on a fixed date as required by the contract, the seller can bring an action for the price. A seller is generally entitled to enforce a lien to retain possession of goods until full payment is made. If the buyer is insolvent, the seller can exercise a right of stoppage in transit to recover goods that are in the possession of a third party carrier. Even if the buyer has received possession and property, the seller can sometimes exercise a right of repossession if the buyer is insolvent or bankrupt.

MyBusLawLab   ADDITIONAL RESOURCES FOR CHAPTER 13

MyBusLawLab provides students with an assortment of tools to help enrich the learning experience, including a Study Plan with Pre- and Post-tests, mini-cases with assessments, and provincial content material, which provides links to relevant cases, legislation, and additional resources.

MyBusLawLab provides the following resources for Chapter 13:

Provincial Material

- **British Columbia:** *Sale of Goods Act*, Consumer Protection Legislation, Lien, Passing of Property, Stoppage in Transit, Terms Implied by Statute
- **Alberta:** Deposits vs. Down Payments, Disclosure Requirements
- **Manitoba and Saskatchewan:** *Sale of Goods Act*—Endnote 1
- **Ontario:** *Consumer Protection Act 2002*, *Sale of Goods Act*
- **Atlantic Provinces:** *Sale of Goods Act*

Review Questions

1. "A knowledge of the *Sale of Goods Act* is important only in those provinces that happen to have the statute." Is that statement accurate and correct? Explain your answer.

2. Briefly explain why knowledge of the *Sale of Goods Act* is important for managing risk.

3. Define a "sale" according to the Act. Does a lease qualify as a sale? Does a gift? Explain your answers.

4. Define "goods" according to the Act. Can a transaction ever fall under the Act if one party provides services? Explain your answer.

5. When, if ever, is it necessary to put a contract for the sale of goods into writing?

6. Explain the *Sale of Goods Act*'s scope of application. Does the Act *always* apply to a sale of goods? Does it apply only if the parties actually choose to use it?

7. "As a general rule, the risk in specific goods that are already in a deliverable state does not pass to the buyer until the seller has received the price." Is that

statement correct? Explain your answer.

8. "As a general rule, if the seller has agreed to do something to specific goods (such as repair or weigh them), property does not pass to the buyer until delivery actually occurs." Is that statement correct? Explain your answer.

9. Explain the differences between a *sale*, an *agreement to sell*, and a *sale or return*.

10. Explain the significance of the concept of unconditional appropriation under a contract for unascertained goods. When does unconditional appropriation occur?

11. The *Sale of Goods Act* implies a variety of terms into a contract. For the purposes of determining the remedies that are available upon breach, each term is classified in one of two ways. Identify and briefly explain the two types of terms. Give examples of each type of term.

12. The Act implies a term that goods must correspond to their "description." Does that requirement apply

to both the identity and the quality of goods? Can goods be bought by description if the buyer selects a particular item off a store shelf?

13. What is meant by the phrase *caveat emptor*? Why is it important to a sale of goods contract? Does the Act entirely eliminate the need to be concerned with that phrase?

14. When are goods considered "merchantable"? Can imperfect goods be merchantable? Outline the situations in which the Act implies a term of merchantability.

15. When are goods considered "fit for their intended purpose"? Explain three limitations to the rule that goods must be fit for their intended purpose.

16. Explain the nature and effect of a deposit.

17. Stoppage in transit is a dramatic remedy, and it is seldom used. Provide two explanations for that fact.

18. The Act allows a court to impose a remedy that occurs under the general law of contract. Outline four possibilities.

19. When will the seller be able to bring an action for the price? How does that type of action differ from an action for damages under a breach of contract?

20. Summarize the differences between a lien, a stoppage in transit, and a repossession. Why might it be true to say that repossession is the most remarkable of those remedies?

Cases and Problems

1. MGM Auto Sales Ltd (MGM), a company situated in Red Deer, Alberta, owned a truck that it wished to sell. A former employee named Bayliss informed MGM of a potential buyer—Frontline Ventures Inc (Frontline), a company situated in Kelowna, British Columbia. MGM had no prior knowledge of Frontline. On June 1, Bayliss arranged a conference call, during which Frontline agreed to purchase the truck from MGM for a price of $15 000. The parties also agreed that Bayliss would drive the truck from Red Deer to Kelowna, and that Frontline would courier a cheque to MGM on June 5. Bayliss did drive the vehicle to Kelowna, but in doing so, he caused a traffic accident that injured Leona Hammerton. That accident occurred on June 4. On June 5, Frontline inspected the truck, recognized that it had not been damaged in the accident, and sent a cheque to MGM as promised. Some time later, Hammerton sued Bayliss for the injuries that she suffered in the accident. Bayliss unfortunately was not insured at the relevant time. Hammerton therefore wants to take advantage of section 17(b) of the *Uninsured Motorists Act*, which states that liability for loss or injury caused by an uninsured driver falls upon the owner of the vehicle that the uninsured driver was operating. It therefore is necessary to determine which company owned the truck on June 4. MGM relies on the fact that the sales contract was created on June 1. Frontline relies on the fact that, within the used vehicle industry, vendors rarely are willing to pass title to a previously unknown buyer until full payment has been received. How would a court likely resolve this case? Explain your answer.

2. Because she and her partner were unable to conceive a child naturally, Miranda Lopez visited Dr Omar Korn, a fertility expert. He suggested artificial insemination using semen collected from a donor. She agreed, and three weeks later, after Dr Korn had obtained semen from an anonymous donor, Mrs Lopez underwent an artificial insemination procedure. In exchange, she paid $1500. The procedure was unfortunately a failure. First, Mrs Lopez did not become pregnant. She does not, however, wish to sue Dr Korn on that basis. As he had explained to her at the outset, there was a chance that the semen would fail to fertilize an egg. Second, Mrs Lopez contracted HIV. The evidence indicates the man who donated the semen carried the virus, which was passed on to Mrs Lopez as a result of the procedure. Mrs Lopez wants to sue Dr Korn under the *Sale of Goods Act* because the semen that he provided was unmerchantable and unfit for its intended purpose. Did the parties enter into a contract for the sale of goods? Explain your answer.

3. Muskoka Fuels Inc required a fuel storage tank that would last for at least 10 years. It contacted Hassan Steel Fabricators Ltd, which is a company with a great deal of experience in the field. Under a contract with Muskoka Fuels, Hassan Steel designed, manufactured, and delivered a tank. After receiving that tank, Muskoka Fuels inspected it, found no sign of problems, and put it into service. Five months later, the purchaser discovered that a substantial amount of fuel had leaked onto the ground through a small hole that had developed at the bottom of the tank. That hole remains something of a mystery. The expert evidence has established that it was caused by "microbally induced internal corrosion." In other words, bacteria had eaten through the metal walls of the tank. Scientists still cannot explain exactly how that process works. At the time of the parties' contract, however, most of the companies that manufacture fuel tanks were aware of the phenomenon and knew that problems could be prevented by installing protective shields inside fuel tanks. Hassan Steel, in contrast, was completely unaware of the entire issue and the tank that it delivered to Muskoka Fuels did not contain a protective shield. The buyer now claims that the seller is liable for breach of contract. The seller, however, relies on the fact that the parties' written contract merely stated the type of tank that it was to create and deliver, the price that was to be paid, and the delivery date. Is Hassan Steel liable to Muskoka Fuels? Explain your answer.

4. Western Environmental Inc decided to close down an oil refinery, which was its only substantial asset. It therefore began to sell off the various pieces of equipment that were located within the refinery. On June 1, it sold a specific piece of pipe to Brendel Industries Co for $250 000. Under the terms of that contract, Brendel immediately paid the purchase price and promised to collect the pipe from Western's refinery within one month. Before Brendel did so, however, Western contacted another oil company, Fink Pipe Inc (Fink) with an offer to sell. Within two days, Fink had paid the purchase price and transported the pipe to its own facilities. A short time later, Brendel began to hear rumours of the deal between Western and Fink. Further investigation revealed a worst-case scenario. Not only had Western resold the same pipe to Fink, it had also ceased operations. Western's president had fled the country with all the company's liquid assets, leaving behind only an empty refinery and a mountain of debts. Brendel realizes that there is no point in suing Western. It has therefore sued Fink for the tort of conversion. Brendel insists that the pipe belongs to it. Furthermore, while admitting that Fink acted honestly when it dealt with Western, Brendel also insists that its own property rights in the pipe have been violated by Fink's actions in taking possession of the pipe. Does Brendel have a good claim in tort law? How does that claim relate to the *Sale of Goods Act*?

5. Karin McClain has been in the business of breeding and selling dogs for 40 years. She takes her job and reputation very seriously. Two years ago, she sold a Samoyed puppy, named Bear, to Martin Pezzente for a price of $350. Bear soon became a much-loved member of Martin's family. It therefore was very upsetting when the dog was diagnosed with a serious medical condition. Although Bear appeared to be in perfect health at the time of purchase, she actually suffered from a congenital defect that was bound to eventually take effect. The veterinarians offered only two options: euthanasia or surgery costing $10 000. Martin chose the latter. Happily, Bear is now in good health. Unhappily, Martin is burdened with the enormous expense. He therefore has sued Karin, claiming that she is responsible, by virtue of her breach of contract, for the veterinarian's bill. How would a court likely resolve the dispute? Explain your answer.

6. Auric Bond was seeking a safe investment for $100 000 that he had inherited from his parents. He contacted Goldcomp Inc, a company that dealt in precious metals. Goldcomp presented a standard form contract to Auric. The relevant portion of that document said:

> Gold is one of the safest investments available, and Goldcomp makes every effort to ensure that your investment is protected as it grows. Goldcomp holds a large amount of gold bullion in its guarded vault. Once you have paid the purchase price, an appropriate percentage of that gold will be allocated to you, and you will receive a certificate verifying your ownership of that gold. You can, at any time, take physical delivery of your purchase by providing Goldcomp with seven days' notice.

Auric agreed to those terms, paid $100 000 to Goldcomp, and received a certificate stating that he was the owner of a certain amount of gold.

Goldcomp recently became bankrupt. Its debts exceed its assets by a 10:1 ratio. Furthermore, it was recently discovered that Goldcomp never actually separated its gold into separate bundles for Auric or its other customers. All of its gold sat in an undifferentiated mass in its vault. Auric has given seven days' notice under the agreement, but because of its bankruptcy, Goldcomp has not delivered any gold to him. In the circumstances, Auric can sue Goldcomp for breach of contract. However, if he does so, he will simply obtain a personal judgment and will have to share Goldcomp's meagre assets with the other creditors. He would be lucky to get $10 000 under that approach. Auric therefore wants to argue that he can take possession of $100 000 worth of gold on the basis that he already has property or ownership in it. Will that argument be successful? Explain your answer.

7. Denise Wharton visited Harris Motors, a car dealership, with a view to buying a new car. While she indicated that she was particularly interested in Cadillacs, she also sought the sales representative's advice. She explained that she was nearing retirement age and was looking for a car that was suitable for long, relaxing drives. She stressed that she wanted a vehicle with a good stereo and a quiet ride. The sales representative showed her several models, but focused on the Cadillac Eldorado Touring Coupe, a luxury vehicle. The sale was finalized when Denise paid $62 000 and drove the Eldorado off the lot. Unfortunately, the sound system soon developed a loud buzzing sound. That sound was almost constant, and it was loud enough to disrupt normal conversation. Not surprisingly, the noise caused Denise a great deal of frustration and disappointment. Her dream car had become something of a nightmare. Over the next two years, she returned the car several times to Harris Motors with the aim of having the problem solved. (Since she was from out of town, those visits to the dealership involved expenses amounting to $2500.) The dealer's mechanics were, however, unable to identify the source of the noise. Denise eventually gave up hope and sold the car to a stranger for $31 000. She now intends to sue Harris Motors under the *Sale of Goods Act*. What provisions should she rely upon and what arguments should she make? If her claim is successful, how will the judge determine the remedy? What losses did Denise suffer? (You may want to reread parts of Chapter 12, which deal with remedies for breach of contract.)

8. Kerasic Lumber Inc agreed to sell planks to Chios Home Supply Ltd. The parties' contract contained the following paragraph:

> Kerasic Lumber will deliver 1000 redwood planks to Chios Home Supply on June 1. Chios Home Supply will pay $7 per plank for a total contract price of $7000. Each plank shall be 3 centimetres thick, between 30 and 35 centimetres wide, and between 3 metres and 3.1 metres in length.

On June 1, Kerasic Lumber delivered 1020 planks to Chios Home Supply. Each plank fell within the terms of the contract with respect to width and length, but about half of the planks were between 3.2 and 3.3 centimetres thick. Chios Home Supply rejected the goods and refused to pay the purchase price. Its motivation for doing so turned on the fact that it had discovered that it could buy the goods from another supplier at a lower price. Kerasic has sued under the contract. As part of its claim, it is able to prove that the planks were free from defects and were entirely fit for Chios's purposes. Will Kerasic win? Provide two reasons for your answer.

9. Syncrude Canada Inc operates a massive tar sands project in Northern Alberta. For the purposes of that project, Syncrude required two devices. First, it contracted to have a mining gearbox designed and delivered by Hunter Engineering Inc. The parties' contract in that instance contained an "express warranty" stating that the device was free from defects. That express warranty, however, was said to be effective for only 12 months following purchase. Second, Syncrude contracted to have an extraction gearbox designed and delivered by Allis-Chalmers Ltd (ACL). The parties' contract in that instance contained two important provisions. Once again, the device was said, under an "express warranty," to be free from defect for a 12-month period. In addition, the contract also stated that the 12-month express warranty was "the only warranty . . . and no other warranty or conditions, statutory or otherwise shall be implied." Although both devices were expected to last for at least ten years, both failed after two years. Syncrude consequently was required to shut down operations while replacement parts were acquired. The resulting financial loss was enormous. Syncrude has now sued both Hunter and ACL for breach of contract. Is a court likely to hold either defendant liable? Explain your answer.

10. The University of Southern Alberta wanted to upgrade its football stadium. Rather than grass, it wanted a field made from a long-lasting, synthetic material that would not easily wear down and that would not discolour under the warm Alberta sun. It also wanted the turf to be purple, rather than green, in order to reflect the school's colours. It explained its needs to Cyber-Turf Inc, an artificial turf company located in Calgary. The sales representative from Cyber-Turf assured the university that it would be able to develop such a product. The parties then entered into a contract. The university agreed to pay $100 000 and Cyber-Turf agreed to manufacture the turf within six months. Approximately six months later, the company informed the university that the new turf was finished and that it was being stored on the company's back lot. The university promised to collect the purple carpet within one month and to provide payment at that time. The company agreed to that arrangement. Two weeks later, however, the Calgary area was hit by a severe rainstorm, followed by six days of intense sunlight and heat. The combined effect of the rain and the sun was to badly discolour portions of the new turf, from bright purple to light blue. Consequently, when the university came to collect the turf a week later, it refused to take delivery. Cyber-Turf, in contrast, insists that it is entitled to the purchase price and that the new turf, whatever its condition, is solely the university's concern. Discuss the parties' rights and liabilities.

11. After upgrading his film studio, Werner agreed to sell his old equipment to Isabelle, a young director who wanted to film a movie beginning on May 1. The equipment consisted of a number of cameras and related items that were valued at $250 000. The parties signed a contract on March 1 that contained this paragraph:

> The seller agrees to deliver the equipment to the buyer's residence on or before April 30. The buyer agrees to pay the purchase price of $250 000 on April 15. The seller will remain the owner of the equipment until full payment has been received or the equipment has been delivered to the buyer, whichever is earlier.

On April 15, Isabelle explained to Werner that she would not be able to pay the price for at least two months. However, she also insisted that she required the equipment by April 30 to begin filming her own movie on May 1. Werner indicated that he was reluctant to hand the equipment over until he received full payment. On April 30, Isabelle repeated her demand. Having done some legal research, she also told Werner that time of delivery was a condition of the contract, and that he could be held liable for any losses that she suffered as a result of late delivery. She also told him that the equipment was already hers because the property in it passed as soon as they signed their agreement. Is she correct? Does the equipment already belong to her? Is Werner required to deliver the equipment before receiving the purchase price? If Werner wants to sue for the purchase price, is he entitled to do so? Explain your answers.

12. In the course of operating a pulp mill, Port Alice Specialty Cellulose Inc (PASCI) required a large amount of oil. For many years, it purchased its oil from ConocoPhillips Co. Last July, ConocoPhillips sold and delivered 30 barrels worth of oil to PASCI. That shipment was added to PASCI's large, under-

ground tank, which already held 60 barrels worth of the same type of oil. The new oil and the old oil became completely mixed. PASCI withdrew 15 barrels of oil from the tank and used it for business purposes. It then became bankrupt and its pulp mill immediately shut down. PASCI has few assets, but it owes a great deal of money to a large number of creditors. It intends to sell the oil remaining in its underground tank and to distribute the sale proceeds amongst all its creditors. ConocoPhillips is one of those creditors because it was not paid for its last delivery of oil to PASCI. ConocoPhillips, however, claims that it does not have to stand in line with PASCI's other creditors. It believes that it is entitled to use a special remedy that will allow it to take back the oil that it delivered, and to walk away from PASCI's financial mess. What remedy does ConocoPhillips have in mind? Do you think that its argument will be successful? Explain your answer.

14 Special Contracts: Negotiable Instruments

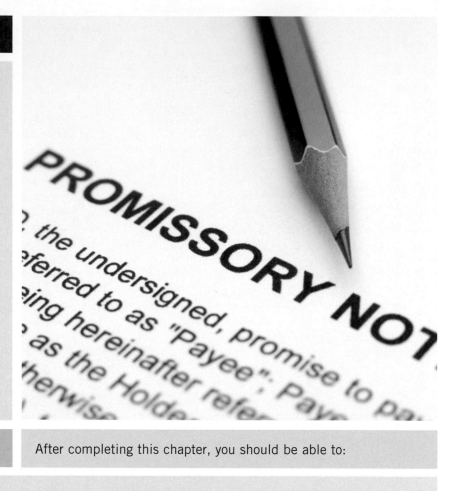

LEARNING OBJECTIVES

After completing this chapter, you should be able to:

❶ Explain why it is often more dangerous to pay with cash than with a negotiable instrument.

❷ Summarize five requirements that a document must satisfy before it will fall within the *Bills of Exchange Act*.

❸ Explain how a cheque works by describing the events that occur between (i) the drawer and the payee, (ii) the drawer and the drawee, and (iii) the drawee and the payee.

❹ Distinguish between overdrawn cheques and countermanded cheques.

❺ Describe the process of certification, and explain how it affects the rights of the parties to a cheque.

❻ Distinguish between a bill of exchange and a cheque.

❼ Explain how a promissory note operates.

❽ Describe the requirements for the negotiation of (i) a bearer instrument, and (ii) an order instrument.

❾ Summarize seven forms of endorsement and explain how each form affects the issue of liability.

❿ Distinguish between (i) immediate parties, (ii) holders, and (iii) holders in due course, and between (i) personal defences, (ii) defect in title defences, and (iii) real defences.

In Chapter 13, we saw that contracts dealing with the sales of goods are governed by special rules that are intended to make the business world operate efficiently. The same is true for contracts that take the form of negotiable instruments. Even if you are not familiar with that term, you certainly are familiar with the underlying concept. In fact, when you pay for something with a cheque, you are dealing with a negotiable instrument.

There are many different ways of making payments. Sometimes it is easiest to use cash.[1] The simplest way of buying a cup of coffee is to hand over, say, $1.75 in coins. Cash, however, can be inconvenient and dangerous. It is inconvenient because it is bulky. The price of a cup of coffee easily fits into your pocket, but the price of a car does not. More significantly, cash is dangerous because it is usually impossible to recover if it is lost or stolen. The essential feature of cash is that it is currency. A $20 bill is valuable in itself—it does not simply represent a right to acquire something else that is valuable. Furthermore, a person can become the owner of cash by honestly paying for it. Suppose I steal $10 000 from your wallet. My dishonesty prevents me from owning that money. However, if I use that cash to buy a stereo from a storekeeper who was unaware of the theft, you no longer own the money; the storekeeper does.[2] Consequently, you cannot retrieve it from them. You can sue me, but like many thieves, I may have disappeared or I may be so poor that I am not worth suing. As a matter of risk management, the lesson of that story is clear: Never carry more cash than you are prepared to do without.

There are other ways of making payments that are more convenient and less dangerous than cash. For instance, credit cards and debits cards can be used. (We briefly examined the use of credit cards and debit cards in Chapter 11.) In this chapter, we will discuss negotiable instruments. A **negotiable instrument** consists of a contract that contains an obligation to pay money. Suppose you buy a car from a dealership. A contract is created—you are required to pay the price, and the dealer is required to transfer the car to you. But how will you pay the price? It would be foolish for you to carry $20 000 in cash from your bank to the car lot.[3] At the same time, however, the dealer wants something more than your simple promise under the sale agreement. You therefore write out a cheque for $20 000. That cheque is a new contract. You have promised that $20 000 will be paid to whoever presents that piece of paper to your bank. Consequently, if your bank refuses to honour the cheque, the dealer can sue you on either the sale contract or the cheque itself.[4] The second option is usually preferable. It is easier to prove the existence of a negotiable instrument than the existence of a sale contract.

a **negotiable instrument** consists of a contract that contains an obligation to pay money

---

[1.] In fact, as we saw in Chapter 11, unless the parties have otherwise agreed, a creditor is entitled to receive payment in legal tender, that is, cash.

[2.] The law allows the storekeeper to become the owner of the $10 000 because it wants cash to flow freely. If the storekeeper were required to determine if I actually owned the $10 000 that I gave them, the business world would grind to halt. Every cash purchase would involve a long, expensive, and perhaps impossible process of proving ownership of the coins and bills that the buyer offered. Different rules apply to things other than money. As we saw in Chapter 13, the general rule is nemo dat quod non habet, "no one can give what they do not have." Consequently, if I stole your car and traded it to my neighbour for their boat, you would probably be entitled to recover the value of the car from them, even if they had acted honestly.

[3.] It might be equally foolish for the dealership to accept cash. If that money were lost or stolen before it could be deposited in a bank, the dealership would suffer the loss. The dealership would be in a safer position if you paid by cheque. If that cheque were lost or stolen, the dealer could ask you to provide another one: *Bills of Exchange Act*, RSC 1985, c B-4, s 155 (Can). In exchange, it would have to indemnify you for any loss that might occur because of the existence of two cheques.

[4.] Your obligation to pay $20 000 under the sales contract was conditionally discharged when you gave the cheque to the dealership. When your bank refused to honour that cheque, however, your obligation under the sales contract was revived.

Understandably, people often do not realize that a cheque is a type of contract.[5] Many of the rules that normally govern contracts do not apply in the same way to negotiable instruments. We note three important differences:

- Consideration: Like all contracts, a cheque is enforceable only if it is supported by consideration. Something of value must be given in exchange for it. However, the requirement of consideration is more easily satisfied in the case of a cheque. As Chapter 8 explained, consideration normally cannot consist of a promise to perform an obligation that is already owed to the same party. However, that rule does not apply to a cheque.[6] In our previous example, the dealership's promise to transfer a car to you acted as consideration twice: first for the sale contract and then for your cheque.

- Privity: Normally, a contract can be enforced only by someone with privity. Chapter 8 explained that a stranger, someone who did not participate in the creation of the agreement, cannot sue on it. Nevertheless, anyone who holds a cheque can sue on it. Suppose the dealership in our earlier example coincidentally owed $20 000 to the Daily Bugle for a newspaper advertisement. Instead of cashing your cheque and using that money to pay its bill, the dealer might simply sell your cheque to the newspaper. The Daily Bugle could then sue you on the cheque, even though it was not originally a party to that contract.

- Assignment: Contractual obligations can generally be assigned to a stranger. As we saw in Chapter 8, however, assignment is a cumbersome process.[7] Furthermore, a person who receives a contractual right through an assignment takes it subject to the equities. The assignee cannot be in a better position than the assignor. Assume that the dealership assigned its rights under the sale contract to the Daily Bugle. If the newspaper sued you for the price, you could use any defence that you could have used against the dealership. Suppose the dealer breached the contract by selling you a car that required $5000 in repairs. If the purchase price was $20 000, you would have to pay only $15 000 to the newspaper. The situation might be different, however, if the dealership sold your cheque to the Daily Bugle. The most remarkable thing about a negotiable instrument is that, depending on the circumstances, it can improve as it is passed from one person to the next. Consequently, the newspaper might be able to recover $20 000 from you even though your car was defective. You would have to sue the dealership for breach of contract if you wanted to be paid $5000 for the repairs.

A negotiable instrument therefore represents a compromise between a simple contract and money. A negotiable instrument is more valuable than a simple contract because, like money, it is negotiable. It can be easily transferred from one party to another in a way that may remove any defects. The Daily Bugle acquired clear title to the cheque that you had given to the car dealership, just as the storekeeper became the owner of the cash that I had stolen from you in our earlier example. At the same time, however, a negotiable instrument is not actually money. It is a contract that is intended to eventually result in the

[5] Although this section refers to cheques, the same observations generally apply to other types of negotiable instruments as well.

[6] Bills of Exchange Act, s 52. The Act also presumes that consideration was given by every person whose signature appears on a negotiable instrument: s 57(1).

[7] For instance, an assignee normally is required (as a matter of risk management, if not as a matter of law) to give notice of an assignment to a debtor. That requirement does not apply to a negotiable instrument.

payment of money. Consequently, it carries the major risk that is associated with every contract: non-performance. While it is often much better to sue on a negotiable instrument than on a simple contract, enforcement is ultimately necessary in either event. And if a cheque is created by a person who simply does not have any assets, it may be a worthless piece of paper.[8] Coins and bills, in contrast, are never worthless. They have value in themselves.

The *Bills of Exchange Act*

L.O. ❶

This chapter is similar to the last one in some respects. Negotiable instruments and sales of goods both involve contracts that are critically important in the business world. Furthermore, because of the need for commercial certainty, both have been codified. As you will recall, when the British Parliament introduced the *Sale of Goods Act* in 1893, it adopted the rules that judges had developed over many years. The legislature's aim was to ensure that the economy ran smoothly. The same process occurred for negotiable instruments. In 1882, the British Parliament enacted the *Bills of Exchange Act*, which formally adopted rules that judges had developed over several centuries. The legislature's intention was to increase economic efficiency by providing business people with a comprehensive set of rules regarding non-monetary payments. The Canadian Parliament once again followed the British model and introduced its own *Bills of Exchange Act* in 1890.[9] With a few exceptions, that statute has hardly changed in more than a century.

Although both statutes were motivated by similar concerns, they are quite different in some ways. The most important difference is that the Bills of Exchange Act is much less flexible than the *Sale of Goods Act*. The *Sale of Goods Act* is a relatively simple statute that provides default rules. The parties are generally free to pick and choose amongst those rules and, even if they accept some and reject others, their contract can still fall within the Act. The *Bills of Exchange Act* is a much longer and more complicated statute. Furthermore, as we will see in the next section, it contains a large number of rules that a contract must satisfy. If those requirements are not met, the Act does not apply. That difference arises because a sale of goods normally involves only two parties, whereas negotiable instruments are designed to be freely transferred amongst many people. Consequently, there is an even greater need for certainty with negotiable instruments. If I did not participate in the creation of a cheque, for instance, I may not be willing to buy it unless I can be assured, by simply looking at that piece of paper, that it is valuable.

Types of Negotiable Instruments

L.O. ❷❸❹❺❻❼

There are many varieties of negotiable instruments. Share certificates, for instance, are sometimes placed into that category. The *Bills of Exchange Act*, however, applies to only three types of negotiable instruments: cheques, bills of exchange, and promissory notes. We will look at each of those separately. But first, we can summarize the five requirements that must always be met before

---

[8.] Interestingly, as we shall see, a cheque may be valuable even if the person who wrote it is penniless. It may be possible to collect money from anyone who endorsed the cheque.

[9.] Bills of Exchange Act, 45 & 46 Vict, c 61. Sales of goods are a provincial matter, but negotiable instruments are a federal matter. Consequently, while each province and territory has its own Sale of Goods Act, there is only one *Bills of Exchange Act*, which applies across the country.

the Act will apply.[10] Notice how each requirement serves the goal of certainty that we just discussed. A negotiable instrument must tell a complete story. A business person cannot be expected to look behind it.

- Signed and written: First, although most contracts can be created orally, a negotiable instrument must be signed and written. The reason is obvious. A promise cannot be clearly passed from one person to the next unless it is in writing.

- Parties identified: Second, the parties must be clearly identified. It must be possible to immediately determine who is required to make the payment. That information is important when the time comes to "cash" the instrument. However, it is also useful in deciding whether to buy a document in the first place. A cheque created by a con artist who holds an account at a bank that is in the process of collapsing is probably not worth the paper it is written on.

- Certain sum of money: Third, the contract must involve an obligation to pay a certain sum of money. The obligation must deal entirely with the payment of money, not with such things as the delivery of goods or the performance of services. It also must be possible to calculate the amount of money by simply looking at the document itself. Consequently, while a negotiable instrument may involve the payment of interest, it cannot, for instance, require the payment of "a reasonable price" or "any money that may be won in a lottery."

- Time of payment: Fourth, the time of payment must be clearly stated. A person buying a negotiable instrument must be able to determine precisely when that piece of paper can be turned into cash.

- Unconditional obligation: Fifth, the contract must contain an unconditional obligation. For instance, if a person paid the price of a car with a cheque, that document could not require payment to be made "if the buyer is satisfied with the vehicle." As always, it must be possible for a person who buys a negotiable instrument to immediately know exactly what they are receiving.

Concept Summary 14.1 summarizes those requirements and compares the essential concepts of a cheque, a bill of exchange, and a promissory note.

Concept Summary 14.1

Nature and Requirements of Negotiable Instruments

Type of Instrument	Nature	Basic Requirements
Cheque	an order by one party (drawer) that directs a bank (drawee) to provide money to someone (payee)	• identify parties • signed and written • certain sum of money • time of payment • unconditional obligation
Bill of exchange	an order by one party (drawer) that directs another party—who may or may not be a bank (drawee)—to provide money to someone (payee)	
Promissory note	a promise by one party (maker) to pay money to someone (payee)	

[10.] A document that does not meet those requirements may still be a valid contract, but it does not fall under the *Bills of Exchange Act*.

FIGURE 14.1   Cheque

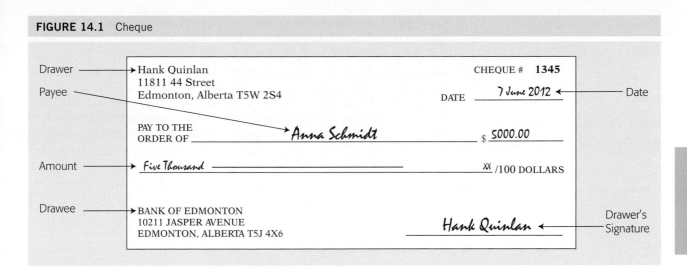

CHEQUES

The most common form of negotiable instrument is a cheque. A **cheque** is created when a person orders a bank to pay a specific amount of money to someone.[11] Suppose Hank Quinlan, an accountant, bought an oak desk from Anna Schmidt for $5000. Hank did not have any money in his pocket, but he did have a chequing account at the Bank of Edmonton. He gave Anna the cheque in Figure 14.1, which shows that (i) Hank is the drawer, (ii) the Bank of Edmonton is the drawee, and (iii) Anna is the payee. The **drawer** is the person who "draws," or creates, the cheque. The **drawee** is the bank that is ordered to pay the money. And the **payee** is the person who is entitled to receive the money from the bank.

To appreciate the effect of that cheque, you must understand the relationships that exist between the parties.

- Hank and Anna: There are two contracts between Hank and Anna. The first is the sale of goods agreement; the second is the cheque itself. By writing that cheque, Hank tried to fulfill his obligation under the sales contract by ordering the Bank of Edmonton to pay $5000 to Anna.

- Hank and the Bank of Edmonton: Hank has a contractual relationship with the Bank of Edmonton. When he opened his chequing account at the bank, he exchanged a large number of promises. For example, he agreed to allow the bank to debit his account—withdraw money from it—whenever he wrote a cheque.[12] In exchange, the bank promised to honour, or pay, cheques that Hank wrote, as long as they appeared in the correct form and he had enough money in his account. Hank ordered the bank to fulfill that promise when he wrote the cheque to Anna. Assuming that everything went well, the bank honoured that cheque, paid $5000 to

a **cheque** is created when a person orders a bank to pay a specific amount of money to someone

the **drawer** is the person who "draws," or creates, the cheque

the **drawee** is the bank that is ordered to pay the money

the **payee** is the person who is entitled to receive the money from the bank

---

[11.] The term "bank" includes some credit unions and trust companies: *Bills of Exchange Act*, s 164. If an instrument is not drawn on a bank, it cannot be a cheque, but it may be a bill of exchange.

[12.] That statement is not entirely accurate. When money is deposited into an account, the bank almost always becomes the owner of the bills and coins that it has received. In exchange, it gives its contractual promise to repay a similar amount when the depositor asks for it. Consequently, in our example, the Bank of Edmonton would not actually withdraw any money from Hank's account after cashing his cheque. Rather, it would simply reduce the amount that it owed to him.

Anna, and deducted that same amount from Hank's account. If the bank improperly refused to pay $5000 to Anna when she presented the cheque to it, it could be held liable to Hank for breach of contract.[13]

- Anna and the Bank of Edmonton: Anna does not have a relationship with the Bank of Edmonton. She is a stranger to the agreement that exists between Hank and the bank. Consequently, she could not sue the bank if it refused to pay $5000 to her. If she wanted that money, she would have to sue Hank on either the cheque or the sales contract.

Most cheques operate smoothly. However, there are five possible complications:

- postdated cheques
- staledated cheques
- overdrawn cheques
- countermanded cheques
- certified cheques

Before we look at those complications, however, it is important to remember that while the bank has a contractual relationship with the drawer, it does not normally owe any obligations to the payee. As a result, the bank may instruct its tellers to use rules that are slightly different from those that we are about to examine. If necessary, the bank will ensure that its contract with the drawer allows for those variations.

Postdated Cheques

Sometimes, a drawer is willing to deliver a cheque immediately, but does not want it to be cashed until later. Assume that while Hank and Anna entered into their sales contract on 1 June 2012, he postdated the cheque to 7 June 2012.[14] A **postdated cheque** is dated in the future. Perhaps Hank was expecting to receive payment from a client on June 3 that would ensure that his chequing account held at least $5000.[15] Anna could not receive payment from the bank until June 7. According to the contract that exists between Hank and the Bank of Edmonton, the bank is allowed to debit his account only if it acts in accordance with his instructions. And in this case, his instructions did not allow Anna to be paid before June 7.

*a **postdated cheque** is dated in the future*

Staledated Cheques

A postdated cheque causes problems if the payee seeks payment too soon. A staledated cheque, in contrast, causes problems if the payee seeks payment too late. A cheque is **staledated** when the payee does not seek payment within a reasonable time. Suppose Anna did not present the cheque to the Bank of Edmonton until 7 June 2013, a whole year later. The bank would probably refuse payment. Banks normally will not honour a cheque that is presented more than six months after the date that appears on it. In that

*a cheque is **staledated** when the payee does not seek payment within a reasonable time*

---

13. For the sake of simplicity, we assume that Anna personally took Hank's cheque to the Bank of Edmonton for payment. She could have endorsed that cheque to her own bank and allowed it to collect the money on her behalf. We will discuss endorsements later.

14. *Bills of Exchange Act*, s 26(d).

15. Postdated cheques are often used if a contract requires instalment payments. For example, if you lease a car for six months, you may be asked for a series of postdated cheques: one for January 1, one for February 1, and so on.

case, Anna would be forced to sue Hank for the $5000, on either the cheque or the sales contract.[16]

Overdrawn Cheques

A cheque is **overdrawn** when the drawer's account does not hold enough money to satisfy it completely. Some people use the term "NSF," or "not sufficient funds." That would occur in our example if Hank's chequing account did not contain at least $5000 when Anna presented his cheque for payment. At that point, the Bank of Edmonton would have an option. It would almost certainly refuse to honour the cheque, in which case Anna would sue Hank for non-payment.[17] However, the bank could treat Hank's overdrawn cheque as his request for a loan, pay $5000 to Anna, and then seek repayment from Hank. Interestingly, that would be true even if the bank failed to realize that Hank's account was overdrawn and paid Anna by mistake.

Countermanded Cheques

As a general rule, a bank can deal with a customer's money only if it has that person's authorization. That rule is important whenever there is a countermand. A **countermand** occurs when a customer orders a bank to refuse payment on a cheque.[18] This is also known as a stop payment order. Returning to our example, assume that Hank noticed that the desk was badly damaged after he took it home. If Anna had not yet cashed his cheque, he might contact the Bank of Edmonton and tell it to stop payment. After all, if he intends to return the desk to Anna, he does not want her to have his money. By countermanding the cheque, Hank would remove the bank's authority to deal with his account. And since the bank would not be willing to give its own money to Anna, it would not pay her $5000 when she presented the cheque.

The ability to countermand a cheque can be very useful. In practice, however, it is limited by two factors:

- First, a bank will not normally accept a countermand unless the drawer gives that order in person and unless the cheque in question is fully described (including the date, the payee, and the amount). Banks require that level of detail because they do not want to stop payment on a cheque incorrectly.

- Second, many bank contracts include a term that allows a bank to debit a customer's account if a countermanded cheque is honoured by mistake. Otherwise, the bank may have to sue the payee if it wants to recover a payment that it made by mistake.[19]

Also note that a cheque is automatically countermanded if the bank is notified that the drawer has died before the payee receives payment.[20]

[16.] Although a bank may not honour a cheque that is presented more than six months after its date, the payee usually has two or six years to sue the drawer. Statutes of limitation say that contracts, including cheques, become unenforceable only after that time: Chapter 11.

[17.] If Hank knew, when he wrote the cheque, that his account did not contain sufficient funds, he could be charged with the crime of false pretences: Criminal Code, RSC 1985, c C-46, s 362(4) (Can).

[18.] *Bills of Exchange Act*, s 167.

[19.] In that case, the bank would sue for restitution under the action in unjust enrichment: Barclays Bank v WJ Simms, Son & Cooke (Southern) Ltd [1980] QB 677. We discussed that cause of action in Chapter 12. The bank could not sue in contract because it does not have a contract with the payee.

[20.] *Bills of Exchange Act*, s 167(b).

Certified Cheques

Although a cheque is a special kind of contract, it is still a promise to pay. And as always, a promise may or may not be kept. Consequently, there is no guarantee that a cheque will actually be cashed. The cheque may be countermanded by the drawer or dishonoured by the drawee. The best way to avoid those problems is through certification.[21] **Certification** occurs when a drawee bank promises to honour a cheque.[22] It normally does so by stamping the word "certified" and the date on the front of the cheque. It then deducts the appropriate amount from the drawer's account, places those funds in a "suspense account," and uses them to honour the cheque when it is presented for payment.

A cheque can be certified by the payee (or holder). Assume that after receiving the cheque from Hank, Anna presented it to the Bank of Edmonton for certification. Perhaps she was travelling to Calgary and felt safer carrying a certified cheque rather than $5000 cash. More commonly, however, a cheque is certified by the drawer. For example, if she was concerned about Hank's ability to pay, Anna might have required him to certify his cheque before giving it to her as payment for the desk.

Whether a cheque is certified by the payee or by the drawer, the consequences are basically the same. Although the law is not entirely clear, the courts generally treat certification as "something equivalent to money."[23] We can see the effects of that rule by continuing on with our example.

- A bank normally owes an obligation only to its own customer. However, once the Bank of Edmonton certified Hank's cheque, it also owed an obligation to Anna. In effect, it promised her that it would honour the cheque. If it later broke that promise, it could be sued by Anna.

- By certifying the cheque, the Bank of Edmonton assured Anna that it would not later dishonour that instrument on the ground that Hank's account was overdrawn. A bank normally will not certify a cheque until after it has transferred funds from the drawer's account into a suspense account. But Anna could demand payment even if the bank certified the cheque in the mistaken belief that Hank's account held enough funds. A bank cannot hide behind its own error; it must fulfill its promise.

- Certification also assured Anna that Hank's cheque could not be countermanded. A drawer is normally entitled to issue a stop payment order any time before a cheque is cashed. However, since certification is treated as "something equivalent" to payment, Hank lost the right to countermand the cheque once the Bank of Edmonton certified it.[24] The bank would have to pay Anna even if Hank objected.[25]

[21.] The *Bills of Exchange Act* does not refer to certification. That procedure is based on American banking law rather than the English statute copied by the Canadian Parliament.

[22.] Banks charge a fee for certification.

[23.] Centrac Inc v CIBC (1994) 120 DLR (4th) 765 at 768 (Ont CA).

[24.] Maubach v Bank of Nova Scotia (1987) 62 OR (2d) 220 (CA). Exceptionally, a bank may allow a certified cheque to be countermanded if the drawer is willing to provide indemnification by promising to provide compensation to the bank if it is sued by the payee.

[25.] An exception may occur when a cheque is certified by the drawer. If the drawer returns the cheque to the bank, the bank will cancel it and return the funds from the suspense account to the chequing account. However, once the drawer actually delivers the cheque to the payee, countermand is no longer possible.

FIGURE 14.2 Bill of Exchange

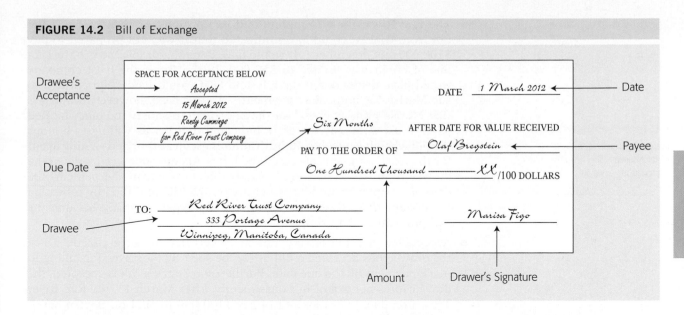

BILLS OF EXCHANGE

A **bill of exchange** is created when one person orders another person to pay a specific amount of money to a third person. Suppose Marisa Figo, who operates a manufacturing plant in Winnipeg, bought a shipment of steel from Olaf Bregstein, an industrialist in Sweden. Although that contract was made on 1 March 2012, the parties agreed that the purchase price of $100 000 was not due until 1 September 2012. Marisa arranged for payment to be made through the Red River Trust Company, with which she held a line of credit.[26] She issued the bill of exchange shown in Figure 14.2.

That bill of exchange looks very similar to a cheque. In fact, a cheque is simply a special type of bill of exchange. The major difference between them is that a cheque must be drawn on a bank, while a bill of exchange may be drawn on a bank or anyone else. We can quickly describe the parties in this case. Marisa was the drawer because she ordered money to be paid from one person to another. The Red River Trust Company was the drawee because it was ordered by one person to pay money to another. And Olaf was the payee because he was intended to receive the money eventually.

We can understand how a bill of exchange works by examining Figure 14.2.

■ Marisa used a basic pre-formatted bill of exchange and filled in the relevant blanks. In effect, she ordered the Red River Trust Company to pay $100 000 to Olaf. Marisa then gave the bill to Olaf. Olaf was not entitled to receive payment immediately, since the parties' contract said that payment for the steel was not due until September 1. Marisa therefore made sure that Olaf could not receive the money from the Red River Trust Company any earlier. Although she created the bill on March 1, she expressly stated that payment was due "Six Months after date."

■ Olaf could have simply kept the bill until September 1. However, he wanted some assurance that he would actually receive $100 000 on that date. He therefore presented the bill to the Red River Trust Company on March 15.

a **bill of exchange** is created when one person orders another person to pay a specific amount of money to a third person

---

26. A line of credit is an amount of money that an institution is willing to lend to a person from time to time.

acceptance occurs when the drawee promises to pay a bill

- The Red River Trust Company had two options when it received the bill from Olaf. It could have indicated that it was not prepared to pay $100 000 on September 1. It would have done so, for instance, if Marisa's line of credit was limited to $50 000. In that case, the trust company would have dishonoured the bill, and Olaf would have been entitled to sue Marisa for immediate payment.[27] In this case, however, it appears that Marisa's line of credit was large enough to satisfy the bill. The Red River Trust Company therefore indicated that it was willing to honour the bill when it came due. Randy Cummings, an authorized signing agent for the trust company, accepted the bill.[28] **Acceptance** occurs when the drawee promises to pay a bill. Randy did so by writing "Accepted," the date of acceptance, and his signature on the bill, and then by returning the document to Olaf.[29] At that point, the trust company became the acceptor rather than simply the drawee.

- Acceptance of a bill is very similar to certification of a cheque. Once the drawee has accepted a bill, it can be sued by the payee for failing to make payment on the due date. Furthermore, once a bill is accepted, the drawer loses control of it. Consequently, after March 15, the Red River Trust Company was required to pay $100 000 to Olaf on September 1, and Marisa lost the ability to cancel the bill.

- Assuming that everything went as planned, Olaf presented the bill to the Red River Trust Company on September 1 and received $100 000. The trust company then required Marisa to repay that amount (undoubtedly with interest).

Note four more things about bills of exchange.

- A bill of exchange, like a cheque, is a contract. Therefore, it is not enforceable unless it is supported by consideration. In this case, Olaf gave consideration for Marisa's bill when he promised to deliver steel to her. That fact is indicated by the phrase "for value received" that appears on the bill.

- A cheque must be payable "on demand."[30] In other words, the drawer must order the drawee to make payment as soon as the payee presents the cheque.[31] A bill of exchange may be payable on demand, in which case it is called a demand draft. However, it can also be a sight draft. This is like a demand draft, except that the payee is not entitled to receive any money until three days after the bill has been presented to the drawee. And finally, as in our example, a bill of exchange can be a time draft, which is payable only on a future date. Although Marisa's bill was dated March 1, Olaf could not obtain payment until "Six Months after date." The date of payment therefore would be September 1.

---

[27] *Bills of Exchange Act*, s 81. Note that Olaf could sue Marisa immediately, even though the bill was not due until September 1.

[28] Marisa also could have asked the Red River Trust Company to accept the bill before she delivered it to Olaf.

[29] *Bills of Exchange Act*, s 38. Note two things about Randy's acceptance: First, he signed "for Red River Trust Company." If he had not used those words, he might have been personally liable as the acceptor. Second, strictly speaking, acceptance requires only the acceptor's signature: s 35(2). However, additional information is usually added to avoid difficulties.

[30] *Bills of Exchange Act*, s 165.

[31] A postdated cheque is payable on demand, but the payee cannot demand payment before the date that appears on the cheque.

- A bill of exchange is usually used for one of two purposes. Both are seen in our example. First, a bill of exchange can be used, like a cheque, to safely transfer funds. Second, because a bill does not have to be payable on demand, it can be used to easily extend credit. In this case, Olaf gave Marisa credit for half of a year. He was not entitled to receive $100 000 until September 1, even though her debt under the sales contract arose on March 1.

- Bills of exchange were traditionally much more common than cheques. Today, however, the situation is reversed. Bills are usually used only in special circumstances, such as international trade between large business enterprises. In our example, Olaf agreed to deliver $100 000 worth of steel from Sweden to Winnipeg.

PROMISSORY NOTES

A cheque or a bill of exchange normally involves an order between three parties: The drawer instructs the drawee to transfer money to the payee. A promissory note is usually a promise between two parties. A **promissory note** is created when one person gives another person a written promise to pay a specific amount of money.[32] The person who is intended to receive the money is once again called the payee. The person who creates the instrument is called the maker.

Suppose on 1 May 2012 Rita Perez agreed to deliver a shipment of sleds to John Chang for $50 000. Because John did not have enough cash to cover the purchase price immediately, Rita agreed to accept instalment payments. The parties assumed that John would be able to pay for the sleds as he resold them in his sporting goods store during the next winter. John therefore gave Rita the promissory note shown in Figure 14.3.[33]

> a **promissory note** is created when one person gives another person a written promise to pay a specific amount of money

FIGURE 14.3 Promissory Note

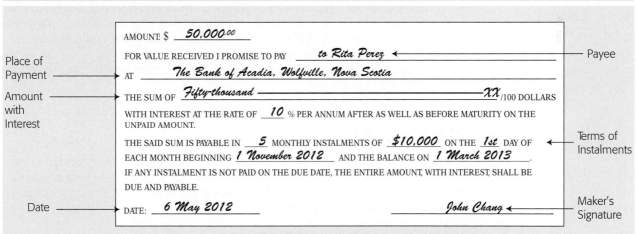

Place of Payment

Amount with Interest

Date

Payee

Terms of Instalments

Maker's Signature

AMOUNT: $ __50,000.⁰⁰__

FOR VALUE RECEIVED I PROMISE TO PAY __to Rita Perez__

AT __The Bank of Acadia, Wolfville, Nova Scotia__

THE SUM OF __Fifty-thousand__ __XX__/100 DOLLARS

WITH INTEREST AT THE RATE OF __10__ % PER ANNUM AFTER AS WELL AS BEFORE MATURITY ON THE UNPAID AMOUNT.

THE SAID SUM IS PAYABLE IN __5__ MONTHLY INSTALMENTS OF __$10,000__ ON THE __1st__ DAY OF EACH MONTH BEGINNING __1 November 2012__ AND THE BALANCE ON __1 March 2013__. IF ANY INSTALMENT IS NOT PAID ON THE DUE DATE, THE ENTIRE AMOUNT, WITH INTEREST, SHALL BE DUE AND PAYABLE.

DATE: __6 May 2012__ __John Chang__

[32.] *Bills of Exchange Act*, s 176(1).

[33.] Although payment was postponed under the promissory note, Rita could have received payment immediately if she had sold the note to a third party. That third party, as the holder of the note, would have been entitled to receive $50 000, plus 10 percent interest, from John starting on November 1.

Examining Figure 14.3 will help us understand promissory notes.

- Although there is no drawee under a promissory note, the document indicated that Rita was entitled to collect the money at the Bank of Acadia in Wolfville, Nova Scotia. John presumably had an account there. If the note did not say anything about the place of payment, Rita could have collected the money at John's office.

- A promissory note is almost always used as a credit instrument. In this case, John was allowed to postpone payment for the sleds. As usually occurs with credit transactions, the promissory note required payment with interest. John promised to pay $50 000 plus 10 percent interest.

- Like a cheque or a bill of exchange, a promissory note can be payable as a lump sum. However, notes are often payable in instalments. That was true in our case. John promised to pay $10 000 per month beginning in November 2012, and to pay the remaining amount on 1 April 2013. As a matter of risk management, John should have made sure that a short receipt was written on the note each time that an instalment was paid. For instance:

$10 000 received in part payment
Rita Perez (1 November 2012)

Without that sort of notation, John might have been forced to make the same payment twice. Assume that Rita received $10 000 on November 1, and then sold the note to an innocent third party. If the payment to Rita was not indicated on the note itself, the third party could probably require John to pay the November instalment again. To encourage commercial transactions, the law usually allows a third party to take a negotiable instrument at face value.

an **acceleration clause** states that the entire amount of the promise becomes due immediately if a single instalment is not paid on time

- An acceleration clause is often found in promissory notes. An **acceleration clause** states that the entire amount of a promise becomes due immediately if a single instalment is not paid on time. There is one in the last line of the pre-formatted note that John used. The explanation for an acceleration clause is quite simple. Suppose John failed to pay the November instalment in a way that made it clear to Rita that the other instalments would fail as well. Without an acceleration clause, she could sue for only $10 000 in November, another $10 000 in December, and so on. An acceleration clause, however, would allow her to immediately claim the entire $50 000 plus interest.

L.O. ❽ ❾

Negotiation

We have focused on situations in which the payee receives money under a negotiable instrument. However, we have also seen that a negotiable instrument can be negotiated, that is, transferred from one party to another. In this section, we examine the process of negotiation.

METHODS OF NEGOTIATION

The process of negotiation depends on whether an instrument is payable to bearer or to order. A **negotiable instrument** is payable to bearer if any person who holds it is entitled to receive payment. A bearer instrument can arise in several ways. We can use the promissory note in Figure 14.3 for illustration.

a **negotiable instrument** is payable to bearer if any person who holds it is entitled to receive payment

- John could have made the note payable "*to Rita Perez or bearer*" or simply "*to bearer.*"

- John could have left the name of the payee blank.[34]

- John could have made the note payable to a fictitious person, such as "*to Sherlock Holmes*," or to a non-person, such as "*to cash*."[35]

- Although the note in Figure 14.3 is an order note, it would have become a bearer note if Rita had delivered it to someone else after endorsing it with her signature and nothing more: "*Rita Perez*."[36] The note would then remain a bearer instrument unless some later party turned it back into an order instrument by using a special endorsement. (We will examine endorsements shortly.)

The important point is that a bearer instrument can be negotiated by the simple delivery, or physical transfer, of the document. An endorsement is unnecessary.

A negotiable instrument is payable to **order** if the party entitled to receive payment is named. For example, the note in Figure 14.3 provides an example because the note is payable "*to Rita Perez*."[37] An order instrument cannot be negotiated unless it is endorsed and delivered to a new party. Suppose Rita wanted to negotiate the note to her sister, Carmen. She could not do so by simply giving that piece of paper to her.[38] She would also have to endorse it by at least signing her name on the back: "*Rita Perez*."

a negotiable instrument is payable to **order** if the party entitled to receive payment is named

LIABILITY

In this section, we will consider several types of endorsements. Before doing so, however, we will briefly discuss how negotiation can affect liability. Staying with Figure 14.3, we assume this series of events.

- John Chang made a promissory note payable "*to Rita Perez*."

- Rita changed that order note into a bearer note by simply signing her name on it before delivering it to her sister, Carmen.

- Carmen sold the note to Vlad Hlinka in exchange for a car. Because the note had become a bearer instrument, Carmen was able to negotiate it to Vlad by simply giving it to him. Vlad changed the instrument back into an order note by delivering it to his business associate, Enya McCall, along with the following endorsement: Vlad Hlinka - Pay to Enya McCall.

- Enya asked John to make payment under the note.

Those events are represented in Figure 14.4 (on the next page).

The primary liability under a promissory note falls on the maker.[39] In this case, John had the initial obligation to pay Enya. One of the most interesting features of a negotiable instrument, however, is that an endorser may also be

---

[34.] In that situation, Rita could have filled in her own name: *Bills of Exchange Act,* ss 30–31.

[35.] *Bills of Exchange Act,* s 20(5).

[36.] *Bills of Exchange Act,* s 66(5). It appears that an instrument that starts as a bearer instrument (for instance, if John made the note "*to bearer*") always remains a bearer instrument: s 20(3).

[37.] The note also would have been payable to order if John had written "*to the order of Rita Perez*" or "*to Rita Perez or order*." Note that the cheque in Figure 14.1 and the bill of exchange in Figure 14.2 are also order instruments.

[38.] An order instrument that is delivered but not endorsed may create an equitable assignment. In that case, however, the person who receives the instrument does not receive any special benefits under the Act: Aldercrest Developments Ltd v Hamilton Co-axial (1958) Ltd (1973) 37 DLR (3d) 254 (SCC).

[39.] The rules discussed in this section generally apply to cheques and bills of exchange as well. Under a cheque, the drawer has the primary liability. Under a bill, the primary liability falls on the drawer at first. However, if a bill is accepted, then the drawee/acceptor has the primary liability: *Bills of Exchange Act,* s 186.

FIGURE 14.4   Liability for Endorsements

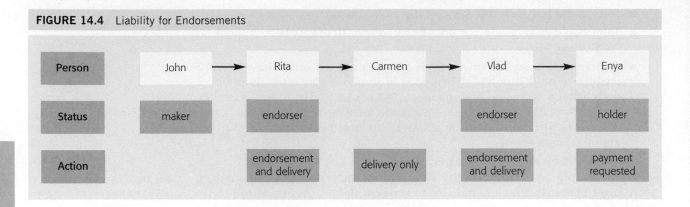

held liable. As a general rule, a person who provides an endorsement promises people who later acquire the instrument that it will be paid.[40]

■ As a result of that rule, Enya might receive full payment even if John was unable to pay a cent. She could sue everyone who endorsed the note: Rita and Vlad. Rita could be held liable even though she did not have any direct contract with Enya. Her responsibility would arise entirely from the fact that she endorsed the note. However, Enya could not sue Carmen.[41] Although Carmen negotiated the note to Vlad, she did so when it was in bearer form. She was therefore able to transfer it to him by delivery alone. And since she did not endorse the note, she did not promise that it would be paid.

■ An endorser who is held liable can sometimes sue a person who negotiated the instrument at an earlier time. Assume that Enya collected payment from Vlad. He might be able to shift that loss to either Carmen or Rita.

■ Unlike Enya, Vlad could sue Carmen even though she did not endorse the note. There are two possibilities: First, the Act would allow Vlad to sue Carmen if she gave him an instrument that (i) was not genuine, (ii) she had no right to transfer, or (iii) she knew was worthless.[42] On our facts, it is unlikely that any of those requirements could be met. Second, Vlad might be able to sue Carmen on the basis of their sales contract if, in exchange for his car, she had promised that she would pay the note if asked to do so.

■ Vlad could sue Rita because she endorsed the note before he acquired it.

■ Now, assume that Enya collected payment from Rita rather than Vlad. Rita could not in turn sue Vlad. Although he endorsed the note, he did so after she did. A person who wants payment on an instrument must look to an earlier party. Consequently, since John was unable to pay, Rita would probably suffer the eventual loss in this case.

The ability to demand payment from an endorser is significant. It is, however, subject to an important limitation. Liability generally cannot be imposed on an endorser unless that person received a notice of dishonour.[43]

---

40. *Bills of Exchange Act*, s 132.

41. *Bills of Exchange Act*, s 136(2).

42. *Bills of Exchange Act*, s 173.

43. *Bills of Exchange Act*, s 95. Since the primary liability for an accepted bill of exchange falls on the acceptor, the notice requirements apply to the drawer as well as the endorsers.

A **notice of dishonour** consists of a statement that the person who was primarily liable on the instrument failed to pay. Note these other things about a notice of dishonour:

a **notice of dishonour** consists of a statement that the person who was primarily liable on the instrument failed to pay

- Notice normally must be given very quickly—usually within one business day.[44]

- Notice does not normally have to be in writing, but it must clearly identify the instrument in question.[45]

- Notice must be given by a holder who wants payment from an endorser. Enya, for example, should have given notice to Vlad and Rita as soon as John refused to pay. Notice must also be given by one endorser who wants payment from another. Vlad, for example, should have given notice to Rita as soon as Enya asked him to pay.

- If notice is not properly given, an endorser is discharged and cannot be held liable on the instrument.

- Notice is not required, however, if (i) the endorser cannot be reached through a reasonable effort, or (ii) the endorser waived the need for notice, for instance, by writing "notice of dishonour unnecessary" beside a signature.[46]

From a risk management perspective, the lesson is clear. If the person who is primarily liable under an instrument is unable to pay, you must give notice as soon as possible to everyone you might want to sue. If you fail to do so, your rights may be lost.

FORMS OF ENDORSEMENT

Several types of endorsement are allowed under the *Bills of Exchange Act*. We will consider seven:

- special endorsement
- identifying endorsement
- qualified endorsement
- conditional endorsement
- accommodation endorsement
- general endorsement
- restrictive endorsement

To better understand each of those possibilities, we return to Figure 14.1 and assume that the following parties dealt with the cheque that Hank Quinlan drew on his account at the Bank of Edmonton: (i) Anna Schmidt, (ii) Jed Leland, (iii) Michael O'Hara, (iv) Isabel Minafer, (v) Elsa Bannister, (vi) Harry Lime, and (vii) Susana Vargas. Figure 14.5 shows the endorsement that each person placed on the cheque.

[44.] *Bills of Exchange Act*, s 96. A delay may be excused if the circumstances were beyond a person's control: s 104. Furthermore, if a notice is sent through the postal system, it merely needs to be mailed by the next day: s 102(2). And finally, notice is deemed to have been given even if it is lost in the postal system: s 103.

[45.] *Bills of Exchange Act*, s 97. A much more formal notice, called a protest, must be given if an instrument is drawn, payable, or accepted in Quebec or outside of Canada: ss 108–125. As a matter of risk management, one should always give notice in writing, which is easy to prove.

[46.] *Bills of Exchange Act*, s 105.

FIGURE 14.5 Endorsements on a Cheque

Anna Schmidt — Pay to Mike O'Hara

Jed Leland—Anna Schmidt hereby identified

Mike O'Hara — pay to Isabel Minafer without recourse

Isabel Minafer — Pay to Harry Lime if he takes me to Vienna

Elsa Bannister — Guarantor for J. Minafer

Harry Lime

Susana Vargas—for deposit only

Special Endorsement

Hank made the cheque payable to Anna. After receiving it, she added a special endorsement.[47] She did so by signing her name on the back of the cheque and by indicating that the money should be paid to Mike O'Hara. Once Mike obtained the cheque from Anna, he replaced her as the only person who was entitled to receive payment.

Identifying Endorsement

Before Mike received the cheque from Anna, however, Jed Leland added an identifying endorsement. Presumably, Mike was reluctant to buy the cheque from Anna because he did not personally know her. Jed, however, knew both parties and was willing to assure Mike that Anna was indeed the payee. Significantly, Jed could not be held liable as a normal endorser. He could be held liable only if the person who negotiated the cheque to Mike was not really Anna Schmidt.

Qualified Endorsement

After receiving the cheque from Anna, Mike transferred it to Isabel Minafer under a qualified endorsement.[48] By stating that his endorsement was "without recourse," Mike indicated that he was not willing to be held liable if the cheque was later dishonoured. Consequently, if Susana Vargas was eventually unable to receive payment from Hank's account at the Bank of Edmonton, she could not sue Mike.

Conditional Endorsement

A cheque must contain an unconditional obligation. Hank, for instance, could not have drafted the cheque payable to "Anna Schmidt if she takes me to Vienna." That order would be conditional on the trip. An endorsement, however, can be conditional.[49] In this case, Isabel has endorsed the cheque "to Harry Lime if he takes

---

[47.] *Bills of Exchange Act,* s 66(3).

[48.] *Bills of Exchange Act,* s 33(a).

[49.] *Bills of Exchange Act,* s 65. The Act also indicates that later parties can assume that the condition was fulfilled.

me to Vienna." Consequently, if Isabel were later sued on her endorsement, she could in turn sue Harry if he did not take her to Vienna.

Accommodation Endorsement

Before Isabel actually delivered the cheque to Harry, Elsa Bannister added an accommodation endorsement.[50] Presumably, Harry was concerned that if he ever tried to sue Isabel on her endorsement, she might not have enough money to pay. Elsa was therefore persuaded to sign as "*Guarantor for I. Minafer.*" That endorsement is called an "accommodation" because it accommodated, or helped, Isabel's effort to negotiate the cheque to Harry. It is also called "anomalous" because it is unusual. A person normally uses an endorsement to negotiate an instrument that they own. In this case, however, Elsa was not trying to transfer her own property. Instead, she was assisting in the transfer of Isabel's property. Elsa nevertheless could be held liable as an endorser.

General Endorsement

After Harry received the cheque from Isabel, he added his general (or blank) endorsement.[51] By simply writing his signature and nothing more, Harry transformed the cheque from an order instrument into a bearer instrument.

Restrictive Endorsement

Finally, after Susana received the cheque from Harry, she added her restrictive endorsement.[52] By writing "*for deposit only,*" Susana prevented the instrument from being negotiated any further. The cheque could be used only to pay funds into Susana's bank account. As a matter of risk management, that sort of endorsement provides good protection against theft.

Defences

Contractual rights can generally be assigned from one party to another. For better or worse, however, the assignee simply steps into the assignor's shoes. Most significantly, the assignee acquires the contract subject to the equities. If sued by the assignee, the debtor can rely on any defence that could also have been used against the assignor.

A negotiable instrument is a type of contract. It is, however, a special type of contract. As a result of the process of negotiation, the rights under an instrument can be easily transferred and they can be improved as they are transferred. Consequently, a defence that could have been used against a payee may not be available against a person who received the instrument by way of negotiation. In this section, we will consider several defences and discover when they apply. The issue of defences is quite complicated. To simplify the discussion, we will use the cheque that appears, front and back, in Figure 14.6. As you can see, it appears that:

- Iman Khan drew a cheque for $9000 on her account at the Island National Bank in favour of Felix Sobers.

L.O. ❿

---

50. *Bills of Exchange Act,* ss 54, 130.
51. *Bills of Exchange Act,* s 66.
52. *Bills of Exchange Act,* s 67.

FIGURE 14.6 Defences

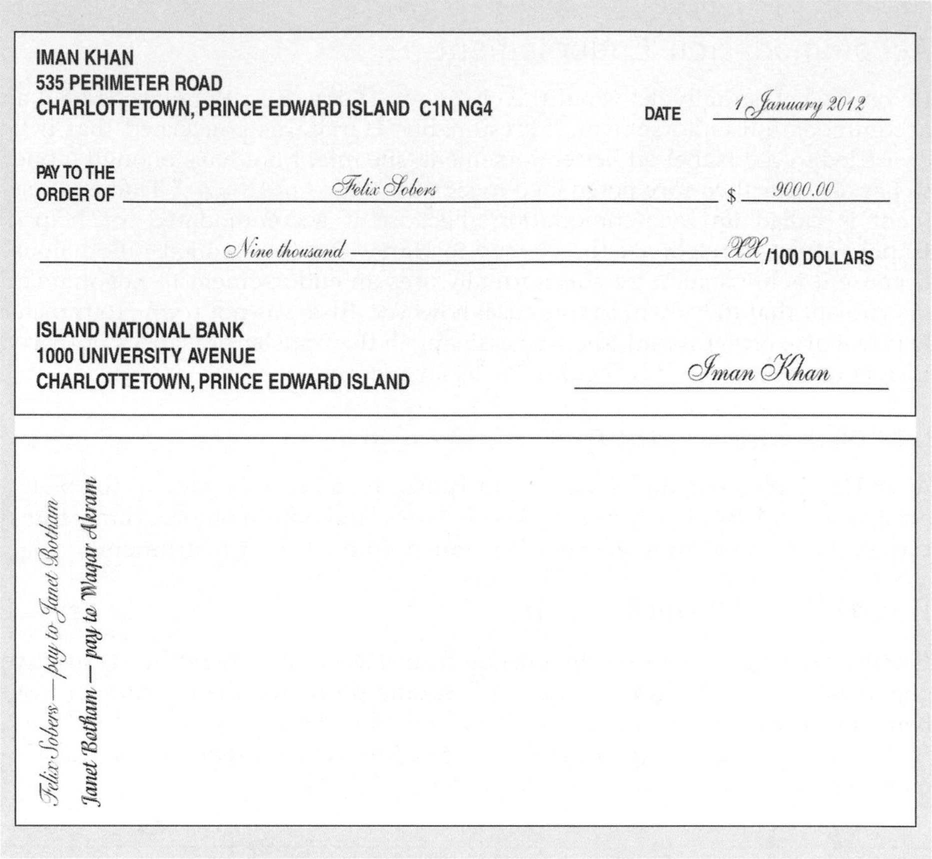

IMAN KHAN
535 PERIMETER ROAD
CHARLOTTETOWN, PRINCE EDWARD ISLAND C1N NG4

DATE *1 January 2012*

PAY TO THE
ORDER OF ___*Felix Sobers*_____ $ ___*9000.00*___

____*Nine thousand*_____ *XX*/100 DOLLARS

ISLAND NATIONAL BANK
1000 UNIVERSITY AVENUE
CHARLOTTETOWN, PRINCE EDWARD ISLAND

Iman Khan

Felix Sobers — pay to Janet Botham

Janet Botham — pay to Waqar Akram

- Felix Sobers specially endorsed the cheque to Janet Botham.
- Janet Botham specially endorsed the cheque to Waqar Akram.
- Waqar Akram now wants payment.

TYPES OF PARTIES

To discuss defences, we need to identify three types of parties: (i) immediate parties, (ii) holders, and (iii) holders in due course.

- **Immediate parties** are parties who dealt directly with each other. In our case, there are three sets of immediate parties: Iman and Felix, Felix and Janet, and Janet and Waqar.

immediate parties are parties who dealt directly with each other

- **A holder** is a person who has possession of a negotiable instrument.[53] In our example, Waqar is the holder. Depending upon the circumstances, he may also be a holder in due course.

a holder is a person who has possession of a negotiable instrument

- **A holder in due course** is a person who acquired a negotiable instrument under specific conditions.[54] While those conditions are complex,

a holder in due course is a person who acquired a negotiable instrument under specific conditions

---

[53.] *Bills of Exchange Act,* s 2.

[54.] *Bills of Exchange Act,* s 55. Unless there is evidence to the contrary, the Act assumes that every holder is a holder in due course: s 57(2).

we can summarize them. Note that they all relate to honesty. Only an honest person deserves the special treatment that the Act gives to a holder in due course.

- Supported by value: The instrument must be supported by value, that is, consideration. Interestingly, Waqar could be a holder in due course even if he did not personally give consideration. It would be enough if someone before him gave consideration for the cheque.[55]

- Complete and regular on its face: The holder must have taken an instrument that was complete and regular on its face. An instrument is not complete if an important part is left blank. That would be true if, for instance, Waqar received a cheque that did not state an amount.[56] And an instrument is not regular if it looks suspicious. That would be the case, for instance, if the cheque contained obvious erasures or alterations.

- Without notice of dishonour: The holder must have acquired the instrument without notice of any previous dishonour. Consequently, Waqar would not be a holder in due course if, for example, he knew or strongly suspected either that the Island National Bank had already refused to honour the cheque or that Iman had countermanded it.

- Good faith and without notice of defect: The holder must have taken the instrument in good faith and without notice of any defect in the title of the person who negotiated it. Waqar therefore would not be a holder in due course if, for instance, he knew or strongly suspected that Iman had been forced or tricked into drawing the cheque, or that Janet had forged Felix's endorsement.

- Before overdue: The holder must have acquired the instrument before it was overdue.[57] As we have seen, an instrument may be due at different times.[58] In our example, the cheque was drawn on January 1 and was payable on demand. As a result, Waqar might not be a holder in due course if he received the document from Janet on May 23. There is usually something suspicious about a cheque that has not been cashed for almost six months.[59]

Note that every person who acquires an instrument after a holder in due course, and who is not involved in any fraud or illegality, is also considered a holder in due course.[60]

Three types of defences are available under the Act: (i) personal defences, (ii) defect in title defences, and (iii) real defences. The availability of each type of defence depends on the type of party involved. Concept Summary 14.2 presents a general overview.

[55.] *Bills of Exchange Act*, s 53. Unless there is evidence to the contrary, the Act presumes that every person who signs an instrument gave value: s 57(1).

[56.] Interestingly, the holder of an instrument generally has the right to fill in any blanks: *Bills of Exchange Act*, s 30.

[57.] *Bills of Exchange Act*, s 69.

[58.] A bill of exchange or promissory note that is payable on a specific day, rather than on demand, is due on that day.

[59.] A promissory note that is payable on demand is not overdue simply because a reasonable length of time has passed: *Bills of Exchange Act*, s 182. That is because a promissory note, unlike a bill or cheque, is normally used to extend credit.

[60.] *Bills of Exchange Act*, s 56.

PART 3

Concept Summary 14.2

Parties and Defences

	Personal Defences	Defect in Title Defences	Real Defences
Immediate party	✓	✓	✓
Holder	✗	✓	✓
Holder in due course	✗	✗	✓

PERSONAL DEFENCES

a **personal defence** is one that affects the parties themselves rather than the instrument

If an action occurs between two immediate parties, the defendant can use any type of defence, including a personal defence. As the name suggests, a **personal defence** is one that affects the parties themselves rather than the instrument. Assume that Waqar presented the cheque to the Island National Bank for payment, but left empty-handed because Iman's account did not contain enough money. He could sue Janet on the cheque because she endorsed it. In response, however, she could raise any defence that arose from her dealings with him. We can consider two common examples:

- Set-off: Janet could set off any debt that Waqar owed to her. Suppose she negotiated the cheque to him because he sold her a car for $9000. A few days later, she sold him a boat for $5000, but he failed to pay. If Waqar sued Janet on the cheque, she could admit liability, set off the price of the boat, and pay only $4000.

- Failure of consideration: Janet could also rely on a failure of consideration.[61] For instance, if the car that Waqar sold to her was defective and required $3000 in repairs, she could admit liability, plead breach of contract, and pay only $6000. After all, she expected to receive a car worth $9000 but received one worth only $6000.

DEFECT IN TITLE DEFENCES

a **defect in title defence** occurs when an instrument is obtained improperly

Defect in title defences are available against an immediate party and against a simple holder. A **defect in title defence** occurs when an instrument is obtained improperly. It is different from a personal defence because it affects the instrument itself.

Suppose Waqar is a holder, but not a holder in due course, because he received the cheque from Janet when it was overdue.[62] Further, suppose the Island National Bank refused to honour the cheque because Iman's account was overdrawn. Waqar could sue Iman as the drawer of the cheque. If he did so, however, she could avoid liability by proving any of the following defect in title defences:

[61.] If consideration was never given in exchange for the cheque, that instrument would be entirely unenforceable.

[62.] To simplify the situation, assume that Janet received the cheque as a gift from Felix. Since she would not be a holder in due course in the examples that follow, Waqar could not become a holder in due course by obtaining the cheque from her: *Bills of Exchange Act*, s 56.

- Fraud or duress: Iman would not have to pay Waqar if she initially drafted the cheque as a result of Felix's fraud or duress.[63] Perhaps Felix tricked her, or threatened her with a beating unless she created the instrument. In that situation, Felix did not obtain good title to the cheque. And since Waqar was not a holder in due course, he did not obtain good title either.

- Illegal consideration: Likewise, Iman would not have to pay Waqar if she issued the cheque to Felix in exchange for illegal consideration. That would be the case if, for instance, Felix promised to deliver drugs to her.

- Drunkenness or insanity: Felix's title also would have been defective if he knew, or should have known, that Iman was drunk or insane when she drafted the cheque.[64] Once again, that defect would affect Waqar as well.

- Absence of delivery: A defect in title can occur when there is an absence of delivery. Suppose Iman completed the cheque as it appears in Figure 14.6 but never actually gave it to Felix. If he took it from her desk without her permission, he would obtain a defective title, as would Waqar.[65]

- No authority: If Iman gave the cheque to Felix with instructions to fill in $7000 as the amount, he would have obtained a defective title if he instead made the cheque out for $9000. He had no authority for what he actually did.

- Discharge or renunciation: Finally, Waqar would have received a defective title if the cheque that he acquired from Janet had been discharged or renounced.[66] Suppose, for instance, that after Iman issued the cheque to Felix, he wrote her a note that said, "You don't really owe this money to me. I therefore won't ask for payment." He nevertheless gave the cheque to Janet, who in turn sold it to Waqar. Because of Felix's renunciation, Iman would not have to pay Waqar. To be safe, of course, she should have asked Felix to return the cheque to her as soon as he renounced his rights.[67]

REAL DEFENCES

A holder in due course cannot be defeated by personal defences or defect in title defences. That person has to worry only about real defences. A **real defence** occurs when an instrument is fundamentally flawed. Such a defence is real in the sense that it affects the res—the thing—itself. It does not simply concern a personal matter between the parties or a defect in one party's title to an instrument.

a **real defence** occurs when an instrument is fundamentally flawed

---

[63.] *Bills of Exchange Act*, s 55(2). Fraud is usually a defect in title defence. However, it may be a real defence if it amounts to non est factum (literally, "this is not my deed"). As we saw in Chapter 10, that defence is available in very limited circumstances. It might work in our case, for instance, if Iman, who was illiterate, infirm, or blind, was tricked into signing the cheque because she thought she was being asked for her autograph.

[64.] Insanity normally creates a defect in title defence. However, it can also lead to a real defence if the person was legally declared to be mentally incompetent: *Bills of Exchange Act*, s 46(1).

[65.] There was a defect in title because Iman did not deliver a completed instrument. However, she would have a real defence if she did not deliver the cheque and if that instrument was incomplete. Perhaps Felix stole it from her desk, filled in the amount (which she had left blank), and gave it to Janet, who sold it to Waqar. In that case, Waqar could not demand payment from Iman, even if he was a holder in due course.

[66.] *Bills of Exchange Act*, ss 139, 141.

[67.] As a matter of risk management, a cheque that has been honoured should have "paid" written on its face. A mere holder cannot sue on a cheque that has been discharged. However, a holder in due course can sue on a discharged or cancelled cheque, as long as that fact is not apparent from the instrument itself: *Bills of Exchange Act*, s 141. Suppose Felix was allowed to keep the cheque even though he had been paid. If Waqar later became a holder in due course, he could force Iman to pay again if the cheque had not been stamped "paid."

Assume that Waqar is a holder in due course and that the Island National Bank has refused to honour the cheque. If Waqar sought payment from someone else, he might be met by a real defence. We have already seen that fraud or duress, drunkenness or insanity, absence of delivery, and discharge or renunciation can lead to either a defect in title defence or a real defence, depending on the circumstances. We also need to consider three more possibilities:

- Minority: Iman would not have to pay if she created the cheque when she was a minor.[68] Waqar could, however, demand payment from either Felix or Janet, on the basis of their endorsements, if they were adults.[69]

- Material alteration: A material alteration may create a real defence.[70] Suppose Felix changed the amount of the cheque from $9000 to $29 000 after he received it from Iman. The effect of that alteration would depend on Felix's skills as a con artist.

  - If the alteration was not apparent to the naked eye, Waqar could enforce the cheque against Iman but only for the original amount of $9000. However, he could also enforce the cheque against Felix or Janet for $29 000. Felix would be liable for that amount because he was the wrongdoer. Janet would be fully liable because she chose to add her endorsement to the cheque after it was altered. She therefore promised to pay $29 000.

  - If the alteration was apparent to the naked eye, Waqar could not enforce it against Iman at all. However, for the reasons that we just discussed, he could enforce it against Felix or Janet for $29 000.

  - Note one more thing about alterations. Look carefully at the cheque in Figure 14.6 and compare it to the cheque in Figure 14.1. As you can see, Iman was sloppy in a way that Hank was not. She left spaces in the cheque that allowed Felix to easily alter the amount. Assume that the Island National Bank honoured the cheque and paid $29 000 to Waqar. Normally, the bank could debit only $9000 from Iman's account because that was the only amount that she authorized. However, since the alteration in this case was caused by Iman's carelessness, the bank could take $29 000 from her account. As a matter of risk management, you should always follow Hank's lead and draft instruments in a way that prevents fraud.

- Forgery: A holder in due course may also be met by a defence of forgery. Suppose someone stole the cheque from Felix, forged his endorsement, and then transferred the instrument to Janet. Although the rules that would apply in that case are complex, the main points can be stated briefly:[71]

  - A person whose signature is forged generally cannot be held liable. Consequently, if the bank refused to honour the cheque, Waqar could not sue Felix.

  - Similarly, a person who signed an instrument before a forgery occurred generally cannot be held liable. Consequently, Waqar would also be unable to sue Iman.

[68.] Although Iman could not be liable to anyone on the cheque, she could be held liable to Felix on the sales contract if he provided her with necessary goods or services, as discussed in Chapter 10.

[69.] *Bills of Exchange Act*, s 47. The same rules apply if a contract is drafted by a corporation that does not have the capacity to incur liability under a negotiable instrument.

[70.] *Bills of Exchange Act*, ss 144–145.

[71.] *Bills of Exchange Act*, ss 48–49.

- However, a person who signed an instrument after a forgery occurred generally can be held liable. Consequently, Waqar could demand payment from Janet, even if she did not know that Felix's signature had been forged. By adding her own endorsement, she promised to pay in any event.

- If the Island National Bank honoured the cheque and paid Waqar, it would have debited Iman's account for $9000. Iman could recover that money from the bank, but only if she promptly notified the bank after learning about the forgery.[72]

- If the bank honoured the cheque, it could recover the amount that it paid from either Waqar (because he received the money) or Janet (because she endorsed the cheque after the forgery), but only if the bank notified them within a reasonable time after it learned of the forgery.

The effect of these rules can be summarized: The person who committed the forgery should bear the loss. However, that sort of person often disappears or does not have enough money. Therefore, the loss usually falls on the first person who endorsed the instrument after the forgery, in this case, Janet.

Consumer Bills and Notes

The *Bills of Exchange Act* has changed very little since it was enacted over 100 years ago. The only substantial alteration was introduced in 1970 to protect consumers. The problem that Parliament wanted to avoid is illustrated in Business Decision 14.1.

Consumer Bills and Notes

Christine used a promissory note to buy $10 000 worth of aluminum siding for her house from Noel's Exteriors Inc. Noel, however, never delivered the goods. In fact, he disappeared altogether. Because Noel was an immediate party, Christine could have relied on his breach of contract if he had sued her on the note. Furthermore, she could have sued him on the sales contract for damages. In the circumstances, that action would have been a waste of time and money.

To make matters worse, Noel sold the note to Mastiff Financing Ltd, which was a holder in due course. When Mastiff sued Christine, she did not have any defence to its claim. Most significantly, since Mastiff was not an immediate party to her, it did not take the instrument subject to the equities. Consequently, Christine could not argue that Noel never delivered the siding. She therefore had to pay $10 000 to Mastiff, even though she received nothing in return.

Question for Discussion

1. How would the new rules regarding consumer instruments (discussed below) affect this situation?

In response to that problem, Parliament added a series of sections to the Act to provide some protection to consumers.[73] The new provisions apply to consumer instruments only. A **consumer instrument** is a bill of exchange,

a **consumer instrument** is a bill of exchange, cheque, or promissory note that is used by a consumer to buy goods or services from a business on credit

---

[72.] If an endorser's signature had been forged, Iman would have to give notice within one year. If her own signature, as the drawer, had been forged, Iman would have to notify the bank within "a reasonable time."

[73.] *Bills of Exchange Act*, ss 188–192.

cheque, or promissory note that is used by a consumer to buy goods or services from a business on credit. Note three things about that definition. First, the instrument must be used for credit purposes. That requirement is satisfied by a promissory note, and by a bill of exchange or cheque that is postdated at least 31 days. Second, the instrument must be used to purchase goods or services from a business person. And third, the instrument must be given by a "consumer," that is, someone who intends to use the purchase for personal, rather than business, purposes.

The front of a consumer instrument must be marked with the words "consumer purchase." The effect of those words is dramatic. Any person, including a holder in due course, who acquires a properly marked consumer instrument takes it subject to the equities. Consequently, if that person sues on the instrument, the consumer can use almost any defence that they could have used against the original seller. The situation is more complicated if an instrument is not properly marked.

- A holder in due course who acquires an instrument without notice that it was used for a consumer purchase does not take it subject to the equities. Consequently, it can be defeated only by a real defence.

- In the hands of any other sort of person, however, an unmarked consumer instrument is void.

- A seller who fails to properly mark a consumer instrument can be fined or imprisoned. The same is true for people who transfer unmarked instruments that they know were used for consumer purchases.

Chapter Summary

A negotiable instrument is a special kind of contract that contains an obligation to pay money. The process of negotiation requires the modification of several general contractual principles, including consideration, privity, and assignment. The *Bills of Exchange Act* codifies the rules for three types of negotiable instruments: cheques, bills of exchange, and promissory notes.

The Act will not apply unless an instrument satisfies five basic requirements. A negotiable instrument must (i) be written and signed, (ii) clearly identify the parties, (iii) contain an obligation to pay a specific sum of money, (iv) clearly state a time of payment, and (v) contain an unconditional obligation. Those requirements are intended to create the level of certainty that is necessary for the process of negotiation.

A cheque is created when a person orders a bank to pay a specific amount of money to someone. It has three parties: (i) the drawer is the person who "draws," or creates, the cheque, (ii) the drawee is the bank that is ordered to pay money, and (iii) the payee is the person who is entitled to receive the money from the bank. Although most cheques operate smoothly, complications can arise if a cheque is (i) postdated, (ii) staledated, (iii) overdrawn, (iv) countermanded, or (v) certified.

A bill of exchange is created when one person orders another person to pay a specific amount of money to a third person. A bill may be payable (i) on demand, (ii) on sight, or (iii) on a specific date. A bill may be accepted by the drawee before it is due. If so, the drawee becomes an acceptor and must honour the bill when it is presented for payment.

A promissory note is created when one person gives another person a written promise to pay a specific amount of money. A promissory note is generally different from a cheque or a bill because (i) it contains a promise rather than an order, and (ii) it involves two parties rather than three. A promissory note (i) is often payable with interest, (ii) is often payable in instalments, and (iii) often contains an acceleration clause.

Negotiation involves the transfer of an instrument from one party to another. A bearer instrument is payable to whoever holds it. It can be negotiated by delivery alone. An order instrument is payable to a named person. It can be negotiated by endorsement and delivery. The primary liability for an instrument is on the drawer in the case of a cheque, the drawer or acceptor in the case of a bill, and the maker in the case of a note. However, liability can usually also be imposed on any person who endorsed the instrument. An endorsement usually creates a promise to pay. There are seven main types of endorsement: (i) special, (ii) identifying, (iii) qualified, (iv) conditional, (v) accommodation, (vi) general, and (vii) restrictive.

For the purposes of defences, there are three types of parties: (i) immediate parties, (ii) holders, and (iii) holders in due course. There are three types of defences: (i) personal defences, which are available against immediate parties, (ii) defect in title defences, which are available against immediate parties and holders, and (iii) real defences, which are available against immediate parties, holders, and holders in due course.

Review Questions

1. "Although the general principles always are the same, each province (and territory) has its own *Bills of Exchange Act*, which must be carefully checked for possible differences. As with the Sale of Goods Act, disputes sometimes are lost by applying the wrong version of the statute." Is that statement true? Explain your answer.

2. What is a "negotiable instrument"? What does the word "negotiable" mean in this context?

3. What is the main advantage of receiving the negotiation of an instrument rather than the assignment of a contract?

4. "A negotiable instrument is only as good as the person who originally created it. If that person has no money, the person who holds the negotiable instrument cannot possibly obtain payment under the instrument." Is that statement true? Explain your answer.

5. "A cheque becomes staledated only when the statutory limitation period lapses." Is that statement correct? Explain your answer.

6. What options does a bank have if a customer writes a cheque on an overdrawn account?

7. What is a "stop payment order"? How is such an order given?

8. Explain the nature and effect of a postdated cheque. Describe a situation in which postdated cheques often are used.

9. "The concept of certification is rather unusual. Unlike other concepts associated with negotiable instruments, certification was not created or codified by the *Bills of Exchange Act*." Is that statement true? What is "certification"? Explain your answers.

10. Which of the following statements is true? (i) "A cheque is a type of bill of exchange." (ii) "A bill of exchange is a type of cheque." Explain your answer.

11. Explain the difference between a demand draft, a sight draft, and a time draft.

12. If you make a promissory note that is payable in instalments, what precaution should you take after you pay each instalment? What is the potential result of not adopting that precaution?

13. What is an "acceleration clause"? When is such a clause used?

14. "Unlike a cheque or a bill of exchange, a promissory note does not create any rights or obligations involving a third party." Is that statement true? Explain your answer.

15. What is the danger of receiving an instrument in bearer form? Explain how you can protect yourself against that danger once you have received the instrument.

16. What is a "bearer instrument"? Explain the ways in which a negotiable instrument may be put into "bearer" form.

17. What is a "notice of dishonour"? When must it be given? What are the consequences of not giving a notice of dishonour?

18. Briefly describe a holder in due course. What types of defences are available against a holder in due course? Why is a holder in due course given special treatment under the *Bills of Exchange Act*?

19. Identify and briefly explain seven types of endorsement.

20. List and briefly explain four types of defences that may act as either defect in title defences or real defences.

Cases and Problems

1. Allan Zimmerman created a contract with Echo Helstrom for the design and manufacture of a custom guitar. Upon delivery of the instrument, Helstrom paid Zimmerman by providing a cheque, drawn in his favour, for $10 000. Zimmerman endorsed that cheque and gave it to Hibbing Music Inc in an effort to discharge a debt of $10 000 that he owed to the company. Before the company could obtain payment on the cheque, however, Helstrom discovered a serious defect in the guitar that she had purchased from Zimmerman. As a courtesy, she contacted Hibbing Music Inc, knowing that it had received the cheque from Zimmerman, and told them that since her guitar was flawed, she was not willing to pay anything more than $7500 on the cheque. (She is correct in at least one sense: in its current condition, the guitar is worth $7500, rather than $10 000.) The company, in contrast, insists that it is not affected by Zimmerman's flawed workmanship and that it is entitled to the full amount of the cheque. How would a court likely resolve the dispute? Explain your answer.

2. Gilles, who is 16 years old but looks much older, bought a snowboard from Eva's Sporting Goods. He paid the $750 price with a promissory note that was payable in three monthly instalments of $250 each. Eva stamped the words "consumer purchase" on the note at the time of the sale. Unfortunately, the board was stolen the first time that Gilles took it to the mountains. He believes that he should no longer be required to pay for something that he no longer enjoys. Not surprisingly, Eva has a different opinion. She believes that Gilles got what he wanted and that he is liable to pay the full price. Is Gilles liable on the note? Explain your answer.

3. Bibi, a lawyer, provided legal advice to Bjorn on a small matter. When he asked her for her fee, she said, "Oh, just pay whatever you think is appropriate." Although the evidence indicates that the reasonable value of Bibi's work was $2500, Bjorn gave her a cheque on February 14 for $15 000. Bibi slipped it into her desk without even looking at the amount. The cheque sat there until December, when Bibi presented it to the drawee bank for payment. The bank refused to honour it, however, because Bjorn's account was overdrawn. Bibi then telephoned Bjorn personally and asked him for payment of $15 000. He refused, claiming that he was temporarily insane when he drafted the cheque: "You should have known that I was on the verge of a complete mental collapse and that I was madly—if irrationally—in love with you. Why else would I give you a cheque for that much money on Valentine's Day? You certainly didn't earn $15 000." And indeed, the evidence indicates that Bjorn was quite obviously insane when he drafted the cheque. Bibi wanted nothing more to do with Bjorn, but she did

want the money. Therefore she sold the cheque to the Bergman Collection Agency, which was entirely unaware of Bjorn's argument when it purchased the instrument from Bibi. Bergman has since learned of Bjorn's argument but claims that it is entitled to payment as a holder in due course. Is that correct? Explain your answer.

4. Roger, who was in the market for a computer, visited Hussein's Electronics with a view to finding a bargain. He was directed to a computer that had been used as a floor model in the store. Although the sales representative was unwilling to provide a warranty, he did assure Roger that the unit could be returned if it did not perform satisfactorily during the first month. He also assured Roger that the price could be dropped by $500 if the computer developed minor problems. Roger agreed on that basis to purchase the computer for either $2000 or $1500, depending upon how well the machine performed. By way of payment, he provided a cheque, which he modified to suit the circumstances. First, he stated the amount of the cheque to be either "$1500 or $2000." Second, although he entered the date of purchase on the cheque, Roger added a notation saying, "payable six months after date." And third, he added a notation to the cheque that said, "payment conditional upon quality of computer." Roger has now used the computer for five weeks without any problems at all. Will Hussein's Electronics, as the payee of his cheque, be able to obtain payment from the drawee bank? Explain your answer.

5. After being badgered for months for payment, Alice Munt attempted to pay her overdue rent by providing her landlord, Revati Singh, with a cheque for $15 000, drawn on her account at the Bank of Cambridge. When Singh presented the cheque for payment, the bank discovered that Munt's account held only $3000 in funds. It therefore dishonoured the cheque and refused payment. Munt was not surprised when she was later told of the events. She had known when she drafted the cheque that her account was overdrawn. By drafting the cheque, she merely intended to "buy time." Explain the legal consequences of Munt's actions.

6. Sam Jasper agreed to sell 4000 litres of animal feed to Kate Hughes, who operates a wildlife park. After receiving the product, but before inspecting it, Kate told Sam that he could collect a cheque, as payment, from on top of the desk in her office. Before Sam did so, however, Kate inspected the feed and realized that it was contrary to the terms of the sale contract. Consequently, although she had completely written out a cheque in Sam's favour, she did not leave it on top of her desk as promised. She instead put it into her desk drawer, with the intention of calling him and explaining her concerns. Before she could do so, however, Sam came by her office while she was out. When he realized that there was no cheque on top of her desk, he looked through the drawers, where he found the cheque

that Kate had drawn. Sam immediately added his general endorsement to the back of that cheque and gave it to Benjamin Gigger as payment for another, unrelated contract. Kate soon discovered the facts and ordered the Bank of Alberta (the drawee) to refuse payment. Because Benjamin could not cash the cheque at the bank, he has sued both Sam and Kate for payment. Will he be successful against either party? What if the cheque that Sam took from the drawer was incomplete because Kate had not filled in the amount (although she had otherwise added all the necessary details, including her signature)? Explain your answer.

7. Officeplus contractually agreed to purchase office furniture from Centrac in exchange for a price of $48 000. That sales contract required payment to be made by way of a certified cheque. Officeplus had a bank account at the Canadian Imperial Bank of Commerce (CIBC). Immediately before the following events occurred, its account balance stood at $173. Officeplus received a cheque for $76 000 from Finlayson Inc that was drawn on Finlayson's account at TD Canada Trust (TD). Officeplus deposited that cheque into its account at CIBC. Although it had not yet actually received payment from TD, CIBC credited Officeplus's account with $76 000. Later the same day, Officeplus drew a cheque upon its own account for $48 000 and asked CIBC to certify it. CIBC, overlooking the fact that it had not yet received payment on the TD cheque, believed that Officeplus had sufficient funds in its account. CIBC therefore certified the cheque and purportedly transferred $48 000 from Officeplus's account into a "suspense account." Officeplus delivered the certified cheque to Centrac. TD then contacted CIBC and explained that the earlier cheque for $76 000 would not be paid because Finlayson did not have sufficient funds in its account. CIBC immediately contacted Centrac and insisted that the certified cheque was invalid because Officeplus did not really hold sufficient funds. Centrac, in contrast, demands that CIBC make payment on the certified cheque. Is CIBC liable to Centrac? If so, is Officeplus or Finlayson or TD liable to CIBC? Explain your answers.

8. Ren/Tex Realty Inc (Ren/Tex) sold several properties on behalf of Erin Amelia Investments Ltd (Erin Amelia). Erin Amelia therefore became contractually obliged to pay a commission of $38 000 to Ren/Tex. Erin Amelia drew a cheque for that amount upon its account at the National Bank of Canada, and then gave that cheque to Ren/Tex on March 16. Two days later, Erin Amelia contacted the National Bank, explained that it was experiencing financial difficulties, and issued a countermand or stop payment order. The bank entered that information into its system. On March 23, Ren/Tex brought the cheque to the National Bank and paid a $7 fee in order to have the cheque certified. The bank should have refused that request because the cheque already had

been countermanded by Erin Amelia. As a result of an honest mistake, however, the teller at the bank overlooked the stop order payment and certified the cheque. On March 26, Erin Amelia learned that the cheque had been certified. It immediately contacted Ren/Tex, said that the cheque could not be used to acquire payment, and insisted that the instrument should be turned over to the bank. Ren/Tex disagreed and, the next day, it presented the certified cheque at the National Bank and demanded payment. The bank refused. It says that that Ren/Tex is not entitled to payment because (i) the cheque was certified by mistake, (ii) the cheque was certified by the payee rather than the drawer, and (iii) the payee knew that the cheque was mistakenly certified before it presented the instrument for payment. Is the National Bank liable to pay Ren/Tex? Explain your answer.

9. In late January, Kurtz Enterprises purchased office supplies from Kilgore Equipment. It paid with a promissory note for $25 000 that was made to the order of Kilgore Equipment and was due on September 1. In June, Kilgore specially endorsed the note and sold it to Willard Financial Inc. On September 1, Willard tried to claim $25 000 from the maker, only to discover that Kurtz Enterprises had disappeared. Over the next week, the president of Willard discussed the situation with her lawyer and accountant. On September 8, she contacted Kilgore Equipment and demanded payment. She took the position that Kilgore was liable on the basis of its endorsement. Is she correct? Explain your answer.

10. Hamilton Co-Axial Ltd was indebted to its president, Hudson Elmore. In payment of that debt, it gave a promissory note to Elmore. That note was made payable to the order of Elmore. Elmore later purchased land from Aldercrest Developments Inc. As payment for the land, Elmore delivered the promissory note to Aldercrest, but he did not endorse the instrument. Before Aldercrest presented the note to Hamilton Co-Axial for payment, Elmore released Hamilton Co-Axial from the debt that previously existed between them and for which the promissory note initially was created. Is Aldercrest now entitled to payment from Hamilton Co-Axial? Explain your answer.

11. Earl Tetley worked as a payroll clerk for Tinwings Inc. Over the course of several months, he defrauded the company of about $250 000. His plan was simple. He drafted cheques, on behalf of the company, that were payable to people who had recently quit or been fired from Tinwings. He then forged the payees' blank endorsements and presented the cheques to the drawee, the Bank of Manitoba. The bank honoured the cheques, paid the money to Earl, and debited Tinwings's account. Tinwings eventually discovered the scheme. Although it normally would have contacted the police immediately, it hesitated to do so because Earl was the company

president's nephew. Tinwings therefore agreed that it would keep the situation quiet as long as Earl repaid the money with interest within 18 months. After a year and a half, however, Earl had made only a token repayment of $5000. Earl has since been convicted and imprisoned for his fraud. Without any other option, Tinwings has now sued the Bank of Manitoba. The company argues that since the endorsements on the cheques were forged, the bank had no authority to debit its account. Is that correct? Explain your answer.

12. Marlon bought a delivery van for his business from Tanita for $20 000. Half of the purchase price was paid with cash, and the other half with a cheque that was payable to bearer. After meeting with Marlon, Tanita took the subway back to her office. Unfortunately, she forgot her purse, which contained both the cash and the cheque that she had received from Marlon, on the subway. After several days of frantic phone calls, it became clear to Tanita that the person who picked up her purse did not intend to return it. Has Tanita necessarily suffered a $20 000 loss? What should she do to minimize the damage? What should Marlon do?

Real Property: Interests and Leases

15

LEARNING OBJECTIVES

After completing this chapter, you should be able to:

❶ Name three types of estates and explain how they differ from one another.

❷ Describe the process of expropriation and explain why it often creates ethical issues.

❸ Distinguish between co-ownership and joint tenancy, and explain why one is often preferred in the business world.

❹ Explain the nature of condominium ownership.

❺ Define "easement" and explain how that type of interest can be created.

❻ Distinguish between dominant tenements and servient tenements, and name two types of interests for which that distinction is important.

❼ Outline the situations in which it is possible to enforce a restrictive covenant against a person who did not participate in its creation.

❽ Distinguish between different types of leases on the basis of how long they last.

❾ Outline the basic difference between an assignment and a sublease.

❿ Define "quiet possession" and explain two ways in which a landlord can break that type of covenant.

real property includes land and any-thing attached to land

In this chapter, we begin our discussion of *real property*. Generally speaking, **real property** includes land and anything attached to land (such as fences and buildings).[1] Lawyers historically went much further and viewed real property rights in terms of the "giant carrot theory," which held that a person who owned a particular piece of land also owned the air up to the heavens and the ground down to the centre of the Earth.[2] The modern approach, however, does not go that far.[3] A landowner can control the airspace only to a reasonable height. While that test is rather vague, it does mean, for instance, that you can complain about a crane swinging over your property, but not about a plane flying safely overhead. Similarly, although there are few cases in the area, a landowner can control the ground only to a reasonable depth beneath the surface.

Despite those limitations, property rights remain critically important to Canadian business, even as our economy continues to move away from its traditional focus on natural products (such as wheat and oil) to new forms of wealth (such as ideas and information). Although a lot of commerce can now be conducted through computers from anywhere in the world, the vast majority of businesses still rely on real property. An Internet bookseller, for instance, requires a warehouse to store its products and at least one office for its personnel. Furthermore, just as a private residence is often a person's most valuable asset, real property often represents the largest part of a business's total wealth.

It is therefore important that you have a basic understanding of real property. However, real property is a notoriously large and complex body of law, which contains a number of specialized areas. For the purposes of risk management, many of those details can be left to the experts. A business person is not required, for instance, to know how to draft a long-term commercial lease. Lawyers are available for that purpose. From a business perspective, it is enough to appreciate the possibilities and to recognize the need for outside assistance.

This chapter is divided into two parts: The first part summarizes the most important types of interests in land. The second describes the essential elements of leasing agreements. Chapter 16 continues the discussion of real property by explaining the process involved in the sale of real property. It also provides an overview of mortgages. Chapter 17 examines personal property.

L.O. ❶❷❸❹❺❻❼

Interests in Land

an **interest in land** is a right that a person can enforce with respect to a particular piece of land

In this section, we consider different types of **interests in land**, that is, rights that a person can enforce with respect to a particular piece of land. Note that we are discussing rights to property *itself*. This is important. Suppose you buy a football stadium from me. Two sets of rights and obligations are created:

---

[1] Land is called "real" property because the owner can recover the *res* (which is Latin for "thing") itself. If someone wrongfully takes your house, the law will evict them and allow you to regain possession. Other types of property are called "personal," because the courts usually will not allow you to recover the thing itself. If someone steals your cow, the law will probably only require the thief to pay you the monetary value of the animal. See Chapter 4.

[2] Lawyers sometimes use the Latin phrase *"cuius est solum, eius est usque ad coelum et ad inferos,"* which means "whoever owns the soil, it is theirs all the way up to Heaven and down to Hell."

[3] *Bocardo SA v Star Energy UK Onshore Ltd* [2011] AC 380 (UK SC).

- First, you and I have a contract. Significantly, we are the only people affected by that agreement. It does not impose rights or obligations on anyone else in the world. Consequently, if I break my promise to transfer the land, I am the only person whom you can sue in contract. Likewise, if you fail to pay the price, I cannot demand the money from anyone other than you.

- Second, once I transfer the property, the stadium belongs to you. If I continue using it for my own purposes, you can get a court order to evict me. Even more significantly, you can exercise the same rights against *anyone else* who interferes with your property rights. That is because property rights are good against the *whole world*, not just the person from whom they are acquired.[4]

ESTATES IN LAND

The most significant interests in land are called *estates*. An **estate** is an exclusive right to possess a property for a period of time. We will consider three varieties:

- fee simple
- life estate
- leasehold estate

an **estate** is an exclusive right to possess a property for a period of time

Fee Simple

A **fee simple** is the largest package of rights that a person can hold in land. Although it technically does not amount to absolute ownership, it comes very close.[5] Consequently, if you enjoy the fee simple in a particular property, you are entitled to possess it for an indefinite duration. You can sell it, lease it, or give it away tomorrow, or you can keep it until you die. And if you do hang on to it for the rest of your life, you are entitled to give it away upon your death. Furthermore, you can generally use or abuse the land however you want. You can maintain it in pristine condition, or you can clear it down to scorched earth.

a **fee simple** is the largest package of rights that a person can hold in land

Although your rights under a fee simple are very broad, they are subject to several important limitations. We mention three:

- First, as we saw in Chapter 5, whenever you possess land, you must avoid committing torts such as occupiers' liability, nuisance, and the rule in *Rylands v Fletcher*. For instance, if you live in a residential suburb, you cannot operate a pig farm in your backyard. The stench would create a nuisance for your neighbours.

- Second, your use of the land is subject to various forms of regulation. For instance, governments are increasingly creating regulations to prevent people from using their properties in ways that hurt the environment.

[4.] That is also true for personal property, which we will discuss in Chapter 17. For instance, as Chapter 4 showed, you can use the tort of conversion against *anyone* who substantially interferes with your car. The entire world must respect your property rights in that vehicle.

[5.] Every piece of the land in Canada is ultimately owned by the Crown, that is, the government. For practical purposes, however, it is generally safe to treat the person with the fee simple as the owner. The Crown's interest is usually relevant only if that person dies without disposing of the property by will *and* without leaving behind any relatives to whom it can be given under *intestacy legislation*. Intestacy means that a person has died without a "testament," or will. In that case, the Crown will take control of the land.

Furthermore, every municipality in Canada uses *zoning and planning* regulations to control the types of activities that occur within certain areas. For example, you probably cannot build a casino on your land if a school is located next door.

expropriation occurs when the government takes property for a public purpose

- Third, your property may be *expropriated*. **Expropriation** occurs when the government takes property for a public purpose, such as the construction of a new bridge or the widening of a highway. You will be entitled to compensation, but you cannot insist upon keeping the land. Similarly, even if the government does not expropriate a section of your land, it may exercise a right to build a sewer system underground or run telephone wires overhead. Expropriation can be particularly controversial in some situations. Consider Ethical Perspective 15.1.

Ethical Perspective 15.1

Expropriation

Molly lives in a house in Come by Chance, Newfoundland, which her family has occupied for six generations. She was recently notified by the provincial government that her property was required for the purpose of constructing a natural gas pipeline that would substantially contribute to the region's economy. She insisted that she would never sell her ancestral home but was told that she had no choice in the matter. While sympathetic to Molly's situation, the government noted several factors that identified her land as the only suitable place for the pipeline. For instance, her land was located near the gas well and the refinery. Furthermore, other nearby areas were especially vulnerable to environmental damage. The government also assured Molly that she would receive fair compensation. She tearfully insists that no amount of money could ever replace her home.

Question for Discussion

1. Is expropriation ethical? On what grounds do you base your answer?

Life Estate

a **life estate** entitles a person to exclusive possession of a property for the duration of a particular life

A *life estate* is similar to a fee simple, but it carries fewer rights. As the name suggests, a **life estate** entitles a person to exclusive possession of a property for the duration of a particular life. The life in question usually belongs to the person who holds the estate, but it can also belong to someone else. Suppose I hold the fee simple in a property and agree to sell a life estate to you. We might agree that the land is yours until you die *or* we might agree that your interest will exist only while my brother is alive. In either event, you will lose control of the property once the relevant life ends. At that time, I will regain control. The property may simply come back to me (or to my estate if I have already died) by way of a **reversion**. Alternatively, if I transfer my reversionary interest to someone else, that person will take the property as a **remainder.**

a **reversion** occurs when the property returns to the person who holds the fee simple

a **remainder** occurs when the property goes to a third party who was selected by the person who holds the fee simple

waste occurs when a property is changed in a way that significantly affects its value

The rights under a life estate are limited in another important way. A person with a fee simple is generally free to use or abuse the property. In contrast, a person with a life estate is normally entitled to the profits that are generated from the land but cannot commit an act of *waste*. **Waste** occurs when a property is changed in a way that significantly affects its value. That includes, for example, digging pits and cutting down trees. A person with a life estate who commits an act of waste can be held liable to the person who holds the reversion or remainder. The rule against waste normally applies, however, only to acts and not to omissions. Consequently, if you purchase a life estate from me, you cannot demolish a building without my permission, but you are not required to spend money to keep that building in good condition.

Life estates are often useful in family situations.[6] Suppose you hold the fee simple in a residential property that you share with your younger sister, who has a disability. While you want your younger brother to eventually inherit that house, you also want to ensure that your sister always has a place to live after you are gone. Consequently, you draft a will that leaves the fee simple to your brother and a life estate for your sister. Upon your death, she will enjoy the use of the property for the rest of her life (assuming that she does not predecease you) and then the land will go to your brother (or his estate if he has died by that point). In the business world, however, life estates tend to be unattractive. Because it is impossible to know when a person will die, and when their interest will come to an end, life estates are usually too unpredictable for business people. Certainty is important in the commercial world.

Leasehold Estate

A **leasehold estate** occurs when a person has exclusive rights to a property for a specific period of time. A lease is like a fee simple or a life interest because it carries the right of exclusive possession. But a lease is also different because it is not defined by a life. A person with a lease can retain the property for only a specific block of time. That block may be long or short—a day or a century, for instance. It may be limited to a single term, or it may be automatically renewed if neither party objects. But in any event, the duration of the lease is established at the outset. We will discuss leases in the last section of this chapter.

a **leasehold estate** occurs when a person has exclusive rights to a property for a specific period of time

Concept Summary 15.1 reviews the main differences between a fee simple, a life estate, and a lease.

Concept Summary 15.1

Fee Simple, Life Estate, and Lease

Type of Estate	Nature and Duration of Estate
Fee simple	right to exclusive possession during own life and right to dispose of property upon death
Life estate	right to exclusive possession during relevant life but no right to dispose of property upon death
Lease	right to exclusive possession during specified period

Shared Ownership

Up to this point, we have assumed that an estate is owned by only one person. However, ownership can also be shared amongst several people. It is therefore important to distinguish *individual ownership* and *shared ownership*. For the purposes of discussion, suppose there is a large piece of land for sale.

- If you buy the east half and I buy the west half, we *do not* share ownership. Rather, the single piece of land is divided in two, and we each

---

[6.] In the family context, life estates are sometimes imposed as a matter of law. For example, a woman was historically entitled upon her husband's death to *dower*, which was a life interest in one-third of any real property in which he held a fee simple. Because of problems associated with that rule, dower has been abolished in Canada. It was replaced with a variety of even more extensive statutory rights.

become the *individual* owner of a separate piece. I can put a fence around my property to keep you out, and you can do the same to me.

- In contrast, if we act together and buy *undivided interests* in a single piece of land, we *do* share ownership. We are both owners of the *same* property. Furthermore, we both own the *whole* property. Consequently, neither one of us can put a fence around any part of the land to keep the other out.[7] One very common example of shared ownership occurs when a couple buys a home together.

There are two important types of shared ownership:

- joint ownership (or *joint tenancy*)
- co-ownership (or *co-tenancy* or *tenancy in common*)

joint ownership occurs when two or more people share exactly the same interest in a property

Joint ownership occurs when two or more people share *exactly* the same interest in a property. Consequently, if you and I are joint tenants with three other people, we each have a 20 percent interest.[8] The most significant feature of a joint tenancy is the *right of survivorship*. The **right of survivorship** means that upon death, a joint tenant's interest automatically passes to the remaining joint tenants. For instance, if I die first, my interest must pass to you and the others—I cannot give it away to anyone else. You and the other joint tenants will then each have a 25 percent interest in the property. That process can be repeated until the last surviving joint tenant takes the whole property.

the right of survivorship means that upon death, a joint tenant's interest automatically passes to the remaining joint tenants

co-ownership occurs when two or more people share an undivided interest in a property

Co-ownership also occurs when two or more people share an undivided interest in a property. However, there are at least two important differences between co-ownership and joint ownership.

- Co-owners do not have to have *exactly* the same interests. Assume, once again, that you and I share ownership with three other people. While our shares must be undivided, in the sense that none of us can assert individual rights over any particular piece of ground, they do not have to be equal. For instance, I may own a 60 percent interest, while you and the other co-owners each enjoy 10 percent interests.[9]
- More significantly, co-owners do not enjoy the right of survivorship. Consequently, if I die first, you and the other co-owners will *not* automatically acquire my interest. I can, for instance, leave my share to a friend, who would then become a co-owner along with you and the others.

The differences between co-tenancy and joint tenancy may affect the type of ownership that you choose for your business. Consider Business Decision 15.1 (on the next page).

severance occurs when a joint tenant deals with the property in a way that is inconsistent with joint ownership

Joint tenants can avoid the right of survivorship through the process of *severance*.[10] **Severance** occurs when a joint tenant deals with the property in a way that is inconsistent with joint ownership. Suppose you jointly owned a cottage along with my sister and me. You then sold your interest to a stranger. You are no longer an owner of any kind. Furthermore, while the stranger has

---

[7.] You and I can use a contract to change the rule between ourselves. For instance, we may agree that, while we share ownership of the whole property, you can put a fence around the east part, and I can put a fence around the west part.

[8.] Each of us is therefore generally entitled to 20 percent of the profits from the land. That rule applies to profits that are received from a *third party* (*eg* by renting the property to an outsider). It might be different, however, if one of us earned profits through our own labour (*eg* by harvesting raspberries).

[9.] I am therefore entitled to 60 percent of the general profits, while you and the others each get 10 percent.

[10.] The law tries to avoid the right of survivorship by assuming, in the absence of evidence to the contrary, that property held under shared ownership is subject to a tenancy in common, rather than a joint tenancy.

Business Decision 15.1

Choice of Shared Ownership

You and your partner have enjoyed great success over the years in a variety of business ventures. As you both near an early retirement at age 60, you decide to enter into one last project. Together you obtain a 75-year lease over a parcel of land on the outskirts of town. You do so with the intention of developing a theme park.

Questions for Discussion

1. Should your shared ownership take the form of a co-tenancy or a joint tenancy?

2. What if the other person is your "partner" in the sense of being the person with whom you have shared an intimate, monogamous, co-habitational relationship for four decades?

3. What if the other person is your "partner" in the sense of being the person with whom, in a purely professional capacity, you have made a great deal of money? Assume that you also have a "partner" of the other sort, with whom you have produced five children.

become *some* kind of owner, he is *not* a joint tenant with my sister and me. He does not have *exactly* the same interest as us, since he acquired his rights after we acquired ours. Consequently, while my sister and I are still joint tenants with respect to each other, we are co-tenants with respect to the stranger.

The right of survivorship can be lost in other ways as well. One of the most significant is through the process of *partition*.[11] **Partition** occurs when there is a division of either the property or its sale proceeds. The parties may agree amongst themselves as to who gets what. But if they cannot do so, they can ask a judge to resolve the matter. The courts generally have broad discretion in deciding whether to physically divide the land, sell the land and divide the proceeds, or refuse relief altogether.[12]

Concept Summary 15.2 summarizes the most important features of shared ownership.

partition occurs when there is a division of either the property or its sale proceeds

Concept Summary 15.2

Shared Ownership

Type of Shared Ownership	Description	Nature of Interests	Effect Upon Death
Joint ownership	two or more people share *the same* undivided interests in a property	each person's interest must be *exactly* the same as the other's (*eg* ownership between two parties must be split 50–50)	right of survivorship: deceased's interest automatically passes to remaining joint tenant
Co-ownership	two or more people share *some* undivided interests in a property	each person may have a different undivided interest (*eg* ownership between two parties may be split 70–30)	no right of survivorship: deceased's interest passes to person named in will or to next-of-kin

---

[11.] It is generally said that a joint tenancy may be severed in three ways. First, as suggested by the preceding paragraph, a new interest may be created that is different from the rest. Second, the parties may agree together to sever their joint tenancy. And third, some other event may have the effect of turning a joint tenancy into a tenancy in common. That may be true, for example, if one party becomes bankrupt, if one party's share is forcibly sold through a court process, or if one joint tenant murders another: *Schobelt v Barber* (1966) 60 DLR (2d) 519 (Ont HC).

[12.] Although the procedures vary between jurisdictions, it is usually possible to bring either form of shared ownership to an end through the process of partition.

PART 4

Condominiums

a **condominium** exists when several people share ownership of some parts of a building, while individually owning other parts

It is sometimes possible to have both individual ownership *and* shared ownership. The most common example involves *condominiums*. A **condominium** exists when several people share ownership of some parts of a building, while individually owning other parts.[13] Although the legislation varies considerably across the country, the basic arrangement is always the same.[14] A building is divided into a number of separate units, plus a variety of common areas (such as hallways, stairwells, parking lots, and tennis courts). The separate units are usually residential, but they may also be used for commercial purposes, such as restaurants and shops. If you purchase a unit in a condominium, you receive three sets of rights:

- First, you receive individual ownership of that particular unit. Your rights closely resemble those of a fee simple, except that you do not have the exclusive right to possess a piece of ground, as well as a portion of the earth below and the sky above. Instead, you have a "flying fee." In other words, while you do have a large bundle of rights, they apply only to the specific unit that is held in the air by the other parts of the building.

- Second, you and the other individual unit owners share ownership of the common areas as tenants in common. As a result, subject to any more specific rules or arrangements that may be created by contract, you can all use those common areas, such as the pool.

- Third, as you can see, a condominium is a small community. And like other communities, it requires decisions to be made and enforced. For those reasons, it will have a *condominium corporation*, which is a non-profit organization that manages the complex. The condominium corporation will create and enforce regulations regarding the individual units (such as rules against keeping dogs) and the communal areas (such as swimming pool hours). As the owner of a separate unit, you are entitled to vote on matters concerning the corporation, such as the creation of by-laws and the election of directors. You are also required to pay condominium fees, which are effectively the community's tax.

NON-POSSESSORY INTERESTS IN LAND

We have examined several property interests that provide a right to possession. Canadian law also recognizes a number of *non-possessory* interests in land. In other words, a person may have rights in a property, without being able to actually possess that property. We will briefly discuss three important possibilities:

- easements
- restrictive covenants
- mineral leases

[13.] The word "condominium" is derived from the Latin words meaning "joint" (*con*) and "control" (*dominium*).

[14.] *Condominium Property Act*, RSA 2000, c C-22 (Alta); *Condominium Act*, RSBC 1996, c 64 (BC); *Condominium Act*, CCSM, c C170 (Man); *Condominium Property Act*, RSNB 1973, c C-16 (NB); *Condominium Act*, RSNL 1990, c C-29 (Nfld); *Condominium Act*, RSNWT 1988, c C-15 (NWT and Nun); *Condominium Act*, RSNS 1989, c 85 (NS); *Condominium Act*, 1998, SO 1998, c 19 (Ont); *Condominium Act*, RSPEI 1988, c C-16 (PEI); *Condominium Property Act*, RSS 1978, c C-26 (Sask); *Condominium Act*, RSY 2002, c 36 (Yuk).

Easements

An **easement** is a right to use a neighbour's land. Most easements are positive. For instance, you might let me drive across your property to reach a road or periodically drain my water reservoir onto your land. While less common, an easement can also be negative. For instance, you might be prohibited from constructing a building that would deprive my house of sunlight, or from cutting down a line of trees that protects my fields from wind erosion.

an **easement** is a right to use a neighbour's land

As our examples suggest, an easement can exist only between neighbours. While our properties do not necessarily have to be touching, they do have to be reasonably close together. I must be able to show that I have the **dominant tenement**, the property that benefits from the easement, and that you have the **servient tenement**, the property that accommodates the easement. As long as those requirements are met, an easement can **run with the land**. That means that it can apply even if different people acquire possession of the affected properties.

a **dominant tenement** is a property that benefits from an easement

a **servient tenement** is a property that accommodates an easement

an easement can **run with the land**, meaning that it can apply even if different people acquire possession of the affected properties

An easement can be created in several ways:

- **Express:** The simplest method is for the parties to expressly agree to create an easement. For example, before selling part of my land to you, I might insist that our contract recognize my right to swim in the pond that will be located on your part of the property.

- **Implied:** An easement can also arise by necessary implication. For instance, I might buy a section of your land without realizing that my new property is completely cut off from the highway. In that situation, the courts will presume, unless there is evidence to the contrary, that we silently agreed that I would be allowed to drive across the remaining section of your property to reach the highway.

- **Prescription:** The law traditionally allowed an easement to be acquired by *prescription*, even if there was no agreement between the parties.[15] Prescription exists in only some jurisdictions in Canada.[16] Although the rules vary from place to place, the basic idea is always the same. An easement by **prescription** is created if land is used in a particular way, for a long time (usually 20 years), without secrecy, without objection, and without permission. Suppose I have openly used a portion of your back lot for a compost heap for decades. You have done nothing about it. The law may now recognize an easement that provides me with the right to continue dumping on your property.[17]

an easement by **prescription** is created if land is used in a particular way, for a long time, without secrecy, without objection, and without permission

- **Statutory:** Statutes often give utility companies and similar organizations the right to bury television cables, dig sewers, and so on. The

---

[15.] In this context, "prescription" is derived from an old English word meaning "establishment of a claim."

[16.] Prescription is generally abolished in those jurisdictions that use a *land titles* system of registration. The aim of that system, which is discussed in Chapter 16, is to provide documents which make it clear, at all times, what interests exist in each piece of land. Interests that arise by operation of law tend to frustrate that goal because they are hidden from view.

[17.] While less common, a *possessory interest* may be acquired through the similar process of *adverse possession*. That may be true if (i) I occupy your land for a long time (usually 10 or 20 years, depending upon the province), (ii) I do so with the intention of excluding you, (iii) I actually do exclude you, and (iv) my possession of your land has been visible, open, notorious, and continuous. If I prove all of those elements, then the land becomes mine. In that situation, lawyers sometimes talk about "squatters' rights." The law wants the land to be owned by the person who will make the best use of it. (The doctrine of adverse possession has generally been modified or abolished in those parts of the country that use the land title system of registration.)

telephone company can, for instance, run wires over your yard even if its office is not located nearby. Although such rights are often called *public easements* or *statutory easements*, they are not true easements because there is no dominant tenement.

It is important to distinguish an easement from a mere *licence*. A **licence** is permission to act in a way that would otherwise be prohibited. For example, if your property is located close to a stadium, you might allow me to park on your lawn while I attend a football game. Unlike an easement, a licence is not an interest in land, it does not run with the property, and it can be revoked at any time (subject to any contractual rights that may exist between the parties). Furthermore, because a licence is not an easement, it does not require the existence of dominant and servient tenements.

a **licence** is permission to act in a way that would otherwise be prohibited

Restrictive Covenants

An easement must be distinguished from a *restrictive covenant*. A **restrictive covenant** is a promise to use a piece of land in a way that benefits one property and burdens another. It is like an easement because it requires a dominant tenement and a servient tenement. In other respects, however, it is quite different. First, while an easement can sometimes arise through prescription, a restrictive covenant can be created only by agreement. Second, a restrictive covenant never allows me to use your land. It merely limits how you can use your own property.[18] Concept Summary 15.3 outlines the major similarities and differences between easements and restrictive covenants.

a **restrictive covenant** is a promise to use a piece of land in a way that benefits one property and burdens another

Concept Summary 15.3

Easements and Restrictive Covenants

	Similarities	Differences
Easements	• non-possessory interest in land • dominant tenement enjoys benefit	• acquisition: agreement or prescription • nature: dominant tenement entitled to use of servient tenement
Restrictive covenants	• servient tenement bears burden • interest may run with the land	• acquisition: agreement only • nature: servient tenement subject to limitations on use and enjoyment of land

Restrictive covenants raise difficult issues of enforcement. Suppose I own several business chains, including one that rebuilds abandoned vehicles. You own a large piece of land, which you use in part to operate a florist shop. You are willing to sell half of that property to me, but you are concerned that I might behave in a way that scares off your customers and hurts the value of your land. Consequently, when drafting the sale contract, we insert two *covenants*, which are promises that are written and placed under seal.

■ Under the first, I promise that I will repaint the buildings on my part of the land every two years.

---

18. That limitation cannot be immoral or against public policy. For example, the courts will not enforce a promise that discriminates against people on the grounds of race or religion.

- Under the second, I promise that I will not use my premises as an auto body shop.

Are those promises enforceable? What if one or both of us later sell our properties—you to Miguel and I to Janet? The answers to those questions depend upon (i) the identity of the parties, and (ii) the nature of the covenant. We consider the three situations shown in Figure 15.1.

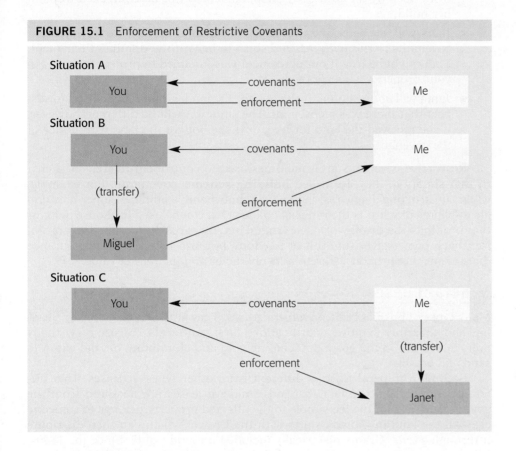

FIGURE 15.1   Enforcement of Restrictive Covenants

- **Situation A:** If we both still own the properties, you can sue me if I break either promise. You are entitled to damages if my breach creates a loss. I might also be forced, through specific performance or an injunction, to actually fulfill my promises.

- **Situation B:** Now assume that while you sold your property to Miguel, I still have mine. A potential problem arises. As we saw in Chapter 8, a contract can usually be enforced only by someone with *privity*, that is, with someone who was a party to the original agreement. However, as we also saw, that rule has exceptions. Perhaps most significantly, contractual *benefits* can generally be *assigned*. Consequently, as long as the original covenants were intended to run with the land, Miguel can sue me if I break either promise.

- **Situation C:** What if you held on to your property, but I sold my property to Janet? If she refused to paint the buildings or if she opened an auto body shop, could you sue her? This situation appears to be similar to the last one, but there is an additional complication. It is generally possible to assign contractual *benefits*, but not contractual *burdens*. The courts are reluctant to impose obligations upon a person simply because they bought a piece of land. Consequently, in deciding whether Janet is caught by the covenants, a judge would look at several factors:[19]

- Janet may be bound by a *negative* covenant, but not by a *positive* one. She could be *prevented* from doing something, but she could not be *required* to do something else. Accordingly, while she could be restrained from opening an auto body shop, she could not be compelled to paint her buildings.[20]

- Janet will *not* be bound unless, as the original parties, we intended our covenants to *run with the land* so as to benefit the dominant tenement. That might be true if our agreement was intended to protect the value of your property, whoever owned it.

- Janet will *not* be bound if she bought the land without any reason to suspect that there was a covenant. The situation will be different, however, if she received the land for free, or if she bought the land with notice of the covenant.

a **building scheme covenant** is a collection of restrictive covenants that are used to control the development of an entire area

Restrictive covenants are sometimes used to control entire areas of a city. In that situation, they are called **building scheme covenants**. For example, when constructing a new residential neighbourhood, a land developer may create a scheme that limits the range of colours that can be used for house paint or that prohibits the display of lawn ornaments. By agreeing to obey such promises, each owner gives up a bit of freedom, but also receives some assurance that the neighbourhood will retain its character and its market value.

Mineral Leases

minerals consist of virtually every substance contained in the ground

Many types of business rely on *mineral leases*. That phrase tends to be misleading and therefore requires clarification. First, **minerals** consist of virtually every substance in the ground, including gold and aluminum, oil and gas, and sand and gravel.

Second, a mineral lease is different from other types of leases. That difference stems from the fact that most mineral leases are acquired from the government, even if the fee simple to the affected property belongs to someone else. All the land in Canada starts with the Crown, which can then distribute it through *grants*. Grants historically included mineral rights. Since the 1880s, however, the government has *reserved* those rights by keeping them for itself. As a result, depending upon where you live in this country, you probably do not have the right to sell the valuable deposits that lie beneath your property. The government does.

a **mineral lease** allows one person to extract and retain something of value from another person's property

As a result of that split between surface rights and mineral rights, a mining operation often requires a complicated set of legal arrangements. Under the common law, the right to extract minerals comes together with an implied right to access and occupy the affected land. The area in question is quite small—just large enough to facilitate the mining operation. After all, the aim of a **mineral lease** is to allow one person to extract and retain something of value from another person's property. In many jurisdictions, however, the traditional common law rights have been altered by statute. It is now common for a statute

[19] *Tulk v Moxhay* (1848) 41 ER 1143 (Ch).

[20] Similarly, as we saw in Chapter 12, courts are more willing to award injunctions than specific performance. An order that *prevents* a person from doing something limits their freedom of choice less than an order that *requires* them to do something.

to require a mining company, having received the government's permission to extract minerals, to create a separate *surface lease* with the surface owner. If the parties are unable to reach an agreement, an administrative tribunal has the ability to create an arrangement that balances the competing interests.

PROFIT À PRENDRE A mineral lease is similar to *profit à prendre*. A **profit à prendre** is a right to take something valuable away from another person's property.[21] That sort of right can apply not only to minerals, but also to other natural things, such as blueberries and moose.[22] Significantly, like a mineral lease, a *profit à prendre* is an interest in land, but not an automatic right to the things in question. Consequently, if you buy a *profit à prendre* with respect to the trees on my property, the timber does not belong to you until you actually harvest it from my land.

a *profit à prendre* is a right to take something valuable away from another person's property

Concept Summary 15.4 reviews various types of non-possessory interests.

Concept Summary 15.4

Non-Possessory Interests in Land

Type of Interest	Description	Dominant Tenement Required?
Easement	a right to use a piece of land in a way that benefits a neighbouring piece of land (*eg* a right to take water from a neighbour's lake)	yes
Restrictive covenant	a restriction that is placed on one property in order to benefit a neighbouring property (*eg* a promise to not construct a building that would block sunlight from entering a neighbour's garden)	yes
Mineral lease	a right to remove minerals from a piece of land (*eg* a right to extract oil from beneath a property)	no
Profit à prendre	a right to take something valuable away from a piece of land (*eg* a right to cut and remove timber from a property)	no

Leases

L.O. ❽ ❾ ❿

We have already seen that a lease is an estate in land that creates an exclusive right to possession. However, given the significant role that leases play in the modern business world, it is necessary to look at them in detail.[23]

A **lease**, or a *tenancy* as it is sometimes called, is a property interest created by contract. Therefore, the usual contractual requirements must be satisfied, including intention to create legal relations, offer and acceptance, and consideration. In addition, while most contracts can be created orally, some leases must be put into print. The legislation varies from jurisdiction to jurisdiction, but

a **lease** is a property interest created by contract

---

[21] The term *"à prendre"* is derived from French and means "a right to take."

[22] *Royal Bank of Canada v Saulnier* (2008) 298 DLR (4th) 193 (SCC).

[23] In this chapter, we are concerned only with leases of land. As we will see in Chapter 17, it is also possible to lease other types of property.

the basic rule is that a lease must be evidenced in writing unless it is for three years or less.[24] Although an oral lease for a longer period is valid, it is generally unenforceable and therefore can be ignored by either party.[25] (As a general rule, to reduce the danger of uncertainty and litigation, you should put *all* of your important contracts into writing.) Because a lease is created by contract, there must be a mutual agreement between two parties: the *landlord* and the *tenant*. The **landlord** is the person with an interest in land who agrees to allow someone else to take possession.[26] The **tenant** is the person who receives the right to possess the property.

DURATION

When a fee simple or a life estate is created, there is no way of knowing exactly how long it will last. The relevant life may continue for decades or end the next day. The maximum duration of a lease, however, must be definite. Consequently, it would not be possible to create a lease that would last "until the Maple Leafs next win the Cup."[27] There are several possibilities:

- **Fixed-term tenancy:** A **fixed-term tenancy** exists when it is possible at the outset to determine when the tenancy will end. The parties may actually specify a date, such as "31 December 2020." Alternatively, if they do not know a specific date at the outset, they may provide a formula that is capable of generating one, such as "the last day of Ramadan in 2020." Even if they initially agreed to a fixed term, the parties can enter into a new lease at the end of the old one. And even if they do not create a new fixed-term lease, a *periodic tenancy* may arise if the tenant remains in possession and the landlord continues to accept rent at regular intervals.

- **Periodic tenancy:** A **periodic tenancy** is also for a fixed period, but it is automatically renewed at the end of each term unless one of the parties provides *notice of termination*. You are probably most familiar with that type of lease, since it is generally used for residential tenancies. The basic term of the lease can be for any length of time. A week, a month, and a year are the most common options. As a general rule, the length of the term mirrors the intervals at which the tenant pays rent. The length of the term usually also mirrors the notice period. Consequently, to terminate a monthly lease, you must provide one clear month's notice.[28] (A longer notice period is required under a residential lease.) A yearly tenancy, however, normally requires only six months' notice.[29]

the **landlord** is the person with an interest in land who agrees to allow someone else to take possession

the **tenant** is the person who receives the right to possess the property

a **fixed-term tenancy** exists when it is possible at the outset to determine when the tenancy will end

a **periodic tenancy** is for a fixed period and is automatically renewed at the end of each term unless one of the parties provides notice of termination

---

[24.] *Law and Equity Act*, RSBC 1996, c 253 (BC); *Statute of Frauds*, RSNB 1973, c S-14, s 7 (NB); *Statute of Frauds*, RSNS 1989, c 442, s 3 (NS); *Statute of Frauds*, RSO 1990, c S.19, ss 1–3 (Ont); *Statute of Frauds*, 1677 (Eng), c 3, ss 1–2 (Alta, Nfld, NWT, Nun, PEI, Sask, Yuk). In Manitoba, the English *Statute of Frauds* has been repealed by RSM 1987, c F158.

[25.] An exception may be created by part performance if the tenant is actually in possession *and* has paid rent.

[26.] Although the landlord typically holds the fee simple in the property, it is also possible for a person with a life estate, or even an earlier lease, to grant a new lease. That last possibility is called a *sublease* and it is discussed below.

[27.] The *maximum* duration must be definite, but a tenancy may end earlier. Therefore, it would be possible to have a lease "for 999 years or until the Maple Leafs next win the Cup." It is enough that the lease is certain to end within 999 years, even though there is a slim chance that it will end earlier.

[28.] Note that the period is one *clear* month's notice. For example, if you want to vacate the premises at the end of July, you must give notice by the end of June. If you wait until the first day of July, your lease will continue until the end of August.

[29.] In New Brunswick, Nova Scotia, and Prince Edward Island, the notice period is only three months.

- **Tenancy at will:** A **tenancy at will** exists if there is no set term and either party can terminate the lease at any time. Because there is no definite duration, it is sometimes said that a tenancy at will is not really a leasehold estate. Nevertheless, there is at least an implicit agreement between the parties, and the tenant is liable to pay rent. Tenancies at will most often arise when the owner of a property allows a potential purchaser to move in before the sale is finalized, or when a tenant remains on the premises with the landlord's consent after the end of a lease.[30]

*a **tenancy at will** exists if there is no set term and either party can terminate the lease at any time*

- Tenancy at sufferance: A **tenancy at sufferance** occurs when a tenant continues to possess the premises at the end of a lease without the landlord's permission. In that situation, there is not really a lease because the parties do not even have an implied agreement. Indeed, a tenant who does not vacate the property within a reasonable time after being asked to do so commits the tort of trespass (as discussed in Chapter 4), and the landlord can take steps to have the tenant forcibly removed. While there is no obligation to pay "rent" (because there is no tenancy), the person in possession is required to pay compensation for the use and occupation of the property.[31]

*a **tenancy at sufferance** occurs when a tenant continues to possess the premises at the end of a lease *without* the landlord's permission*

ASSIGNMENTS AND SUBLEASES

As a tenant, you may find that you do not want to occupy the premises for the full length of your lease. Perhaps you have been transferred to another city and no longer require an apartment. Perhaps your business has fallen on hard times and you no longer can afford to rent a warehouse. You have several options:

- You might persuade your landlord to terminate the lease early. That is unlikely to happen, however, unless you also introduce the landlord to a new tenant.
- Even if you cannot escape your lease, you might be able to *assign* it. As we saw in Chapter 8, an **assignment** occurs when you transfer your contractual rights to a third party. That third party (the *assignee*) would step into your shoes (at least for some purposes) and become the tenant. That possibility is subject to four limitations:

*an **assignment** occurs when a contractual party transfers its rights to a third party*

  - Although contractual rights can generally be assigned, your lease may either prohibit an assignment or require your landlord's consent (which, your lease may also say, cannot be withheld "unreasonably").[32] Such provisions are very common. Landlords want control over the people who occupy their premises.
  - Second, an assignment would not necessarily include all the terms in the lease. The assignee would be bound by only the *real covenants*. **Real covenants** include promises that are directly related to the land

real covenants include promises that are directly related to the land, but not promises that are merely personal obligations

[30] However, if the landlord continues to receive rent from the tenant at regular intervals, a court may recognize the creation of a periodic tenancy, with the result that notice must be given in a timely manner to terminate the new lease.

[31] If the landlord does accept "rental" payments, a court may recognize the implied creation of a periodic tenancy.

[32] To protect tenants, some jurisdictions have legislation to that effect unless the parties expressly say otherwise: *Landlord and Tenant Act*, CCSM, c L70, s 22 (Man); *Landlord and Tenant Act*, RSNB 1973, c L-1, s 11 (NB); *Commercial Tenancies Act*, RSNWT 1988, c C-10, s 11 (NWT and Nun); *Commercial Tenancies Act*, RSO 1990, c L.7, s 23 (Ont); *Landlord and Tenant Act*, RSPEI 1988, c L-4, s 12 (PEI); *Landlord and Tenant Act*, RSS 1978, c L-6, s 13 (Sask); *Landlord and Tenant Act*, RSY 2002, c 131, s 11 (Yuk).

(such as the obligation to pay rent or repair the premises), but not promises that are merely personal obligations (such as the original tenant's promise to buy goods from the landlord).

- Third, an assignment would not necessarily protect you from liability. If your assignee did not fulfill the lease, the landlord could normally demand relief from you. You could ask your landlord to release you from responsibility, but the landlord would probably refuse. You should therefore ensure that your assignment requires the assignee to honour the lease *and* to compensate you for any money that you may have to pay to the landlord.

- Fourth, an assignment must cover the entire term of a lease. If it falls short, even by one day, then it cannot be an assignment—but it may be a *sublease*.

- A **sublease** occurs when a tenant grants a lease to a third party.[33] In that case, the third party would not step into your shoes. You would continue to be the tenant under the original lease, but you would also be a landlord under the sublease. Your sublease might apply to the whole property or just one section of it. Similarly, it might contain the same terms as the original lease, but it need not do so. Once again, however, the original lease probably prohibits subleasing or requires you to obtain your landlord's consent.

> a **sublease** occurs when a tenant grants a lease to a third party

COMMERCIAL LEASES

Generally speaking, there are two types of leases: *commercial* and *residential*. We will focus on the former, and discuss the latter briefly at the end of this chapter.

Standard Covenants

> a **commercial lease** occurs when premises are rented for a business purpose

A **commercial lease** occurs when premises are rented for a business purpose. Although some modifications have been introduced by statute or by the common law, the basic contractual rules apply, and the parties are generally free to set their own terms. In fact, there often is some scope for negotiations even if a commercial lease is based on a standard form agreement. (We discussed standard form agreements in Chapter 9.) Consequently, depending upon the circumstances, a commercial lease may consist of a book-length document (for the long-term lease of an office tower) or a few words written on the back of an envelope (for temporary use of a patch of ground as a souvenir kiosk during a festival). Nevertheless, certain *covenants*, or promises, are standard.

Perhaps the most obvious covenant is the tenant's obligation to pay *rent*. Although that concept may seem obvious, it is important to appreciate a number of specific points:

- **Express or implied:** The parties will normally set the rent in advance. But even if they do not expressly agree on a price, the law will normally require the payment of a "reasonable" amount.

- **Calculation of rent:** In residential leases, the rent is usually set at a flat rate that reflects the type of tenancy. For instance, a periodic tenancy

---

[33.] It is often difficult to distinguish between an assignment and a sublease. There is no magic in words. A court will base its decision on the substance of the transaction, rather than the language that the parties used.

for an apartment may require the tenant to pay $1000 per month to the landlord. The rent provision in a commercial lease is often more complicated. For instance, the rent may be based on the size of the premises. An accountant in a business complex may pay $10 per square foot for an office. If the unit has 1000 square feet, then the rent will be $10 000 per year. Alternatively, the rent may be calculated on the basis of the profits that the tenant earns on the premises. For instance, a store in a shopping mall may be required to pay 10 percent of its gross profits. If the store earns $400 000 during a particular year, then the landlord is entitled to receive $40 000. Commercial leases often are classified, from a different perspective, as either *gross* or *net*. A *gross lease* requires the tenant to pay a single sum, which is intended to cover both rent and costs (such as utilities, taxes, and operating expenses). Many landlords dislike that arrangement, however, because they are forced to bear the full burden of any increased costs (such as when electricity rates rise). A *net lease* therefore requires the tenant to separately pay rent *and* a proportion of costs. If costs rise, then the burden is shared proportionately by the landlord and the tenant.

- **Rent review:** Many commercial leases last for long periods. Very often, however, it would be unreasonable to use the same rent for the entire time. Commercial leases therefore often allow for periodic reviews. The parties may agree, for instance, that they will negotiate a new rent every five years. They may also agree that the new rate will reflect prevailing market values or some percentage of the tenant's profits. And because the parties may not be able to reach an agreement, the lease may also require disputes to be sent to an arbitrator. (Arbitration was discussed in Chapter 2. A sample of a rent review arbitration clause can be found on MyBusLawLab for Chapter 2.)

- **Independent obligation:** Perhaps surprisingly, the obligation to pay rent is generally independent of other obligations in the lease. As a result, a tenant has no right to refuse to pay rent even if (for instance) the landlord fails to honour a promise to keep the property in good repair. In that situation, the tenant is expected to pay the rent and sue the landlord for breach of contract.

In addition to an obligation to pay rent, a tenant usually has a number of physical obligations. Because the common law rules regarding the actual condition of the property are so slim, almost every commercial lease establishes a more detailed set of rights and obligations. A landlord usually is required to merely look after the building's structure, as well as any *common areas* that are available to various tenants.[34] The tenant, in contrast, is obligated to maintain the premises themselves. It must treat the property in a "tenant-like manner" by doing things such as unplugging blocked toilets.[35] Because the landlord will want to maintain control over the property, the lease will also severely restrict the tenant's ability to undertake renovations. And, as will be discussed in Chapter 17, any permanent renovations to the building are likely to be considered *fixtures*, which presumably become the property of the landlord, even if the tenant paid for them.

One of the landlord's most important obligations requires *quiet possession*. A covenant for **quiet possession** prohibits the landlord from interfering with

a covenant for **quiet possession** prohibits the landlord from interfering with the tenant's enjoyment of the premises

---

[34.] The associated costs are shared proportionately between the landlord and the tenant under a *net lease*.

[35.] *Warren v Keen* [1954] 1 KB 15 (CA).

the tenant's enjoyment of the premises.[36] That covenant can be broken in a number of ways. (Notice that the concept of *quiet* possession usually has nothing to do with the absence of noise.)

- The landlord may be unable to grant an effective lease because, for example, the property is still occupied by another tenant.
- The landlord may disturb the tenant's use of the premises by, for example, allowing carbon monoxide to seep up from a parking lot, or habitually using a jackhammer that causes an intolerable amount of noise and vibration.
- While the landlord is not responsible for another tenant's *wrongful* behaviour, they may be liable for granting a lease with an incompatible use by, for example, allowing a bowling alley to operate directly over a relaxation clinic.

Depending upon the circumstances, a court may respond to a breach of a covenant for quiet possession in various ways. It may:

- award an injunction requiring the landlord to remedy the interference
- allow the tenant to discharge the lease and recover compensatory damages
- allow the tenant to have a reduction in rent

Unless the parties agree otherwise, the landlord is required to pay the *taxes* associated with a property. And while neither party is generally obligated to obtain *insurance* over the premises, the landlord normally does so to protect its investment. In some cases, the lease will shift the expense of that insurance to the tenant. And as a matter of risk management, the tenant should, in any event, obtain insurance coverage for the things that they store on the premises and for any damage that they may cause to outsiders. For instance, a fire may not only destroy the contents of the rental unit, but also spread to a neighbouring property.

Remedies

A commercial lease is created by contract and therefore supports the usual contractual remedies if there is a breach. We referred to several options in Chapter 12, including compensatory damages, injunctions, and discharge. Several special forms of relief, including eviction and distress, may be available to a landlord if the tenant commits a serious breach. Two are especially important:

eviction or **right of re-entry** allows a landlord to resume possession of the premises

forfeiture occurs when a tenant loses its interest in a property

- **Eviction:** If the tenant commits a serious breach, such as not paying the rent, the landlord may be entitled to exercise a right of eviction (sometimes called a **right of re-entry**) to resume possession of the premises before the end of the lease. That remedy often creates hardship for the tenant because it results in a **forfeiture**, which means the tenant loses their interest in the property. Consequently, even if a tenant has committed a serious breach, a court may grant relief from forfeiture by allowing the tenant to make amends and retain possession of the property. Each jurisdiction has detailed legislation regarding evictions.

distress occurs when the landlord seizes the tenant's belongings and sells them to pay the rent

- **Distress:** If a tenant is not evicted for failing to pay the rent, they may be subject to the remedy of *distress*. **Distress** occurs when the landlord seizes the tenant's belongings and sells them to pay the rent. Once again, each jurisdiction has detailed legislation on this point.

Finally, it is important to note that some of the rules that normally govern contractual remedies may not apply to commercial leases. As we discussed in

---

[36.] A landlord is, however, entitled to inspect the premises occasionally for signs of damage and abuse.

Chapter 12, a person who suffers a breach of contract can claim *expectation damages* for the benefit they should have received under the agreement. Those damages are reduced, however, to the extent that the plaintiff unreasonably failed to *mitigate* a loss. Suppose I agree to buy a car from you for $9000. I later refuse to go through with that deal when I learn that the car is worth only $6000. It seems that your expectation damages are $3000, which was your expected profit. However, you will be entitled to only $2000 if I can prove that you could have resold the car to someone else for $7000. You are responsible for the other $1000 because you unreasonably failed to mitigate that loss by selling the car to a third party.

That same rule may not apply to commercial leases. Although the cases are inconsistent, the Supreme Court of Canada has suggested that if a tenant wrongfully vacates the premises, the landlord can sometimes let the premises sit empty and recover the value of the rent that would have been paid over the entire tenancy.[37] Does that seem fair? How would you respond to the dispute in You Be the Judge 15.1?

You Be the Judge **15.1**

Commercial Leases and Mitigation

Archer Holdings Ltd owns a shopping centre in a suburban area. Although a number of smaller shops rent space in the mall, the "anchor" (that is, the main tenant) is Bainsbury Foods, a grocery store. Bainsbury signed a lease with Archer for a fixed term of 15 years. Business was brisk for the first 12 months, but after a downturn in the economy Bainsbury began to lose a lot of money as a result of operating in that particular location. Consequently, two years into the lease, it removed its stock and equipment, transferred its employees to other outlets, and closed its doors in Archer's mall.

Archer has resumed control of the vacated space, but has made no effort to find another anchor. The evidence indicates that, despite the downturn in the economy, a replacement tenant could be found if the landlord were willing to reduce the rent by 25 percent. Bainsbury admits that it breached the contract but insists that it should not be responsible for 13 years of full rent on a property that it no longer occupies.

Question for Discussion

1. Do you agree with Bainsbury's argument? Explain your answer.

Risk Management: Lease or Purchase

We have now examined the most important aspects of *leasing* land. In the next chapter, we will consider the possibility of *purchasing* land. The choice between those two options may be amongst the most difficult that a business must make. And, as always, successful risk management requires information. Concept Summary 15.5 therefore identifies some of the most important advantages and disadvantages for each option.[38] As you will see, the decision to lease or purchase a business property is, in some ways, similar to the decision that must be made in renting or buying a home. Early in life, when resources are limited and the future is uncertain, it often makes sense to pay for the right to use someone else's property. As time passes, however, finances improve, long-term plans are fixed in place, and it usually makes more sense to acquire ownership.

[37] *Highway Properties Ltd v Kelly Douglas & Co* (1971) 17 DLR (3d) 710 (SCC). Damages are reduced, however, to the extent that the landlord does limit their loss by renting the property to a third party.

[38] Many of the same considerations made when dealing with personal property, such as cars and computers, equally apply to decisions made about commercial property. There may be some differences, however. For instance, it is common for a vehicle leasing agreement to allow the customer to buy the vehicle at the end of the lease period. If so, the total cost will certainly be substantially higher than it would be under a simple purchase. It is uncommon to have that sort of term in a leasing agreement for land.

Concept Summary 15.5

Risk Management: Lease or Purchase[39]

	Lease	Purchase
Cost	• lower immediate costs • tax-deductible rent • permanent and ongoing expense	• higher immediate costs (price, down payment, legal fees, transfer tax) • purchase expense ends when price paid in full
Cash flow	• leasing usually available even if limited cash flow and poor credit rating • lower monthly expenses allow resources for other business needs (hiring, acquiring equipment, and so on)	• initial expenses require substantial cash and usually strong credit rating • often higher monthly expenses
Obligations	• minimal obligations contained in lease • most burdens fall on landlord	• full burden of obligations arising from ownership (*eg* ongoing maintenance, tort liability, property taxes, environmental regulations)
Investment	• no lasting benefit after end of lease	• increasing equity as price paid • eventual absolute ownership
Flexibility	• short-term lease allows for quick growth or downsizing	• long-term commitment • more difficult and costly to change premises
Control	• limited opportunity for renovations • untimely disruptions from landlord's renovations • subject to landlord's rules on usage	• complete control over property, structures, and timing of renovations
Market change	• rent not (immediately) affected by market changes	• increased value of property if market rises • decreased value of property if market drops

RESIDENTIAL LEASES

a **residential lease** provides a place to live

Although it shares the same basic purpose as a commercial lease, a *residential lease* is different in some respects. A **residential lease** provides a place to live. The law therefore is much more willing to become involved in the landlord–tenant relationship. It may be acceptable to allow two businesses to freely negotiate the terms of their agreement. It seems unfair and unrealistic, however, to expect a residential tenant to do the same. In that situation, there is probably a great difference in bargaining power between the parties, especially when accommodation is scarce. Almost by definition, a residential tenant has limited resources. People with large amounts of money usually buy, rather than rent, so that their payments create an investment. Consequently, every jurisdiction in Canada has extensive legislation that regulates residential tenancies by requiring some terms, prohibiting others, providing mechanisms for resolving disputes, and so on.[40]

It is impossible for us to consider that legislation in detail.[41] We can, however, note several important differences between residential and commercial leases:

■ **Termination:** In the commercial context, it is usually possible to terminate a periodic tenancy by giving notice equal to the length of one

---

[39.] T Andersen "The Buy or Lease Dilemma" *Ottawa Business Journal* (1 December 2008).

[40.] *Residential Tenancies Act*, SA 2004, c R-17.1 (Alta); *Residential Tenancy Act*, RSBC 1996, c 406 (BC); *Residential Tenancies Act*, CCSM, c R119 (Man); *Residential Tenancies Act*, SNB 1975, c R-10.2 (NB); *Residential Tenancies Act*, 2000, SNL 2000, c R-14.1 (Nfld); *Residential Tenancies Act*, RSNWT 1988, c R-5 (NWT and Nun); *Residential Tenancies Act*, RSNS 1989, c 401 (NS); *Residential Tenancies Act*, 1997, SO 1997, c 24 (Ont); *Rental of Residential Property Act*, SPEI 1988, c 58 (PEI); *Residential Tenancies Act*, RSS 1978, c R-22 (Sask); *Landlord and Tenant Act*, RSY 2002, c 131 (Yuk).

[41.] See C Bentley *et al* *William & Rhodes Canadian Law of Landlord and Tenant* 6th ed looseleaf (1988).

term. Residential notice periods, however, tend to be much longer, for example, 60 or 90 days for a monthly lease. Likewise, in the residential context, a periodic tenancy may automatically arise at the end of a fixed-term lease unless notice was given.

- **Rental rates:** Commercial parties are generally free to agree upon any price. Residential leases, in contrast, are governed by rent control mechanisms that prevent landlords from gouging tenants.
- **Distress:** A commercial landlord may be entitled to seize and sell a tenant's belongings if rent is not paid. However, that right usually is not available against a residential tenant.
- **Repair and maintenance:** Unlike a commercial landlord, a residential landlord has a statutory obligation to repair and maintain the property.
- **Mitigation:** Although a commercial landlord may be relieved of the need to mitigate when a tenant wrongfully vacates a property, a residential landlord is generally required to take reasonable steps to minimize the losses that result from a breach.

Chapter Summary

Real property includes land and things attached to land. A defining feature of property interests is that they are generally enforceable against the whole world and not merely against the person from whom they are acquired.

An estate in land involves the right to exclusive possession. A fee simple entitles a person to exercise rights over a piece of property for life and to dispose of it after death. A life estate lasts only as long as the relevant life; upon death, the property either reverts to the person from whom it was obtained or passes as a remainder to someone else. A lease provides the right to exclusive possession and therefore qualifies as an estate in land. However, its duration is not measured by anyone's life—a lease must be for a definite duration.

Ownership in a piece of land can be shared between two or more people. With co-ownership, two or more people share an undivided interest in a property. With joint ownership, two or more people share exactly the same interests in a property. Joint ownership includes the right of survivorship. Joint ownership can be turned into co-ownership through the process of severance. Shared ownership can be brought to an end through the process of partition. In a condominium, several people share ownership of some parts of a building, while individually owning other parts.

An easement is a right to use a neighbour's land. An easement must exist between two neighbouring properties—the dominant tenement and the servient tenement. An easement may be created expressly or implicitly. In some jurisdictions, it can also be created through prescription. A statutory or public easement is not really an easement because it does not require a dominant tenement. A licence is permission to act in a way that would otherwise be prohibited, but it is neither an easement nor an interest in land.

A restrictive covenant is a promise to use property in a way that benefits the dominant tenement and burdens the servient tenement. A restrictive covenant can be created only by agreement. The enforcement of a covenant depends upon (i) the identity of the parties and (ii) the nature of the covenant.

A mineral lease allows a person to extract and retain minerals from another person's property. It is similar to a *profit à prendre*.

A lease (or tenancy) is contractually created between the landlord and the tenant. Its maximum duration must be definite. A fixed-term tenancy exists when it is possible at the outset to determine when the tenancy will end. A periodic tenancy is also for a fixed period, but it is automatically renewed at the end of each term unless one of the parties provides notice to quit. A tenancy at will exists when there is no set term and either party can terminate the lease at any time. With a tenancy at sufferance, a tenant continues to possess the premises at the end of a lease without the landlord's permission. The parties do not really have a lease because they do not have an agreement.

Tenants can sometimes assign their rights under a lease to a third party, who then becomes the tenant. A tenant may also sublease a property. If so, that person remains a tenant under the original lease but also becomes a landlord under the sublease. Many leases either prohibit assignments and subleases or require the landlord's consent.

With a commercial lease, premises are rented for a business purpose. The parties are generally free to negotiate the terms. Some promises or covenants, however, are standard. If a tenant breaks a commercial lease, the landlord may be entitled to use the special remedies of eviction and distress. In some situations, a landlord can claim contractual relief without the need to mitigate its losses.

A residential lease provides a place to live. Every jurisdiction in Canada has extensive legislation regulating residential tenancies. They all require some terms, prohibit others, and provide mechanisms for resolving disputes.

MyBusLawLab   ADDITIONAL RESOURCES FOR CHAPTER 15

MyBusLawLab provides students with an assortment of tools to help enrich the learning experience, including a Study Plan with Pre- and Post-tests, mini-cases with assessments, and provincial content material, which provides links to relevant cases, legislation, and additional resources.

MyBusLawLab provides the following resources for Chapter 15:

Provincial Material

- **British Columbia:** Adverse Possession and Prescriptive Easements, Builders' Liens, Distress for Rent, Condominiums, Expropriation, Fixtures, Partition of Property, Strata Title, Residential Leases, Commercial Leases, Trespass to Land

- **Alberta:** *Alberta Land Stewardship Act (2010)*, Builders Liens, *Land Assembly Project Area Act (2009)*, Commercial Leases, Condominiums, Distress, Enforcement of Judgments, Fixtures, Garnishment, Limitations of Actions, Residential Tenancies, Restrictive Covenants, Personal Covenants, *Surface Rights Amendment Act (2009)*

- **Manitoba and Saskatchewan:** Condominiums, Conservation Easements, Residential Tenancies Information

- **Ontario:** Adverse Possession, Condominiums, Consumer Leases, Matrimonial Homes, Reserve Funds, Restrictive Covenants, Assignment of Tenancy, Assignment of Rents, Ontario Rental Housing Tribunal, Distress, Fixtures, Leasehold Improvements, Overholding, *Residential Tenancies Act*, Landlord and Tenant Legislation

- **Atlantic Provinces:** Condominium Legislation, Crown Leases and Grants, Expropriation, Landlord and Tenant, Residential Tenancies

Review Questions

1. What is the "giant carrot theory"? Do Canadian courts apply that concept? Explain your answer.

2. "The Crown, or the government, is the true owner of every piece of land in Canada." Is that statement true? Explain your answer.

3. "A private person who owns a piece of land has complete control over that property." Is that statement true? Provide three illustrations in support of your answer.

4. "It is impossible to know today when the current Queen of England will die. For that reason, it is impossible to have either a life estate or a lease that is set up to last as long as the Queen lives." Is that statement true? Explain your answer.

5. Explain why life estates are generally unattractive in a commercial context.

6. Describe the right of survivorship. Explain when and how it applies. Describe two ways in which that right can be brought to an end.

7. Explain the process of partition. Provide an example of when it would be desirable to use that process.

8. "Ownership of land can be shared only if all the interested parties have exactly the same interests." Is that statement true? Explain your answer.

9. What does it mean to say that an interest "runs with the land"? Provide two examples of interests that run with the land.

10. Briefly explain the nature and purpose of a "condominium corporation."

11. Explain the meaning of "adverse possession."

12. "A public easement is not really an easement." Is that statement correct? Explain your answer.

13. Describe a licence and explain how it differs from an easement.

14. What is the difference between positive and negative covenants? Provide an example of each. In the context of restrictive covenants, why does the law draw that distinction?

15. What is a "building scheme covenant"?

16. What is a *"profit à prendre"*? If you have a *profit à prendre*, do you automatically own the things to which it applies?

17. Explain why a tenancy at sufferance is not really a tenancy at all, and why a tenancy at will may not really be a true lease either.

18. Explain the difference between the assignment of a lease and the creation of a sublease.

19. Describe two special types of remedies that may be available to a landlord under a commercial lease if the tenant fails to pay rent.

20. Explain five general differences between commercial leases and residential leases. Why have the legislatures felt the need to introduce those changes?

Cases and Problems

1. Serena and Douglas were joint tenants of a piece of land. Although Serena did not take much interest in the property, Douglas saw its potential value in the rental market. He therefore leased the property to Marcus Inc for $50 000 per year. Because Douglas did not want Serena to know about the lease, he persuaded Marcus Inc that there was no need for a written agreement. Marcus Inc occupied the property for five years, during which it paid a total of $250 000 in rent to Douglas. The land now sits empty. Serena died two months ago. Shortly before she passed away, however, she discovered the details of the rental arrangement that Douglas had created with Marcus Inc, and she demanded a share of the profits. Douglas refused. The situation became more complicated upon Serena's death because she left a will that gave everything she owned, including her interest in the land, to her sister, Rumana. Discuss the rights and liabilities that may affect Douglas, Serena, and Rumana.

2. Raj owned the fee simple in a piece of land known as Blackacre, which contained a small shopping mall. Although he had no children of his own, he was especially fond of his nephew, Ludwig, and his niece, Elise. Raj wanted to ensure that they enjoyed the benefit of Blackacre, especially after he died. He therefore created the following arrangement: Beginning immediately, and for the rest of Raj's life, Ludwig was entitled to enjoy a life estate in Blackacre. Upon Raj's death, Elise (who is 25 years younger than Ludwig) would become entitled to enjoy a life estate in the property. Although all the parties were initially happy with that arrangement, difficulties arose after the economy went into a recession and the shops that had been operating in the shopping mall on Blackacre began leaving the premises. Within six months, the entire mall was empty. Despite protests from Elise, Ludwig did nothing to protect the value of the property, even though vandals were smashing windows and trespassers had begun to use the parking lot as a garbage dump. Has Ludwig done anything wrong? Aside from Elise, is there anyone who might be concerned about the condition of Blackacre?

3. Because of a number of problems that have arisen under the existing law, the provincial government intends to enact new legislation governing condominiums. Section 67(2) of that statute states, "Unless otherwise agreed, all common areas shall be shared amongst the individual unit owners as joint tenants." Explain the difficulties that this provision would create. How could those difficulties be avoided?

4. Igor Cvokic purchased Lorenzo's Pizza for $40 000. The purchase price included a lease of the premises for three years. The landlord was John Belisario. Unfortunately, Cvokic and Belisario did not get along, largely because of the unreasonable nature of the lease. (The lease, for example, did not provide the tenant with parking or storage space.) Following a series of disagreements, Cvokic (i) began an action against Belisario, alleging several breaches of contract, and (ii) advertised the business for sale. A potential buyer offered to purchase Lorenzo's Pizza for $27 000, but that sale was conditional upon the landlord's consent to an assignment of the lease. Belisario, however, refused to consent to the assignment unless Cvokic terminated his lawsuit. Because Cvokic refused to do so, the condition was not satisfied, and the potential buyer refused to complete the sale. Has Belisario done anything wrong? Identify and explain a common lease clause that would help Cvokic in this instance.

5. Stanley Simpson was a leading businessman and philanthropist in Kelowna, British Columbia, in the first half of the twentieth century. One of his ventures, a sawmill, burned down in 1944. Simpson had no other property nearby and none of his other businesses were in any way related to the sawmill. Consequently, rather than rebuild the sawmill or put the land to other profitable use, Simpson sold the land to the city at a price that was far less than market value. As part of that sale, however, he included two sets of conditions to the sale: (i) the land could be used only for municipal purposes, the buildings on the land had to be attractive, and the grounds had to be suitably landscaped, and (ii) the city could not, at any time, sell the property or use it for either commercial or industrial purposes. Those conditions were registered against title as "restrictive covenants." For many years, the city used the land purchased from Simpson for a city hall and a civic centre. Recently, however, the city has formed the intention to sell the property to a real estate developer, who plans to build condominiums and retail shops on the site. Stanley Simpson is no longer alive, of course, and his old business assets are now owned by a company that is in agreement with the city's plans. Simpson's family and friends, in contrast, have created a group known as Save the Heritage Simpson Covenant Society. The Society insists that the restrictive covenant must be enforced and that the city's plans must be prevented. Will the Society be successful? Did Simpson create a valid restrictive covenant when he sold the land to the city? Is there any other basis on which the Society might win the case?

6. Cloudy Hill Road runs through a part of the Town of Trent Valley. The plaintiffs consist of a number of people who own cottages that are located immediately to the east of Cloudy Hill Road. The defendant is Fall River Farms Inc, which owns a large farm immediately to the west of Cloudy Hill Road. The defendant also owns the land on which Cloudy Hill Road runs. The road has fallen into a very bad

condition. The town has announced that the road requires significant upgrades. The plaintiffs are willing to contribute to the cost of repairs, but only if they have legally enforceable rights to use the road in order to get to their cottages. (Another road exists for that purpose, but it is very inconvenient to use.) The defendant, in contrast, refuses to pay a cent toward road repairs, and they have announced that they no longer are willing to allow the plaintiffs to use the road free of charge. The defendant's lawyer recently delivered a letter to each of the cottage owners. The important part of the letter says, "In exchange for a fee of $10 000, Fall River Farms Inc will grant permission to you and your immediate family to use Cloudy Hill Road for 50 years. The road may be used for personal purposes only, and the rights acquired under this agreement cannot be transferred to any other person." The plaintiffs argue that the defendant's position is unlawful, unrealistic, and unfair. They point out that they (and the previous owners of the cottages) have used Cloudy Hill Road for at least 40 years. During that time, the defendant never used the road for its own purposes, never asked the plaintiffs to pay a fee, and never even complained that the plaintiffs were using Cloudy Hill Road to access their cottages. (It also is true that Fall River Farms Inc never actually gave the cottagers permission to use the road.) If you were a cottage owner, would you accept the offer that you received from Fall River Farms Inc? What is likely to happen if that offer is not accepted? Explain your answer.

7. BiNovo Group Inc owns a shopping mall in the business area of a large city. In 2010, it signed a lease to allow Horseshoe Corp to operate a restaurant, known as The Georgia Peach, in the mall. The parties' contract contained the terms usually found in a commercial lease. The agreement was to run for 10 years, but the lessee held an option to renew the lease for two more 10-year periods. Rent was set at $100 per square metre. The lease allowed the rent to be increased each year, but only in accordance with increases in the market price. Within weeks of opening the restaurant, Horseshoe ran into serious financial difficulties. To BiNovo's relief, Horseshoe was able to find a replacement. By agreement of all the parties, Tyrus Cobb Ltd stepped into Horseshoe's place and assumed control of the premises and the restaurant business.

The next five years were uneventful. Two issues then combined to create a problem. First, as a result of difficulties associated with its other business ventures, Tyrus Cobb found it necessary to sell The Georgia Peach to raise cash. It was confident that things would go well after it persuaded Carnival Properties Inc to buy its business and its lease for $500 000. That plan was complicated, however, when BiNovo announced that it was unwilling to substitute Carnival Properties for Tyrus Cobb. According to BiNovo, Carnival Properties was an "undesirable tenant" because it was unlikely to pay its rent on time. That allegation is absurd. Carnival

Properties is one of Canada's biggest companies. Amongst other business ventures, it owns a large number of restaurants and it has never failed to pay rent on time. Tyrus Cobb and Carnival Properties therefore believe that there must be another reason for BiNovo's position. They claim that BiNovo simply was not willing to honour the terms of the lease that it signed in 2010. That allegation now seems to be true. Because BiNovo would not allow Carnival Properties to substitute for Tyrus Cobb, the original lease was terminated. The next day, BiNovo agreed to lease the same premises to Carnival Properties. The terms of the new lease are the same as the terms of the old lease, with one exception. Although the market rate for rent is still $100, Carnival Properties is required to pay a lump sum of $100 000, plus rent of $120 per square metre. Rent may be increased each year, in accordance with market rates plus 10 percent. Tyrus Cobb has successfully sued BiNovo for breach of contract. What is the most likely explanation for that action? Explain your answer.

8. Solomon Holdings Ltd entered into an agreement with Kostal Sporting Goods Supplies Inc. The agreement provided a formula for calculating monthly rent based on a combination of the market value of the premises and the net profit generated by Kostal's sale of sporting goods. The document also contained the following provision:

> Kostal shall have exclusive possession of the premises for a single five-year period commencing the first day of January in the next calendar year.

The agreement proceeded as planned. At the end of the five-year period, however, Kostal remained in the premises and continued to pay rent according to the formula established in the agreement. Solomon received such payments for nearly three years without objection. Recently, however, Kostal has discovered an alternative location at a lower rental price. On the first day of July, it provided Solomon with written notice that it intended to vacate the premises by August 1. Solomon was generally agreeable to that proposal, but it insisted that Kostal was liable to pay rent for August, as well as July. Which party is correct? Explain your answer.

9. Takahana Sushi, a Japanese restaurant, rented its premises from Gunnar Schultz. The contract signed by the parties was very brief. For our purposes, these are the relevant provisions:

- Schultz promises to provide Takahana with quiet possession.
- Takahana shall pay an annual rent of $36 000, payable monthly in equal instalments.
- This lease shall be for a single fixed term of 10 years.

Three months after taking possession of the premises, Takahana was informed by a public health inspector that the property was unfit for use as a restaurant because the plumbing in the toilets was defective. The cost of the necessary replacement was about $50 000. Takahana asked Schultz to make the necessary repairs. Schultz, however, refused because the lease did not require him to make repairs. He expressed some sympathy for Takahana's position, and indicated that he would not object if the tenant replaced the defective plumbing. He also insisted, however, that he was entitled to full rent for the remainder of the 10-year term. At that point, Takahana left the premises, relocated to a new building, and refused to continue paying rent to Schultz. Which party will prevail in this dispute? Explain your answer.

10. Juliet Hwong is the owner and operator of Fashion Hair Culture. That business operates out of rented premises. The original lease ran for a period of five years. After two years, the landlord sold the property to Yip Cheung. Hwong and her lawyer wrote to Cheung to confirm the fact that the lease would continue to operate. Along with that letter, the lawyer included a document titled "Renew Lease Contract Agreement." That document stated that Hwong was entitled, at the end of the original lease, to renew the lease for an additional five-year period. Although Hwong was the only person to sign that document, Cheung did agree, during several conversations, that the lease was renewable for a further five-year period. When the original lease expired, Hwong claimed that she was entitled to renew the lease for another five years. Cheung, however, now insists that the option to renew is invalid and that the premises must be vacated. How is a court likely to resolve the dispute? Explain your answer.

11. Wilson Hum leased a commercial property to Frank Mosher for use as a pizzeria. The parties' agreement contained three important provisions:

- During the term of the lease, the tenant shall not sell, assign, or sublet or part with possession of the said premises or any part thereof without the written consent of the landlord. Such consent shall not be unreasonably withheld.

- During the term of this lease, the tenant shall keep the premises in good repair, both interior and exterior. Damage by fire or other circumstances beyond the tenant's control is excepted.

- This lease shall be for a fixed term of five years. Annual rent of $30 000 shall be paid in equal monthly instalments.

Frank operated the pizzeria for two years, but he soon tired of the business. However, his friend Janine Gallant indicated that she would be willing to take control of the business for the three years remaining under the lease. Frank wrote to Wilson to seek consent for an assignment of the lease. At the same time, he provided documentation that established that Janine had good credit and was experienced in the food sales industry. Although Wilson simply ignored the request, Frank proceeded to assign his interest under the original lease to Janine. Unfortunately, for reasons that were completely unforeseeable at the time of the assignment, Janine's personal life fell into turmoil. As a result, she totally lost interest in the pizzeria. She failed to pay the rent and she allowed the property to fall into very poor condition. By the time that Wilson discovered that state of affairs, Janine had become destitute. She had no assets and was clearly not worth suing. Wilson therefore insists that Frank is responsible for paying the overdue rent and for the cost of repairing the premises. Do paragraphs (b) and (c) of the lease still apply to Frank? Explain your answer.

12. Igor Polska, an entrepreneur with varied interests, entered into two contracts with Ishtla Singh. The first was for the sale of goods. Ishtla promised to pay $5000 for a rare book. The second contract was for the rental of a property. Ishtla agreed to take possession for a one-year term beginning on the first day of July. The total rent was to be $36 000, paid in equal monthly instalments. Ishtla moved into the premises on the first day of July and paid $3000 in rent. Within two days, however, she informed Igor that she intended to remain only until the end of that month. She also told him that she had found another copy of the same book elsewhere at a lower price, and that she therefore was unwilling to pay the $5000 as promised. Igor nevertheless insists that he is entitled to the full value of both contracts, which he calculates to be $38 000 ($5000 for the book and $33 000 for the property). Ishtla believes that Igor's position is unreasonable. She relies on the fact that she has already introduced him to one person who is willing to pay $4000 for the book and to another who is willing to occupy the property immediately under a monthly tenancy at a rent of $2000. Is Igor correct? Explain your answer. Do you require additional information to calculate the full value of Ishtla's liability?

16

Real Property: Sales and Mortgages

LEARNING OBJECTIVES

After completing this chapter, you should be able to:

❶ Explain the basic differences between a registry system and a land titles system, and indicate which system operates in your jurisdiction.

❷ Describe the concept of indefeasibility and its underlying principles.

❸ Describe five types of unregistered interests that may be enforceable against the owner of a registered interest.

❹ Explain the risk management issues that arise in the purchase of land.

❺ Outline the purpose of an agreement of purchase and sale and explain the role of the conditions that are frequently contained in that type of agreement.

❻ Describe the remedies that may be available if an agreement of purchase and sale is breached.

❼ Describe a mortgage and identify the mortgagor and the mortgagee.

❽ Outline the basic difference between a mortgage under a registry system and a mortgage under a land titles system.

❾ Describe a subsequent mortgage and explain the risk management issues that are associated with that type of arrangement.

❿ Describe four types of remedies that may be available to a mortgagee if a mortgagor does not fulfill the terms of a mortgage.

In Chapter 15, we began our discussion of real property by describing a variety of interests and by examining one important type of transaction: the lease. In this chapter, we discuss another important type of transaction: the sale. We also consider a form of financing that is often used to facilitate the purchase of land: the mortgage. First, however, it is necessary to briefly explain the registration systems that operate in Canada.

Registration Systems

L.O. ❶ ❷ ❸ ❹

A variety of interests may simultaneously exist in a single piece of land: a fee simple, a life estate, a lease, an easement, a restrictive covenant, and so on. We will discover even more possibilities in this chapter. As a matter of risk management, it is necessary to keep track of all of those interests. If you intend to purchase a particular property, you will want to know exactly what you are getting for your money. You certainly would not want to pay for a fee simple and then discover that you received only a life estate. Likewise, if you enjoy the benefit of a restrictive covenant, you would want to advertise that fact to a potential buyer of the servient tenement. Otherwise, the new owner might not be bound by the covenant. In either event, you will be able to rely upon one of two *registration systems*, depending upon where in Canada you live. A **registration system** documents the existence of interests in land.

*a **registration system** documents the existence of interests in land*

REGISTRY SYSTEM

A *registry system* (or *deeds registration system*, as it is sometimes called) is used in the four Atlantic provinces, as well as parts of Manitoba and Ontario.[1] A **registry system** provides an opportunity to inspect and evaluate documents that may affect real property. Suppose you are interested in buying a cottage from me, but you are not sure that I actually own it. Before you go ahead with the purchase, you will visit the registry office, search through all the relevant records, and try to satisfy yourself that I am at the end of a good **chain of title**—that is, a series of transactions in which ownership was validly passed from one person to the next. Theoretically, it is possible to trace that chain all the way back to the time when the government held the land. Fortunately, as a result of legislation, it is only necessary to go back a much shorter period, for example, 40 years.

*a **registry system** provides an opportunity to inspect and evaluate documents that may affect real property*

*a **chain of title** is a series of transactions in which ownership was validly passed from one person to the next*

The task of *searching title* nevertheless is often difficult and hazardous. Consequently, it is usually best left to someone with expertise in the area, such as a lawyer specializing in real estate. The records may be unclear or misleading. Mistakes may be made, and errors may be overlooked for decades, only to be later discovered after many people have relied on the appearance of a good title.

Continuing with our example, suppose I thought that I had purchased the cottage 15 years ago from Alison. She in turn believed that she had inherited it from her uncle. In fact, her uncle's will actually left the property to her brother. Consequently, my chain of title is defective. Even though the records for the last 15 years seem to indicate that the property is mine, it really belongs to someone else (presumably Alison's brother). Furthermore, one of the defining features of the registry system is that the government's role is passive. It provides access to the documents, but it does not guarantee their accuracy. Therefore, even if

---

[1.] There is, however, a gradual shift toward land titles systems in a number of those jurisdictions.

you pay the price, you cannot get good title to the cottage from me. Because of that possibility, you may want to purchase *title insurance*, which provides a source of compensation if our transaction does not include everything promised. (Insurance is considered in detail in Chapter 17.)

From a risk management perspective, the registry system leaves something to be desired. Although it does not happen often, a simple oversight during a title search may have disastrous consequences. You may end up paying a lot of money without actually getting any land in exchange. That is one reason for hiring a lawyer to assist in the purchase of land. It is the lawyer's job to ensure that the seller actually has a good chain of title. If the lawyer makes a mistake, you will not be able to get the land, but you will be able to sue the lawyer.

There is another point to note about risk management. If I did have a good chain of title, and if we did go through with the sale, you (or your lawyer) should return to the registry office as soon as possible to register the transfer documents. If that does not happen, you might actually lose the cottage. After selling the land to you, I might dishonestly sell it again to a third party named Tre. The general rule under a registry system is that competing claims are resolved by the *timing* of registration. If Tre did not have notice of your earlier transaction, and if he gave valuable consideration for his purchase, he gets the cottage if he registers before you. You can bring an action against me for damages, but you cannot get the property from Tre. In contrast, if you register your transfer first, you will provide Tre and the rest of the world with notice of your rights. Your claim to the land therefore cannot be defeated.

LAND TITLES SYSTEM

To avoid many of the problems associated with the registry system, the three western-most provinces, the territories, and large parts of Manitoba and Ontario operate under a *land titles system* (or *Torrens system*, as it is sometimes called).[2] A **land titles system** does more than simply provide an opportunity to inspect and evaluate documents. It generates certificates of title that virtually guarantee the validity of the interests that are listed.

The key to a land titles system is the doctrine of *indefeasibility*. **Indefeasibility** means that, with very few exceptions, the interests that are included in a certificate of title cannot be defeated. That doctrine is based on three principles. To illustrate this, we return to our earlier example.

> a **land titles system** generates certificates of title that virtually guarantee the validity of the interests that are listed

> **indefeasibility** means that, with very few exceptions, the interests that are included in a certificate of title cannot be defeated

> the **mirror principle** states that all the interests listed in a certificate of title generally are valid

- **Mirror principle:** The **mirror principle** states that all the interests listed in a certificate of title generally are valid. The certificate reflects reality. For example, when I purchased the land from Alison 15 years ago, the land titles office examined the transfer documents and issued a new certificate of title that named me as the owner. (It also would have listed any other type of interest that existed, such as an easement or a mortgage.) You are entitled to rely upon that certificate when buying the cottage from me. That is true even if my chain of title was defective because Alison never really inherited the property from her uncle.

> the **curtain principle** states that the only valid interests in a property generally are the ones listed in the certificate of title

- **Curtain principle:** The **curtain principle** states that the only valid interests in a property generally are the ones that are listed in the certificate of title. Consequently, it is unnecessary for you to "lift the curtain" and look behind the certificate of title to determine whether anyone else has rights in the property. By the same token, even though Alison's

---

[2.] Sir Robert Torrens, an Australian politician, developed the land titles system partially on the basis of a ship registration system that he had encountered as a marine customs collector.

brother at one time was entitled to the cottage, his rights were lost when the land titles office issued a certificate of title naming me as the owner. The curtain fell on him.

■ **Insurance principle:** The **insurance principle** states that a person who suffers a loss as a result of an error in the system generally is entitled to compensation. The land titles system includes an *assurance fund* that helps people like Alison's brother. Although he cannot get the cottage back, he is entitled to a payment of money.

the insurance principle states that a person who suffers a loss as a result of an error in the system generally is entitled to compensation

Mortgage Fraud

For the most part, the land titles system is efficient and fair. Errors occasionally occur, but historically they have been rare. In a 25-year period in British Columbia, for example, the system saw only 100 successful claims against the assurance fund, despite processing 18 500 000 land transfers.[3] Unfortunately, the situation appears to be changing. Fraud has become a pressing problem, especially in Ontario.

The key feature of the land titles system is the principle of indefeasibility. Regardless of the underlying facts, registered interests are effective and enforceable. Registration is reality. Unfortunately, the strength of the system is also its greatest weakness. If a person is improperly removed from title, the only source of relief may be a claim against the assurance fund. And to make matters worse, a successful action against the fund often involves many years and great expense. A victim of fraud may be required to exhaust all other potential sources of relief before claiming against the assurance fund.[4]

A typical case of mortgage fraud is surprisingly simple in operation. An innocent person owns Blackacre, a piece of land. A rogue steals the landowner's identity, forges the necessary documents, and arranges to transfer Blackacre to an accomplice. Once registered as the new owner of Blackacre, the accomplice borrows money from a bank. As security for the loan, the bank takes a mortgage over Blackacre. The criminals disappear with the money and the bank begins proceedings to enforce its mortgage against Blackacre. At that point, the original owner of Blackacre finally discovers the fraud. The courts are then left with a difficult situation. The bank and the original owner are both entirely innocent. Who shall bear the loss? Even if title is returned to the original owner, the bank's mortgage remains a validly registered interest, which it will want to enforce in order to be repaid on the loan.

Some courts have held that the principle of indefeasibility requires a decision in favour of the bank.[5] The resulting hardship to the original owner, however, has led judges and legislators to seek ways of protecting the landowners. The land titles legislation may be amended to ensure that the original owner recovers title. Procedures may be tightened to make it more difficult for criminals to steal identities and forge documents. The land titles system may be restricted to individuals directly involved in transactions, rather than being entirely open to the public, as it is currently. If a bank carelessly allows fraud to occur, it may be held responsible for the resulting losses.[6] Most significantly of all, however, the courts have begun to reconsider the principle of indefeasibility. Case Brief 16.1 examines an important decision.

[3.] "Title Security in British Columbia" in *BC Land Title & Survey* www.ltsa.ca/land-title/security-of-land-title.

[4.] *Rabi v Rosu* (2006) 277 DLR (4th) 544 (Ont SCJ).

[5.] *Household Realty Corp Ltd v Liu* (2005) 261 DLR (4th) 679 (Ont CA).

[6.] *Rabi v Rosu* (2006) 277 DLR (4th) 544 (Ont SCJ).

Case Brief 16.1

Lawrence v Wright (2007) 278 DLR (4th) 698 (Ont CA)

Susan Lawrence was astonished to learn that she no longer owned the house in which she had lived for 30 years. She had been the victim of mortgage fraud. An impostor, posing as Lawrence, had stolen her identity and forged her signature in order to transfer title to another criminal named Thomas Wright. Wright then mortgaged the property to the bank as security for a large loan. When the truth finally emerged, and it was clear that Wright would not repay the loan, a dispute arose between Lawrence and the bank. The bank graciously dropped its claim to immediately evict Lawrence, but it insisted that it was entitled to enforce its mortgage, possibly by foreclosure or forced judicial sale of the property. (Those remedies are discussed later in this chapter.) Since the Ontario Court of Appeal had very recently held that a registered mortgage is indefeasible in such circumstances, the trial judge agreed with the bank.[7]

On this occasion, however, the same court saw things differently and consequently reversed its position. Three types of innocent parties were distinguished:

- the *original* owner, who is victimized by the rogue
- the *intermediate* owner, who deals directly with the rogue
- the *deferred* owner, who deals with the intermediate owner, rather than the rogue

The crucial point, the court explained, is that the intermediate owner is the only one of the innocent parties to deal with the rogue and therefore is the only one in a position to discover the fraud. The original owner has no knowledge of the facts until it is too late. And the deferred owner deals only with the intermediate owner, who honestly holds a registered interest.

On that basis, the court adopted the new concept of *deferred indefeasibility*. The principle of indefeasibility is deferred, or postponed, until an interest is registered in favour of a person who did *not* deal with the rogue. In contrast, an interest registered in favour of a person who *did* deal with the rogue, is defeasible—it may be defeated by the original owner. One result of that approach is that intermediate parties are encouraged to act very carefully when lending money and taking mortgages. Extra efforts should be made to ensure that a person who claims to own the land actually is the proper landowner.[8]

Applying those rules to the facts, the court found that Lawrence was the original owner and that the bank, having dealt with Wright, was the intermediate owner. (There was no deferred owner in *Lawrence v Wright* because the bank had not sold the property to anyone.) Since the bank, as the intermediate party, could have discovered Wright's fraud, its mortgage was invalid and it was directed to seek compensation from the assurance fund.[9] At the end of the story, Lawrence once again enjoyed the position of having the only registered interest in the land.

UNREGISTERED INTERESTS

Although the land titles system was designed to avoid uncertainty, a certificate of title is not entirely indefeasible. In some circumstances, an interest in land may be effective even if it is not registered. That is also true under a registry system. Consequently, when buying the cottage from me, you should conduct more than a single search at the land titles or land registry office. There are other places to look. Furthermore, unless you have expertise in this area, you should leave those tasks to your lawyer. Consider these common examples:

- **Short-term leases:** A short-term (say, three-year) lease may be enforceable against a purchaser even if it is not registered. For that reason, you should inspect the premises for any signs of tenants.

- **Prescription and adverse possession:** As we discussed in Chapter 15, it is sometimes possible for a person to acquire an interest in land as a result of a long period of use or occupation. That is true under registry

[7] *Household Realty Corp Ltd v Liu* (2005) 261 DLR (4th) 679 (Ont CA).

[8] Although the court referred to "owners," any registered interest holder qualifies for the same position.

[9] Significantly, however, the courts in *Lawrence v Wright* held that the bank was *not* guilty of negligence in its dealings with the rogue. As a result, the burden was placed on the bank, not because it had done anything wrong, but rather merely because it had an opportunity to discover Wright's fraud.

systems and even under some land titles systems. Consider that fact when you inspect the premises. Look for signs of "squatters."[10]

■ **Public easements:** As we saw in Chapter 15, a utility company or similar body may have the right to bury cables beneath a property or to run wires above it. Consequently, your lawyer should look for signs of activity on the land and perhaps contact the organizations in question.[11] If an easement does exist, its exact location should be determined. A house that sits directly beneath a tangle of power lines may, for instance, be difficult to resell.

■ **Unpaid taxes:** As a landowner, I am required to pay taxes on my property. If I fail to do so, the government may be entitled to seize and sell the land to raise the necessary money. Furthermore, its right to do so may continue to exist even after I have transferred the cottage to you. Before you buy, therefore, your lawyer should search the municipal and provincial records to ensure that there are no outstanding taxes.

■ **Unpaid creditors:** Your lawyer should also search the records in the sheriff's office to determine whether there are any *writs of execution* (or *writs of seizure and sale*) against me. A **writ of execution** is a document that allows a court's judgment to be enforced. Suppose someone successfully sued me in tort. If they filed the writ with the sheriff, that officer might have the power to seize and sell any property registered in my name to pay my debt.[12] And significantly, as long as the writ was filed while I was still the owner, the seizure and sale could take place even after I transferred the property to you. To keep the property, you would have to pay my debt.[13]

a **writ of execution** is a document that allows a court's judgment to be enforced

Is it fair that those interests can be enforced against you, even though they were not registered, and even though you were unaware of them when you bought the land from me? Consider Ethical Perspective 16.1.

Ethical Perspective **16.1**

Unregistered Interests in Land

Unregistered interests in land often are a trap for unsuspecting purchasers. Why are they enforced? Does enforcement seem fair to the purchaser? For the person with the unregistered interest? For society?

Questions for Discussion

1. Is it fair to enforce an unregistered short-term lease against a purchaser? Would it be fairer to refuse enforcement?

2. Is it fair for the courts to enforce rights acquired through prescription or adverse possession against a purchaser? Do you think that

the rule exists for the benefit of the unregistered rights holders or for society?

3. Who benefits from the enforcement of unregistered public easements? Does enforcement seem fair to you?

4. Is it fair that a purchaser may be held liable for municipal taxes that were owed by the vendor? Do you think that the rule exists to help the vendor? Who benefits from the rule?

5. Why should a purchaser be held responsible for a writ of execution that was filed against the vendor? Is it fair to prefer the rights of the person who holds the writ over the purchaser?

---

10. A "squatter" is a person who occupies a piece of land without any right or permission to do so.

11. Private easements are generally enforceable only if they are registered.

12. The governing rules, which are quite complicated, vary amongst jurisdictions. In some instances, the power to seize and sell arises only when the writ is filed with the registry office.

13. You would then be allowed to sue me for the same amount, but I may not have it. If I did, I presumably would have paid the judgment myself.

L.O. ❺ ❻

Land Sales

Ownership of land can be passed between people in a variety of ways. We have already mentioned several possibilities, including expropriation, gifts, and adverse possession. From a business perspective, however, the most important possibility is *sale*. A **sale** occurs when ownership is transferred in exchange for consideration.

*a **sale** occurs when ownership is transferred in exchange for consideration*

RISK MANAGEMENT

The general rule for the purchase of land is *caveat emptor*: "let the buyer beware." As with the purchase of most types of chattels, the buyer must make sure that the property is in good condition. The vendor normally has no obligation to reveal facts that would cause a reasonable purchaser to either demand a lower price or walk away from the deal altogether. There are exceptions, however, especially if land is being purchased as a home. In that situation, a vendor cannot cover up or hide a defect. Going even further, the vendor must actually tell the purchaser about a latent or hidden defect that could cause the property to be dangerous or unfit as a home. That would be true if, for instance, the vendor knew that the foundations of the house were sinking into the ground, or that the basement frequently flooded.[14] Interestingly, a court may also hold a real estate agent equally liable for carelessly failing to ensure that the vendor properly disclosed the existence of such a defect.[15]

The sale and purchase of land is complicated by a number of other facts as well. That is true for both residential and commercial properties. As we saw in the last section, a variety of people—other than the vendor—may have interests in the land. Other dangers also exist. As a matter of risk management, many of those dangers can be managed, if not completely eliminated, by hiring certain types of experts. To better understand that point, assume that you are interested in buying a factory from me. You should enlist the help of the following people:

■ **Real estate agent:** Even if my property appeals to you, there may be others that better suit your needs. Given the time and expense involved in a real estate transaction, it is highly unlikely that you would want to relocate after only a few years in my factory. A real estate agent can search the market for alternatives and help you find the right property in the first place. An agent can also put you into contact with the other people you will need to safely purchase a property.

■ **Lawyer:** It is important that you hire a lawyer. In addition to conducting the searches that we previously discussed, a lawyer will perform a large number of other tasks, including (i) communicating with the seller or the seller's lawyer, (ii) verifying which secondary pieces of property are included in the sale (such as machines in the factory), (iii) ensuring that local by-laws will allow you to use the land for your intended purpose, (iv) obtaining insurance coverage for the property, (v) checking mortgage arrangements (if any), and (vi) preparing, filing, and registering the formal documents that are needed for the transfer. It is also very

---

[14.] It has even been suggested that a vendor may be liable for failing to disclose to a purchaser with young children that a nearby neighbour has been convicted of possessing child pornography: *Dennis v Gray* (2011) 333 DLR (4th) 376 (Ont SCJ).

[15.] *Krawchuk v Scherbak* (2011) 332 DLR (4th) 310 (Ont CA).

common for the lawyer to secure the services of other professionals on this list.

- **Appraiser:** It is often difficult to determine the correct price for a property. Several factors can affect the value of land, including the condition of the buildings, the value of neighbouring properties, accessibility to public transport, the uses that are permitted under zoning regulations, and the municipality's plans for future development in the area. Consequently, before agreeing to a price, you should get an opinion from a professional appraiser.

- **Surveyor:** During the course of negotiations, I will provide a *legal description* of my property, which includes its precise size and location. That description, however, may be inaccurate. For instance, it might overlook the fact that my building *encroaches* upon a neighbour's land by a few metres. (We discussed the tort of trespass in Chapter 4.) A survey would reveal that fact. Since you would not be willing to pay full market value for a property that could lead you into a lawsuit, you would likely refuse to go ahead with our sale unless I either obtained the neighbour's consent to the encroachment or reduced the price.

- **Inspector:** You are concerned about the physical condition of the premises, especially since the value of the property is affected by its state of repair. Furthermore, a dangerous structure could expose you to liability by causing injuries or deaths amongst your employees or guests. (We discussed the torts of occupiers' liability, nuisance, and *Rylands v Fletcher* in Chapter 5.) And even if no one is hurt, health and safety regulations might eventually require you to spend a lot of money fixing the defects. For those reasons, you should hire an inspector to check the premises for potential problems.

- **Environmental auditor:** Depending upon the nature of my business, you might be concerned by the possibility that my factory has leaked toxic substances into the environment. Even if no one is killed or injured as a result, you may eventually be required, as the owner of the premises, to pay a substantial amount of money for a cleanup operation. An environmental auditor could identify that possibility.

One final, perhaps cynical, observation is appropriate. We opened this section by discussing the need for risk management. The individuals in the preceding list could minimize the risks by identifying potential problems at the outset. However, by hiring those people, you would also create a safety net for yourself. Suppose you discover an underground pool of hazardous waste on the property shortly after our deal closed. If you sue me for the cost of the cleanup, I might honestly say that I simply do not have the money to pay damages. Therefore, you will need another source of compensation. If you had hired an environmental auditing company, you might now be able to sue it for breach of contract or for the tort of negligence because it failed to detect the problem. As we discussed in Chapter 6, a professional can be held liable for doing a job carelessly. And furthermore, even if the environmental auditor does not have a lot of money, they very likely have liability insurance.[16]

As we have seen, the purchase of land creates a number of risks. Concept Summary 16.1, on the following page, provides a checklist of some of the dangers you should guard against. (You may do all the work yourself or ask your lawyer to take care of the issues.)

[16.] When purchasing my factory, you should also have considered buying *property insurance* that would cover the cost of an environmental cleanup. Chapter 17 explains property insurance.

Concept Summary 16.1

Risk Management and the Purchase of Land

Danger	Precaution
• subsequent purchaser acquiring interest in same property	• registration as soon as possible to provide notice or obtain certificate of title
• short-term leases	• inspection of property to discover tenants
• rights to use or occupation of land created through prescription or adverse possession	• inspection of property to discover signs of use or occupation
• public easements	• inspection of property to discover activity • inquiries to utility companies and similar organizations
• unpaid taxes creating a right of seizure and sale	• search of municipal records
• unsatisfied writs creating a right of seizure and sale	• search of sheriff's records
• payment of excessively high price	• valuation of property by a professional appraiser
• misdescription of property	• description of land and buildings by a professional surveyor
• defects in building and equipment	• inspection by an engineer and similar professionals
• toxic or hazardous substances	• inspection of property by an environmental auditor

AGREEMENT OF PURCHASE AND SALE

Transactions involving commercial properties are often complicated by the fact that the parties are dealing with several matters at the same time. For instance, if you are buying my factory, you may also want to obtain the equipment in it.[17] You may even be interested in acquiring my business as a whole, including my customer lists and the name of my company. However, we will focus on the sale of the real property itself. That sale is created by an **agreement of purchase and sale**.

An agreement of purchase and sale is a contract and therefore must satisfy all of the usual contractual elements, including an intention to create legal relations, an offer and acceptance, and consideration. Furthermore, although most types of contracts can be created orally, a contract for the sale of an interest in land must be evidenced in writing.[18] And as always, the parties must agree on all of the important terms. That does not mean, however, that the **vendor** (the person selling the land) and the **purchaser** (the person buying the land) must settle every point at the outset. It is very common for an agreement of purchase and sale to include *conditions*.

A **condition** (or **condition precedent**) is a requirement that must be satisfied before the transaction can be completed.[19] It does not prevent the creation of a contract, but it does suspend the parties' obligations to complete the deal. As a matter of risk management, that may be important. As a general rule, a contract, once created, must be performed even if the agreement turns out to have

an **agreement of purchase and sale** is a contract for the sale of land

the **vendor** is the person who sells the land

the **purchaser** is the person who buys the land

a **condition** or **condition precedent** is a requirement that must be satisfied before the transaction can be completed

---

17. Chapter 17 explains that, when you buy land, you are generally entitled to the *fixtures*, which are things that are attached to the land.

18. As Chapter 10 explained, although a contract for a sale of land that is not evidenced in writing is valid, it cannot be enforced by either party.

19. As we saw in Chapter 11, there are different types of "conditions precedent."

unexpected costs. And in the context of land sales, there are various factors that may have that effect. Several possibilities might arise in our earlier example.

- If my building was partially constructed on someone else's land, you might agree to buy the property from me, but only on the condition that I obtain my neighbour's permission for the encroachment.

- If a heap of toxic waste sits at the back of my lot, you might make our agreement conditional upon my ability to remove the hazard and obtain a clean report from an environmental auditor.

- If you intend to use the property differently than I did, you might make the sale conditional upon your ability to obtain zoning permission for the proposed activity.

- If you are unsure that you can afford to buy my land, you might make our agreement conditional upon your ability to obtain financing on reasonable terms.

If any condition is not met, then our sale will not be completed.[20] Nevertheless, one of us might still be held liable. Most conditions expressly or implicitly require at least one party to act in a certain way. For instance, I might be required to use my best efforts to obtain my neighbour's consent to the encroachment or to remove the toxic substances from the land. You might be required to use your best efforts to obtain zoning permission or arrange financing. Those requirements are known as *subsidiary obligations*. If a condition fails because of a lack of effort on a subsidiary obligation, the other party may be entitled to damages. Consider how you would respond in You Be the Judge 16.1.

You Be the Judge **16.1**

Agreement of Purchase and Sale and Conditions[21]

OK Detailing Ltd owns a piece of land. Dynamic Transport Ltd wants to buy part of it. The parties therefore entered into an agreement of purchase and sale. Dynamic promised to pay $250 000 and OK Detailing promised to transfer a specific portion of its property. There is, however, a problem. At the time of entering into that agreement, both parties knew that the sale could not proceed without permission under the *Planning Act* to subdivide the property into two lots. Unfortunately, their agreement does not expressly say that the sale is conditional on that fact. Nor does it expressly impose an obligation upon either party to obtain the planning approval.

Since the parties signed their agreement, the value of the land has increased from $250 000 to $400 000. OK Detailing realizes that it entered into a very bad bargain and is anxious to find some way out of it. It therefore argues that the sale cannot be completed because the planning authority has not approved the necessary subdivision.

In response, Dynamic notes that OK Detailing has not even applied for permission to subdivide its property.

Dynamic also argues that it would be unfair if the vendor could avoid the sale by simply refusing to seek planning approval.

The only relevant sections of the *Planning Act* state:

> 19(1) A person who proposes to carry out a division of land shall apply for approval of the proposed subdivision.

> 19(2) A subdivision means a division of a land by means of . . . transferring an interest in land to another person.

Questions for Discussion

1. Do the parties have a valid agreement?

2. If so, is the performance of that agreement subject to a condition?

3. If so, which party, if either, has an obligation to satisfy that condition?

4. What relief, if any, should be available if that obligation is not met?

[20.] In some circumstances, it is possible for the person who was intended to benefit from the condition to waive the need for satisfaction and to insist upon the completion of the sale: *Beauchamp v Beauchamp* (1972) 32 DLR (3d) 693 (Ont CA). Chapter 11 discusses the concept of waiver.

[21.] *Dynamic Transport Ltd v OK Detailing Ltd* (1978) 85 DLR (3d) 19 (SCC).

CLOSING

Once all conditions attached to the sale have been satisfied, the parties' transaction can be *closed*, or completed. At that point, it is important to ensure that any statements made regarding the property continue to be accurate. That may be a problem if new information becomes available between the time that the contract was created and the time that it is to close. If, for instance, the vendor learns that the property is contaminated by radioactive materials, the purchaser must be told. Unless the parties can work out a way to deal with the issue, the purchaser is entitled to cancel the contract.[22] Of course, the vendor may be held liable for keeping quiet and allowing the purchaser to buy a defective property.

It is common for *adjustments* to occur at the time of closing. For instance, if the vendor has already paid the annual property tax, the price will be increased to reflect the fact that the purchaser will enjoy the benefit of that payment for the remainder of the year. The purchaser's lawyer will also conduct one last search at the various offices to ensure that competing interests have not been filed or registered against the land at the last minute. And at that point, the vendor's lawyer will provide the purchaser's lawyer with the formal document that is needed to convey ownership in the property. In jurisdictions under a registry system, a *deed* (or *deed of conveyance*) is used. In jurisdictions under a land titles system, a document called a *transfer* is used. The purchaser's lawyer will promptly register the deed or transfer to protect the client's rights. The lawyer will generally also help with the paperwork that is needed to obtain insurance coverage on the property and may notify the municipality, the utility companies, and so on of the change in ownership.

REMEDIES

In most situations, an agreement of purchase and sale ends with a successful closing. The vendor receives full payment and the purchaser receives clear title. Occasionally, however, problems arise. The parties are entitled to rely upon the usual remedies for breach of contract that were discussed in Chapter 12. For instance, the plaintiff is normally entitled to recover the value of the property that it expected to obtain. Furthermore, at least historically, the courts would order *specific performance*. In other words, instead of being restricted to the monetary value of the property, the plaintiff could obtain the property itself by forcing the defendant to go through with the sale. That remedy was justified by the belief that every piece of land was unique, with the result that money could never truly provide an adequate substitute for actual performance.[23] Recently, however, the Supreme Court of Canada has adopted a different view. Case Brief 16.2 (on the next page) discusses its decision.

We mention two more special remedies that may be available under a contract for the sale of land:

- A *purchaser's lien* is generally created whenever the purchaser pays money to the vendor. For example, before the completion of a transaction, the vendor often requires payment of a deposit or part of the price.

[22.] *Wile v Cook* (1986) 31 DLR (4th) 205 (SCC).

[23.] Given that explanation, it seems strange that vendors can also demand specific performance. After all, a vendor is normally interested in receiving only the payment of money under a sale. Consequently, monetary damages should normally be an adequate remedy if the purchaser refuses to complete the sale. It might be different, however, if the vendor had a special or non-monetary reason for wanting to complete the sale: *Hoover v Mark Minor Homes Inc* (1998) 75 OTC 165 (Gen Div).

Case Brief 16.2

Semelhago v Paramadevan (1996) 136 DLR (4th) 1 (SCC)

The plaintiff agreed to buy a house from the defendant for $205 000. As the closing date approached, however, the defendant said that he was not willing to go through with the sale. The plaintiff sued for breach of contract. By the time of trial, the property had increased in value to $325 000. The judge held that the purchaser was entitled to choose between (i) an order for specific performance and (ii) monetary damages that would place the plaintiff in the position that he would have enjoyed if the sale had been completed. The plaintiff chose the second option and therefore received about $120 000 from the defendant.

The defendant appealed all the way to the Supreme Court of Canada. Justice Sopinka agreed with the result reached at trial. In doing so, however, he rejected the traditional view that specific performance is almost *always* available for a contract dealing with the purchase of land.

While the common law traditionally regarded every piece of land to be unique, that is no longer true, given the nature of modern real estate developments. Residential, business, and industrial properties are all mass-produced much in the same way as other consumer products. If a deal falls through for one property, another is frequently, though not always, readily available.

The court therefore introduced a new rule that limits specific performance to situations in which the plaintiff has legitimate grounds for saying that monetary damages would not provide an adequate remedy.

On the facts before him, Justice Sopinka saw nothing special about the property in question. Nevertheless, since both parties had assumed that the property was unique, he did so as well.

If the deal later falls through, the purchaser will want a refund. A **purchaser's lien** allows the purchaser to have the land sold in order to satisfy the outstanding debt. In practice, however, property is seldom sold under a lien. In most instances, the vendor simply repays the money. And in other cases, the purchaser may wait until the vendor voluntarily sells or mortgages the land to someone else, and then take part of the proceeds.

a **purchaser's lien** allows the purchaser to have the land sold to satisfy the outstanding debt

■ A *vendor's lien* is similar. Occasionally, a person may be willing to sell land on credit, without insisting upon full payment at the time of closing. In that situation, there is a danger that the purchaser will later refuse to pay the remaining amount even though it has already received ownership. The law therefore provides a **vendor's lien**, which allows the vendor to have the property sold to satisfy the outstanding debt.[24]

a **vendor's lien** allows the vendor to have the property sold to satisfy the outstanding debt

Note that a lien is a form of *security*. (Chapter 23 discusses security.) That means that the lien holder may be entitled to priority over other types of claimants. Business Decision 16.1 illustrates this.

Business Decision 16.1

Vendor's Lien and Priority

Sukie Petroutsas sold a piece of land worth $90 000 to Anthony Sidhu. Anthony paid $30 000 at the time of closing and promised to pay the remaining $60 000 within two years. Unfortunately, shortly after obtaining ownership of the property, Anthony's business began to falter. He was unable to make any more payments to Sukie. And to make matters worse, he also incurred $120 000 in debts to other creditors. Anthony's only significant asset is the land that he bought from Sukie.

Questions for Discussion

1. Assume that Sukie has exercised her unpaid seller's lien and has had the property sold for $90 000. How much of that amount will she receive? How much will Anthony's other creditors receive?

2. What would likely happen if Sukie did not have the right to exercise an unpaid seller's lien? Assuming that Anthony sold the land to pay his debts, how much would Sukie receive? How much would the other creditors receive?

[24.] A lien should be registered as an interest in the property. If it is not, it can be defeated if a person buys the land from the purchaser without notice of the vendor's claim.

L.O. ❼❽❾❿

Mortgages

The purchase of land is often the largest single transaction that a person or business will ever complete. Real property tends to be very expensive, especially if it is located in a commercially desirable area or if it contains a development, such as an apartment complex or a shopping mall. Consequently, the purchaser can seldom pay the full price from pre-existing resources. It is usually necessary to obtain a loan. A lender, however, will be reluctant to extend *credit* (that is, provide money in exchange for a mere promise of repayment) without some form of *security*. A bank, for instance, is unlikely to lend you the $5 000 000 that you need to buy a new factory unless you have something that the bank can take or sell if you do not repay your debt. The purchase of land is therefore usually financed through a *mortgage*. Broadly speaking, a **mortgage** is an interest in land that provides security for the repayment of a debt.[25] The person who borrows the money and provides an interest in land is the **mortgagor**. The person who lends the money and acquires an interest in land is the **mortgagee**. Take a moment to repeat those terms. They are often confused.

A mortgage can be used in several ways:

- The previous example presents a typical situation. The same property was involved in two transactions. First, you bought the factory from the vendor. Second, to pay for that purchase, you granted a mortgage over your newly acquired asset as security for a bank loan.[26]

- The two transactions can, however, be distinct. For instance, if you already own a factory, but wish to buy new equipment, you might borrow money for that purchase by allowing the lender to take a mortgage over the land. You would be using one asset (the factory) to acquire another (the equipment).

- Our examples to this point have involved three parties. You bought property from one person and borrowed money from another. But often, there are only two parties. For instance, in the first case, the vendor presumably received full payment when the sale closed. You paid with the money that you borrowed from the bank. Under a different arrangement, however, the vendor could have allowed you to take the factory on credit. And to secure your promise to pay the price in the future, the vendor themself could have taken a mortgage over the property that it just sold to you.

In any event, the basic operation of the mortgage itself remains the same. Figure 16.1 illustrates the process. (Some of the features of that diagram are discussed below.)

a **mortgage** is an interest in land that provides security for the repayment of a debt

the **mortgagor** is the person who borrows the money and provides the interest in land

the **mortgagee** is the person who lends the money and acquires the interest in land

---

[25] Although less common, a mortgage can also be created by using other types of property, such as cars and boats, as security for a loan.

[26] It is highly unlikely that the bank would give credit for the full value of the property. The reason is risk management. Suppose the bank allowed you to borrow $5 000 000 on the basis that your new factory was worth that much when the mortgage was created. A downturn in the economy might have two effects: (i) it might prevent you from repaying the loan, and (ii) it might cause the value of the land to collapse. Consequently, at the end of the story, the bank might be left holding a property worth only $3 000 000, even though it had given you $5 000 000. It would suffer a loss of $2 000 000.

FIGURE 16.1   Mortgage

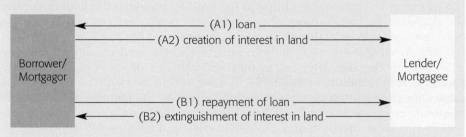

(A1) The lender provides money to the borrower.
(A2) In exchange, the mortgagor creates an interest in land in favour of the mortgagee.
(B1) The borrower repays the loan to the lender.
(B2) In exchange, the mortgagee cancels the interest in land that it received from the mortgagor.

NATURE OF MORTGAGES

Although we have provided a general definition of a mortgage, the specific rules are different in every jurisdiction. The most important differences depend upon whether the security is given under a land titles system or a registry system.

Registry System and Land Titles System

If the land in question is held under a land titles system, a mortgage *creates* a *charge* over the property. A **charge** occurs when the mortgagor agrees that the land will be available to the mortgagee if the debt is not repaid. As we will discuss, the mortgagee is required to remove that charge if the loan is repaid and if the other terms of the parties' agreement are satisfied.

> a **charge** occurs when the mortgagor agrees that the land will be available to the mortgagee if the debt is not repaid

However, if the land in question is held under a registry system, then a mortgage does not merely create a charge; it actually involves a *conveyance of title*. In exchange for the loan, the mortgagor transfers the property to the mortgagee, who then becomes the legal owner.[27] The mortgagor is, however, entitled to have the title reconveyed if the mortgage is fulfilled.

Subsequent Mortgages

Under the registry system, the mortgagee acquires the *legal title* to the property. But the mortgagor is not left without anything—they receive an *equitable interest* in the land. That interest arises because the borrower enjoys the *equity of redemption*. As Chapter 1 explained, there were traditionally two types of courts: courts of law and courts of equity. The courts of law initially adopted a very harsh approach to mortgages. If the mortgagor did not repay the loan within the required time, the mortgagee could keep the property for themselves *and* sue for the late payment. Not surprisingly, the results of that rule were often grossly unfair. A mortgagor who missed the repayment schedule by even

---

[27.] In most cases, the mortgagor holds the fee simple to the property at the outset. However, it is also possible to mortgage other interests in land, such as a lease or even an easement: *Russell v Mifflin (SW) Ltd* (1991) 89 Nfld & PEIR 168 (Nfld SC TD).

the **equity of redemption** entitles the mortgagor to recover legal title to the land by repaying the loan even after the due date

a single day could lose their land forever and still be liable for the debt. The courts of equity therefore created the **equity of redemption**, which entitles the mortgagor to recover legal title to the land by repaying the loan even after the due date.[28] The two types of court are now combined, but the distinction between legal and equitable rights remains important.

The mortgagor therefore holds an interest in the land under either a land titles system (because they retain the legal title) or under a registry system (because they acquire an equitable interest). That is significant because it allows for the creation of *subsequent mortgages*. As the name suggests, a **subsequent mortgage** is one that takes effect after the initial mortgage. Suppose you own a large piece of land, called Greenfield, that is worth $500 000. To acquire a new fleet of trucks, you borrow $300 000 from the Primus Bank and give a mortgage over Greenfield as security for that loan. At that point, the bank acquires either legal title or a charge, and you enjoy the equity of redemption. Your interest in the land, or your *equity*, is worth $200 000. That is a valuable property interest in itself. Consequently, you might be able to use it if you later want to buy a new computer system for $100 000. To secure a loan in that amount from the Nether Bank, you could grant a second mortgage over your interest in Greenfield.

a **subsequent mortgage** is one that takes effect after the initial mortgage

As you might expect, subsequent mortgages raise a number of interesting risk management issues.

VULNERABILITY OF MORTGAGORS Although subsequent mortgages can help you raise additional funds, they also carry an obvious danger. If you have two mortgages, you also have two outstanding loans. And if you fail to repay either one of them, you may lose your land.

VULNERABILITY OF SUBSEQUENT MORTGAGEES If a mortgagor does not repay a loan, the mortgagee may be entitled to *foreclose*, that is, permanently keep the land for themselves. And in doing so, the mortgagee will extinguish not only the mortgagor's equity of redemption, but also the interest held by any subsequent mortgagee.[29] After all, if the mortgagor no longer has an interest in the property, there is nothing that the subsequent mortgagee can use as security. Consequently, in our previous example, Nether Bank is in a vulnerable position. If you fail to fulfill your first mortgage, Primus Bank could foreclose on Greenfield. And while Nether Bank could still sue you for repayment of its loan, it would probably have little chance of success. It no longer has any security, and since you were unable to repay Primus Bank, you presumably do not have much money. To avoid that result, Nether Bank would be required to prevent foreclosure by paying off your outstanding debt to Primus Bank. Not surprisingly, because of that possibility, Nether Bank would almost certainly charge a higher rate of interest than Primus Bank. A subsequent mortgagee will demand additional compensation for the additional risks that it faces.

In theory, it is possible to have any number of subsequent mortgages. However, very few lenders are willing to stand worse than second, since a subsequent mortgagee faces the danger of foreclosure by any of the earlier mortgagees.

[28.] Although a mortgage under a land titles system does not involve the transfer of ownership to the lender, it is still common to use the term "equity of redemption" to describe the borrower's right to re-acquire clear title to the property upon fulfillment of the mortgage.

[29.] Subsequent mortgagees are also treated less favourably in other situations. For instance, if the property is sold rather than foreclosed, the first mortgagee will be paid off completely before a subsequent mortgagee can claim any part of the sale proceeds.

PRIORITY OF MORTGAGES Mortgages generally take priority in the order that they are registered, not necessarily in the order that they are created. Suppose Primus Bank received all the relevant documents from you on Monday but did not take them to the land registry office until Friday. If Nether Bank received all its documents from you on Tuesday and filed them promptly, it would take first priority as long as it did not have notice of your earlier transaction with Primus Bank. That could be important. Suppose the economy collapsed, the value of Greenfield slumped to $250 000, and the land was sold to satisfy your debts. Nether Bank would be entitled to the full amount of its loan ($100 000) and Primus Bank would receive only half of its loan ($150 000 out of $300 000). The lesson is clear. As a matter of risk management, a mortgagee should register their interest as soon as it is created, because registration provides notice to the whole world.

Disposition of Interests

Since we have been discussing the people who may be involved in a mortgage, it is appropriate to briefly mention two more possibilities:

- **Disposition by mortgagee:** A mortgagee may wish to sell their rights to a third party. Although they are entitled to do so, the parties should act carefully. A mortgage is a *property interest* that is created by *contract*. The mortgagee can use a simple *assignment* to transfer their *contractual* rights (such as the right to demand repayment). (Chapters 8 and 15 discuss assignments.) But the third party will not acquire the *security* unless they also receive the mortgagee's property interest— either title (under a registry system) or a charge (under a land titles system). Furthermore, as soon as the appropriate transfer takes place, the third party should promptly register their interest.[30] They should also notify the mortgagor of the assignment.[31] Figure 16.2 illustrates the basic process.

- **Disposition by mortgagor:** The distinction between the proprietary and contractual aspects of a mortgage is also important when a mortgagor sells their interest. Suppose a third party wants to buy a piece of land that is already subject to a mortgage. The third party might pay for the property partially by providing cash and partially by promising to pay the balance of the vendor's loan.[32] Figure 16.3 illustrates the basic process.

You should notice two more points about that arrangement: First, as long as the lender registered their mortgage, the land will still be subject to that security, even though it is in the third party's hands. Consequently, if the loan is not repaid, the land can still be used to satisfy the debt. Second, the general

---

[30] If the third party fails to register its interest, it can be defeated if another person later buys the mortgagee's interest and registers first.

[31] The mortgagor is required to pay only once. If they pay the original mortgagee before receiving notice of the assignment, they are not required to make the same payment again to the third party assignee. (The third party can, however, sue the original mortgagee for their improper receipt of that payment.)

[32] Alternatively, the third party might arrange to discharge the existing mortgage by repaying the loan on the mortgagor's behalf. In that situation, the third party would probably finance their purchase by giving a new mortgage over the property as security for a bank loan. The choice between assuming an existing mortgage and creating a new one is usually based on whether the third party can get a new loan with better terms than are contained in the existing mortgage.

FIGURE 16.2 Disposition by Mortgagee

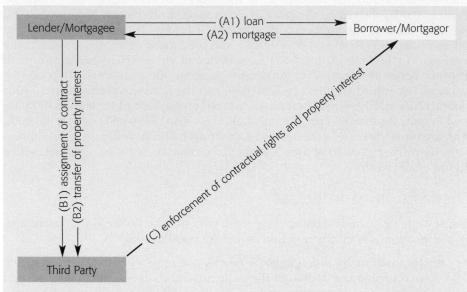

(A1) The lender loans money to the borrower.
(A2) The borrower creates a mortgage by giving the lender a proprietary interest in a piece of land. The borrower is the mortgagor and the lender is the mortgagee.
(B1) The lender/mortgagee assigns to a third party the contractual right to demand repayment of the loan from the borrower/mortgagor.
(B2) The lender/mortgagee transfers its proprietary interest to the third party.
(C)   The third party enforces the contractual rights and the proprietary interest against the borrower/mortgagor.

FIGURE 16.3 Disposition by Mortgagor

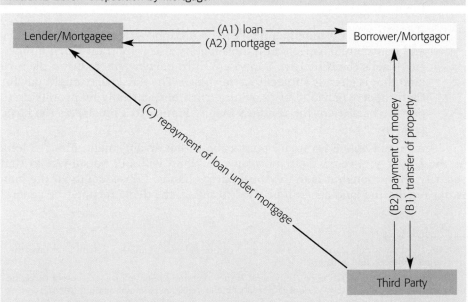

(A1) The lender loans money to the borrower.
(A2) The borrower creates a mortgage by giving the lender a proprietary interest in a piece of land. The borrower is the mortgagor and the lender is the mortgagee.
(B1) The mortgagor sells its property interest to a third party. The mortgagor is now also the vendor.
(B2) The third party satisfies part of the purchase price by paying money to the vendor/mortgagor.
(C)   The third party satisfies the rest of the purchase price by repaying the loan that the vendor/mortgagor received from the lender/mortgagee.

rule states that it is possible to assign contractual rights but not contractual obligations. As a result, even though they no longer have an interest in the land, the original mortgagor (now the vendor) can be sued if the third party does not repay the loan as promised).

TERMS OF THE CONTRACT

Because a mortgage is created by contract, the parties are generally free to include any terms that are appropriate. Certain types of covenants (promises) are, however, standard. (Sample mortgage documents can be found on **MyBusLawLab**.) With respect to the mortgagee, the most important term concerns the duty to discharge the mortgage once the debt has been repaid. They will do so by either reconveying title to the mortgagor (under a registry system) or by registering a *cessation of charge* (under a land titles system). The mortgagor tends to have more obligations.

- **Repayment:** The borrower must repay the debt according to the parties' agreement. That will generally mean that payments must be made on certain days, in certain amounts, and with a certain amount of interest. Furthermore, it is very common for a mortgage to contain an **acceleration clause**, which requires the mortgagor to immediately repay the full amount of the loan if they miss a single payment. It is easy to see why a mortgagee would insist upon such a clause. Once the contract is breached, the mortgagee does not want to wait and see if it will be breached again. They want to bring the matter to an end immediately.[33] An acceleration clause can be contrasted with a *prepayment privilege clause*. The mortgagor sometimes repays the loan earlier, or in larger instalments, than initially agreed. In most circumstances, the mortgagee will impose a financial penalty (or a *bonus*) on the mortgagor for doing so. After all, while the mortgagee wants the loan to be repaid, they also want the interest to build up as much as possible. To avoid that problem, the mortgagor may insist upon a **prepayment privilege** that allows early or additional payments to be made without penalty.

  > an **acceleration clause** requires the mortgagor to immediately repay the full amount of the loan if they miss a single payment

  > a **prepayment privilege** allows early or additional payments to be made without penalty

- **Taxes:** If the mortgagee has registered their interest, its security is reasonably safe. However, even a registered interest can sometimes be defeated. For example, the government may be entitled to seize and sell a piece of land if the taxes on that property have not been paid. The mortgagor is therefore usually required to promise to pay the taxes. Indeed, to ensure that payment actually occurs, the mortgagee may insist upon receiving an appropriate amount of money so that they can pay the taxes themself.

- **Insurance:** The mortgagee's security is only as valuable as the property itself. For instance, a mortgage over an office complex that is worth $1 000 000 provides sufficient protection for a $600 000 loan. The situation will be much different, however, if the building burns to the ground and leaves the land with a market value of only $200 000. To protect themself against that danger, the mortgagee will require the

---

[33.] An acceleration clause can create hardship. It might be unfair, for instance, to demand full payment from a mortgagor who simply missed a single payment because of illness. The courts therefore sometimes grant relief from acceleration if the borrower puts the loan back on track.

mortgagor to purchase adequate insurance for the property. (Chapter 17 considers insurance policies in more detail.) Furthermore, the mortgagee will insist upon being named as a beneficiary of that insurance policy. Therefore, if the building is destroyed, the lender will effectively receive repayment of the loan from the insurance company.

■ **Waste:** For similar reasons, mortgages usually contain a clause that prohibits the borrower from committing an act of waste. As we saw in Chapter 15, waste occurs when a property is changed in a way that significantly affects its value.

REMEDIES FOR DEFAULT

A mortgage typically comes to an end when the borrower fulfills the terms of the parties' agreement, and the lender discharges their interest in the land. Difficulties do occasionally arise, however, especially during economic recessions or depressions. The most common source of problems is the mortgagor's failure to repay the loan. As we saw with respect to the equity of redemption, our legal system has struggled to find ways of fairly balancing the parties' interests in that situation. The mortgagor is often vulnerable and in need of protection. But at the same time, the mortgagee has a legitimate interest in recovering the debt that they are owed, by using their security if necessary. There is no obvious way to resolve that tension. Not surprisingly, the rules vary significantly amongst jurisdictions. Each province and territory has legislation that governs the remedies that are available in the event of default.[34] There are generally four possibilities:

■ suing on the covenant
■ possession of the property
■ foreclosure
■ sale

Suing on the Covenant

A mortgagee has both property rights and contractual rights. To enforce repayment of the loan, they are entitled to use the security interest that they hold in the mortgagor's land. But they are not required to do so. In most circumstances, they have the option of simply suing the mortgagor for the outstanding amount. There are, however, certain limitations on that right. Most significantly, legislation in Alberta, British Columbia, and Saskatchewan generally prevents an action from being brought against an individual or against a corporation that has not *waived* its statutory protection.

Possession of the Property

Under a registry system, the mortgagee becomes the legal owner of the property. In theory, they are therefore entitled to possession at the outset. Almost invariably, however, the parties' agreement states that the mortgagor is allowed to occupy the premises unless they go into *default* by breaching the contract. In theory, the situation is somewhat different under a land titles system because the mortgagee merely acquires a charge, rather than ownership. They therefore

---

[34.] Given the large number of statutory provisions that are involved, citations are not provided.

have no natural right to possess the land. In practice, however, the situation is much the same. The parties' agreement generally states that the borrower's right to occupy the premises may be lost in the event of default.

The mortgagee's right to possession is, however, far less attractive than it might seem.

- Most mortgagees are financial institutions that have little interest in occupying land. As a general rule, banks want "the money, not the mud." They do not want the problems associated with the possession of real property.

- A mortgagee who takes possession acquires a number of responsibilities. They must keep the property in good repair and cannot commit acts of waste. They must also take reasonable steps to generate income from the property. And when they do generate income (such as rent), they are generally required to use that money to reduce the mortgagor's debt.[35]

- The mere fact that the mortgagee took possession does not prevent the mortgagor from later exercising their equity of redemption (assuming that it is still available), repaying the amount that is due under the loan, and resuming possession of the property.

For those reasons, the mortgagee normally will not take possession of the property unless the mortgagor has either abandoned it or is acting in a way that will decrease its value.

Foreclosure

To understand the remedy of *foreclosure*, we must once again look at the history of mortgages. The mortgagee was traditionally entitled to keep the land that had been transferred into their name if the mortgagor was even a single day late with a payment. Because the effects of that rule were often unfair, the Court of Chancery created the equity of redemption, which allowed the mortgagor to recover the property by repaying the loan at a later date. In time, however, that led to complaints by mortgagees. They could never be sure that they were entitled to keep the land that they had acquired. A mortgagor was often allowed to redeem a property years after the loan had become due. The Court of Chancery therefore created a new rule that allowed mortgagees to apply for orders for foreclosure. **Foreclosure** (from the Latin words meaning "to close from outside") is a procedure for extinguishing the mortgagor's equity of redemption.

Once again, the remedy tends to be more attractive in theory than in practice.[36] Although the details vary between jurisdictions, the procedure tends to be quite drawn out. And surprisingly, it often lacks finality. After the mortgagee applies for foreclosure, the court initially grants an order *nisi* (Latin for "unless") as a way of informing the mortgagor and any subsequent mortgagees that the equity of redemption may be foreclosed unless the outstanding debt is repaid.[37] If that does not occur within the required period (usually six months), the court will grant a final order of foreclosure. But even at that point the mortgagee is not necessarily entitled to the property forever. As long as the lender

foreclosure is a procedure for extinguishing the mortgagor's equity of redemption

---

[35.] The mortgagee is, however, entitled to deduct a reasonable amount for repairs and expenses.

[36.] The concept of foreclosure is best suited to a registry system, in which the mortgagee receives legal title at the outset. However, the same terminology and essentially the same procedures are used under a land titles system, in which the lender starts with only a charge.

[37.] Foreclosure will extinguish both the mortgagor's equity of redemption and a subsequent mortgagee's security interest.

still holds the land, the borrower can apply to the court to have the foreclosure set aside in exchange for repayment of the loan.

There are other reasons why foreclosure is often not a satisfactory remedy:

■ Mortgagees tend to be lending institutions that are not particularly interested in owning land. They want money.

■ Foreclosure often seems unfair from the perspective of the mortgagor and any subsequent mortgagees. The mortgagor will lose the property and the subsequent mortgagees will lose their security. Furthermore, the mortgagee may be overcompensated. Suppose you borrow $60 000 from a bank by mortgaging a property that is worth $100 000. Some time later, you buy $20 000 worth of goods from a supplier. Because that purchase is made on credit, you are required to give a second mortgage over your land. Your business then experiences financial difficulties, and you are unable to repay either creditor. If the bank is able to foreclose, it will receive land worth $100 000, even though it was owed only $60 000 at the outset. By the same token, you will effectively pay $100 000 to discharge a debt of $60 000. And the holder of the second mortgage will lose their security. For that reason, mortgagors and subsequent mortgagees can seek a court order that requires the mortgagee to proceed by way of *sale*, rather than foreclosure. The mortgagee also has the option of requesting a sale.

Sale

*the remedy of **judicial sale** occurs when the mortgaged property is sold under a judge's order*

The remedy of **judicial sale** occurs when the mortgaged property is sold under a judge's order. Although the rules vary from place to place, the process is carefully controlled. It is done under the authority of the court or another government official (the registrar of titles), who must approve the terms of the sale. In some jurisdictions, the court or the registrar of titles may set the minimum price for which the land can be sold.

The sale proceeds are used to repay the loan that was granted by the first mortgagee.[38] If there is money left over, it is used to satisfy the claims of subsequent mortgagees. And if any money *still* remains at that point, it is paid to the mortgagor.[39] However, if the sale proceeds are insufficient to cover the debts, there is a *deficiency*, and the mortgagee may be entitled to sue the mortgagor for the shortfall.[40]

The use of sale varies significantly between jurisdictions. In Nova Scotia, the courts insist upon it rather than foreclosure. Similarly, although foreclosure is available in Alberta, Saskatchewan, and the parts of Manitoba that are under the land titles system, the courts prefer a sale to be attempted first. The mortgagee is entitled to foreclose only if the attempted sale did not generate a reasonable offer. In the rest of the country, the lender generally has a greater choice between remedies.

*a **power of sale** is a contractual right that allows the mortgagee to sell the land in order to obtain payment*

As an alternative to seeking a court-ordered sale, the mortgagee can sometimes exercise a *power of sale* that is contained in the parties' agreement. A **power of sale** is a contractual right that allows the mortgagee to sell the land

---

[38] The mortgagee is also entitled to the payment of interest and compensation for the costs associated with enforcing their rights.

[39] If the mortgagee forecloses and later sells the property to a third party, the mortgagor and the subsequent mortgagees are usually not entitled to a share of the sale proceeds, even if those proceeds exceed the amount that was owed under the first mortgage.

[40] Some jurisdictions generally prohibit the mortgagee from suing the mortgagor on the covenant.

in order to obtain payment. The mortgagee is responsible for getting a reasonable price for the property. If they fail to do so, they can be held liable for the shortfall. Although quite common in some places (especially Ontario), that type of term is severely restricted in others (especially Alberta).

Combination of Remedies

The preceding remedies can often be used in combination. For example, if the mortgagor has abandoned the property, the mortgagee may take possession of the land to prevent it from losing value, and then have it sold. As we have seen, some jurisdictions allow the mortgagee to sell the property and then sue the mortgagor on the covenant for any outstanding debt. And quite often, a financial institution will obtain a property by way of foreclosure and then sell it for its own benefit. Banks, as we have said, usually want "the money, not the mud."

Finally, before leaving this section, consider Concept Summary 16.2, which briefly describes the remedies that may be available under a mortgage.

PART 4

Concept Summary 16.2

Remedies for Mortgage Default

Remedy	Nature	Limitations
Sue on the covenant	mortgagee sues mortgagor for payment of debt	
Possession	mortgagee takes possession of property	• mortgagee usually "wants money, not mud" • severely restricted in Western Canada • mortgagee required to maintain land and generate income from land • mortgagor may later exercise equity of redemption
Foreclosure	mortgagee extinguishes mortgagor's equity of redemption	• lengthy and complicated procedure • limited availability in some jurisdictions • mortgagee usually "wants mud, not money" • potential unfairness to mortgagor and subsequent mortgagee if value of land exceeds amount of debt
Sale	property sold under judge's order—debt paid from sale proceeds	• mortgagee not entitled to retain sale proceeds in excess of debt

Chapter Summary

A registration system documents interests in land. Two registration systems operate in different parts of the country. A registry system provides an opportunity to inspect and evaluate documents that may affect real property. It provides access to the documents, but it does not guarantee their accuracy. A land titles system does more than simply provide an opportunity to inspect and evaluate documents. It generates certificates of title that virtually guarantee the validity of the interests that are listed on those certificates. Although both systems are based on registration, some types of unregistered interests are enforceable.

The sale of land is a complicated matter involving a large number of people performing a variety of tasks. As a matter of risk management, the purchaser should retain various professionals. A sale occurs through an agreement of purchase and sale that is created by the vendor and the purchaser. Such agreements often contain conditions that suspend the parties' obligations to complete the deal. A sale closes when the vendor provides the purchaser with the formal document needed to actually convey ownership in the property. As a matter of risk management, the purchaser should register that document as soon as possible. If an agreement of purchase and sale is breached, the innocent party may be entitled to a variety of contractual remedies, including specific performance or a lien.

A mortgage is an interest in land that is created to provide security for the payment of a debt. The person who borrows the money and gives an interest in land is the mortgagor. The person who lends the money and acquires an interest in land is the mortgagee. Under a land titles system, a mortgage creates a charge over the property. Under a registry system, a mortgage involves a conveyance of title. In either event, the mortgagor enjoys an equity of redemption. The mortgagor can use the equity of redemption to create subsequent mortgages.

A mortgage involves both an interest in land and a contractual relationship between the parties. The contract imposes various obligations on the mortgagee and the mortgagor.

If the mortgagor defaults, the mortgagee may be entitled to a variety of remedies, including an action on the covenant, possession, foreclosure, and sale.

MyBusLawLab   ADDITIONAL RESOURCES FOR CHAPTER 16

MyBusLawLab provides students with an assortment of tools to help enrich the learning experience, including a Study Plan with Pre- and Post-tests, mini-cases with assessments, and provincial content material, which provides links to relevant cases, legislation, and additional resources.

MyBusLawLab provides the following resources for Chapter 16:

- Sample Agreement for Purchase and Sale of Land (located in British Columbia)

Provincial Material

- **British Columbia:** Conveyance of Land, Cost of Borrowing, Credit Reporting, Land Title and Survey Authority, Power of Attorney, Property Taxes, Riparian Rights, Real Estate Agents
- **Alberta:** Foreclosures, Land Titles System, Real Estate Agents, Spousal Interests in Land (Dower Rights), Title Insurance
- **Manitoba and Saskatchewan:** Registry System (Manitoba) and the Land Titles System, Mortgage Legislation
- **Ontario:** Charge, Discharge, Dower—Family Law Legislation, Electronic Registration, Foreclosure, Judicial Sale, *Land Registration Reform Act,* Land Registration Reform, Land Titles, Real Estate Agent, Real Estate Fraud, Registry Systems, Title Insurance, *Mortgages Act*, Personal Covenant, Power of Sale, Ontario Real Estate Association
- **Atlantic Provinces:** Chattel Mortgages, Conditional Sales, Mortgage Brokers, Power of and Court-Ordered Sales, Real Estate Agents, Title Insurance

Review Questions

1. What is the major difference between a registry system and a land titles system? Why is it necessary to trace a good chain of title under the former but not the latter?

2. Explain why Sir Robert Torrens is important to land law in Canada.

3. Explain the basic meaning of "indefeasibility" and describe the three principles upon which it is based.

4. Briefly explain the difference between "immediate indefeasibility" and "deferred indefeasibility."

5. List five types of unregistered interests that may be enforced against a person who purchases land. In each instance, briefly explain why enforcement is allowed without registration.

6. "The concept of *caveat emptor* does not always apply when land is bought and sold." Is that statement true? Explain your answer.

7. What does it normally mean if someone says that a purchase and sale of land is subject to a "condition precedent"? Provide a few examples of common conditions precedent.

8. Why did the Supreme Court of Canada decide that specific performance should not always be available under an agreement for the purchase of land?

9. What is a "purchaser's lien"? What is a "vendor's lien"? Describe situations in which each type of remedy would be available.

10. Briefly explain the concept of a charge that arises in the context of mortgages.

11. Can a mortgage be used to finance the purchase of something other than the land that is being mortgaged? Illustrate your answer with an example.

12. The mortgagee receives an interest in land. Is that interest the same under both a registry system and a land titles system? Explain your answer.

13. "A mortgage involves a difficult tension between the rights of the mortgagor and the rights of the mortgagee." Discuss that statement in light of the history of the equity of redemption and the remedy of foreclosure.

14. What is a "subsequent mortgage"? How is a subsequent mortgage related to the equity of redemption?

15. Identify and briefly explain four types of obligations that are usually imposed upon a mortgagor.

16. "A purchaser of land has no need to worry if the land is already subject to a mortgage. As long as the purchaser did not personally create the mortgage, the mortgagee can sue only the person who actually obtained the loan that is associated with the mortgage." Is that statement true? Explain your answer.

17. What is an "acceleration clause"? What is a "prepayment privilege"? Which would you prefer to insert into a mortgage agreement if you were a mortgagor? What if you were a mortgagee?

18. Briefly explain the concept of "waste" that applies in the case of a mortgage of land. (You may find it useful to refer back to Chapter 15.)

19. Explain the consequences of foreclosure. How does foreclosure relate to the equity of redemption? Does foreclosure always allow the mortgagee to permanently retain the land in question?

20. Describe a situation in which the mortgagor and a subsequent mortgagee would prefer the remedy of sale to the remedy of foreclosure by the first mortgagee.

Cases and Problems

1. Five years ago, Megarry Inc owned a large piece of land. It subdivided that property into ten equal parts and sold three of them, as a single unit, to Cheshire Ltd. (Each of the three parts was individually described.) The transfer documents were immediately registered. Although Cheshire had initially intended to construct a number of warehouses on its new property, it soon developed economic difficulties. Since it no longer has any use for the property, Cheshire recently sold it to the Burns Corp. Shortly after that sale closed, Burns began to survey the land with a view to building a shopping mall. When Burns began construction, however, Megarry's lawyer sent a letter stating that her client still owned part of the property that Burns was in the process of developing. After some investigation, the parties agreed that Cheshire accidentally registered itself as owner of four parcels, rather than three. That mistake was overlooked, both at the time of the original sale and at the time of the recent resale by Cheshire to Burns. Who owns the disputed fourth section of the property? Do you require additional information to answer that question?

2. The neighbourhood known as Pettytown is in the midst of a resurgence. The area was first settled following World War II. In that era, small houses usually were built on large lots. After a period of decline, the neighbourhood once again is trendy and desirable. In contrast to the past, however, most homeowners now prefer very large houses. As a result, every metre—indeed, every centimetre—may be treated as precious land. This case involves two adjacent properties, known as Blackacre and Whiteacre, each of which originally was 20 metres wide. In 1962, the two individuals who owned the properties co-operated to build a fence between Whiteacre and Blackacre. As a result of a mutual mistake, the fence was located incorrectly. The fenced area of Whiteacre was 19 metres wide, while Blackacre was 21 metres wide. Cantera Sdeo purchased Blackacre in 1997 and discovered the mistake within a short time. In 2004, Connolly Wright purchased Whiteacre with the intention of demolishing the existing house and constructing a much larger replacement. After reading the original survey and plan of the property, Wright developed a plan that assumed a property 20 metres in width. He therefore announced his intention to tear down the existing fence. Because Sdeo strongly objected to that proposal, Wright waited until Sdeo was out of town for a weekend before demolishing the fence and moving ahead with his construction project. Although Wright's new house on Whiteacre is located within the 19-metre boundary, a new fence sits at the 20-metre mark. Furthermore, Wright's workers frequently left materials on the disputed one-metre strip during the construction phase. Discuss the law that governs the disputed piece of land and explain how a court probably would resolve the case.

3. Darren Munt is an unsophisticated man who has spent most of his adult life working as a custodian in an elementary school. Recently, he decided to use the money that he had inherited from his father to create a company that would sell books and DVDs over the Internet. Because he had no experience in that field, he visited Jenny Schmidt, the lawyer who had handled his father's estate. Jenny agreed to help Darren in exchange for a hefty fee. Several weeks later, she informed him that she had found a property with a building that would be suitable for a warehouse. They briefly toured the premises together. Darren was excited about the prospect but expressed concern "about all the little details." Jenny assured him that she had extensive experience in real estate matters and promised that, for a price, she would "do all the legwork."

Jenny contacted the owner of the property. Two months later, the deal closed, and Darren acquired the fee simple to the premises. Shortly after he took possession, however, he became aware of a number of problems. (i) His neighbour complained that the warehouse, which had been built only three years earlier, was located partially on their land. (ii) As a result of discussions with other people in the business, Darren realized that he had grossly overpaid for the property. (iii) He discovered that the building's foundations were cracked and that its roof was in serious danger of collapse. (iv) He was notified by government officials that a large pool of blood was buried only several metres underground on a part of the property that was adjacent to a river. The government explained that the land had previously been used as a slaughterhouse. Fearing that the water supply might become contaminated, the government has demanded a cleanup. (v) Several ex-employees of the slaughterhouse informed Darren that they had been injured on the job as a result of the previous owner's carelessness. They also informed him that they had successfully sued the former owner, and that they had filed writs of execution against the property two days before Darren's sale had closed. (vi) And finally, Darren soon became aware that while he might be able to store merchandise in the warehouse, he could not process Internet orders from the same premises. Although he had not noticed them when he briefly visited the property with Jenny, and although they had not been registered against title, power lines had been installed directly overhead by a utility company. Those lines cause electrical interference with computer equipment.

Discuss Darren's situation from a risk management perspective. Is there any obvious solution to his various problems? Explain your answer.

4. Mark Minor owns a unique property in the Town of Leitch. Several appraisers have stated that no other property in the vicinity is comparable in terms of either size or features. The lot is very large and, unusually for a suburban property, it features a large stand of trees, as well as a permanent pond. The property is located at the end of a paved road and therefore experiences little traffic. Despite all of those benefits, however, the property has attracted very few potential buyers. Aside from the fact that the economy is in recession, it is well known within the community that the property previously was used as an abattoir and that it contained a blood pit at the site where a slaughterhouse once existed. Mark Minor therefore was delighted, four years ago, when Ann Hoover agreed to purchase the property for $150 000. Their contract contained two important paragraphs:

> 2(a) This sale is conditional upon the vendor obtaining planning permission to allow for a residential dwelling to be built upon the property. Failure to satisfy this condition before the date of closing will render the agreement null and void.

> 3 The vendor at their own cost and expense shall locate, empty, and fill with sand any blood pit now existing on the property.

Prior to the closing date, Mark Minor obtained the required planning permission. Also before the

closing date, he removed the blood pit from the property and filled in the resulting hole with fresh landfill. When the closing day arrived, however, Ann Hoover refused to complete the sale. She relied on the fact that, contrary to paragraph 3, Mark Minor did not "empty and fill with sand any blood pit." He removed it instead. Mark Minor explains that he eliminated the problem by an even more effective process and that he is entitled to specific performance of the agreement. He also suggests that Hoover's real reason for refusing to close the sale stems from the fact that, because of market conditions, the property is now worth only $110 000. How would a court most likely resolve the dispute? Explain your answer.

5. Bamidele Diop entered into an agreement of purchase and sale with Elton Singh. Under the terms of that contract, she immediately paid $50 000 and promised to pay the remainder of the $500 000 price within six months. In exchange, Elton promised to transfer title to the property, known as White Oaks Landing, to Bamidele within three months. Create additional facts that would subsequently lead to the enforcement of (i) a purchaser's lien and, alternatively, (ii) a vendor's lien. Explain the nature and effect of each type of lien.

6. Since Sharon Krawchuk owned a house that she wanted to sell, she hired Wendell Aitch to act as her real estate agent. Zoriana Scherbak appeared as a potential buyer. While looking around the house, Zoriana noticed a crack in the foundations and asked if the building had experienced any recent problems. Since she was concerned about flooding in the basement, she also asked if the local sewer system worked well. After that meeting, the vendor completed a Seller Property Information Sheet (SPIS) that described the property. The SPIS observed that the foundations had settled in one corner, but also said that the building had not suffered any problems in the past 17 years. The SPIS also stated that basement flooding was not a problem. The real estate agent was with the vendor when the SPIS was completed. Since he did not have any first-hand knowledge of the house, he simply assumed that the vendor's statements on the SPIS were accurate. Unfortunately, they were not. As the purchaser discovered shortly after buying the house and taking possession, and as the vendor knew all along, the building was continually sinking and causing significant problems. Furthermore, after her basement flooded, the purchaser learned that the local sewer system failed several times a year. The purchaser is now faced with a set of expensive repairs. She would like to sue. Is a vendor generally required to disclose defects? If not, did an obligation to disclose defects arise as an exception in this case? If the vendor cannot afford to pay full damages, is any other option available to the purchaser? Explain your answer.

7. Dominion Instruments Inc purchased an office complex from Premium Holdings Ltd for $1 000 000. Under the terms of that agreement, Dominion paid

$400 000 immediately and gave a mortgage under which it promised to pay the remaining amount, with interest, in a lump sum five years after the date of closing. Although the time for payment has now arrived, Dominion has offered only $300 000 to Premium, along with a renewed promise to pay the outstanding amount within one year. Dominion has explained that its financial position is weaker than expected on account of a trade dispute with the United States regarding government subsidies on the manufacture of musical instruments. However, it has also demonstrated that the situation will almost certainly be rectified within 12 months. Premium, however, insists that it is entitled to obtain clear title to the property by foreclosing at once. There is, therefore, a tension between the parties' interests. Discuss that tension by tracing the historical development of the rules regarding foreclosure and redemption.

8. Seyed Rabi was the victim of identity theft. A pair of criminals hacked into his computer and acquired all of his personal and financial information. By forging Seyed's signature on a land transfer document, they were able to transfer title to his house into their own names. They then went to a bank, borrowed $500 000, and gave a mortgage over the property as security for the loan. Of course, after receiving the cash, they disappeared, rather than repay the loan. Since it had not been repaid, the bank began legal proceedings against the property. Seyed was entirely unaware of the fraud until the bank's lawyer and real estate agent showed up at his front door and insisted that the house was theirs for the taking. Seyed says that that is ridiculous. Since he had neither transferred title to the rogues, nor done anything wrong, he insists that he is not responsible for the bank's problems. The bank, in contrast, explains that it honestly believed that the mortgage was valid and insists that, since the property is located in a Torrens system, it has acquired indefeasible title. It has threatened Seyed that he will lose the property unless he repays the loan that gave rise to the mortgage that is registered against title. Which party is likely to win? Explain your answer.

9. Russ Roberts stole $100 000 from his employer, a company named Mifflin Inc. He used that money to build a house on a piece of land that was owned by his father. Although Roberts and his father had never formalized their arrangement with a written document, the relationship effectively was one of landlord and tenant. Roberts paid his father a small sum of money (usually around $2500) each year in exchange for the right to occupy the land. Mifflin Inc eventually discovered the theft and learned what Roberts had done with the money. The company demanded repayment of the $100 000, plus interest. It also insisted that Roberts provide security for his repayment of the debt by creating a mortgage over the land that he occupied. When the company attempted to enforce the mortgage, however, Roberts insisted that the security was invalid.

He argued that since he did not own the property, he could not impose a mortgage upon it. How would a court likely resolve the dispute? Explain your answer.

10. The Newton Widget Company owned two properties, each of which contained a factory. After recognizing the need to modernize its operations, it requested a loan of $500 000 from the Bank of the Rockies. The bank agreed but insisted on taking a mortgage over both properties as security. Even with the loan, Newton found it very difficult to afford the computerized equipment that it intended to purchase. It therefore decided to cut back on other expenses. It accordingly stopped paying its property taxes and cancelled the insurance contract that previously provided compensation for any loss or damage that occurred to its land, buildings, or equipment. In an effort to streamline its production of widgets, it also levelled one of its factories, which was valuable but in need of repair and costly to maintain. It then consolidated all its operations into the single factory. Up to this point, Newton has made mortgage payments as required under the parties' agreement. The bank nevertheless feels aggrieved. Why? Has Newton done anything wrong? Explain your answer.

11. Ahmad Vaughan borrowed $50 000 from Sarah Jamal. The parties' agreement required Ahmad to repay the loan in monthly instalments of $1000. As security, Sarah took a mortgage over Ahmad's nightclub, which was worth $200 000. Unfortunately, because of the unusual nature of his business dealings, Ahmad frequently experienced tremendous fluctuations in his monthly income. What would be the likely outcome if, three months into the agreement, Ahmad received a large amount of money and attempted to repay the entire outstanding balance immediately? What if, instead, Ahmad suffered an economic setback and was unable to pay three consecutive instalments? If Sarah did not want to use her security to enforce repayment, is there any way that she could nevertheless sue Ahmad for immediate repayment of the entire outstanding balance? Explain your answer.

12. Srijan owned a large piece of land, called Greyland, in an area that he believed would soon be re-zoned to allow for industrial developments. In preparation for a business venture that he planned to launch, he borrowed $1 000 000 from the Bank of London and in exchange granted a first mortgage over Greyland. At that time, Greyland had a market value of $1 700 000. Unfortunately, the economy soon went into recession and Srijan's financial situation took a turn for the worse. In an attempt to keep his business alive, he borrowed $300 000 from the Bank of Ottawa, and in exchange granted a second mortgage over Greyland. As the recession grew deeper, however, Srijan found it impossible to repay either of his loans. The Bank of London then foreclosed on the land. At the time of foreclosure, it seemed as though all three parties were losers. Srijan lost his property, the Bank of Ottawa lost its security, and the market

value of the land that the Bank of London obtained through foreclosure had fallen to $900 000. Within a couple of years, however, the recession had passed and property values had skyrocketed. Consequently, the Bank of London was eventually able to sell Greyland to an unrelated corporation for $2 000 000. Srijan and the Bank of Ottawa now feel cheated. They note that the Bank of London received $2 000 000 even though it lost only $1 000 000 on its loan.

Their lawyers argue that it would be fairer to split the $2 000 000 three ways: (i) $1 000 000 to the Bank of London, (ii) $300 000 to the Bank of Ottawa, and (iii) $700 000 to Srijan. That approach would put each of the parties back into their original positions. Will a court agree with that argument? Explain your answer. As you do so, think about the risks that each of the parties accepted by entering into the mortgage agreements.

Personal Property: Bailment and Insurance

17

LEARNING OBJECTIVES

After completing this chapter, you should be able to:

❶ Distinguish between real property and personal property, and between tangible property and intangible property.

❷ Describe four ways in which personal property rights can be acquired and four ways in which they can be brought to an end.

❸ Define the term "bailment" and list the three elements of a bailment.

❹ Explain the nature of a lien and a right of sale.

❺ Explain five factors that a judge will consider in determining how a reasonable person would have acted in a bailment.

❻ Describe the scope of liability for a common carrier, and outline three sets of defences that may be available to a common carrier.

❼ Describe the process of sub-bailment.

❽ Distinguish between third party insurance and first party insurance by giving an example of each.

❾ Explain the concept of indemnification and explain how it is related to the ideas of an insurable interest, excessive insurance, and insufficient insurance.

❿ Describe the process of subrogation.

real property is immoveable

personal property is moveable

Having looked at *real property* in the last two chapters, we can now turn to *personal property*. Although complications occasionally arise, the basic distinction is straightforward.[1] **Real property** is immoveable, and **personal property** is moveable. You cannot carry a piece of land around with you, but you can take a cat or a car from one place to the next. Another distinction is that real property is usually permanent, whereas personal property tends to be transitory. Different owners will come and go, but a particular piece of land will always exist (unless, for instance, it falls into the ocean following an earthquake). In contrast, cats and cars come into the world through birth and manufacture, and eventually pass away through death and destruction. A third distinction is beginning to disappear. Historically, wealth was concentrated in real property. Position and power in society depended upon the ownership of land. Increasingly, however, wealth is held in other forms of property. Bill Gates is proof of that.

tangible property is a thing that can be touched

intangible property is a thing that cannot be touched

The general concept of personal property can be broken down into several other categories. The most important distinction is between *tangible* and *intangible* property. **Tangible property** is a thing that can be touched. You can, for example, pick up your cat and sit in your car. Such things are sometimes called *goods* or *chattels*.[2] **Intangible property** is a thing that cannot be touched. For instance, while you can physically hold a cheque, your real concern, as we saw in Chapter 14, is with the rights that that piece of paper represents. You cannot put your hands around those rights. At most, you can require the debtor to fulfill an obligation.[3] As we will see in Chapter 18, much of our new economy consists of a special type of intangible property known as intellectual property, which includes copyrights, patents, and trademarks.

L.O. ❶   Acquiring Personal Property Rights

Personal property rights are usually acquired through the *intention* of one or more people. For instance, you probably bought this text. The bookseller intended to transfer ownership in exchange for a payment of money. The same sort of process occurs when you rent something, such as a moving van. Your rights once again arise from a contractual arrangement. The only major difference between purchasing and renting is that you receive a smaller package of rights when you rent. You cannot keep the vehicle indefinitely. You must return it at the end of the agreed period.

Property rights are not always acquired through contract. Sometimes you can get something for nothing. Assuming that the other person intends to give, and that you intend to receive, you can become the owner of a gift once it is delivered to you. Going further, you may be able to acquire property rights even if you act alone. There is some truth in the old saying that "possession is nine-tenths of the law." Sometimes, things have no owner at all. That is true, for instance, of a fox that is running wild or an intentionally abandoned bicycle by

---

[1] The concept of "property" can be defined in different ways for different purposes. As a result, legislation may classify a certain type of thing as "property," even if the more general definition of "property," as developed by the courts over the years, would not necessarily reach the same conclusion: *Royal Bank of Canada v Saulnier* (2008) 298 DLR (4th) 193 (SCC).

[2] The word "chattel" comes from the same source as the word "cattle." The root word first referred to moveable wealth generally, and then to livestock specifically. The overlap is understandable. Domesticated animals were once a primary form of wealth.

[3] For that reason, lawyers refer to intangible property as *choses in action*. A chose in action is a "chose" (the French word for "thing") that can be enforced only through legal action. A piece of tangible property is a *chose in possession*, because it is a thing that can be possessed.

the side of the road. In that situation, you can acquire ownership of the thing by taking possession of it with the intention of controlling it for yourself. [4] There is also some truth in the old saying "finders keepers," but not "losers weepers." Suppose you find property that someone else has lost.[5] By intentionally taking control of that thing, you will acquire rights that are effective against everyone *except* the true owner.[6] Consequently, if I take that property from you, you can sue me in tort (as explained in Chapter 4) even if it is clear that you are not the true owner.[7] In the business world, however, a finder's rights may depend upon the circumstances. Although the law is rather unclear, it appears that an occupier is entitled to things that are found in the private, but not the public, parts of its premises.[8] Case Brief 17.1 discusses the leading decision.

Case Brief 17.1

Parker v British Airways Board [1982] 2 WLR 503 (CA)

Alan Parker found a gold bracelet in the executive lounge at Heathrow Airport in London. He turned the bracelet over to the British Airways Board, which leased the airport, but made it clear that he wanted it back if the true owner did not come forward. The owner never appeared, and the board sold the jewellery for £850. Instead of paying that money to Parker, however, it kept it on the basis that it was entitled to anything found on its premises. Parker was understandably upset and sued.

The court ordered the board to pay the money to Parker. The judge agreed that an occupier is entitled to personal property *if* it is found in an area over which the occupier had a "manifest intention" to exercise control. That might be true, for instance, if Parker had discovered the bracelet under a desk in an office. On the facts, however, the item was discovered on the floor of a publicly accessible waiting area.

Some rights can be acquired through an act of creation. An author enjoys copyright as a result of writing a new book. And for somewhat different reasons, the owner of a cow acquires rights to any calves that are born. As both of those examples illustrate, property and property rights sometimes arise when none previously existed.

Losing Personal Property Rights

L.O. ❷

Personal property rights do not last forever. For example, you will lose all of your rights to this book if you sell it to someone else. And if you rent it to a classmate for a term, you will no longer enjoy the right to immediate possession (but you will gain a right to a payment). More dramatically, since you cannot own something that does not exist, your rights will be lost if this book is destroyed in a fire. And while we have already seen that your rights will continue to exist even if this book is *lost* or *stolen*, the situation will be different if you *abandon* the text with an intention of giving up control.

---

[4] *Pierson v Post* 3 Cai 175 (NY SC 1805).

[5] Perhaps surprisingly, the same rules apply even if you *steal* something, rather than find it. While you do not acquire any rights against the true owner, you do acquire rights in the property that can be enforced against everyone else in the world: *Costello v Chief Constable of Derbyshire Constabulary* [2001] 1 WLR 1437 (CA).

[6] Although a finder acquires substantial rights, they may also incur some obligations. A finder may be required to make a reasonable effort to locate the true owner and preserve the goods.

[7] *Armory v Delamirie* (1722) 93 ER 664 (KB).

[8] There are other limitations. You cannot, for instance, acquire property rights in something that you discover while trespassing on another's land.

a fixture is a chattel that has been sufficiently affixed, or attached, to land or a building

Rights can also disappear if your personal property becomes attached to, or mixed with, land or other chattels. Although there are several possibilities, we will focus on the most common situation, which involves *fixtures*.[9] A **fixture** is a chattel that has been sufficiently affixed, or attached, to land or a building.[10] The important point is that once a chattel becomes a fixture, it belongs to the owner of the land. Suppose you bought a dishwasher to use in your apartment. Although the decisions are frustratingly inconsistent, a court would be influenced by the following factors in deciding whether the machine became a fixture:

- **Degree of attachment:** A chattel is more likely to be considered a fixture if it is attached to a building rather than merely sitting under its own weight. Consequently, if you simply wheeled a dishwasher into the corner of the kitchen, it would presumably remain yours. However, if you installed it under the kitchen counter with screws and plumbing, it might be a fixture and therefore belong to your landlord.

- **Purpose of attachment:** A court would be even more concerned with the objective intention served by placing the dishwasher in the apartment. The key issue is whether a reasonable person would believe that the dishwasher became part of the building. If it was installed to enhance the value of the apartment, then it is probably a fixture. However, if it was merely done to make better use of the dishwasher itself, then it is less likely to be a fixture.

- **Tenants' fixtures:** There are special rules that would apply because your apartment was rented. The courts are concerned that tenants might unfairly lose ownership over things that they add to their premises. Consequently, even if the dishwasher did become the landlord's fixture, you could turn it back into your chattel if you removed it, within a reasonable time after the end of the lease, and without doing irreparable damage to the apartment. The same rule applies to trade fixtures. For instance, you probably could remove shelves and signs that you installed in a warehouse that you rented for storage.[11]

Concept Summary 17.1 reviews some of the ways in which ownership in personal property may be acquired or lost.

Concept Summary 17.1

Acquiring and Losing Ownership of Personal Property

Acquiring Personal Property	Losing Personal Property
purchase through contract with previous owner	*sale* through contract to new owner
gift received from previous owner	*gift* through intention and delivery to new owner

(Continued)

[9] Similar rules apply when two chattels are joined together. For example, I may apply paint to your boat or tires to your car; my stallion may impregnate your mare and produce a foal; my grapes may become mixed with your grapes in a single barrel of wine; and my sheep may become mingled within your flock. Although the precise rules depend upon the situation, the courts will always try to strike a fair balance between our competing interests.

[10] A building is usually a fixture itself because it is attached to land. Interesting issues sometimes arise with mobile homes.

[11] Since the issue of fixtures is almost always addressed in a lease, the parties can generally create their own terms. The basic rules discussed in the text, however, are usually followed.

(continued)

first possession of things that were never owned or that were abandoned	*abandonment* with intention to give up rights
finding of lost property (good against everyone *except* true owner)	*fixture* of chattel to land or a building (subject to right of tenant's fixtures)
creation of new property	

Bailment

L.O. ❸❹❺❻❼

Many things can be done with personal property. We discussed a number of examples earlier in this text. For instance, contractual rights can be assigned, goods can be sold, and cheques can be negotiated. Another important type of arrangement, known as a **bailment**, occurs when one person temporarily gives up possession of property with the expectation of getting it back.[12] The person who delivers the property is the **bailor**. The person who receives it is the **bailee**.

A bailment may arise in a variety of ways. A *consignment* provides a good example. A **consignment** occurs when an owner gives property to another person for the purpose of selling it. The owner is called the *consignor* and the person making the sale is called the *consignee*. When the consignee sells the property on behalf of the consignor to a purchaser, ownership passes directly from the consignor to the purchaser. The consignee only ever had control and possession of the property for the purpose of making the sale—they were never the owner. Other examples of bailment include:

- renting a circular saw from a hardware store
- shipping furniture with a moving company
- delivering a machine to a shop for repairs
- placing equipment in a storage unit
- leasing a vehicle from a dealership
- borrowing a book from a library
- sending a package by courier
- lending a lawnmower to a neighbour

Those illustrations cover a lot of ground. Some arise in business contexts, others more informally. Some involve payments of money; others do not. They are all considered bailments, however, because they all satisfy the same requirements:

- one person voluntarily delivers property to another
- for a particular purpose
- with the intention that the property will be returned or disposed of as directed

Although the second and third requirements are usually straightforward, the first element occasionally causes problems. As a general rule, a bailment exists only if one person intends to deliver control and possession of property to another person.[13] It is, however, sometimes difficult to distinguish between a *bailment* and a *licence*. A **licence** is simply permission to do something that would otherwise be

a **bailment** occurs when one person temporarily gives up possession of property with the expectation of getting it back

the **bailor** is the person who delivers property

the **bailee** is the person who receives property

a **consignment** occurs when an owner gives property to another person for the purpose of selling it

a **licence** is permission to do something that would otherwise be wrongful

---

12. The word "bailment" comes from the French word *bailler*, which means "to deliver."

13. That requirement is sometimes relaxed. For instance, a finder is often classified as a *quasi-bailee* (that is, *sort of like* a bailee) even though the person who lost the property did not voluntarily deliver possession and control of the goods. Likewise, if you leave your jacket in a store, the proprietors may be considered to be a type of bailee, at least if they pick it up with the intention of taking control of it.

PART 4

wrongful. The need to draw that distinction may arise if, for instance, you park your car on my parking lot.[14] If we have merely created a licence, then you are entitled to park on my land, but you have not given me control and possession of your car. I therefore am not obliged to protect your vehicle. If, in contrast, I did receive control and possession of your car under a bailment, then I will have some obligation to take care of your vehicle. The distinction between a licence and a bailment is therefore critically important in terms of risk management.

In deciding whether a relationship is a bailment or a licence, it is necessary to ask how a reasonable person would view the parties' intentions. A bailment will exist if, according to the reasonable person, the parties intended for possession and control of the chattel to be substantially handed over. Otherwise, there is only a licence. Following our earlier example, Concept Summary 17.2 reviews several factors that a court would consider in deciding whether a parking lot involves a bailment or a licence. (Notice in particular that the mere payment of money by a car owner does not necessarily create a bailment.)

Concept Summary 17.2

Parked Car—Bailment or Licence?

- Did the car owner pay a substantial amount of money to an attendant (suggesting a bailment) or merely put a few coins into a machine (suggesting a licence)?
- Was the parking lot self-serve (suggesting a licence) or were there attendants on duty (suggesting a bailment)?
- Did the car owner keep the keys (suggesting a licence) or hand them over to attendants (suggesting a bailment)?
- If attendants collected the keys, did they merely put them in a safe place (suggesting a licence) or did they use them to drive the car (suggesting a bailment)?
- Did the car owner choose the specific parking spot (suggesting a licence) or was that decision made by attendants (suggesting a bailment)?
- Was the parking lot simply an open space (suggesting a licence) or was it enclosed with a controlled entrance and exit (suggesting a bailment)?
- Had the parking lot previously dealt with the car owner in such a way as to imply that it would (suggesting a bailment) or would not (suggesting a licence) assume substantial possession and control of the vehicle?
- Was there a sign or a ticket stub indicating that cars were left at the owners' risk (suggesting a licence) or would the reasonable person believe that the parking lot assumed some responsibility (suggesting a bailment)?

Business Decision 17.1 explores the difference between a bailment and a licence.

Business Decision 17.1

Parking Lot: Bailment or Licence?[15]

You own and operate a restaurant. You also own and operate a nearby parking lot. On most nights, when business is reasonably relaxed, you simply allow customers of your restaurant to use that parking lot free of charge. But on special occasions, when the restaurant is very busy, you hire three or four attendants to maintain order in the parking lot. While some customers insist upon parking themselves, most are happy to hand over their keys, to allow the attendants to deal with parking, and to collect their vehicles at the end of the night. In either event, there is no charge for parking.

That system has generally worked well. Recently, however, you have been sued by Martin Miller. Miller was a customer of your restaurant during a particularly busy evening last winter. He was happy to accept an

(Continued)

[14.] Although the parking cases are the most common, there are many other examples. The same issue may arise, for instance, if you hang your coat in my cloakroom as you enter my restaurant.

[15.] *Martin v Town 'n' Country Delicatessen Ltd* (1963) 42 DLR (2d) 449 (Man CA).

(continued)

attendant's offer to park his vehicle but very upset at the end of the night when his car could not be found. As the police later discovered, Miller's car had been stolen, taken on a joy ride, and crashed into a tree. After recovering his car, Miller had to spend $5000 repairing damage that the thief had caused. Since the thief cannot be identified, Miller has sued your restaurant. He claims that a bailment was created when the attendant offered to park his car, and that there was a breach of that bailment relationship when the restaurant failed to reasonably protect his vehicle. You have argued in response that Miller simply enjoyed a licence to park his car on your property, and that you therefore were not obligated to guard his vehicle.

Questions for Discussion

1. Is a court more likely to find a bailment or a licence? Explain your answer.

2. What could you have done to clearly prevent a bailment from arising?

3. If the court finds that there was a bailment relationship between your restaurant and Miller, will you continue to do business the same way in the future? If not, what changes will you make?

LIABILITY OF BAILORS

Most bailments occur without incident. The bailor delivers the property to the bailee, it is held for the intended purpose, and then returned in good condition. Exceptionally, however, difficulties arise on one side or the other. We consider the bailor's liability in this section and the bailee's in the next.

Consider a situation involving a lease. Suppose you are in the business of renting heavy machinery to construction firms. If you *sold* the same equipment, your transaction would be caught by the *Sale of Goods Act*, and you might be required, amongst other things, to ensure that it was fit for its intended purpose. (We discussed the *Sale of Goods Act* in Chapter 13.) A lease, however, is not a sale. It is a bailment because you expect that the property will be returned to you at the end of the transaction. Nevertheless, the law requires you, as a bailor who is receiving consideration for the use of your property, to use reasonable care in providing appropriate machines.[16] Consequently, if a backhoe collapses and injures a worker, you might be held liable if you knew, or should have known, of the defect that caused the accident. You might also be required to provide a special warning regarding any unusual dangers, unless the bailee was already familiar with the type of equipment it was renting.

The other major basis of liability arises from a bailor's failure to pay a charge. Suppose you deliver your car to a garage for repairs or leave your furniture in a storage unit. You are expected to pay for the benefit that you receive from the mechanic or the warehouse. To ensure that you do so, the bailee is entitled to exercise a *lien* over your property.[17] A **lien** is the bailee's right to

a **lien** is the bailee's right to retain possession of property until the bailor pays a debt

---

[16.] The lease itself can impose additional obligations upon the bailor or reduce the obligations that are normally imposed by the law.

[17.] Every province and territory has legislation that provides such rights to people who warehouse or store goods: *Warehouseman's Lien Act*, RSA 2000, c W-2, s 3 (Alta); *Warehouse Lien Act*, RSBC 1996, c 480, s 2 (BC); *Warehousemen's Lien Act*, CCSM, c W20, s 2 (Man); *Warehouseman's Lien Act*, RSNB 1973, c W-4, s 2 (NB); *Warehousers' Lien Act*, RSNL 1990, c W-2, s 3 (Nfld); *Warehouse Keepers Lien Act*, RSNWT 1988, c W-2, s 2 (NWT); *Warehousemen's Lien Act*, RSNS 1989, c 499, s 3 (NS); *Warehouse Keepers Lien Act*, RSNWT 1988, c W-2, s 2 (Nun); *Repair and Storage Liens Act*, RSO 1990, c R.25, s 4(1) (Ont); *Warehousemen's Lien Act*, RSPEI 1988, c W-1, s 2 (PEI); *Warehouse Keepers Lien Act*, RSY 2002, c 226, s 2 (Yuk). Similar rights are given to people who repair or improve goods. However, the scope of mechanic's lien legislation varies between jurisdictions. See *eg Possessory Liens Act*, RSA 2000, c P-19, s 2 (Alta); *Repairers' Lien Act*, RSBC 1996, c 404, s 2(1) (BC); *Repair Shops Act*, CCSM, c R90, s 1 (Man); *Liens on Goodsand Chattels Act*, RSNB 1973, c L-6, s 2 (NB); *Mechanics' Lien Act*, RSNL 1990, c M-3, s 6(1) (Nfld); *Garagekeepers' Lien Act*, RSNWT 1988, c G-1, s 2(1) (NWT); *Mechanics' Lien Act*, RSNS 1989, c 277, s 6(1) (NS); *Garagekeepers' Lien Act*, RSNWT 1988, c G-1, s 2(1) (Nun); *Repair and Storage Liens Act*, RSO 1990, c R.25, s 3(1) (Ont); *Mechanics' Lien Act*, RSPEI 1988, c M-4, s 2 (PEI); *Garage Keepers Lien Act*, RSY 2002, c 99, s 2(1) (Yuk). A number of other statutes also confer rights on more specific types of people, such as threshers and woodsmen.

retain possession of the property until the bailor pays a debt. Note that the bailee is entitled only to *retain* your property. If you somehow honestly recover your goods, the lien usually disappears. If a lien is exercised, and if you do not respond to it in a timely manner, the bailee may also be entitled to exercise a statutory *right of sale*. Although the exact requirements vary between jurisdictions, a **right of sale** allows a bailee to sell the bailor's property to obtain payment of the bailor's debt. If the sale proceeds are larger than the debt, the bailor is entitled to the extra money.[18]

a **right of sale** allows a bailee to sell the bailor's property to obtain payment of the bailor's debt

LIABILITY OF BAILEES

A bailee's primary obligation is to return the property, in good condition, to the bailor at the end of the arrangement. A bailment, however, exposes the bailor to considerable risk. Suppose you deliver your truck to me. The vehicle might become lost, damaged, or destroyed. Furthermore, those events may occur while I am in possession. Since you would have little way of knowing exactly what happened to your truck, you might find it difficult to satisfy the usual requirements of, say, the tort of negligence. (We discussed the tort of negligence in Chapter 6.) The general rule in private law requires the plaintiff to prove that the defendant wrongfully caused a loss. But in our situation, I am the only one with access to all the facts. The courts have therefore developed a special rule in this situation. If the bailor proves that goods were lost or damaged during a bailment, then the *burden of proof* shifts to the bailee. At that point, I would be required to prove that I was not to blame. If I could not do so, I would be held liable, even though you did not actually show that I was responsible for your loss. Although that rule provides a great benefit to the bailor, it is available only if the court is satisfied that the loss occurred during the bailment and that a shift in the burden of proof would not be unfair to the bailee. Consider the issue in You Be the Judge 17.1.

You Be the Judge **17.1**

Shifting the Burden of Proof[19]

Wong Aviation Ltd rented a Cessna airplane to Douglas Taylor one morning in late October. The weather was cold, visibility was limited, and the air was turbulent. Taylor took off with the intention of flying the plane in a tight circle around the Toronto Island Airport. Unfortunately, he and the aircraft disappeared without a trace. Although there is no positive evidence whatsoever regarding the disappearance, the evidence indicates that, given the weather conditions, it would have been possible for Taylor to lose control of the plane even if he did not act negligently.

Wong Aviation has sued Taylor's estate for $250 000, the value of the Cessna. Wong admits that it cannot succeed in a simple claim in negligence because it has no basis for positively proving, on a balance of probabilities, that Taylor carelessly caused the loss. Therefore, it has based its action on the contract of bailment that was created when Taylor rented the plane. In doing so, Wong believes that it can shift the burden of proof. More specifically, it argues that since it has established that the property was lost during the bailment, to avoid liability, the defendant must prove that the loss was not caused by Taylor's lack of care. The defendant could not discharge that burden—no one has any idea what happened to Taylor and the aircraft.

Questions for Discussion

1. Under what conditions is the burden generally shifted in the context of a bailment?

2. Are those conditions satisfied in this case?

3. Would it be fair to shift the burden in any event?

[18.] Note that statutory liens and rights of sale are generally limited to bailees who repair and store property. For instance, while common carriers have the ability to exercise a common law lien, they do not have a right of sale.

[19.] *Taylor Estate v Wong Aviation Ltd* (1969) 3 DLR (3d) 55 (SCC).

Notice that even if the burden of proof does shift, the bailee is not generally required to *guarantee* the safety of the bailor's property.[20] Liability will arise only from a failure to take reasonable care. But how much care must be used to avoid liability? Although the courts traditionally applied different standards of care to different types of bailments, they have moved toward a situation in which most bailees simply have to act as a reasonable person would act in similar circumstances.[21] Depending upon the circumstances, a reasonable person might exercise more or less caution and care. Several factors are especially important:[22]

- **Contract, custom, and statute:** If a bailment is contained within a contract, the parties are generally free to agree upon the level of care that the bailee must use. The court may also formulate the standard of care to reflect a practice that is customarily used in a certain type of business. Diamond merchants, for instance, use greater care than people who deal in bricks. Similarly, the standard may be affected by legislation.

- **Benefit of the bailment:** Greater care must be used if a bailment is entirely for the benefit of the bailee. That would be the case if I borrowed a truck from you, as a friend, because I was moving to a new apartment. In contrast, a lower level of care may be acceptable if a bailment is entirely for the bailor's benefit. Perhaps I had possession of your vehicle simply because I allowed you, as a favour, to park it in my garage while you were on vacation.

- **Gratuity or reward:** A bailee's burden also depends upon whether it was *gratuitous* (free of charge) or for *reward* (for payment). If I were using your truck to move my furniture, I would have to exercise more care if I did not pay for that privilege. After all, I was getting something for nothing. However, if I rented the truck from you, a court might be more lenient, since the transaction benefitted you too.

- **Value and nature of the property:** A reasonable person's behaviour is influenced by the nature and value of the property. I would be expected to behave more cautiously if the truck that I borrowed from you was a fragile and priceless antique rather than a sturdy, but well-used, pick-up.

- **Bailee's expertise:** I might be expected to exercise greater care if I claimed to have special experience or training in handling the property. For instance, the standard would be higher if you stored your truck in my commercial parking complex rather than the garage attached to my house.

The expectation under the general standard of care can be quite demanding, especially if there is a gratuitous bailment entirely for the bailee's benefit. In exceptional circumstances, however, the bar is set even higher: The bailee is treated as an *insurer*. In other words, the bailee can be held liable even if they were *not* careless. The bailor is entitled to compensation simply because

---

[20.] We will see an exception that applies to common carriers. Furthermore, the defence of reasonable care is not available in a case of *deviance*, where the bailee dealt with the bailor's property in an unauthorized way. For instance, if you left your furniture in my storage facilities while you were abroad for a year, I might, without your permission, let my brother use it for a few months. If so, I could be held liable even if I was not directly at fault for the fact that the goods were lost or damaged: *England v Heimbecker* (1977) 78 DLR (3d) 177 (Sask Dist Ct).

[21.] That is a general trend in the law. We saw a similar development for the tort of occupiers' liability in Chapter 5.

[22.] While it is important to know which factors affect the content of the standard of care, you should not become too caught up in the exercise. The distinctions between situations are even harder to apply than they are to describe. At the end of the day, a judge usually adopts a common sense approach to all the facts.

their property has been lost or damaged. We will consider the most important example in the business context: *common carriers*.[23]

Common Carriers

a **common carrier** is a company that offers to deliver any goods for any person in exchange for a standard price

A **common carrier** is a company that offers to deliver any goods for any person in exchange for a standard price (assuming that it has available space). That definition can apply to companies that transport by trains, trucks, ships, or airplanes. Notice, however, that a company must do more than commonly carry goods for money. It must also offer its services without reserving the right to refuse to deliver some goods while taking others. Railways, for instance, are often common carriers. In contrast, a moving company is a *private carrier*, rather than a common carrier, if its owner frequently turns away work that involves particularly heavy lifting. An airline that reserves the right to refuse some sorts of goods is also a private carrier.

A private carrier is liable only if it fails to exercise the level of care that is reasonably expected from someone in its line of work. A different rule applies to common carriers, for largely historical reasons. In ancient times, unscrupulous carriers often agreed to transport goods but then delivered the property to highwaymen in exchange for a share of the loot. A *shipper* (a person who shipped the property) usually found it difficult to prove carelessness because they had no way of knowing exactly what happened. The loss occurred while the goods were out of their possession. To remedy that problem, the courts held that a common carrier was generally liable for any loss or damage, even if they were not personally at fault. The shipper merely had to prove that (i) the carrier was a common carrier, (ii) the property was given to the carrier in one condition, and (iii) the property either was not properly delivered to its destination or was delivered to its destination in worse condition.

That basic rule is still applied. Furthermore, a common carrier has very few defences.

an **act of God** is a natural catastrophe

- **War and act of God:** A carrier is not liable if goods are harmed as a result of war or **an act of God**, which is a natural catastrophe, such as an earthquake or flood. In either event, however, the carrier may be held responsible if it carelessly exposed the shipper's property to danger. A trucker, for example, might damage goods as a result of unreasonably driving under treacherous weather conditions.

an **inherent vice** is a defect in the goods themselves

- **Inherent vice and shipper's fault:** The shipper's goods may have suffered damage as a result of an **inherent vice**, which is a defect in the goods themselves. For instance, cattle may die in transit because they were already diseased when they were brought on board. Similarly, the carrier is not responsible for loss or damage that is the shipper's fault. The person sending the property might, for example, improperly pack crystal bowls or fail to label their container as "fragile."

an **exclusion clause** is a contractual term that protects one party from liability

- **Exclusion clause:** By far the most important defence arises from the use of *exclusion clauses*. As we discussed in Chapters 9 and 12, an **exclusion clause** is a contractual term that protects one party from

---

23. A similar set of rules applies to innkeepers, who are people who offer food and lodging to the public without reserving a general right to turn away travellers: *Innkeepers Act*, RSA 2000, c I-2 (Alta); *Hotel Keepers Act*, RSBC 1996, c 206 (BC); *Hotel Keepers Act*, CCSM, c H150 (Man); *Innkeepers Act*, RSNB 1973, c I-10 (NB); *Innkeepers Act*, RSNL 1990, c I-7 (Nfld); *Hotel Keepers Act*, RSNWT 1988, c H-5 (NWT); *Tourist Accommodations Act*, SNS 1994–95, c 9 (NS); *Hotel Keepers Act*, RSNWT 1988, c H-5 (Nun); *Innkeepers Act*, RSO 1990, c I.7 (Ont); *Tourism Industry Act*, RSPEI 1988, c T-3.3 (PEI); *Hotel Keepers Act*, RSS 1978, c H-11 (Sask); *Hotel and Tourist Establishments Act*, RSY 2002, c 113 (Yuk).

liability. Common carriers typically use standard form agreements that contain provisions along the following lines: "The carrier's liability is limited to $50 per package for any damage howsoever caused," or "The carrier shall be liable only for damage caused by negligence."[24] As usual, judges interpret such clauses narrowly and insist that they be sufficiently drawn to a shipper's attention before a contract is created. Furthermore, in the present context, exclusion clauses must be approved by the Canadian Transport Commission to ensure that customers are treated fairly. Within those limitations, however, exclusion clauses provide an important mechanism for risk management for both parties. The carrier is relieved of responsibility, and the shipper is alerted to the fact that it should purchase property insurance.

SUB-BAILMENT

We need to briefly consider the concept of *sub-bailment*. As the name suggests, a **sub-bailment** occurs when property that is already held under a bailment is transferred into a further bailment. Suppose you deliver property to me and that I then deliver it to someone else. You are called the *original bailor*. I am called the *bailee/bailor* (because I am the bailee under the original bailment, but the bailor under the sub-bailment). And the third party is called the *sub-bailee*. That sort of arrangement arises quite often in the business world. Three simple examples will illustrate the point:

> a **sub-bailment** occurs when property that is already held under a bailment is transferred into a further bailment

- I own a general repair shop. You deliver a television to me with instructions to fix the speakers. Because I do not have the proper equipment to deal with that problem, I deliver the television to another company, with instructions that is should be returned to me once the job is done.

- I own a trucking company. You deliver a load of kitchen fixtures to me for shipment from Vancouver to Charlottetown. When I arrive at the east coast of New Brunswick, I learn that the Confederation Bridge, which links Prince Edward Island to the mainland, is closed for repairs. I therefore deliver the goods to a local ferry company for the last leg of the journey across the water.

- You manufacture heavy machinery. I operate a local construction supply company. My stock includes several vehicles that I have leased from you, including a bulldozer. As part of my business, I sublease that bulldozer to a construction firm for use on a particular project.

Figure 17.1 illustrates the process of sub-bailment.

FIGURE 17.1 Sub-Bailment

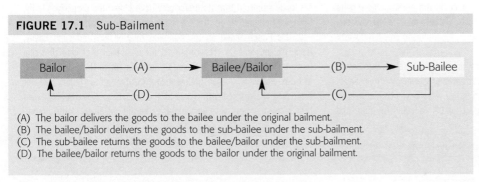

(A) The bailor delivers the goods to the bailee under the original bailment.
(B) The bailee/bailor delivers the goods to the sub-bailee under the sub-bailment.
(C) The sub-bailee returns the goods to the bailee/bailor under the sub-bailment.
(D) The bailee/bailor returns the goods to the bailor under the original bailment.

---

24. In the second situation, since the burden of proving the defence is on the common carrier, they would have to prove that they had not been careless.

A bailee is allowed to place the property into a sub-bailment only with the bailor's consent. A bailment contract may expressly state that the bailee is entitled to deliver the goods to a third party. However, the courts also often recognize implied consent from the circumstances. It is common for a court to assume that a person who delivers an automobile to a mechanic for repairs, or a package to a carrier for shipment, agrees to allow the bailee to transfer the property to a third party to complete the task if necessary. If a bailee places property into a sub-bailment without the bailor's permission, they can be held responsible for any resulting loss. They may even be held liable for the tort of conversion if their conduct seriously interferes with the bailor's ownership. (The tort of conversion was discussed in Chapter 4.)

The most important issue concerning sub-bailment arises if property is lost or damaged while it is in the sub-bailee's possession. As a general rule, that party is expected to use reasonable care in dealing with the goods. There are two possible actions if they fail to do so:

- A claim may be brought by the bailee/bailor, even though that party did not own the property and merely enjoyed a right of possession under the original bailment. If that claim is successful, then the bailee/bailor normally receives the damages from the sub-bailee on behalf of the original bailor.

- The original bailor may also be entitled to sue the sub-bailee. That is true only if (i) the original bailor expressly or implicitly agreed to the sub-bailment, and (ii) the sub-bailee knew, or ought to have known, that they received possession of goods that were already held under a bailment.[25]

The situation can become quite complicated if property passes through a series of bailments and sub-bailments, especially if some of those arrangements involve exclusion clauses. Case Brief 17.2 provides a useful summary of the entire area.

Case Brief 17.2

Punch v Savoy's Jewellers Ltd (1986) 26 DLR (4th) 546 (Ont CA)

Lenore Punch, who lived in Sault Ste Marie, received a ring from her aunt as a gift. It was a family heirloom that was worth more than $11 000. Because the ring was in need of repair, Ms Punch took it to a local shop, Savoy's Jewellers. Savoy realized that it could not perform the repairs itself and consequently sent the ring, by registered mail, to Harry Walker Jewellery in Toronto. In doing so, however, it purchased only $100 worth of insurance on the ring.

Harry Walker fixed the ring and was prepared to return it to Savoy. Because of a postal strike, however, it obtained permission from Savoy (but not from Ms Punch) to send the ring by CN Railway's courier service rather than by registered mail. A driver for CN collected the ring, and an employee for Harry Walker signed a shipping form that contained a provision that limited CN's liability for any loss to $100. Unfortunately, the ring disappeared. Although the exact cause of the loss was unknown, CN freely admitted that its driver may have stolen the property. (Oddly, CN never bothered to discuss the matter with its employee.)

Ms Punch relied on the bailment relationship and sued Savoy, Harry Walker, and CN. The Ontario Court of Appeal first held that she had implicitly consented to Savoy's sub-bailment to Harry Walker, and to Harry Walker's sub-sub-bailment to CN. Although Ms Punch had not discussed the matter with Savoy at the outset, she presumably knew that a sub-bailment was possible and she did not object. Furthermore,

(Continued)

[25.] Even if the bailor did not initially consent to the sub-bailment, it can subsequently *ratify* that arrangement. In other words, it can later adopt the bailee/bailor's act of placing the property into a sub-bailment as having been performed on its behalf.

(continued)

she admitted that if she had been asked, she would have consented. And finally, the evidence indicated that Savoy's use of a sub-bailment was common in the jewellery business.

Next, the court stated that since the ring disappeared while it was held on bailment, the burden of proof shifted from Ms Punch. Each defendant consequently could be held liable unless they established that its carelessness had *not* caused the loss. None of the defendants were able to do so. Indeed, the evidence pointed in the opposite direction. Savoy carelessly failed to purchase adequate insurance coverage for the ring. It should have been more cautious, especially since it agreed to allow Harry Walker to return the ring by way of a courier service with which it had no experience. Harry Walker was also careless. It should have explored the possibility of obtaining better insurance coverage. And CN was careless because it allowed the ring to disappear while in its possession, probably through theft by its own employee.

Finally, the court held that the exclusion clause contained in CN's shipping document might be effective against Harry Walker, but not against Savoy or Punch. The exclusion clause was contained in a contract. And, as we saw in Chapter 8, contractual terms can generally be enforced only between contractual parties—in this case, CN and Harry Walker. An exception may be created if a bailor agrees to be bound by a term. On the facts of this case, however, neither Savoy (as the bailor/bailee) nor Ms Punch (as the original bailor) even knew about the exclusion clause.

The defendants were therefore all liable to Ms Punch. She was entitled to recover from any or all of them up to the full value of her ring. (She could not, of course, recover complete compensation three times over.) Between themselves, the defendants were equally liable. CN tried to limit its liability with regard to Harry Walker, but the Court of Appeal narrowly interpreted the exclusion clause and found that it was ineffective because it did not cover losses created through theft.

Personal Property, Risk Management, and Insurance

L.O. ❽ ❾ ❿

Personal property raises interesting risk management issues. In one sense, property rights are very strong. They usually exist until their owner intentionally disposes of them.

- If you lose your property, you can recover it from me even though, as a finder, I acquired rights against everyone else in the world.

- If a thief steals your goods and sells them to me, I may be liable for the tort of conversion even if I acted in the reasonable belief that the thief was the true owner. (See Ethical Perspective 4.1.) As a general rule, people cannot give more than they actually have.[26] I could not buy from the thief something that still belonged to you.

In a number of other respects, however, personal property rights are quite fragile:

- Even if I found your goods, you cannot sue me unless you know that I have your property. However, personal property is easily moved from one place to another. And while there are registration systems for keeping track of some chattels (such as vehicles), it is often impossible to locate goods that have gone missing.

- Personal property may be damaged innocently or in a way that does not support a valuable cause of action. Your computer may be ruined by an electrical storm that causes a power surge, or it may be crushed by a common carrier under a shipping contract that contains an effective exclusion clause.

---

[26] The rule of *nemo dat quod non habet* (or *nemo dat* for short) is subject to several exceptions. The most important occurs if value is given in exchange for *money* rather than *goods*. Suppose a thief stole $5000 in cash from you. If I bought that money from the thief by selling a car to him, I can obtain ownership of the money. That exception is based on the need for cash to pass freely through the commercial world.

Those sorts of concerns create the need for risk management. Some strategies are *proactive* because they reduce the risk of loss in the first place. For instance, security systems can prevent thefts, and training programs can help employees avoid accidents. Perhaps the most important form of risk management, however, is *insurance*.

In Chapter 3, we discussed the need for *liability insurance,* which involves an insurance company's contractual promise to pay damages on behalf of a person who incurs liability. In exchange for that promise, the insured party pays a price, called a *premium*. Since an employer may be vicariously liable for an employee's torts, liability insurance is often a matter of survival. Few businesses have sufficient assets to pay for all the damage that they may cause in the course of their operations.[27] In this chapter, we look at another significant form of insurance: *property insurance*. **Property insurance** is a contract in which an insurance company, in exchange for a premium, promises to pay money if property is lost, damaged, or destroyed.[28] The basic difference between the two types of insurance is reflected in the fact that liability insurance is often called *third party coverage*, whereas property insurance is often called *first party coverage*.

> **property insurance** is a contract in which an insurance company, in exchange for a premium, promises to pay money if property is lost, damaged, or destroyed

- **Third party coverage:** Liability insurance provides third party coverage because, in one sense, it is aimed at providing compensation to someone outside of the insurance contract.[29] The insurance company's obligation is triggered only if the insured party is accused of wrongfully inflicting a loss upon someone else.

- **First party coverage:** Property insurance provides first party coverage because it does not require the involvement of an outsider. The insurance company's obligation to pay is triggered by a loss to the insured party itself.

Figure 17.2 illustrates the difference between third party and first party insurance.

Although the rules are complex, we can briefly summarize the essential points that arise in connection with property insurance:

SCOPE OF COVERAGE

First, as a matter of risk management, it is critical to understand the scope of coverage that is provided by an insurance policy. You get only what you pay for.[30]

[27.] A business with sufficient assets may *self-insure*. Most businesses purchase insurance coverage year after year, even if they seldom incur liabilities. As an alternative, however, some businesses save the money that they would have used to purchase insurance, and use it instead to satisfy the liabilities that do occasionally arise.

[28.] Although insurance is a type of contract, it is governed by special rules. Most significantly, while you generally are not required to volunteer information when you negotiate an agreement, the situation is different when you purchase insurance. Insurance is a contract of *utmost good faith*. You are therefore required to voluntarily disclose any facts that might affect the risks for which you are seeking coverage. If you fail to do so, your contract may be void.

[29.] That statement is not strictly accurate. Liability insurance is actually intended to protect the insured party against the risk of being held liable to a third party. The important point, however, is that such coverage necessarily requires the involvement of a third party. Furthermore, a practical effect of liability insurance is that the third party is much more likely to receive compensation. The insurance company usually has enough money to pay damages even if the insured party does not.

[30.] And sometimes not even that much. In an effort to save money, unscrupulous insurance companies occasionally refuse to pay for losses that fall within the policies that they have sold. In doing so, they commit a breach of contract. To discourage that practice, a court may award punitive damages, as well as compensatory damages, against an insurance company: *Whiten v Pilot Insurance Co* (2002) 209 DLR (4th) 257 (SCC) ($1 000 000 in punitive damages).

FIGURE 17.2   Third Party and First Party Insurance

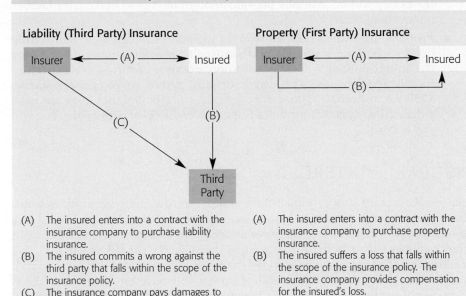

Liability (Third Party) Insurance

Property (First Party) Insurance

(A)   The insured enters into a contract with the insurance company to purchase liability insurance.

(B)   The insured commits a wrong against the third party that falls within the scope of the insurance policy.

(C)   The insurance company pays damages to the third party on behalf of the insured for losses caused by the "insured's" wrong.

(A)   The insured enters into a contract with the insurance company to purchase property insurance.

(B)   The insured suffers a loss that falls within the scope of the insurance policy. The insurance company provides compensation for the insured's loss.

Most insurance contracts are based on standard form agreements (as discussed in Chapter 9) that cover common events, such as fires, storms, and thefts. That basic coverage, however, is subject to restrictions. Standard fire insurance, for instance, may not cover accidents that arise from the storage of explosives or from riots. As a general rule, you can obtain extra protection for those events, but you will have to pay higher premiums. At the same time, however, an insurance contract is subject to the same rules of interpretation that generally govern contractual terms. We discussed those rules in Chapter 9. And as we saw there, the *contra proferentem* rule states that any ambiguities in a standard form contract will be read in favour of the customer rather than the insurance company. You should take a minute to review that material.

INDEMNIFICATION

Second, property insurance is never profitable. At most, it provides **indemnification**, which is reimbursement for a loss that has occurred. And it seldom offers even that much relief.

indemnification is reimbursement for a loss that has occurred

■   There are different ways of calculating the loss that occurs when property is lost, damaged, or destroyed. Suppose a piece of equipment in your factory is badly damaged in a fire. Your policy may entitle you to replace it with a new machine. It is more likely, however, that your insurance company is merely obligated to pay the value that your equipment had the moment before it was destroyed. And if your equipment had been in use for some time before the accident, its *depreciated value* would probably be far less than the cost of a replacement.[31]

---

31. Insurance policies also often give the insurer the option of paying to repair, rather than replace, damaged property. An insurance company will choose the cheaper alternative.

Consequently, unless you can find a suitable second-hand substitute, the policy will not actually provide enough money to make your factory operational again.

- Property insurance policies usually include *deductibles*. A **deductible** occurs when the insurer is not required to provide indemnification for the initial part of a loss. A common example involves cracked automobile windshields. The driver usually agrees to pay, for instance, $250 toward repair. You can always ask for a policy that does not have a deductible and that provides full replacement cost. But again, you will pay accordingly.

a **deductible** occurs when the insurer is not required to provide indemnification for the initial part of a loss

INSURABLE INTEREST

You cannot obtain property insurance unless you have an *insurable interest*. That requirement is needed to avoid "moral hazards." Suppose you could buy coverage over my car. You would have an incentive to destroy my vehicle. Even though you would not actually suffer a loss (because the car belongs to me), you would be entitled to a payment under the insurance policy. The law therefore prevents you from obtaining insurance unless you have an *insurable interest*. An **insurable interest** exists if you benefit from the existence of the property and would be worse off if it were damaged. Consistent with the goal of indemnification, you can be protected only from a loss that you could actually suffer. However, you do not necessarily have to *own* the property in question. The Supreme Court of Canada has held, for instance, that you can have an insurable interest in a corporation's property if you own a substantial number of shares in that company. Any loss to the business would also be harmful to you.[32]

an **insurable interest** exists if a person benefits from the existence of the property and would be worse off if it were damaged

EXCESSIVE AND INSUFFICIENT INSURANCE

Since property insurance is limited to indemnification, it is important to avoid excessive insurance. There is nothing to be gained from purchasing the same coverage from two insurers. Suppose you insured the full value of your building, worth $500 000, against the risk of fire with both Insurance Company A and Insurance Company B. Even if your building were entirely destroyed by fire, you would be able to collect only $500 000, not $1 000 000. The premium that you paid to one of the companies therefore would be a waste of money. That extra payment would simply provide a benefit to the insurers. The doctrine of **contribution** states that if two parties are equally liable, they share the loss between themselves. Consequently, if you recovered $500 000 from Company A, it could demand $250 000 from Company B. In effect, the companies would enjoy a bargain at your expense. Each would be liable for only $250 000 even though it had charged you for $500 000 in coverage.

the doctrine of **contribution** states that if two parties are equally liable, they share the loss between themselves

Just as it is important to avoid *excessive* coverage, it is also important to avoid *insufficient* coverage. That proposition is especially important in one context. To encourage you to buy as much coverage as possible, insurance companies often put *co-insurance clauses* into their policies. A **co-insurance clause** states that if you do not maintain a certain level of coverage you may be held partially responsible if you suffer a loss of a *lesser* extent. We can demonstrate that difficult rule by using a simple example. Suppose you buy only $6000 worth of insurance even though your equipment is worth $10 000. The policy contains

a **co-insurance clause** states that if an insured party does not maintain a certain level of coverage it may be held partially responsible if it suffers a loss of a lesser extent

---

[32] *Kosmopoulos v Constitution Insurance Co* (1987) 34 DLR (4th) 208 (SCC).

FIGURE 17.3   Co-Insurance

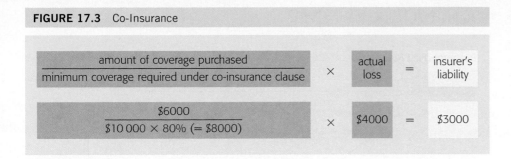

a co-insurance clause that requires coverage for at least 80 percent of the value of your machine.

- If an accident occurs and the damage to your machine is worth *at least* 80 percent of its value (say, $9000), you will be entitled to receive $6000, which is the full extent of the benefit that you bought.

- However, if an accident occurs and the damage to your machine is worth *less than* 80 percent of its value (say, $4000) then you will be a co-insurer to the extent that you did not buy enough coverage. Since you bought only 75 percent of the protection required under the co-insurance clause (that is, $6000 coverage rather than $8000 coverage), you can recover only 75 percent of your loss (that is, $3000 of the $4000 loss). Figure 17.3 shows the relevant calculation.

SUBROGATION

There is one more point to make in connection with indemnification. So far, we have ignored the possibility that the property protected under a policy may be *wrongfully* damaged by a third party. Suppose I destroy your factory by carelessly starting a fire. Generally speaking, the rights that you enjoy under your policy are not affected by the fact that I committed a tort against you. You will still receive compensation from your insurance company. But because your policy limits you to indemnification, you *cannot* also sue me in tort. If you did, you might recover twice for the same loss—once from me and once from the insurer. That is not to say, however, that I will not have to pay for my wrong. The terms of your policy will entitle your insurance company to *subrogation*. The doctrine of **subrogation** allows your insurance company to stand in your shoes and acquire the rights that you have against me. Consequently, after indemnifying you, your insurance company will, at its own cost, bring an action against me for negligently burning down your factory. Figure 17.4 illustrates the process of subrogation.

Are the effects of the doctrine of subrogation fair? Consider Ethical Perspective 17.1.

subrogation allows an insurance company to stand in the insured party's place and acquire any rights that it may have against a third party

OTHER FORMS OF BUSINESS INSURANCE

Before leaving this topic, it is important to note that there are many types of insurance policies in addition to those that we have discussed. Some are especially important to the issue of risk management in the business world. In determining which are appropriate for a particular business, you should consult an insurance broker.

- Although property insurance may allow a business to replace or repair equipment and facilities that have been lost, damaged, or destroyed,

PART 4

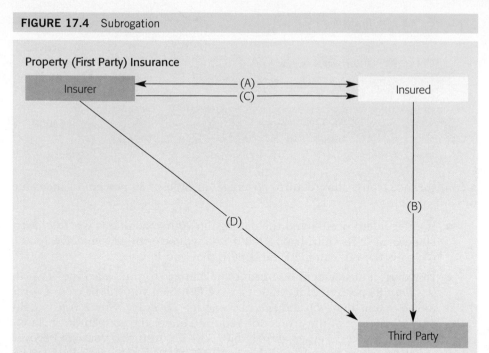

FIGURE 17.4   Subrogation

Property (First Party) Insurance

(A)   The insured enters into a contract with the insurance company to purchase property insurance.
(B)   The insured suffers property damage as a result of a wrong committed by the third party.
(C)   The insurance company indemnifies the insured for the loss that occurred.
(D)   The insurance company is subrogated to the insured's rights in tort law and recovers damages from the third party.

Ethical Perspective **17.1**

Subrogation

Questions for Discussion
Answer these questions on the basis of the preceding example of subrogation:

1. Would it be unfair if you were entitled to both claim indemnification from the insurer and sue me for damages in tort? If you could have obtained damages from me if you had not purchased a policy, then why did you pay the premium to the insurance company? Was the policy really a benefit to you? Explain your answer.

2. Assume that (i) you paid $10 000 in premiums, (ii) you received $100 000 in indemnification, and (iii) your insurer recovered $100 000 in damages from me as a result of being subrogated to your rights in tort. Is it fair that the insurance company can retain the money that you paid in premiums even though it did not eventually suffer any loss in return? Explain your answer.

---

business interruption insurance
provides coverage for losses incurred as a result of downtime

there will usually be a delay before operations return to normal after an accident. And that delay may be very costly. Consequently, **business interruption insurance** is quite common. As the name suggests, this insurance provides coverage for losses incurred as a result of downtime. It can include, for instance, compensation for lost profits, wasted expenditures, and relocation expenses.

■ A similar issue arises as a result of computer saboteurs. The release of a single virus can easily cost the global economy billions of dollars as websites crash and hard drives are erased. Although the insurance industry is still coming to terms with that problem, it is possible for a business to purchase *hacker insurance*. **Hacker insurance** provides protection from the economic consequences of computer saboteurs. Because of the potential size of the losses, however, coverage tends to be expensive and therefore is often practical only for enterprises that rely heavily upon the Internet, such as eBay and Amazon.

■ A business may suffer a substantial economic loss if an important member of its organization dies or becomes incapacitated. Although that person will be missed, a company may find it easier to adjust to the loss if it has access to funds with which it can hire and train a replacement. **Key person insurance** provides such a fund as protection against the loss of important members of a business.

■ Many businesses also help to arrange **life, health, and disability insurance** for employees and their families, which provides protection for employees in the event of health problems. Typically, the employer and the employee reach an agreement in which both contribute to the cost of the premium. The employer's portion is part of the employee's total remuneration package. Such arrangements are advantageous to employees because, while they could individually purchase insurance for themselves, the costs of group coverage are substantially lower.[33]

■ *Bonds* are used to provide comfort in some business contexts. A **fidelity bond** provides coverage when an employee steals money, equipment, or other assets from a business or one of its clients. *First party fidelity* covers the company's own property. *Third party fidelity* covers property belonging to a client. A **surety bond** is used to assure a client that they will be financially protected if a job is not performed as promised. For instance, you may be concerned about a construction company's ability to complete a new building on time. If so, you might insist upon a surety bond that would allow you to receive compensation from an insurance company if the project is delayed.

hacker insurance provides protection from the economic consequences of computer saboteurs

key person insurance provides protection against the loss of important members of a business

life, health, and disability insurance provides protection for employees in the event of health problems

a **fidelity bond** provides coverage when an employee steals money, equipment, or other assets from a business or one of its clients

a **surety bond** is used to assure a client that they will be financially protected if a job is not performed as promised

PART 4

[33.] An injured employee may also be entitled to benefits under workers' compensation schemes: Chapters 3 and 26.

Chapter Summary

Broadly speaking, there are two types of property: real property and personal property. Personal property is either tangible or intangible. Personal property rights can be acquired in various ways: contract, gift, finding, and creation. They can also be lost in various ways: contract, destruction, abandonment, and fixture.

A bailment occurs when one person temporarily gives up possession of property with the expectation of getting it back. The person who delivers the property is the bailor, and the person who receives it is the bailee. Bailments arise in many circumstances, including leases for personal property.

A bailor may be liable for delivering goods that are not fit for the bailee's purpose. A bailor may also be liable to pay a price in exchange for the benefit of the bailment.

If they fail to do so, the bailee may be entitled to exercise a lien and a right of sale.

A bailee's primary obligation is to return the property to the bailor in good condition. If the bailee fails to do so, the burden of proof may shift, and the bailee may be held liable unless they prove that they were not carelessly responsible for the loss or damage to the bailor's property. In rare circumstances, the standard of care is higher, and the bailee is treated as an insurer of the bailor's goods. That rule applies to common carriers.

A sub-bailment occurs when property that is already held under a bailment is transferred into a further bailment. In that situation, the sub-bailee may be held liable if the property is lost or damaged.

Insurance is one of the most important forms of risk management in business. Liability insurance, which we examined in Chapter 3, is sometimes called third party insurance because, in one sense, it is aimed at providing compensation to someone outside of the insurance contract. Property insurance, on the other hand, is sometimes called first party insurance because it does not require the involvement of an outsider and because the insurance company's obligation to pay is triggered by a loss to the insured party themself.

Basic property insurance policies are usually limited in scope. Furthermore, insurance merely provides indemnification for a loss. There are different ways in which to calculate losses for the purpose of insurance. Insurance benefits are often subject to deductibles.

Insurance is available only to a person who has an insurable interest in property. An insurable interest exists if a person benefits from the property and would be worse off if it were damaged or lost.

Businesses should avoid obtaining excessive insurance and insufficient insurance. Excessive insurance often provides a benefit to the insurance companies as a result of the doctrine of contribution. Insufficient insurance often gives rise to the problem of co-insurance.

The process of subrogation allows an insurance company to stand in the insured party's place and acquire any rights that the insured may have against a third party.

Besides liability insurance and property insurance, a business may wish to purchase other types of insurance, including business interruption insurance; hacker insurance; key person insurance; life, health, and disability insurance; fidelity bonds; and surety bonds.

MyBusLawLab   ADDITIONAL RESOURCES FOR CHAPTER 17

MyBusLawLab provides students with an assortment of tools to help enrich the learning experience, including a Study Plan with Pre- and Post-tests, mini-cases with assessments, and provincial content material, which provides links to relevant cases, legislation, and additional resources.

MyBusLawLab provides the following resources for Chapter 17:

Provincial Material

- **British Columbia:** Lien, Warehouse Lien, Repairers' Lien, Hotel Keepers, Insurance Corporation of British Columbia (ICBC), Health Insurance

- **Alberta:** *Alberta Insurance Act,* Common Carriers, Innkeepers' Liability, Insurance, Mechanics Liens, Possessory Liens, Warehouse Liens, Sale of Goods, Subrogation

- **Manitoba and Saskatchewan:** Innkeepers/Hotel Keepers, Common Carriers, Insurable Interest in a Life, Warehouse Storage

- **Ontario:** Common Carriers, *Consumer Protection Act 2002*, Pawnbrokers, Repair and Storage Liens, Warehousing, Innkeepers' Liability, Good Faith, Insurance Legislation, Subrogation, Duty to Disclose

- **Atlantic Provinces:** *Innkeepers' Act,* Insurance Legislation, *Mechanics' Lien Act*, Subrogation

Review Questions

1. "Finders keepers, losers weepers." Is that statement accurate, in whole or in part? Explain your answer.

2. There are different ways of classifying personal property. Use examples to explain the difference between tangible and intangible property, and between choses in possession and choses in action.

3. Identify and briefly explain four ways in which personal property rights can be acquired.

4. What is a "consignment"?

5. "You are always entitled to keep property that you find on someone else's premises." Explain the extent to which that statement is correct.

6. Identify and briefly explain four ways in which personal property rights can be lost.

7. What is a "fixture"? To whom does a fixture belong? Explain the factors that will influence a court's decision as to whether a chattel has become a fixture.

8. Define the term "bailment," and list the three elements of a bailment. Which party is the bailor, and which party is the bailee?

9. Define the word "licence" and explain how that idea applies within the law of bailment.

10. "Since the bailor is simply delivering possession of goods to the bailee, the bailor never has an obligation with respect to the quality of the property." Is that statement true? Illustrate your answer with an example.

11. Explain how the concept of a lien is important to some types of bailment.

12. Why does the law sometimes shift the burden of proof when the bailor complains that property has not been returned in a timely manner or in good condition? Briefly describe the situation in which the burden of proof will shift.

13. Explain the concept of deviance and explain how it is related to the defence of reasonable care that exists in a case of bailment.

14. Define the phrase "common carrier." Is every business that transports goods for a price a common carrier? Explain your answer.

15. "A common carrier is an insurer of bailed goods." What does that statement mean? Will a common carrier always be held responsible if goods are lost or damaged while in its possession? List three types of defences that a common carrier can use against a bailor. In practical terms, which type of defence is the most significant? Explain your answer.

16. Explain the process of sub-bailment and identify the parties that are involved in that process. Is a bailee always entitled to place goods into a sub-bailment?

17. Use examples to explain the difference between third party insurance and first party insurance.

18. Define the term "indemnification." Explain how the concept of indemnification affects the ideas of (i) an insurable interest, (ii) excessive insurance and insufficient insurance, and (iii) contribution and co-insurance.

19. Briefly explain the concept of "subrogation" in the context of property insurance.

20. Aside from basic property insurance and liability insurance, identify and briefly explain five specialized types of insurance that are important in business.

Cases and Problems

1. Abe Costello has a lengthy criminal record for car theft. Some time ago, a police officer observed him driving through a red light. When the officer demanded Costello's driver's licence and car registration, it became clear that the car was not registered. Further investigation also revealed that all the car's unique identifying elements (such as its serial number and engine identification number) had been expertly removed. Finally, upon opening the vehicle's trunk, the officer discovered tools used for breaking into cars, as well as a kit for forging car registration numbers. The officer confiscated the vehicle and Costello was charged with theft. Those criminal charges, however, were eventually dropped. Because of the "special modifications" done to the vehicle, the Crown prosecutor was unable to determine the car's original owner. It therefore was impossible to prove that Costello was guilty of theft. Several days later, the police were shocked when Costello demanded possession of the car. As the Chief of Police explained, "We all know that it isn't really his car, so we won't be giving it back to him." Assuming that the general common law rules apply, who is entitled to the car? Explain your answer.

2. The Lazy Lion Restaurant was owned and operated by Leon Lowe. Although the property upon which the restaurant was located was owned by Lowe, it was also subject to a mortgage in favour of Ursula Aust. Likewise, although Lowe owned most of the equipment that was located within the restaurant, the main oven was subject to a conditional sales agreement that Lowe had created with Jeremy Froelich. (Froelich did not register that agreement under any personal property security legislation, as discussed in Chapter 23.) That conditional sales agreement stated that while Lowe was immediately entitled to possession and use of the oven, Froelich retained ownership until the purchase price was paid in full. The agreement also stated that if Lowe failed to make a monthly payment, Froelich was entitled to re-acquire possession of the oven and to sue for damages. For reasons of safety and efficiency, Lowe had the oven bolted to the floor and actually incorporated into the adjacent wall. Exhaust shafts and electrical cords that were attached to the oven were similarly firmly built into the surrounding area.

The Lazy Lion unfortunately failed within two months of opening. That created a number of difficulties. On a personal level, Lowe was financially ruined. As a result, he was unable to meet his monthly payment requirements under the conditional sales agreement with Froelich. And for the same reason, he defaulted on his mortgage payments to Aust. Before Froelich was able to take any action, Aust began proceedings to exercise her right of foreclosure under the mortgage and to acquire ownership of the property (as explained in Chapter 16). A dispute consequently has arisen between Froelich and Aust. Aust claims that she is entitled to the entire mortgaged property, including the oven. Froelich claims that he continues to own the oven under the terms of the conditional sales contract and that he consequently is entitled to re-acquire possession of it. Who is right? Explain your answer.

3. Helen Cottee visited Franklin's Hardware Store and purchased a number of items. Because of the size and weight of those items, a store clerk provided Helen with a shopping cart to allow her to more easily transport the goods from the store to her car. While she was pushing the cart across the parking lot, however, one of its wheels fell off. The cart collapsed on Helen, causing extensive injuries. Helen brought an action against Franklin's seeking

compensation for the accident. Will she succeed? Explain your answer.

4. Ben Wicks was a tremendously successful cartoonist whose work appeared in over 270 newspapers worldwide. He produced thousands of drawings during his career, and he wanted to keep them all. He insisted, for example, that the publishers of his cartoons return his cartoons to him. He also charged his children with the responsibility of collecting his published works into scrapbooks. Two green garbage bags full of his drawings were stored at a house belonging to his son, Vincent. When Vincent moved house, however, he mistakenly left the bags behind. The new owner, Richard Harnett, found the bags and sold two of the cartoons to an art gallery for $425. Although Ben Wicks had died by that time, his estate demanded that Harnett hand over the drawings, together with his profit of $425. Harnett, in response, insists that "finders keepers, losers weepers." How would a court likely decide the dispute? Explain your answer.

5. Babe Ruth hit 60 home runs in 1927. Roger Maris hit 61 in 1961. Mark McGwire hit 70 in 1998. But in 2001, Barry Bonds surpassed them all. He wrote his name in the baseball record book with 73. His final home run that season also went into the law books. The game was held on October 7 in San Francisco. In anticipation of catching the record-setting ball, fans crowded into the outfield stands. Amongst them were Alex Popov and Patrick Hayashi. In the bottom of the first inning, Bonds connected with a knuckleball and sent it over the right field wall. The video evidence clearly shows the ball starting to enter the upper portion of Popov's outstretched baseball glove. Popov did not, however, have a chance to complete the catch. He was immediately swallowed up by the crowd and tackled to the ground. A mob descended on Popov with the obvious intention of seizing control of the ball. In the commotion, several other fans, including Hayashi, were knocked to the ground. A short time later, Hayashi crawled from the melee, stood up with the ball in his hand and was quickly whisked away by security personnel. A dispute then arose regarding ownership of the record-setting ball. There is no suggestion that Hayashi had participated in any of the violence. Popov did insist, however, that he had already acquired ownership of the ball by the time that Hayashi grabbed it off the ground. He also insisted that Hayashi therefore committed the tort of conversion (discussed in Chapter 4) when he took possession of the ball. The motivation for the lawsuit was, of course, profit. Although a baseball is normally worth only a few dollars, collectors are willing to pay a fortune for historical memorabilia. (For instance, the ball that Mark McGwire hit to set the record in 1998 was purchased for US$3 200 000.) Who owned the ball? Hayashi? Popov? Or perhaps the party (Major League Baseball) that had purchased the ball in the first place? Explain your answer.

6. Occidental & Atlantic (OA) is a shipping company that offers to deliver goods for anyone anywhere in the world. Mediterranean Imports Ltd wished to have $500 000 worth of silk sent from a port in northeast Italy to Halifax. It entered into a contract with OA that included the following provisions:

■ The carrier shall use whichever route is the most appropriate in the circumstances.

■ The carrier's liability for loss or damage caused by fire, storm, or act of God shall be limited to $500 per shipment.

■ Any disputes arising between the parties shall be resolved under the laws of Canada.

Shortly before the journey began, an armed conflict erupted in a region of the Balkans, which lies to the east of Italy. Although carriers regularly passed through the affected area when transporting goods from northeastern Italy to North America, most carriers chose to adopt alternative routes during the course of the conflict. The captain of OA's vessel, however, realized that any deviation from the standard course would be costly and therefore decided to proceed as usual. Unfortunately, the entire cargo of silk was lost when OA's ship was caught in crossfire and sank. Mediterranean Imports did not purchase first party insurance for its property and therefore is anxious to recover compensation from OA. Is it entitled to do so? Explain your answer.

7. Bobcat Marina operates a marina and dock in a resort area. Because its owner was cautious, it wanted to purchase the "widest possible insurance policy." After discussing its needs with Lloyd's of London Insurance Co, Bobcat purchased a policy that contained two important paragraphs:

■ You are insured against physical loss of or physical damage to the equipment, buildings, and contents specified in Section 2 of the Certificate if they are accidentally lost, stolen, destroyed, or damaged during the Period of Insurance other than by an excluded cause.

■ You are not insured against loss or damage caused by theft or malicious damage to property unless such property is contained in a securely locked building.

Other sections of the policy defined the terms "equipment," "buildings," and "contents" that appear in paragraph 2.1, but the policy does not define the word "property" that appears in paragraph 2.2. In addition to its dock, Bobcat's business premises also contains a large number of items, ranging from deck chairs, batteries, and picnic tables, to ice machines, gas pumps, and boat racks.

Late one night, a disgruntled ex-employee of Bobcat broke into the marina, vandalized several pieces of equipment, and drove the company's forklift off its dock and into the water. The dock and the forklift suffered extensive damage. Lloyd's insists that the resulting losses are not covered by the insurance policy because, contrary to the exclusion clause in paragraph 2.2, the forklift was not "contained in a securely locked building." Is Bobcat Marina entitled to be indemnified for the damage caused to the dock and the forklift? Explain your answer.

8. The plaintiff, Parvanh Backmirzie, owned two Persian rugs that she wanted to sell. She brought the rugs to a shop, called La Moquette Fine Rugs, which was owned by the defendant, Cathy Rinaldi. The parties agreed that the defendant would attempt to sell the rugs, on the plaintiff's behalf, at a price of $4850 each. The defendant was entitled to receive a 20 percent commission if and when the rugs were sold. Although the rugs did not attract the attention of any potential buyers, the defendant did notice two men who acted suspiciously while visiting her shop. The defendant immediately contacted the plaintiff, explained that the rugs probably were not going to sell, and warned the plaintiff that the two men appeared to be "casing" the shop in preparation for stealing the rugs. The plaintiff agreed that she should collect the rugs, but said that she was busy for the next few days. Two days later, the defendant closed her shop at the end of the day, turned on the security alarm, and hid the rugs under other merchandise. The store was burgled that night and the two rugs were stolen. Neither party had insurance to cover the loss. The plaintiff now claims that the defendant is liable for failing to properly safeguard the rugs. Provide an analysis of the legal issues raised by the facts. Describe the parties' relationship. How much care was the defendant required to exercise?

9. Western Paper Inc's warehouse was located next to Thames Explosives Ltd's factory. As a result of a careless manufacturing process, a fire erupted in Thames' premises and soon spread next door. By the time the blaze was contained by the local fire department, $100 000 worth of Western's product had been destroyed. Western had purchased from Fortress Insurance first party coverage that entitled it to compensation for losses attributable to fire. Thames had purchased from Sentinel Insurance third party coverage that entitled it to complete protection from losses that it carelessly inflicted as a result of careless manufacturing processes. Explain how the insurance policies will apply in this case. Who will ultimately pay for the loss created by Thames and sustained by Western? Explain your answer.

10. Horst and Jurgen Romani grew up in Europe. As an adult, Horst immigrated to Vancouver. Jurgen remained behind and, while in France, developed an idea for a perfume company. He then began to purchase the necessary supplies and equipment. As his project neared fruition, he asked his brother to join him in the venture. Although Horst was initially skeptical, he was eventually persuaded and agreed to meet the expenses associated with transporting Jurgen and his materials from France to Canada. Horst also gave his brother $11 000 to purchase additional materials. Once they were reunited in British Columbia, the pair informally agreed that they would create a company named Roma France Ltd to manufacture and distribute perfume in this country. They did not, however, actually go through the process of incorporation.

Furthermore, while all the property was stored in Horst's basement, it still belonged to Jurgen. Horst nevertheless purchased a fire insurance policy for it. In fact, a fire did occur and destroyed all the equipment and supplies that the brothers had intended to use in their business. The insurance company, however, has refused to honour the policy on the grounds that the property in question belonged to Jurgen, with the result that Horst did not have an insurable interest in it. Is the insurer's argument persuasive? Explain your answer.

11. Nocturna Mattress Ltd kept a large inventory of beds in its warehouse. As a matter of internal management, it tried to keep about $60 000 worth of stock on hand at all times. It purchased property insurance from Citadel Insurance. That policy contained a co-insurance clause that called for the insured to hold 80 percent coverage. Nocturna nevertheless chose to pay for only $30 000 worth of coverage. As a result of a cycle of heavy snowfall and warm weather, Nocturna's warehouse was flooded, and much of its inventory sustained irreparable water damage. It therefore has made a claim under its policy with Citadel. How much will Nocturna receive if (i) the total loss was valued at $50 000, (ii) the total loss was valued at $40 000, and (iii) the total loss was valued at $30 000 and the policy also contained a $5000 deductible? Explain your answers.

12. The plaintiff, Socratis Reppas, is a goldsmith. The defendant, Shahram Mirkalami, is an auctioneer. The parties' relationship began 10 years ago. They developed a practice under which the plaintiff delivered jewellery to the defendant, together with a minimum price. The defendant then attempted to sell the goods. By way of profit, the defendant was entitled to keep sale proceeds in excess of the plaintiff's minimum price. Any jewellery that did not sell was to be immediately returned to the plaintiff. The relationship was very informal. The plaintiff kept a running list of items handed over to the defendant, but otherwise business was done on the basis of spoken words and handshakes. The situation unfortunately fell apart last year. The plaintiff had a list of 40 items that the defendant had neither returned nor provided sale proceeds for. After considerable argument, the defendant accounted for 27 of the items, but he now denies ever receiving the remaining 13 pieces of jewellery. How would a court resolve the dispute? Explain how a judge would deal with the general lack of evidence and the issues of proof.

PART 4

18 Intellectual Property

LEARNING OBJECTIVES

After completing this chapter, you should be able to:

❶ Demonstrate how businesses can generate value from ideas.

❷ Explain the competing interests that intellectual property laws seek to balance.

❸ Determine whether a particular creation is protected under copyright legislation.

❹ Outline the protection offered under trademark law, and determine whether an action for trademark infringement may succeed.

❺ Distinguish between trademark infringement and passing off.

❻ Discuss the patentability of inventions, and identify possible grounds of infringement.

❼ Explain how the international patent system streamlines the process for patent protection across multiple jurisdictions.

❽ Explain how intellectual property law protects industrial designs.

❾ Describe the nature of confidential information and the remedies available when confidentiality is breached.

❿ Discuss trade secrets as a means of protecting ideas.

In recent years many entrepreneurs have come to believe that the power of ideas—not just the tangible goods derived from them—can transform the way we do business. A business that fully capitalizes on its ideas can create "global competition—not just for running shoes and laptop computers, but also for bank loans and other services that cannot be packed into a crate and shipped. A world in which innovation is more important than mass production. A world in which investment buys new concepts or the means to create them, rather than new machines."[1] Consider, for example, the powerful ideas of four under-graduates from Harvard College named Mark, Eduardo, Dustin, and Chris, who developed a "hot or not" social media website called facesmash.com in 2004. With a minor name change and eight years of development, their ideas (remember, relatively few tangible goods were required) were valued at $104 billion, resulting in one of the largest IPOs in history, just behind companies such as VISA Inc and General Motors.

Intellectual property is a key enabler of Facebook and other emerging business models. Intellectual property provides a means of generating value from ideas. We begin this chapter with an examination of ideas as a form of property. We then investigate the central legal mechanisms by which ideas and other non-tangible assets can be controlled and harnessed for profit: intellectual property laws. There are several types of intellectual property law that are reviewed in this chapter: copyright, trademarks, patents, industrial designs, and a related area of law known as trade secrets (sometimes called confidential information). Two additional, and more narrow, categories—integrated circuit topography and plant breeders' rights—are not discussed here.

Ideas as Property

L.O. ❶

THE NATURE OF IDEAS

When we talk about property, usually we are talking about tangible objects—things that can be picked up, passed around, trampled upon, traded, bought, or sold. Running shoes, laptop computers, and other forms of tangible property are capable of *exclusive possession*. **Exclusive possession** characterizes an individual's ability to exercise power over a thing to the exclusion of all others. I can keep you from wearing my sneakers by tying them to my feet. I can stop you from using my laptop computer by locking it in my office. Exclusive possession is possible in the case of tangible goods because they occupy space and can therefore remain in the sole control of those who possess them.

Ideas are different. Exclusive possession of ideas is impossible. I can try to keep my ideas secret but, once they are known to others, I cannot tie them to my feet or lock them in a room. Nor can I prevent you from coming up with the very same idea. In addition to being non-exclusive, ideas are also *non-rivalrous*. Something is **non-rivalrous** when my possession and enjoyment of it does not diminish your ability to do the same. For example, think about a television broadcast. The fact that I have turned on my TV set to watch a show does not interfere with your ability to do the same. Ideas can be

exclusive possession characterizes an individual's ability to exercise power over a thing to the exclusion of all others

a thing is **non-rivalrous** when my possession and enjoyment of it does not diminish your ability to do the same

PART 5

[1.] J Browning & S Reiss *Encyclopaedia of the New Economy* (2002) at 1.

disseminated *en masse*. And, in the age of Twitter, you don't need a broadcast studio to do so.

THE ECONOMICS OF IDEAS

When the creator of an idea has the sole aim of spreading its gospel, the fact that ideas are non-rivalrous is seen as a benefit. However, many creators of ideas have additional motives. As the saying goes, "Information wants to be free. It also wants to be expensive."[2] For example, why would the creators of books—whose livelihoods depend upon the number of copies sold—spend years writing, while passing up other financial opportunities, if they knew that anyone could easily reproduce their book without their permission, without cost or sanction? There is far less incentive for creators of ideas to toil in their creation if those ideas, once developed, can be universally possessed without compensation.

Running shoes and laptops are property—they are bought and sold. My incentive to make shoes or laptops depends largely on the *natural scarcity* of those items. **Natural scarcity** occurs when the supply of a natural resource is inadequate. Because natural resources are finite, the market value of those resources usually increases when supplies become inadequate. Ideas are not usually subject to natural scarcity. Because ideas are non-exclusive and non-rivalrous, they can be possessed by the world at large at virtually zero cost without any loss of enjoyment. Therefore, ideas are not as easily bought and sold as running shoes and computers. To create a market for them, an *artificial scarcity* must be introduced. **Artificial scarcity** occurs when an idea is rendered exclusive and rivalrous, thereby rendering its supply inadequate. Businesses depend upon the creation of an artificial scarcity to increase the value of their ideas and other business-related information, and to encourage investment in creation and innovation. The means by which such artificial scarcity is introduced into the marketplace of ideas is through the laws of intellectual property. Intellectual property is a lifeline for modern businesses.

L.O. ❷❸❹❺❻❼❽

Intellectual Property Law

Intellectual property law aims to protect products of the mind. Although it does this to provide incentives to creators, intellectual property recognizes that creators should not be able to monopolize their ideas indefinitely. To allow a monopoly of ideas would grind human progress to a halt. Creators must be able to build on the creative works and ideas of those who came before them. In 1676, for example, Sir Isaac Newton famously acknowledged his debt to Robert Hooke, who came before him: "If I have seen further it is by standing on ye shoulders of Giants." Consequently, **intellectual property law** is a set of rules that aims to balance the rights of a creator against the public interest. They provide time-limited monopolies to certain types of innovations, goods, and services in exchange for sharing them with the public. The tension between these sometimes competing interests is readily apparent when a court is asked to establish a new legal precedent. Consider the decision in Case Brief 18.1.

natural scarcity occurs when the supply of a natural resource is inadequate

artificial scarcity occurs when an idea is rendered exclusive and rivalrous, thereby rendering its supply inadequate

intellectual property law is a set of rules that aims to balance the rights of a creator against the public interest

---

[2.] S Brand *The Media Lab: Inventing the Future at MIT* (1988) at 202.

Case Brief 18.1

Théberge v Galérie d'Art du Petit Champlain (2002) 210 DLR (4th) 385 (SCC)

Claude Théberge, an internationally known Quebec painter, sued a gallery for making an illegal copy of his work. The gallery had purchased a poster from Théberge and, using sophisticated technology, literally lifted the ink right off the poster and transferred it to canvas. No copies of the work were made, and the poster was blank once the process was complete.

The Supreme Court of Canada held that, because no copy had been made in the transfer process, there was no infringement of copyright. In reaching its decision the court emphasized the importance of balance in copyright law, noting the danger to our society if the balance in copyright tilts too far toward copyright owners: "Excessive control by holders of copyrights and other forms of intellectual property may unduly limit the ability of the public domain to incorporate and embellish creative innovation in the long-term interests of society as a whole, or create practical obstacles to proper utilization."

The *Thébergev Galérie d'Art du Petit Champlain* case marked the first time our Supreme Court placed such significant emphasis on user rights, the public interest, and balance in intellectual property law. The court seemed to affirm the principle that stronger intellectual property protection does not necessarily create greater incentives for the creation of original works and may, in fact, be contrary to the long-term interests of society.

The tension between the public interest and private rights—the idea that information wants to be both free and expensive—is a recurring theme of intellectual property law.

COPYRIGHT

Copyright does not protect ideas, but rather the manner in which ideas are expressed. It rewards and protects an author's efforts by giving the author an exclusive right to publish or otherwise control the distribution of a creative work. Copyright is a creature of statute. The *Copyright Act* provides creators with both economic and moral rights as incentive to produce creative expression.[3] The Act presents a balance between promoting expressive works for public consumption while, at the same time, providing various means of compensating authors for their effort. The Supreme Court described this intricate balance in the *Théberge* case: "In crassly economic terms it would be as inefficient to overcompensate artists and authors for the right of reproduction as it would be self-defeating to undercompensate them."

Many people are under the mistaken impression that a copyright must be registered in order to be enforceable. In fact, although copyrights can be registered, copyright protection arises automatically upon the creation of an original work in a fixed medium. To protect the creative process, the law prohibits others from copying an author's work for a specified period of time to allow the author to benefit from the work, whether or not the author registers the copyright. Unless ownership of the copyright is somehow transferred to another person or waived, only the author is permitted to produce or reproduce a work, and only the author can authorize others to do the same.

copyright does not protect ideas, but rather the manner in which ideas are expressed

PART 5

Requirements for Copyright Protection

For a work to enjoy copyright protection in Canada, it must be a work recognized under the *Copyright Act* and meet three requirements:

- The work must be *original*.
- The work must be *fixed*.

---

[3] *Copyright Act*, RSC 1985, c C-42 (Can).

■ The author of the work must be *connected to Canada* (or to a World Trade Organization, Berne, Rome, or Universal Copyright Convention member state).

original work is work that is not copied from any other source but derived through the exercise of the author's (non-trivial and non-mechanical) skill and judgment

ORIGINALITY The "originality" requirement is perhaps a lower threshold than the term might imply. In copyright law, **original work** is work that is not copied from any other source but derived through the exercise of the author's skill and judgment. The author's efforts in this regard must not be so trivial as to be a purely mechanical exercise. For example, when you take notes in your business law class, even if the main ideas all come from the professor, your notes will probably count as "original" so long as you have organized them in a way that makes sense to you, using your own headings and cutting out any confusing points. The same would not be true if you simply copied every single word of the lecture verbatim.[4]

FIXATION Although the Act does not expressly stipulate this, copyright is usually restricted to the expression of a work in a fixed medium. For example, a choreography must have its scenic arrangement fixed, usually in writing. Likewise, a broadcast must be recorded on tape or some other medium while being transmitted. There is a similar requirement for computer programs. The aim of such requirements is to add certainty to the law. By insisting that an author is capable of identifying the work and demonstrating that it persists in some medium, the courts ultimately prevent improper claims of spontaneous activities (such as oral conversations) from enjoying copyright protection.[5]

AUTHOR'S CONNECTION TO CANADA A work is subject to Canadian copyright law only if its author has some connection to Canada. All work created in Canada is protected. However, work created outside of Canada by a Canadian national or an ordinary resident of Canada is also protected. Because of a number of international treaties, copyright eligibility extends even further. Any author of an original work who is a citizen of, or ordinarily resident in, a country that is subject to the Berne Copyright Convention, the Rome Convention, the Universal Copyright Convention, or the World Trade Organization is protected by Canadian copyright law regardless of where the work was created. This is an important point for business owners, who must take care to minimize the risk of their employees copying foreign material under the mistaken impression that it is not subject to Canadian law.

Forms of Expression That Are Protected

There are several ways in which an author can express an idea. The *Copyright Act* refers specifically to seven forms of expression that are protected. Figure 18.1 provides examples of each.

Some forms of expression are not protected by copyright. Slogans, short phrases, titles, names, and factual information are not generally subject to copyright law. Factual information is considered to be part of the public domain. Where a business report or recipe contains factual information, it is the expression of the information that is subject to protection, not the facts themselves; "were the law otherwise . . . everybody who made a rabbit pie in

---

[4.] See *Ladbroke (Football) Ltd v Williams Hill (Football) Ltd* [1964] 1 All ER 465 (HL). See also *CCH Canadian Ltd v Law Society of Upper Canada* (2004) 236 DLR (4th) 395 (SCC).

[5.] See *Gould Estate v Stoddart Publishing Co* (1996) 30 OR 520 (Gen Div); *Canadian Admiral Corp v Rediffusion Inc* [1954] Ex CR 382.

FIGURE 18.1 Seven Forms of Expression Protected by Copyright

	Examples of Copyright Material
literary works	stories, textbooks, instruction manuals, compilations, translations, computer programs, poems, lyrics independent of/without music
dramatic works	films, videos, DVDs, screenplays, choreography, scenic arrangements, recitals
musical works	compositions, melodies, harmonies, sheet music
artistic works	paintings, drawings, photos, sculptures, engravings, maps, charts, architectural works
performances	acting, dancing, singing, drumming
sound recordings	records, cassettes, compact discs, digital music
communication signals	broadcast signals

Source: Industry Canada *A Guide to Copyrights* (2010) at 4.

accordance with the recipe of Mrs Beeton's cookery book would infringe the literary copyright in that book."[6]

Copyright Ownership and Economic Rights

Our discussion of copyright has so far focused on the perspective of the author. Copyright provides important economic rights in creative expression. Although the author of a work is generally the initial copyright owner, these economic rights can be unbundled into several discrete rights, many of which can be bought, sold, licensed, or given away. This gives copyright holders—whether it is the initial author or someone else—a multitude of business opportunities. Figure 18.2 summarizes these rights.

While the author of a work is *generally* the first copyright owner, an important exception occurs in the employment context. Generally, the copyright in a work created by an employee in the course of employment is owned by the employer. For example, copyright in a government brochure developed by a public servant belongs not to the brochure's creator but to the Crown. Note that the rule does not generally cover independent contractors. To obtain ownership, businesses that engage independent contractors to generate the expression of ideas should stipulate in their contracts that copyright is held by the business and not the contractor.

Recall that the copyright owner has the legal power to prevent others from copying the work. Some authors and artists are interested in exploiting such power for monetary gains, but others are not. Those who, for any reason, are not interested in monetary gains can use their legal power to prevent others from gaining access to their work. For example, American author JD Salinger once used the law of copyright to block the publication of his private letters.[7]

[6.] *Cuisenaire v South West Imports Limited* [1969] SCR 208.

[7.] *Salinger v Random House Inc* (1976) 811 F2d 90 (2d Cir).

FIGURE 18.2 The Bundle of Rights Held by the Copyright Owner

the right to *produce, reproduce, perform, or publish a work*
the right to *translate* a work
the right to *convert* a dramatic work into a novel, non-dramatic work, or sound recording
the right to *convert* a non-dramatic or artistic work into a dramatic work through public performance
the right to *communicate* a work by telecommunication
the right to *reproduce, adapt,* or *present* a work by film or photograph
the right to *present* an artistic work at a public exhibition (works created after June 7, 1988)
the right to *create* a sound recording of a musical work
the right to *license* computer software
the right to *reproduce* any performance that has been fixed
the right to *fix* any performance that has not yet been fixed
the right to *reproduce, license, or publish* sound recordings
the right to *fix* or reproduce broadcast signals
the right to *authorize* another broadcaster to simultaneously retransmit the signal

Source: Industry Canada *A Guide to Copyrights* (2000) at 3–4.

royalties are monetary compensation given to an author in exchange for the use of their intellectual property

an **advance on royalties** is an interest-free incentive that is paid to the author before the completion of a work and is later deducted from the sum of royalties

copyright collectives are organizations that administer certain rights granted by the copyright system on behalf of copyright owners who are members of the collective

Salinger also exploited the power of copyright law in the usual manner by transferring aspects of the copyright he owned to a book publisher in exchange for *royalties*. **Royalties** are monetary compensation given to an author in exchange for the use of their intellectual property. Royalties are usually expressed as a percentage of the publisher's receipts from the sales associated with the copyrighted material. Some publishers even offer an author an incentive to write by way of an *advance on royalties*. An **advance on royalties** is an interest-free incentive that is paid to the author before the completion of a work and that is later deducted from the sum of royalties.

A number of creative business methods have been implemented to allow copyright holders to monetize their copyrights. Licensing schemes have been developed to both (i) allow people to use copyrighted material without having to seek permission and (ii) provide compensation to the copyright owner for use of the material. For example, it is now permissible in Canada to make a copy of a musical recording for private use without seeking authorization (such as burning a CD from your digital library to listen to in your car). This is made possible by a blank audio recording media levy.[8] Instead of trying to stop private copying, a compensation scheme transfers a percentage of revenue from the sale of blank recordable media back to the copyright owners through *copyright collectives*. **Copyright collectives** are organizations that administer certain rights granted by the copyright system on behalf of copyright owners who are members of the collective. In the case of the audio recording media levy, the Canadian Private Copying Collective is responsible for collecting the levy. The monies collected are ultimately redistributed to performing artists, composers and lyricists, music publishers, and record companies through their own collectives, such as the Society of Composers, Authors and Music Publishers of Canada (SOCAN). In 2008 the Canadian Federal Court of Appeal ruled that digital audio recording devices such as iPods and MP3 players are not subject to such a levy.[9]

[8.] See Part VIII, 'Private Copying,' *Copyright Act*, RSC 1985, c C-42 (Can).

[9.] See *Apple Canada Inc et al v Canadian Private Copying Collective et al* (2008) FCA 9.

Duration of Copyright

Copyrights do not last forever. Unlike property in tangible objects—which continues to exist until such objects are given away, sold, consumed, or ruined—the bundle of rights inherent in copyright *always* comes to an end. When it does, the work is said to pass into the *public domain*. The **public domain** is the realm of works that belong to the community at large and that can be used by anyone. For example, the works of Shakespeare are in the public domain; the song "Happy Birthday" is not.[10] In Canada, the duration of copyright generally lasts for the life of the author and then for 50 years following the end of the calendar year in which the author dies. In the European Union and the United States, the general duration of copyright has changed to last for the life of the author plus 70 years.

the **public domain** is the realm of works that belong to the community at large and that can be used by anyone

Moral Rights

In addition to the bundle of economic rights that constitute copyright, the creation of an original work also gives rise to a separate package of *moral rights*, which are legally enforceable.[11] Moral rights are considered to be so important that they cannot be bought or sold—they are retained by the author even if ownership in a copyright is subsequently transferred to someone else. **Moral rights** include (i) the right of attribution, (ii) the right of integrity over a work, and (iii) the right to be associated (or not associated) with a work.

moral rights include the right of attribution, the right of integrity over a work, and the right to be associated (or not associated) with a work

The right of attribution allows authors to ensure that their names are attached to the work. It also allows an author to remain anonymous or to work under a pseudonym. In either case, the attribution right prevents others, even if they own the copyright, from using the work and claiming it as their own.

The right of integrity provides an author with a further degree of control over the work after it is sold. It allows an author to prevent others from distorting, mutilating, or otherwise modifying the work where doing so would prejudice the author's honour or reputation. A famous Canadian artist exercised that right by forcing a shopping mall to remove Christmas decorations from his sculptures.[12] Note that the right of integrity in a work is not always easy to enforce. Often what one party sees as the distortion or modification of a work is perceived as free speech by another, or as an exercise of a right in the tangible property. Although the distortion of a work is sometimes grounds for a lawsuit, the courts will not always view the total destruction of a work as prejudicing the author's reputation.

The fact that an author retains moral rights in a work even after it is sold is offset by the fact that moral rights can be waived by the author. This is an important consideration for businesses that buy and sell copyrighted content. From a risk management perspective, a business should consider whether to include a contractual condition requiring an author to waive their moral rights. In some circumstances, this will provide the business with a greater ability to control the content that it has purchased with no strings attached.

Copyright Infringement

Since the owner has an exclusive right to control the use of a work (as well as all associated economic rights outlined in Figure 18.2), anyone who makes an

---

[10.] Purchased for $15 million by Warner/Chappell in 1990, "Happy Birthday" is said to generate nearly $2 million in annual royalties in the United States alone and is expected to continue doing so until its copyright expires in 2030: R Brauneis "Copyright and the World's Most Popular Song" *GWU Legal Studies Research Paper No 1111624*: <http://ssrn.com/abstract=1111624>.

[11.] The name derives from the French *droits moraux*, which is better understood as a "personal right."

[12.] *Snow v Eaton Centre Ltd* (1982) 70 CPR (2d) 105 (Ont HCJ).

a **copyright infringement** occurs when a person other than the owner makes an unauthorized or unlicensed use of all or a substantial part of a work with no legal basis for doing so

unauthorized or unlicensed use of all or a substantial part of that work is said to have committed a **copyright infringement** unless they have a legal basis for doing so. For example, even though the owner has a right of public performance, you are permitted to reproduce songs in a private performance without running afoul of the law. For instance, you are legally permitted to sing "Happy Birthday" in your basement at your son's birthday party. The same would not be true if his birthday party is being broadcast on national television. Unless you pay a licensing fee to perform the song in public, you are infringing copyright. There are numerous forms of copyright infringement. Figure 18.3 outlines some examples.

The digital world poses unique opportunities and challenges for copyright owners. On one hand, digital works can be distributed by copyright owners to millions of people on the Internet or on peer-to-peer networks at minimal cost. On the other hand, digital technologies have made it easier for individuals to infringe copyright works and to share the infringing copies with millions of other people through a simple click of a mouse. After a decade of deeply contested nationwide debate on copyright reform, the governor general of Canada granted royal assent to *The Copyright Modernization Act* on June 29, 2012.[13]

a **technological protection measure** is any effective technology, device, or component that, in the ordinary course of its operation, controls access to a work

Following in the footsteps of the United States's *Digital Millennium Copyright Act*, Canada's *Copyright Modernization Act* adopts a number of new measures that provide significant additional protection against copyright infringement in the digital medium.[14] One important example is a new provision that protects digital locks (referred to in the Act as a *technological protection measure*). The Act defines a **technological protection measure** as "any effective technology, device or component that, in the ordinary course of its operation . . . controls access to a work."[15] Section 41.1 provides new legal remedies for copyright owners who use digital locks to protect their content, creating new forms of infringement for those who tamper with those locks. The provision is controversial because it operates even if alleged lock breakers never infringe copyright and, even if they have a legal right of access to the content secured by the lock.

FIGURE 18.3 Examples of Copyright Infringement

Infringement	Not Infringement
reprinting an article without the copyright owner's permission	quoting a few lines of the article in a research paper (fair dealing)
playing records at a dance without the copyright owner's permission	playing records at home
giving a public performance of a modern play without permission	giving a public performance of a play by Shakespeare (no copyright exists—public domain)
photocopying articles for a class of students without permission	obtaining permission from the author and paying a fee to them (if requested) to use an article
taping your favourite band at a music concert without permission	borrowing a DVD from a friend to copy onto a blank DVD for private use (a royalty payment to the owner of the song rights was paid when the blank DVD was purchased)

Source: Adapted from Industry Canada *A Guide to Copyrights* (2000) at 6.

[13.] This is the short title for a bundle of copyright reforms enacted in *An Act to Amend the Copyright Act* (The Copyright Modernization Act *[CMA]*), *SC 2012, c 20*.

[14.] *Digital Millennium Copyright Act* (*DMCA*), 17 USC (1998).

[15.] *Copyright Modernization Act*, SC 2012, c 20, s 41.

It remains to be seen whether the digital lock provision and a number of other new measures enacted to protect copyright owners against infringement will maintain copyright's delicate balance, or whether the net effect of Canada's copyright reform will unduly impair citizens' ability to access information through an excessive locking up of digital content.[16] The recent measures protecting copyright owners against infringement are summarized below in Figure 18.4.

The law of copyright protects not merely whole works but also substantial parts of a work against infringement. The notion of a *substantial part* is as much a qualitative judgment as it is a quantitative one. The general principle is that copyright owners cannot protect every particle of a work, where the taking of that piece would not undermine the overall value of the work. For example, borrowing 60 lines of code in a software routine that consists of 14 000 lines was

FIGURE 18.4   Measures Protecting Copyright Owners against Infringement in *The Copyright Modernization Act*

Provision	Its Effect
Technological protection measures (digital locks)	• protects copyright owners by creating an absolute restrictionon the circumvention of digital locks and other copyright access controls • makes breaking a digital lock illegal even if access to the work is permissible under copyright law • results in intention having no effect on liability
File sharing/ISP Liability	• protects copyright owners by holding peer-to-peer file sharing sites and Internet service providers (ISPs) accountable for copyright infringements committed by their customers • bases liability on whether the service provider enables public access to copyrighted materials knowingly or intentionally
Notice-and-notice	• protects copyright owners through a clarification of the role of ISPs in copyright enforcement • requires ISPs to notify customers of suspected copyright infringement upon receipt of notice from a copyright owner. Failure to comply may result in an award of statutory damages against the ISP in the order of $5000–$10 000.
Statutory damages for commercial and non-commercial infringements	• protects copyright owners by creating two distinct categories of damage awards: commercial and non-commercial; commercial infringements range from $500–$20 000 per work infringed
Performer/sound recordings	• confers a new right for copyright owners to make performances and sound recordings available to the public over the Internet
Ownership of photographs and commissioned artwork	• protects photographers by harmonizing their works with literary, dramatic, musical, and artistic works while, at the same time, permitting those who commission the creation of photographic works to use them for private or non-commercial purposes

PART 5

[16.] For discussions about the potential implications of these developments, see <www.speakoutoncopyright.ca> and <www.michaelgeist.ca/content/view/6544/125/>

held not to infringe copyright.[17] On the other hand, taking just a few important bars from the chorus of a pop song may be substantial.

The Right to Use Another's Works

As Ethical Perspective 18.1 illustrates, "all rights reserved" is not the motto of every copyright owner. As an antidote to the "all rights reserved" approach, intellectual property law aims to balance the rights of copyright owners with the public interest in having adequate access to the material. Therefore, copyright law provides a number of broad exemptions. For example, music may be performed without permission or licence at an event held for an educational or charitable purpose, or any activity incidental to it.[18] Likewise, what might otherwise amount to a copyright infringement is often excused where a person has good cause to deal with the material as a matter of public interest.

Ethical Perspective **18.1**

Creative Commons and Open Source

In response to what some see as an overemphasis of owner rights in the *Copyright Act*, there has been a significant increase in alternative copyright licensing tools. One such tool is Creative Commons Canada; another is open-source licences. Creative Commons Canada operates a website that offers artists a number of options for constructing and attaching copyright licences to their works. Creators can, for example, choose to permit others to copy, modify, and share their works, provided that credit is given to the artists and the works are not put to commercial use. These alternative licences allow copyright holders to disseminate their works without the strict limitations of the *Copyright Act*. It is important to note that these alternative schemes still rely on copyright law—both its protections (to enforce compliance) and its exceptions (to allow users the freedom to experiment with content in new and innovative ways).

A company has recently started a new record label. Many of its artists have expressed an interest in Creative Commons Canada. The company is anxious to know how those new copyright licensing tools might affect its business. Visit Creative Commons Canada's website at http://creativecommons.org and answer the following questions.

Questions for Discussion

1. Are there any moral aspects to the decision of whether to reserve only some rights, rather than all rights? Would the decision to reserve only some rights always be disadvantageous from a business perspective?

2. Does the issue of moral rights come into play? Explain why or why not.

3. The record label is concerned that none of the licences would meet its business needs. Is this true? Explain why or why not.

4. Recommend one of the Creative Commons Canada licences for the record label to consider, and explain why it might be a good fit for its digital repository.

fair dealing encompasses several enumerated categories of legitimate use of a work, including private study, research, criticism, review, or news reporting

The most well-known exemption is *fair dealing*. **Fair dealing** encompasses several enumerated categories of legitimate use of a work, including private study, research, criticism, review, or news reporting. Whether a particular dealing is "fair" is a matter to be determined by a court. In making its determination, a court must first decide whether the activity falls within one of the enumerated categories of fair dealing. If it does, the court will then consider the following six factors: (i) the purpose of the dealing; (ii) the character of the dealing; (iii) the amount of the dealing; (iv) whether there were alternatives to copying; (v) the nature of the work; and (vi) the effect of the dealing on the work. Drawing a bright line between fair dealing and infringement is not always possible. However, once an act of copying is deemed "fair dealing," it is not understood merely as a defence to copyright infringement but as a broader "user right" that enables public access. Business Decision 18.1 provides an illustration.

[17.] *Delrina Corp v Triolet Systems Inc* (1993) 47 CPR (3d) 1 (Ont Gen Div), aff'd (2002) 17 CPR (4th) 289 (Ont CA). This decision was not based merely on the actual percentage copied but also on the fact that "their extent was so slight, and their effect so small, as to render the taking perfectly immaterial."

[18.] *CAPAC v Kiwanis Club of West Toronto* [1953] 2 SCR 111.

Business Decision 18.1

CCH Canadian Ltd v Law Society of Upper Canada (2004) 236 DLR (4th) 395 (SCC)

In March 2004, the Supreme Court of Canada issued a significant ruling regarding originality, fair dealing for research, and liability for authorizing copyright infringement. The Law Society of Upper Canada (LSUC) operated a law library. The library offered a custom photocopy service whereby the library would copy materials and deliver them to patrons in person, by mail, or by fax. LSUC also provided and maintained self-service photocopiers in its library. It posted a notice near the copiers, which stated that LSUC was not responsible for any infringement of copyright.

The plaintiff, CCHCanadian Ltd, was a publisher of legal materials, including court decisions with headnotes. Headnotes typically consist of keywords and a short summary of a court decision. Like many other legal publishers, CCH created original headnotes, which it placed at the beginning of the reported court decisions. CCH claimed that LSUC was infringing copyright by copying the headnotes, along with the court decisions, and faxing them to patrons. CCH also claimed that, by providing self-service photocopiers, LSUC was liable for authorizing its patrons' infringement of copyright.

With respect to CCH's infringement claims, the court found in favour of LSUC. The court held that LSUC was not infringing copyright by copying and sending materials to its patrons. The court adopted a large and liberal interpretation of fair dealing for "research." The court held that "research" is not limited to non-commercial or private contexts, and that LSUC was engaged in fair dealing for the purpose of the "research" of its patrons. Although LSUC was not engaged in its own research, its activities were carried out for the sole purpose of research and were a necessary and integral part of the research of its patrons.

The court also held that LSUC did not authorize copyright infringement by maintaining self-service photocopiers in its library: "[A] person does not authorize copyright infringement by authorizing the mere use of equipment (such as photocopiers) that could be used to infringe copyright. In fact, courts should presume that a person who authorizes an activity does so only so far as it is in accordance with the law." The court went on to add that "even if there were evidence of the photocopiers having been used to infringe copyright, [LSUC] lacks sufficient control over [its] patrons to permit the conclusion that it sanctioned, approved or countenanced the infringement."

Questions for Discussion

1. CCH invests significant resources in the production and publication of its headnotes. Given that their primary function is to assist in legal research and that they are used by almost all lawyers from time to time, can you think of a different business model that publishers of headnotes might adopt instead of suing their potential clients for copyright infringement?

2. Is there any real difference between what LSUC was doing and what university students do when they make copies of their textbooks for their friends?

The Copyright Modernization Act, discussed above, expands the purposes relating to fair dealing to include three additional categories: education, parody, and satire. Section 29.21 of the Act creates a new fair dealing exception for content generated by non-commercial users (the "mashup" exception). This exception has important ramifications for business models that incorporate user-generated content, which we examine in greater detail in Chapter 19. Section 29.22 of the Act provides that consumers have the right to reproduce for a private purpose any work or protected subject matter if the source copy was legally obtained (the "format-shifting" provision). This allows music and other works subject to copyright, once purchased, to be moved from one device to another. Section 29.23 permits individuals to make a fixation of a communication signal or to reproduce a work, sound recording, or performance being broadcast for the purpose of privately viewing the work at a later time (the "time-shifting" exception). This allows people to enjoy the works they have purchased as part of a broadcast whenever it is convenient for them, just as they were previously able to do with video recorders.

TRADEMARKS

A **trademark** is a word or words, symbol, or design that is used to distinguish one person's goods or services from another's in the marketplace. While copyright is meant to protect the expression of ideas, trademarks

a **trademark** is a word or words, symbol, or design that is used to distinguish one person's goods or services from another's in the marketplace

protect the image and reputation of the business, its brand recognition, and the goodwill that it has developed. Viewed from the consumer perspective, trademarks are necessary to distinguish the origin of goods and services. In serving the public interest, a trademark is "a guarantee of origin and inferentially, an assurance to the consumer that the quality will be what he or she has come to associate with a particular trade-mark (as in the case of the mythical 'Maytag' repairman). It is, in that sense, consumer protection legislation."[19]

Following on the heels of the statutory expansion of fair dealing in the *Copyright Modernization Act*, the Supreme Court of Canada released its most important interpretation of fair dealing in the history of Canadian copyright law in July 2012. In a series of five cases now referred to asCanada's "copyright pentalogy," the Supreme Court reaffirmed its earlier position in *CCH* (see Business Decision 18.1 above), prescribing fair dealing as a "user right" that enables significant access to copyrighted works.[20] In the two decisions that focused on fair dealing, the Supreme Court endorsed a low threshold for coming within fair dealing categories such as "research" or "private study." For instance, in *SOCAN v Bell Canada*, the Supreme Court ruled that the purpose of "research" in a given case is to be interpreted broadly and from the perspective of the user, not the service provider. In *Alberta (Education) v Access Copyright*, the Supreme Court held that "research" is not limited to a scholarly inquiry but carries over to lifelong learning and even daily information seeking. Similarly, "private study" does not require isolation or solitude but can occur in a classroom or as a group activity. Consequently, teachers who reproduce excerpts from textbooks and other copyrighted materials are protected by fair dealing when distributing them to students as part of their classroom studies. Likewise, online music providers who allow their subscribers to listen to 30-to-90-second "previews" of copyrighted songs are able to claim fair dealing against copyright collectives seeking royalties. From a risk management perspective, coming to terms with the expansion of fair dealing will be important for businesses that operate on narrow and restrictive copyright policies.

Why Trademark Law is Important to Businesses

The success of any product or service frequently depends upon the public's perception of the business that offers it. The fact that the product or service is the finest in the land is often irrelevant. If your competitor has a stronger market presence or brand recognition, and its products or services are more easily distinguished from the rest, your business could be in trouble. Consumers are often inclined to choose products or services with familiar names or symbols, especially where those names and symbols are associated with desirable qualities. In fact, the marketing and protection of trade names, trademarks, logos, and package designs to distinguish the origin of a ware or service is often as important to a business as the products or services it represents.

[19.] *Mattel Inc v 3894207 Canada Inc* [2006] 1 SCR 772 at para 2.

[20.] *Rogers Communications Inc v Society of Composers, Authors and Music Publishers of Canada*, 2012 SCC 35; *Alberta (Education) v Canadian Copyright Licensing Agency (Access Copyright)*, 2012 SCC 37; *Entertainment Software Association v Society of Composers, Authors and Music Publishers of Canada*, 2012 SCC 34; *Society of Composers, Authors and Music Publishers of Canada v Bell Canada*, 2012 SCC 36; *Re Sounds v Motion Picture Theatre Associations of Canada*, 2012 SCC 38.

Trademark law is also meant to protect businesses that invest in brands and similar forms of corporate identification. Like other forms of intellectual property, trademarks can be sold, licensed, or otherwise exploited for profit. In fact, this is a fundamental premise of franchising and other business structures. But trademark law does not entitle the owner or licensee of the mark to exclusive use in the same way that copyright and patent do. Depending upon the type of trademark used, only goods or services that are registered or associated with the trademark are protected. For example, the law cannot stop me from using the word "Coke" in this sentence. But I cannot use the word "Coke" in association with a drink product that I wish to sell.

Acquiring a Trademark

Trademark protection is gained in Canada both through the common law and by way of statute. Both methods require prior use before trademark rights will be recognized. The *Trade-mark Act*[21] allows businesses to gain national protection of marks in use by registering these marks with the Canadian Intellectual Property Office (CIPO). The *Trade-mark Act* places a number of limitations on what marks are registrable as trademarks in Canada and provides a list of marks that are prohibited because of their resemblance to national and international departments and organizations.

Registered trademarks allow companies to associate their marks with particular goods and services in a national registry. Companies can then refer to the registry when coming up with new names and marks. The list also serves to deter companies from assuming names that may infringe the trademarks of their competitors. The legal protections of trademarks encourage businesses to invest in branding to make their marks more easily recognized and more easily remembered by consumers. By registering the use of a name or mark, your company is protected across Canada for 15 years (and the trademark can be renewed indefinitely with continued use).

As with copyright registration, trademark registration is not absolute proof of ownership, but it does provide the registrant with certain advantages. In the case of a dispute, the fact that a trademark has been registered will shift the onus of proving ownership in the use of the mark to the challenger. Since businesses often engage in lengthy and expensive fights over the use of names and marks, a prudent risk manager will register, in Canada and other countries where the company does business, all variations on the names and marks used to represent its goods and services in the marketplace.

The scope of protection for an unregistered mark is much narrower. While trademark law protects companies who spend time and effort creating unregistered brand recognition, the common law doctrine of passing off protects such marks only in the geographic area where the company has established a reputation. Outside of that geographic area, other companies are generally free to use the same mark.

Three basic categories of marks can be registered by businesses: *ordinary marks*, *certification marks*, and *distinguishing guises*.

- ■ **Ordinary marks** are words, symbols, or designs that distinguish the goods or services of a business. Sometimes, the words are names (for example, Tom's House of Pizza® in Figure 18.5) and other times slogans (for example, "Pizza Made to Perfection"™).

ordinary marks are words, symbols, or designs that distinguish the goods or services of a business

---

[21.] *Trade-marks Act*, RSC 1985, c T-13 (Can).

FIGURE 18.5   Tom's House of Pizza

certification marks identify goods or services that meet a standard set by a governing organization

distinguishing guises identify the unique three-dimensional shape of a product or its package

- **Certification marks** identify goods or services that meet a standard set by a governing organization (for example, "Recognized by the Canadian Dental Association").
- **Distinguishing guises** identify the unique three-dimensional shape of a product or its package.

Canada's *Trade-marks Act* does not specifically require or prohibit the use of symbols such as ® (registered trademark) or ™ (unregistered trademark). Still, businesses ought to use these symbols appropriately, especially if that use might find its way into another jurisdiction. A misleading use of the mark may not be prohibited in Canada (such as using the label ® on an unregistered mark), but it is prohibited in other jurisdictions, including the United States.

As a result of ongoing consultations on changes to the Regulations of the *Trade-marks Act* by the CIPO, non-traditional marks such as sound marks, motion marks, and holograms may soon be deemed registrable. Registrations of such marks are already possible in other jurisdictions, such as the United States. Business Decision 18.2 investigates some of these recent developments in trademark law.

In contemplating the policy implications of permitting non-traditional marks, it is important to consider the relationship between copyright and trademark law. Recall that a Canadian copyright generally lasts for the life of

Business Decision 18.2

Do Trademarks Roar?

For years the CIPO has refused all applications for sound marks. Its basis for doing so was that section 30(h) of the *Trade-marks Act* requires "a drawing of the trade-mark and such number of accurate representations of the trade-mark as may be prescribed." Metro-Goldwyn-Mayer Studio Inc. (MGM) has been using the sound of the roaring lion in the Canadian marketplace since the early 1900s and has been trying for more than 20 years to register this sound as a trademark in Canada.[22] Recently, the Federal Court of Canada ruled that this sound can be registered as a trademark in Canada.[23] On this basis, the CIPO subsequently released new conditions for applications for sound mark registration:

The application for the registration of a trade-mark consisting of a sound should:

1 state that the application is for the registration of a sound mark;

2 contain a drawing that graphically represents the sound;

3 contain a description of the sound; and

4 contain an electronic recording of the sound.[24]

Questions for Discussion

1. From a business perspective, discuss the reasons why registering a trademark consisting of a sound might be beneficial for your company.

2. Can you think of any reasons why the decision to permit the registration of trademarks consisting of sound might harm certain businesses?

---

the author and then for 50 years following the end of the calendar year in which the author dies. Trademarks, on the other hand, last for 15 years but can be renewed *indefinitely* with continued use. As such, it is possible that businesses might use trademarks to try to extend intellectual property protection in sounds beyond what copyright law previously permitted, since copyrights are time limited whereas trademarks offer the possibility of perpetual protection.

Trademark Infringement and Passing Off

The most common type of trademark infringement is when a company represents its business, goods, or services as someone else's through a confusingly similar mark or name. This type of behaviour could give rise to the tort of **passing off**. This cause of action protects both registered and unregistered trademarks. To succeed, the business claiming that its mark or name has been illegitimately used must prove three things: (i) that the business had established a reputation or goodwill in its name, mark, or logo, (ii) that the impostor represented itself in a manner that resulted in a misrepresentation or confusion to the public, and (iii) that the established business suffered or is likely to suffer harm. The test for passing off normally requires expert witness to determine if confusion is present. Survey data can be useful to determine whether the public was confused.[25]

Confusion in the marketplace is also grounds for one business to oppose another's attempt to register a trademark in the first place. You Be the Judge 18.1 provides an opportunity to consider the scope of such opposition.

passing off occurs when a company represents its business, goods, or services as someone else's through a confusingly similar mark or name

---

[22.] Canadian Trade-marks Database. Canadian Trade-mark Data. Accessed 26 June 2012 <www.ic.gc.ca/app/opic-cipo/trdmrks/srch/vwTrdmrk.do?lang=eng&status=&fileNumber =0714314&extension=0&startingDocumentIndexOnPage=1>.

[23.] *Metro-Goldwyn-Mayer Lion Corp v Attorney General of Canada et al* (1 March 2012), Ottawa T-1650-10 (FC).

[24.] CIPO Practice Notice. 28 March 2012 <www.cipo.ic.gc.ca/eic/site/cipointernet-internetopic.nsf/ eng/wr03439.html>.

[25.] *Kirkbi AG v Ritvik Holdings Inc* [2005] 3 SCR 302.

You Be the Judge **18.1**

Confusion in the Marketplace[26]

A woman in Montreal has successfully registered the trademark "Barbie's" in connection with a small chain of restaurants. The restaurant is targeted toward adults and serves bar and grill–type food, much of which is barbecued. In response, Mattel, manufacturer of Barbie dolls, opposes the restaurant's trademark registration pursuant to the *Trade-mark Act.* Although Mattel has not registered or used the name in association with restaurants or catering services, it claims that use of the mark "Barbie's" will create confusion since its mark, Barbie, has become so famous that it is associated with any ware or service bearing its name.

Questions for Discussion

1. Do you think that the general public would confuse a restaurant called "Barbie's" with wares or services associated with the doll? Why or why not?

2. Recall that one of the purposes of trademark law is to provide a guarantee of origin, or an assurance to consumers that something's quality will be what they have come to associate with a particular trademark. Would the use of "Barbie's" by the restaurant owner undermine this form of consumer protection?

In the Internet context, Canadian courts have held that the mere registration of a domain name can be a misrepresentation to the public for the purposes of the second element of a passing-off action.[27] Disputes involving domain names are discussed in detail in Chapter 19.

A successful trademark registration gives the owner a number of additional rights. Trademark law is meant to protect the owner against infringements of those rights.

- The first and most obvious kind of infringement occurs when an exact imitation of the trademark is used without permission. A typical example is the *knock-off*. A knock-off is an item for sale that looks very much like a product made by the trademark holder and that is represented by a similar mark. It is usually of inferior quality.

- A second kind of infringement occurs not through imitation, but when some other mark has the effect of confusing consumers. Often such infringements involve similar words, phrases, or symbols.

trademark depreciation occurs when one person uses the mark of another to depreciate the value of its goodwill

- A third kind of infringement, known as **trademark depreciation** occurs when one person uses the mark of another to depreciate the value of its goodwill. According to the owner of the trademark for Perrier mineral water, this occurred when a Canadian company started selling a bottled water product known as "Pierre Eh!" The court agreed.[28]

- A fourth kind of infringement occurs when a foreign party imports an authentically branded product (*not* a knock-off) into Canada as though it were the authorized Canadian distributor. If the Canadian distributor holds a registered trademark for the product in Canada, the foreign party will usually have to seek permission to import the product even if it holds the trademark in other jurisdictions.

[26.] *Mattel Inc v 3894207 Canada Inc* [2006] 1 SCR 772.

[27.] *Law Society of British Columbia v Canada Domain Name Exchange Corp* (2002) 4 BCLR (4th) 373 (BSC).

[28.] *Source Perrier SA v Fira-Less Marketing Co* [1983] 2 FC 18 (FCTD).

Trademark infringement gives rise to a number of legal remedies:

- Typically, the trademark holder will claim damages resulting from the infringement of its exclusive right to use the mark. Damages can also be claimed when the illegitimate use of the trademark has injured its reputation and diminished the value of its goodwill. Damages will be applied in the same manner as they are in tort law. (Tort damages were discussed in Chapter 3.)

- Sometimes the trademark holder does not suffer damages but claims that the trademark infringer has been unjustly enriched through the illegitimate use of the mark. If a profit has been earned as a result of the infringement, the court may order an *accounting of profits*, requiring the infringer to transfer profits made through the use of the mark to the trademark holder. (The account of profits was discussed in Chapter 12.)

- One of the more common and important remedies sought by trademark holders is an *injunction*. When an injunction is appropriate, the court will make an order restraining the infringer from continuing to do business in a manner that involves the illegitimate use of the mark. (Injunctions were discussed in Chapters 3 and 12.)

- Sometimes the infringing party is ordered to *deliver up* the infringing materials—that is, to turn over goods bearing the mark to the trademark holder or to otherwise dispose of them.

PATENTS

The Patent Bargain

Many inventors believe that the chief value of a *patent* is that it gives them the time needed to develop and market their ideas. A **patent** grants a time-limited monopoly, allowing the inventor to exclude others from making, using, or selling a new and useful invention or improvement to an invention for a period of up to 20 years from the date of filing an application. Patents provide an incentive for research and development. With patent protection, inventors can be confident that the effort and money spent on creating new products will not be undermined by speedy copycat manufacturers trying to take advantage of the invention once it hits the marketplace. Patents allow inventors to recoup their research and development investments by having the ability to stop competitors from entering the market for a limited time.

patents grant a time-limited monopoly to inventors, allowing them to exclude others from making, using, or selling their inventions or improved versions of their inventions for a period of up to 20 years from the date of filing the applications

At the same time, the *patent system* also plays an important part in serving the broader public interest. Because a clear description of the invention must be filed with the patent office before a patent is granted, the patent system plays a pivotal role in the way that information and knowledge are shared. In exchange for fixed-term monopolies, patentees must disclose their inventions to the public. This is commonly calledthe **patent bargain**. This disclosure allows other inventors to access and build upon the innovations in the patent. The patent office (and its website) is also a critical resource for businesses, researchers, academics, journalists, and others interested in keeping up with technological development. Given the breathtaking pace of innovation, businesses can regularly monitor the state of the art. Failing to do so may result in a waste of time and money. According to recent statistics, roughly 10 percent of all research and development in Canada results in duplicating patented technologies.[29]

the **patent bargain** gives the patent holder a fixed-term monopoly in exchange for disclosing the invention to the public

---

[29.] Industry Canada *A Guide to Patents* (2000) at 15.

Businesses should therefore develop the habit of searching patent literature before developing new technologies to avoid "reinventing the wheel."

Patentability

Not just any idea can be patented. Patent law protects inventions, which are defined in the *Patent Act* as "any new and useful art, process, machine, manufacture or composition of matter."[30] The Act also allows patents for "new and useful improvements" of existing inventions. In fact, 90 percent of patents granted in Canada are for such improvements.[31] Note that "useful" here does not mean that the invention must achieve some public benefit. It has always been thought that it is up to the market, not the patent office, to determine which inventions are useful.[32]

A patent is available only if it can be demonstrated that the proposed invention is:

- patentable subject matter
- novel
- non-obvious
- useful

PATENTABLE SUBJECT MATTER Think of a patent as the *embodiment of an idea*. Just as one cannot copyright an idea (only its expression), one cannot patent a newly discovered natural law, scientific principle, or abstract theory. Other matters are unpatentable on the basis of public policy. For example, one cannot patent a medical treatment, although one can patent a drug used for the treatment of a disease.

It is said that business methods are generally unpatentable in Canada, although, arguably, some have been allowed through indirect means. With reference to jurisprudence in the United States,[33] the Canadian Patent Appeal Board (CPAB) recently denied an appeal by Amazon.com over its "one-click" ordering system. The CPAB spoke in strong language against business method patents, stating that "since patenting business methods would involve a radical departure from the traditional patent regime, and since the patentability of such methods is a highly contentious matter, clear and unequivocal legislation is required for business methods to be patentable."[34]

The patentability of computer software is also a difficult question in Canada. Computer software patents are permitted in the United States and have become highly profitable assets for software makers, particularly when the patented product is in broad use or is needed as a component for other software companies to build upon. The importance of software patents is demonstrated in the tremendous increase in patent litigation involving software in the United States. However, software patents have generated a great deal of controversy because of their potential to lock down areas of technological development and obstruct software innovation. In Canada, the patent office has indicated that computer programs are not themselves patentable *per se*, because they are considered to

---

30. *Patent Act*, RSC 1985, c P-4 (Can).

31. Canadian Intellectual Property Office *A Guide to Patents* (2007) at 4.

32. For example, patents continue to be granted for lethal weapons. This approach was reinforced by Parliament in 1994 when it removed the requirement that inventions have *no illicit object in view*: *Patent Act*, RSC 1985, c P-4, s 27 (Can).

33. *In re Bilski* (2008) 545 F3d 943 (Fed Cir)

34. Decision 1290 of Commissioner of Patents, dated 5 March 2009.

FIGURE 18.6 Forms of Patentable Inventions

Form	Example
product	a knife
composition	chemicals that remove rust from knife blades
apparatus	a machine that makes knife handles
process	a method of assembling knives

Source: Industry Canada *A Guide to Patents* (2010) at 4.

be a mere scientific principle or abstract theorem. The presence of a computer program in an invention will therefore neither add nor subtract from the patentability of the invention. However, inventions incorporating a computer program can be patented where its subject matter is patentable and the computer program has been integrated with it—even where, for example, the hardware element of the invention is relatively minor.[35] That said, in light of the Amazon "one-click" decision in Canada and a related decision in the United States, the patentability of software also remains in dispute. Further guidance from both the Supreme Courts in Canada and the United States is needed to clarify what elements are necessary to transform software into patentable subject matter.

One striking difference in the Canadian approach to patentable subject matter is that, unlike the United States and other countries, Canada does not allow patents for higher life forms.[36] How long this will remain the case is an open question given that Canadian courts have determined that protection of a patented gene or cell extends to its presence in a whole plant, even while the plant itself, as a higher life form, cannot be patented.[37]

Given the broad range of patentability permitted by the *Patent Act*, a patentable invention may come in a number of forms, as Figure 18.6 shows.

NOVELTY The novelty criterion does not mean that an inventor must prove that no one else has ever come up with the idea or built a similar product. **Novelty** means that the invention has not previously been disclosed and become known, or otherwise made available, to the public. Even if the invention is novel in the sense that it is the first of its kind in the world, if the inventor made the invention available to the public before filing a patent application, its patentability would be jeopardized.[38] Typical examples of such disclosures are (i) delivering a presentation about the invention at a conference or trade show, (ii) displaying the invention in a public place, or (iii) showing the invention to someone without requiring confidentiality.

The novelty requirement makes it crucial for business managers to institute safeguards against premature disclosure of products under development.

novelty means that the invention has not previously been disclosed and become known, or otherwise made available, to the public

---

[35.] *Re Motorola Inc Patent Application No 2 085 228* (1998) 86 CPR (3d) 71 (PAB).

[36.] *Harvard College v Canada (Commissioner of Patents)* [2002] 4 SCR 45.

[37.] *Monsanto Canada Inc v Schmeiser* [2004] 1 SCR 902.

[38.] In Canada, and some other jurisdictions, there is a one-year grace period before filing during which a business can disclose: *Patent Act*, RSC 1985, c P-14, s 28(1) (Can). However, disclosure before filing can prevent patentability in other countries.

PART 5

Although some legal mechanisms exist to protect *trade secrets*, prudent managers prevent the risk of untimely disclosure by including confidentiality clauses in employment contracts and by developing and distributing company policy on trade secrets.

It is also important for businesses to file a patent application as soon as the essential elements of the invention are complete. As a result of recent changes to the Act, if your business is working on a new invention, but a speedier competitor files it at the patent office before you do, your invention will not be seen as novel—even if you invented it first. This system has become known as a *first-to-file* (as opposed to a *first-to-invent*) system. This creates an incentive for businesses to file early and repeatedly in order to protect the core of their inventions as they are developed.

NON-OBVIOUS   The second requirement is that the invention or improvement must be *non-obvious*. **Non-obvious** means that the item for which a patent is sought would not have been immediately obvious to technicians fluent in similar technologies. It must be capable of provoking a "Why didn't I think of that!" reaction from other designers in the field. Note that the non-obvious requirement does not entail complexity. Simple inventions can suffice. After all, someone patented the spoon straw, depicted in Figure 18.7. It is a feature of many great inventions that they appear obvious only after their discovery. Inventors seeking patents must therefore think very carefully about how to present their work as a non-obvious improvement of the current state of the art. According

non-obvious means that the item for which a patent is sought would not have been immediately obvious to technicians fluent in similar technologies

FIGURE 18.7   Patent CA 901307: Combination Drinking Straw and Spoon

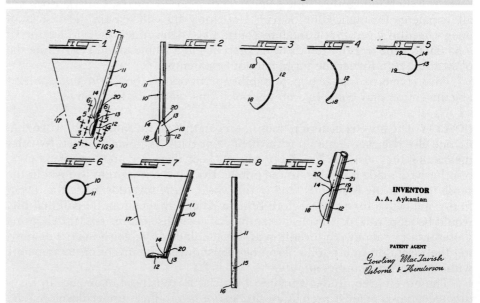

Patent CA 901307: Combination Drinking Straw and Spoon

Not all patents stem from complex ideas. Indeed many of the most ingenious inventions result from a relatively unsophisticated leap of logic that was non-obvious at the time of conception. The Spoon-Straw illustrates how two simple yet effective snips of plastic can result in significant utility. Once the market need was determined, the inventor quickly assembled this drawing on a plane ride home from a meeting with the Coca-Cola corporation.

Reproduced by permission of Ardashus A. Aykanian.

to the Supreme Court of Canada, the proper approach is to look at all similar inventions and ask if a technician would, "in the light of the state of the art and of common general knowledge as at the claimed date of invention, have come directly and without difficulty to the solution taught by the patent."[39] If so, the invention is obvious and therefore not subject to patent. If not, the non-obviousness criterion has been established.

UTILITY   The very definition of an invention implies that it serves some practical purpose. Product development merely for the sake of scientific curiosity is insufficient for patent purposes. The **utility requirement** precludes products that have no useful function or that do not work from being patented. For example, if a manufacturing process has the effect of ruining the very items it is said to produce, it will be unpatentable.[40] The utility requirement does not, however, preclude the patenting of a wasteful, unsafe, primitive, or commercially useless product.[41] As we have seen, it is up to the market and not the patent office to determine the value of the invention.

> the **utility requirement** precludes products that have no useful function or that do not work from being patented

Patent Infringement

A successful patent registration gives the registrant a number of economic rights, most notably, the exclusive right of "making, constructing and using the invention and selling it to others to be used."[42] **Patent infringement claims** are the means by which patent holders enforce the monopoly on their inventions. With patents in hand, inventors can commence a patent infringement case against anyone who uses their inventions for commercial purposes. Patent litigation has been on the rise in recent years, particularly in the United States. Because the US market is often the most important market for Canadian companies, having a US patent and avoiding infringing the US patents of other companies can become key risk management issues for Canadian businesses. Infringing a patent can result in millions of dollars in damages, even in cases that settle, and may in some cases threaten the very survival of a business.

> **patent infringement claims** are the means by which patent holders enforce the monopoly on their inventions

The Federal Court of Canada hears the vast majority of this country's patent disputes. Defendants will usually claim that (i) the disputed patent is not valid under the criteria for patentability and/or (ii) they are not infringing the patent. To determine if the contested patent is valid, the court first goes through a process of **claims construction** to interpret from the patent what area of innovation the patent is claiming as the invention. Using this "fenced-off" area, the court will then determine if the patent is valid in terms of its subject matter, novelty, non-obviousness, and utility. Finally, if the court determines that the patent is valid, it will proceed to determine if the defendants are infringing the claims of the patent. The courts will ask if the infringing product "appropriates its substance" (or "pith and marrow"). The infringing product need not be exactly the same as the protected invention, but to infringe the patent the defendant must use "the essential teachings of the claims compared to the prior art."[43]

> **claims construction** is used to determine the area of innovation a patent protects as the invention

---

39. *Apotex Inc v Sanofi-Synthelabo Canada Inc* 2008 SCC 61 at paras 52–54.

40. *TRW Inc v Walbar of Canada Inc* (1991) 39 CPR (3d) 176 (FC CA).

41. D Vaver *Intellectual Property* (1997) at 138.

42. *Patent Act*, RSC 1985, c P-14, s 42 (Can).

43. D Gervais & E Judge *Intellectual Property: The Law in Canada* (2005) at 442.

Similar to copyright and trademark, patent infringement gives rise to a number of legal remedies:

- Typically, the patent holder will claim that the illegitimate use or sale results in damages. Again, this remedy will be applied in the same manner as it is in tort law. Damages might be calculated in part on the basis of the royalty that the infringer would have had to pay to the patent holder for use of the invention and whether the infringement began during the patent application stage. Recently, the Federal Court of Canada granted punitive damages to a patentee.[44] Given the unusual nature of this order in Canadian patent law, it remains to be seen whether this case will mark a trend toward an increase in awards of punitive damages.

- Sometimes, the patent holder does not suffer damages directly but claims that the infringer has been unjustly enriched through the illegitimate use of the patented object or process. If there has been a profit as a result of the infringement, the court may order an accounting of profits, requiring the infringer to transfer profits made through the use of the patent to the patent holder.

- Another common remedy is injunctive relief. When an injunction is successfully sought, the court will order the infringer to stop doing business in a way that interferes with the patent holder's rights.

- The patent holder may also ask for delivery of the infringing products.

Exploiting a Patent

Patents can be exploited by their owners or licensees. However, it is important to note that, unlike copyright, there is no provision in the *Patent Act* which provides that an employer will own inventions patented by employees in the course of employment. Patent ownership clauses are therefore critically important in the employment context. Unless a clause in the employment contract states otherwise or the inventor was hired to invent and the invention was created in the course of their duties, the patent belongs to the employee.[45] This is true even if the employee uses time and materials belonging to the employer.

Once a patent is obtained, it is like any other type of property. Valuation of a business includes its portfolio of patents. Inventors often include their patents along with other assets when trying to arrange corporate financing. As well, owners of patents can engage in a series of business decisions to gain revenue from their research and development. What is the best means of profiting from this asset? There are usually several options:

- In some cases, the patent owner will choose to develop and market the product. By doing so, the owner retains full control over the invention. This choice allows the owner to select the image and branding of the product, its availability in the marketplace, pricing, profit margins, and so on. Retaining full control of the products also means assuming all the risks. Even after years of research and development during the patenting process, it is possible to miscalculate what will happen in the market.

- If the owner of a patent is unable or unwilling to assume the risk, another option is to license the patent. Licences permit other businesses to bring the product to the market in exchange for royalties. Various licensing

---

[44.] *Eurocopter v Bell Helicopter Textron Canada Limited* 2012 FC 113. <http://decisions.fct-cf.gc.ca/en/2012/2012fc113/2012fc113.html>

[45.] *Comstock Canada v Electec Ltd* [1991] 38 CPR (3d) 29.

schemes allow smaller businesses with information-based assets to create capital without large investments or expenditures. They can be granted in any jurisdiction where a patent is held. **Exclusive licences** transfer all the patent rights to a single licensee for the agreed period of time with only title remaining with the patent holder. **Non-exclusive licences** can be granted to one or many licensees on a variety of different terms.

- The owner may choose to sell the patent outright. Although this usually requires assigning all rights as inventor, the owner receives, in return, a lump sum without incurring any risk in the marketplace. Sometimes, however, it is difficult to know how to determine the value of the patent, especially when the product has not yet been marketed.

exclusive licences transfer all the patent rights to a single licensee for the agreed period of time with only title remaining with the patent holder

non-exclusive licences can be granted to one or many licensees on a variety of different terms

The Right to Use Another's Patent

Although the economic rights obtained by a patent are generally given a wide range of application, there are limits. As we have seen, the patent system aims to balance private rights with the public interest. Even if you hold a patent, you cannot prevent me from building an exact replica of your machine for my own private research, as long as I am not exploiting your invention for profit. However, most companies in the business of improving existing inventions usually enter into mutually beneficial agreements with the original patent holder, rather than working secretly without the patent holder's knowledge and consent.

I have a right to use your patented invention for experimental purposes and other non-commercial uses. Like the fair dealings doctrine in copyright law, the lines are not always clear, and litigation is often required to balance private rights against the public interest. Similarly, although it is usually an infringement to make or construct a patented item, users have the right to repair and, in some cases, modify them. Although excessive modification might approach reconstruction, there is a public interest in permitting repairs if they conserve resources. There are other circumstances in which users have the right to use a patented product. For example, to obtain governmental approval, a patented product may be used when necessary for public health or safety reasons.

International Patent System

Patents are inherently territorial. However, the seemingly borderless reach of innovation and its tremendous impact on the world's economy have pushed the patent regime to become a much more global affair. While there is no such thing as an "international patent," treaties signed by much of the industrialized and developing world have harmonized many of the governing rules. Such treaties and conventions have become invaluable to inventors and businesses from Manitoba and Menlo Park to Mumbai and Madrid.

The *Paris Convention for the Protection of Industrial Property* is one of the oldest and most important treaties dealing with a range of intellectual property matters including trademarks, industrial designs, and patents. With regard to patents, signatories of the *Paris Convention* prohibit member states from discriminating against other nationals when granting patents within their domestic system. In addition, inventors from a member state are granted a period of 12 months in which to claim priority back to their originating application within other member states. This allows a patentee to first file in Canada and then wait up to a year before having to file in other countries. As a result, there

PART 5

is no longer any need to file applications simultaneously in multiple jurisdictions, reducing the cost of gaining wide protection while providing time for a patentee in Canada to work the patent and amass funds before deciding if further protection in other jurisdictions is needed.

Newer international treaties such as the *Patent Cooperation Treaty* (PCT) and the *European Patent Convention* (EPC) have further streamlined the process for gaining protection in multiple jurisdictions by allowing a single application in one language. These instruments also offer a more cost-effective approach for patent applicants and decrease the need for multiple decisions on patentability, reducing repetition in the work of national patent examiners and the overall strain on national patent offices.[46]

INDUSTRIAL DESIGNS

The success of a manufactured product often depends not only on its usefulness but also on its visual appeal. Because a distinctive product can be considered an intellectual asset, some manufacturers invest time and effort in the look of their product. An **industrial design** consists of the features of shape, configuration, pattern, or ornament applied to a finished article to improve its aesthetic appeal. Because the *Industrial Design Act* seeks to protect only the visual appeal of an object, you will not be permitted to register designs that are purely functional in nature, that have no fixed appearance, or that are not clearly visible, such as those hidden from view.[47] Nor can you register the use of particular materials or colours. Although the use of particular materials or colours can certainly enhance the visual appeal of an object, no one is entitled to a monopoly on these alone. In some cases, however, a unique pattern that is created through the arrangement of certain contrasting tones will qualify.

Unlike copyright and trademark, an industrial design is protected only if it is registered. The *Industrial Design Act* protects registered original designs for up to 10 years by preventing others from making, importing for trade or business, renting, or selling the design. Once the 10-year term has expired, the design falls into the public domain, and anyone is free to make, rent, import, or sell it. It is useful to mark all registered designs with the proprietor's name and a "D" in a circle. Doing so will entitle the registrant to seek monetary damage awards from anyone who infringes the design. A failure to mark the design will limit the remedy to an injunction if the infringer is able to prove that they were unaware, and had no reasonable grounds to suspect, that the design was registered.[48] Registrants must enforce their rights within three years of the alleged infringement.

As with other forms of intellectual property, businesses can commercially exploit industrial designs in several ways. Design rights can be assigned to others in exchange for cash, merchandise, or credit. They can also be licensed. The advantage of licensing the design is that ownership of the design is retained. As well, an entrepreneurial designer may, for example, license the design to a number of parties (i) by geographic region to give the licensee exclusive rights to market the design within that region, or (ii) across Canada but for different periods of time.

industrial design consists of the features of shape, configuration, pattern, or ornament applied to a finished article to improve its aesthetic appeal

---

46. "Protecting Your Inventions Abroad: Frequently Asked Questions About the Patent Cooperation Treaty" *World Intellectual Property Organization* (WIPO) (March 2012) at 11. <www.wipo.int/pct/en/basic_facts/faqs_about_the_pct.pdf>.

47. *Industrial Design Act*, RSC 1985, c I-89 (Can).

48. *Industrial Design Act*, RSC 1985, c I-89, s 7 (Can).

Confidential Information and Trade Secrets   L.O. ❾ ❿

Although patent law is an important means of protecting the value generated by ideas, sometimes there are situations where a business may not wish to disclose its ideas to the public. In these circumstances, there are other means of legally protecting and exploiting business-related information.

CONFIDENTIAL INFORMATION

Although potentially risky, the easiest means of protection is to keep an idea or business-related information a secret. Since some secrets must be told in order to maintain a profitable business, it is important to build a relationship of trust around it by creating conditions of *confidentiality*. **Confidential information** is material exchanged in a relationship that prohibits its recipient from sharing it or otherwise using it to take advantage of the person who communicated it. The advantage of being able to prove that someone has used or disclosed your confidential information is that you can sue for *breach of confidence*. A **breach of confidence** occurs when a person who has been entrusted with confidential information uses that information improperly. The plaintiff must prove (i) that the information was of a confidential nature, (ii) that it was disclosed to the defendant in circumstances giving rise to an obligation of confidence, and (iii) that there was a misuse or unauthorized use of the information.[49] As in the case of intellectual property, the cause of action for breach of confidence supports a broad range of remedies, including injunctions, delivering-up, an account of profits, and compensatory damages.

The courts recognize that information may be confidential for a variety of reasons. Very often, however, it is difficult to decide whether knowledge acquired in the course of employment is confidential or merely common industry know-how. This problem is compounded by the fact that the technology sector is rapidly evolving. What was one company's trade secret or confidential information yesterday can be general industry knowledge in a matter of days or weeks. In situations of doubt, an employer should consider inserting a detailed confidentiality provision into an employee's contract. Such a clause should apply during the tenure of employment and after the employee leaves the business.

Customer lists are typically considered confidential information and should be protected by contract. Even in the absence of a contract, employees are normally prohibited from using or disclosing customer lists or other confidential information after they leave their employment. However, some courts have drawn a distinction between the actual taking of a list and merely recalling customer names through the use of a phone book or other means. Subject to a contract or a fiduciary duty, employees are often permitted to compete with their former employer by recalling customer names from memory and then soliciting the business of those customers.[50]

To prove that information is confidential in nature, one must be able to demonstrate that the information was not generally known to a substantial number of people. There is no specific test to determine whether information is known to a substantial number of people. A judge will consider all the facts to determine whether information can still be considered confidential despite some degree of disclosure. In some cases, an idea, formula, or process may be confidential, even if parts of it are generally known to a substantial number

confidential information is material exchanged in a relationship that prohibits its recipient from sharing it or otherwise using it to take advantage of the person who communicated it

breach of confidence occurs when a person who has been entrusted with confidential information uses that information improperly

PART 5

---

49. *Lac Minerals Ltd v International Corona Resources Ltd* (1989) 61 DLR (4th) 14 (SCC).

50. *Valley First Financial Services Ltd v Trach* (2004) 30 BCLR (4th) 33 (CA).

of people, as long as it is original as a whole. The confidentiality requirement is most easily met by telling all recipients of the information that it is secret and must not be disclosed. However, it is usually sufficient if the information is disclosed under circumstances that imply confidence. The final requirement entails proof that there has been a misuse of the information. Even if the claimant has not suffered any financial loss, the court may award relief simply because a secret was disclosed against that person's wishes.[51]

TRADE SECRETS

a **trade secret** is a special type of confidential information, such as a formula, pattern, device, or compilation of information, that is used to obtain a business advantage over competitors

Trade secrets are a special type of confidential information, such as a formula, pattern, device, or compilation of information, that is used to obtain a business advantage over competitors who do not know or use it. A famous example of a trade secret is the mixture of 11 secret herbs and spices in Kentucky Fried Chicken (KFC) said to be told by Colonel Harland Sanders to only two living souls: his wife, Claudia, and the head of the three-person syndicate that purchased KFC back in 1964. A business can help protect its trade secrets through non-disclosure agreements in its employment contracts and contracts for services. Other non-legal measures involve establishing strict information access controls within an organization. For example, it is said that, to this day, KFC franchisees are not told what is in the seasoning mix. Instead, they are required to buy the seasonings premixed from the Kentucky Fried Chicken Corporation.

Not surprisingly, relying on trade secrets creates certain risks:

- Even if you create such obligations contractually, it is possible for your employees and independent contractors (or anyone they might tell) to register your trade secret as though it were their own intellectual property. Despite your ability to prove that those information-based assets belong to you, you will still be forced to spend time and energy fighting to get back what is yours, and you may be forced to reveal the information in the process.

- Even if you effectively protect your trade secrets by way of contracts with your employees, your secrets may be vulnerable after an employee quits or is terminated, and your remedies may be purely contractual. Although you can protect your secrets by way of contractual restrictions that continue to apply after an employee leaves your business, disgruntled employees may nevertheless disclose your trade secrets to others.

- Even if your employees and independent contractors are completely trustworthy, protecting ideas and business-related information exclusively by way of trade secrets runs the risk that someone else might independently discover the trade secret. If that happens, there is nothing to prevent that person from registering it as intellectual property or otherwise making it available to the public.

Although it can be risky to use trade secrets as the *sole* means of protecting ideas and business-related information, trade secrets do have advantages. For example, in contrast to patents and copyrights, trade secrets do not involve a public disclosure of ideas, nor are they limited by a term. Businesses can exploit trade secrets indefinitely, so long as the information is still secret. This principle of trade secrets has allowed KFC to exploit its secret recipe for decades.

Concept Summary 18.1 summarizes the five main types of protection of intellectual works that we have discussed in this chapter.

[51.] *Cadbury Schweppes Inc v FBI Foods Ltd* (1999) 167 DLR (4th) 577 (SCC).

Concept Summary 18.1

Differentiating between the Five Main Types of Protection of Intellectual Works

	Copyright	Trademarks	Patents	Industrial Designs	Trade Secrets
Basis	statutory	statutory and common law (passing off)	statutory	statutory	common law
Registration	not mandatory but beneficial	not mandatory but beneficial	mandatory	mandatory	registration not possible
What it protects	original forms of expression (*eg* dramatic, literary, software, musical)	marks used in association with particular businesses, wares, and services	useful, non-obvious, and novel inventions that are patentable subject matter	features, such as shape and pattern, that appeal to the eye as applied to a finished article	secret information
Term of protection	generally life of the author plus 50 years	renewable in perpetuity, unless mark is not used and then it is expunged	maximum of 20 years from the date of filing application	maximum of 10 years from the date of registration	indefinite, so long as secrecy is maintained

Chapter Summary

Traditionally, the value of tangible goods and services was determined in the market according to their natural scarcity. Because ideas and other business-related information are non-exclusive and non-rivalrous, their value is dependent on the creation of an artificial scarcity. This is achieved through intellectual property laws.

Intellectual property laws seek to balance private rights and the public interest through an incentive system for creators and entrepreneurs by granting time-limited monopolies on various intellectual constructs, their expression, and their functionality. This requires a delicate balance between the rights of intellectual property owners and the public. In addition to moral rights, authors are awarded copyright in their works, allowing them to prevent unauthorized copying and distribution. Exceptions are carved out for fair dealing and works that have fallen into the public domain. A copyright may be bought, sold, licensed, or given away. Moral rights may not be sold, but they may be waived. To qualify for protection, a work must be original, in fixed form, and created in a copyright convention member state. A work must also fit into one of the enumerated categories outlined in the *Copyright Act*.

The law of trademarks is especially important for businesses and consumers because it connects products and services to their originator. Trademark owners are protected as long as the mark is used against competitors who try to confuse consumers through illegitimate use of the mark, thereby diluting its value. Businesses are encouraged to register trademarks to increase the geographic range of their application. Unlike copyrights, registered trademarks do not automatically apply to countries that have intellectual property agreements with Canada.

The granting of a patent for an invention allows the inventor to exclude others from making, using, or selling the invention for a period of 20 years from filing an application. Unlike trademarks, patents cannot be renewed. The patent bargain plays an important role in encouraging innovation, while ensuring the sharing of information and knowledge between businesses. Patent law protects original inventions and improvements to already existing inventions. Much like the fair dealing doctrine in copyright law, the public retains the right to use patented inventions for experimental and non-commercial purposes. Given the increasing importance of international patent protection, the process for obtaining patents in multiple jurisdictions has recently been streamlined through a series of international treaties.

Industrial design law protects the distinctive visual appeal of manufactured articles. Original designs are protected for up to 10 years by preventing others from making, importing for trade or business, renting, or selling the design. After 10 years, the design falls into the public domain. Like the patent system, priority is based on the timing of registration, regardless of who came up with the design first.

Businesses can further protect ideas and business-related information by using legal and non-legal measures to protect confidential information and trade secrets. In determining the confidentiality of the information, courts will consider the degree to which the information had been disclosed to the public and the extent of the alleged infringer's duty of confidentiality. A special type of confidential information known as a trade secret can be used to obtain a business advantage over competitors who do not know or use it. Although it can be risky to use trade secrets as the *sole* means of protecting ideas and business-related information, trade secrets do have advantages.

MyBusLawLab ADDITIONAL RESOURCES FOR CHAPTER 18

MyBusLawLab provides students with an assortment of tools to help enrich the learning experience, including a Study Plan with Pre- and Post-tests, mini-cases with assessments, and provincial content material, which provides links to relevant cases, legislation, and additional resources.

MyBusLawLab provides the following resources for Chapter 18:

- Business Decision 18.1W—Unbundling Copyright

Provincial Material

- **Alberta:** *Copyright Act*, Trade Name/Trademark

Review Questions

1. Distinguish between "non-exclusive possession" and "non-rivalry," and discuss how these features of ideas create a need for intellectual property law.

2. How does the scarcity of an asset affect its value? How can a prudent business manager increase the value of ideas and business-related information?

3. In what sense can intellectual property law be understood as an attempt to "balance" interests? How might *The Copyright Modernization Act* affect the balance? Explain your answer.

4. Name five forms of expression protected by copyright and give examples of each.

5. What are the requirements for copyright protection? Explain each requirement, and provide an example.

6. Name three changes to copyright law as a result of *The Copyright Modernization Act*. Give examples of the impact of these changes on businesses.

7. One of the most significant changes in *The Copyright Modernization Act* is the digital lock provision. How might the new digital lock rules affect Canadian businesses? Consider both the perspectives of creators and users.

8. Who owns the copyright in a work created in the course of employment? How might a prudent business manager ensure that the employer is recognized as the copyright holder?

9. Explain the concept of "moral rights." How can a prudent business manager ensure that these rights will not conflict with copyrights held by the business?

10. Must a copyright be registered to be enforceable? Explain your answer.

11. List three kinds of trademark, and give an example of each.

12. What is "passing off"? How is it relevant to trademark law?

13. What are the advantages of registering a trademark?

14. Can non-traditional marks (such as sound marks, motion marks, and holograms) be registered with the Canadian Intellectual Property Office? If so, what must the application for the registration of a trademark contain?

15. What legal remedies are available for trademark holders in a judicial finding of trademark infringement by another party?

16. Like copyright, patent law attempts to create a balance between private rights and the public interest. What does this balance in patent law look like in a business setting and how does it benefit businesses?

17. Outline three ways a patent owner can exploit the patent for financial gain. Briefly discuss the advantages and disadvantages of each option.

18. Explain the purpose of the protection afforded to industrial designs. Is registration required? Explain your answer.

19. Other than intellectual property laws involving trademarks, copyright, patents, and industrial designs, name two means by which businesses can protect ideas and business-related information. Outline the elements needed to succeed in an action for breach of confidence.

20. Discuss some of the advantages and risks of using trade secrets as a means to protect ideas and business-related information.

Cases and Problems

1. The Beautiful Boy Modelling School hired Keith to prepare commercial artwork for its company materials. Upon completion of the work, Keith invoiced the school for $1600 and was promptly paid. Later, when he realized that the modelling school was using the artwork more extensively than he was originally led to believe, Keith sued the school and its president, Dan, for copyright infringement. Dan, who was not only beautiful but also a lawyer, argued that Keith's allegation of copyright infringement fails because his contract did not contain any limitations on the use of the work by the modelling school. Moreover, Dan argued that common business practices establish that in the case of work for hire, the commercial artist assigns all copyrights to the employer unless explicit restrictions are included as part of the terms of employment. What factors can the courts consider in determining whether the school has infringed Keith's copyright? How could Dan, as a prudent business manager, have avoided this situation?

2. Talia sold her famous sculpture *Angst of a Bicycle Tire* to the owners of a new downtown shopping mall for a substantial price. The owners installed the sculpture in the foyer of the mall to the delight of both Talia and mall patrons. Years later, the mall owners allowed one of its tenants to use the sculpture to promote a bicycle tire sale. As part of the promotion, some of the sculpture's tires were adorned with the tenant's corporate logo as well as details of the sale. Talia, who was not consulted, was outraged. She sued, calling for the restoration of her sculpture to its original form. On what basis, if any, have the mall owners infringed Talia's intellectual property rights? How could the mall owners have avoided this situation altogether? Explain your reasoning.

3. Lindsay is a game designer who created a new board game using rods of different colours and lengths to help children learn math. The game has become an important tool within classrooms in the Maritime provinces as a math learning aid. As part of the instructions for the board game, Lindsay provides a detailed manual that explains how teachers can use the game to encourage children to learn math. Byron, a competitor, decided to mimic the game and has recently come out with a similar teaching tool using very similar rods of various lengths and colours. Because he thought his game was "self-evident," Byron's game does not come with an instruction manual. This has helped reduce costs, allowing Byron's game to capture a sizeable share of the market. Incensed upon learning that Byron has "stolen her idea," Lindsay decides to bring an action for copyright infringement. Is she likely to succeed? Explain your reasoning.

4. The Cameron Library for the Intellectually Gifted has one of the most comprehensive libraries of rare books in Canada. It has a public facility in Vancouver where it permits patrons to review rare books in the library. Although the Cameron Library does not permit patrons to sign out the priceless works, it does provide self-serve photocopiers and digital scanners that patrons can use to copy materials. Upon request, the library will also scan and email materials to individual patrons outside the Vancouver area. This service is called the Email Service. A Cameron Library policy states that copying in the library and copying for the Email Service is permitted for research purposes. Recently, however, Dr Allworth, the author and owner of copyright in a book at the Cameron Library, discovered that his book had been copied by patrons in the library. He also learned that the library has scanned and emailed a portion of his book under the Email Service. He immediately commenced an action for copyright infringement against the library. You work at the Cameron Library and have been asked to provide an opinion as to whether it has committed a copyright infringement through its Email Service.

5. With reference to the facts described in the previous problem, explain whether the Cameron Library would be liable for the patrons' use of the self-service copiers and scanners to infringe Dr Allworth's copyright.

6. Natalie Smith is the founder of Natalie's Natural Beauty Products Inc. Her company imports, sells, and distributes olive oil–based skin care and body care products manufactured in Turkey exclusively for Smith. Smith filed a trademark application, hoping to operate her business under the trademark Natalie's Naturals. Larkin Industries already sells juices under the trademark Naturals and other marks that include Naturals, such as Naturals Classique. Larkin opposes the application and alleges that Smith is infringing its trademark rights by using a confusingly similar design. Smith's beauty products are generally sold in upscale grocery and specialty stores, whereas Larkin's juice is generally carried at mainstream grocery stores.

   The Court of Appeal decides in favour of Smith's company, finding that confusion was unlikely. The court also finds that Larkin filed an unnecessary injunction application, sent threatening letters, and engaged in overly complicated litigious conduct, which the court believes is menacing and abusive behaviour. Larkin successfully appeals the order, but Larkin's conduct has also resulted in substantial public criticism. As a result of media attention by local newspapers and bloggers, #naturals becomes the most locally hashtagged term on Twitter. Because of this onslaught of negative publicity, Larkin has offered a large settlement to Smith's company.

PART 5

Do you agree with the decision that Natalie's Naturals is not confusingly similar to Naturals juice products? Explain your answer. Consider the impact of social media in this case. How do you think social media is changing the face of business management? If you were part of Naturals' management, what steps would you take to avoid a similar situation in the future?

7. Four Horsepeople Technologies Inc is launching new Internet marketing software. Its product uses advanced algorithms to create and place advertisements faster and in more convenient locations on a website than its competitors' software. As well, it is thought that its advanced interface will be well received within the arts community. With the proper push, Four Horsepeople's branded marketing software may become the new standard in web advertising. Discuss how Four Horsepeople should make use of the three major branches of intellectual property—copyright, trademarks, and patents—to ensure its place in the market.

8. Backside Health Corp, the manufacturer and retailer of a very successful home-exercise device called Buns of Fury, is distressed by the emergence of a competitor marketing a strikingly similar product named Ferocious Buttocks. The Ferocious Buttocks machine is sold at a lower price than Buns of Fury on account of the substandard materials used in its construction. Backside Health wants to sue the competitor on the basis of trademark infringement. How should it characterize the alleged infringement? What remedies may be available? Briefly outline each remedy and discuss which are preferred.

9. Quickcopter, a helicopter manufacturer, has contracted your intellectual property firm for assistance in filing a statement of claim against its competitor Boss Helicopter (Boss). Quickcopter alleges that Boss has copied its patented design for a helicopter landing gear. Boss has produced 21 units that allegedly infringe Quickcopter's patent. The invention is intended for light helicopters and is composed of two skids, each of which has longitudinal ground support assurance and is connected to a front crosspiece and a rear crosspiece, which are themselves attached to the aircraft by connecting devices. Quickcopter believes that Boss should have known about the existence of its patent, given that Boss is a sophisticated corporate entity that employs thousands of engineers and highly skilled personnel. Assuming the court finds in favour of Quickcopter, explain what remedies it should ask the court to impose against Boss. Indicate what additional information, if any, the court would consider when deciding which remedies to impose.

10. The patent for Uncle Jimmie's Toy Blocks® has recently expired. Its design method included an array of tiny cylindrical studs on each block's top surface that interlock with precision-fitted perforations in the bottom of other blocks. Recognizing that the patent has finally expired, KT's Building Blocks™ (a competitor of Uncle Jimmie) releases a new set of building blocks that are compatible with Uncle Jimmie's. KT's blocks have a completely different visual appeal but function exactly the same. Disappointed that its patent protection has expired, Uncle Jimmie has expeditiously registered an industrial design on Uncle Jimmie's Toy Blocks® and is also considering a lawsuit claiming that KT is trying to pass off its blocks as his. Will either of these strategies allow Uncle Jimmie to continue his monopoly in the interlocking toy block market? Explain your reasoning.

11. Louis Saint Chicken has sued its closest competitor, Bistro Poultry, for misappropriation of trade secrets, and former employee Nicolette Lemar for breach of confidence with regard to Louis's secret dipping sauce. Nicolette, who worked for Louis as a supervisor in its sauce laboratory for the last seven years, was recently recruited as Vice-President of Research and Development at Bistro. Subsequently, Bistro began to produce and sell a chicken wing garlic sauce suspiciously similar to Louis's own world-famous dipping sauce. Louis alleges that, during the course of her employment, Nicolette was exposed to trade secrets with respect to its formula for its chicken wing sauce. There was no contractual clause barring Nicolette from disclosing the ingredients of the sauce or from undertaking future employment within the industry. What must Louis prove to succeed in its claim against Nicolette? How can Louis better protect itself against the occurrence of a similar incident in the future?

12. Wotherspoon World Industries (WWI) is one of Canada's largest stock photography businesses. WWI supplies cutting-edge digital photographs to advertisers, magazines, newspapers, journals, book publishers, businesses, and governments across Canada. WWI typically retains copyright in its photographs and grants each entity a non-exclusive licence for specific uses of the images. WWI employs a number of salespeople who have access to WWI's detailed and comprehensive customer list. WWI guards this secret customer list very closely. However, WWI does not have a confidentiality clause in its contracts with its salespeople. WWI believes that it can build better trust and loyalty with its salespeople by not using formal contracts. Recently, WWI learned that one of its former salespeople had opened a business in direct competition with WWI and that the salesperson was soliciting the business of all of WWI's customers. When WWI checked its electronic records, it learned that the former salesperson had viewed and printed a copy of WWI's customer list the day before he quit. WWI believes that the salesperson took a copy of the confidential customer list. What must WWI show in order to succeed in a claim against the former salesperson? Does it make a difference if the salesperson did not actually take a copy of the customer list but instead merely recalled customers and contacts from memory?

Weblinks

Canadian Intellectual Property Office (CIPO) www.cipo.ic.
gc.ca/eic/site/cipointernet-internetopic.nsf/eng/home

CIPO was created to administer the intellectual property
system in Canada and to provide information on intellectual property. Its website links to the web pages of each
subsection of intellectual property law.

**Canadian Intellectual Property Policy: Laws and
Regulations—Industry Canada** http://strategis.ic.gc.ca/epic/
internet/inippd-dppi.nsf/en/h_ip00007e.html

This site provides links to Canadian legislation regulating
patents, copyright, trademarks, and industrial design.

Canadian Patent Database http://brevets-patents.ic.gc.ca/
opic-cipo/cpd/eng/introduction.html

This online searchable database lets you search, retrieve,
and inspect over 1 500 000 Canadian patent documents.

Canadian Trade-Marks Database http://strategis.ic.gc.ca/
cipo/trademarks/search/tmSearch.do

This trademarks database allows you to search by trademark, status, application number, and registration number.

Canadian Trade-marks Journal www.ic.gc.ca/cipo/
tradejournal.nsf/tmmain-eng?readform

This CIPO web page archives the *Canadian Trade-marks
Journal*, which operates under the authority of the *Trademark Act* and publishes applications for trademarks for
public comment and opposition.

Copyright Board of Canada www.cb-cda.gc.ca

This site provides information on public hearings, recent
decisions of the board, links to copyright collectives, and
general information on copyright.

Creative Commons Canada http://creativecommons.org

Creative Commons is a non-profit organization that allows
creators to share their works with others, and to use the
works of others that have been issued under a Creative
Commons licence. Creative Commons has a worldwide
presence, including in Canada. This website contains
information about the organization, including short animated movies that explain the history and concepts behind
Creative Commons.

Intellectual Property Institute of Canada (IPIC) www.ipic.ca

IPIC is a professional organization concerned with patents,
trademarks, copyright, and industrial design. It maintains a
list of intellectual property agents and lawyers.

**Intellectual Property Policy Directorate—Industry
Canada** www.ic.gc.ca/eic/site/ippd-dppi.nsf/eng/home

This directorate is responsible for reviewing and modernizing federal intellectual property laws. Its website

provides news, research papers, laws and regulations,
treaties, and links related to intellectual property.

**International Intellectual Property Policy: International
Treaties— Industry Canada** http://strategis.ic.gc.ca/epic/
internet/inippd-dppi.nsf/en/h_ip00008e.html

This web page provides basic information on the international intellectual property treaties that Canada has
signed and links to their full text.

PATSCAN—Patent and Trademark Searching www.patscan.ca

This site provides patent and trademark searches for university and industry, intellectual property resources, and
database access.

Recording Industry Association of America (RIAA) www.riaa.
com/index.php

RIAA represents the joint interests of many American film
and music studios. Its site provides information on industry news, copyright, freedom of speech, licensing and
royalties, piracy, audio technologies, and the interaction
of music and the Internet.

**Society of Composers, Authors and Music Publishers of
Canada (SOCAN)** www.socan.ca

SOCAN collects and administers tariffs for music copyrights.
Its website provides information on events, news, and other
resources for music consumers, creators, and publishers.

US Copyright Office http://lcweb.loc.gov/copyright

This US government website provides a wealth of US
copyright information, publications, legislation, announcements, and a searchable registration database.

US Patent and Trademark Office (USPTO) www.uspto.gov

This US Department of Commerce site allows users to search
patents and trademarks, order copies, apply for patents, register trademarks, pay fees, and monitor file progress.

World Intellectual Property Organization (WIPO) www.wipo.
org/index.html

This website provides information on intellectual property,
WIPO activities and services, and links to treaties, decisions, and publications.

19 Electronic Commerce

LEARNING OBJECTIVES

After completing this chapter, you should be able to:

❶ Outline the business problems arising from the domain name system and understand the Canadian Internet Registry Authority Dispute Resolution Policy and its remedies.

❷ Explain the key components of a website's terms of use and privacy policy, and articulate how these can be used to reduce business risk in electronic commerce.

❸ Evaluate the benefits and the risks of allowing user-generated content on a website.

❹ Understand the concept of intermediary liability as it pertains to Internet service providers and online service providers.

❺ Outline some general strategies that have been adopted in existing and proposed electronic commerce legislation to ensure business certainty in online transactions.

❻ Discuss the contractual issues specific to automated electronic commerce and the legislative method for correcting keystroke errors.

❼ Discuss the jurisdictional implications of transacting in a global medium and explain how to minimize exposure to liability online.

❽ Formulate strategies for managing the legal risks, responsibilities, and costs associated with privacy breaches.

❾ Describe the core principles of consumer protection and the potential benefits they provide.

❿ Understand the ramifications of identity theft and describe the risks and responsibilities arising from spyware, spam, phishing, and telemarketing.

On 1 January 2007, nearly 90 years into its annual tradition of naming its "Person of the Year," *Time* magazine made a rather unusual choice. Previous winners had included the likes of Mahatma Gandhi, Adolf Hitler, Elizabeth II, John F. Kennedy, and Martin Luther King, Jr, not to mention business greats such as Walter Chrysler, Ted Turner, Andy Grove, Jeff Bezos, and Bill Gates. Reflecting its choice for 2006 with cover art depicting a computer screen in the form of a mirror, the magazine pronounced, "for seizing the reins of the global media, for founding and framing the new digital democracy, for working for nothing and beating the pros at their own game, *Time's* Person of the Year for 2006 is you."[1]

The decision to celebrate the Internet, its users, and the impressive business of user-generated content (that is, content produced by everyday people) proved to be quite controversial. Some critics wondered whether it would have been more appropriate to give the award to innovators who had created the applications that made possible a participatory Internet, such as Chad Hurley and Steve Chen (*YouTube*) or Mark Zuckerberg (*Facebook*). However, the magazine had its reasons: "It's a story about community and collaboration on a scale never seen before. It's about the cosmic compendium of knowledge *Wikipedia* and the million-channel peoples' network *YouTube* and the online metropolis *MySpace*. It's about the many wrestling power from the few and helping one another for nothing and how that will not only change the world, but also change the way the world changes."[2]

Without question, such changes have also had dramatic effects in the business world. The year of *Wikipedia*, *YouTube*, and *MySpace* also signalled a significant resurgence in electronic commerce. As one example of the potential for personalized electronic commerce, consider the fact that the annual global revenue from **ringtones**—very short songs and sounds that can be downloaded to a cellphone or email device to indicate an incoming call or text message— now stands at over $2 billion.[3]

From a business perspective, the Internet has been a key communications platform for electronic commerce for at least one and a half decades. In this context, **electronic commerce** refers to technology-mediated transactions between two businesses or between a business and a customer across a communications network. Electronic commerce makes many transactions easier and more affordable. Electronic commerce facilitates businesses in reaching more customers in more places. It enables the speedy formation and performance of contracts. And it can reduce expenses associated with business development and product marketing.

Although the communication element of electronic commerce greatly enhanced and facilitated business right off the mark, most transactions in the early days of the Internet still involved the physical transportation of goods, services, or information from one place to another (think *Amazon. ca*). However, as network technologies and bandwidth capacities began to improve toward the end of the Internet's first decade, the digital transmission of many goods and services no longer required physical interaction or transportation (think *iTunes*). This possibility, as well as the advent of user-generated content sites, such as *Flickr* and *YouTube*, and social networking

a **ringtone** is a very short song or sound that can be downloaded to a cellphone or email device to indicate an incoming call or text message

electronic commerce refers to technology-mediated transactions between two businesses or between a business and a customer across a communications network

PART 5

---

[1]. L Grossman "Time's Person of The Year: You" *Time* (13 December 2006).

[2]. *Ibid*.

[3]. B Ray "Ringtones Still Netting $2.1bn for Music Biz" *The Register* (11 November 2011) <www.theregister.co.uk/2011/11/11/ringtone_sales/>.

sites, such as *Facebook* and *Twitter*, have undoubtedly transformed many business models, creating new schemes for advertising and new ways to manage, motivate, and monitor employees. How do these new ways of doing business affect the way that we manage legal risk? Do those who manage legal risk need to think differently about electronic commerce as compared with other modes of doing business?

These are not easy questions. In many instances the legal issues are the same. Likewise, some of the once difficult issues arising in the early days of electronic commerce are by now straightforward, everyday commercial transactions. For example, previous uncertainties about how (not) to generate an online offer (or how its acceptance may be communicated) are now clear-cut.[4]

However, there are other issues more specific to electronic commerce that were not easily dealt with by existing laws. This resulted in the development of specialized legislation, discussed below, the purpose of which is to enable electronic commerce by removing various legal impediments. While it is tempting to think exclusively about the Internet when thinking about electronic commerce, the legal considerations are in fact much broader. Important laws, policies, and guidelines are in full-scale development with respect to a range of technologies associated directly or indirectly with electronic commerce. As a matter of risk management, a business that relies on information technology or is otherwise engaged in electronic commerce must stay abreast of these developments.

This chapter examines how law has responded to various technological changes in the business world. Given the relative novelty of this area of law, there is no single, comprehensive chronology, or structure to adhere to. In this chapter, we track the issues in the order that they might be encountered when a business moves into the electronic commerce environment. For that reason, we begin with the legal issues that arise when a business sets out to acquire a domain name for its website or other purposes. We then look at a number of risks attendant on hosting a website and some best practices for managing those risks through the development of terms of use, privacy policies, and policies regarding the use of user-generated content. Website owners and other online businesses are often intermediaries to an electronic transaction even if they are not involved in buying or selling goods or services themselves. This raises a number of unique legal issues pertaining to Internet service providers and other online service providers, which are also canvassed here.

Next, we investigate how the law treats business transactions that take place online, focusing on contract formation and rules regarding automated transactions. Because online transactions are often global in nature, we follow this with a discussion of the risks inherent in doing business in more than one jurisdiction. In an age of globalism and the rapid infiltration of technology, it is also important to understand the risks arising from the proliferation of data flows about individuals, businesses, and corporations. Personal and corporate information is regularly collected, used by, and disclosed to third parties. This trade in information generates a number of legal risks that businesses must face concerning identity theft and other privacy breaches.

[4.] They are, therefore, more appropriately examined in our general chapter on contract formation. See Chapter 7.

After examining these issues, we end this chapter by looking at consumer protection rules and guidelines, including codes of practice and recently proposed or enacted legislation regarding a range of consumer protection issues that businesses need to know about involving identity theft, spam, spyware, phishing, and telemarketing.

Domain Names

L.O. ❶ ❷

When a business decides to engage in electronic commerce, one of the first choices to be made is "where" it will locate itself online. Although a key benefit of electronic commerce is that geography is less important, the marketing slogan "location, location, location" is still relevant on the Internet. Perhaps the most important real estate in cyberspace is the *domain name*. A **domain name** locates the Internet protocol (IP) address associated with one or more websites belonging to an organization or other entity on the Internet. For example, by entering www.pearsoncanada.ca into a web browser or by entering the name "Pearson Canada" in a search engine, you will locate the website of the company Pearson Canada, the publisher of this book.[5] Because of the enormous number of domain names on the Internet, several national and international organizations administer their registration and use.[6]

a **domain name** locates the Internet protocol (IP) address associated with one or more websites belonging to an organization or other entity on the Internet

In the world of real estate, a person may buy a piece of land with a view to re-selling it at a profit. A similar sort of activity can happen on the Internet although, from a legal perspective, it does not involve property. A **cybersquatter** purchases a potentially valuable domain name in which they have no legitimate claim with the intention of later selling it to the highest bidder. Not all attempts to sell a domain name are illegitimate. For example, some entrepreneurs register domain names for common English words (such as drugstore.com or furniture.com) in the hope of reselling them to companies that are interested in dealing with the relevant products online. Domain names are typically registered on a first-come, first-served basis. The first person to register it has the right to re-sell it. This can be big business. For example, sex.com was reportedly sold for $12 million, while business.com sold for $350 million.[7]

a **cybersquatter** purchases a potentially valuable domain name in which they have no legitimate claim with the intention of later selling it to the highest bidder

Problems arise, however, when a domain name is not merely a common word but rather a name in which someone else asserts a proprietary interest. Although the regulating authorities have received complaints about thousands of domain names, the disputes usually fall into four groups.

1. A person may innocently or justifiably register a domain name that is later disputed. For example, if your newborn nephew is named Ed Pearson, you might register the domain www.pearsoned.ca and post pictures of him at that address. You may receive a complaint from Pearson Canada, which holds a proprietary interest in that name by way of trademarks still held associated with its former name: Pearson Education.

[5.] Like many other international companies, Pearson Canada has registered several other domain names, such as www.pearsoneducation.com.

[6.] For instance, dot-ca (as in www.pearsoned.ca) is administered by the Canadian Internet Registry Authority (CIRA).

[7.] R Weisman "Is America.com a $12m Name Like Sex.com?" *Boston Globe* (19 May 2008); N Gonzalez "Business.com Sells for $350 Million," *TechCrunch* (26 July 2007) <http://techcrunch.com/2007/07/26/businesscom-sells-for-350-million>.

2. A person may register a domain name that resembles a trademark to which both parties claim a commercial right. For example, if you hold the US trademark Pearson International, you may register www.pearsoninternational.ca. If so, you may receive a complaint from the Greater Toronto Airport Authority, which believes that, as operator of Pearson International Airport and holder of a similar registered Canadian mark, it has a stronger claim to that domain name.[8]

3. A person may be guilty of **registration in bad faith**. For example, you might try to be the first to register www.pearsoncanada.ca, either to prevent Pearson Canada from using it, to profit from its use by selling it to Pearson at a price far exceeding its cost, or to use it to confer an advantage to Pearson's competitors.

4. A person may register a domain name not for the purpose of re-selling it but to create a "click farm." A **click farm** is a large group of websites that link to one another in order to multiply the number of incoming links to each website, thereby increasing the index ranking for search engines. By populating each site in the group with click-through advertising, the click farm can inflate Internet rankings and generate substantial advertising revenues.

registration in bad faith occurs when a domain name is registered to prevent someone with a legitimate proprietary interest from using it to force them to buy it at a price far exceeding its cost or to use it to the benefit of a competitor

a **click farm** is a large group of websites that link to one another in order to multiply the number of incoming links to each website, thereby increasing the index ranking for search engines

As discussed in the previous chapter, there are some circumstances in which a business may wish to commence trademark infringement or passing-off litigation against an offending party. However, litigation may require a considerable investment of time and money. That is especially true if the cyber-squatter lives in a different legal jurisdiction in some distant part of the world. These costs may be out of proportion to the value of securing the domain name. As a result, domain name registry authorities have adopted expedited procedures for resolving disputes over claims to a particular domain name in a way that can avoid the litigation process entirely. This is achieved through *online dispute resolution (ODR)*. As we discussed in Chapter 2, alternative dispute resolution (ADR) allows parties to settle their argument without involving a court. In the domain name context, ODR can resolve disputes far more quickly and cost-effectively than court systems. Although it is still open to a business to bring a claim in court for trademark infringement, there is no need to do so if the only goal is to secure the domain name.

All registrants within the dot-ca domain, such as pearsoncanada.ca, are governed by the Canadian Internet Registry Authority (CIRA).[9] As such, they are contractually required to adhere to the **CIRA Dispute Resolution Policy** (CDRP), a framework for the resolution of disputes between dot-ca domain name registrants and trademark owners alleging bad faith registration of domain names. All proceedings are administered by dispute resolution service providers approved by CIRA (currently either the British Columbia International Commercial Arbitration Centre or Resolution Canada Inc).[10] Domain name disputes can be resolved by these ODR providers much more quickly than a protracted trademark dispute in the courts.

CIRA Dispute Resolution Policy (CDRP) is a framework for the resolution of disputes between dot-ca domain name registrants and trademark owners alleging bad faith registration of domain names

A business with a presence in Canada or holding Canadian trademarks that wishes to commence a dispute against a dot-ca registrant may file a written complaint in either French or English. The registrant has 20 days to respond.

---

8. Though a domain name may resemble a trademark, these are two distinct concepts. A trademark is a more extensive right to use a particular word and extends beyond the use of that term in a domain name. See Chapter 18 for further explanation on the protection granted to trademarks.

9. Canadian Internet Registration Authority <www.cira.ca>.

10. Canadian Internet Registration Authority, *CDRP* <www.cira.ca/legal/cdrp>.

The arbitral panel will issue its decision based on the written submissions and evidence provided by the parties and will normally make its decision within 28 days of being appointed. In many cases, no response is ever filed. In such cases, the panel will make a decision based on the complainant's information. One significant disadvantage of domain name dispute resolution is that the only remedy available is cancellation or transfer of the domain name from the cybersquatter to the business. Damages and legal costs are not available as they are in court proceedings. Cybersquatters who are willing to abandon a domain name may therefore operate with relatively little to no fear of the consequences of domain name arbitrations.

A business wishing to pursue a claim regarding a domain name should consider a number of risk management factors in determining whether to bring court or arbitration proceedings. The first factor to consider is whether dispute resolution is appropriate at all. Domain name dispute resolution is typically designed to handle only a narrow category of cases—clear cases of bad-faith cybersquatting. Disputes between two companies with competing trademark rights to a name will normally not be suited for resolution by ODR. If both litigation and dispute resolution are options, then the claimant will need to consider a number of factors including (i) the strength of the trademark, (ii) the evidence available about the cybersquatter, (iii) the urgency of resolving the dispute, (iv) the acceptable costs of resolution, and (v) the ultimate objectives, such as whether the business merely wants a transfer of the domain name or whether it also wants money damages for trademark infringement. Generally speaking, dispute resolution can be an efficient and low-risk way to resolve a domain name dispute where a strong case can be made out on paper. If credibility is an issue, evidence against a cybersquatter is lacking, or a claimant wants an injunction and an award of money damages for trademark infringement, then litigation in court may be preferable.

As a matter of risk management, the best strategy is to avoid domain name difficulties altogether. While that is not always possible, businesses can take steps to minimize the potential for domain name disputes. For instance, as a component part of its overall intellectual property strategy, a business should register trademarks and business names as domain names as early as possible to avoid time-consuming and potentially expensive interactions with a cybersquatter. These **defensive domain name registrations** might include registering domain names that correspond to company names, brand names, slogans, and product names. While dot-com, dot-net, and dot-org domain names tend to be the most popular domain names, a business should also consider the various country-code domain names that it might wish to register, for example, dot-ca or dot-us. Note that a registered trademark or business name will not guarantee your business a proprietary interest in a particular domain name.

Business Decision 19.1 **provides an example of a domain name dispute.**

defensive domain name registrations is the registration of trademarks and business names as domain names as early as possible to avoid time-consuming and expensive interactions with a cybersquatter

Business Decision **19.1**

Domain Name Dispute Resolution

Freemantle Media is an international production company. One of its flagship programs is the hit television series American Idol, a reality show premised on a singing competition. By the end of the show's first season in 2002, each episode attracted between 4.5 and 5.5 million Canadian viewers. In 2006 and 2007, FreemantleMedia registered trademarks in Canada for the American Idol name and logo. Freemantle Media already owned *americanidol.com*. However, when the acquisitions manager attempted to register the *americanidol.ca* domain name in late 2009, she was surprised to learn that someone else had already registered it. Worse, when entering *americanidol.ca* into her web browser, the

(Continued)

(continued)

manager was automatically re-directed to a website with pay-per-click links to American Idol's competitors.

The acquisitions manager conducted a WHOIS search at http://cira.ca (a database used to determine the owner of a domain name or IP address) and discovered that the registrant was an individual in Canada named Dave Leather. Leather had registered the domain name in 2003. All attempts to negotiate a suitable arrangement with the registrant failed.[11]

Questions for Discussion

1. From a business perspective, do you think that Freemantle Media should commence an action for trademark infringement or simply seek an order for the transfer of the americanidol.ca domain name?

2. What dispute resolution provider(s) can Freemantle Media use if it decides to seek a claim to its dot-ca domain name and what is the legal device that determines this?

3. What could FreemantleMedia have done to avoid this situation?

Concept Summary 19.1 summarizes domain name business strategies.

Concept Summary 19.1

Business Strategy Regarding Domain Names

- Avoid disputes by registering key trademarks, product names, and business names as domain names before someone else does (*eg* register key domain names *prior* to the launch of the relevant business or product, if possible).

- Consider registering generic domains (*eg* dot-com) and country-code domains (*eg* dot-ca) for the countries where you do business.

- If a dispute arises regarding a domain name, consider whether dispute resolution is an option.

- When deciding whether to pursue dispute resolution or litigation, consider factors such as the strength of the trademark, the evidence available about the cybersquatter, the urgency of resolving the dispute, the cost you are willing to incur, and your objectives.

L.O. ❸

Websites

a website is a collection of web pages containing text, images, videos, music, and sometimes other business assets that are hosted on one or more web servers, usually accessible via the Internet

Once the appropriate domain name has been acquired, the next thing a business must do is build a *website*. A **website** is a collection of web pages containing text, images, videos, music, and sometimes other business assets that are hosted on one or more web servers, usually accessible via the Internet. Online businesses need to think of their websites as an integrated whole, recognizing that there is as much potential for legal risk in its links to external websites or its use of external databases as there is on the website's main banner.

Corporate websites usually display business logos, associated trademarks, and brand-related images. Often, they contain mission statements and other information about the history and operations of the business. Products and services are usually described, sometimes in the form of frequently asked questions (FAQs). Many companies provide biographies of key executives and employees in the organization. Corporate websites often have news items and press releases and provide lists of key clients, projects, and partnerships. Some also include postings for employment opportunities, annual reports, and other investor information. Given the vast amount of information published on a corporate website, a business must be carefully attuned to potential liabilities that it might incur—even if it never conducts a single online transaction. These liabilities include disputes about copyright and trademarks, claims of fraudulent or innocent misrepresentation, defamation, discrimination, securities disclosures, and possibly even negligence or criminal infractions. We will not discuss the potential legal consequences of these in detail because their online occurrence

---

11. *CIRA Decision 2010-00146* <www.cira.ca/assets/Uploads/00146-americanidol.ca3.pdf>.

is usually treated in the same manner as it would be in other circumstances contemplated in our discussions of the law of torts, contracts, and public law in previous chapters in this book.

Consequently, the remainder of our discussion will focus on three important aspects of a website and how those aspects can be used to mitigate risk in electronic commerce:

- terms of use
- privacy policy
- user-generated content

TERMS OF USE

Not all websites contain *terms of use*. **Terms of use** define the legal relationship between visitors to a website and its owner; they stipulate the conditions under which a visitor may use or contribute to information or products on the site. These terms (sometimes called "terms of service" or "terms and conditions") are usually posted in a separate document identified by a hyperlink on the main page of a website. Companies post them to create a contract that binds all visitors to their websites' terms. Although many businesses do not realize this, terms of use are a crucial means of protecting the interests of the business.

Typical terms of use include provisions concerning the following:

- product descriptions
- pricing policies
- limitations on the use of goods and services
- legal relationship between visitor and business
- general responsibilities of visitor and business
- code of online conduct
- passwords and security
- privacy
- information sharing with advertisers and third party websites
- copyright and trademark notices
- intellectual property rights and licences
- disclaimers, waivers, limitations, and exclusions of liability
- jurisdiction and dispute resolution
- other boilerplate provisions (for example, indemnity, entire agreement, severability of terms, non-transferability)

Given the potential import of such provisions, it is essential for a business to ensure that its terms of use are legally binding—even if nothing is ever bought or sold online. Fortunately, ensuring that the terms are binding is not difficult, as long as the business carefully considers the basic rules of contract formation discussed in Chapter 7. In particular, the business must construct its website so that the terms of use are understood as part of a unilateral offer that can be accepted by the performance of some condition (namely, use of the website). The offeror should also ensure that acceptance of its offer to use the site includes an explicit promise by the offeree to abide by its terms. This can be accomplished by including in the terms of use language such as the following: "By accessing or using our website, you signify that you have read, understood,

terms of use define the legal relationship between visitors to a website and its owner; they stipulate the conditions under which a visitor may use or contribute to information or products on the site

and agreed to be bound by these Terms of Use, whether or not you are a registered member of the site."

As is the case with more traditional standard form agreements, the central issue arising in typical contractual disputes over the terms of use is whether the business provided reasonable notice of the terms. (See our previous discussion of the ticket contracts in Chapter 9.) A website owner wishing to ensure that notice has been adequately provided will require visitors to click "I agree" after viewing the terms and conditions as a pre-condition of using the site. Much like someone who is given the opportunity to read the terms of a paper-based standard form contract but decides to sign it without reading it, visitors who click "I agree" will later be precluded from claiming that they didn't have adequate notice of the terms.

In *Rudder v Microsoft*, two law students argued that one of Microsoft's terms of use (stipulating that disputes arising from the use of the website must be resolved by courts in the State of Washington) was not binding because of a lack of notice since the "fine print" could not be viewed in its entirety from the main page of the site. The court refused this argument, stating that the law students were given the opportunity to read the terms of use before they clicked on the button that said, "I agree." According to the court, the students' claim was no different from saying that only the terms and conditions appearing on the signature page of a printed document should apply. The court also said that ignorance of the relevant term was no excuse, because Microsoft's agreement required potential members to view its terms on two occasions and to signify acceptance on each occasion. In fact, the second display of the terms advised users, "If you click 'I agree' without reading the membership agreement, you are still agreeing to be bound by all of the terms... without limitation."[12]

Establishing and ensuring that visitors comply with the terms of use is most easily achieved in the context of online services that require the payment of fees or a form of registration. A **registration process** requires the visitor to provide some form of identification, such as a name, email address, or credit card number, and, for many websites, additional personal information. In exchange, the website assigns a password or some other means of authenticating visitors so that they can gain secure access to the website. During a registration process, the business can also stipulate the terms of use and require individuals to click "I agree" (or an equivalent phrase indicating acceptance) before finalizing the registration in order to ensure that they are part of the overall agreement between the parties. Registration also ensures a means of identifying, locating, and communicating with a person who is in violation of the terms. Although a carefully orchestrated registration process is usually sufficient to ensure that the terms of use are binding, it is not always necessary. There are many ways to provide notice of the terms of use without requiring visitors to register, and many potential customers prefer not to register or otherwise provide nonessential personal information.

Businesses will sometimes want to bind their customers to terms and conditions set out on their websites regardless of whether those customers ever visit or use their websites. This was precisely the situation in *Kanitz v Rogers Cable Inc*, where an Ontario court had to decide whether unilateral changes made by Rogers regarding the price of its cable/Internet services were enforceable given that the only notice of the fee change was provided in a hyperlink posted on its corporate website.[13] Although Kanitz claimed never to have seen the notice or to have known of its existence, the court held that the changes to the contract

a **registration process** requires the visitor to provide some form of identification, such as a name, email address, or credit card number, and, for many websites, additional personal information

---

[12.] *Rudder v Microsoft* (1999) 47 CCLT (2d) 168 (Ont SCJ) at para 17.

[13.] *Kanitz v Rogers Cable Inc* (2002) 58 OR (3d) 299 (SCJ).

were enforceable because the original contract stated that the defendant could make changes if it sent customers a notice by email, by postal mail, or via its website. Although the court noted that the defendant could have done more to notify its customers of the changes to the contract, the defendant's posting of the changes on its website was found to be sufficient, given the wording of the original contract.[14] The decision in the *Kanitz* case suggests that businesses may be able to make binding changes to a contract if they reserve the right to do so and then fulfill any notice requirements set out in the contract. To manage risk, however, businesses should strive to make contractual terms and changes to such terms as conspicuous as possible.

Rudder, Kanitz, and the more recent Supreme Court of Canada decision in *Dell Computer* demonstrate that the terms of use on a website can be used to create effective contracts that protect business interests online and off.[15] In fact, many consumer groups argue that the incredible power and reach of these unilateral contracts can lead to unfair, one-sided agreements that favour a business at the expense of its customers.[16] From the perspective of risk management, while businesses must act to protect their interests, it is bad business practice to create terms of use that obfuscate unfair or unconscionable terms. A court will find a way to protect consumer interests if it feels that a business is operating unfairly by burying important consumer information or using other means to conceal hidden terms or practices. This is something to keep in mind when developing business practices and policies.

PRIVACY POLICIES

With a domain name in hand, a website set up, and the terms of use in place, businesses must also consider a number of information policy issues, including informational privacy. In the online setting, businesses rely extensively on personal information to identify, develop, and maintain relationships with customers. **Personal information**, in this context, is information about an identifiable individual. According to the Office of the Privacy Commissioner of Canada it includes:[17]

personal information is information about an identifiable individual

- name, age, weight, height
- medical records
- income, purchases, and spending habits
- race, ethnic origin, and colour
- blood type, DNA code, fingerprints
- marital status and religion
- education
- home address, personal email or other electronic address, and phone number
- opinions, evaluations, comments, social status, or disciplinary actions

14. *Ibid.*

15. *Dell Computer Corp v Union des consommateurs* (2007) 284 DLR (4th) 577 (SCC).

16. See *eg* Canadian Internet Policy and Public Interest Clinic (CIPPIC), *Projects and Cases: Consumer Protection Online.*

17. Office of the Privacy Commissioner of Canada *Fact Sheet: Complying with the Personal Information Protection and Electronic Documents Act* (June 2005) <www.priv.gc.ca/resource/fs-fi/02_05_d_16_e.asp>.

privacy laws set limits on the extent to which businesses can collect, use, or disclose personal information in the course of their activities

Online businesses regularly buy, sell, trade, or share personal information and other marketing data that facilitates communications with new customers who they believe are predisposed toward their goods and services. Consumers often surrender those details without consent and, sometimes, without even knowing it. **Privacy laws** set limits on the extent to which businesses can collect, use, or disclose personal information in the course of their activities. Although privacy laws are meant to protect individual rights, they also recognize the needs of businesses to gather, store, and share personal information for legitimate business purposes. Businesses need to carefully consider their obligations under those laws and should proactively attend to trends and changes in privacy protection legislation. Figure 19.1 contains a list of risk-minimizing strategies for businesses that collect personal information. More often than not, respecting consumer privacy is good for business. Limiting the types of personal information that a business collects from its customers will minimize exposure to liability and reduce compliance costs.

Canada's private sector privacy laws are complicated by our Constitution, which gives Parliament the power to make laws relating to the "regulation of trade and commerce," and gives the provinces the exclusive power to make laws relating to "property and civil rights in the province."[18] Since privacy laws protect civil rights by limiting trade and commerce, the regulation of privacy clearly overlaps with these federal and provincial powers. Consequently, the Government of Canada enacted the *Personal Information Protection and Electronic Documents Act (PIPEDA)* in an attempt to ensure a significant overlap between federal and provincial privacy laws. Since January 2004, this federal law has applied across Canada; however, provinces have the ability to enact "substantially similar" privacy laws, in which case the federal law will not apply to certain activities and organizations within those provinces. To date, only British Columbia, Alberta, and Quebec have created their own business

FIGURE 19.1   Strategies for Minimizing Privacy Compliance Risks and Costs

• Gain a clear understanding of how your business and technology might collect, use, or disclose personal information. Talk to your information technology employees and involve them in your privacy compliance plans.
• Appoint a person or a team of people to be responsible for privacy issues. Ensure that all of your employees receive adequate training in privacy.
• Consider strategies for limiting, as much as possible, the collection of personal information— especially information of a sensitive nature.

• Before dealing with personal information, always ask how a reasonable person would view the situation.
 • Ask the following questions before dealing with personal information:
   • Is it necessary to meet a specific need?
   • Is it likely to be effective in meeting that need?
   • Is the loss of privacy proportional to the benefit gained?
   • Is there a less privacy-invasive way of achieving the same result?

• Whenever possible, obtain consent before dealing with personal information. And, of course, always comply with the consent requirements under *PIPEDA* and similar statutes.
• Consider encrypting or otherwise removing identifiers from personal information where possible.

[18.] *The Constitution Act, 1867* (UK), 30 & 31 Victoria, c 3, ss 91(2) and 92(13).

sector privacy laws.[19] As with many other laws governing electronic commerce, businesses that operate in multiple jurisdictions need to be aware of the legal discrepancies between jurisdictions.

The legislation in Quebec, Alberta, and British Columbia all carry out the same basic functions as *PIPEDA*, namely, to govern the means by which private sector organizations handle personal information. All three jurisdictions take a balanced approach meant to recognize both the right of individuals to have their personal information protected and the need of organizations to collect information for purposes that are reasonable. The legislation in Alberta and British Columbia provide individuals with the opportunity to request access to their own personal information and includes provisions regarding the correction and care of personal information by organizations. In either province, a privacy commissioner is given the power to review decisions made by businesses that deny individuals access to their own personal information or that refuse requests for corrections to personal information. Individuals in Alberta and British Columbia may also make a complaint to the commissioner if they believe their personal information has been collected, used, or disclosed without proper authority or without their consent. Unlike *PIPEDA* and the Quebec legislation, the Alberta and BC Acts do not require consent where an employee's personal information is collected, used, or disclosed only for the purpose of the employment relationship, as long as the employee is notified in advance, and as long as the collection, use, or disclosure is reasonable, considering the purpose.[20] The Quebec legislation (which was enacted 10 years earlier than the Alberta and BC Acts) is similar in most of the above respects but is even more expansive, applying to all private sector organizations, and not just with respect to commercial activities. Quebec's Commission d'accès à l'information can issue binding orders requiring compliance with the legislation. The Civil Code of Quebec also creates liability for breach of the principal requirements of the Quebec legislation, for which individuals may claim damages in a court action. This right of action, which does not exist in other provinces, creates additional privacy risks for businesses operating in Quebec that are not compliant with basic privacy principles.

Regardless of which province a business is in and whether the provincial or federal privacy law applies, it is safe to say that:[21]

- If your business wants to collect, use, or disclose personal information about people, you should obtain their consent, except in a few specific and limited circumstances.
- You can use or disclose people's personal information only for the purpose for which they gave consent.

---

[19] *Personal Information Protection Act*, SBC 2003, c 63 (BC); *Personal Information Protection Act*, SA 2003, c P-6.5 (Alta); *Act Respecting the Protection of Personal Information in the Private Sector*, RSQ 1993, c P-39.1 (Que). Ontario has enacted "substantially similar legislation" for the health sector but not the business sector: *Personal Health Information Protection Act*, SO 2004, c 3, Sched A. The fact that businesses are subject to either the federal *PIPEDA* or a provincial equivalent may raise a question of constitutional authority. We discussed the division of powers between the two levels of government in Chapter 1.

[20] Bill C-12, *Safeguarding Canadians' Personal Information Act* (1st Sess 41st Parl 2011) proposes to expand the circumstances in which personal information under *PIPEDA* can be collected, used, or disclosed without the individual's knowledge or consent: when the personal information is produced during the course of employment; when the information is necessary to manage an employment relationship; and when the information is related to certain types of "business transactions" (that require a confidentiality agreement stating that the personal information can be used only for the transaction). As of the writing of this chapter, Bill C-12 remains at the first reading stage in Parliament.

[21] Office of the Privacy Commissioner of Canada *Fact Sheet: Complying with the* Personal Information Protection and Electronic Documents Act (June 2005) <www.priv.gc.ca/resource/fs-fi/02_05_d_16_e.asp>.

- Even with consent, you have to limit collection, use, and disclosure to purposes that a reasonable person would consider appropriate under the circumstances.

- Individuals have a right to see the personal information that your business holds about them, and to correct any inaccuracies.

- There is oversight, through the Privacy Commissioner of Canada or one of the provincial commissioners, to ensure that the law is respected, and that redress is available if individuals' rights are violated.

Of course, many businesses have no reason to collect personal information in the first place and we would be suspicious of them if they tried to do so. The hot-dog vendor on the street does not need to know my name or age. The downtown bookstore does not need my postal code. Online sellers might need my name and address if they are delivering physical goods to me, but may need only an email address if they are sending e-books or electronic tickets. Although the publication of a privacy policy is not required by law, from a risk management perspective, it is prudent for every business that has a website or that otherwise engages in the collection, use, and disclosure of personal information to formulate a carefully crafted privacy policy that accurately reflects business practices and adequately respects federal and provincial private sector privacy laws. The courts have begun to provide businesses with guidance on how to meet their obligations under *PIPEDA*.[22]

USER-GENERATED CONTENT

user-generated content refers to various kinds of online media, including photographs, videos, podcasts, comments, articles, and blogs that are produced and posted by visitors to a website

In addition to deciding how a business will deal with information that it posts about itself and information that it collects, uses, and discloses about others, some website owners must also consider a range of issues that arise with user-*generated content*. **User-generated content** refers to various kinds of online media, including photographs, videos, podcasts, comments, articles, and blogs that are produced and posted by visitors to a website. Many businesses allow visitors to post content in order to increase website traffic, draw a broader audience to the site, increase its brand awareness, and boost customer loyalty. To fully enjoy these and other benefits of user-generated content, it is important for the website owner to have the appropriate permissions from the visitors who made the contributions. The best way to achieve this is through a carefully drafted clause in the website's terms of use which, amongst other things, licences the use of the posted material to the website owner. Rather than requiring the visitor to surrender ownership of the material, which users may find offensive, a more prudent approach gives the website owner a non-exclusive though unlimited licence to "use, copy, edit, publish, and distribute the material, in any media, as well as the right to use the contributor's name, likeness, and performance."[23]

Although user-generated content can add value to a website, it also has the potential to generate liability and risks. These include:

- loss of brand identity
- liability for posting illegal content
- claims of false advertising[24]

[22.] For example, the Federal Court has noted a requirement for human checks of informational accuracy prior to the transmission and disclosure of personal information in some circumstances: *Nammo v TransUnion of Canada Inc* 2010 FC 1284. See also *Eastmond v Canadian Pacific Railway* (2004) 16 Admin LR (4th) 275 (FCTD), and *Englander v Telus Communications* (2004) 247 DLR (4th) 275 (FCA).

[23.] K Brown "Website User-Generated Content: Avoiding the Pitfalls" (30 April 2008) 4 *Co-Counsel: Technology Law Quarterly* 1 at 1–2.

[24.] *Ibid*.

Loss of Brand Identity

Although businesses can definitely benefit from the user-generated contributions made by visitors to their websites, there is always the possibility that the website could lose control over its **brand identity**, that is, how the business wishes consumers to perceive the company, organization, and its goods or services. For example, the Canadian Broadcasting Company allows its readers, listeners, and viewers to post online comments on many of its news items. While opening up the dialogue to the general public generates interest, readership, and, in some cases, "customer" loyalty, it is also possible for contributors to do some damage. Losing control over brand identity has an important legal dimension because it can undermine corporate trademarks and the means by which consumers are able to distinguish between goods or services in the marketplace. To avoid losing control over their intellectual property, businesses allowing user-generated content ought to consider whether it is appropriate to either moderate the content contributed by visitors or to let the visitors themselves inform the business about, for example, offensive or other inappropriate content posted by others. A **website moderator** examines and sorts contributions, flagging and, in some cases, deleting those which are irrelevant, disparaging, obscene, illegal, or insulting, with a view to providing quality assurance regarding the usefulness of outside contributions. Moderation systems range from sites that allow users to self-moderate to sites that employ human or automated moderators with certain delegated powers to enforce business policies or an online community's rules on behalf of the owner of the site. From a risk management perspective, it is not enough to simply monitor user-generated content, nor is it always desirable. A website that allows visitors to contribute content must carefully define acceptable and prohibited conduct and content in its terms of use and, where appropriate, in its privacy policy.

brand identity is how a business wishes consumers to perceive the company, organization, and its goods or services

a **website moderator** examines and sorts contributions, flagging and, in some cases, deleting those which are irrelevant, disparaging, obscene, illegal, or insulting, with a view to providing quality assurance regarding the usefulness of outside contributions

PART 5

Liability for Posting Illegal Content

In addition to protecting their reputation, intellectual property, and brand, business owners must be mindful that visitors to their websites might post content or contribute in ways that interfere with the legal rights of other businesses. As we shall see in the section that follows, one potential risk is that a visitor will post content about a third party who later claims the content is disparaging and false. Similarly, a website that allows user-generated content risks the possibility that a visitor might post content that infringes the copyright or trademark rights of another business. In the past, these risks were usually incurred only by information intermediaries such as Internet service providers; however, as more and more businesses seek to obtain the advantages of user-generated content, they must also be prepared to bear these burdens. In addition to moderating their websites, another important means businesses can use to reduce exposure to liability is by contemplating various possibilities explicitly in a website's terms of use. In particular, the terms of use should:

- require visitors contributing content to the site to warrant that the contributors themselves own all rights to the materials submitted
- provide explicit guidelines for the use of trademarks, names, and likenesses of other people, as well as materials subject to copyright by third parties
- prohibit visitors from posting any material in violation of the guidelines

- permit the website to remove materials in violation of the terms of use
- require visitors to indemnify the website owner for all user-generated content[25]

Claims of False Advertising

Even if user-generated content is acceptable and appropriate, its presence on a corporate or electronic commerce website runs the risk of blurring the corporate message with the views of its devoted consumers. One risk, in particular, is that user-generated content on a website could lead to claims of misrepresentation or false advertising about a company or its competitors' products or services. Consider Ethical Perspective 19.1.

Ethical Perspective **19.1**

Viral Sandwich Slander?

Doctor's Assoc Inc v QIP Holders 38 Media L Rep 1616 (D Conn 19 February 2010)

In an attempt to capitalize on the growing popularity of *YouTube*-style videos, Quiznos (a toasted sandwich franchise operation) decided to hold a contest amongst its consumer base to make the best commercial depicting Quiznos sandwiches as superior to the sandwiches of Subway, its chief competitor. The purpose of the contest was to generate brand loyalty as well as some entertaining homegrown commercials that would draw web traffic to Quiznos' promo site, meatnomeat.com, in exchange for the prospect that the lucky winner's video would be featured on VH1 and on a giant screen in Times Square on New Year's Eve. To give contestants guidance, Quiznos provided four sample videos showing that Subway sandwiches had no meat or less meat than Quiznos sandwiches. More than 100 contestants entered, resulting in many humorous submissions. For example, one of the videos showed two men in a sandwich-punting competition. While the first punter booted the light and airy Subway sandwich clear across a parking lot, so meat-heavy was the Quiznos sub that the second punter fell to the pavement when he attempted to kick it. Another video portrayed a wife arriving home with a Quiznos sandwich for her husband and a Subway sandwich for her dog. The winning video depicted a pinewood derby race between two sub-shaped cars. The much meatier Quiznos sub—more meat equalling more momentum—literally smoked past the Subway derby car,

which was reported by the *New York Times* to "topple over in defeat."[26] Not impressed by the disparaging manner in which its products were depicted, Subway sued for misrepresentation and false advertising.

Although these ads appear to be no different from the multitude of commercials in which one company bashes a competing brand of another (think PC v Mac, Coca-Cola v Pepsi), there is an important difference here. In this case, Quiznos disclaimed liability for false advertising on the basis that the uploaded commercials were generated by its customers. According to Quiznos, "We're just facilitating consumers who go out and create their own expression in the form of a commercial... there can't be an element of deception if everyone knows the videos were created by consumers for the sake of entering a contest."[27]

Questions for Discussion

1. Do you think that brands should be permitted to make fun of each other in public ad campaigns? Where do you draw the line?

2. What role, if any, did Quiznos play in the creation of the user-generated content uploaded to the contest website? Was Quiznos unethical in its role in the production of that content?

3. What should Quiznos have done differently?

---

[25] *Ibid* at 3.

[26] The winning video of the competition can be viewed online at the following link: www.myspace.com/video/allready/quiznos-vs-subway/37240080. The video that shows two men in a sandwich-punting competition can be found at "Quizno's v. Subway Kick," *Spike* (12 June 2002) <www.spike.com/video-clips/f0ax42/quiznos-vs-subway-kick>. The video depicting a woman bringing home a Quiznos sandwich for her husband and a Subway sandwich for her dog is found at "Quizno's Ummm," *Spike* (25 November 2006) <www.*spike*.com/video-clips/z4at0q/quiznos-ummm>.

[27] In denying Quiznos's motion for summary judgment, the court ruled that Quiznos was sufficiently involved in the creation and distributions of the videos and could therefore be held legally responsible for them: <http://pub.bna.com/eclr/06cv1710_021910.pdf>. The case settled shortly after this decision, thereby preventing further development of the law with regard to false advertising claims and user-generated marketing messages.

Intermediary Liability

L.O. ❹

Although user-generated content and other novelties in the online environment can sometimes change the rules of the game, for the most part, liability issues in electronic commerce are much the same as in the offline context. The core elements of proof in a defamation case, for instance, are identical whether the tort is committed in person or over the Internet. The same is true for misrepresentation, false advertising, trademark infringement, and the like.[28] However, electronic commerce may also generate new forms of liability for certain kinds of online businesses because of the role that *online intermediaries* play in various online relationships. The Quiznos example discussed in the preceding section illustrates this possibility. Although Quiznos disclaimed liability on the basis that it was merely a conduit for and not the author of the disparaging advertisements about Subway, intermediaries in electronic commerce—including websites that host user-generated content—may attract liability even if they do not exclusively or directly cause harm. A second example of a potentially new form of liability is explored in Case Brief 19.1.

Case Brief **19.1**

Crookes v Newton 2011 SCC 47

Jon Newton owned and operated a website containing commentary about issues such as free speech on the Internet. Many of the articles he posted contained hyperlinks to other websites. Wayne Crookes sued Newton on the basis that two of the hyperlinks on his website connected to material that defamed Crookes. By linking to the information, claimed Crookes, Newton was in effect republishing the defamatory material. The Supreme Court of Canada disagreed, finding that hyperlinking in and of itself does not constitute a republication of the content to which it refers. Hyperlinks are generally content-neutral, as the author of the hyperlink has no control over the content to which it points.

The entire court agreed, however, that if a hyperlinker presents content from the hyperlinked material in a way that it actually repeats the defamatory content, that activity would constitute a republication of the defamatory material and the hyperlinker might be at risk of legal liability. However, in a concurring opinion, Chief Justice McLachlin and Justice Fish went further by suggesting that a hyperlink should be read contextually. If the hyperlink can be read as an adoption or endorsement of the content it links to, the hyperlink may constitute a republication of the defamatory material.

An **online intermediary** is a party that enables or facilitates an online transaction between others. Think about all the things that need to happen before you can sell me stuff that is advertised on your website. First, you need to have a website, which means someone has to agree to host your website. Second, I need access to your website, which means that unless I am fortunate enough to own an Internet server, someone needs to provide me with access to the Internet. I also need an email account. So do you. Someone is probably in the business of storing or managing most of that data. Therefore, many kinds of businesses *intermediate* our online transactions. They are all considered online intermediaries. In fact, you might even be one. If your business provides employees with access to the Internet or email, then you are an online intermediary in any and all of their transactions. Other online intermediaries might include courier companies or financial intermediaries such as banks or

an online intermediary is a party that enables or facilitates an online transaction between others

---

[28.] As discussed above, one possible exception occurs at the intersection between domain names and trademarks. Trademark disputes give rise to at least one novel form of liability in electronic commerce: A bad faith registration of a domain name may result in the transfer of the registration to a trademarked holder.

credit card companies. Here, we will focus on two different kinds of online intermediaries:

- Internet service providers
- online service providers

INTERNET SERVICE PROVIDERS

an **Internet service provider (ISP)** provides others with access to the Internet

An **Internet service provider (ISP)**, sometimes called an *"Internet access provider,"* provides others with access to the Internet. Suppose you start a business that provides Internet access for a flat fee. What happens if one of your customers uses your service to defame someone, download obscene materials, or breach copyright? As an intermediary, can you be held accountable? Generally speaking, the law says "no." Internet access providers, such as telephone companies, are usually given special treatment because they are in the business of supplying the "pipeline" for the communication, not monitoring the content that flows through it. This legal immunity is part of a trade-off that is based on the **common carriage principle**, which precludes the owner of key social infrastructures (such as a railway or a phone system) from discriminating amongst users of that infrastructure, or using the infrastructure to confer upon itself an undue advantage.[29] The common carriage principle is especially important in industries, such as telecommunications, that are characterized by monopolies or oligopolies. The incumbents in these industries can control the development of competition by denying their competitors access to their facilities. Because ISPs are generally considered to be common carriers, they are not usually held accountable for the actions of their clients while using those services.[30]

the **common carriage principle** precludes an owner of key social infrastructures from discriminating amongst users of that infrastructure, or using the infrastructure to confer upon itself an undue advantage

Until relatively recently, common carriage in telecommunications also entailed the separation of carriage from content. Policy changes in Canada have increasingly done away with this separation, however, with the result that the owners of the "pipes" have converged with the producers of content (as in the case of Rogers Communications and the former BellGlobeMedia). This has created an inherent potential for a conflict of interest, since carriers have an incentive to prioritize their own content over that of their competitors.

network neutrality means that all information sent across the Internet should be treated equally, with no privileges, degradation of service, or prioritization based on the content's source, ownership, or destination

For this reason a number of Internet companies, such as Google and Yahoo!, as well as a number of academics and public interest advocates, have supported a corollary to the common carriage principle known as *network neutrality*.[31,32] The principle of **network neutrality** states that all information sent across the Internet should be treated equally, with no privileges, degradation of service, or prioritization based on the content's source, ownership, or destination. In other words, the Internet should act as a set of pipes through which data flows from sender to receiver without any intervention by the pipe owners.

---

29. These rules are codified in the *Telecommunications* Act, SC 1993, c 38, ss 27(2) and 36, which apply to all electronic communications and are enforced by the Canadian Radio-television and Telecommunications Commission (CRTC).

30. This is not to say that an ISP is immune from all forms of liability. For example, an employee may download obscene materials in the workplace. By allowing the employee to create a hostile work environment, the employer may be held liable under human rights legislation, especially if the employer adopted a policy of monitoring employee conduct online but failed to enforce the policy.

31. See eg T Wu "Why You Should Care about Network Neutrality" *Slate Magazine* (1 May 2006) <www.slate.com/id/2140850>; T Wu "Network Neutrality, Broadband Discrimination" (2003) *Journal of Telecommunications and High Technology Law* 2 at 141.

32. See eg Canadian Internet Policy and Public Interest Clinic (CIPPIC), *Net Neutrality: FAQ and Resources* <www.cippic.ca/en/net-neutrality>.

Unfortunately, not all ISPs have adopted these principles. A number of businesses have taken it upon themselves to remove or block access to certain data for their own purposes.[33] A failure to comply with the net neutrality principle can have serious business repercussions, especially if the transmission of your business data is treated as a lesser priority. You Be the Judge 19.1 illustrates a number of policy issues raised by the net neutrality debate.

You Be the Judge **19.1**

ISPs and the Network Neutrality Principle

More than 60 million people around the globe play the *World of Warcraft* or the *Call of Duty* video games on a regular basis. The most recent iteration of the *Call of Duty* series earned $1 billion in sales within 16 days of its release.

In 2011, people playing *World of Warcraft* and *Call of Duty* online found that they were having trouble with their Rogers Internet connections. An investigation was launched in October 2011 by the Canadian Radio-television Telecommunications Commission (CRTC) after they received a formal complaint from the Canadian Gamers Organization.[34] While the *Telecommunications Act* and CRTC Regulations allow ISPs such as Rogers to throttle (that is, to traffic shape) peer-to-peer network traffic, companies are not permitted to throttle real-time or time-sensitive traffic such as online chatting and gaming. Reporting on 20 January 2012, the CRTC found that Rogers was throttling some of its Internet traffic in violation of federal net neutrality rules.[35]

Questions for Discussion

1. Should Rogers be permitted to unilaterally limit network access for certain users or businesses? Why or why not?

2. The CRTC states that throttling is permissible in certain circumstances. What criteria should be used to shape Internet traffic?

3. Is network neutrality good for small businesses?

The legality of interfering with Internet data transfers remains murky. A recent CRTC decision considered whether **traffic shaping**, the practice of altering the speed of certain users' broadband services on the basis of the type of application being used, constitutes an interference with Internet data. While the CRTC concluded that some network management is reasonable and is not in violation of the *Telecommunications Act*, it also introduced a mixed-model approach to network management. Larger ISPs are permitted to charge fees based only on data transmission *speeds* rather than on the amount of data transmitted.[36] In contrast, the Federal Communications Commission in the United States has taken a stronger stand against such interference, prohibiting

traffic shaping is the practice of altering the speed of certain users' broadband services on the basis of the type of application being used

PART 5

---

[33] In 2005, Canada's second-largest telecommunications corporation, TELUS Inc, found itself in a labour dispute with some of its unionized workers. A website called Voices for Change was launched to publicize some of the workers' grievances, as well as to post pictures of replacement workers crossing the picket line. TELUS responded by blocking access to the site on its Internet backbone, which meant that not only were TELUS's own million or so customers denied access, but so were thousands of other customers of ISPs who bought wholesale network access from TELUS. In blatant disregard of the net neutrality principle, TELUS's actions also resulted in over 700 *other* websites being blocked, even though they were completely unrelated to the union. Those sites happened to share the same IP address as that of the Voices for Change website.

[34] Rita Trichur, "CRTC finds evidence of throttling on Rogers Internet service" *Globe and Mail* (20 Jan 2012), <http://www.theglobeandmail.com/news/technology/tech-news/crtc-finds-evidence-of-throttling-on-rogers-internet-service/article2310196>.

[35] A letter from the CRTC to Rogers ordered that the company respond directly to the CRTC or comply with Canadian law: <www.crtc.gc.ca/eng/archive/2012/lt120120.htm>.

[36] The public consultations resulted in Telecom Regulatory Policy CRTC 2009-657 <www.crtc.gc.ca/eng/archive/2009/2009-657.htm>. In early 2011, the CRTC called for the outright establishment of usage-based billing: Telecom Decision CRTC 2011-44 <www.crtc.gc.ca/eng/archive/2011/2011-44.htm>. However, late 2011 saw the introduction of a mixed-model compromise approach: L Payton, "CRTC Offers Compromise on Usage-Based Billing," *CBC News* (15 November 2011) <www.cbc.ca/news/canada/story/2011/11/15/pol-crtc-ubb-decision.html>.

Internet giant Comcast from discriminatorily throttling the transfer speed of particular kinds of data (including transmissions from peer-to-peer file sharing systems such as *BitTorrent*) in the service of network management.[37]

In addition to having the capacity to interfere with Internet communications, ISPs have considerable power over businesses and individuals insofar as they store and have access to sensitive business information, including, in some cases, details of private communications and other online activities. Let's say that you own a small business that has purchased a telecom package providing Internet access, website hosting services, multiple email addresses, and a two-year lease on a dozen wireless mobile devices. Imagine that the police want to gain access to your business email or to monitor the use of one of your wireless devices. Can your ISP help the police by providing them with particulars about your account and subscriber information without your consent?

Historically, none of this could be done without a court order. However, recently proposed legislation would require a mandatory back door that police could use to intercept certain telecommunications with a properly obtained warrant. The proposed legislation would also provide law enforcement agencies with an expedited means of obtaining *subscriber information* associated with your account *without* a warrant and *without* your permission.[38] According to the recently proposed bill, **subscriber information** includes the "name, address, telephone number, and electronic mail address of any subscriber to any service provider's telecommunications services and the Internet protocol address, mobile identification number, electronic serial number, local service provider identifier, international mobile equipment identity number, international mobile subscriber identity number, and subscriber identity module card number that are associated with the subscriber's service and equipment."[39] If a designated police officer requests such information from your telecom service provider during the course of an investigation, your telecom provider will be obliged to provide the subscriber information—no questions asked—and will have a legal duty not to tell you about it. A number of businesses and privacy advocates have raised concerns about the "information grab" this bill would enable at the discretion of the police and without court supervision. The proposed legislation puts ISPs—no longer able to ensure the confidentiality of their customers' communications and online interactions—in an awkward position.

ONLINE SERVICE PROVIDERS

ISPs are not the only businesses that take on liability as information intermediaries. As the Quiznos case illustrates, other forms of intermediary liability are also possible for a broader range of *online service providers*. An **online service provider** offers goods or services, beyond mere Internet access, in exchange for something of value. Quiznos, for example, intermediated hosting services and offered prizes in exchange for videos that promoted its brand. Other more typical electronic commerce examples of online service providers include blog

subscriber information includes the name, address, telephone number, and electronic mail address of any subscriber to any service provider's telecommunications services and the Internet protocol address, mobile identification number, electronic serial number, local service provider identifier, international mobile equipment identity number, international mobile subscriber identity number, and subscriber identity module card number that are associated with the subscriber's service and equipment

an **online service provider** offers goods or services, beyond mere Internet access, in exchange for something of value

---

[37.] Federal Communications Commission Memorandum and Order FCC 08-183 (20 August 2008).

[38.] Bill C-30, *An Act to Enact the Investigating and Preventing Criminal Electronic Communications Act and to Amend the Criminal Code and Other Acts,* 1st Sess 41st Parl 2012 (which subsequently died on the order page at the end of the Parliamentary session); previously introduced as Bill C-52, *An Act Regulating Telecommunications Facilities to Support Investigations,* 3rd Sess 40th Parl 2011 (died on order paper); also previously introduced as Bill C-47, *An Act Regulating Telecommunications Facilities to Support Investigations,* 2nd Sess 40th Parl 2009 (also died on the order paper).

[39.] *Ibid,* s 16(1).

hosts, email suppliers, bulletin board operators, online auctions, anonymous re-mailers, social networking sites, and commercial websites. Many ISPs act as both an ISP and an online service provider.

Online service providers usually enter into contracts with visitors or subscribers that are governed by their terms of use. Online service providers can be held liable if they are in breach of those agreements. Risk can also be managed by inserting exclusion clauses into contracts. Such clauses do not protect an online service provider from liability to a third party. Since third parties are not covered by those exclusion clauses, they may sue the service provider *as an intermediary*. (We discussed exclusion clauses and privity of contract in Chapter 8.) For example, when a customer uses *Facebook* or *Twitter* to distribute a defamatory statement or to breach copyright, the plaintiff may sue both the customer and the online service provider. The plaintiff may also commence a lawsuit to compel the service provider to reveal the identity of the customer if an alleged wrong was committed using a pseudonym. It is important to recognize, however, that you do not have to be an Internet giant to expose your business to these kinds of lawsuits. In general, risk managers will want to shield their online businesses against liability for such things as (i) publishing defamatory remarks, (ii) distributing materials that infringe copyright, (iii) disclosing personal information, (iv) infringing trademarks, (v) participating in computer mischief, and (vi) possessing or distributing child pornography.

Unfortunately, very few Canadian lawmakers have squarely addressed these issues. Canadian businesses are therefore often in the precarious position of relying on the courts to correctly interpret and apply the *SOCAN* decision outlined in Case Brief 19.2.[40] One province that has legislatively intervened is Quebec. According to section 27 of its *Act to Establish a Legal Framework for Information Technology*, service providers acting as intermediaries are not required to monitor the information communicated on their networks or in the documents stored on them, nor are they required to report communications or documents that may be used for illegal activities.[41] Even if a service provider chooses to monitor or report, its decision to do so will not automatically result in intermediary liability if illegal content is later found on its site. Section 36 of the Act states that service providers acting as intermediaries are not generally responsible for the illegal acts of service users; however, it also states that a service provider may incur liability if it *participates* in acts performed by service users.[42]

What about online service providers in other provinces? How can you shield your business from intermediary liability?

■ You should have a clear contract with each user. Each user should be required to clearly consent to the *terms of use* contained in that contract. And those terms should allow you to claim *indemnification* from a user if you are ever held liable for something that they posted.[43]

■ Those *terms of use* should clearly explain, with examples, which uses are acceptable and which are unacceptable. While you should not commit yourself to monitoring content, you should reserve the right to remove

---

[40.] As of this chapter's writing, the federal government has proposed legislation that would introduce notice-and-takedown provisions: Bill C-11, *An Act to Amend the Copyright Act*, 1st Sess 41st Parl 2011 (in second reading as of 2012).

[41.] *An Act to Establish a Legal Framework for Information Technology* SQ 2001 c 32 (Que).

[42.] For example, liability may be imposed if the service provider (i) sends a document, (ii) selects or alters the information in a document, (iii) determines who transmits, receives, or has access to a document, or (iv) stores a document longer than is necessary for its transmission.

[43.] Indemnification would require the user to compensate you for any losses that you suffered (eg where you were successfully sued as an intermediary by a third party).

content where the content is in violation of your terms of use or where you wish to remove it for other reasons at your discretion.

■ You should, whenever possible, set up your business so that you can demonstrate that it merely acts as a conduit or pipeline for the materials that pass through the system.

■ If your business is sued, you should try to convince the court that legislation in Quebec and the United States is not binding; it is based on sound policies that should be adopted. The Supreme Court of Canada's decision discussed in Case Brief 19.2 may also be helpful.

Case Brief 19.2

Society of Composers, Authors and Music Publishers of Canada v Canadian Association of Internet Providers (2004) 240 DLR (4th) 193 (SCC)

The Society of Composers, Authors and Music Publishers of Canada (SOCAN) is a collective society that administers Canadian copyright in music for Canadian and foreign copyright owners. SOCAN collects royalties from radio stations that play copyrighted songs that SOCAN is responsible for administering. In this case, SOCAN tried to collect royalties from Canadian ISPs on the basis that ISPs infringed the right of copyright owners to communicate their works to the public and to authorize such communication.

The Canadian Association of Internet Providers (CAIP) opposed SOCAN's attempt to collect royalties from ISPs. CAIP argued that ISPs do not communicate copyright works or authorize such communication. According to CAIP, ISPs are merely conduits for communications and do not regulate the content of communications passing over their networks.

The Supreme Court of Canada held that ISPs are not liable to pay SOCAN royalties when they merely function as content-neutral conduits. That is true when ISPs do not have knowledge of the infringing content and when, from a technical and economic standpoint, they cannot practically monitor the vast amount of content passing over their networks. "Caching" (the temporary storage) of content by an ISP is a conduit function because it is content-neutral and motivated by the need to deliver faster and more economical Internet access service. The court did not, however, rule out the possibility that ISPs might have to pay royalties when they act as more than mere conduits.

Finally, the court held that an ISP does not "authorize" an infringement merely because it knows that a user *might* use its facilities to commit infringement.

L.O. ❺❻ Online Transactions

More than a decade ago, it was recognized that successful online transactions require consistent laws from place to place. If every jurisdiction had a different set of rules, it would be impossible to achieve certainty in electronic commerce. As a result, the United Nations Commission on International Trade Law (UNCITRAL) encouraged countries to create uniform legislation governing online transactions based on a single model—the *United Nations Model Law on Electronic Commerce*.[44] The model law is not really a law. It does not create rights, powers, obligations, or immunities. It merely provides a model for the creation of a consistent set of laws. Ultimately, it is up to each government to decide how much of the model to adopt. In Canada, electronic commerce legislation has been adopted on a province-by-province basis through a similar model law process. A special working group of the Uniform Law Conference of Canada created its own model law based on the UN model—the *Uniform Electronic Commerce Act (UECA)*.[45] *UECA* likewise has no legal force. It has,

---

[44] *United Nations Model Law on Electronic Commerce* <www.uncitral.org/uncitral/uncitral_texts/electronic_commerce/1996Model.html>.

[45] *Uniform Electronic Commerce Act (UECA)* <www.ulcc.ca/en/us/index.cfm?sec=1&sub=1u1>.

however, formed the basis for most provincial laws governing online transactions. These laws provide a common framework for online transactions.

CONTRACT FORMATION

Amongst other things, these laws aim to remove uncertainty about online contract formation by stipulating rules that govern *where* and *when* a message is said to be *sent* or *received*.

Most provinces follow the UECA approach, which prescribe a set of default rules that deem messages to be sent from the sender's place of business and received at the recipient's place of business.[46] Suppose your place of business is in Alberta, but you send a message through your Internet server in Manitoba, while you are travelling in the Yukon. Without legislation, it might plausibly be said that your message was sent from any one of those three places. Because the *UECA* stipulates "place of business" as determinative, it is clear from a legal perspective that the message will be deemed as sent from Alberta unless the parties expressly agreed to the contrary. Electronic Commerce legislation therefore eliminates the uncertainty and promotes commerce by consistently choosing one of those possibilities while leaving it open to the parties to stipulate different rules if they so choose.

The *UECA* approach also contains clear default rules that determine *when* a message is *sent* or *received*. A message is deemed *sent* when it leaves the sender's control. Consequently, once you push a button and can no longer stop the message from being sent, that message is considered sent, even if it is never received. A message is deemed *received* when it reaches an information system in the control of the person to whom it is sent. That rule can be tough on recipients because they can be held responsible for messages even if they have never actually read them. A recipient can claim that a particular message was never received by proving, for instance, that it could not be downloaded from the server. The best way for a business to avoid disputes about the transmission of its messages is to either require acknowledgment that communications have been received or invoke a system of automated confirmation.

It is crucial to note that electronic commerce legislation does not change the common law rules regarding the communication of acceptance. As we saw in Chapter 7, contractual acceptance must be communicated to be effective. Furthermore, the time and the place of the acceptance depend upon the *medium of communication*. Electronic commerce legislation has quite purposefully avoided the issue of instantaneous versus non-instantaneous communication, recognizing that the decision about whether to treat a particular electronic transmission as similar to a phone call or first-class mail depends upon the circumstances and must be determined on a case-by-case basis.

It is important to recognize that the rules eliminating uncertainty about where and when a message is sent or received are merely default rules. In other words, parties can choose, by mutual consent, to adopt rules that are different from those set out in provincial legislation. This choice is important from a risk management perspective. Risk managers need to think carefully about the nature and circumstances of their online transactions to ensure that online contract formation rules are appropriate to their circumstances. If the default rules set out in provincial legislation are not appropriate to your online transactions, you will need to work with lawyers to create suitable rules and ensure that both parties consent to them.

---

46. The rules are more complicated if a company has several places of business or no place of business. For a more elaborate discussion of these and other rules pertaining to email, see C Morgan & J Saulgrain *Email Law* (2008).

Most provinces have adopted *UECA* as a model for their electronic commerce legislation.[47] Many provinces have adopted that model entirely or with minor variations.[48] Others have attempted to overcome the same problems by other means. Although it is impossible to provide a detailed comparison of each jurisdiction's approach, we can mention a few important differences.

The most substantial differences occur in New Brunswick and Quebec. For example, unlike that of most of the other provinces, the New Brunswick legislation does not regulate the process of offer and acceptance, and the Quebec legislation is much more extensive than its counterparts. It contains, for example, a number of detailed provisions regarding the consultation and transmission of documents that have legal implications for third parties, such as online service providers. As a matter of risk management, businesses that are not confined to a single province or territory should seek professional advice on the relevant legislation to avoid difficulties.

Businesses often transact online with governments. This trend is sure to increase as federal and provincial governmental departments further embrace the online environment. Electronic commerce legislation in most provinces therefore contains a number of provisions regarding electronic documents that are sent to government.[49] Some of these provisions protect governments from being swamped by electronic documents that arrive in various incompatible formats. A government can, for instance, specify the formats that it is willing to accept.[50] From a risk management perspective, businesses that transact with governments online should ensure that they are compliant with all government procurement procedures in order to ensure success in the contract formation process.

AUTOMATED TRANSACTIONS

With advances in hardware and software, online transactions are increasingly automated. **Automation** in electronic commerce reduces the need for human intervention. This is said to increase efficiency by freeing up time for employees and managers to do other work. With automation, the cornerstone of traditional contract theory, the notion of *consensus ad idem* (a "meeting of the minds"), becomes more difficult to apply. Electronic commerce transactions may not be created and performed exclusively by humans. Many transactions are initiated and completed by computer software programs and do not easily fit within traditional notions of contract. In fact, part of the point of developing technologies that automate electronic commerce is to allow transactions to take place without any need for humans to review or even be aware of particular transactions. As demonstrated by Case Brief 19.3, a business must take care in the way that it designs and implements automated services.

automation in electronic commerce reduces the need for human intervention

47. *Electronic Transactions Act*, SA 2001, c E-5.5 (Alta); *Electronic Transactions Act*, SBC 2001, c 10 (BC); *Electronic Commerce and Information Act*, CCSM, c E55 (Man), amending *Manitoba Evidence Act*, CCSM c E150 (Man) and amending *Consumer Protection Act*, CCSM, C200 (Man); Bill 70, *Electronic Transactions Act*, 3d Sess, 54th Parl, 2001 (NB); *Electronic Commerce Act*, SNS 2000, c 26 (NS); *Electronic Commerce Act*, SO 2000, c 17 (Ont); *Electronic Commerce Act*, SPEI 2001, c 31 (PEI); *Act to Establish a Legal Framework for Information Technology*, SQ 2001, c 32 (Que); *Electronic Information and Documents Act*, SS 2000, c E-722 (Sask); *Electronic Commerce Act*, SY 2000, c 10 (Yuk).

48. This is true of Alberta, British Columbia, Manitoba, Nova Scotia, Ontario, Prince Edward Island, Saskatchewan, and the Yukon.

49. For the purposes of *UECA*, the term "government" does not include Crown corporations, but it may include municipalities if the provincial or territorial legislature so decides.

50. Some jurisdictions, including Ontario, Nova Scotia, and the Yukon, have adopted those provisions. Others, including British Columbia and New Brunswick, have not.

Case Brief 19.3

Zhu v Merrill Lynch HSBC 2002 BCPC 0535

Zhu was a stock trader who used Merrill Lynch's NetTrader automated online stock trading system to buy and sell stocks. Immediately after selling stocks on one occasion, Zhu attempted to cancel the sale. He received an automated confirmation that some stocks had already been sold but that the sale of the remaining stocks was cancelled. In fact, the remaining stocks had also been sold. Zhu did not know this and sold the remaining stocks through another transaction. This meant that Zhu had sold the same stocks twice. Zhu had to buy back the stocks under the second transaction. However, by the time he was required to do that, the price of the stock had increased, causing him a loss of nearly $10 000. Merrill Lynch argued that the cancellation notice did not indicate that the cancellation was successful and that Zhu should have called to confirm that the cancellation was complete before making further sales.

The court held that Zhu was entitled to rely on the online prompts: "Surely common sense dictates that 'cancelled' means 'cancelled' and [Zhu] is entitled to treat that as a confirmation that his cancellation has been completed. It strikes me that [Merrill Lynch's] system could easily have issued a prompt saying 'cancellation pending' or 'please wait until advised that cancellation is completed before placing another order.'" Because of the high risk of loss of investment funds, the court also held that Merrill Lynch owed its customers a higher duty of care and performance in providing the automated online service. This decision suggests that businesses providing online services should design their systems and automated notices in a way that consumers can readily understand. This is particularly important for services where there is a high risk of loss to customers.

Most provincial electronic commerce statutes allow contracts to be created by automated electronic devices.[51] However, it may be dangerous to rely on such systems. Most of the statutes also say that transactions are unenforceable when purchasers make a keystroke error when dealing with an automated system. A **keystroke error** occurs when a person mistakenly hits a wrong button or key. For instance, you may order 1000 items instead of 100, or you may hit the "I agree" button instead of the "I decline" button. An automated system normally cannot recognize subsequent messages that you send in an attempt to correct a mistake. It will simply fill your order as originally received. The legislation may allow you to escape the consequences of your error in certain circumstances. Basically, you must prove that (i) the automated system did not provide an opportunity to prevent or correct the error, (ii) you notified the other party of the error as soon as possible, (iii) you took reasonable steps to return any benefit that you received under the transaction, and (iv) you have not received any other material benefit from the transaction. An online business can avoid those sorts of situations by creating an automated mechanism to correct such errors. The simplest tactic is to require the purchaser to confirm the order by repeating the important steps (for instance, by re-typing the number of items that the purchaser wants to receive).

Automation can facilitate online transactions. It can also be misused. One example is a practice known as **spamming**, an abuse of automated messaging systems to send unsolicited bulk messages to large numbers of consumers without their consent. Spam messages can cause widespread damage to businesses and individuals alike, sometimes because of wasted time and resources spent reading and filtering through spam messages, and sometimes because of embedded software code that does damage to computers and other business assets. These issues will be further considered in this chapter in the section on consumer protection.

a **keystroke error** occurs when a person mistakenly hits a wrong button or key

spamming is an abuse of automated messaging systems to send unsolicited bulk messages to large numbers of consumers without their consent

PART 5

[51.] *UECA*, s 21, states, "A contract may be formed by the interaction of an electronic agent and a natural person or by the interaction of electronic agents."

L.O. ❼   Jurisdiction

Although speedy and efficient, online transactions do not always proceed smoothly. Problems cannot always be avoided, and disputes cannot always be settled. Litigation may be inevitable, especially if a business is engaged in global e-commerce. In that situation, it may not be enough to comply with local laws. Website owners and operators must also consider the possibility of being dragged into court in some remote place. They must factor that possibility into the cost of doing business. And while it is expensive to ensure compliance in foreign legal systems, it is sometimes even more expensive to become embroiled in a faraway legal battle. For this reason, the question of *jurisdiction* becomes important. **Jurisdiction** refers to the ability of a court from a particular place to hear a case. Although the issue of jurisdiction can arise in any kind of case, it is particularly important in electronic commerce.

jurisdiction refers to the ability of a court from a particular place to hear a case

Suppose you have a company located in Los Angeles that offers free software downloads and a group of consumers living in Quebec bring an action against you in Canada, claiming that the software contained *spyware* that caused harm to their machines.[52] Can the consumers sue in Canada? Or, suppose you have a company in Toronto that allows your customers to download movies from your Canadian website subject to Canada's copyright laws and that *Disney Enterprises Inc* wants to sue you in New York, claiming that it holds copyright as well as the exclusive distribution rights in the United States. Should New York law apply, even though your company is registered and operates only in Canada? And if a New York court says it should, is a Canadian court obliged to enforce a US judgment here in Canada?

There are several circumstances in which a court may assert jurisdiction over an out-of-country defendant. First, it can assert jurisdiction if the defendant is physically present within the territory over which the court has jurisdiction. Second, it can do so in situations where the foreign resident consents to the hearing. Third, a court might assert jurisdiction if it is determined that the court is competent to hear the matter in question.[53] Competence can be determined through the application of at least one of the three following methods:

- a real and substantial connection test
- a passive versus active test
- an effects-based approach

In Canada, the courts usually apply a **real and substantial connection test**. They ask whether the plaintiff's cause of action and the effects of the defendant's conduct are sufficiently linked to the place in which the plaintiff wants to sue.[54] Unfortunately, the courts have not fully developed their application to the electronic commerce context.[55]

a **real and substantial connection test** asks whether the plaintiff's cause of action and the effects of the defendant's conduct are sufficiently linked to the place in which the plaintiff wants to sue

---

[52.] We discuss spyware in greater detail in our examination of identity theft and consumer protection.

[53.] *Desjean v Intermix Media Inc* (2007) 28 BLR (4th) 315 (FC) at para 23; *Club Resorts Ltd v Van Breda* 2012 SCC 17, [2012] SCJ No 17.

[54.] The Supreme Court in Club Resorts Ltd outlined presumptive factors that support the existence of jurisdiction in a tort case under the real and substantial connection test. These factors include whether the defendant lives in the province where jurisdiction is sought, whether the defendant carries on business in that province, whether the tort was committed in that province and whether a contract connected to the dispute was made in the province. The decision does not touch on how or whether these presumptive factors would apply in an e-commerce context, but the clarification of the real and substantial connection test in Club Resorts Ltd may affect the outcome of e-commerce jurisdictional disputes.

[55.] The Supreme Court of Canada has held that relevant connecting factors in the *real and substantial connection test* include the locations of the content provider, the host server, the intermediaries, and the end user: *Society of Composers, Authors and Music Publishers of Canada v Canadian Association of Internet Providers* (2004) 240 DLR (4th) 193 (SCC).

Courts may also examine the online interaction to determine (i) the level of interactivity between the parties and (ii) the commercial nature of the exchange of information that occurs on the website.[56] Under this **passive versus active test**, a court looks at the way in which each party does business online. Is the company merely posting information, or does it require customers to interact through the exchange of information online? Does its website send email to particular places? Does it encourage customers from foreign places to call by providing a local or toll-free number? The more interactive a website is in a particular country, the more likely that a court in that country has jurisdiction to hear a case. This occurrence raises an important point for risk management. If a company does not want to be involved in litigation in a particular place, it should avoid interacting online with people in that place.

Several courts have moved away from a test that examines the specific characteristics, or the *potential impact*, of a particular website. Instead, they have adopted a broader **effects-based approach** that focuses on the *actual impact* that a website has in the place where jurisdiction is being sought. This type of approach has been used in a few instances in Canadian courts.[57] To the extent that the courts are tempted to look at where the harm is done rather than *how* it is done, it will be very difficult for businesses to insulate themselves from possible liability in remote jurisdictions.

One way a business can seek to protect itself from liability in specific jurisdictions is to avoid *targeting a location*.[58] **Targeting a location** means specifically choosing to create business relationships with people within that location. A business that targets individuals or corporations within a particular place is more likely to have the courts in that place take jurisdiction.

Given their depth and breadth, it is worth pausing to reflect briefly on these three approaches to jurisdiction in light of the two examples that we started with. Returning to the case involving the consumers in Quebec who wanted to sue the Los Angeles–based company for bundling spyware into their free software downloads, imagine that the Los Angeles–based company did not host its website or servers in Canada, had an English-only website, had no Canadian employees, no offices, agents, or bank accounts in Canada, held no Canadian assets, did not advertise, market, or solicit goods in Canada, and did not pay Canadian taxes. On these facts, one might expect that a court would have some difficulty in finding that the LA company had any real and substantial connection to Canada.[59] Likewise, it would be hard to characterize the defendant, on these facts, as targeting Canada or Quebec consumers in any specific way. Rather, the website is more easily characterized as passive, engaging only those Canadians who happen to find their way to the website and download the free software without requiring any registration or further interaction. On these facts, it would be difficult to convince a Canadian court to assert jurisdiction.

By contrast, let's return to the other example involving the Toronto-based business that allows its US customers to download movies from its website. Imagine in this instance the Canadian website was designed specifically to use the Internet as the means of entering the United States and to make its services available to New York residents who wished to download American films that, within the United States, are subject to its copyright laws. Imagine as

a **passive versus active test** requires a court to look at the way in which the parties do business online

an **effects-based approach** focuses on the actual impact that a website has in the place where jurisdiction is being sought

targeting a location means specifically choosing to create business relationships with people within that location

PART 5

---

[56] *Zippo Manufacturing Co v Zippo Dot Com Inc* 952 F Supp 1119 (WD Pa 1997); *Braintech Inc v Kostiuk* (1999) 171 DLR (4th) 46 (Ont CA).

[57] *Bangoura v Washington Post* (2004) 235 DLR (4th) 564 (Ont SCJ).

[58] M Geist "Is There a There There? Toward Greater Certainty for Internet Jurisdiction" (2001) *Berkeley Tech Law Journal* 1345.

[59] See *eg Desjean v Intermix Media Inc* (2007) 28 BLR (4th) 315 (FC).

well that the website contracted with a US service provider in order to process Internet payments online. Finally, imagine that it incorporated in Delaware so that payments could be made within the United States and then transferred to the Canadian company. On these facts, one might have a much easier time persuading a court that there was a real and substantial connection between the Canadian website and the State of New York.[60] The plaintiff's cause of action and the effects of the defendant's conduct seem sufficiently linked to the place in which the plaintiff wants to sue. Likewise, these facts reveal an active interaction between the Canadian website and an American customer base, encouraging them to download from Canada to take advantage of uncertainty in Canadian copyright law. When one considers the actual impact that the Canadian website might have in New York and other nearby states, and when one considers who is targeted and where actual harm was done, it is not difficult to imagine a finding that a New York court is an appropriate jurisdiction to hear the matter.

Although these two cases help illustrate the three approaches to jurisdiction adopted and applied by Canadian courts, it is useful to remember that all three tests for jurisdiction are designed to allow significant flexibility in their general application and cannot be reduced to a fixed formula.[61]

Concept Summary 19.2 examines ways in which businesses can manage Internet jurisdiction risks.

Concept Summary 19.2

Managing and Minimizing Internet Jurisdiction Risks

- Assess, minimize, and eliminate any connections your business might have with jurisdictions in which you do not wish to face potential liability. These connections might include physical assets, bank accounts, country-code domain names, host servers, and intermediaries.

- Consider inserting a jurisdiction clause into contracts that requires any disputes arising from the agreement to be heard by the courts in a specified place in accordance with the laws of that place. Recall that such a clause will be effective only if adequate notice is given and if the other party is capable of agreeing to it.

- Use *geo-location* targeting technologies. **Geo targeting** is the method of determining the physical location of a website visitor and delivering (different) content to that visitor based on location. This can be done through an analysis of information provided by visitors during a registration process or through a determination of their **Internet protocol addresses**, numerical identifiers assigned to network devices for communication between different nodes in the network. Such technologies allow a company to manage the legal risks of e-commerce by restricting the geographical area in which it does business. For example, for legal or business reasons, a website based in Canada might wish to sell goods to customers in Canada and the United States but not European countries. Geo-location technologies can help to achieve this end, thereby minimizing the possibility of legal liability in non-targeted countries.

geo targeting is the method of determining the physical location of a website visitor and delivering (different) content to that visitor based on location

an **Internet protocol address** is a numerical identifier assigned to network devices for communication between different nodes in the network

Identity Theft

Our discussion of jurisdiction demonstrates the business risks associated with an inability to determine *where* one is said to be doing business. Another set of risks is incurred with the inability to determine *who* one is said to be doing business with.

Some business transactions are anonymous. When I walk into your tavern, order a beer, drop ten dollars on the bar, and tell you to keep the change, you probably don't care who I am. Certainly, your business does not depend upon it. The same cannot be said in electronic commerce. Given that an important

---

[60.] *Disney Enterprises v Click Enterprises Inc* (2006) 267 DLR (4th) 291.

[61.] *Ibid* at para 19.

aspect of doing business online is to transact at a distance, often without any pre-existing business relationship, electronic transactions sometimes require *authentication*. **Authentication** is a process through which certain attributes of a user or potential customer are verified. For example, the ability of a business to authenticate the creditworthiness of its clients is important in transactions where an expensive good or service is provided prior to the completion of payment.

Although often unnecessary and excessive, the usual means by which this is achieved is through the collection and use of *personal identifiers*. **Personal identifiers** are tokens, numbers, or digital representations that can be uniquely associated with an individual. Typical examples include name, date of birth, driver's licence, health card, social insurance number, passport, fingerprint, iris scan, password, or digital certificate. These and other personal identifiers are convenient means by which one can obtain a credit card or bank account, redirect mail, establish an account for mobile devices, rent vehicles, secure accommodations or employment, or gain access to sensitive medical information. They can also be misused in a manner that permits an imposter to assume the identity of another without his or her knowledge or consent. This is often referred to as **identity theft**—the unauthorized collection and use of your personal information, usually for the purposes of committing some wrong.[62]

Identity theft has a range of negative impacts for citizens, consumers, and governments. The damage done to individual victims can be enormous, expensive, and enduring. Typical scenarios involve victims battling with creditors years after an identity thief racks up a series of debts. When the thief is able to infiltrate several of the victim's financial institutions over a longer period of time, say, six months or a year, sometimes to the tune of $250 000 or more, it is not uncommon for victims to spend several thousand hours setting the matter straight. Although the accumulated debt and lost hours are possible to quantify, how do you put a price on the nightmare experience discussed in Ethical Perspective 19.2?

authentication is a process through which certain attributes of a user or potential customer are verified

personal identifiers are tokens, numbers, or digital representations that can be uniquely associated with an individual

identity theft is the unauthorized collection and use of your personal information, usually for the purposes of committing some wrong

PART 5

Ethical Perspective **19.2**

What's in a Name?

For 19 years, Daniel Friedland, a Philadelphia bookkeeper, has not been entirely himself. That is because authorities have determined that, Friedrich Himmel, an Austrian immigrant in East Los Angeles, has been him, too. The real Daniel Friedland has lived a low-key, law-abiding life with his wife and children in the City of Brotherly Love. But, recently, he has brushed up against the law on a couple of occasions. For reasons unknown to him, he had a tough time getting credit a few years back. More recently, he was served with a warrant for his arrest. What eventually came to light was hard to believe, even for Friedland himself.

Twenty years ago, Friedland lost his wallet during a trip to Los Angeles. He thought nothing of it at the time, other than the hassle of having to replace his birth certificate, social security card, and driver's license. It turns out that Himmel used Friedland's lost identifiers nearly

19 years ago, when arrested and convicted of driving under the influence of alcohol in Los Angeles. Since that time, Himmel has been convicted of a series of crimes under Friedland's identity: vandalism (18 years ago), burglary (15 years ago), leaving the scene of an accident (7 years ago), and making a bomb threat (3 years ago). For much of that time, Himmel had a California driver's license in Friedland's name. Prosecutors are trying to learn when it was first issued and how.

Friedland first suspected a problem five years ago when he was denied a credit card because of what one creditor referred to as "fraudulent activity." The next year he received a letter from an insurer for an accident he was never in. He received a similar letter for a different incident two years later. When he reported these matters to the LA police, he was told that unless he had the true name of the perpetrator there was

(Continued)

[62] Office of the Privacy Commissioner of Canada *Fact Sheet: Identity Theft* <www.priv.gc.ca/resource/fs-fi/02_05_d_10_e.asp>.

(continued)

nothing that could be done. Problems continued right up until the time of the warrant for his arrest. Friedland was ultimately at the mercy of the LA police. "Me and my wife have been stressed out about this for a long time," he told them. "My credit has gone downhill. I cannot believe this has been going on for 19 years."

Questions for Discussion

1. How would you describe the kinds of harm that victims of identity theft suffer?

2. Are criminal charges against Himmel an adequate legal remedy? What other kinds of laws should be available to Friedland in this situation?

The prospect of identity theft can also be devastating to businesses, large and small. For large institutions such as banks and credit card companies, preventing and undoing the damage of identity theft requires a cumbersome and expensive bureaucracy. The associated costs are inevitably passed on to consumers, inflating the price of goods and services. Identity theft can also be costly to small and medium-sized enterprises. Most businesses depend upon credit facilities to assure smooth cash flow. Likewise, most small and medium-sized businesses are supported by bank loans backed by personal guarantees of individuals, family members, and even key partners and executives. In a business context, some of the potential harms of identity theft include:[63]

- Lost work time and earnings: The average victim of identity theft spends more than 60 hours recovering from each instance of theft. According to the Canadian Anti-Fraud Centre, over 18 000 Canadians reported being victims of identity theft in 2010. In the United States, that number exceeds 8 million. According to a 2008 study by the McMaster eBusiness Research Centre, victims of identity theft in Canada overall spent more than 20 million hours and $150 million to resolve the frauds resulting from identity theft.

- An adverse impact on cash position: The average out-of-pocket cost to the identity theft victim is about $631 per incident, money that would otherwise be available for debt service and other obligations.

- An inability to get a clean audit and accurate credit report: These credentials are critical to support other financial needs, such as liquidity for a small business owned by the borrower.

- Adverse tax implications: If employment is gained by another individual using the business owner's name and social insurance number, the victim may appear responsible for more taxes.

- General disruption: This can result in a business owner's inability to generate income or make timely loan payments.

Reducing the risk of identity theft requires at least a rudimentary understanding of its two core elements: (i) how identity thieves collect personal identifiers without authorization and (ii) how they misuse that information once it is collected.

[63.] Canadian Anti-Fraud Centre *Annual Statistical Report 2010* <www.antifraudcentre-centreantifraude.ca/english/documents/Annual%202010%20CAFC.pdf>; McMaster eBusiness Research Centre *Measuring Identity Theft in Canada: 2008 Consumer Survey* <www.business.mcmaster.ca/IDTDefinition/WP23%20exec%20summ.htm>; J S Schultz, "The Rising Cost of Identity Theft for Consumers, 2011" *New York Times*: Bucks (9 February 2011) <http://bucks.blogs.nytimes.com/2011/02/09/the-rising-cost-of-identity-theft-for-consumers>; Y Ross "Identity Theft Can Devastate Your Business," *All Law* (2004) <www.alllaw.com/articles/business_and_corporate/article27.asp>.

COLLECTION OF PERSONAL IDENTIFIERS

To perpetrate a fraud, an identity thief will usually require the acquisition of a few different personal identifiers from different sources. These can be harvested from a variety of sources, such as unshredded garbage or recycled paper, discarded hard drives that have not been properly wiped of data, lost wallets, and discarded or unopened electronic mailboxes.[64] In many of these instances, the possession and even the surreptitious collection of another's personal identifiers is not illegal. As we shall see, the wrongdoing is usually triggered by the fraudulent misuse of those identifiers. There are, however, a few types of collection that can be legal.[65] We will briefly mention two of these: *spyware* and *phishing*.

Spyware is software that has been surreptitiously installed on a computing device in order to intercept or otherwise control a user's interaction with that device without knowledge and consent. "Rootkits," "zombies," "screen-scrapers," "hijackers," "tricklers," and other such software can be used not only to secretly monitor user behaviour, but also to collect, use, and distribute various types of personal information.[66] For example, a screen-scraper that captures images of your computer screen (for example, while you are doing online banking) can be used to mine personal identifiers that could be used to obtain a credit card in your name under false pretenses.

Although spyware is an effective tool in an identity thief's arsenal, the more prevalent trend is a practice known as *phishing*. As the name implies, the object is to set some bait, cast a line, wait, and hope to reel something in.[67] From a legal perspective, **phishing** is a fraudulent means of acquiring personal identifiers, such as usernames, passwords, and credit card details, by masquerading as a trustworthy entity in an electronic communication. Phishing is usually done online or by phone, sometimes directing recipients to enter personal information at a phony website whose appearance is virtually identical to the legitimate one, under the pretense that those identifiers are needed to "update" or "reactivate" an account. For example, in 2007 a flood of spam that mimicked communications from the Canada Revenue Agency encouraged unknowing recipients to forward sensitive personal information to the spammer, allegedly to comply with the requirements of Canadian tax law.[68]

spyware is software that has been surreptitiously installed on a computing device in order to intercept or otherwise control a user's interaction with that device without knowledge and consent

phishing is a fraudulent means of acquiring personal identifiers, such as usernames, passwords, and credit card details, by masquerading as a trustworthy entity in an electronic communication

PART 5

MISUSE OF PERSONAL IDENTIFIERS

Once just a few identifiers are collected, it becomes relatively easy to consolidate them to obtain others. For example, in most provinces, a thief who is able to obtain a victim's legal name and date of birth can apply for a replacement driver's licence. With this and other information, one can set up or take over hydro, telephone, cable, and cellphone accounts, through which information

---

64. Canadian Internet Policy and Public Interest Clinic (CIPPIC) ID *Theft: FAQ* <www.cippic.ca/en/identity-theft-faq#faq_general_what-is-identity-theft>.

65. The legality of these techniques will be further discussed below in the section on consumer protection.

66. CIPPIC *Spyware and Other Potentially Unwanted Technologies* <www.cippic.ca/en/spyware> and <www.cippic.ca/projects-cases-spyware/>.

67. It is speculated that the strange spelling ("ph") is an allusion to "phreaking," a term used to designate a clique of early hackers said to be "phone-freaks" (*Wikipedia* <http://en.wikipedia.org/wiki/Phreaking>).

68. CBC News "Canada Revenue Agency Issues Alert about Email Scams" (2 November 2007) <www.cbc.ca/news/story/2007/11/02/cra-scam.html>.

can be gleaned to obtain a bank account or credit cards, which can be used to set up still other accounts. With the right set of identifiers, a thief can obtain prescription medicine, health care, and even avoid arrest.

The *Criminal Code* therefore contains a number of offences that prohibit personation, forgery and fraud, theft of government-issued identification documents, making or uttering a forged document, assuming identities for financial gain, and assisting someone else in obtaining false information.[69] Numerous other statutes create offences for improper use or disclosure of specific types of information.[70] Businesses can avoid significant risk by setting up processes that will prevent and deter such crimes. Meanwhile, as will be discussed in more detail below, the federal Department of Justice is currently seeking to create new offences that will directly address identity theft in an information age.

Given that identity theft laws remain underdeveloped, there are a number of self-help measures that businesses and consumers can adopt, as indicated in Figure 19.2.

FIGURE 19.2 Reducing the Risk of Identity Theft[71]

Business

• Shred paper records that are no longer needed.	• Ensure adequate security for electronic data, including access control mechanisms and encryption of data.
• Monitor the web to ensure that no spoofs of your website exist that could be used for phishing expeditions.	• If your website is spoofed, search domain names to determine a web hosting service or ISP and register a complaint immediately.
• Monitor software updates for security "holes" to avoid improper access to customer data.	• Implement a fraud detection and prevention program.
• Have a strategy in place to manage a possible breach in a timely and effective manner.	• Seek help from financial institutions (which are often willing to help businesses put fraud prevention programs in place); fraud prevention is especially important for businesses that conduct "card-not-present" transactions because they can be liable for customer fraud (even if the card issuer has approved that customer).
• Request more than one form of identification when a customer is paying with a cheque or credit card in face-to-face transactions.	• Conduct regular overviews of your business's credit report to ensure accuracy and make sure that only those activities you have authorized are included.
• Conduct employee background checks.	• Limit the sending of personal information via mail to clients to reduce the risk of that information being misappropriated by mail thieves.
• Before discarding electronic equipment, use scrubbing software or destroy hard drives to permanently delete the information stored on them.	*(Continued)*

[69] *Criminal Code of Canada*, RSC 1985, c 46, s 403 (personation); ss 366–378 (forgery); ss 380(1) and (2) (fraud); s 57 (use of forged passport); s 58 (fraudulent use of certificate of citizenship), s 342 (theft and unauthorized or fraudulent use of credit cards).

[70] For instance, s 141 of the federal *Employment Insurance Act*, SC 1996, c 23, makes it an offence to make fraudulent or deceptive use of or to manufacture social insurance cards.

[71] These tips were compiled from advice offered in the following documents: Public Safety Canada *Advice for Consumers: Identity Theft* (2011) <www.publicsafety.gc.ca/prg/le/bs/consumers-eng. aspx>; Government of Alberta *Identity Theft Tip Sheet* (2001); Public Safety Canada *Phishing: A New Form of Identity Theft* (2011) <www.publicsafety.gc.ca/prg/le/bs/phish-eng.aspx>; Public Safety Canada *Advice for Retailers: Identity Theft* (2011) <www.publicsafety.gc.ca/prg/le/bs/retailers-eng. aspx>; Consumer Measures Committee *Business Identity Theft Checklist* <http://cmcweb.ca/eic/site/ cmc-cmc.nsf/eng/fe00095.html>; Privacy Rights Clearinghouse *Coping with Identity Theft:* Reducing the Risk of Fraud <www.privacyrights.org/fs/fs17-it.htm>; and Canadian Internet Policy and Public Interest Clinic Identity *Theft: Frequently Asked Questions (Organizations)* (2007) <www.cippic.ca/en/ identity-theft-faq>.

FIGURE 19.2 Reducing the Risk of Identity Theft *(continued)*

Consumer

• Sign all credit cards upon receiving them and shred any that you do not use.	• Leave social insurance card, passport, and birth certificate in a secure spot at home.
• Provide social insurance number only when absolutely necessary.	• Know your billing cycle and check regularly to ensure accuracy of all transactions by cross-referencing them with receipts.
• Notify issuing credit card company immediately if any discrepancies appear.	• Follow up immediately on bills that do not arrive when expected.
• Use a locked mailbox with a deposit slot, if possible.	• Shred all credit card receipts and statements that are no longer needed and insist that businesses you deal with do the same.
• Do not give out more information than is needed; and ask why the information is being sought if you do not think it is relevant to your transaction.	• Request an authentication requirement prior to any inquiries or changes to your accounts.
• Seek out credit card programs that offer fraud protection.	• Check your credit report once a year by contacting at least one major credit reporting agency.
• Avoid disclosure of personal information by telephone, mail, or Internet unless you initiated contact (to ensure legitimacy of the organization requesting the information).	• Do not transmit personal information on voicemail.
• Avoid disclosure of personal information without knowing the purpose for its collection, who it will be shared with, and how it will be stored.	• Avoid choosing obvious passwords, such as maiden name, date of birth, or names of children.
• Beware of onlookers or video equipment when entering passwords or PINs at public terminals.	• Take advantage of privacy enhancing technologies such as digital signatures, data encryption, or anonymizing services.
• Install and maintain strong firewall and anti-virus protection on your computer and other electronic devices.	• Use password protection on documents containing personal data.
• When disposing of your computer, permanently destroy all data by either physically destroying the hard drive or by using scrubbing software.	• Ignore unexpected email and do not click on links from banks or credit card companies seeking confirmation of personal information.
• Install access control devices, such as passwords or biometrics, on electronic devices.	• Ensure compliance with the federal *Personal Information Protection and Electronic Documents Act* and substantially similar provincial privacy legislation.
• Minimize collection of personal data to that which is necessary to achieve purpose.	• Store paper-based customer data, such as credit card or bank account numbers, in a secure location.

PART 5

Privacy Breaches

L.O. ❽

Ironically, although there are currently no laws preventing thieves from collecting or disclosing another's personal information, privacy laws prevent businesses from doing so without knowledge and consent. As noted in our discussion of privacy policies, Canada's federal and provincial privacy laws also require businesses to limit the collection, use, and disclosure of personal information to that which is reasonably necessary. By doing so, privacy laws can be said to help to reduce the risk of identity theft. Privacy laws further reduce the risk of identity theft by requiring businesses to act as the custodians of the personal information they collect and keep in their possession, requiring that businesses establish appropriate security measures, and requiring that information which is no longer needed be destroyed in a secure manner.

It is one thing for businesses to be aware of, to comprehend, and to put into operation these obligations; it is quite another thing to determine the appropriate

a **privacy breach** occurs whenever there is an unauthorized collection, use, or disclosure of personal information

course of action when things go wrong.[72] A **privacy breach** occurs whenever there is an unauthorized collection, use, or disclosure of personal information. While this obviously applies to businesses that collect personal information without consent, it also applies to situations in which personal information is stolen, lost, or mistakenly disclosed by a business that was legitimately in possession of that information. An important element of risk management is to ensure that privacy breaches are not a consequence of faulty information management procedures or negligence. Since customers and employees expect businesses to safeguard their personal information, one would likewise expect that they might also wish to be informed whenever a significant privacy breach occurs.

Privacy breaches appear to be on the rise. According to the Identity Theft Resource Center (ITRC), public and private sector organizations reported 157 breaches in 2005. In contrast, 662 breaches were reported in 2010, and 419 breaches were reported in 2011.[73] As a result, nearly 38 million personal records were exposed over that two-year period.[74] From a business perspective, perhaps the most important statistical data reveals that the majority of breaches stemmed from acts or omissions of business personnel and subcontractors, resulting in accidental exposure, lost laptops, or missing portable storage devices. In other words, *most privacy breaches are preventable.* By taking simple measures, such as installing password protection and encrypting sensitive data, businesses can drastically reduce the risk of privacy breaches. Hacking, which accounted for 26 percent of data breaches, is also preventable by hardening software through updated anti-virus and anti-spyware programs. Businesses can further reduce risk by inculcating a culture of privacy and data security in the workplace that includes implementing a system of well-understood internal controls, instituting various security protocols, providing regular training, and offering employee incentive programs.[75] However, as You Be the Judge 19.2 illustrates, such measures are not always sufficient.

You Be the Judge 19.2

Payment Processing and Security Breaches

Heartland is a payment processing company in the United States. As one of the largest credit card processors in the world, it also offers debit, cheque, payroll, online payment, and other transactional services around the globe. Heartland processes more than 11 million transactions a day, amounting to over $80 billion in transactions a year. At some point in 2008, the company was alerted by Visa and MasterCard of suspicious activity surrounding processed card transactions. On 20 January 2009, Heartland disclosed to the public that unknown intruders had broken into its systems and planted malicious software to steal card data. Heartland announced that they would be working hand in hand with various law enforcement agencies to examine the affected software and determine the exact number of identified instances of breach. Soon afterwards, it was discovered that the data stolen included the digital information encoded onto the magnetic strip built into the backs of credit and debit cards.

The Heartland breach is considered to be the largest security breach in history, based on its impact. More than 130 million accounts

(Continued)

---

[72] An excellent checklist for such occasions is available at the following: Office of the *Privacy Commissioner of Canada Privacy and Your Business: Privacy Breach Handbook* (2008) <www.priv. gc.ca/resource/pb-avp/pb_hb_e.asp>.>.

[73] Identity Theft Resource Center, Data Breaches <www.idtheftcenter.org/artman2/publish/lib_survey/ITRC_2008_Breach_List.shtml>. It is worth noting that the vast majority of breaches remain internal and are therefore not reported or accounted for.

[74] Although these are US statistics, there is reason to believe that the numbers are proportionately similar in Canada.

[75] W Gross "2008 Security Breaches Exceed 2007 Total" (2008) 4 *Co-Counsel: Technology Law Quarterly* 3 at 45–46.

(continued)

were affected, dwarfing the 2006 TJX security breach that affected just over 40 million accounts, and exceeding the 2011 Sony PlayStation Network breach that saw about 75 million records compromised.[76]

In the years that followed, Heartland settled with several parties. Hefty financial settlements were reached in consumer class actions, and with the major credit card companies, resulting in an excess of $100 million in breach-related settlement payments. In March 2010, computer hacker Albert Gonzalez was convicted for his role in the breaches of Heartland and other companies. The court found that Gonzalez and an uncharged accomplice selected targets from a list of Fortune 500 companies, one of which was Heartland. After acquiring information on the payment-processing system used by Heartland, Gonzalez then uncov-

ered vulnerabilities in the system that he could exploit. While Gonzalez claimed that he played only a minor role in the Heartland breach, he was eventually fined $25 000 and sentenced to 20 years in prison.[77]

Questions for Discussion

1. How could Heartland have prevented or mitigated the security breach? What degree of responsibility should Heartland have toward its affected consumers?

2. What steps should Heartland have taken upon discovery of the breach?

3. How does the threat of security breaches affect small businesses?

Consumer Protection

L.O. ❾ ❿

Our discussion of identity theft and privacy breaches clearly illustrates that businesses and their customers expose themselves to significant risks in the e-commerce environment. We end this chapter by considering one means of reducing some of those risks—the adoption and implementation of consumer protection principles. These principles are important to consumers and businesses alike. By adopting them alongside the privacy practices described earlier, a business can enhance its reputation, strengthen consumer confidence, and ultimately increase sales. This is particularly important in electronic commerce, where consumer confidence is relatively low and markets remain underdeveloped. This section describes an established code of practice and then outlines key laws and regulations that have either been proposed or recently implemented. Although the law and policy in this area is only now beginning to emerge and is in flux during the writing of the fourth edition of this book, prudent risk managers should proactively attend to the changing regulatory environment, particularly when setting up new electronic commerce ventures, so as to avoid higher compliance costs when new laws come into effect.

CODE OF PRACTICE

Although some provinces have amended existing consumer protection legislation in light of electronic commerce, full-scale law reform has only recently

---

[76] *United States of America v Albert Gonzalez* 18 USC 371 and 1349 < www.wired.com/images_blogs/threatlevel/2009/08/gonzalez.pdf>; E Chung "PlayStation Data Breach Deemed in 'Top 5 Ever'" CBC News (27 April 2011) <www.cbc.ca/news/technology/story/2011/04/27/technology-playstation-data-breach.html>; J Vijayan "TJX Data Breach: At 45.6M Card Numbers, It's the Biggest Ever" *Computer World* (29 March 2007) <www.computerworld.com/s/article/9014782/TJX_data_breach_At_45.6M_card_numbers_it_s_the_biggest_ever>.

[77] K Zetter "Hacker Sentenced to 20 Years for Breach of Credit Card Processor" *Wired* (26 March 2010) <www.wired.com/threatlevel/2010/03/heartland-sentencing Gonzalez had also been previously convicted in the breach of TJX. In their analysis of TJX, the privacy commissioner of Canada and the information and privacy commissioner of Alberta found that the company collected too much personal information, kept it too long, and relied on weak encryption technology to protect it. Of particular concern was TJX's practice of collecting and retaining information not necessary to its business: Office of the Privacy Commissioner of Canada and Office of the Information and Privacy Commissioner of Alberta *Report of an Investigation into the Security, Collection and Retention of Personal Information: TJX Companies Inc/Winners Merchant International LP* <www.privcom.gc.ca/cf-dc/2007/TJX_rep_070925_e.asp>.

commenced. Its origins date back to 1999, when Industry Canada (a branch of the federal government) set up a working group to develop and promote a code of practice ultimately titled *Canadian Code of Practice for Consumer Protection in Electronic Commerce.*[78] This Code is not law, but it reflects a number of the legal obligations described throughout this chapter and is the precursor to emerging law and policy discussed in the section that follows. Another perspective on the Code is to see it as a set of best practices for ethical and effective business. Compliance will likely minimize legal risks in a number of areas. Federal, provincial, and territorial ministers responsible for consumer affairs endorsed the Code in 2004. The Code remains open for endorsement by private sector organizations and consumer organizations. Figure 19.3 summarizes its key provisions.

Although the eight principles set out in Figure 19.3 go a long way as voluntary means of protecting consumers in the online environment, there has been

FIGURE 19.3 Key Provisions of the Canadian Code of Practice for Consumer Protection in Electronic Commerce

1.	Information provision	Consumers should be provided with clear and sufficient information to make informed choices about whether and how to make a purchase. Online businesses should fairly and accurately describe their goods and should avoid jargon, using plain language whenever possible. Businesses should clearly distinguish marketing material from the terms and conditions of sale and should disclose their legal identities, business address, and any geographic limitations on where a product or service is for sale.
2.	Language	When an online business offers products or services in a given language, it should use that language to provide all of its material information about itself, its policies, its products or services, and the terms of the transaction. When information or support is not available in that language, that fact should be stated by the vendor in the language used to conduct the transaction.
3.	Contract formation and fulfillment	Vendors should take reasonable steps to ensure that the consumer's agreement to contract is fully informed and intentional. The consumers should be provided with an opportunity to correct or cancel the order before it is accepted and filled. A vendor who cannot deliver a product within the time frame originally specified should promptly notify consumers and give them the option of cancelling their order at no charge, except where unreasonable.
4.	Online privacy	An online business should set up its data collection system with a view to respecting and protecting its customers' privacy in compliance with Canadian privacy laws.
5.	Security of payment information	Vendors and intermediaries should take reasonable steps to ensure that transactions in which they are involved are secure. An online business should use technologies and procedures that are consistent with industry standards to safeguard payment and personal information that is collected as a result of a transaction.
6.	Complaint handling resolution	Consumers should have access to fair, timely, effective, and affordable means of resolving problems with any transaction. An online business should have resources for handling consumer complaints efficiently and effectively. Vendors should offer an internal complaints-handling process that is easily accessible, available to consumers free of charge, and easy to use. It should deal with complaints within 7 business days, endeavour to resolve or address complaints within 45 days, and record and monitor complaints.
7.	Unsolicited email	Vendors should not send unsolicited email to consumers without consent. In any marketing email, vendors should provide a return address and a simple way for consumers to indicate that they do not wish to receive such messages. Online businesses should avoid spamming or sending unsolicited emails to a large number of people.
8.	Communications with children	Vendors have a social responsibility to determine whether they are communicating with a child in any given transaction. Vendors should not exploit children's lack of experience or sense of loyalty, and they should not exert pressure on children to urge their parents to purchase products or services. Vendors should take reasonable steps to avoid monetary transactions with children and should not collect personal information from children except where express parental consent has been obtained.

[78.] Industry Canada *Canadian Code of Practice for Consumer Protection in Electronic Commerce* (2004). This document is based on the *Recommendation of the OECD Council Concerning Guidelines for Consumer Protection in the Context of Electronic Commerce* (1999). It is excerpted from the Canadian Standards Association's *Model Code for the Protection of Personal Information* (1999).

a push to create specific legislation regarding a number of consumer protection issues, including some already mentioned in this chapter, such as (i) identity theft, (ii) spam, spyware, and phishing, and (iii) telemarketing. We will now briefly discuss each of these.

Identity Theft

In late 2009, the Government of Canada passed legislation to address identity theft by adding new provisions not covered by existing provisions in the *Criminal Code*.[79] These amendments focus on the preparatory stages of identity theft, making it an offence to obtain, possess, transfer, or sell the identity documents of another person. This new focus responds to the problems with traditional theft-related property offences, which pertain to tangible things that the owner is deprived of, making it difficult for information to be characterized as *property* unless it has a legitimate commercial value (such as intellectual property). Another reason for the new law has to do with the electronic nature of the transactions involved in identity theft. Whereas identity fraud prior to the advent of the Internet usually involved one person stealing a physical identity token (for example, a credit card) and then using it for his or her own gain, current technologies enable the involvement of numerous people along a continuum of criminal activity, trading information with no single individual committing each and every element of the fraud.

The new legislation creates general offences for illegally possessing or trafficking in government documents or identity information, and numerous other provisions relating to identity theft and fraud. The penalties for these new offences include prison sentences, in some cases for up to a maximum of five years. The *Act* also creates specific offences for using or copying credit card data and for mail-related offences. Another element of the legislation is a provision granting a restitution order, wherein the offender may be required to pay the victim any reasonable amount spent to restore his or her identity, including correcting his or her credit history or rating, and replacing identity documents.

Spam, Spyware, and Phishing

When we looked at automated transactions, we mentioned spam and its ability to cause widespread damage. The actual costs of spam—estimated by one study in the range of $100 billion per year—are borne mostly by businesses, consumers, and ISPs and almost never by those who send it.[80] Some studies estimate that as much as 90 percent of all email traffic is spam, leading to bandwidth overloads, strains on server capacity, and a loss of user productivity.[81] Spam can also be used to spread spyware, computer viruses, Trojan horses, or other malicious software that can do serious damage to computers, servers, and networks. As we already have seen, it is also deployed in conjunction with phishing techniques to perpetrate identity theft. Despite being a widely detested nuisance, spam remains economically viable simply because advertisers have no operating costs beyond the management of their mailing lists, and because,

[79] *An Act to Amend the Criminal Code (Identity Theft and Related Misconduct)*, SC 2009, c 28.

[80] International Telecom Union ITU *Study on the Financial Aspects of Network Security: Malware and Spam* (2008) <www.itu.int/ITU-D/cyb/cybersecurity/docs/itu-study-financial-aspects-of-malware-and-spam.pdf>.

[81] Symantec, *MessageLabs Intelligence: 2010 Annual Security Report* <www.inteco.es/file/27gHxrzWsYyeyRTFYq8MuQ >; also see M Geist "Senator's Anti-Spam Bill Is Welcome News," *Toronto Star* (19 May 2008) <www.thestar.com/business/article/427246—senator-s-anti-spam-bill-is-welcome-news>.

without specialized legislation, it is difficult to hold senders accountable for their mass mailings.

However, in December 2010, the Canadian government passed Bill C-28, *Canada's Anti-Spam Legislation (CASL)*.[82] Its aim is to promote electronic commerce by regulating activities that discourage consumers from using electronic means of carrying out commercial activities. *CASL* prohibits the sending of commercial email (or other electronic messages, such as text or instant messaging) without the informed consent of the recipient. This means that your business cannot send me commercial emails unless you have my prior consent to do so. Likewise, the legislation necessitates various form and content requirements for commercial email. For example, even if you have my consent to send bulk messages, your business would be required to identify itself and provide an accurate subject header that allows me to easily determine the purpose of the message. Misleading or misrepresentative electronic messages are prohibited and can result in jail terms of up to 14 years. *CASL* also requires that commercial email senders establish an easy way for recipients to opt out of (that is, "unsubscribe" from) receiving future messages. It also prohibits the creation of phishing websites and email address–harvesting tools. Some of these offences are subject to fines as high as $10 000 000 or prison terms. Significantly, the legislation creates a right of private action for citizens who wish to seek injunctions against spamming activity or to sue spammers for the actual costs of spam, awarding up to $200 per individual occurrence and up to $1 000 000 per day. Already passed into law, *CASL* is expected to come into force in 2013.

Telemarketing

Long before spam was ever an issue, consumers expressed a distaste for unwanted phone calls to their homes from companies and other organizations seeking to survey, sell, or solicit donations from them. These days, given the ease in obtaining consumer information and customer lists, and the ability to automate calls with voice-activated and speech-recognition software, telemarketing is a big business. Like spam, it is generally perceived by consumers and many businesses as unwanted and is often negatively associated with various scams and frauds, such as pyramid schemes and deceptively overpriced products and services.

The Government of Canada has enacted telemarketing laws by amending section 41 of the *Telecommunications Act* to permit the CRTC to administer and oversee a national Do Not Call List (DNCL). Now in full operation, the DNCL rules require that businesses must cease solicitations within 31 days of a consumer registering their phone or fax number on the DNCL.[83] Moreover, if a consumer states during the course of a call or through a communication with the telemarketer that they do not want further calls, the telemarketer must add that consumer to its own internal DNCL on pain of financial penalties up to $15 000 per occurrence. The CRTC has also set out specific rules regarding

---

[82.] *The Act was originally referred to as the "Fighting Internet and Wireless Spam Act [FISA]" but is now referred to as "CASL." The long title is An Act to Promote the Efficiency and Adaptability of the Canadian Economy by Regulating Certain Activities That Discourage Reliance on Electronic Means of Carrying Out Commercial Activities, and to Amend the Canadian Radio-television and Telecommunications Commission Act, the Competition Act, the Personal Information Protection and Electronic Documents Act and the Telecommunications Act, SC 2010, c 23.*

[83.] *Unsolicited Telecommunications Rules Framework and the National Do Not Call List Telecom Decision* CRTC 2007-48; *Delegation of the Commission's Investigative Powers with Regard to Unsolicited Telecommunications Rules Complaints,* Telecom Decision CRTC 2008-6.

the form, content, and conduct of telemarketing as well as a list of organizations that are exempted from the DNCL rules. Given the substantial financial penalties that can be incurred, it is important for businesses using telemarketing services to know and understand these rules. Interested students can learn more about them on the CRTC website.[84]

[84.] CRTC *Telemarketing at a Glance* (20 April 2009) <www.crtc.gc.ca/eng/INFO_SHT/t1030.htm>.

Chapter Summary

Electronic commerce involves technology-mediated business transactions, a mode of doing business that has expanded dramatically in scope and complexity in recent years. While the legal risks attendant on electronic commerce are in many respects the same as in traditional commerce, businesses relying on information technology need to be aware of legal developments that respond to various technological changes in the business world.

One of the first business decisions to be made concerns the acquisition of a domain name. Given the potential value of domain names as virtual storefronts, businesses anticipating an online presence should proactively register company names, products, and slogans as domain names in the appropriate top level and country-code domains. In dealing with cybersquatters, dot-ca businesses should understand the mechanisms of the CDRP and its potential remedies prior to engaging in traditional litigation.

Developing and hosting websites generates considerable legal risk. One important means of mitigating risk is the careful development of a website's terms of use. Terms of use become legally binding on website users when they function as a unilateral offer by which the offeree (the website visitor or customer) explicitly promises (usually with a "click") to abide by the terms. Clear notice of the terms of use is required and is most easily achieved by allowing access by way of a subscriber registration process. Privacy policies are a second important element of business websites. Federal regulations in the *Personal Information Protection and Electronic Documents Act (PIPEDA)*, in conjunction with privacy laws in certain provinces, require businesses to ensure that adequate steps have been taken to protect personal information through a set of 10 "fair information practices." Although privacy policies are not required by law, they are useful for minimizing privacy compliance risks and costs. The touchstone of any privacy policy should be a commitment to minimal collection, and informed and meaningful consent in the collection and use of personal information. Thirdly, user-generated content poses special problems for online companies, notably loss of brand identity, liability for posting illegal content, and claims of false advertising. These issues are best dealt with by defining acceptable content in the terms of use and then by actively moderating the material that is posted in user-accessible areas of the site.

An online intermediary is a party that facilitates online transactions between other parties. The emergence of online intermediaries has created a range of new liability risks. In some cases, the actions of website visitors can attract liability to the intermediary. Internet service providers (ISPs) are generally not held accountable for the actions of visitors to their sites because of the common carriage principle, which mandates that providers of network access should be neutral as to content. But where an ISP breaches net neutrality, or distributes its own content, it may find itself liable for the content that flows through its network. In contrast to ISPs, online service providers may be legally liable both for their own online actions and those of their customers. In general, risk managers will want to shield their online businesses against liability for such things as (i) publishing defamatory remarks, (ii) distributing materials that infringe copyright, (iii) disclosing personal information, (iv) infringing trademarks, (v) participating in computer mischief, and (vi) possessing or distributing child pornography. Carefully drafted terms of use and monitoring of content are the chief protections against these risks, but online businesses should be aware that their potential liability may increase to the extent that they invite user content or exercise editorial control over communications on their sites.

Online transactions are subject to specific e-commerce laws that aim to remove uncertainty about contract formation. The co-ordination of model laws at both the international and national level has facilitated the global implementation of uniform laws at the provincial level. Amongst other things, Canada's model law, the *Uniform Electronic Commerce Act*, sets out a series of default rules that determine when and where electronic communications are said to occur. Those rules can be adjusted by mutual consent, usually by way of a contract. Automated electronic commerce promises to dispense with the need for human supervision in the contract-formation process. Although most provincial legislation contemplates a method for rectifying keystroke errors, managers should incorporate safety mechanisms into their electronic contracts to protect their businesses against liability for computer-generated errors.

The global reach of electronic commerce means that compliance with local laws no longer provides sufficient protection from legal risk. Website owners and operators must consider the possibility that they may be dragged into a court battle in some remote jurisdiction. In resolving matters of jurisdiction, Canadian courts consider whether there is a real and substantial connection between the cause of action, its effects, and the location in which the action has been commenced. Other considerations may include the passivity or interactivity of a website and the actual effects of the alleged transgression on the location where jurisdiction has been sought. Targeting strategies, including the use of both technological measures and terms of service specifying legal jurisdiction, will reduce the risk of a business being sued successfully in a foreign court.

The advent of the Internet has facilitated a new wave of fraudulent activities that are specific to electronic commerce. Identity thieves collect personal identifiers and use them to exploit the credit or goodwill of businesses and individuals. Likewise, businesses that collect, use, or disclose the personal information of their customers expose themselves to liability where personal information that they have collected is used or released without authorization. Privacy breaches are on the rise and can be extremely costly, not just to the victims but to the person or business who experienced the breach. The best safeguards against these risks include strictly limiting the amount of private information a business collects and stores, and attending carefully to the security of any such data.

Finally, electronic commerce has attracted the attention of consumer protection advocates and government agencies, resulting in new regulations and guidelines to protect the public from potential abuses. The *Code of Practice for Consumer Protection in Electronic Commerce* contains suggestions for ethical and effective business practices. Compliance with it is likely to reduce or minimize legal risks in a number of areas. The Code paved the way for existing and emerging legislation that deals with issues such as identity theft, network neutrality, spam, and telemarketing. Compliance with its provisions and attention to trends and changes in the regulatory environment are an important means of establishing and maintaining trusting relations with customers and ensuring responsible and ethical e-business practice.

MyBusLawLab   ADDITIONAL RESOURCES FOR CHAPTER 19

MyBusLawLab provides students with an assortment of tools to help enrich the learning experience, including a Study Plan with Pre- and Post-tests, mini-cases with assessments, and provincial content material, which provides links to relevant cases, legislation, and additional resources.

MyBusLawLab provides the following resources for Chapter 19:

Provincial Material

- **British Columbia:** Electronic Transactions, Privacy Rights
- **Alberta:** Electronic Contracts, Identity Theft
- **Manitoba and Saskatchewan:** *Consumer Protection Act*—Internet Agreement Legislation, Electronic Transactions, *Freedom of Information and Protection of Privacy Act* (FIPPA), *Internet Consumer Contracts and Consumer Protection Act, Personal Health Information Act, Privacy Act*
- **Ontario:** Amending Electronic Contracts, *Consumer Protection Act,* E-Commerce Legislation, Education, Electronic Contracts, Freedom of Information and Privacy Legislation, Identity Theft, Municipalities, Personal Health Protection Information Legislation, Private Sector Employees
- **Atlantic Provinces:** Electronic Commerce Legislation, Electronic Signatures, Internet Sales Contracts, *Personal Information Protection and Electronic Document Act*

Review Questions

1. What is a defensive domain name registration? How does it compare to cybersquatting?

2. Describe three typical disputes arising from the domain name registration system and provide an example of each. How can business managers avoid domain name disputes?

3. What factors should a business consider when choosing between dispute resolution and litigation in the context of a domain name dispute?

4. Why might a court find that a provision in your terms of use is not binding on a visitor to your website?

5. What is "personal information" and when should a company decide not to collect certain types of personal information?

6. Discuss three kinds of liabilities and risks associated with allowing user-generated content on your website.

7. What is "network neutrality" and how might it affect a business?

8. What is the difference between an "online service provider" and an "Internet service provider"?

9. As an online service provider in Newfoundland and Labrador, describe how you can shield yourself from possible liability as an online intermediary.

10. What are the relevant contract formation rules governing the sending and receiving of electronic documents? As a risk manager, what steps can you take to avoid related disputes?

11. Explain the complexities associated with automated electronic commerce. How can a business safeguard against the undesirable consequences of keystroke errors?

12. Why might a business want to avoid targeting a particular jurisdiction, and what steps can it take?

13. Name and discuss the variables that a court may consider in deciding whether a specific online interaction falls under its jurisdiction.

14. What is "phishing" and how might it affect a legitimate business?

15. Describe several simple measures that a business could adopt to reduce the risk of a privacy breach.

16. Is the *Canadian Code of Practice for Consumer Protection in Electronic Commerce* legally binding in Quebec and New Brunswick? In which provinces should businesses adhere to the Code of Practice and why?

17. What is "spyware" and how might it have a negative impact on a business?

18. What can happen to an entrepreneur who sends an email to his existing clients (with consent) if its subject header is misleading? Can the recipient sue or is it up to law enforcement agencies to charge the sender?

19. What must a Canadian business do to comply with the law once it decides to engage in a telemarketing campaign?

20. What steps can consumers take to reduce the number of calls they receive from telemarketers? Is there a way for a business or a consumer to ensure that no telemarketers will call?

Cases and Problems

1. BuyEvenMoreStuff Inc is a company incorporated under the laws of Minnesota. It is also the registered owner of several Canadian trademarks, including Hire-a-Dweeb®, DweebCity®, DweebMobile®, and DweebsforHire®. These trademarks, which have been held for nearly 10 years, are part of a famous brand campaign for a house-call service for people in need of computer support. A subsidiary company known as BuyEvenMoreStuff Canada Ltd, a national supplier of electronics products, holds an exclusive licence to use these trademarks in Canada. When the Canadian company decided to start advertising its computer help services online, it learned that its preferred dot-ca domain name, *dweebs4hire*.ca, had been registered two years earlier by a small company operating in Saskatoon known locally as Hire-a-Dweeb. The Saskatchewan-based business also provides computer help and has been advertising its services for the past year on a website registered under the domain name *dweebs4hire.ca*. After finding the contact information of the registrant by way of a WHOIS search, the national marketing manager for the big box store phoned the registrant and was told by the owner of the Saskatchewan business that she was a former employee of BuyEvenMoreStuff Canada. During the discussion, the registrant proclaimed that she was not a cybersquatter because she legitimately registered the domain name first and because she had no intention of selling the domain name to anyone for any price.

   Does BuyEvenMoreStuff have a claim against the registrant that is likely to succeed? What remedy would you advise, and how should the electronics supplier go about getting it?

2. Ejay's Éclairs is a small, exclusive pastry shop that has recently decided to use its website to deliver catered goods locally on Prince Edward Island. With the hope of cutting down on roaming charges, Ejay has designed an online ordering system that automatically forwards orders to her mobile email device. Worried that some orders may slip between the cracks, Ejay wants to add a provision to the terms of use on her website to exclude liability for any late or undelivered orders, minimizing her exposure to a refund plus a gift certificate. At the same time, Ejay does not want to burden her customers with an online registration process. What legal principles are at play? How should Ejay set up her website to ensure that the terms are effective?

3. ShareEverythingForever is large social networking company with a Canadian office located in Ontario. They have hired you to revamp the social network's privacy policy. Your new boss asks you to locate and carefully analyze the privacy policies of two major social networking services and compile a

list of the following: (i) the three terms that are the most important, (ii) the three terms that are the least important, and (iii) any missing terms that ought to be included. Name the two policies you considered, listing the domain names where they can be found, and perform the analysis as requested. What reasons informed your selection? Do you think any of those terms will be controversial from the perspective of the public?

4. After witnessing all the publicity that Quiznos received through its user-generated advertisement contest (see Ethical Perspective 19.1), Giant Giovanni's Subshop has decided to give Quiznos a little taste of its own medicine. It wants to host a contest for user-generated videos that say why Giant Giovanni's subs are even better than Quiznos subs. It plans to have even better prizes and better exposure for the contestants' submissions. In order to avoid lawsuits, the board of directors has asked its director of marketing, Dorota, to draw up a set of rules of conduct for appropriate submissions as well a series of additional strategies for diminishing the prospect of liability. Dorota needs help. How would you advise her?

5. Catharina is about to create a small start-up ISP somewhere in Canada. Like other ISPs, her company will offer a number of services, including blog hosting, photo-sharing, bulletin boards, and the like. As a small business, one of her chief concerns is liability for her client's content. Given these concerns, where in Canada should she set up shop, and why? What other strategies can she adopt to minimize legal risk?

6. You are the information manager of an electronic mailing service, BadNews.ca. Your primary customers are collections agencies. BadNews.ca assists these agencies by locating debtors and delivering legal notices to them prior to the repossession of their assets. You were operating under the assumption that simply sending an email message would fulfill the written notice requirements set out in the provincial legislation that regulates the collection of debts. Recently, however, you discovered that the law requires such notices to not merely be sent but to actually be received. You have been asked to determine whether your current approach would succeed in provinces that have enacted electronic commerce legislation based on Canada's *Uniform Electronic Commerce Act*. Prepare a brief memo explaining the rules governing the sending and receiving of electronic messages. Make sure that your memo provides some advice indicating the best way to avoid disputes with intended recipients.

7. You are the owner of a small digital content provider based in Brandon, Manitoba. Your content is marketed under your Canadian registered trademark, dFOX. As well, you are the registered owner of the dFOX.com and dFOX.ca domain names. It has come to your attention that a US software company is advertising its newest voicemail-bot under the name dFOX on its website, codeworks.com. Code Works does not have a registered trademark for the dFOX product in the United States or anywhere else. The Code Works site is targeted to Americans and explicitly warns that its voicemail-bot software may work only with US telecommunications hardware. The site has a US-only 1-888 number but allows transactions to be completed online from anywhere in the world. The terms and conditions say that the warranty for the product is valid only for sales in the United States. You decide to write a demand letter to Code Works, insisting that it cease using your trademark immediately. In the letter, you indicate that, for the past several weeks, customers confused by Code Work's use of your mark have flooded your web server, causing email transmission problems and irreparable damage to some of your corporate hardware. Code Works ignores your demand and continues to market dFOX voicemail-bots on its website. You decide to go to a Manitoba court to seek a remedy for trademark infringement and economic loss. Outline the jurisdictional issues and tests you will be facing. What will your argument be? What can you expect Code Works to argue? As a risk manager for Code Works, how can you seek to avoid legal liabilities in foreign jurisdictions?

8. Marie-Sophie is the owner of *Tixe*—one of Canada's most exclusive online luxury stores for women. Paul is the vice-president in charge of online security, and he has retained you to provide legal advice. In the past six months, *Tixe* has been attacked by hackers on two occasions. Before this, the system had never been hacked before. While the hacking attacks diverted some staff and technology resources for a short time, the *Tixe* online operations were not affected and no business was lost. Marie-Sophie is very concerned about the attacks, however, and has instructed Paul to ensure that the situation does not reoccur.

You are aware that vulnerabilities in *Tixe's* online ordering system likely contributed to the fact that the attacks were not stopped at an earlier stage. You also know that although those vulnerabilities could be fixed and would stop the hackers, the fix would be expensive and might slow down overall system performance. Paul thinks he has a better solution; he wants to catch the hackers in the act by installing a key-logging program on the computer of every user who visits the *Tixe* website. This program would be invisible to all but the most sophisticated computer users, and it would keep track of every key that users press on their computers. That information would be relayed back to *Tixe*, where Paul could monitor it for suspicious patterns or activities. Paul thinks this is a real win–win solution because the hackers would be caught and *Tixe* could also use the information it gathers for marketing or other purposes. Your job is to advise Paul about whether his proposed solution is acceptable for the company from a legal perspective in light of *Tixe's* obligations under *PIPEDA*. Do you think there are problems with his system from a privacy perspective? If so, how might those problems be addressed?

9. Radhika is an employee of the TransCanadian Savings and Loan Corporation. After coming back from picking up her lunch one day, having left her office door wide open, as always, she noticed her laptop had been stolen from its docking station. Realizing that sensitive and personal information for more than 800 of her customers was contained on her machine, she immediately told her supervisor. The bank duly reported the theft to the Office of the Privacy Commissioner of Canada.

   Carmen was a customer of the bank. Almost three months later, he received a letter from the bank in which he was merely advised to contact the institution about a "current matter." Only when he called the bank was he informed of the theft and the potential security risk to his credit information. He was then advised to contact two credit bureaus and have an alert put on his file.

   During an investigation, it came to light not only that the laptop had been left unattended in the employee's office, but also that the office door did not have a lock on it. Further, Radhika's office was located on a corridor accessible to a public area by a door that was always unlocked during business hours. The bank also admitted that Radhika had not followed the company's data backup requirements or its security procedures regarding laptop computers.

   Analyze and discuss the above privacy breach in light of the bank's obligations pursuant to PIPEDA. What are the potential risks that Carmen faces now that his personal information has been stolen? What steps might the bank have taken to avoid this situation?

10. Stevie is a computer programmer who makes applications for popular smartphone devices. Her newest application is called ThreeTriangle and it allows users to share their current location using the GPS capability built into compatible smartphones. The application also allows users to upload and share photos, status messages, and the like. One of Stevie's primary concerns is liability for the content uploaded by users. Advise Stevie on some of the appropriate strategies that she can adopt to minimize legal risk.

11. Having taken a business law class in university, Frieda was asked to lead in the development of an appropriate email business practice policy statement for her company. Although her company does not buy or sell anything that is illegal, they do engage in mass-marketing strategies that include the transmission of bulk email. Frieda remembers hearing about an anti-spam law, but she doesn't remember the details. Write a memo for Frieda briefing her on the law's key elements and informing her of what her company should and should not do when sending bulk email.

12. Adrie is a young entrepreneur who lives in British Columbia. He owns several businesses. Recently, having been disturbed during dinner for the third night in a row by telemarketers, he decided that he would set up a business that would help people avoid these annoying calls by registering them for Canada's Do Not Call List. A lover of irony, Adrie thought that the most effective way to get customers was to call them during dinner and explain to them that, if they subscribed to his services, this would be the last annoying call they would ever receive. When Adrie called you one night, you made it clear that you no longer wanted to hear from him and demanded that you be taken off of his call list. What is Adrie required by law to do and what are the potential penalties if he fails to do so? Under what circumstances could Adrie be allowed to continue calling you?

What? Your Kindle Ate Your Homework?

As you read these words, what are you holding in your hands? Is it a shiny new textbook? A used book? A photocopy? An electronic reader?

As every university and college student is painfully aware, required textbooks can be extremely expensive. Canadian students can shell out as much as $1000 per year on course materials. And the price of textbooks is rapidly rising. According to one US study, textbook prices increased 6 percent per year between 1986 and 2004—twice the rate of inflation. Although no comparable research has been conducted in Canada, the conclusions from the US study are applicable here: Textbooks are a significant and swiftly escalating expense with serious implications for access to education and government student assistance programs.

A 2009 investigative report by the *Toronto Star* revealed how some students are coping with these sky-rocketing costs. Instead of starting the semester in coffee shops, they hang out at copy shops. An undercover reporter from the *Star* joined them, posing as a student in 12 copy centres in Toronto. The reporter entered each store with a new textbook and asked whether he could get copies of the entire text, an act in clear violation of copyright law. Ten of the twelve stores agreed to copy the entire book; for many of them, copyright infringement seemed to be business as usual.

From the perspective of the copyright owners, such widespread copying represents a significant amount of lost revenue. In response, Access Copyright (a copyright collective consisting of publishers and other copyright owners) has successfully sued copy centres for hundreds of thousands of dollars. Access Copyright had also commenced an action against Business Depot seeking $10 million in damages for facilitating copyright infringement through its photocopying services. Without much fanfare, the case was quietly dismissed by the courts a few years later.

Although the traditional "copyfight" is alive and kicking, other publishers have taken a different tack. Not confident that litigation would solve their problems in the long term, a few publishers and distributors have generated interesting new business models employing technologies at the forefront of electronic commerce. In the spring of 2009, Amazon.com launched the latest version of its e-book reader, the Kindle DX. With an e-ink screen that "reads like paper," this wireless device can download a bestseller in about a minute and can store 3500 books and documents. It reads aloud, lets you jot handwritten notes in the margins of any page, and its battery lasts for days.

The Kindle DX launch included a pilot project with several textbook publishers and US universities exploring distribution models for e-textbooks. The pilot program was modest in scale, and in the autumn of 2009, 300 students from several American universities downloaded schoolbooks onto their Kindles. The pilot project sparked a considerable uptake of e-book readers and tablet computers across the country, from elementary schools to universities. From the publishers' perspective, electronic distribution offers numerous features that may help spur wide-scale adoption in the future. Like Apple's iPad line of tablets, Amazon's Kindle e-reader uses digital rights management (DRM) to create a "digital lock" that tethers e-textbooks to an individual e-reader. DRM-enabled e-textbooks cannot easily be copied or transferred to a different machine. This will effectively eliminate the copy shop problem while, at the same time, putting an end to the used textbook market. Those same digital locks could also enable innovative revenue streams based on a rental or pay-per-use model. For example, a student could rent an e-textbook at a lower cost than purchasing it; the book would auto-delete after an agreed-upon period of time or number of uses. Likewise, e-textbooks can be un-bundled so that students do not have to buy the whole book when a professor assigns only one or two chapters. Some suggest that these models could potentially offer a win–win scenario for businesses and students, where the infringement of publishers' copyrights becomes difficult while textbook costs are significantly reduced.

As promising as they might seem, however, those very same digital locks pose a threat to consumer rights. The flipside of preventing infringement is limiting access, and there is nothing preventing DRM from being used to restrict access to and use of a work that would be perfectly legal in the paper-based world. For example, many student budgets currently rely on money obtained from re-selling textbooks, defraying their own book costs for the coming semester. Although this practice is perfectly legal, DRM could make it next to impossible. By eliminating the ability to sell, lend, or even give away their books, DRM can be used to change the rules regarding access to and ownership of books.

The broad power of DRM was dramatically illustrated in July 2009 when reports started to circulate online that Amazon was remotely auto-deleting copies of George Orwell's 1984 and *Animal Farm* from law-abiding Kindle owners. Apparently, a publisher had been selling electronic copies for the Kindle not knowing that George Orwell's works were in the public domain in some jurisdictions but still protected by copyright in others. Fearing serious sanction from the copyright owners after selling many e-copies, Amazon capitulated. Using DRM to trespass within the digital libraries of all Kindle customers, Amazon electronically "seized" Orwell's books. It was a classic Orwellian moment, the author himself having predicted in 1949 a day when the "Ministry of Truth" could make information appear and disappear on a whim.

From strange to stranger, a high-school student subsequently commenced a class action lawsuit against Amazon for breach of its Terms of Service, claiming in essence that his Kindle ate his homework. The student was reading *1984* for an advanced-placement class and had to turn in a journal on each hundred pages. With the loss of the digital book, he claims that his page count was thrown off and his notes were "rendered useless because they no longer referenced the relevant parts of the book."

While "the Kindle ate my homework" might sound like a silly excuse to a teacher not in the know, this case is important in a number of respects. First, the Kindle's Terms of Service do grant book buyers the "right to keep a permanent copy of the applicable Digital Content and to view, use, and display such Digital Content an unlimited number of times." Second, consumers who purchase the Kindle are not getting what they expect—namely, a device that has the same basic properties as a hard copy, minus the paper. Consumers learned the hard way that the Kindle's DRM gives Amazon the power to track, monitor, and erase. Just like Big Brother.

Jeff Bezos, CEO of Amazon, recognized that it was time to grovel to his consumer base, admitting that Amazon's actions were "stupid, thoughtless, and painfully out of line with our principles." He promised that Amazon would "use the scar tissue from this painful mistake to help make better decisions going forward." What he didn't promise was to remove the digital locks or re-write its DRM so that the Ministry of Truth's auto-delete functionality would no longer exist. Amazon also won't say much about whatever else is lurking in the Kindle.

What we do know is that copyright law in the age of the Kindle and the iPad is no longer merely about ownership of the means of (re)production. It is also about access to knowledge, personal privacy, the citizen's right to read anonymously, and consumers' rights to control the devices that they own.

While the future of e-book readers hangs in the balance, Canada's policymakers are under immense pressure from the United States to adopt new copyright laws that would make it illegal for consumers to tamper with DRM. Whether e-readers become the dominant method of distributing textbooks or simply one more way in which academic material is accessed, it seems clear that technology has the potential to deeply alter the landscape of the textbook industry, just as it has almost every other enterprise that revolves around intellectual property.

Questions to Consider

1. Is the soaring cost of textbooks a proper excuse for copyright infringement? Should copyright laws have broader exemptions for education?

2. Access Canada has decided to sue the intermediaries (copy shops) rather than the alleged infringers themselves. Why would it do this? Is this model better or worse than the record industry's approach of suing music fans for copyright infringement?

3. From a business perspective, do you think Amazon took the right approach after finding out that it had distributed *1984* without the copyright owner's permission? What other options were at its disposal?

4. If Canadian copyright policymakers are adamant about creating anti-tampering laws that protect DRM from being hacked, what kinds of balancing provisions should they include to protect consumers against an excessive use of digital locks?

ADDITIONAL RESOURCES

The Star: Textbook Piracy Thriving around City's Campuses **www.thestar.com/article/568628**
This *Toronto Star* report investigated the scope of textbook photocopying in Toronto.

An Economic Analysis of Textbook Pricing and Textbook Markets **www.eric.ed.gov/PDFS/ED497025.pdf**
This link contains a PDF copy of the Koch Report, which examined textbook pricing in the USA.

The New York Times: As Classrooms Go Digital, Textbooks May Become History **www.nytimes.com/2009/08/09/education/09textbook.html?pagewanted=1&_r=1&em**
With the emergence of lower cost e-readers and netbook computers, e-textbooks have come to be seen as viable only recently. This story discusses the future of the textbook industry and pays particular attention to e-textbooks and efforts to produce (and use) open-source textbooks.

Ars Technica: Amazon Supersizes Kindle for Textbooks, Newspapers **http://arstechnica.com/gadgets/news/2009/05/amazon-supersizes-kindle-for-textbooks-newspapers.ars**
Ars Technica, an online news outlet focusing on the computer industry, covered the Amazon press conference in which the Kindle DX was unveiled. This article provides technical details on the device, as well as describing Amazon's intentions of entering the textbook market.

The New York Times: Amazon Erases Orwell Books from Kindle Devices **www.nytimes.com/2009/07/18/technology/companies/18amazon.html?_r=1**
The New York Times published this article on the controversy surrounding Amazon's decision to remotely delete content from Kindles.

Boing Boing: Jeff Bezos's Kindle Apology **http://boingboing. net/2009/07/23/jeff-bezoss-kindle-a.html**
Here, noted author and commentator on intellectual property law and policy Cory Doctorow reproduces and discusses Amazon.com CEO Jeff Bezos's apology for the remote deletion of legitimately purchased copies of George Orwell's works.

CBC: Amazon Sued for Wrecking Teen's Kindle Work **www.cbc.ca/technology/story/2009/07/31/tech-amazon-lawsuit-student-1984-kindle-gawronski.html**
This article provides more details on the goals behind the class action lawsuit being launched against Amazon.

The Chronicle of Higher Education: This Could Be the Year of E-Textbooks **http://chronicle.com/article/The-Year-of-E-Textbooks-/48305/**
This article suggests that the number of textbooks available electronically has reached a "critical mass" that, in combination with the increasing availability and functionality of e-readers, will lead to them rapidly increasing in popularity. The article outlines the pros and cons such a development may have on academic institutions and students.

Copyright Consultations **http://copyright.econsultation.ca**
The official website for the Canadian copyright consultations provides information on the reform and consultation process and gives access to the submissions themselves. (It stopped accepting submissions on 14 September 2009.)

20 Agency and Other Methods of Carrying on Business

LEARNING OBJECTIVES

After completing this chapter, you should be able to:

❶ Explain how an agency relationship can be created.

❷ Distinguish between the actual authority of agents to enter into contracts on behalf of their principals and their apparent authority to do so.

❸ Describe situations in which a principal will be bound by a contract entered into by an agent without any authority from the principal.

❹ Describe situations in which an agent's fiduciary duty to act in the best interests of a principal and their duty of care protect the principal.

❺ Identify the obligations that a principal owes to their agent even if the principal has not expressly agreed to them.

❻ Identify events that will terminate an agency relationship.

❼ Describe practical and legal strategies that a principal can use to manage the risk that their agent will bind it to obligations that they have not authorized.

❽ Explain the circumstances in which a principal may be liable for the torts of their agents.

❾ Explain how questions may arise as to whether a person is an agent in several kinds of business relationships.

❿ Describe the special legal requirements imposed on agents working in some sectors that are designed to protect people who deal with them.

In business, one person often represents another for a specific purpose. Stockbrokers are independent business people, but they represent you to execute your purchases and sales of shares. A manager employed by a car dealership represents the dealership when negotiating the terms under which the dealership will sell you a new car. In each case, the person acting on behalf of someone else is called an **agent**. The person being represented is called the **principal**. **Agency** is the legal relationship between the principal and the agent. A principal may agree to be represented by an agent because the agent can achieve the principal's business purpose more effectively than the principal on their own. You may use a travel agent because the agent can get you a better price or routing for a trip. Senior managers in a business may delegate responsibility for negotiating some contracts with outsiders to particular employees because that is more efficient than having the senior managers negotiate all the contracts. It may be more efficient for the office manager to have the power to buy office supplies than to limit that power to the president.

an **agent** is a person who acts on behalf of someone else for some specific purpose

a **principal** is a person whom an agent represents for some specific purpose

an **agency** is the legal relationship between a principal and an agent

Sometimes, the agent has authority to bind the principal to a contract. In the car dealership example, the manager likely has authority to agree to the terms on which the dealership will sell you the car. Sometimes, however, a question will arise as to whether the manager has acted within the authority the dealership has granted. On the one hand, if the dealership has not authorized the manager to give you a price reduction of more than 10 percent, it will not want to be bound to sell you the car if the manager agreed to give you a 20 percent discount. On the other hand, as the person negotiating the contract with the agent, you will want to be able to rely on the manager having authority to bind the dealership if the manager offers you the discount. The legal rules of agency govern the circumstances in which an agent's actions bind the principal and, as a result, define when you can rely on an agent having authority to contract with you. These rules have a significant impact on the risks for principals and third parties when they deal through agents and define the risk management strategies available to each. The rules regarding the scope of an agent's authority to contract are one of the important subjects of this chapter.

Agents do not always have authority to enter into legal obligations on the principal's behalf. They may represent the principal's interests only in some other way. If you are selling your house, for example, your real estate agent will not usually have the authority to commit you to selling for a particular price, but the agent will be responsible for finding prospective purchasers and assisting with the sale process. Even in these situations, however, agents are subject to legal standards of behaviour that are designed to protect principals from some of the risks to which their agents may subject them. For example, agents must not be negligent in carrying out their responsibilities. Principals have a much more limited set of obligations to their agents, such as to reimburse them for expenses they incur on the principals' behalf. In this chapter, we discuss these basic standards of behaviour.

Agency relationships arise in many business settings. Agency relationships in partnerships and corporations are discussed in detail in Chapters 21 and 22. In this chapter, we discuss agency issues that arise in other commercial contexts, such as joint ventures and franchises. In some agency relationships, the general legal standards of behaviour for agents have been found to be insufficient to protect people dealing with agents. As a result, some agency relationships are governed by special statutes. For example, legislation addresses the risk that stockbrokers may not have sufficient assets to pay claims against them by their clients. This chapter provides a basic overview of some of these statutory regimes.

L.O. ❶❷❸❹   Basic Rules of Agency
CREATION OF AN AGENCY RELATIONSHIP

There are several ways to create an agency relationship. One of the most common is by express agreement. The principal and the agent enter into a contract that sets out the terms on which the agent is appointed, including the scope of the agent's authority and the agent's remuneration. In those provinces where the *Statute of Frauds* is still in force, the contract must be in writing if the relationship is to last longer than one year. (Provincial writing requirements were discussed in Chapter 10.) As well, the agreement must be in writing if the agent is going to have the authority to sign cheques on behalf of the principal.[1] The listing agreement that you sign with a real estate agent is an example of an agency relationship that is created by express agreement.[2] What is commonly called a *commercial representation agreement* is also a kind of express agency. A **commercial representation agreement** occurs when a manufacturer of goods agrees to allow someone to sell its goods on its behalf. For example, a manufacturer of sportswear could allow an individual to enter into contracts with retail sporting goods stores for the purchase of its clothes. Figure 20.1 illustrates the creation of agency.

A business relationship created by express agreement may have the effect of making someone your agent, even if that person is not referred to by that name. If you authorize a lawyer to act on your behalf in closing a real estate transaction, the lawyer is acting as your agent.

One of the most important contexts in which agency issues arise is the corporation. As we will discuss in Chapter 21, corporations are separate legal entities that can act only through human beings. Individuals acting on behalf of a corporation are acting as its agents. The directors and officers of a corporation as well as its salespeople, purchasing clerks, and other employees may all have authority to act as agents of the corporation for particular purposes. The agency rules discussed in this chapter apply to corporations and people acting on their behalf. We sometimes use examples involving corporations to illustrate these rules. Chapter 22 provides a more detailed discussion of the particular ways in which agency rules apply to corporations as well as the issues associated with what are referred to as "agency costs" in a corporation.

> a **commercial representation** agreement occurs when a manufacturer of goods agrees to allow someone to sell its goods on its behalf

---

FIGURE 20.1   Creation of Agency

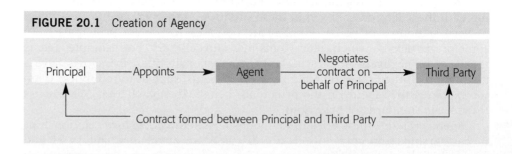

[1.] *Bills of Exchange Act*, RSC 1985, c B-4 (Can). Cheques were discussed in Chapter 14.

[2.] In some provinces, listing agreements with real estate agents must be in writing: *eg Real Estate Act*, RSA 2000, c R-5, s 22 (Alta); *Real Estate Trading Act*, SNS 1996, c 28, ss 26, 27 (NS); *Real Estate and Business Brokers Act*, 2002, SO 2002, c 30, s 33(3) (Ont), and *Ontario Reg* 580/05 made under that Act, ss 11–15.

When an agency is created through an express agreement, usually the agreement describes the authority given to the agent. The authority a principal gives an agent to act on its behalf is called **actual authority**. An express grant of *actual authority* could be given in an employment contract with the agent through a resolution of the corporation's board of directors or in an agency agreement. Actual authority can also be granted less formally, such as through an oral delegation of authority by a principal. Appointing an agent to a particular position, such as sales manager, that has certain authority in the principal's organization gives the agent the actual authority of that position. As well, agents will be considered to have implied powers to do what is necessary to fulfill the responsibilities of their position, even though these powers are not expressed anywhere.

actual authority exists when the principal authorizes the agent to act on its behalf

An agency relationship can also arise without the principal taking any action to appoint the agent and give them specific authority. An agency relationship exists when a principal represents, or holds out, someone as their agent in discussions with a third party. That person will have the authority to deal with the third party that is suggested by the principal's actions, even if that person was never properly appointed by the principal as an agent. The authority created when the actions of the principal give a third party the reasonable impression that the agent has authority to act on behalf of the principal is called **apparent authority**. *Apparent authority* could be created by a statement to you by the president of a corporation that the sales manager has authority to sign contracts to buy office supplies for the corporate principal. A contract created by an agent within their apparent authority is just as enforceable as if the agent had actual authority.

apparent authority exists when the principal creates the reasonable impression that the agent is authorized to act on the principal's behalf

Finally, agency can arise as a matter of law. For example, under partnership law, each partner is an agent of the partnership and can bind the partnership to obligations that arise in connection with carrying on the business of the partnership in the usual way. We will discuss partnerships in Chapter 21.

Ratification

Even if an agency relationship does not exist, a person can still enter into an agreement that ultimately binds someone else in limited circumstances. Suppose Gary has no authority to act on your behalf. Nevertheless, Gary purports to enter into a contract to buy you a tablet computer from a third party, telling the third party that he is your agent. Perhaps Gary knows that you wanted to buy a tablet computer and hopes that you will reward him if he negotiates a good price for you to buy one. Since Gary has no authority to act for you, the contract he has negotiated is not binding on you. However, you could agree to **ratify** the contract by choosing to accept the contractual obligation. If you do so, the contract will become binding upon you. It will be as if you had given Gary authority to act on your behalf before he started negotiating with the third party.

a contract is **ratified** when someone accepts a contract that was negotiated on their behalf but without their authority

For ratification to be effective, it must meet these requirements:

- It must be clear. Ratification can, however, be either *express* or *implied* from behaviour. In the previous example, your ratification of the contract would be implied if you took delivery of the tablet computer and used it.[3]
- It must occur within a *reasonable time* after the creation of the contract. What is reasonable depends upon the facts. If someone without your

PART 6

[3.] *Findlay v Butler* (1977) 19 NBR (2d) 473 (QB); *Canada Trust Co v Gordon* [1978] 5 WWR 268 (Sask QB).

authority purported to act on your behalf to enter into a fire insurance contract on a building that you owned, you could not ratify it after the building had burned down.[4]

- The principal must accept the *whole contract* or none of it. For example, if you had developed some software and someone purported to license the software to a third party on your behalf, you could not accept the royalties under the licence without also accepting the other obligations in the licence agreement, such as providing technical support to the licensee.

- The principal must have been *identified* by the agent. An agent cannot make a contract, either on their own behalf or on behalf of some person the agent has not yet identified, and then try to find someone to ratify it.[5]

- The principal must have had the legal *capacity* to enter into the contract both at the time the agent created the contract and at the time of ratification. Children who are minors or mentally disabled persons are examples of persons who have no capacity or limited capacity to contract. We discussed capacity to contract in Chapter 10.

What happens if an agent without authority purports to enter into a contract on behalf of a principal but the principal does not ratify it?[6] In that situation, the agent is not personally liable to the third party under the contract *unless* the third party and the agent intended the contract to be binding on the agent personally. When the agent is liable is discussed in more detail below.

WHEN IS THE PRINCIPAL LIABLE?

Most disputes about agency relate to the scope of the agent's authority. Did the agent have authority to enter into the agreement that the third party is trying to enforce against the principal? In the example referred to in the chapter introduction, a dispute might arise if the manager of the car dealership agreed to give you a 20 percent discount off the list price of a new car but the dealership subsequently refused to give you the discount because it had given the manager authority to offer a maximum discount of 10 percent. The rules regarding when a principal is liable in contract balance the interests of the principal with the interests of third parties seeking to enter into contracts with the principal.

- On the one hand, a principal does not want to be bound to a contract that an agent purports to enter into on their behalf if the contract was outside the authority that the principal granted to the agent.

- On the other hand, a third party who enters into a contract with an agent on behalf of a principal does not want to spend too much time or money investigating whether the principal has actually given authority to the agent to enter into the contract. They want to be able to rely on commonly accepted indicators of authority, such as a letter of introduction from a principal's president on the principal's letterhead. Where it looks as if the person is an agent of the principal with authority to enter into the contract, the third party wants to be able to rely on the agent having such authority.

[4.] *Portavon Cinema Co Ltd v Price and Century Insurance Co Ltd* [1939] 4 All ER 601 (KB).

[5.] If an agent *does* have authority to act on behalf of a principal but does not tell the third party that, the third party may hold the "undisclosed principal" or the agent liable, as discussed below.

[6.] In this situation, an agency relationship never arises in a technical legal sense. There never really was an "agent" or "principal." These terms nevertheless are used here for convenience to identify the parties.

In large transactions, each party to the contract will do a significant amount of investigation to satisfy themselves that the person executing a contract on behalf of the other party has authority to do so and, as a result, that the contract is enforceable. These investigations will be backed up by documentation demonstrating that such authority exists, such as certified copies of resolutions of a corporation's board of directors authorizing the people signing the contract to enter into the transaction on the corporation's behalf, and lawyers' opinions regarding their authority. In most situations, however, the size of the transaction simply does not justify incurring the costs associated with these kinds of risk management strategies.

As we saw above, an agent may have received *actual authority* from the principal to enter into commitments on their behalf in many ways, such as by entering into a contract with the principal that gives the agent authority, or by being appointed to a position in the principal's organization that has certain authority. However the agent acquires actual authority, the principal is bound by any obligation that the agent creates within the scope of that authority. That is true whether or not the third party knows the exact scope of the agent's actual authority.[7]

A third party usually does not know—and has no easy way of finding out—the extent of an agent's actual authority. That information is often contained in a document to which the third party does not have access, such as the principal's internal business records or the agent's employment contract. As a result, a third party is permitted to rely on words or conduct by the principal that indicate to the third party that the agent has authority to enter into the contract that the third party wants to enforce. As discussed above, when the principal's actions create the reasonable impression that the agent is authorized, that gives the agent *apparent authority*. If a car dealer tells you that a particular person has authority to negotiate to sell you a car on behalf of the dealership, then that would give that person the apparent authority to do so. The principal is liable to a third party under any contract that an agent creates within the scope of the agent's apparent authority.[8]

Apparent authority is not necessarily connected with actual authority. In practice, however, they often overlap. Suppose you are the office manager of a business that is being conducted through a corporation. You want to buy a photocopier for that business. You may have actual authority to do so under the terms of your employment contract with the corporation. You may also have apparent authority because the corporation's president wrote a letter to the photocopier supplier saying that you were authorized to buy the photocopier. Nevertheless, one form of authority can exist without the other. That would be true, for instance, if the president's letter were inaccurate because your employment contract said that only the vice-president was authorized to buy office equipment. In such a case, you would have apparent, but not actual, authority. It is impossible to list every form of behaviour that can create apparent authority. Significantly, only the principal's conduct—not the agent's—is relevant. When the principal actually tells the third party that the agent is authorized to contract, apparent authority will be established. But less direct forms of communication may also be enough for a third party to reasonably believe that an agent has authority. For example, permitting a lawyer to defend a lawsuit may give that lawyer apparent authority to settle the claim on your behalf. If the lawyer is found to have that

---

[7] *Freeman & Lockyer v Buckhurst Park Properties (Mangal) Ltd* [1964] 2 QB 480 (CA).

[8] That form of authority is sometimes described as "ostensible authority," "agency by estoppel," or "agency by holding out." Estoppel was discussed in Chapter 8. Holding out in the context of partnerships is discussed in Chapter 21.

authority, you will be bound by the settlement agreement, even if you never gave the lawyer actual authority to settle.[9] You could, however, sue your lawyer if the lawyer exceeded the scope of the authority that you did give.[10]

If a principal allows an agent to act as if they had authority, such behaviour may be a representation that the agent has that authority.[11] Case Brief 20.1 illustrates how apparent authority can arise without any express representation by the principal.

Case Brief 20.1

Spiro v Lintern [1973] 3 All ER 319 (CA)

John owned a house. He directed his wife, Iris, to list the property with a real estate agent but did not give her authority to sell the house. Iris entered into a contract to sell the house to a third party, Lintern. John was aware of what his wife had done but did nothing about it. He even permitted Lintern to come to the house with his architect to plan some repairs. At the time of the contract, Lintern had no idea that Iris was not the owner of the house. John eventually refused to sell, arguing that Iris had no authority to sell his house. The court held that, by allowing Iris to act as she had, John had given her apparent authority to sell the house. John, acting as a principal, had represented to Lintern that Iris was his agent with authority to sell his house.

usual authority allows a person appointed to a particular position to exercise the authority normally associated with that position

Putting someone in a particular position constitutes a representation that the person has the **usual authority** for that position. This kind of apparent authority is referred to as *usual authority*. What is "usual" is determined by reference to the authority of agents in similar positions in similar businesses. Agents with titles such as vice-president, treasurer, and secretary, however, may have widely varying degrees of authority in different industries and even within industries. In the car dealer example discussed in the introduction, if the dealer appointed a person as the "sales manager" of the dealership and allowed that person to use an office that had that title on the door, you would be able to enforce any contract with the dealership that was negotiated by that person so long as it was within the usual authority of a car dealership sales manager.

A principal will be bound by contracts within the agent's apparent authority only if the third party relied on that appearance of authority. As a practical matter, reliance is seldom hard to prove. But a third party cannot enforce a contract if they knew, or should have known, that the agent did not have authority.[12]

Finally, where the principal is not an individual but a business organization, one more requirement must be satisfied. The individual whose conduct constitutes the representation on behalf of the principal that the agent has authority to contract must be someone who is permitted to make such a representation under the allocation of responsibility within the business organization. Continuing with the car dealership example, if the sales manager of the dealership has the authority to decide at what prices the dealership will sell its cars, the sales manager could represent to you that a salesperson has authority to give you a 20 percent discount. You could rely on such a representation as giving the salesperson

---

[9.] *Sign-O-Lite v Bugeja* [1994] OJ No 1381 (Gen Div).

[10.] As your agent, the lawyer has a duty to follow your instructions and has a fiduciary duty to you. Both of those duties would be breached if the lawyer agreed to the settlement without your consent.

[11.] *Freeman & Lockyer v Buckhurst Park Properties (Mangal) Ltd* [1964] 2 QB 480 (CA).

[12.] *Hazelwood v West Coast Securities Ltd* (1975) 49 DLR (3d) 46 (BC SC), aff'd (1976) 68 DLR (3d) 172 (CA).

apparent authority to grant you the discount. You could not rely on a representation from the salesperson alone if the salesperson did not, in fact, have authority to grant you the discount. In some circumstances, however, you might be able to argue that the dealership had represented that the salesperson had authority by allowing the salesperson to offer such discounts.

Concept Summary 20.1 summarizes the circumstances in which a principal is bound by the acts of an agent on their behalf.

Concept Summary 20.1

When a Principal Is Bound by the Acts of an Agent

- Agent acts within the scope of the actual authority given by the principal to the agent created by
  - express delegation to the agent
  - appointing the agent to a position with that authority
  - implication from the circumstances
- Agent acts within the scope of the apparent authority created by the principal's representation to a third party, which may consist of the
  - principal's statement or conduct
  - principal acquiescing to the agent acting with that authority
  - principal appointing the agent to a position that would usually have that authority
- Agent enters into a contract on behalf of an identified principal but without the principal's authority, and the principal subsequently ratifies the contract.

WHEN IS THE AGENT LIABLE?

Normally, an agent is not liable personally for contracts that they negotiate because it is usually clear that they were contracting on behalf of an identified principal. However, the agent and the third party may agree otherwise. And even if the contract does not expressly provide for liability, a court may decide that the parties implicitly intended the agent to be liable.[13] The agent can also be held personally liable if they gave the third party the impression that they were the principal. That can happen if the agent fails to disclose that they were acting on behalf of a principal. If the third party later discovers that the person they dealt with was only an agent, and if that agent did have authority to act on behalf of the **undisclosed principal**, the third party can hold either the agent or the principal liable, but not both.[14] Therefore, to avoid the risk of personal liability, an agent should clearly explain their own role and disclose the existence of the principal to the third party.

An agent will be responsible for any loss that a third party suffers as a result of a contract negotiated with them if the agent knew they were not authorized to act on the principal's behalf and acted fraudulently.[15] Even if the agent did not act fraudulently, they may still be liable to the third party for a *breach of warranty of authority*. A **breach of warranty of authority** occurs if an agent

an **undisclosed principal** exists when the agent purports to contract without disclosing that they are acting on behalf of a principal

a **breach of warranty of authority** occurs if an agent indicates that they are authorized to act for a principal when they are not

---

13. The agent will be liable only if there is clear evidence that the parties intended the agent to be liable: *Petro-Partners v Eastside Management 94 Inc* [1999] OJ No 2269 (CA).

14. The undisclosed principal can also enforce the contract against the third party.

15. *Doiron v Devon Capital* (2003) 38 BLR (3d) 82 (Alta CA); *Keddie v Canada Life Assurance Co* (1999) 179 DLR (4th) 1 (BC CA). Fraud and the tort of deceit were discussed in Chapter 5.

indicates that they are authorized to act for a principal when they are not. Liability arises even if the agent honestly, but mistakenly, thought that they had the principal's authority.[16] As a result, the third party does not bear the risk of loss when they were misled by the agent.

THE AGENT'S DUTIES TO THE PRINCIPAL

When an agent is appointed by contract, their responsibilities may be set out in some detail. They must comply with those duties and follow any instructions given by the principal. The agent can be held responsible for failing to do so. In one case, a principal appointed an agent to insure a ship. The agent failed to do so. When the ship was lost, the agent was liable to the principal for the loss that the insurance would have covered.[17] Furthermore, an agent may have duties that are not mentioned in the contract but that arise from circumstances related to the contract. For example, an agent who receives goods to sell may have the duty to insure them while they are in their possession.

In general, an agent's obligations cannot be delegated to anyone else—they are personal obligations. This rule recognizes that a principal often puts great trust in the judgment and skill of their agent. There are important practical qualifications to this general rule. For instance, if a law firm or a business enterprise is appointed as an agent, responsibility necessarily is delegated to individuals within that organization. If you hired an advertising firm as an agent to place newspaper advertisements on your behalf, the actual task of negotiating for the advertisements would have to be given to some person within the firm.

Because an agency relationship exposes the principal to the risk of being held liable in unwanted ways, the common law also imposes two other types of duties on agents that reduce the principal's risk: a fiduciary duty and a duty of care.

Fiduciary Duty

a **fiduciary duty** requires an agent to act in good faith and in the best interests of the principal

Agents have a **fiduciary duty** to act in good faith and in the best interests of their principals, in most circumstances.[18] While the precise content of that duty depends upon the facts, one of its key requirements is that agents avoid situations in which their personal interests conflict with the best interests of their principals. For instance, if you were appointed to negotiate a contract for the sale of your principal's land, you could not sell that property to yourself. There would be an obvious conflict of interest. You would be acting for the principal as the seller *and* for yourself as the buyer.[19] You would be tempted to favour your own interests over the principal's, such as by agreeing to a lower price.

A conflict of interest would also arise if, without your principal's knowledge, you arranged for the property owned by your principal to be sold to someone with whom you have a relationship.[20] Suppose I agreed to pay you $5000 if you found a suitable piece of land for me. You then arranged for me to buy your principal's property for $200 000. There is a risk that your desire to

---

[16] *Yonge v Toynbee* [1910] 1 KB 215 (CA).

[17] *Turpin v Bilton* (1843) 134 ER 641 (CP).

[18] *R v Kelly* (1992) 92 DLR (4th) 643 (SCC). We discuss the fiduciary duty that partners in a partnership owe each other in Chapter 21 and the fiduciary duty that directors and officers owe to a corporation in Chapter 22.

[19] *Aaron Acceptance Corp v Adam* (1987) 37 DLR (4th) 133 (BC CA).

[20] *Andrews v Ramsay* [1903] 2 KB 635.

obtain $5000 from me may have interfered with your obligation to find the best deal possible for your principal. You have breached your fiduciary duty in this situation. You would have to pay the $5000 finder's fee over to your principal.[21] It would not matter if $200 000 was an entirely fair price for the land and that you did your best to ensure that your principal got the best price—the fiduciary duty may be breached even if the principal did not suffer any loss. That rule is imposed because of the need to ensure that agents never have any incentive to act in their own interests at the expense of their principals'. You would be entitled to keep the $5000 only if you had explained the entire situation to your principal, who then allowed the sale to be completed.

The fiduciary duty involves several other obligations:

■ An agent must disclose to their principal any information that may be relevant to the principal's interests.[22] For example, if you are appointed to buy cars, you must reveal any bargains that you find to your principal.

■ An agent cannot personally profit from the unauthorized use of information or opportunities that arise as a result of the agency relationship.

■ An agent cannot compete with the principal. Consequently, if you are appointed to sell goods for your principal, you cannot also sell the same kind of goods for yourself or for the principal's competitor.

An agent's fiduciary duty may, however, be displaced by the principal's instructions. If your principal specifically tells you to act in a certain way, you must do so, even if you think some other course of action would be in the principal's best interests.[23]

Duty of Care

Every agent owes its principal a *duty of care*. The **duty of care** requires an agent to take reasonable care in the performance of their responsibilities. The precise content of that duty depends upon what the agent agreed to do and the circumstances surrounding the relationship between the agent and the principal.[24] If that duty is breached, the agent must compensate the principal for any loss that they suffer. The principal may be denied recovery, however, if they knew that the agent was incompetent or unqualified.[25] If you appointed someone to be your agent to buy an apartment building and you knew that the agent had no ability to identify defects in building structure, you could not hold the agent liable for any loss you suffered because a building that the agent bought for you had structural defects.

Case Brief 20.2 illustrates how an agent must understand the scope of their obligations, ensure that they are able to fulfill those obligations, and alert their principal to any deficiency in their skills. Case Brief 20.3 provides a recent example of the duty of a real estate agent in relation to the disclosure of problems with a property.

the **duty of care** requires an agent to take reasonable care in the performance of their responsibilities

PART 6

[21.] *Raso v Dionigi* (1993) 100 DLR (4th) 459 (Ont CA).

[22.] *McCullough v Tenaglia* (1998) 40 BLR (2d) 222 (Ont Gen Div).

[23.] *Bertram v Godfray* (1830) 12 ER 364 (PC); *Volkers v Midland Doherty Ltd* (1995) 17 DLR (4th) 343 (BC CA). Also, in some cases, the nature of the relationship between the agent and the principal may mean that no fiduciary duty arises: *Hunt v TD Securities Inc* (2003) 66 OR (3d) 481 (CA).

[24.] *Tonks v Aetna Life Assurance Co of Canada* (1992) 98 DLR (4th) 582 (Ont Gen Div).

[25.] *Hillcrest General Leasing Ltd v Guelph Investments Ltd* (1971) 13 DLR (3d) 517 (Ont Co Ct) (negligence in selecting sub-agent).

Case Brief 20.2

Fine's Flowers Ltd v General Accident Assurance Co of Canada (1977) 81 DLR (3d) 139 (Ont CA)

Fine's Flowers appointed an insurance agent to obtain "full coverage" for its garden business. The agent obtained insurance against a number of business risks—but not damage to plants caused by freezing as a result of a heating system failure. Unfortunately, that is exactly what happened. Fine's sued the agent for breach of contract and negligence.

The Court of Appeal held that the agent's undertaking to obtain "full coverage" created an obligation to ensure that Fine's was insured against all foreseeable and normal risks. The agent was liable for failing to fulfill its contractual duty to obtain adequate insurance and for breaching its duty of care to Fine's by failing to warn Fine's about the gap in coverage.[26]

Case Brief 20.3

Krawchuk v Scherbak 2011 ONCA 352

Krawchuk contracted with Wedell to act as her real estate agent. Wedell was also the agent for the Scherbaks, who were seeking to sell their house. In the disclosure form that the Scherbaks filled out regarding their home, they indicated that they were unaware of any plumbing or foundation problems. In fact, as the Scherbaks knew, the house was sinking and the sewage drains backed up several times per year. The Court of Appeal held the Scherbaks liable for negligent misrepresentation. The court also held the real estate agent liable for negligent misrepresentation

for passing on the representation of the Scherbaks without taking reasonable steps to ensure that it was accurate or recommending that Krawchuk have a home inspection done. Wedell's duty of care required her to go beyond relying on the Scherbaks' statement, because the problems with the house were obvious to her: the floors were sloping, there were cracks in the walls, and the house was underpriced because of its well-known foundation and plumbing problems.

THE PRINCIPAL'S DUTIES TO THE AGENT

Like an agent, a principal must fulfill any obligation that is set out in the agency contract. Furthermore, a principal generally must satisfy certain obligations that are imposed by law.

- Unless the parties agreed that the agent would work for free, the principal must pay reasonable remuneration for the agent's services.[27]
- A principal has an obligation to indemnify the agent for liabilities and expenses that are reasonably incurred in connection with the agency relationship. Suppose you are asked to obtain insurance for your principal. You do so and pay the first premium on the principal's behalf. The principal must reimburse you for that expense. A principal is not, however, under any obligation to the agent if an agent acts illegally or in breach of the agency agreement.[28]

TERMINATION

There are several ways to terminate an agency relationship:

- Either party gives the other notice of termination.

---

[26] Fine's could not recover compensation for the same loss twice. It was required to elect between damages for breach of contract and damages for negligence.

[27] *Banfield, McFarlane, Evan Real Estate Ltd v Hoffer* [1977] 4 WWR 465 (Man CA).

[28] *Duncan v Hill* (1873) LR 8 Ex 242, cited in GHL Fridman *Law of Agency* 7th ed (1997) at 202.

- An event occurs that results in termination under the terms of the agency contract.

- The agent is appointed for a specific project or a particular period, and the project is completed or the period expires, even if the agency contract does not provide for termination in these circumstances.

- Performance of the agency becomes impossible.

- The principal loses the capacity to contract as a result of death, insanity, or bankruptcy. (Capacity to contract is discussed in Chapter 10.)

That last ground can create practical difficulties if the agent is unaware that the principal has lost capacity. Since the principal cannot be liable for obligations that arise after the incapacity occurs, a third party may try to hold the agent personally responsible. The agent may be liable for breach of warranty of authority in these circumstances.

Because an agency relationship may be terminated by notice from either party, the relationship can be very fragile. For that reason, agency agreements often require a reasonable notice period before termination. Furthermore, if an agent is an employee, the law states that the agency–employment relationship can be terminated only for just cause, or with either reasonable notice or compensation in lieu of notice.[29] Consequently, the nature of the parties' relationship will determine the rules that apply to termination.

Risk Management Issues

L.O. ❺❻❼❽

Before concluding our general discussion of agency, it is appropriate to discuss how principals can manage their risk of liability in contract and tort that results from using agents.

CONTRACTS

A principal is liable for contracts created on their behalf by an agent with either actual or apparent authority. The principal's risk of being bound to unwanted contracts is more easily managed with respect to *actual authority*. The principal can use an agency agreement to clearly state what the agent is and is not authorized to do. That document should be carefully drafted to ensure that it is broad enough to allow the agent to do a proper job, but not so broad as to permit the agent to create unintended liabilities.

Risks associated with *apparent authority* can also be managed, but not as easily. The principal must carefully monitor how it communicates, directly and indirectly, with third parties to avoid giving an agent apparent authority to create unwanted obligations to third parties.[30] The principal must also realize that apparent authority may exist even after the actual agency relationship has come to an end. If a third party dealt with the agent before the agency relationship was terminated and that third party was unaware of the termination, they may be able to enforce any new agreements that the agent purports to enter into against the principal. To avoid that possibility, the principal should notify all of their customers whenever they terminate an agent's authority.

[29.] The characteristics of the employment relationship are discussed in Chapter 26. The question of when an agent should be considered an employee is considered in *Renmar Sales Agency Inc v 806897 Ontario Inc* [1999] OJ No 3956 (SCJ).

[30.] When the agent acts outside the actual authority given by the principal, but in circumstances in which the third party can rely on apparent authority, the third party can hold the principal liable; however, the principal may also be able to sue the agent for breach of the agency agreement.

TORTS

If an agent commits a tort, the principal is vicariously liable to the victim if (i) the agent was an employee, and (ii) the tort was committed within the course of employment.[31] The basic rules for vicarious liability were discussed in Chapter 3. In Chapter 26, we will discuss the rules that determine when a person is, in law, an employee.

A principal may be liable even if an agent was not an employee. In general, if the agent is acting within the scope of their actual or apparent authority, the principal is liable for the agent's fraud or negligent misrepresentation.[32]

As we have seen, a principal is exposed to substantial risks whenever they use an agent. Often, the best strategy for avoiding such risks is to carefully select, train, supervise, and require reporting from agents. You Be the Judge 20.1 illustrates the importance of that strategy. Ethical Perspective 20.1 addresses the appropriateness of using criminal penalties as a way of reducing the risk that agents will not fulfill their duties to their principals.

You Be the Judge 20.1

Authority of Insurance Brokers[33]

Horne carried on business as an insurance broker on behalf of several insurance companies, including Canada Life. Under his contract with Canada Life, he was authorized to solicit customers for life insurance and various other products, but he was not authorized to incur any liability for Canada Life without prior approval from the company.

In 1990, Horne met Keddie, who was seeking to make an investment. He told her that he was a Canada Life broker operating under the name Royal Pacific Consulting. On Horne's advice, Keddie purchased a $375 000 Canada Life annuity contract. Horne subsequently gave Keddie a folder containing information about the annuity. The folder had a picture of the Canada Life building in Toronto on the front, and the name and address of Canada Life on the back.

In 1992, Keddie was interested in making another investment. Horne convinced her that she should purchase another Canada Life annuity. Keddie gave Horne a cheque for $300 000 payable to Royal Pacific Consulting. Horne invested $105 000 in an annuity offered by another financial institution and kept the remaining $195 000 for himself. Horne later gave Keddie a folder similar to the first one that contained information about the annuity inside. However, whereas the earlier policy simply referred to "Canada Life," the new policy statement referred to "Royal Pacific Group Representing the Canada Life/NN Financial Group."

There was no evidence as to how Horne got the folders. There was, however, evidence that he had been provided with a large quantity of material from Canada Life, including application forms and brochures. The only information that Keddie had about Horne's relationship to Canada Life was based on what he had told her.

When Horne eventually stopped making payments to her, Keddie successfully sued him for fraud. Unfortunately, Horne no longer had any assets and therefore could not satisfy that judgment. Keddie then sued Canada Life, alleging that Horne was Canada Life's agent and Canada Life was liable for his fraud.

Question for Discussion

1. Should Keddie succeed against Canada Life?

[31.] If the principal is forced to pay compensation to the tort victim, it is generally entitled to recover that amount from the agent-employee. Often, however, the principal does not exercise that right.

[32.] When an agent has made a negligent misrepresentation, the third party may be able to rescind the contract, even when the principal did not authorize, or even forbade, the misrepresentation: *Betker v Williams* [1992] 2 WWR 534 (BC CA).

[33.] *Keddie v Canada Life Assurance Co* [1999] BCJ No 2165 (CA); *Doiron v Devon Capital* (2003) 38 BLR (3d) 82 (Alta CA).

Ethical Perspective 20.1

Agent's Criminal Liability[34]

Over a two-year period, almost three dozen investors purchased shares in two companies on the advice of Hudec. The majority of the investors received no information about the companies and relied exclusively on Hudec's advice. Hudec continued to play a role in advising the investors from time to time as to the status of their investments. He later admitted that one company had given him $43 000 and the other 79 000 shares in return for directing his clients to them. He also later admitted that he did not tell any of the investors that he had received benefits from those companies.

Hudec was found guilty under the *Criminal Code* for accepting "secret commissions" from the companies in which his clients were advised to invest without his clients' knowledge and consent. He knew that he was an agent for his clients. The court found that the clients were entitled to know that Hudec was receiving benefits from the companies in question. If they had known, they might have invested elsewhere.

Questions for Discussion

1. Is it appropriate for agents to be held criminally liable in these circumstances?

2. Should liability depend upon whether the investors lose their investments?

3. Why would civil liability to compensate for any investor losses not be sufficient?

Business Relationships in which Agency Issues Arise

L.O. ❾ ❿

Agency arises in a variety of business arrangements. We will look at agency in partnerships in Chapter 21. Agency in corporations is discussed in Chapter 22. In this section, we will consider several other business situations that can involve agency relationships: joint ventures and strategic alliances, distributorships, and franchises. At the end of this section, we will discuss the special statutory rules applicable to agents in certain businesses.

JOINT VENTURES AND STRATEGIC ALLIANCES

A *joint venture* is not a distinct form of business organization. In fact, it is not a relationship that has a precise legal meaning. A **joint venture** is simply any legal arrangement in which two or more parties combine their resources for a limited purpose, for a limited time, or both. For instance, a small exploration company may own the rights to mine gold from a certain area but not have the financial resources it needs to actually build the mine. The smaller company could enter into a joint venture with a larger mining company that does have sufficient resources. That joint venture could operate through a corporation in which each party has an investment as a shareholder or through a partnership in which each party is a partner. Alternatively, the parties to the joint venture could have their relationship governed exclusively by contract.

Strategic alliance describes an even more broadly defined category of relationships. A **strategic alliance** is any arrangement in which two or more parties agree to co-operate for some purpose. That arrangement can be formal or informal and can involve varying degrees of co-operation. Sometimes a joint venture or partnership may be referred to as a strategic alliance. "Strategic alliance" may also be used, for example, to describe an arrangement in which the parties (i) conduct a research project together, (ii) jointly market products, or (iii) share information.

a **joint venture** is a legal arrangement in which two or more parties combine their resources for a limited purpose, a limited time, or both

a **strategic alliance** is any arrangement in which two or more parties agree to co-operate for some purpose

---

34. *R v Hudec* [1992] OJ No 2992 (HCJ). The relevant provision of the *Criminal Code*, RSC 1985, c C-46 (Can), is s 426.

The rules of agency applicable to joint ventures and strategic alliances that operate as partnerships or corporations have already been referred to in this chapter and are discussed in Chapters 21 and 22 in more detail. If a joint venture or strategic alliance is purely contractual, the participants are not automatically agents for each other. They may, however, agree to set up an agency relationship. Joint venturers often agree that each will have authority to create obligations for both parties in connection with the joint venture business. When that is done, the precise scope of the agency relationship should be clearly stated in the joint venture agreement. Even if no *actual authority* is given in the joint venture agreement, one joint venturer's actions may provide the other joint venturer with apparent authority. A third party may be entitled to rely on the actions of one joint venturer that represent that the other joint venturer has authority to contract on behalf of the joint venture. Imagine that Sam and Anna have entered into a joint venture that they call Sam and Anna's Homes, to build and sell some houses. Anna goes to a bank to borrow money to finance construction of the homes. Sam tells the bank that he is involved in the project and agrees to the loan to Anna. Sam's actions might be found to constitute a representation to the bank that Anna had authority to borrow the money on behalf of the joint venture with the result that Sam could be responsible for the loan along with Anna.

DISTRIBUTORSHIPS

a **distributorship** exists when one business enters into a contract to sell another's product

A **distributorship** exists when one business enters into a contract to sell another's product. In addition to selling the basic product, a distributor may also agree to perform some of the tasks that would normally be performed by the manufacturer or supplier. The distributor may, for example, provide warranty service.

A distributorship does not normally involve an agency relationship. The parties can agree that the distributor acts on behalf of the supplier when they deal with customers for some purposes. Usually, however, the distributor buys the supplier's products and then resells them on their own behalf. In fact, most distributorship agreements expressly state that the distributor is *not* an agent and has no authority to bind the supplier. Suppliers do not want to be exposed to the risk of unwanted obligations negotiated by the distributor. For that reason, suppliers must be concerned about avoiding the creation of *apparent authority*. If a distributor is made to look like an agent of the supplier, a customer may acquire rights against the supplier, regardless of what the distributorship agreement says.

FRANCHISES

a **franchise** is a purely contractual relationship under which the franchisor gives the franchisee the right to operate its "business system" in return for a set of fees

A **franchise** is a purely contractual relationship under which the franchisor gives the franchisee the right to operate its "business system" at a particular location in return for a set of fees. Franchise agreements often contain these major provisions, among others:

- a licence that allows the franchisee to use the franchisor's trademark[35]
- obligations of the franchisor to assist in the operation of the franchised business (by providing training, uniforms, and so on)

[35.] A licence gives permission to act in a way that would otherwise be prohibited by rights held by the licensor.

■ obligations of the franchisee to maintain certain standards and follow certain rules in carrying on the franchise business and to pay fees based, in part, on the volume of sales[36]

We often think of franchises in the fast-food context, but they are common in many other areas, such as retailing. A franchisee may appear to the public to be an agent of the franchisor. A franchise could be set up as an agency relationship, whereby the franchisee conducts business on behalf of the franchisor. In practice, however, franchise agreements invariably provide that the franchisee is not an agent of the franchisor. This is done to minimize the risk to the franchisor of liability arising out of the activities of franchisees. A franchisor may still be held liable in some circumstances. (See the discussion of liability for negligence in Chapter 6.) Typically, the franchise agreement will include a commitment by the franchisee to indemnify the franchisor for any liability that it incurs as a result of the operation of the franchised business by the franchisee.

AGENTS GOVERNED BY SPECIAL STATUTES

Some kinds of agents are governed by special statutes that are intended to protect the people with whom they deal. Lawyers, real estate agents, insurance agents, stockbrokers, and travel agents are all subject to regulation that complements the basic common law rules that we have discussed reflecting the significant risks consumers face in their dealings with these agents.

For example, real estate agents advise people on one of the most important financial decisions they make—buying a house. In recognition of the risks that people are exposed to when they rely on real estate agents in connection with such decisions, a person must be either licensed to work as a real estate agent or employed by a licensed agent.[37] Licensing bodies established under provincial legislation try to ensure that agents meet certain standards for competence, honesty, integrity, and financial responsibility. They enforce specific rules relating to trading (including prohibiting agents from supplying false information), handling clients' money, advertising, and disclosure of any personal interest that an agent may have in the transaction. For instance, real estate agents are required to tell their clients about any compensation they will receive from another party to the transaction.

Regulatory regimes for agents often have a complaints process. Anyone concerned about the actions of a real estate agent can file a complaint with the licensing body, which has the power to inspect the agent's premises and records. If it discovers wrongdoing, it may subject the agent to disciplinary proceedings, which can lead to the suspension or revocation of the agent's licence, or even criminal charges. Typically, licensing bodies do not have the power to award damages.

Similar regimes apply to insurance agents and travel agents.[38] Stockbrokers are governed by more comprehensive regulation, which includes standards for

---

[36.] Some provinces have special statutes to protect franchisees against exploitation by franchisors: *eg Franchises Act*, RSA 2000, c F-23 (Alta); *Arthur Wishart Franchise Disclosure Act, 2000*, SO 2000, c 3 (Ont); *Franchises Act*, SNB 2007, c F-23.5 (NB); *Franchises Act*, RSPEI 1988, c F-14.1 (PEI).

[37.] In Ontario, for example, licensing is under the *Real Estate and Business Brokers Act*, SO 2002, c 30. Since 1997, the legislation governing real estate agents in Ontario has been administered by the Real Estate Council of Ontario, a non-profit body created by statute. Real estate agents in Alberta are regulated under the *Real Estate Act*, RSA 2000, c R-5, and in Nova Scotia under the *Real Estate Trading Act*, SNS 1996, c 28.

[38.] *Eg Registered Insurance Brokers Act*, RSO 1990, c R.19 (Ont); Insurance Agents and Adjusters Regulation, Alta Reg 122/2001 (Alta); *Travel Industry Regulation*, BC Reg 296/2004 (BC); *Travel Industry Act*, SO 2002, c 30, Sch D (Ont).

internal financial controls, insurance, and requirements to ensure that firms have sufficient capital to remain solvent.[39] The Canadian Investor Protection Fund covers customers' losses of securities and cash balances resulting from the insolvency of a brokerage firm.

Business Decision 20.1 asks you to decide how best to structure a particular business relationship, including the use of agency arrangements.

Business Decision **20.1**

Methods of Carrying on Business

You are a new manufacturer of tennis rackets and you are looking for someone to help you sell your product in a particular territory. Jordan has worked for several years as a distributor of in-line skates in the territory and sells to many of the same retailers that you would like as customers. You want to enter into some kind of relationship with Jordan to help you sell to those retailers.

Questions for Discussion

1. What are the options for structuring your relationship with Jordan?

2. What are the advantages and disadvantages of each option?

[39.] *Eg Securities Act,* RSBC 1996, c 418 (BC); *Securities Act,* RSO 1990, c S.5 (Ont).

Chapter Summary

In an agency relationship, an agent represents a principal for some specific purpose. That purpose may include the creation of contracts between the principal and third parties. Agency relationships themselves are often created by a contract between the principal and the agent. They exist as a matter of law in partnerships. Agency can be created by the principal granting actual authority to a person to be an agent to act on the principal's behalf or by the principal representing that a person has the authority of an agent. This second type of authority is called apparent authority. Even if a person is not an agent when an obligation is purportedly created on behalf of an identified principal, that obligation can become binding on the principal if the principal ratifies it.

The principal is liable for a contract entered into by an agent on their behalf if it is within either the actual authority or the apparent authority to contract given by the principal. An agent is not normally personally liable for contracts entered into on behalf of a principal unless the agent and third party have agreed that the agent will be liable. If an agent purports to enter into a contract on behalf of a principal but has no authority to do so, the agent may be liable to the third party for breach of warranty of authority.

An agent is required to fulfill any obligations to the principal created under the agency agreement. An agent also has a fiduciary duty to act in the principal's best

interests in most cases and a duty of care to act reasonably when performing the agency obligations. A principal must also comply with the obligations specified in the agency agreement. In the absence of an express provision to the contrary, a principal must pay reasonable remuneration and indemnify the agent for any reasonable expenses.

An agency relationship can be terminated in several ways, including notice from either party. If the agent is an employee, additional statutory and common law rules regarding termination must be observed.

A principal can manage the risk of becoming liable on account of the unauthorized acts of an agent by limiting the agent's actual authority, by being careful about how they represent the agent's authority to third parties, and by carefully selecting, training, supervising, and requiring reports from their agents.

A principal is liable for torts committed by agents within the scope of the agent's actual or apparent authority. In most cases, such vicarious liability arises only when agents are employees of the principal.

An agency relationship can exist in the context of some methods for carrying on business, such as a contractual joint venture or a strategic alliance. Generally, distributorships and franchises are not agencies. Some agency businesses, such as real estate agents, are subject to special regulatory schemes designed to protect the public and consumers.

MyBusLawLab   ADDITIONAL RESOURCES FOR CHAPTER 20

MyBusLawLab provides students with an assortment of tools to help enrich the learning experience, including a Study Plan with Pre- and Post-tests, mini-cases with assessments, and provincial content material, which provides links to relevant cases, legislation, and additional resources.

MyBusLawLab provides the following resources for Chapter 20:

■ Business Decision 20.1W—When Is the Government Liable as Principal?

Provincial Material

■ **British Columbia:** Power of Attorney, Real Estate Agents, Collection Agents, Travel Agents

■ **Alberta:** Franchises, Liability for Agent's Tortious Conduct, Agency by Necessity, Enduring Power of Attorney, Personal Directives, Real Estate Agents, Insurance

■ **Manitoba and Saskatchewan:** Real Estate Agency Rules

■ **Ontario:** Agency by Necessity, Fiduciary Duty, Franchising Legislation, Parental Liability, Powers of Attorney, Real Estate Agents

■ **Atlantic Provinces:** Franchise Legislation

Review Questions

1. Why would you appoint an agent to act on your behalf? What are the risks of using an agent?

2. Describe three ways that a principal can be held liable for the actions of an agent.

3. You have a business leasing photocopiers. You are negotiating a contract with Zoltan, who is acting on behalf of Bridgeworks Manufacturing Inc. You have visited Zoltan at the offices of Bridgeworks, and he is listed in the corporation's directory as the President. This title also appears on his office door. Does Zoltan have authority to lease five photocopiers from you on behalf of Bridgeworks?

4. You negotiate an agreement under which Tom is to rent Ellen's ski chalet. Tom did not know you were doing this but is happy with the deal that you have arranged when you tell him about it. Has a contract been created between Tom and Ellen for the rental of the chalet? If not, how could one be created?

5. The president of a corporation you are dealing with tells you that Alton has authority to sell you one of the corporation's cars. You find out that the president was mistaken, because Alton's employment contract says that he does not have this authority. Can you rely on the president's statement to enforce a contract with the corporation that you negotiated with Alton?

6. You are negotiating to rent an apartment from Island Property Management Inc. The person you are dealing with is Arif. Arif says that he can offer you a discount of 50 percent off the advertised rent. If you were concerned that Arif did not have the authority to give you this discount, what would you do about it?

7. How would your answer to the previous question differ if, instead of renting an apartment, you were negotiating with Arif to buy a business from Island Property Management Inc worth $10 000 000?

8. You have entered into a contract with Azam to supply your business with stationery. You have known Azam for a long time and find him to be a reliable supplier of office supplies, though you have never bought paper from him before. A few days later, Azam discloses that he was acting as an agent for a paper manufacturer that you have never heard of. Can you enforce the contract against the paper manufacturer? Can you enforce it against Azam? Can the paper manufacturer enforce the contract against you?

9. You negotiated a contract with an agent, but later found out that the agent had no authority to contract on behalf of the principal. Assuming that the principal is not liable, do you have any claim against the agent?

10. If you appointed an agent to buy a car for you at a car auction, what concerns would you have about actions of the agent that you had not authorized, such as agreeing to a higher price than you were prepared to pay? How would you deal with those concerns?

11. Allan has appointed you as an agent to sell his line of ski jackets to retailers. Another manufacturer asks you to carry its line of ski jackets as well. Can you agree to carry the other line?

12. If you were a real estate agent acting on behalf of someone who wanted to purchase a house and the seller told you that the basement was dry but you noticed water stains on the basement drywall, what should you do?

13. You entered into a contract with your nephew under which you gave him the power to buy you a new television. You know that your nephew is incompetent, but you want to give him an opportunity to make some

money. The nephew buys a television on your behalf, paying the price with money you gave him. On his way to deliver the television to you he negligently drops it on the road and it smashes to pieces. Is your nephew liable to you for the cost of the television?

14. You contracted with Lana to act as your agent in purchasing lumber. That contract does not say that she is entitled to be paid. Are you required to pay her a fee? Are you required to pay her expenses for travelling to visit lumber producers to acquire lumber for you?

15. At 9:00 am, you instruct your stockbroker to buy 1000 shares of Bolt Networks Inc as soon as possible at the current market price of $10. The stockbroker forgets to place your order until the next day when the price has gone up to $15. Do you have any claim against the agent?

16. Describe the ways in which an agency can be terminated by the principal.

17. Explain the situations in which a principal can be held liable for torts committed by their agent. Is there anything that the principal can do to reduce the risk of liability?

18. You are a principal who wants to terminate the agency agreement under which Shazad sells products on your behalf. Would you be worried that Shazad would be able to commit you to contracts after the termination? If so, what could you do about it?

19. Are the parties to a contractual joint venture, a strategic alliance, a distributorship, and a franchise agreement in an agency relationship?

20. You have recently bought a house with the help of a real estate agent you had hired. After the transaction, you found out that the house belonged to the agent's brother. You are now concerned that you may have paid too much. What could you do?

Cases and Problems

1. Magda is an artist. She entered into a contract with Karl under which she gave Karl the authority, for six months, to try to find a buyer for one of her paintings. After three months, Karl had not been able to sell the painting and offered to buy it himself. Magda and Karl entered into a contract under which Karl agreed to buy the painting for $5000. The contract provided that he would pay $1000 at the time the contract was signed and the balance within 30 days. After the expiry of 30 days, Karl did not pay the balance. Is Karl liable to Magda for breaching his obligations as an agent?

2. Tatiana was looking for a BMW to lease. She went to Reston Sales and Leasing Inc and met with Joe Reston, the manager and sole owner of the business. After some discussion, Reston said he could arrange for a two-year lease on the car that Tatiana wanted from Corporate Leasing Inc. Though nothing in Tatiana's dealings with Reston had indicated that he was acting for Corporate Leasing, Tatiana said that if the terms were acceptable to her, she would contract with Corporate Leasing. Reston telephoned Corporate Leasing and, after Corporate Leasing did a credit check on Tatiana, it faxed Reston a lease agreement. Tatiana signed the agreement that provided for a fixed term of two years with no right to cancel before the end of the term. After signing the agreement, she asked Reston if she could have the right to cancel the agreement on written notice from her. Reston said she could and confirmed this in writing. After six months, Tatiana lost her job and wrote to Corporate Leasing cancelling the lease. Corporate Leasing says that cancellation is not permitted under the terms of the lease. Can Tatiana cancel the lease?

3. Jennifer is an agent of MB Forest Products Inc. Under her agency contract, she has authority to buy raw logs from independent logging companies. While Jennifer is visiting some logging companies in the interior of British Columbia, MB goes bankrupt. A day later, Jennifer, who is not aware of the bankruptcy, signs a contract on behalf of MB with ForCan Logging Ltd for the purchase of 1000 logs. The contract is at a very favourable price for ForCan. Can ForCan enforce the contract against MB? Does ForCan have any rights against Jennifer?

4. You are negotiating an agreement with Salim to buy some watches from the corporation that Salim works for, Alpha Watch Corp. The president has told you that Salim is the "manager of sales." Would you be able to hold the corporation liable for a contract that you negotiated with Salim if (i) Salim is the manager of sales, (ii) Salim is not the manager of sales but you did not know that when you entered the contract, or (iii) Salim is not the manager of sales and you found out before you entered into the contract? Explain your answer in each situation.

5. Geomedia Inc helps retailers promote sales by arranging to distribute advertising flyers to consumers, usually in the form of newspaper inserts. Red Rose Inc sells arts and crafts supplies across Canada. In the past, it managed its own advertising by contracting with the *Regina Post* to distribute its flyers. Recently, Red Rose hired Geomedia to act as its agent to distribute flyers. It then faxed an announcement to the *Regina Post* that said, "From this point forward, Geomedia will be managing all media distribution for Red Rose." The *Regina Post* interpreted that fax to mean that it would be contracting with Geomedia rather than Red Rose.

   The *Regina Post* subsequently received several orders from Geomedia that involved advertisements for Red Rose. Those orders, printed on Geomedia letterhead, said, "Please bill Red Rose care of Geomedia." The *Post* published those ads but has not been paid. To make matters worse, Red Rose has gone bankrupt. Is the *Post* entitled to recover payment from Geomedia?

6. Koh agreed to provide cleaning services for one year to Mid-Town Management Inc, which operates several large office buildings in Saskatoon. The contract price was much cheaper than what other cleaning services were offering. In its dealings with Mid-Town, Koh always made clear that it was acting on behalf of a principal in contracting to provide the services, though it never identified who that principal was. In fact, Koh was acting on behalf of Down-Town Realty Inc, a competitor of Mid-Town's. After six months, Koh stopped providing the services. Is Koh liable to Mid-Town for breach of contract? Explain your answer.

7. Novak contracted with Janus, a real estate agent, to find a commercial property for Novak to operate as a nursing home. Janus suggested that Novak buy a small apartment building that he owned. Eventually, Novak agreed to pay $800 000 for the building in December 2015. In connection with re-financing the building shortly after the sale, Novak had an appraisal of the building done. The appraiser said the building was worth only $700 000. Novak also discovered that Janus had paid only $500 000 when he bought the building in December 2014. In 2016, Novak received an offer of $1 000 000 for the building, but still thinks that he paid too much. What should Novak do?

8. Trusty Resources Ltd is a producer of natural gas. Trusty entered into a contract with Power Marketing Inc to find a purchaser of Trusty's gas that would commit to a long-term purchase agreement. Trusty entered into a 15-year supply agreement with Clean Energy Inc, a purchaser found by Power. The agreement provided that Trusty would pay Power a fee for each unit of gas purchased under the contract. For five years, Clean Energy purchased gas under the contract and Trusty paid Power the agreed fee. After five years, Clean Energy wanted out of the agreement because the price that it had to pay under the agreement was too high. Trusty agreed to terminate the contract at the end of the sixth year. Halfway through the sixth year, Clean Energy and Trusty agreed that Clean Energy would no longer be obliged to purchase gas under the contract in return for a payment to Trusty of $100 000. Does Trusty have any liability to Power for the fees that would have been paid if the contract had continued for the full 15-year term? What about if the contract had continued until the end of the sixth year?

9. Porter entered into a contract with Hip Sports Inc under which Hip agreed to sell Porter's basketball shoes as its agent. Hip was authorized to enter into contracts to sell the shoes on Porter's behalf and Porter agreed to pay (i) a commission of 10 percent of the sale price of the shoes, and (ii) all of Hip's advertising expenses. Hip represented several other lines of products.

Hip planned to advertise Porter's shoes through a flyer campaign. The going rate for having flyers produced was $5000. However, Hip was able to negotiate a discount of $1000 because it did a high volume of business with the flyer producer for its other clients. Hip saw no reason to pass that benefit on to Porter since it was granted on the basis of *all* the business that Hip did with the flyer company—for Porter and for other clients. Hip therefore charged Porter the full $5000. Is Hip liable to give Porter the benefit of the discount?

10. Sal and Vasu entered into an agreement to buy an apartment together, hold it for a year or so, and then resell it. They called their contract a "joint venture agreement." It provides that each will contribute half the price and be entitled to half the proceeds of the sale. During the time they own the apartment, they will hire a property manager to run it. They will each pay half of the expenses of the building, including the property manager's fee, and receive half of the rents. If Sal hired a landscaping service to maintain the gardens at the apartment, would Vasu be liable to the service for half the fees?

11. Sharif owned 10 percent of the shares of Orca Environmental Consulting Inc. Jenna, the lawyer for Orca, approached Sharif, telling him that she represented "a group of investors" who were interested in purchasing Sharif's shares. Jenna made an offer, accompanied by a deposit, and Sharif accepted it. There was no "group of investors." Jenna had thought that she would be able to put together a group after she had negotiated the purchase from Sharif. She could not do so and the purchase was never completed. Is Jenna personally liable for failing to purchase Sharif's shares? What is the legal basis of liability?

12. Able has acted as an agent for Solon Corp for several years. Solon was in the business of selling security services. Able's contract required him to seek customers for Solon's services. In the course of working with Solon, Able learned a great deal about the security business and the sophisticated software that Solon uses. Able wants to use this knowledge to start up his own security service business. Can he do so?

21 Basic Forms of Business Organizations

LEARNING OBJECTIVES

After completing this chapter, you should be able to:

❶ Explain how a sole proprietorship is created and how it operates.

❷ Describe the advantages and disadvantages of using a sole proprietorship to carry on business.

❸ Identify and apply the factors that determine when a partnership comes into existence.

❹ Describe strategies for minimizing the risk of being a partner.

❺ Identify the key elements of a partnership agreement.

❻ Distinguish between general and limited partnerships.

❼ Describe the process of incorporating and organizing a corporation.

❽ Describe the implications of the separate legal existence of the corporation.

❾ Explain the division of power amongst the shareholders, directors, and officers to manage and control the corporation.

❿ Identify the basic characteristics of shares of a corporation.

Every business involves risks. A manufacturer, for example, faces the risk that no one will buy its products, or that its products will hurt someone. But who bears those risks? In part, the answer depends upon the type of organization that is carrying on the business. We will focus on four possibilities:

- sole proprietorship
- general partnership
- limited partnership
- corporation[1]

In each type of organization, the law strikes a different balance between the interests of the categories of people who have a stake in the operation of the business (identified in Figure 21.1). Significantly, the law determines the extent to which individual entrepreneurs benefit when their businesses prosper and the extent to which they are responsible for losses when they do not. By affecting the risk to entrepreneurs in this way, the law influences incentives for entrepreneurs to start and continue to carry on their businesses.

Business organizations law also addresses the risks that other stakeholder groups experience in their relationships with businesses—but only to a limited extent. For the most part, other types of laws govern the relationships between the business and non-shareholder stakeholders. These are discussed in other chapters of this book.[2] For example, business organizations law governs when a business is bound by a contract that creates an obligation to a creditor. But the nature and effect of the contract are governed by contract law.

The law governing business organizations also provides a structure for the *operation* of businesses, focusing on the relationship that owners and managers have with the business and with each other. It establishes the rights and

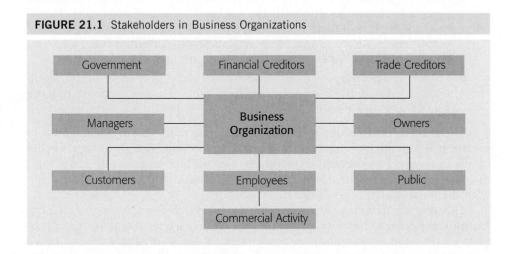

FIGURE 21.1 Stakeholders in Business Organizations

---

[1] Other more specialized forms of business organizations, such as real estate investment trusts are beyond the scope of this book. Trusts were briefly discussed in Chapter 8.

[2] The rights and obligations of employers and employees are discussed in Chapters 26 and 27. The relationships between a business and its trade creditors (such as suppliers of goods and services), financial creditors (such as banks), and customers are examined in chapters of this book dealing with contract, tort, property, commercial, and criminal law, and secured transactions. Businesses are subject to various forms of direct regulation to protect the public interest, as discussed in Chapter 25.

obligations of owners to manage the business themselves and to monitor and control others who manage on their behalf. When management acts in a manner contrary to the best interests of the business, it provides remedies to business owners. In this way, business organizations law addresses the risks that business owners face as a result of actions by managers.

L.O. ❶ ❷

Sole Proprietorships

The *sole proprietorship* is the simplest form of business organization. A **sole proprietorship** comes into existence when a person starts to carry on business on their own, without adopting any other form of business organization, such as a corporation. If you agree to cut your neighbour's grass for money each week, you are carrying on business as a sole proprietor.

a **sole proprietorship** exists when a person carries on business on their own, without adopting any other form of business organization

As a sole proprietor, you could enter into a contract to *employ* someone else to cut your neighbour's grass, but you remain the sole owner of the business and the only person responsible for its obligations. Both legally and practically, there is no separation between the sole proprietorship business organization and the individual who is the sole proprietor. A sole proprietor cannot be an employee of the business because you cannot contract with yourself.

The sole proprietor gets all the benefits and bears all the burdens of the business. This has several important implications in terms of the relationships between the business and its other stakeholders:

- The sole proprietor is exclusively responsible for performing all contracts entered into in the course of the business, including contracts with customers, suppliers, employees, and lenders.
- The sole proprietor is exclusively responsible for all torts committed personally in connection with the business. That person is also vicariously liable for all torts committed by employees in the course of their employment. As we saw in Chapter 3, vicarious liability occurs when an employer is held liable for a tort that was committed by an employee.
- For income tax purposes, the income or loss from the sole proprietorship is included with the income or loss from other sources in calculating the sole proprietor's personal tax liability.

The main advantage of a sole proprietorship is that it is simple and easy to set up. It is equally easy to dissolve: The sole proprietor simply stops carrying on the business. Just because you stop carrying on business, however, does not mean that you cease to be liable for the obligations that arose in connection with the business while you were carrying it on.

unlimited personal liability of a sole proprietor means that third parties may take all the sole proprietor's personal assets to satisfy the business's obligations

The main disadvantage of a sole proprietorship is *unlimited personal liability*. **Unlimited personal liability** means that third parties may take all the sole proprietor's personal assets—not just those of the business—to satisfy the business's obligations. As the scale of the business and the related liabilities increase, this exposure to personal liability becomes an increasingly important disincentive to using a sole proprietorship. Suppose your grass-cutting business was wildly successful. You had contracts to cut 1000 lawns each week and had hired 100 students to do the work. As a sole proprietor, you would be personally responsible for all the work and to each employee. If one of your customers was not happy with the work and demanded a refund, or if an employee whom you fired sued you for wrongful dismissal, the liability would be yours alone. While you could try to manage the liability risk through contracts and insurance, incorporation is often a less expensive and more effective strategy.

Another problem with sole proprietorships is raising money. Every business needs investment to grow. Since it is not possible to divide up ownership of the sole proprietorship, the only method of financing is for the sole proprietor to borrow money directly. An advantage of other forms of business is that they permit a wider range of financing possibilities. Limited financing options and unlimited personal liability mean that sole proprietorships are used only for relatively small businesses.

LEGAL REQUIREMENTS FOR SOLE PROPRIETORSHIPS

There are few rules for carrying on a sole proprietorship. The name of a sole proprietorship must be registered if that name is something other than, or more than, the proprietor's personal name. For example, Amman Malik would not have to register if he carried on a grass-cutting business under his own name. But he would have to register if he used the name "Malik's Gardening Services" or "Superior Gardening Services."[3] Registration must be completed in every province or territory in which the sole proprietorship carries on business. Registration does not create any ownership interest in the business name. The sole proprietor's interest may be protected, however, under provincial passing-off laws and federal trademarks law, which are discussed in Chapter 18.

A second requirement, which applies to all forms of business organization including sole proprietorships, is that a *business licence* is necessary for some types of activities. A **business licence** is government permission to operate a certain kind of business. For example, most municipalities require taxi-driving businesses and restaurants to obtain licences. Provincial governments have enacted licensing requirements for many types of businesses, including real estate agents, car dealers, and securities brokers. Sole proprietors are also subject to the same regulatory requirements as businesses carried on by any other form of business organization, such as labour and environmental standards.

> a **business licence** is government permission to operate a certain kind of business

General Partnerships

L.O. ❸ ❹ ❺

Where people pool their resources, knowledge, or skills, they may carry on business as a *general partnership* (or, more simply, a *partnership*). A **general partnership** is a form of business organization that comes into existence when two or more persons carry on business together with a view to a profit. Partnership arises automatically by operation of law when a relationship meeting these criteria begins. No formalities are required, although the partnership may have to register its name and obtain a business licence. Imagine that you and James agree to develop a business together: James agrees to buy a lawnmower and look for homeowners who want their lawns cut, and you agree to cut the lawns. The profits are split between the two of you. You and James have created a partnership. Even if you and James never made any money, you would still have formed a partnership so long as your goal was to make money.

> a **general partnership** is a form of business organization that comes into existence when two or more persons carry on business together with a view to a profit

PART 6

[3.] This is the requirement in most provinces: *eg Business Names Act*, RSO 1990, c B.17, s 2(2) (Ont); *Business Names Registration Act*, RSS 1978, c B-11 s 4(1) (Sask).

CHARACTERISTICS OF GENERAL PARTNERSHIPS

Like sole proprietors, partners carry on business on their own behalf. Although the business can do some things in the name of the partnership, such as hold title to land or be sued, the partnership is not legally separate from the partners. That fact has several consequences:

- A partner cannot be employed by the partnership.
- All benefits of the partnership business accrue directly to the partners.
- All partners, even those who did not consent to a particular obligation, are personally liable for all the obligations of the business, including torts committed by a partner or an employee of the partnership in the course of the firm's business.

Just like a sole proprietor, partners have unlimited personal liability. If a partnership is liable for an obligation, each partner is liable to the full extent of the obligation. *All* of a partner's *personal* assets—not just those that the partner committed to the business—may be seized to satisfy a partnership debt.

This characteristic of partnership means that its creditworthiness is partially based on the creditworthiness of the individual partners. For example, assume that Eli and Taylor are equal partners in a restaurant business. The partnership has asked you to supply $200 000 worth of restaurant equipment today but wait 90 days for payment. Suppose you provide the equipment but are not paid on time. If the business's assets are worth only $100 000, you could get a judgment against the partnership and seize those assets *and* then seek to recover the remaining money from Taylor and Eli personally. You could try to collect $50 000 from each, or $100 000 from either.[4] The risk that you will not be able to recover what you are owed is reduced because you could seize not just the assets held by the business, but also the assets held by the partners personally.

To determine the liability of partners for income tax, the income (or loss) of the partnership is calculated by adding up all revenues of the partnership business and deducting all expenses. A share of the income (or loss) is allocated to each partner according to the partner's entitlement to share in the profits of the business. The partner's share of any business income must be included in their personal income, even if those profits were re-invested in the business and were not actually paid to the partner.

PARTNERSHIP LEGISLATION AND PARTNERSHIP AGREEMENTS

The courts in England developed the law of partnerships, and it was codified in the English *Partnerships Act* of 1890. All provinces, other than Quebec, have partnership legislation based on that English statute.[5] These short acts often do not provide a satisfactory set of rules for organizing a partnership today. For that reason, partners often use a contract, called a **partnership agreement**, to supplement or modify the rules governing their relationship. Legal issues

a **partnership agreement** is a contract between partners regarding the operation of the partnership

---

4. If you collect $100 000 from Eli, he can recover $50 000 from Taylor, unless they had some other arrangement between them.

5. *Eg Partnership Act*, RSBC 1996, c 348 (BCPA) (BC); *Partnership Act*, RSNS 1989, c 334 (NSPA) (NS); *Partnerships Act*, RSO 1990, c P.5 (OPA) (Ont).

concerning the partnership are usually resolved on the basis of both the legislation and the partnership agreement.

CREATING A PARTNERSHIP

A partnership comes into being when two or more persons *carry on business together* with a view to profit.[6] Sometimes, it is unclear if a partnership relationship that fits this definition exists. A number of factors must be considered. The most important is the sharing of *profits*. The focus on profit sharing is related to the requirement that partners must *carry on business together*. If you are compensated only out of revenues, you have a stake only in how much the business can sell. In contrast, if you are sharing profits, you must be concerned with the entire business operation, including the management of expenses. When you have a financial stake in the management of the business through sharing profits, a court is likely to find that the business is being carried on for your benefit and that you are a partner in the business.

A partnership does not *necessarily* exist simply because the parties share profits, however. People may share profits *without* carrying on business together, such as in the following situations:

- A loan is to be repaid out of the profits of the borrower's business.
- An employee's remuneration varies with the employer's profits, such as in a profit-sharing arrangement.
- The purchaser of a business agrees to pay some of the business's profits to the seller as part of the purchase price.

Since profit sharing is not conclusive, other factors must be considered to determine whether a partnership exists:

- The idea of carrying on business together usually suggests the existence of an enduring relationship. There is probably no partnership if two competitors simply co-operate on an isolated transaction, as when a pair of software companies split the cost of a particular research project. The courts have held, however, that a partnership *may* arise even in relation to a single, time-limited activity.[7]
- A partnership is less likely to be found to exist if the people involved are merely passive investors, such as where they simply jointly own an apartment building and collect rent.[8] The situation may be different, however, if co-ownership of real estate is combined with active participation in its management and a sharing of profits.[9] These facts suggest that the co-owners are engaged in carrying on a business.
- A person who describes themself as a partner or allows someone else to do so is likely to be found to be a partner. A person who permits their name to be used as part of the firm name will also likely be found to be a partner.

In the final analysis, to determine whether a partnership exists, a court will look at a number of factors, including those identified in Concept Summary 21.1. You Be the Judge 21.1 discusses the question of the existence of a partnership.

[6] *BCPA*, s 2; *NSPA*, s 4; *OPA*, s 2.

[7] *Spire Freezers Ltd v The Queen* (2001) 196 DLR (4th) 210 (SCC).

[8] *AE Lepage Ltd v Kamex Developments Ltd* (1977) 78 DLR (3d) 223 (Ont CA). See also *Hickman Motors Ltd v The Queen*(1997) 148 DLR (4th) 1 (SCC); *Spire Freezers Ltd v The Queen*(2001) 196 DLR (4th) 210 (SCC).

[9] *Volzkhe Construction v Westlock Foods Ltd* (1986) 70 AR 300 (CA).

Concept Summary 21.1

Factors Suggesting the Existence of a Partnership

- sharing profits
- sharing responsibility for losses, including guaranteeing partnership debts
- jointly owning property
- participating in management, including having signing authority for contracts and bank accounts, and enjoying access to information regarding the business
- holding oneself out as a partner, or allowing others to do so

You Be the Judge 21.1

Is There a Partnership?[10]

Groscki and Durocher were chartered accountants. Groscki ran a business giving tax advice and providing accounting services, which he operated out of premises that he owned. In 1989, he entered into an agreement with Durocher under which Durocher agreed to review financial statements and prepare tax returns for Groscki's clients for $20 an hour plus $913 a month. They agreed that Durocher would not be classified as an employee but as an independent contractor. That allowed Durocher to deduct certain expenses in connection with his work against his income for tax purposes. Over time, Durocher assumed more responsibility for managing the business and supervising the staff. Groscki increasingly worked on other business ventures. In 1993, the name on the business letterhead and its sign was changed to say "Groscki and Durocher." Nevertheless, Durocher was never given signing authority for the business bank account and did not have access to the financial records of the business. In 1993, Durocher loaned $25 000 to Groscki for the business. In 1994, Durocher terminated his relationship with Groscki. Durocher argued that some of the firm's business belonged to him because he and Groscki are partners.

Questions for Discussion

1. What factors support the conclusion that the relationship between Groscki and Durocher was a partnership?

2. What factors suggest that it was not a partnership?

3. Is there anything else that you would like to know to answer these questions?

RISK AND LIABILITY IN GENERAL PARTNERSHIPS

How Partnership Liabilities Arise

Provincial partnership statutes determine when a partnership incurs liabilities.[11] The basic rule is that each partner is an agent of the partnership when acting in the usual course of the partnership business.[12] If you and James formed a partnership as described above and James bought gas for the lawnmower used in the business, the obligation to pay for the gas would bind the partnership. An exception exists if a partner did not have authority to act in a particular way (perhaps because of a restriction in the partnership agreement) *and* the other party either knew that that partner lacked authority or did not know that they were dealing with a partner.

[10.] *Groscki v Durocher* [1999] OJ No 2052 (SCJ), aff'd [2001] OJ No 39 (CA).

[11.] *Eg OPA*, ss 6–19.

[12.] The rules of agency that we discussed in Chapter 20 apply to partners, subject to the rules in the applicable partnership statute.

This rule effectively places the risk of unauthorized behaviour by one partner on all the partners. Partners are also liable for torts, such as negligence, that their fellow partners commit in the ordinary course of the partnership business.

Managing the Risk That a Business Relationship Will Be Found to Be a Partnership

Business people need to know whether they are entering a relationship that might be found to be a partnership. As partners, they will have unlimited personal liability for the obligations of the firm, including liability for unauthorized acts and torts of other partners that bind the firm. An entrepreneur may be willing to accept these risks, either because the risks can be managed or because they are outweighed by the benefits of being a partner, such as a share in expected profits or the ability to deduct partnership losses for personal tax purposes. Other people who are involved with a business, such as lenders, will want to avoid these risks. For that sort of person, being found to be a partner may have unanticipated, and even disastrous, financial consequences.

As a matter of risk management, you should examine a proposed relationship carefully to determine whether you would be entering into a partnership. The following list of dos and don'ts provides advice regarding how to proceed.

Do:

- insist that the contract governing the relationship state that the relationship is not a partnership[13]
- negotiate to restructure the business organization so that it is a not a partnership
- insist upon sufficient compensation to reflect any residual risk that you may be found to be a partner

Don't:

- enter the relationship without seeking advice from a lawyer

Managing Liability Risk If You Are a Partner

There are several legal rules and practical strategies that can help to manage the risks associated with being a partner.

First, each partner owes a *fiduciary duty* to the others.[14] The **fiduciary duty** requires a partner to act honestly and in good faith with a view to the best interests of the partnership. Compliance with the duty reduces the risk of unwanted liability. Partners must never put their personal interests ahead of those of the partnership. For instance, a partner cannot sell a piece of property to the partnership for an unfairly high price. A partner is also prohibited from competing with the partnership or using the name, property, or business reputation of the partnership to obtain a personal benefit. A partner who breaches the fiduciary duty must pay any resulting profits to the partnership.[15] Case Brief 21.1 provides an example of a partner obtaining a personal benefit.

the **fiduciary duty** requires a partner to act honestly and in good faith with a view to the best interests of the partnership

---

[13.] Partnership status cannot be avoided, however, by a simple statement in a contract to that effect: *Lansing Building Supply Ltd v Ierullo* (1990) 71 OR (2d) 173 (Dist Ct). A court will consider how the parties actually acted under their agreement to determine whether a partnership exists.

[14.] *BCPA*, s 22 (1). Although there is no general expression of the duty in the *OPA* and some other partnership statutes, it is well established that the fiduciary duty is a guiding principle of partnership law: *Hitchcock v Sykes* (1914) 23 DLR 518 (SCC).

[15.] These obligations are specifically addressed in provincial partnership statutes: *BCPA*, ss 32–33; *NSPA*, ss 32–33; and *OPA*, ss 28–30.

Case Brief 21.1

Rochwerg v. Truster (2002) 112 DLR (4th) 498 (Ont CA)

A partner in a firm of accountants became a director of one of the firm's clients. He also purchased 8000 common shares in the client for what was a fair price at the time and acquired options to purchase an additional 24 000 common shares for a nominal price. The partner disclosed the directorship to his partners and paid the director's fees he received to the partnership. He did not disclose his investment because he believed that it was a private transaction. Ultimately, the Ontario Court of Appeal decided that his duty required him to disclose the investment. He was also required to account for the profits he made from the shares and options because they were a benefit derived from the partnership business. It was not necessary to show that the partnership suffered a loss as a result of the partner's activities.

Second, a partnership agreement can be used to manage the risk of liability. Each partner's authority can be limited and subject to control and monitoring mechanisms. For instance, restrictions can be placed on who can write cheques or sign contracts. Note that when a partner fails to follow the rules and creates a liability to a third party, the firm may still be liable. These mechanisms are designed to reduce the risk that the liability will be created in the first place. When a liability is created by a partner in breach of partnership agreement requirements, the agreement may require the offending partner to compensate the others for any amount that they must pay to a third party. That is called a *right to indemnification*.[16]

Third, partners can take practical steps to reduce the risk of partnership liability. Some partnerships involve only a small number of people who know each other very well. A natural relationship of trust and confidence reduces the risk of unwanted liability. Where each partner is involved in the business on a daily basis, opportunities for informally monitoring each other exist. In that situation, there is relatively little risk of unauthorized activity. Those protections break down, however, as a partnership grows. The business becomes larger and more impersonal. In large law and accounting firms, for example, few partners are actively involved in all aspects of the business. Formal monitoring mechanisms therefore must be established through increasingly elaborate partnership agreements.

The lack of informal protections in large partnerships, coupled with an explosion in the number and size of professional liability claims, encouraged professionals to lobby governments to change the law. In most provinces, certain professional partnerships, such as lawyers and accountants, are not permitted to carry on business using a corporation to limit their personal liability, but they can now agree to become a special form of general partnership, called a *limited liability partnership*. In a **limited liability partnerships**, individual partners are not personally liable for the professional negligence of their partners and some other obligations if certain requirements are met.[17] Most large law and accounting firms have now become limited liability partnerships.

in a **limited liability partnership**, individual partners are not personally liable for the professional negligence of their partners and some other obligations if certain requirements are met

---

[16.] If some partners pay more than their share of a partnership debt, they can claim reimbursement from the other partners. That right, provided for in partnership statutes, is also a form of indemnification. An individual partner may seek to minimize the risk associated with liability as a partner by holding the partnership interest in a corporation. Partnerships may limit liability to their customers and others by using contract provisions. Insurance may also be a good mechanism for dealing with some risks.

[17.] *Eg Limited Liability Partnerships Act*, SO 1998, c 2 (Ont); *Partnership Act*, RSA 2000, c P-3 (Alta); *Partnerships Amendment Act*, 2004, SBC 2004, c 38 (BC). The degree to which partners are protected against liability varies from province to province.

The partnership remains liable for all obligations, but once the firm's assets are exhausted, no claim can be made against individual partners—other than the one who is responsible for the negligence. A limited liability partnership is the same as a general partnership in all other respects.

Managing Liability Risk When You Are Not a Partner

Generally you are *not* liable as a partner for partnership liabilities that arose before you joined, or after you left, the firm. However, you *may* be liable for a partnership obligation, if you **hold yourself out as a partner** or allow someone else to do so even if you were never a partner and someone relied on it when they dealt with the partnership.[18] Suppose you are not a partner but you allow your name to be associated with a partnership. Thinking you are a partner, a bank lends money to the partnership because it believes that you are personally creditworthy. The bank can seek repayment from you because it relied on your *apparent* membership in the firm when deciding to make the loan.[19] You are also at risk if, for instance, you allow your name to appear on the partnership's letterhead, invoices, or business sign. You cannot be held liable, however, unless you actually *hold yourself out* as a partner or *know* that your name was being associated with the partnership and do nothing about it.[20]

    The issue of holding out often arises when a partner leaves a firm. In most cases, you want to avoid responsibility for any debts that arise *after* that time. Two groups of clients should concern you:

- Clients who dealt with the firm *prior* to your departure. These clients may honestly continue to rely on your creditworthiness when dealing with the firm. You will continue to be liable to them for partnership obligations until they learn of your departure.

- Clients who deal with the firm for the first time *after* your departure, or who never knew that you were a member of the firm. These clients cannot hold you liable unless you were held out to be a partner when they did business with the partnership.[21]

    To manage those risks, you should ensure that clients who dealt with the firm before you left receive actual notice of your departure. You should also ensure that your name is deleted from the partnership registration filed with the provincial government. A notice published in a local paper may also be desirable, especially if the nature of the firm's business makes notice to each client impractical. You should allow the firm to continue using your name only if the partnership agrees to indemnify you for any liabilities that you might incur as a result.

INTERNAL ORGANIZATION OF THE PARTNERSHIP

Since partnerships involve more than one person, partners need rules to settle basic issues regarding their relationship, such as what each partner will do for the business, what their entitlements to profits will be and how decisions will be made for the firm. The partnership legislation in each jurisdiction provides

holding yourself out as a partner occurs when you represent yourself as a partner or allow someone else to do so

---

18. *BCPA*, s 16; *NSPA*, s 17; *OPA*, s 15.

19. *Bet-Mur Investments Ltd v Spring* (1994) 20 OR (3d) 417 (Gen Div).

20. You cannot be held liable simply because you carelessly failed to realize that your name was being associated with the firm: *Tower Cabinet Co v Ingram* [1949] 1 All ER 1033 (DC).

21. *BCPA*, s 39; *NSPA*, s 39; *OPA*, s 36. In Ontario, publishing notice of your departure in the *Ontario Gazette* is sufficient to avoid liability to new clients of the firm.

default rules in partnership statutes are a kind of standard form agreement for the internal organization of a partnership that applies unless the partners agree to some other arrangement

default rules—a kind of standard form agreement for the internal organization of a partnership that applies unless the partners agree to some other arrangement. Because default rules can be changed, they give partners great flexibility to customize the partnership's structure to fit their particular needs.

The default rules governing partners' relations presume that all partners are *equal* in terms of their financial interest *and* their rights to participate in management. In practice, that is hardly ever the case. Partners typically make unequal contributions of capital and services to the business, and their respective shares in the profits reflect those unequal contributions. Also, except in the smallest partnerships, partners generally delegate certain management functions to particular partners or committees. It is too cumbersome to have all partners involved in all management decisions. As a result, the default rules usually need to be altered by a partnership agreement to ensure that the rules governing the partnership are consistent with the partners' needs and expectations. The following default rules are the most important ones in provincial statutes:[22]

- Each partner shares equally both in the capital of the partnership and in any partnership profits. They must also contribute equally to any losses incurred.

- Each partner is entitled to be indemnified for payments that they make in the ordinary course of the partnership business.

- A partner is not entitled to interest on capital that they contribute.

- Each partner has a right to participate in the management of the partnership business.

- Each partner has equal access to the partnership books.

- Decisions about ordinary matters related to the partnership are decided by a majority of the partners, but unanimous consent is required for admission of a new partner, expulsion of a partner, or any change in the nature of the partnership business.

- Any variation of the default rules requires unanimous consent.

DISSOLUTION OF PARTNERSHIPS

dissolution is the termination of the partnership relationship

Dissolution is the termination of the partnership relationship. Partnerships can be dissolved easily. Unless the partners agree otherwise, a partnership terminates when:

- one partner gives notice of termination to the others

- a partner dies or becomes insolvent[23]

- the partnership is set up for a specific purpose or for a limited time, such as to operate a gardening business for one summer, and that purpose has been achieved or that time expires[24]

Partnership agreements often provide that some period of notice is required for a partner to leave and that the departure, death, or insolvency of a partner does not terminate the partnership. A partner can always apply for a court order dissolving a partnership. The main ground for dissolution by a court is that it is just and equitable to dissolve the partnership. This may occur where the partners can no longer agree on how to run the partnership business.[25]

[22.] *BCPA*, ss 21–34; *NSPA*, ss 22–34; and *OPA*, ss 20–31. These rules vary slightly from one province to another.

[23.] *BCPA*, ss 29, 36(1); *NSPA*, ss 29, 36(1); *OPA*, ss 26, 33.

[24.] *BCPA*, s 30; *NSPA*, s 38; *OPA*, s 27.

[25.] *BCPA*, s 38; *NSPA*, s 30; *OPA*, s 34. Other specific grounds are also set out in the statutes.

Partnership legislation provides a basic framework of rules to deal with the claims that arise upon dissolution. First, debts and liabilities to persons who are not partners are paid from the assets of the partnership. Second, debts to partners are paid. Third, capital invested by the partners is returned to them. Finally, if anything is left, it is paid out to the partners according to their respective rights to profits. The statutory scheme with respect to what partners are entitled to on dissolution may be modified or fleshed out in a partnership agreement.[26]

Concept Summary 21.2 identifies some of the most important issues to be considered in drafting a partnership agreement in light of the default rules in partnership statutes.

Concept Summary 21.2

Key Issues to Address in a Partnership Agreement

Issue	Content
Name	What is the name of the partnership? Who will be entitled to use it if the partnership breaks up?
Membership of partnership	What criteria will be used for admission and expulsion of partners? What process will be required to admit or expel a partner?
Capitalization	What will be the financial contributions of the partners (usually called capital) now and in the future?
Profits	How will the profits be shared between the partners? On what basis will they be paid to partners?
Management	How will the partnership make decisions? What monitoring and control procedures will be put in place to guard against unauthorized liability and negligence by partners? How will disputes be resolved?
Dissolution	What limits will be placed on the right of dissolution? Will death, insolvency, or resignation of a partner terminate the partnership for all partners?

Business Decision 21.1 asks you to consider whether a partnership is an appropriate form of business organization in a specific situation.

Business Decision **21.1**

Creation of a Partnership

Melvin and Erin have known each other since childhood and trust and respect each other. They have an idea for a new business—Ramps R Us. They have noticed that many businesses around the town where they live do not have adequate access for people in wheelchairs. They believe that they could make money by supplying low-cost ramps to businesses. Melvin has experience with metal fabrication, and Erin has worked for several years in retail marketing. Their plan is that Erin will get orders from local businesses, and that Melvin will construct and install the ramps. To get started, they need $100 000 for the metal-fabricating equipment, rent, and initial marketing expenses.

Melvin has a new car, owns his house, and has $50 000 in savings, which he is willing to contribute to the business. He is the sole supporter of two small children. He also currently operates as a sole proprietor under the name of Mel's Metal. Mel's Metal has made a few wheelchair ramps

in the past. Mel intends to continue working full time at Mel's Metal, at least initially. He will work in the new business at nights and on weekends.

Erin is single and has no dependants. She has no cash and no source of income at the moment. She also has substantial outstanding debts to various financial institutions.

Erin wants to be able to make commitments to prospective customers without having to consult Melvin. Even though Melvin trusts Erin and will be busy with his work at Mel's Metal, he does not want Erin to be able to bind the business without his consent.

Question for Discussion

1. What are the advantages and disadvantages of using a partnership to carry on this business?

---

26. *BCPA*, s 47; *NSPA*, s 47; *OPA*, s 44.

L.O. ❻   # Limited Partnerships

All jurisdictions in Canada recognize a special form of partnership called a *limited partnership*.[27] Limited partnerships allow people to become partners but avoid unlimited personal liability so long as they restrict their involvement in the partnership business. There are three essential distinctions between limited partnerships and general partnerships:

- First, in general partnerships, all partners have unlimited personal liability. But in **limited partnerships**, while at least one of the partners, called a *general partner*, has unlimited liability, at least one other, called a *limited partner*, has liability limited to the amount of their investment. Suppose you invested $5000 in a limited partnership as a limited partner. The partnership is sued by an unpaid creditor. All the partnership assets *and* the personal assets of the general partner can be used to satisfy that debt. Your liability, however, is limited to the amount of your investment—$5000.

- Second, limited partnerships come into existence only when a partnership declaration is filed with the appropriate government authority. A general partnership comes into existence as soon as the partners start carrying on business together with a view to a profit.

- Third, limited partners can be employees of the limited partnership. They will, however, lose the limit on their liability if they participate in controlling the business or if they allow their names to be used in the firm name (but not if they merely provide management advice). In practice, it is often difficult to know when advice ends and control begins. For instance, in many limited partnerships, the general partner is a corporation. In such a case, one individual may be both a limited partner in the partnership and a senior employee of the corporation. That person may manage the limited partnership, but in the capacity of an employee of the corporation. Since that limited partner is not in control of the business in a *personal* capacity, they may still have limited liability.[28]

Apart from these distinctions, most of the rules applicable to general partnerships apply to limited partnerships. Limited partnerships are usually attractive to passive investors who want to be treated as partners so they can share in profits and deduct any partnership losses against their other income for tax purposes. Otherwise, they want their liability limited.

L.O. ❼❽❾❿   # Corporations

The corporation is the most common form of business organization. It is used for all types and sizes of businesses, from one-person operations to large multinationals. In this chapter, we will introduce the basic characteristics of the corporation and the process of incorporation. We will restrict our discussion to general business corporations, excluding state-owned entities

---

[27.] *Eg BCPA*, Part 2; *Limited Partnerships Act*, RSNS 1989, c 259 (NS); and *Limited Partnerships Act*, RSO 1990, c L.16 (Ont).

[28.] *Nordile Holdings Ltd v Breckenridge* (1992) 66 BCLR (2d) 183 (CA). The circumstances in which a limited partner loses limited liability are more restricted under Manitoba's *Partnerships Act*, CCSM c P30, s 63.

and specialized corporations, such as banks and charities, that are governed under their own legislation. In Chapter 22, we will consider the legal rules for corporate governance.

INCORPORATION PROCESS

Unlike sole proprietorships and general partnerships, corporations do not come into existence simply because one or more people start doing business. A corporation is created only when certain documents are filed with the appropriate government office under either the federal *Canada Business Corporations Act* (*CBCA*) or similar legislation in each province or territory.[29] Once incorporated, the company is governed by the laws of the jurisdiction where incorporation occurred. The corporate laws in Alberta, Saskatchewan, Manitoba, Ontario, Quebec, New Brunswick, and Newfoundland and Labrador follow the federal model more or less closely.[30] Though the structure of the corporate law rules in British Columbia, Nova Scotia, and Prince Edward Island are somewhat different from the *CBCA*, their effect is similar in many respects.[31] Under the *CBCA* and the provincial Acts that follow it, the main filings required to incorporate are:

- articles of incorporation
- a name search report on the proposed name of the corporation
- the fee

The **articles of incorporation** set out the fundamental characteristics of the corporation: its name, the class and number of shares authorized to be issued, the number of directors, any restriction on transferring shares, and any restriction on the business that the corporation may conduct.[32] The name search shows the names used by other business organizations in Canada that are similar to the proposed name of the corporation. A corporation cannot have a name that is confusingly similar to another business name. Once the required documents are properly filed along with the fee, the responsible official issues a certificate, which is then attached to the articles. That official document certifies that the corporation was incorporated on the date of the certificate.

The actual process of filing the requisite documents and receiving a certificate of incorporation is straightforward and can be done online in most jurisdictions. However, since tax planning and other issues can arise in connection with incorporation, it is often wise to seek professional advice.

Upon incorporation, a corporation can start doing business. The business may be entirely new, or an existing business may be transferred to it. Several more steps are required, however, before the corporation is fully organized. The directors named in the articles must have a meeting and pass a resolution to issue shares to the shareholders. The directors also usually adopt arrangements

the **articles of incorporation** set out the fundamental characteristics of the corporation

---

[29.] *Canada Business Corporations Act*, RSC 1985, c C-44 (Can).

[30.] *Business Corporations Act*, RSA 2000, c B-9 (Alta); *The Business Corporations Act*, RSS 1978, c B-10 (Sask); *Corporations Act*, CCSM c C225 (Man); *Business Corporations Act*, RSO 1990, c B.16 (Ont); *Business Corporations Act*, RSQ, c S-31.1 (Que); *Business Corporations Act*, SNB 1981, c B-9.1 (NB); *Corporations Act*, RSNL 1990, c. C-36 (Nfld & Lab).

[31.] *Business Corporations Act*, SBC 2002, c 57 (*BCBCA*) (BC); *Companies Act*, RSNS 1989, c 81 (*NSCA*)(NS); *Companies Act*, RSPEI 1988, c C-14 (*PEICA*) (PEI).

[32.] The equivalent of articles under the *NSCA* is the memorandum of association; under the *BCBCA*, it is an incorporation agreement that contains a notice of articles, combined with some elements of articles under the *CBCA*; under the *PEICA*, it is the letters patent.

for carrying on the formal legal business of the corporation.[33] The directors decide, among other things:

- the notice to be given for meetings of directors and shareholders
- what constitutes a quorum for meetings
- who can sign contracts on behalf of the corporation
- what officers the corporation will have

a **general by-law** sets out the arrangements for carrying on the legal business of the corporation

Those arrangements are typically set out in a **general by-law**.[34] To take effect, a by-law must be passed by the directors, but it continues to be in effect only if it is passed by the shareholders at their next meeting.

a **shareholders' agreement** is a contract between shareholders that customizes their relationship

If a corporation has few shareholders, the final organizational step is usually the creation of a *shareholders' agreement*. A **shareholders' agreement** is a contract between shareholders that customizes their relationship by providing rules that are better suited to their particular needs. Shareholders' agreements are discussed in Chapter 22.

a **minute book** is a book in which corporate records are kept

The corporation must maintain the articles of incorporation, by-laws, minutes of shareholders' meetings, including any resolutions passed, and any shareholders' agreement at its registered office, usually in a **minute book** (a book in which corporate records are kept), though electronic records are now permitted. Shareholders and creditors must be given access to those documents. Articles of a corporation, as well as any other documents (such as annual information filings) that are filed with the government agency responsible for the corporation, are maintained by the agency in a publicly accessible record.

A corporation does not have to register under provincial business names legislation unless it uses a name other than its corporate name.[35] However, it may require a business licence. Also, if a corporation wants to conduct business outside of the province or territory where it was incorporated, it may need an extra-provincial corporation licence from the government of the jurisdiction where it wants to operate to allow it to carry on business. Corporations incorporated under the *CBCA*, however, have a right to carry on business throughout Canada. No licence is required.

CHARACTERISTICS OF CORPORATIONS

Separate Legal Existence

Unlike a sole proprietorship and a partnership, a corporation has a *separate legal existence*. The corporation *itself* carries on business, owns property, possesses rights, and incurs liabilities (including liability for crimes and torts). In most ways, a corporation has the same rights, powers, and privileges as a natural person. Shareholders have a bundle of rights in relation to the corporation through their ownership of shares. Shareholders do not, however, own the business that is carried on by the corporation, or the property belonging to it. This contrasts with sole proprietors and partners, who carry on the business, own the property of the business, possess its rights, and are responsible for its liabilities directly.

[33.] Corporate statutes set default rules for the governance of the corporation that apply if the directors do not adopt different arrangements.

[34.] Many of the provisions contained in a by-law are included in the articles under the *BCBCA* and the *NSCA*.

[35.] *Eg Business Names Act*, RSO 1990, c B.17 (Ont).

Separate legal existence of corporations has three important implications:

- First, a shareholder can be an employee or a creditor of the corporation.[36] The shareholder and the corporation are two distinct entities that can contract with each other.

- Second, because it is a distinct entity, the corporation is unaffected if a shareholder dies or withdraws from the business.

- Third, the corporation is treated as a separate tax payer for income tax purposes. Income or losses from the corporation's business are attributed to the corporation, and it is liable for the applicable tax. Shareholders are taxed only when they personally receive something from the corporation, such as a *dividend*. A **dividend** is a payment of cash or property by the corporation to shareholders that is authorized by the directors. The payment of dividends is one way that shareholders receive a return on their investment in the corporation. Concept Summary 21.3 summarizes the taxation of the main forms of business organization discussed in this chapter. Taxation of corporations and their shareholders is further discussed in Chapter 25.

a **dividend** is a payment of cash or property by the corporation to shareholders that is authorized by the directors

Concept Summary 21.3

Taxation of Income of Business Organizations

Sole Proprietorship	Partnership	Corporation
Income (or loss) from business added to (or deducted from) individual sole proprietor's taxable income	Income (or loss) from business calculated for partnership but added to (or deducted from) individual partner's taxable income • in proportion to partner's entitlement to profits • whether or not cash distributed to partner	Income (or loss) from business added to (or deducted from) corporation's taxable income • shareholders pay tax only on distributions actually received from corporation (*eg* dividends)

It is often said that shareholders have *limited liability* for the obligations of the corporation. Strictly speaking, however, shareholders have *no liability* for a corporation's obligations. To obtain shares, shareholders provide the corporation with money, property, or services. Shareholders are said to have **limited liability** because they cannot lose more than they invest in the corporation in return for their shares. Creditors, employees, and other claimants against the corporation can demand to be paid out of the corporation's assets. But once the corporation's assets are exhausted, the creditors and other claimants cannot claim against the shareholders personally. In the worst case, if all the assets of the corporation are taken by creditors, then the shareholder's shares may be worth nothing. They will have lost all their investment—but nothing more. Limiting the risk for shareholders in this way—a key characteristic of the corporation—is intended to encourage entrepreneurship and shareholder investment.

limited liability means that shareholders cannot lose more than they invest in the corporation in return for their shares

Limited liability effectively shifts some of the risk of loss from the shareholders to the creditors and other stakeholders of a corporation. Creditors can recover what is owed them only from the assets owned by the corporation. If a corporation has few assets, creditors may refuse to lend money to it unless a creditworthy shareholder provides a *personal guarantee* for the corporation's debt. If a shareholder gives such a guarantee and the corporation defaults, the shareholder is personally liable for the corporation's obligation. (Chapter 22

[36.] *Salomon v Salomon & Co* [1897] AC 22 (HL).

discusses how shareholders may incur personal liability as directors and officers when they act in that capacity; Chapter 23 discusses guarantees.)

While the courts generally adhere to the concept of limited liability, they sometimes disregard the separate legal existence of the corporation to impose personal liability on a shareholder for a corporation's obligation. In other words, they **pierce the corporate veil**.[37] For instance, a judge may permit a creditor of a corporation to claim directly against a controlling shareholder if the corporation has insufficient assets to satisfy the creditor's claim. Disregarding the corporation in this way does not destroy its separate existence for all purposes, only for the *limited purpose* of granting relief to the creditor directly against the shareholder.

It is very difficult to predict when a court will pierce the corporate veil, although usually there must be some kind of serious wrongdoing or unfairness or both. When a business has been incorporated to do something (or facilitate the doing of something) that would be illegal or improper for the individual shareholders to do personally, the courts have disregarded the separate existence of the corporation. When a corporation was used to disguise a fraud, as in Case Brief 21.2, the rationale for piercing the corporate veil is compelling. Ethical Perspective 21.1 presents a case in which the arguments for piercing the corporate veil are not as clear.

> a court may **pierce the corporate veil** by disregarding the separate legal existence of the corporation to impose personal liability on a shareholder for a corporation's obligation

Case Brief 21.2

Big Bend Hotel Ltd v Security Mutual Casualty Co (1979) 19 BCLR 102 (SC)

Kumar operated a hotel that was destroyed in a fire. Kumar decided to acquire another hotel but knew that he would be turned down for fire insurance because of the suspicious circumstances surrounding the fire. He therefore incorporated Big Bend Hotel Ltd and had it acquire the hotel and apply for the insurance. Subsequently, the new hotel burnt down. The insurance company refused to pay when it found out that Kumar was the sole shareholder of Big Bend Hotel. The corporation sued for payment of the insurance proceeds. (Property insurance was discussed in Chapter 17.)

The court denied the corporation's claim. It held that the insurance company would not have issued the policy to Kumar. Even though the corporation was a distinct legal person from Kumar, it was being used solely to disguise the real person behind the corporation. The insurance company should be able to disregard the separate personality of the corporation and treat the policy as if it had been applied for by Kumar directly. On that basis, the insurance company did not have to pay because Kumar had fraudulently failed to disclose the prior fire loss.

Ethical Perspective **21.1**

Limited Liability[38]

Carleton operated a taxi business using a number of separate corporations, each of which owned two cabs. Carleton owned all the shares of each corporation and managed the corporation's business. Each corporation maintained the minimum amount of third party liability insurance coverage required by law at the time: $10 000. Walkovszky was hit by a taxicab owned by one of Carleton's corporations and suffered serious injuries. She sued the corporation that owned the cab and was awarded compensatory damages in an amount that far exceeded $10 000. However, because the defendant corporation had no assets other than the cabs, which were not worth much, she could not actually collect much more than the $10 000 that was available under the corporation's insurance policy.

Questions for Discussion

1. Is it appropriate for a person to carry on a taxi business through a corporation with assets that are insufficient to meet the reasonably foreseeable liabilities resulting from car accidents?

2. Should the court disregard the separate legal existence of the corporation and hold Carleton personally liable?

---

37. *Littlewoods Mail Order Stores Ltd v Inland Revenue Commissioners* [1969] 3 All ER 855 (HL).
38. *Walkovszky v Carleton* (1966) 223 NE 2d 6 (NY CA).

Separation of Ownership and Management

There is a legal distinction between those responsible for the management of a corporation—the directors and officers—and the shareholders. By a majority vote, the shareholders elect a **board of directors** to manage or supervise the management of the corporation. In most cases, the directors delegate the responsibility for managing the corporation to the **officers** that they appoint, such as a president. The directors then monitor and supervise the officers' management of the corporation's business. Shareholders do not participate, as shareholders, in management. Unlike partners, they are not agents of the firm. In many corporations, especially small ones, however, these legally distinct roles are played by the same people: the shareholders are also the directors and officers. But in larger businesses, directors and officers are unlikely to hold all the shares of a corporation. Very large corporations, such as Research In Motion Limited, have thousands of shareholders, including the officers and directors. The separation of ownership and management creates a number of issues regarding internal relationships in the corporation that are discussed in Chapter 22. The most important is how shareholders can ensure that management acts in their interests.

> a **board of directors** consists of the individuals elected by shareholders to manage the corporation

> **officers** are the people to whom the board of directors delegates responsibility for managing the corporation

Corporate Finance

Corporations are financed in two basic ways:

- **equity**—the shareholders' investment in the corporation in return for shares
- **debt**—loans that have been made to the corporation by shareholders, commercial lenders, or other creditors

> **equity** is what the shareholders have invested in the corporation in return for shares

> **debt** consists of loans that have been made to the corporation

There is a basic difference between equity and debt. Debt is a claim for a *fixed amount*. In contrast, the **shares** issued in connection with an equity investment usually represent a claim to the *residual value* of the corporation after the debts and all other claims against the corporation have been paid. The value of that residual claim depends upon the value of the corporation's business.[39] If the value of the business exceeds the total amount of the other claims against it, then the shares will have a positive value. If the value is not as much as the claims, the shares are worthless. Valuing a business is complex and imprecise because it is determined by numerous factors that change over time. The value of a business depends, in part, upon the value of the tangible assets owned by the business, which may be difficult to assess. Increasingly, it also depends upon intangible assets, which are even harder to value. How much is Microsoft's copyright in Windows worth? Most businesses are worth more as a **going concern**, that is, as an operating unit, than as a collection of assets that will be sold piecemeal. The prospect for future growth in the business's income is usually a significant factor affecting value. Because businesses are hard to value, the residual claim that shares represent is also difficult to value. Shares are attractive because their value increases with the value of the business. Unlike debt, there is no limit on what they may be worth; nor, however, is there any guarantee that they will have any value at all.

> **shares** represent a claim on the *residual value* of the corporation after the claims of all creditors have been paid

> the **going concern** value represents the value of a corporation as an operating unit

There is another critical difference between debt and equity. If a debt obligation is not repaid, there is a breach of contract. The creditor can sue for damages and even force the corporation into bankruptcy. (Bankruptcy is discussed in Chapter 24.) But if an obligation to a shareholder, such as a dividend payment,

---

[39]. The value of shares also depends on the expected dividends that will be paid on the shares. Dividends are discussed below.

is not met, the shareholder cannot put the corporation into bankruptcy. In fact, there may not be any remedy at all, as will be discussed in Chapter 22. Since shareholder rights are not as easily enforced as debt-holder rights, and because the value of shares depends upon the residual value of the corporation after everyone else gets paid, shares are a much riskier investment than debt.

A corporation can have different classes of shares with a wide range of names and characteristics. The specific name and bundle of characteristics are set out in the articles. The bundle determines both the nature of the financial claim created by the share and the role that the share gives the shareholder in corporate governance. Every corporation must have shares that provide at least three basic rights:

- to vote for the election of directors
- to receive dividends when declared by the board of directors
- to receive the property that remains after a corporation has been dissolved and all prior claims have been satisfied

These basic rights do not have to be attached to any *single* class of shares; they can be allocated to different classes, so long as all shareholders in a particular class have the same rights. In practice, most corporations have one class of shares, called **common shares**, that includes all three basic rights. A corporation may also have *preferred shares*. Usually **preferred shares** are entitled to receive fixed dividends on a regular basis. Those shares enjoy two kinds of preferences: (i) dividends must be paid on preferred shares before any dividends are paid on common shares, and (ii) on dissolution, the investment in preferred shares is repaid before the residual value is distributed to the holders of common shares. Preferred shares are therefore less risky than common shares. On the other hand, they usually have no voting rights and no claim to the residual value of the corporation after the amount invested has been repaid.

The particular bundle of rights given to a class of shares can be designed to make them attractive to prospective investors. The flexibility of equity financing is a significant advantage of the corporation over other forms of business organization. Also, in the absence of restrictions on share transfer in a shareholders' agreement or the articles, shares are freely transferable. By comparison, in most cases, partnership interests cannot be transferred without the consent of all partners.

common shares usually carry the rights to vote, to receive dividends, and to receive the remaining property of the corporation upon dissolution

usually **preferred shares** are entitled to receive fixed dividends on a regular basis and a return of the amount invested before any payments are made to common shares

Chapter Summary

The sole proprietorship is the simplest form of business organization. It comes into existence whenever a person begins carrying on a business on their own. A sole proprietor has unlimited personal liability for the obligations of the business and is solely entitled to its benefits. Sole proprietorships (and other forms of business organization) may have to register under provincial business names legislation, and obtain a business licence.

A partnership comes into existence when two or more people start to carry on business together with a view to a profit. Partnerships are governed by special statutes in each province that provide (i) default rules governing the relations of partners to each other, and (ii) mandatory rules governing the relationship of the partnership to out-

siders. Partners are personally responsible for the obligations of the business and are entitled to the benefits from it. Each partner is considered an agent of the partnership who is capable of creating partnership obligations within the usual course of the firm's business.

The risks associated with unlimited personal liability, and the ability of all partners to bind the partnership, are addressed legally by the fiduciary duty owed by each partner to the partnership. Provisions in partnership agreements may be used to provide additional protections. In smaller partnerships, these legal protections are supplemented by informal monitoring of each partner by the other partners who work in the business. A limited partnership is a special form of partnership in which at least one partner's liability is limited to the amount the partner has invested in the partnership.

A corporation is formed when certain documents are filed with the appropriate government authority. A corporation is legally separate from its shareholders and managers. The corporation alone is responsible for the obligations of the business that it carries on and is solely entitled to the benefits from the business. Shareholders have an interest in the corporation represented by their shares. They elect directors who have responsibility for managing the business and affairs of the corporation. Directors usually delegate some of their management responsibility to officers.

A corporation can be financed in two ways. Equity is what the shareholders have invested in the corporation in return for shares. Debt consists of loans that have been made to the corporation. Shares represent a claim to the residual value of the corporation after all others with claims against the corporation are paid. Because they rank last, shares are a riskier investment than debt.

MyBusLawLab   ADDITIONAL RESOURCES FOR CHAPTER 21

MyBusLawLab provides students with an assortment of tools to help enrich the learning experience, including a Study Plan with Pre- and Post-tests, mini-cases with assessments, and provincial content material, which provides links to relevant cases, legislation, and additional resources.

MyBusLawLab provides the following resources for Chapter 21:

■ Business Decision 21.1W—Partnership Tax Losses and the Creation of a Partnership

Provincial Material

■ **British Columbia:** Sole Proprietorships, Partnerships, Limited Partnerships, Limited Liability Partnerships, Business Corporations, Incorporation, Business Names, Corporate Name Registration

■ **Alberta:** *Business Corporations Act,* Incorporation, Limited Liability Partnerships, Limited Partnerships, Partnerships in Alberta, Pre-Incorporation Contracts, Income Trusts, Other Incorporated Bodies, Professional Corporations, Taxation of Corporations, Unlimited Liability Corporations, International Partnerships, NUANS Reports, *Alberta Investment Management Corporation Amendment Act (2011),* Corporate Management, Directors' Liability

■ **Manitoba and Saskatchewan:** Business Names, Process of Incorporation, Non- share Capital Corporations, Partnerships, Separate Legal Entity, Shareholders

■ **Ontario:** Annual Filing, Articles of Incorporation, Business Names, Fiduciary Duty, Limited Liability Partnerships, Limited Partnerships, Multi-Disciplinary Partnerships, Not-for-Profit Corporations, Ontario Corporations, Partnership Agreements, Professional Corporations, Promoters, Reporting Issues, Registration of Partnerships, Securities Legislation

■ **Atlantic Provinces:** Business Corporation Legislation, Business Names, *Co-operative Associations Act,* Extra-Provincial Registration, Limited Liability Partnerships, Non-Profit Corporations, Partnership Legislation, Professional Corporations, Public–Private Partnerships, Unlimited Liability Corporations

Review Questions

1. How does business organizations law address risk?
2. What do you have to do to create a sole proprietorship?
3. Who is responsible for the obligations of a business that is carried on by a sole proprietor? What does this mean in practice for sole proprietors?
4. What are the major limitations of the sole proprietorship?
5. When does a sole proprietorship have to register its name under provincial law?
6. Why should a creditor of a partnership be concerned about the creditworthiness of the partners?
7. What are the criteria for the creation of a partnership?
8. If you were a draftsperson employed by a firm of architects who were carrying on their business as a partnership and you received a share of the profits of the business as part of your compensation, would you be a partner in the partnership?
9. If you were entering a business relationship and did not want to be a partner, what could you do?
10. How does the fiduciary duty that each partner owes the others help to protect partners against the risk of unwanted liabilities?

11. If you are a partner, how do you protect yourself against the risk of other partners creating unauthorized obligations for the firm?

12. What is a "limited liability partnership" and how is it different from a limited partnership?

13. Sarah is a partner in a partnership that carries on an engineering consulting business. She will retire on January 1. Does she need to worry about any liabilities incurred by the partnership after she retires? Is there anything that she can do to manage her risk?

14. What kind of rules does provincial partnership legislation provide for the internal organization of partnerships? How are these rules addressed in a partnership agreement?

15. How is a corporation created and organized? Why would you need a lawyer to advise you on creating a corporation?

16. What key documents define the characteristics of a corporation?

17. When does a corporation need a licence to operate in a particular province?

18. "A corporation is a separate legal entity." What does that statement mean?

19. Describe the legal separation of ownership and control in a corporation. Does it always exist in practice?

20. What are the differences between debt and equity from an investor's point of view? From the corporation's point of view?

Cases and Problems

1. Oren and Jenna carry on their business of buying and selling real estate as a partnership. Each is entitled to 50 percent of the profits from the business. Oren bought and sold a parcel of real estate in the name of the partnership without Jenna's permission or knowledge. Oren took for himself the full amount of the profits from the sale ($100 000). Is there a legal basis for Jenna to claim compensation from Oren? If so, how much is she entitled to receive?

2. Carol carried on a consulting business as a sole proprietorship. She met Steven Stevenson at a conference. Steven told Carol that he was a "senior litigator and partner" in a mid-sized Saskatoon law firm and gave her a business card that set out his name and the name "Stevenson, Smith, Jones, and Khan, Barristers and Solicitors." Steven asked Carol to do some work for the firm. Carol did the work and sent a bill for $20 000 to Steven. While providing the services, Carol received letters from Steven on paper bearing, at the top, the same firm name as the business card and the full names of Stevenson, Smith, Jones, and Khan at the bottom. Steven did not pay. Carol sued Steven along with Smith, Jones, and Khan. Assuming that Steven and the three other individuals named on the letterhead were not partners, will Carol succeed in holding them liable for her account? What else would you need to know to answer the question?

3. You are the president of a large steel manufacturer and all of your corporation's legal work is done by one of the largest law firms in the country, Osman & Co. Your company regularly relies on opinions from Osman & Co in making million-dollar business decisions. You have never worried about receiving bad advice from the firm because, if the firm was negligent and gave the wrong advice, the firm's insurance and the assets of all its rich partners would be available to satisfy any judgment in your favour. Today, you receive in the mail an announcement that Osman & Co is becoming a limited liability partner-

ship. Would you have any concerns about this change and, if so, what might you do about it?

4. Ben and Stephanie decided to open up a restaurant. Stephanie contributed a building that she owns, in which the restaurant will operate, that is worth $300 000 and Ben contributed $100 000 for renovations. The parties agreed orally that once the restaurant is open, Stephanie will manage the restaurant on a day-to-day basis, while Ben will keep the books for the business. They have also agreed that they will share the profits from the business. The renovations take three months during which both Ben and Stephanie are involved in supervising the work. The restaurant opens on January 1. The restaurant business is not successful and does not make any profits. Neither Ben nor Stephanie received any financial benefit from the restaurant's operations. Then, Stephanie and Ben began to disagree about what to do. On April 1, Stephanie locks Ben out. Based on these facts, what is the nature of the relationship between Ben and Stephanie? What relief should Ben seek?

5. Bobby was one of several limited partners in a limited partnership called Typecast Limited Partnership, as well as the sole shareholder and president of a corporation named Live Magazine Inc, which was the general partner of Typecast. In his capacity as president of Live Magazine, he acted as the manager of the limited partnership. On behalf of the limited partnership, Bobby negotiated a contract with Gold Dust Graphics Ltd to supply printing services worth $50 000. GoldDust paid the $50 000 to Typecast, but the limited partnership failed to perform the services. Gold Dust sued the limited partnership and got a judgment for $50 000, only to discover that neither Typecast nor the general partner, Live Magazine, has any assets. Can Gold Dust seek to recover its $50 000 from Bobby?

6. Samron, Amir, and Laura have carried on a florist shop business as a partnership for 10 years. The partnership uses the name "Samron, Amir, & Laura

Flowers." The business has a line of credit with a local bank, but the business has drawn only $25 000 of the total of $50 000 available. The partnership also has three long-term suppliers of flowers as well as many loyal corporate customers who order substantial amounts of flowers each year. Amir is 60 and has decided to retire from the partnership business. What liability risks would Amir have in connection with the business after his retirement and how should he deal with them? Are there any other financial issues that Amir should consider in connection with his retirement?

7. For over five years, Rick was the CEO of JB Guitars Inc, a corporation operating a chain of retail guitar stores. He had gained tremendous practical experience and decided to start his own business selling guitars. He had entered into an agreement with JB Guitars when he first started working there under which he promised that he would not carry on a competing business for two years after he ended his employment with JB Guitars. To avoid breaching that contract, Rick incorporated a corporation named Generation X Guitars Inc to carry on the business. He is the sole shareholder, director, and president. Rick's old employer claims that the new corporation is just a way of getting around the non-competition agreement and has sued for a court order prohibiting Generation X Guitars from carrying a business competing with JB Guitars. Will JB Guitars be successful?

8. Tryon Medical Services Inc is a corporation in a partnership with Jordan. The sole business of the partnership has been leasing premises that the partnership owns to Elton Medical Clinic. Elton rented the premises for 30 years and then moved out when its lease expired. A real estate agent has advised the partnership that finding another tenant would be extremely difficult, if not impossible, without a very large investment in renovating the premises. Jordan, who is about to retire, does not want to make that investment and thinks that selling the building would be the best strategy. Tryon wants to hold on to the building, make the investment, and try to find a new tenant. The partnership agreement between Tryon and Jordan provides that it cannot be terminated by notice from a partner. Could Jordan get a court order to dissolve the partnership?

9. Lucia and Olga have decided to buy some commercial real estate through a corporation. The corporation will buy commercial properties, earn money from rent paid by tenants to cover the operating costs, and then sell the properties for a profit. Lucia is an experienced real estate developer and will run the business, making all the decisions relating to the acquisition of the properties, the management of them, and their eventual sale. Because the success of the business will depend on her management, Lucia is anxious to have any returns she receives from the business depend on its success. Lucia will not be investing any money in the business. Her friend, Olga, has $500 000 that she will invest in the business. Olga will have no management role in the business but would like a fixed annual return of 10 percent on her investment. Describe the different kinds of shares that Olga and Lucia would want.

10. Alice has been carrying on a sporting goods business in Ottawa as a sole proprietorship under the name A-Sport since 1999. By the spring of 2012, she was unable to cover the substantial costs associated with the business. By September 2012, she had sold many of her personal assets, including her house, to pay the expenses of the business. Alice is very worried that she will lose the business and not be able to support her daughter, since she is a single mother and has no other source of income.

In September 2012, Alice met Mario at a trade show. Mario carries on a successful business as a sole proprietor. The key to his success has been a combination of innovative inventory management techniques and the use of aggressive television advertising. Mario is married with three children.

Alice and Mario decide to carry on the A-Sport business in Ottawa together. Mario has $100 000 available to invest in Alice's business and has substantial other assets, including three store premises and a warehouse in Toronto. They agree on the following.

- Alice will contribute all of her interest in the A-Sport business.

- Mario will contribute $100 000 in cash.

- Alice will manage the A-Sport stores on a day-to-day basis, while Mario will be responsible for marketing and inventory management. Mario will continue to spend most of his time in Toronto looking after his business there.

- All major decisions for the business will require the agreement of both Mario and Alice.

What issues should Alice and Mario address before going into business as a partnership?

11. Based on the facts in Problem 10, how would these issues be addressed differently if Alice and Mario were to set up a corporation to accomplish their business objectives?

12. You are the manager of a National Bank branch. Janis, a wealthy business person, who runs several successful restaurants in town, has asked for a loan to support a new business venture. She wants to incorporate a new corporation to carry on a business selling gelato from a kiosk at a local skating rink. She wants the bank to lend the corporation $20 000 to cover the start-up costs. What concerns would you have about this loan to the corporation and how might they be addressed in light of what we have discussed in this chapter?

22 Legal Rules for Corporate Governance

LEARNING OBJECTIVES

After completing this chapter, you should be able to:

❶ Describe the rights of shareholders and how they are exercised.

❷ Outline the legal remedies available to shareholders when management acts contrary to their interests.

❸ Identify common situations in which the personal interests of directors and officers may be in conflict with the best interests of the corporation.

❹ Explain the legal standard of care that management must observe when making business judgments.

❺ Identify the liability risks associated with being a director or officer and some strategies that can be used to manage these risks.

❻ Explain the ways in which securities law and corporate law overlap.

❼ Explain how the allocation of power contemplated in corporate law amongst shareholders, directors, and officers does not always operate in practice.

❽ Explain what is meant by corporate social responsibility.

❾ Determine whether a corporation's employee has authority to enter into a contract on behalf of the corporation.

❿ Explain when a corporation will be liable for torts and crimes because of the actions of people working on its behalf.

In this chapter, we discuss the basic legal rules for corporate governance in Canada. We begin with a discussion of the corporate governance rules that define when management is accountable to shareholders. Without sufficient accountability, shareholders will not invest. However, accountability obligations must not be so great that they interfere with management's ability to do its job, or discourage capable people from becoming managers.

We start by laying out the basic distribution of power and responsibility amongst directors, officers, and shareholders as set out in the *Canada Business Corporations Act (CBCA)* and most other corporate statutes in Canada.[1] Next, we look at the standards for management behaviour that are imposed by corporate statutes to address the risk that managers will act to benefit themselves at the expense of shareholders. Those standards include the fiduciary duty and duty of care. We look at the remedies that shareholders can use to enforce those standards and ensure management accountability as well as the strategies that management may adopt to manage its risk of liability for breaching those standards. In some circumstances, the legal rules for corporate governance are not effective to ensure that management is accountable to shareholders. We discuss some recent reforms to securities law that are intended to address the challenges for shareholders in this regard.

Management also has responsibilities to non-shareholder stakeholders, such as employees, creditors, and the public. In this chapter, we look at the extent to which management must take into account the interests of these stakeholders under corporate law. We also discuss situations in which corporations become liable to particular people in contract, tort, and criminal law as a result of the actions of individuals on their behalf, and the implications that these liability rules have for corporate organization and risk management. Rules defining when someone can bind a corporation to a contract, for example, affect how corporations organize their contract approval process to reduce the risk that contracts are entered into without proper authorization. Another important aspect of the governance scheme for business is government regulation to protect the public. Many regulatory statutes impose personal liability on corporate managers. The rules that impose fines on directors for misleading advertising caused by corporate activities are one example. These rules and some other forms of regulation are discussed in Chapter 25.

Management and Control of the Corporation

L.O. ❶

In Canadian corporate statutes, power and responsibility in the corporation are allocated amongst different groups of people:

- **Shareholders** are entitled to the assets of the corporation that remain after all the creditors are paid on its dissolution. Their only powers are

shareholders are the residual claimants to the assets of the corporation and elect the directors

---

[1.] *Canada Business Corporations Act*, RSC 1985, c C-44 (*CBCA*) (Can); *Business Corporations Act*, RSA 2000, c B-9 (*ABCA*) (Alta); *Corporations Act*, CCSM, c C225 (*MCA*) (Man); *Business Corporations Act*, SNB 1981, c B-9.1 (*NBBCA*) (NB); *Corporations Act*, RSNL 1990, c C-36 (*NLCA*) (Nfld & Lab); *Business Corporations Act*, RSO 1990, c B.16 (*OBCA*) (Ont); *Business Corporations Act*, RSS 1978, c B-10 (*SBCA*) (Sask). In subsequent notes, references will be made to illustrative provisions, rather than to all statutes. As noted in Chapter 21, corporate statutes in British Columbia, Quebec, Nova Scotia, and Prince Edward Island are based on different models. Nevertheless, most of the discussion in this chapter is equally applicable to corporations incorporated in those jurisdictions.

FIGURE 22.1 Relationship of Shareholders, Directors, and Officers

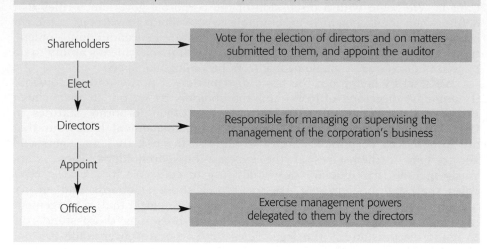

to vote for the election of directors, to appoint the auditor, and to vote on proposals made to them. In most cases, each share has one vote. As shareholders, they do not participate in managing the business of the corporation.[2]

- **Directors** are responsible for managing or supervising the management of the business of the corporation and its internal affairs, including issuing shares, declaring dividends, and calling shareholder meetings.

- **Officers** are appointed by directors and usually exercise substantial management powers delegated to them by the directors.

Figure 22.1 shows the relationships amongst these three groups of people. In corporations with few shareholders, the same people may be the shareholders, directors, and officers. These are sometimes referred to as **private corporations** and often the scale of their business is small.[3] As the scale of the corporation's business increases these groups are less likely to overlap. In larger corporations that have distributed their shares to the public, often referred to as **public corporations**, the directors and officers are usually shareholders, but most shareholders are other people not involved in the corporation's business. Another critical difference, as discussed below, is that public corporations are subject to burdensome requirements under provincial securities law.

How Shareholders Exercise Power

For most purposes, shareholders must act collectively. How this is done depends upon whether the corporation is a public corporation or a private one. Usually shareholder actions take place at meetings. Directors

directors are responsible for managing or supervising the management of the business of the corporation and its internal affairs

officers are appointed by the directors of a corporation and usually exercise substantial management powers delegated to them by the directors

private corporations have few shareholders and the same people may be the shareholders, directors, and officers

public corporations are corporations that have distributed their shares to the public with only a few shareholders involved in the corporation as directors and officers

---

[2] Certain fundamental changes to the corporation, such as selling all of its assets, must be approved by shareholders. Shareholders can also make proposals to have matters discussed at shareholder meetings.

[3] Some private corporations carry on very large businesses, but most carry on smaller businesses. Often when businesses reach a certain size, they need to raise money to grow further by issuing their shares to the public and becoming public corporations.

are responsible for calling shareholder meetings.[4] Directors are obligated to call *annual meetings* at least every 15 months. At an **annual meeting** (i) directors are elected, (ii) the auditor is appointed for the coming year, and (iii) financial statements for the past year are discussed. Directors must ensure that shareholders receive advance notice of the meeting, along with information regarding these three items and any other business. Shareholder meetings may take place at other times to conduct other business. In public corporations, meetings are an important opportunity to question and criticize management, as well as to discuss and vote on proposals made to shareholders. In private corporations where most shareholders are also directors, shareholder meetings may be only a formality. Corporate statutes permit any business that must be done at a meeting to be recorded in written resolutions and signed by all shareholders. Such signed resolutions are commonly used as an alternative to meetings in corporations with few shareholders and are just as effective as actions taken at a meeting.[5]

> at an **annual meeting**, shareholders elect directors, appoint an auditor, and review the annual financial statements

Only a small percentage of shareholders of public corporations attend shareholders' meetings in person. Shareholders can participate without attending by appointing a *proxy*, who need not be a shareholder, to represent them at the meeting and vote their shares. The **proxy**, or **proxy holder**, has all the powers of the shareholder at the meeting, but must vote in accordance with any direction given by the shareholder.

> a **proxy**, or **proxy holder**, is a person designated by a shareholder to vote at a shareholders' meeting

For all public corporations, management must send the shareholders a form of proxy allowing them to appoint a proxy holder.[6] The form is sent along with a **management proxy circular**, a document that contains management proposals and information regarding the proxy, the business to be dealt with at the meeting, and certain other information. The information provided by the circular enhances shareholders' ability to ensure that management is acting in their interests and to make informed choices regarding how to vote.

> a **management proxy circular** is a document sent to the shareholders that contains management proposals and information regarding the proxy, the business to be dealt with at the meeting, and certain other information

Dissident shareholders are those who disagree with management proposals. They may try to encourage their fellow shareholders to vote against management. Dissident shareholders are entitled to obtain a list of shareholders and their addresses from the corporation and to use this information to contact other shareholders.[7] With some exceptions, dissident shareholders must send out a **dissidents' circular** with information on their identity, their relationship to the corporation, and their interest in the proposal.[8] Dissidents' circulars are relatively rare in the Canadian marketplace. The costs of complying with the disclosure requirements are often too high.

> **dissident shareholders** disagree with management proposals

> a **dissidents' circular** is a document sent to all shareholders by shareholders who seek the votes of other shareholders against management

At the meeting, voting is usually by a show of hands, but any shareholder may require that each vote be recorded on a ballot that is collected and counted.[9] Approval is usually by an ordinary majority vote.

[4.] *Eg ABCA*, s 142; *Business Corporations Act*, SBC 2002, c 57 (*BCBCA*) (BC), s 167; *CBCA*, s 143.

[5.] *Eg ABCA*, s 141; *BCBCA*, ss 180, 182(2); *CBCA*, s 142.

[6.] *Eg OBCA*, s 111. All corporations with more than 50 shareholders incorporated under the *CBCA* must meet this requirement (*CBCA*, s 149).

[7.] *Eg ABCA*, s 21(3), (9); *CBCA*, s 21(3), (9); *OBCA*, ss 145, 146.

[8.] *Eg OBCA*, s 112; RRO 1990, Reg 62, ss 33–36; *CBCA*, s 150(1)(*b*); *CBCA Regulations*, SOR/2001-512, ss 57, 63, 64.

[9.] *Eg ABCA*, s 140; *CBCA*, s 141.

SHAREHOLDERS' ACCESS TO INFORMATION

Shareholders need information about the corporation to monitor management and to exercise their rights as shareholders effectively. A corporation must maintain these records and allow shareholders access to them:[10]

- articles
- by-laws
- minutes of meetings of shareholders and shareholders' resolutions
- a share register showing the owners of all shares

Shareholders as well as creditors may examine and copy these records during business hours. Minutes of directors' meetings and directors' resolutions must be maintained as well, though these records cannot be inspected by shareholders or creditors.

The annual financial statements of the corporation prepared by management are the most important information shareholders receive. For public corporations, these are usually contained in an annual report. Annual statements must be audited by an independent accountant who determines whether the statements were prepared in accordance with generally accepted accounting principles and fairly present the financial results of the corporation for the year.[11] The auditor bases their opinion on an evaluation of the financial records of the corporation. Shareholders may unanimously agree to dispense with the audit requirement. This is commonly done in small private corporations where all the shareholders are closely involved in its business and do not consider the protection of an independent assessment of the corporation's financial statements to be worth the expense.

SHAREHOLDERS' AGREEMENTS

If a corporation has few shareholders, they often use a shareholders' agreement to create an arrangement for governing the corporation that is different from the arrangement that occurs under the statute. They may:

- change shareholder voting entitlements and the role of shareholders in management
- change shareholder approval requirements
- create rules for share transfers

Voting and Management

Shareholders may want to allocate decision-making power amongst themselves in a way that is different from the allocation that would result from the number of shares each holds. Suppose Ellen and Phillipe decide to set up a corporation to carry on a business of distributing computer software. Phillipe will contribute the $100 000 needed to set up the business and will be the sales manager. Ellen will contribute some software she has developed. Because of his large financial contribution, Phillipe will get 80 percent of the

---

[10] *Eg ABCA*, ss 20, 21; *CBCA*, ss 20(1), 21; *OBCA*, ss 145, 146. Articles and by-laws were discussed in Chapter 21.

[11] Most public corporations have adopted International Financial Reporting Standards for fiscal years beginning on or after 1 January 2011.

shares, while Ellen will get 20 percent. If each share has one vote, Phillipe would have enough votes to determine who will be on the board. He does not have to include Ellen. But what if Phillipe and Ellen consider themselves to be in a relationship in which each should have an equal say and each wants to be on the board?

They could address this in a shareholders' agreement. Both could agree that they will vote their shares to elect both of them as directors. Ellen and Phillipe may also agree that all shareholder decisions must be approved unanimously.

The *CBCA* and the statutes modelled on it also permit all the shareholders of a corporation to agree to alter the allocation of power between directors and shareholders. Such a **unanimous shareholders' agreement** may "restrict, in whole or in part, the powers of the directors to manage the business and affairs of the corporation." Shareholders who are party to such an agreement have all the powers, as well as the duties and liabilities, of a director to the extent of the restriction. The directors are relieved of their powers, duties, and liabilities to the same extent. Where the shareholders are running the business, in practice, a unanimous shareholder's agreement gives them the power to manage directly.[12]

> a **unanimous shareholders' agreement** is an agreement of all shareholders to transfer some or all of the directors' powers to themselves

Share Transfer

L.O. ❷

In corporations with few shareholders, share transfer is a problem. Typically, the business is tied up with the individuals who are the shareholders. To continue with our example, Ellen would probably have difficulty selling her shares if she leaves the business because the business would have trouble operating without her expertise. Another problem with finding a buyer for an interest in a small corporation is that such interests are inherently hard to value. There is no market, such as the Toronto Stock Exchange, to establish prices.

Share transfers are also difficult for non-financial reasons. Shareholders do not want other shareholders to be able to sell their shares to just anyone. They want some restrictions on share transfer so that they can control who becomes involved in the business as a shareholder. At the same time, all shareholders want minimal restrictions on their ability to sell their own shares.

It is common to deal with share transfers in a shareholders' agreement by prohibiting transfers except in accordance with specified procedures. Often transfers are permitted upon compliance with a **right of first refusal**. If Ellen wanted to sell her shares, a right of first refusal would require her to offer them first to Phillipe at a price set by her. Phillipe would then have a limited time to purchase her shares. If Phillipe does not purchase her shares, Ellen may offer them for sale to someone else at the same price for a limited time. The requirement to sell at the *same price* discourages Ellen from setting an unreasonably high price for her shares in the first place.

> **right of first refusal** is the right for shareholders to be offered shares that one shareholder wants to sell first before they are offered to non-shareholders

A shareholder agreement may also contain a *shotgun buy-sell* provision. A **shotgun buy-sell** is a share transfer mechanism that forces one shareholder to buy out the other. If Ellen offers all of her shares to Phillipe at a price she specifies, Phillipe must then either (i) buy all of Ellen's shares, or (ii) sell all of his

> a **shotgun buy-sell** is a share transfer mechanism that forces one shareholder to buy out the other

---

12. *Eg ABCA*, s 146; *CBCA*, s 146; *OBCA*, s 108. There are many unresolved issues with respect to how a corporation that is subject to a unanimous shareholders' agreement will function. For example, does it still need to have directors if the shareholders have removed all of their powers and liabilities?

shares to her at that price. Either way, one of them ends up with all the shares in the corporation. This drastic mechanism can be used to break a deadlock between shareholders.

Shareholder Remedies

Corporate statutes provide shareholders with a variety of remedies in situations where their interests have been injured by acts of the corporation or its directors.

DERIVATIVE ACTION

a **derivative action** is an action by a shareholder on behalf of a corporation to seek relief for a wrong done to the corporation

The value of shareholders' investment will be reduced if the corporation suffers a loss. For this reason, shareholders may seek a court's permission to pursue relief on the corporation's behalf for breach of fiduciary duty or any other wrong done to the corporation if the directors fail to do so. In practice, the directors may not act if the wrong is a breach of duty by the directors themselves. The action commenced by a shareholder on behalf of the corporation is called a **derivative action** and any damages or other relief goes to the corporation. A derivative action is one way for shareholders to ensure that directors and officers comply with their duties to the corporation.[13]

RELIEF FROM OPPRESSION

the **oppression remedy** allows a shareholder to claim relief from an act or omission by the corporation or its directors that oppresses or unfairly disregards or prejudices the interests of the shareholder

When actions or omissions by the corporation or the directors have oppressed or unfairly disregarded or prejudiced their interests, shareholders may claim relief under the **oppression remedy**.[14] Relief from oppression is obtained by shareholders directly. The courts have interpreted their authority to provide relief broadly. In fact, the oppression remedy is one of the most flexible and effective shareholder remedies in the world. The courts have said that relief is available when the *reasonable expectations* of shareholders about management behaviour have not been met. Relief can include anything the court decides is necessary to remedy the problem, including ordering the corporation to buy the oppressed shareholder's shares and orders against other shareholders. These are examples of behaviour that the courts have found oppressive:[15]

- approval of a transaction lacking a valid corporate purpose that is prejudicial to a particular shareholder
- failure by the corporation and its controlling shareholder to ensure that a transaction between them was on terms that were comparable to the terms that would have been negotiated by parties who were not related to each other
- actions that benefit the majority shareholder to the exclusion or the detriment of minority shareholders

---

[13.] *Eg CBCA*, s 239; *OBCA*, s 246; *NBBCA*, s 164.

[14.] *Eg BCBCA*, s 227; *CBCA*, s 241; *NBBCA*, s 166. Creditors and anyone else may seek permission from a court to bring an oppression action.

[15.] *Arthur v Signum Communications Ltd* [1991] OJ No 86 (Gen Div), aff'd [1993] OJ No 1928 (Div Ct); *Ford Motor Co. of Canada v Ontario Municipal Employees Retirement Board* [2006] OJ No 27 (CA).

- lack of adequate and appropriate disclosure of information to minority shareholders
- planning to eliminate minority shareholders[16]

OTHER SHAREHOLDER REMEDIES

Shareholders may seek other remedies, such as a court order that directs compliance with the governing statute or the rectification of corporate records that contain errors. On an application by a shareholder, a court may even direct that the assets of the corporation be sold, its creditors paid off, any remaining money distributed to the shareholders, and, finally, the corporation's existence terminated. This extreme remedy is called **liquidation and dissolution**, or **winding up**. It may be ordered when it is "just and equitable" to end the corporation's existence. For example, a court may order the winding up of a corporation with two equal shareholders who cannot agree on how the corporation should carry on business.[17]

Another remedy is available for a shareholder who disagrees when at least two-thirds of shareholders approve certain fundamental changes to the corporation, such as specific major amendments to the articles, and the sale of all, or substantially all, the assets of a corporation outside of the ordinary course of business. Shareholders who vote against such changes are entitled to have their shares bought by the corporation for their fair value.[18] This **dissent and appraisal right** allows a change approved by most shareholders to go ahead, while permitting those who strongly disagree to exit the corporation.

under a **liquidation and dissolution**, or **winding up**, the corporation's assets are sold, its creditors paid off, any remaining money distributed to the shareholders, and the corporation's existence terminated

the **dissent and appraisal right** entitles shareholders who dissent from certain fundamental changes to have the corporation buy their shares

How Directors and Officers Exercise Power

L.O. ❸❹❺

DIRECTORS

Under the *CBCA*, the first directors of a corporation are those named in the articles of incorporation. These directors hold office until the first meeting of shareholders, which must be held within 18 months of incorporation.[19] At that meeting and others at which an election is required, shareholders must, by simple majority vote, elect directors. Some corporate statutes impose Canadian residency requirements for some proportion of directors. Under the *CBCA*, it is 25 percent for most corporations.[20]

Directors exercise their power collectively, primarily at meetings, with each director getting one vote. However, a written resolution signed by all directors is as effective as a resolution passed at a meeting. In public corporations, a significant amount of work is done by committees of the board. Typical committees include an audit committee to supervise financial reporting by the corporation and manage the relationship with the corporation's auditors, and a committee to make recommendations to the full board regarding officer

PART 6

[16.] Relief from oppression and other shareholder remedies may be pursued as class actions in some cases. Class actions were discussed in Chapter 2.

[17.] Liquidation and dissolution may be ordered in other circumstances: *Eg CBCA*, ss 213–214; *OBCA*, s 207.

[18.] *Eg BCBCA*, ss 237–247; *CBCA*, s 190; *NBBCA*, s 131; *NLCA*, ss 300, 301. The specific events triggering the dissent and appraisal right are listed in the applicable statute.

[19.] *CBCA*, s 133. Similar rules apply under provincial statutes: *eg OBCA*, s 119.

[20.] *CBCA*, s 105(3). Similar rules apply in provinces with statutes modelled on the *CBCA*.

compensation. As well, while directors may be actively engaged in management in private corporations, in public corporations, management is delegated to the officers, with directors remaining responsible only for making high-level policy decisions and overseeing management. As Chapter 21 explained, the corporation's by-laws typically contain its rules for calling and conducting meetings, such as the required quorum and who is the chair. Corporate statutes provide some default rules if the corporation has not set its own.

OFFICERS

Nothing in Canadian corporate legislation addresses what officers a corporation should have or what they are to do. Most corporations have officers called the chief executive officer (CEO), president, and secretary. A common corporate structure gives the CEO overall responsibility for running the corporation's business, while the day-to-day operations are delegated to others who report to the CEO. A corporate secretary is usually a lawyer, employed by the corporation, who is a senior officer with extensive responsibility for compliance with a wide range of legal requirements, including corporate law obligations. Directors can be officers, but they need not be.

Corporate statutes give directors the power to designate offices, such as president, and to specify the duties of those offices. Usually this is done in a by-law passed by directors and approved by shareholders just after incorporation. After setting up the offices, the directors appoint people to fill them. Directors can delegate any of their powers to one or more officers, except for certain key powers relating to the internal management of the corporation. Issuing shares, declaring dividends on shares, and repurchasing the shares of the corporation are functions that cannot be delegated.[21]

L.O. ❻

Management's Duties to the Corporation
FIDUCIARY DUTY

the **fiduciary duty** is the duty of officers and directors to act honestly and in good faith with a view to the best interests of the corporation

The **fiduciary duty** is the most important legal standard of behaviour for officers and directors. Section 122(1)(a) of the *CBCA* defines this duty:

> Each director and officer in exercising his powers and discharging his duties shall . . . act honestly and in good faith with a view to the best interests of the corporation.

What the fiduciary duty requires in specific situations can be elusive. The duty to act honestly is straightforward: directors and officers cannot defraud the corporation, such as by stealing corporate assets. Beyond acting honestly, directors and officers must try to do what is best for the corporation and must not put their personal interests ahead of the interests of the corporation.

The fiduciary duty is owed to the corporation, not to the shareholders or to employees, customers, suppliers, creditors, the public, or any other corporate stakeholder. It is often difficult, however, to define what the interests of the corporation are. For example, is it in the corporation's best interests to pay high wages or to keep wages as low as possible? While high wages may lead to happy, productive workers, it may reduce cash flow available to pay

---

[21.] *Eg ABCA*, s 115(3); *CBCA*, s 115(3); *OBCA*, s 127(3).

off creditors. Does the obligation of management to act in the best interests of the corporation require it to try to accommodate the divergent interests of employees and creditors?

In the past, Canadian courts often treated the interests of the corporation as defined by the interests of shareholders: Whatever maximized the value of shareholders' investment in the corporation's shares was regarded as being in the best interests of the corporation. Recently, the Supreme Court of Canada rejected this view. The court said, "it may be legitimate, given all the circumstances, to consider . . . the interests of shareholders, employees, suppliers, creditors, consumers, governments and the environment" in determining the best interests of the corporation.[22] In resolving any conflicts between the interests of stakeholders, the court said that directors' duty requires them to treat all stakeholders fairly and "to act in the best interests of the corporation, viewed as a good corporate citizen."

The fiduciary duty's main purpose is to prevent directors and officers from benefitting themselves when their personal interests and their duty to the corporation conflict. It protects the investment of shareholders in the corporation by prohibiting directors and officers from favouring their interests at the corporation's expense. We will discuss the most common situations in which such conflicts may arise and the strategies that can be used by directors and officers to avoid breaching their duty.

Transacting with the Corporation

A conflict of interest arises when a director or officer contracts with the corporation. Suppose you have an opportunity to sell goods to a corporation of which you are a director. If, as a director, you are responsible for negotiating the contract on behalf of the corporation, you have a serious conflict of interest. Your duty binds you to do whatever is in your power to get the lowest price for the corporation. At the same time, your personal interest is in selling for the highest price. Even if you are not directly involved in the negotiations on behalf of the corporation, as a director, you may be in a position to influence the corporation's decision making either directly, as a member of the board if the contract must be approved by the board, or indirectly, by virtue of your relationship with the corporation and its personnel. A conflict still exists and may result in an unfavourable transaction for the corporation.

Historically, because of the inevitable conflict between duty and personal interest, a fiduciary was prohibited from participating personally in any transaction with the corporation. This creates a practical problem where the best price or the only source of supply is a director or officer or a business related to a director or officer. This problem often arises in transactions between corporations with common ownership that do business with each other. Imagine that there are two corporations under common ownership and one supplies the raw materials that the other uses in its manufacturing business. This may be a good arrangement for each corporation, but if one person is a director of both, that person has a conflict of interest and transactions between them would be a breach of that person's fiduciary duty.

The solution to this problem in the *CBCA* and most other Canadian statutes is to permit a transaction between the corporation and a director or officer (or a business related to them) *if procedural safeguards are observed*. The director or officer must give adequate notice of their interest to the board and may not vote

---

22. *BCE Inc v 1976 Debentureholders* [2008] 3 SCR 560, citing *Peoples Department Stores (Trustee of) v Wise*, [2004] 3 SCR 461.

on the approval of the contract by the board of directors. As well, the contract must be fair and reasonable to the corporation. In practice, notice regarding the interest should be recorded in the minutes of the board meeting at which the contract is approved. Compliance with these requirements is the only way to avoid a fiduciary breach. If this scheme is not complied with, the corporation may refuse to complete the transaction.[23]

Taking Corporate Opportunities

A conflict between personal interest and fiduciary duty arises when a fiduciary considers taking advantage of some project or opportunity in which the corporation has an interest. This situation arises frequently because a principal task of management is to choose the projects the corporation should invest in, such as acquiring an asset, establishing a business, or signing a contract. If fiduciaries were permitted to invest personally in projects being considered by the corporation, there is a risk that they would take for themselves valuable investment opportunities that they should have tried to obtain for the corporation. The fiduciary duty prohibits fiduciaries from taking an opportunity belonging to the corporation. If they breach their duty, any personal profit from the opportunity must be paid over to the corporation. This obligation to account for profits is intended to eliminate any incentive for the fiduciary to take the opportunity in the first place.

Whether a breach of fiduciary duty will be found in any case depends upon several factors. In addition to those cited in *Canadian Air Services* (see Case Brief 22.1), the courts have said that these factors indicate that an opportunity belongs to the corporation:

- **Significance of opportunity:** The opportunity would have represented a major component of the corporation's business if acquired or was a unique opportunity rather than merely one of many considered by the corporation.

Case Brief 22.1

Canadian Air Services Ltd v O'Malley (1974) 40 DLR (3d) 371 (SCC)

Canadian Air Services Ltd (Canaero) was in the business of mapping and geographic exploration. O'Malley, the president, was given responsibility for obtaining a contract to map Guyana. After working on this project for some time, he resigned from Canaero and incorporated his own business, Terra Surveys Ltd, to perform work similar to what he was doing for Canaero. The government of Guyana asked for bids to map the country and accepted Terra's bid over Canaero's. Canaero sued O'Malley, alleging that he had breached his fiduciary duty to Canaero by taking the benefit of an opportunity belonging to the corporation.

The Supreme Court of Canada held that O'Malley did breach his duty. The court cited several factors that showed that the opportunity to map Guyana belonged to Canaero.

- **Specific nature of opportunity:** It was an opportunity that the corporation had been actively pursuing, rather than one that was simply in the same general area as the corporation's business. Although the ultimate contract was different in some respects, it was substantially the same opportunity that Canaero had been working on through O'Malley.

- **Maturity of opportunity:** It was also a mature opportunity in the sense that Canaero had done extensive work in preparing for it.

The court also decided that O'Malley's close relationship to the opportunity while at Canaero supported a conclusion that he should be prohibited from taking it. O'Malley learned about the opportunity through his position, did the preparatory work relating to the opportunity as an officer of Canaero, and negotiated for it on behalf of the corporation.

[23] *Eg CBCA*, s 120; *OBCA*, s 132.

- **Private opportunity:** The opportunity was not publicly advertised or otherwise widely known, but was one to which the fiduciary had access only by virtue of the fiduciary's position in the corporation.

- **No rejection:** The opportunity had not been rejected by the corporation before the fiduciary acquired it.[24]

Competition by Directors and Officers with the Corporation

In general, it is not a breach of fiduciary duty to terminate one's relationship with a corporation and go into competition with it. Otherwise, the fiduciary duty might become an unreasonable restraint on a person's ability to earn a living. However, a fiduciary may not compete with the corporation while remaining in a fiduciary relationship with it. As Case Brief 22.1 showed, if you are a fiduciary, you cannot quit to take an opportunity that you developed while working for the corporation. Using a corporation's confidential information for personal gain would also be a breach of the fiduciary duty. Any competing fiduciary will be forced to pay over all profits from the competing business to the corporation.[25]

DUTY OF CARE

The second important legal standard of behaviour for management is the **duty of care**, which the *CBCA* defines in these terms:[26]

> Every director and officer of a corporation in exercising his powers and discharging his duties shall . . . exercise the care, diligence and skill that a reasonably prudent person would exercise in comparable circumstances.[27]

The degree of care required by this standard depends upon the facts of each case. In all cases, however, directors must have at least a basic understanding of the business. A director who does not have this minimal level of understanding should acquire it or resign.[28]

In addition to a basic level of competence, the duty of care requires some monitoring of the business by directors. The duty does not require a detailed inspection of the daily activities of the corporation, but directors must keep informed about the corporation's policies and its business, and regularly attend board meetings.

The reference to a person "in comparable circumstances" means that the duty has a subjective element. If you have significant knowledge or experience, you have to meet a higher standard of care.[29] The standard of care also depends

the **duty of care** requires every director and officer to exercise the care, diligence, and skill that a reasonably prudent person would exercise in comparable circumstances

---

[24.] *Peso Silver Mines Ltd v Cropper* (1965) 56 DLR (2d) 117 (BC CA), aff'd 58 DLR (2d) 1 (SCC). In this case, a rejection by the board of an opportunity was held to be sufficient to allow a board member to take the opportunity himself.

[25.] *Bendix Home Systems Ltd v Clayton* (1977) 33 CPR (2d) 230 (Ont HCJ); *Taylor v. Oakes* [2001] 2 BCLC 749 (Ch Div).

[26.] *CBCA*, s 122(1)(b). Provincial statutes, other than those in Nova Scotia and Prince Edward Island, also impose a duty of care: *eg BCBCA*, s 142(1)(b) and *OBCA*, s 134(1)(b).

[27.] In Chapter 6, we discussed the duty of care (and a standard of care) that applies under the tort of negligence.

[28.] *Peoples Department Stores (Trustee of) v Wise* (2004) 244 DLR (4th) 564 (SCC).

[29.] *Re Standard Trustco Ltd* (1992) 6 BLR (2d) 241 (Ont SC).

upon a person's position. For example, all public corporations must have an audit committee to review their financial statements and their financial reporting process. Directors who serve on this committee have more opportunity to examine the financial affairs of the corporation than other directors. Therefore, more is expected of them in terms of monitoring these affairs and warning other directors about problems.

Not being involved in some aspect of the corporation's business, however, does not relieve directors of their duty altogether. For example, one director, say, a chartered accountant who is also the chief financial officer, may be responsible for dealing with the financial side of a corporation's business. However, the other directors are still required to comply with a standard of care in relation to financial matters. If another director learns that the corporation failed to properly withhold income tax from employee wage payments and remit the tax to the Canada Revenue Agency, that director must do everything reasonably possible to ensure that the corporation puts in place procedures to prevent a recurrence. This might include requesting a board meeting to discuss the problem, inquiring into the problem, designing a solution, and monitoring to ensure that the solution is put into effect.[30]

The courts have been reluctant to find a breach of the duty of care when this involves second-guessing management on issues of general business judgment, such as whether a particular deal was the best one for the corporation. They have acknowledged their lack of business expertise and that it is unfair for them to evaluate business decisions when they have the benefit of hindsight. Courts often say that they do not want to set the standard for the duty of care so high that it inhibits business people from doing their jobs or discourages people from becoming directors and officers at all. As a result, business decisions are not a breach of duty as long as they fall within the range of reasonable alternatives that were available in the circumstances. For this rule to apply, the process for making the decision must also be reasonable. For example, managers must ensure that decisions are based upon adequate information and advice. The approach taken by courts to business decisions is sometimes referred to as the **business judgment rule**.[31]

PROTECTION FOR CREDITORS

Directors and officers do not have a duty to creditors of the corporation. For the most part, creditors are left to protect themselves by contract. Chapter 23 describes risk management strategies for creditors. Some recent cases have held, however, that the duty of care and the fiduciary duty may provide some protection to creditors.[32] There are also specific corporate law provisions that benefit creditors, such as rules that try to ensure that the corporation's money and assets are not distributed to shareholders, directors, officers, or employees if that would threaten the corporation's ability to pay its creditors. For example, directors cannot authorize either the payment of a dividend to a shareholder or the corporation's purchase of a shareholder's shares unless there are reasonable grounds for believing that the corporation could pay its liabilities to its

the **business judgment rule** is a rule that courts should defer to the business decisions of directors and officers where they acted reasonably and the decision was within the range of reasonably available alternatives

---

30. *Fraser v MNR* [1987] DTC 250 (TCC).

31. The business judgment rule was endorsed by the Supreme Court of Canada in *BCE Inc v 1976 Debentureholders* [2008] 3 SCR 560.

32. *Peoples Department Stores (Trustee of) v Wise* (2004) 244 DLR (4th) 564 (SCC) and *BCE Inc v 1976 Debentureholders* [2008] 3 SCR 560. As noted above, in a few cases, such as the *BCE* case, creditors have been permitted to seek relief from oppression by using the corporate law remedy.

creditors as they become due, and that some other financial tests have been satisfied.[33] Directors are personally liable to the corporation if they authorize such payments where these tests are not met. Even though the main purpose of these provisions is to protect creditors, they are not enforceable directly by creditors. The directors' obligation not to authorize payments if the tests are not met, and to compensate the corporation if they do, is owed to the corporation. Only the corporation can enforce those obligations.

Other Sources of Personal Liability for Directors and Officers

Directors and officers are subject to a wide range of other potential liabilities in connection with corporate activity. Governments have imposed personal liability on directors and officers, including fines and imprisonment, as a way of encouraging their corporations to comply with laws relating to income tax remittance, environmental protection, and other regulatory objectives.[34] Some of these laws are discussed in Chapter 25. Furthermore, directors and officers are increasingly being held personally responsible for torts, such as the tort of inducing a breach of contract by their corporations, which are discussed in Chapter 5.

Managing Liability Risk for Directors and Officers

L.O. ❼

Exposure to all the sources of liability discussed above creates a strong disincentive to becoming a director or officer of a corporation. Corporate statutes provide some defences that may be relied upon to manage risk. Especially in large corporations, officers and directors must rely on the advice of experts. Directors and officers are not liable for breach of their duty of care or some other duties under the statute if they reasonably rely on financial statements or reports of lawyers, accountants, and other professionals.[35] As well, to offset liability risks, a corporation can reimburse directors and officers for any expenses that they *reasonably* incur in connection with the defence of any civil, criminal, administrative, or investigative proceeding that is connected to their position with the corporation. This reimbursement, called an **indemnity**, is mandatory if the directors or officers:

indemnity is compensation paid by a corporation to a director or officer for costs incurred in connection with performing their duties

- were not found to have committed any fault
- complied with their fiduciary duty
- had reasonable grounds for believing their conduct was lawful[36]

Even when a director or officer is found to have committed a fault, a corporation may still decide to provide indemnification if the other two criteria

---

33. *Eg CBCA*, ss 34–36, 42, 118; *OBCA*, ss 30–32, 38, 130.

34. *Eg Income Tax Act*, RSC 1985, c 1 (5th Supp) (Can), s 227.1; *Canadian Environmental Protection Act*, SC 1999 c 33 (Can), s 280; *Environmental Protection Act*, RSO 1990, c E.19 (Ont), s 194; *Employment Standards Act, 2000*, SO 2000, c 41 (Ont), Part XX.

35. *Eg BCBCA*, s 157; *CBCA*, s 123(4); *ABCA*, s 123(3). This defence is not expressly provided for under the *NLCA*.

36. *Eg ABCA*, s 124; *CBCA*, s 124; *OBCA*, s 136.

You Be the Judge 22.1

Consolidated Enfield Corporation v Blair (1995) 128 DLR (4th) 73 (SCC)

Blair was the president and a director of Consolidated Enfield Corporation. At Enfield's annual meeting, a slate of nominees proposed by management, and including Blair, stood for election. Canadian Express Ltd, a major shareholder, nominated a candidate for director to replace Blair. Canadian Express had enough votes to ensure that its candidate would be elected. After the votes on the election of directors were cast, the corporation's lawyers advised Blair that he, as chair, had to make a ruling on the results of the vote, even though his own election was at stake, and that the votes cast by Canadian Express against Blair were invalid. He took the advice and ruled (i) that the votes cast for the Canadian

Express nominee were invalid, and (ii) that the management slate was elected. In subsequent legal proceedings, a court ruled that the votes cast in favour of the Canadian Express nominee were valid, and so Blair had not been re-elected. Blair claimed indemnification from Enfield for his legal costs in connection with these proceedings.

Questions for Discussion

1. Should Blair be entitled to indemnification in these circumstances?

2. What arguments may be made for and against indemnification?

are met. Indemnification may include amounts not directly relating to the defence, such as money paid to settle an action or satisfy a judgment. You Be the Judge 22.1 asks you to apply these rules regarding indemnification.

Indemnification commitments are only as good as the ability of the indemnifier to pay. If there is a risk that an indemnifying corporation may not have enough money to pay, a director or officer may seek a guarantee, perhaps from a shareholder, to provide greater security. It has become common for directors and officers to ask their corporations to pay for insurance to compensate them if they are held liable. Corporations are permitted to obtain such insurance covering any liability. None of the restrictions on the availability of indemnities apply to insurance. Insurance policies, however, have their own limitations imposed by insurers, and insurance is expensive.

Ethical Perspective 22.1 asks you to think about when a corporation should pay an indemnity. Business Decision 22.1 requires you to consider what protection an indemnity provides and what other strategies you could use as a director to protect yourself.

Ethical Perspective 22.1

Indemnification for Liabilities under Regulatory Statutes

Governments have tried to strengthen environmental and other regulatory schemes by imposing liability on directors and officers. This has raised questions about when indemnification and insurance to cover these liabilities should be available. On the one hand, with the range and seriousness of potential liability increasing, indemnities and insurance become more important as a way of ensuring that competent people are willing to become officers and directors. On the other hand, the intended effect of imposing liability on directors and officers is to discourage businesses from acting illegally. If directors and officers are insulated from this liability by

indemnification and insurance, the effectiveness of the legislative scheme is reduced.

Question for Discussion

1. In one case, several officers were convicted of the offence of failing to take all reasonable care to prevent the corporation from permitting the unlawful discharge of wastes. The judge ordered the officers to pay fines.[37] Should the corporation indemnify the officers by paying their fines for them?

[37.] *R v Bata Industries* (1992), 9 OR (3d) 329 (1995), aff'd 127 DLR (4th) 438 (CA).

Business Decision 22.1

Joining a Board of Directors

You run an environmental consulting business, and your major client is Medex Inc, which has carried on a business of collecting and disposing of medical waste since 2000. Jamal is the majority shareholder, CEO, and chair of the board of directors of Medex. He has asked you to join the board as its fifth member and to go on the environmental compliance committee, which the board intends to set up.

Questions for Discussion

1. What concerns would you have about accepting this offer?

2. What strategies could you adopt to minimize these risks?

Concept Summary 22.1 identifies sources of corporate liability and strategies for risk management.

Concept Summary 22.1

Director and Officer Liability and Risk Management

Sources of Personal Liability for Directors and Officers	Strategies Available to Manage Liability Risk
General standards of behaviour • fiduciary duty • duty of care • oppression remedy	Diligence • regularly attending board meetings • keeping informed and acting when put on notice of problems • conducting a risk assessment • establishing compliance policy and monitoring systems, including timely reporting and education • seeking advice • being sensitive to conflicts of interest • following corporate law procedures in connection with any transaction in which a director or officer has a personal interest
Examples of specific liability risks • environmental offences and liability under other statutes • failure to remit employee withholdings of income tax • authorizing dividends and share buy-backs when solvency and other financial tests not met	
	Indemnification
	Insurance
	Resignation

Securities Regulation

L.O. ❽

Some aspects of securities laws provide rules for corporate governance that supplement the corporate law rules discussed above. **Securities** include shares and a wide range of other kinds of claims issued by corporations and other business organizations. Each province has laws that regulate buying and selling securities within its territory.[38] The goals of securities regulation are to protect investors from unfair, improper, or fraudulent practices and to ensure that the markets in which securities are traded function fairly and efficiently. To

securities include shares and a wide range of other kinds of claims issued by corporations and other business organizations

PART 6

[38.] *Eg Securities Act*, RSO 1990, c S-5 (Ont); *Securities Act*, RSBC 1996, c 418 (BC).

achieve this goal, securities law imposes standards for the behaviour of managers of public corporations.[39]

For example, securities laws impose requirements regarding the disclosure that corporations must make. Before a corporation issues securities to the public, management of the corporation must prepare and make public an extensive disclosure document that describes the characteristics of the securities and the corporation's business. This document is called a **prospectus**. Once a corporation has issued shares to the public, management must also disclose to the public any **material change** to the corporation's business operations or capital, meaning a change that could significantly affect the value of its shares. These changes would include environmental problems that affect the corporation, such as a toxic waste spill. Other securities rules specify the disclosure that a corporation must make in connection with shareholder meetings. These securities rules substantially overlap corporate law rules. Both are intended to ensure that shareholders have adequate information to make an informed decision regarding the exercise of their voting rights and whether they should sell or continue to hold their shares.

Recently, securities law rules for corporate governance have expanded in all provinces. A few best practices for corporate governance are now mandatory, such as having an audit committee, responsible for overseeing the financial statement preparation and financial reporting process, the members of which are independent of management. Independent directors can monitor management behaviour more effectively. Other best practices, such as having a board with a majority of independent directors, are not mandatory, but corporations must disclose whether they have adopted the practice or explain why they have not.[40] Exemptions ensure that the burden of securities law requirements does not fall on small corporations with few shareholders.

> a **prospectus** is an extensive disclosure document that management of a corporation must prepare and make public before the corporation issues securities to the public that describes the characteristics of the securities and the corporation's business

> **material change** to the corporation's business operations or capital is a change that could significantly affect the value of its shares

L.O. ❾ # Corporate Governance in Practice

Corporations vary in size. At one extreme, a corporation may have only a single shareholder, who is also the sole director and officer. At the other, a large public corporation may have thousands of shareholders spread out around the world and more than 20 directors, some of whom work as managers in the corporation. The operation of the legal rules for corporate governance varies significantly depending upon where a corporation is on this continuum.

If one person is the sole shareholder, director, and officer, the allocation of rights and responsibilities contemplated in corporate statutes is a mere formality and generally irrelevant. Even if the sole shareholder elects other directors, it will be the shareholder who ultimately makes management decisions. If there are a few shareholders, usually they will also be the managers. The legal arrangements for management are likely to be set out in a shareholders' agreement and may be quite different from what the corporate statute provides.

As the number of shareholders increases, not all of them will be involved in management. In such a situation, it is often said that the managers act as

---

[39.] Securities laws also deal with the licensing of securities market participants, such as stockbrokers, and impose liability on insiders of corporations and others who trade in their corporation's securities by using information that has not been publicly disclosed. See JA VanDuzer, *The Law of Partnerships and Corporations*, 3d ed (2009), c 12.

[40.] National Instrument 52–110 (Audit Committees); National Instrument 58–101 (Disclosure of Corporate Governance Policies); and National Policy 58–201 (Corporate Governance Guidelines).

agents of the shareholders in managing the corporation. The relationship of managers to shareholders is not the same kind of agency that is discussed in Chapter 20. Unlike most agents, a manager in a corporation does not have the power to make commitments on behalf of shareholders or to represent them. But a manager in a corporation does act like an agent of the shareholders in some ways. Where shareholders do not manage the business of the corporation themselves, managers do so on their behalf.

This separation between shareholders and management gives rise to what are sometimes referred to as "agency costs." There are two kinds of agency costs:

- **Costs caused by management misbehaviour:** Managers may be tempted to act in ways that benefit themselves at the expense of the corporation, such as by paying themselves excessive salaries. The reduction in share value that such actions cause will affect management if they are shareholders. But any loss experienced by management will be much less than the benefit they receive because the loss in share value resulting from their actions is spread amongst all shareholders. For example, imagine that a manager pays herself an excessive bonus of $100 000. She receives 100 percent of the benefit (the full $100 000), but her loss as a shareholder is limited. The value of all shares are reduced by $100 000 because the residual value of the corporation is $100 000 less after the bonus is paid. The manager's share in that loss is limited to that proportion of the loss that her shares represent out of the total of all shares that have been issued by the corporation. If she has 10 percent of the shares, she suffers 10 percent of the reduction in share value resulting from the excessive bonus payment.

- **Costs associated with monitoring management and seeking legal remedies for misbehaviour:** To reduce the risk of management misbehaviour, shareholders may spend time and money trying to detect misbehaviour with a view to discouraging such behaviour and seeking relief when it occurs through the shareholder remedies discussed above.

The legal standards imposed on directors and officers by the fiduciary duty, duty of care, and oppression remedy are intended to reduce these agency costs. These standards prohibit management misbehaviour, and corporate law provides ways to seek relief when the standards are breached. Shareholder power to elect directors and vote on management proposals can also be used to keep management accountable.

As the size of a corporation grows, however, the effectiveness of these legal rules diminishes. In a large corporation, shareholders are at a disadvantage partly because they do not have enough information to understand and evaluate management's performance. Even if some are willing and able to gather sufficient information and analyze it, they may find it difficult and expensive to mobilize other shareholders, who are spread around the country or the world, to take action. The relatively small financial stake of most individual shareholders will discourage them from incurring these costs. In practice, shareholders rarely work together to vote against proposals made by management or to pursue shareholder remedies through litigation. As a result, shareholders' legal rights may not be very useful.

Another problem with the legal corporate governance scheme is that it is designed to ensure only that the *board of directors* is accountable to shareholders. Little attention is paid to the accountability of *officers*, who run corporations in practice. In large public corporations, the board of directors has tended to be dominated by the full-time professional managers of the corporation.

Recent securities law reforms to the rules for corporate governance in both Canada and the United States are designed to improve the accountability of management to shareholders by improving the effectiveness of board oversight of management. Requirements for independent directors are one example. As discussed in the previous section, in Canada, some best practices for corporate governance are now mandatory. Others are voluntary, but corporations must disclose to what extent they comply and explain any non-compliance. Some of these new requirements are backed up by criminal penalties.[41]

Securities law reforms that encourage management accountability to shareholders raise an important question: What effect will they have on the willingness of management to take into account the interests of others affected by a corporation's activities, such as creditors, employees, the local community, and society generally? In the next section, we discuss management's responsibility to address these interests.

L.O. ⑩ Corporate Social Responsibility

Canadian corporations have an enormous and multi-dimensional impact on society in Canada and abroad. Decisions taken by management on a day-to-day basis affect not only the profitability of the corporation and the value of shareholder investments, but also (i) the stakes of others with financial claims against the corporation, including employees, creditors, customers, and suppliers, (ii) the interests of the community in which the corporation operates, including the quality of the local environment, and (iii) in some cases, society at large. All those with a stake in what a corporation does have a common interest in the financial success of the corporation, measured by the value of its shares. Often, maximizing shareholder value, at least in the long run, will have the effect of increasing the security of the claims that creditors, employees, suppliers, and customers have against the corporation. This is because maximizing shareholder value means maximizing the assets of the corporation above what is required to pay those claims. In most situations, maximizing this surplus makes it more likely that all stakeholder claims will be paid. As well, the community in which a corporation operates benefits from the direct employment that a successful corporation generates and economic benefits associated with local spending by employees. Some studies also show that corporate behaviour that is designed to achieve a social purpose, such as improved environmental protection, can be profitable for corporations and their shareholders in some situations.[42]

Sometimes, however, the value of the shareholders' investment in the business of the corporation may be maximized only at the expense of other stakeholder interests. Shutting down a money-losing plant to preserve corporate profitability is one example. The laid-off workers and the community in which they live may suffer greatly from such a decision, which is designed to safeguard shareholders' financial interests. Seeking to maximize profits by scrimping on pollution-control technology is another example of management imposing a cost on society for the benefit of shareholders.

[41.] More details regarding recent changes to corporate governance rules can be found on MyBusLawLab on the Updates and Other Resources page.

[42.] M Kerr, P Janda & C Pitts, *Corporate Social Responsibility: A Legal Analysis* (2009) at 32–45.

We try to prevent some kinds of adverse social effects by direct regulation. Regulation has inherent limits, however. No regulatory scheme responds comprehensively and perfectly to all the possible harms caused by corporations. As well, there is always a gap between standards set and their enforcement. Where Canadian corporations operate abroad there are a variety of additional challenges with respect to regulation of their activities. Canada has been reluctant to legislate standards that have an effect outside the country. One result of these imperfections in direct regulation is that it is commonplace to hear claims that corporations should take into account the effects of their actions on society beyond the specific requirements of regulations. Pursuing a commitment to environmental protection and sustainability as well as going beyond what the law requires to ensure that a corporation takes responsibility for the impact of its actions on the environment, consumers, employees, the local community, and other affected stakeholders is often referred to as **corporate social responsibility (CSR)**.

Of course, managers of corporations do take social interests into account. Some corporations have adopted ethical codes of conduct to guide their actions with a view to ensuring that they are sustainable. Typically these are not binding. In part, increased concern by management with the social impact of its decisions is being driven by market forces. Some institutional shareholders, such as a few pension funds and mutual funds, are adopting policies about what corporations to invest in that take into account the social impact of a corporation's activities. As well, consumers' preferences regarding the corporations that they buy from are increasingly influenced by their views regarding the sensitivity of corporate management to the social impact of the corporation's actions.

Legal rules for corporate governance play a small role in relation to CSR. As discussed above, to comply with their fiduciary duty to act in the best interests of the corporation, managers may take into account the interests of stakeholders other than shareholders. Ultimately, however, the extent to which management does take the social impact of its decisions into account and how they do so depends substantially upon the individual managers and their ethics. Ethical Perspective 22.2 asks you to think about another approach to using legal rules for corporate governance to encourage management to act in a socially responsible way.

corporate social responsibility (CSR) means pursuing a commitment to environmental protection and sustainability as well as going beyond what the law requires to ensure that a corporation takes responsibility for the impact of its actions on the environment, consumers, employees, the local community, and other affected stakeholders

PART 6

Ethical Perspective **22.2**

Mandatory CSR Reporting

It is easy to find examples of situations in which significant injuries to stakeholders as well as losses to the corporation could have been avoided if management had been more sensitive to the social impact of its decisions. In the late 1980s, a Canadian mining corporation, Placer Dome Inc, began operating a mine in the Philippines without having first contracted for an independent assessment of the social and environmental impact of its operations, even though such an assessment had been proposed by a minority shareholder. Within eight years, the mine was closed and several employees faced criminal charges relating to the disastrous environmental effects of the mine. If the corporation had done

a proper social and environmental impact assessment, it may have been able to avoid these problems.

It is challenging, however, to design appropriate legal rules that require management to take social impacts into account in its decision making. Rules cannot be just window dressing, but, at the same time, cannot be so burdensome that they distract management from focusing on the successful operation of the corporation's business. Many have suggested that the best approach would be to require corporations to disclose how they take into account the social consequences of their activities. That way management can do what it thinks best for its

(Continued)

(continued)

business, and shareholders and consumers can make choices with clear and consistent information regarding a corporation's social responsibility record. Because of the effects of these choices on the corporation's business, management would have a stronger incentive to manage in a way that is responsive to the views of the corporation's stakeholders.

In 2004, the Canadian Institute of Chartered Accountants published a report that clarified when the environmental and social effects of business activities should be considered material for financial reporting purposes under securities law, meaning that disclosure would be required by a corporation in its financial statements.[43] However, a 2008 study by the Ontario Securities Commission found that public company disclosure regarding the impact of climate change on their operations was inadequate. In 2010, the organization of Canadian securities commissions, the Canadian Securities Administrators, released a guide clarifying when public companies should disclose a change relating to environmental matters, such as a risk of an environmental liability.[44] Beginning in 2011, for financial years beginning after 1 January 2011, public companies are to disclose the following information in the management's discussion and analysis sections of their annual reports to shareholders:

- the financial and operational effects of environmental protection requirements on the capital expenditures, profit or loss, and competitive position of the company in the current financial year and the expected effect in future years

- any social or environmental policies that are fundamental to the company's operations, such as policies regarding the company's relationship with the environment or with the communities in which it does business, or human rights policies, including the steps the company has taken to implement them

- risk factors relating to the company and its business, such as, among other things, environmental and health risks[45]

Questions for Discussion

1. What are the likely costs and benefits of these steps that require reporting on CSR in Canada?

2. Are there other matters that should be disclosed?

Corporate Liability

The rules governing a corporation's liability for contracts, crimes, and torts determine how a corporation is legally affected by the behaviour of people acting on its behalf. These rules influence how the corporation organizes itself to participate in the marketplace. For example, the rules that determine when a corporation is liable in tort for acts of its employees determine how a corporation supervises employees in their interactions with customers to minimize the risk of liability. These rules also affect the risks for people dealing with the corporation because they define when the corporation will be held responsible for its behaviour with regard to them.

LIABILITY FOR CONTRACTS

an **agent** of a corporation is a person who is authorized to act on behalf of the corporation

actual authority is authority that is actually given to an agent by a corporation

A corporation becomes liable to perform contracts only as a result of actions by **agents**, who act on its behalf. Salespeople, purchasing clerks, directors, and officers may all be considered agents of the corporation for specific purposes. As discussed in Chapter 20, an agent can bind a corporation only if the corporation has given the agent one of these types of authority:

- **Actual authority:** The agent is actually authorized by the corporation to enter into the obligation in question.

[43] CICA, "Financial Reporting Disclosures about Social, Environmental and Ethical (SEE) Issues" (November 2004) at 11–12, <www.nrtee-trnee.com/eng/publications/capital-markets/cica-see-issues-eng.pdf> (accessed 24 April 2012); and Canadian Performance Reporting Board, "Building a Better MD&A - Climate Change Disclosures" (October 2008), <www.cica.ca/download.cfm?ci_id=35203&la_id=1&re_id=0> (accessed 24 April 2012).

[44] OSC Staff Notice 51-716 – Environmental Reporting (27 February 2008) and CSA Staff Notice 51-333 – Environmental Reporting Guidance (27 October 2010).

[45] National Instrument 51-102 – for financial years beginning on or after 1 January 2011.

■ **Apparent (or ostensible) authority:** The corporation represents that the agent has authority to bind the corporation to the obligation in question. For a third party to rely on apparent authority, the representation must have induced the third party to enter into the disputed contract with the corporation.[46]

the **apparent (or ostensible) authority** is created by a representation on behalf of the corporation that an agent has authority to bind the corporation

Many corporations are complex organizations that have various types of agents with different kinds of authority. Often it is difficult for people seeking to contract with a corporation to determine whether the individuals they are dealing with have authority to act on the corporation's behalf. Consequently, most corporate statutes prevent corporations from avoiding liability, by relying on internal corporate restrictions that affect the authority of the agent to bind the corporation or that require some procedure to be followed before a contract can be created. The result is that the risk of unauthorized conduct falls upon the corporation. The **indoor management rule** states that a corporation cannot rely on any provision in its articles or by-laws, or in any unanimous shareholder agreement, that creates a defect in the agent's authority to defeat a claim that the corporation is bound to a contract. As well, a corporation cannot claim that a person held out by a corporation as an officer, director, or agent has not been duly appointed or does not have the authority that a person in that position usually has in the business of the corporation.[47]

the **indoor management rule** states that a corporation cannot rely on any provision in its articles or by-laws, or in any unanimous shareholder agreement, that creates a defect in the agent's authority to defeat a contractual claim

A person cannot enforce a contract against a corporation, however, if that person knew that there was a defect in the agent's authority or if they should have known of that defect. Suppose you are a customer of a shoe manufacturer. The corporation's sales representative purports to sell you $1 000 000 worth of inventory. If you know that sales representatives are not allowed to enter into contracts for more than $500 000, the contract would be unenforceable.

LIABILITY FOR CRIMES

The consequences of imposing criminal liability on corporations are different from those of imposing criminal liability on individuals, because corporations have "no soul to damn; no body to kick."[48] Corporations will be concerned about the effect of a criminal conviction on their reputation, but the threat of a conviction may not deter them from misbehaving to the same extent as it would deter an individual. Also, criminal penalties are problematic. Imprisonment of the corporation itself (as distinct from its officers and directors) is impossible. If a fine is imposed on a corporation, its shareholders and all those with financial claims against the corporation, including employees, may suffer. Despite those distinctive characteristics of criminal punishment for corporations, they can be held criminally responsible. The practical issue is how to determine when a corporation has committed a crime.

There are three broad categories of offences, each with different rules about what is required for corporate liability:

■ **Absolute liability offences** occur when the accused engages in an act prohibited by law. Corporate liability arises when a person commits the prohibited act on behalf of the corporation. The acts of employees in the course of their employment will satisfy this test. If an employee drove a company truck that did not meet mandatory safety standards,

an **absolute liability offence** is committed by a corporation when a person acting on behalf of the corporation commits an act prohibited by law

---

46. *Freeman & Lockyer v Buckhurst Park Properties (Mangal) Ltd* [1964] 2 QB 480 (CA).

47. *Eg CBCA*, s 18; *OBCA*, s 19; *NBBCA*, s 15.

48. Lord Thurlow, quoted by G Williams *Criminal Law: The General Part* 2d ed (1961) at 856.

for example, and that was an absolute liability offence, the corporation would be held liable.

■ A **strict liability offence** also occurs when a person, acting on behalf of the corporation, commits an act prohibited by law. Unlike an absolute liability offence, however, the *defence of due diligence* is available for a strict liability offence. That means that liability does not arise if the accused acted reasonably in the circumstances. A corporation can rely on this defence if a person with responsibility for establishing corporate policy in the relevant area of the corporation's affairs used due diligence. That person is described as a **directing mind** of the corporation. The care exercised by that person is considered to be the care exercised by the corporation itself.[49] If a due diligence defence was available to the corporation in the trucking example above, and if the corporation's trucking manager had exercised the required level of care to ensure that the truck met the safety standards, likely the corporation would not be liable. Absolute and strict liability offences usually form part of a regulatory scheme, such as those protecting public health, safety, and the environment.

■ Most criminal offences, such as fraud, are committed only if the accused had some degree of knowledge or intention, referred to as ***mens rea*** (or "guilty mind"), when they performed the prohibited act. Under the traditional common law rules, a corporation may be liable under this category of offence if the person who had the *mens rea* to commit the crime was a directing mind of the corporation. The person who was the directing mind can be held *individually* responsible as well.

The *Criminal Code* has broadened the category of people whose actions can trigger corporate liability. The category now extends to any senior officer, meaning any person who either plays an important role in setting the corporation's policies or is responsible for managing an important aspect of the corporation's activities.[50]

A corporation may have many senior officers. Each person responsible for a discrete aspect of the corporation's business—whether that aspect is defined functionally, geographically, or otherwise—may incur criminal liability for the corporation. It is not only the president or the board of directors who may do so. In *Waterloo Mercury Sales*, liability was imposed on a corporation operating a car dealership because the used car sales manager had fraudulently caused odometers on used cars to be turned back.[51] In this case, the employee with *mens rea* had authority to *design and supervise* the performance of corporate policy relating to used cars. Before amendments to the *Criminal Code* in 2003, corporate liability was not triggered if the crime was committed by a person who had authority only to *carry out* policies that someone else in the corporation created.[52] As a result of the amendments, however, liability may be imposed even if the person who acted did not have authority to set policy in an area as long as they were responsible for management in that area.

The *Criminal Code* also provides that corporate liability can arise where the actions constituting the crime were innocently committed by employees or other lower-level representatives of the corporation, so long as a senior officer had the required guilty mind. If a senior officer directed employees to deal in

---

49. *R v Sault Ste Marie* (1978) 85 DLR (3d) 161 (SCC).

50. *An Act to Amend the Criminal Code (criminal liability of organizations)*, SC 2003, c 21 (Can), s 2.

51. *R v Waterloo Mercury Sales Ltd* (1974) 49 DLR (3d) 131 (Alta Dist Ct).

52. *R v Safety-Kleen Canada Inc* (1997) 145 DLR (4th) 276 (Ont CA).

Margin notes:

a **strict liability offence** is committed by a corporation when a person acting on behalf of the corporation commits an act prohibited by law unless a person who is a directing mind of the corporation acted reasonably in the circumstances to prevent the offence

a **directing mind** of a corporation is a person who has responsibility to establish corporate policy in the area in which the offence occurred

a ***mens rea*** offence arises upon the commission of an act prohibited by law by a person who had the degree of knowledge or intention required for the offence

stolen goods, the corporation would be liable, even though the employees had no knowledge that the goods were stolen. As well, a corporation can be held liable if a senior officer knew employees were going to commit a crime but failed to take all reasonable measures to stop them.[53]

Note that a corporation will not necessarily escape liability merely because it had a policy *against* the behaviour that constituted the crime. In *Waterloo Mercury Sales*, the dealership had a policy against turning back odometers. The court still imposed liability. The lesson is clear. In some situations, the best that a corporation can do by way of risk management is to adopt clear policies *and* hire responsible people to carry them out. Concept Summary 22.2 provides an overview of the rules regarding corporate criminal liability.

Concept Summary 22.2

Corporate Criminal Liability

Type of Offence	Requirements for Corporate Liability
Absolute liability	• person acting on behalf of the corporation commits prohibited act
Strict liability	• person acting on behalf of the corporation commits prohibited act
	• but subject to defence that person who is directing mind took reasonable steps to prevent offence
Mens rea	• person acting on behalf of the corporation commits prohibited act and
	• senior officer
	• had required intention or knowledge to commit offence, or
	• knew an employee would commit offence and failed to take all reasonable steps to prevent offence

LIABILITY IN TORT

A corporation may be liable in tort in two ways. It may be directly liable when a person who is a directing mind of the corporation has committed the tort. Alternatively, it may be vicariously liable for acts of employees in the course of their employment, as discussed in Chapter 3.

[53] *An Act to Amend the Criminal Code (criminal liability of organizations)*, SC 2003, c 21 (Can), s 22.2. The *Criminal Code* amendments expand the scope of corporate liability in other ways as well, and create rules for the liability of non-corporate forms of organizations, including partnerships.

Chapter Summary

Shareholders are the residual claimants to the assets of the corporation, but their only power is to vote for the election of directors, on proposals made to them, and on the appointment of an auditor. Corporate law requires that shareholders have access to certain information to allow them to monitor management and exercise their rights as shareholders. Shareholders may enter agreements to exercise their powers differently from what is provided in the governing corporate law and to create rules to govern share transfers. When shareholder agreements are unanimous, they may transfer some or all of the directors' powers and responsibilities to the shareholders. Shareholders have several remedies to seek relief from the actions of the corporation and management, including the oppression remedy.

Directors are responsible for managing the business of the corporation or supervising its management. Officers are appointed by the directors and exercise powers delegated to them. Directors and officers are subject to a fiduciary duty to act honestly and in the best interests of the corporation. Fiduciaries may not (i) be involved personally in transactions with the corporation (unless certain safeguards in the corporate statute are observed), (ii) personally take opportunities belonging to the corporation, or (iii) compete with the corporation. Directors and officers also have a duty to exercise the care, diligence, and skill that a reasonably prudent person would exercise in comparable circumstances. The business judgment rule means that directors and officers will be found to have complied with their duty if what they did falls within the range of reasonable alternatives that were available in the circumstances.

In general, creditors do not benefit from corporate law protections and must negotiate for protection in their contracts with the corporation. Some corporate law provisions limit the ability of corporations to distribute their assets to shareholders if that would prejudice creditors.

Directors and officers are subject to a wide range of statutory liabilities as well. They can manage their liability risk by relying on others in some circumstances. As well, they can obtain indemnification from the corporation and insurance coverage to provide compensation for costs that they incur in carrying out their duties.

Securities rules supplement corporate law rules for corporate governance. The main goals of securities law are to protect investors and ensure that securities markets function fairly and efficiently. Securities law imposes corporate governance requirements, including obligations regarding disclosure to shareholders, that go beyond corporate law to ensure that management is accountable to shareholders. The legal scheme for corporate governance under both corporate and securities law is less effective in public corporations because of the practical inability of shareholders to take advantage of legal accountability mechanisms. Corporate social responsibility (CSR) is an increasingly important consideration for managers, but, apart from (i) specific regulatory requirements, (ii) securities requirements regarding the disclosure of environmental and some other matters related to CSR, and (iii) permission to take stakeholder interests into account under the fiduciary duty, legal rules do not impose CSR requirements.

A corporation's responsibilities are defined, in part, by the legal rules that determine when it is liable for contracts and for crimes and torts. Corporations are liable for contracts made by persons with actual or apparent authority to contract on their behalf. A corporation is liable for crimes and torts committed by a person who is the directing mind of the corporation, and in some other circumstances.

MyBusLawLab   ADDITIONAL RESOURCES FOR CHAPTER 22

MyBusLawLab provides students with an assortment of tools to help enrich the learning experience, including a Study Plan with Pre- and Post-tests, mini-cases and assessments, and provincial content material, which provides links to relevant cases, legislation, and additional resources.

MyBusLawLab provides the following resources for Chapter 22:

- Business Decision 22.1W—Fiduciary Duties and Hostile Takeover Bids

Provincial Material

- **British Columbia:** British Columbia Environmental Legislation, Liability of Management, Liability of Shareholders, Shareholder Remedies, Derivative Actions, Corporate Dissolution, Oppression Remedy, Due Diligence Defence and Limited Liability
- **Alberta:** Shareholders' Remedies, Oppression Remedy
- **Manitoba and Saskatchewan:** Directors, Environmental Liability, Personal Liabilities of Directors and Officers, Corporate Internal Liability, Securities Commission, Shareholders
- **Ontario:** Business Judgment Rule, Conflict of Interest, Corporate Governance, Corporate Social Responsibility, Directors' and Officers' Duties, Directors' Liability, Directors' and Officers' Liability, Disclosure, Environmental Protection Legislation, Fiduciary Duty, Legislation Imposing Directors' Liability, Prospectus, Insider Trading, Oppression Remedy, *Sarbanes-Oxley Act*, Secondary Market Liability, Codes of Conduct, Toronto Stock Exchange
- **Atlantic Provinces:** Business Corporation Legislation, Derivative Actions and the Oppression Remedy, Directors' Liability, Environmental Legislation, Securities Commissions

Review Questions

1. Describe the differences between the roles played by shareholders, directors, and officers in a corporation.

2. How does corporate law try to facilitate shareholders' exercise of their rights?

3. Assume a corporation had two shareholders holding 10 percent and 90 percent of the corporation's shares. Both shareholders want an equal say in any major decision about the corporation's business. Do these shareholders need a shareholders' agreement? If so, what would be its main provisions?

4. What is a "shotgun buy-sell"?

5. Why is the oppression remedy more useful to shareholders than the derivative action?

6. You own 20 percent of the shares of Ermine Inc and Adam owns the remaining 80 percent. Adam is the sole director and runs the business on a day-to-day basis while you are a passive investor. If Adam has not sent you financial statements or held a shareholders' meeting for three years, what could you do?

7. How does a corporation get its first directors? Its next directors?

8. Are there restrictions on the directors' ability to delegate management responsibility to officers?

9. "The fiduciary duty of directors and officers is owed to the corporation." Explain that statement.

10. Is a director of a corporation allowed to be involved personally in a transaction with the corporation? If so, when?

11. Joelle is a director of Gold Assets Corp, a gold mining company. At a board meeting, Joelle hears about a mining claim that a prospector wants to sell to Gold Assets Corp. The board is presented with many such offers each year and decides not to buy the prospector's claim. Can Joelle buy it?

12. What is the significance of a person's position and personal characteristics in determining what the director's duty of care requires?

13. Explain how the duty of care applies to business judgments made by directors and officers.

14. Describe one way in which corporate law protects creditors.

15. What limits are there on the ability of a corporation to indemnify its directors for costs incurred in defending an action to which they were made a party only because they were directors?

16. In what ways do securities law and corporate law rules overlap?

17. Why do the legal mechanisms by which shareholders keep directors accountable to them not work very well in large corporations with many shareholders?

18. What are the main legal requirements that management of a corporation must fulfill to help ensure that its decisions are consistent with corporate social responsibility?

19. What must a person dealing with a corporation establish to enforce a contract with the corporation?

20. Who is the "directing mind" of the corporation? What is the significance of this concept in relation to corporate liability for crimes? For torts?

Cases and Problems

1. Carl owns 51 percent of the shares of Probex Inc, which carries on a successful building supplies business. At the last shareholders' meeting, Carl elected Morris, Ellen, and himself as the directors of the company. Morris, Ellen, and Carl appointed Carl as the CEO of the company. The corporation's business has been slow this year. Both Morris and Ellen believe that the current slowdown of the business is a direct result of Carl neglecting his duty as CEO to oversee the day-to-day operations of the business.

   By outvoting Carl at the next directors' meeting, Morris and Ellen replace Carl as CEO with Philip. Carl is furious and tells Morris and Ellen that since he owns 51 percent of the company, they had no right to replace him, especially since he elected them. Carl further advises them that, as the controlling shareholder, he is reclaiming his position as CEO of Probex. Is Carl entitled to be the CEO of the corporation? What can he do to ensure that he is appointed to this office?

2. Claire, Stephan, and Gopa decided to go into business together to provide consulting services. Each invested $100 000 in return for one-third of the shares in a corporation that will carry on the business. There was an oral understanding, but no written contract, as follows:

   ■ Gopa would not be involved in the day-to-day decision making related to the business.

   ■ Claire and Stephan would be elected as the directors and appointed as the president and vice-president of the corporation.

   ■ All major decisions of the corporation, including selling the business, would require the consent of all shareholders.

   For several years, the business operated on this basis, but in 2011 Claire and Stephan decided to sell all the assets of the business. They called a shareholders' meeting to vote on the sale. Gopa did not agree with the sale, but she was outvoted at the meeting. Now that the sale has been approved, is there anything Gopa can do about it?

3. Crook was employed as the scrap manager for Canada Labs Inc (Canlab). In that capacity, Crook regularly sold waste gold generated by the experimental work conducted by Canlab to Golden Corona Mines Inc for recycling. Corona also sold gold, although Canlab had never been one of its customers.

Crook devised a scheme to make himself wealthy. One day, he sent a purchase order on a Canlab order form to Corona for $1 000 000 in gold. Because Corona had not sold gold to Canlab in the past, it called Smith, the manager of purchasing for Canlab, to ask if the gold order from Crook was authorized. Smith, who was responsible for all purchases made by Canlab, said she would check into it. She called Crook, and he convinced her that the gold was needed for a particular set of experiments. Smith was too busy to inquire further and forgot to call Corona back. Corona called Smith several more times, but Smith did not call back. In frustration, after five days, Corona called Crook who, of course, confirmed that Corona should send the gold.

Corona did send the gold to Canlab. It was received by Crook, who then skipped the country with it. Corona sued Canlab for payment for the gold. On what basis could Canlab be liable to pay for the gold? Are any defences available to Canlab?

4. Jordan is an accountant with a national firm. He is also a director of Bear-Tech Inc, a producer of communications equipment, and a member of the audit committee of Bear-Tech. In the committee's review of the financial statements prepared by management for the most recently completed financial year, Jordan noticed that the statements failed to refer to certain transactions. The audit committee was told by the chief financial officer that they did not need to be disclosed in the statements. The audit committee recommended to the board that it approve the statements. The board did so and disclosed the statements to the public. Subsequently, the chief financial officer realized that the transactions should have been disclosed in accordance with generally accepted accounting principles. The result of the omission of the transactions was that the financial statements overstated the corporation's income for the year by 20 percent. Bear-Tech disclosed the error and the shares of the corporation dropped in value. Did Jordan breach an obligation to the corporation by failing to ensure that the transactions were disclosed in the financial statements?

5. Xena was the original shareholder and sole director of Aberdeen Consulting Ltd. She held 10 shares. The corporation was profitable, but it needed more capital to engage in new business projects. To raise capital, Xena has issued 20 shares of Aberdeen to Raju for $1000 per share.

Upon reviewing the corporation's financial statements, Raju discovers that the corporation has a consulting contract with a company controlled by Xena. The contract fees are much higher than the usual market rate for consulting services and have substantially reduced the profits of the business. Raju decides that, at the next shareholders' meeting when Xena's term expires, he will elect himself as director, terminate the contract, and put the business of the corporation on a much stronger financial footing. Upon hearing of this plan, Xena, as director, issues herself an additional 20 shares. At the shareholders' meeting, much to Raju's surprise, Xena outvotes him, re-electing herself as director. Raju is outraged and certain that something must be done to remedy this terrible situation. Is there anything Raju can do?

6. Apex Ltd has been having financial difficulties. The directors of Apex are concerned that the corporation is not going to be able to pay its obligations to creditors at the end of the month. Nevertheless, one of the directors, Alvaro, who is also the controlling shareholder, has asked the directors to declare a dividend. If you were one of the other directors, what do your obligations require you to take into consideration in relation to the decision the board is being asked to make? What should you do?

7. Florence Industries Ltd, based in Alberta, manufactures household cleaning products. Its president, Ebenezer, entered into negotiations with Second Class Disposal Services Inc for a service contract. Second Class promised Ebenezer that its disposal services, which were much less expensive than those of other disposal businesses, met all legal requirements. Ebenezer was satisfied by these assurances and signed the contract without further investigating Second Class or its track record.

Three months into the contract, Florence Industries was accused of dumping industrial waste into the Bow River, contrary to the Alberta *Water Resources Act*, and Ebenezer was accused of authorizing the dumping. This statute provides that an accused who exercised reasonable care to prevent the corporation from disposing of the waste can avoid liability.

Assuming that industrial waste was dumped into the Bow River on behalf of Florence Industries by Second Class, discuss whether Ebenezer *or* Florence Industries can be held liable under the *Act*.

8. New Technology Co is a public company whose shares are widely held and listed on the Toronto Stock Exchange. In the last year, the corporation's business has struggled, and its share price has fallen from an all-time high of $150 to $15. Over the same period, its competitors have done well, and their shares have increased in value. This month, it was announced that the board of directors had decided that the president should be given a $10 000 000 bonus. Assume that you bought 1000 shares at the peak of the market for $150 000 and your shares are now worth only $15 000. You are very angry that, while the shareholders are suffering, the president is getting this enormous bonus. What can you do?

9. PVRCo Inc is a distributor of PVRs. The corporation has 10 shareholders, including Frances and her two sons, who together hold 60 percent of the shares and are also the directors of the corporation. The sons run the business. Frances has no experience in business and is not involved in any way. She pays no attention to what is going on, although she regularly attends board meetings. In 2012, the sons started taking large amounts of money out of the business in the form of loans to themselves.

   When the financial statements for 2014 were prepared, they showed that shareholder loans had ballooned from nil to $1 000 000 in a year, when revenues of the business had been only $2 000 000 over the same period. The board of directors approved the statements in June 2015. Frances was at the meeting but did not look at the statements. Within two months, the corporation was not paying its debts, and one of its creditors obtained a court order appointing a receiver to take control of the business. The receiver discovered the loans to the sons. The sons are now insolvent. Frances, however, has substantial personal assets. Is there any way that the receiver, acting on behalf of the corporation, can seek relief against Frances?

10. Corrine has been a real estate developer in the City of Ottawa for more than 20 years. She regularly buys and sells properties. In 2014, Corrine agrees to go into business with Akbar who has experience buying and selling property in the small towns that surround Ottawa. They agree to set up a corporation to carry on a business of buying and selling property outside of Ottawa. They each will contribute $1 000 000 in return for 50 percent of the shares of the corporation. Each will be a director. The corporation buys and sells several properties over the next two years. In 2016, Corrine hears from an old friend about a very small property for sale just outside of Ottawa in Blackburn Hamlet. The price is a real bargain, $50 000. She wants to buy it herself. Can she? What should she do?

11. Simone is a director of Pace Computers Ltd. She is also the sole shareholder and director of Simtronics Supply Inc, which sells parts for personal computers. At a Pace board meeting, Simone suggests that Pace could get its parts inventory for less money from Simtronics than from its current supplier. Is there anything preventing Pace from entering into a supply contract with Simtronics? Should Simone take any steps to ensure that no legal problems arise?

12. Sureet has just been appointed a director and the CEO of Astra Corp, which carries on dry cleaning businesses at locations across Canada. The shares of Astra Corp are listed for trading on the Toronto Stock Exchange. Sureet wants the business to be known as an excellent employer and good corporate citizen. He plans to cause the corporation to adopt a policy of paying its employees 25 percent more than is paid by its competitors and to give generously to local charities in every city in which Astra carries on business. He is convinced that this strategy will be a good one for the business in the long run. He will be able attract and keep good employees, which is hard to do in the dry cleaning industry. Also, he thinks that his strategy will be attractive to customers. He acknowledges, however, that it will be costly and, at least for the first few years while the reputation of the corporation improves, is likely to result in lower profits and less cash flow available for creditors. His chief financial officer has advised him, however, that there will be no significant increase in the risk that creditors will not be paid. Should Sureet adopt this strategy? What process should he follow to do so?

23 Secured Transactions

LEARNING OBJECTIVES

After completing this chapter, you should be able to:

❶ Explain how financial institutions and other creditors can manage the risk of default by people who have obligations to them.

❷ Describe ways for a business to finance the acquisition of assets that are equivalent to borrowing money and giving the lender a security interest in the asset acquired.

❸ Explain how a creditor can obtain a security interest in all of the property that the debtor owns, including property acquired in the future.

❹ Describe the advantages of the current rules protecting security interests for creditors.

❺ Describe the kinds of security interests that are not covered by the general rules protecting security interests of creditors.

❻ Explain the steps that a creditor should take to protect their security interest in a debtor's property most effectively.

❼ Outline the risks for a person who acquires property from someone who has previously given security interests to a creditor in that property, and explain how to manage them.

❽ List the steps that should be followed by secured creditors to enforce their rights against the personal property of debtors.

❾ Describe the obligations that a creditor owes to a debtor when they seize the debtor's property.

❿ Identify situations in which one person's guarantee of another person's credit obligation becomes unenforceable.

We all rely on credit, at least some of the time. If you promise to pay later to get something now, you are a *debtor*, the person who owes a credit obligation. The person who allows time to pass before requiring you to pay is the *creditor*. If you buy furniture and do not have to pay for it until next year, you are a debtor who owes a credit obligation to the furniture store. Credit in various forms is essential for many business activities. A bank loan may be necessary for a store to be able to add floor space and grow its business. An agreement from a supplier of the store's inventory to defer payment for 60 days so some of the inventory can be sold may be the only way for the store to be able to pay for the inventory.

Risk Management Strategies for Creditors

L.O. ❶

No matter how honest and reliable a debtor is, creditors, such as the furniture store, the bank, and the supplier mentioned in the examples above, all face the risk that the debtor will not pay. They have two main ways of managing that risk:

- security interests
- guarantees

A **security interest** allows a creditor to seize some of a debtor's personal property if a debt is not repaid, usually without the delay and expense of going to court. Suppose you want to borrow money from a bank to buy a new delivery truck. The bank will decide whether to lend you the money based largely on your ability to repay the loan. What if, after examining your income and expenses, the bank still has concerns about your ability to make the payments? The bank would be more willing to give you credit if it received your permission to seize and sell the truck if you failed to repay the loan. Giving the bank this permission is called granting a security interest in the truck. Property that is subject to a security interest is called **collateral**. A creditor that has a security interest is called a **secured party**.

A **security interest** gives the bank advantages over an ordinary creditor. If the bank has a security interest in the truck, it is entitled to seize the collateral, dispose of it, and use the money it receives to pay off your debt. If the bank did not have a security interest, it would have to sue you for the unpaid debt and then get an order to seize your property. Even if its lawsuit were successful, it would take time and money. In any case, the bank may not be able to seize the property if it is subject to a security interest held by another creditor.

A security interest can be given over any type of property to any type of creditor. Personal property, as discussed in Chapters 17 and 18, includes both *tangible* property (assets that can be touched), such as cars, and *intangible* property (assets that cannot be touched), such as corporate shares, life insurance policies, some kinds of licences, and intellectual property. In this chapter, we will discuss the creation, registration, and enforcement of security interests in personal property. We will not discuss security interests in *real property*, such as mortgages, which we examined in Chapter 16.

Another way for a creditor to reduce the risk associated with non-payment is to obtain a *guarantee*. A **guarantee** is a contractual promise by a third party, called a *guarantor*, to satisfy the principal debtor's obligation if that debtor fails to do so. Suppose you persuade a friend to act as the guarantor of the loan you got from the bank to buy the truck. If you fail to

a **secured party** is a creditor with a security interest

collateral is property that is subject to a security interest

a **security interest** allows a creditor to seize some of a debtor's personal property if a debt is not repaid

a **guarantee** is a contractual promise by a third party to satisfy the principal debtor's obligation if the debtor fails to do so

PART 7

repay that loan, the bank can demand payment from your friend. In some situations, however, the law recognizes that the debtor and the creditor may act in ways that unfairly hurt the interests of the guarantor. For instance, if the debtor agrees to pay a higher rate of interest on the debt, the guarantor's potential liability is increased. If that occurs after the guarantee is signed and without the guarantor's consent, the law may release the guarantor from liability. Our discussion of guarantees will focus on what is required for a guarantee to be valid and the situations in which guarantors are relieved of their obligations.

L.O. ❷ ❸

How Security Interests Are Created

An early form of security interest was what we now call a "pawn" or "pledge." In return for a person lending you money, you give them temporary possession of some of your property as security for the loan. You agree that if you fail to pay the loan, the lender can sell the property and apply the money received against your debt. If you repay the loan, you get your property back. Because this form of secured loan transaction requires the physical transfer of a piece of property, there is a natural limit on its use. In practice, a debtor often needs to use the property given as security in its business. Eventually, the law developed to permit the creation of security interests by contract that did not require a transfer of possession. This permitted a much wider range of more efficient secured financing alternatives, as discussed below.

GRANTING A SECURITY INTEREST IN A SPECIFIC ASSET

In a lending transaction, the debtor often agrees to provide the creditor with ownership, or some other form of security interest, in a specific piece of its personal property. In our example in the introduction, you gave the bank an interest in your truck. From the creditor's perspective, that arrangement is attractive because the collateral is identified, making it easy to determine its value, and it is relatively easy to enforce the security interest. The bank knows that the collateral was worth, say, $50 000 when you bought it and, to enforce its rights, it simply has to seize the vehicle if you fail to repay the loan. When the debtor transfers title in a specific asset to a secured party, the transaction is sometimes called a **chattel mortgage**. (In Chapter 17, we considered the source of the word "chattel" and examined rules regarding the acquisition and loss of chattels.) Security interests may also be created in specific assets without transferring title or ownership to the creditor in the ways discussed below.

a **chattel mortgage** is a transaction in which a debtor gives a creditor title to some specific personal property to secure the performance of an obligation it owes to the creditor

Conditional Sales

A *conditional sale* is another kind of transaction in which a security interest is created in a specific asset. In the commercial world, a buyer is often allowed to postpone paying at least part of the purchase price. As security for that debt, the seller may retain an interest, usually in the form of ownership, in the goods that are being sold. The buyer gets *possession* of the goods immediately, but they do not *own* them until they pay the full price. This arrangement is called a **conditional sale.**

a **conditional sale** occurs when the seller retains ownership of the goods to secure payment of the purchase price by the buyer

Conditional sales are very common in consumer transactions where a person buys furniture or other household items but defers payment until some time in the future. They are also quite common where two businesses have an ongoing relationship for the purchase of goods. For instance, a manufacturer may retain a security interest in the equipment that it supplies to a distributor. In each case, the security interest is taken to secure the payment of the purchase price. If the buyer defaults, the seller can take back the goods. Usually, the buyer is responsible for any damage to the goods. Sometimes, the buyer may be required to buy insurance to cover the goods while payment is pending. The seller may require that they be named as the beneficiary under that insurance policy.

SPECIAL CASES There are two kinds of transactions that are similar to conditional sales which are often used to create security interests:

- consignment
- lease

A **consignment** occurs when the owner of goods transfers possession, but not ownership, to someone else. The owner is called the **consignor**. The person who receives possession of the goods is called the **consignee**. There are many business reasons for creating a consignment:

- The consignee may be examining the goods for possible purchase.
- The consignee may have agreed to try to sell the goods on the consignor's behalf. This is what we usually mean when we say goods are held by someone "on consignment." A children's used-clothing store may take clothes on consignment from a parent, offer them for sale, and then pay the parent a percentage of the purchase price if the clothes are sold.

In a true consignment, the consignee is not bound to pay for the goods until they do something, such as selling them to a third party. However, the term "consignment" is also sometimes used to refer to a situation in which the "consignee" has already agreed to pay for the goods and the "consignor" holds on to ownership to secure full payment of the price. In effect, that transaction is a conditional sale, not a true consignment. Retention of ownership under the consignment is a form of security interest.[1]

A lease can also operate like a conditional sale and as an alternative to a secured loan. Suppose you want to buy a truck for $50 000. You could acquire the truck in at least three different kinds of secured transactions, including a lease:

- The seller might agree to a conditional sale in which it gives you time to pay but retains ownership of the truck until you have paid the full price, plus interest, in 60 monthly instalments of, say, $1000 that blend payment of the price and interest.
- You could borrow $50 000 from a bank, agreeing to repay that amount, plus interest, in 60 blended monthly instalments of $1000. As security for your promise to pay those monthly instalments, you could give the bank an interest in the truck.
- You could acquire the truck in a financing transaction set up as a lease. Under a **lease**, the lessor retains ownership of an asset but gives possession of it to the lessee for a period of time in return for the lessee's

a **consignment** occurs when the owner of goods transfers possession, but not ownership, to someone else

the **consignor** is the owner of goods who transfers possession of the goods, but not ownership, to someone else

the **consignee** is the person who receives possession of the goods, but not ownership

a **lease** is a relationship where the lessor retains ownership of an asset but gives possession of it to the lessee for a period of time in return for the lessee's promise to make regular payments

---

[1] In *Re Stephanian's Carpets Ltd* (1980) 1 PPSAC 119 (Ont SC), it was held that if a consignee has an unrestricted right to return the goods under the consignment, the consignor does not have a security interest.

promise to make regular payments. When used for financing, the lessor's ownership of the leased asset is a security interest. Its purpose is to secure the lessee's obligation to make the lease payments and help the lessor manage the risk of default. To acquire the truck in a lease financing transaction, you could enter into an arrangement with a lessor, who would buy the truck that interests you. In order for you to acquire the truck, the lessor would then agree to lease that vehicle to you for 60 months in exchange for your promise to make monthly payments of $1000. The lessor would also give you an option to purchase the truck at the end of the 60 months. Since you have paid the full purchase price plus interest, the option price could be nominal, say $1.

All three of these transactions are equivalent ways to finance your acquisition of the truck. With the bank financing, you get ownership of the truck at the outset, which you use as collateral for the bank loan. The bank makes its decision to lend the money to you based on two factors: (i) its assessment of your ability to make the loan payments, and (ii) its assessment of its own ability to acquire and sell the truck if you fail to make the payments.

In the lease financing and the conditional sale, you do not get ownership of the truck at the outset. The lessor or the seller owns the truck. But you do get the right to possess and use the vehicle, just as if you were the owner. In a conditional sale, you receive ownership when you have made all the payments. Under the lease, you have an option to obtain ownership after making all the payments. The lessor and the conditional seller will make their decisions to enter into a transaction with you based on the same two factors as the bank: their assessment of (i) your ability to make the monthly payments and (ii) their own ability to acquire and sell the truck if you fail to make those payments.

This example has shown how a lease of an asset can be structured to have the same financial characteristics as a conditional sale or a secured bank loan to fund the purchase of the asset:

- The same amount of credit is extended to you in each transaction—$50 000 (the price of the truck).
- You are obligated to repay the price of the truck *plus* some interest. Consequently, while the truck costs only $50 000, you must make 60 monthly payments of $1000 each for a total of $60 000.
- You give up an interest in the vehicle to secure your payments.
- You will own the truck at the end of the arrangement. The only distinctive characteristic of the lease financing is that you must actually exercise your option to buy the vehicle for $1. Of course, it would be economically irrational for you *not* to exercise that option unless the truck was so badly damaged that it was worth less than $1.[2]

Assignment of Accounts Receivable

One specific asset in which business debtors often give a security interest is *accounts receivable*. Most businesses sell some of their products on credit. For instance, customers may be given 30 or 60 days to pay for goods or services they have bought. The amounts that a business is entitled to collect from its

---

[2.] In practice, option prices are usually more than $1. Even when the option price is substantial, however, a lease transaction may be functionally equivalent to a conditional sale or a bank-financed purchase if the price is at, or less than, the likely market value of the leased goods at the end of the lease term.

customers are its **accounts receivable**. Those accounts usually represent a substantial asset, which can be used as security if the business wants to borrow money. The business can give the bank an **assignment of accounts receivable**, which would allow the bank to collect the debts (or "book debts") owing to the business if the loan is not repaid.

When a debtor makes an assignment of accounts receivable to a creditor, typically, the debtor is allowed to collect their own accounts receivable and to carry on business as usual. The creditor steps in and demands payment from the debtor's customers only if the debtor fails to fulfill their obligations to the creditor. (We discussed assignments of accounts receivable in Chapter 8.) Figure 23.1 illustrates the process of assigning accounts receivable as security.

accounts receivable are the amounts that a business is entitled to collect from its customers

an **assignment of accounts receivable** allows a creditor to collect debts owing to a debtor if the debtor does not fulfill their obligations to the creditor

---

FIGURE 23.1 Assignment of Accounts Receivable

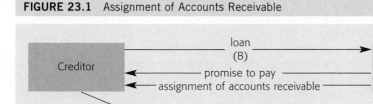

(A) The debtor has accounts receivable consisting of money owing to the debtor by its customers.
(B) A creditor gives a loan to the debtor. As security for its debt, the debtor gives an assignment of its accounts receivable to the creditor.
(C) If the debtor fails to fulfill its obligations to the creditor, the creditor is entitled to collect money from the debtor's customers.

GRANTING A SECURITY INTEREST IN ALL OF THE DEBTOR'S ASSETS

A creditor may not be satisfied with a security interest in specific identified pieces of personal property. To get maximum protection against a debtor's failure to pay, banks and other financial institutions often take a security interest in *all* of the debtor's assets with a **general security agreement**. The security interest in such an agreement typically covers assets of the debtor at the time that the security agreement becomes effective and assets that the debtor acquires *after* that time.

Before modern provincial personal property security legislation (PPS legislation) was created, creditors often used a *floating charge* to take security in after-acquired property.[3] A **floating charge** is a security interest that *hovers*

a **general security agreement** provides a creditor with a security interest in *all* of the debtor's assets

a **floating charge** is a security interest that *hovers* above the debtor's assets until some event causes the charge to become *fixed* or *crystallized* on those assets

PART 7

[3.] *Eg Personal Property Security Act*, RSA 2000, c P-7 (APPSA) (Alta); *Personal Property Security Act*, RSBC 1996, c 359 (BCPPSA) (BC); *Personal Property Security Act*, CCSM, c P35 (*MPPSA*) (Man); *Personal Property Security Act*, SNB 1993, c P-7.1 (*NBPPSA*) (NB); *Personal Property Security Act*, SNL 1998, c P-7.1 (*NLPPSA*) (Nfld & Lab); *Personal Property Security Act*, SNS 1995–96, c 13 (*NSPPSA*) (NS); *Personal Property Security Act*, RSO 1990, c P.10 (*OPPSA*) (Ont); *Personal Property Security Act*, RSPEI 1998, c P-3.1 (*PEIPPSA*) (PEI); *Personal Property Security Act*, SS 1993, c P-6.2 (SPPSA) (Sask). Quebec's *Civil Code* also provides for security interests, but its rules remain distinct. Our discussion is based on the rules in the other provinces.

above the debtor's assets until some event causes the charge to become *fixed* or *crystallized* on those assets. A contract creating a floating charge usually states that the charge descends and becomes fixed only if the debtor misses a payment and a notice of default is given by the creditor. Until then, the debtor can carry on business, including buying and selling assets, without regard to the floating charge. However, once the relevant event occurs, the debtor can sell its assets only *subject to the creditor's charge*. That means that a purchaser of the debtor's assets does not own them outright—the creditor's interest continues to exist in them.

Floating charges are not often used anymore because PPS legislation allows a creditor to take a similar but more effective sort of security interest. A secured party's interest can attach to all of the debtor's current and after-acquired property as soon as the property is acquired by the debtor without any requirement for crystallization. With some important exceptions, that interest continues to exist even if the debtor disposes of their property to a third party. Since it is not in either party's interest to freeze the debtor's operations, however, the debtor typically will be given permission in the security agreement to carry on business as usual, including selling inventory and replacing worn-out equipment. People who buy from the debtor in these circumstances get the goods free of the security interest of the creditor.[4]

SPECIAL SECURITY INTERESTS OF BANKS

In Canada, banks can be incorporated only under the federal *Bank Act*.[5] Section 427 of the Act allows banks to take a special kind of security in certain types of assets, which other creditors cannot take. Banks may take section 427 interests *in addition* to the other sorts of security interests described above, and often do take more than one type of security for a single obligation.

Banks may take section 427 security interests only in the types of assets listed in the Act. These include the goods of retailers, wholesalers, and manufacturers, as well as mining and forest products. Banks cannot take this special kind of interest in either consumers' assets or the assets of most businesses providing services.

Under the Act, there is a special registration system for these interests. For the registration to be effective, the bank must get the debtor to file a "notice of intention" to give security to the bank at the branch of the Bank of Canada closest to the debtor's place of business.

The main advantage of a section 427 security interest for banks is that a single registration applies to all the debtor's assets, no matter where they are located. In contrast, the PPS legislation of a province is effective only with respect to assets in that province. Consequently, a section 427 security interest is less burdensome to register if the debtor has assets in several provinces. Another advantage of section 427 interests is that they will prevail over some other forms of security interests in the same collateral.[6]

Concept Summary 23.1 reviews the common ways in which security interests are created.

---

[4] For more information about what happens to security interests under PPS legislation when collateral is transferred, see below under the heading "Security Interests When Collateral Is Transferred."

[5] *Bank Act*, SC 1991, c 46 (Can).

[6] The precise relationship between interests created under the federal *Bank Act* and those created under provincial legislation is not always clear, as discussed below.

Concept Summary 23.1

Common Ways Security Interests Are Created

Conditional sale	The seller of goods retains title, or some other form of security interest, to secure future payment of the purchase price by the buyer.
Security interest in a specific asset	The debtor gives a security interest in some of their personal property to a creditor to secure performance of an obligation owed by the debtor (*eg* a chattel mortgage).
Assignment of accounts receivable	A person (the assignor) who is owed a debt (the account receivable) assigns it to someone else (*eg* a bank) to secure performance of an obligation owed by the assignor to the bank.
Security interest in all of the debtor's assets, including after-acquired property	The debtor gives a security interest in all of their personal property, including all property acquired by the debtor after the date that the security agreement is created, to a creditor to secure performance of an obligation owed by the debtor (a general security agreement).
Special security interests of banks created under the *Bank Act*	The debtor gives a bank a security interest in certain types of property described in the Act. A single registration protects this interest in the debtor's assets wherever they are in Canada.

Provincial Rules for Secured Transactions

L.O. ❹❺❻❼❽❾

Despite their different forms, each method of creating a security interest discussed above has the same function: to give the creditor an interest in the debtor's property to secure the debtor's performance of an obligation. Each method helps the creditor to manage the risk that the debtor will fail to perform. Historically, the security interests created by each method were governed by special legislation or common law rules. Each had different remedies and enforcement procedures. Different types of security interests had to be registered in different places. That situation was inconvenient for a business considering extending credit for at least two reasons:

- Even within a single province, a potential creditor who wanted to know whether a debtor had already given a security interest in a particular asset to another creditor had to search separate registries for each type of registered interest.

- A secured party had to search for security interests separately in every province where the debtor had assets that it offered as security.

It is still necessary for secured parties to search in every province where the debtor has assets that they have offered as security. And, in some cases, it may be difficult to tell which provincial laws apply, such as when a truck that is collateral moves between provinces. Within each province, however, PPS legislation now integrates the common law and statutory rules for security interests into a single system. The details of the provincial systems differ slightly. But *most* security interests are now governed by one set of provincial rules under the provinces' PPS legislation.

FACILITATING RISK MANAGEMENT FOR CREDITORS

The unified approach under PPS legislation allows creditors to assess and manage risks more easily and accurately. It provides a simple and inexpensive system for secured parties to register their interests. Provincial registers can be

priority of a secured creditor's claim is the ranking of the creditor's right to enforce its claim against a piece of collateral compared to the claims of other secured creditors in the same collateral

searched online to determine what security interests a debtor has granted, and PPS legislation establishes a clear set of rules for determining the **priority**, or ranking, of competing claims to the same collateral. Provincial legislation also provides a single system of default rights that applies to almost all types of security interests. In all these ways, the PPS legislation provides greater certainty for creditors.

SCOPE OF APPLICATION

Provincial PPS legislation applies to all security interests in personal property created by agreement between a debtor and a secured party.[7] A security interest is defined simply as an interest in personal property that secures the payment or performance of an obligation. This functional definition was intended to catch all kinds of security interests that arise by agreement, regardless of their form. It includes, for instance, interests created by conditional sales, assignments of accounts receivable, and general security agreements.

Leases

One difficult, but important, issue is how to determine whether a lease transaction creates a security interest. As discussed earlier, a lease of goods can be used as a substitute for a secured loan to finance the acquisition of goods. It can also be a real lease: the lessor simply grants the lessee temporary possession in return for fixed regular payments over some period of time. Whether the lessor's title functions as a security interest depends upon the terms of the lease and circumstances of the transaction. PPS legislation avoids the problem of determining when a lease creates a security interest by providing that any lease of personal property that has a term of over one year is subject to the province's PPS legislation.[8]

If a lease is subject to provincial PPS legislation, the priority of the lessor's security interest is determined by the legislation. If a lease is not subject to the PPS legislation, the lessor's ownership of the leased assets typically gives it a claim ranking ahead of all other creditors of the lessee, including those who have registered under the legislation. This is always the lessor's preferred result.

Exceptions

The rules in provincial PPS legislation do not apply to all forms of interests in personal property.[9] Rights created by statute, rather than agreement, are not caught. The following are the most important statutory rights:

the **right of distress**, or **distraint**, allows a landlord to seize property that is on the rented premises and belongs to the tenant, sell it, and use the sale proceeds to pay the outstanding rent

- A landlord under a commercial lease of real property usually enjoys the *right of distress*, or *distraint*, if the tenant has not paid its rent (as discussed in Chapter 15). The **right of distress**, or **distraint**, allows a landlord to seize property that is on the rented premises and belongs to the tenant, sell it, and use the sale proceeds to pay the outstanding rent. Normally, that right cannot be used against non-commercial tenants.

- *Deemed trusts* that are created under some statutes for the benefit of the government are exempt from the application of provincial PPS

---

7. *Eg BCPPSA*, s 2(1); *NBPPSA*, s 3(1); *OPPSA*, s 11(2).

8. *Eg BCPPSA*, s 3(c); *NBPPSA*, s 3(2)(b); *NSPPSA*, s 4(2)(b); *OPPSA*, s 2(c).

9. Exceptions are provided for in PPS legislation: *eg BCPPSA*, s 4; *NBPPSA*, s 4; *OPPSA*, s 4.

legislation. Under such a **deemed trust**, some assets of a business are deemed as a matter of law to be held for the benefit of the government and cannot be used for the business. The most important deemed trust is the provision of the *Income Tax Act* that states that tax deductions from employee wages by employers are deemed to be held in trust for the government. As a result, the government beneficially owns the funds, and they must be remitted to the Canada Revenue Agency.[10]

under a **deemed trust,** some assets of a business are deemed as a matter of law to be held for the benefit of the government and cannot be used for the business

■ *Liens* for people who provide repair or storage services are usually excluded from PPS legislation. A person who is in possession of personal property for the purpose of either repairing or storing it can retain the property until the owner pays the price of the repairs or storage. For instance, a mechanic who fixes your car can keep the vehicle until you pay the repair bill. The mechanic's right against your car is like a security interest since it is used to reduce the risk that the mechanic's bill will not be paid. It is different from a security interest, however, because it arises without you, as the debtor, consenting. That right, called a **lien**, usually exists only if the person providing the goods or services is in possession of the property. In some situations, however, a *non-possessory lien* may be available.[11]

a **lien** allows a person who has not been paid to retain possession of goods that the person has repaired or stored until payment is made

Creditors with these kinds of claims do not have to register under PPS legislation, and, in most cases, they have priority over security interests that are subject to the legislation.

The interests of banks under section 427 of the *Bank Act* represent a sort of hybrid. In Ontario, the courts have said that a bank may register these interests under PPS legislation and take advantage of whatever rights registration may provide in terms of priority over other creditors. Banks do not have to register, however. They may choose to register only under the special system set up under the *Bank Act* and enforce their rights under that statute.[12] In other provinces, PPS legislation provides that it does not apply to section 427 interests.

PROTECTING SECURITY INTERESTS UNDER PPS LEGISLATION

As we saw in Chapter 8, ccontracts usually can be enforced only against those who are parties to them. That rule of *privity* generally applies to contracts that create security interests. Under PPS legislation, however, a security agreement may be effective against third parties, including other secured parties, if the security interest meets the requirements for **attachment** in the PPS legislation. In some cases, security interests are even enforceable against people who acquire collateral from the debtor.[13] This protects creditors against the risk that their claims will not be paid because the debtor transferred the collateral to someone else.

attachment allows a security interest to be enforced against third parties

---

[10.] *Income Tax Act*, RSC 1985 (5th Supp), c 1, s 227(4) and (4.1) (Can). The equitable concept of the trust was discussed in Chapter 1.

[11.] *Repair and Storage Liens Act*, RSO 1990, c R.25 (Ont). Even though they are not generally subject to PPS legislation, the statutes in some provinces state that repair and storage liens prevail over interests that are subject to the legislation: *eg* OPPSA, s 31. As well, the Ontario *Repair and Storage Liens Act* sets out certain requirements for a lien and creates some exceptions to its priority: ss 7(3) and 16(1)(c) and (d). Repairers and storers may register their liens under the Ontario PPS legislation. Liens were discussed in Chapter 17.

[12.] *Re Bank of Nova Scotia and International Harvester Credit Corp of Can Ltd*(1990) 73 DLR (4th) 385 (Ont CA); *Royal Bank of Canada v Sparrow Electric Corp* (1997) 143 DLR (4th) 385 (SCC).

[13.] See below under the heading "Security Interests When Collateral Is Transferred."

Attachment

Attachment occurs when three requirements are met:

- The debtor signs a written security agreement containing a description of the collateral or the secured party gets possession of collateral.
- The secured party gives some value, such as a loan, to the debtor.
- The debtor has some rights in the collateral.[14]

Perfection

perfection of a security interest usually occurs when a security interest has attached and the secured party has registered the interest under PPS legislation

To fully protect the priority of its claims to a debtor's assets, a secured party must *perfect* its security interest. **Perfection** usually occurs when a security interest has attached and the secured party has registered under PPS legislation. It is also possible, though less common, for a secured party to perfect its security interest by taking possession of the collateral.[15]

To perfect by registration, the secured party must file a **financing statement** with the registrar responsible for administering the PPS legislation in that province. The registrar will note the time and date of registration. That information is used to determine the priority of the secured party's interest in relation to any other security interest under PPS legislation. A security interest perfected by registration has priority over all *subsequently* registered security interests in the same collateral, but not over *previously* registered security interests. Registration also ensures that the existence of a security interest is disclosed to people who search the register, including other potential creditors. Registration continues for a period of time chosen by the registering secured party. Registration fees increase with the duration of the registration.[16]

a financing statement is the document that is filed to register a security interest under PPS legislation

The financing statement identifies the debtor, the secured party, and the general nature of the security interest. Paper financing statements are scanned and stored in an electronic database. Financing statements can also be filed

---

Business Decision 23.1

Registration before Attachment

Lenders generally file a financing statement to register their security interest *before* closing the financing transaction. Imagine that Keeshon Construction Ltd and the Royal Bank discussed a loan from the bank to Keeshon of $1 000 000. The loan was to be secured on all of Keeshon's assets. They arranged that the loan and security agreements would be signed and the money advanced on 19 September 2014.

In anticipation of the loan, the bank registered a financing statement against Keeshon on September 15. The bank was able to register its still-to-be-created security interest in this way because filing a financing statement does not require filing a copy of the agreement creating the security interest. Four days later, as anticipated, the parties signed the loan and security agreements and the bank gave Keeshon a cheque for $1 000 000.

The bank's security interest attached in all of Keeshon's assets as soon as the security agreement was signed and value was given by the bank on September 19. Perfection occurred at the same time because the financing statement relating to the interest had already been filed. For perfection to occur, there must be attachment plus a registration, but the order in which the two requirements are met does not matter.

Question for Discussion

1. Why would the bank want to register its interest as soon as possible?

[14.] *Eg BCPPSA*, s 12; *OPPSA*, s 11(2).

[15.] *Eg* under the *OPPSA*, perfection is possible through registration (s 23) or possession (s 22).

[16.] In Ontario, a registration for up to 25 years can be obtained for $8 per year.

directly in electronic form. This *notice filing system* means that the secured party can register before the security agreement is created. Business Decision 23.1 illustrates the benefits of that last feature of the notice filing system.

PRIORITIES UNDER PPS LEGISLATION

A great advantage of PPS legislation is that it provides a system for determining who prevails when more than one secured party claims an interest in the same collateral. The relative priority of claims is often critically important. A debtor in default on their credit obligations usually does not have enough assets to pay off all of their creditors, so it matters whose security interest ranks first. A clear system of priorities helps creditors to manage their risks in two ways. At the time they make a decision about granting credit, they can find out what security interests the debtor has already given that will rank ahead of theirs. Anyone can find out about prior registrations as soon as they are registered by searching the register. With the benefit of this information, creditors can decide whether to advance credit to the debtor. Later, if there is a default, it is usually easy for the creditor to figure out whose security interest ranks first.

A key feature of PPS legislation is that all security interests are treated the same way regardless of their form. It does not matter, for example, whether one security interest consists of ownership of a piece of collateral retained by a conditional seller and another is a security interest of a bank in the same collateral under a general security agreement. The basic rule is that the first to register has the best claim. It makes no difference if a subsequently registered secured party knew about another secured party's interest that was registered earlier or that attachment occurred after registration.[17] In Business Decision 23.1, the relevant date for determining the bank's priority in any contest with another secured party is the date of its registration, 15 September 2014, even though perfection did not occur until September 19. If another secured creditor had obtained and perfected by registration a security interest in Keeshon's assets on September 18—before the bank had advanced any money—it would still rank behind the bank. PPS legislation considers only the date of registration in the interests of certainty.

An **unperfected security interest**, meaning a security interest that has not been perfected, is subordinate to:

an **unperfected security interest** is a security interest that has not been perfected

- any perfected interest
- other unperfected interests that attached earlier
- any lien created under any law
- any creditor who has both successfully obtained a judgment against the debtor and taken steps to enforce it by seizing the debtor's property[18]

Unperfected interests are also ineffective against anyone who represents the debtor's creditors and has control of the debtor's assets, such as a trustee in bankruptcy.[19] Secured creditors of a bankrupt debtor can enforce perfected security interests against the trustee. An unperfected security interest, however, is treated as an unsecured debt. As Chapter 24 discusses, wwhen a debtor

---

[17.] *Robert Simpson Co v Shadlock* (1981) 119 DLR (3d) 417 (Ont HCJ). The rules are different where the secured party has perfected by taking possession of the collateral. In that case, the first to take possession or register prevails: *BCPPSA*, s 35; *NBPPSA*, s 35; *OPPSA*, s 30.

[18.] *Eg OPPSA*, s 20; *SPPSA*, s 20.

[19.] *Eg OPPSA*, s 20; *SPPSA*, s 20.

becomes bankrupt, a creditor with an unsecured debt is entitled only to share in whatever assets are left after the creditors with perfected security interests enforce their rights to the debtor's collateral. Each unsecured creditor will receive a share of the debtor's remaining assets equal to the proportion that the debt owed to that creditor represents of the debtor's total unsecured debt. For example, assume that a debtor owes $1 000 000, but it has assets worth only one-tenth of that amount, $100 000, and there are no creditors with perfected security interests. If you, as an unsecured creditor, are owed $50 000, you will receive only one-tenth of what you are owed: $5000. If you were the only secured creditor with a perfected security interest, you would be entitled to seize $50 000 of the debtor's assets, forcing the unsecured creditors to share the remaining $50 000. As a matter of risk management, you should perfect your interest.

Purchase Money Security Interests

Banks and other financial institutions typically use a general security agreement to take a security interest in *all* of the debtor's property, including property acquired after the loan is made and the general security agreement has been entered into. Security interests that include after-acquired property can be troublesome to a debtor who wants to acquire new assets on credit.

Suppose a farm equipment distributor takes a bank loan, giving the bank a security interest in all of its assets, both present and future. The bank files a financing statement to register its security interest under PPS legislation. The distributor now wants to purchase goods from a manufacturer. Since it has little money, it wants to buy on credit. The manufacturer may not agree to sell on credit unless it can take an effective form of security to reduce its risk associated with non-payment by the distributor. However, all of the distributor's assets, including any subsequently acquired from the manufacturer, are *already* subject to the bank's perfected security interest. That means that the manufacturer's security interest would necessarily rank second at best. The first priority of the bank's security interest in after-acquired property may jeopardize the distributor's ability to acquire new assets for the business.

Because this is a frequent problem, PPS legislation provides a special priority rule that applies in such circumstances. When a security interest in collateral is taken by a seller of personal property to secure payment of the purchase price, the seller's security interest can be given priority over all other security interests in the same collateral given by the debtor. This is called a **purchase money security interest (PMSI)**. A PMSI can also be acquired by a lender, such as a bank, if (i) they lend money to the debtor to acquire an asset, (ii) the debtor actually uses that money to acquire that asset, and (iii) the debtor uses that asset as collateral for the loan.[20]

In either case, to obtain the PMSI super-priority, the secured party must register their interest within 15 days of the debtor getting possession of the collateral.[21] Suppose you want to buy a car on credit from a car dealer, but you have already given your bank a security interest in all of your property, including after-acquired property. The car dealer could get a PMSI in the car and rank ahead of the bank if they registered their financing statement to perfect their security interest within 15 days of when you get possession of the car.

a **purchase money security interest (PMSI)** is a security interest in a particular asset given by a debtor to a secured party that either sells that asset to the debtor or finances the debtor's acquisition of that asset

---

[20.] PMSIs are defined in *OPPSA*, s 1, and their super-priority is granted in *OPPSA*, s 33. It is possible for creditors to enter into an agreement to fix the priority of their security interests in a way that is different from what PPS legislation would provide. Where a secured party agrees to a lower priority, the agreement is called a "subordination agreement."

[21.] *Eg BCPPSA*, s 34; *NBPPSA*, s 34; *OPPSA*, ss 20(3), 33.

Special rules apply to PMSIs in **inventory**, those goods held for sale or lease by the debtor. They must be registered *before* the debtor gets possession of the collateral, and notice must be given to any secured party who previously filed a financing statement indicating an interest in inventory. Case Brief 23.1 illustrates these rules.

inventory consists of goods held for sale or lease

SECURITY INTERESTS WHEN COLLATERAL IS TRANSFERRED

As explained above, one key protection for secured parties in PPS legislation is that a security interest in personal property may continue to exist even when the property is transferred by the debtor to someone else.[22] The buyer of the property has to respect the secured party's interest, even if they did not know about the interest. If the debtor defaults, the property could be seized from the buyer. While the buyer will be able to sue the seller for what they paid plus any damages they suffer, that action may not be very useful. If the secured party has been driven to actually enforce a security interest, the debtor presumably has little money.

Case Brief 23.1

Clark Equipment of Canada Ltd v Bank of Montreal (1984) 4 PPSAC 38 (Man CA)

In 1977, the Bank of Montreal made a loan to Maneco Equipment Ltd. As security for the loan, the bank obtained a security interest in all property currently owned or acquired in the future by Maneco. It registered its interest in 1977 by filing a financing statement.

Maneco's business was selling and leasing equipment produced by Clark Equipment of Canada Ltd. In 1978, Clark entered into an agreement to finance the acquisition of its equipment by Maneco. On 7 September 1978, Clark gave notice to the bank that it would have a PMSI in the equipment that Maneco would acquire from Clark as inventory. Clark filed a financing statement in relation to this interest on 20 September 1978. Subsequently, in 1979, 1980, and 1981,

Maneco acquired three pieces of equipment from Clark but did not pay for them.

In June 1981, Maneco defaulted on its loan, and the bank seized the equipment. Clark claimed that it had first claim to the equipment because it had a PMSI that ranked ahead of the bank's previously registered security interest.

The court held that the requirements for a PMSI had been met: (i) Clark's interest had been perfected by registration before Maneco got possession of the collateral, and (ii) Clark had given notice to the bank of its PMSI claim in Maneco's inventory. Clark was therefore entitled to seize the equipment.

Buyers will want to avoid this kind of risk. For each sale, a buyer could search the register maintained under PPS legislation to make sure that the seller has not granted a security interest in the goods they want to buy. However, that strategy would be expensive and time-consuming, and it would not disclose unregistered interests. If that were the only strategy for avoiding risk, people would be discouraged from making many commercial transactions. Consider the problem of having to do a search every time you bought something at a store. Because of that difficulty, PPS legislation contains exceptions to the general rule that a secured creditor's security interest in collateral follows the collateral into the buyer's hands.[23] An exception arises if

---

[22.] *Eg OPPSA*, s 25(1)(a); *SPPSA*, s 28(1)(a). Provincial PPS legislation also requires that secured parties make a new filing, called a "financing change statement," within a specified time after they find out about a transfer of collateral. That document, which names the buyer, is needed to maintain the perfection of the secured party's interest: *eg OPPSA*, s 48.

[23.] *Eg OPPSA*, ss 25(1)(a), 28; *SPPSA*, ss 28(1)(a), 30.

■ the secured party has permitted the debtor to sell or otherwise deal with the collateral, or

■ the debtor sells the collateral in the ordinary course of the debtor's business.

In either of the situations, the buyer receives the collateral free of any security interest given by the seller, even if the security interest is perfected and the buyer knows it. The only time that the buyer is not protected is when (i) the sale was a breach of the security agreement between the seller and a secured party, and (ii) the buyer knew it. Imagine that a debtor had given a security interest in their truck to the bank. The security agreement said that the debtor could not sell their truck. You bought the debtor's truck even though you knew about the prohibition on selling it. The bank would be able to enforce its security interest against you.

The first exception is hard to rely on because a buyer seldom knows the content of the security agreements that exist between the seller-debtor and that party's creditors. Consequently, the key question from the buyer's perspective is usually whether the sale occurred in the ordinary course of the seller-debtor's business. A buyer who is in doubt on that question should search the register that is maintained under the PPS legislation to make sure that what they are buying is not subject to a security interest.

A buyer does not have to worry about unperfected security interests. PPS legislation provides that unperfected interests are not effective against a buyer who had no knowledge of the interest.[24] This is another good reason for secured parties to register their interests.

Concept Summary 23.2 reviews the priority rules under PPS legislation.

Concept Summary 23.2

Priority of Security Interests in an Asset under PPS Legislation

1. Purchase money security interest in the asset*	Rights of certain creditors with claims outside the scope of PPS legislation (*eg* landlord's distress rights) may have priority over security interests subject to PPS legislation.
2. Perfected security interests in the asset ranked in order of the time of registration*	
3. Unperfected security interests in the asset ranked in order of the time of attachment* but subordinate to claims by • a trustee in bankruptcy or other representative of creditors of the debtor • a creditor with a judgment against the debtor • buyers of the asset without knowledge of security interest	

*None of these interests are enforceable against a person who acquires the asset in a manner permitted under the security agreement or in the ordinary course of the seller's business (unless sale was a breach of the security agreement and the person knew it).

ENFORCEMENT OF SECURITY INTERESTS

PPS legislation creates rules governing the enforcement of security interests by secured parties, including rules protecting the interests of debtors.

---

24. *Eg OPPSA*, s 20(1)(c); *SPPSA*, s 20(1)(d).

Default by the Debtor

A secured party can take possession of the collateral only when the debtor has defaulted on its obligations. A **default** occurs when

- the debtor fails to pay or to perform any other obligation secured under the security agreement, or
- an event occurs that is defined as a default in the security agreement

Security agreements often define default to include a failure to maintain

- the collateral in good working order
- insurance on the collateral

A security agreement may give the debtor a period, such as 30 days, to remedy the default. The creditor cannot take steps toward enforcement until that period expires.

default occurs if the debtor fails to pay or to perform any other obligation secured under the security agreement, or an event occurs that is defined as a default in the security agreement

Taking Possession

The secured party's first step when a debtor defaults is to take possession of the collateral. Possession may not be taken by force.[25] If the debtor resists, the secured party must seek a court order for possession. Once a secured party has taken possession of collateral, it has an obligation to take reasonable care of it.[26]

To take possession of the collateral, the secured party must give reasonable notice to the debtor.[27] What is reasonable varies from no notice at all to a few days. No notice would be appropriate if, for example, the debtor had no prospect of paying, and the collateral was at risk. Imagine, for example, that the collateral consisted of a truckload of ripe peaches. If collateral consists of accounts receivable, the secured party can simply give notice to the person obligated to make payment to the debtor that all future payments should be made directly to the secured party.[28]

Disposition of Collateral

Once the secured party has obtained possession of the collateral, it usually wants to sell it and apply the proceeds of the sale toward the outstanding debt. There are few legal rules regarding such sales. The secured party may advertise the sale to the public or enter into a private agreement with a buyer. They must give at least 15 days' notice of the sale to the debtor and others with an interest in it.[29] Alternatively, the secured party may decide to lease the collateral to someone or do something else. Whatever it decides to do, the secured party must act in a manner that is commercially reasonable.[30]

---

[25] *R v Doucette* (1960) 25 DLR (2d) 380 (Ont CA). Any method permitted by law may be used: *OPPSA*, s 62(a).

[26] *Eg BCPPSA*, s 17; *NBPPSA*, s 17; *OPPSA*, s 17.

[27] *Ronald Elwyn Lister Ltd v Dunlop Canada Ltd* (1982) 135 DLR (3d) 1 (SCC). There are special notice requirements when a secured party intends to enforce its security interest against an insolvent debtor provided for in the *Bankruptcy and Insolvency Act*, RSC 1985, c B-3 (Can). See Chapter 24.

[28] *Eg BCPPSA*, s 57; *NBPPSA*, s 57; *OPPSA*, s 61.

[29] *Eg OPPSA*, s 63; *SPPSA*, s 59.

[30] *Eg OPPSA*, s 63; *SPPSA*, s 59.

What is commercially reasonable depends upon the circumstances. In general, the secured party must take reasonable care to ensure that they obtain the fair value of the collateral and do not act negligently. In some cases, the secured party will be obliged to either advertise the sale to ensure that a competitive bidding process takes place or obtain a professional valuation to ensure that the collateral is not sold for less than it is worth.

The requirement for the secured party to act in a commercially reasonable manner protects the debtor. The secured party is interested only in recovering what they are owed, plus any expenses that they incurred as a result of enforcing their rights. Since the secured party cannot keep any excess money, they might be tempted to sell the collateral quickly for less than it is worth, so long as the price will cover what is owed to them. Consider the case in You Be the Judge 23.1.

When a secured party sells the collateral, they can keep from the proceeds (i) the amount they are owed on the debt and (ii) any reasonable expenses they incurred while seizing and disposing of the collateral. Any amount left over must be paid to the debtor. If there are other secured parties, however, proceeds may have to be paid to them rather than the debtor, in accordance with the priorities rules in the PPS legislation. If the secured party does not recover all that they are owed, the debtor remains liable for any deficiency.

You Be the Judge **23.1**

Commercial Reasonableness and the Disposition of Collateral[31]

Copp and Piccininni carried on a dental practice together through a corporation. For that practice, the corporation leased equipment from Medi-dent Services Ltd under a number of long-term leases. Copp and Piccininni got into a fundamental disagreement about how to run the practice. Everything stopped, including the payments to Medi-dent. Eventually, Medi-dent seized the equipment. At that time, Medi-dent was owed $31 000 under the leases.

On 18 April 1990, Medi-dent gave a notice to the corporation, as well as to Piccininni and Copp, that it would sell the equipment at a public or private sale after May 14 if the full amount of the indebtedness was not paid before that date. Piccininni contacted Medi-dent immediately after the seizure and offered to buy the equipment himself for $31 000.

Medi-dent readily agreed since that was a simple and inexpensive way to get its money out. The sale was concluded on May 15.

Copp subsequently challenged the sale on the basis that it was not commercially reasonable. Copp argued that Medi-dent had not had a valuation done, nor had it tried to sell the equipment through a competitive bidding process. He also produced evidence that the equipment had a fair market value of at least $79 000.

Questions for Discussion

1. Did Medi-dent act in a commercially reasonable manner?

2. What should Medi-dent have done?

When a Secured Party Can Keep the Collateral

Sometimes, a secured party will decide to keep the collateral after it has taken possession. Suppose the secured party runs an electrical contracting business. It sold some extra wiring it had on hand to another electrical contractor on credit and took a security interest in the wiring to secure the payment of the purchase price. If the buyer defaulted and the seller took possession of the wiring, the seller might want to keep the wiring to use in their own business.

Under PPS legislation, if the seller decides to keep the wiring, they give up any claim they have against the buyer for payment of the price. Therefore, the

---

[31.] *Copp v Medi-dent Services Ltd* (1991) 3 OR (3d) 570 (Gen Div).

seller would have to be satisfied that the goods are worth at least the amount of the buyer's obligation before they would want to keep the collateral. Before the seller can keep the collateral, however, they must give notice to the buyer and any other secured party with a security interest in the collateral. If anyone objects to the seller keeping the collateral, it has to be sold. Objections most commonly arise when the collateral is worth more than the debt owed to the secured party.[32]

When a Debtor Can Get the Collateral Back

The Ontario PPSA permits a debtor to **redeem collateral**—recover it back from a secured creditor who has seized it—only if the debtor has (i) fulfilled all the secured obligations, and (ii) paid all of the secured party's reasonable expenses.[33] In Ontario, a debtor does not have any right to cure a default and put the credit obligation back into good standing by making only their missed payments. Unless the secured party agrees, the debtor must redeem the collateral before the debtor can get it back. Secured parties who rank behind the secured party in possession of the collateral can also redeem it.

In other provinces, the debtor can redeem the collateral but can also get the collateral back by remedying all of their defaults, including making any missed payments, plus paying the secured party's expenses.[34] This is called **reinstating the collateral**. Some loan agreements include an **acceleration clause** providing that upon default by the debtor the full remaining amount of the debt becomes due. In provinces where reinstatement is permitted, such acceleration clauses are not enforceable.

Concept Summary 23.3 reviews the rules for enforcing security interests.

redeeming collateral means recovering the collateral from a secured creditor who has seized it by fulfilling all obligations owed to the secured party and paying any expenses the secured party has incurred

reinstating the collateral means the debtor gets the collateral back from a secured party that has seized it by remedying all of its defaults plus paying the secured party's expenses

an **acceleration clause** provides that upon default by the debtor the full remaining amount of the debt becomes due

Concept Summary 23.3

Steps in Enforcing a Security Interest

1. Debtor defaults.
2. Secured party takes possession of collateral.
3. Secured party retains collateral in full satisfaction of the debtor's obligation, *or*

   Secured party disposes of collateral and applies proceeds to debtor's debt, *or*

   Debtor gets collateral back (i) by redeeming it, meaning the debtor pays all outstanding amounts owed to the secured party, or (ii) in some provinces, by reinstating it, meaning the debtor pays the amounts owing at the time of default. To reinstate or redeem, the debtor must also pay the expenses of the secured party.
4. Debtor remains liable for any deficiency.
5. Any surplus is distributed in accordance with the scheme of priority in the relevant PPS legislation.

Special Rules for Consumers

Consumers are especially vulnerable to creditors who engage in unfair credit practices or aggressive enforcement of credit arrangements, including security interests. As a result, consumers are protected by an array of special rules under

---

[32] *Eg OPPSA*, s 65(2)–(7).

[33] *OPPSA*, s 66(1).

[34] *Eg SPPSA*, s 62; *MPPSA*, s 62.

PPS legislation and consumer protection legislation. For example, in many provinces, creditors are required to provide consumers with a disclosure statement before they enter into a credit agreement setting out prescribed information regarding items such as the interest rate, payment obligations, and costs. If disclosure is not made, the agreement is not enforceable.[35] With respect to enforcement, a conditional seller may not take possession of the property sold to a consumer if the consumer has paid at least two-thirds of the purchase price.[36]

L.O. ⑩   Guarantees

As we have seen, a creditor can reduce the risk of non-payment by taking security in the debtor's assets. A creditor can also reduce that risk by obtaining a *guarantee*, meaning a contractual promise by a third party, called a *guarantor*, to satisfy the principal debtor's obligation if the debtor fails to do so. For example, if you were going to borrow money to buy a car, the bank might ask your parents to sign a guarantee of your obligation to make the loan payments. Your parents' guarantee would mean that if you failed to pay, the bank could demand payment from them.[37] A bank might also ask for a guarantee if the borrower is a corporation with few assets or is starting a new business. A guarantee from a shareholder with substantial personal assets may convince the bank to make the loan. The obligation under a guarantee is typically independent of the debtor's obligation, meaning that, after the debtor has defaulted, it is not necessary for the creditor to take steps against the debtor to enforce the debtor's obligation before making demand on the guarantor for performance. Figure 23.2 illustrates how a guarantee works.

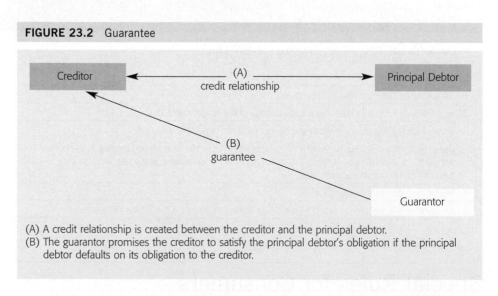

FIGURE 23.2   Guarantee

(A) A credit relationship is created between the creditor and the principal debtor.
(B) The guarantor promises the creditor to satisfy the principal debtor's obligation if the principal debtor defaults on its obligation to the creditor.

[35.] *Consumer Protection Act, 2002*, SO 2002, c 30, Sch A, ss 79, 93 (Ont), *Regulation under the Consumer Protection Act, 2002* O Reg 17/05, s 63; *Business Practices and Consumer Protection Act*, SBC 2004, c 2, s 84 (BC).

[36.] *Consumer Protection Act, 2002*, SO 2002, c 30, Sch A, s 25 (Ont); *BCPPSA* s 58(3). If collateral is consumer goods, the debtor has a right to reinstate the collateral in Ontario: *OPPSA*, s 66(2), (3). Other special provisions relating to consumer goods under the *OPPSA* include ss 12(2)(b), 45(2), 57, and 66. Consumer protection is discussed in Chapter 25.

[37.] There are many business situations in which guarantees may be sought and given, but the rules in each case are always the same as those described in this section.

A guarantor may be relieved of liability if the guarantor's risk is increased without the guarantor's consent. That occurs in four main situations:

- The contract between the creditor and principal debtor is modified, without the consent of the guarantor, in a material way that is prejudicial to the guarantor.[38] This commonly occurs when the creditor and the debtor agree to increase the size of the loan or the rate of interest to be paid by the debtor. In either event, the guarantor's exposure is increased. When this happens, the guarantor is released from liability.[39]

- The creditor breaches their contract with the principal debtor in a way that affects the guarantor's risk. Suppose a loan agreement stated that the debtor's failure to send the creditor annual financial statements was a default, but also that the creditor could take no action on the default for 30 days. If the creditor initiated enforcement proceedings when the statements were only one day late, and refused to accept the statements on the following day in breach of its obligations, the guarantor would be released. The creditor's action eliminated the debtor's right to cure the default.

- The creditor does something that decreases the value of the collateral that the principal debtor gave as security. In this case, the guarantor's obligation is reduced to the extent that the creditor diminished the value of the collateral. In some cases, the guarantor may be relieved of liability altogether.[40] Suppose the security was a shipment of pork bellies that were worth more than the debt. The bank took possession, but then let the goods sit for an unreasonable time. The pork became rancid and unsellable.[41]

- The creditor breaches the contract of guarantee. This might occur if, for instance, the contract required the creditor to notify the guarantor before demanding payment, but the creditor failed to do so.

In general, the guarantor can resist enforcement of the guarantee by using any defence that the principal debtor could use against the creditor. Suppose the creditor sold a television to your brother, and you signed a guarantee of your brother's obligation to pay the purchase price. If the television did not work, and your brother was entitled to refuse to pay the price, you could also refuse to make payment under the guarantee. Typically, however, the contract that creates the guarantee is a standard form that will require the guarantor to waive those defences, as well as all the grounds that we discussed in the previous bullet points that would relieve the guarantor of responsibility.[42] Finally, if a guarantor pays off the debt owed to the creditor, it can seek payment from the principal debtor.

A guarantee is often a significant obligation from which the guarantor may get little direct personal benefit.[43] The courts have held that a guarantee will not be enforceable if the guarantor does not understand the nature of the

---

[38.] *Reid v Royal Trust Corp of Canada* (1985) 20 DLR (4th) 223 (PEI CA).

[39.] *Manulife Bank of Canada v Conlin* [1996] 3 SCR 415.

[40.] The failure by a creditor to perfect its security interest in property of the principal debtor resulted in the guarantor being relieved of liability in *First City Capital Ltd v Hall* (1993) 11 OR (3d) 792 (CA).

[41.] *Bank of Montreal v Korico Enterprises Ltd* (2000) 190 DLR (4th) 706 (Ont CA).

[42.] These sorts of waivers are enforceable but are interpreted strictly against the creditor: *Bank of Montreal v Korico Enterprises Ltd* (2000) 190 DLR (4th) 706 (Ont CA).

[43.] Typically, the consideration received by the guarantor for giving the guarantee is credit being granted to the principal debtor.

obligations being undertaken. This is why guarantees must be in writing to be enforceable in every province except Manitoba.[44] Likewise, in some situations, courts have insisted that guarantors receive independent legal advice regarding the obligations that they are assuming, especially if they are in a vulnerable position and the guarantee exposes them to great risk.[45] Ethical Perspective 23.1 illustrates this issue.

Ethical Perspective 23.1

Informed Consent of Guarantor

Aline carries on a trucking business and is negotiating a loan of $100 000 from her bank. The bank is concerned that Aline will not be able to make her payments and asks her for security. Aline says that she does not have any assets to give as collateral. However, she also says that she lives with her grandmother, who has a portfolio of stock worth about $500 000. The bank suggests that if Aline could get her grandmother to guarantee Aline's debt and give a security interest in the stock portfolio to secure her obligation under the guarantee, it would make the loan.

Aline comes back to the bank several days later with her grandmother. When the banker tries to explain what she is committing herself to, the grandmother says she does not want to be worried about the details but just wants to help her granddaughter. The grandmother signs a guarantee and a security agreement that gives the bank a security interest in her stock portfolio. She does so without reading or receiving any explanation of either document.

Question for Discussion

1. Should the bank worry that the grandmother might not have fully appreciated the nature of the legal obligations to which she was committing herself? What difference would it make if the grandmother's sole source of income is what she receives from her stock portfolio?

---

44. In Alberta, a guarantee must be acknowledged before a notary public to be enforceable: *Guarantees Acknowledgement Act*, RSA 2000, c G-11, s 3.

45. *Bertolo v Bank of Montreal* (1986) 33 DLR (4th) 610 (Ont CA).

Chapter Summary

In a credit transaction there is a risk that the creditor will not be paid by the debtor. To reduce that risk, a creditor may take a security interest in the debtor's personal property. A security interest allows the creditor to seize and sell the collateral if the debtor does not fulfill their obligations. An alternative way to manage the risk of default for the creditor is to obtain a guarantee of the debtor's obligations from a third party.

Security interests can be created by agreement between the debtor and a creditor in several ways: (i) a security interest may be given by the debtor in a specific identified asset, including accounts receivable. These transactions may be structured as conditional sales, leases, and consignments; (ii) a debtor may give a security interest in all of their property including after-acquired property; and (iii) a debtor may give a security interest to a bank under the *Bank Act*. A conditional sale, a lease, and a consignment are forms of transaction that may be used to finance the acquisition of an asset.

Each province has personal property security (PPS) legislation that creates rules for the creation, registra-

tion, priority, and enforcement of security interests in personal property. These rules make it more likely that secured creditors will be able to obtain and enforce their security interests in a cost-effective and predictable way. PPS legislation applies to every transaction that creates a security interest, subject to some exceptions. These include legal rights such as landlords' distraint rights and deemed trusts in favour of the Canada Revenue Agency. Under PPS legislation, secured parties may perfect their interests in collateral if they have attached by registering a financing statement or taking possession of the collateral. PPS legislation creates rules for determining the priority of security interests. For registered security interests, priority is determined by the date of registration. An important exception to this rule is the super-priority given to secured parties who supply goods to the debtor or directly finance their acquisition by the debtor. These purchase money security interests (PMSIs) have priority over all other security interests created by the debtor in the goods if certain requirements are met. Security interests usually follow the collateral into the hands of anyone who buys it from the debtor. To protect buyers, a security interest does not follow the collateral when (i) the sale is in the ordinary course of the debtor's business, (ii) the sale was permitted by the secured party, or (iii) the secured party's interest was unperfected, and the buyer was unaware of it.

Three steps are followed in the enforcement of a security interest by a secured party following default by a debtor: (i) the secured party takes possession of collateral, (ii) the secured party retains collateral or disposes of it, or the debtor redeems it, and (iii) after disposition, any surplus is distributed in accordance with the priority of any

other security interests in the collateral under PPS legislation. The debtor receives any remaining surplus and is liable for any deficiency. Creditors have an obligation to act in a commercially reasonable manner when they take possession of a debtor's assets. This obligation governs how creditors deal with these assets.

Creditors can also reduce the risk of non-payment or non-performance by acquiring a guarantee from someone other than the principal debtor. Guarantors are released from liability when the creditor or the principal debtor acts in certain ways that prejudice the guarantor's position without the guarantor's consent.

MyBusLawLab   ADDITIONAL RESOURCES FOR CHAPTER 23

MyBusLawLab provides students with an assortment of tools to help enrich the learning experience, including a Study Plan with Pre- and Post-tests, mini-cases with assessments, and provincial content material, which provides links to relevant cases, legislation, and additional resources.

MyBusLawLab provides the following resources for Chapter 23:

Provincial Material

- **British Columbia:** Builders' Liens, Collection Agents, *Creditor Assistance Act,* Debt Collection, Liens, Enforcement of Security Interests, *Personal Property Security Act*, Perfection and Priority of Security Interests, Personal Property Registry

- **Alberta:** *Builders' Lien Act,* Consumer Credit, Debt Collections, Guarantees, Liens, Loan Transactions, Personal Money Security Interest, Personal Property Registry, *Personal Property Security Act*

- **Manitoba and Saskatchewan:** *Personal Property Security Acts*, Builders' Liens, Seizing Goods

- **Ontario:** Attachment, Bulk Sales, Construction Liens, Debt Collection Process, Financing Statement, Personal Property, *Personal Property Security Act*, Purchase Money Security Interest, Registration, Security Interest, Sale of Collateral, Consumer Credit, Limitation Periods

- **Atlantic Provinces:** Construction Liens, Consumer Credit, Personal Property Security Legislation

Review Questions

1. Why would a creditor be interested in obtaining a security interest?

2. Describe how a pledge can be used to give a security interest. What is a limitation on the use of a pledge to create security interests?

3. Describe four other ways in which a creditor can obtain a security interest in the specific property of a debtor.

4. When is a consignment the same as a conditional sale?

5. How can a lease be like a secured loan to finance the acquisition of an asset?

6. What is a floating charge and how is it different from the kind of security interest created in a general security agreement?

7. Why is the security that banks may take under the *Bank Act* different from other types of security interests?

8. How does provincial PPS legislation improve the ability of creditors to manage the risks associated with debtors' defaults compared to the rules that were in place before the enactment of such legislation?

9. Salvatore carries on an excavation business in British Columbia. He has just agreed to lease a bulldozer from Condon Leasing Inc for two years. Should Condon register its interest under the British Columbia PPS legislation?

10. What types of interests are not subject to PPS legislation? What problems does this pose for secured parties?

11. When does a security interest "attach"? What is the legal significance of attachment?

12. What advantage does a secured party obtain by perfecting its security interest? When should a secured party perfect?

13. If a manufacturer wanted to sell their product on credit to a dealer who had already given a bank a security interest in all of their current and future property, could the manufacturer obtain a security interest in the product they supplied that would rank ahead of the bank's? Assume that the bank's security interest is perfected.

14. If you were buying a boat from a friend, would you have any concerns about whether your friend had given a security interest in the boat to a creditor? If so, what would you do about it? Would your answer be any different if you were buying the boat from a boat dealership?

15. Describe the kind of protection that an attached but unperfected security interest has.

16. What must happen before a secured party can seize collateral?

17. When does a creditor's obligation to act in a commercially reasonable manner arise, and what does it require?

18. What rights does a debtor have once the secured party has taken possession of the collateral following a default?

19. Janet guaranteed Eldon's debt of $18 000 to the Bank of Montreal on 1 January 2014. Eldon's loan agreement with the bank provided that he was to pay back $1000 every month for 20 months. On 1 February 2014, Eldon and the bank agreed that the loan amount would be increased to $25 000 with the same monthly payment of $1000 but for 28 months. Does this agreement have any effect on Janet's obligations under her guarantee?

20. Is it necessary for a person to understand the nature of the obligations being undertaken in a guarantee for the guarantee to be enforceable against that person?

Cases and Problems

1. City Manufacturing Corp produces solar panels and sells them to dealers across Canada on credit. City's sole shareholder is Jerome, who has made an enormous amount of money in a number of high-tech businesses. City is negotiating to borrow $100 000 from TD Bank. The bank has some concerns regarding City's ability to repay the loan. If you were advising the bank, what are all the strategies that you could suggest to manage the risk that City would not repay the loan?

2. Tornado Tyres Inc borrowed $1 000 000 from National Bank. As security for its loan, Tornado gave National a security interest in all personal property that it owned at the time that it entered into the security agreement or acquired later. National registered a financing statement relating to its interest on 1 January 2013. In June 2014, Tornado ran into financial difficulty and failed to remit to the Canada Revenue Agency $50 000 that it had withheld from employee wages for income tax. Tornado also stopped making its loan payments to National.

   Acting under its security agreement, National seized all of Tornado's assets, including the $50 000 that was in Tornado's bank account at National. National has checked and there are no other security interests registered under the PPS legislation. Is there any reason that National should not apply the $50 000 against the liability of Tornado under the loan? Would it make any difference to your answer if National had never properly registered its interest under the PPS legislation?

3. In June 2013, Cory leased a $50 000 truck from Superior Leasing Inc for the snowplowing business he carried on in Toronto. The lease allowed Cory to use the truck for three years in return for monthly lease payments of $1000. There is no option to purchase the truck at the end of the term. Superior did not file a financing statement in relation to its interest in the truck. Cory had also borrowed $40 000 from the Bank of Toronto and had given the bank a security interest in all of his property. The bank properly registered a financing statement relating to this interest on 1 January 2014. Who is entitled to the truck if Cory defaults on his payments to both the bank and Superior?

4. Erin bought a new car for her catering business from Davis Motors Inc for $20 000. Under the terms of the purchase, Erin paid $5000 down and agreed to pay the balance in regular monthly instalments. To secure her obligation, Erin gave Davis a security interest in the car. Erin defaulted on the payments when she had just $3000 left to pay. Acting under its security agreement, Davis repossessed the car. The manager of Davis liked Erin's car and offered to buy it from Davis for $7500. Davis agreed. When Davis received the money from the manager, it applied $3000 to the loan and paid the balance of $4500 to Erin. Erin is unhappy because she recently saw an identical car advertised for $10 000.

   Is there any basis upon which Erin could complain about what Davis has done?

5. Samra had agreed to guarantee a loan of $50 000 that her brother, Amman, had received from the Bank of Vancouver. Amman had entered into a general security agreement with the bank giving it a security interest in all his personal property, which included several vehicles and some jewellery. After Amman had paid back $25 000, he approached the bank asking for permission to sell one of his rings to a friend for $5000. He convinced the bank that his remaining personal property would be more than enough to cover the amount of the debt still unpaid. The bank agreed. Amman and the bank signed an

agreement releasing the bank's security interest in the ring, and Amman sold it.

Two years later when $5000 remained to be paid, Amman defaulted on his loan. The first thing that the bank did was to ask Samra to pay under her guarantee the amount of the payments that Amman had missed. Does Samra have to pay?

6. Goldie bought a new refrigerator from Cool Refrigerators Ltd, a retail appliance dealer, under a conditional sales agreement. In the contract, Goldie was given the right to possession of the refrigerator in return for promising to make six equal monthly payments of $150. Cool was to retain ownership of the refrigerator until the full price was paid. The contract also stated that if Goldie failed to make a payment, the total of all the outstanding payments became immediately due upon notice from Cool. Moreover, Cool was entitled to take possession of the refrigerator. Goldie has failed to make any payments after the initial instalment. What can Cool do? Describe all the steps that Cool would have to take to enforce its interest.

7. Senf Mustard Manufacturing Inc borrowed $75 000 from Lucia Lending Inc. As security for the loan, Senf agreed that Lucia could have possession of some gold bullion that it owned. Senf agreed that Lucia could sell the gold to pay off Senf's debt if Senf defaulted. Subsequently, Senf borrowed $100 000 from Metro Bank. Senf gave the bank a security interest in all of its property. The bank properly registered a financing statement relating to this interest. Whose security interest in the bullion ranks first if Senf defaults on his payments to both Lucia and the bank?

8. Elena operates a computer consulting business. She has a small number of large clients whom she bills monthly. Elena is seeking a loan from Northern Bank. How could Northern manage its risk that Elena will default on a loan from Northern if the business has no significant physical assets?

9. Elmira Bakery Inc operates a bakery business. Elmira entered into a general security agreement with Brunswick Bank on 1 January 2014 to provide security for a loan from the bank. On 1 April 2014, Elmira defaulted on the loan. At that time the outstanding balance was $50 000. The bank seized the equipment at the bakery. The bank has put an advertisement in a local newspaper asking for offers for the equipment. The advertisement says that the bank will sell at the best price offered. Alcon Bakeries Inc offers $65 000 for the equipment, and this is the only offer received by the bank. Can the bank sell the equipment to Alcon?

10. Giovanni Boats Inc has a line of credit with Imperial Bank in Vancouver. The line of credit is secured on all the assets that Giovanni has or later acquires. The bank filed a financing statement to register its security interest under the British Columbia PPS legislation on 1 March 2013. In June 2013, Giovanni bought a boat from West-End Marina under a conditional sales contract for $15 000. That contract provided that Giovanni would make regular monthly payments for five years. West-End retained ownership of the boat as security for Giovanni's obligations to make the payments. West-End assigned its interest in the boat and the conditional sales contract to Springliner Finance Corp.

At the end of three years Giovanni defaulted on its payments under the conditional sales agreement and on its obligations to the bank. The bank has seized the boat. What should Springliner do? Is there anything that Springliner could have done to better protect its interests?

11. Gilles has a restaurant business that he operates as a sole proprietorship. He has a line of credit with ScotiaBank that is secured by a general security agreement. The bank has perfected its security interest by filing a financing statement under the applicable PPS legislation. Gilles was moving and decided to put some of his furniture in storage for a few months. He agreed to pay Ace Storage Inc $100 per month for 12 months in return for a storage locker. He paid for the first month but made no other payments. At the end of the 12 months, Gilles went to get his furniture. Ace refused to give it to him until he paid his bill. Gilles has also defaulted on his line of credit. Who is entitled to the furniture—ScotiaBank or Ace?

12. Global Realty Inc owned an office building. It leased the fourth floor to Jensen Corp for two years beginning 1 January 2013. Sarah Jensen, the president and sole shareholder of Jensen Corp, gave Global a personal guarantee of all of Jensen Corp's obligations under the lease. By June 2013, Jensen Corp was having difficulty with its obligations and wanted to sublet part of the fourth floor. The lease permitted Jensen Corp to sublet so long as the landlord, Global, consented. The lease also provided that Global's consent could not be unreasonably withheld. Jensen Corp found five different possible tenants, but Global would not consent to any of them. Global did not give any reason for its refusal. Eventually, Jensen Corp defaulted on its lease payments and Global demanded payment from Sarah Jensen under her guarantee. Is Sarah Jensen obliged to pay?

24 Dealing with Bankruptcy and Insolvency

LEARNING OBJECTIVES

After completing this chapter, you should be able to:

❶ Identify the main legal options by which an insolvent business can deal with its creditors.

❷ Explain why creditors may be better off if the person who owes them money becomes bankrupt.

❸ Distinguish between bankruptcy and insolvency of a debtor.

❹ Describe how the bankruptcy of a consumer differs from the bankruptcy of a corporation.

❺ Identify the participants involved in a bankruptcy and the roles they play.

❻ Identify the property of a debtor that is exempt from distribution to creditors upon bankruptcy.

❼ Identify three categories of creditors and describe the rights of each to share in the debtor's assets upon bankruptcy.

❽ Explain the principle that creditors should be treated equally upon bankruptcy.

❾ Identify pre-bankruptcy transactions involving the debtor's assets that can be set aside upon bankruptcy.

❿ Describe the advantages and disadvantages to the debtor and their creditors of restructuring an insolvent debtor compared to bankruptcy.

An unavoidable part of any business venture—as we stress throughout this book—is risk. In this chapter, we focus on the risk of business failure. More than 80 percent of small businesses in Canada fail during the first five years of operation.[1] The liquidation during the past decade of several well-established companies, such as Nortel, reminds us that big business is not immune from the risk of failure either.

Canadian law provides several procedures for dealing with a business's failure. In all of them, the usual ways in which creditors pursue their claims, such as by suing in court, are superseded by a collective process in which the interests of all creditors are addressed fairly and equitably.

One procedure for dealing with business failure is *bankruptcy*. When a person's debts exceed their assets or they cannot meet their liabilities as they come due, often described as being **insolvent**, they may become formally **bankrupt**, either by assigning themselves into bankruptcy or as a result of a creditor applying to a court for a bankruptcy order against them. Upon bankruptcy, all legal proceedings against a debtor are subject to a **stay**, meaning that they are suspended and superseded by the bankruptcy proceeding. The bankrupt's assets are then *liquidated*. **Liquidation** is the sale of the debtor's assets in return for money, which is "liquid" and can be distributed to the bankrupt's creditors. Once that distribution has occurred, the law prohibits new claims from being launched against the bankrupt for any pre-existing debt. Eventually a debtor may be either *discharged* or, in the case of a corporation, its existence terminated. **Discharge** is the release of a debtor from bankruptcy status. After discharge, a debtor is free of all of their pre-bankruptcy debt, subject to certain limited exceptions.

One goal of this procedure is to provide for the orderly and predictable distribution of the debtor's assets amongst their creditors. Another is to provide debtors who are individuals with a fresh start through their discharge from bankruptcy. This is one way in which the risks of business activity are mitigated for entrepreneurs. Nevertheless, significant costs remain for debtors going bankrupt. Corporate and consumer bankrupts will usually find it difficult to re-establish their credit. But bankruptcy may not mark the end of a debtor's career, as it often did in the past. Bankruptcy law tries to balance rehabilitation of the debtor with protecting the legitimate interests of creditors in getting paid.

Another method of dealing with financial distress is for the debtor to make a *proposal* to creditors. A **proposal** is a court-approved arrangement between a debtor and their creditors providing for a restructuring of the debtor's debts and other financial affairs outside of formal bankruptcy. If the proposal is successful, the debtor continues to operate their business in most cases. If not, the debtor is placed into bankruptcy. Proposals are used to provide time and a process by which a business can be restructured under court supervision in situations where the creditors are more likely to recover more of what is owed to them if the debtor continues their business than if the assets are sold in a liquidation.

When a business is in financial difficulty, both debtors and creditors must make strategic choices. Fundamentally, creditors must assess whether it is more likely that they will get paid if the debtor is permitted to continue their business than if their assets are liquidated and the proceeds are shared

a person is **insolvent** when their debts exceed their assets, or they cannot meet their liabilities as they come due

a person becomes **bankrupt** by assigning themselves into bankruptcy or as a result of a creditor applying to a court for a bankruptcy order against them

a **stay** is a suspension of legal proceedings against a debtor

liquidation is the sale of the debtor's assets in return for money, which is "liquid" and can be distributed to the bankrupt's creditors

discharge is the release of a debtor from bankruptcy status

a **proposal** is a court-approved arrangement between a debtor and their creditors providing for a restructuring of the debtor's debts and other financial affairs outside of formal bankruptcy

PART 7

[1.] F Zaid *Canadian Franchise Guide* (1983) at 1:401.

amongst all creditors. Creditors sustain significant monetary and non-monetary costs in pursuing debtors. The aggravation and expense of collecting overdue debts can cause creditors to hesitate before strictly enforcing their right to payment and ultimately applying to have a bankruptcy order made against the debtor. Creditors may also hesitate for fear of suffering intangible losses during the bankruptcy process, particularly the loss of business synergies, established relationships, and accrued **goodwill**—a business's favourable and valuable public reputation. A creditor that acts too quickly and too harshly can be viewed poorly in the business community. Creditors may stand to gain more by adopting a flexible attitude. The outcome of these strategic calculations will depend upon the circumstances. For instance, a debtor may be so important in the community that creditors feel unable to "pull the plug," at least for a period of time.

> **goodwill** is a business's favourable and valuable public reputation

A debtor in financial distress must decide whether to approach their creditors with a restructuring proposal or to cut their losses and get a fresh start through bankruptcy. If a debtor decides to try to continue, they must choose whether they want to proceed through direct negotiations with creditors or by making a proposal. Depending upon the personal relationship the debtor has with their creditors and the prospects to turn the business around, the debtor may have more or less flexibility in this regard. The debtor may also use the threat of an assignment in bankruptcy to play for time. Typically, debtors will retain the services of a lawyer or accountant who specializes in insolvency to advise them regarding these choices.

Well-developed bankruptcy and insolvency laws help to reduce uncertainty for debtors and creditors and provide tools for risk management. They give creditors a better sense of the risks that arise when they extend credit, by providing a detailed set of rules to govern the repayment of creditors when a business becomes bankrupt and the process through which insolvent businesses may be restructured to facilitate repayment. They also provide debtors with several alternatives for their rehabilitation. To parties on both sides of the credit transaction, bankruptcy and insolvency laws provide predictability regarding what will happen in the event of financial failure.

L.O. ❶   Authority to Regulate Bankruptcy and Insolvency

Canada's Constitution assigns the power to enact bankruptcy legislation exclusively to the federal government. (The division of legislative authority between the federal and provincial governments was discussed in Chapter 1.) The federal *Bankruptcy and Insolvency Act* (*BIA*) provides a framework to administer the bankruptcy process, various kinds of proceedings in bankruptcy (assignments and applications by creditors for a bankruptcy order), non-bankruptcy alternatives (proposals), detailed regulations concerning the administration and distribution of the debtor's property, the duties of a bankrupt, and miscellaneous related matters.[2]

[2.] *Bankruptcy and Insolvency Act*, RSC 1985, c B-3 (Can).

Bankruptcy and Insolvency Law

Prior to the enactment of modern bankruptcy law, a creditor's only option was to sue a debtor for non-payment. (The process by which creditors enforce their judgments in discussed in Chapter 2.) However, news of a single suit often triggered a legal stampede by creditors, all trying to claim the same assets of the debtor. Once all the claims came before the court together, it was often difficult to determine which *claims* were valid and which creditors should rank ahead of others. The response eventually developed by the courts was to halt all claims against the debtor in these circumstances, pool their remaining assets, and provide for the liquidation and distribution of the proceeds to creditors. Once the proceeds of the liquidation were distributed, no further claims could be brought against the bankrupt for debts previously incurred. Even though creditors often received far less than the face value of their loans under this approach, this judicial innovation had several advantages:

- A single proceeding prevented a race to the courts with the first creditor to obtain a judgment getting the right to execute their judgment against all the debtor's assets while the next judgment creditor could execute only against what was left. All creditors were treated on the same basis by a single judge, who heard all the evidence of the debtor's various debts. In this context, creditors have an incentive to work co-operatively with the debtor and one another to maximize recovery of the amounts owed, rather than trying to be the first one to make a claim.

- The proceeding was efficient in that it avoided the multiplication of enforcement costs for creditors and provided for the orderly disposition of the debtor's assets in a way that was more likely to realize their value than the uncoordinated disposition of assets as individual creditors sought execution of their judgments.

- Because the debtor was exposed to only one set of legal proceedings, their assets were not depleted by paying for lawyers to defend a variety of claims. Money that would have gone to the debtor's lawyers went to creditors instead.

- The bankrupt was given a fresh start. Although the stigma of bankruptcy was harsh, the bankrupt's rehabilitation could begin as soon as they were discharged.

Over time some of those procedures changed, but on the whole they still apply in Canada today under the *BIA*.

The *BIA* is the most important statute relating to bankruptcy and insolvency. Broadly speaking, the *BIA* tries to achieve a number of objectives simultaneously. It aims to:

- provide for a timely, orderly, and equitable distribution of the bankrupt's assets to creditors in accordance with clear rules establishing the priority of creditor claims

- provide for the rehabilitation of debtors through a discharge that frees them from prior debts and obligations in appropriate circumstances

- limit the possibility of discharge for certain debts that are considered socially important, such as family support obligations and student loans

- deter and redress fraudulent pre-bankruptcy transfers by debtors and transfers that prefer particular creditors over others
- promote confidence and certainty in the credit system
- promote national uniformity of laws in a field of importance to Canadian business

The *BIA* applies to all Canadian businesses, subject to some important exceptions. It does not apply to banks, insurance companies, trust companies, or railways—key economic institutions that are dealt with under separate statutes. In addition, farmers and fishers cannot be placed into bankruptcy. That reflects a policy decision based on the highly volatile nature of the farming and fishing industries.

The Act is by far the most commonly looked-to statute concerning financial distress and failure in Canada, but it is not the only one. The federal *Companies' Creditors Arrangement Act (CCAA)* allows a debtor to seek a stay of all claims pending the acceptance of a reorganization plan that restructures the debts and other financial aspects of the debtor's business.[3] Unlike bankruptcy, which is essentially a regime dealing with the liquidation of the debtor's assets and the distribution of the proceeds to creditors, a restructuring under the *CCAA* preserves the business by reducing or adjusting the claims of creditors through a reorganization of its debt. Restructuring may also be accomplished through proposals under the *BIA*.

Finally, the federal *Winding-Up and Restructuring Act* applies to the liquidation of federally incorporated corporations, banks, and insurance companies.[4] Later in this chapter, we will discuss how those statutes interact with the *BIA*.

A number of provincial statutes apply to debtor–creditor relations. These statutes, like the provincial personal property security statutes discussed in Chapter 23, are enacted by the provinces under their constitutional jurisdiction over property and civil rights.[5] In case of conflict, the *BIA* prevails. For instance, an early version of the Ontario *Employment Standards Act* purported to give priority to unpaid wages over all other claims. The applicable section of the Act was held to be inapplicable in the event of a bankruptcy because it directly conflicted with the *BIA*, which subordinates wage claims to the claims of secured creditors.[6]

BANKRUPTCY AND INSOLVENCY UNDER THE *BANKRUPTY AND INSOLVENCY ACT*

To understand the *BIA*, it is necessary to appreciate the difference between *bankruptcy* and *insolvency*.

Insolvency is the inability of a debtor to meet their financial obligations to their creditors. Many businesses operate in, or near, a state of insolvency from time to time on account of lags in payment and the level of debt they carry. Insolvency is defined in the *BIA* as any of the following:

insolvency is the inability of a debtor to meet their financial obligations to their creditors.

[3.] *Companies Creditors' Arrangement Act*, RSC 1985, c C-36 (Can).

[4.] *Winding-Up and Restructuring Act*, RSC 1985, c W-11 (Can).

[5.] Provincial statutes that apply to businesses in financial distress also include provincial fraudulent conveyances statutes (*eg Fraudulent Conveyances Act*, RSO 1990, c F.29) and the business corporations laws discussed in Chapters 21 and 22.

[6.] *Re Lewis Department Stores Ltd* (1972) 17 CBR (NS) 113 (Ont Reg).

- The debtor is unable to meet their liabilities as they become due.

- The debtor has ceased paying their current obligations in the ordinary course of business as they generally become due.

- The aggregate of the debtor's property is not, at a fair valuation, sufficient or, if disposed of, would not be sufficient to enable payment of all obligations due and becoming due.[7]

Bankruptcy is the legal status of a person who has either made an **assignment** in bankruptcy (a procedure by which a debtor voluntarily becomes bankrupt) or had a bankruptcy order made against them by a court or other official based on a creditor's application. In order for a person to be the subject of a bankruptcy order, they must have committed an "act of bankruptcy." That act of bankruptcy usually involves being insolvent.[8] The simple fact that a debtor is insolvent is not sufficient, however, for a person to be legally bankrupt. In practice, creditors are often prepared to wait well beyond mere insolvency to begin bankruptcy proceedings. They may adopt that attitude to maintain business relationships, preserve assets, and avoid the expense of legal action.

Figure 24.1 illustrates the methods of entering bankruptcy. We will examine the procedures for creditor applications for bankruptcy orders and assignments in detail later in the chapter.

bankruptcy is the legal status of a person who has either made an assignment in bankruptcy or had a bankruptcy order made against them by a court or other official based on a creditor's application

an **assignment** is a procedure by which a debtor voluntarily becomes bankrupt

FIGURE 24.1 Two Methods of Entering Bankruptcy

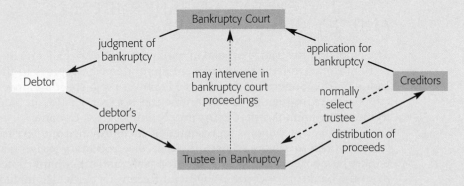

1. **Assignment**: the debtor assigns its available property to the trustee for eventual distribution to creditors

Debtor → transfer of assets → Trustee in Bankruptcy → distribution of proceeds → Creditors

2. **Application by creditor for bankruptcy order**: creditors apply to the court for order that debtor is bankrupt (must be owed at least $1000 and debtor must have committed an act of bankruptcy)

Bankruptcy Court

judgment of bankruptcy

application for bankruptcy

may intervene in bankruptcy court proceedings

Debtor

Creditors

debtor's property

normally select trustee

distribution of proceeds

Trustee in Bankruptcy

PART 7

[7.] *BIA*, s 2(1).

[8.] *BIA*, s 42, sets out nine other possible "acts of bankruptcy." These include conduct by the debtor that shows an intention to frustrate the legitimate collection efforts of their creditors, such as fraudulently disposing of their assets to defeat their creditors, and acts that show insolvency, such as a declaration of insolvency or a default on a proposal.

L.O. ❹ # Corporate and Consumer Bankruptcy

In 2010, almost 100 000 Canadians entered bankruptcy. Of these, more than 95 percent were consumers and 4 percent were corporations. In 2010, total liabilities for bankrupt corporations amounted to $8.6 billion, or $2 105 756 per bankrupt, while total liabilities of consumer bankrupts were only $11 billion, or $118 936 per bankrupt.[9]

Because of the marked difference in the size and scope of consumer and corporate bankruptcy, there are some different rules for each type of bankruptcy proceeding. Two differences are especially important:

- Proposals by corporations to their creditors to settle their obligations require the approval of a majority of creditors in each class of creditors, and those creditors must represent at least two-thirds of the value of the claims in that class. The division of creditors into different classes is discussed below. Consumer debtors can make a simplified form of proposal that needs to be approved by only a majority of all creditors.

- Corporate debtors are rarely discharged from bankruptcy unless they pay all of their debts. However, first-time consumer debtors who demonstrate responsible behaviour are usually discharged within nine months.

Apart from these differences, there are few explicit distinctions between corporate and consumer bankruptcy.[10] This chapter focuses on corporate bankruptcy. Nevertheless, because consumer bankruptcies have become increasingly common, we will consider their distinctive characteristics from time to time.

L.O. ❺ # Officials Involved in Bankruptcy Procedures

Bankruptcy procedures are distinct from ordinary court procedures. A number of specialized officials play important roles in the bankruptcy process. In this section, we describe who these people are and what they do. Figure 24.2 provides an overview.

SUPERINTENDENT OF BANKRUPTCY AND OFFICIAL RECEIVERS

The chief administrative official in bankruptcy in Canada is the Superintendent of Bankruptcy, a federal government appointee who reports to the Minister of Industry. The Superintendent has wide powers to inspect and investigate bankrupts' estates, to regulate and examine the work of trustees in bankruptcy, and to intervene in bankruptcy court proceedings across Canada.

The Superintendent is represented in each province and territory by a number of *Official Receivers*, whose offices receive voluntary assignments, copies of bankruptcy orders against debtors, proposals, and other bankruptcy documents from the bankruptcy court. An Official Receiver's tasks also include examining bankrupts, chairing first meetings of creditors, and generally monitoring trustees' performance.

[9.] Office of the Superintendent of Bankruptcy Canada, *Annual Statistical Report for the 2010 Calendar Year* (2010). There were also some 43 468 proposals filed in 2010 by debtors with total liabilities of almost $7 billion.

[10.] *BIA*, s 66.11, defines a "consumer debtor" as an insolvent natural person whose total debts, excluding those secured by their principal residence, do not exceed $250 000.

FIGURE 24.2   Officials in Bankruptcy Procedures

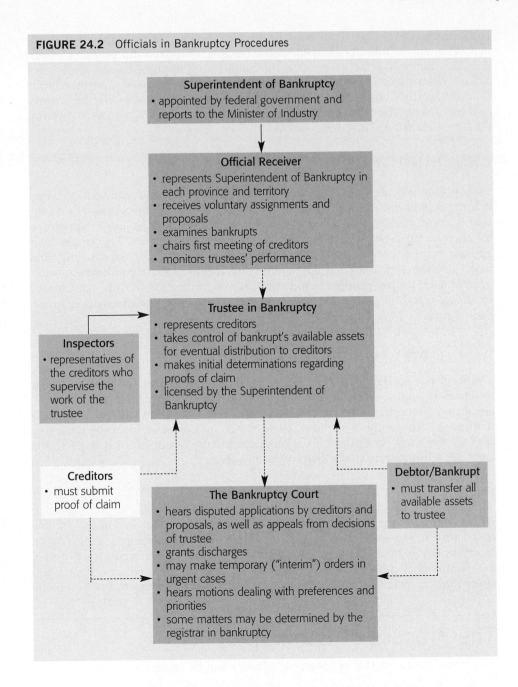

TRUSTEE IN BANKRUPTCY

Creditors in a bankruptcy are usually represented by a *trustee*, who gathers in and liquidates the debtors' assets and distributes the proceeds to creditors. The trustee is a private person licensed by the Superintendent who assumes control of the debtor's assets once appointed by a court (in the case of a bankruptcy order) or by the Official Receiver (in the case of an assignment). Typically, trustees are accountants or are employed by corporate trustees, such as Deloitte and Touche, and are members of the Canadian Association of Insolvency and Restructuring Professionals. As we saw in Chapters 1 and 8, a trustee is someone who has possession of property for the benefit of someone else. In the bankruptcy context, a trustee becomes the legal owner of the bankrupt's property. The trustee takes possession of the bankrupt's assets and prepares essential documents in connection with the bankruptcy, reports on the bankrupt's affairs, determines if creditors' proofs of claim will be allowed, and then, after liquidation, distributes the proceeds to creditors in accordance with the priority of their claims. The trustee's claim to be paid for that work is a preferred claim. Preferred claims are discussed below.

BANKRUPTCY COURT

Most provinces call their provincial superior court a "bankruptcy court" when it hears a bankruptcy case. There is no formally separate system of courts for that purpose. Most bankruptcy courts are staffed by regular judges appointed for their competence in bankruptcy and commercial matters. The judges hear appeals from decisions of the Registrar in Bankruptcy (discussed below) and make decisions on disputed applications by creditors for a bankruptcy order against a debtor, on proposals and applications for discharge from bankruptcy by debtors, and on motions relating to conflicts regarding the priority of creditors' claims.

REGISTRAR IN BANKRUPTCY

The Registrar in Bankruptcy is like a deputy judge with the power to (i) hear unopposed applications by creditors for bankruptcy orders and proposals, (ii) grant discharges, (iii) make interim orders in cases of urgency, (iv) hear disputes about creditors' proof of their claims and appeals from the decisions of a trustee, and (v) deal with various administrative questions related to the trustee's administration of a bankrupt's property.[11]

INSPECTORS

Under the *BIA*, the creditors have the right to appoint a maximum of five inspectors to supervise the trustee in managing the bankrupt's property. In practice, the inspectors are usually employees of the largest creditors, but they have a fiduciary duty to act in the best interests of all the creditors. Their decisions may be reviewed by the bankruptcy court if fraud or partiality is shown.

L.O. ❻❼❽❾ # The Process of Bankruptcy

As we saw earlier in this chapter, bankruptcy can be triggered in two ways:

- *voluntarily*—by assignment of the debtor
- *involuntarily*—by application of creditors for a bankruptcy order against the debtor

ASSIGNMENT INTO BANKRUPTCY BY THE DEBTOR

Even before creditors have decided to take court action, the debtor may decide that their financial situation is so serious that an assignment may be appropriate.

[11.] *BIA*, s 192(1).

Assignment is the most commonly used bankruptcy procedure in Canada.[12] If the debtor is a corporation, the directors must call a meeting to authorize the corporation to assign itself into bankruptcy. A debtor must be insolvent to file an assignment. Assignments are filed with the Official Receiver in the locality of the debtor. Formally, the Official Receiver appoints a trustee. Often, the debtor selects the trustee first, and the trustee assists the debtor with the documents necessary to make the assignment. The Official Receiver then appoints that person as trustee unless there is some objection from the debtor's creditors.

After taking possession of the bankrupt's property, the trustee meets with the debtor to prepare a long-form statement of affairs and a notice of the first meeting of creditors, which is chaired by the Official Receiver. At that meeting, the trustee advises creditors on how they intend to liquidate the assets and distribute the proceeds. The rules regarding gathering in and liquidating assets and distributions to creditors are discussed later in this chapter.

APPLICATION BY CREDITORS FOR A BANKRUPTCY ORDER

To obtain a bankruptcy order against a debtor, a creditor or creditors acting together must prove that the debtor owes at least $1000. Furthermore, they must prove that the debtor committed an act of bankruptcy within the past six months. As noted, the most common act of bankruptcy is the insolvency of the debtor, in the sense that the debtor has ceased to meet their liabilities as they become due. A creditor making an application often makes a fresh demand for payment to provide clear evidence in support of the creditor's application. The creditor also needs evidence from other creditors that the debtor has ceased to meet their liabilities "generally," and therefore will *examine* other creditors for that purpose. Because that examination is informal, being outside or prior to a court action, there is no guarantee that the other creditors will co-operate.

Submitting an Application for a Bankruptcy Order

An application for a bankruptcy order must be filed in the court having jurisdiction in the locality of the debtor. Once submitted, it becomes an action on behalf of and binding on all the creditors. The bankruptcy action supersedes all individual actions by creditors. An application for a bankruptcy order will include an affidavit, a voluntary written statement made under oath that supports the statements made in the application, as well as a notice that sets the date for the hearing of the matter before the registrar or a bankruptcy judge. An application by a creditor for a bankruptcy order is often resisted by the debtor. If the debtor is defending the application they may submit a notice disputing the allegations and cross-examine a representative of the creditor with a view to showing that the allegations in the affidavit are not true.

An undisputed application for a bankruptcy order may be heard by the Registrar in Bankruptcy who, after examining the documents, may grant the application if satisfied that the requirements of the *BIA* have been met. Disputed applications for bankruptcy orders are heard by a bankruptcy judge. The main issues before the judge are usually whether the debtor has committed the alleged act of bankruptcy and whether the debts claimed by the creditors are valid.

Case Brief 24.1 deals with one aspect of bankruptcy procedure: the requirement to commence proceedings in the debtor's locality.

[12.] An insolvent person must owe at least $1000 to make an assignment.

Case Brief 24.1

Re Malarctic Hygrade Gold Mines Ltd (1966) 10 CBR (NS) 34 (Ont SCJ)

In Canada, bankruptcy proceedings must be started in the debtor's "locality." That requirement occasionally causes problems because the debtor's locality may appear to be in several places. For example, the places where the debtor is physically located, where the debtor carries on business, where the majority of their assets are situated, and where their creditors reside may all be different. The *BIA* focuses on the place where the debtor carries on business, where they reside, or sometimes where the greater part of the bankrupt's property is located.

Malarctic Hygrade Gold Mines Ltd carried on a substantial amount of business prospecting for gold in northern Quebec. It had creditors there and was making plans to expand operations in that province. However, the head office of the company was in Ontario, the company was incorporated in Ontario, the company's books were located in Ontario, and the company's share register was in Ontario.

The court decided that, in all the circumstances, Ontario was the debtor's locality. That decision illustrates the importance of the *legal* presence of a debtor when other factors are conflicting or inconclusive.

The Bankruptcy Order

If the court or the registrar decides to allow the application for a bankruptcy order, it usually orders the debtor to release all of their assets to the court or to a court-appointed agent, usually a trustee in bankruptcy. This order is often accompanied by a notice directing the bankrupt, or their representative, to make themselves available to be examined by the trustee.

Under the bankruptcy order, the trustee becomes the temporary manager of the debtor's business under the supervision of the inspectors appointed by the creditors. The trustee's main responsibility is to gather in all the property of the debtor and apply it toward payment of the creditors. The trustee therefore must (i) obtain the keys, passwords, and operating authorities of the bankrupt, (ii) take possession of the bankrupt's assets, and (iii) notify insurers, banks, sheriffs, and landlords about the change in management. The trustee must also tell the Official Receiver which of the bankrupt's officers will answer questions and perform the obligations that are imposed upon the bankrupt by the *BIA*. That officer is usually the person who oversaw the bankrupt party's day-to-day operations before the bankruptcy occurred.

The Official Receiver examines or questions the bankrupt's officer about the causes of the bankruptcy, the whereabouts of creditors, and the status of debts. That information is written into a *statement of account*, which the trustee uses to plan and perform the liquidation of the bankrupt's assets.

DISTRIBUTION OF ASSETS

Once the trustee has taken possession of the bankrupt's property, the trustee must liquidate the property and then distribute the proceeds to the bankrupt's creditors. As discussed below, some assets are exempt and continue to belong to the bankrupt. As well, the *BIA* provides rules regarding how assets are to be distributed to creditors.

Exempt Property

Generally speaking, all of the bankrupt's assets are available for distribution to the creditors; however, individual consumers who enter bankruptcy are entitled to certain exemptions that ensure they do not become destitute. Since both federal and provincial governments have the power to designate exempt property, the entitlements vary slightly between jurisdictions.[13] In addition to specific assets, bankrupts are entitled to keep wages that they earn during bankruptcy, but only up to a maximum set by the Official Receiver.[14] Corporate bankrupts are not entitled to exempt property. In Ontario, individuals are allowed to keep the following assets:

- tools of their trade worth up to $11 300
- necessary clothing worth up to $5650
- one motor vehicle if needed for work worth up to $5650
- their principal residence
- food, fuel, household furniture, and appliances worth up to $11 300
- farm property
- statutory pension benefits, insurance proceeds, and certain registered retirement savings plan assets

Creditors' Entitlements upon Bankruptcy

Bankruptcy occurs because a debtor cannot pay their debts. As a consequence, bankruptcy typically results in creditors getting less than the full amount of their claims. For instance, if you owe me $2000, I may receive only $1000 if you become bankrupt. In fact, for the lowest ranking creditors, the average recovery upon bankruptcy is only about 5 percent of their claim. Most professional creditors, such as banks, deal with this risk by obtaining security in the debtors' assets, as discussed below. As well, the interest rate charged on a bank loan reflects the bank's assessment of two risks: (i) that the debtor will not be able to repay the loan and (ii) that the amount it will actually be able to recover if the debtor becomes bankrupt will be less than the amount of the debt. If these risks are too great, the bank may simply refuse to make the loan.

CATEGORIES OF CREDITORS   Under the *BIA*, creditors' entitlements on bankruptcy depend upon whether they are *secured* or *unsecured*.[15] As we saw in Chapter 23, a **secured creditor** is a creditor who has a security interest in a particular asset of the debtor, such as a tractor or accounts receivable, or all of the debtor's assets under a general security agreement. The creditor is "secure" in the sense that there are definite assets that it can look to for payment in the event of a bankruptcy. For this reason, creditors may be willing to make secured loans even in situations of advanced financial distress. Secured credit is privileged under the *BIA*. That privilege exempts the creditor from the stay of legal proceedings that arises upon bankruptcy.[16] The secured creditor can take possession of a secured asset for themselves or dispose of it immediately.[17]

a **secured creditor** is a creditor who has a security interest in a particular asset of the debtor or all of the debtor's assets

---

[13.] *BIA*, s 67(1)(b). All property that is exempt from seizure by creditors under the law of the province in which the debtor resides is exempt from distribution.

[14.] The amount is calculated by a formula. In general, a family of four in which the bankrupt was the sole income earner with a monthly income of $4000 would be required to contribute approximately $263 monthly to the trustee for distribution to creditors. Those payments stop when the bankrupt is discharged.

[15.] Certain claims get paid even before secured creditors, including claims by the Canada Revenue Agency and by certain suppliers, such as farmers. Some claims, including the wages of spouses who are employed by the bankrupt, are deferred, meaning that they are paid only after all unsecured claims are paid.

[16.] *BIA*, s 244(1), allows a secured creditor to enforce their security against a debtor 10 days after giving notice of intent to enforce.

[17.] As discussed in Chapter 23, under provincial personal property security legislation, upon bankruptcy a secured creditor can rely on their security interest only if it is perfected.

This is a critical advantage. Unsecured creditors can wait years for their share of the bankrupt's assets to be paid upon completion of the bankruptcy proceeding, or they may not be paid at all. Secured creditors enjoy another form of protection as well. If the property that the debtor gave to a creditor as security is worth less than the debt owed, the secured creditor can apply the proceeds realized from the property against the debt and then claim for the balance as an unsecured creditor.

Suppose Nancy borrowed $250 000 from Mark and gave Mark a security interest in her dump truck to secure the loan. Nancy has now defaulted on the loan and has made an assignment in bankruptcy.

- **Enforcing the security:** Mark can enforce his security in one of two ways. As we saw in Chapter 23, he may be entitled to simply seize and retain the dump truck. However, that option may create difficulties. For instance, he may insist that the vehicle is worth only $200 000, leaving a deficiency of $50 000. Nancy's trustee in bankruptcy, in contrast, may claim that the truck is worth $220 000, leaving a deficiency of only $30 000. If the parties cannot eventually agree, the court may order the truck to be sold.[18] Indeed, to avoid such complications, creditors typically proceed directly to a sale of the collateral. Mark might also proceed directly to sale simply because he does not have any need for a dump truck.

- **Suing for the deficiency:** Whether or not the truck is sold, Mark is entitled to register a proof of claim as an ordinary unsecured creditor for the deficiency. While he is entitled to the full value of his security, he is unlikely to recover the full amount of the deficiency. As a bankrupt, Nancy has more debts than assets, and Mark will have to share her inadequate assets with her other creditors.

- **Being accountable for any surplus:** Mark cannot, in any event, recover *more than* the value of Nancy's debt to him. If, for instance, she owed $250 000, but he sold the truck for $275 000, he would have to pay the extra $25 000 to her trustee in bankruptcy.

Sometimes it is difficult to know whether a creditor qualifies as a secured creditor. You Be the Judge 24.1 provides an example of this problem.

You Be the Judge 24.1

Is the Creditor a Secured Creditor?[19]

Seiberling Rubber Co was a creditor of Sklar who obtained a judgment against Sklar in the amount of $14 000. Seiberling began execution proceedings and registered the judgment in the land registry office against some real estate owned by Sklar. Based on the registration, Seiberling had a charge on the land, the right to require that the property be sold, and the proceeds applied to pay its debt. Subsequently, Sklar made an assignment in bankruptcy.

Question for Discussion

1. Is Seiberling a secured creditor of Sklar?

---

18. *BIA*, ss 127–35.

19. *Re Sklar and Sklar* [1958] SJ No 21 (QB).

All creditors who do not have a security interest are unsecured creditors. The *BIA* divides unsecured creditors into two categories. A **preferred creditor** is a creditor who is preferred in relation to all other unsecured creditors. Employees owed unpaid wages and governments with claims to taxes normally fall into this category.[20] Those bearing the administrative costs of carrying out the bankruptcy, such as the trustee, are also in this category. They are "preferred" because they are deemed deserving enough to enjoy priority over other unsecured creditors.

Finally, there is the residual category of **general unsecured creditors**, who are neither secured nor preferred. This is normally the largest class of creditor. Ordinary suppliers of goods and services, small lenders, and other creditors are grouped together and paid out of whatever is left over after the other higher priority claims are satisfied. Depending upon the size of the bankrupt's estate, there is frequently little or nothing remaining. Unsecured creditors must take this risk into account when deciding whether to lend.

Concept Summary 24.1 summarizes the different types of creditors examined in this section.

a **preferred creditor** is a creditor that is preferred in relation to all other unsecured creditors

general unsecured creditors are all creditors that are neither secured nor preferred

Concept Summary 24.1

Classes of Creditors

Secured		Creditors whose interests are "secured" by assets of the debtor, such as a piece of equipment, inventory, or accounts receivable. If the debtor defaults on the loan, the creditor can claim the asset and, if the amount realized on its disposition or its value is less than the amount of the debt, claim for the balance of the debt owing as an unsecured creditor.
Unsecured	Preferred	Creditors who are "preferred" in relation to other general creditors by operation of law. Creditors who are owed wages, taxes, rent, and support payments, and those bearing the administrative costs incurred in carrying out the bankruptcy, such as the trustee, fall into this category.
	General	The residual class of creditor. These creditors are paid out of the debtor's assets remaining after all prior claims are satisfied.

CREDITOR EQUALITY One key point concerning the treatment of creditors upon bankruptcy is the principle of creditor equality. This has two aspects:

- **Stay:** All unsecured creditors are subject to a stay of court proceedings against the debtor once the debtor is bankrupt. This means that they cannot bring independent actions against the bankrupt for debts owed at the time that the bankruptcy proceeding is commenced. It also means that any other proceedings that they previously began are stayed in favour of the bankruptcy action. The stay guarantees procedural equality amongst creditors.

- *Pro rata* **sharing:** In the event of a bankruptcy, all creditors in the same class recover on a *pro rata* basis. Each creditor is entitled to a share of all of the debtor's assets based on how much the creditor is owed as a proportion of the total amount owed to all creditors. Suppose the debtor has assets of $100 000 but owes $600 000 to unsecured creditor A and

---

[20.] *BIA*, s 136. Since 2008, employees have been entitled to up to six months' wages to a maximum of $3531 (for 2012) when their employer goes bankrupt from a fund created under the *Wage Earner Protection Program Act*, SC 2005, c 47.

$400 000 to unsecured creditor B. A will get $60 000 because the proportion that its debt represents of the debtor's total debt is 60 percent ($600 000/$1 000 000 = 60 percent), and 60 percent of $100 000 is $60 000.[21]

UNDISCHARGED DEBT   Individual debtors who are first-time bankrupts are automatically discharged from bankruptcy after nine months if (i) there is no objection by a creditor, the trustee, or the Superintendant and (ii) the debtor attends mandatory counselling sessions. In all other circumstances, a longer period must elapse prior to a discharge and, often, a court must decide if the debtor is to be discharged. If the debtor has been engaged in dishonest conduct, creditors are receiving less than $0.50 for each $1.00 of debt, or for a variety of other reasons, a court may refuse a discharge.[22] Corporate debtors are rarely discharged unless they have repaid all of their debts, which is uncommon.

Most of the bankrupt's debts are *released* once the bankrupt is discharged. That means that the debtor does not have to pay them to the extent that any money is still owing. There is, however, a class of debts that are non-dischargeable. These are debts that, for policy reasons, the debtor is not permitted to walk away from. Debts in this category include fines, spousal and child support orders, judgments against the debtor for assault and misrepresentation, and student loans made under federal or provincial statutes. Ethical Perspective 24.1 discusses the dischargeability of student loans.

Ethical Perspective **24.1**

Discharging Student Loans in Bankruptcy—Think Again

Like cars and laptop computers, loans have become an increasingly common part of student life. Many students need loans to complete their studies. Many students also want to know if they can discharge—get rid of—their student loans by entering bankruptcy.

Until October 1997, student loans were fully dischargeable. Soaring student bankruptcy rates, however, forced the federal government to rethink the law. In June 1998, the *BIA* was amended to limit the availability of discharges. Since 2008, student loans cannot be discharged if the bankruptcy occurred when the bankrupt was a student or within seven years after full- or part-time studies cease. However, the *BIA* provides that a bankrupt can be discharged from student loans

if the court is satisfied that the person (i) acted in good faith, and (ii) will continue to experience financial difficulties that will likely prevent repayment.[23] The current law reflects the fact that while bankruptcy is an opportunity to "clean the slate," it is rarely a cure-all. In many cases, student loans remain payable.

Question for Discussion

1. Should students be able to discharge their student loans in bankruptcy?

PROOF OF CREDITORS' CLAIMS   To be officially recognized in the bankruptcy process, each creditor must prove their claim before a bankruptcy official. The claim process is designed to identify the pool of potential claimants, to eliminate ineligible claims, and to streamline the bankruptcy process. Unsecured creditors must, by a certain date, submit a proof of claim setting out the amount at issue, how it arose, and whether the bankrupt has any counterclaim against the creditor. Failure to do this usually makes it impossible for a creditor to pursue a claim.

---

[21] How attempts by individual creditors to get paid a disproportionate amount are dealt with are discussed in the next section of this chapter under the heading "Prohibited Pre-Bankruptcy Transactions."

[22] *BIA*, ss 168.1–174.

[23] *BIA*, ss 178(1)(g), 178(1.1).

PROHIBITED PRE-BANKRUPTCY TRANSACTIONS

In the period leading up to bankruptcy, debtors and creditors may both be tempted to engage in behaviour that puts them in a better position when bankruptcy happens. Debtors may try to transfer assets to related companies, friends, or relatives in the hope that they can somehow escape distributing them to their creditors and continue to benefit from them. Such transfers will usually be made for less than their true value, even for free or for nominal payment. Likewise, debtors may attempt to **prefer**, or favour, some creditors over others by paying certain debts in advance of bankruptcy. Directors of a corporate debtor, for example, might be keen to pay off any creditors whose debts they have guaranteed. Creditors may encourage debtors to pay them before bankruptcy so that they do not have to share the debtor's assets with other creditors.

to **prefer** a creditor means that a debtor has paid the creditor but not others in advance of bankruptcy

That sort of behaviour undermines the equality of creditors and decreases the assets available for distribution. Courts therefore developed rules for transfers at undervalue and preferences; the trustee can apply to a court for a declaration that these transactions are void and have any assets distributed in this way delivered to the trustee. Those doctrines are now contained in the *BIA*.

- **Void transfer at undervalue:** Any transfer of the debtor's assets at undervalue made within a one-year period before bankruptcy may be declared void by a court if the debtor was insolvent at the time of the transfer (or was made so by the transfer) and the debtor intended to defraud a creditor. If the debtor and the other party to the transfer were not dealing at arm's length, perhaps because they were husband and wife or affiliated companies, any transaction at undervalue may be declared void if it occurred within five years of the date of the initial bankruptcy and the same criteria are met. As well, any non-arm's-length transfer at undervalue that occurred within a year of bankruptcy may be declared void.[24]

- **Void preference:** A transfer of the debtor's assets to a creditor within three months of bankruptcy is void if the aim of the transfer was to prefer that creditor over others. As well, a non-arm's-length transfer between related parties less than one year prior to bankruptcy may be voided if the effect is to give a preference to someone over other creditors.[25]

LIABILITY OF DIRECTORS OF BANKRUPT CORPORATIONS

When a corporation goes bankrupt and does not have enough money to pay its creditors, its directors are usually not liable for the deficiency. Nor do directors owe a fiduciary duty to creditors to act in their interests.[26] However, a bankrupt corporation's directors may be liable if they have given personal guarantees for the company's debts or if a statute imposes liability upon them. For instance, the *Canada Business Corporations Act* imposes liability on the directors of a

---

[24.] *BIA*, s 96.

[25.] *BIA*, s 95. Creditors may also be able apply to a court to set aside dispositions by a debtor under provincial fraudulent conveyances legislation where the debtor sells assets for less than they are worth to related parties with the intention of defeating the claims of creditors. *Eg Fraudulent Conveyances Act*, RSO 1990, c F.29.

[26.] This point was confirmed by the Supreme Court of Canada in *BCE v 1976 Debentureholders*, 2008 SCC 69, where the court held that while corporate directors owe a duty of care to creditors, that duty does not include a fiduciary duty to act in their interests.

PART 7

bankrupt corporation for up to six months' wages for employees.[27] To cover such liability, many directors of large corporations today maintain insurance.

L.O. ⑩   # Proposals

A proposal is an offer by a debtor to their creditors to restructure their claims against the debtor. In most cases, the debtor continues to operate their business, but the proposal provides for the orderly repayment of the debtor's obligations over time. Proposals are an alternative to bankruptcy and must be approved by creditors and the court. Usually the proposal process is commenced by the debtor filing a notice of intention to file a proposal with the Official Receiver. Once such a notice of intention is filed, all actions of creditors are stayed. No actions may be commenced or continued. Unlike the stay that arises when the debtor becomes bankrupt, the stay arising in relation to a proposal applies to secured creditors as well.[28] This stay gives the debtor time to develop a plan to put to their creditors. The following are some of the most important kinds of provisions included in proposals:

- A *composition* is an agreement between a debtor and their creditors under which the creditors agree to accept, in satisfaction of their claims, less than the amount that is owing to them.

- An *extension of time* prolongs the time available for repayment to creditors. That may happen alone or together with a composition.

- A *scheme of arrangement* is a situation where the debtor's assets are vested in, or controlled by, a trustee for the benefit of creditors while the proposal is being performed.

- Under a *liquidation proposal*, the debtor agrees to sell assets and distribute the proceeds. One benefit of that procedure is that the debtor themself can assist in the recovery of receivables, meaning debts owed to the debtor by others. Under a bankruptcy, that job is performed by the trustee. Collection may be facilitated if done by the debtor. Often, however, creditors do not have confidence in the debtor to perform this function.

- A *share exchange* occurs when a debtor corporation offers to exchange its shares for outstanding debt. That procedure is sometimes called a "debt–equity swap."

A creditor may be willing to accept less than the full value of a debt when the alternatives are even less attractive. If the creditor enforces their rights to the letter, they will have to spend much time and expense in litigation. In addition, in doing so, the creditor may scare away the debtor's customers, making the debtor's business conditions even more difficult. The ultimate result may be the debtor's bankruptcy, with the likely result that the creditor would not receive full payment in any case. A creditor may consent to a proposal if the creditor thinks that the debtor, by continuing to operate, will be able to pay more than the creditor would receive on the debtor's bankruptcy. Creditors'

[27.] *Canada Business Corporations Act*, RSC 1985, c C-44, s 119 (Can). For the directors to be held liable, the employees must prove their claims within six months of the assignment or the bankruptcy order.

[28.] *BIA*, s 244. There are some important exceptions to the application of the stay to secured parties. The stay does not apply if the secured party is already in possession of the debtor's assets or if they have given a notice of intention to enforce their security interest more than 10 days before the notice of intention to make a proposal is filed.

reputations are important too, especially for major creditors. A debtor would rather deal with Bank A, which has a reputation for fairness and flexibility, than Bank B, which has a reputation for squeezing debtors as hard as possible.

To obtain creditor approval, a debtor often makes a variety of commitments to their creditors. For example, the debtor may agree to:

- repayment at a higher rate of interest in the future
- a restructuring of their operations in ways desired by the creditors
- heightened scrutiny of their affairs by creditor representatives
- some combination of these and other commitments

FORM AND APPROVAL REQUIREMENTS

A proposal can be made by a bankrupt, an insolvent person, a trustee in bankruptcy, or some other creditor representative, such as someone appointed to liquidate the debtor's assets; but, most often, the proposal is made by an insolvent debtor who is not yet bankrupt. Usually the debtor files a notice of intention to file a proposal with the Official Receiver and then consults with their creditors to develop the proposal. Depending upon the outcome of those consultations, they may then file a formal proposal with a licensed trustee in bankruptcy at a later date. The trustee files a copy with the Official Receiver. The debtor has 30 days from the filing of the notice of intention to file the proposal itself, but the bankruptcy court can extend that time by periods of 45 days. The court cannot, however, extend the original 30-day period by more than five months.

In drafting the proposal, the debtor prepares a plan that takes into account the general business conditions and the wishes of its creditors. The debtor has a strong incentive to be realistic, given that a proposal is likely to hurt their credit rating less than bankruptcy and will usually leave the debtor in control of the business.

The trustee has responsibilities with respect to proposals. The trustee's initial responsibility is to conduct an appraisal of the business of the debtor to assess their financial situation and to report the results of the assessment to the creditors. Where a notice of intention has been filed, the trustee assists the debtor in the preparation of the proposal. The trustee is also responsible for monitoring the debtor's business on an ongoing basis until the proposal is approved or the debtor is bankrupt, and for filing reports with the creditors and the court prior to the court hearing at which the proposal will be considered.

For the purposes of voting on the proposal, creditors are categorized in classes according to their common interests. There may be, for example, a class of unsecured creditors with claims under $1000 and another with claims above that amount. The *BIA* does not define classes of preferred and unsecured creditors for the purposes of the proposal. Creditors will be concerned that the class they are in is not dominated by creditors with different interests from their own, since each class must approve the proposal. If a proposed classification is unfair, creditors will likely object and the matter may be brought to court. The debtor has the option of applying directly to the court for a determination of the appropriate classes.

The *BIA* does not require secured creditors to be dealt with under a proposal. The debtor may deal with them separately; however, when secured creditors are included in a proposal, they must be placed in the same class if they are secured against the same assets.

Besides dividing creditors into classes, proposals must meet other requirements. For example, the proposal must ensure that the ranking of creditors is respected. Consequently, secured creditors must recover the value of their security before payment is made to general unsecured creditors.

Once the proposal is submitted, it must be considered and voted on at a meeting of creditors within 21 days. The trustee is responsible for calling the meeting. Creditors can request, at any time, that the proposal proceedings be terminated on the basis that the debtor is not acting in good faith or that there is little real chance that the proposal will be accepted.[29]

For the proposal to be formally approved, it must receive the support of at least half of the creditors in each class, and those creditors must hold at least two-thirds of the face value of the debtor's debt in that class. Once the proposal is approved, it binds all creditors covered by its terms, including those who may have voted against it. A court must then decide whether to approve the proposal within 15 days. Court approval is normally given if creditor approval is obtained, but the court must be satisfied that the terms of the proposal are reasonable and for the benefit of the creditors as a whole.[30]

If the creditors do not vote in favour of the proposal, the debtor is automatically deemed to be bankrupt. The Official Receiver steps forward and conducts the first meeting of creditors and the regular bankruptcy procedure, as described above, applies.[31]

Other Statutes Dealing with Financial Distress and Failure

The *BIA* is not the only statute that deals with financial distress and failure. There are some provincial statutes that regulate general debtor–creditor relations, such as statutes relating to fraudulent conveyances, business corporations, and personal property security. Some may provide more favourable options for debtors or creditors than a bankruptcy or proposal under the *BIA*. In the relevant circumstances, they should be carefully considered.[32] For example, if the real problem with a debtor is that they have fraudulently given their assets away to a related party, such as a spouse, it may be that an application to set aside the transaction under provincial fraudulent conveyances law would be simpler and provide a more expeditious solution than bankruptcy proceedings.[33]

One important alternative is a court-approved arrangement under the *Companies' Creditors Arrangement Act* (*CCAA*), which can be used by insolvent corporations that have total outstanding debts exceeding $5 000 000. This amount includes the total of all claims against affiliated corporations. In most cases, arrangements seek to get creditors to reduce the amount of their claims in exchange for a restructuring of the business operations that will permit the debtor to operate more efficiently and profitably. As a result, the prospects for repayment are improved. The process under the *CCAA* is similar to that which is available for the restructuring of insolvent corporations in the United States under Chapter 11 of the US Bankruptcy Code.[34]

The benefit of applying under the *CCAA* is that, in general, the rules governing the *CCAA* restructuring process may be customized to meet the specific

---

[29] *BIA*, s 50(12).

[30] *BIA*, s 59(2).

[31] The procedure for consumer proposals is somewhat simpler.

[32] For instance, many provincial statutes allow a creditor to claim priority for both a debt *and* the costs associated with recovering that money through execution proceedings to enforce a court judgment. Creditors in bankruptcy are governed by *BIA*-set priorities and normally recoup only a small percentage of their court costs: *Royal Bank v R* (1981) 40 CBR (NS) 27 (Ont Div Ct).

[33] *Eg Fraudulent Conveyances Act*, RSO 1990, c F.29.

[34] Pub L No 95-598, 92 Stat 2549 (6 November 1978).

needs of the debtor and their creditors, with the result that the *CCAA* is thought to be better able to address the wide variety of complex issues that arise in restructuring large businesses. Under the *BIA*, more of the rules are specified in the statute. For this reason, and because the role of the courts is more limited, *BIA* proposal proceedings are, generally, cheaper. As a result, they are more attractive to small and medium-sized businesses. The flexibility of the *CCAA* means that it is a better choice to deal with the challenges of an insolvency that crosses international borders.[35]

Business Decision 24.1 demonstrates another element of the flexibility of restructuring under the *CCAA*.

Insolvent banks and insurance companies cannot use either the *BIA* or the *CCAA*. These businesses can be restructured under only the *Winding-Up and Restructuring Act* (*WURA*). Federally incorporated corporations and some provincial companies that are insolvent may also use this Act. If proceedings have been commenced under the *BIA*, they preclude the application of the *WURA*. The *WURA* differs considerably from the *BIA* in both substance and procedure. In general, the procedures under the *WURA* are much less detailed and have not been regularly updated, as compared to the *BIA*. Because of its limited application and outdated nature, the *WURA* has been rarely used in recent years.

Business Decision 24.1

Insolvency and the *CCAA*

In *Re Stelco*,[36] where the existence of insolvency was disputed by the corporation's union, the judge appeared to open the door to a more liberal "reasonable foreseeability" test for insolvency under the *CCAA*. The judge held that a financially troubled corporation can be insolvent for *CCAA* purposes if it reasonably expects to be unable to meet its obligations within a certain amount of time. The judge based his decision on the practical consideration that, as the financial condition of the debtor grows worse, it often becomes increasingly difficult for the debtor to assemble a survival package. In the judge's view, rescuing corporations in financial distress and avoiding liquidation is an important objective of the legislation and so the court should be flexible in interpreting the requirement for insolvency.

While this interpretation has not yet been adopted by every Canadian court, it may be the start of a trend toward recognizing that businesses do not need to be on their "last legs" to take advantage of *CCAA* restructuring. The decision is also consistent with international trends. In the United States and elsewhere, similar laws require only that a company demonstrate "financial distress" to qualify for restructuring protection. The decision should help companies manage their financial risks in a more proactive way.

Questions for Discussion

1. Explain the idea behind court-authorized restructuring. What problems does it avoid?

2. What are three advantages of a more liberal approach to corporate restructuring under the *CCAA*? What are three disadvantages?

---

35. The *CCAA* has some features in this respect that are found in Chapter 15 of the US Bankruptcy Code.

36. *Re Stelco Inc* (2004) 48 CBR (4th) 299 (Ont SCJ).

Chapter Summary

A key aspect of risk management is planning for the possibility of business failure. In Canada, bankruptcy and insolvency law provides several procedures for debtors and creditors to choose from in dealing with business failure. Making strategic choices regarding the use of these procedures is an important aspect of risk management. Sometimes a creditor will be better off if a debtor is bankrupt, because bankruptcy provides an orderly and cost-effective process for the payment of creditors. Before a debtor goes bankrupt, there is a risk for a creditor that other creditors will take the debtor's assets.

The main Canadian statute relating to bankruptcy and insolvency is the *Bankruptcy and Insolvency Act (BIA)*. Insolvency is an inability of a debtor to meet their financial obligations to their creditors. Bankruptcy is a legal status that can arise in two ways: assignment or an application by creditors for a bankruptcy order. An assignment is a voluntary act by the debtor to place themself in bankruptcy. An application by creditors for a bankruptcy order is a request by creditors to the court to place the debtor in bankruptcy. In both cases, the benefit of bankruptcy status for the debtor is to provide a stay of creditor actions and a limit on recovery against the debtor.

Consumer bankruptcies involve less money than corporate bankruptcies but are much more numerous. Also, unlike corporate bankrupts, consumer bankrupts are usually discharged from bankruptcy, even if not all of their debts are paid in full. When bankrupts are discharged, they cease to be liable for their pre-bankruptcy obligations, with a few exceptions.

The chief administrative official in bankruptcy is the Superintendent of Bankruptcy. The Superintendent is represented in each province and territory by a number ofOfficial Receivers, whose offices receive assignments and other bankruptcy documents.Creditors in a bankruptcy are usually represented by a trustee, who gathers in and liquidates the debtors' assets and distributes the proceeds to creditors.

Some of the debtor's assets are exempt from distribution, including the debtor's clothing, tools of the trade, and household furniture up to a maximum value. The trustee distributes the proceeds of the assets available for distribution first to secured creditors with an interest in the assets, and then to preferred creditors, such as the trustee. The remainder is distributed to the remaining general creditors on a *pro rata* basis to the extent that the debtor's assets permit. Creditors in each class must be treated equally. Certain transactions by the debtor prior to bankruptcy may be set aside by a court. These include settlements of property for free or a nominal payment, and payments that prefer one creditor over others.

The *BIA* also provides for a third procedure outside bankruptcy in the form of a proposal. A proposal involves an arrangement between the debtor and their creditors in which the parties agree to compromise or rearrange debts. A proposal must be approved by at least half of the creditors in each class, representing at least two-thirds of the value of the debt represented by that class and the court. A proposal offers significant advantages to a debtor. In most cases, it permits the debtor to remain in possession of their assets and carry on their business. As well, a proposal does not stigmatize the debtor as a bankrupt. An alternative court-supervised procedure for restructuring corporations with debts exceeding $5 000 000 is provided under the *Companies' Creditors Arrangement Act*.

Each procedure has its own advantages. The ultimate choice of procedure is dictated by various factors, including the prospects for the debtor to carry on business successfully in the future and pay their debts, given the nature of the business, the relationship between the debtor and their creditors, and general economic conditions. Where the prospects for the debtor to carry on their business successfully are good and the debtor's creditors have confidence in the debtor, a proposal may be desirable. If the prospects for the business are poor, creditors may decide to proceed directly and swiftly to an application to have the debtor found to be bankrupt.

MyBusLawLab ADDITIONAL RESOURCES FOR CHAPTER 24

MyBusLawLab provides students with an assortment of tools to help enrich the learning experience, including a Study Plan with Pre- and Post-tests, mini-cases with assessments, and provincial content material, which provides links to relevant cases, legislation, and additional resources.

MyBusLawLab provides the following resources for Chapter 24:

- Business Decision 24.1W—Trustees and Environmental Liability
- Business Decision 24.2W—Selling Assets: A "Good Price" or Simply the "Best"?
- Business Decision 24.3W—International Bankruptcy

Provincial Material

- **British Columbia:** Fraudulent Transfer of Property
- **Alberta:** Bankruptcy and Insolvency, Fraudulent Conveyances, Fraudulent Preferences
- **Manitoba and Saskatchewan:** Exempt Property in Bankruptcy, Fraudulent Transfers and Conveyances
- **Ontario:** Assignment and Preferences, Fraudulent Conveyances, Limitation Periods
- **Atlantic Provinces:** Fraudulent Conveyances and Preferences

Review Questions

1. Bankruptcy law overcame problems that arise when an insolvent debtor has multiple creditors. What were they?

2. How is "insolvency" different from "bankruptcy"?

3. What are the purposes of bankruptcy? How are these purposes different from the purposes of proposals?

4. Against whom does the "stay" operate in bankruptcy? What does it stay?

5. Identify and briefly describe the statutes that deal with businesses in financial distress.

6. How does the law differ between commercial and consumer bankruptcies?

7. Describe the role of the trustee in bankruptcy. Who does the trustee represent? Who regulates the trustee?

8. When might a debtor want to make an assignment into bankruptcy?

9. When might a creditor want to apply to have a bankruptcy order made against a debtor?

10. What is the procedure for filing an application for a bankruptcy order? What is its effect?

11. What is "exempt property" under the *BIA* and what is its purpose? Who is responsible for defining what property is exempt under the law?

12. What is the effect of the bankruptcy of a debtor on a secured creditor of that debtor?

13. What is the significance for an unsecured creditor of being a general creditor or a preferred creditor?

14. What is a "discharge from bankruptcy"? What debts are non-dischargeable? Why?

15. If you were a debtor in financial difficulty who thought that your creditors were likely to seek a bankruptcy order against you in the next few months, could you protect some of your assets against your creditors by transferring them to your spouse for $1?

16. Jerome has just made an assignment in bankruptcy. He had started a restaurant business as a sole proprietorship but, despite his best efforts, it failed. He could not pay off all his creditors. He is very embarrassed because he has never had a business failure before. What is the likelihood that Jerome will be discharged as a bankrupt?

17. What concerns would you have if you were the director of a corporation that was about to be the subject of a bankruptcy order?

18. What are the circumstances in which a creditor would be interested in supporting a debtor who was making a proposal under the *BIA*?

19. What are some of the advantages of a proposal for a debtor?

20. Who can take advantage of an arrangement under the *CCAA*? Explain when an action under the *CCAA* may be preferred over action under the *BIA*.

Cases and Problems

1. Elaine runs the Five Brothers restaurant in Niagara Falls. She has given the bank a general security interest on the restaurant property that she owns in exchange for a loan of $200 000. The restaurant is not successful and, because of a recent decline in tourism, has a fair market value of only $150 000. If Elaine decides to make an assignment, what can the bank do to recoup its loan?

2. Bengt Norsson lives in Toronto. He works as a carpenter and drives his truck to work at various sites every day. Unfortunately, he does not really like his job and gambles on the side. Bengt gambled away thousands of dollars recently and is contemplating an assignment in bankruptcy. If he does make an assignment, will he lose everything?

3. Amanda decides to incorporate her business of homemade organic soaps and body lotions. She causes the corporation to borrow $2500 in 2014 from a bank, and her good friend Sharon agrees to lend the corporation a further $5000 in 2015 in exchange for a promise to be paid back with interest. On top of this, she approaches her uncle to personally lend her $500 for the business. In 2015, the corporation makes an assignment in bankruptcy without paying back any of its debts. What will the creditors be entitled to if there are no other creditors and the corporation's total assets are $5000? How would the answer be different if the bank had a security interest in all of the corporation's assets?

4. Belinda and Joe previously lived together. After a disagreement, Belinda and her daughter, Marianna, moved out 18 months ago. She has an order from a British Columbia court against Joe, under which he is required to pay $1200 a month to her for support. Joe sends cheques for seven months and then stops making payments. Can Belinda apply for a bankruptcy order against Joe? If so, how would her claim rank compared to the claims of Joe's other creditors?

5. Kerry's Bagels Inc is a corporation that is owned and operated by Paul Kerry in Victoria, British Columbia. Bagels were a popular item in the late 1990s but recently the trend has been toward wraps and Italian-style sandwiches, and Kerry's Bagels sales have fallen off. In June 2014, Paul found that

he was unable to fund his payroll of 12 employees because of continuing financial difficulties. At the same time, however, he arranged for funds to be paid by the corporation to himself as his wages as president of the company. On 10 September 2014, less than a month after paying the funds to himself, Paul decided he had had enough and he caused Kerry's Bagels to make an assignment in bankruptcy. The trustee has now come forward and wants to know whether the wage payment by the corporation to Paul could be challenged under the *BIA*.

6. Jodie is a well-known local business person who has a flour supply business. She loaned $10 000 to Kelly, one of her customers, to help Kelly renovate the building where she operates her bakery business in September 2014. The business has struggled since. After repaying $1000 of the loan, in January 2015, Kelly stopped making the $250 monthly payments they had agreed on. Should Jodie apply for a bankruptcy order against Kelly? What else would you want to know if you were Jodie to help you to decide what to do?

7. Dalfen Courier Inc has a package delivery business. It has a loan of $50 000 from ScotiaBank that is secured on all the assets of the business. It also bought two trucks on credit and still owes the seller $50 000. The seller's claim is secured on the trucks and has priority over the bank. The value of all the assets of Dalfen is $60 000. Dalfen's basic business is successful but it cannot always make the $500 monthly payments that it is required to make to each of these two creditors. Dalfen wants to make a proposal under which the creditors agree to reduced payments of $250 per month each. If you represented ScotiaBank, would you recommend approving such a proposal? Would your advice be different if you represented the truck seller?

8. MIR Networks is in financial trouble. It is a large business with more than $500 000 000 in assets. In the past few years it has expanded beyond its core telephone switch business into new areas, including personal computers and telephone handsets both in the United States and Canada. These new business activities have lost so much money that MIR is now insolvent. Creditors are demanding payments that MIR has no funds to make. The management of MIR thinks that the corporation could return to profitability if it could temporarily delay its payments to its creditors so that it could sell off the computer and telephone handset divisions and concentrate on its core business. What should management of MIR do?

9. Janetti Inc, a Montreal sweater manufacturer, concludes a security agreement with Bank Y in which it gives the bank a security interest in all of Janetti's accounts receivable in exchange for a loan of $1 million. Janetti then files for bankruptcy, and the bank gives notice that it seeks to realize on its security. Bank Y recovers only $300 000 from the accounts and wants to know if it can claim the balance of its loan in some way. What if, instead, it were able to recover $1.2 million?

10. Jaco Inc operates a small struggling technology business in Toronto. Jaco wants to make a proposal to its creditors—a bank, a private lender, and its landlord—to accept a deferral of the amounts that they are owed until the technology that Jaco has been working on has been tested and sold. How should Jaco proceed to try to get its creditors to agree to this?

11. Bluebird Finance of Saskatoon offered Rubina Naderi a $50 000 loan to start a dressmaking business. The loan was to be secured by a "floating charge" over all of Naderi's assets. The floating charge would crystallize only at the moment that Rubina was declared bankrupt. Rubina went into business in a Saskatoon mall and began making payments to repay the loan; however, her efforts were not enough. After several months she went out of business and assigned herself into bankruptcy. She wonders if Bluebird Finance remains a secured lender, given that she owes it less than the full $50 000.

12. Joseph Inc, a retail fashion chain, contemplates making a proposal to its creditors. It is thinking about making the proposal to both secured and unsecured creditors in the form of an arrangement or a debt–equity swap. Is it necessary for Joseph to include secured creditors in its proposal?

Government Regulation of Business

25

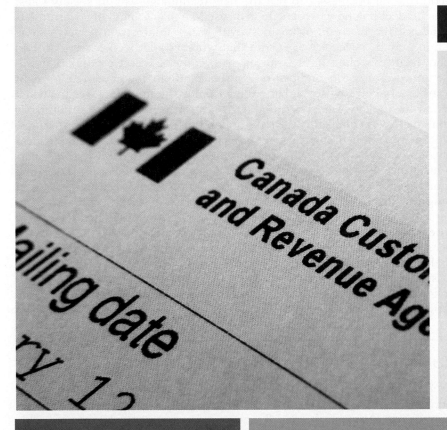

LEARNING OBJECTIVES

After completing this chapter, you should be able to:

❶ Describe the different types of taxation in Canada.

❷ Distinguish the taxation of business income earned by a corporation and distributed to an individual shareholder from the taxation of business income earned by that individual directly.

❸ Explain why competition is important.

❹ Explain why Canada needs a government agency to protect competition.

❺ Describe how the common law treats agreements not to compete.

❻ Explain the difference between a reviewable matter and a criminal matter under the *Competition Act*.

❼ Describe the restrictions that the *Competition Act* imposes on the activities of a dominant firm.

❽ Identify practices engaged in by a manufacturer with its customers that may raise concerns under the *Competition Act*.

❾ Identify the ways in which governments protect consumers against false, misleading, and deceptive representations by businesses.

❿ Describe the main categories of consumer protection requirements imposed on business and when they are applied.

Canada's federal and provincial governments regulate businesses to achieve particular policy objectives, such as environmental protection. How they do so determines whether Canada is an attractive place to invest and work. The main reason for regulation is that sometimes businesses seeking to promote their own interests will operate in ways that are contrary to the overall interests of society. A manufacturing business might, for example, continue to use an old production technology that creates high levels of toxic emissions rather than a newer, cleaner technology, in order to save money. A government might decide that requiring all businesses to use the new technology was in society's best interests. In deciding how to regulate in a case like this, Canadian governments must balance the interests of business with other interests in society. Some regulation may be necessary to ensure that workers and people living around the manufacturer's plant have clean air to breathe. Excessive regulation will impose unnecessary costs on business. In this example, the government might try to strike a balance by subsidizing the costs for the manufacturer to switch to the new technology. Understanding what governments regulate, and how, is essential to properly managing the risks of liability under regulatory provisions.

We have examined some aspects of government regulation of business already. One of the ways in which governments ensure that businesses operate in accordance with the standards they set is through licensing. Licensing of certain agents, such as real estate agents, was discussed in Chapter 20 and licensing was discussed generally as a requirement for starting some kinds of businesses in Chapter 21. (For example, licences are required for dealing in securities, providing health services, and selling liquor.)Chapter 22 discussed the rules for corporate governance, including the interests that management must take into account when making decisions. In Chapter 26, we will look at labour standards. In this chapter, we focus first on federal and provincial taxation followed by two specific areas of regulation that affect most businesses: the protection of competition in the marketplace and the protection of consumers.[1]

L.O. ❶ ❷   # Taxation

The drafters of Canada's Constitution set out to create a strongly centralized country. The federal government was therefore given the power to make laws for the purpose of raising money "by any mode or system of taxation." This broad power was designed to allow the federal government to pay for big projects, such as railways and harbours, that were vital to the development of the country as a whole. The provinces, in contrast, were given jurisdiction over more localized matters, such as the administration of justice, health care, and education, which were local and, at the time, less costly. The provinces' taxation power was therefore restricted to the imposition of direct taxes. A direct tax is a tax imposed directly on the person who has to pay it, such as income tax. By comparison, an indirect tax is a tax levied on one person with the expectation that it will be passed along to another person. For example, if a province imposed a tax on goods sold to retail stores with the expectation that retailers would pass on the burden of the tax to consumers, then that tax is indirect.[2]

---

[1] Examples of other aspects of business that are subject to regulation include product standards and occupational health and safety standards.

[2] Sales taxes that are charged directly to consumers at the point of sale have been found to be direct taxes within provincial jurisdiction (*Atlantic Smoke Shops v Canlon* [1943] AC 550 (JCPC)).

Since 1867, the growing complexity of Canadian society and the demands on different levels of government have expanded the areas of activity for which the provinces are responsible. Much of the federal government's tax revenue is now redistributed to the provinces to pay for increasingly expensive social programs (such as health care). In addition, the federal government is committed to a system of transfer payments that is designed to equalize conditions between rich and poor provinces.

Today, governments at all levels recognize the need to make Canada attractive to business people. Consequently, they aim to ensure that business taxes are at a level that is competitive with the tax burden in the United States and other countries, and they have introduced a number of tax-related incentives designed to attract and retain research-intensive industries. These moves demonstrate how tax can be an important instrument of government policy regarding business. Understanding the effect that different transaction structures and methods of carrying on business have on the taxes that businesses have to pay is a critical aspect of business planning.

TYPES OF TAXATION

Governments levy several types of taxes in Canada. The most important of these is income tax, which is levied on individuals both by the federal and provincial governments. In general, the federal government charges the highest percentage of income tax, while the provinces charge a lesser percentage. For example, in 2012, the federal personal income tax had four basic rates:

- 15 percent on the first $42 707
- 22 percent on the next $42 707 (up to $85 414)
- 26 percent on the next $46 992 (up to $132 406)
- 29 percent on amounts over $132 406

For individuals who reside in Ontario, for 2012, the province imposed an additional 5.05 percent on the first $39 020, 9.15 percent on the next $39 023, and 11.16 percent on any amount over $78 043. For corporations, basic combined federal and provincial corporate income tax rates varied between 29 and 35 percent, depending upon the province. Rates for the first $500 000 earned by certain Canadian-controlled corporations are lower, ranging on average between 12 and 19 percent. This is a special rate intended to benefit small businesses.[3]

Every province, except Alberta, has a provincial sales tax. The amount of tax varies from province to province and item to item. In 1991, the federal government also introduced its own sales tax, the goods and services tax (GST), which now stands at 5 percent and is applied on top of provincial sales taxes. In Nova Scotia, New Brunswick, and Newfoundland and Labrador as well as, since July 2010, Ontario and British Columbia, the GST is combined with a provincial sales tax into a harmonized sales tax (HST). Purchasers must pay GST/HST on almost all goods and services supplied commercially. Most health and educational services are exempt, as is the re-sale of your home. Consumers pay the tax when they buy something. The seller is then responsible for remitting it

---

[3.] To be eligible for this special rate, a corporation must be a Canadian-controlled private corporation, meaning, generally, a corporation that was incorporated in Canada and is not controlled by non-residents or a public corporation (*Income Tax Act*, RSC 1985, c 1, s 125(7), (5th Supp) (Can)). Such corporations are entitled to other tax benefits as well.

to the government. Businesses also pay the GST/HST on most purchases they make for the purposes of their business. Usually, they can claim a tax credit to recover the GST/HST paid on those purchases.

In addition to income and sales taxes, Canadian governments also levy taxes on property, consumption, and payroll. Property taxes are an important source of revenue for municipal governments. Consumption taxes, also known as "excise" taxes, are levied on non-essential goods, such as cigarettes, alcohol, and gasoline, often constituting a significant portion of the cost of these items. Payroll taxes are levied on most workers' salaries and are used to fund employment insurance, the Canada Pension Plan, and workers' compensation. Finally, capital gains taxes are levied on the proceeds realized from some sales of assets at a price above their cost. In general, capital gains result from sales that occur outside the ordinary course of business. Only a portion of capital gains are taxed, while all income from sales in the ordinary course of business is taxed.

TAXATION OF CORPORATIONS AND SHAREHOLDERS

One of the most important business planning issues is whether to use a corporation to carry on a business. As we discussed in Chapter 21, one of the benefits to a business person of carrying on business through a corporation is that only the corporation is liable for the obligations of the business, including tax. Corporations are solely responsible for the tax on the income earned by the businesses that they carry on. Distributions to shareholders, such as dividends, are taxed in the shareholder's hands only when they are paid to the shareholder.

Often the key issue in choosing to incorporate a business is whether it will result in less total tax being paid on income compared to an individual earning the same income directly. For example, if Sandro carries on business directly, all the income from his business will be taxed in his hands. If he carries on business using a corporation in which he is the sole shareholder, the corporation will pay the tax on the income. But what happens when the corporation distributes that income to Sandro through a dividend? In that case, Sandro has to pay tax on the dividend, too, which is a form of double taxation. In general, the federal government has tried to set up the tax rules so that the same overall amount of tax is paid on income earned by a business regardless of whether it is carried on by an individual directly or through a corporation.[4] This is done by giving a special tax treatment to dividends paid by corporations to shareholders. Figure 25.1 provides an example that illustrates how this works in Canada. The basic idea is that the income earned in the corporation and paid out as a dividend is treated as if it had been earned directly by Sandro. He must calculate his tax owing as if the income earned in the corporation were his income and then reduce the amount he actually pays by taking a credit for the taxes already paid by the corporation. The result is that the cash he ends up with after all the taxes are paid is the same, regardless of whether he earns the money directly or through a corporation. In many situations, however, there may be advantages to earning the money in a corporation. In the example in Figure 25.1, the corporate tax rate is lower than Sandro's individual rate. As a result, as long as Sandro does not need the money, he can save tax by leaving it in the corporation. As well, there are a variety of special tax rules that make it beneficial to use a corporation in particular situations. For example, as noted above, the first $500 000 of annual income earned by certain Canadian-controlled private corporations is taxed at special low rates of between 12 and

---

[4.] This approach is called "integration."

FIGURE 25.1   Example of Taxation of Business Income Earned by Sandro Directly and Through a Corporation

Assume that Sandro's individual tax rate is 30% and the corporate tax rate is 25%				
Case 1 Income earned directly by Sandro		**Case 2** Income earned by Sandro's corporation and the full amount left after the corporation pays tax is distributed to Sandro as a dividend		
Income from the business received by Sandro	$1000	Income from the business	$1000	
		Subtract corporate tax @ 25%	−$250	
		Amount remaining is paid to Sandro as a dividend	$750	
Subtract Sandro's individual tax paid on $1000 @ 30%	−$300	For the purposes of calculating Sandro's taxable income, the dividend is considered to be increased to the amount earned by the corporation (adding back corporate tax paid of $250)	$1000	
		Sandro's individual tax paid on $1000 @ 30%	−$300	
		Add tax credit for corporate taxes paid	$250	
		Subtract net tax paid on dividend	−$50	
Total cash received by Sandro after tax ($1000 − $300 = $700)	$700	Total cash received by Sandro after tax ($750 − $50 = $700)	$700	

19 percent. These low rates increase the benefit of using a corporation to carry on a small business. The advice of an accountant is usually needed in order to decide when using a corporation would be beneficial from a tax point of view.

INCOME TAX ADMINISTRATION AND AUDITS

The principal source of tax law in Canada is the federal *Income Tax Act* (*ITA*).[5] The Act is administered by the Canada Revenue Agency (CRA). Most provinces other than Quebec levy their personal income tax on the basis of taxable income calculated under the federal Act. Some provinces have enacted separate income tax statutes under which they collect provincial taxes.

Each year, CRA receives tax returns from more than 23 million individual Canadians and registered trusts, and more than 1.5 million corporations. It collects in excess of $300 billion. For most individuals who work as salaried employees, employers directly withhold their taxes from salaries throughout the year and remit them to the government, facilitating collection and reducing the risk of fraud. All filers of tax returns must report their total income, which is reduced by the deductions claimed to determine taxable income. The tax that must be paid is reduced by federal and provincial personal tax credits available for such things as child-care expenses.

The administration of the federal *ITA* inevitably gives rise to complex disputes that require specialized expertise for their resolution. Taxpayers who

5. *Income Tax Act*, RSC 1985, c 1 (5th Supp) (Can).

PART 8

dispute the amount that the CRA's Notice of Assessment says they owe must launch an administrative appeal. This process involves discussions with CRA. If the administrative appeal fails, the dispute may be taken to the Tax Court of Canada. Appeals from the Tax Court may be taken to the Federal Court of Appeal, and then, with the court's permission, to the Supreme Court of Canada. (The court structure and the appeal process were described in Chapter 2.)

Every year some individuals and businesses are selected by the CRA for audits. An **audit** is a detailed examination of a taxpayer's annual income and tax payable. The *field audit* is the main tool in the CRA's audit program. The **field audit** is usually a detailed examination of books and records conducted by CRA representatives at the taxpayer's place of business. When the audit is completed, the CRA auditor may propose to adjust the tax payable by reassessing the taxpayer's return. If the taxpayer disagrees, they can appeal in the usual manner.

> an **audit** is a detailed examination of a taxpayer's annual income and tax payable
>
> a **field audit** is usually a detailed examination of books and records conducted by CRA representatives at the taxpayer's place of business

L.O. ❸❹❺❻❼❽

Competition

Competition is vital to maintain the efficiency and adaptability of the Canadian economy for the benefit of consumers. In a competitive market, firms compete for consumers' business by lowering their prices, improving product or service quality, or both. Competition encourages innovation and other changes in the way businesses operate to reduce costs or otherwise improve efficiency. Some marketplace behaviour by individual businesses or groups of businesses that is intended to promote their commercial interests, however, can injure competition and be detrimental to consumers. An agreement by all sellers in a market to charge a price that is higher than the price that would result if they competed with one another is an example. As well, if competition were completely free, the most efficient firm might drive all the others out of the market. If a monopoly were created in this way (or in any other way), there is a significant risk that the monopolist would abuse its position by raising prices above the level that would exist if the market were competitive. The law intervenes in the market to prevent such abuse.

The preservation of competition is dealt with in a limited way in the common law. Like other countries, Canada has adopted specific legislation that deals with anti-competitive behaviour much more comprehensively.

COMPETITION AND THE COMMON LAW

Under the common law, agreements that unreasonably restrain trade cannot be enforced. (Chapter 10 discussed contractual commitments in restraint of trade.) Examples of agreements that restrain trade include a person's commitment not to compete with their former employer and a business's undertaking to its usual supplier not to buy products from a competitor of the supplier. Restraint of trade agreements such as these are not necessarily invalid, but the courts scrutinize them carefully to ensure that they do not unreasonably restrict competition. For example, imagine that Yasmin had sold her car repair business in Lethbridge, Alberta, to Javier. As part of the sale, Yasmin had agreed not to start up a car repair business in Lethbridge for two years. A court could refuse to enforce this agreement if it determined that such a broad restriction was not reasonably necessary to protect the interests of the business. A court might decide that the interests of the business would be adequately protected so long as Yasmin did not set up a competing business within a kilometre of her old business, because customers of her old business would not travel any farther to have their cars repaired. As a result, non-competition agreements must be carefully and reasonably drafted. Because courts will not always enforce agreements to restrain trade, however, their utility as a risk management device is reduced. Also, a challenge to a restraint of trade clause may be brought only by the party to the contract who is subject to the constraint. The common law provides no relief where parties are co-operating to restrain competition.

As Chapter 5 explained, the common law also allows actions in tort for conspiracy and unlawful interference with trade. Those actions are, however, difficult to prove and rarely successful. They require the plaintiff to prove that the defendant deliberately inflicted a loss on the plaintiff by either (i) conspiring with another party to restrain trade, or (ii) inducing a breach of contract.

THE *COMPETITION ACT*

Because of the limited scope of the common law, the federal government long ago enacted legislation to protect competition. The main piece of federal legislation regulating competition today is the *Competition Act*.[6] It aims to restrict anti-competitive practices and stimulate competitive conduct. The Act includes provisions relating to agreements amongst competitors to fix prices as well as abusive behaviour by a dominant firm and mergers that reduce competition. It also contains prohibitions on misleading advertising and other consumer protection provisions that are discussed in the following section on consumer protection.

The *Competition Act* is administered by the Commissioner of Competition, who oversees the operation of the Competition Bureau in Ottawa. The Bureau is an independent law enforcement agency of the federal government that investigates complaints and monitors the marketplace. The Commissioner is responsible for enforcement of the Act and three other standard-setting statutes.[7] The Act categorizes anti-competitive conduct as *civilly reviewable*, or *criminal*. Criminal and civil matters have distinct procedures and remedies.

- **Criminal matters:** These are serious matters that always threaten competition. Criminal matters include agreements to lessen competition, such as by fixing prices, bid-rigging, and employing deceptive marketing practices. After an investigation by the Competition Bureau, the Commissioner refers criminal matters to the Attorney General for prosecution in court.

- **Civilly reviewable matters:** Civilly reviewable matters, also known as **reviewable matters**, must be reviewed in each case to determine whether they have an anti-competitive effect. Reviewable matters include mergers, abuse of dominant position, refusal to deal, exclusive dealing, tied sales, market restriction, and price maintenance.[8] If the Commissioner determines that any conduct is a reviewable matter and is having an anti-competitive effect, it may be referred to the Competition

reviewable matters are actions by firms in the market that must be reviewed to determine whether they have an anti-competitive effect

---

[6] *Competition Act*, RSC 1985, c C-34 (Can).

[7] *Consumer Packaging and Labelling Act*, RSC 1985, c C-38 (Can); the *Textile Labelling Act*, RSC 1985, c T-10 (Can); and the *Precious Metals Marking Act*, RSC 1985, c P-19 (Can). These statutes all deal with some aspect of consumer or industrial protection.

[8] Other reviewable matters include specialization agreements (*Competition Act*, ss 85–90)—agreements where one business agrees to stop producing a product on the condition that another company stops producing a product of its own in return—and delivered pricing (ss 80–81)—prices that are based on a refusal to deliver goods to a customer in a particular location on the same terms that the supplier delivers goods to other customers.

Tribunal, which is an administrative tribunal composed of judges and lay members, including economists. The tribunal has the power to impose a number of remedies aimed at stimulating competition. Those remedies include (i) an order to stop the anti-competitive practice, (ii) the dissolution of mergers, and (iii) an order requiring entities that are contemplating a merger to be "held separate." Appeals from the tribunal's orders can be taken to the Federal Court of Appeal.

■ **Dual category matters:** Misleading advertising may be dealt with as a criminal or civil matter. If the Commissioner determines that the behaviour was committed intentionally or recklessly, the issue can be referred to the Attorney General for prosecution. Otherwise, the Commissioner may decide to refer the matter to the Competition Tribunal.

The ways in which different kinds of activities are addressed under the *Competition Act* are summarized in Concept Summary 25.1 and Figure 25.2.

Concept Summary 25.1

Major Criminal Offences and Civilly Reviewable Matters under the *Competition Act*

Nature of Offence/Matter	Activity
Criminal offences • Always anti-competitive	**Agreements to restrict competition:** agreeing with a competitor to fix product price or supply or to allocate sales, territories, customers, or markets
	Bid-rigging: agreeing not to submit a bid in response to a call for tenders or submitting a bid based upon a prior agreement as to what the bid would be
	Deceptive telemarketing: making a misrepresentation or failing to make a required disclosure when using the telephone to promote the sale or use of a product or to promote some other business interest
	Misrepresentations regarding multi-level marketing plans: making a representation regarding the compensation that a participant in such a plan may receive that is not fair and reasonable or based on compensation that has actually been received
	Pyramid selling: creating a scheme in which participants pay to participate and receive benefits only when they persuade others to join the scheme
Civilly reviewable matters • Must review to determine whether have anticompetitive effect	**Abuse of dominance:** a firm that has substantial control over a "class or species" of business engaging in a practice of anti-competitive acts
	Mergers: acquiring a "significant interest" in or control over a business of a competitor, supplier, customer, or some other person
	Refusals to deal: refusing to sell to a customer who is willing to meet the usual trade terms
	Exclusive dealing: requiring a customer to deal only, or primarily, in products designated by the supplier as a condition of agreeing to supply the customer
	Tied sales: refusing to sell to a customer unless the customer either acquires another product or does not distribute a product associated with another business
	Market restriction: limiting the market in which the purchaser may resell a product
	Price maintenance: attempting to influence upward the price at which the supplier's customer resells its product or refusing to supply a product to a customer because of the low pricing policy of that customer
	Bait and switch: advertising a product for a very low price but telling customers who come to the store that the advertised product is no longer available but a different, higher-priced alternative is in stock
Dual matter	**Misleading advertising:** making a representation to the public that is false or misleading in some material way for the purpose of promoting the supply of a product or a business interest

FIGURE 25.2 Enforcement Process under the *Competition Act*

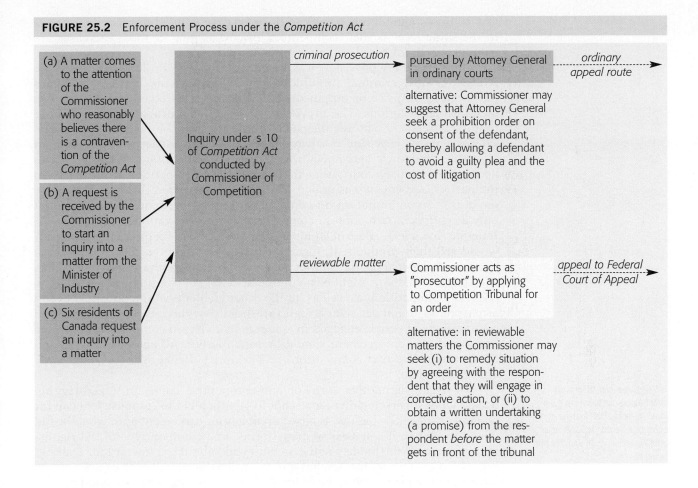

Co-Operation amongst Competitors

Co-operation amongst competitors is the opposite of competition. Section 45 of the *Competition Act* makes it a crime for a person to agree with a competitor to:

- fix, maintain, increase, or control the price or the supply of a product
- allocate sales, territories, customers, or markets for the production or supply of a product
- fix, maintain, control, prevent, lessen, or eliminate the production or supply of a product

However, proving such an agreement is difficult. Because direct proof of an agreement is difficult to obtain, the existence of an agreement may be inferred from the actions of the parties, even without evidence that they communicated with each other. The evidence of the agreement must, however, satisfy the criminal standard of proof—establishing the existence of an agreement beyond a reasonable doubt.[9]

Consumers often make allegations of conspiracy when gas stations uniformly raise their prices to the same level within a very short time. The *Competition Act*, does not, however, prohibit such conscious parallel behaviour.

[9.] *Competition Act*, s 45(3).

Gas stations (and all other types of business) are entitled to raise their prices to the same level as their competitors' prices, as long as those increases are voluntary and not based on an agreement.

The conspiracy provision was amended, effective in 2010, to create the straightforward criminal prohibition on all agreements between competitors relating to price or output described above. This change is intended to facilitate prosecutions. The previous version of this provision had required that the agreement between the parties unduly lessen competition. The courts interpreted this provision in a way that required the parties to the agreement to realize that their agreement would lessen competition.[10] As well, it was necessary to satisfy courts that the lessening of competition resulting from the parties' agreement was undue. The courts interpreted this requirement to mean that *some* limitation on competition is permitted, and concluded that only a *significant* reduction in competition meets the statute's requirement.[11] Imagine that a few sellers of laptop computers agree to fix prices at which they would sell their products. If, together, these sellers represented only a small portion of the market for laptops and competition by the remaining sellers was unaffected, there might be no undue lessening of competition. Proving the effect on competition, as well as all the other elements of the offence, beyond a reasonable doubt set such a high threshold that there were few successful prosecutions of people engaged in agreements to lessen competition. With the new provision, enforcement should be much easier. All agreements between competitors to restrict competition are a criminal offence. They are inherently anti-competitive.

Bid-rigging is another form of anti-competitive collusion.[12] **Bid-rigging** occurs when a person either agrees not to submit a bid in response to a call for tenders or submits a bid that is based upon a prior agreement as to what the bid would be. While it can assume many forms, one common type of bid-rigging occurs when all the bidders agree on who will submit the lowest bid. That bid is likely to be the winning bid, but it is at a price that is higher than what would have been the lowest bid if the bidders were competing with one another. The winning bidder may kick back some of the benefits associated with the contract to the other bidders. Bid-rigging is an offence, no matter what the effect on competition; however, it often will limit competition. Where all bidders are involved in a bid-rigging agreement, the government or private entity making the call for tenders ends up paying more than it should and often these costs will be passed on to the public. .

bid-rigging occurs when a person either agrees not to submit a bid in response to a call for tenders or submits a bid that is based upon a prior agreement as to what the bid would be

Abuse of Dominant Position

The existence of a firm with a very high market share, or even a monopoly in a market, is not, by itself, a basis for intervention by the Competition Bureau. *Abuse of dominant position* by such a firm, however, is a reviewable practice under the *Competition Act*. An **abuse of dominant position** occurs any time (i) a firm has substantial control over a "class or species" of business and (ii) engages in a practice of anti-competitive acts, and (iii) the practice has had or is likely to have the effect of lessening competition substantially.[13] Abuse of dominance is reviewable because of the risk that a dominant firm will exploit

abuse of dominant position occurs any time a dominant firm engages in a practice of anti-competitive conduct that results in a substantial lessening of competition

PART 8

---

10. *R v Nova Scotia Pharmaceutical Society* [1992] 1 SCR 606.

11. *Ibid.*

12. *Competition Act*, s 47.

13. *Competition Act*, s 79.

its market power to restrict competition by other businesses in the marketplace to benefit itself. For example, a dominant firm may try to eliminate its competitors so that it can charge higher prices.

While the Act does not define "dominance," the Bureau has not taken enforcement action against a dominant firm unless its market share is above 85 percent. In addition, the Bureau has said that it will not generally be concerned if the allegedly dominant firm has a market share of less than 35 percent.[14]

To establish abuse of dominance, it is necessary to prove that there has been a substantial lessening of competition as well as market dominance. For the purpose of drawing conclusions regarding whether a firm is dominant in its market and the likely impact of an action on competition, it is necessary to define the market. This requires identifying both the relevant product and the geographic area in which the product is being sold. For some products, the relevant market may be local, such as restaurant services: Most people will not leave their local community to eat at a restaurant. For other products, such as oil, the market may be global. The questions in an abuse of dominance case are whether the firm is dominant in the market for the identified product and whether its actions affected competition in that market. In assessing the impact that a practice has had on competition, the Competition Tribunal must also consider to what extent the impact is the result of superior competitive performance by the dominant firm.

The *Competition Act* does not define "anti-competitive acts" either, but section 78 lists several examples of actions that may limit competition, including the following:

- selling products at a price that is lower than their cost for the purpose of disciplining or eliminating a competitor
- adopting product specifications that are incompatible with products produced by any other supplier and are designed to prevent others from entering a market or to eliminate others from a market
- buying up of products to prevent the erosion of existing price levels

One case involving alleged abuse of dominance began in mid-1997 with an investigation of the marketing and selling practices of HJ Heinz, a well-known manufacturer of baby food with a large share of the market. The Bureau was concerned about Heinz's practice of (i) making large, lump-sum payments to retailers that did not stock competitor's brands, (ii) entering into multi-year contracts for exclusive supply with retailers, and (iii) providing discounts conditional on the retailer agreeing to be supplied by Heinz exclusively. In 2000, Heinz settled the matter with the Bureau by promising to stop such practices. You Be the Judge 25.1 asks you to decide whether an abuse of dominance has occurred.

Mergers

Competition may be reduced when two or more business entities combine their operations in some way, even though the combined business may be more efficient. Business combinations are commonly referred to as *mergers*. Mergers may occur through a variety of different types of transactions, such as the acquisition of shares or assets of a business. Section 91 of the Act defines a

14. Competition Bureau, *Enforcement Guidelines on the Abuse of Dominance Provisions* (2009).

You Be the Judge 25.1

Canada Pipe Company Ltd v Commissioner of Competition (2004) 30 CPR (4th) 429 (Fed CA)

Canada Pipe Company Ltd produces cast iron pipe and related fittings for drain, waste, and vent (DWV) applications used in the construction of buildings. The company had a loyalty program under which customers could obtain substantial rebates and price reductions on their orders if they ordered all of their DWV products from Canada Pipe. A quarterly rebate of between 7 percent and 15 percent was given if a distributor bought only Canada Pipe products in the quarter. An additional rebate of 4 percent was paid if the distributor stayed in the program for a full year. Distributors could leave and restart the program at any time. While some other firms supply DWV products, Canada Pipe has between 80 percent and 90 percent of the market and is the only firm with a national presence. It is hard for new competitors to enter the market because of the costs of setting up a new DWV manufacturing facility. Nevertheless, over the period investigated prices had declined and some new firms had entered the market.

In November 2002, the Commissioner filed an application to the Competition Tribunal for an order directing Canada Pipe to stop its loyalty program on the basis that the program was an abuse of dominance. The Commissioner alleged that the loyalty program was anti-competitive because it locked in distributors by imposing high costs on them if they left. It was argued that the effect was to limit the possibility of entry by competing firms.

Questions for Discussion

1. What has to be shown for an abuse of dominance to be established?

2. Do you think the loyalty program described is an abuse of dominance?

3. What additional information would you need to decide?

---

a merger is the acquisition by one business of a significant interest in another business

merger broadly as the acquisition by one business of a "significant interest" in or control over a business of a competitor, supplier, customer, or some other person. A *significant interest* does not necessarily require control to be acquired. A supplier's interest in a distributor under a long-term supply contract could be a significant interest. Where the Commissioner determines that "a merger is likely to lessen competition substantially in a trade, industry or profession," the Commissioner may apply to the Competition Tribunal for an order prohibiting the merger from taking place, or, if it has already taken place, dissolving the merger, requiring the disposition of assets or some other action to preserve competition.[15]

There are three basic types of mergers:

- **Vertical merger:** A combination of complementary businesses at different stages of production or distribution, such as a supplier and a customer

- **Horizontal merger:** A combination of businesses at the same stage of production or distribution, such as competitors

- **Diversification merger:** A combination of businesses that have little or no relationship to each other, such as a meat-packing business and a lumber mill

In terms of their impact on competition, in most cases only horizontal mergers raise concerns. Where competitors merge, competition is reduced. Competition could also be reduced in a vertical merger between a manufacturer and a distributor if the manufacturer has a large share of the market for a particular product and, as a result of the merger, decides not to supply other distributors. Competition will rarely be affected by a diversification merger. The only question when there is a reduction in competition is whether the

---

[15.] *Competition Act*, s 92

reduction is substantial. This requires an assessment of the likely market share of the merged entity and the likelihood that it will be able to unilaterally exercise market power, such as by raising prices. The Bureau has stated that it is unlikely to challenge a merger on the basis of a concern related to unilateral exercise of market power when the post-merger market share of the merged entity would be less than 35 percent.[16] Whether the merged firm will be able to exercise market power will depend upon the characteristics of the market.

Several specific factors that must be taken into account in analyzing the effect of a merger on competition include the following:

- the extent to which other products or competitors, including foreign competitors, provide effective competition to the businesses of the parties to the merger
- whether the business of a party to the merger has failed or is likely to fail
- whether the merger will result in the removal of a vigorous and effective competitor
- the extent to which barriers block entry into a market, including
  - tariff and non-tariff barriers to international trade
  - inter-provincial barriers to trade
  - regulatory control over market entry (such as licensing)

In addition to a merger's effect on competition, the *Competition Act* requires that the impact of the merger on efficiency be considered. Efficiencies could result, for example, from a pooling of the resources of the merged firms or from the fact that a larger business can produce products at lower cost. The Competition Tribunal cannot make an order in relation to the merger if the benefits from the gains in efficiency will be greater than the cost associated with the effects on competition that are likely to result from the merger.[17] Case Brief 25.1 provides an example of a situation in which the tribunal decided that the benefits of the efficiency gains outweighed the negative impact on competition. Any business engaged in planning a merger must take into account the risk that the transaction will be challenged by the Commissioner, which means the business must analyze the merger's competitive impact and any offsetting efficiency gains.

Case Brief 25.1

Canada (Commissioner of Competition) v Superior Propane Inc 2003 FCA 53

Superior Propane Inc proposed its merger with ICG Propane Inc. Both were suppliers of propane in a number of markets in Canada. The Commissioner challenged the merger before the Competition Tribunal on the basis that it would cause a substantial lessening of competition. In some areas, the merger would result in a virtual monopoly for the merged firm. The tribunal found that there would be a substantial lessening of competition but refused to prohibit the merger because of the significant efficiencies that would result, such as cost savings, improved customer service, and an improved position in the energy market. The tribunal determined that these efficiencies could be valued at $29.2 million, thus outweighing the likely costs associated with anti-competitive effects, such as price increases to consumers, which the tribunal valued at only $6 million. This case was the first to thoroughly consider the significance of efficiency gains.

PART 8

[16.] Competition Bureau, *Merger Enforcement Guidelines* (2011).

[17.] *Competition Act*, s 96.

The *Competition Act* requires advance notice to the Bureau of certain large transactions so that the Bureau can decide whether or not it should challenge the transaction under the merger provisions. It is much simpler to stop a merger from happening than to deconstruct one after the fact. Notification is required in relation to a broad range of proposed transactions where (i) the value of the assets or the target firm itself exceeds $73 million, and (ii) the combined assets or revenues of the parties and their affiliated entities exceed $400 million.[18] The merger may not be completed until the expiry of a waiting period to permit the Commission to investigate the merger. It is possible to seek an advance ruling from the Bureau regarding whether a proposed merger will raise concerns under the merger provisions.[19] Obtaining such a ruling is a common way of managing the risk that the Commissioner will take action under the merger provisions.

Refusal to Deal and Other Reviewable Distribution Practices

In a competitive market, a person is usually free to decide to whom and on what terms they will sell their products. They may even decide not to sell to a particular person. In general, these kinds of choices raise no issue under the *Competition Act*. The Act does prohibit a supplier from **refusing to deal** with a prospective customer where the customer is willing to meet the usual trade terms and would be substantially affected or unable to carry on its business as a consequence of its inability to obtain supplies of a product because there is insufficient competition among suppliers of the product. In these circumstances, the Competition Tribunal can order a supplier to sell the product to the customer.[20]

Similar kinds of distribution practices, such as *exclusive dealing*, *tied selling*, and *market restriction*, are not forbidden but are reviewable and may be the subject of a Competition Tribunal order prohibiting the practice where there is an adverse effect on competition because it is engaged in by a major supplier or is widespread in the market.[21]

- **Exclusive dealing** occurs when, as a condition of agreeing to supply a customer, a supplier requires the customer to deal only, or primarily, in products designated by the supplier. Such arrangements often arise in franchising, where a franchisor requires that the franchisee obtain all of their supplies from the franchisor.

- **Tied selling** occurs when a supplier will sell a customer their product only if the customer either (i) acquires another product or (ii) does not distribute a product associated with another business (usually a competitor). For example, imagine that a supplier of machinery requires their customers to buy a certain brand of industrial lubricant from it as a condition of supplying the machinery.

refusing to deal is refusing to sell to a customer who is willing to meet the usual trade terms

exclusive dealing occurs when, as a condition of agreeing to supply a customer, a supplier requires the customer to deal only, or primarily, in products designated by the supplier

tied selling occurs when a supplier will sell a customer their product only if the customer purchases or does not purchase another product

---

[18.] The thresholds are set out in ss 109–110 of the *Competition Act*. The transaction size threshold is calculated each year based on a formula which adjusts the amount by reference to the annual change in Canadian GDP. In 2008–2009, the Bureau commenced 239 merger examinations. One case was resolved through a consent order of the Competition Tribunal and no contested challenge to a merger was initiated before the Competition Tribunal (*Annual Report of the Commissioner of Competition 2008–2009* [2009]).

[19.] *Competition Act*, ss 102–103. The Bureau issued 134 advanced ruling certificates in 2008–2009 (*Annual Report of the Commissioner of Competition 2008–2009* [2009]).

[20.] *Competition Act*, s 75.

[21.] *Competition Act*, s 77.

■ **Market restriction** occurs when a supplier restricts the market in which the purchaser may resell a product. This would occur where a manufacturer prohibits retailers from selling its products beyond a given geographic region, to particular customers or otherwise.

A reviewable practice of *price maintenance* was created with amendments to the *Competition Act* in 2009. **Price maintenance** occurs when a supplier attempts to influence upward the price at which their customer resells their product or refuses to supply a product to a customer because of the low pricing policy of that customer. Even a suggestion of a retail price by a wholesale supplier can be price maintenance unless the supplier makes clear that the customer is not obliged to accept the suggestion and will not suffer in its business dealings with the supplier if it does not do so. A supplier might engage in retail price maintenance to stop a customer from discounting its product and, as a result, affecting the product's reputation. Like other reviewable practices, price maintenance may be the subject of an order by the Competition Tribunal if it has an adverse effect on competition.[22] This would likely occur only where it was engaged by a supplier with a very large market share or a monopoly. Where price maintenance is found, the tribunal can order that the practice be stopped or that a customer be supplied with the supplier's product. The tribunal cannot make an order, however, if the customer was making a practice of (i) using the supplier's products as loss leaders (meaning not for the purpose of making a profit on selling those products but for purposes of advertising), (ii) engaging in misleading advertising related to the supplier's products, or (iii) not providing the level of servicing that purchasers of the supplier's products might reasonably expect. Business Decision 25.1 asks you to apply the rules for reviewable distribution practices.

market restriction occurs when a supplier restricts the market in which the purchaser may resell a product

price maintenance occurs when a supplier attempts to influence upward the price at which their customer resells their product or refuses to supply a product to a customer because of the low pricing policy of that customer

Business Decision **25.1**

Avoiding Competition Law Issues in Setting Up a Dealer Network

You are the marketing manager for Blue Sky Solar Panels Inc, a new business that manufactures and sells solar panels. You have just joined the company and are very excited about its prospects because the company has a patent on a new technology that makes the conversion of solar energy into electricity extremely efficient. Blue Sky is quickly becoming the market leader in Canada because of this advantage. Your team has developed a marketing strategy for you to consider. They propose that you set up a dealer network throughout Canada. Their strategy includes the following elements:

■ Each dealer will have the exclusive right to sell Blue Sky products in a defined territory and will not be permitted to sell into any other territory. This element is intended to give each dealer an opportunity to maximize sales in its own territory.

■ Blue Sky will set the re-sale price to prevent discounting and brand deterioration as well as to ensure that no dealer has an incentive to sell in the other's territory.

■ Each dealer will obtain all spare parts for Blue Sky products from Blue Sky and not from any third party supplier in order to maintain quality.

Questions for Discussion

1. Is there any legal reason that you should not approve these strategy elements for Blue Sky?

2. Is there anything more that you would like to know in order to answer this question?

---

[22] *Competition Act*, s 76.

Compliance, Enforcement, and Risk Management

The Commissioner enjoys broad discretion in enforcing the Act. Often, in the interests of achieving a quick and cost-effective end to anti-competitive behaviour, the Commissioner seeks to resolve problems by using alternatives to a criminal prosecution or a contested application to the Competition Tribunal. These may include arranging an information visit, obtaining a written undertaking of the person engaged in the behaviour to stop, or seeking a consent order from the Competition Tribunal. If the person engaged in the anti-competitive conduct does not co-operate or if there is evidence of a continuing violation, the Commissioner may resort to more formal enforcement procedures.

Especially for firms that have a large market share, educating employees regarding the requirements of the *Competition Act* is an important way to manage risk. Many large firms have developed **competition compliance manuals** that describe the *Competition Act* rules in an accessible way with industry-specific examples in order to raise awareness among employees and ensure compliance with the Act.

competition compliance manuals are documents, prepared by firms, that describe the *Competition Act* rules in an accessible way with industry specific examples as a way of raising awareness among employees and ensuring compliance with the Act

Private Action under the *Competition Act*

In addition to enforcement by the Commissioner, private parties have a limited right to bring an action against anti-competitive conduct under the Act. Section 36 allows a civil action for damages by a person who has suffered a loss because of anti-competitive conduct that is either a criminal act or is in violation of a court or Competition Tribunal order. In addition, the *Competition Act* has been amended recently to provide for a more limited private right of action in cases of refusal to deal, exclusive dealing, tied selling, market restriction, and re-sale price maintenance. In such cases, the law requires that the complainant must first obtain the tribunal's permission to take action by showing that they are directly and substantially affected by the behaviour in question. If successful before the tribunal, the complainant is allowed to obtain only a cease-and-desist order against the defendant, *not* damages. The complainant is, however, permitted to request reimbursement of their legal costs.[23] These private rights of action have been rarely used.

L.O. **9** **10**

Consumer Protection

We describe people who buy goods and services for their own use, rather than for use in a business or for re-sale, as **consumers**. Consumers are perceived as vulnerable in their dealings with businesses for a variety of reasons. They often lack the ability to fully assess whether the products they buy meet their needs or have defects. These challenges are much greater than they used to be. In today's market, consumers often cannot evaluate goods they purchase because the goods are complex technological products or the packaging prevents consumers from examining them. Because sellers are not usually the producers of the goods, they may not be able to answer consumers' questions or detect and remedy any defects in the products. These challenges are particularly great for transactions concluded over the Internet. As well, consumers are parties to increasingly complicated credit arrangements through credit cards and vendor financing arrangements that they may not understand. Finally, consumers are often unable to bargain effectively with businesses to get the best terms, especially where they

consumers are people who buy goods and services for their own use, rather than for use in a business or for re-sale

---

[23.] *Competition Act*, s 103.1.

are under pressure from the seller. This problem is more likely to occur in particular situations, such as if consumers are dealing with salespeople at their door instead of in a store. For all these reasons, federal and provincial governments have intervened to protect consumers through legislation.[24]

In previous chapters, we discussed some ways that consumers are protected. Using tort law to protect consumers from sellers' negligence was discussed in Chapter 6. We discussed the circumstances in which courts will not enforce clauses in contracts that exclude the liability of the seller in Chapter 10. In Chapter 13, we discussed the implied promises that sellers make to buyers in sale of goods transactions under the *Sale of Goods Act*.[25] Some provinces have even made the requirements of the *Sale of Goods Act* mandatory in transactions with consumers.[26] In Chapter 19, we discussed some of the protections for consumers contracting online. In addition to these protections, all provinces and the federal government have established minimum standards for the information that consumers receive to help them make informed decisions, prohibited certain kinds of unfair practices engaged in by businesses when they are transacting with consumers, and created specific requirements for particular kinds of transactions in which consumers are most vulnerable. These rules apply to all sales, including services and financing transactions. Unfortunately, the approach adopted in different Canadian jurisdictions has not been consistent or comprehensive. We will look at three key areas:

■ misleading advertising and other deceptive marketing practices, such as making false statements about a product to get people to buy it or making untrue statements about availability of repair services related to the product

■ product regulation to ensure the maintenance of minimum standards for quality, safety, and labelling

■ regulation of business conduct toward consumers, including disclosure of the true cost of credit

MISLEADING ADVERTISING AND OTHER DECEPTIVE MARKETING PRACTICES

One important source of consumer protection legislation is the *Competition Act*. That statute prohibits misleading advertising and a broad range of other deceptive marketing practices targeted at consumers.

Misleading advertising occurs when a person makes a representation to the public that is false or misleading in some material way for the purpose of promoting the supply of a product or a business interest. A representation can take almost any form, including information marked on packaging, a statement made by an individual in a store or over the telephone, and advertising. "Material"

misleading advertising occurs when a person makes a representation to the public that is false or misleading in some material way for the purpose of promoting the supply of a product or a business interest

---

[24.] With respect to some kinds of services, consumers are at a significant disadvantage because they typically do not have enough knowledge to evaluate the quality of the service. Legal and medical services are examples. The government protects consumers by setting and enforcing standards for legal, medical, and other practitioners.

[25.] In Chapter 10, we discussed using requirements for contracts to be in writing to protect consumers.

[26.] *Eg Sale of Goods Act*, RSBC 1996, c 410 (BC), s 20; *Consumer Protection Act*, SO 2002, c 30 (Ont) s 9. Some provinces have extended these promises so that they may be enforced by any person that the seller might reasonably foresee would use the product (*eg Consumer Protection Act*, SS 1996, c C-30 (Sask)). As discussed in Chapter 13, the *Sale of Goods Act* generally permits buyers and sellers to agree that the implied promises that the Act creates do not apply and, in any case, they only apply between the buyer and the seller.

simply means that the representation could influence the consumer's decision to purchase the product. It is not necessary to prove that any person was actually deceived or misled by the representation. What is misleading is determined objectively, looking at the general impression created by the representation as a whole, including all of its visual elements. A representation may be misleading with respect to the price of a product, the product characteristics, the supplier, or some other matter. If a supplier of a car tells you that it is new when, in fact, it is used but has been reconditioned, that is a material misleading misrepresentation.

Misleading advertising is a criminal offence under the *Competition Act* if the representation was made knowingly or recklessly. It may be punished by up to 14 years in prison and a substantial fine. As noted above, misleading advertising is a dual category matter. If it is pursued civilly as a reviewable matter, the supplier can avoid liability if it exercised *due diligence* to prevent the offence. The **defence of due diligence** is available if the person responsible for the advertisement acted with reasonable care to ensure that it was not misleading.[27] Most cases of misleading advertising are pursued civilly. Relief can be pursued by individuals and businesses and remedies include an order of the Competition Tribunal to stop the advertising as well as damages. The Commissioner may also seek such an order and the payment of a financial penalty. The *Competition Act* identifies several other reviewable practices relating to advertising:

the **defence of due diligence** is available to a person charged with misleading advertising if the person acted with reasonable care to ensure that it was not misleading.

- a seller makes a representation to the public regarding the performance, efficacy, or length of life of a product that is not based upon an adequate and proper test

- a seller makes a representation to the public concerning the price at which it ordinarily supplies a product and has not sold a substantial volume of the product at that price or a higher price within a reasonable period of time before or after making the representation

Case Brief 25.2 provides an example of a business that claimed benefits for its products without a proper test.

Case Brief 25.2

lululemon athletica[28]

The popular exercise wear seller lululemon athletica advertised its VitaSea seaweed-based clothing as providing various health benefits upon contact with moisture. lululemon claimed that the fabric would release minerals and vitamins into the skin that would, among other things, moisturize the wearer's skin, promote skin cell regeneration, enhance the skin's blood supply, and reduce stress. After a study was published disputing the existence of any of these benefits, the Commissioner commenced an investigation.

Within 48 hours, lululemon agreed to remove all unsubstantiated claims from its VitaSea products, to remove all references to "VitaSea technology" from its website and in-store advertising, and to make sure that none of its employees gave information to customers regarding the health claims. lululemon also agreed to review all of its advertising to make sure that it complied with all relevant requirements.

telemarketing is using the telephone to promote the sale or use of a product or to promote some other business interest

The practice of *deceptive telemarketing* may also be an offence. **Telemarketing** is using the telephone to promote the sale or use of a product or to promote some other business interest. It is an offence to engage in

---

27. *Competition Act*, ss 52 (criminal offence) and 74.01 (reviewable matter).

28. "Competition Bureau Takes Action to Ensure Unsubstantiated Claims Removed from lululemon Clothing" (16 November 2007) <www.competitionbureau.gc.ca/eic/site/cb-bc.nsf/eng/02517.html>.

telemarketing unless callers doing it identify themselves, explain the purpose of the call, and describe the product at the beginning of the call. Fair, reasonable, and timely disclosure must also be made of the price of any product and any material terms applicable to its delivery. Misrepresentation by telemarketers is an offence. Certain additional requirements are imposed with respect to contests, lotteries, and some pricing schemes carried out through telemarketing. For example, a telemarketer cannot invite you to participate in a contest without telling you the number and approximate value of the prizes, and of any fact within the telemarketer's knowledge that affects materially your chances of winning. A person can avoid a conviction if they exercised due diligence to prevent the commission of the offence. If convicted, a person is liable for up to 14 years of imprisonment and a fine at the discretion of the court.[29] In practice, fines of $1 000 000 and jail sentences have been imposed.

A final category of marketing offences relates to *multi-level marketing plans*. A **multi-level marketing plan** is a scheme in which participants receive compensation for supplying a product to another participant in the plan, who, in turn, receives compensation for supplying the product to a third participant in the plan. For example, imagine that you are offered the right to be a distributor of a product. For each product you sell, you will receive a portion of the proceeds. You can also make money by finding other people who will buy the product from you and try to sell it to others. These kinds of plans are not necessarily illegal. It is an offence to make any representation relating to the compensation that may be received under such a plan to a prospective participant, unless the representation is fair and reasonable and relates to information known by the person making the disclosure regarding compensation that has actually been received by participants. These kinds of arrangements often collapse if there is no market for the products and the compensation of participants depends upon finding new participants to sell to. In many cases, at some point, no new participants can be found. Again, a due diligence defence is available to any person who gets someone else involved in such an arrangement.[30]

Pyramid selling is a form of multi-level marketing. It can occur in several variations. In one variation each participant in the pyramid-selling scheme pays for a right to receive compensation for each new participant they recruit who, in turn, receives compensation on the same basis. For example, you pay me for the right to participate in a scheme for selling pots and pans. In turn, you will receive payments from people whom you persuade to join the scheme. And they, in turn, will receive payments from the people whom they enlist, and so on. A pyramid selling scheme like this is a criminal offence.[31] The maximum penalty for pyramid selling and misrepresentations regarding multi-level marketing plans is five years in prison and a fine at the discretion of the court.

Many other types of deceptive marketing practices are only reviewable practices. For instance, goods cannot be offered for sale under a *bait and switch*. A store engages in a **bait and switch** when it advertises a product for a very low price but tells customers who come to the store that the advertised product is no longer available but a different, higher-priced alternative is in stock. This tactic

a **multi-level marketing plan** is a scheme in which participants receive compensation for supplying a product to another participant in the plan, who, in turn, receives compensation for supplying the product to a third participant in the plan

pyramid selling occurs when people pay to participate in a scheme in which they receive benefits in exchange for persuading other people to join the scheme

a **bait and switch** occurs when a store advertises a product for a very low price but tells customers who come to the store that the advertised product is no longer available but a different, higher-priced alternative is in stock

[29.] *Competition Act*, s 52.1. The Canadian Radio-television and Telecommunications Commission has created a do-not-call list. Telemarketers cannot call any consumer who is registered—unless they are a registered charity or a political party, or have an existing business relationship with the consumer. If they call a consumer who has registered, they may be fined.

[30.] *Competition Act*, s 55.

[31.] *Competition Act*, s 55.1. The *Competition Act* creates a number of additional, more specific offences: s 53 prohibits sending a person a notice of winning a prize if the person is required to do something or incur a cost to receive the prize; s 54 prohibits a seller from refusing to allow someone to buy a product at the lowest of two prices indicated for the product.

relies on the fact that many people will buy the more expensive item, rather than waste the trip and go home empty-handed. Likewise, products cannot be promoted on the basis of false testimonials or product-testing.[32] With respect to all these reviewable deceptive practices, the Commissioner may seek a court order prohibiting the conduct and imposing an administrative penalty (such as a fine) of up to $750 000 for an individual and $10 000 000 for a corporation. Ethical Perspective 25.1 asks you to make a choice about an advertising campaign in which the risk that it would be an offence or a reviewable practice is small.

Ethical Perspective **25.1**

Choices about Advertising

Assume you work in the marketing department of a large power tool manufacturer. You have been asked to review an ad prepared by an outside advertising agency that shows a woman using some of your company's products. The ads are for a drill and a circular saw. They feature the caption, "So light and easy to use, even a woman can do it." You are not worried that the ad is misleading. Independent tests have verified that your company's tools are lighter than your competitor's products, and your design team has adopted some innovations that make the tools easy to use. However, you are worried about whether the ads are sexist.

You know that Advertising Standards Canada (ASC) publishes the Canadian Code of Advertising Standards. ASC is a not-for-profit corporation established by the advertising industry; most of the large companies in Canada are members. ASC helps to ensure the integrity and viability of advertising through industry self-regulation, in part through a public complaints process. Complaints are reviewed by consumer response councils and where a violation of the Code is found, the determination is made public and the advertiser is directed to change or remove the ad. Such a direction is not legally binding. Under the heading "Unacceptable Depictions and Portrayals," the Code says:

Advertisements shall not
(a) condone any form of personal discrimination, including that based upon race, national origin, religion, sex or age; . . .
(c) demean, denigrate or disparage any identifiable person, group of persons, firm, organization, industrial or commercial activity, profession, product or service or attempt to bring it or them into public contempt or ridicule.

Questions for Discussion

1. Should you approve the ad, confident that it is neither a criminal offence nor a reviewable practice under the *Competition Act* because it is not misleading?

2. What do you think would be the consequences if a complaint were made and a consumer response council found the ad was contrary to the Code?

3. Is there any way to manage the risk of a complaint being made?

OTHER FEDERAL LEGISLATION RELATING TO STANDARDS, PACKAGING AND LABELLING

A key element of product marketing is how the product is packaged and labelled. Suppliers try to design product packages and labels to be attractive to consumers. The federal government has a number of statutes to ensure that labelling provides accurate information so that consumers can compare products and make informed purchasing decisions.[33] Other federal statutes establish specific standards for products themselves:[34]

■ The *Consumer Packaging and Labelling Act* requires pre-packaged consumer products to bear labels that provide accurate information in English and French. Labels must clearly identify the common name of

---

[32.] *Competition Act*, s 74.01.

[33.] We discussed how warning labels can be used to manage the risk of suppliers being found negligent in Chapter 6.

[34.] *Eg* the *Motor Vehicle Safety Act*, SC 1993, c 16 (Can), applies to motor vehicles made or imported into Canada. Its provisions deal with safety features and procedures in case of vehicle recall.

the product, the quantity, and the name and principal place of business of the manufacturer. Certain listed products, such as wine and peanut butter, must be sold in standardized containers. Misleading or false representations on labels are prohibited. For example, your business's label for a food product cannot say how many servings that package contains unless it also says how big the servings are.[35]

- Under the *Textile Labelling Act*, each piece of clothing must bear a label that states the materials used and the name of the dealer. Detailed requirements apply to how materials are described. Misleading or false representations regarding the material, either on labels or in advertising, are prohibited. You cannot use a picture on a label that falsely suggests that a particular kind of fibre is in the clothing. For example, a picture of a sheep on the label of a sweater would not be permitted if the sweater contained no wool.[36]

- The *Hazardous Products Act* lists inherently dangerous products, such as lead-based paints, glues, and industrial chemicals, that can be produced and handled only according to standards set out in the Act and the regulations under the Act.[37] For example, the regulations set standards for the labelling and use of mattresses, tents, baby pacifiers, and cellulose insulation, among other things.

- The *Food and Drugs Act* deals with many aspects of food, drugs, and cosmetics, including their processing, storing, and labelling. The Act imposes penalties on businesses that sell food, cosmetics, or drugs that are adulterated, or that produce or store these products in unsanitary conditions. The Act also sets standards for product labelling, including the listing of ingredients and dating for products with limited shelf life.[38]

PROVINCIAL CONSUMER PROTECTION LEGISLATION

Each province has enacted consumer protection legislation that complements the federal measures described above by dealing with a range of specific situations involving consumers. Provincial laws prohibit a broad range of false, misleading, and exaggerated claims by businesses in a way that overlaps with the protections in federal law. However, the provincial statutes provide that the consumer is not responsible under any contract entered into where there has been such a claim, and the consumer can claim relief in addition to the remedies offered under federal law, including damages.[39] As well, provincial legislation regulates other aspects of the conduct of businesses in specific situations. New legislation enacted within the past few years has attempted to update consumer protection to address Internet-based contracting. While there is significant diversity in the scope and content of rules across the country, several key elements of the approach taken in most provinces may be identified:

- *Written contracts with prescribed disclosure are required for certain types of contracts*—To ensure that consumers know what kind of deal they

[35.] *Consumer Packaging and Labelling Act*, RSC 1985, c C-38 (Can).

[36.] *Textile Labelling Act*, RSC 1985, c T-10 (Can).

[37.] *Hazardous Products Act*, RSC 1985, c H-3 (Can).

[38.] *Food and Drugs Act*, RSC 1985, c F-27 (Can).

[39.] *Eg Consumer Protection Act*, 2002, SO 2002, c 30, s 18 (Ont); *Fair Trading Act*, RSA 2000 c F-2, ss 7, 15 (Alta).

are getting, some contracts must be in writing and provided to the consumer. These include contracts in which consumers are likely to find themselves under pressure, such as when a salesperson comes to their house, and contracts in which it is hard for the consumer to understand the value of what they are paying for, such as contracts requiring payment in advance for future services, such as a one-year gym membership that a consumer pays for today, and time-share agreements. Contracts concluded over the Internet are subject to the same rules.[40]

■ *A limited right to rescind contracts exists in certain circumstances*—This right is granted to consumers in relation to the same contracts as covered in the previous point (contracts entered into where the salesperson comes to your house, some contracts involving payments in advance for services in the future, time-share contracts, and contracts concluded over the Internet) and for the same reasons. The right to rescind is usually exercisable only during a cooling-off period that lasts a few days, running either from the time the contract is entered into or the time a written record of the agreement is delivered. The goal is to ensure that consumers have an opportunity to get out of the contract after fully considering the obligations that they are assuming.[41]

■ *There is no obligation to pay for unsolicited goods*—If you receive goods you did not order, you do not have to pay for them or return them. You can even use them. These provisions seek to ensure that a consumer cannot be pressured to pay for goods just because the seller sends them to the consumer.[42]

■ *Credit terms must be fully disclosed*—Anyone providing goods or services on credit must give the consumer a written statement showing all financing charges and the effective annual percentage rate of interest for the credit transaction. The statement must also explain how any extra charges would be calculated if the consumer failed to make the payments. A borrower is not bound unless the required disclosure is made.[43] Some statutes require additional, more specific disclosure for some complex transactions, such as leases and time-share contracts.[44] These provisions enable borrowers to make informed choices regarding whether to enter into a credit obligation. Consumers can compare financing costs and look for the best rates.

---

[40] Eg *Consumer Protection Act, 2002*, SO 2002, c 30, ss 22, 27, 42, 46 (Ont); *Business Practices and Consumer Protection Act*, SBC 2004, c 2, ss 19, 20, 23, 24, 48 (BC). The *Fair Trading Act*, RSA 2000, c F-2, ss 35, 37 (Alta), *Time Share and Points-based Contracts and Business Regulation*, Alta Reg 105/2010, s 2, and *Internet Sales Contract Regulation*, Alta Reg 81/2001, ss 4, 5 deal with contracts concluded with a salesperson who comes to your house, time-share contracts and Internet sales, respectively.

[41] Eg *Consumer Protection Act, 2002*, SO 2002, c 30, ss 28, 35, 40, 43, (Ont) (cooling-off period 10 days or 7 days for Internet agreements); *Business Practices and Consumer Protection Act*, SBC 2004, c 2, ss 21, 25, 26, 39 (BC) (cooling-off period 10 days or 7 days for Internet contracts).

[42] Eg *Consumer Protection Act, 2002*, SO 2002, c 30, s 13 (Ont); *Consumer Protection Act*, RSNS 1989 c 92, s 23 (NS); *Business Practices and Consumer Protection Act*, SBC 2004, c 2, s 12 (BC).

[43] Eg *Consumer Protection Act, 2002*, SO 2002, c 30 (Ont), ss 77–81; *Consumer Protection Act*, RSNS 1989 c 92, s 17 (NS); *Business Practices and Consumer Protection Act*, SBC 2004, c 2, ss 81–93 (BC); *Fair Trading Act*, RSA 2000 c F-2, ss 58–101 (Alta). The *Interest Act*, RSC 1985, c I-18, s 4 (Can), requires that interest rates in written contracts be expressed in annual percentages.

[44] Eg *Consumer Protection Act, 2002*, SO 2002, c 30, ss 27, 89 (Ont), and Ontario Reg 17/05.

Chapter Summary

Governments tax businesses and individuals to fund government operations. In addition to income and sales taxes, Canadian governments levy taxes on property, consumption, and payroll. Corporations must pay taxes on the income that they earn. Special tax rules try to ensure that the overall tax paid on income is the same in most cases, whether it is earned through a corporation and distributed to the individual shareholders, or earned by the individuals directly.

The Canadian government seeks to promote competition and protect consumers. Competition promotes innovation, lower prices, and improved product quality. Some marketplace behaviour can hurt competition. The common law protects competition in a limited way. Under the common law, agreements that unreasonably restrain trade, such as a commitment not to compete with a former employer, cannot be enforced by a party to the agreement. Because of the importance of competition and the limitations of the common law, the *Competition Act* prohibits a wide range of activities that harm competition and establishes the Competition Bureau to enforce the Act. That Act prohibits some kinds of behaviour that always threaten competition. Other behaviour is prohibited only when it has an anti-competitive effect. The Act makes it a criminal offence to enter into agreements to restrict competition and to rig bids. It also requires the review of many other transactions, including the abuse by a firm of its dominant position in a market through anti-competitive acts.

Other reviewable distribution practices include exclusive dealing, tied selling, market restriction, and price maintenance. These reviewable practices may be prohibited by an order from the Competition Tribunal if they have anti-competitive effects. Mergers are also reviewable. Some mergers may be beneficial to Canadian society because the merged firm is more efficient, but mergers may also lessen competition substantially. If the merged entity has enough market power, there is a risk that it will use that power to engage in anti-competitive activity. The Commissioner of Competition may seek an order from the Competition Tribunal stopping the merger or, if it has already occurred, dissolving it. The Competition Bureau must be notified of major business acquisition transactions in advance.

Consumers benefit from various kinds of protection. The *Competition Act* contains provisions dealing with misleading advertising, deceptive marketing, and telemarketing. Other federal laws attempt to protect consumers through the regulation of industrial or commercial activities, including setting standards for consumer packaging and labelling, and food and drug safety. Provincial consumer protection legislation complements federal law by providing additional remedies to consumers who are affected by false, misleading, or deceptive representations by sellers. As well, provincial laws require some contracts to be in writing, allow consumers to get out of contracts within a short period after entering into them, and insist on disclosure of the full cost of credit.

MyBusLawLab   ADDITIONAL RESOURCES FOR CHAPTER 25

MyBusLawLab provides students with an assortment of tools to help enrich the learning experience, including a Study Plan with Pre- and Post-tests, mini-cases with assessments, and provincial content material, which provides links to relevant cases, legislation, and additional resources.

MyBusLawLab provides the following resources for Chapter 25:

- You Be the Judge 25.1W—Can Mergers Be Efficient?
- Environmental Impact Assessments
- Environmental Remedies
- International Environmental Protection: Climate Change and the Kyoto Protocol

Provincial Material

- **British Columbia:** Credit Reporting, Collection Agents, Consumer Protection Legislation, *Sale of Goods Act*, Dishonest Trade Practices, Cooling-Off Period, British Columbia Environmental Legislation, Consumer Taxes, Cost of Borrowing, Credit Cards, Direct Sales Contracts, Distance Sales Contracts, *Business Practices and Consumer Protection Act*

- **Alberta:** *Alberta Competitiveness Act (2011)*, *Alberta Corporate Tax Amendment Act (2010)*, *Alberta Health Act (2010)*, *Carbon Capture and Storage Statutes Amendment Act (2010)*, *Dangerous Goods Transportation Act (2010)*, Environmental Legislation, *Fisheries (Alberta) Amendment Act (2009)*, Occupational Health and Safety, *Consumer Protection Acts*, *Fair Trading Act*, Gift Cards, Securities Commission, Dishonest Trade Practices

- **Manitoba and Saskatchewan:** *Business Practices Act*, Consumer Protection Legislation, Consumer Protection Legislation—Disclosure of Restrictions, Environmental Legislation, False or Exaggerated Claims

- **Ontario:** Agreements to Share Power, *Consumer Protection Act 2002*, Environmental Protection Legislation, Payday Loans, Unfair Business Practices

- **Atlantic Province:** *Consumer Product and Liability Act*, Payday Loans, Public Utilities Board

PART 8

Review Questions

1. What are the basic types of taxation in Canada?

2. Describe the difference between the tax treatment of income from a business that is earned directly by an individual and the same income earned by a corporation and distributed to the individual as a shareholder.

3. What is the administrative procedure followed by the Canada Revenue Agency to audit tax filings?

4. Why is it necessary to have a law protecting competition?

5. Identify the common law actions that can be brought for anti-competitive behaviour, and explain why a purely common law approach to anti-competitive behaviour is insufficient

6. Jerome was a salesperson for Edge Electronics Inc, which makes smartphone handsets and sells them only in Canada. He signed an agreement that said, among other things, that if he left his job, he would never work for any other handset manufacturer anywhere in the world, ever. Is this non-compete provision enforceable?

7. Who is the "Commissioner of Competition"?

8. What is the distinction between a criminal matter and a reviewable matter under the *Competition Act*?

9. Is it illegal if two competitors agree not to compete with each other?

10. Salome has control of all the driving lesson businesses in Ottawa. Is this contrary to the *Competition Act*?

11. If the Competition Bureau is dealing with a complaint about an anti-competitive act by a dominant firm, how will it assess whether the firm is dominant?

12. Why are mergers reviewable under the *Competition Act*?

13. If your corporation were planning a merger that would be subject to notification under the *Competition Act*, is there any way to manage the risk that the merger might be challenged under the Act?

14. Noel holds the rights to sell franchises for an international fast-food restaurant chain in Canada. He will agree to sell a franchise to someone only if they agree to buy all of their food supplies from him. Is Noel in breach of the *Competition Act*?

15. Can the *Competition Act* be invoked by individuals? If so, what remedy can they obtain if they are successful?

16. Why do Canadian governments not require consumers to look after their own interests in the contracts that they enter into?

17. If you were a marketing manager for a chain of grocery stores, would you approve a print ad that said that prices for apples were 40 percent lower than the regular price of $4 per kilogram if, in fact, your stores never sold apples at the higher price?

18. Gini has a business producing eye makeup. Are there any rules that she must comply with regarding the packaging and labelling of her product?

19. Would it be a good strategy to send samples of your products to consumers and ask them to pay for the product if they like it?

20. Are there any circumstances in which consumers can get out of a contract that they have entered into?

Cases and Problems

1. Cesar is considering incorporating the consulting business that he has been carrying on for the past several years as a sole proprietorship. He will be the sole shareholder and director of the corporation. Will he reduce the tax that is paid on the income from the business if it is earned in the corporation?

2. Lisa Inc produces what has become the most popular brand of tablet computer. Lisa supplies about 90 percent of the market for this product worldwide. All retailers want to stock Lisa's tablets. Lisa sells to many distributors but has decided not to sell its tablets to discount electronics chains because it wants to encourage people to go to its own corporate-owned stores and non-discounting retailers. Low Price Electronics is one of the distributors that Lisa will not sell to, even though Low Price is willing to meet Lisa's sales terms. If you were the president of Low Price, what could you do?

3. Javier carries on a business of selling shoes at a store in a shopping mall. Cecilia also operates a shoe store in the same mall. While they are competitors, they are also friends. They decide that they could both make more money if they did not compete with each other aggressively. In the past, whenever one of them had a sale, usually the other would immediately put their shoes on sale, often with better discounts from the regular retail prices. They agreed that they would not have sales that offered more than 10 percent off the regular retail price. They think that they would each sell just as many shoes but earn more income with this arrangement. Is the agreement between Javier and Cecelia illegal? What is likely to be the effect on competition?

4. Casino Inc produces and sells a low-calorie artificial sweetener called Spartan that is a substitute for sugar. Casino's Spartan has about 90 percent of the market. It thinks that it can get 100 percent of the market if it reduces its prices for about six months to $5 per kilogram, a price close to its cost of production. Its main competitor, Asoh Inc, has higher costs and will not

be able to compete by selling its product at that price. Casino thinks that Asoh will have to go out of business or stop selling its sweetener if Casino adopts this temporary low-pricing policy. Selling at that price will significantly limit Casino's profits, but Casino is confident that it can more than recover those lost profits by raising its prices after Asoh has left the market. Is this a rational strategy? Is it legal?

5. Prado Shoes Inc manufactures very expensive, high-quality women's shoes, which it sells to retail stores throughout Canada. Universal Shoes Inc has a large chain of shoe stores in Alberta. One of its marketing strategies is to compete aggressively on price, even when pricing its Prado shoes. Prado is unhappy that Universal is discounting its shoes because it feels discounting tarnishes Prado's brand image as a high-end shoe. It also makes Prado's other shoe retailer customers unhappy. Prado tells Universal that it has to sell Prado's shoes at or above the suggested retail price or Prado will stop selling to Universal. Universal is unhappy about this demand. Is there anything that Universal can do about it under the *Competition Act*?

6. Cinefed Inc operates the largest film exhibition business in Ontario. Cinefed has theatres in every significant town and city in the province. Aside from a few independent theatres, the only competitor of Cinefed in Ontario is Starfilm Ltd, which is much smaller. Over the past few weeks, Cinefed has been negotiating with the owners of Starfilm to buy Starfilm's business for $100 000 000. Cinefed is hoping that by combining the two businesses, it can get a better price from US film distributors. It might also be able to charge higher prices to its customers. Together, Cinefed and Starfilm would be worth more than $500 000 000 and would control 90 percent of the film exhibition market in Ontario. Would this transaction raise any concerns under the *Competition Act*?

7. S&A Electronics, a high-volume retail sales outlet, advertises its products in local newspapers and flyers at very low prices with claims that the products are "priced to move!" However, the stores often have very few of these items in stock and S&A's sales staff routinely attempt to convince potential customers to buy other, higher-priced products instead. Sales staff tell customers that the store is sold out of the items on sale and unable to order more, when in fact the wholesaler has plenty in stock and an order could easily be filled. Some customers seeking the advertised products receive rain checks that are never honoured and others are simply told that S&A has run out of the product. If you were a competitor of S&A and discovered these facts, what could you do to address these practices?

8. For a number of decades, the six manufacturers of microscopes in Canada operated under an informal agreement that required no competition on price, but high competition in performance and service. The manufacturers in the arrangement often re-designed their products and generally maintained the technology of their products at world-class levels. Could

this agreement be the subject of action under the *Competition Act*? What would have to be proven?

9. Nancy and Bob Brown ran a successful locksmithing and security business in Perth, Ontario, a town of about 6000 people, for 17 years. They were well-known and highly respected in the community. The Browns were thinking of retiring and decided to sell their company to Vladimir Markovic, who had just moved to Perth. As a term of the sale, the Browns signed a non-compete agreement with Markovic that prohibited them from operating a similar business within 100 kilometres of Perth for 10 years. After being out of the business for a year, however, the Browns set up a new business in Ottawa, about 85 kilometres away, selling locksmithing and security services. Markovic wants to know if the non-compete clause can be enforced.

10. Shazad was looking for a new pair of skis. He went to the website of Downhill Specialists Inc, found the skis he wanted, and ordered them through the website for $400. He was very pleased with the purchase because Downhill said that it did not require any payment for one year and that, after a year, Shazad could pay $50 per month for eight months. Shazad missed the first payment and Downhill sent a demand for the full price of $400 plus interest of $25 and a charge for collection of $25. The right to demand the full price, interest, and a collection charge had not been communicated to Shazad. Is Shazad bound to pay the full amount plus the interest and the collection charge?

11. Manuel Inc produces and sells its own popular brand of photocopiers and printers. It also is an investor in a paper company called Bondar Inc. Manuel is considering adopting a marketing strategy under which it would agree to sell its products only if the buyer agrees to buy all of their copier and printer paper from Bondar. To make this attractive to customers, Manuel has arranged for Bondar to offer a discounted price to Manuel's customers. The increase in Bondar's sales will benefit Manuel as an investor in Bondar. Is there any legal reason that Manuel should not adopt this strategy? Is there anything more that you would like to know in order to answer this question?

12. Orton Inc sells car parts to hardware stores and garages across Canada. It grants its customers the following discounts from the unit price of individual products set out in its price list:

- discounts of 10 percent for individual orders exceeding certain volumes
- discounts of 5 percent on any orders that exceed certain aggregate volumes over a six-month period
- discounts of 5 percent based on a commitment not to buy parts from any other supplier for a year (the commitment is not binding but if the customer honours it, the discount will be granted)
- discounts of 15 percent based on the purchase of specified volumes of other products sold by Orton

Do any of these discounting practices raise legal concerns?

Should Consumers Be Allowed to Commit to Arbitrating Their Disputes with Businesses?

On 3 April 2003, Dell Computer Corp made a mistake. The pages on its website that advertised the Axim X5 300 MHz and Axim X5 400 MHz handheld computers listed the prices as $379 and $549, but on the pages where the handhelds could be actually be ordered, the prices were listed as just $89 and $118. When Dell discovered the error on April 5, it blocked access to the order pages but did not take them down or correct them while it figured out how to deal with the problem. On April 7, Dell corrected the error, posted a notice of the price correction, and announced that it would not process orders for the handhelds at $89 or $118.

Olivier Dumoulin, a Quebec resident, was told by a friend about the low prices for the handhelds on the morning of April 7. The friend also sent him "deep links" that enabled him to get directly to the blocked order pages. Before Dell had corrected its error, Dumoulin used these links to order an Axim X5 300 MHz for $89. In total, 394 Quebec consumers ordered more than 500 of the two handhelds at the low prices that appeared on the order pages between Friday, April 3, and Tuesday, April 7, with one customer ordering 40 units. Normally, weekend sales of these units in Quebec were between one and three.

When Dell refused to deliver handhelds for the $89 and $118 prices, Dumoulin, along with other customers and the Union des consommateurs (a Quebec consumer protection organization), filed an application to commence a class action against Dell on behalf of all Quebec consumers who had purchased Dell handhelds at the prices mistakenly included on the order pages of Dell's website. Dell's response was that the contract entered into by consumers who purchased its computers included a provision under which they agreed to resolve all disputes with Dell through arbitration instead of the courts, so the application to commence a class action should be dismissed. Dell's website included a hyperlink at the bottom of every page marked "Terms and Conditions of Sale" that provided access to all of its terms of sale, including the arbitration provision. Dumoulin and the Union argued that the arbitration clause was "null" and not binding on various grounds, including that Dell had not done enough to bring the provision to the attention of consumers. As a consequence, they argued, the arbitration provision should not be considered part of the contract.

First the Quebec Superior Court and then the Court of Appeal held that the arbitration provision could not be enforced against Mr Dumoulin and other consumers and that the class action could proceed. Dell appealed to the Supreme Court of Canada, and in 2007 the Supreme Court allowed the appeal. A majority of the court held that the parties were free to contract to have their disputes dealt with exclusively in arbitration. The court found that because the arbitration clause was sufficiently accessible to customers it formed part of their online contract. To read the clause, a customer needed only to click once on the hyperlink. The Supreme Court also concluded that the possibility that a consumer could pursue a claim through a class action did not provide the consumer with any additional rights. This is because a consumer cannot pursue a claim through a class action unless the consumer is already entitled to bring such a claim as an individual. As a result, taking away the possibility of a class action through an agreement to arbitrate is not unfair. The court dismissed the motion to authorize the class action and referred the parties to arbitration.

On 9 November 2006, just before the decision was released, the Quebec government amended Quebec's consumer protection law to prohibit provisions in contracts with consumers that force them to resolve their disputes only through arbitration or that prevent them from initiating class actions. The provisions came into force in December 2006 but were not retroactive. Ontario had previously amended its *Consumer Protection Act, 2000*, in 2005 to make provisions requiring arbitration or waiving class action rights unenforceable. Not all other provinces, however, have specific provisions dealing with arbitration and class actions like those of Ontario and Quebec. Recently, the British Columbia Court of Appeal confirmed that clauses in contracts with consumers in that province that require arbitration are enforceable.[45]

Questions to Consider

The decision of the Supreme Court in Dell endorses the freedom of parties to contract and the enforcement of agreements to arbitrate. (Arbitration and class actions are discussed in Chapter 2. The contract law issues raised in the *Dell* case are discussed in Chapters 9 and 10. The application of contract law to Internet-based contracts is dealt with in Chapter 19.) Resolution of disputes through arbitration where commercial parties have agreed to arbitrate is strongly encouraged by the courts and by Canadian arbitration legislation. Enforcing arbitration agreements increases certainty and predictability in commercial relationships where parties have chosen to arbitrate.

In *Dell*, the Supreme Court extended the courts' policy of enforcing arbitration agreements to consumer contracts. The legislatures in Ontario and Quebec, however, have decided that consumers should not be free to commit themselves to resolving disputes in arbitration. If the situation in *Dell* had occurred in Quebec or Ontario today, the consumers would have won and been able to proceed with their class action. One effect of the Ontario and Quebec reforms is that the strategy of avoiding the risk of being subject to class action proceedings and the costs and procedures of judicial dispute resolution

---

[45.] *MacKinnon v National Money Mart Company* 2009 BCCA 103.

through an agreement to arbitrate is no longer available to businesses in their dealings with consumers in these two provinces.

1. Is legislation that makes some specific kinds of contract provisions, including agreements to arbitrate, unenforceable by businesses in all cases the best way to protect consumers? Would it be better for businesses and consumers if it were left up to the courts to decide whether to refuse to enforce contracts on the basis that they are unfair, taking into account the unique circumstances of each case?

2. Is it ever a good idea to permit consumers to agree that disputes with a business can be resolved only by arbitration? Should the answer depend upon the nature of the arbitration process?

3. The Supreme Court decided that taking away the right of a consumer to initiate a class action through an agreement to arbitrate is not unfair. Do you agree with the court? What arguments might be made in favour of protecting a consumer's ability to make a claim through a class action?

4. In light of the changes to consumer protection legislation in Ontario and Quebec, how would you modify your online agreement if you were Dell?

ADDITIONAL RESOURCES

Canadian Internet Policy and Public Interest Clinic www. cippic. ca/documents/consumer-protection/archive/

This website is maintained by one of the organizations that participated in the *Dell* case as an intervenor. It provides an archive of all the main documents filed in the case, including the submissions of pro-arbitration organizations such as the London Court of International Commercial Arbitration, as well as consumer organizations such as the Union des consommateurs.

Dell Corporation Inc. www1.ca.dell.com/content/topics/global. aspx/services/service-contracts/service-contracts? c=ca&l=en&s=bsd &cs=cabsdt1&~ck=anavml&redirect=1

This website provides the terms and conditions that Dell is currently using in its consumer contracts. It still provides for arbitration of disputes with people who purchase its products but states that consumers benefit from any protections applicable by virtue of consumer protection legislation in their jurisdiction.

Manitoba Law Reform Commission www.manitobalawreform.ca/ pubs/pdf/115-full_report.pdf

This link provides access to an extensive study completed in 2008 by the Manitoba Law Reform Commission on mandatory arbitration clauses and consumer class action proceedings. The report considers how mandatory arbitration clauses are dealt with in consumer protection legislation in Canadian jurisdictions as well as in the United States, the European Union, New Zealand, and Australia. The Commission recommends that Manitoba reform its consumer protection law to follow the approach in Ontario and Quebec.

26 Individual Employment

LEARNING OBJECTIVES

After completing this chapter, you should be able to:

❶ Develop business strategies to ensure that pre-employment practices comply with employment legislation.

❷ Distinguish between employees and dependent and independent contractors.

❸ Explain the difference between non-competition and non-solicitation covenants.

❹ Outline the circumstances in which a business is liable to third parties for the conduct of its employees and describe three ways in which a business can improve the supervision of its employees.

❺ Identify five employer obligations imposed by employment standards legislation.

❻ Discuss human rights in the workplace.

❼ Explain the basic statutory measures designed to ensure safety in the workplace.

❽ Distinguish between summary dismissal, wrongful dismissal, and constructive dismissal, and define just cause for dismissal as well as the notice periods that must be provided when dismissing an employee without cause.

❾ Distinguish between severance packages and settlement packages, and explain the effect of a signed release.

❿ Discuss the possible post-employment obligations of employees in the absence of contractual obligations.

In this chapter, we will consider the three main phases of the employment relationship. First, we will consider *pre-employment matters*, including recruiting, hiring, and the employment contract. Then we will examine *employer obligations* and *worker protection* mechanisms imposed by statute and see how the employment relationship is maintained. Finally, we will investigate issues that arise when the employment relationship breaks down, including the termination of employment and *post-employment practices*, such as severance, settlement packages, and ongoing obligations.

Pre-Employment Matters

L.O. ❶ ❷

JOB DESCRIPTIONS

Before hiring for a position, an employer should define their requirements in a job description. A **job description** is a written list of the employment duties of a particular job. A well-drafted job description makes it easy for an employer to find the right person for the job. When included in an advertisement for a position, a job description also saves considerable time and money by reducing the number of applicants. It also functions as a standard of measurement that can be used to discipline or, if necessary, dismiss an employee who is not living up to the employer's expectations. Although not technically a legal document, a job description that is poorly drafted is a liability. If the job description is too narrowly drafted, it can provide leeway for an employee to refuse certain tasks on the basis that they fall outside of their job. One way to manage this risk and achieve flexibility is to include a provision near the end of the job description that acknowledges that the job may include additional duties as assigned by the employer.

> a **job description** is a written list of the employment duties of a particular job

ADVERTISING POSITIONS

After drafting a proper job description, many employers advertise the position. Advertising not only allows employers to select from a broad and diverse applicant pool, but also provides the appearance of impartiality during the hiring process. However, there are risks associated with advertising. For instance, an advertisement may violate human rights legislation. Consider the example in Business Decision 26.1.

Business Decision 26.1

Advertisements and Human Rights

Giuseppe's Pizza needs to hire someone to answer the phones and take walk-in orders. Since Giuseppe regularly advertises in the local classified ads for delivery drivers, he decides to run his usual ad:

> Giuseppe's is now hiring. Good wages, flexible hours, and free pizza (while on the job). Call Giuseppe's today! Valid driver's licence required.

Although this ad may seem perfectly reasonable, it probably violates human rights legislation. Since the ad is for a phone attendant—not a driver—requiring a valid driver's licence may discriminate against certain people who might otherwise apply for the job. For

example, someone with a visual impairment might be perfectly well qualified for the job even though they may not be able to drive. By advertising a valid driver's licence as a requirement for the job, Giuseppe's has unintentionally discriminated against persons on the basis of physical disability.

Questions for Discussion

1. How could Giuseppe's Pizza have avoided that problem?

2. Would Giuseppe's Pizza lose anything if it re-wrote its advertisement to comply with human rights legislation?

APPLICATION FORMS AND INTERVIEWS

employment application forms are useful to screen job candidates for the necessary qualifications

A successful advertisement will generate many job applications. To fill positions with appropriate people, employers need more information, often obtained through application forms and personal interviews. **Employment application forms** are useful to screen job candidates for the necessary qualifications. However, employers must be careful not to ask questions that are too invasive. Questions must relate to the applicant's ability to do the job. Unrelated questions may violate provincial human rights legislation or privacy legislation, as discussed later in this chapter. Figure 26.1 lists several kinds of information that may be sought in an application form or an interview, and, as a matter of risk management, suggests questions that should and should not be used.

FIGURE 26.1 Managing Risk in Employment Applications and Personal Interview Questions

Information Sought	Do not ask:	Do ask:
Name	What is your Christian name?	What is your first name?
Emergency contact	Who should be contacted in case of an emergency? What is your relationship with this person?	Who should be contacted in case of an emergency?
Eligibility for work	What is your nationality?	Are you legally entitled to work in Canada?
Education	What schools did you attend?	What is the highest level of education you have attained?
Ability	Describe any disabilities you may have.	Are you able to perform the following duties? If not, what is the nature of accommodation that you require?
Availability	What religious holidays do you celebrate?	Are you available for shift work? If not, what accommodations are necessary?
Languages	What is your mother tongue?	What languages do you speak?
Mobility	Are you married?	Are you able to transfer to another city?
Associations	Do you have any memberships in clubs or other organizations?	Do you have any memberships in clubs or other organizations that do not reveal your gender, race, religion, ancestry, or place of origin?

Source: Rearranged and reprinted with permission from RS Echlin & CM Thomlinson For Better or *for Worse: A Practical Guide to Canadian Employment Law* (1996) at 14–20.

STATEMENTS MADE DURING HIRING

When the employer has selected an applicant, the parties usually negotiate the terms of employment. Both sides need to be careful to avoid making false statements that could amount to misrepresentations, as discussed in Chapter 9. A misrepresentation by either party could allow the other to walk away from the employment contract with impunity. If a misstatement is negligent or fraudulent, it could even lead to a cause of action in tort or criminal law. Case Brief 26.1 illustrates the possible consequences of an employer's misrepresentation.

Case Brief 26.1

Queen v Cognos Inc (1993) 99 DLR (4th) 626 (SCC)

Queen, an accountant, had a good job with decent pay but was looking for something different. He saw an advertisement in a Calgary newspaper for a job with Cognos, a high-tech company. Queen applied for the job. During his interview, Queen was told that the position was a permanent one and that the successful applicant would play a lead role in developing a new accounting software program. The interviewer failed to mention that the entire project—including the budget for the lead position and the hiring of additional staff—was subject to further approval. Queen took the job. Soon after, Cognos decided to slash the funding allocated to the project. Consequently, no other staff members were hired and, as a result, Queen's job became much less significant.

After being dismissed 18 months later, Queen sued Cognos for negligent misrepresentation, claiming that he never would have agreed to leave his former position if Cognos had not inflated the significance of the project and Queen's role in it.

The Supreme Court of Canada agreed with Queen. It held that employers have a duty during employment interviews to exercise reasonable care and diligence when making representations about the nature of an employment opportunity. It is not enough that the interviewers be honest. They owe a further duty to make sure that their representations are accurate.

NATURE OF THE WORK RELATIONSHIP

Our discussion has focused on the employment relationship. However, not all work- or service-related contracts are contracts of employment. Nor are all workers considered to be employees.

Employees

An **employee** is a person who contractually agrees to work under the control and direction of an employer. Employees are legally protected in some ways that other workers are not. For example, an employee is entitled by both statute and common law to reasonable notice before being dismissed. The failure to give such notice entitles the employee to sue. The same is not true for workers who lack employee status.

an **employee** is a person who contractually agrees to work under the control and direction of an employer

Independent Contractors and Consultants

One kind of worker who lacks the legal status of an employee is an *independent contractor*. An **independent contractor** contractually agrees to work but is *not* controlled by another person in how they accomplish a task. Independent contractors and consultants are not entitled to many of the rights that employees enjoy, including those discussed later in this chapter: reasonable notice of termination, statutory termination and severance pay, overtime pay, vacation pay, and statutory holiday pay. However, they benefit in other ways through various tax advantages conferred by the *Income Tax Act*, and, unlike employees, are not subject to wage deductions pursuant to the *Employment Insurance Act* and the *Canada Pension Plan*.

an **independent contractor** is a person who contractually agrees to work but who is not controlled by another person in how they accomplish a task

Being an independent contractor involves a trade-off. Independent contractors and consultants do not owe the same loyalty as employees. Subject to the terms of their contracts, they have more freedom in deciding when to work, how to work, where to work, for whom to work, and so on. As communication and networking technologies continue to improve, employers are becoming more willing to relinquish control of those choices. This significantly reduces the costs generally associated with employee protection. It can also reduce the overall financial risk of employing a large number of workers. For example, time and resources permitting, a business can hire an independent contractor for a specific or time-limited project without taking on the responsibility of hiring a full-time employee.

Although employee and independent contractor contracts will often state explicitly whether the person is hired as an employee or not, it is sometimes difficult to distinguish between employees and independent contractors or consultants. Such contractual designations are, however, not decisive; instead, the true nature of the relationship must be determined through a series of questions. One test asks how much control is exercised by the party paying for the work. The **control test** is based on four significant factors: (i) the employer's authority to select individuals for employment, (ii) the employer's ability to decide the payment scheme, (iii) the employer's ability to control and direct the type, manner, and timing of the work, and (iv) the employer's right to discipline the worker. The more control that can be exercised, the more likely the worker will be considered an employee.[1]

Since highly skilled professional employees are not always subject to direct supervision, the degree of control is not always a determining factor. Therefore, courts have considered such other factors as (i) who owns the equipment used to perform the job, (ii) whether the worker had the chance to profit, (iii) who risks any loss, (iv) the regularity of the work, and (v) whether the worker has the authority to delegate performance of the work. Courts have also recently considered the overall role that the worker plays in the organization. The **organization test** attempts to determine whether the work is an integral part of the overall business.

Recently, courts have begun to identify a third category of worker, called the *dependent contractor*. This category lies somewhere between employee and independent contractor. A **dependent contractor** is someone who generally meets the test for an independent contractor, but who has had a long-standing and exclusive relationship with their employer. This exclusivity can entitle the worker to certain rights that are not otherwise owed to contractors, such as reasonable notice of termination. As a matter of risk management, employers should consider whether they have an exclusive relationship with their contractor that resembles an employer–employee relationship, entitling the contractor to expect reasonable notice of termination.[2]

Given the variety of factors that judges take into account, it is difficult to ensure that a particular worker will be considered an independent contractor, a dependent contractor, or an employee. Concept Summary 26.1 provides a recap of these various factors. Figure 26.2, on the following page, offers a number of tips for companies that want to set up independent-contractor relationships.

---

the **control test** may determine whether a worker is an employee or an independent contractor based on the degree of control exercised by the party paying for the work

the **organization test** attempts to determine whether a person's work is an integral part of the overall business

a **dependent contractor** is someone who generally meets the test for an independent contractor, but who has had a long-standing and exclusive relationship with their employer

---

[1.] RS Echlin & CM Thomlinson *For Better or for Worse: A Practical Guide to Canadian Employment Law* (1996), at 43–44.

[2.] *McKee v Reid Heritage Homes*, 2009 ONCA 916, [2009] OJ 5489; *Marbry Distributors Ltd v Avrecan International Inc* (1999), 171 DLR (4th) 436 (BCCA).

Concept Summary 26.1

Judicial Considerations in Determining the Nature of the Work Relationship

The Control Test	Additional Considerations
Does the employer have authority to select individuals hired by the worker?	Who owns the equipment used to perform the job?
Does the employer decide the payment scheme?	Did the worker have a chance to profit from particular outcomes?
Does the employer control or direct the type, manner, and timing of the work?	Who risks the loss associated with particular outcomes?
Does the employer have authority to discipline the worker?	How regular is the work?
Is there authority to delegate the tasks to other workers?	Does the worker work for other employers as well?
Is the work an integral part of the overall business?	

FIGURE 26.2 Risk Management Strategy: Ensuring an Independent Contractor Relationship

- Expressly state in the written contract that the party performing the services is not an employee and is not entitled to any of the statutory protections afforded to employees.
- Do not take any statutory deductions, such as income tax, employment insurance, Canada Pension Plan, or workers' compensation off the worker's pay.
- Do not provide vacation pay, statutory holiday pay, or overtime pay.
- Do not provide benefits such as health care plans, stock options, or bonuses.
- Do not provide a company uniform, business cards, a company vehicle, company equipment (such as a computer, a desk, voicemail or email, or office space).
- Do not provide bookkeeping, invoicing, or secretarial services.
- Do not provide performance reviews or disciplinary measures. (This does not preclude a termination provision in the contract.)
- Expressly allow the worker to set their own work schedule.
- Expressly allow the worker to work for competitors or to generate income from other sources.
- Encourage the worker to set up a company, sole proprietorship, or a partnership with a GST/HST number.

Source: Rearranged and reprinted with permission from RS Echlin & MJ MacKillop *Creative Solutions: Perspectives on Canadian Employment Law* (2000) at 17.

The Employment Contract

L.O. ❸

Once a business has decided which applicant it wants to hire as an employee, it typically will make an offer of employment. The process leading to a binding employment contract is governed by the same rules that apply for contracts generally, as discussed in Part 3.

The employment contract is an essential tool in the risk management strategy of any business. Although not required by law, employment contracts should normally be in writing to avoid disputes, and should clearly describe the obligations of the employee and employer. Any number of issues can be addressed in an employment contract, including terms of pay, salary, job description, and benefits. Employment contracts will often require the employee to agree to read and abide by all of the employer's policies and procedures. In addition to these important issues (discussed later in this chapter) there are at least two other key issues that should be specifically addressed in many employment contracts: *non-competition/non-solicitation* and *confidentiality*. Trade secrets and confidentiality obligations (discussed in Chapter 18) are often important. Here we focus on non-competition and non-solicitation clauses.

NON-COMPETITION AND NON-SOLICITATION

a **non-competition clause** is a form of restrictive covenant that prohibits or restricts an employee's ability to work for a competitor or to start a business that would compete with the employer

a **non-solicitation clause** is a form of restrictive covenant that prohibits the employee from soliciting the customers of the employer, but otherwise leaves the employee free to compete

Generally speaking, a **non-competition clause** is a form of restrictive covenant that prohibits or restricts an employee's ability to work for a competitor or to start a business that would compete with the employer. A **non-solicitation clause** is a form of restrictive covenant that prohibits the employee from soliciting the customers of the employer, but otherwise leaves the employee free to compete. These covenants typically are specifically meant to apply after the breakdown of the employment relationship. For example, a non-competition clause might prohibit the employee from working for a competing business within 100 kilometres of the employer's place of business for a period of five years after termination of the employment relationship.

Courts typically view non-solicitation clauses as adequate means of protecting business interests. By contrast, non-competition clauses can be excessive and are therefore viewed with caution. When non-competition clauses are used, employers must be limited in their geographic and temporal application.

In certain circumstances, courts will refuse to enforce non-competition, non-solicitation, or confidentiality clauses in an employment contract. Unreasonable covenants in restraint of trade, for example, can be contrary to public policy. If so, they may be illegal and unenforceable, as discussed in Chapter 10. In the employment context, where employers can often exert power over employees, restrictive covenants are construed more strictly against the employer. Given the risk that such terms may be found unenforceable, knowledge of the law and special care are required when crafting such clauses.

In the employment context, courts will consider three factors in deciding whether to enforce a restrictive covenant:[3]

- whether the employer has a *proprietary interest* worthy of protection
- whether the *temporal* and *geographic restrictions* are broader than would reasonably be required to protect the employer's proprietary interest
- whether the covenant *restricts competition generally*, or merely bars solicitation of the former employer's clients

An employer might have a proprietary interest in its trade connections with clients or customers. This can be particularly important where customers of a business are long-term or repeat customers. However, the general rule is that courts are reluctant to enforce a non-competition covenant where a mere non-solicitation covenant would have adequately protected the employer's proprietary interest.

Exceptions to the general rule will be made where the temporal and geographic limits in a non-competition covenant are reasonable. There are no hard and fast rules for deciding what is reasonable, although shorter time frames and smaller geographic scopes are advisable. The circumstances of each case must be taken into account. For example, a two-year non-competition clause might be reasonable in the insurance industry but not for high-tech employees—two

---

3. *Elsley v JG Collins Insurance Agencies Ltd* (1978) 83 DLR (3d) 1 (SCC).

years at "Internet time" might be unreasonable given how quickly technology is evolving and the need for workers to keep up to date in their area of work.

It is important to note that an employer who terminates employment without cause usually cannot enforce restrictive covenants against the employee. Additionally, where an employment contract does not include a restrictive covenant, the former employee is generally free to compete with the employer and solicit the employer's clients upon termination of their employment.[4] Concept Summary 26.2 highlights several ways to manage risk through the use of restrictive covenants. Business Decision 26.2 offers an opportunity to reflect on the use of restrictive covenants more generally.

Concept Summary 26.2

Managing Risk through the Use of Restrictive Covenants in an Employment Contract

- Know the law and draft your restrictive covenants with the legal requirements in mind.

- Define the proprietary interest you are trying to protect through the clause (*eg* your trade connection with your clients).

- Consider whether to include non-competition, non-solicitation, and confidentiality clauses. Consider whether a non-solicitation clause would be sufficient to protect your interest, rather than a non-competition clause.

- When drafting a non-competition clause, bear in mind the circumstances of your industry and the employee, and draft the restriction to be reasonable, both temporally and geographically. Do not be too broad.

- Be aware that if you repudiate the employment contract, you may not be able to enforce its restrictive covenants.

Business Decision 26.2

Restrictive Covenants[5]

Pedja owned a Vancouver-based insurance company, which he sold to another company, Insure Co, for a tidy profit. As part of the sale, Insure Co agreed that Pedja would continue to be employed as a broker with the new company. The parties entered an employment contract that included a non-competition covenant restricting Pedja from working as a broker in the Metropolitan City of Vancouver for a period of three years if he were to leave Insure Co. A few years later, when Pedja's employment contract was set to expire, he went to work as a broker for a different insurance company in Richmond, a city on the outskirts of Vancouver, also considered a suburb of the City of Vancouver. Insure Co subsequently sued Pedja for breaching the non-compete covenant. Pedja claims that he has not breached the covenant because he is working outside of the restricted geographical area of the "Metropolitan City of Vancouver." The parties never discussed what the "Metropolitan City of Vancouver" includes.

Questions for Discussion

1. What was the purpose of this restrictive covenant?

2. What could you as an employer do to prevent a dispute like this one from arising? Re-draft the non-compete clause for this situation, creating one that would protect the interests of Insurance Co.

Employers' Obligations and Worker Protection Legislation

L.O. ❹ ❺ ❻ ❼

We now survey some of the more important obligations that employers owe to their employees and others: *third party liability*, *supervision*, and *statutory protection*.

---

4. *RBC Dominion Securities Inc v Merrill Lynch Canada Inc* [2008] SCJ No 56 (SCC).

5. Based on *Shafron v KRG Insurance Brokers (Western) Inc* 2009 SCC 6.

THIRD PARTY LIABILITY

vicarious liability occurs when an employer is held liable for an employee's tort

A worker's status is important to the company that commissioned the work if that person causes damage to a third party. As we saw in Chapter 4, the injured third party can sue both the individual worker and the company. **Vicarious liability** occurs when an employer is held liable for an employee's tort. That doctrine is, however, subject to two important restrictions:

- The doctrine does *not* apply to *independent contractors*.[6]
- The doctrine applies to an employee's torts only if the employee was acting in the course of employment.

To determine whether an employee was acting in the course of employment, a court will look at several factors. The location of the incident, the time of day, and the fact that company equipment was involved are important considerations, but they are not always conclusive.[7] The fundamental issue is whether the harmful act occurred while the employee was carrying out assigned duties. You Be the Judge 26.1 focuses on that issue.

You Be the Judge 26.1

Cole v California Entertainment Ltd [1989] BCJ No 2162 (BC CA)

Wayne Cole and some friends entered Club California wearing matching red bomber jackets bearing the crest *Victoria Kick Boxing Club*. A doorman named Wolf explained the club's dress code and said that they would have to take off their jackets if they wanted to enter. The group exchanged words with Wolf and other staff members. The club owner then instructed the bouncers to clear the entrance. When the altercation moved outside, the club owner went back into his office and closed the door. Cole and his friends left the club along with four bouncers and walked to a nearby parking lot. Wolf challenged one of Cole's friends to a fight. A brawl broke out. Eventually, Wolf went after Cole who, being a lot smaller, backed away and said he did not want to fight. But Wolf

kept coming. He grabbed Cole by the front of his jacket and hurled him through the plate-glass window of a nearby store, pulled him out, and threw him against a car parked in front of the store. Wolf kept punching until two people pulled him off Cole. Cole staggered across the street and collapsed. He was later taken to the hospital.

Questions for Discussion

1. Did the fight fall within the owner's instructions to clear the club's entrance?

2. Was Cole injured within the course of Wolf's employment?

SUPERVISION

The risk of vicarious liability and other workplace hazards imposes certain responsibilities on employers to supervise their employees; however, even the most conscientious employer cannot stand guard around the clock. There are other ways in which employees can be controlled, including:

- employment policy manuals
- performance reviews
- promotion or progressive discipline

[6.] A company may be held liable for failing to exercise reasonable care when hiring an independent contractor. In that case, the company's liability is not based directly on the independent contractor's wrong, but rather on its own wrongful act in hiring an inappropriate worker.

[7.] Some provinces (such as British Columbia) have legislation that makes the registered owner of a motor vehicle vicariously liable for the accidents of any authorized driver of the vehicle, whether an employee or not: *Motor Vehicle Act*, RSBC 1996, c 318, s 86 (BC). In such cases, the fact that a company vehicle was used is determinative.

Employment Policy Manuals

The basis of a good employment relationship is communication. Employers can use an **employment policy manual** to explain the conduct expected of employees in the course of their employment. A carefully drafted policy manual also details the manner in which its policies will be implemented, applied, and enforced, and should be accompanied by a form requiring employees to indicate that they have read and understood the manual and will comply with all of its terms, subject to dismissal for cause. A clear policy manual may therefore allow an employer to demonstrate cause for dismissal of an employee. For instance, if a policy manual provides clear instructions on what employees are and are not allowed to do on the Internet, an employer can more readily determine when Internet usage is inappropriate, and what sort of Internet usage may justify summary dismissal.[8] Ethical Perspective 26.1 illustrates the legal importance of a policy manual.

an **employment policy manual** explains the conduct expected of employees in the course of their employment

Ethical Perspective **26.1**

Poliquin v Devon Canada Corporation, 2009 ABCA 216, [2009] AJ No 626

Poliquin was employed by Devon for over 25 years until his termination. For the majority of his employment, Poliquin had supervisory responsibilities over other employees. Following his termination, Poliquin brought an action seeking damages for wrongful dismissal. Poliquin had been an exemplary employee and had received positive performance appraisals throughout his time with Devon. Devon argued that, despite this being Poliquin's first incident requiring discipline, he was dismissed for cause for violation of the company's Code of Conduct.

Specifically, Poliquin was dismissed for accepting free services from suppliers, which is explicitly forbidden in the Code. He also used Devon's computer equipment and Internet to view and transmit pornographic and racist material, in further violation of the Code of Conduct. There was additional evidence that Poliquin even forwarded some of this offensive material to other Devon employees.

The judge found that while Poliquin's actions were "beyond inappropriate," his case deserved to go to trial because Devon's disciplinary

actions were disproportional, particularly in light of Poliquin's exemplary record. On appeal of this decision, a subsequent judge found that a trial was not necessary and precluded Poliquin from pursuing his wrongful dismissal action. The judge found that Poliquin's conduct demonstrated that he was gravely deficient in some of the qualities needed to perform the core of his job. In particular, he demonstrated exceptionally poor judgment and an unwillingness to obey and enforce Devon's Code of Conduct. This entitled Devon to dismiss him with cause.

Questions for Discussion

1. Do you find it fair that that the appellate judge dismissed Poliquin's wrongful dismissal action largely because of Poliquin's poor judgment? What additional information might you require to make this decision?

2. Can you recommend terms to include in Devon's Code of Conduct that might help the company avoid a similar situation in the future?

Performance Reviews

Another way to direct the behaviour of employees is to conduct regular *performance reviews*. A **performance review** is an evaluation of an employee that provides feedback about the quality of their work. Most performance reviews are conducted in person; however, employers should have a standard written evaluation form to guide the process (i) to ensure that all employees are treated the same, and (ii) to provide a written record in case the employment relationship breaks down. If an employer has recorded a string of poor performance reviews in an employee's file, it is difficult for the employee to argue that they were wrongfully dismissed. It is also important to note that a properly conducted performance review can be used to identify and correct workplace problems in their infancy.

a **performance review** is an evaluation of an employee that provides feedback about the quality of their work

---

[8.] *See Poliquin v Devon Canada Corporation*, 2009 ABCA 216, [2009] AJ No 626. This case is discussed in more detail in Ethical Perspective 26.1.

Promotion and Progressive Discipline

Employee behaviour can be directed through rewards and punishments. Employers should recognize employees who consistently perform well and consider them for *promotion* to higher positions. This both rewards productivity and sets a behavioural benchmark for other employees. A **promotion** usually entails new duties on the part of the employee, whether or not it includes a pay raise.

a **promotion** usually entails new duties on the part of the employee, whether or not it includes a pay raise

When an employee has received a number of poor performance reviews or is otherwise misbehaving in the workplace, the employer should consider a *progressive discipline program*. A **progressive discipline program** involves a series of disciplinary steps that may progress from verbal or written warnings, through degrees of suspension, to dismissal.[9] It is useful to explain such a program in the employment policy manual. Suspension is a drastic measure and must be used only in appropriate circumstances. However, when there is a plausible basis for commencing an investigation and the employer carries it out in good faith, courts have held that a brief period of suspension is a reasonable course of conduct.[10]

a **progressive discipline** program involves a series of disciplinary steps

STATUTORY PROTECTION

The employment relationship traditionally was governed exclusively by the law of contract. Today, however, workers are also protected by various statutory schemes that courts will construe broadly in order to safeguard workers. Much of the legislation falls under provincial jurisdiction and varies in detail among provinces.[11] Sophisticated employers usually hire human resource experts or employment law specialists to navigate the intricacies of these statutory measures. We will discuss five statutory regimes: *employment standards, human rights, employee privacy, occupational health and safety, and workers' compensation.*

Employment Standards

Employment standards legislation requires an employer to meet minimum obligations, which apply only to employees and not to independent contractors or consultants. An employer cannot generally contract out of the legislation's minimum obligations. If an employment contract fails to meet those requirements, the employer must nevertheless compensate the employee according to the legislation. Furthermore, the legislation establishes *minimum standards*. If an employment contract actually provides the employee with greater protection, the employer cannot use the statute to reduce those rights. We briefly consider minimum standards in connection with holidays; wages; work hours, overtime, and rest days; leaves; and vacations.

Holidays Every jurisdiction requires employers to pay employees for specific public holidays. This does not mean that employees cannot be asked to work on these days, as long as they are adequately compensated for doing so. Some provinces, such as British Columbia, Manitoba, Nova Scotia, and Prince Edward Island, entitle employees to public holidays only if they have worked 15 or more days in the month preceding the public holiday. Other provinces,

---

[9.] Echlin & Thomlinson *For Better or for Worse* (1996) at 116.

[10.] *Pierce v Canada Trust Realtor* (1986) 11 CCEL 64 (Ont HCJ).

[11.] Federal legislation governs some employees, including those in federal government, transportation, shipping, radio, and banking. The division of legislative authority between the federal and provincial governments was discussed in Chapter 1.

such as Newfoundland and Labrador, New Brunswick, and Ontario, allow certain kinds of employers, such as those in hospitals or the hotel and restaurant industry, to require their employees to work on public holidays. Usually, these employees are entitled to additional compensation for working on those days.

Wages Every province has set a minimum wage. Minimum-wage legislation ensures that an employee's pay increases in line with the cost of living. The minimum wage is determined on an hourly basis, but it also applies to employees who are compensated in other ways. In such cases, it is up to the employer to ensure that the statutory minimum is met. Some jurisdictions have set different minimums for different categories of employees. For example, Alberta's standard minimum wage does not apply to certain professions, such as bartenders and other salespersons who earn commission. Ontario sets a lower minimum for workers under 18 years of age. And the Northwest Territories limits the amount of earnings that an employer can deduct from the minimum wage of an employee requiring room and board. The typical minimum wage varies substantially between provinces and is influenced by such factors as the level of industry, the cost of living, and the political beliefs of the government in power.

Work Hours, Overtime, and Rest Days Every jurisdiction regulates the number of hours that an employee can be asked to work. In most jurisdictions, this varies from 40 to 48. An employee can refuse to work more than that without fear of disciplinary action. Employees who choose to work more are entitled to overtime pay. In most provinces, the minimum rate of pay for overtime is 1.5 times the employee's regular wages. In a few provinces, the minimum rate is 1.5 times the minimum wage. A minimum daily rest period is also imposed in most provinces. Employees are typically entitled to 30 minutes for every 5-hour period worked, as well as 8 to 11 hours of consecutive rest in any 24-hour period. Legislation also grants workers time for additional short rest periods such as time taken for personal medical needs, for breastfeeding infants, and for religious worship.

Leaves Many jurisdictions entitle employees to unpaid leaves of absence. In some jurisdictions, bereavement leave is available for employees who grieve the loss of a loved one; sometimes it is paid, sometimes not. Employees are also entitled to take time off to vote in elections. Every jurisdiction entitles women who have fulfilled a minimum service requirement to a leave of absence during and after pregnancy. Some provinces also offer parental leave to both/either parent(s) of a newborn in specified circumstances and within certain time frames. Although most parental leaves are unpaid, many employers continue to offer benefits, which may include part pay. Other employers offer no benefits, leaving the pregnant employee to claim employment insurance. Women who take pregnancy leaves are entitled to return to their jobs after the leave and do not lose seniority in their position. If it is impossible to reinstate the employee to her previous position, she must be provided with a comparable job with equivalent wages and benefits.

Vacations Employees are entitled to paid vacation and statutory holidays. In most jurisdictions, the length of paid vacation depends upon years of service. Vacation allowance often begins to accrue from the first day of service, but employees are often required to work a full year before taking a paid vacation. The legislation usually provides a minimum of two weeks and sometimes allows employees to postpone vacations. Employees do not have a right to take vacations whenever they want—the employer may usually set the dates. As a practical matter, however, flexibility should be allowed, especially since most employees regard vacations as very important.

According to employment standards legislation, employers are usually required to keep accurate records as evidence that they have met the minimum statutory requirements. For example, employers must keep records of wages paid, hours worked, and vacations accrued. If a dispute arises and no accurate records have been kept, the employer risks having an employment standards referee defer to the recollection of the employee. If so, the employer may have to meet the statutory minimum for a second time if the employee's evidence is incorrect.

Human Rights

Both provincially and federally, special statutory provisions deal with human rights in the employment context. As we saw in connection with job advertising, such legislation is remedial in nature. Its main purpose is not to punish the employer, but to provide a remedy to the employee who has been discriminated against.

discrimination is treating someone differently on the basis of a ground prohibited by human rights legislation

Discrimination, in this context, is treating someone differently on the basis of one of the grounds prohibited by human rights legislation, including race, ancestry, place of origin, colour, ethnic origin, citizenship, age, sex, sexual orientation, disability, record of criminal offences for which a pardon has been granted, marital status, family status, and religion.[12] Case law has further extended human rights protections for drug and alcohol dependency,[13] pregnancy and childbirth,[14] marital status,[15] and mental illness.[16]

direct discrimination occurs when an employer adopts a rule or practice that treats a person differently on the basis of a prohibited ground

indirect discrimination occurs when an employer's seemingly neutral practices and policies have disproportionate adverse consequences for a person on the basis of a prohibited ground

Discrimination can either be *direct* or *indirect*. **Direct discrimination** occurs when an employer adopts a rule or practice that treats a person differently on the basis of one of the prohibited grounds. For example, if an employer refuses to hire a woman because she may decide to get pregnant, this would be direct discrimination. **Indirect discrimination** occurs when an employer's seemingly neutral practices and policies have disproportionate adverse consequences for a person on the basis of a prohibited ground. For example, Giuseppe's Pizza refused to hire Aruna as a receptionist because she does not have a valid driver's licence. If Aruna does not have a licence because of a visual impairment, Giuseppe's Pizza is indirectly discriminating against her on the basis of a disability, which is a prohibited ground of discrimination.

BFOR, or a *bona fide* **occupational requirement**, justifies discrimination that would normally be prohibited

An employer is not necessarily liable merely because they discriminated against an employee. Human rights legislation recognizes a number of defences. The nature of some jobs justifies discrimination that would normally be prohibited. The acronym for that sort of defence is **BFOR**, *bona fide* **occupational requirement**.[17] To defend against a claim of discrimination, an employer must be able to demonstrate that the allegedly discriminatory requirement is rationally connected with job performance, that it was adopted with an honest and good faith belief in its necessity, and that the requirement is indeed reasonably necessary to the accomplishment of a legitimate work-related purpose.[18] For

---

[12.] See *eg Human Rights Code*, RSBC 1996, c 210, s 13 (BC); Saskatchewan *Human Rights Code*, SS 1979, c S-24.1, s 9 (Sask); *Alberta Human Rights Act*, RSA 2000, c A-25.5, preamble (Alta); *Human Rights Code*, RSO 1990, c H.19, s 5 (Ont); *Human Rights Act*, RSNB 1973, c H-11, preamble (NB); *Human Rights Act*, SNWT 2002, c 18, preamble (NWT).

[13.] *Entrop v Imperial Oil Ltd* (2000) 50 OR (3d) 18 (Ont CA).

[14.] Discrimination based on pregnancy and childbirth is generally treated as an offshoot of "sex" discrimination. See *Brooks v Canada Safeway Ltd* [1989] 1 SCR 1219 (SCC) at 1241–1250.

[15.] *B v Ontario (Human Rights Commission* ([2002] 3 SCR 403 (SCC).

[16.] In *Lane v ADGA Group Consultants Inc* 2007 HRTO 34 (CanLII), bipolar disorder was ruled to be a disability and therefore a protected ground against discrimination.

[17.] The wording in some provinces is "*bona fide* occupational qualification" (BFOQ).

[18.] *British Columbia (Public Service Employee Relations Commission) v British Columbia Government Service Employees' Union*, 1999 SCC 48, [1999] 3 SCR 3 (*Meiorin* for short).

example, requiring a candidate for a firefighting job to meet some minimum requirement of physical ability is justified if the employer believes that such a requirement is truly necessary to carry out the job duties safely. If the job involves climbing a ladder while carrying a heavy object, then the requirement would be justied. It would not be justied if the position were a desk job.

Harassment is a form of discrimination in the workplace. **Harassment** involves any demeaning or offensive conduct connected to a prohibited ground of discrimination. As with other forms of discrimination, harassment can occur even if the conduct was not intended to be demeaning or offensive. **Sexual harassment** involves unwelcome or objectionable sexual advances, or any sexual comment, gesture, or conduct that the offender knew (or should have known) was unwelcome. In many jurisdictions, including Ontario, Manitoba, New Brunswick, Prince Edward Island, and the federal jurisdiction, employers have an obligation to take reasonable pro-active steps to prevent sexual harassment. An employer who fails to do so is vicariously liable for the acts of their employees.

> **harassment** involves any demeaning or offensive conduct connected to a prohibited ground of discrimination
>
> **sexual harassment** involves unwelcome or objectionable sexual advances, or any sexual comment, gesture, or conduct that the offender knew (or should have known) was unwelcome

The *duty to accommodate* is often used to remedy some forms of discrimination under human rights legislation. The **duty to accommodate** requires an employer to make adaptations to the workplace to meet the needs of an employee who would not otherwise be able to work there. These include wheelchair access, Braille signage, ergonomic workstations, modified terms and conditions of employment, and temporary job assignments. Note that the scope of an employer's duty to accommodate is not absolute but is limited to situations where it would not cause *undue hardship* to the employer. For instance, in a case of chronic absenteeism caused by illness, undue hardship will be met when the proper operation of the business is excessively hampered, or when the employee remains unable to work for the reasonably foreseeable future even though the employer has tried to accommodate them.[19] Courts have avoided setting rigid rules as to when undue hardship has been met, but relevant factors can include (i) the cost of the accommodation, (ii) the ease of its implementation, (iii) health and safety requirements, (iv) whether outside sources of funding are available to assist in making the accommodation, (v) whether the accommodation will disrupt a collective agreement, and (vi) whether the accommodation will affect the morale of other employees.[20] Safety risks to the public should be given significant weight when employers are analyzing undue hardship and the scope of their duty to accommodate. In this regard, employers are entitled to rely on their own observations regarding the employee, without the need to defer exclusively to medical experts.[21]

> the **duty to accommodate** requires an employer to make adaptations to the workplace to meet the needs of an employee who would not otherwise be able to work there

It is sometimes hard to know when there is a duty to accommodate, but it is generally up to employees to express their need to be accommodated.[22] They also have a duty to take reasonable steps to assist their employers in making those accommodations.[23] The employee is not entitled to a perfect solution—if the employer has made a reasonable adaptation to the workplace or can show undue hardship, then they may have discharged their duty to accommodate.

[19.] See *Hydro-Québec v Syndicat des employées de techniques professionnelles et de bureau d'Hydro-Québec, section locale 2000* (SCFP-FTQ) 2008 SCC 43.

[20.] Echlin & Thomlinson *For Better or for Worse* (1996) at 164–166.

[21.] See *Oak Bay Marina Ltd v British Columbia (Human Rights Commission)* (2002) 217 DLR (4th) 747 (BC CA).

[22.] *Emrick Plastics v Ontario (Human Rights Commission)* (1992) 90 DLR (4th) 476 (Ont Div Ct).

[23.] *Central Okanagan School District No 23 v Renaud* (1992) 95 DLR (4th) 577 (SCC).

Concept Summary 26.3 summarizes how businesses can manage risk associated with human rights law.

Concept Summary 26.3

Managing Risk in Association with Human Rights Law

- Know the relevant provincial and federal laws, and be pro-active, not reactive, in meeting your obligations.
- Be clear about job requirements and the BFOR for each position to ensure that any discrimination can be justified.
- Adopt employment policies and procedures that reflect and comply with human rights legislation.
- Institute informal complaints procedures and appoint a person in the workplace to investigate potential human rights complaints in a neutral way.

Employee Privacy

In Chapter 19, we discussed online privacy, outlining the general requirements of privacy laws. However, a number of specific issues regarding privacy laws arise in the employment context. For example, Canada's federal private sector privacy law, the *Personal Information Protection and Electronic Documents Act (PIPEDA)*, defines "personal information" as information about an identifiable individual but does not include the name, title, business address, or telephone number of an employee in an organization. Privacy laws do not regulate the collection, use, or disclosure of this kind of information.

Privacy laws in British Columbia and Alberta contain an employment-related exception not expressly found in *PIPEDA*.[24] In the case of the BC law, employers are permitted to collect, use, and disclose an employee's personal information without the employee's consent for purposes reasonably required to establish, manage, or terminate an employment relationship. The employer is, however, required to notify the employee of the purposes.

As another example of the overlap between privacy and employment, *PIPEDA* and the laws in British Columbia and Alberta all provide whistleblower protections for employees. This protection prohibits an employer from dismissing, suspending, demoting, or disciplining an employee who in good faith reports the employer for violating privacy laws.

Employee privacy in the workplace is also a very important consideration in relation to the surveillance of employees. Employers often have good reasons to use surveillance cameras or other monitoring devices. That sort of equipment can be used as a tool to prevent, deter, or investigate fraud or theft. However, employers should collect only information that is relevant to their legitimate business interests to avoid the risk of infringing an employee's privacy rights.[25] For instance, an employer may wish to install a monitoring device into a company car to ensure that it is being regularly maintained, but the employer should avoid monitoring where employees go in the car during their personal time. Employers should inform their employees of their surveillance policies: of when an employee might be monitored and to what extent. Surveillance in the workplace can also have an adverse effect on employee morale, particularly when it is targeted directly at employees rather than the business premises in general. Pervasive surveillance may make all employees—even those doing

---

[24.] *Personal Information Protection Act*, SBC 2003, c 63, s 16; *Personal Information Protection Act*, SA 2003, c P-6.5, s 15.

[25.] *International Union of Elevator Constructors, Local 1 v Otis Canada Inc* [2010] BCCAAA No 121.

excellent work—feel like they are not trusted, and it may, as a result, adversely affect their job performance. Surveillance in the workplace can also be illegal.[26]

The Privacy Commissioner of Canada and the courts have developed a four-part test for determining whether surveillance complies with the requirements of *PIPEDA*: (i) Is the surveillance necessary to meet a specific organizational need? (ii) Is the surveillance likely to be effective in meeting that need? (iii) Is the loss of privacy proportional to the benefit gained? (iv) Is there a less invasive way of achieving the same end?

Organizations considering surveillance measures in the workplace should bear in mind how they would answer each of these questions. For example, it might be difficult to justify a comprehensive camera surveillance system on the basis that it will prevent theft when the workplace has had virtually no incidents of theft. In such a case, there might be no specific need. And even if there were a need, it may not warrant comprehensive surveillance. Unless the threat of misconduct was particularly strong, the benefit to the employer would not be proportional to the employees' loss of privacy. Finally, even if the risk of theft were substantial, it might be possible for the employer to adopt less invasive ways of achieving the same end, for example, by providing employees with desk drawers that lock.

Occupational Health and Safety

Every employer must meet minimum standards for workplace health and safety. Health and safety legislation is aimed at preventing accidents, injuries, and industrial diseases. That is accomplished by reducing risks through educational and punitive measures. Many jurisdictions require the creation of workplace advisory groups composed of workers and managers. Employees have the right to refuse to work in unsafe conditions. The employer is then required to investigate the problem. An employee who is not satisfied with the investigation may take up the matter with the workplace advisory group and, ultimately, with the responsible governmental agency. In exceptional circumstances, an unsafe workplace may be shut down.

In most jurisdictions, a serious violation of occupational health and safety standards can be a crime. The first conviction under the *Criminal Code* occurred in 2008 when unsafe work conditions led to the death of an employee, resulting in a conviction for criminal negligence and a corporate fine of $110 000.[27] A violation of a health and safety inspector's order may also be criminal. Companies and individuals may, however, use the defence of *due diligence*. **Due diligence** occurs when the accused took every reasonable precaution to avoid violating the safety standard.

due diligence occurs when the accused took every reasonable precaution to avoid violating the safety standard

Workers' Compensation

While occupational health and safety legislation is aimed at preventing workplace injuries, workers' compensation schemes (which we discussed in Chapter 3) were created to redress injuries that do occur by financially compensating injured workers. Many workplace injuries may be addressed through tort actions. However, there are at least two difficulties with formal litigation: First, it is very expensive.

---

26. For example, *Criminal Code*, RSC 1985, c C-46, s 184, prohibits the interception of a private communication where it is reasonable for the originator of the communication to expect that it will not be intercepted.

27. G Hamilton "Safety Ruling Likely to Set Legal Precedent: Company Fined" *National Post* (18 March 2008) at A6.

Second, it operates on an all-or-nothing basis. If the defendant wrongfully caused the injury, the plaintiff receives full compensation. Otherwise, the plaintiff does not receive any relief. Workers' compensation schemes use a much simpler and less expensive procedure. Furthermore, they provide some compensation even if a worker cannot prove that someone else was at fault.[28]

Workers' compensation schemes are funded through compulsory contributions by employers. The amount that an employer must contribute depends upon the industry in which it is involved—more dangerous industries naturally carry higher rates.

Workers' compensation schemes provide benefits in several circumstances:

- A *partial disability* allows the worker to continue performing in some capacity. Compensation for partial injuries is based on the difference between the worker's pre-accident earning capacity and post-accident earning capacity.

- A *total incapacity* prevents the worker from performing in any capacity. Workers who suffer a total, though temporary, disability are paid a portion of their pre-accident earning capacity while they are unable to work.

- If a worker is *killed* in the course of employment, their dependants are entitled to compensation. For a spouse, some provinces provide periodic payments until the spouse remarries or reaches the age of 65. In other provinces, the spouse receives a lump-sum payment equal to the amount that the worker would have received if they had been permanently injured rather than killed. The worker's children are also entitled to compensation until they reach the age of majority. In some provinces, dependent children are entitled to a further amount toward post-secondary education.

Termination of Employment

L.O. ❽ ❾ ❿

An employer's obligations do not last forever. They sometimes end abruptly—an employee may retire, resign, or be fired, or a company may cease to exist. We end this chapter by examining some issues that arise when the employment relationship breaks down. We will (i) look at an employer's right to dismiss employees who are in serious breach of their employment obligations, (ii) explore the rights of employees under the law of wrongful dismissal, (iii) examine the concept of constructive dismissal, (iv) consider the obligations of an employee who wishes to resign, and (v) survey post-employment practices, such as restrictive covenants and confidentiality, severance packages and settlements, and post-employment obligations.

SUMMARY DISMISSAL

Employees sometimes misbehave on the job. If they do not perform their duties properly, they may be in breach of their employment contracts. As with other contracts, if the employee commits a serious breach, the employer may be entitled to terminate the contract. In the language of employment law,

---

[28.] In Chapter 3 we discussed how workers' compensation legislation generally prevents employees from suing their employer in tort for workplace injuries. Some provinces, including British Columbia, Manitoba, New Brunswick, and Ontario, provide exceptions to this legislation in specific situations, such as when an employer negligently maintains defective machinery or when the injury was caused by another employee.

the employer is entitled to a self-help remedy known as *summary dismissal*. **Summary dismissal** occurs when an employer dismisses the employee and thereby terminates the employment relationship without notice. That remedy is available only if the employer has just cause. **Just cause** means that the employer was justified in firing the employee without notice; it is usually limited to situations of repeated misconduct. It is also limited to certain types of breach, including:

- absenteeism
- substance abuse (while on the job)
- incompetence and carelessness
- dishonesty and disobedience
- conflicts of interest
- criminal behaviour

summary dismissal occurs when an employer dismisses the employee and thereby terminates the employment relationship without notice

just cause means that the employer was justified in firing the employee without notice

Absenteeism

The employment contract requires the employee to regularly attend work during specified hours. If those hours are not expressly stated in the contract, the courts will imply a term that is in line with the employer's normal hours of business. Although the failure to report for work on a single occasion will not usually constitute grounds for dismissal, repeated *absenteeism* will.[29] **Absenteeism** is an unauthorized failure to report for work that is not the product of an illness. When absenteeism hurts its business interests, the employer may be justified in terminating the employee.

absenteeism is an unauthorized failure to report for work that is not the product of an illness

Under some circumstances, a repeated pattern of lateness will also constitute grounds for dismissal. After recognizing a pattern of lateness, the employer must clearly warn the employee that such behaviour will not be tolerated. A similar tactic should be applied in dealing with employees who repeatedly leave work early or before the end of their shifts. Before dismissing an employee on the basis of absenteeism or lateness, an employer should document a pattern of conduct as well as a series of warnings. The document should state that the employee did not have a legitimate reason for being absent or late.

Substance Abuse

Some employees have been known to come to work under the influence of alcohol or other drugs. This may be grounds for dismissal. However, the employer in these situations may still have the duty to accommodate the employee or offer rehabilitation or other help to impaired employees.

- First, courts consider whether the employee's job performance was impaired. The mere smell of alcohol on the breath of the employee is insufficient to warrant dismissal.
- Second, courts consider whether the employee's abuse of alcohol or other drugs threatened the safety of the workplace. It may be possible to dismiss a forklift operator who is drunk on the job, but perhaps not a typist who is inebriated at an office party.
- Third, courts consider whether the employer's business reputation has been harmed by the employee's conduct.

[29.] *Bowie v Motorola Canada Ltd* (1991) 44 CCEL 307 (Ont Gen Div).

■ Fourth, courts consider whether the employer had a policy in place that prohibited such conduct and if it was known, or ought to have been known, by the employee.

Courts tend to be more lenient if it appears that the employer *condoned* the employee's conduct. **Condonation** occurs whenever an employer fails to reprimand an employee for their misconduct. If a business maintains an extremely permissive attitude in the workplace, its *apparent* condonation may deprive it of the authority to dismiss a drunken employee. To avoid that risk, a business should implement and enforce a clearly worded policy that defines acceptable and unacceptable conduct.

condonation occurs whenever an employer fails to reprimand an employee for their misconduct

Incompetence and Carelessness

Employers are often dissatisfied with workers' performance. That alone does not mean that employees have breached their employment obligations. One situation where poor performance does justify dismissal occurs when an employee is *incompetent*. **Incompetent** employees lack basic skills or qualifications, or are otherwise unable to perform their assigned jobs. To prove incompetence, the employer must do more than show that a job could have been done better; it must prove that the employee fell below a standard of basic competence.

incompetent employees lack basic skills or qualifications, or are otherwise unable to perform their assigned jobs

A good risk manager will notify an employee that their work is substandard, and state that such shoddy performance will not be tolerated in the future. The employer should (i) clearly identify the problems with the employee's work, (ii) establish a review process to help the employee improve, and (iii) inform the employee that a continued substandard performance will result in termination.

Dishonesty and Disobedience

An employment relationship imposes a duty on the employee to be faithful and honest. When dishonesty causes the employer to lose trust and confidence in the employment relationship, it is grounds for dismissal. In fact, the nature of some jobs requires an even higher standard of honesty. Employees who hold positions of trust, such as senior managers in financial institutions, are generally obligated to act in the best interests of the business. Although honesty is usually required only when the employee is acting in the course of their employment, courts have sometimes allowed an employer to dismiss an employee for dishonest conduct outside of the course of employment.[30] For example, courts have permitted summary dismissal in cases where an employee engages in unfair competition with the employer, whether during work hours or otherwise.[31]

Not every act of dishonesty will justify dismissal, however. Employers must consider whether, on a balance of probabilities, the evidence indicates that the employee has been dishonest. If so, the employer must then consider whether the nature and degree of the dishonesty justifies dismissal. The test is whether the employee's dishonesty gives rise to a breakdown of the employment relationship.[32]

Two common forms of dishonesty are *employee fraud* and *employee theft*. **Employee fraud** occurs when an employee intentionally deceives the employer in a way that is detrimental to its interests. The employee can be dismissed if the

employee fraud occurs when an employee intentionally deceives the employer in a way that is detrimental to its interests

---

30. *Marshall v Pacific Coast Savings Credit Union* (1992) 44 CCEL 261 (BC CA).

31. *Knowlan v Trailmobil Parts and Services Canada Ltd* [2006] BCJ No 457 (SC).

32. *McKinley v BC Tel (2001) 200 DLR* (4th) 385 (SCC).

nature of the fraud is incompatible with a continuing employment relationship. However, an employer should carefully assess a situation of alleged fraud to ascertain whether the employee was intentionally deceptive or simply exercised poor judgment, as poor judgment may not justify termination.[33] **Employee theft** occurs when an employee steals from the employer. The law implies a term in every contract that prohibits employee theft. Since loyalty and honesty are at the core of the employment relationship, a single incident of theft may justify termination.

Disobedience is also a ground for dismissal. **Disobedience** occurs when an employee repeatedly and deliberately defies a supervisor's clear instructions or, without reasonable excuse, refuses to perform. The employment relationship is based on the idea that the employer controls and directs the work of its employees. A repeated failure to follow instructions not only results in unaccomplished tasks, but also undercuts the authority of the employer and generally lowers employee morale. Likewise, a repeated pattern of severe disrespect, or insulting behaviour directed at the employer or supervisors, may be grounds for dismissal, unless there is a reasonable excuse, such as provocation.[34]

> **employee theft** occurs when an employee steals from the employer

> **disobedience** occurs when an employee repeatedly and deliberately defies a supervisor's clear instructions or refuses to perform without reasonable excuse

Conflicts of Interest

An employee is required to avoid a *conflict of interest*. A **conflict of interest** occurs when an employee acts in a way that conflicts with the employer's best interests. An employee cannot, for example, (i) carry on a business that competes with the employer, (ii) accept personal gifts or other advantages from a party who conducts business with the employer, (iii) have personal dealings with the employer's clients, customers, or suppliers, or (iv) provide confidential information acquired during the course of employment to a competitor in exchange for some benefit. An employee may argue that the conduct in question did not *actually* hurt the employer. The lack of harm may be irrelevant, however, especially if the employer imposed a policy that prohibited the conduct in question, or if it was expressly prohibited by the employment contract.[35]

> a **conflict of interest** occurs when an employee acts in a way that conflicts with the employer's best interests

Criminal Behaviour

In addition to dishonest acts such as fraud or theft, other criminal conduct during the course of employment can lead to dismissal. Typical examples are physical assault and property offences. When an employee commits a crime on the job, they may be dismissed as soon as charges have been laid—even before there has been a conviction. As a matter of risk management, however, the employer should not dismiss an employee until a thorough investigation shows that a crime has been committed. A false allegation could lead to a punitive damage award.[36]

[33.] *Leitner v Wyeth Canada* 2010 ONSC 579.

[34.] For example, see *Thompson v Lex Tec Inc* [2001] OJ No 3651 (Ont CA), in which an employee's use of profanity and shoving his supervisor were not grounds for immediate dismissal because he had a reasonable excuse of being provoked by his supervisor both historically and during this incident. The court also relied on the fact that this was his only instance of poor judgment on an otherwise pristine work record.

[35.] *Ennis v Canadian Imperial Bank of Commerce* (1989) 13 CCEL 25 (BC SC).

[36.] *Conrad v Household Financial Corp* (1992) 115 NSR (2d) 153 (SC TD), aff'd 45 CCEL 81 (SC AD).

Concept Summary 26.4 reviews the grounds for summary dismissal.

Concept Summary 26.4

Grounds for Summary Dismissal

- absenteeism, lateness, and leaving work without permission
- substance abuse while on the job
- incompetence and carelessness
- dishonesty and disobedience
- conflicts of interest
- criminal behaviour

WRONGFUL DISMISSAL

Reasonable Notice

Summary dismissal is an exception to the general rule. An employee may be summarily dismissed only in the sort of exceptional circumstances we have discussed. Normally, the common law and provincial employment standards legislation require an employer to provide an employee with some reasonable period of notice before terminating the employment relationship. The notice period gives the employee an opportunity to receive income while looking for another job.

It is not always possible to provide reasonable notice. If the employer fails to do so, the employee is usually entitled to *money in lieu of notice*. Sometimes an employer will offer to pay that amount and ask the employee to leave immediately. Other times, the end is not so smooth. **Wrongful dismissal** occurs when an employee is dismissed without cause and without reasonable notice or money in lieu of notice. Although an employer generally cannot be forced to retain a particular employee, they may be held liable if they fire that person without cause and without reasonable notice or money in lieu of notice. In that situation, the employee may sue to recover not only money owed in lieu of notice, but also damages for the loss of commissions, bonuses, or benefits. Recently, courts have also considered whether an employee should be compensated for lost training. For instance, if an employee is wrongfully dismissed from an apprenticeship and therefore loses the ability to enter a particular profession, the employee may be entitled to compensation for that loss.[37]

The "reasonable notice period" depends upon the circumstances. Employment standards legislation always states a minimum notice period. Most jurisdictions require at least two weeks' notice for employees who have been at a job for two years. Employees who have been at a job for 10 or more years are often statutorily entitled to four to eight weeks' notice, depending upon the jurisdiction. Note that these are the minimums, and courts often require much longer notice periods.[38] Judges sometimes try to determine the length of the notice period that the parties themselves would have set if they

wrongful dismissal occurs when an employee is dismissed without cause and without reasonable notice or money in lieu of notice

---

[37] *Marchen v Dams Ford Lincoln Sales Ltd* 2010 BCCA 29.

[38] In *Machtinger v HOJ Industries Ltd*, [1992] 1 SCR 986, the Supreme Court of Canada emphasized that minimum notice requirements do not displace the common law requirement that employers must give *reasonable* notice. Thus, depending upon the circumstances of each case, an employee might be entitled to more than the statutory or contractual minimum notice.

had addressed the issue when they created their contract.[39] Usually, however, the courts look at such factors as (i) the employee's age, (ii) the nature of the position held, (iii) the length of service, (iv) the salary level of the employee, and (v) the employee's likelihood of securing alternative employment. It is generally accepted, however, that the upper limit, even for the most senior executives, should not exceed 24 months.

Disputes about dismissal and reasonable notice can be hurtful and stress inducing. What happens if dismissal results in mental distress for an employee? Until recently, courts were willing to simply extend the notice period as a means of punishing employers for bad behaviour around the time of dismissal.[40] However, the Supreme Court has since rejected this approach in a case called *Honda Canada*.[41] As a result, the notice period cannot be lengthened in order to compensate employees for mental distress arising from bad faith dismissal. Now, damages can be awarded only on the basis of proof that (i) an employer acted in bad faith during dismissal, (ii) the employer's bad behaviour was the cause of foreseeable mental distress, and (iii) the employee suffered actual psychological damage. *Honda Canada* therefore draws a bright line between reasonable notice and psychological damages flowing from bad faith discharge. It remains to be seen how *Honda* will affect the number of lawsuits for bad faith discharge. One likely outcome, however, is that though it may be more difficult to prove actual psychological harm, employers who are egregious in their manner of dismissal could be liable for significantly more in damages than they have in the past.[42]

Mitigation

Even when employees are wrongfully dismissed, they cannot sit idle while they sue their former employers for damages. Employees must mitigate their damages by promptly taking reasonable steps to minimize the losses flowing from their dismissal. Normally, this means that they must (i) seek reinstatement and/or the grounds for its refusal, and (ii) make reasonable efforts to seek out new employment.[43] They will not be compensated for damages that they could have avoided through reasonable efforts at mitigation. Nor will employees be compensated for damages that they did avoid through mitigation. For example, if the employer should have given six months' notice, resulting in a payment of $40 000, and the employee was able to get another job and earn $10 000 within six months, then the former employer would be required to pay only $30 000. (We discussed mitigation in Chapters 3 and 12.)

WRONGFUL RESIGNATION

There is also an implied term in employment agreements that requires employees to give their employers reasonable notice before quitting. An employer is entitled to a reasonable amount of time in which to find a replacement, or to mitigate the loss in some other way. This period is not necessarily the same

---

[39] *Lazarowicz v Orenda Engines Ltd* (1960) 26 DLR (2d) 433 (Ont CA).

[40] *Wallace v United Grain Growers Ltd* (1997) 152 DLR (4th) 1 (SCC) at 33.

[41] *Honda Canada Inc v Keays* (2008) SCC 39.

[42] See eg *Altman v Steve's Music Store Inc* 2011 ONSC 1480 at para 132. Ms Altman established that she had suffered mental distress to the point of clinical depression as a result of Steve's bad faith discharge and was therefore awarded $35 000 as compensation for her distress.

[43] Refusing an employer's offer of continued employment may be seen as a failure to mitigate. See *Evans v Teamsters Local Union No. 31* (2008) SCC 20 at 32.

as the period that an employer would be required to give if they wished to terminate the contract. However, industry norms may provide some guidance in determining how much notice an employee must give. Employees may be liable to their former employer for losses sustained as a result of a wrongful resignation.

CONSTRUCTIVE DISMISSAL

constructive dismissal occurs when an employer fundamentally changes the nature of a person's job

An employer may try to avoid a notice period by making a situation so intolerable that the employee simply quits. The law responds to that tactic through the doctrine of *constructive dismissal*. **Constructive dismissal** occurs when an employer fundamentally changes the nature of a person's job. The three most common changes amounting to constructive dismissal are (i) a reduction in salary or benefits, (ii) an alteration in job status or responsibility that changes the nature of the employee's position, or (iii) a change in geographical location. If constructive dismissal can be proved, the employee is treated as though they had been dismissed without notice and consequently will be entitled to damages in lieu of notice. Case Brief 26.2 offers an example.

Case Brief 26.2

Miller v ICO Canada Inc 2005 ABQB 226

After nearly 30 years in the oil pipe transportation business the Miller family decided to sell their company. Included in the deal was written confirmation that Norman Miller would retain employment with the new owners in the capacity of "special project supervisor." This position included various management responsibilities integral to business operations. In the years following the sale, numerous changes were made to Norman's employment duties. He was no longer responsible for projects and was removed altogether from the corporate consultation process. His new business cards identified him as "foreman," resulting in a further deterioration of his relationship with management. After being told that he was interfering with corporate decision making, Norman's desk was removed from his office one day while he was at lunch. Norman continued to work, using his briefcase on his lap as a work surface. His files were eventually placed in a cardboard box, his security pass was taken away, and his office space was re-assigned to the foremen's room. After experiencing a nervous breakdown resulting in hospitalization, Norman sent a letter to his employer stating that the way he had been treated amounted to constructive dismissal.

The court agreed. While some changes in his employment were justified on the basis of a corporate re-organization, the end result was that Norman had clearly been demoted in a manner that altered the nature of his employment. The court further found that it was foreseeable that his continued mistreatment would result in psychological harm.

SEVERANCE PACKAGES AND SETTLEMENTS

a **severance package** is a payment meant to cover everything that is due to the employee at the time of termination

severance pay is the amount owed to a terminated employee under employment standards legislation

Fortunately, most employment relationships do not end with the employer's complete disregard for the employee's welfare. Many employers offer a **severance package**, a payment meant to cover everything that is due to the employee at the time of termination. It is called a "severance" package because it includes severance pay. **Severance pay** is the amount owed to a terminated employee under employment standards legislation. A severance package may also include (i) salary, commissions, or bonuses owing, (ii) benefits owing, (iii) contributions to the Canada Pension Plan, (iv) contributions to registered retirement savings plans or private pension plans, (v) an automobile allowance, (vi) vacation pay and sick leave, (vii) stock options, (viii) employee discounts and staff loans, and (ix) reference letters.

Sometimes an employer and employee negotiate the items to be included in the package so that it includes more than is required by legislation. This is called a *settlement package*. A **settlement package** is what the employer gives to the employee to bring an employment dispute to an end. As a matter of risk management, the employer should deliver the settlement package only after the employee has signed a *release*. A **release** is the employee's written promise to release the employer from any possible legal claims that the employee might have against the employer. Like other contracts, a release is effective only if the employer provides new consideration—something more than what the employee was already owed under the employment contract and the employment standards legislation.

a **settlement package** is what the employer gives to the employee to bring an employment dispute to an end

a **release** is the employee's written promise to release the employer from any possible legal claims that the employee might have against the employer

POST-EMPLOYMENT OBLIGATIONS

Generally speaking, the employer's obligations come to an end when the employment contract is terminated. However, there are two exceptions where ongoing obligations arise: First, the employment contract itself might provide for ongoing obligations. For example, an employer might include a provision that would relocate an employee in the event of an unexpected termination of employment. Second, employers can incur ongoing obligations as part of a settlement package when resolving a dispute with an employee. For example, as part of a settlement, an employer might agree to make periodic payments for a specific time period.

The situation is quite different for employees. Earlier we discussed why an employer should ensure that an employment contract imposes clear non-competition, non-solicitation, and confidentiality obligations on an employee. Those obligations are usually written to survive the termination of the employment relationship. Where there is no enforceable non-competition or non-solicitation clause, employees are entitled to solicit clients of their former employer and to compete, provided they do so in a fair manner and provide reasonable notice of resignation. They are allowed to make arrangements for their new business while they are still employed. And while they cannot physically remove customer lists belonging to their employer, they can commit those lists to memory and later recall the customers' names with the help of a phone book.

In cases involving key or senior former employees, or in situations of manifest unfairness, courts may impose restrictive obligations on former employees. Key employees and senior employees usually owe fiduciary duties to their employer that survive termination of the employment relationship. This means that they may be restricted in their ability to compete for former clients. Situations of manifest unfairness may also justify restrictions, even for regular employees, and are usually quite obvious.

Chapter Summary

Before hiring an employee, an employer should draft a job description that accurately defines the duties attached to the position. Any advertisements should refer only to *bona fide* occupational requirements. When obtaining additional information from job applicants, employers must be careful to limit their questions to those relating to the applicant's ability to do the job. Both the employer and applicant should avoid misstatements during contract negotiations. The contract should be in writing.

Not all work- or service-related contracts are contracts of employment, nor are all workers employees. One way to test the nature of the work relationship is by determining how much control is asserted by the party paying for the work. Another test determines whether the work is an integral part of the overall business of the organization. Employment contracts are essential tools for risk management and should usually include non-competition or non-solicitation clauses. The risk of vicarious liability and other workplace hazards imposes responsibilities on employers to supervise their employees. Risk management requires employment policy manuals, performance reviews, and promotion or probation.

Statutory protection for workers includes (i) employment standards, which are concerned with holidays, wages, work hours, overtime, rest periods, leaves, and vacations; (ii) human rights, which are concerned with discrimination, harassment, and the duty to accommodate; (iii) privacy laws, which protect employees' privacy; (iv) occupational health and safety standards, which are concerned with the prevention of accidents, injuries, and industrial diseases through educational and punitive measures; and (v) workers' compensation—which is concerned with redressing workplace injuries through an accident compensation scheme that is funded by compulsory contributions from employers. Because of the complexity of employment law, many employers hire trained human resource personnel or employment law specialists.

An employer's obligations may end abruptly. Summary dismissal occurs when an employer dismisses an employee without providing notice. It is allowed when the employer can establish just cause. Just cause may exist if an employee is guilty of (i) absenteeism, (ii) substance abuse, (iii) incompetence and carelessness, (iv) dishonesty and disobedience, (v) a conflict of interest, or (vi) criminal behaviour. The best way for a business to avoid being perceived to condone employee misconduct is to implement and enforce a clearly worded policy that defines the limits of acceptable and unacceptable conduct.

The common law and provincial employment standards legislation generally require an employer to provide employees with some reasonable period of notice before terminating an employment relationship. Employees are also required to give reasonable notice before quitting. Wrongful dismissal may arise if an employee is dismissed without cause and without reasonable notice or money in lieu of notice. Employees are under a duty to mitigate their losses flowing from a wrongful dismissal. The notice period may be further extended by a court in the case of bad faith dismissal. Constructive dismissal may arise if an employer fundamentally changes the nature of a person's job to force that person to quit.

Some employers put together a severance package when terminating an employee. A severance package is meant to cover everything that is due to the employee at the time of termination. That package will include severance pay, which is the amount that is owed to a terminated employee under employment standards legislation. Some employers provide their employees with additional items in their severance packages. If an employer wants to end the relationship amicably, they may offer the employee a settlement package, which generally includes more than the statutory minimums and is negotiated in return for the employee's willingness to sign a release, which effectively terminates the employment relationship and any potential disputes arising from it.

Without an enforceable contractual non-competition or non-solicitation clause, employees are generally free to compete with their former employers and to solicit customers. However, they must not do so in a manner that is manifestly unfair.

MyBusLawLab   ADDITIONAL RESOURCES FOR CHAPTER 26

MyBusLawLab provides students with an assortment of tools to help enrich the learning experience, including a Study Plan with Pre- and Post-tests, mini-cases with assessments, and provincial content material, which provides links to relevant cases, legislation, and additional resources.

MyBusLawLab provides the following resources for Chapter 26:

- Business Decision 26.1W—Mandatory Vacation Dates

Provincial Material

- **British Columbia:** Discrimination in the Workplace, Privacy Rights, *Employment Standards Act*, Workers' Compensation, Occupational Health and Safety, Child Employment, Leave of Absence, Minimum Wage, Termination and Lay-Off, Termination of Temporary Employees, Termination of Probationary Employees, Unfair Labour Practices, Worker Pay

- **Alberta:** Conditions of Employment, Constructive Dismissal, Cooling Off Period for Employees, Crown's Right to Recover Health Care Costs, Good Faith, Duty to Accommodate, Employment Standards, *Employee Standards (Reservist Leave) Amendment Act (2009)*, Summary Dismissal, Termination and Layoffs, Workers' Compensation, *Workers' Compensation Amendment Act (2011)*, Wrongful Dismissal

- **Manitoba and Saskatchewan:** Employment Standards (Minimum Standards in Legislation), Human Rights, Vicarious Liability and Motor Vehicles, Vicarious Liability of Employees, Workers' Compensation, Reasonable Notice (Statutory Minimums)

- **Ontario:** Bad Faith, Discrimination, Duty to Accommodate, Employment Equity, Employment Standards, Human Rights, Mandatory Retirement, Occupational Health, Pay Equity, Workers' Compensation

- **Atlantic Provinces:** *Employment Standards Act*, Occupational Health and Safety

Review Questions

1. What are the benefits and risks of advertising a position?

2. Name an occupational requirement that might appear to be discriminatory. Give an example of how such a requirement might be justified as a *bona fide* occupational requirement.

3. What is the difference between an employee, an independent contractor, and a dependent contractor? What are the risks when a business chooses to make exclusive use of a particular contractor?

4. What is the risk if an employer makes an inaccurate statement during the hiring process?

5. Give two examples of enforceable restrictive covenants that employers might seek from employees and describe their purpose in doing so.

6. Provide four examples of basic workplace issues that an employment policy manual should address.

7. What is the value of giving employees regular performance reviews?

8. When is the suspension of an employee a reasonable course of conduct?

9. Name several statutory regimes that have been created to protect employees. Give an example of each.

10. What factors might cause the provincial minimum wage to change periodically?

11. Distinguish between direct discrimination and indirect discrimination.

12. What is a BFOR and how can it be used to defend against a case of direct discrimination?

13. Can harassment be found to have occurred even if the conduct in question was not intended to be demeaning or offensive? Why?

14. Give two examples of how a risk manager can help to prevent violations of human rights legislation.

15. Can an employer from Alberta discipline an employee who has reported that the employer breached provincial privacy legislation? Why or why not?

16. What are the core differences between workers' compensation schemes and occupational health and safety legislation? How are such schemes funded?

17. List six forms of employee misconduct that are considered to be just cause for a summary dismissal.

18. What factors should employers consider in determining a reasonable notice period for dismissing an employee? Is there a cause of action that exists for employees who feel that they have not been provided with reasonable notice of dismissal?

19. Define "constructive dismissal." What are the three most common kinds of changes that amount to constructive dismissal? What are the legal implications of proving constructive dismissal?

20. What can an employer do to prevent a terminated employee from bringing a legal claim against them?

Cases and Problems

1. William Lee has been employed as a farmhand at Jean-Louis Mushroom Farms for four years. Following a decline in the value of mushrooms, Jean-Louis was forced to unilaterally alter the terms of William's pay slightly, reducing it to the current minimum wage. Jean-Louis also decided that it was necessary to abolish his custom of allowing employees to eat as many mushrooms as they desire while at work. Despite the fact that William's wage underwent only a minor reduction, William refuses to work for minimum wage and has brought an action for the balance of wages owing at his previous hourly rate. William is relying on his employment contract as well as past payment accounts, which prove his previous rate of pay. Discuss the factors that affect minimum pay rates. Is Jean-Louis justified in lowering William's wages if they continue to meet minimum wage requirements? Explain.

2. NumbersMagic Inc alleged that its bookkeeper, Chris Ginsberg, had stolen from it. The company made a claim against its insurer, Neverpay Insurance Ltd, to

recover the loss. Neverpay refused the claim on the basis that the policy stated that:

> In the event of loss and/or damages which can be attributed, even in part, to the acts of an employee, Neverpay Insurance will not be held responsible for compensating the company for said losses and/or damages.

The issue is whether Chris was a company employee at the time of the thefts. The evidence indicates that he performed basic bookkeeping services for the company, worked regular hours out of the NumbersMagic offices, and was subject to the direct supervision of a company manager. Chris was not a member of a recognized professional association, and his duties were those normally associated with a bookkeeper, not a professional accountant. Consequently, Chris was paid on an hourly basis— he did not set fees depending upon the nature of services he performed. He had no shares in the company, nor any incentive-based remuneration. No deductions were made from his cheques, nor did he receive holiday pay or any other company benefits. Apply both the control test and the organization test to determine whether Neverpay Insurance will likely have to make a payment under the policy. Support your position.

3. Patinski worked full time as an equipment operator at Modern Dairy. To help make ends meet she also took on part-time work, maintaining a disposal site for the Municipality of Simmonsville. Five years ago, she was approached by a city councillor to consider work on a full-time basis. During their discussions, the councillor promised Patinski that she could have the job as long as she wanted, even though no such term was contemplated in their written contract. With more than double her previous pay and total job flexibility Patinski thought this was a no-brainer and instantly quit from Dairy. She went out and bought a used 977 High Efficiency Caterpillar tractor to cut down her total hours. Though it cost her a pretty penny, she was happy to make the purchase, thinking she had the same job security as all other municipality employees. Each year, like magic, Patinski renewed her contract with the municipality for a specific term of 12 months. The contract outlined the services Patinski was to render for pay, stating that she was to use her own equipment and hire her own labourers, and that no deductions were to be made from her pay. Recently, without notice, the municipality informed Patinski that it would not renew the contract for next year. If Patinski sues for money in lieu of two months' notice, will she win? Why or why not?

4. You are a manager at a factory that manufactures bike frames. You supervise workers at the factory by periodically walking around and observing productivity. However, you cannot be in all places at once. Therefore, in addition to your personal supervision, the employees are required to punch time-cards so you know when they come and go from the factory. Of course, you also keep detailed records about how many bike frames are produced by each employee at the factory. The factory has turned a reasonable profit every year under this system. Despite these measures and the relative success of the factory, Billy Buckston, the owner of the factory, has recently put pressure on you to boost profits. He wants you to increase the performance of the factory workers. He thinks that they are not working fast enough and suggests that you install closed-circuit cameras in the factory to manage employee productivity. These cameras would be linked to a computer in your office where you could watch over every worker in the factory at all times. Through the sound system installed in the factory, you would then be able to yell directions at any workers who were not working fast enough. Do you think Mr Buckston's idea would be justified in light of Canada's privacy laws? In particular, do you think the cameras would be effective in achieving Mr Buckston's goal of increasing productivity? Can you think of any other less privacy-invasive ways of trying to achieve the same goal?

5. WeBuildIt Construction Ltd hired Danele, an architect and construction manager, to build part of a tuna-canning plant. Danele was responsible for completing the project for a fixed sum. Her arrangement required her to employ workers and purchase materials, subject to the budgetary approval of WeBuildIt. The overall supervision of the workers remained under the direction of WeBuildIt's chief architect, Marty McPencil, who provided instruction to Danele and four other construction managers involved in the project. Following Marty's instructions, Danele designed and installed a giant metal tuna on the outside of the building. On the opening day of the plant, the giant tuna fell and killed a fisherman who had just delivered his week's catch to the plant. The fisherman's wife is now seeking to recover damages from both Danele, who oversaw the installation of the giant tuna, and WeBuildIt Construction Ltd. Discuss the potential liability resulting from this situation.

6. Following the conclusion of his contract, Puneet is seeking to recover overtime pay for time worked in excess of a 48-hour week. The facts are as follows: His contract is silent as to the number of hours to be worked in consideration for stated remuneration. His tendered record of the exact number of hours worked, although detailed, is uncorroborated. He has already been paid well in excess of the minimum hourly rate for all recorded hours worked. He is not a farmer or an emergency worker of any kind. Puneet has approached you to represent him in this matter. What legal issues does this scenario raise? What type of employment legislation is relevant to the resolution of this dispute? Does Puneet have a legal basis upon which to make this claim?

7. Elsa was a favourite among all employees at Grocers Group, where she worked for nearly eight years. During that time, Elsa got married. Her manager knew that Elsa wanted children and hoped that she would remain enthusiastic about returning to her job when she announced, one day, that she was pregnant. Elsa's group insurance plan at Grocers provided weekly benefits for loss of pay on account of accident or sickness. Elsa was told that this provision covered pregnant employees, subject to an exclusion "during the period commencing the tenth week prior to the expected week of confinement and ending with the sixth week after the week of confinement." During that 17-week period, pregnant women, even if they suffered from an ailment totally unrelated to pregnancy, were not entitled to any compensation under the plan. When Elsa had to miss work because of illness during her pregnancy, she was denied weekly benefits during the disentitlement period. Fortunately, she was able to receive some limited benefits under the provincial *Employment Insurance Act*. Elsa believes that her insurer's policy is discriminatory and is seek-

ing to file a complaint with her provincial Human Rights Commission. What should she argue and do you think a human rights tribunal will find in her favour?

8. Sylvan was employed as the garage manager for Tough Lucy's Trucking Ltd for seven years. During that time, he reported directly to the owner, Lucy LaRue. Sylvan proved to be an exemplary manager. He was known for his charm and got along well with other employees. However, according to several witnesses, Lucy seemed to think that Sylvan was not getting along with one employee in particular, namely Lucy's 24-year-old nephew, whom she had hired to be the garage bookkeeper. Upon arriving to work one snowy January day, Sylvan was informed by Lucy that, on account of financial difficulties, Lucy would take over as garage manager and Sylvan would be re-assigned to drive a company manure truck. There was no evidence that the garage was anything but profitable. The change in Sylvan's position involved a considerable change in responsibility as well as a lower salary, longer working hours, and substantially smellier working conditions. Sylvan was flabbergasted and appealed to Lucy on the basis of their long and pleasant working relationship. Lucy told him he could take it or leave it. Sylvan refused, resigned, and commenced a lawsuit. What is Sylvan's cause of action? What will he have to prove to win? Do you think that he will succeed? How might Lucy have otherwise achieved her purpose without risking a lawsuit?

9. Shortly after his high-school graduation, Sweyn agreed to help his older sister, Svetlana, and her husband construct their home. The first day, Sweyn wore tennis shoes instead of proper boots. Although the issue was raised by another person who was on the construction crew, nothing was done about it. Since Sweyn had been driven to the construction site by Svetlana, he had no way to acquire adequate footwear, and his sister did not offer to drive him home. In fact, she and the rest of the crew seemed eager to commence work immediately. After walking through wet cement for several hours, Sweyn's feet began to turn yellow. Everyone knew that this was likely happening, but no one told Sweyn to stop working. Svetlana's husband said that Sweyn could continue working and would be fine as long as he washed his feet off, which he did. However, Sweyn suffered severe burns to his feet. He was on crutches for several weeks and has had trouble walking ever since. Sweyn has sued Svetlana. He contends that, during the construction project, he was effectively her employee, and therefore she had breached her duty of care as an employer when she brought Sweyn onto the work site without providing him with proper work boots. Do you think that the minimal standards set out by occupational health and safety legislation apply in this case? Explain your position. What kind of evidence would Svetlana need to prove to invoke a defence of due diligence?

10. A few years ago, Chuckie Norris was promoted from a forklift operator to parts manager at Trailrocks Inc. Ever since, he has learned much about how to run a dealership. His natural curiosity and common-sense approach led the company president to offer him an opportunity to do just that. Norris applied for the necessary credit, but his bank denied the application because Norris lacked collateral. Norris decided to find a business partner in order to get the loan. After doing some homework, his new partner suggested that Norris continue working at Trailrocks while they set up a competing dealership. After seeing the potential profits of striking out on their own, Norris agreed. Norris led Trailrocks and its customers to believe that he would open a dealership with a partner so that he could maintain his current job. Norris failed to mention that they would in fact be competing with Trailrocks. While putting the competing business in place, Norris was sold some of Trailrocks' inventory at discount. Since Trailrocks believed the store would be part of its chain, it also allowed Norris access to its database of customer information. After the opening, when Trailrocks finally figured out that the new dealership was a competitor, it instantly fired Norris. Since Norris had never signed a non-competition clause, he decided to sue Trailrocks for wrongful dismissal. Was Norris's behaviour just cause for his summary dismissal? Is it necessary for Trailrocks to prove fraud to justify the dismissal?

11. For the past 10 years, Gurpreet has been employed as an investment analyst at BucksCorp, one of Canada's largest financial institutions. Gurpreet signed an employment contract with BucksCorp that includes the following restrictive covenant:

> For a period of two years after the termination of employment, as a result of either the employee's resignation or dismissal with cause, the employee under this contract shall not conduct any business with any of BucksCorp's clients or affiliates.

Gurpreet was unhappy in her work and felt that BucksCorp was treating her poorly. One day, Gurpreet received a very generous employment offer from SkyBank, a competing financial institution. Gurpreet resigned from BucksCorp and happily started working for SkyBank. Gurpreet works in an industry where clients develop very close relationships with their brokers. Soon after she began her new job, some of Gurpreet's old BucksCorp clients contacted her, hoping to move their business to SkyBank in order to continue working with her. She agreed and the clients left BucksCorp. Angered by this new development, BucksCorp began a lawsuit against Gurpreet claiming that she breached the restrictive covenant in her employment contract. Discuss the factors that the court will consider when deciding whether to enforce this restrictive covenant. Can Gurpreet somehow avoid liability for BucksCorp's claim?

12. Aisha had been a faithful employee of HydroCorp for several years when she developed an illness that caused severe migraine-like headaches. She began to experience regular episodes during which she could not work. Her affliction could last for days at a time, and she would be exhausted afterwards, finding it difficult to return to her full working capacity immediately. As a result of her affliction, she missed more than half of her regular workdays in one year. HydroCorp allowed her to temporarily perform lighter duties upon her return in order to accommodate her exhaustion, and allowed her to take sick days as needed. Eventually her doctor recommended that she stay home from work indefinitely. Upon learning that Aisha would not return to her duties in the foreseeable future, HydroCorp sent her a letter giving two weeks' notice of her termination. HydroCorp explained that its decision was based on Aisha's inability to work on a regular basis and HydroCorp's belief that her attendance at work would not increase. Aisha has come to you for advice. She hopes to file a complaint with her provincial human rights tribunal alleging that HydroCorp failed to meet its duty to accommodate her. Discuss whether or not you believe that HydroCorp met its duty explain and why or why not.

Organized Labour

LEARNING OBJECTIVES

After completing this chapter, you should be able to:

❶ Distinguish between individual employment and organized labour.

❷ Understand the nature and function of collective bargaining.

❸ Explain the collective bargaining process and the manner in which bargaining rights are acquired.

❹ Describe provisions typically contained in a collective agreement.

❺ Discuss the nature and function of grievance arbitration.

❻ Identify three typical employee grievances in the context of organized labour.

❼ Describe several remedies typically awarded by labour arbitrators.

❽ Distinguish between the jurisdiction of labour arbitrators and courts.

❾ Compare and contrast strikes and lockouts.

❿ Explain the strategies and legalities of picketing and boycotts.

In this chapter, we will investigate the features of organized labour that distinguish it from individual employment and consider their impact on the legal aspects of doing business. We will then consider collective bargaining and examine the trade union, the instrument through which collective bargaining is achieved. We will discuss the aim of bargaining through unions: the establishment and maintenance of a collective agreement. We will look at the system of grievance arbitration that is used in connection with disputes under a collective agreement, and conclude with a survey of the legal treatment of such industrial conflicts as strikes, picketing, lockouts, and boycotts.

L.O. ❶❷❸

Collective Bargaining

Not all work relationships are *individual* relationships between workers and their employers. In fact, much of the Canadian labour force is organized and governed *collectively*. Therefore, we distinguish *employment law* from *labour law*. As we saw in Chapter 26, employment law is the system of rules that governs the relationship between individuals and their employers. **Labour law** is the system of rules that governs collective relations between management, trade unions, their members, and the institutions involved in such relations.[1]

> **labour law** is the system of rules that governs collective relations between management, trade unions, their members, and the institutions involved in such relations

NATURE AND FUNCTION OF COLLECTIVE BARGAINING

The practice of collective bargaining took root primarily during the Industrial Revolution in Britain. Between the late eighteenth and mid-nineteenth centuries, large populations stopped farming, abandoned rural life and agrarian society, and began working in cities for employers in factories and other industrial settings. Workplace conditions in these new industrial settings were often appalling, and wages were low. Practically slaves, individual employees had little or no power against the captains of industry. Only by banding together were workers able to exert meaningful influence on their employers. Collective action has evolved into a number of contemporary workplace practices, which are discussed throughout this chapter.

While collective power can be used to escape intolerable working conditions, it can also be used to illegitimately intimidate and coerce employers (consider, for example, the plight of a ship's captain when its crew members engage in a mutiny). At one time, participating in organized labour was a crime in Canada. Eventually, the right to organize gained legal recognition, first in Britain in 1867, and not long after in the United States. In 1872, Canada adopted the *Trade Union Act*, which decriminalized collective bargaining. Workers could no longer be threatened with jail sentences simply for trying to improve working conditions. But even then, there were roadblocks. Workers who tried to organize unions were initially confronted with economic reprisals from their employers. Today, trade unions are recognized as a legitimate way of empowering individual workers and enforcing their collective rights.

Labour law aims to find an appropriate balance between slavery and mutiny by imposing a system of rules around *collective bargaining*. **Collective bargaining** is the process through which an employer and a *trade union* seek to negotiate a *collective agreement*. A **trade union** is an organization of employees

> **collective bargaining** is the process through which an employer and a trade union seek to negotiate a collective agreement

> a **trade union** is an organization of employees formed to regulate the relations between the employer and the collective of employees

---

[1.] HW Arthurs, DD Carter, J Fudge, HJ Glasbeek, & G Trudeau *Labour Law and Industrial Relations in Canada* 4th ed (1993) at 32.

formed to regulate the relations between the employer and the collective of employees. A **collective agreement** is a document containing the terms of employment, as well as the rights and duties of the employer, the trade union, and the employees. In most jurisdictions, the collective agreement of any organized group of workers can be enforced only through an arbitration procedure that has been started by either the employer or the union.

At common law, trade unions have no distinctive legal personality; legal rights and duties belong exclusively to individual members. This has been modified by legislation in all Canadian jurisdictions, which grants unions legal status. Industries regulated by the federal jurisdiction are governed by the *Canada Labour Code*.[2] Other industries are regulated by similar provincial legislation, each of which establishes a statutory tribunal usually known as a *labour relations board*. A **labour relations board** administers labour relations legislation within a jurisdiction.

Not every worker is entitled to the benefits and protections of collective bargaining. Each jurisdiction defines which employees are eligible to bargain collectively. Most jurisdictions use the term "employee" in the context of organized labour almost the same way as in the context of individual employment. However, there are differences in its meaning. For example, a corporate manager is usually an employee in the context of employment law, but not in the context of collective bargaining. Corporate managers are excluded from the right to bargain collectively for policy reasons: the law is designed so that managers can retain their loyalty to their employer and keep an arm's-length relationship between employees and management.[3]

There is no definitive test to determine who is a manager and who is an employee, but factors typically considered include (i) the nature of the organization, (ii) the person's position in the organizational structure, (iii) the extent of the person's authority over other workers, and (iv) the proportion of that person's work that is non-managerial.[4] Managers are not the only workers who are ineligible to bargain collectively. Other workers excluded from the collective bargaining process or limited in how they can collectively bargain may include public employees, such as firefighters and police, as well as such professional employees as doctors, dentists, and lawyers.[5]

ACQUISITION OF BARGAINING RIGHTS

Just as some employees are ineligible to bargain collectively, some employee organizations are not qualified to take part in the collective bargaining process. For example, many employee associations that organize primarily for social or recreational purposes are not qualified to bargain collectively. In addition to being qualified, the organization must be recognized by the jurisdiction's labour relations board as an *appropriate bargaining unit*. An **appropriate bargaining unit** is a group of workers recognized by the labour relations board as having a

> a **collective agreement** is a document containing the terms of employment, as well as the rights and duties of the employer, the trade union, and the employees

> a **labour relations board** administers labour relations legislation within a jurisdiction

> an **appropriate bargaining unit** is a group of workers recognized by the labour relations board as having a common interest in the outcome of negotiations

---

[2.] *Canada Labour Code*, RSC 1985, c L-2.

[3.] GW Adams *Canadian Labour Law* (2008) at 6.180.

[4.] HW Arthurs *et al Labour Law and Industrial Relations in Canada* 4th ed (1993) at 214.

[5.] The *Canadian Charter of Rights and Freedoms* protects the rights of employees to associate in order to achieve collective goals. Therefore, federal and provincial legislation cannot eliminate the ability of workers to collectively bargain. However, the *Charter* does not protect any particular methods of collective bargaining, so employees may be restricted in how they are allowed to negotiate. See *Ontario (Attorney General) v Fraser* 2011 SCC 20. The government may also be able to justify a reasonable limitation of this right under s 1 of the *Charter*. We discussed the *Charter* in Chapter 1.

a **bargaining agent** is a trade union that is legally recognized as representing the interests of a bargaining unit

voluntary recognition occurs when the employer agrees to recognize a trade union as the bargaining agent for its employees

a **membership drive** aims to persuade a majority of employees in an appropriate bargaining unit to become union members

a **certified bargaining agent** acquires exclusive bargaining rights on behalf of a bargaining unit

the **duty to bargain in good faith** imposes an obligation on both parties to make every reasonable effort to successfully negotiate a collective agreement

common interest in the outcome of negotiations. It is important to distinguish the bargaining unit—the constituency of workers—from its *bargaining agent*. A **bargaining agent** is a trade union that is legally recognized as representing the interests of the bargaining unit.

A trade union can become recognized as a bargaining agent for a particular bargaining unit through *voluntary recognition* by the employer. **Voluntary recognition** occurs when the employer agrees to recognize a trade union as the bargaining agent for its employees. Voluntary recognition occurs more frequently in industries where job duration is temporary, such as the construction industry. The downside of voluntary recognition is that such arrangements are often challenged by employees who do not want to be represented by the bargaining agent agreed to by the employer.

The more common method of acquiring bargaining rights is through a *membership drive*. The aim of a **membership drive** is to persuade a majority of employees in an appropriate bargaining unit to become union members. In most provinces, a union that secures the required number of members automatically becomes a **certified bargaining agent** and thereby acquires exclusive bargaining rights on behalf of the bargaining unit. This is commonly achieved by way of a majority vote. In Alberta and Nova Scotia, however, voting is mandatory, regardless of the success of a membership drive. In other jurisdictions, a vote is necessary if the membership drive fails to recruit a majority of employees. And in some jurisdictions, employees who do not want to be represented by a particular union may, under some circumstances, complain to the labour relations board.

COLLECTIVE BARGAINING PROCESS

Once a union has acquired the bargaining rights for an appropriate bargaining unit, it must negotiate with the employer to reach a collective agreement that protects the collective interests of the employees. A business that does not want its employees to organize, or that does not want to deal with the employees' chosen bargaining agent, may try to delay the creation of a collective agreement. That tactic sometimes threatens the very survival of the union as the bargaining agent.

Once a bargaining unit has selected and certified its bargaining agent, that union has the exclusive right to bargain on behalf of its members. Even if a collective agreement has not yet been created, other unions cannot attempt to bargain on behalf of the employees in that bargaining unit, even if some of those employees would prefer to be represented by another bargaining agent. Likewise, individual employees are prohibited from bargaining for themselves with their employer.[6]

One controversial obligation in the collective bargaining process is the *duty to bargain in good faith*. The **duty to bargain in good faith** imposes an obligation on both parties to make every reasonable effort to successfully negotiate a collective agreement. An employer or a union that intentionally tries to thwart the negotiation process violates that duty. Some people believe that either party should be entitled to negotiate as forcefully as it wants, and that the point of collective bargaining is to match the economic strength of the collective against that of the employer. Remember, however, that the aim of labour law is to strike a balance between slavery and mutiny. The duty to bargain in good faith is a reminder that the entire process will break down if both parties feel free

---

[6.] *Syndicat catholique des employés des magasins de Québec Inc v Cie Paquet Ltée* (1959) 18 DLR (2d) 346 (SCC).

to engage in tactics that are inherently destructive of the employer–employee relationship. The duty has therefore been interpreted by most labour relations boards as an obligation about the manner in which negotiations are conducted, not about the actual content of particular proposals. The duty to bargain in good faith includes (i) the duty to meet with the other party, (ii) the duty to engage in full and informed discussion, (iii) the duty to supply information, and (iv) the duty to complete negotiations.[7] As Case Brief 27.1 illustrates, it is not always easy to determine whether there has been a violation of this duty.

Case Brief 27.1

PIPSC v Canada (Treasury Board) (2008) 92 CLAS 399

Knowing that the collective agreement governing the Applied Science and Patent Examination bargaining unit was due to be renegotiated, a letter was sent by the Professional Institute of the Public Service of Canada (PIPSC) requesting contact information for all members of that bargaining unit to keep them abreast of developments in the collective bargaining process. The request sought considerable personal information, including employee names, positions, and their personal telephone and fax numbers, postal and email addresses. Because a number of bargaining units within the union were seeking the same information, the employer told the union that it would consider all information requests together and formulate a single response applicable to all bargaining units. After nearly half a year passed without further reply, the union filed a complaint with the labour relations board, claiming that the employer had failed to bargain in good faith, and that its failure to provide the con-

tact information was an unfair labour practice. The employer responded by claiming that the delay was in part due to logistical difficulties in obtaining accurate information and in part due to privacy concerns arising from the disclosure of personal information collected for other purposes.

The labour relations board held that the employer's failure to provide a timely response did violate its duty to make a reasonable effort to enter into a collective agreement. Union members had a right to be informed about potential strike or ratification votes, and the employer's failure to respond was an unfair labour practice. At the same time, concerns about the accuracy and privacy of the information sought persuaded the labour relations board that the employer need not simply hand over all personal information. Instead, both parties were ordered to begin negotiations regarding the appropriate sharing of information.

Collective Agreements

L.O. **❹**

There are three essential requirements for any collective agreement:

- It must be in writing.
- It must be entered into by the employer and a trade union with a signature indicating the agreement of each party.
- It must contain provisions respecting the terms and conditions of employment.[8]

Although it is tempting to think of the collective agreement as a multi-party contract, there are several important differences between collective agreements and contracts. Collective agreements are enforceable not by common law but by labour legislation. Furthermore, labour legislation in most jurisdictions dictates the inclusion of particular statutory provisions that make the character of a collective agreement quite different from a common law contract. Some authors have suggested that the collective agreement is a kind of labour relations "constitution."[9] The following are some of the standard provisions.

[7.] HW Arthurs *et al Labour Law and Industrial Relations in Canada* 4th ed (1993) at 259–63.

[8.] G Adams *Canadian Labour Law* (1985) at 671.

[9.] HW Arthurs *et al Labour Law and Industrial Relations in Canada* 4th ed (1993) at 676.

STRIKE AND LOCKOUT PROVISIONS

To promote industrial stability, most jurisdictions in Canada require collective agreements to prohibit strikes and lockouts while the collective agreement is binding. Consequently, some otherwise legitimate labour practices become unlawful. Exceptions to this approach are found in Nova Scotia and Quebec, where strikes and lockouts are permitted during a collective agreement so long as the agreement contains a clause contemplating this possibility.[10] Business Decision 27.1 provides an opportunity to reflect on the general approach.

Business Decision **27.1**

The Lockout Provision[11]

To cut costs, SecureHome Alarm Company decided to reduce the work hours of certain employees from full time to part time. Employees were given the option under the collective agreement to accept the reduced work hours, "bump" a junior employee and take their position (this chapter discusses "bumping" in more detail later), or elect to be laid off. But before the employees had an opportunity to make their decision, SecureHome reduced all of their hours to part time. When employees showed up to work and were informed of their new hours, some replied that they had not yet decided to accept the part-time schedule and walked out.

SecureHome brought an application to the labour relations board for a declaration that the employees who left work were engaging in an illegal strike. The union asserted that by reducing the work schedules to part time, SecureHome was engaging in an illegal lockout.

The board determined that the employee's refusal to work part time did not constitute an unlawful strike because they had been given the option to elect to be laid off. However, because the employees who chose to leave work were essentially electing to be laid off, the union's counterclaim that SecureHome had locked them out was dismissed.

Questions for Discussion

1. Do you agree with the labour relations board?

2. How might management have achieved its desired result without causing a grievance?

GRIEVANCE PROVISIONS

Since strikes and lockouts are prohibited during a collective agreement, most jurisdictions in Canada set out other mechanisms for resolving disputes about the interpretation, application, administration, or alleged violation of a collective agreement. The most common mechanism is the process of *grievance arbitration*.[12] Some collective agreements have a very detailed grievance provision that sets out the entire procedure step by step. Others are completely silent on the issue, in which case, attention must be directed to the applicable labour legislation. Labour relations boards sometimes amend arbitration provisions that are inadequate and, in some cases, impose a statutory "model arbitration" clause. Therefore, business managers who employ organized labour should include in their collective agreement a procedure that they like (for example, a provision that requires arbitration decisions to be released within a specified period of time).

[10.] *Trade Union Act*, RSNS 1989, c 475, s 48 (NS); *Labour Code*, RSQ, c C-27, s 107 (QB).

[11.] Based on *Brinks Canada Lts* (1992) 92 CLLC (CLRB).

[12.] The Supreme Court of Canada held in *Weber v Ontario Hydro* [1995] 2 SCR 929 that unionized employees cannot sue their employers regarding matters that are addressed in a collective agreement. Business managers should be aware that in these cases, grievance arbitration will be final and binding. If the collective agreement does not stipulate that grievance arbitration is final and binding, provincial labour legislation might fill this gap by making such a stipulation. See *eg Labour Relations Act*, SO 1995, c 1, Sch A, s 48 (Ont).

UNION SECURITY CLAUSES

Every jurisdiction permits the inclusion of a *union security clause*. A **union security clause** is meant to strengthen the position of the union by providing it with a means of being paid—whether by its membership or otherwise. Usually a union is remunerated through the payment of union dues. Unions typically adopt one of these three structures:

- First, the union might decide to operate as a *closed shop*. A **closed shop** requires that management hire only people who are already members of that union.

- A second approach is a *union shop*. In a **union shop**, management may hire workers from outside the union, but the new workers are required to become union members in the early stages of their employment.

- A third approach is the *dues shop*. A **dues shop**, sometimes called an "agency shop," requires a person who is hired to pay union dues, but does not require that person to join the union.[13]

In some jurisdictions, an employer is required to include a union security clause in a collective agreement if the union requests it. To ignore such a request is considered to be a breach of the duty to bargain in good faith and is grounds for complaint to the labour relations board. Concept Summary 27.1 reviews these three approaches.

a **union security clause** is meant to strengthen the position of the union by providing it with a means of being paid

a **closed shop** requires that management hire only people who are already union members

a **union shop** requires workers to become union members in the early stages of their employment

a **dues shop** requires a person who is hired to pay union dues, but does not require that person to join the union

Concept Summary 27.1

Union Security: The Means by Which a Union Will Be Remunerated

Closed shop	Employers cannot hire a person unless they are already a union member in good standing.
Union shop	Employers cannot hire a person unless they promise to become a union member in good standing when starting employment.
Dues shop	Employers cannot hire a person unless they promise to pay union dues (though actual union membership is optional).

Grievance Arbitration

L.O. ❺❻❼❽

To understand the arbitration process, it is important to be aware of the four general categories of labour disputes that can arise: *recognition disputes*, *jurisdictional disputes*, *interest disputes*, and *rights disputes*.

Recognition disputes typically relate to the acquisition of bargaining rights and especially to the appropriateness of the bargaining unit. If a bargaining agent purports to represent a group of employees, the employer may dispute the bargaining agent's right to do so, for example, on grounds of the scope or terms of a voluntary recognition agreement.

Jurisdictional disputes can arise in a number of different ways. For example, there may be a dispute as to whether particular workers come under the

[13.] This form of union payment is accomplished through a clause in the collective agreement known as a "check-off." Requiring all employees to pay into the union regardless of whether they are members of the union can also be referred to as the "Rand formula."

jurisdiction of federal or provincial labour laws.[14] This kind of situation can arise in areas such as shipping, where many workers are under federal jurisdiction, but workers on the wharves, or in warehouses nearby, are under provincial jurisdiction. There may also be a dispute as to whether an arbitrator or a labour board has jurisdiction to decide a particular substantive issue.

Interest disputes are not defined by the nature of the dispute, but rather by the nature of the process for resolving the dispute. In other words, under an interest dispute, a mediator or an arbitrator may hear presentations from the employer and the workers and then informally attempt to reach a resolution to the dispute through compromise. This is not strictly a legal process.

Rights disputes are traditional forms of disputes as to, for example, the respective rights and obligations of the parties under a collective agreement or labour laws. Unlike interest disputes, rights disputes are resolved through a stricter form of adjudication, including the arbitration process described in the next sections.

ARBITRATION PROCESS

grievance arbitration is an external method of resolving labour disputes that cannot be resolved by the parties alone

Most collective agreements contain an *internal* procedure for dealing with employee grievances. In addition, labour law provides an *external* method of resolving such disputes: *grievance arbitration*. **Grievance arbitration** is an external method of resolving labour disputes that cannot be resolved by the parties alone. Usually the process begins with the union notifying the employer of the dispute and their attempt to resolve it internally. If a settlement cannot be reached between the employee and management, the parties will engage in arbitration.

It is important to distinguish between (i) disputes brought before an arbitration panel, and (ii) disputes brought before the labour relations board. The labour relations board usually hears disputes about the violation of labour relations legislation. An arbitration panel or sole arbitrator hears and resolves disputes about the collective agreement. The role of arbitration is therefore to resolve a dispute between employee and management under an existing collective agreement.

The parties to a collective agreement are jointly responsible for appointing an arbitrator. If the matter can be resolved by a sole arbitrator, the parties must agree to that person's selection. If a panel of arbitrators is required, each party selects its own arbitrator to sit as a member on the panel, and then the parties jointly select a third member to chair the panel. If the parties cannot reach an agreement, legislation usually provides that the Minister of Labour shall appoint arbitrators. The cost of the proceedings, including the expense of the arbitrators, is generally shared equally by both parties. Management and unions must therefore be careful to budget for these expenses.

arbitral jurisprudence is the body of existing arbitration decisions

If the collective agreement is insufficient to resolve the dispute, arbitrators look to outside sources, including (i) the traditional rules of interpretation, (ii) the labour legislation itself, and (iii) *arbitral jurisprudence*. **Arbitral jurisprudence** is the body of existing arbitration decisions. Although arbitrators do not strictly adhere to the doctrine of precedent (that is, follow decisions from earlier cases), previous arbitral decisions often play an important role in decision making. (The doctrine of precedent was discussed in Chapter 2.) Usually, arbitrators follow a previous decision that is relevant unless they think it is wrong. Finally, arbitrators may apply many of the principles of equity.

[14.] See *eg NIL/TU, O Child and Family Services Society v BC Government and Service Employees' Union*, 2010 SCC 45.

To determine whether the grievance is a proper subject for arbitration, some arbitrators allow the parties to make preliminary submissions before the formal hearing begins. An employer can make several arguments to try to end the grievance before the matter is formally heard. They may, for instance, argue that (i) the grievor is not a person covered under the collective agreement, (ii) the issue falls outside the scope of the collective agreement, or (iii) the submission of the grievance fell outside of the required time limits.[15]

TYPICAL GRIEVANCES

Business people who will be operating in an organized labour environment need to know about the most typical grievances. We briefly consider three basic grounds of complaint: *discipline and discharge*, *seniority*, and *compensation*.

Discipline and Discharge

Like individual employment contracts, collective agreements often say how employee misconduct will be treated. One main difference is that disciplinary procedures are generally spelled out in the collective agreement. Disciplinary measures usually include suspensions, formal warnings, and sometimes demotion. Extreme misconduct leads to discharge. Another difference is that many collective agreements provide that the employer is allowed to discipline or discharge an employee only if there is just cause. Where such a provision exists, an arbitrator will interfere with the employer's handling of a disciplinary matter only if the arbitrator believes that cause was lacking. Where a collective agreement does not contain such a provision, arbitrators will not usually interfere with an employer's decision to take action. For more leeway, business managers should therefore try to avoid a just cause provision.

It is sometimes difficult to tell whether an employer's particular conduct is of a disciplinary nature. *Demotion* is a typical example. **Demotion** occurs when an employer transfers an employee to a lower-rated job. Often employers demote employees on account of their misconduct. In this context, demotion is a form of discipline and is subject to review if the collective agreement contains a just cause provision. What if an employee is demoted because of their incompetence? This is generally seen as a non-disciplinary demotion and is not subject to review by an arbitrator. Sometimes the line between disciplinary and non-disciplinary demotion is difficult to draw, as You Be the Judge 27.1 demonstrates.

demotion occurs when an employer transfers an employee to a lower-rated job

You Be the Judge **27.1**

Demotion[16]

TJ, an employee of Sun-Time Snacks Ltd, brought a grievance through his union claiming that he had been demoted because of his absenteeism. Many of TJ's absences were due to legitimate illnesses and injuries, most of which were sustained while playing soccer. TJ had recorded an absenteeism percentage of just over 15 percent, which was three times the company average. Once TJ was made aware that his excessive absenteeism was a problem, he promised to retire from playing soccer. However, the employer decided to demote TJ anyway.

Sun-Time characterized its decision to demote TJ as a non-disciplinary response to excessive absenteeism from a position that

(*Continued*)

[15.] HW Arthurs *et al Labour Law and Industrial Relations in Canada* 4th ed (1993) at 332.

[16.] This case is based on *Sun-Rype Products Ltd and Teamsters Local No 213* (1997) 67 LAC (4th) 301.

required an "above average attendance" record. Because of the training necessary to safely do TJ's work, finding a replacement for TJ when he was sick or injured was near impossible. The union argued that the demotion was disciplinary and could be justified only on the basis of culpable behaviour. The union argued that the employer had essentially treated TJ's involvement in soccer as behaviour for which he could be disciplined.

Questions for Discussion

1. Do you agree with the employer's characterization of TJ's demotion as non-disciplinary or with the union, which claims that TJ's demotion was disciplinary?

2. What additional information might you require before making a decision?

3. Do you think Sun-Time's ultimate decision to demote TJ was justified despite his promise to retire from soccer, which was the main cause of his absenteeism problems?

Seniority

A complaint that often arises in grievance arbitration is that an employer has acted without proper regard to an employee's *seniority*. The concept of seniority is central to virtually every collective agreement.[17] **Seniority** grants preferences to certain employees based on their accumulated length of service. Not only does seniority define who is eligible for certain monetary benefits, it also provides a way of determining which employee is entitled to job promotion and which employee is subject to a transfer or lay-off. Seniority provisions in collective agreements are usually one of two types: (i) *non-competitive clauses* and (ii) *competitive clauses*.[18] **Non-competitive clauses** require seniority to be the determining factor, as long as the more senior person is competent. **Competitive clauses** require seniority to be the determining factor only when the skill and ability of the competing employees are relatively equal.

Many collective agreements contemplate bumping. **Bumping** occurs when a senior employee who is about to be laid off is allowed to invoke their seniority and replace an employee in a junior position. In many instances, this sets off a chain reaction. The junior person who was just bumped asserts their seniority against a still more junior person, and so on. Most collective agreements either explicitly or implicitly provide that an employee who has elected to bump into a lower position does not forfeit the right to return to their previous job if it is eventually recalled. Collective agreements that include bumping rights usually carry a minimum requirement that the senior person be capable of doing the junior person's job. However, if the junior position requires a specialized skill, the senior employee is usually entitled to the necessary training to learn that skill.

Business managers involved in negotiating a collective agreement should realize that employees may want to use the bumping procedure in reverse. **Bumping up** is an application of seniority rights in the context of promotion. Prudent business managers will not want a system of promotion that is based solely on seniority. To avoid that risk, management should negotiate an exclusive right to make appointments in a manner that applies seniority rights differently in promotions than in lay-offs.[19]

seniority grants preferences to certain employees based on their accumulated length of service

non-competitive clauses require seniority to be the determining factor, as long as the more senior person is competent

competitive clauses require seniority to be the determining factor only when the skill and ability of the competing employees are relatively equal

bumping occurs when a senior employee who is about to be laid off is allowed to invoke their seniority and replace an employee in a junior position

bumping up is an application of seniority rights in the context of promotion

[17] DJM Brown & D Beatty, *Canadian Labour Arbitration* 3d ed (2000) 6:000.

[18] HW Arthurs *et al Labour Law and Industrial Relations in Canada* 4th ed (1993), p. 343.

[19] DMJ Brown & DM Beatty *Canadian Labour Arbitration* 3d ed (2000) at 6:2340.

Compensation

Compensation is a ground of complaint that often leads to grievance arbitration. Like the individual employment scenario, typical complaints involve (i) equal pay for equal work, (ii) unilateral change in wages, (iii) overtime pay, and (iv) entitlement to benefits. One issue that arises more often in the context of organized labour is *retroactive pay*. **Retroactive pay** is money that is owed by the employer to the employee as a result of a collective agreement that is deemed to come into effect some time before the date of its creation. The law generally presumes that wage increases apply retroactively. Although most employers are willing to comply with collective agreements for retroactive wages in the form of back-pay, disputes often arise about whether employees are also entitled to other benefits as of that date. Traditionally, arbitrators have drawn a distinction between monetary and non-monetary provisions.[20] Therefore, they usually require clear language that expressly includes benefits before awarding them retroactively.[21]

retroactive pay is money that is owed by the employer to the employee as a result of a collective agreement that is deemed to come into effect some time before the date of its creation

A business sometimes has to decide whether to offer back-pay to people who were employees at the time the collective agreement retroactively became effective but ceased to be employees before the agreement was signed.

ARBITRATION AWARDS

Arbitrators often enjoy the ability to select from amongst a range of remedies. Three remedies are especially important:

- **Damages:** An arbitrator may award compensatory *damages* to a party that has suffered a loss. We examined the general rules of compensatory damages in Chapters 3 and 12. We also examined the issue in the employment context in Chapter 26.

- **Compliance order:** In appropriate circumstances, an arbitrator may grant a declaration of a party's rights by way of a *compliance order*. A **compliance order** usually requires a specific obligation in the collective agreement to be fulfilled or a particular course of conduct to be brought to an end.

a **compliance order** usually requires a specific obligation in the collective agreement to be fulfilled or a particular course of conduct to be brought to an end

- **Reinstatement:** An arbitrator may have the power to *reinstate* employees who were discharged without cause. Similarly, unless labour legislation or the collective agreement provides otherwise, arbitrators generally have the power to substitute a lesser penalty in the case of a suspension or discharge.[22]

An arbitrator's authority to award remedies is, however, limited by both the labour legislation and the terms of the collective agreement. Consequently, if the parties want to allow arbitrators broad power in resolving grievances, they must consider this in negotiating the collective agreement. That is true, for example, with respect to the remedy of *rectification*. **Rectification** is the process by which a contract is rewritten to better reflect the actual agreement contemplated by the parties. According to the Supreme Court of Canada, arbitrators do not have the power to rectify a collective agreement unless that agreement expressly gives them the power to do so.[23]

rectification the process by which a contract is rewritten to better reflect the actual agreement contemplated by the parties

---

[20.] *Onesimus Community Resources* (1994) 39 LAC (4th) 289 (Thorne); *Sturgeon General Hospital* (1974) 6 LAC (2d) 360 (Taylor).

[21.] *Toronto Hospital* (1995) 49 LAC (4th) 1 (Thorne); *York Regional Board of Education* (1990) 11 LAC (4th) 345 (Marszewski).

[22.] *Heustis v New Brunswick Electric Power Commission* (1979) 98 DLR (3d) 622 (SCC).

[23.] *Port Arthur Shipbuilding Co v Arthurs* (1968) 70 DLR (2d) 283 (SCC).

ENFORCEMENT OF ARBITRATION AWARDS

Although arbitrators have the power to order awards, they do not have the power to enforce them. Labour legislation in each jurisdiction therefore provides that arbitration orders are to be filed with the courts and enforced in the same way as a judicial order.

L.O. ❾ ❿

Industrial Conflict

Disputes under a collective agreement are usually resolved through grievance arbitration. However, if the parties reach an impasse before establishing a collective agreement or after it is no longer in effect, one party may decide to use economic pressure to persuade the other to make the appropriate concessions. The most common practice used by employees is a *strike*, while employers often respond by *locking out* their employees. Strikes and lockouts sometimes lead to secondary activities, such as *picketing* and *boycotts*. We finish this chapter by briefly considering *strikes*, *lockouts*, *picketing*, and *boycotts*. We will discuss both lawful and unlawful industrial action.

STRIKES

a **strike** is a cessation of work, resulting from a concerted activity, that has a common purpose designed to limit or restrict output

The term *strike* is not consistently defined across Canada, providing labour boards and courts some flexibility when deciding whether or not employee action constitutes a strike. Most statutory definitions of a **strike** require that there be (i) a cessation of work, (ii) resulting from a concerted activity, (iii) that has a common purpose, (iv) designed to limit or restrict output. Some jurisdictions, such as Alberta, Manitoba, and Nova Scotia, require a fifth element: (v) the common purpose is to compel the employer to accept certain terms and conditions of employment.

Although employees who go on strike usually do so in a clear way, less obvious activities may also constitute a strike. Consider Case Brief 27.2.

Although striking is a fundamental practice in the labour movement, neither the common law nor the *Canadian Charter of Rights and Freedoms*

Case Brief 27.2

Canada Post Corp v Canadian Union of Postal Workers [2011] CLAD No 146

Numerous letter carriers employed by Canada Post Corporation filed grievances through their union in response to the elimination of approximately 11 routes. The additional work from these routes was added to existing routes that many of the grievors now found difficult to keep up with. The new routes also caused more overtime, which attracted increased monitoring by the supervisors.

One employee, who felt particularly strained by the difficulty of keeping up with her new route, called the union president to the worksite to address some of their concerns. When the president arrived at the worksite, he found that the union members were very upset and needed

someone to vent to. Many of the employees went to the lunchroom to air their concerns. The employees returned to work approximately one hour after the meeting started. Subsequently, a one-day suspension was imposed on all the employees who had attended the meeting, which Canada Post considered to be an illegal work stoppage.

An arbitrator concluded that the one-hour meeting fell within the definition of a strike and that such a work stoppage could not take place under the terms of a collective agreement. Since all the mail was delivered on time on the day in question and the employer did not suffer an economic loss, the arbitrator felt that the one-day suspension was reasonable.

expressly identifies a general right to strike.[24] If there is a right to strike, it is limited to those circumstances in which striking is not otherwise prohibited under the governing labour legislation.

A strike is generally lawful if it is designed to gain economic objectives and if it starts after the statute's compulsory conciliation procedures have been exhausted. In contrast, a strike typically is unlawful if it (i) occurs while a collective agreement is in force, (ii) takes place during a statutory freeze period, (iii) begins before certain bargaining procedures have been exhausted, (iv) is designed to gain sympathy and bring pressure on a secondary employer, or (v) is undertaken for the purpose of a political protest.[25]

Most jurisdictions require union members to vote before striking. Usually, a strike is permitted only if a majority votes in favour of striking. It is usually necessary for the union to give notice of the vote to the employer and, in some cases, to the Ministry of Labour. Typical notice periods do not exceed 72 hours.

Although workers are sometimes free to strike, they may not have any guarantee that they will be able to return to their jobs afterwards.

- Some strikes put employers out of business permanently. When that occurs, there are no such jobs to return to.
- In other instances, some employees may lose their positions because their union could not negotiate positions for them under the new collective agreement.
- Even if a business can withstand the financial hardship of a strike, employees sometimes cannot. Although some unions provide strike pay to their members, some employees cannot afford to live on that lower amount and are therefore forced to look for other jobs.
- Alternatively, rather than looking for a new job, some workers are willing to abandon the strike and return to their jobs.

In most jurisdictions, if an employee's position remains intact after a strike has ended, that employee has the right to be reinstated. But the right to reinstatement is not absolute. Employers have grounds to discharge an employee during a strike if the worker engaged in serious misconduct, such as sabotage against company property or violence on a picket line.

LOCKOUTS

The flip side of an employee strike is an employer *lockout*. A **lockout** occurs when an employer closes the workplace, or refuses to continue to employ its workers, with the intention of compelling them to agree to certain conditions of employment. A number of high-profile lockout situations have occurred in major league sports, such as the 2011 National Basketball Association lockout. Note that there is a subjective element to the definition of a lockout. For the business closure to be classified as a lockout, the employer must have intended to use it to compel its employees to agree to its terms. In some instances of industrial conflict, it is hard to tell what the employer's intentions are in shutting down operations. Industrial conflict often coincides with economic hardship for the business. The employer is free to make sound business decisions to suspend or cease operations altogether, and such decisions must be distinguished from closures designed to force concessions from a union. Consequently, if a business can show that its decision to shut down was

a **lockout** occurs when an employer closes the workplace, or refuses to continue to employ its workers, with the intention of compelling them to agree to certain conditions of employment

---

[24] As explained in Chapter 1, the *Charter* does not contain protection for economic or property rights.

[25] HW Arthurs *et al* *Labour Law and Industrial Relations in Canada* 4th ed (1993) at 276.

irrevocable, it is better able to argue that it did not shut down with the intention of forcing an agreement.[26]

As is true of strikes, some lockouts are lawful, while others are not. The strategy of compelling workers to accept the employer's terms is completely legitimate if it is carried out within the statutory requirements that govern lockouts. If the lockout (i) begins only after the negotiation and conciliation procedures prescribed by statute have been exhausted, and (ii) does not involve any other unlawful activity, a business's management team can choose to shut down operations to achieve its bargaining position.

PICKETING

Picketing is used as a response to a variety of situations including strikes, lockouts, and boycotts. **Picketing** involves:

picketing involves the presence of one or more persons, the communication of information, and the intention to secure a sympathetic response from some third party

- the presence of one or more persons
- the communication of information
- the intention to secure a sympathetic response from some third party[27]

Well-meaning picketers try to distribute information in a peaceful way to convince customers, other companies, the employees of other companies, and even potential replacement workers to support their strike. Picketers often ask people not to cross picket lines. If successful, that tactic interferes with the employer's ability to carry on business in spite of the strike. Unfortunately, while picketing is usually a peaceful communicative process, discussions between picketers and those nearby occasionally get emotionally charged and even violent.

Picketing is generally governed by the courts, because most issues that arise in a picketing dispute are based in either criminal or tort law. The torts mentioned in this paragraph were discussed in detail in Part 2 of this book. Since picketing is a form of communication, picketers must be careful with the message they are sending—false statements about an employer may be defamatory. When picketing behaviour leads to physical injury, picketers may be sued for either battery or negligence or can be subject to criminal liability. Sometimes, when picketing interferes with another's property rights, picketers can be sued for the torts of nuisance or trespass. For this reason, many picketers are careful to picket on public property, where an employer has little recourse unless the picketers are actually blocking a public passage way.

secondary picketing exerts pressure on a business indirectly by threatening or imposing sanctions against some third party

Picketers expose themselves to additional liability when they engage in the practice of _secondary picketing_. **Secondary picketing** exerts pressure on a business indirectly by threatening or imposing sanctions against some third party. When picketers exert secondary pressure, they exceed the primary purpose of picketing, namely the peaceful communication of information about the strike. Picketing of this sort is prohibited by statute in some provinces.[28] As well, it

---

[26.] _Doral Construction Ltd_ (1980) OLRB Rep Mar 310; _Westinghouse Canada Ltd_ (1980) OLRB Rep Apr 577.

[27.] AWR Carrothers "Recent Developments in the Tort Law of Picketing" (1957) 35 _Can Bar Rev_ 1005.

[28.] In _RWDSU Local 558 v Pepsi Cola Canada Beverages (West) Ltd_ (2002) 208 DLR (4th) 385, the Supreme Court of Canada affirmed that (unless prohibited by statute) secondary picketing is generally lawful, as long as it does not involve tortious or criminal conduct. Asked to determine whether picketing the homes of Pepsi-Cola's management was unlawful, the court applied the "wrongful action" approach, focusing on the character and effects of the activity rather than merely its location. The court held that the conduct of union members amounted to disorderly conduct, accompanied by threats of harm, in an effort to make members of Pepsi's management refrain from doing what they had every right to do. Given its tortious nature, the conduct of the union members was held to be unlawful.

sometimes gives rise to a cause of action in tort for *inducing breach of contract*. (The tort of inducing breach of contract was discussed in Chapter 5.) When picketers intentionally induce a breach of contract, they wrongfully interfere with the economic relations between the employer and a third party. If the courts find that the aim of secondary picketing is not merely to communicate information but to induce a breach of contract, they may issue an order that brings the picketing to an end. Third parties caught in the crossfire of an industrial conflict might sometimes have to protect their own interests, as Ethical Perspective 27.1 illustrates.

Ethical Perspective **27.1**

Interforest Ltd v Weber [1999] OJ No 3637, 180 DLR (4th) 176

The production employees of Interforest commenced a legal strike at the Interforest plant. The company maintained limited production by hiring summer students and new employees as well as through the use of managerial employees. Certain union members began picketing at the residences of many of Interforest's managers and new employees. Picketers marched in front of the employees' homes for periods of time ranging from 20 minutes to more than an hour. The picketers carried signs with such messages as "The IWA is on strike" and "Negotiate don't dictate." In addition, they carried signs personally tailored to the specific employee whose home was being picketed. For example, a sign might say, "'John Doe' is a scab and proud of it." Some of the residents allege that the picketing was also accompanied by obscene gestures, offensive comments to the residents' children, vandalism to motor vehicles, the slashing of tires, and, in one case, the scattering of nails over an employee's driveway, and in another, vandalism on the side of an employee's house.

An injunction was granted limiting the proximity of picketing around the employees' homes. The picketers were ordered not to picket within a 500-foot radius of where the property lines of the Interforest employees intersect with the public sidewalk or roadway. The court found this order to appropriately balance legal rights and to interfere as little as possible with the fundamental rights and freedoms of union members to convey information.

Questions for Discussion

1. Do you think that the union members exceeded their right to convey information?

2. Do you think the court was correct in allowing the union members to picket outside of a 500-foot radius from Interforest's employees' homes?

BOYCOTTS

Boycotts are often created by way of secondary picketing. A **boycott** occurs when people refuse to interact with a business, or to handle goods that are associated with that business, as support for a collective bargaining position. Although a boycott may involve picketing, it need not. Some boycotts are carried out through advertising or telephone campaigns designed to appeal to members of the public or other union members. Regardless of the manner of the campaign, boycotts are economically dangerous. By definition, boycotts interfere with the interests of parties who are not directly involved in the industrial conflict. In some instances, businesses are forced to suffer financially even though they have absolutely nothing to do with the labour dispute. Not only are innocent third party businesses affected by a boycott, such campaigns also cause harm to the employer—often even greater harm than would be caused by direct picketing.

The economic effect of strikes, lockouts, picketing, and boycotts has led to a response by both federal and provincial governments to temporarily revoke the right of some public sector groups to strike. In some instances, this has even led to wage control.[29] A number of jurisdictions have recently felt the need to invoke back-to-work legislation that forces workers to return to their

> a **boycott** occurs when people refuse to interact with a business, or to handle goods that are associated with that business, as support for a collective bargaining position

---

[29.] AWR Carrothers *Collective Bargaining in Canada* (1986) at 108–125.

jobs while their labour disputes are settled through compulsory arbitration, as was recently seen when the federal government ordered postal workers back to work in 2011.[30] These rather drastic measures demonstrate governments' desire to keep the economy productive. Occasionally, when a large enough sector of organized labour is involved in an industrial dispute, there is a clash of wills. On such occasions, the matter is no longer merely a legal dispute between a business and its employees, but a political battle involving the public interest.

Concept Summary 27.2 reviews how businesses can manage the risks regarding industrial conflict.

Concept Summary 27.2

Managing Risk in Association with Industrial Conflict

- If your workers strike, consider your ability to argue that the strike is unlawful because, for example, the workers have not exhausted bargaining procedures or because the purpose of the strike is political protest. Be aware of vote and notice requirements too.

- If you wish to lock out employees to achieve your bargaining position, ensure that you comply with statutory requirements.

- If your workers engage in picketing and ask other workers at your business not to cross the picket lines, consider whether you could argue that the other workers are engaging in an unlawful strike. Monitor pickets for any evidence that workers are engaged in criminal or tortious conduct. Watch for evidence of secondary picketing that may give rise to a cause of action against the workers in tort.

- Have a strategy in place for dealing with strikes, pickets, lockouts, and boycotts. For example, you can protect your business by training management staff to be able to perform a wide variety of tasks. This knowledge can be essential to the survival of your business in the event that unionized workers go on strike.

[30.] "Canada Post Back-to-Work Bill Clears House," *CBC News* (25 June 2011) at <www.cbc.ca/news/politics/story/2011/06/25/canada-post.html>.

Chapter Summary

Not all work relations are individual relationships. A substantial portion of Canadian industry is organized and governed collectively under labour legislation. Labour law is the system of rules that govern collective relations between management, trade unions, their members, and the institutions in such relations. The collective nature of organized labour distinguishes it from other kinds of work.

Labour law aims to find an appropriate balance between employer and employee objectives by imposing a system of rules on collective bargaining. Collective bargaining is the process by which an employer and a trade union seek to negotiate a collective agreement. A collective agreement is a document containing the terms of employment and the rights and duties of the employer, the trade union, and the employees. Not every worker is entitled to the benefits and protections of collective bargaining. Each jurisdiction defines those employees who are eligible to bargain as a collective and those who are not.

In addition to being eligible, employees who wish to bargain collectively must be recognized by the jurisdiction's labour relations board as an appropriate bargaining unit. Once recognized as such, the bargaining unit must choose a trade union to act as its bargaining agent. As soon as its bargaining agent has been selected and certified, that union has the exclusive right to bargain on behalf of its members. As its bargaining agent, the trade union must try to represent the interests of all the employees in the bargaining unit. One of the more controversial obligations in the collective bargaining process is the duty to bargain in good faith. This duty imposes an obligation on both parties to make every reasonable effort to successfully negotiate a collective agreement. Collective agreements typically include strike and lockout provisions, grievance provisions, and union security clauses.

Most businesses that employ organized labour put into place an internal procedure to deal with employee grievances. In addition to the internal grievance procedure that is usually stipulated in collective agreements, labour law provides an external method of resolving such disputes through a process known as grievance arbitration. Grievance arbitration is the final stage in the attempt to resolve an industrial dispute under an ongoing collective agreement. Typical grievances issues are discipline and discharge, seniority, and compensation. Disciplinary measures include suspensions, formal warnings, and demotion. The concept of seniority is central to almost every collective agreement. Not only does seniority define who is eligible for certain monetary benefits, it also provides a way for determining which employee is entitled to job promotion and which employee is subject to a transfer or lay-off. Typical complaints about compensation concern equal pay for equal work, a unilateral change in wages, overtime pay, entitlement to benefits, and retroactive pay.

The authority of an arbitrator to award remedies is limited in scope by both the labour legislation and the terms of the collective agreement. Arbitrators usually have the power to award damages, issue compliance orders, and reinstate employees to their previous positions. Although arbitrators have the power to order such awards, they do not have the power to enforce them. The enforcement of arbitration awards is carried out by a court of competent jurisdiction.

When industrial disputes arise before or during the negotiation of a collective agreement, one party may decide to use economic pressure to convince the other party to make the appropriate concessions. The most common practice used by employees is a strike. Employers often respond in such situations by locking out their employees. Strikes and lockouts sometimes lead to secondary activities, such as picketing and boycotts. A strike or lockout is generally lawful if it is designed to gain economic objectives and if it is timely. Although workers are permitted to strike in certain circumstances, they do not always enjoy a guarantee that they will be able to return to their previous jobs afterwards. Under some conditions, an employer is permitted to shut down operations to convince employees to accept its bargaining position. In extreme cases, an industrial conflict may force a business to shut down operations permanently. Picketing is a mechanism used in response to a variety of situations including strikes, lockouts, and boycotts. Secondary picketing exerts pressure on a business indirectly by threatening or imposing sanctions against some third party. Boycotts interfere with the interests of parties who are not directly involved in the industrial conflict. Businesses that are the victim of secondary picketing and boycotts often have recourse in the courts.

MyBusLawLab ADDITIONAL RESOURCES FOR CHAPTER 27

MyBusLawLab provides students with an assortment of tools to help enrich the learning experience, including a Study Plan with Pre- and Post-tests, mini-cases with assessments, and provincial content material, which provides links to relevant cases, legislation, and additional resources.

MyBusLawLab provides the following resources for Chapter 27:

- Business Decision 27.1W—Retroactive Pay to Former Employees

Provincial Material

- **British Columbia:** Essential Services, Union Certification and Decertification, Collective Bargaining, Mediation and Arbitration, Strikes, Lockouts and Picketing
- **Alberta:** *Labour Relations Act*
- **Manitoba and Saskatchewan:** Labour Relations Boards
- **Ontario:** Public Sector and Essential Services, Labour Relations
- **Atlantic Provinces:** Labour Relations Legislation

Review Questions

1. Distinguish labour law from employment law. On what basis can organized labour be differentiated from other kinds of work?
2. What role do corporate managers play in the collective bargaining process?
3. Describe the test that is used to determine whether a person is a manager or an employee.
4. How does a trade union become recognized as the bargaining agent for a particular bargaining unit?
5. What is the first step when a union and management reach an impasse while negotiating a collective agreement?
6. What are the different elements of the duty to bargain in good faith? Why does labour law impose such a duty?
7. List the three essential requirements of an enforceable collective agreement. Are there other provisions that one of the parties can insist on including?

8. Name and describe two types of union security clauses and identify their common purpose in a collective agreement.

9. Name four general categories of labour disputes that can arise. Which type of dispute will typically be resolved through a more formal arbitration process?

10. Define "arbitral jurisprudence." How much deference must a labour arbitrator show to previous arbitration decisions?

11. Give three examples of disciplinary measures that an employer may take in the context of organized labour.

12. What is the purpose of a "just cause" provision? Are employers or employees more likely to want a just cause provision in a collective agreement? Why?

13. What is the difference between the terms "bumping" and "bumping up"? Why might a risk manager want to negotiation a collective agreement that does not allow for bumping up?

14. When might an employee be entitled to retroactive pay? Does this generally include benefits as well as wages?

15. Do labour arbitrators and labour relations boards generally have remedial powers similar to those of judges? Be specific. Is it possible to expand or limit the authority of labour arbitrators? What about labour relations boards?

16. How are arbitration awards enforced?

17. List the four requirements common to most statutory definitions of a strike. What is a fifth requirement in some jurisdictions?

18. What is the defining feature of a lawful employer lockout? Why can this factor sometimes be difficult to isolate?

19. Distinguish picketing from secondary picketing. Under what circumstances could these practices involve unlawful activity?

20. Why might a provincial or federal government invoke back-to-work legislation? What purpose does this form of legislation serve?

Cases and Problems

1. Local 54 has retained James Love to represent it in a grievance against Dilated Peoples Optical Inc. The union is grieving the employer's decision to exclude from the bargaining unit the position of dilation officer, which the employer decided to move from Edmonton to San Francisco. Dilated Peoples argued that dilation officers are excluded from the bargaining unit based on the collective agreement, which specifies that only staff "employed in the offices located in Edmonton" are to be included in the bargaining unit. Local 54 responded with the argument that the words used in the collective agreement were meant to be descriptive rather than limiting. Which interpretation do you think should prevail? Explain your reasoning.

2. The collective agreement between the United Train Conductors of Canada (Local 49) and Rails and Trails Inc (R&T), a private railway system, has come up for renewal. The parties are finding it difficult to come to an agreement on an issue related to health benefits, and the negotiations appear to be getting nowhere. Both parties are concerned that there might soon be a strike or a lockout. It has recently come to Local 49's attention that some R&T managers are being trained as conductors, and are even driving trains containing passengers as part of their training. R&T claims that training managers as conductors has always been its practice so that managers can better understand the positions that they supervise. However, since the recent manager-training program began, R&T has seemed unwilling to listen to Local 49 and has held more firmly than usual to its bargaining position. The union has accused R&T of breaching its duty to bargain in good faith by training the managers to replace the unionized employees. Describe what the duty to accommodate entails. What argument can R&T make to support its claim that the manager training is not a breach of its duty? What argument can the union make to support its claim?

3. Six years ago, after nearly 31 years of teaching at Green Grass Elementary School, Linnea decided it was time to retire. Four years prior to her retirement, the Saskatchewan government had been looking to cut costs by reducing the number of senior teachers. Green Grass School's bargaining unit had entered into a new collective agreement with the province that implemented a retirement incentive policy with the local school board. Under the guidelines listed in the retirement incentive policy, retired teachers were to receive a retirement bonus. In the ensuing years, the province was forced to gut the number of school boards in the province from 83 to 27, necessitating a completely different management structure. Linnea was disappointed to learn, upon retirement, that the new school board management refused payment of the retirement incentive bonus, but she decided not to pursue the matter at the time. Having recently discovered that her roof needs replacement, Linnea has decided it might be worthwhile contacting her old union to see if it would grieve on her behalf to collect the several thousand dollars she lost out on when she was refused the retirement bonus. The union has agreed and is seeking the amount she would have been entitled to plus six years of interest. What steps can Linnea's old employer take to avoid paying the bonus? What arguments can the employer make to convince the arbitrator that no such order should be made?

4. Local 393, a trade union representing employees of an Internet start-up company, is upset by a recent business decision made by the start-up. The plan is to transform many of the employees currently working in head office into teleworkers—requiring them to perform their jobs from home via the Internet. The employees are concerned because the collective agreement provides certain corporate benefits only to those employees who are "working at corporate headquarters." In adopting this cost-saving measure, the chief operating officer (COO) of the start-up has relied on a labour relations board decision that defined "headquarters" as the main office, or centre of control, in any organization. The COO agrees with the board that the main office is rightly considered the headquarters. The employees, however, argue that the Internet has decentralized the corporate structure in a way that makes the designation of headquarters meaningless; therefore, they are entitled to the benefits provided for in the collective agreement whether they are located in the corporate office tower or are connected to it through the Internet. Is the board bound to follow its previous decision? Create an argument on behalf of the employees indicating why the board should not be bound to its previous decision. Explain your reasoning.

5. During a recent slowdown in the global lumber market, BigTree Sawmill decided to shut down core operations for six weeks to save money. It informed the union of its plans and provided a list of "machine service" jobs that would continue during the shutdown to provide necessary repair and maintenance to the mill. A number of employees applied to work these positions. Nathaniel, who has worked at the mill for 17 years, was turned down. Nathaniel had previously worked in a similar "machine service" position, but that was several years before BigTree had switched from using Acme machines to its more sophisticated and efficient Plan B equipment. The two employees hired for the positions have each worked at the mill for 11 years. During that time they have both worked on the newer Plan B gear, which required a few days of special training. The collective agreement includes a clause that reads, "BigTree Sawmill recognizes the principle of seniority, competency considered." Nathaniel wants to grieve the decision not to hire him for the temporary service position. Describe the argument that Nathaniel should make. How should BigTree Sawmill respond? Who do you think the arbitrator will agree with and on what basis?

6. Local 861 has brought a grievance against ESPO Broadcasting on behalf of one of its former employees, Addey Farberino. The grievance alleges that employees who resigned during the term of the first collective agreement, but before ratification of a retroactive wage increase, were entitled to the wage increase recently issued by ESPO. The union alleges that it had proposed specific entitlement of retroactive pay to anyone who had been an employee under the first collective agreement but that the proposal had somehow been dropped during the course of negotiations. The union claims that it allowed the specific proposal to be dropped because it had relied on a general presumption of retroactivity for wages and benefits. Nothing in the collective agreement explicitly contemplates this presumption. What position should management at ESPO take?

7. Khalil was transferred to a remote workplace contrary to the collective agreement between his union and his employer, Self Scientific Inc. Khalil filed a grievance. Although Self Scientific is prepared to reimburse Khalil for automobile and parking expenses, it argues that an arbitrator does not have the authority to provide any further remedies and, therefore, is not in a position to order payment of salary in lieu of travel time. Does Self Scientific's argument have any merit? Is the arbitrator limited to remedies set out in the terms of a collective agreement?

8. Peter & Harvey Furs and Local 275 had previously entered into a collective agreement that explicitly prohibited strikes and lockouts before the end of the calendar year. However, on July 30, the union applied to the labour relations board to request a strike vote, referring to the labour legislation that stated, "Employers are prohibited from imposing conditions in contracts of employment which would restrain employees from exercising rights under this Act."

   Peter & Harvey has countered by seeking an order to prevent the strike vote by its employees. To support its position, it made reference to another section of the relevant legislation which provides that "This section does not affect agreements between employer and union."

   Prepare an argument for the resolution of these two apparently contradictory provisions, first arguing on behalf of the employer and then on behalf of the union. Explain your reasoning in each case.

9. Randall's Motorcycle Shop employed the 208 members of LOCO 666. Until recently, every union member was employed on a full-time basis. Unfortunately, because of financial difficulties, Randall determined that he would have to unilaterally change the status of some employees to part time to remain in business. In announcing his intention to the union, Randall stated that those employees with seniority would be given the opportunity to bump junior persons into the part-time positions. When they heard about these arrangements, several unruly junior employees refused to accept part-time status and threatened Randall with physical harm if he refused to reinstate everyone to a full-time position. Many of them also left work in the middle of their shifts. Randall wants a declaration that those employees who left mid-shift engaged in an illegal strike. In turn, the union is seeking a declaration that Randall had imposed an illegal lockout. Your business consulting firm has been called upon to mediate this dispute in an attempt to find a resolution without having to take matters before the labour relations board. You have wisely chosen to meet with each of the parties separately before making any recommendations. What will you say to each party? How will you try to reach some sort of consensus?

10. Deepak works for the city hospital as a supervising nurse in his unit. His hospital was recently forced to reorganize some of its units in response to budgetary cutbacks. In the reorganization, the supervisory position that Deepak held was eliminated from the hospital. Deepak was reassigned to another position in the same unit at the same rate of pay. The collective agreement between the hospital and the nurses' union includes a provision that expands the definition of "layoff" to include a reduction of the nurse's work hours or reassignment to a different area. Should a layoff occur, the nurse is entitled to use a bumping provision in the collective agreement to secure a junior position. Deepak's union filed a grievance, arguing that he was laid off because he was displaced from his area of assignment, and therefore should have been entitled to his layoff rights in the collective agreement. Deepak would have preferred to bump a junior employee from a position on the unit that he thought would be more enjoyable, rather than take the one assigned to him by the hospital. The hospital argued that its management rights include the right to re-assign workers as needed, and that Deepak did not qualify for bumping rights because he was not laid off. Should Deepak be able to bump the junior employee for a position he would prefer? Support your position.

11. Robots Inc has lawfully locked out its unionized factory workers after exhausting negotiation and conciliation procedures prescribed by the applicable labour relations statute. Despite the lockout, Robots Inc has been able to continue supplying machinery to large automotive manufacturers, largely through accumulated inventory. These car makers are the biggest customers of Robots Inc. The workers are furious that they have been locked out, because they thought that their position during negotiations was quite reasonable. They are also getting desperate because they have been locked out for six months and are facing severe financial hardship. Picketing has not proven effective in getting media attention or in pressuring Robots Inc to come back to the negotiating table. The workers want to get their message out and want to get media attention to their plight. However, they want to do so in a lawful manner. What course of action would you suggest?

12. Meg's Party Supplies and Addison's Authentic German Beer Steins operate out of the same warehouse. Addison's employees are unionized and are engaged in a legal strike seeking to change their hours of employment and overtime pay. They have set up a picket line along the public sidewalk adjacent to the warehouse parking lot. Meg's employees are not unionized but are refusing to come to work because they do not want to cross the picket line. Delivery trucks bringing party supplies to Meg's business have been slowed down near the loading dock by Addison's employees, who have blocked the thoroughfare. In some instances, Addison's employees have yelled at the truck drivers and banged on the doors and roofs of their trucks with stainless steel beer mugs when truckers have tried to bypass the picket line. As a consequence of their discomfort with the picketing behaviour, a number of drivers have refused to deliver to the warehouse. This, in conjunction with a number of late deliveries and the worker shortage because of the picketing, has caused Meg to be late in filling some party supply orders. She has also lost a number of lucrative contracts. Having nothing to do with Addison's labour dispute, Meg thinks someone should have to pay for her contractual woes and would like to sue to recover her lost money. Meg has come to you, as a member of her risk management service providers, for advice. Whom can she sue and on what grounds?

There (But without the Grace of God) Goes "Cisco Fatty": Social Networks and the Workplace

In precisely 139 characters, Connor Reilly wrote off part of her future. Not altogether atwitter about her recent job offer, the 22-year-old Berkeley graduate student in information management posted the following to her social network: "Cisco just offered me a job! Now I have to weigh the utility of a fatty paycheck against the daily commute to San Jose and hating the work."

Too bad she didn't know at the time that her default settings would broadcast her message not only to her friends but also to the entire *twittosphere*. Unfortunately for her, one of the 15 million visitors to twitter.com was a Cisco employee who saw her post and tweeted in response: "Who is the hiring manager? I'm sure they would love to know that you will hate the work. We here at Cisco are versed in the web."

In addition to finding herself the subject of ridicule in front of an online audience of millions, Connor (dubbed "Cisco Fatty") eventually lost out on a decent job at the pre-hiring stage. She is not alone. Many potential employees and long-time personnel have learned the hard way that online social networks blur the line between an employee's public and private life. Employers have also learned that these sites—even if used only after hours—can have a significant impact on employment law issues such as workplace privacy and summary dismissal.

One Canadian grocery chain called "Farm Boy" experienced all of this first-hand, making international headlines when a group of its employees started a *Facebook* group called "I Got Farm Boy'd." The group describes itself as a place "for current and past employees of Farmboy Inc. to share experiences, discuss topics and even have a place to express their opinion as guaranteed under the *Canadian Charter of Rights and Freedoms*." Unfortunately, the group's discussion has turned out to be somewhat less lofty than its stated objectives. Even the *Charter* (inapplicable to private employers) could not guarantee that the opinions expressed on the site would be immune from sanction. For example, one recently promoted supervisor admitted that he was the "worlds worst service supervisor, just goes to prove how messed up farm boy is. Like who in their right mind would promote me. I am the worst employee, I am always late, and I slack off all the time."

Spelling and grammar mistakes notwithstanding, his employer decided to take him at his word. On 13 January 2007, he and several other employees were promptly dismissed without notice. As discussed in Chapter 18, although employees do have privacy rights in and outside of the workplace that preclude excessive surveillance and places limits on the collection, use, or disclosure of certain personal information without consent, it is unclear whether privacy protections will apply when employees disclose information to public groups. When employees admit to criminal behaviour (such as theft or harassment), cast doubt upon their honesty, or say things that damage the reputation of the employer, their admissions can be considered just cause for dismissal.

Although the comments on the "I Got Farm Boy'd" group may not seem much different from the banter that often takes place when employees socialize around the water cooler or at the pub, posting such confessions on the Internet creates a (potentially) persistent public record, which can lead to serious repercussions. Employees using *Facebook* to discuss the workplace sometimes have a false sense of security, mistakenly thinking that the group is accessible only to members approved by an administrator. It is prudent to keep in mind, however, that the culture of online social networks is primarily about information sharing. Even if the information is meant to be kept within an enclosed circle of "friends," it would be imprudent not to expect leakage. Some seepage occurs when "friends" share with others outside the circle. Information is also frequently shared with third party providers pursuant to the site's terms of service that are usually either unread or misunderstood by users of those sites. In the end, what happens on *Facebook* doesn't necessarily stay on *Facebook*.

These considerations are not limited to social networks such as *Facebook* and *Twitter*. Perhaps the most celebrated example of someone losing their job because of something that was said online belongs to Heather B Armstrong, who was fired from her web design job in 2002 after blogging about her job and co-workers on her own website. Her story has become so well known that she is even the source of a popular culture name for this phenomenon: "getting dooced" (based on her website, dooce.com). The range of behaviour for which employees have been "dooced" also varies wildly. In New York, a paramedic was fired after posting pictures of a murder scene on *Facebook*, an obviously egregious act. Less flagrant is the story of a woman fired because a posted photo of her office desk revealed to her boss that she was too disorganized. Perhaps most typical of all, though, is what happened to a young intern working for a North American bank who asked his manager for a day off, supposedly for a family emergency. In actuality he used the time to attend a Halloween party, photos of which were posted to *Facebook*. His manager promptly discovered them and forwarded a picture of the intern, in full costume, to the rest of the office before terminating him for dishonesty.

It is likely that that our cultural, ethical, and legal expectations regarding the appropriate level of scrutiny afforded to an employee's digital footprint will evolve as participation in various online environments becomes increasingly ubiquitous and people voluntarily share more and more personal information. What is already clear, however, is that our so-called virtual lives are not entirely separate and distinct from our work lives.

Questions to Consider

1. Given that absolute privacy is almost impossible to guarantee on the Internet, and that information leakage can occur even in "private" groups, is it reasonable that an employee may be subject to summary dismissal based on online conduct otherwise unrelated to the workplace? Are there ever any situations in which employees should be able to claim a reasonable expectation of privacy in their online conduct?

2. Many potential employers are requiring job candidates to consent to third party screening of *Facebook* accounts as a condition of being interviewed for the job. Do you think that this is a prudent practice for employers? Will the information learned from online social networks necessarily facilitate a determination of whether a job candidate is suitable for the position?

3. Online social networks such as *Facebook* have provided a platform for a growing number of social movements. If you were a socially active employee seeking to organize workers and create a bargaining unit, do you think that these sites would be an appropriate vehicle for discussions about unionization? What about for promoting a union once it has been established?

ADDITIONAL RESOURCES

Dooce **www.dooce.com**

When Heather B Armstrong was fired for content posted to her personal website, it was only the start of her blogging career. Today, her site is read by thousands daily and in 2009 she was listed by Forbes magazine as one of the 30 "Most Influential Women in Media."

Businessweek: Employers, Get Outta MyFacebook **www.businessweek.com/debateroom/archives/2008/03/employers_get_o.html**

Businessweek ran this story containing arguments for and against the appropriateness of employers considering applicants' social networking activity when making hiring decisions.

Ottawa Sun: Workers fired over Internet postings **http://cnews.canoe.ca/CNEWS/Canada/2007/01/17/3394584-sun.html**

This article, originally published in the *Ottawa Sun*, broke the Farm Boy story.

Wrongful Dismissal & Employment Law: Use Facebook with Caution **www.toronto-employmentlawyer.com/facebook-and-workplace-consequences**

Daniel A Lublin is a Toronto employment lawyer who maintains a site on Canadian employment law. Here he comments on the practical realities facing employees and employers who make use of social networking sites.

Norton Rose: Off-Duty, Online and Out of Work **www.nortonrose.com/news/47481/off-duty-online-and-out-of-work-web-20-in-the-non-workplace**

Norton Rose, a large international law firm with offices in Canada, here briefly discusses the challenges posed in evaluating off-duty conduct in an online environment.

Appendix to Chapter 9

Boilerplate Terms

Standard form agreements often include a number of boilerplate terms. A **boilerplate term** is a standard provision that can be reused in various contractual settings in a virtually unchanged form. Boilerplate clauses often help to provide a framework for commercial agreements. Without them, many of the parties' substantive rights that are contained in an agreement would have little meaning. Lawyers have come to rely on boilerplate terms to satisfy clients who require contracts to be drafted in a hurry at as little expense as possible. Because they play such an important role in many business transactions, we will briefly consider some of the more common types of boilerplate terms:

- exclusion clauses
- *force majeure* clauses
- confidentiality clauses
- arbitration clauses
- jurisdiction clauses
- entire agreement clauses

Exclusion Clauses

Many standard form agreements contain exclusion clauses, terms that are designed to protect one party from various sorts of legal liability. (An example of an exclusion clause is on the following page.) Exclusion clauses may be perfectly legitimate as long as they meet certain requirements. See the section on exclusion clauses in Chapter 9.

A difficult question arises if the party trying to rely on an exclusion clause acted in a way that deprived the other party of substantially the whole benefit of a contract. Suppose you own a factory and enter into a contract with a security company to patrol your building on a regular basis. The security company's standard form contract excludes liability against "burglary, theft, fire, or any other cause." Although these are the very things that you are seeking to avoid in your decision to hire security, you figure that the low monthly fee makes the risk of agreeing to exclude liability seem reasonable. While making the required rounds one day, the security guard decides to light a small fire, which eventually burns out of control and destroys your entire factory. Should the security company be able to take advantage of the exclusion clause, even though it failed to perform the fundamental term of the contract—to secure, rather than to destroy, your factory? To allow the security company to rely on the clause seems unjust, since it was the security company's misperformance of the contract that ultimately deprived you of its entire benefit.

The Supreme Court of Canada has held that an exclusion clause should generally be enforced according to its true meaning, even if the party relying on the exclusion clause has failed to live up to its end of the bargain and thereby deprived the other party of substantially the whole benefit to be obtained under the contract. However, it also held that an exclusion clause will not be enforced if it is "unconscionable" or if it would be "unfair or unreasonable" to enforce the exclusion clause.[1]

EXCLUSION CLAUSE: THE GREAT CANADIAN ADVENTURE COMPANY

The Great Canadian Adventure Company:

I, _____, hereby acknowledge and agree that in my participation in adventure activities by The Great Canadian Adventure Company:

1. I will not hold The Great Canadian Adventure Company, its officers, directors and employees responsible for any injury, death, accident, illness, delay, personal loss, personal property damage or other loss sustained by me and hereby release The Great Canadian Adventure Company, its officers, directors and employees due to any cause whatsoever, including without limitation, negligence on the part of The Great Canadian Adventure Company or its employees. I further agree to indemnify The Great Canadian Adventure Company and its employees for any and all legal fees (on a solicitor and his own client basis) or costs which may be incurred in defending any lawsuit or claim I may bring against them.

2. AND I DO HEREBY ACKNOWLEDGE AND AGREE THAT:

    (a) I will participate in adventure activities entirely at my own risk. Participation in any outdoor activity and travel in natural, outdoor environments involve inherent risks, dangers and hazards. These risks may include, but are not limited to: natural disasters, forces of nature, weather conditions, rugged or steep terrain, avalanches, rock fall, slippery footing, water, isolation from medical facilities, difficult evacuation, equipment failure, mechanical breakdown, human error and accidents. These and other risks may cause serious injury, illness, death, personal property damage or personal losses.

    (b) That this Waiver of all Claims, Release from Liability and Assumption of Risk is binding on myself, my heirs, my executors, administrators, personal representatives and assigns.

    (c) That the term "adventure activities" as used in the Waiver of all Claims, Release from Liability and Assumption of Risk includes without limiting the generality of that term, training sessions, programmes and events that are in any way authorized, sanctioned, organized or operated by The Great Canadian Adventure Company.

    (d) I understand that by signing this release I may be forever prevented from suing or otherwise claiming against The Great Canadian Adventure Company, its officers, directors and employees for certain loss or damages, whether for property loss or personal injury, that I may sustain while participating in adventure activities.

    (e) I understand that the included itinerary is a general guideline of what can be expected on my adventure trip, but is NOT a contract. Factors such as weather conditions, mechanical breakdown, flight cancellations, medical emergencies, political unrest, natural disasters or other uncontrollable circumstances can alter my trip.

    (f) I will not hold The Great Canadian Adventure Company responsible for extra costs incurred by me which include, but are not limited to: extra

---

[1] *Hunter Engineering Co v Syncrude Canada Ltd* (1989) 57 DLR (4th) 421 (SCC).

meals, personal costs, or rebooking of commercial transportation in the event of unforeseen or uncontrollable circumstances.

I confirm that I have carefully read this agreement and understand its terms as acknowledged by my signature below.

Dated at _____ on _____, 20___.

Participant's Name:_____ Participant's Signature:_____

Witness's Name:_____ Witness's Signature:_____

* Minors, under 18 years old, must have parent or legal guardian witness the form. Note: All participants in your party are required to read and sign a waiver before a booking/reservation can be confirmed. All waiver forms must be witnessed and dated. Any participants under 18 years old must also have their parent or legal guardian sign the waiver.

Force Majeure Clauses

Another way for the parties to limit their potential liability is through the use of a *force majeure* clause. *Force majeure* literally means a superior or irresistible force, such as a flood, stormy weather, or war. A **force majeure clause** aims to protect the parties when part of the contract cannot be performed because of some event that is outside of their control and could not have been prevented by their exercise of due care. Sound risk-management principles dictate the use of such clauses. Unlike exclusions clauses, which ought to be drafted as narrowly as possible, an effective *force majeure* clause will be drafted as broadly as possible to include as many unpredictable events as are imaginable.

FORCE MAJEURE CLAUSE: O'BRIEN'S ENCYCLOPEDIA OF FORMS[2]

Where the Seller is unable to make delivery of any portion of the Items covered by this contract due to a labour dispute, accident, fire, war, government regulation or any cause whatsoever beyond the control of the Seller, the Seller shall not be liable for such liability to make delivery if, within a reasonable time, it notifies the Buyer by prepaid post of the cause of such inability and that the contract for the undelivered portion of the Items is cancelled or that it will make delivery of such Items at a future date to be named in the notice of and the Buyer may within _____ days after the date of mailing such notice, notify the Seller by prepaid post that it will accept the delivery of the Items pursuant to the terms of the Seller's notice or cancel the undelivered portion of the contract but upon the Buyer's failure to so notify the Seller the undelivered portion shall be cancelled.

Confidentiality Clauses

In many business transactions, one or both parties want to prevent the disclosure of certain information to third parties. Business people generally do not want competitors or other customers to learn about such things as payment

2. *O'Brien's Encyclopedia of Forms: Commercial and General,* 11th ed looseleaf vol 4 (1998) 39.21–39.22.

schedules, business operations, or trade secrets. When confidential treatment is warranted, the parties might choose to include a **confidentiality clause**. Unlike the *force majeure* clause, an effective confidentiality provision should be drafted narrowly to apply to only specific, limited information. A good confidentiality clause requires that materials be expressly designated as confidential by the party seeking confidential treatment and that the other party to the agreement have sufficient time to register objections. It provides that information is presumed not to be confidential and that the burden lies with the party seeking confidential treatment to justify such treatment.

CONFIDENTIALITY CLAUSE: LIBLICENSE, YALE UNIVERSITY LIBRARY

It is understood and agreed by the parties that specific reports and other disclosures required by this agreement, and any changes which may be effected thereto, are considered by both parties to be sensitive. Such information will not be disclosed by either party to third persons except as may be required by law.

Arbitration Clauses

Parties often recognize that future disputes about the terms of an agreement could result in costly litigation. To avoid having to litigate such disputes, they sometimes insert an **arbitration clause** into a contract.[3] Arbitration clauses outline who should act to resolve the dispute and what method of arbitration should be used. Business people should consider these features of arbitration clauses:

- First, like exclusion clauses, a well-drafted arbitration clause is drafted in a clear, straightforward manner. By keeping the clause simple, one reduces the risk of hindering the arbitration process.

- Second, an effective arbitration clause stipulates how the expenses incurred in the course of arbitration are to be divided.

- Third, the clause determines, in advance, the number, qualifications, and role of the arbitrators.

- Fourth, an effective clause settles the procedural aspects of the arbitration, including the order in which the parties will present their case and the amount of time allowed for each presentation.

- Fifth, a well-constructed clause ensures that any information discussed at the arbitration will be kept confidential.

- Sixth, the clause contemplates whether the parties will require written reasons in support of the decision and whether there are avenues of appeal available to the parties.

Most of these details may not be specifically enumerated in the arbitration clause itself. They are often prescribed by reference to a document external to the contract, such as a set of rules or guidelines published by some arbitration institute.

[3.] Arbitration was discussed in Chapter 2; arbitration clauses are discussed in Chapter 28W on MyBusLawLab (www.pearsoned.ca/MyBusLawLab).

ARBITRATION CLAUSE: BC INTERNATIONAL COMMERCIAL ARBITRATION CENTRE

All disputes arising out of or in connection with this contract, or in respect of any legal relationship associated therewith or derived therefrom, shall be referred to and finally solved by arbitration under the rules of the British Columbia International Commercial Arbitration Centre. The appointing authority shall be the British Columbia International Commercial Arbitration Centre. The case shall be administered by the British Columbia International Commercial Arbitration Centre in accordance with its "Procedures for Cases under BCICAC Rules." The place of the arbitration shall be Vancouver, British Columbia, Canada.

Jurisdiction Clauses

Parties that are not interested in arbitration as an alternative method of dispute resolution might still decide that it is worthwhile to contemplate where the court battle will take place, should there be one. A **jurisdiction clause** predetermines the locale of the court and whose law will apply in the event of a legal dispute between the parties. Such a clause is especially useful for situations where the parties are not governed by the same jurisdiction. As discussed in Chapter 19, jurisdiction issues are particularly important for the e-commerce aspects of a business, and there a number of steps a business should take to manage risk in this area. If a business has a centralized structure, based in a single jurisdiction, it is usually wise to insert a jurisdiction clause.[4] Such a clause will help to ensure that those involved in the litigation process, whether as lawyers or witnesses, are not required to travel to other jurisdictions to sue or be sued.

JURISDICTION CLAUSE: TYPICAL WEBSITE

This user agreement is governed by the laws of the Province of Ontario, Canada. You hereby consent to the exclusive jurisdiction and venue of courts in Middlesex County, Ontario, Canada in all disputes arising out of or relating to the use of this website. Use of this website is unauthorized in any jurisdiction that does not give effect to all provisions of these terms and conditions, including, without limitation, this paragraph.

Entire Agreement Clauses

When parties to a contract negotiate both orally and in writing, it is sometimes difficult to know which communications are to be incorporated as terms of the contract. One way to avoid uncertainty is to use an entire agreement clause. An **entire agreement clause** is a provision stating that the entire agreement between the parties is contained within the four corners of the contract. Such a clause ensures that none of the exceptions to the parol evidence will operate to defeat the written document. The principles of risk management therefore

---

[4.] We discuss that situation in Chapter 28W on MyBusLawLab (www.pearsoned.ca/MyBusLawLab).

require business people to determine whether the standard forms they are signing contain an entire agreement clause. If so, they must ensure that every single aspect of the agreement is captured in the written document.

ENTIRE AGREEMENT CLAUSE: O'BRIEN'S ENCYCLOPEDIA OF FORMS[5]

This Agreement constitutes the entire agreement between the Lessor and Lessee and the Lessee acknowledges that there are no promises, inducements, representations, collateral warranties, warranties, conditions, options or terms, oral or written, express or implied or otherwise, made by or on behalf of the Lessor or operating in favour of the Lessee with respect to any aspect of the Equipment (including, without limitation, its condition, design, capabilities, operation, use, suitability, fitness, durability, quality, merchantability, or history (e.g., new, used, reconditioned) or with respect to the appropriate treatment of this Agreement or payments to be made pursuant thereto for the Lessee's accounting or tax purposes, other than as may be expressly stated in this Agreement.

Summary

Standard form agreements often include a number of boilerplate terms, which can be reused in various contractual settings. Exclusion clauses seek to protect one party from various sorts of legal liability. To be effective, they must be drafted in unambiguous language; the party against whom the exclusion clause is meant to operate must be given reasonable notice; and both parties must agree that the clause is part of the contract. *Force majeure* clauses aim to protect the parties from events beyond their control. Confidentiality clauses prevent disclosure of certain information to third parties. Arbitration clauses outline who should act to resolve a dispute and what method of arbitration should be used. Jurisdictional clauses predetermine the locale of the court and whose law will apply in the event of a legal dispute between the parties. Entire agreement clauses state that the entire agreement between the parties is contained within the contract, preventing the assertion of oral terms.

[5.] *O'Brien's Encyclopedia of Forms: Commercial and General,* 11th ed looseleaf vol 4 (1998) 39.21–39.22.

Full Case Analysis

The purpose of this feature is to teach the art of reading court decisions. That is not as easy as it may sound. Judgments are a unique form of literature. Judges write in a particular style and for a particular audience. They use specialized jargon and they often assume a great deal of background knowledge. As a result, it may be difficult for a businessperson to determine why a case came to trial or how it has been resolved.

To some extent, understanding judgments is simply a matter of practice and experience. The more judgments one reads, the easier they are to decipher. It also is important, however, to know what to look for. Because most judges follow the same approach to judgment-writing, certain elements appear in virtually every case. Those elements are a key to understanding.

It also is important to view each case in context. Even though it sometimes seems that courts are concerned with dry technicalities, every case involves some sort of human drama. The parties typically have gone to the trouble and expense of appearing in court because the plaintiff wants something—usually money—from the defendant. A good case analysis therefore contains not only legal rules and reasons, but also a summary of the parties' relationship. It often is the human aspects that make a case memorable or interesting.

For the purposes of illustration, we will rely upon the Supreme Court of Canada's decision in *Mustapha v Culligan of Canada Ltd*. You can find the case, which is quite short, online at http://scc.lexum.umontreal.ca/en/. As you read through the judgment, try to pull out everything that is important, but nothing more. A good case analysis is both *exhaustive* and *succinct*. It is exhaustive because it explains all of the essential elements of the parties' dispute and the court's decision. At the same time, however, a good case analysis is succinct because it leaves out everything that is unnecessary.

Two documents appear below. The first is a Sample Case Analysis for *Mustapha v Culligan*. Although there is no magic formula for *briefing* or analyzing cases, this sample demonstrates a common method of breaking down a judgment into its core parts. The second document provides a set of Notes. It explains the different headings that appear in the Sample Case Analysis and it suggests some strategies for understanding judgments.

Sample: Case Analysis
STYLE OF CLAUSE

Mustapha v Culligan of Canada Ltd (2008) 293 DLR (4th) 29 (SCC), aff'g (2006) 275 DLR (4th) 473 (Ont CA), rev'g (2005) 32 CCLT (3d) 123 (Ont SCJ)

FACTS

- M purchased bottled water from C for 15 years
- M was unusually vulnerable to psychological injury
- C delivered a sealed bottle of water to M containing parts of 2 dead flies
- M became obsessed with the "revolting implications" of C's water for the health of his family

- M developed a major depressive disorder with associated phobia and anxiety
- M's psychological condition required medical care and hurt his business

NATURE OF CLAIM

- tort of negligence (breach of contract also pleaded)

JUDICIAL HISTORY

Superior Court of Justice (trial)
- C liable to M in negligence
- damages: $80 000 general + $24 174.58 special + $237 600 business loss

Court of Appeal
- appeal allowed
- M's injury not reasonably foreseeable — no duty of care in negligence

COURT AND JUDGES

- Supreme Court of Canada — unanimous — McLachlin CJC

RATIO DECIDENDI

- a loss is too remote if harm to ordinary person was not reasonably foreseeable

REASONS

- negligence requires duty of care, breach of standard of care, injury, and causation
  - *duty of care:* established category between manufacturer and consumer
  - *breach:* C carelessly provided contaminated water
  - *injury:* M suffered serious and prolonged psychological injury
  - *cause in fact:* M would not have suffered injury but-for C's breach
- cause in law or remoteness is based on test of reasonable foreseeability
  - trial erred in applying *subjective* test based on M's actual circumstances
  - test is *objective:* was injury to *ordinary person* reasonably foreseeable?
    - unfair to require precautions against peculiar or extreme possibility
    - unfair to burden C with M's unusual risk of psychological harm
- C liable if *ordinary* person would have suffered *some* psychological harm
  - "must take the plaintiff as it finds him for purposes of damages"
  - C liable for M's *full* loss if ordinary person would suffer *some* loss
- no reasonably foreseeable risk to ordinary person — M's loss too remote

NOTES

- remoteness test is *subjective* if defendant knows of plaintiff's special vulnerability
- M's loss was also not reasonably foreseeable for purposes of *breach of contract*

Notes
STYLE OF CLAUSE

The **style of cause** is the name of the case: *Mustapha v Culligan of Canada Ltd*. In Canada, the style of cause is written in *italics*. If the judgment is from a trial court, then the plaintiff appears first and the defendant appears second. (In a criminal case, the style of cause reads *R v Jones*, where *R* stands for Regina or the Queen, and the named individual is the accused.) If the judgment is from an appellate court, then the appellant usually appears before the respondent.

the **style of cause** is the name of a case

The style of cause usually is followed by a set of *citations*. A **citation** is a formula, containing numbers and abbreviations, identifying a reporting series that contains the case. A list of reporting series appears inside the front cover of *Managing the Law;* see "How to Read a Citation." The citation also identifies the court or courts that have been involved with the dispute.

a **citation** is a formula, containing numbers and abbreviations identifying a reporting series that contains the case

In this instance, the citation reads: (2008) 293 DLR (4th) 29 (SCC), aff'g (2006) 275 DLR (4th) 473 (Ont CA), rev'g (2005) 32 CCLT (3d) 123 (Ont SCJ). (There are many case reports in Canada, and *Mustapha v Culligan of Canada Ltd* appeared in several. We have kept this citation short in the interests of simplicity.) Expressed in plain language, the citation reveals the following information:

- The Supreme Court of Canada released a judgment in 2008 that appears at page 29 in volume 293 of the fourth series of the Dominion Law Reports.
- The Ontario Court of Appeal also released a judgment, in 2006 that appears at page 473 in volume 275 of the same reporting series.
- The Ontario Superior Court of Justice, which is a trial court, released a judgment in 2005 that appears at page 123 in volume 32 of the third series of Canadian Cases on the Law of Torts. (Although the editors of the DLR decided not to publish the trial judge's decision, that judgment appeared in several other reporting series, including the CCLT.)

The citation also describes how the case was treated on appeal. The term *"aff'g"* indicates that the Supreme Court of Canada was *affirming* the decision of the Ontario Court of Appeal, while the term *"rev'g"* indicates that the Ontario Court of Appeal had *reversed* the Ontario Superior Court of Justice.

FACTS

Most judgments begin with a narrative of the events that caused the parties to appear in court. Sometimes the story is quite long. One of the keys to a good case analysis lies in the ability to recognize which facts are *really* important. A fact is really important if it directly affects the court's ultimate decision. Beyond that, a fact also may be important if it helps to explain the parties' motivations or if helps to distinguish the parties' dispute from some earlier case.

In the case of *Mustapha v Culligan of Canada Ltd*, the story is memorable even though its essential elements are quite simple. As the next section (Nature of Claim) demonstrates, the plaintiff sued for the tort of negligence. The statement of facts therefore should identify all of the information that is essential to that claim (There was also a claim for breach of contract, but it received very little attention in the Supreme Court of Canada. The court explained that the lack of reasonable foreseeability was equally fatal in both tort and contract. We therefore will not discuss the contractual action.).

- The fact that the defendant sold bottled water to the plaintiff established not only a contract, but also a duty of care for the purposes of the action in negligence.

- The fact that the sealed bottle of water contained parts of dead flies established that the defendant breached its obligation in contract and negligence.

- The fact that the incident caused the plaintiff to develop psychological conditions established that the defendant's breach *in fact* caused the plaintiff to suffer some form of loss or injury.

NATURE OF CLAIM

A lawsuit may take many forms. Indeed, it is common for a single case to involve several causes of action. It therefore is important to identify the basis upon which the plaintiff has sued the defendant. In this instance, the plaintiff sued for both the tort of negligence and breach of contract, but the court focused almost entirely on the first claim.

JUDICIAL HISTORY

If a judgment is given by a trial judge, then there are no previous judgments to identify and no judicial history to describe. Our case, however, was decided on appeal—first by the Ontario Court of Appeal and then by the Supreme Court of Canada. The final decision cannot be understood without some sense of what happened in the courts below.

As explained in Chapter 2, appellate courts do not hear cases in the same way as trial courts. For the most part, a trial judge's findings of *fact* are immune from review (unless they contain a "palpable and overriding error" or are entirely unsupported by the evidence). Appellate courts therefore focus on issues of *law*.

In the earlier stage of this case, the trial judge in the Ontario Superior Court of Justice held the defendant liable and awarded damages under several heads. *General* damages, of $80 000, were awarded to compensate the plaintiff for losses that occurred in the natural course of things and that could not be given a precise dollar figure. *Special* damages, of $24 174.58, were awarded to compensate the plaintiff for the particular losses and expenses, such as medical costs, that he actually suffered as a result of the incident. And finally, *loss of business* damages, of $237 600, were awarded to compensate the plaintiff for the fact that his condition caused him to lose income.

The Ontario Court of Appeal, in the second stage of this case, allowed the defendant's appeal on the ground that the plaintiff's injury was not *reasonably foreseeable*, with the result that the defendant did not owe the claimant a duty of care in negligence. The Court of Appeal's judgment was then appealed to the Supreme Court of Canada.

COURT AND JUDGES

The judgment that we are looking at was delivered by McLachlin CJC in the Supreme Court of Canada. As explained in Chapter 2, the Supreme Court of Canada stands at the top of every judicial hierarchy in Canada. As a result, if a similar situation arises in the future, the decision in *Mustapha v Culligan of Canada Ltd* will be treated as a *binding precedent*. Every court in the country, except the Supreme Court of Canada, must apply its *ratio*.

An appellate court always contains more than one judge—usually an odd number so as to prevent the possibility of a tie. If one of those judges disagrees with the *majority* decision, it is possible to write a **dissenting opinion** or **dissent** that provides a different set of reasons and *ratio*, along with a different conclusion. Alternatively, an appellate judge may write a **concurring** judgment that agrees with the majority on the outcome, but disagrees on the *ratio* or reasons.

a **dissenting opinion** or **dissent** provides a different set of reasons and *ratio*, along with a different conclusion

write a **concurring** judgment agrees with the majority on the outcome, but disagrees on the *ratio* or reasons

In this instance, all nine members of the Supreme Court of Canada agreed on a single *unanimous* judgment that was written by the Chief Justice of Canada, McLachlin CJC.

RATIO DECIDENDI

The **ratio decidendi** (meaning "grounds for deciding") is the basis upon which a case is resolved. Judgments often contain much more information than is strictly necessary. Everything that is not essential to the decision is called *obiter dicta* or *dicta* (meaning "something said in passing"). The distinction between *ratio* and *dicta* is critically important. As a matter of precedent, the *ratio* of a decision is binding on lower courts, but the *dicta* is not. Often, however, it also is necessary to distinguish between different types of *dicta*. Even if a judge's statements are *dicta*, they may be highly persuasive (even though it are not technically binding). Whether or not *dicta* actually are persuasive depends upon a number of factors, including the level of the court, the reputation of the judge, and the relevance of the statement.

the **ratio decidendi** or **ratio** s the basis upon which a case is resolved

obiter dicta or **dicta** means "something said in passing"

Unfortunately, it often is difficult to precisely identify the *ratio* of a case. It usually is possible to interpret the *ratio* broadly or narrowly. The binding part of a case therefore may be stated broadly or it may be expressed in terms that are tied very tightly to the underlying facts.

In *Mustapha v Culligan of Canada Ltd*, the ratio generally involves the idea that liability will not occur under the tort of negligence if the loss was not reasonably foreseeable because the plaintiff, unlike an ordinary person, was unusually vulnerable to injury. In other words, the defendant will not be liable if the loss was too *remote*.

We might therefore state the *ratio* this way: a loss is too remote if harm to ordinary person was not reasonably foreseeable.

Notice that the *ratio* in the Supreme Court of Canada is different than the *ratio* in the Ontario Court of Appeal, even though both courts arrived at the same outcome. The Court of Appeal said that since the plaintiff's injury was not reasonably foreseeable, the defendant did not owe a *duty of care*. The Supreme Court of Canada, in contrast, said that because the plaintiff's loss was not reasonably foreseeable, it was too *remote*. Duty of care and remoteness are different issues. The duty of care determines whether the defendant was required to act carefully toward the plaintiff. The concept of remoteness determines whether — even if the defendant owed a duty of care to the plaintiff, even if the defendant breached that duty, and even if that breach in fact caused the plaintiff to suffer an injury — that injury was reasonably foreseeable and therefore open to liability.

REASONS

The *ratio* of a case states the essential rule that the court employed to resolve the dispute. In addition, a court will provide **reasons** that explain the formulation and application of the *ratio*. The reasons also explain the court's view on other issues that exist within the case.

In this instance, McLachlin CJC began by explaining that the tort of negligence contains four elements and that the plaintiff had satisfied three and a half of them. The defendant owed a *duty of care* and breached the *standard of care*, and the plaintiff suffered an *injury or loss*. The element of *causation*, however, consists of two parts. The plaintiff had shown that his injury was *caused in fact* by the defendant's breach. That left the issue of *cause in law* or, as it sometimes is called, *remoteness*.

The court explained that *cause in law* is a rule of fairness. Even if a loss in fact is caused by a breach of the standard of care, it may be so unusual that it would be unjust to impose liability. With that in mind, the courts have long decided the issue of remoteness by means of a test of *reasonable foreseeability*. A loss is reasonably foreseeable if it is a "real risk" and not "far-fetched."

As the court further explained, that test of reasonable foreseeability is applied *objectively* rather than *subjectively*. The trial judge in this case wrongly asked whether there was a reasonably foreseeable risk that the plaintiff, being unusually vulnerable to psychological injury, might suffer harm if the defendant breached the standard of care. The proper approach instead asks whether it was reasonably foreseeable that a person of "ordinary fortitude" would have suffered an injury in the same circumstances. After all, while the defendant can be expected to guard against injuries that are reasonably foreseeable in the normal course of things, it is impossible (or at least unreasonably difficult) to guard against a risk that exists only because the plaintiff is peculiarly vulnerable.

Finally, the court explained that a tortfeasor "must take the plaintiff as it finds him for purposes of damages." In this case, the defendant was not liable at all because there was no reasonable foreseeability of harm to an ordinary person. The plaintiff's injury was too remote. The result would have been much different, however, if at least *some* injury to an ordinary person had been reasonably foreseeable. If that had been true, then the defendant would have been liable for *all* of the plaintiff's injury, even though the plaintiff suffered to a much greater degree because of his unusual vulnerability to harm. As lawyers sometimes say, "In for a buck—in for a bundle." That rule is thought to be fair because, given the risk that exists for the ordinary person, the defendant should have taken sufficient care to avoid injury.

NOTES

The final section of the case analysis contains miscellaneous comments, ideas, and concepts that may arise in the course of a judgment: important *dicta*, new terminology, unresolved issues or questions, and so on.

In this instance, the court said that while the test for remoteness generally is objective, it may be tailored to the plaintiff's specific circumstances *if* the defendant actually knows of the claimant's unusual vulnerability to harm.

The court also said that the claimant's action for breach of contract failed for essentially the same reason as his action for the tort of negligence: in either event, his injury was not reasonably foreseeable.

Index